The Slang and Jargon of Drugs and Drink

by
RICHARD A. SPEARS

The Scarecrow Press, Inc.
Metuchen, N.J., & London
1986

Library of Congress Cataloging-in-Publication Data

Spears, Richard A.
The slang and jargon of drugs and drink.

Includes bibliographies and index.
1. Substance abuse--Terminology. 2. Substance abuse--Dictionaries. 3. English language--Jargon. 4. Substance abuse--Slang--Dictionaries. 5. English language--Slang--Dictionaries. I. Title. [DNLM: 1. Alcohol Drinking--dictionaries. 2. Drugs--dictionaries. 3. Substance Abuse--dictionaries. WM 13 S741s]
HV4998.S64 1986 394.1 85-26277
ISBN 0-8108-1864-7

Manufactured in the United States of America

Acknowledgments

I am grateful to the many people who have contributed attestations of the entry words. This includes various students in my courses and individuals who have sent me lists of words by mail. Included in the latter group are Angela Douglas, Grant Gallup, Tom Hicks, and Jay W. Kaiser. The correspondence with Jay Kaiser extends over a number of years and covers hundreds of terms. I am deeply indebted to him for his help.

Thanks also to my colleagues Morris Goodman, and Rae Moses for valuable advice on the project and its execution.

Without the advice, criticism, and copy editing of my wife Nancy, this volume would not exist. For all that and more, I am very grateful.

Contents

Introduction

This is a collection of the terms used for drugs, alcohol, and tobacco. Most of the terms are known primarily in the U.S., but many terms from other English-speaking countries are included. Spanish has also become an important source for drug terms, and many entries are Spanish or of Spanish origin. The time period covered is from about 1700 to the present, with most of the drug terminology appearing during the past century. In addition to the obvious words and phrases, terms for doctors, police, arrests, and similar matters are also included. Terms for specific mixed-drinks, and most of the special medical, psycho-therapeutic, legal, or pharmaceutical terms are omitted.

The entries are based on material collected from existing published material and from many individuals who know something about drugs and drinking. No dictionary of slang terms is complete. Although this is the largest collection of terms related to drugs, alcohol, and tobacco in print, it does not contain all of the eligible terms. There must be thousands of terms for drugs, alcohol, and tobacco which come and go without ever being brought to the attention of a word collector. The kind of slang, jargon, and word play recorded here is often restricted to to a short period of time or to a limited geographical area. On the other hand, not all slang is here today and gone tomorrow. Much of it has been around for decades or even centuries, and many terms are in use within the community of drinkers and drugs users long before they became known to the rest of the population.

Most dictionaries of slang and similar linguistic phenomena are "retrospective." Such dictionaries include most of what has already been published in existing dictionaries. Usually, such dictionaries are augmented with the author's own collection of terms. This dictionary is retrospective and augmented. It differs from most of the others of this type in that it acknowledges the source of each word and thereby distinguishes the author's newly-glossarized terms from those already glossarized. Although there are relevant sources which have not been used in the preparation of this work, there are a number of hitherto untapped sources represented in the word list. In addition, sources such as JWK: 1981 and ADC: 1975-84 have provided much original and corroborative material.

This dictionary attempts to relate various themes, such as the use of color in marijuana terms, through the use of cross-referencing. In general it seeks to redefine and integrate the expressions and definitions found in all the various sources, new and old, published and unpublished. Many of the terms for drug use have been borrowed from alcohol and tobacco terms. These similarities in vocabulary become apparent in this dictionary. The long lists of synonyms and related subjects provide additional clues to the interrelation of themes and concepts. A directory for these lists can be found on the last two pages of the book. At each entry, the reader is presented with sufficient information to estimate when a term was actually used as slang or jargon. There is also an indication of where a term has been used in the English-speaking world, or at least where it has been written down.

In addition to the printed glossaries and dictionaries, the list of sources for the entries includes persons who use (or have used) alcohol, narcotics, or tobacco addictively. The "Affluent Drug Culture" is also represented by material gathered from persons between 15 and 22 years old, some users and some simply aware of the drug and alcohol use around them. Other contributors include academics, a clergyman, and assorted individuals who choose anonymity.

Guide To The Dictionary

Alphabetical Order

The entry words or phrases are alphabetized in absolute alphabetical order. This means that spaces, hyphens, and punctuation are ignored in the alphabetizing process.

The Use of Various Type Faces

The entry words or phrases appear in **bold sans serif type.** Alternate spellings and related forms of the entry appear in sans serif type. *Slanted sans serif type* indicates a word which is defined in this dictionary. *Italic type* is used for foreign words and to set off a word or a phrase being referred to. Entry words which can be italicized are marked with an asterisk.

The Form of the Entry

Entries may be defining entries or cross-referencing entries. Defining entries contain alternate forms (if any), definitions or identifications, cross-referencing, and an indication of the source(s) of the entry word or phrase. Where an entry has more than one sense, the senses are numbered. Cross-referencing entries refer the reader to another entry for more information.

Parts of Speech

The part of speech of an entry word or phrase is usually indicated by the grammatical form of the definition or identification. Occasionally, part-of-speech terminology is used in citing derived forms of an entry word or phrase.

Source Codes

Source codes have two major forms. (1) 2 or 3 letters. Examples: ADD, DU, OED. (2) 2 to 4 letters (including "&") followed by a colon, followed by the year of publication. Examples: DA: 1857, DCCU: 1972, DST: 1984, W&F: 1975. All source codes are defined in the Source Index (p. 563).

Some entries can be dated only by the year of publication of the work in which they appear. For more specific dating, either form may be preceded by a date (a specific year) in parentheses, followed by a colon. For example: (1923): ADD, (1968): W&F: 1975. In these instances, the date in parentheses has been stated or implied in the source which follows the date. For instance, (1968): W&F: 1975 means that a given word appeared in print in 1968 according to Wentworth and Flexner's work which was published in 1975.

Occasionally the name of an author is mentioned in the definition or discussion of an entry. Source codes are indexed by author in the section titled Authors Cited which starts on page 576.

Some source codes refer to individuals or groups who have provided attestations for various entries. These persons are also identified in the Source Index.

Attestations

The source codes found within square brackets in each defining entry, i.e., "[U.S., W&F: 1975]" indicate where an entry has appeared in print before, or what person(s) attested to its use. The goal is to have at least two sources for each sense, if possible. It is believed that the first source cited (or only source cited) is the earliest attestation available from the sources listed in the Source Index which starts on page 563. Not every attestation found in the works listed in the Source Index is listed for each entry. Multiple editions of a work have been used to make the dating more specific. It is reasonable to assume that enlarging the list of sources would produce more terms and earlier dates for many already-collected terms. The author's attestations, indicated by RAS: 1974-1985, are usually not listed unless they represent the first or second attestation of an entry.

Country of Use or Origin

Where the evidence indicates the country of origin or use, that is indicated before the source code. If it not possible to place a term geographically, no country has been listed. It can be assumed that many of the terms marked "U.S." are known throughout the English-speaking world.

Cross-referencing

Six cross-referencing devices are used. Each is explained in the section on Terms and Abbreviations. *Cf.* and (*q.v.*) indicate a casual reminder of the existence of relevant terms which may assist the reader. It is not assumed that most people will consult the terms thus indicated. "See" is a stronger suggestion to look up the word indicated. Usually the "see" entry contains additional information. "See also" indicates an entry which is only marginally related to the entry you are consulting. "RT:" refers the reader to a list of related terms. "RS:" refers to reader to a list of related subjects. There is a directory for these lists beginning on page 584.

Terms and Abbreviations

The following terms and abbreviations are used in the body of the dictionary. Cross-referencing to terms enclosed in square brackets refers to entries in the body of the dictionary. All other cross-referencing is to terms within this list.

abbreviation a shortening of a word of phrase. The can be done by deleting words or by replacing words with initials. Examples: [*L.S.D.*, *NORMAL*]. See the following.

acronym an abbreviation of a phrase where the initial letters of the words in the phrase are pronounced as if they were one word. Typically, acronyms are capitalized, but usually not followed by periods. Example: [*NORMAL*] from "National Organization for the Reform of Marijuana Laws."

akin to related to in some way, semantically or formally.

also 1. the word *also* enclosed in parentheses, immediately after an entry, introduces a list of forms which are related to the entry. These variants may be spelling variants, capitalization variants, or simple equivalent words or phrases. If there are subentries, the *also* in this position applies to each subentry. 2. an *also* which follows the numeral indicating a subentry applies only to the subentry whose numeral it follows.

Amerindian native or indigenous American; American Indian.

argot the French equivalent of *cant* (*q.v.*).

asterisk (*) follows an entry or subentry which is usually recognized as a foreign word and is therefore often italicized.

Aust. Australian.

backslang a form of slang where the letters of a word are placed in reverse order and then pronounced as one word. Example: [*reeb*] from [*beer*].

BF: refers to the writing of Benjamin Franklin. Franklin published lists of expressions meaning "drunk." BF: 1722 or BF: 1737 in the text of an entry introduces the original spelling or phraseology of the Franklin entry.

blend a combination of two or more words. See *portmanteau*.

Boontling a species of slang, jargon, and catch phrases used by the people of Boonville, California, 1880–1920.

Br. British.

c. *circa*, about, approximately.

calo (or caló) A Spanish Language cant. Terms so labeled get into U.S. use through Mexican or Puerto Rican Spanish.

cant criminal and underworld jargon which flourished in Britain from the 1600s through the 1800s, and in the U.S. in the 1800s. Similar to French ***argot***.

catch phrase a frequently-repeated phrase which draws attention to the speaker or to what the speaker is doing.

Cf. (always *Cf.*) an abbreviation of Latin *confer,* "compare." *Cf.* precedes a list of one or more entries in this dictionary which can be consulted to help in the understanding of the word at hand. The *Cf.* cross-references may lead to antonyms, synonyms, or related concepts.

Cockney the pronunciation and dialect of the working class residents of the East End of London, especially their rhyming slang. See ***rhyming slang***.

colloquial having to do with expressions typically found in spoken language, rather than edited, written language.

dialect having to do with nonstandard expressions which are usually found in specific parts of a country.

drug culture the community of drug users and addicts, particularly recreational drug users since the 1960s.

dysphemism a word or phrase which degrades the person or thing it stands for.

elaboration a word or phrase which is built on another expression, e.g. [***barbecue***] is an elaboration of [***bar***].

equals sign (=) indicates a definition inside of an entry. For example, ***bush = marijuana,*** bush, which is defined as marijuana.

euphemism a relatively mild or polite expression which is substituted for a harsher expression.

eye-dialect the use of special, nonstandard spelling to represent or signify dialect pronunciation.

GEN: generic for something. The word or expression following GEN: is a definition of the entry word which is more general than the drug jargon definition.

initialism an abbreviation consisting of the initial letter(s) of an expression in which each letter is pronounced separately. In this volume, each such letter is capitalized and followed by a period. Example: [***L.S.D.***].

jargon specialized vocabulary used by a particular group of people.

juvenile having to do with expressions used by children or expressions used by adults talking to children.

mock in imitation of, e.g., "mock-Chinese," in imitation of Chinese.

nonce having to do with a word which was made up and used only once.

N.Z. New Zealand.

p. present; up to the present.

Pig Latin a type of play language found in the U.S. It was frequently used in the underworld in the early part of this century. Example: [*ea-tay*] "tea."

play on punning on something.

portmanteau a word formed from the parts of other words, [*ginters*] is a portmanteau of [*gin*] and "jitters." Also called a *blend*.

q.v. refer to the indicated entry. Always seen as (*q.v.*) following the word to which it refers.

recurrent nonce a word or expression which is thought to have been coined repeatedly over the years. See *nonce*.

rhyming slang a variety of slang synonym consisting of two words, the second of which rhymes with the standard English synonym. For example: [*needle and pin*] stands for [*gin*]. Frequently, the second word of the pair is omitted, i.e., [*needle*] stands for [*gin*]. Also called *Cockney Rhyming slang*.

Romany (also spelled Romani) the language of the Gypsies.

RS: related subjects are listed at the indicated entry. See page 584 for a directory.

RT: related terms are listed at the indicated entry. See the Synonym Directory on page 584.

See consult the entry indicated by "See" for further information.

See also Consult the entry indicated by "See also" for similar material.

Shelta a variety of language (jargon) spoken by itinerants (tinkers, etc.) in some parts of Ireland and England.

slang a wide range of varieties of *colloquial* vocabulary and speech styles not usually accepted in edited, written language.

spoonerism a linguistic structure containing a pair of words which have interchanged initial consonants, eg, [*jober as a sudge*] from [*sober as a judge*].

truncation a shortening of a word or a phrase.

U.S. United States of America.

word-of-choice the most likely word in a given context.

WWI World War One.

WWII World War Two.

ziph a special kind of underworld jargon used especially in the context of narcotics. [*mizake the mizan*] is ziph for [*make the man*]. Still extant.

A

A. 1. *acid* (*q.v.*), the hallucinogenic drug *L.S.D.* (*q.v.*). RT: *L.S.D.* [U.S., EEL: 1971, W&F: 1975, YKB: 1977] 2. (also **A.s**) amphetamine in liquid or pill form. The plural refers to capsules or tablets of amphetamine. RT: *amps*. [U.S., RB: 1967, AHC: 1969, W&F: 1975] 3. alcohol; liquor. RT: *booze*. [U.S., RDS: 1982]

Ab. (also **ab**, **A.B.**, **abb.**, **A.B.C.**) an abscess at the site of an injection of narcotics. Caused by unsterile drugs and needles or by the subcutaneous injection of opium. *Cf. cave, Chicago leprosy, crater, raspberry*. [U.S., BD: 1937, DWM: 1938, VJM: 1949, M&D: 1952, EEL: 1971] See also *corn*.

abbot (also **abbott**) a capsule of *Nembutal* (TM; *q.v.*), a barbiturate. From the manufacturer's name, Abbott Laboratories. RT: *nemb*. [U.S., EEL: 1971, RDS: 1982]

A.B.C. an abscess at the site of an injection of narcotics. *Cf. Ab*. [U.S., (1922): JES: 1959, BVB: 1942]

Abe a five-dollar bag of drugs. GEN: a five-dollar bill (in underworld jargon). Named for the picture of Abraham Lincoln on a five-dollar bill. *Cf. nickel bag*. RS: *load*. [U.S., SNP: 1977]

A-bomb 1. a tobacco or marijuana cigarette laced with heroin, opium, or some other powerful drug. Short for *atom bomb* (*q.v.*). GEN: something very powerful. [U.S., RRL: 1969, EEL: 1971, W&F: 1975] 2. a nickname for a mixture of powerful drugs; a potent marijuana cigarette. [U.S., (1965): ELA: 1982, JH: 1979]

A-bomb juice strong liquor; moonshine. RT: *rotgut*. [U.S., D&D: 1957]

aboriginal having to do with undiluted liquor. RT: *neat*. [Br., B&L: 1890, F&H]

about drunk alcohol intoxicated; tipsy. Similar phrases are: **about full, about had it, about half drunk, about shot, about to cave in, about to go under**. RT: *drunk*. [PD: 1982]

about gone (also **about right**) alcohol intoxicated. *Cf. far gone, gone, half gone*. RT: *drunk*. [U.S., MHW: 1934, BVB: 1942]

absorb to drink alcohol; to drink alcohol to excess. RT: *guzzle*. [1900s, DSUE]

abstinence syndrome the symptoms experienced when withdrawing from drugs or alcohol. [JF: 1972]

a-buzz alcohol intoxicated. *Cf. buzzed, buzzy.* RT: *drunk.* [U.S., MHW: 1934, BVB: 1942]

Acapulco marijuana; a grade of marijuana. See *Acapulco gold.* [U.S., D&B: 1970c]

Acapulco gold a potent grade of brownish-gold marijuana presumably from Mexico. The term is widely known outside the drug culture and is almost a generic slang term for high-quality marijuana. *Cf. Acapulco, gold.* RT: *pot.* [U.S., (1965): ELA: 1982, (1967): DNE: 1980, DCCU: 1972, W&F: 1975, DNE: 1980, EAF: 1980, NIDA: 1980, ADC: 1981]

Acapulco gold paper marijuana cigarette rolling paper made from a leaf of marijuana. RT: *paper.* [U.S., (1974): ELA: 1982]

Acapulco red a reddish-brown marijuana presumably from Acapulco, Mexico. *Cf. Panama red.* See other red marijuanas listed at *red.* RT: *pot.* [U.S., M&V: 1973, R&P: 1982]

accessories marijuana smoking equipment. A code word used in advertising. See *tea accessories.* [U.S., RAS: 1983]

ace 1. a marijuana cigarette; a single marijuana cigarette. *Cf. deuce.* RT: *joint.* [U.S., MB: 1938, A&T: 1953, RRL: 1969, W&F: 1975] 2. a capsule or pill of amphetamine or barbiturate. Black slang. [U.S., EAF: 1980] 3. phencyclidine, *P.C.P.* (*q.v.*). RT: *P.C.P.* [U.S., ELA: 1984]

aced alcohol intoxicated. GEN: out-maneuvered, beaten. RT: *drunk.* [PD: 1982]

acelerante* amphetamines; *speed* (*q.v.*). From the Spanish word meaning accelerating. RT: *amps.* [U.S., NIDA: 1980]

acid lysergic acid diethylamide, *L.S.D.* (*q.v.*). The drug is usually consumed orally or on crackers, sugar cubes, or bits of blotter paper. The term is widely known outside the drug culture. *Cf. cid, sid.* RT: *L.S.D.* [U.S., S&W: 1966, W&F: 1967, RRL: 1969, DCCU: 1972, DNE: 1973, MW: 1976, EAF: 1980, NIDA: 1980, ADC: 1981] See also *paper acid.*

acid cube *L.S.D.* (*q.v.*) on a sugar cube. RS: *dose.* [U.S., HSD: 1984]

acid-dropper an *L.S.D.* (*q.v.*) user. *Cf. acid.* [U.S., M&V: 1967, H&C: 1975]

acid freak an *L.S.D.* (*q.v.*) user, especially an early, cultish user. *Cf. acid-dropper, acidhead.* [U.S., RRL: 1969, EEL: 1971, W&F: 1975]

acid funk a depression induced by the use of *L.S.D.* (*q.v.*). [U.S., RB: 1967, EEL: 1971, RDS: 1982]

acidhead an *L.S.D.* (*q.v.*) user. See list at *head.* RS: *user.* [U.S., W&F: 1967, RRL: 1969, DCCU: 1972, DNE: 1973, MW: 1976]

acid lab any location where ***L.S.D.*** (*q.v.*) is manufactured. *Cf.* ***speed lab.*** [U.S., EEL: 1971, RDS: 1982]

acid mung (also **mung**) an uncomfortable feeling after taking the hallucinogenic drug ***L.S.D.*** (*q.v.*). Described as feeling like one has an oily face. *Cf.* ***mungy.*** [U.S., EEL: 1971] See also ***acid funk.***

ácido* acid, ***L.S.D.*** (*q.v.*). Spanish for ***acid*** (*q.v.*). RT: ***L.S.D.*** [U.S., EEL: 1971, NIDA: 1980]

acid pad a place to consume ***L.S.D.*** (*q.v.*). Sometimes used for a place to consume any drugs or a place with psychedelic decorations. An **acid party** is held there. See ***pad.*** [U.S., EEL: 1971, W&F: 1975]

acid-rapping experimenting with ***L.S.D.*** (*q.v.*) in order to learn how much one can safely take. Essentially, arguing with the hallucinogenic drug L.S.D. [U.S., (TW: 1968)]

acid rock a style of rock music inspired by L.S.D. or with lyrics which pertain to L.S.D. use. The rock group *The Grateful Dead* is said to be the inspiration for the term. Now used outside the drug culture, especially in pop music jargon. [U.S., RB: 1967, (TW: 1968), RRL: 1969, DCCU: 1972, DNE: 1973, W&F: 1975, MW: 1976]

acid scene a place where ***L.S.D.*** (*q.v.*) is used; the setting where L.S.D. is used. *Cf.* ***scene.*** [U.S., RG: 1970]

acid test a mass introduction to the use of ***L.S.D.*** (*q.v.*). A classic acid test of the 1960s included psychedelic effects such as black light and strobes. Soft drinks spiked with L.S.D. were served as refreshments. [U.S., JBW: 1967, (TW: 1968), RRL: 1969]

acid toking the taking of ***L.S.D.*** (*q.v.*). *Cf.* ***acid, toke.*** [U.S., (DNE: 1980)]

acid trip a session of L.S.D. use. May include exotic visions and hallucinations. See ***trip.*** [U.S., DNE: 1973, RDS: 1982]

acid zonk the ***come down*** (*q.v.*) from an acid trip; the aftereffects of an acid trip. *Cf.* ***zonked.*** [U.S., (TW: 1968)]

acrophobia the fear of a marijuana high. From the medical sense: fear of altitudes. *Cf.* ***high.*** [U.S., BR: 1972]

action the drug-selling business; opportunities to purchase drugs. GEN: any activity; any illicit activity. [U.S., M&V: 1967, RRL: 1969, EEL: 1971]

action, in 1. having to do with a person engaged in the selling of drugs or a person willing to sell drugs. *Cf.* ***operating.*** [U.S., RRL: 1969, H&C: 1975] 2. having to do with a person who is currently taking drugs. [U.S., H&C: 1975]

activated tipsy; alcohol intoxicated. RT: ***drunk.*** [PD: 1982]

active principle the stimulant or depressant properties of a drug. ***T.H.C.*** (*q.v.*) is the active principle of marijuana. Not slang. [U.S., RRL: 1969]

A.D. 1. (also **Ad.**, **Add.**) a drug addict or habitual drug user. Some sources claim that this is from D.A. (district attorney), and that the letters have been reversed to avoid confusion (CM: 1970, W&F: 1975). This is probably an abbreviation for addict. RT: *junky*. Not necessarily argot. [U.S., (1920s): JES: 1959, DWM: 1938, BVB: 1942, CM: 1970, EEL: 1971, W&F: 1975] 2. (usually **Ad.**) *P.C.P.* (*q.v.*). RT: *P.C.P.* [U.S., (1970): FAB: 1979]

Adam's ale (also **Adam**, **Adam's wine**) water, the only drink that Adam had. The terms are occasionally revived for special effect. [(1643): F&H, FG: 1785, D&D: 1957]

addict a person physically addicted to a drug; a person mentally habituated to drug use; any drug user. *Cf. addiction*. RT: *junky*. Standard English. [1900s, (1909): OEDS]

addicted habituated to something, especially drug or alcohol use. *Cf. addiction*. This term is usually reserved for physically addictive drugs such as alcohol, opium, heroin, and morphine. GEN: habituated to a practice (1561): OED. Standard English. [since the 1600s, (1612): OED; with reference to drugs, 1900s]

addiction habituation to a drug. Addiction to a drug includes physical and psychological dependence. Most uses of the term also imply that the user develops a tolerance to the drug and requires increasingly larger doses to sustain the habit. The sudden cessation of drug use brings on withdrawal symptoms. The term has been used to refer to opiate and barbiturate addiction and is being used increasingly for any drug dependence. See a list of terms at *habit*. GEN: habituation to a practice. Standard English. [in reference to drugs, 1900s]

addled alcohol intoxicated. **Addled** = *rotten* (*q.v.*). RT: *drunk*. [BF: 1737]

ad-it See *attic*.

admiral of the red a drinker or a habitual drunkard whose face is red from drink. Refers to the red ensign, a red signal flag. See *flying the ensign*. RT: *sot*. [Br., JCH: 1887, B&L: 1890; listed in BVB: 1942, D&D: 1957] See also *tap the admiral*.

adrip alcohol intoxicated; dripping with alcohol. *Cf. a-buzz*. RT: *drunk*. [U.S., BVB: 1942]

afflicted alcohol intoxicated. RT: *drunk*. Probably revived during prohibition. [BF: 1737, DSUE, BVB: 1942]

affliction drunkenness; habitual drunkenness or alcoholism. [U.S., BVB: 1942]

affluence of incohol, under the alcohol intoxicated. A jocular spoonerism in imitation of drunken speech. [1900s, DSUE]

Afghani (also **afghani**) hashish oil, an alcohol extract of marijuana, presumably from Afghanistan. Based on the name of the Asian country. RT: *oil*. [U.S., (1976): ELA: 1982, YKB: 1977, DEM: 1981]

afloat alcohol intoxicated. *Cf. adrip.* RT: *drunk.* [Br., late 1800s, F&H; listed in MGH: 1915]

African black a potent grade of marijuana, presumably from Africa. RT: *pot.* [U.S., RG: 1970, IGA: 1971, W&F: 1975, RDS: 1982]

African bush hashish. *Bush* (*q.v.*) = cannabis. RT: *hash.* [U.S., JH: 1979]

African Woodbines marijuana cigarettes. Woodbine is a British brand name of cigarettes. RT: *joint.* [Br., M&J: 1975]

Africa speaks strong beverage alcohol imported from Africa. Can refer to cheap red wine, fortified wine, or other potent alcohol. RT: *rotgut.* [Aust. and New Zealand, SJB: 1943, DSUE]

after-dinner man (also **afternoon man**) a tippler; one who starts drinking after lunch. **Afternoon man** since the early 1600s (F&H). RT: *sot.* [Br., early 1800s, F&H, DSUE]

after-hours spot (also **after-dark spot**) a nightclub open later than other such establishments, presumably illegally. RT: *dive.* [U.S., D&D: 1957]

against it, up addicted to a narcotic, usually heroin. GEN: having to face adversity. RT: *hooked.* [U.S., BVB: 1942, DSUE]

against the stem, up (also **up against the gonger**) addicted to opium. *Stem* (*q.v.*) = opium pipe. RS: *hooked.* [U.S., late 1800s, DSUE]

aged in the cuspidor having to do with inferior liquor. A play on *aged in bond.* Cuspidor = spittoon. [U.S., BVB: 1942]

agent a police officer; a narcotics agent. RS: *fuzz.* [U.S., D&B: 1970c]

age of pain prohibition; the prohibition era. *Cf. alcoholiday, dry era, eighteenth amusement, Methodist hellinium, Prohibition Error.* [U.S., BVB: 1942]

aglow alcohol intoxicated. A variant of *lit* (*q.v.*). RT: *drunk.* [PD: 1982]

agonies the extreme discomforts of drug withdrawal. *Cf. horrors.* GEN: pain and suffering. [U.S., JTD: 1971]

agur-forty strong whiskey; inferior liquor. A play on *aqua fortis* (*q.v.*) = nitric acid. RT: *rotgut.* [U.S., JSF: 1889]

A-head 1. an *acidhead,* a user of acid, i.e., *L.S.D.* (*q.v.*). See list at *head.* RT: *user.* [U.S., EEL: 1971, W&F: 1975] See also *B-head, C-head.* 2. a habitual user of amphetamines or stimulants. RT: *user.* [U.S., RRL: 1969, CM: 1970, W&F: 1975]

ah-pen-yen opium. See *pen-yen.*

aimies defined as amphetamines. Possibly an error. [G&B: 1969, ELA: 1984]

aimless Amy *amyl nitrite* (*q.v.*). RT: *snapper.* [U.S., JH: 1979]

A.I.P. heroin grown in Afghanistan, Iran, or Pakistan for export to the U.S., via Turkey. RS: ***heroin***. [U.S., RDS: 1982]

airplane 1. a truncation of ***jefferson airplane*** (*q.v.*), a device used to hold the butt of a marijuana cigarette. *Cf.* ***roach***. RT: ***crutch***. [U.S., ADC: 1975] 2. to breathe in marijuana smoke through the nose. [U.S., D&B: 1970c]

airs, in one's alcohol intoxicated. (BF: 1737: He's in his Airs.) RT: ***drunk***. [BF: 1737]

alba de narco* a state or federal narcotics officer. Spanish. RS: ***fuzz***. [U.S., EEL: 1971]

alc (also **alk**) beverage alcohol; any alcohol. RT: ***booze***. BVB: 1942 list only **alk**. [Br., (1930): DSUE; U.S., BVB: 1942]

alchy 1. beverage alcohol; any alcohol. *Cf.* ***alc***. See ***alky***. RT: ***booze***. [U.S., (1846): DAE, BVB: 1942, W&F: 1960] 2. an alcoholic; a drunkard. RT: ***sot***. See ***alky***.

alcohol 1. a soluble and flammable liquid obtained by fermentation of sugars and starches. Standard English. [since the 1600s, (1672): MW: 1983] 2. any intoxicating liquor which contains some proportion of alcohol. Standard English. [18–1900s, (1879): OED]

Al Cohol alcohol; beverage alcohol. Possibly a play on *Al Capone*, a notorious criminal. *Cf.* ***Al K. Hall***. RT: ***booze***. [U.S., BVB: 1942]

alcohol abuse overindulgence in alcohol; alcoholism. Euphemistic in the latter sense. Compare to ***drug abuse***. Not slang. [U.S., popular since the 1970s]

alcoholic a person physically addicted or psychologically habituated to alcohol. Originally meant having to do with alcohol. Formerly euphemistic, now the word-of-choice for such a person. [since the late 1800s, (1891): OEDS] See also ***beeroholic***.

alcoholic constipation a drinking habit; an insatiable need for alcohol. A jocular expression derived from *can't pass a hotel*. ***Hotel*** (*q.v.*) = bar. [Aust., SJB: 1945]

alcoholiday 1. a drinking spree; a holiday devoted to drinking. RT: ***spree***. [U.S., MHW: 1934, BVB: 1942] 2. prohibition; a holiday from drinking alcohol. RT: ***prohibition***. [U.S., BVB: 1942]

alcoholism a physical, emotional, and social disability caused by the excessive drinking of alcohol or an addiction to alcohol. Standard English. [since the mid 1800s, (1860): OED] See also ***affliction, alcohol abuse, alecie, apple palsy, barrel fever, beeriness, blind staggers, boskiness, bottle fever***.

alcoholist an alcoholic; a drunkard. RT: ***sot***. [(1888): OEDS]

alcoholize to take a drink of alcohol; to get oneself drunk. RT: ***irrigate, mug oneself***. [U.S., BVB: 1942]

alcoholized alcohol intoxicated. RT: ***drunk***. Possibly nonce. [U.S.,

BVB: 1942]

Alderman Lushington liquor; a personification of alcohol. *Cf. lushington*. RT: *booze*. [Aust., B&L: 1890, F&H]

ale an alcoholic beverage fermented from malt and hops. It is similar to beer but more heavy-bodied. [since about 900, OED] Synonyms and nicknames for ale: *angel's food, apple fritter, barley-bree, barley broth, barley-corn, bass, beggar boy's, beggar boy's ass, belsh, berpwater, bitter, bitter ale, bitter beer, bitters, brewer's fizzle, choc, daily mail, day and night, giggle and titter, happy sale, hum, hum cap, humming bub, humming liquor, humming October, knock down, knock-me-down, lush, mad dog, malt liquor, merry-go-down, nap, nappy, nappy ale, October, old boy, pharaoh, pharo, porter, porter's ale, porter's booze, ship in full sail, ship in sail, stingo*.

alecie intoxication with ale. A play on *lunacy*. RS: *drunk*. [late 1500s, F&H]

alecied drunk on ale; alcohol intoxicated. RS: *drunk*. [listed in F&H (at *screwed*)]

ale draper a keeper of an alehouse. RS: *bartender*. [Br., 15–1800s, OED, F&H]

ale pock (also **ale pocks**) a sore from drinking to much ale. RS: *gin bud*. [(1601): OED, listed in BVB: 1942]

alfalfa tobacco. RT: *fogus*. Underworld use (W&F: 1960). [U.S., W&F: 1960] See also *hay*.

Alice B. Toklas (also **Alice B. Toklas brownies**) a brownie (a small square of chewy chocolate cake) with marijuana in it. Alice B. Toklas, the companion of Gertrude Stein, devised the recipe. *Cf. brownies, fudge, funny brownies, grass brownies*. [U.S. drug culture, (1969): ELA: 1982, EEL: 1971, RDS: 1982]

alight alcohol intoxicated. *Cf. lit*. RT: *drunk*. [U.S., BVB: 1942]

alkali whiskey, especially bootleg whiskey. RT: *whiskey*. [U.S., W&F: 1960]

alkee stiff (also **alki stiff**) a hobo who drinks liquor habitually. Stiff = hobo. RS: *sot*. [U.S., EK: 1927]

alkeyed (also **alkeyed up**) alcohol intoxicated. A play on the *alco* of alcohol. The same as *alkied* (*q.v.*). *Cf. keyed*. RT: *drunk*. [U.S., D&D: 1957, W&F: 1960]

Al K. Hall alcohol; a personification of alcohol; a disguise of alcohol. *Cf. Al Cohol*. RT: *booze*. [U.S., BVB: 1942]

alki See *alky*.

alki bum a drunkard. See *alky bum*.

alki cooker an illegal distiller. See *alky cooker*.

alkie a drunkard; an alcoholic. See *alky*.

alkied (also **alkied up**) alcohol intoxicated. *Cf. alkeyed*. RT: *drunk*. [U.S., BVB: 1942, W&F: 1960]

alki hall alcohol; beverage alcohol. *Cf. Al K. Hall.* RT: *booze.* Hobo use. [U.S., MHW: 1934, BVB: 1942]

alki king a leader in the illegal liquor racket during prohibition. RT: *bootlegger.* [U.S., BVB: 1942, VJM: 1949]

alki man (also **alki peddler**) liquor dealer or source for illegal liquor during prohibition. RT: *bootlegger.* [U.S., BVB: 1942]

alki up to drink alcohol; to drink alcohol excessively. RT: *irrigate.* [U.S., BVB: 1942]

alky (also **alkee, alki**) **1**. beverage alcohol; any alcohol. RT: *booze.* [U.S., (1844): SBF: 1982, VWS: 1929, DWM: 1931, GI: 1931, VJM: 1949, GOL: 1950, W&F: 1960] 2. a heavy drinker; a drunkard. Probably short for *alcoholic.* RT: *sot.* [U.S., DUS, RAS: 1970; Aust., (1964): GAW: 1978]

alky bum (also **alki bum**) a drunkard; a hobo drunkard. The same as *alkee stiff* (*q.v.*). *Cf. smoke bum.* [U.S., BVB: 1942, D&D: 1957]

alky cooker (also **alki cooker**) an illegal distiller of alcohol during prohibition. Probably someone who reclaims drinkable alcohol from denatured alcohol. RT: *bootlegger.* [U.S., DWM: 1931, MHW: 1934, VJM: 1949, D&D: 1957]

alky driver a smuggler or seller of illegal alcohol during prohibition. RT: *bootlegger.* [U.S., BVB: 1942]

alky-soaked alcohol intoxicated. RT: *drunk.* [U.S., BVB: 1942, D&D: 1957]

all arms and legs (also **legs and arms**) having to do with weak beer or ale. A colloquial expression meaning bodiless. [Br., 18-1900s, F&G: 1925, DSUE]

all at sea alcohol intoxicated. GEN: confused, undecided. RT: *drunk.* [late 1800s, F&H; listed in BVB: 1942]

alleviator alcohol; a drink of alcohol. *Cf. medicine.* RT: *nip.* [Br., early 1800s, F&H, DSUE; Aust., SJB: 1945]

alley juice diluted methyl alcohol drunk for its intoxicating properties. The term may refer to alcohol derived from any source such as Sterno (= canned heat) or antifreeze. From the prohibition era. RT: *methyl.* [U.S., 1920s, H&C: 1975, SNP: 1977]

alley oops a covert sale of drugs carried out in an alley, away from the gaze of the police. *Cf. ob sale.* [U.S., JWK: 1981]

all fucked up alcohol intoxicated. GEN: confused, distraught. RT: *drunk.* [PD: 1982]

all geezed up 1. alcohol intoxicated. *Cf. geezed, geezer.* RT: *drunk.* See *geezed.* [U.S., HNR: 1934, D&D: 1957, W&F: 1960] 2. drug intoxicated. RT: *stoned.* See *geezed.* [U.S., JES: 1959, H&C: 1975]

all gone alcohol intoxicated. *Cf. far gone, gone.* RT: *drunk.* [U.S.,

MHW: 1934, BVB: 1942]

all het up alcohol intoxicated. LIT: all heated up. *Cf. hot*. GEN: angry, excited. RT: *drunk*. Dialect in some areas, slang in others. [U.S., BVB: 1942]

all in (also **all out**) alcohol intoxicated. *Cf. weary*. GEN: worn out, exhausted. RT: *drunk*. [PD: 1982]

all keyhole (also **all keyholed**) alcohol intoxicated. Probably a play on *al-co-holed*. *Cf. keyholed*. RT: *drunk*. [Br., 1800s, F&H, DSUE]

all lit up drug intoxicated. *Cf. lit up*. RT: *stoned*. [U.S., DWM: 1936, BVB: 1942]

all mops and brooms alcohol intoxicated. *Cf. mops and brooms*. RT: *drunk*. [Br., late 1800s, F&H; listed in BVB: 1942]

all pink elephants alcohol intoxicated. RT: *drunk*. [PD: 1982]

all schnozzled up alcohol intoxicated. RT: *drunk*. [PD: 1982]

all there alcohol intoxicated. *Cf. there*. RT: *drunk*. [U.S., BVB: 1942]

all wet alcohol intoxicated. *Cf. wet*. GEN: uninformed, silly. RT: *drunk*. [U.S., BVB: 1942, D&D: 1957]

almost froze alcohol intoxicated; very drunk. *Cf. frozen, froze his mouth*. RT: *drunk*. [BF: 1722]

alocados* barbiturates. Spanish meaning thrills, wild ones. RT: *barbs*. [U.S., NIDA: 1980]

alpha powder any powdered, addictive narcotic, e.g., morphine, heroin. RS: *powder*. [U.S., JES: 1959, H&C: 1975, SNP: 1977]

alter (also **alter**) an opium pipe. RT: *hop stick*. [U.S., JES: 1959]

altitudes, in one's (also **in the altitudes**) alcohol intoxicated. *Cf. high*. RT: *drunk*. [cant, (1630): OED, BE: 1690, F&H, DSUE; listed in BVB: 1942]

altogethery alcohol intoxicated. RT: *drunk*. [(1816): DSUE, JRW: 1909]

Amanita muscaria a poisonous mushroom containing the alkaloid muscarine which can cause hallucinations. This mushroom and others of the genus *Amanita* are sometimes confused with those of the genus *Psilocybe* resulting in the death of the person who eats them. See *psilocybin*. *Cf. magic mushrooms*. [in drug culture use, RRL: 1969, YKB: 1977]

amarilla* 1. "yellow"; barbiturates, probably Nembutal. *Cf. yellows*. RT: *barbs*. The Spanish word for yellow. [U.S., NIDA: 1980] 2. (also **la amarilla***) marijuana. RT: *pot*. Colombian Spanish. [U.S., RDS: 1982]

amber brew, the beer. *Cf. the liquid amber*. RT: *beer*. [U.S., BVB: 1942]

am-dray a dram (1/16 of an ounce) of a powdered drug. Pig Latin for dram. RS: *load*. [U.S., VJM: 1949]

amies capsules of *Amytal* (TM; *q.v.*), a barbiturate. RT: *blue.* [U.S., YKB: 1977] See also *amy.*

ammunition liquor. *Cf. shot.* RT: *booze.* [U.S., BVB: 1942]

amoeba phencyclidine, *P.C.P.* (*q.v.*), an animal tranquilizer. RT: *P.C.P.* [U.S., YKB: 1977]

among the Philistines drunk. See *been among the Philistines.*

amp See *amps, ampule.*

amped hyperactive due to amphetamines; high on amphetamines. *Cf. amps.* RS: *stoned.* [U.S., RG: 1970, IGA: 1971, NIDA: 1980]

amphetamine a general class of chemicals used as a central nervous system stimulant. See a list of slang and jargon terms at *amps.* Standard English. [(1938): OEDS]

amphets amphetamines. RT: *amps.* Not necessarily drug argot. [U.S., RDS: 1982]

amps 1. glass ampules of a liquid drug, such as *Methedrine* (TM; *q.v.*) or *amyl nitrite* (*q.v.*). Also singular. See *box of L.* [W&F: 1967, BTD: 1968, M&V: 1973] 2. amphetamines; amphetamine tablets or capsules. The opposite of *damps* (*q.v.*) = barbiturates. [U.S., H&C: 1975, ADC: 1981] Nicknames and other terms for amphetamines: *A., ace, acelerante, amphets, amps, A.M.T., amy, anfetamina, B., bam, bambinos, bambita, bams, B-bomb, beaners, beans, benj, bennies, benny, benz, benzadrina, Benzedrine, benzies, biphet, Biphetamine, black and white, black beauties, blackbirds, black Cadillac, black mollies, black widow, blancas, blue, blues, bombida, bombido, booster, booster pills, bottle, bottles, brain burners, brain tickler, brother Ben, brown, brown and clears, brown bomber, brownies, browns, bumblebees, California turnarounds, camioneros, carceleras, carga, cartwheel, Catholic aspirin, chalk, chaulkers, chicken powder, Christian, Christina, coast-to-coasts, cockle burrs, M.s, copilot, copilotas, copilot ben, copilots, corazónes, crank, cranks, crink, cris, cristal, cristales, cristian, cristina, Cristine, crosses, crossroads, cross tops, crystal, D.A.S., dex, Dexedrine, dexie, dexo, dexy, dice, Didrex, diet pills, doe, dolls, dominoes, double-crosses, drin, drivers, duraznos, Durophet, Durophet M, dynamite, eye-opener, fives, footballs, forwards, four-way hit, French blue, garbage, glass, go-fasters, goies, go-pills, gorilla biscuits, grads, grease, green dragon, greenies, green meanies, hearts, helpers, hi-ball, horse heads, horse hearts, jam, jam Cecil, jelly babies, jelly beans, jolly beans, jug, juice, L.A., L.A. turnabouts, L.A. turnarounds, leaper, leeper, lid-poppers, lid-proppers, lift pills, lightning, liquid bam, marathons, met, metanfetamina, meth, Methedrine, minibennies, molly, morenas, motherdear, negrillos, nigger minstrels, nuggets, orange, pa'arribas, pap pills, peaches, pep-em-ups, pepper-uppers, pep pills, peps, píldora de fuerza, pink and greens, propper, purple hearts, purple passion, rhythms, rippers, road dope, root, rosas, roses, saltos mortales, skyrockets, sparkle plenties, sparkler, speckled birds,* *speckled eggs, speed, speedball, speed demon, speeder, splash, splivins, strawberry, stuka, sunflower seeds, sweets, tangerine, tens, thrusters, thrusts, truck drivers, truckers, turnabouts, upper, uppers, uppies, ups, velocidad, verdosas, wake up, water, West-Coast turnarounds, white, white cross, whites, whities, widow, zings, zooms.*

ampule (also amp, ampoule) a small, sealed glass container used to hold liquid medicinal substances, usually a single dose. Standard English. [(1886): MW: 1983]

A.M.T. (also AMT) amphetamines. RT: *amps*. [U.S., RRL: 1969, SNP: 1977]

amuck (also amock) alcohol intoxicated. From *amok*, a frantic, suicidal run practiced in Malaya. RT: *drunk*. [U.S., BVB: 1942, EEL: 1971]

amy 1. (also amy joy, amyl, amys) *amyl nitrite* (*q.v.*), a vasodilator drug which causes the blood vessels to expand when it is inhaled. Often seen as amyl nitrate. RT: *snapper*. [U.S., RRL: 1969, EEL: 1971] 2. amphetamines. RT: *amps*. [U.S., ELA: 1984]

amyl nitrite an *inhalant* (*q.v.*) drug which causes the small blood vessels to dilate. It is used as a sexual stimulant (especially among homosexuals) and is said to increase the intensity of orgasm. It is sold in glass ampules which are broken to allow the drug to vaporize and be inhaled. *Cf. butyl nitrite*. RT: *snapper*. The drug was discovered in the mid 1800s and is sometimes called amyl nitrate. [(1857): RRL: 1969]

amyls ampules of *amyl nitrite* (*q.v.*). RT: *snapper*. [U.S., RAS: 1983]

amys *amyl nitrite* (*q.v.*). See *amy*.

Amytal a protected trade name for amobarbital (barbiturate) in a variety of forms. The drug is a central nervous system depressant. Most slang and jargon terms refer to blue capsules of *Amytal* (TM) sodium. RT: *blue*. See *barbs* for a list of terms for barbiturates. [(1926): OEDS, in current use; consult a pharmaceutical reference for more information]

anchored in Sot's Bay (also moored in Sot's Bay) alcohol intoxicated. Probably of nautical origin. RT: *drunk*. *Cf. over the bay*. [late 18–1900s, DSUE, WG: 1962]

anfetamina* amphetamines. RT: *amps*. Spanish. [U.S., NIDA: 1980]

angel cocaine. *Cf. heaven dust, stardust*. RT: *cocaine*. [Aust., SJB: 1945]

angel altogether a drunkard. Akin to *full-blown angel* (*q.v.*). *Cf. altogethery*. RT: *sot*. Possibly nonce. [West Indian, (c. 1876): F&H]

angel dust 1. a mixture of cocaine, morphine, and heroin for smoking or injection. RS: *set*. [U.S., M&V: 1973] 2. synthetic heroin. Probably refers to *P.C.P.* (*q.v.*). [U.S., W&F: 1975] 3. (also **angel hair, dust of angels**) phencyclidine, P.C.P.; P.C.P. mixed with other powdered drugs such as L.S.D. The term has become the word-of-choice for P.C.P. RT: ***P.C.P.*** [U.S., RRL: 1969, EEL: 1971, W&F: 1975, DNE: 1980, NIDA: 1980, JWK: 1981] 4. any smokable substance (marijuana, parsley, tobacco) laced with *P.C.P.* (*q.v.*), an animal tranquilizer. [U.S., RRL: 1969, JWK: 1981] 5. finely-chopped marijuana. RS: ***pot.*** [U.S., M&V: 1973, SNP: 1977]

angel foam champagne. RT: ***cham.*** [U.S., BVB: 1942]

angel hair (also **angel mist**) phencyclidine; *P.C.P.* (*q.v.*), an animal tranquilizer. *Cf.* ***angel dust.*** RT: ***P.C.P.*** [U.S., YKB: 1977, DEM: 1981, ELA: 1984]

angel puke *P.C.P.* (*q.v.*). A dysphemism for ***angel dust*** (*q.v.*). RT: ***P.C.P.*** [U.S., (1970s): FAB]

angel's food ale; potent ale. RS: ***ale.*** [late 1500s, DSUE]

angel teat (also **angel tit**) a mellow whiskey. From a term meaning high-quality food or drink. Distiller's use. RS: ***whiskey.*** [U.S., (FH: 1946), BVB: 1953, D&D: 1957]

angie cocaine. *Cf.* ***angel.*** RT: ***cocaine.*** [Aust., SJB: 1945]

Angola black a potent black variety of cannabis from Angola. RT: ***pot.*** [U.S., ELA: 1982]

anhalonium From *Anhalonium lewinii,* an old name for *Lophophora williamsii,* the Mexican cactus which produces mescaline. Probably late 18-1900s. [MW: 1934]

animal 1. (also **the animal**) *L.S.D.* (*q.v.*). The same as ***the beast*** (*q.v.*). See ***crackers.*** RT: ***L.S.D.*** [U.S., SNP: 1977] 2. phencyclidine, *P.C.P.* (*q.v.*). RT: ***P.C.P.*** [U.S., ELA: 1984]

animal crackers small, animal-shaped biscuits impregnated with the hallucinogenic drug *L.S.D.* (*q.v.*). *Cf.* ***crackers.*** RT: ***L.S.D.*** [U.S., RDS: 1982]

animal tranquilizer (also **animal**) phencyclidine, *P.C.P.* (*q.v.*). Phencyclidine was formerly used as an animal tranquilizer until its sale was banned. RT: ***P.C.P.*** [U.S., YKB: 1977]

anotherie another drink; a second drink. *Cf.* ***nip.*** [Aust., SJB: 1966]

another nail in one's coffin another drink; a second drink. RS: ***nip.*** [Br., FG: 1823; listed in M&J: 1980] See also ***coffin nail.***

ante-lunch a drink before noon. RT: ***nip.*** [U.S., JSF: 1889, BVB: 1942]

ante-Volstead having to do with liquor produced before prohibition. The Volstead Act was the law which established national prohibition. Such alcohol was presumably purer and stronger. [U.S., MHW: 1934]

anti-abstinence liquor. RT: ***booze.*** [U.S., BVB: 1942]

antidote a hypodermic syringe. Something to counteract drug craving. RT: ***monkey pump***. [U.S., H&C: 1975]

antifogmatic a drink of alcohol allegedly taken to counteract fog, either atmospheric or mental fog. BHH: 1856 lists ***fogmatic*** (*q.v.*) with the same meaning. RT: ***nip***. [U.S., (1815): RHT: 1912, listed in BVB: 1942]

antifreeze 1. heroin. RT: ***heroin***. [U.S., W&F: 1975] 2. beverage alcohol; any alcohol derived from any source such as antifreeze; inferior alcohol. RT: ***booze***. Heard on the television program M*A*S*H, 1970s. [U.S., 1900s, RAS: 1978, N&S: 1983] 3. automobile antifreeze used as an ***inhalant*** (*q.v.*) by a ***huffer*** (*q.v.*). [Br., BTD: 1968]

antifreezed alcohol intoxicated. RT: ***drunk***. [PD: 1982]

antiseptic alcohol intoxicated. Sterile due to the excessive alcohol. RT: ***drunk***. [PD: 1982]

Anyone out? Are there dealers around? Are there drugs available? RS: ***How are you going to act?*** [U.S., JWK: 1981]

anything drugs; a term of avoidance for the word dope. *Cf.* ***stuff***. Black use. [U.S., ADC: 1975]

anywhere possessing, using, or selling drugs as in ***Are you anywhere?*** (*q.v.*). [U.S., M&W: 1946, RRL: 1969, IGA: 1971]

A.O.B. "alcohol on breath." A police or medical notation. [U.S., S&E: 1981, RDS: 1982]

aped alcohol intoxicated. RT: ***drunk***. [U.S., RB: 1915, MHW: 1934]

apostle a prepared opium pellet. RT: ***opium***. Probably early 1900s. [U.S., ELA: 1984]

appetizer a drink of alcohol. RT: ***nip***. [Br., late 1800s, F&H]

apple 1. a capsule of ***Seconal*** (TM; *q.v.*), a barbiturate; any barbiturate capsule or tablet. Seconal (TM) is red. Usually in the plural. RT: ***barbs***. Black slang. [U.S., EAF: 1980] 2. a nonaddict. The same as ***square apple*** (*q.v.* at ***square John***). RT: ***square***. [U.S., LVA: 1981]

apple brandy an alcoholic beverage distilled from apple cider. RT: ***brandy***. [U.S., (1780): OEDS, M&C: 1905]

apple fritter ale, a ***bitter*** (*q.v.*). Rhyming slang. RT: ***ale***. [Br., late 18-1900s, DRS]

apple jack ***apple brandy*** (*q.v.*); any liquor; any strong alcoholic drink; prohibition alcohol. Used occasionally now for ***hard cider*** (*q.v.*). RT: ***booze***. [U.S., (1816): OEDS, M&C: 1905]

apple palsy drunkenness; intoxication from ***apple brandy*** (*q.v.*). [U.S., FBL: 1898, D&D: 1957]

apps drug-taking apparatus: needles, syringes, cooking tools. RT: ***outfit***. New York City Puerto Rican use. [U.S., JWK: 1981]

aprobarbs a truncation of aprobarbital, a barbiturate compound.

RS: *barbs*. From medical jargon. [U.S., SNP: 1977]

apron someone who sells and serves liquor at a bar. RT: *bartender*. [U.S., BVB: 1942, DB: 1944, GOL: 1950]

aqua-duck a prohibitionist. RS: *dry*. [U.S., BVB: 1942]

aqua fortis liquor. From a term for nitric acid. See *agur-forty*.

aqua vitae the water of life, liquor. RT: *booze*. [Br., 1800s, F&H, and nonce]

aras (also **aris**) a bottle; a bottle of beer. A truncation of *Aristotle* which is rhyming slang for *bottle*. [Aust., SJB: 1966]

Arctic explorer (also **Artic explorer**) a cocaine user; a user of powdered drugs. Arctic refers to *snow* (*q.v.*) = cocaine. *Artic* is a misspelling or a phonetic representation. See similar terms at *winter wonderland*. RT: *kokomo*. [U.S., (1920s): JES: 1959, BVB: 1942, H&C: 1975]

ardent (also **the ardent**) liquor. Refers to the heat it produces. From *ardent spirits* (*q.v.*). RT: *booze*. [(1833): OED, JRW: 1909; U.S. Army, Civil War, DST: 1984]

ardent spirits liquor. RT: *booze*. [(1833): OED, BWG: 1899, SBF: 1976]

Are you anywhere? (also **Is you anywhere?**) Are you a drug user?; Do you have drugs which you can sell me? The *also* is from M&W: 1946. *Cf. How are you going to act?* for similar questions. [U.S., (1953): ELA: 1982, (RRL: 1969), LVA: 1981]

Are you holding? (also **Are you carrying?**) Do you have drugs which you can sell me? *Cf. hold*. RS: *How are you going to act?* [U.S., (1935): OEDS, M&D: 1952, RRL: 1969, RG: 1970]

arf-a-mo a cigarette; a short work break for smoking. From *half a moment*. [Br. military, WWI DSUE]

arf an arf (also **arf-and-arf**) a drink mixture, half ale and half porter. [Br. (Cockney), (1830): DSUE, JRW: 1909]

arf arf an arf (also **arfarfanarf**) alcohol intoxicated; very drunk. PD: 1982 lists **arfarfanark** in error. RT: *drunk*. [Br. (Cockney), JRW: 1909]

arid hound a prohibitionist. RT: *dry*. [U.S., BVB: 1942]

aristippus canary wine. From the name of a Greek Philosopher. RS: *wine*. [cant, (1627): OED, F&H]

Aristotle (also **arry**) a bottle. Rhyming slang. See *aras*. [Br., late 18-1900s, DRS]

arm 1. a measurement of hashish or *dagga* (*q.v.*). *Cf. elbow*. RS: *load*. [South African, (1977): JB: 1980] 2. a police officer. See *arm of the law*.

arm of the law (also **arm, long arm of the law, long limb of the law**) a police officer. RT: *fuzz*. [U.S., BVB: 1942]

armour, in (also **in one's armour**) alcohol intoxicated; fighting drunk. RT: ***drunk***. [cant, BE: 1690, FG: 1823, BVB: 1942]

arm squirt a hypodermic syringe. RT: ***monkey pump***. [U.S., early 1900s, DU]

army brew beer with a 3.2% alcohol content, sold in Army Post Exchanges. RS: ***queer-beer***. [U.S. Army, WWII, DST: 1984]

army disease morphine addiction. RT: ***habit***. From medical morphine addiction during the civil war. [U.S., mid 18-1900s, RRL: 1969]

Aroma (also **Aroma of Man**) the brand name of ***amyl nitrite*** (*q.v.*) or ***butyl nitrite*** (*q.v.*) sold as a room deodorizer. [U.S., YKB: 1977, ELA: 1984]

around the bend drug intoxicated. GEN: far gone. *Cf.* ***bent***. RT: ***stoned***. [U.S., AP: 1980]

arreador* a drug seller. From Spanish meaning foreman, overseer, cattle herder. RT: ***dealer***. [U.S., EEL: 1971, JH: 1979]

arry See ***Aristotle***.

arseholed alcohol intoxicated. RT: ***drunk***. [PD: 1982]

arsenal a supply of drugs packaged and concealed in the rectum; a rectal stash; any drug supply. A play on *arse*. *Cf.* ***turd***. RT: ***stash***. [U.S., JES: 1959, JTD: 1971, H&C: 1975] See also ***whammer***.

artesian beer; ***stout*** (*q.v.*). RT: ***beer***. [Aust., late 18-1900s, F&H, SJB: 1945]

Arthur Duffy (also **Arthur K. Duffy**) a faked convulsive drug withdrawal symptom performed to get drugs from a sympathetic physician. *Cf.* ***Duffy***. RT: ***brody***. [U.S., early 1900s, DU]

artichoke ripe a tobacco pipe; to smoke a pipe. Rhyming slang. JCH: 1859 attests the verb sense. [Br., JCH: 1859, DRS; U.S., M&B: 1944]

artillery a hypodermic syringe, a medicine dropper, needles, or any equipment used in the injection of drugs, i.e., used in shooting drugs. See ***heavy artillery, light artillery***. RS: ***monkey pump***. [U.S., (1931): DU, DWM: 1933, VJM: 1949, W&F: 1960, DCCU: 1972, JH: 1979; Br., BTD: 1968]

artillery man 1. a (male) drunkard. Because he takes many shots of alcohol. RT: ***sot***. [Br., F&H, (1903): DSUE] 2. an addict who injects drugs. RT: ***bangster***. [U.S., early 1900s, DU]

as good conditioned as a puppy alcohol intoxicated. Conditioned = housebroken. RT: ***drunk***. [BF: 1737]

ashes marijuana. Possibly refers to burned out marijuana. RT: ***pot***. [U.S., YKB: 1977, ELA: 1982] See also ***green ashes***.

as it came from its mother having to do with undiluted alcohol. RT: ***neat***. [Br., late 1800s, F&H] See also ***mother's milk***.

ask for cotton (also **ask for the cotton, beg for cotton**) for an addict to be so down-and-out that he is reduced to asking for some other addict's used straining cotton. *Cf.* ***boot and shoe.*** [U.S., DWM: 1938]

aspirin hound a person addicted to aspirin, either addicted to the pills or to smoking it. RS: ***user.*** [U.S., GOL: 1950]

aspirin smoke a tobacco cigarette containing crushed aspirin. *Cf.* ***nail.*** [U.S., M&V: 1973, RDS: 1982]

asskash (also **asscache**) a supply of drugs hidden in the rectum. A linguistic blend of *ass* and *cache*. RS: ***stash.*** [U.S., JES: 1959, ELA: 1984]

ass, on one's alcohol intoxicated. GEN: down-and-out, done-in. RT: ***drunk.*** [Aust., SJB: 1943]

atom bomb (also **A-bomb**) a marijuana cigarette laced with heroin. RT: ***set.*** [U.S., (1962): ELA: 1982, H&C: 1975]

atombombo a cheap, potent wine; very strong ***bombo*** (*q.v.*). RT: ***wine.*** [Aust., SJB: 1966]

atop Mt. Shasta high on marijuana. See ***from Mt. Shasta.***

atshitshi marijuana; ***dagga*** (*q.v.*). RT: ***pot.*** Probably from Afrikaans. [South African, (1977): JB: 1980]

attic (also **ad-it**) a drug addict. Eye-dialect or deliberate mispronunciation. RT: ***junky.*** [U.S., JES: 1959]

auger in to pass out from drinking too much alcohol. [U.S., WWII, W&F: 1960]

Augustus Owsley authentic ***L.S.D.*** (*q.v.*); the best quality L.S.D.; the best quality of anything. See ***Owsley*** for further comments on the name. RT: ***L.S.D.*** [U.S., W&F: 1975]

Aunt Emma morphine. From the initial M. RT: ***morphine.*** [U.S., EEL: 1971, JH: 1979]

Aunt Hazel heroin. *Cf.* ***witch hazel.*** Based on the H of heroin. RT: ***heroin.*** [U.S., JES: 1959, H&C: 1975, SNP: 1977]

auntie opium. Probably akin to ***Aunt Nora*** (*q.v.*). RT: ***opium.*** [U.S., JES: 1959, SNP: 1977]

Aunt Mary marijuana. Based on the M of ***marijuana.*** *Cf.* ***Mary.*** RT: ***pot.*** [U.S., JES: 1959, H&C: 1975, SNP: 1977]

Aunt Nora a water-soluble powdered drug; any narcotic. The N of *Nora* indicates narcotics. RT: ***powder.*** [U.S., JES: 1959, H&C: 1975, SNP: 1977]

aurora borealis phencyclidine, ***P.C.P.*** (*q.v.*). RT: ***P.C.P.*** [U.S., ELA: 1984]

author an addict known to be able to write acceptable prescriptions. The same as ***scribe.*** [U.S., JWK: 1981] See also ***line of the old author.***

autograph an injection of drugs. RT: ***shot.*** [U.S., JES: 1959, H&C: 1975]

avec spirits used to lace coffee; any beverage alcohol, usually brandy. From the French expression *café avec*. *Avec* = with (in French). Compare to ***coffee-and habit***. RT: ***brandy***. [Br., WWI, F&G: 1925, B&P: 1965]

avispa* barbiturate tablets or capsules. RT: ***barbs***. From the Spanish word for wasp. [U.S., NIDA: 1980]

avs the law of averages; chance. General drug-oriented street talk. [U.S., JWK: 1981]

awash alcohol intoxicated. *Cf.* ***adrip***. RT: ***drunk***. [U.S., BVB: 1942, DNE: 1973]

away from the habit (also away) off drugs, temporarily or permanently. RT: ***off***. [U.S., DWM: 1938, JWK: 1981]

awry-eyed (also orie-eyed) alcohol intoxicated. RT: ***drunk***. [U.S., DWM: 1931, BVB: 1942]

awsley a misspelling of ***Owsley*** (*q.v.*). [U.S., RG: 1970]

ayahuasca a hallucinogenic substance. The same as ***yage*** (*q.v.*). [U.S., RRL: 1969, YKB: 1977]

azul* the police; a police officer. RS: ***fuzz***. From the Spanish word for blue. [U.S., EEL: 1971, W&F: 1975, RDS: 1982]

azulillos* barbiturates. Spanish meaning blues = ***Amytal*** (*q.v.*). RT: ***barbs***. [U.S., NIDA: 1980]

B

B. 1. ***Benzedrine*** (TM; *q.v.*). RT: ***benz***. [U.S., M&D: 1952, W&F: 1960, CM: 1970] 2. (also **bee**) a matchbox measurement of marijuana. From the *B* in *box*. RS: ***load***. [U.S., (1967): ELA: 1982, EEL: 1971, RDS: 1982]

babo ***Nalline*** (TM; *q.v.*), a ***narcotic antagonist*** (*q.v.*). It makes one ***clean*** (*q.v.*). Babo (TM) is the brand name of a cleaning powder. *Cf.* ***Nalline***. [U.S., (M&V: 1954), JBW: 1967, IGA: 1971, LVA: 1981]

baby 1. a bottle of liquor. From its size and fragility. [U.S., MHW: 1934, BVB: 1942] 2. (also **baby buds**) marijuana. Because it is used by babies, i.e., drug beginners. *Cf.* ***baby bhang, schoolboy***. RT: ***pot***. [U.S., (1960): ELA: 1982, RRL: 1969, EEL: 1971, D&B: 1978] 3. a small or beginning heroin habit. RT: ***habit***. [U.S., RRL: 1969] See also ***blue babies***.

baby bhang marijuana. *Cf.* ***bhang***. RT: ***pot***. [U.S., JH: 1979]

baby doll probably a ***barbiturate*** (*q.v.*). Braddy (HB: 1955) states "Heart stimulant; possibly an alteration of barbital." See ***dolls***. [U.S., HB: 1955]

baby-sit to sit with and guide a person who is having an L.S.D. experience. RT: ***sitter***. [U.S., W&F: 1960, IGA: 1971, D&B: 1978]

baby sitter a guide for an L.S.D. trip; a ***sitter*** (*q.v.*). [U.S., RDS: 1982]

bacca (also **baccer, bacco, baccy, backa, backer**) tobacco. RT: ***fogus***. These are all dialect. [Br. and U.S., (1792): OEDS, DSUE, BVB: 1942]

bacca chew a hunk of chewing tobacco. RT: ***quid***. [17–1900s, DSUE]

Bacchi plenus* alcohol intoxicated. RT: ***drunk***. LIT: full of Bacchus. [Br., 1800s, F&H; listed in BVB: 1942]

Bacchus (also **bacchus**) wine; beverage alcohol. The god of wine and the growing of grapes. RT: ***booze, wine***. [U.S., BVB: 1942]

Bacchus-bulged full of liquor; bulging and distended with drink. Similarly: **Bacchus-butted** = fat in the rump from gluttony. [PD: 1982]

bacco tobacco. *Cf. bacca.* RT: *fogus.* [(1792): OEDS]

baccy tobacco. *Cf. bacca.* RT: *fogus.* [Br., (1859): OEDS]

back a dose of one drug taken immediately after a dose of a different drug. Compare to *front.* [Br., BTD: 1968]

backdoor artist a drug addict who cheats other addicts. GEN: a cheater, a sneaky person. RS: *junky.* [U.S., D&B: 1970c, IGA: 1971]

backed up drug intoxicated. RT: *stoned.* [U.S., H&C: 1975]

backer tobacco. *Cf. bacca.* RT: *fogus.* [Br., (1848): DSUE; U.S., LWP: 1908]

backey (also **backy**) tobacco. *Cf. bacca.* RT: *fogus.* [Br., (1823): OEDS, DSUE]

backtrack to pull a needle out slightly and reinsert into a vein for an injection of narcotics. *Cf. back up.* [U.S., JES: 1959, JBW: 1967, IGA: 1971, LVA: 1981]

back up 1. to refuse to go through with a drug transaction. The same as colloquial *back out.* [U.S., DWM: 1938] 2. to draw a little blood out of a vein as in a *verification shot* (*q.v.*) or to mix the blood with the drug bit by bit. This enables the drug user to control and prolong the *rush* (*q.v.*). See *jack off.* [U.S., M&V: 1967, RRL: 1969] 3. to use a tourniquet (or a substitute) to make a vein stand out for an injection of narcotics. [U.S., DWM: 1936, BVB: 1942]

backwards 1. a barbiturate; a depressant drug, especially a tranquilizer given to calm a person coming out of an *L.S.D.* (*q.v.*) trip. The opposite of *forwards* (*q.v.*). RT: *barbs.* [U.S., S&W: 1966, JH: 1979, ADC: 1981, LVA: 1981] 2. a drug habit which one has returned to. [U.S., RRL: 1969, W&S: 1977] 3. having to do with the state of someone who is feeling the effects of a barbiturate. [U.S., EEL: 1971]

bacon the police; a police officer. RT: *fuzz.* Based on *pig.* Black use. [U.S., ADC: 1975]

bad having to do with very good or potent drugs; having to do with anything which is powerful or intense. Bad is also used in its literal sense. The term is widely known outside the underworld and it is assumed to be of black origin. *Cf. decent, intense, primo, righteous, wicked.* [U.S., RRL: 1969, IGA: 1971, JWK: 1981]

bad acid 1. impure or low-potency *L.S.D.* (*q.v.*). RS: *blank.* [U.S., H&C: 1975] 2. peyote. Implies that peyote is a poor substitute for L.S.D. or that peyote is a very good substitute for L.S.D. Probably an error. See *bad.* RS: *peyote.* [U.S., SNP: 1977]

bad bundle a wet, overly diluted, or impure measure of heroin. *Cf. bundle.* RT: *blank.* [U.S., EEL: 1971]

bad coke inferior or heavily diluted, powdered cocaine. RT: *blank.* [U.S., JWK: 1981]

bad craziness serious negative effects from drug use. Compare to *good sick*. [U.S., JH: 1979]

bad dope very good dope. See *bad*. [U.S., RRL: 1969]

bad go a bad drug deal; low-quality drugs or inferior drugs. RT: *blank*. [U.S., HB: 1955, EEL: 1971]

bad grass phencyclidine, *P.C.P.* (*q.v.*), an animal tranquilizer. *Bad* (*q.v.*) = good. *Cf.* *supergrass, superweed*. RT: *P.C.P.* [U.S., NIDA: 1980]

bad green badly-cured marijuana which has bad effects on users. RS: *blank*. In *On The Road*, by Jack Kerouac. [JK: 1957]

bador* *ololiuqui* (*q.v.*), a hallucinogenic compound derived from morning glory seeds. Said to be an Aztec word for *little children*. [U.S., RRL: 1969, YKB: 1977]

bad scene a *setting* (*q.v.*) for an L.S.D. trip which will lead to a bad experience. *Cf.* *acid scene*. The expression has referred to any type of bad situation since the 1950s. [U.S., S&W: 1966, EEL: 1971, JWK: 1981]

bad seed (also **the bad seed**) peyote cactus. RS: *peyote*. [U.S., RRL: 1969, IGA: 1971]

bad shape, in (also **in a bad way**) alcohol intoxicated. GEN: sick; injured. [U.S., BVB: 1942]

bad trip a bad experience with a drug, usually, the hallucinogenic drug *L.S.D.* (*q.v.*). *Cf.* *trip*. Has become widely used for any bad experience. Compare to *good trip*. [U.S., RRL: 1969, EEL: 1971, DCCU: 1972, W&F: 1975] Slang terms for a bad drug experience: *bad trip, bum bend, bum kicks, bummer, bum trip, burn trip, downer, down trip, drag, freak-out, horrors, low, negative, panic trip, trip*.

bag 1. a bag, folded paper, balloon, condom, or coin envelope containing drugs. Usually refers to a bag of heroin or a plastic bag of marijuana. A smaller portion is a *half bag* (*q.v.*). RS: *load*. [U.S., W&F: 1967, G&B: 1969, EEL: 1971, DNE: 1973, MA: 1973, MW: 1976, EAF: 1980, JWK: 1981] 2. any drug at all as in the question *What's your bag?* = What kind of drug do you prefer? [U.S., RRL: 1969] 3. to package marijuana or powdered drugs in bags. *Cf.* *cap*. [U.S., EEL: 1971, IGA: 1971] 4. a dose, ration, or supply of drugs regardless of how the substance is packaged. [U.S., W&F: 1967, RRL: 1969, ADC: 1981] 5. to buy drugs. RS: *score*. [U.S., ADC: 1975]

baggage drugs; narcotics. RS: *dope*. [U.S., BVB: 1942]

bagged 1. (also **in the bag**) alcohol intoxicated. RT: *drunk*. [U.S., W&F: 1967, PE: 1980] 2. having to do with drugs sold packaged or wrapped (in clear plastic) rather than in capsules. [U.S., JWK: 1981] 3. arrested. In the way game is bagged when it is caught. RT: *busted*. [U.S., JWK: 1981]

baggie 1. a street dealer who sells only small amounts in plastic bags. RS: *dealer*. [U.S., JH: 1979] 2. a plastic food storage bag of marijuana. RT: *load*. [U.S., (1967): ELA: 1982]

bag, in the drunk. See *bagged*. [U.S., AP: 1980, PE: 1980, BW: 1984]

bag lady (also **bag woman**) a female drug seller. *Cf. bagman*. RT: *dealer*. [U.S., W&F: 1975]

bagman a drug supplier or seller; a drug pusher. *Cf. bag lady*. RT: *dealer*. There are numerous additional specific meanings in underworld jargon. [U.S., TRG: 1968, RRL: 1969, EEL: 1971, W&F: 1975]

bagman's blood cheap red wine. RS: *wine*. [Aust., SJB: 1966]

bag of beer a quart of beer. *Cf. bucket of beer* (at *bucket of suds*). RT: *beer*. [Br., JRW: 1909]

bail of hay a large quantity of marijuana. Bail = *bale* (*q.v.*). RS: *load*. [U.S., G&B: 1969]

baked 1. alcohol intoxicated. See list at *cooked*. RT: *drunk*. [U.S., ADC: 1975] 2. drug intoxicated. *Cf. fried*. RT: *stoned*. [U.S., ADC: 1981, ADC: 1984]

baking soda base *free base* made with baking soda rather than ether as a solvent. [U.S., ELA: 1984]

bala* a capsule of *Seconal* (TM; *q.v.*) barbiturate. Spanish for ball, bullet. *Cf. bullet*. RT: *barbs*. [U.S., SNP: 1977]

balderdash an unpleasant mixture of different kinds of drink; adulterated or inferior drink. RS: *rotgut*. Also means a mixture of anything, and is used as an exclamation. [(1611): OED, BE: 1690, FG: 1823, B&L: 1890; listed in BVB: 1942]

bald face (also **bald-face whiskey**) inferior, home-brewed whiskey; strong whiskey. Probably refers to whiskey in bottles with no labels. RT: *moonshine*. [U.S., (1840): OEDS, B&L: 1890, BVB: 1942, D&D: 1957]

baldfaced having to do with undiluted liquor. RT: *neat*. [listed in F&H (at *neat*)]

bale (also **bale of hay**) a large amount of marijuana; a kilogram of marijuana or hashish. RS: *load*. [U.S., RRL: 1969, EEL: 1971, D&B: 1978]

ball 1. a wild party; a drinking bout. RT: *spree*. Now refers to any good time. [U.S., W&F: 1960, S&W: 1966, TRG: 1968, M&J: 1975] 2. a drink of liquor. Similar to *highball*. RT: *nip*. [listed in F&H, BVB: 1942] 3. to absorb drugs through the genitals, specifically the vagina. Usually refers to cocaine or amphetamines. From *ball* = to copulate. [U.S., JTD: 1971, W&F: 1975] 4. to nod off or enjoy heroin or other drugs. [U.S., JWK: 1981]

ball-dozed alcohol intoxicated. A pun mixing *ball* (*q.v.*) = drink, and *bulldozed* = a beating administered with a cowhide strap. *Cf.*

bulldozed. RT: *drunk*. [Aust., SJB: 1943]

ball of fire brandy; a snifter of brandy. GEN: a dynamic person; a powerful, burning food or drink. RT: *brandy*. [Br., FG: 1823, F&H, DSUE; listed in BVB: 1942]

balloon 1. a balloon, condom, or finger stall into which a drug, usually heroin, is packed for swallowing, concealing in the rectum, or in the vagina. In the plural, heroin in general. Now used for cocaine and other powdered drugs. Sometimes *balloon* is used in print as a euphemism for *condom*. See *body-packing*. [U.S., GS: 1959, M&V: 1967, RRL: 1969, EEL: 1971, W&F: 1975] 2. to put heroin into balloons. *Cf. bag*. [U.S., D&B: 1970c] 3. a saloon. Rhyming slang. See *balloon car*.

balloon car (also **balloon**) a saloon bar, a fancy public bar. Rhyming slang. RS: *bar*. [Br., late 18-1900s, DRS]

balloon juice soda water; aerated water. This term is also slang for gas. [Br., mid 1800s, JRW: 1909]

balloon juice lowerer a total abstainer from liquor. LIT: a soda water drinker. RT: *dry*. Contrived slang. [Br., JRW: 1909]

balloon room a place where people gather to smoke marijuana. Because one gets high there. *Cf. balloon*. RT: *pad*. [U.S., DB: 1944, W&F: 1960]

balloons See *balloon*.

balm of Gilead (also **balm**) illicit whiskey; beverage alcohol. *Cf. alleviator*. RT: *booze*. [U.S., JWC: 1905, MHW: 1934, BVB: 1942]

balmy alcohol intoxicated. GEN: crazy, giddy. *Cf. balm, balm of Gilead*. RT: *drunk*. [U.S., (1850): DAE; listed in BVB: 1942]

balot* opium; heroin. Possibly from Spanish *balota*, a small ball used in voting, i.e., a ballot. This may refer to pellets of opium or heroin capsules. [U.S., SNP: 1977]

bam 1. amphetamines. RT: *amps*. From Spanish *bombita* = little bomb. [U.S., RRL: 1969, CM: 1970, EEL: 1971, JWK: 1981] 2. a mixture of barbiturates (b-) and amphetamines (-am). The etymology is probably apocryphal. RT: *set*. [U.S., EEL: 1971, W&F: 1975] See also *bams*.

bambalacha* (also **bambalache***) marijuana. Probably from Spanish. RT: *pot*. [U.S., RPW: 1938, M&V: 1954]

bambalacha rambler a marijuana smoker. RT: *toker*. [U.S., (1937): JES: 1959, H&C: 1975]

bambalache* marijuana. See *bambalacha*.

bambinos amphetamine capsules. Possibly a translation of *jelly babies* (*q.v.*). Possibly from **bombita** (*q.v.*). RT: *amps*. [U.S., D&D: 1966]

bambita* amphetamine capsules; methamphetamine in ampules. The same as *bombita* (*q.v.*). RS: *amps, speed*. [U.S., ADC: 1975, H&C: 1975]

bamboo 1. an opium pipe. The stem of a Chinese opium pipe is made of bamboo. RT: *hop stick.* [U.S., (1920): DU, DWM: 1936, VJM: 1949, GOL: 1950] 2. an opium smoker; an opium addict. RT: *campfire boy.* [U.S., BVB: 1942, VJM: 1949] See also *suck bamboo.*

bamboo juice rice wine sold in "bottles" made of bamboo segments. RS: *booze.* [U.S., WWII, W&F: 1960]

bamboo-puffer an opium smoker; an opium addict. RT: *campfire boy.* [U.S., (c. 1890): JES: 1959, BVB: 1942, DU]

bamboozled 1. alcohol intoxicated. GEN: confused. RT: *drunk.* College use. [U.S., BHH: 1856] 2. addicted to drugs. RT: *hooked.* [U.S., JES: 1959, H&C: 1975]

bambs barbiturates. See *bam.* RT: *barbs.* [U.S., C&H: 1974]

Bambu a brand of cigarette rolling papers. Used in making marijuana cigarettes. RT: *paper.* [U.S., (1950s): ELA: 1982, RRL: 1969]

bameba (also **ba-me-ba, bamidy-bam, bomb-ne-bomb**) beer brewed in Saigon and drunk during the Vietnamese War. From the Vietnamese word for "33," the trademark of the beer. RT: *beer.* [U.S. military, Vietnamese War, DST: 1984]

bammy (also **bammies**) marijuana; a marijuana cigarette; inferior marijuana. Probably from *bambalacha* (*q.v.*). RT: *pot.* [U.S., (1954): DUS, RDS: 1982]

bams 1. amphetamines; amphetamine capsules. See *bam.* 2. (also **bambs**) barbiturate capsules; 15 mg capsules of pentobarbital (SNP: 1977). *Cf. yellow bams* (at *yellow angels*). RT: *barbs.* [U.S., SNP: 1977] 3. a mixture of a stimulant and a depressant, an amphetamine and barbiturate. See *bam.* RS: *set.* [U.S., EEL: 1971, W&F: 1975] 4. marijuana cigarettes; weak marijuana cigarettes. RS: *joint.* [U.S., M&H: 1959]

Banana a trade name for a cigarette rolling paper for making marijuana cigarettes. RT: *paper.* [U.S., ELA: 1984]

banana splits ampules of *amyl nitrite* (*q.v.*). Named for the odor of the substance. RT: *snapper.* [U.S., BR: 1972]

banana with cheese a marijuana cigarette doctored with *free base.* RS: *set.* [U.S., ELA: 1984]

Ban Apple a trade name for *amyl nitrite.* RS: *snapper.* [U.S., ELA: 1984]

B. and S. brandy and soda. RT: *brandy.* Colloquial rather than slang. [Br., (1868): F&H; listed in BVB: 1942, D&D: 1957]

bane, the brandy. A play on *ruin* (DSUE). See *blue ruin.* RT: *brandy.* [18-1900s, DSUE]

Banette a hypodermic syringe. From the brand name of a hypodermic syringe. RT: *monkey pump.* [U.S., H&C: 1975]

banewort *belladonna* (*q.v.*) [U.S., YKB: 1977]

bang 1. the potency of the alcohol in liquor; the effect of potent liquor. [U.S., BVB: 1942] 2. an injection of a drug, especially morphine or heroin. RT: *shot*. [U.S., DWM: 1936, BD: 1937, VJM: 1949, GOL: 1950, W&F: 1960, RRL: 1969, CM: 1970, EEL: 1971] 3. to inject a drug. RT: *shoot*. [U.S., (1920s): DU, DWM: 1938, M&D: 1952, W&F: 1960, RRL: 1969, DCCU: 1972] 4. a dose or ration of a drug; a fix. RS: *load*. [U.S., PRB: 1930, MHW: 1934] 5. a puff of a marijuana cigarette. *Cf. hit*. RT: *toke*. [U.S., 1900s, (1929): OEDS] 7. a snort of cocaine. [U.S., CM: 1970, RDS: 1982] 8. the *rush* (*q.v.*) after an injection of drugs into a vein; any drug rush. RS: *rush*. [U.S., A&T: 1953, M&V: 1954] 9. the flowering tops of the marijuana plant. The same as *bhang* (*q.v.*). [U.S., JES: 1959]

bang a pitcher to drain a drinking vessel or pot. One bangs it when one sets it down empty. RT: *irrigate*. [Br., 18–1900s, DSUE]

bang a reefer to smoke a marijuana cigarette. *Cf. bang*. RT: *hit the hay*. [U.S., GOL: 1950, A&T: 1953]

banged up to the eyes alcohol intoxicated. RT: *drunk*. [U.S., BVB: 1942]

banger a hypodermic syringe. Used to *bang* (*q.v.*) (= inject) drugs. RT: *monkey pump*. [U.S., GOL: 1950]

banging taking heroin; injecting heroin. *Cf. bang*. [U.S., M&D: 1952]

bang in the arm an injection of narcotics. RT: *shot*. [U.S., DWM: 1936, BVB: 1942]

bang room (also **bing room**) a place where drugs are used; a place where drugs are injected. *Cf. bang*. RS: *pad*. [U.S., (1931): DU]

bangster one who injects drugs; a mainline drug addict. *Cf. bang*. [U.S., (1917): JES: 1959, (1929): OEDS, PRB: 1930, GOL: 1950, A&T: 1953] The following list includes terms for drug users and addicts who inject drugs of any type, in any fashion: *artillery man, bangster, barb freak, booter, boot man, channel swimmer, cotton shooter, gutter, hit man, hype, hypo, hypo juggler, hypo smecker, jab artist, jabber, jab-popper, junkie, keek, liner, mainliner, mainline shooter, needle fiend, needle freak, needle jabber, needle knight, needle man, needle nipper, needle pusher, oiler, pinch hitter, pinhead, pleasure shooter, pricked-arm, prodder, railroader, safety pin mechanic, sharp shooter, shooter, skinner, skin-popper, skin-shooter, speed freak, speedhead, straight shooter, vein-shooter, V.S.*

bang up to inject oneself with a drug; to inject a drug to support one's addiction. See *bang*. RT: *shoot*. [U.S., early 1900s, DU]

banjaxed alcohol intoxicated. GEN: demolished, ruined (HSD: 1984). RT: *drunk*. [PD: 1982]

banji marijuana. A type grown in the Middle East. RT: *pot*.

[U.S., D&B: 1978, RDS: 1982] See also ***ganji*** at ***ganga***.

bank bandit pills (also **bank bandits**) barbiturates or depressant capsules. RT: ***barbs***. [U.S., RRL: 1969, LVA: 1981]

baptized (also **baptised**) **1**. having to do with an alcoholic drink which has been diluted with water. VJM: 1949 lists **baptized booze**. *Cf.* ***christen***. RS: ***cut***. The string of citations is a classic example of the way cant material has been copied from one source to another down through the ages. [(1636): OED, FG: 1785, FG: 1823, GWM: 1859; listed in MHW: 1934, RDS: 1982] **2**. alcohol intoxicated; saturated with alcohol. RT: ***drunk***. Probably nonce. [U.S., S&E: 1981]

bar 1. any raised counter over which liquor is sold or served; the room or entire establishment in which a liquor-serving counter is located. A special sense of bar meaning barrier. Now standard English. [since the late 1500s, (1592): OED] (This entry continues after the following list.) See ***sly grogshop*** for illegal shops. See ***speak*** for prohibition speakeasies. See ***dive*** for low and unsavory drinking establishments. This list includes places where liquor is sold by the drink: *after-hours spot, balloon, balloon car, bar, barbecue, barley bar, bar parlour, barrelhouse, battle cruiser, bazaar, beeratorium, beer barrel, beer cellar, beer flat, beer garden, beer hall, beer joint, beer mill, beer parlor, beer stube, beertorium, benzinery, bevvy-ken, Bierstube, bistro, blind pig, blind tiger, blue pig, boose-casa, boosing-ken, booze benderie, booze-casa, booze crib, booze foundry, booze joint, boozer, boozerie, boozery, booze shunter, boozeteria, boozing-ken, bottle factory, bottle joint, brass rail, break o' day drum, bubbery, bub factory, bub joint, bucket shop, budge ken, budging-ken, bunch of grapes, canteen, cash bar, clinic, club, cocktail lounge, comfort station, confectionary, creep dive, creep joint, cross-drum, deadfall, deadhouse, dive, diving bell, doggery, drinkateria, drinkatorium, drink den, drinkery, drum, drunkery, filling station, fillmill, flash case, flash drum, flash ken, fuddle factory, gargle factory, gashouse, gin dive, gin flat, gin mill, ginnery, gin palace, grocery, groggery, grog mill, grogshop, gut bucket, guzzery, guzzle crib, guzzlery, guzzle shop, halfway house, happy shop, honka-tonk, honky-tonk, hoocherie, hooch house, hop joint, hotel, hurdy-gurdy, hush-house, hushie, hush joint, imbibery, inkpot, Jack Tar, jimmy, jinny, joint, joker, jook, jook house, juice-joint, juke-joint, key club, leggery, leg joint, little church round the corner, lounge, low talk, lush crib, lush dive, lush drum, lushery, lush house, lushing crib, lushing ken, lush ken, lush panny, marijuana bar, mooch joint, moonlight inn, moonshinery, mop-up, mug house, near and far, nineteenth hole, oasis, o-be-joyful works, open bar, patter crib, pig, piss factory, pub, public, public bar, public house, Q.T., red nugget, red onion, refreshery, roadhouse, rub-a, rub-a-dub, rub-a-dub-dub, rubbedy, rubbity, rum house, rummery, rum mill, rum shop, saloon, scatter, schooner, shanty, shebang, shebeen, shinery, shock joint, shoe* *polish shop, shypoo, shypoo joint, shypook, shypoo shop, skee joint, sluice house, sluicery, sly groggery, sly grog joint, sly grogshop, smoke joint, sneakeasy, sneaker, sneakery, sneakie, sotto voce parlor, speak, speakeasy, speaker, speaketeria, speakie, spot, spun joint, suck casa, suck crib, sudsery, suds joint, tap, tappeteria, tap room, there you are, thirst-aid station, Tom and Jerry shop, walloper, water hole, watering hole, watering place, whiskey hole, whiskey house, whiskey joint, whiskey mill, whisper joint, whisper low, whisper parlor.* 2. a solid brick of marijuana or hashish held together with sugar or honey. [U.S., (1967): ELA: 1982, G&B: 1969, EEL: 1971, JWK: 1981]

barb 1. a hypodermic needle with a bent or barbed point; a dull hypodermic needle. *Cf. blunt.* RS: *needle.* [U.S., RRL: 1969, H&C: 1975] 2. barbiturates; a barbiturate capsule. See *barbs.*

barbecue 1. a place where illegal booze is sold in secret. An elaboration of *bar.* RT: *sly grogshop.* [U.S., AH: 1931, MHW: 1934] 2. a fatal injection of narcotics. The same as *hot shot* (*q.v.*). [U.S., S&W: 1973]

barbed wire See *barbwire.*

barber's cat an emaciated opium addict. GEN: a sickly person (British). There are numerous other slang meanings. RT: *junky.* [U.S., (1936): DU]

barb freak a barbiturate user; one who habitually uses alcohol and barbiturates together; someone who injects barbiturates. RS: *user.* [U.S., M&V: 1973, YKB: 1977, LVA: 1981]

Barbidex a combination of amphetamines and barbiturates. RS: *set.* [Br., BTD: 1968; U.S., RDS: 1982]

Barbie doll (also **barbies**) a barbiturate tablet or capsule. A play on *barb* = barbiturate. *Dolls* (*q.v.*) = pills. *Cf. Ken doll.* RT: *barbs.* [U.S., JH: 1979, HSD: 1984]

barbitone a hypnotic drug similar to the barbiturates. *Cf. Veronal.* [(1914): OEDS]

barbiturate a chemical substance which is derived from barbituric acid. The drug is used as a sedative and a hypnotic. It is a central nervous system depressant. See a list of slang and jargon terms at *barbs.* [U.S., (1928): OEDS]

barbitúrico* barbiturates. RT: *barbs.* From Spanish. [U.S., (NIDA: 1980)]

barbs barbiturates; barbiturate capsules. [U.S., JBW: 1967, RRL: 1969, EEL: 1971, DCCU: 1972, W&F: 1975, YKB: 1977, (DNE: 1980), NIDA: 1980, JWK: 1981] Nicknames and slang terms for barbiturates: *abbot, alocados, amarilla, amies, Amytal, apple, aprobarbs, avispa, azulillos, backwards, bala, bam, bambs, bams, bank bandit pills, bank bandits, Barbie doll, barbies, barbitúrico, barbs, blockbuster, blue, bluebirds, blue bullets, blue clouds, blue devils, blue dolls, blue dots, blue heavens, blue horse, blue jackets,* *blues, blue tips, blue velvet, blunt, bomber, border, border red, brain tickler, bullet, bullethead, busters, Canadian bouncer, canary, candy, cardenales, Christmas roll, Christmas tree, colorado, courage pill, damps, devil, diablo rojas, dolls, double-blue, double-trouble, down, downer, downie, downs, dreamer, fender-benders, F-forties, forties, gangster pills, G.B., goofball, goofers, gorilla pills, green dragon, gumdrop, hors d'oeuvres, idiot pills, jacket, jack-ups, ju-ju, juju, Ken doll, King Kong pills, King Kong special, lay-back, lillys, Luminal, M and Ms, maní, marshmallow reds, Mexican jumping beans, Mexican red, muscle relaxer, neb, nebbies, nem, nemb, nembies, Nembutal, nemish, nemishes, nemmie, nimbie, nimbles, nimby, pa'abajos, pájaro azul, peanuts, phenies, phennies, phenobarb, phenobarbital, phenos, pink ladies, pinks, prescription reds, pula, purple hearts, purple passion, rainbows, R.D., red, red and blues, redbirds, red bullets, red devils, red dolls, red jackets, red lillys, reds, rojas, rojita, roll of reds, round head, sec, seccies, seccy, secky, Seconal, secs, seggies, seggy, sex, sleepers, sleeping pills, softballs, stoms, stoppers, stum, stumble-bumbles, stumblers, stumbles, stums, suckonal, T., thrill-pills, tooeys, tooies, tooles, toolies, tootsie, trues, tuies, Tuinal, tus, twos, Veronal, whites, yakenal, yellow, yellow angels, yellow bams, yellow birds, yellow bullets, yellow dolls, yellow jackets, yellows, yukenal, 40s.*

bar-bug one who frequents bars; a *bar-fly* (*q.v.*). RS: *sot.* [U.S., D&D: 1966]

barbwire (also **barbed wire**) any strong whiskey. RT: *rotgut.* [U.S., D&D: 1957]

bare-footed having to do with undiluted beverage alcohol. *Cf. naked.* RT: *neat.* [Br., B&L: 1890, F&H]

bar-fly 1. a person who frequents bars. *Cf. bar-bug.* [U.S., (1910): DA, (1928): W&F: 1960] 2. a drunkard. RT: *sot.* [U.S., BVB: 1942, VJM: 1949, W&F: 1960]

barhopping going from bar to bar, drinking at each one. See *pub-crawl.* [U.S., D&D: 1966, HSD: 1984]

barkeep 1. to tend a bar; to act as bartender. [MHW: 1934, BVB: 1942] 2. someone who serves drinks at a bar. RT: *bartender.* [U.S., (1712): MW: 1983, (1846): DA]

barley beer. *Cf. oil of barley.* RT: *beer.* [Br., 1800s, F&H; U.S., BVB: 1942, DC: 1972] See also *oil of barley.*

barley bar a beer joint; a beer parlor. RS: *bar.* [U.S., BVB: 1942]

barley-bree a strong alcoholic drink such as scotch whiskey or ale. Scots for *barley-brew.* [(1786): OED, (Robert Burns)]

barley broth strong ale or beer. RT: *ale, beer.* [(1593): OED; listed in BVB: 1942]

barley-corn beer or ale in *Sir John Barleycorn* (*q.v.*).

barley juice beer. *Cf. barley broth.* RT: *beer.* [U.S., BVB: 1942]

barley pop beer. *Pop* (*q.v.*) = a carbonated drink. RT: *beer.* CB radio slang. [U.S., EE: 1976]

barley sick alcohol intoxicated. RT: *drunk*. [OED, BVB: 1942]

barley wagon a beer truck. Citizens band radio slang. [U.S., AP: 1980]

barley water beer. A play on the term for a weak broth made from barley. RT: *beer*. [U.S., BVB: 1942]

barley wine a high-quality and potent beer. RT: *beer*. [U.S., BVB: 1942]

barmaid a female bartender or bartender's helper; a waitress in a drinking establishment. RT: *bartender*. [since the 1600s, (1658): MW: 1983]

barman a male bartender. RT: *bartender*. [since the early 1800s, (1837): OED]

barmecide morphine. From *Barmecide,* the name of a character in *The Arabian Nights*. The original term has nothing to do with *-cide* = kill. RT: *morphine*. [U.S., JES: 1959, H&C: 1975]

barmy alcohol intoxicated. From an older slang use = slightly crazy. RT: *drunk*. [U.S., BVB: 1942]

barnecide Probably an error for or a (foreign) dialect pronunciation of *Barmecide* (*q.v.*), the name of a character in *The Arabian Nights*. [U.S., SNP: 1977]

bar of soap (also **bars of soap**) dope; drugs. Rhyming slang. RS: *dope*. [(1940): DRS, A&T: 1953]

bar parlour a saloon bar; the well-appointed public bar in a drinking establishment. RS: *bar*. [Br., (1876): OED]

bar-polisher a drunkard. Someone who keeps the bar polished by using it. RT: *sot*. [U.S., BVB: 1942]

barrel 1. to drink to excess. RT: *guzzle*. [U.S., GI: 1931, MHW: 1934] 2. a drunkard. *Cf. tank*. RT: *sot*. [U.S., BVB: 1942] 3. (usually **barrels**) *L.S.D.* (*q.v.*) in tablet form. RT: *L.S.D.* [U.S., EEL: 1971, YKB: 1977]

barrel bum See *barrelhouse bum*.

barrel dosser a drunkard; a frequenter of a *barrelhouse*. Dosser = sleeper, one who sleeps (in a place). RT: *sot*. [U.S., EK: 1927, GI: 1931]

barreled (also **barreled up**) alcohol intoxicated. RT: *drunk*. [U.S., W&F: 1960, HSD: 1984]

barrel fever 1. drunkenness. *Cf. have barrel fever*. [U.S., MHW: 1934, BVB: 1942] 2. a hangover; sickness from a bout of drinking. [B&L: 1890, MHW: 1934] 3. the delirium tremens. RT: *D.T.s*. [FG: 1811, FG: 1823, GWM: 1859, F&H, GI: 1931, SJB: 1943, VJM: 1949]

barrel goods beverage alcohol; home-brewed alcohol; prohibition alcohol. *Cf. dry goods*. RS: *booze*. From the prohibition era. [U.S., VR: 1929, AH: 1931]

barrelhouse 1. a cheap saloon; a place where beer is sold from the barrel; any saloon. RT: *dive*. [U.S., (1882): SBF: 1976, JSF: 1889, EK: 1927, AH: 1931, HS: 1933, VJM: 1949, GOL: 1950, CM: 1970] 2. a place where illegal beverage alcohol is manufactured and sold by the barrel. RS: *sly grogshop*. [U.S., GOL: 1950]

barrelhouse bum (also **barrel bum, barrelhouse stiff, barrel stiff**) a vagrant drunkard; a wino; any drunkard. The type of drinker who is found in a *barrelhouse* (*q.v.*). RT: *sot*. [U.S., (1920): W&F: 1960, CS: 1927, EK: 1927, VJM: 1949]

barrelhouse drunk alcohol intoxicated; very drunk. RT: *drunk*. [U.S., GI: 1931, BVB: 1942]

barrels the hallucinogenic drug *L.S.D.* (*q.v.*). See *barrel*.

bartarian someone who sells and serves liquor at a bar. *Cf. fermentarian*. RT: *bartender*. Contrived slang, never in wide usage. [U.S., BVB: 1942]

bartender one who tends a bar; someone who serves liquor at a bar. Standard English. [since the early 1800s, (1836): DA] Terms for someone who sells and serves liquor by the drink: *ale draper, apron, barkeep, barmaid, barman, bartarian, bartender, beer jerker, beer-jugger, beer slinger, beertender, beggar maker, blind pigger, booze fencer, booze heister, booze pusher, brother bung, bung, bung starter, dive-keeper, draper, drinkologist, fizzical culturalist, gin miller, jigger boy, mixer, mixologist, pour man, pour-out man, publican, saloonist, skinker, tapster, tapstress, tippler*.

base See *free base*.

baseballing (also **basing, free basing**) using *free base* (*q.v.*), a highly-purified form of cocaine. [U.S., RAS: 1978]

base binge a session or *run* spent using *free base*. [U.S., ELA: 1984]

base burner a drink of whiskey. RT: *nip*. [U.S., (1850-1900): RFA]

baseman someone who is using *free base*, i.e., "on base." Part of a set of words on the theme of baseball. A **first baseman** gets the first use of the *free base*, then the **second baseman**, etc. RT: *user*. [U.S., ELA: 1984]

bash 1. a drinking bout; any wild party; a night on the town. RT: *spree*. To get drunk is to go **on the bash** in New Zealand. [Aust., Canadian, and U.S., DSUE, D&D: 1957, W&F: 1960, SJB: 1966] 2. marijuana. Possibly an error. *Cf. bush*. RT: *pot*. [U.S., IGA: 1971, WCM: 1972]

bashed alcohol intoxicated. GEN: crushed, struck. RT: *drunk*. [U.S., D&D: 1973]

bashings cigarette makings, finely-cut tobacco and rolling papers. RT: *freckles*. [Aust. military, SJB: 1966]

bash the turps to go on a drinking spree. *Cf. on the turps*. RS:

irrigate. [Aust., SJB: 1945]

basing See *baseballing*, *free basing*.

basketballs 250 mg capsules of *Placidyl* (TM; *q.v.*). RT: *plass*. [U.S., JWK: 1981]

bass 1. (usually **Bass**) a brand name of a British ale. RT: *ale*. [since the mid 1800s, SOD] 2. a bottle (fifth) of hard liquor. Bigger than a *bream* (*q.v.*) or a *perch* (*q.v.*). College slang. [U.S., GU: 1975]

bass attack a beer or ale drinking bout. From Bass (brand) ale, punning on *gas attack*. RT: *spree*. [Aust. military, WWI, WHD: 1919, cited in SJB: 1966]

bast an error for *blast* (*q.v.*) [U.S., H&C: 1975]

basted 1. alcohol intoxicated. A play on *sauce* (*q.v.*) and *saturated* (*q.v.*). See *cooked* for a list of cooking terms meaning drunk. RT: *drunk*. [U.S., MP: 1928, MHW: 1934, W&F: 1960] 2. drug intoxicated. RT: *stoned*. [U.S., ADC: 1975]

bat 1. a drinking bout. From *batter*. *Cf. on a bat*. RT: *spree*. [U.S., (1848): DAE, F&H, MHW: 1934, EEL: 1971] 2. a drunkard; a person on a spree. From sense one. RT: *sot*. [U.S., BVB: 1942] 3. a fat marijuana cigarette. Compares the cigarette to a baseball bat. RT: *joint*. [U.S., ADC: 1975]

batch a drinking bout; a great intake of alcohol. Probably from *bat* (*q.v.*). RT: *spree*. [Br., FG: 1823]

bathtub gin inferior and illegal, homemade gin during the prohibition era. RS: *gin*. The term is still known. [U.S., BVB: 1942, D&D: 1957]

bato marijuano* a marijuana-smoker (male); a marijuana-smoking thug. RT: *toker*. From Spanish. [U.S., EEL: 1971, RDS: 1982]

bat, on a on a drinking bout; on a drinking tirade. *Cf. bat*. RT: *spreeing*. [U.S., (1848): SBF: 1976, AH: 1931, W&F: 1960, DCCU: 1972]

bato narco* a drug user (male). RT: *user*. Spanish. [U.S., EEL: 1971, RDS: 1982]

bats 1. (also **batty**) alcohol intoxicated; confused and drunk. GEN: crazy. RT: *drunk*. [U.S., BVB: 1942] 2. the delirium tremens. Akin to *bats in the belfry*. RT: *D.T.s*. [U.S., DU, VJM: 1949]

batster a person (usually male) on a drinking bout; a habitual drunkard. *Cf. bat*. RT: *sot*. [U.S., BVB: 1942]

batted 1. alcohol intoxicated. RT: *drunk*. [U.S., BVB: 1942] 2. (also **batted out**) arrested. RT: *busted*. [U.S., M&V: 1954]

batter a spree. See *on the batter*.

battered alcohol intoxicated. In the same class as *bashed*, *blasted*, *crashed*, *fractured*, *smashed*. *Cf. batter*. RT: *drunk*. [U.S., (c. 1848): SBF: 1976, BHH: 1856, F&H, BVB: 1942]

batter, on the alcohol intoxicated; on a binge. RT: *drunk*. [(1839): OEDS]

battle cruiser a bar; a *pub* (*q.v.*). Rhyming slang for *boozer* (*q.v.*). RS: *bar*. [HSD: 1984]

batty (also **bats**) alcohol intoxicated; drunk and crazy. GEN: crazy. RT: *drunk*. [U.S., BVB: 1942]

bawdy-house-bottle a small liquor or beer bottle. [cant, BE: 1690, FG: 1785]

bayonet a hypodermic syringe; a hypodermic needle. The metaphor is obvious and it is supported by *Bay State* (*q.v.*), or *Banette* (*q.v.*). RT: *monkey pump*. [U.S., JES: 1959, H&C: 1975]

bay, over the alcohol intoxicated. *Cf. anchored in Sot's Bay, half seas over*. RT: *drunk*. [U.S., (1830): SBF: 1976]

Bay State a hypodermic syringe, the brand name of a hypodermic syringe used generically. Uses a screw-on needle. RT: *monkey pump*. [U.S., DWM: 1936, A&T: 1953]

bazaar a bar in a pub. Rhyming slang. RS: *bar*. [Br., late 18-1900s, DRS]

B.B. 1. (also **B.B.s**) a "blue bomber," a 10 mg tablet of Valium. RT: *vals*. [U.S., RAS: 1977] 2. "base burnout," debilitation from the excessive use of *free base*. [U.S., ELA: 1984]

B-bomb 1. a *Benzedrine* (TM; *q.v.*) inhaler, a device for inhaling Benzedrine. RT: *benz*. [U.S., RRL: 1969, EEL: 1971] 2. in the plural, amphetamines in general. Possibly a play on *A-bomb* (*q.v.*). RT: *amps*. [U.S., NIDA: 1980]

bead moonshine whiskey; beverage alcohol; an alcoholic drink. This liquor makes many small bubbles or beads when shaken. [Br., 1800s, F&H; U.S., HK: 1917, BVB: 1942]

beam, on the (also **beaming**) under the effects of marijuana; set straight by marijuana use. Alludes to a pilot flying on a radio beacon. RT: *wasted*. [U.S., TRG: 1968, D&B: 1978]

bean See *beans*.

beaned up *high* (*q.v.*) on amphetamines. *Cf. beans*. [U.S., MT: 1971]

beaners (also **beans**) amphetamines; amphetamine capsules. *Cf. jelly beans*. RT: *amps*. [U.S., ADC: 1981]

beanhead (also **bean head**) a drug user who uses pills habitually. The same as *pillhead* (*q.v.*). See the list at *head*. RT: *user*. [U.S., M&V: 1973]

beano a drinking bout; any spree. Probably from *beanfest* which is a general term for a celebration. RT: *spree*. [Br., 18-1900s, SOD, DSUE, M&J: 1975; listed in BVB: 1942]

beans 1. capsules of *Benzedrine* (TM; *q.v.*). Probably punning on *benz* (*q.v.*). RT: *benz*. [U.S., M&V: 1967, EEL: 1971] 2. capsules of any amphetamine. *Cf. jelly beans*. RT: *amps*. [U.S., SH: 1972,

YKB: 1977, EAF: 1980, NIDA: 1980] 3. capsules of *Methedrine* (TM; *q.v.*). RT: *speed*. [U.S., ADC: 1975] 4. capsules of mescaline. RS: *peyote*. [U.S., YKB: 1977, NIDA: 1980] 5. any capsules of a drug. *Cf. juice and beans*. [U.S., TRG: 1968]

bean trip intoxication from *Benzedrine* (TM; *q.v.*); a sustained high from Benzedrine, possibly with hallucinations. *Cf. beans*. [U.S., M&V: 1967, H&C: 1975]

beanup a drug user who habitually uses *Methedrine* (TM; *q.v.*). *Cf. bean, beanhead*. [U.S., ADC: 1975]

bear a capsule of a drug. Possibly an error for *bean* (*q.v.*). [U.S., W&F: 1975]

beargered alcohol intoxicated. RT: *drunk*. [Br., JCH: 1859, B&L: 1890, F&H; listed in BVB: 1942]

bearing the ensign alcohol intoxicated. See *ensign-bearer*. RT: *drunk*. [U.S., BVB: 1942]

beast, the 1. alcohol; liquor in general. *Cf. creature*. [U.S., BVB: 1942] 2. (also **beast**) the hallucinogenic drug *L.S.D.* (*q.v.*). RT: *L.S.D.* [U.S., JBW: 1967, YKB: 1977, NIDA: 1980, KBH: 1982]

beat 1. having to do with counterfeit or bogus drugs. [U.S., RRL: 1969] 2. to cheat someone in a drug deal; to sell *beat* (sense one) drugs to someone. [U.S., M&V: 1967, RRL: 1969, MA: 1973, JWK: 1981] 3. having to do with marijuana ashes or marijuana after the smokable substance is exhausted. GEN: exhausted (M&W: 1946). *Cf. cashed*. [U.S., ADC: 1975, ADC: 1981] 4. sick; down-and-out due to lack of drugs. Said of an addict. [U.S., M&V: 1973]

beat artist 1. an addict whose typical means of getting money to support a habit is to rob someone. *Cf. maggot*. [U.S., JWK: 1981] 2. a drug seller who sells bogus drugs. *Cf. beat*. [U.S., M&V: 1973, JWK: 1981]

beatnik (also **beater**) a (usually male) member of the youth subculture which flourished in the 1950s. Though not primarily a drug-using subculture, marijuana and some pills were used, in addition to alcohol. [U.S., (1958): OEDS, DCCU: 1972]

beat pad a place where marijuana is used; a place where bad marijuana is sold. RS: *pad*. [U.S., MB: 1938, D&D: 1957]

beat pounder a police officer who patrols on foot, i.e., one who pounds a beat (= route). Not limited to drug argot. *Cf. pounder*. RS: *fuzz*. [U.S., BVB: 1942]

beat the eight ball to use heroin; to attempt to use heroin and not get addicted. To avoid getting behind the eight ball. [U.S., EEL: 1971]

beat the gong to smoke opium. *Cf. kick the gong*. RT: *suck bamboo*. [U.S., DWM: 1936, VJM: 1949, W&F: 1960]

beat the weeds (also **beat a weed**) to smoke a tobacco cigarette. Possibly a play on *beat the bushes*. *Weed* (*q.v.*) = cigarette. [U.S.,

BVB: 1942, D&B: 1970c]

beautiful having to do with a very satisfying drug. *Cf. decent.* [U.S., JWK: 1981]

beautiful lady *belladonna* (*q.v.*). The entry word is a translation of the Italian *belladonna.* RT: *belladonna.* [U.S., YKB: 1977]

bee 1. (also B.) a matchbox of marijuana; a small measure of marijuana. RS: *load.* [U.S., G&B: 1969, EEL: 1971, W&F: 1975] 2. one's drug habit; one's drug addiction. The habit and the bee can both sting if not treated with care. See *bee that stings.* [U.S., RRL: 1969]

bee bites injection sites; scars from injections of drugs. See *bitten by white mosquitoes. Cf. tracks.* [U.S., BR: 1972]

bee-drinker a *B-girl* (*q.v.*).

been among the Philistines (also been among the Philippians) alcohol intoxicated. *Cf. philistine.* RT: *drunk.* [BF: 1737]

been at an Indian feast alcohol intoxicated. RT: *drunk.* [BF: 1737]

been at a ploughing match alcohol intoxicated. *Cf. plowed.* RT: *drunk.* [Br., 1800s, F&H]

been at Barbadoes (also been at Geneva) alcohol intoxicated; tipsy. Barbadoes (now spelled Barbados) refers to rum. *Geneva* (*q.v.*) = gin. RT: *drunk.* [BF: 1737]

been before George alcohol intoxicated. RT: *drunk.* [BF: 1737]

been bitten by a barn mouse (also been bit by a barn mouse) alcohol intoxicated. RT: *drunk.* [17–1800s, F&H]

been crooking the elbow alcohol intoxicated. *Cf. elbow-crooker.* RT: *drunk.* [Br., 1800s, F&H]

been drowning the shamrock alcohol intoxicated. A reference to Irish whiskey. RT: *drunk.* [Br., 1800s, F&H]

been flying rather high alcohol intoxicated. *Cf. high.* RT: *drunk.* [Br., 1800s, F&H]

been had arrested. GEN: cheated. RT: *busted.* [U.S., JBW: 1967, EEL: 1971]

been having the eyes opened alcohol intoxicated. *Cf. eye-opener.* RT: *drunk.* [Br., 1800s, F&H]

been in the bibbing plot alcohol intoxicated. RT: *drunk.* [BF: 1737]

been in the cellar alcohol intoxicated. Refers to drinking the alcohol stored in the cellar. See *beer cellar.* RT: *drunk.* [BF: 1737]

been in the sauce have been drinking; alcohol intoxicated. *Sauce* (*q.v.*) = liquor. RT: *drunk.* [PD: 1982]

been in the sun (also standing too long in the sun) alcohol intoxicated. RT: *drunk.* [BF: 1737, F&H, JRW: 1909, BVB:

1942]

been lapping in the gutter alcohol intoxicated. RT: *drunk*. [Br., 1800s, F&H]

been lifting the little finger alcohol intoxicated. RT: *drunk*. [Br., 1800s, F&H]

been looking through a glass alcohol intoxicated, i.e., has been looking through the bottom of a drinking glass. RT: *drunk*. [Br., 1800s, F&H; listed in BVB: 1942]

been making fun alcohol intoxicated. *Cf. funny*. RT: *drunk*. [Br., 1800s, F&H]

been on sentry alcohol intoxicated. *Cf. on sentry*. RT: *drunk*. [Br., 1800s, F&H]

been talking to Herb and Al been using marijuana and drinking alcohol. *Herb* (*q.v.*) = marijuana. Al = alcohol. [U.S., ADC: 1981]

been talking to Jamie Moore alcohol intoxicated. RT: *drunk*. [Br., 18-1900s, F&H, DSUE]

been to a funeral alcohol intoxicated. RT: *drunk*. [BF: 1737]

been to France (also been to Jericho) alcohol intoxicated. RT: *drunk*. [17-1800s, BF: 1737, DSUE] See also *been at Barbadoes, been at Geneva*.

been to Mexico have been drinking; alcohol intoxicated. RT: *drunk*. [PD: 1982]

been too free with Sir John Strawberry (also been too free with Sir Richard) alcohol intoxicated. RT: *drunk*. [BF: 1737]

been too free with the creature alcohol intoxicated. See *creature*. [BF: 1737]

been to the salt water alcohol intoxicated. See *salt, salted*. RT: *drunk*. [BF: 1737]

been trying Taylor's best alcohol intoxicated. RT: *drunk*. [Br., 1800s, F&H]

been with Sir John Goa alcohol intoxicated. RT: *drunk*. [BF: 1737]

beer 1. a light alcoholic drink made from fermented malt and hops. Not slang or jargon in this sense. [since c. 1000, OED] (This entry continues after the following list.) Nicknames and slang terms for beer: *army brew, artesian, bameba, ba-me-ba, bamidy-bam, barley, barley broth, barley-corn, barley juice, barley pop, barley water, barley wine, belch, belsh, berps, berpwater, bevie, bevvy, bevy, birra, bitter, bivvy, bock, bock beer, bomb-ne-bomb, bottled bellyache, bottled sunshine, brew, brewer's fizzle, brew-ha, brewski, brewsky, brown bottle, brown food, brown stone, bub, bumclink, bumy juice, bung juice, bunker, catch up, chalk, Charley Freer, chill, choc, clink, cold blood, cold coffee, cold sody, colonial, colonial tangle, Colorado Kool-Aid, Crimea, dimey, down, drafty,*

Dutch milk, Dutch suds, eer-bay, er-bay, far and near, foam, forty-weight, frosty, froth, gatter, German conversation water, goog, grog, gusto, heavy wet, honey, hootawater, hops, hum cap, humming bub, John Barleycorn, joy-juice, kero, ketchup, knock down, knock-me-down, koolaid, lace, lace curtain, liquid bread, loogan, lube, lush, malt, milk, muddy water, nap, nappy, near-beer, neck oil, needle beer, never fear, Oh my!, Oh my dear!, oil of barley, oyl of barley, pale, pharaoh, pharo, pig's, pig's ear, pig sweat, piss, piss-maker, pong, pongellorum, pongelo, pongelow, ponjello, porter's beer, pot of O., pot o' reeb, purge, queer-beer, red steer, reeb, rosin, sailor's champagne, shandy, sheep-dip, sheep-wash, shot beer, shypoo, Sir John Barleycorn, sissy beer, skat, skit, sloosh, slops, sludge, small beer, squaw piss, squirt, stingo, strike-me-dead, suck, suds, super-suds, swipes, swizzle, tanglefoot, tangleleg, taps, the amber brew, the liquid amber, thick, three-two, tiger beer, tiger sweat, toilet water, top o' reeb, turpentine, turps, wallop, wet one, whip-belly, whip-belly vengeance, wildcat beer, yell. 2. to drink beer; to drink a beer. *Cf. booze.* RS: *irrigate.* [(1780): OED, F&H, BVB: 1942] 3. (also **beer up**) to get oneself drunk on beer. *Cf. beer-up.* RS: *mug oneself.* BVB: 1942 lists **beer up**. [1700s, F&H, BVB: 1942]

beer-a-bumble bad beer; weak beer. Beer so bad that one could not hold enough to get drunk. The bumble is a rumbling in the bowels. RT: *queer-beer.* [Br., FG: 1823]

beerage people made rich through the sale of beer; brewery owners. Based on *peerage. Cf. maltimillionaire.* [Br. and U.S., JRW: 1909, MHW: 1934]

beeraholic See *beeroholic.*

beerathon a *beer-blast* (*q.v.*); a beer-drinking contest. *Cf. beer fest.* RT: *spree.* [U.S., BVB: 1942, D&D: 1957]

beeratorium (also **beertorium**) a beer parlor; a beer hall. RS: *bar.* Contrived slang. [U.S., MHW: 1934, BVB: 1942]

beer barrel 1. a beer parlor; a *barrelhouse* (*q.v.*). RS: *bar.* [U.S., BVB: 1942] 2. a beer drunkard; a drunkard. RT: *sot.* Both senses from the literal sense, a barrel for beer. [Br. and U.S., 18-1900s, F&H, BVB: 1942]

beer belly 1. (also **beer gut**) an enlarged abdomen from drinking beer or some other beverage alcohol to excess. *Cf. Milwaukee goiter.* [U.S., (c. 1900): SBF: 1976, (1920): W&F: 1960, D&D: 1957] 2. a heavy drinker (male); a beer alcoholic; an alcoholic. RT: *sot.* [U.S., LP: 1971a]

beer-bibber a beer drinker; a beer alcoholic. RS: *sot.* [(1840): OED, (Dickens)]

beer-blast a beer-drinking party; a beer binge. RT: *spree.* [U.S., K&M: 1968]

beer bottle a rotund, red-faced man, presumably from drinking much beer. RS: *sot.* [JRW: 1909]

beer-bust a beer-drinking spree; a beer binge. W&F: 1967 also lists **beerburst**. RT: ***spree***. [U.S., BVB: 1942, D&D: 1957, W&F: 1967, DCCU: 1972, DNE: 1973]

beer cellar a tavern. RT: ***bar***. *Cf.* ***been in the cellar***. [U.S., (1732): DA]

beer-drink a beer-drinking session. RS: ***spree***. [South African, (1895): OEDS]

beer-eater a beer drinker; a beer drunkard. RT: ***sot***. [Br., JRW: 1909]

beer fest (also **beer-blast, beer-bust**) a beer-drinking spree; a beer binge. RT: ***spree***. [U.S., BVB: 1942, D&D: 1957]

beer flat a speakeasy in someone's apartment; a place where liquor, gambling, and prostitution is available; a speakeasy. *Cf.* ***gin flat***. From the prohibition era. RT: ***sly grogshop***. [U.S., BVB: 1942, GOL: 1950]

beer freak a heavy beer drinker; a person (usually a youth) who prefers beer to marijuana. RT: ***sot***. Compare to ***acid freak, barb freak, downer freak, kick freak, meth freak, pill freak***. [U.S., D&B: 1971]

beer garden an outdoor area adjacent to an inn or tavern where beer is served at tables. From the German *Biergarten*. [U.S., (1868): SBF: 1976, GAS: 1941]

beer hall a beer parlor; a barrelhouse. RT: ***bar***. [U.S., since the 1800s, (1882): DA]

beer heister a beer drinker; a beer drunkard. RT: ***sot***. [U.S., D&D: 1957]

beerified drunk on beer. RT: ***drunk***. [U.S., BVB: 1942]

beerily (also **beery**) drunk on beer. A play on *cheerily*. RS: ***drunk***. See ***beery***.

beer, in intoxicated with beer. *Cf.* ***in liquor***. RT: ***drunk***. [(1631): OED, DSUE, BVB: 1942]

beeriness drunkenness. [Br., 1800s, F&H]

beer jerker 1. a bartender. Not limited to one who serves beer. RT: ***bartender***. [U.S., (1863): SBF: 1976, (1873): DA, BVB: 1942] 2. a beer tippler; a beer drunkard. RT: ***sot***. [U.S., JSF: 1889, F&H]

beer joint a beer hall; a barrelhouse. RS: ***dive***. [U.S., BVB: 1942, D&D: 1957, W&F: 1960]

beer joint widow the wife of a beer-drinker. [U.S., D&D: 1957]

beer-jugger a barmaid. RT: ***bartender***. [U.S., JRW: 1909]

beer mill a beer hall; a tavern serving beer. *Cf.* ***gin mill***. RS: ***bar***. [U.S., (1879): DA]

beer-muddled tipsy; intoxicated with beer. *Cf.* ***muddled***. RT: ***drunk***. [Br., mid 1800s, OED]

beerocracy people who get rich from manufacturing and selling beer; brewery owners. Patterned on *bureaucracy*. *Cf. beerage*. See *maltimillionaire*. [(1881): OED, MHW: 1934, D&D: 1957]

beerocrat a member of the *beerocracy* (*q.v.*). From the prohibition era. [U.S., BVB: 1942]

beeroholic (also **beeraholic**) a heavy beer-drinker; a beer-drinking alcoholic. Based on *alcoholic*. RS: *sot*. [Aust. and U.S., RAS: 1980, BH: 1980]

beer, on the 1. intoxicated with beer. RT: *drunk*. [Br., 1800s, F&H] 2. on a beer-drinking binge. RT: *spreeing*. [Br., JRW: 1909]

beer parlor a beer hall; a barrelhouse. RT: *bar*. [U.S., BVB: 1942]

beer shunter a beer tippler. See *brandy shunter*.

beer slinger 1. a bartender. *Cf. beer jerker*. RT: *bartender*. [U.S., (1875): SBF: 1976, B&L: 1890] 2. a beer drinker; a beer drunkard. RT: *sot*. [Br., late 1800s, F&H, DSUE]

beer-soaked alcohol intoxicated; intoxicated with beer. RT: *drunk*. [PD: 1982]

beer street the throat. *Cf. gin lane*. [JRW: 1909]

beer stube a beer parlor; a beer hall. From German *Bierstube*. RS: *bar*. [U.S., BVB: 1942]

beer swiper a beer drinker; a beer drunkard. RT: *sot*. [Aust., WWI, WHD: 1919, cited in SJB: 1945]

beertender someone who sells and serves liquor, especially beer, at a bar. RT: *bartender*. [U.S., BVB: 1942]

beertorium See *beeratorium*.

beer-up 1. a beer-drinking party; a beer-bust. RT: *spree*. [Aust., (1857): GAW: 1978, SJB: 1943; U.S., W&F: 1960] 2. to guzzle beer. See *beer*.

beery (also **beerily**) intoxicated with beer; cheerfully drunk on beer. RT: *drunk*. [Br. and U.S., (1857): F&H, JCH: 1887, MHW: 1934, K&M: 1968]

bee that stings (also **bee**) a drug habit; drug withdrawal symptoms. RT: *habit*. [U.S., M&V: 1967, H&C: 1975]

beezle See *bezzle*.

beezy-weezies a hangover. RT: *hangover*. [U.S., BVB: 1942]

befuddle to make oneself or someone else drunk. See *fuddle*.

beggar boy's ass (also **beggar boy's**) Rhyming slang for *bass*, i.e., Bass Ale, a British brand. RT: *ale*. Note that this is not *arse* but the nonstandard British *ass*. [Br., 18-1900s, DRS]

beggar maker an alehouse; an alehouse keeper. RS: *bartender*. [Br., FG: 1785]

behind acid using acid; under the influence of the hallucinogenic drug *L.S.D.* (*q.v.*). *Cf. get behind it*. [U.S., RRL: 1969, RG: 1970,

ADC: 1975]

behind juice alcohol intoxicated; addicted to alcohol. RT: *drunk*. [U.S., JHF: 1971]

behind P.C.P. using *P.C.P.* (*q.v.*) on a regular basis; habituated to P.C.P. use. [U.S., (1970s): FAB: 1979]

behind the cork alcohol intoxicated. *Cf. corky*. RT: *drunk*. [U.S., RM: 1942, W&F: 1960]

behind the stuff (also **behind stuff**) addicted to heroin. RT: *hooked*. [U.S., M&V: 1967, H&C: 1975]

belch beer; ale; inferior beer; any fermented malt beverage. RT: *beer*. BE: 1690 lists *belsh* (*q.v.*). [Br., BE: 1690, FG: 1785, B&L: 1890, F&H; listed in BVB: 1942]

belcher 1. a beer drinker. [(1876): F&H] 2. a hard drinker; a drunkard. RT: *sot*. [1800s, F&H; listed in BVB: 1942]

belch-guts a drunkard. RT: *sot*. [Br., 1800s, F&H; listed in BVB: 1942]

belladonna a compound derived from the belladonna (*Atropa belladonna*) plant used as a medicine. Italian for *beautiful lady* (*q.v.*). [(1788): OED] Synonyms and related terms: *banewort, beautiful lady, deadly nightshade, death's herb, horror drug*.

belly habit 1. an addiction to a narcotic; an addiction strong enough to lead to withdrawal symptoms, such as stomach cramps, when the drug is not available. RT: *habit*. [U.S., CM: 1970, H&C: 1975] 2. an oral drug habit; an addiction to drugs in pill form; an addiction to orally-taken opium. RT: *habit*. [U.S., M&W: 1946, BVB: 1953, M&V: 1954]

belly up 1. (also **belly up to the bar**) to move up to the bar (and order a drink). [U.S., BVB: 1942] 2. alcohol intoxicated. A synonym of *dead* (*q.v.*). RT: *drunk*. [PD: 1982]

belly vengeance inferior beer or ale; weak beer that only causes gastric upset. *Cf. queer-beer*. [Br., JCH: 1887, F&H; listed in BVB: 1942]

belly wash (also **gullet wash**) 1. a weak or inferior alcoholic beverage. RT: *rotgut*. [U.S., JM: 1923, HNR: 1934, W&F: 1960] 2. a dysphemism for any soft drink. [U.S., EHB: 1900]

belong to be addicted to a drug. Either to belong to the drug or to belong to the addicts' fraternity. *Cf. in*. RS: *hooked*. [U.S., LVA: 1981, RDS: 1982]

below the mahogany alcohol intoxicated. An elaboration of *under the table* (*q.v.*). RT: *drunk*. [PD: 1982]

belsh any fermented malt beverage. From *belch* (*q.v.*). RT: *beer*. [cant, BE: 1690]

belt 1. a drink of an alcoholic beverage. RT: *nip*. [U.S., (1921): SBF: 1982, W&F: 1960, DCCU: 1972] 2. (also **belt down**) to take a drink of an alcoholic beverage; to get a drink under one's belt.

RT: *irrigate*. [U.S., (1846): SBF: 1982, D&D: 1957, W&F: 1960] 3. an injected dose of an addictive drug. RT: *shot*. [U.S., H&C: 1975] 4. the rush or jolt from an injection of a drug. RT: *rush*. [U.S., BD: 1937, DWM: 1938, RRL: 1969] 6. marijuana; a marijuana cigarette. RT: *joint*. Not now known. [U.S., W&F: 1960] 7. a trouser belt used as a *tie* (*q.v.*). [U.S., MA: 1973]

belted alcohol or drug intoxicated. GEN: struck, clobbered. RT: *drunk, stoned*. [U.S., RRL: 1969, RDS: 1982]

belt the grape to drink heavily and become intoxicated. Does not necessarily refer to wine. RT: *mug oneself*. [U.S., (1931): PE: 1980, D&D: 1957, W&F: 1960]

belula* marijuana. RT: *pot*. Spanish. [calo, JBR: 1973]

belyando sprue marijuana. The term is a variant of, or an error for *Belyando spew*. Sprue is the name of a disease (psilosis) which includes among its symptoms a sore mouth, a raw tongue, and a loss of weight. This also describes the state of some heavy marijuana smokers. Belyando is the name of a river in Queensland, Australia. The spew version refers to the vomiting of Belyando spew (the disease) which is better known medically as gastric spirochetosis. (Baker lists it as Australian slang and defines it as a rural sickness). The most likely connection is the common name of the disease: grass sickness, where *grass* (*q.v.*) = marijuana. RS: *pot*. [U.S., SNP: 1977]

bemuse to intoxicate oneself or another person with alcohol. *Cf. befuddle*. RS: *mug oneself*. [Br., (1847): OED, B&L: 1890; listed in BVB: 1942]

bemused alcohol intoxicated. RT: *drunk*. [Br., (1735): OED; listed in BVB: 1942]

bencher (also **bench-whistler**) one who sits on tavern benches and tipples; a drunkard. RT: *sot*. [Br., 1800s or earlier, F&H]

bend to drink much liquor; to tipple, to bend the elbow in drinking. RT: *irrigate*. [Br. (Scots), (1758): OED; listed in BVB: 1942] See also *bent*.

bender 1. a riotous drinking bout. GEN: any bout or spree. RT: *spree*. [U.S., (1827): OEDS, (1846): DA, GWM: 1859, BWG: 1899, LWP: 1908, DCCU: 1972] 2. a single drink of an alcoholic beverage. From the bending of the elbow. *Cf. bend, elbow-bending*. RT: *nip*. [Br., 1800s, F&H; listed in BVB: 1942] 3. a person participating in a riotous drinking bout; a hard drinker; a drunkard; a tippler. Possibly from *hellbender* (*q.v.*). RT: *sot*. [Scots, (1728): OED; U.S., RHT: 1912, BVB: 1942] 4. a marijuana smoker. One who gets *bent* (*q.v.*) frequently. RT: *toker*. [U.S., VJM: 1949] 5. a spree of drug use. *Cf. binge*. [U.S., A&T: 1953]

bender, on a on a riotous drinking bout; on a protracted, solitary drinking binge. See *bender*. [U.S., (1827): OEDS, (1846): SBF: 1976, AH: 1931, MHW: 1934, W&F: 1960, D&D: 1973]

bending and bowing drug intoxicated; experiencing euphoria from a drug, probably heroin. *Cf. leaping and stinking.* See *nodding out.* [U.S., DWM: 1938, BVB: 1942, (A&T: 1953)]

bending an elbow taking a drink; on a drinking bout. RT: *spreeing.* [U.S., (1850–1900): RFA]

bend, on a (also **on the bend**) on a drinking bout. See *bend, bender.* [Br. and U.S., (1887): OEDS, F&H]

bend one's elbow (also **bend the elbow**) to take a drink of an alcoholic beverage; to drink alcohol to excess. *Cf. bending an elbow.* RT: *irrigate.* [(1880): SBF: 1982, JAWB: 1943, DCCU: 1972, M&J: 1975]

bend the habit (also **bend the needle**) to reduce the intake of addictive drugs without stopping altogether, i.e., without breaking the habit. See *break the habit.* RS: *kick.* [U.S., JES: 1959, H&C: 1975]

benj *Benzedrine* (TM; *q.v.*). A variant of *benz* (*q.v.*).

bennied up *high* (*q.v.*) on *bennies* (*q.v.*) (= amphetamines). The same as *beaned up* (*q.v.*). RS: *stoned.* [U.S., (MT: 1971)]

bennies *Benzedrine* (TM; *q.v.*) capsules. The plural of *bennie* and *benny.* RT: *benz.* [U.S., D&D: 1957, GS: 1959, RRL: 1969, M&J: 1975, NIDA: 1980]

benny (also **bennie**) **1.** a capsule of *Benzedrine* (TM; *q.v.*); Benzedrine; a Benzedrine inhaler. RT: *benz.* [U.S., (1945): W&F: 1960, M&D: 1952, M&V: 1954, TRG: 1968, CM: 1970, EEL: 1971, DCCU: 1972; Br., DSUE, BTD: 1968] **2.** a state of intoxication from *Benzedrine* (TM; *q.v.*). *Cf. benny jag.* [U.S., TRG: 1968, W&F: 1975] **3.** marijuana. Possibly an error. RT: *pot.* [M&J: 1975]

benny chaser a cup of coffee. Refers to drinking coffee after taking a *benny* (*q.v.*). CB radio slang. [U.S., MT: 1971, EE: 1976]

benny jag a state of intoxication from *Benzedrine* (TM; *q.v.*) amphetamines; a benny high. *Cf. jag.* [U.S., M&V: 1954, D&D: 1957]

benser Probably an error for *bender* (*q.v.*). [U.S., VJM: 1949]

bent 1. tipsy; alcohol intoxicated. Suffering from a *bender* (*q.v.*). RT: *drunk.* [U.S., (1833): DA, MHW: 1934, W&F: 1960, DCCU: 1972] **2.** drug intoxicated. *Cf. tween the knees.* See *straight.* RT: *stoned.* [U.S., RRL: 1969, EEL: 1971, W&F: 1975, JWK: 1981]

bent and broken alcohol intoxicated. An elaboration of *bent* (*q.v.*). RT: *drunk.* [PD: 1982]

bent out under the influence of *L.S.D.* (*q.v.*). RS: *stoned.* [U.S., JHF: 1971]

bent out of shape 1. alcohol intoxicated, having been on a *bender* (*q.v.*). RT: *drunk.* [U.S., DCCU: 1972, W&F: 1975] **2.** drug intoxicated. RT: *stoned.* [U.S., TRG: 1968, EEL: 1971, W&F:

1975, S&F: 1984]

benz (also **benj**) *Benzedrine* (TM; *q.v.*). A general slang term in use since WWII. [U.S., 1940s-p., RRL: 1969, EEL: 1971] Nicknames and slang terms for Benzedrine: *B.*, *B-bomb*, *beans*, *benj*, *bennies*, *benny*, *benz*, *benzadrina*, *benzies*, *brother Ben*, *copilot ben*, *crosses*, *drin*, *hearts*, *hi-ball*, *minibennies*, *peaches*, *roses*, *whites*.

benzadrina* 1. *Benzedrine* (TM; *q.v.*); amphetamines. Some Spanish use. RT: *benz*. Attested as gay slang. [U.S., BR: 1972] 2. (also **Benzadrina***) a heavy user of benzedrine or amphetamines in general. [U.S., BR: 1972]

Benzedrine a protected trade name for amphetamine sulfate in capsules and tablets. The drug is a central nervous system stimulant. In drug jargon, the term may be used for stimulants other than Benzedrine (TM). RT: *benz*. [(1933): OEDS; in current use; consult a pharmaceutical reference for more information]

benzies *Benzedrine* (TM; *q.v.*) capsules. The same as *bennies* (*q.v.*). RT: *benz*. [U.S., YKB: 1977]

benzine rotgut whiskey. RT: *rotgut*. [U.S., D&D: 1957]

benzinery a low tavern; a saloon. *Cf. benzine*. RT: *dive*. [U.S., D&D: 1957]

Bernice (also **bernese**, **Bernies**, **Bernies flake**, **Burnese**) crystallized cocaine for snorting. The term does not always appear capitalized. It is intended be used as a personification and a disguise. *Cf. Al K. Hall*, *Dr. Hall*, *old Steve* for other personifications. Possibly the term is based on *burnies*, referring to crystals of cocaine added to a tobacco cigarette and smoked. Possibly from a cocaine preparation made up by a Dr. Burney. RT: *cocaine*. [U.S., (1914): DU, DWM: 1933, MHW: 1934, DWM: 1936, W&F: 1960, RRL: 1969, EEL: 1971, YKB: 1977, NIDA: 1980]

berper a drinker; a drunkard. *Cf. belcher*. RT: *sot*. [U.S., BVB: 1942]

berps beer. *Cf. German conversation water*. RT: *beer*. [U.S., BVB: 1942]

berpwater beer; ale; champagne. *Cf. berps*. [U.S., BVB: 1942]

berries, the wine. *Cf. grapes*. RT: *wine*. Black slang. [U.S., EAF: 1980]

besotted alcohol or narcotic intoxicated. RT: *drunk*, *stoned*. [(1831): OED]

Bethesda gold a weak variety of marijuana. RT: *pot*. [U.S., (1969): ELA: 1982]

betting on a horse addicted to morphine. *Horse* (*q.v.*) usually refers to heroin. RT: *hooked*. [U.S., JES: 1959, H&C: 1975]

bev an alcoholic drink. From *beverage*. RS: *booze*. [(1937): DSUE]

beverage alcohol ethyl alcohol in some drinkable form. Standard English. [1900s, K&M: 1968]

beverage wine natural, unfortified table wine. RS: *wine*. [1900s or earlier, K&M: 1968]

bevie See *bevvy*.

bevvied alcohol intoxicated. Done-in by *bevvy* (*q.v.*). RT: *drunk*. [Br., PW: 1974, M&J: 1975]

bevvy (also **bev, bevie, bevy**) 1. beer; any alcoholic drink. RT: *beer*. [Br., B&L: 1890, F&G: 1925, B&P: 1965, SSD; listed in BVB: 1942] 2. to drink beer; to drink any alcohol, perhaps to excess. *Cf. beer*. RT: *irrigate*. [Br., B&L: 1890, DU]

bevvy-ken a tavern; a beerhall. Ken = a hangout (in cant). RS: *bar*. [cant (Lincolnshire), POS: 1979]

bevvy-merchant a heavy drinker; a drunkard. RT: *sot*. [cant (Lincolnshire), POS: 1979]

bevy See *bevie*.

beware alcoholic drink. Possibly a Cockney pronunciation of *bever* from *beverage*. [Br., (1840): DSUE]

bewildered alcohol intoxicated. GEN: confused. RT: *drunk*. [U.S., BVB: 1942]

bewitched alcohol intoxicated. RT: *drunk*. [BF: 1737, BVB: 1942, W&F: 1960] See also *water-bewitched*.

bewottled alcohol intoxicated. RT: *drunk*. [PD: 1982]

bezzle 1. (also **beezzle**) to drink greedily; to do away with anything. From *embezzle*. [(1604): OED] 2. (also **bezzler**) a drunkard; a heavy drinker. RT: *sot*. [(1592): OED]

bezzled alcohol intoxicated. RT: *drunk*. [PD: 1982]

B-girl a bar-girl who works in bars soliciting drinks. Usually assumed to be a prostitute. *Cf. bee-drinker*. [U.S., BVB: 1953, W&F: 1960]

bhang 1. (also **bang**) the leaves, stems, and fruit of a marijuana plant. RT: *pot*. From Hindi. The word has been in English since the late 1500s. [U.S., JES: 1959, RRL: 1969, EEL: 1971, D&B: 1978] 2. (also **baby bhang**) any form of marijuana. RT: *pot*. [U.S., D&D: 1957, YKB: 1977] 3. an infusion of marijuana in tea or some other beverage. [U.S., RRL: 1969, ADC: 1981] 4. a marijuana cigarette; the smoking of a marijuana cigarette. RT: *joint*. [M&J: 1975]

bhang ganjah marijuana; marijuana resin. RT: *pot*. [U.S., EEL: 1971]

B-head a barbiturate user. RS: *user*. [U.S., JH: 1979] See also *A-head, C-head*.

bhong See *bong*.

bib-all-night a person who drinks all night; a drunkard. *Cf. Billie-born-drunk.* RT: *sot.* [(1612): F&H]

bibber (also **bibbler, wine-bibber**) a drunkard; a tippler. RT: *sot.* [(1536): OED, F&H]

bibble to drink constantly; to tipple. RT: *irrigate.* [(1583): OED]

Bible 1. a book of cigarette papers. RT: *paper.* [U.S., (1850–1900): RFA] 2. the *PDR (q.v.).*

bibulous alcohol intoxicated; having to do with a tippler or an alcoholic. RT: *drunk.* [(1861): OED]

bidgee an alcoholic drink containing methyl alcohol. RT: *methyl.* [Aust., SJB: 1943]

Bierstube See *beer stube.*

biffy alcohol intoxicated. *Cf. buffy.* RT: *drunk.* [Br., 1900s, DSUE]

big bag a large bag of heroin. RS: *load.* [U.S., RRL: 1969, RDS: 1982]

big bloke cocaine. Rhyming slang for *coke (q.v.). Cf. Billie Hoke.* RT: *cocaine.* [U.S., (1920): DU, DWM: 1938, M&B: 1944, W&F: 1967, EEL: 1971]

big boy heroin. *Cf. boy.* RT: *heroin.* [U.S., RDS: 1982]

big-C. cocaine. *Cf. C.* RT: *cocaine.* [U.S., JES: 1959, IGA: 1971, YKB: 1977, NIDA: 1980]

big chief 1. mescaline. RS: *peyote.* [U.S., RRL: 1969, EEL: 1971] 2. *L.S.D. (q.v.). Cf. chief.* RT: *L.S.D.* [U.S., EEL: 1971, JH: 1979]

big-D. 1. *L.S.D. (q.v.).* RT: *L.S.D.* [U.S., RRL: 1969, EEL: 1971, W&F: 1975, YKB: 1977, NIDA: 1980] 2. *Dilaudid* (TM; *q.v.*) painkiller. *Cf. D., dees, D.s.* See *little-D.* [U.S., YKB: 1977]

big daddy heroin. RT: *heroin.* Used in the movie *$Dollars,* 1972. [U.S., RAS: 1984]

big fish See *the big man.*

biggy alcohol intoxicated. (BF: 1737: He's Biggy.) RT: *drunk.* [BF: 1737]

big-H. heroin. *H. (q.v.)* = heroin. RT: *heroin.* [U.S., EEL: 1971, DCCU: 1972, GU: 1975, W&F: 1975, YKB: 1977, NIDA: 1980]

big Harry (also **Harry**) heroin. A personification of *heroin.* RT: *heroin.* [U.S., W&F: 1975, SNP: 1977]

bighead a headache and other ill-effects from a drinking bout. *Cf. biggy.* RT: *hangover.* [F&H, BVB: 1942, D&D: 1957, W&F: 1960]

big John the police; a policeman. *Cf. Johnny Law.* RT: *fuzz.* [U.S., JBW: 1967, EEL: 1971, W&F: 1975, EAF: 1980]

big-M. morphine. *M. (q.v.)* = morphine. RT: *morphine.* [U.S., JES: 1959, H&C: 1975, SNP: 1977]

big man, the (also **big fish**) a big dealer; the head of a large drug operation; the primary dealer in a particular location. [U.S., DWM: 1936, RRL: 1969]

big-O. opium. *O.* (*q.v.*) = opium. RT: ***opium***. [U.S., D&D: 1957, W&F: 1960]

big reposer an alcoholic beverage; a drink of liquor. RT: ***booze***. [Br., 1800s, F&H]

Big Three the three major intoxicants of the 1980s: alcohol, cocaine, and marijuana. RS: ***dope***. [U.S., RAS: 1984]

big time heroin; having to do with the use of heroin; having to do with heroin addiction. GEN: powerful, serious, felonious. RT: ***habit***. [U.S., EEL: 1971]

biled (also **boiled**) alcohol intoxicated. A dialect pronunciation of ***boiled*** (*q.v.*). Possibly a truncation of ***biled owl, biled as an owl***. RT: ***drunk***. [U.S., BVB: 1942]

biled as an owl alcohol intoxicated. See ***biled***.

biled owl (also **boiled owl**) a drunkard; an alcoholic. See ***biled***. RT: ***sot***. [U.S., 1900s, MHW: 1934, BVB: 1942]

bilge water bad beer; weak beer. RT: ***queer-beer***. [Br. and U.S., 18–1900s, F&H, DSUE, BVB: 1942, D&D: 1973]

billiard drinker a tippler; a drunkard. Refers to having a glass of liquor handy while playing billiards. RT: ***sot***. [U.S., D&D: 1957, W&F: 1960]

Billie-born-drunk a long-time drunkard; a man who has been drunk as long as anyone can remember. May also apply to a drinker of methyl alcohol. RT: ***sot***. [Br., JRW: 1909]

billied addicted to or dependent on cocaine. From the personification of cocaine, ***Billie Hoke*** (*q.v.*). *Cf.* ***cocainized***. [U.S., JES: 1959, H&C: 1975]

Billie Hoke (also **Billie Hoak**) cocaine. Rhyming slang for ***coke***. *Cf.* ***big bloke***. RT: ***cocaine***. [U.S., (1940): JES: 1959, H&C: 1975]

bim a police officer. Origin unknown. RS: ***fuzz***. [U.S., ELA: 1982]

bimmy a drunkard. RT: ***sot***. [U.S., GOL: 1950]

binder a glass of brandy at the end of a drinking session. This may refer to binding a friendship or to stabilizing the bowels. *Cf.* ***caulker, settler***. [Br., (1899): DSUE]

bindle a packet, bundle, ration, or dose of drugs. GEN: a hobo's bundle of possessions. RS: ***load***. [U.S., HNR: 1934, DWM: 1936, BD: 1937, GOL: 1950, M&D: 1952, W&F: 1960, TRG: 1968, EEL: 1971]

bindle bum a hobo addicted to a drug. GEN: a hobo. *Cf.* ***bindle***. RS: ***junky***. [U.S., (1920s): JES: 1959, DU]

Bindle Kate a female drug addict. RT: ***junky***. [U.S., early 1900s, JES: 1959]

bindle stiff a narcotics addict. GEN: a hobo. RT: ***junky***. [U.S., (1901): MW: 1983, GI: 1931, VJM: 1949]

bindle stiffened intoxicated by narcotics; addicted to drugs. *Cf.*

bindle. RT: ***hooked***. [U.S., JES: 1959, H&C: 1975]

bing 1. a packet of a drug; a dose of a drug; an injection of a drug; a puff of a marijuana cigarette. See ***bang***. *Cf.* ***dose, shot***. [U.S., BD: 1937, DWM: 1938, D&D: 1957, W&F: 1960] 2. a drug ***rush*** (*q.v.*) or jolt. RT: ***rush***. [U.S., DWM: 1938]

binge 1. to drink heavily; to soak with alcohol. From a British dialect term meaning soak. RT: ***irrigate***. [(1854): OEDS, B&L: 1890] 2. a bout of riotous drinking; a protracted bout of solitary drinking. RT: ***spree***. [Br. and U.S., (1854): OEDS, B&L: 1890, (1889): SBF: 1976, F&G: 1925, MHW: 1934, VJM: 1949, W&F: 1960, B&P: 1965] 3. a protracted bout of cocaine use. [U.S., S&F: 1984]

binged alcohol intoxicated. *Cf.* ***bingoed***. RT: ***drunk***. [Br. and U.S., HNR: 1934, DSUE]

bingle 1. a drinking bout; a riotous bash. RT: ***spree***. [Aust., SJB: 1945] 2. narcotics; a large supply of dope. RS: ***dope***. [U.S., GOL: 1950, A&T: 1953, D&D: 1957, W&F: 1960] 3. a seller of drugs. RT: ***dealer***. [U.S., GOL: 1950, A&T: 1953, RDS: 1982]

bingle biff a dope smuggler. RS: ***mule***. [U.S., HNR: 1934]

bingo 1. brandy; liquor. RT: ***booze***. [cant, BE: 1690, FG: 1785, GWM: 1859, JCH: 1887; listed in MHW: 1934] 2. an injection of drugs; a dose of drugs. RT: ***shot***. [U.S., BD: 1937, DWM: 1938, VJM: 1949] 3. allegedly to inject a drug. Probably an error for the noun form (sense two). [U.S., RDS: 1982]

bingo boy a brandy drunkard; an alcoholic. *Cf.* ***bingo, bingo mort***. RT: ***sot***. [cant, BE: 1690, FG: 1785, FG: 1811, GWM: 1859, B&L: 1890, (1946): W&F: 1960, VJM: 1949]

bingoed (also **bingo'd**) alcohol intoxicated; drunk on brandy. *Cf.* ***binged***. RT: ***drunk***. [Br., (1920s): DSUE]

bingo mort a drunken woman; a female alcoholic. Mort = a woman (in cant). RT: ***sot***. [cant, NCD: 1725, FG: 1785, FG: 1811, GWM: 1859, B&L: 1890; listed in MHW: 1934]

bing room (also **bang room**) a place where drugs are sold and injected; a dope den. *Cf.* ***bing***. RT: ***pad***. [U.S., GI: 1931, MHW: 1934, VJM: 1949]

biphet a truncation of ***Biphetamine*** (*q.v.*). Compare to ***amphets***. RS: ***amps***. [U.S., RDS: 1982]

Biphetamine a protected trade name for a combination of amphetamine and dextroamphetamine in capsule form. The drug is a central nervous system stimulant. Most slang terms for this drug refer to the black, white, or black and white capsules. RT: ***amps***. [in current use; consult a pharmaceutical reference for more information]

birdcage hype (also **birdhouse hype**) a low type of addict inhabiting a flop house. *Bird cage* refers to the wire netting used to separate sleeping cubicles in a flop house. Partridge (DU): "A destitute drug addict..." BD: 1937 lists **bird-cage hyps**. RT: *junky*. [U.S., BD: 1937, DWM: 1938]

birdie powder (also **birdie stuff**) any powdered narcotics; a mixture of powdered narcotics. Such powders make one fly. RT: *powder*. [U.S., BVB: 1942, A&T: 1953, EEL: 1971]

birdie power an error for *birdie powder* (*q.v.*). [U.S., VJM: 1949]

bird's eye (also **eyespeck**) a small amount of drugs; a small pack of drugs; a very small pellet of opium. Just the amount of a powdered drug which would cover a bird's eye, or a pill the size of a bird's eye. *Cf. dose*. [U.S., DWM: 1936, BD: 1937, VJM: 1949, M&D: 1952, TRG: 1968, EEL: 1971, W&F: 1975]

birdwood 1. a tobacco cigarette. RT: *nail*. [U.S., BVB: 1953] 2. marijuana. RT: *pot*. [U.S., DB: 1944, RDS: 1982]

birra* beer; booze. From Spanish. RT: *beer*. [U.S., EEL: 1971]

biscuits 1. *methadone* (*q.v.*). *Cf. medicine*. RT: *dolo*. [U.S., YKB: 1977, DEM: 1981] 2. peyote; peyote cactus. A truncation of *dog biscuits* (*q.v.*). RT: *peyote*. [U.S., JWK: 1981] See also *dog food*.

bistro a small nightclub; a tavern. From French. RT: *bar*. [(1921): MW: 1983, BVB: 1942, W&F: 1960]

bit by a barn weasel alcohol intoxicated. *Cf. been bitten by a barn mouse*. RT: *drunk*. [late 16–1700s, DSUE]

bitches' wine champagne. Refers to champagne as a woman's drink. RT: *cham*. [Br., mid 1800s, F&H, DSUE]

bite 1. the addictive power of a drug. *Cf. bee, bee that stings*. [U.S., JES: 1959, H&C: 1975] 2. an unpleasant sting in the mouth or gullet from drinking strong whiskey or from smoking cheap tobacco. [U.S., mid 1900s, MW: 1983]

bite into the brute (also **bite the brute**) to get drunk on purpose. The brute = liquor. See *creature*. RT: *mug oneself*. [U.S., WM: 1927, AH: 1931, MHW: 1934]

bite one's lips to smoke marijuana. RT: *hit the hay*. [U.S., JES: 1959]

bite one's name in to tipple. *Cf. bite into the brute*. RT: *irrigate*. [Br., 18–1900s, DSUE; listed in BVB: 1942]

bit high, a alcohol intoxicated; tipsy. *Cf. high*. [BVB: 1942, M&J: 1975]

bit lit, a alcohol intoxicated; tipsy. *Cf. lit*. RT: *drunk*. [Br., (1925): DSUE]

bit o' beef a chunk of chewing tobacco. Probably rhyming slang for *leaf*. Not listed in DRS. *Cf. bit of leaf*. RT: *quid*. [Br., JRW: 1909]

bit of blink beverage alcohol; a serving of liquor. Rhyming slang for *drink* (*q.v.*). RS: *nip*. [Br., JRW: 1909, DRS]

bit of leaf tobacco; a ration of tobacco. RT: *fogus*. Prison use. [Br., (1876): DSUE, B&L: 1890]

bit of tape beverage alcohol. *Cf. tape.* RT: *booze.* [U.S., BVB: 1942]

bit on, a alcohol intoxicated; tipsy. RT: *drunk.* [Br., B&L: 1890, F&H; listed in BVB: 1942]

bitten by white mosquitoes habituated to cocaine use. Probably refers to marks from injections. *White mosquitoes* (*q.v.*) = cocaine. *Cf. cocainized.* [U.S., JES: 1959, H&C: 1975]

bitter a glass of *bitters* (*q.v.*); a glass of beer with high hop content. *Cf. bitter beer.* [Br., (1856): OEDS, F&H]

bitter beer (also **bitter ale**) a fermented malt beverage with a high hop content. Not slang. [Br., (1856): OEDS, K&M: 1968]

bitters 1. an aromatic tincture of specific plant materials. A component of various mixed drinks. [(1713): OED, M&C: 1905] 2. the cheapest grade of British ale. RS: *ale.* [since the mid 1800s, (1856): OED]

bit under, a alcohol intoxicated; tipsy. *Cf. under.* RT: *drunk.* [U.S., BVB: 1942]

bivvy beer; a pot of beer. See *bevvy.* RT: *beer.* [Br. (Cockney), JCH: 1887, F&H, JRW: 1909]

biz 1. a small bag of drugs; a portion of drugs. From *business* (*q.v.*). RS: *load.* [U.S., DWM: 1938, EEL: 1971] 2. the drug selling business. [U.S., H&C: 1975] 3. (also **biz stuff, bizz, the biz**) equipment or apparatus for injecting drugs. From *business* (*q.v.*). RT: *outfit, monkey pump.* [U.S., DWM: 1938, A&T: 1953, RRL: 1969, EEL: 1971]

B.J.s the delirium tremens, the *blue Johnnies* (*q.v.*). RT: *D.T.s.* [Aust., 1800s, F&H]

black 1. opium. Short for *black stuff* (*q.v.*). RT: *opium.* [U.S., VJM: 1949, IGA: 1971] 2. a potent variety of hashish, probably from Africa. Probably from *black hash* (*q.v.*). RT: *hash.* [U.S., (1975): ELA: 1982]

black acid *L.S.D.* (*q.v.*). *Cf. acid.* RT: *L.S.D.* [U.S., RG: 1970]

black and tan *Durophet* (TM; *q.v.*), an amphetamine and barbiturate compound. The same as *black and white* (*q.v.*). RT: *set.* [Br., BTD: 1968, M&J: 1975]

black and white 1. a specific amphetamine, probably a *Biphetamine* (TM; *q.v.*) capsule. RT: *amps.* [U.S., EEL: 1971, ADC: 1981] 2. an amphetamine and a barbiturate taken together; *Durophet* (TM; *q.v.*). RT: *set.* [U.S., EEL: 1971, ADC: 1981; Br., BTD: 1968, M&J: 1975] 3. (also **black and whites**) the police; a black and white police patrol car. RT: *fuzz.* [U.S., JBW: 1967, M&V: 1967, EEL: 1971, M&V: 1973, EAF: 1980]

black and white minstrel an amphetamine and a barbiturate capsule taken together. May also refer to *Biphetamine* (TM; *q.v.*) amphetamine capsules which come in black, white, and black and white. May also refer to *Durophet* (TM; *q.v.*). *Cf. black and tan,* *black and white, minstrels, nigger minstrels.* RT: *set.* [U.S., EEL: 1971; Br., BTD: 1968, M&J: 1975]

black beauties (also **Black Beauties**) amphetamine capsules; *Biphetamine* (TM; *q.v.*) capsules. Also used for capsules of mixed amphetamine and barbiturate. RT: *amps.* [U.S., RRL: 1969, CM: 1970, EEL: 1971, M&V: 1973, YKB: 1977, NIDA: 1980]

blackbirds amphetamine capsules. Probably *Biphetamine* (TM; *q.v.*) capsules. RT: *amps.* [U.S., H&C: 1975, YKB: 1977]

black bombers *Durophet* (TM; *q.v.*), an amphetamine and barbiturate compound. RS: *set.* [Br., (1963): DSUE, BTD: 1968, M&J: 1975; U.S., EEL: 1971]

black bottle an opiate; narcotics in general. In the world of tramps, *black bottle* referred to a bottle of poison which physicians were alleged to have kept around to put unsuspecting hobos out of their misery. [U.S., EK: 1927, GI: 1931]

black Cadillac an amphetamine in a black capsule. *Cf. Cadillac.* RT: *amps.* [U.S., NIDA: 1980]

black Columbus (also **Columbus black**) marijuana. Probably akin to *Colombo* (*q.v.*). RT: *pot.* [U.S., RG: 1970, IGA: 1971]

black dog the delirium tremens. RT: *D.T.s.* [Br., (1861): F&H]

blackfellow's delight rum. Blackfellow = an Australian aborigine. RT: *rum.* [Aust., SJB: 1943]

black ganja resin from the lower branches of the cannabis plant. *Cf. ganga.* RT: *pot.* [U.S., D&B: 1978]

black gold potent marijuana. RT: *pot.* Possibly nonce. [U.S., (1946): ELA: 1982]

black gungeon (also **black gungi, black gunion, black gunnion, black gunny**) cannabis; marijuana. Sometimes defined as Indian marijuana. *Cf. ganga.* RT: *pot.* Black slang. [U.S., RRL: 1969, CM: 1970, EEL: 1971, EAF: 1972, RDS: 1982] See also *African black.*

black hash 1. a mixture of hashish and opium. RS: *set.* [U.S., H&C: 1975] 2. hashish. *Cf. black oil.* See *black.* RT: *hash.* [U.S., ADC: 1981]

blackjack 1. a leather bottle or jug lined with pitch. [(1591): OED, BE: 1690, K&M: 1968] 2. whiskey; sweetened rum; hard liquor. RT: *booze.* [U.S., (1863): OEDS] 3. paregoric cooked down and injected. *Cf. black stuff.* RS: *goric.* [U.S., M&V: 1967, SNP: 1977] See also *apple jack.* 4. (usually **Black Jack**) a trade name for *amyl nitrite.* RS: *snapper.* [U.S., ELA: 1984]

blackjacked alcohol intoxicated. RT: *drunk.* [PD: 1982]

black mo a potent, black variety of marijuana. Possibly a pronunciation variant of *black moat* (*q.v.*). Possibly akin to *mota* or *muta.* Attested as black use. RT: *pot.* [U.S., EAF: 1972]

black moat (also **black mold, black mole, black monte, black mota,**

black mote) a potent, black variety of marijuana. Possibly akin to *black mo* (*q.v.*), or *mota* and *muta*. RG: 1970 defines it as marijuana cured with sugar and buried in the ground. Attested as black use. RT: *pot*. [U.S., RG: 1970, IGA: 1971, JHF: 1971, EAF: 1972, JLD: 1977, EAF: 1980]

black mollies amphetamines in black capsules. Named for a tropical fish. RT: *amps*. [U.S., YKB: 1977]

black oil *hash oil* (*q.v.*), an alcohol extract of hashish. *Cf. cherry leb, red oil, son of one, The One*. RT: *oil*. [U.S., YKB: 1977, DEM: 1981]

black pills pellets of opium prepared for smoking. RS: *opium*. [U.S., (1910): DU, RRL: 1969, EEL: 1971]

black Russian (also **black russian**) a dark, potent hashish. RT: *hash*. [U.S., RRL: 1969, EEL: 1971, YKB: 1977, NIDA: 1980]

black shit opium. Opium is nearly black and of a gummy consistency. RT: *opium*. [U.S., M&V: 1967, H&C: 1975]

black silk opium. See *Chinese needlework, embroidery*. RT: *opium*. [U.S., early 1900s, DU]

black smoke opium. RT: *opium*. [U.S., early 1900s, DU]

black smoker an opium addict. *Cf. black smoke*. RT: *campfire boy*. [U.S., early 1900s, DU]

black spot a place where opium is sold and smoked. RT: *opium den*. [U.S., BVB: 1942, VJM: 1949]

blackstrap 1. a thick, sweet port wine. See *blackstrap alchy*. RT: *port*. [cant, FG: 1785, FG: 1823, JCH: 1887, JRW: 1909] 2. a mixture of beverage alcohol and molasses. VR: 1929 defines it as alcohol made from molasses. See *blackstrap alchy*. [U.S., JSF: 1889, BVB: 1942]

blackstrap alchy (also **blackstrap alky**) prohibition alcohol distilled from molasses. Blackstrap = molasses. RT: *moonshine*. [U.S., AH: 1931, MHW: 1934]

black stuff 1. opium; reprocessed opium. *Cf. brown stuff*. The same as *yen-shee* (*q.v.*). [U.S., DWM: 1936, VJM: 1949, M&D: 1952, W&F: 1960, RRL: 1969, CM: 1970, EEL: 1971] 2. *laudanum* (*q.v.*). [U.S., M&V: 1954] 3. *paregoric* (*q.v.*) boiled down and injected. *Cf. blackjack*. RS: *goric*. [U.S., M&V: 1967] 4. brown Mexican heroin. RS: *heroin*. [U.S., M&V: 1967]

black tabs *L.S.D.* (*q.v.*). RT: *L.S.D.* [U.S., KBH: 1982]

black varnish a dysphemism for British Navy *stout* (*q.v.*). *Cf. salmon and trout*. RT: *stout*. [Br., WG: 1962] See also *coffin varnish*.

black velvet a mixture of champagne and *stout* (*q.v.*). [Br. (Anglo-Irish), 1900s, SSD] See also *blue velvet*.

black whack phencyclidine, *P.C.P.* (*q.v.*). RT: *P.C.P.* [U.S., ELA: 1984]

black widow (also **widow**) a capsule of amphetamine. May refer to a black *Biphetamine* (TM; *q.v.*) capsule. Named for the poisonous spider. RT: *amps*. [U.S., GU: 1975]

blah alcohol intoxicated; very drunk. GEN: detached; confused; bland. RT: *drunk*. [(1930): DSUE]

blancas* amphetamine tablets, *Benzedrine* (TM; *q.v.*). Spanish for *whites* (*q.v.*). RT: *amps*. [U.S., M&V: 1967, NIDA: 1980] See also *blanco*.

blanco* (also **blanca***, **La dama blanca***) heroin. Spanish (calo) for white. *White* (*q.v.*) = heroin. RT: *heroin*. [U.S., JBR: 1973, RRL: 1974, NIDA: 1980]

blanco y negro* "black and white," a trade name for one of many brands of marijuana cigarette rolling paper. RT: *paper*. [U.S., ELA: 1984]

blank 1. an empty capsule; a *cap* (*q.v.*). [U.S., H&C: 1975; Br., BTD: 1968] 2. (also **blanks**) white, non-narcotic powder sold as heroin or some other drug; low grade or adulterated drugs of any kind. [U.S., JBW: 1967, M&V: 1967, RRL: 1969, CM: 1970, EEL: 1971, MA: 1973, W&F: 1975, JWK: 1981] (This entry continues after the following list.) Terms for bogus or adulterated drugs: *bad acid, bad bundle, bad coke, bad dope, bad go, bad green, blank, bootleg, bunk, caca, catnip, cold shot, coolie mud, crap, dead bang, dog, dummy, flea powder, garbage, hot stuff, jaloney, jell, kaka, leather dew, lemon, lemonade, Lipton's, Lipton Tea, manteca, Mexican brown, queer, sucker weed, sugar, talcum powder, turd, turkey*. 3. to sell bogus capsules to a drug user. [U.S., JH: 1979] 4. heroin. Probably a misreading of sense two. [U.S., YKB: 1977, DEM: 1981]

blanked (also **blank-ed**) alcohol intoxicated; drunk or tipsy on *vin blanc*. A play on the *blanc* of *vin blanc*. RT: *drunk*. [U.S. and Br., F&G: 1925, HNR: 1934, RAS: 1984]

blanket a tobacco or marijuana cigarette rolling paper. *Cf. tumblings and blankets*. RT: *paper*. [U.S., DWM: 1935, GOL: 1950]

blanks See *blank*.

blast 1. a party; a riotous drinking bout. RT: *spree*. [U.S., TRG: 1968, DNE: 1973] 2. to inject a drug; to take a drug. RT: *shoot*. [U.S., D&D: 1957, DCCU: 1972] 3. to smoke marijuana; to take a deep draw on a marijuana cigarette. Akin to *blast off* in rocketry. JES: 1959 lists **blast Mary Jane to kingdom come**. RT: *toke*. [U.S., (1943): ELA: 1982, GOL: 1950, (M&D: 1952), RRL: 1969, CM: 1970, D&B: 1978] 4. a puff or a draw of a marijuana cigarette. *Cf. toke*. [U.S., EEL: 1971] 5. the kick or rush from taking or injecting a drug. RT: *rush*. [U.S., EEL: 1971, JWK: 1981]

blast a joint (also **blast a stick**, **blast the weed**) to smoke a marijuana cigarette. RT: *hit the hay*. [U.S., JES: 1959, TRG: 1968, EEL: 1971]

blasted 1. alcohol intoxicated. RT: *drunk*. [U.S., MHW: 1934, EEL: 1971, DCCU: 1972, ADC: 1984] 2. drug intoxicated. RT: *stoned*. [U.S., JBW: 1967, EEL: 1971, DCCU: 1972, ADC: 1981, S&F: 1984]

blaster a drug novice. *Cf. J.C.L.* RT: *user*. [U.S., D&D: 1957]

blasting smoking marijuana. [U.S., M&D: 1952]

blasting party (also blast party) a party where marijuana is smoked. [U.S., D&D: 1957, W&F: 1960, RRL: 1969, EEL: 1971, DCCU: 1972]

blast the roach to smoke marijuana; to smoke the butt end of a marijuana cigarette. *Cf. blast, roach*. RT: *hit the hay*. [U.S., GOL: 1950]

blazer See *blue blazer*.

bleary-eyed alcohol intoxicated; showing signs of drink. GEN: tired, exhausted. *Cf. weary*. RT: *drunk*. [U.S., AH: 1931, BVB: 1942]

bleed the monkey (also suck the monkey) to steal rum from a cask. Monkey = cask. See *monkey pump*. Sometimes the rum was sucked out through a straw. [Br. naval, 18–1900s, F&H, WG: 1962] See also *tap the admiral*.

blewed See *blued*.

blimped alcohol intoxicated; swollen with drinking. *Cf. globular*. RT: *drunk*. [U.S., D&B: 1971]

blind 1. (also blinded) alcohol intoxicated; *blind drunk* (*q.v.*). RT: *drunk*. F&H refer to a use by John Taylor (the water poet). [(1630): F&H, DSUE, MP: 1928, GI: 1931, W&F: 1960, AP: 1980] 2. drug intoxicated. RT: *stoned*. [U.S., NAM: 1953, D&B: 1978, JWK: 1981]

blind as a mole alcohol intoxicated. *Blind* (*q.v.*) = drunk. BVB: 1942 also list blind as a bat, blind as a beetle, blind as an owl. RT: *drunk*. [U.S., BVB: 1942]

blind as Chloe (also drunk as Chloe) alcohol intoxicated. *Cf. blind*. [late 1700s, DSUE]

blind drunk very heavily intoxicated with alcohol. [(1830): SBF: 1976, (1845): F&H, BVB: 1942, W&F: 1960]

blinded alcohol intoxicated. RT: *drunk*. See *blind*.

blinder 1. a bad cigar or cigarette. RT: *seegar*. [Br. (Cockney), 1900s, DSUE] 2. strong beverage alcohol. *Cf. blind*. RT: *rotgut*. [U.S., BVB: 1942]

blinders alcohol intoxicated. *Cf. blind*. RT: *drunk*. [Br., (1930): DSUE]

blind munchies the need to eat after getting high on marijuana. *Cf. M.M.s, munchies*. [U.S., RRL: 1969, (D&B: 1978)]

blindo (also blind-o) 1. alcohol intoxicated; tipsy. *Cf. blindo*. [Br., DSUE, F&G: 1925; listed in BVB: 1942] 2. a drinking bout. RT:

spree. [Br., mid 18-1900s, DSUE]

blindo-blotto alcohol intoxicated. *Cf. blind, blindo, blotto*. [U.S., HNR: 1934, BVB: 1942]

blind-pickings cigar and cigarette butts picked up off the street. *Cf. blinder*. RT: ***brad***. [Aust., early 1900s, DSUE]

blind pig (also **blind pigger**) an illicit or concealed saloon; a ***speakeasy*** (*q.v.*). At a carnival or fair, a sign on a tent or building inviting people to see a blind, blue, or spotted pig or tiger, indicated that liquor would be served inside. The use of this term expanded greatly in the U.S. during prohibition. RT: ***sly grogshop, speak***. [U.S., (1840): SBF: 1976, AH: 1931, MHW: 1934, VJM: 1949, W&F: 1960; Br., DSUE]

blind pigger 1. a ***blind pig*** (*q.v.*). 2. the proprietor of a blind pig; the operator of a speakeasy. RT: ***bartender***. [U.S., (1894): DAE, D&D: 1957]

blind staggers drunkenness; the state of being drunk. [Aust. and U.S., DSUE, SJB: 1943]

blind tiger 1. an unlicensed rural saloon. RT: ***sly grogshop***. [Aust., SJB: 1945] 2. (also **tiger**) an illicit tavern or saloon; a speakeasy. In the 1800s it was possible to purchase liquor clandestinely in such a place. At carnivals, circuses, and fairs, the advertisement of a blind, striped, blue, or one-eyed pig, tiger, etc. would indicate such an opportunity. *Cf.* ***blind pig***. RT: ***speak***. [U.S., (1857): DA, LWP: 1908, AH: 1931, VJM: 1949, D&D: 1957, W&F: 1960] 3. illicit whiskey; inferior whiskey. RT: ***rotgut***. [U.S., RDS: 1982]

blink 1. a cigarette butt. RT: ***brad***. [F&G: 1925, HNR: 1934, SJB: 1945, M&J: 1975] 2. to drink. Rhyming slang. Not listed in DRS. *Cf. flicker*. RT: ***irrigate***. [Br., 1800s, F&H; listed in BVB: 1942]

blink-blonk white wine. From French ***vin blanc***. *Cf. plink-plonk* (at *plonk*). RS: ***wine***. [Br., WWI, DSUE]

blink, on the alcohol intoxicated; on a drinking spree. From a colloquial expression meaning out of order. *Cf.* ***blink***. RT: ***drunk***. [U.S., AH: 1931, MHW: 1934]

blinky ***free base*** (*q.v.*). Origin unknown. [U.S., ELA: 1984]

blissed out 1. alcohol intoxicated. RT: ***drunk***. [PD: 1982] 2. in a heavenly euphoria from ***Quaalude*** (TM; *q.v.*); drug intoxicated with Quaaludes. RS: ***stoned***. [U.S., RAS: 1980]

bliss out to become euphoric by taking Quaaludes or by smoking marijuana. *Cf. cap out*. [U.S., RAS: 1980]

blithered alcohol intoxicated. RT: ***drunk***. [Aust., SJB: 1943]

blitzed 1. alcohol intoxicated; very drunk. Named for a WWII bombing blitz. RT: ***drunk***. [U.S., E&R: 1971, DCCU: 1972, W&F: 1975, ADC: 1981] 2. drug intoxicated. RT: ***stoned***. [U.S., E&R: 1971, ADC: 1981, RDS: 1982]

blixed mildly drug or marijuana intoxicated. RT: *wasted*. [U.S., JWK: 1981]

bloak See *bloke*.

bloat a drunkard. *Cf. whiskey bloat*. RT: *sot*. [U.S., (1861): OEDS, B&L: 1890, JSF: 1889, F&H, BVB: 1942]

bloated alcohol intoxicated. See *blimped*. GEN: swollen. RT: *drunk*. [Br., F&H (at *screwed*); U.S., MGH: 1915, MHW: 1934, D&D: 1957, W&F: 1960]

bloater a drunkard; a tippler. *Cf. bloat*. RT: *sot*. [U.S., BVB: 1942]

blob a glass of beer. RS: *nip*. [Br. military, F&G: 1925, B&P: 1965]

block 1. a cube of morphine, either crude or processed morphine. *Cf. cube*. RS: *load*. [U.S., BD: 1937, DWM: 1938, VJM: 1949, RRL: 1969] 2. a compressed block of hashish or marijuana; a kilo of marijuana. *Cf. brick*. RS: *load*. [U.S., (1966): ELA: 1982, EEL: 1971, M&V: 1973] 3. crude opium. RS: *opium*. [U.S., RRL: 1969]

blockade (also **blockade liquor, blockade whiskey**) untaxed whiskey; illicitly distilled whiskey. RS: *moonshine*. The term became prominent during prohibition but dates from the 1800s. [U.S., (1867): RHT: 1912, HK: 1917, VR: 1929, BVB: 1942]

blockader an illegal distiller of whiskey; a liquor smuggler. *Cf. blockade*. RT: *bootlegger*. [U.S., HK: 1917, ADD]

blockage illegal whiskey. RS: *moonshine*. From the prohibition era. [U.S., AH: 1931, MHW: 1934]

block and block alcohol intoxicated. Probably the same as **blockablock** and **chockablock** = full, block-to-block as with nautical tackle. RT: *drunk*. [BF: 1737]

block and fall alcohol intoxicated; drunk and irritated. RT: *drunk*. [Br. (Anglo-Irish), 1900s, DSUE]

blockbuster 1. a barbiturate; *Nembutal* (TM; *q.v.*). From the nickname of a powerful bomb used in WWII. *Cf. blitzed*. RT: *nemb*. [U.S., RRL: 1969, YKB: 1977, NIDA: 1980, ADC: 1981] 2. a mass of severely constipating fecal material. From the constipation caused by opium addiction. *Cf. yen-shee baby*. [U.S., M&V: 1967]

blocked 1. alcohol intoxicated. *Cf. block and block*. RT: *drunk*. [U.S., EEL: 1971] 2. drug intoxicated. RT: *stoned*. [U.S., (1968): ELA: 1982, EEL: 1971]

bloke 1. (also **bloak**) a drunkard; a tippler. RT: *sot*. [U.S., (1914): MGH: 1915, BVB: 1942, W&F: 1960] 2. cocaine. Rhyming slang for *coke*. From *big bloke* (*q.v.*). RT: *cocaine*. [U.S., W&F: 1967, EEL: 1971]

bloker a cocaine addict. *Cf. bloke*. RT: *kokomo*. [U.S., JES: 1959, H&C: 1975]

blond hash (also **blond, blond hashish**) 1. a mild, golden hashish. RT: *hash*. [U.S., RRL: 1969, ADC: 1975] 2. a weak variety of marijuana, golden in color. May be the same as sense one. RS: *pot*. [U.S., H&C: 1975, SNP: 1977]

blond Lebanese a light, golden hashish from Lebanon. *Cf. Lebanese hash, leb hash*. RT: *hash*. [U.S., ADC: 1975]

blood and thunder port wine and brandy mixed. From an oath (DSUE). [Br., mid 18-1900s, DSUE]

blood-sucker a physician. Probably refers to the drawing of blood for clinical testing and diagnosis. RT: *croaker*. [U.S., DWM: 1938]

blooey alcohol intoxicated. *Cf. flooey*. RT: *drunk*. [U.S., BVB: 1942]

blorphs *blue morphone* (*q.v.*). Possibly (blue) elixir of morphine sulfate. [U.S., JWK: 1981]

blossom nose a drunkard; a tippler. From the sore and reddened nose some drinkers get. *Cf. brandy blossom*. RT: *sot*. [U.S., MHW: 1934, BVB: 1942]

blotted alcohol intoxicated. Having soaked up alcohol like a blotter. RT: *drunk*. [U.S., BVB: 1942]

blotter 1. (also **blot**) a drunkard who soaks up alcohol like a blotter. *Cf. sponge*. RT: *sot*. [U.S., JAS: 1932, W&F: 1960] 2. (also **blotter acid**) a bit of paper (blotter) impregnated with the hallucinogenic drug *L.S.D.* (*q.v.*). Sheets of paper are soaked in a dilute solution of L.S.D., and then cut up into small squares and sold. *Blotter* is often stamped with a logo or "trademark" such as a *red dragon* (*q.v.*). [U.S., E&R: 1971, ADC: 1975, YKB: 1977, RAS: 1983] 3. cloth or filtering material which has been used to strain a drug solution as it is sucked into a syringe or a medicine dropper. [U.S., JES: 1959, H&C: 1975] 4. a drug solution retrieved from *cotton* (*q.v.*) or filtering cloth. [U.S., JES: 1959, H&C: 1975]

blotto 1. alcohol intoxicated; dead drunk. RT: *drunk*. [Br. and U.S., (1905): SBF: 1976, (1919): OEDS, F&G: 1925, MP: 1928, JAR: 1930, AH: 1931, D&D: 1957, B&P: 1965, SSD, ADC: 1984] 2. strong drink; hard liquor. RS: *rotgut*. [Br. military, WWI, DSUE]

blow 1. (also **blow-out**) a riotous drinking bout. GEN: a feast (1924): OEDS. RT: *spree*. [Br., B&L: 1890, M&J: 1975] 2. to inhale any powdered drug, including snuff. Now used primarily for cocaine. [U.S., (1924): JES: 1959, (BD: 1937), RRL: 1969, W&F: 1975, JWK: 1981, ADC: 1984] 3. an inhaled dose of a powdered drug. [U.S., A&T: 1953, W&F: 1967] 4. cocaine. *Cf. superblow*. RT: *cocaine*. [U.S., ADC: 1975, YKB: 1977, ADC: 1984] 5. to smoke marijuana. RT: *hit the hay*. [U.S., (1944): ELA: 1982, M&W: 1946, (M&D: 1952), RRL: 1969, EEL: 1971, M&V: 1973, W&F: 1975] 6. (also **blow a shot**) to miss the vein when injecting a drug. From the general slang expression meaning to ruin an opportunity. See *blow a fix*. [U.S., RRL: 1969]

blow a bine to smoke a cigarette; to smoke a Woodbine (TM) cigarette. [Canadian, WWII, MMO: 1970]

blow a cloud to smoke a cigar, cigarette, or pipe. [(1600s): JCH: 1887, GWM: 1859; listed in BVB: 1942]

blow a fill allegedly to smoke opium. Possibly an error for *blow a pill* (*q.v.*). [U.S., RRL: 1969]

blow a fix to miss a vein while injecting and lose the drug in the skin. The same as *blow a shot*. [U.S., W&F: 1967]

blow a pill to smoke opium. *Pill* (*q.v.*) = an opium pellet. RT: *suck bamboo*. [U.S., M&V: 1954, H&C: 1975]

blow a shot to miss a vein while injecting and lose the drug in the skin; to waste a solution of narcotics. See comments at *blow* (sense five). [U.S., DWM: 1936, BD: 1937, DWM: 1938]

blow a stick to smoke a marijuana cigarette. *Cf. stick*. RT: *hit the hay*. [U.S., JBW: 1967, RRL: 1969, EEL: 1971, W&F: 1975]

blow a vein to ruin a portion of a vein for further injections. [U.S., RG: 1970, IGA: 1971, JHF: 1971, H&C: 1975]

blow coke (also **blow Charlie, blow dust, blow the coke**) to sniff (snort) cocaine. RT: *snort*. [U.S., MHW: 1934, VJM: 1949, GOL: 1950, DCCU: 1972]

blow dust to sniff (snort) cocaine. *Dust* (*q.v.*) = cocaine. See *blow coke*.

blowed away 1. (also **blowed**) alcohol intoxicated. RT: *drunk*. F&H list only **blowed**. [Br., F&H; U.S., BVB: 1942, D&B: 1970c] 2. drug intoxicated. *Cf. blow*. RT: *stoned*. [U.S., RAS: 1978]

blower 1. a cocaine user. RT: *kokomo*. [U.S., VJM: 1949] 2. a cigarette. RT: *nail*. [Canadian, MMO: 1970] 3. cocaine. Refers to the snorting of powdered or crystallized cocaine. RT: *cocaine*. [U.S., JH: 1979]

blow gage (also **blow gauge**) to smoke marijuana. *Cf. gage*. RT: *hit the hay*. Black slang. [U.S., CM: 1970, EAF: 1980]

blow grass (also **blow hay**) to smoke marijuana. *Cf. grass, hay*. RT: *hit the hay*. [U.S., TRG: 1968, EEL: 1971, W&F: 1975]

blow horse to sniff (snort) heroin. *Horse* (*q.v.*) = heroin. RS: *snort*. [U.S., RDS: 1982]

blowing 1. inhaling (snorting) powdered drugs. See *blow*. [U.S., DWM: 1936] 2. smoking marijuana. *Cf. blow*. RT: *hit the hay*. [U.S., M&D: 1952]

blow it to smoke marijuana. *Cf. light up*. RT: *hit the hay*. [U.S., EEL: 1971]

blow jive to smoke marijuana. *Jive* (*q.v.*) = marijuana. RT: *hit the hay*. [U.S., TRG: 1968, W&F: 1975]

blown away 1. (also **blown**) alcohol intoxicated. GEN: killed. *Cf. blown up*. W&F: 1960 date the word **blown** at c. 1850. RT: *drunk*. [U.S., W&F: 1960, ADC: 1981] 2. drug intoxicated; debilitated by frequent drug use or marijuana smoking. RT: *stoned*. [U.S., ADC: 1975, RDS: 1982]

blown out drug intoxicated. RT: *stoned*. [U.S., DCCU: 1972, W&F: 1975]

blown up alcohol intoxicated. *Cf. blimped*. RT: *drunk*. [U.S., D&D: 1957, W&F: 1960]

blow one's mind to become euphoric or dysfunctional due to a drug, usually the hallucinogenic drug *L.S.D.* (*q.v.*). Now general slang for overwhelm. [U.S., AHC: 1969, EEL: 1971, DCCU: 1972]

blow one's roof (also **blow one's top**) to smoke marijuana. RT: *hit the hay*. [U.S., GOL: 1950, A&T: 1953]

blow one up to light up and smoke a tobacco cigarette. [U.S., HS: 1933, MHW: 1934, GOL: 1950]

blow-out a spree; a bash. See *blow*. RT: *spree*. [U.S., BVB: 1942, M&J: 1975, RDS: 1982]

blow pot to smoke marijuana. *Pot* (*q.v.*) = marijuana. RT: *hit the hay*. [U.S., GS: 1959, TRG: 1968, W&F: 1975]

blow smoke to smoke marijuana. RT: *hit the hay*. [U.S., (1973): DNE: 1973]

blow snow to sniff (snort) cocaine. *Snow* (*q.v.*) = cocaine. RT: *snort*. [U.S., GOL: 1950, A&T: 1953]

blow tea to smoke a marijuana cigarette. *Cf. tea*. RT: *hit the hay*. [U.S., TRG: 1968, W&F: 1975]

blow the bag to inhale chemical vapors from a paper or plastic bag. The vapors produce a high. [U.S., EEL: 1971]

blow the coke to sniff (snort) cocaine. See *blow coke*.

blow the meet to fail to meet with a drug seller. Compare to *make a meet* at *make a buy*. *Blow the scene* was used in general slang to mean "leave the area," through the mid 1950s. [U.S., DWM: 1938, BVB: 1942]

blowtop a marijuana smoker. RT: *toker*. [U.S., (1948): ELA: 1982]

blow weed to smoke marijuana. *Cf. weed*. RT: *hit the hay*. [U.S., M&V: 1967, H&C: 1975]

blowzy alcohol intoxicated. RT: *drunk*. [U.S., BVB: 1942]

blue 1. alcohol intoxicated. RT: *drunk*. [U.S., (1818): DA, (1838): DAE, BVB: 1942, SJB: 1943] 2. an amphetamine tablet; a *Dexamyl* (TM; *q.v.*) tablet. This may be an error since Dexamyl is green. The term may refer to the *Amytal* (TM; *q.v.*) component of *Dexamyl* (TM; *q.v.*). See sense three. [U.S., EEL: 1971] 3. an *Amytal* (TM; *q.v.*) capsule. [U.S., M&V: 1967, RRL:

1969, EEL: 1971, YKB: 1977, EAF: 1980, NIDA: 1980] (This entry continues after the following list.) Terms and nicknames for Amytal: *amies, blue, blue angel, bluebirds, blue clouds, blue devils, blue dolls, blue dots, blue heavens, blue jackets, blues, blue tips, blue velvet, double-blue, jack-ups, pájaro azul.* 4. some variety of the hallucinogenic drug *L.S.D.* (*q.v.*). See *blue acid, blue angelfish, blue barrel, blue babies, blue cheer, blue dragon, blue flag, blue heaven, blue mist, blue pyramids, blue vials.* See also *French blue, heavenly blue, light blue.* 5. a police officer; the police. *Cf. azul.* RT: *fuzz.* Black use. [U.S., EAF: 1980] 6. a 10 mg tablet of *Valium* (TM; *q.v.*). See *blues.* [U.S., JWK: 1981]

blue acid the hallucinogenic drug *L.S.D.* (*q.v.*). Named for its blue color on white blotter or sugar cubes, or for the blue hallucinations claimed by its users. RT: *L.S.D.* [U.S., RRL: 1969, IGA: 1971, YKB: 1977]

blue angel a capsule of *Amytal* (TM; *q.v.*) barbiturate. RS: *barbs.* [U.S., RG: 1970, EEL: 1971, EAF: 1980]

blue angelfish a bit of blotter containing a drop of the hallucinogenic drug *L.S.D.* (*q.v.*). The blotter is stamped with a blue angelfish. RT: *L.S.D.* [U.S., ADC: 1981]

blue babies the hallucinogenic drug *L.S.D.* (*q.v.*). RT: *L.S.D.* [Canadian, MMO: 1970]

blue barrel a blue tablet of the hallucinogenic drug *L.S.D.* (*q.v.*). *Cf. barrel.* RT: *L.S.D.* [U.S., RG: 1970, EEL: 1971]

bluebirds capsules of *Amytal* (TM; *q.v.*), a barbiturate. *Cf. blue.* [U.S., JBW: 1967, M&V: 1967, RRL: 1969, EEL: 1971, YKB: 1977, NIDA: 1980] See also *redbirds.*

blue blazer (also **blue blazes**) beverage alcohol; a particular alcoholic drink. RT: *booze.* [U.S., MHW: 1934]

blue bombers 10 mg tablets of Valium. They are blue in color. *Cf. B.B.* RT: *vals.* [U.S., RAS: 1978]

blue boys (also **blue coats**) the police. RT: *fuzz.* Black use. [U.S., BVB: 1942, EEL: 1971, EAF: 1980]

blue bullets barbiturates, probably *Amytal* (TM; *q.v.*). RT: *blue.* [U.S., RG: 1970, IGA: 1971, NIDA: 1980]

blue caps one or more blue capsules impregnated with *L.S.D.* (*q.v.*). RT: *L.S.D.* [U.S., S&R: 1972]

blue chair (also **blue chairs**) the hallucinogenic drug *L.S.D.* (*q.v.*). Possibly a dialect pronunciation of *blue cheer* (*q.v.*). RT: *L.S.D.* [U.S., H&C: 1975]

blue cheer *L.S.D.* (*q.v.*); L.S.D. mixed with methamphetamine. From the brand name of a laundry detergent. RS: *L.S.D.* [U.S., D&B: 1970c, EEL: 1971, W&F: 1975, YKB: 1977, KBH: 1982]

blue cheese hashish. Possibly from the gummy consistency of hashish. RT: *hash.* [U.S., JES: 1959, H&C: 1975]

blue clouds capsules of *Amytal* (TM; *q.v.*) barbiturate. RS: ***blue***. [U.S., SNP: 1977]

blued (also **blewed**) alcohol intoxicated. *Cf.* ***blue***. RT: ***drunk***. [Br., JCH: 1887, F&H, DSUE; U.S., MHW: 1934]

blue de Hue a variety of marijuana used by the military in the Vietnamese war. Hue is a city in South Vietnam. RT: ***pot***. [U.S. military, 1960s-70s, ELA: 1982]

blue devils 1. the delirium tremens. RT: ***D.T.s***. [Br., (1822): DSUE, JCH: 1887, F&H; U.S., BWG: 1899, VJM: 1949, DCCU: 1972] 2. barbiturate capsules, *Amytal* (TM; *q.v.*). RS: ***barbs***. [U.S., (1944): HLM: 1982, JBW: 1967, DCCU: 1972, W&F: 1975, YKB: 1977, NIDA: 1980]

blue dolls capsules of *Amytal* (TM; *q.v.*) barbiturate. RS: ***blue***. [U.S., RG: 1970, SNP: 1977] See also ***red dolls, yellow dolls***.

blue dot 1. (also **blue jackets**) a barbiturate capsule, *Amytal* (TM; *q.v.*). RT: ***blue***. [U.S., NIDA: 1980, ELA: 1984] 2. (also **blue dots**) a blue tablet impregnated with the hallucinogenic drug *L.S.D.* (*q.v.*). RT: ***L.S.D.*** [U.S., EEL: 1971, ADC: 1981, KBH: 1982]

blue doubledomes *L.S.D.* (*q.v.*). *Cf.* ***domes***. RT: ***L.S.D.*** [U.S., KBH: 1982]

blue dragon a bit of white blotter impregnated with L.S.D. and stamped with a blue dragon. RT: ***L.S.D.*** [U.S., ADC: 1981]

blue-eyed alcohol intoxicated. *Cf.* ***blue***. GEN: innocent; appearing innocent. RT: ***drunk***. [U.S., (1850): W&F: 1960]

blue fascists the police. RT: ***fuzz***. [U.S., IGA: 1971]

blue flag the hallucinogenic drug ***L.S.D.*** (*q.v.*). RS: ***L.S.D.*** [U.S., W&F: 1975]

blue flats (also **flat blues**) the hallucinogenic drug ***L.S.D.*** (*q.v.*). RT: ***L.S.D.*** [U.S., H&C: 1975, ADC: 1981]

blue heaven (also **blue heavens**) 1. a capsule of *Amytal* (TM; *q.v.*). RS: ***blue***. [U.S., M&V: 1954, RRL: 1969, EEL: 1971, W&F: 1975, MW: 1976, YKB: 1977, EAF: 1980, NIDA: 1980] 2. the hallucinogenic drug ***L.S.D.*** (*q.v.*). *Cf.* ***blue***. [U.S., YKB: 1977, NIDA: 1980]

blue horrors the delirium tremens. *Cf.* ***blue devils, blue Johnnies***. RT: ***D.T.s***. [Br., late 1800s, DSUE]

blue horse barbiturates, probably *Amytal* (TM; *q.v.*). *Horse* (*q.v.*) = heroin. RT: ***barbs***. [U.S., SH: 1972]

blue jeans the hallucinogenic drug ***L.S.D.*** (*q.v.*). *Cf.* ***blue***. RT: ***L.S.D.*** [U.S., EEL: 1971]

blue jeans and T-shirts a mixture of *Talwin* (TM; *q.v.*) and *Pyribenzamine* (TM; *q.v.*). See ***T.s and blues***. A (reverse) disguise for the T and B sequence in ***T.s and blues***. RS: ***set***. [U.S., RAS: 1982]

blue Johnnies the delirium tremens. *Cf. B.J.s.* RT: *D.T.s.* [Aust., 1800s, F&H]

blue mist *L.S.D.* (*q.v.*); a sugar cube impregnated with L.S.D. From the blue tint of the chemical. RT: *L.S.D.* [U.S., C&H: 1974, YKB: 1977]

blue mornings seeds of a blue morning glory variety. RT: *seeds.* [U.S., RDS: 1982]

blue morphone morphine or a derivative of morphine. Possibly elixir of morphine. *Cf. blorphs, B.M.* [U.S., JWK: 1981]

bluenose a prohibitionist. GEN: a prig. RT: *dry.* [U.S., BVB: 1942]

blue pig 1. whiskey; illicit whiskey; inferior whiskey. RT: *whiskey.* [U.S., (1840): SBF: 1982, JRW: 1909, MHW: 1934, D&D: 1957] 2. an illicit liquor establishment; a speakeasy. RS: *speak.* [U.S., BVB: 1942]

blue pyramids the hallucinogenic drug *L.S.D.* (*q.v.*). *Cf. blue.* RT: *L.S.D.* [U.S., ADC: 1975]

blue ribbon (also **blue ribband**) gin. *Cf. blue tape.* RT: *gin.* [cant, FG: 1811, FG: 1823, DSUE]

blue-ribbon army teetotallers; abstainers RS: *dry.* [Br., JRW: 1909]

blue ribboner (also **blue ribbonite**) a teetotaller; a member of the *blue-ribbon army* (*q.v.*). RT: *dry.* [Br., (1878): SOD, JRW: 1909]

blue-ribbon faker a teetotaller; a member of the *blue-ribbon army* (*q.v.*). Faker = a hustler (in cant). RT: *dry.* [Br., (1822): DSUE, JRW: 1909]

blue ruin gin; bad gin; inferior hard liquor of any kind. The DRS suggests that it is rhyming slang for *gin.* SBF: 1982 lists **blue rum** (1831). Possibly a play on *blue ribbon* (*q.v.*). RT: *gin, rotgut.* [FG: 1811, GWM: 1859, W&F: 1960, RDS: 1982]

blues 1. (also **the blues**) the delirium tremens. *Cf. blue devils, blue Johnnies.* RT: *D.T.s.* [Br. and U.S., FG: 1811, DRS, (1827): DAE, GWM: 1859, JCH: 1887, B&L: 1890, BVB: 1942] 2. barbiturate capsules, *Amytal* (TM; *q.v.*). *Cf. blue angel, bluebirds, blue devils, blue heaven, blue velvet.* See *blue.* 3. 10 mg tablets of Valium. *Cf. B.B., blue bombers.* RT: *vals.* [U.S., JWK: 1981] 4. *Dexamyl* (TM; *q.v.*). See *blue.*

blue sage marijuana; a marijuana cigarette; hashish. RT: *pot.* [U.S., (1943): OEDS, BVB: 1953, A&T: 1953]

blues and reds (also **reds and blues**) capsules of *Tuinal* (TM; *q.v.*). *Cf. red and blues.* RT: *tooies.* [U.S., JHF: 1971, DEM: 1981]

blue saze a marijuana cigarette. Possibly a (foreign) dialect pronunciation of *blue sage* (*q.v.*). Probably an error for *blue sage.* [U.S., SNP: 1977]

blues, in the drunk and depressed; alcohol intoxicated. *Cf. blues.* RT: *drunk.* [Br., 1800s, F&H]

blue sky blond potent Colombian marijuana. RT: *pot.* [U.S., ELA: 1982]

blue splash L.S.D. on a bit of blotter paper. RT: *L.S.D.* [U.S., ELA: 1984]

blue star morning glory seeds used as a hallucinogen. From the color variety name. RT: *seeds.* [U.S., YKB: 1977]

blue stone any inferior hard liquor, bad gin or whiskey. Blue stone = vitriol, i.e., copper sulfate. RT: *rotgut.* [Br., 18-1900s, (1880): F&H; listed in BVB: 1942]

blue tape gin. The same as *blue ribbon.* RT: *gin.* [cant, FG: 1785, FG: 1811, FG: 1823, F&H; listed in BVB: 1942]

blue tips *Amytal* (TM; *q.v.*) barbiturates. RS: *blue.* [U.S., RG: 1970, IGA: 1971, W&S: 1977]

blue velvet 1. barbiturates; a barbiturate capsule, *Amytal* (TM; *q.v.*). RS: *blue.* [U.S., M&V: 1967, H&C: 1975] 2. an injection of paregoric and *Pyribenzamine* (TM; *q.v.*), an antihistamine. RS: *set.* [U.S., JBW: 1967, EEL: 1971, W&F: 1975] 3. a mixture of *Terpin Hydrate* (TM; *q.v.*) with codeine and *Pyribenzamine* (TM; *q.v.*). RS: *set.* [U.S., RRL: 1969, RG: 1970] See also *black velvet.*

blue vials the hallucinogenic drug *L.S.D.* (*q.v.*). *Cf. blue.* RT: *L.S.D.* [U.S., H&C: 1975, SNP: 1977]

bluey a methyl alcohol drinker. From the blue skin color due to cyanosis. RS: *sot.* [Aust., 1900s, DSUE] See also *bluies.*

bluies (also **blueys**) *Drinamyl* (TM; *q.v.*). *Cf. blue.* [Br., (1963): DSUE, M&J: 1975]

blunt 1. a barbiturate capsule; *Seconal* (TM; *q.v.*) capsule. RT: *sec.* [U.S., EAF: 1972] 2. a hypodermic syringe. RT: *monkey pump.* Black slang. [U.S., EAF: 1980]

B.M. *blue morphone* (*q.v.*). *Cf. blorphs.* [U.S., JWK: 1981]

bo marijuana; Colombian marijuana. From *Colombo* (*q.v.*). *Cf. boo.* See *bo-bo* at *bo-bo bush.* RT: *pot.* Black use. [U.S., ADC: 1975, ADC: 1984]

bob gin. *Cf. Tom.* RT: *gin.* [Br., (1740): F&H]

Bob, Harry, and Dick hungover. Rhyming slang for *sick.* GEN: sick. RS: *hangover.* [JRW: 1909]

bo-bo bush (also bo-bo) marijuana; hashish. *Cf. bo, Colombo, bo-bo bush.* RT: *hash, pot.* [U.S., DWM: 1936, VJM: 1949, RG: 1970]

bo-bo jockey a marijuana smoker. *Cf. bo, bo-bo bush.* RT: *toker.* [U.S., JES: 1959, H&C: 1975]

bock (also **bock beer**) a strong, dark beer which is the first beer drawn from the vats each spring. Ultimately from German *Eimbeck,* the name of a German town. Not slang. [U.S., mid 1800s-p., SBF: 1976]

body carrier See *body-packer.*

body drug (also body) an addictive drug; a drug which causes physical dependence. [U.S., RB: 1967, AHC: 1969, RRL: 1969, EEL: 1971] See also *head drug*.

body hangover a severe and debilitating hangover. RT: *hangover*. [U.S., D&B: 1970c]

body, out of one's having to do with the feeling of leaving one's body under the effects of a drug. Patterned on *out of one's head*. RS: *stoned*. [U.S., EEL: 1971]

body-packer (also **body carrier**) a person who practices *body-packing*, i.e., swallowing packets of drugs in order to smuggle them into the country. See *internal, swallower*. [U.S., RAS: 1982]

body-packing the practice of smuggling cocaine into the U.S. by runners who to swallow a large number of rubber-wrapped packages of the drug in Colombia, fly to Florida and vomit and excrete the packages for a smuggler's agent. A broken package can cause death. See comments at *Colombian roulette*. [U.S., RAS: 1982]

body trip a drug *trip* (*q.v.*) which has powerful physical side effects. See *body drug*. [U.S., M&V: 1973]

Bogart (also **bogard**) to monopolize a communal marijuana cigarette; to hold a communal marijuana cigarette so long that one drools on it. The same as *Humphrey* (*q.v.*). M&V: 1967 claims that violence is used in monopolizing the cigarette. Named for the movie tough guy, Humphrey Bogart. [U.S., M&V: 1967, RRL: 1969, EEL: 1971, EAF: 1980, ADC: 1981, ADC: 1984]

boggy drug intoxicated. GEN: muddled, confused, or perhaps, damp. RT: *stoned*. [U.S., S&E: 1981]

bogue inferior; sick; having drug withdrawal sickness. [U.S., W&F: 1967, RRL: 1969, CM: 1970, EEL: 1971, DCCU: 1972, MA: 1973]

boiled (also biled) alcohol intoxicated. *Cf. boiled owl, parboiled*. RT: *drunk*. See list at *cooked*. [U.S., (1886): SBF: 1976, GI: 1931, MHW: 1934, D&D: 1957; Aust., (1918): DSUE]

boiled as an owl alcohol intoxicated. The same as *biled as an owl*. RT: *drunk*. [U.S., BVB: 1942]

boiled corn whiskey; corn whiskey. RT: *whiskey*. [U.S., (1836): DA]

boiled owl (also **biled owl**) a drunk person, usually male. From the mental image of an owl, staring straight ahead, firmly boiled, or from the expression *tough as a boiled owl*. RT: *sot*. [JRW: 1909, BVB: 1942]

boilermaker 1. a mixture of light and dark ales. [Br., (1920): DSUE] 2. a glass of beer with a shot of whiskey in it. [U.S., D&D: 1957, W&F: 1960] 3. whiskey with a beer *chaser*. Less common than the previous sense. [U.S., BVB: 1953]

boilermaker's delight inferior whiskey; moonshine. RT: *rotgut.* [U.S., HS: 1933, MHW: 1934, D&D: 1957, W&F: 1960, RDS: 1982]

boiling drunk alcohol intoxicated. From *boiling mad. Cf. boiled.* RT: *drunk.* [Br., B&L: 1890]

boil out to attempt to end a case of drug addiction by stopping one's drug intake suddenly. Found in *take the boil-out* (*q.v.* at *take the cure).* RT: *kick.* [U.S., BVB: 1942, VJM: 1949]

Bo Jimmy marijuana. RT: *pot.* Black use. [U.S., ADC: 1984]

bokoo soused alcohol intoxicated. From French *beaucoup. Cf. soused.* RT: *drunk.* [U.S. WWI, MHW: 1934]

bolsa* a bag of narcotics; a ten-dollar bag of marijuana. The Spanish word for bag. RS: *load.* [U.S., RRL: 1969, EEL: 1971, CG: 1980]

Bolt a trade name for *amyl nitrite* (*q.v.*). RS: *snapper.* [U.S., ELA: 1984]

boluf an error for *bolus* (*q.v.*). [U.S., H&C: 1975]

bolus 1. a pill of opium. From a Latin word for pill. GEN: a pill, pellet. [(1603): MW: 1983, JES: 1959] 2. a physician. RT: *croaker.* [U.S., (c. 1850): W&F: 1960]

bomb 1. high potency heroin. *Cf. P.* RS: *heroin.* [U.S., RRL: 1969, MA: 1973, JWK: 1981] 2. a large, thick marijuana cigarette. *Cf. torpedo.* RT: *joint.* [U.S., RRL: 1969, D&B: 1978] See also *A-bomb, B-bomb.* 3. a lethal dose of a drug. *Cf. hot shot.* [U.S., RRL: 1969, RDS: 1982]

bombed out (also bombed) 1. alcohol intoxicated. RT: *drunk.* [U.S., (1940): SBF: 1976, W&F: 1967, DCCU: 1972, DNE: 1973, GU: 1975, MW: 1976, ADC: 1984] 2. drug intoxicated; totally incapacitated by a drug. RT: *stoned.* [U.S., RRL: 1969, CM: 1970, EEL: 1971, DNE: 1973, W&F: 1975, MW: 1976, JWK: 1981]

bomber 1. (also bombers) a barbiturate capsule. *Cf. B-bomb.* [U.S., DU, RRL: 1969] 2. a large, thick marijuana cigarette. *Cf. bomb, torpedo.* RT: *joint.* [U.S., M&D: 1952, W&F: 1960, RRL: 1969, CM: 1970, EEL: 1971, EAF: 1972] 3. a powerful grade of marijuana. RT: *pot.* [U.S., (D&B: 1978)]

bombita* (also bambita, bombida, bombido, bombito) 1. heroin and cocaine taken together. LIT: little bomb. RS: *set.* [U.S., ADC: 1975] 2. (also bombidos) an amphetamine capsule. RT: *amps.* [U.S., W&F: 1967, M&V: 1973, YKB: 1977, NIDA: 1980] 3. an ampule of amphetamine; a vial of *Desoxyn* (TM; *q.v.*). [U.S., JBW: 1967, RRL: 1969, EEL: 1971, JHF: 1971]

bomb-ne-bomb beer. See *bameba.*

bombo 1. a weakly alcoholic punch served cold. [Br., B&L: 1890] 2. a cheap wine; a cheap fortified wine. *Cf. atombombo.* RS: *wine.* [Aust., (1930): DSUE, SJB: 1945] 3. a wine drunkard; a wine drinking hobo. RT: *wino*. [Aust., SJB: 1966] 4. whiskey. [Aust., (1919): DSUE] See also *bumbo*.

bombo-basher a *wino* (*q.v.*). *Cf.* *bombo*. RS: *sot*. [Aust., SJB: 1966]

bonaroo (also bonarro) having to do with good-quality narcotics. From an old prison term meaning essentially *of better quality*. Possibly from French *bonnet rouge* (DU) referring to red hats worn by French prison convicts who had more privileges than others. There is no explanation of how this got into English. *Cf.* *bad, decent, wicked*. [U.S., DU, M&V: 1954, EEL: 1971]

bonche a group of marijuana smokers. *Cf.* *cofradia*. EEL: 1971 lists boncha. Cuba and New York City use (M&V: 1973). [U.S., M&V: 1954, EEL: 1971]

bone a marijuana cigarette. RT: *joint*. [U.S., ADC: 1981]

bone-clother port wine. Because it puts weight on a person. RS: *wine*. [JRW: 1909]

boned alcohol intoxicated. RT: *drunk*. [Br., (1937): DSUE]

bone dry 1. a prohibitionist. RT: *dry*. [U.S., BVB: 1942, D&D: 1957] 2. sober; having given up drinking. RT: *sober*. [1900s, K&M: 1968]

bonfire a cigarette; a cigarette butt. RT: *nail, brad*. [WWI, F&G: 1925, BVB: 1942, DB: 1944]

bong (also bhong) 1. a marijuana smoking device which cools the smoke by passing it through water. Widely known outside the drug culture. [U.S., (1971): ELA: 1982, ADC: 1975, D&B: 1978, DNE: 1980, JWK: 1981] (This entry continues after the following list.) Terms for devices used for smoking drugs: *bong, bowl, carburetor, chamber pipe, chillum, cock pipe, dope pipe, dugout, grass mask, grass pipe, hash cannon, hash pipe, Hawaiian pipe, hooka, hookah, horn, hubble-bubble, hubbly-bubbly, hukka, icer, isomerizer, jay-pipe, joystick, J-pipe, marcia, narghile, one-hit bowl, one-hitter, party bowl, pipe, poopkie, power hitter, resinator, roach pipe, sherm, sherman, shotgun, slave master, steamboat, steamroller, toke pipe, toker, tote, water pipe, wood*. 2. to smoke marijuana or other drugs with a bong or other device. RS: *hit the hay*. [U.S., ADC: 1975] 3. a puff or a hit of marijuana taken through a bong. Usually plural. RT: *toke*. [U.S., ADC: 1981]

bongo (also bongo'd, bongoed) alcohol intoxicated. RT: *drunk*. [U.S., BVB: 1942, D&D: 1957, W&F: 1967, DCCU: 1972]

bonita a baby laxative used to dilute heroin or cocaine; milk sugar. Mexican Spanish. *Cf.* *mannitol*. [U.S., M&V: 1967, RRL: 1969, JWK: 1981, S&F: 1984]

bonkers alcohol intoxicated; tipsy. GEN: crazy, giddy. RT: *drunk*. [Br., (1920): DSUE, WG: 1962, SSD]

boo (also bu) marijuana; a marijuana cigarette. Some sources state that this is from the word *jabooby*. *Cf.* *bo*. RT: *joint, pot*.

[U.S., (1930): CM: 1970, (1965): DNE: 1973, AHC: 1969, EEL: 1971, W&F: 1975, MW: 1976, D&B: 1978, EAF: 1980; Br., BTD: 1968, M&J: 1975]

boo-gee a bit of paper (tissue paper) or cloth used to tighten the joint between a hypodermic needle and a glass medicine dropper, or between an opium pipe bowl and the pipe stem. *Cf. gee.* RT: *gasket.* [U.S., DWM: 1938, BVB: 1942]

book a thin, flat folded paper container of a drug. RT: *load.* [U.S., M&H: 1959]

Book, The The Physician's Desk Reference, a reference book of drug information. See *PDR*. So-called in the novel *The Valley of the Dolls.* [U.S., JH: 1979]

boom marijuana; *dagga* (*q.v.*). Possibly a play on *bhang* (*q.v.*), i.e., "bang." Partridge (DU) is probably correct in suggesting that this is the Dutch word for tree as in *tree of knowledge* (*q.v.*). RT: *pot.* [South African, late 18-1900s, DU, JB: 1980]

boom boy a marijuana smoker. *Cf. boom.* RT: *toker.* Mentioned in JB: 1980 at *roker.* [South African, JB: 1980]

boomer an addict who moves frequently; a drifter. From railway worker's jargon (Maurer). GEN: a laborer who follows every *boom* such as an oil boom. There is considerable disagreement as to what boomer means outside drug argot. It always refers to some kind of a transient male, however. *Cf. globetrotter.* [U.S., EK: 1927, M&V: 1967]

boom tea a tea brewed from marijuana leaves. *Cf. boom.* [South African, (1971): JB: 1980]

boo-reefer marijuana; a marijuana cigarette. *Cf. boo, bu.* RT: *pot, joint.* [U.S., DC: 1972]

boose See *booze.*

boose-casa (also booze-casa) a pub. *Cf. boose* (at *booze*). RS: *bar.* [cant, JCH: 1887]

boosing-ken a saloon. RS: *bar.* See *boozing-ken.* [GWM: 1859]

boost and shoot an addict who *boosts* (= steals, shoplifts) in order to get money to buy drugs. Possibly a play on *boot and shoe* (*q.v.*). RT: *junky.* [U.S., S&W: 1973]

booster 1. an addict who shoplifts to pay for drugs. RS: *junky.* [U.S., DWM: 1931, JWK: 1981] 2. an amphetamine. RT: *amps.* [U.S., JH: 1979] 3. a bit more of a drug taken to prolong the high. [U.S., IGA: 1971]

booster pills amphetamine capsules. Because they raise your spirits. RT: *amps.* [U.S., EEL: 1971]

booster shooter an addict who shoplifts to pay for drugs. The same as *booster* (*q.v.*). RT: *junky.* [U.S., JH: 1979]

booster stick a tobacco cigarette whose end is dipped into marijuana resin before it is smoked. Its power is boosted by the resin. [U.S., M&V: 1967, H&C: 1975]

boot 1. to smuggle liquor or sell it illegally; to *bootleg* (*q.v.*). [U.S., 1920s, BVB: 1942] 2. the kick or charge from alcohol. [U.S., BVB: 1942] 3. a kick from a drug, usually an injected drug. *Cf. kick.* RT: *rush.* [U.S., BD: 1937, DWM: 1938, M&H: 1959, TRG: 1968] 4. (also **boot shot**) a manner of injecting a drug wherein blood is drawn back into the syringe to dilute it. This can be repeated in order to delay and prolong the peak of the *rush* (*q.v.*). [U.S., W&F: 1967, IGA: 1971, DCCU: 1972, MA: 1973] 5. to inject drugs into the bloodstream as described in sense two: to inject, pause, dilute, inject etc. *Cf. jack.* [U.S., RRL: 1969, EEL: 1971, M&V: 1973, JWK: 1981] 6. some material, usually paper or cloth, used to make an airtight seal between a hypodermic syringe or medicine dropper and a hypodermic needle. RT: *gasket.* [U.S., M&V: 1967]

boot and shoe (also **boot and shoe dope fiend, boot and shoer, boots and shoes**) a down-and-out addict or alcoholic. [U.S., DWM: 1936, BD: 1937, M&H: 1959]

boot and shoot allegedly an addict who shoplifts to get money to buy drugs. Probably an error for *boost and shoot* (*q.v.*). [U.S., RRL: 1969, RDS: 1982]

booter 1. a bootlegger. RT: *bootlegger.* [U.S., BVB: 1942] 2. an addict who injects in a manner which will delay the rush. See *boot.* RS: *bangster.* [U.S., M&V: 1967, JWK: 1981]

bootician a bootlegger; an illicit liquor dealer. A play on *beautician* and *bootlegger.* RT: *bootlegger.* [U.S., BVB: 1942]

bootie a bootlegger. RT: *bootlegger.* [U.S., BVB: 1942]

booting taking boot shots; using an injection technique which maximizes the drug's effect. Done with a variety of drugs including heroin and cocaine. The same as *flushing* (*q.v.*). *Cf. boot, boot shot.* [U.S., JWK: 1981, S&F: 1984]

bootlace a thin twist of tobacco. RT: *fogus.* Prison use. [Br., early 1900s, DSUE]

bootleg 1. to manufacture, distribute, or sell illicit alcohol, especially whiskey. This sense is from the prohibition era, although the word itself is older. [U.S., (1906): DA, MHW: 1934] 2. bad whiskey; illicit whiskey; any illegal alcohol. RS: *moonshine, rotgut.* [U.S., MHW: 1934, VJM: 1949, D&D: 1957] 3. having to do with bootlegging or contraband material. [U.S., B&L: 1890] 4. phony drugs; homemade drugs. RT: *black.* [U.S., ELA: 1984]

bootlegger an illicit liquor manufacturer, dealer, or smuggler. Widely known during prohibition. [U.S., (1850): SBF: 1976, DWM: 1931, GI: 1931, BVB: 1942] Terms for someone who sells or transports liquor illegally: *alki cooker, alki king, alki man, alki peddler, alky cooker, alky driver, blockader, booter, bootician, bootie, bootlegger, booze baron, booze gob, booze heister, booze* *hustler, boozelegger, booze runner, boozeteer, bung starter, duck, finger, hoocher, hootcher, legger, moonlighter, moonshiner, moonshiner's gopher, pint peddler, pirate, puller, rummy, rum runner, runner, shiner, stick, whiskey legger, white liner.*

boot man an addict who injects and withdraws repeatedly to control the rush. *Cf. boot, booter.* In communal drug injecting such a person can monopolize the needle while everyone else is kept waiting. [U.S., JWK: 1981]

boot shot an injection of an addictive drug where blood is withdrawn, mixed with the drug in the syringe (or medicine dropper) and injected again. See *boot, booting, boot man.* [U.S., JWK: 1981]

boot the gong around 1. (also **kick the gong around**) to smoke opium. Boot = kick. RT: *suck bamboo.* [U.S., GOL: 1950, A&T: 1953] 2. to smoke marijuana. RT: *hit the hay.* [U.S., GOL: 1950]

boot the habit to get rid of one's drug addiction. Boot = kick. The same as *kick the habit* (*q.v.*). RT: *kick.* [U.S., GOL: 1950]

booze (also **boose, bouse, bouz, bouze, bowse, bowze**) 1. (also **booze up**) to drink alcohol to excess; to go on a bash. RT: *guzzle.* [since the 1300s, OED] 2. any beverage alcohol. [(1732): OED, (1880s): SBF: 1982] The following list contains terms for beverage alcohol: *A., A-bomb juice, Africa speaks, agur-forty, alc, alchy, Al Cohol, alcohol, Alderman Lushington, ale, alk, alkali, alkee, Al K. Hall, alki, alki hall, alky, alleviator, alley juice, ammunition, angel foam, angel's food, angel teat, angel tit, anti-abstinence, antifogmatic, antifreeze, apple brandy, apple fritter, apple jack, aqua fortis, aqua vitae, ardent, ardent spirits, aristippus, army brew, artesian, atombombo, avec, Bacchus, bagman's blood, bag of beer, balderdash, bald face, bald-face whiskey, ball of fire, balm, balm of Gilead, bamboo juice, bameba, ba-me-ba, bamidy-bam, B. and S., barbed wire, barbwire, barley, barley-bree, barley broth, barley-corn, barley juice, barley pop, barley water, barley wine, barrel goods, bass, bathtub gin, bead, beer, beer-a-bumble, beggar boy's, beggar boy's ass, belch, belly vengeance, belly wash, belsh, benzine, berps, berpwater, bev, beverage alcohol, beverage wine, bevie, bevvy, bevy, beware, bidgee, bilge water, binder, bingo, birra, bitches' wine, bit of tape, bitter, bitter ale, bitter beer, bitters, bivvy, blackfellow's delight, blackjack, blackstrap, blackstrap alchy, black varnish, black velvet, blinder, blind tiger, blink-blonk, blockade, blockade whiskey, blockage, blood and thunder, blotto, blue blazer, blue blazes, blue pig, blue ribband, blue ribbon, blue ruin, blue rum, blue stone, blue tape, bob, bock, bock beer, boiled corn, boilermaker, boilermaker's delight, bomb-ne-bomb, bombo, bone-clother, boose, bootleg, booze, bosom friend, bottled bellyache, bottled earthquake, bottled sunshine, bounce, bourbon, bouse, bowse, bowze, boxcar, boy, brandy, brave maker, breaky leg, brew, brewer's fizzle, brew-ha, brewski, brewsky, Brian O'Flinn, Brian O'Linn, Brian O'Lynn, brightener, Bristol milk, British champagne, brown, brown bottle,* *brown food, brown plaid, brown stone, brush whiskey, bub, bubb, bubbles, bubble water, bubbly, buck, bucket, budge, bug juice, bug poison, bumble whiskey, bumbo, bumclink, bumy juice, bun, bung it in, bung juice, bunk, bunker, burps, bush girlfriend, busthead, bustskull, cactus juice, cane, canebuck, cane corn, cane spirit, canned heat, Cape brandy, caper juice, Cape smoke, catch up, catgut, catlap, cat's water, cawn, celebration water, cement water, chained lightning, chain lightning, chalk, cham, chammy, chamois, champers, charged water, Charley Freer, Charley Frisky, Charley Randy, cheer, cheerer, cheerer-upper, cherry bounce, chill, choc, choke dog, Christmas cheer, cinder, clap of thunder, clink, coal tar, cocktail, cocky's joy, coffin nail, coffin varnish, cold blood, cold coffee, cold cream, cold sody, cold tea, colonial, colonial tangle, Colorado Kool-Aid, comfort, comfortable waters, condensed corn, conk-buster, conversation fluid, conversation water, cool Nantz, corker, corn, corn coffee, corn husk, corn juice, corn likker, corn liquor, corn mule, corn spirits, corn squeezings, corn whiskey, corn wine, corroboree water, cougar milk, courage, cowboy cocktail, crank, crater, crawrot, crazy water, cream, cream of the valley, cream of the wilderness, creature, creature comfort, Crimea, crimson dawn, crooked whiskey, cup of cheer, cup that cheers, curse of Scotland, cut alchy, cutthroat, dad and mum, dago, dago red, daily mail, damp, damper, dancing girl, day and night, deadeye, death promoter, dee-horn, dehorn, demon rum, demon vino, derry-down-derry, devil's eyewater, dew, diddle, didn't ought, dido, digester, dimey, dishwater, Doctor Hall, do-it fluid, donk, down, drafty, drain, dram, Dr. Hall, drink, drops, drudge, drugstore whiskey, dry, dry goods, duck, Dutch courage, Dutch milk, Dutch suds, dynamite, dyno, earthquake, earthquake protector, eer-bay, elevator, embalming fluid, English burgundy, er-bay, ethyl alcohol, evidence, eye-opener, eyewash, eyewater, family disturbance, far and near, favorite vice, feke, fine, fine and dandy, finger and thumb, firewater, fiz, fizz, flapper likker, flash of lightning, flowing bowl, foam, fogram, fogrum, foot juice, forbidden fruit, formaldehyde, forty-rod, forty-rod lightning, forty-rod whiskey, forty-two caliber, forty-weight, fox head, freight, French article, French cream, French elixir, frisky whiskey, frog's wine, frosty, froth, fuddle, fuel, fun milk, fun water, fusel oil, fustian, gage, gargle, gas, gatter, gauge, gay and frisky, gee, geezer, Geneva, Geneva courage, Geneva liquor, German conversation water, giant killer, giddy water, giggle and titter, giggle goo, giggle juice, giggle soup, giggle water, gin, gin and it, glass, golden cream, good creature, good creature of God, good-natured, good-natured alcohol, good-natured alk, goog, Gordon, Gordon water, grapes, grapes of wrath, grappa, grapple the rails, grappo, gravedigger, greased lightning, Greek fire, groceries, grog, gullet wash, Gunga Din, gunpowder, gurgle, gusto, gut rot, gutter, gut warmer, guzzle, hair curler, half and half, hall, happy juice, happy sale, hard cider, hard liquor, hard stuff, hardware, hard water, Harry Champers, headache, heart's ease, heavy, heavy brown, heavy wet, hell broth, hen wine, hi-ball, highball, highland frisky, high octane, high-toned tonic, high voltage, hod of mortar, hogwash, Holland tape, home-brew, homespun, honey, honeydew, honey dip, hooch, hoochinoo, hootawater, hootch, hootchenoo, hops, horse brine, horse liniment, hot bottle, hot bozel, hot bozzle, hot stuff, Huckleberry Finn, hum, hum cap, humming bub, humming liquor, humming October, hundred proof, idiot oil, ignant, ignant oil, ignite oil, ignorant oil, ill-natured, ill-natured alcohol, I'm so, I'm so frisky!, in and out, Indian liquor, Indian whiskey, infernal compound, in-jay, ink, inside dope, invigorator, Irish, Irish aqua vitae, Irish dew, it, jack, jack-a-dandy, jackass, jackass brandy, Jack Dandy, jackey, jacky, jake, jango, Japanese dogs, J.D., Jersey lightning, jig-juice, jig-water, jinny, John Barleycorn, John Hall, jollop, Jon Hall, joy-juice, joy water, juice, jump-steady, jungle-juice, juniper, juniper-juice, junk, Kentucky corn, Kentucky dew, Kentucky fire, Kentucky horn, kero, ketchup, kickapoo joy-juice, kill-cobbler, kill-devil, killemquick, kill-grief, killmequick, kill-priest, kill-the-beggar, King Alky, kingdom come, King Kong, knock down, knock-me-down, knockout drops, kong, koolaid, kudu milk, lace, lace curtain, Lady Dacre's wine, lag, lage, lamp oil, lap, lapper, laughing soup, laughing water, legs and arms, leth bringer, light blue, lightning, lightning flash, light stuff, light wet, likker, Lincoln's Inn, lip-trap, liquid bread, liquid courage, liquid fire, liquid fuel, liquid joy, liquid lightning, liquor, little brown jug, liver destroyer, London Milk, long wine, loogan, lotion, lube, lubrication, lunatic broth, lunatic soup, lush, mad dog, madman's broth, magic, malt, malt liquor, max, McCoy, M.D., mecks, medicine, merry-go-down, Merry Widow, meth, metho, meths, methyl, Mexican milk, milk, Minnehaha, misery, moisture, mokus, monkey swill, moon, mooney, moonlight, moonshine, moony, moose milk, mother's milk, mother's ruin, mountain dew, mouthwash, muddler, muddy water, mule, mur, mustika, mutiny, myrrh, nanny goat sweat, nantz, nap, nappy, nappy ale, naturalized alky, near-beer, neaters, neck oil, nectar, nectar of the gods, needle, needle and pin, needle beer, Nelly, Nelly's death, Nelson's blood, never fear, nig, nigger gin, nigger pot, ninety-weight, nippitate, nippitato, nippitatum, nose paint, o-be-joyful, October, Oh my!, Oh my dear!, oil, oil of barley, oil of joy, old boy, old man, old man's milk, old redeye, old red goofy, old shoes, old Tom, ould Tom, oyl of barley, pack, painkiller, paint, paint remover, pale, paleface, panther, panther juice, panther piss, panther pizen, panther's breath, panther's piss, panther's pizen, panther sweat, pass whiskey, penitentiary highball, pepper-upper, P.G.A., pharaoh, pharo, phlegm-cutter, phlegm-disperser, physic, pick and choose, pig iron, pig's, pig's ear, pig sweat, pimple and blotch, pimple and wart, pinch-gut vengeance, pine top, pink-eye, pinkie, pink lady, pink tea, pinky, pish, piss, piss-maker, pissticide, pizen, plink, plinkety-plonk, plink-plonk, plonk, pluck, plunk, point blank, poison, pong, pongellorum, pongelo, pongelow, ponjello, pop, popskull, pop wine, port, porter, porter's ale, porter's beer, porter's booze, pot, potato soup, potato water, poteen, potheen, pot of O., pot o' reeb, potsheen, poverty, prairie dew, prescription, prescription whiskey, prune juice, pruno, punk stuff, purge, quartern o' bry, quartern o' finger, queer, queer-beer, queer belch, queer booze, queer bub, queer lap, quill, quin, rag water, railroad, railroad whiskey, rain in Spain, raisinjack, rat poison, rat-track whiskey, razors, real A.V., real goods, real mokoy, real stuff, red, red biddy, red disturbance, redeye, red fustian, redhead, red ink, red liquor, red ned, red ribbin, red ribbon, red ruin, red steer, red tape, red tea, reeb, repeal milk, rerun, rerun alky, resin, ribbon, right sort, rise and shine, River Ooze, River Ouse, roasting-ear wine, roger, rooje, rookus juice, rosie, rosin, rosy, Rosy Loader, rot, rotgut, rotto, rouge, royal poverty, rub-a-dub, rubbydub, ruby, ruin, rum, rye, rye sap, sagebrush whiskey, sailor's champagne, salmon and trout, sangaree, satin, sauce, scamper juice, scat, schoolboy Scotch, scooch, scoop, scorching fluid, scorpion Bible, Scotch, Scotch tea, scrap iron, screech, seafood, sentimental water, serum, shake-up, sham, shammy, shampers, shampoo, shandy, sheep-dip, sheepherder's delight, sheep-wash, shellac, sherry, shicker, shikker, shine, shine liquor, shinny, ship in full sail, ship in sail, shoe polish, shoestring, short dog, shorty, shypoo, silk and twine, silken, silken twine, silly milk, silo drippings, Simon, Simon Pure, Sir John Barleycorn, sissy beer, skag, skat, skee, skilly, skimish, skink, skit, sky, sky blue, slim, slip-slop, sloe gin, sloosh, slop, slops, slosh, sludge, slumgullion, sly grog, small beer, smash, smile, smoke, snake, snakebite medicine, snakebite remedy, snakehead whiskey, snake juice, snake medicine, snake poison, snake water, snap-neck, snapps, snaps, sneaky Pete, snops, snopsy, soda-pop wine, something, something cool, something damp, something short, something wet, soother, soothing syrup, soul destroyer, sparkle, speedball, spirits, splash, spodiodi, sprang, spud, squaw piss, squeeze, squirrel, squirrel dew, squirrel whiskey, squirt, staff naked, staggering juice, stagger juice, staggers, stagger soup, stagger water, stark naked, steam, Sterno, Sterno Club, stim, sting, stingo, stinkibus, stinkious, stinko, stout, strike-me-dead, string and twine, strip-me-naked, strong and thin, strong drink, strong stuff, strong waters, stuff, stump, stump likker, stump rum, stump water, stupor juice, suck, suction, suds, suet, sugar candy, super-suds, swag, swamp dew, swamp root, swicky, swig, swill, swipe, swipes, swizzle, tanglefoot, tangleleg, Taos, Taos lightning, tape, taps, tarantula juice, taste, tea, the amber brew, the bane, the berries, the bottle, the bubbly, the clear McCoy, the crater, the creature, the demon rum, the evidence, the glass, the grapes, the hot bozzle, the jug, the liquid amber, the real McCoy, the real thing, The River, the sma' still, thick, thick and thin, thimble and thumb, thin drink, third rail, three-two, throat gag, tickle brain, tiger beer, tiger eye, tiger juice, tiger milk, tiger piss, tiger's milk, tiger sweat, tip, tipple, titley, tittery, tittey, titty, toddy, toilet water, Tom, Tom Thumb, tongue loosener, tongue oil, tonic, tonsil bath, tonsil oil, tonsil paint, tonsil varnish, tonsil wash, tornado juice, torn thumb, torpedo juice, toth, touse, trade whiskey, treacle, turpentine, turps, twankay, twine, two and over, unsweetened, upper cut, usquebaugh, van blank, van blank Anglais, van blonk, van rooge, varnish, varnish remover, veeno, vice, vin blink, vinegar blink, vinegar-de-blink, ving blong, vino, vin ruge, vin sisters, vitriol, Volstead exile, wallop, wampo, wanks, water-bewitched, waterbury watch, water of life, weeno, wet goods, wet one, wet stuff, wet-thee-through, what it takes, whip, whip-belly, whip-belly vengeance, whiskey, whistle-belly vengeance, whistle wetter, white, white coffee, white eye, white face, white fustian, white horse, white lace, white lady, white lightning, white lime, white line, white liquor, white mule, white ribbin, white ribbon, white satin, white stuff, white tape, white velvet, white whiskey, white wine, white wool, whoopee, whoopee-water, Who shot John?, wibble, wildcat, wildcat beer, wildcat whiskey, wild mare's milk, wine, wino, wish-wash, witch piss, woofle water, woozle water, wring-jaw, yadnarb, yakky-dak, yard of satin, yell, yocky-dock.*

booze artist a drunken person; a drunkard. RT: *sot.* [Aust., (1920): DSUE, SJB: 1945]

booze baron the leader of a bootlegging operation. From the prohibition era. RS: *bootlegger.* [U.S., BVB: 1942, VJM: 1949]

boozeblind alcohol intoxicated. RT: *drunk.* [U.S., (1850-1900): RFA, RDS: 1982]

booze blues the after-effects of excessive drinking. *Cf. blues.* RT: *hangover.* [U.S., BVB: 1942]

booze bout a riotous drinking bout. RT: *spree.* [U.S., BVB: 1942]

booze bum a drunkard; a *wino* (*q.v.*). RT: *sot.* [U.S., BVB: 1942, D&D: 1957]

booze crib (also **guzzle crib**) a pub; a low drinking establishment. *Cf. lush crib, patter crib, suck crib.* RT: *dive.* [cant, late 1800s, DU]

boozed (also **boosed, boozed up, bowzed**) alcohol intoxicated. *Cf. booze.* RT: *drunk.* [(1850): OED, (1886): RML: 1950, F&H, MGH: 1915, MP: 1928, D&D: 1957]

boozed as the gage (also **has boozed the gage**) alcohol intoxicated. (BF: 1737: [He's] Booz'd the Gage.) RT: *drunk.* [BF: 1737]

booze fencer a pub operator; a pub bartender. Fence = sell. RS: *bartender.* [cant, JRW: 1909]

boozefest a bash; a riotous drinking bout. RT: *spree.* [U.S., (AH: 1931), BVB: 1942, D&D: 1957]

booze fight a drinking bout. RS: *spree.* [U.S., (1922): DA, BVB: 1942]

booze fighter 1. a drug addict. RT: *junky.* A person (usually a hobo) who fights alcoholism by using drugs. [U.S., EK: 1927, W&F: 1960] 2. a drinker; a drunkard. RT: *sot.* [U.S., (1903):

DA, AH: 1931, MHW: 1934]

booze foundry (also booze benderie, booze joint, booze spot) a place where illicit liquor is sold; a speakeasy. RT: *sly grogshop, speak.* [U.S., AH: 1931, MHW: 1934]

booze freak a drunkard; someone who prefers alcohol to drugs. *Cf. booze fighter.* See *freak.* RT: *sot.* [U.S., D&B: 1970c]

booze gob 1. a heavy drinker; a drunkard. Gob = mouth (in British slang). RT: *sot.* [U.S., MHW: 1934] 2. a liquor smuggler or bootlegger who smuggles by sea. Gob = sailor. RT: *bootlegger.* [U.S., BVB: 1942]

booze guzzler a heavy drinker; a drunkard. RS: *sot.* [U.S., BVB: 1942, D&D: 1957]

booze heister (also booze hister) 1. a heavy drinker; a drunkard. RT: *sot.* [U.S., BVB: 1942, VJM: 1949, D&D: 1957] 2. someone who sells and serves liquor at a bar. [U.S., MHW: 1934, BVB: 1942] 3. a liquor smuggler; a bootlegger who hijacks liquor shipments. RT: *bootlegger.* [U.S., AH: 1931, BVB: 1942]

booze hitter a drunkard; a tippler. RT: *sot.* [U.S., BVB: 1942]

booze hound a drunkard; a heavy drinker; an alcoholic. RT: *sot.* Heard on the U.S. television program M*A*S*H, 1970s. [Aust., SJB: 1945; U.S., (1926): SBF: 1976, BVB: 1942, VJM: 1949]

booze hustler a *bootlegger* (*q.v.*); a liquor smuggler. RT: *bootlegger.* [U.S., D&D: 1957]

booze, in alcohol intoxicated. RT: *drunk.* [U.S., BVB: 1942]

booze it up (also booze it) to drink excessively; to drink to intoxication. RT: *mug oneself.* [16-1900s, DSUE, BVB: 1942, AP: 1980]

booze king a heavy drinker; a drunkard. RT: *sot.* [Aust., SJB: 1945] See also *booze baron.*

boozelegger a *bootlegger* (*q.v.*); a liquor smuggler. RT: *bootlegger.* [U.S., BVB: 1942, D&D: 1957]

booze mopper a heavy drinker; a drunkard. RT: *sot.* [M&J: 1975]

booze, on the on a protracted drinking bout. RS: *spreeing.* [Aust. and Br., late 18-1900s, DSUE]

booze pusher the proprietor of a pub or tavern. RS: *bartender.* [Br., JRW: 1909]

boozer (also booser) 1. a heavy drinker; a drunkard; an alcoholic. RT: *sot.* [(1611): DSUE, F&H, (1890s): SBF: 1976, BVB: 1942, VJM: 1949, D&D: 1957] 2. a pub; a tavern. RS: *bar.* [JRW: 1909, BVB: 1942, B&P: 1965]

boozerie See *boozery.*

boozeroo a riotous drinking bout. *Cf. jamberoo* (at *jamboree*). The *-eroo* ending is thought to be from American English. RT: *spree.* [New Zealand, JAWB: 1943]

booze runner a *bootlegger* (*q.v.*); a liquor smuggler. Similar to *rum runner* (*q.v.*). RT: *bootlegger*. [U.S., early 1900s, DU]

boozery (also **boozerie**) a saloon; a tavern. RS: *bar*. [U.S., AH: 1931, BVB: 1942]

booze shunter 1. a heavy beer drinker. *Cf. brandy shunter*. RT: *sot*. [Br., JRW: 1909] 2. a pub; a tavern. RS: *bar*. [Br., JRW: 1909]

booze stiff a drunkard; a hobo drunkard. Stiff = hobo. RS: *sot*. [U.S., VJM: 1949]

boozeteer a *bootlegger* (*q.v.*); a booze racketeer. RT: *bootlegger*. [U.S., BVB: 1942]

boozeteria a saloon; a tavern. *Cf. beeratorium*. RS: *bar*. [U.S., BVB: 1942]

booze the jib to drink to excess. Jib = jaw, mouth. RT: *guzzle*. [Br., (1837): DSUE]

booze-up 1. a drinking bout. *Cf. beer-up*. RT: *spree*. [Aust., (1897): DSUE, SJB: 1943; U.S., BVB: 1942, (1968): DNE: 1973] 2. to drink liquor. See *booze up* at *booze*.

boozey (also **boosey**, **boozy**) alcohol intoxicated. (BF: 1737: [He's] Boozy.) RT: *drunk*. See *boozy*. [(1529): OED, BF: 1722, BF: 1737, FG: 1785, JCH: 1887, B&L: 1890, BWG: 1899, BVB: 1942, SSD]

boozician a heavy drinker; a drunkard; a drunken person. RT: *sot*. [Aust., SJB: 1945]

boozified alcohol intoxicated. RT: *drunk*. [U.S., BVB: 1942]

boozify to drink to excess; to drink to inebriation. RT: *guzzle, mug oneself*. [U.S., BVB: 1942]

boozing-ken (also **boosing-ken**) an alehouse; a drinking den. Ken (from *kennel*) = house (in cant). RT: *dive*. [cant, TH: 1567, BE: 1690, FG: 1785, FG: 1823, B&L: 1890]

boozington a heavy drinker; a drunkard; a drunken person. *Cf. lushington, swipington, thirstington*. RT: *sot*. Prison use. [Aust., (1860): DSUE, F&H, SJB: 1945]

boozy (also **boosy**, **boozie**, **boozey**, **bousey**, **bousy**) alcohol intoxicated; tipsy; showing the effects of drink. RT: *drunk*. [in various spellings since the early 1500s, (1529): OED, M&C: 1905]

boozy-woozy alcohol intoxicated. *Cf. woozy*. RT: *drunk*. [U.S., BVB: 1942]

bop a drug in pill form; a dose of a drug. A synonym of *hit* (*q.v.*). *Cf. drop a bop*. [U.S., HER: 1971, DCCU: 1972]

boraccho (also **borracho**) alcohol intoxicated. Spanish *borracho* = a drunkard. RT: *drunk*. [U.S., D&B: 1970c, EEL: 1971]

borachio (also **boracho**, **borrachio**) a drunkard; a drunken person. LIT: a wine bag. BE: 1690 lists boracho. See the previous entry. RT: *sot*. [Br., BE: 1690, F&H]

Bordeaux hammer a headache from drinking Bordeaux wine; a hangover. A jocular nonce expression. RT: *hangover.* [(1576): OED]

border (also border red) a weak secobarbital capsule manufactured in Mexico. *Cf. Seconal* (TM). From *South of the border,* i.e., Mexico. RS: *sec.* [U.S., EEL: 1971, EAF: 1980]

boredom beater a marijuana pleasure smoker. Probably never argot. RS: *toker.* [U.S., HB: 1955]

boshy alcohol intoxicated; tipsy. Probably a drunken imitation of *bosky* (*q.v.*). RT: *drunk.* [U.S., (1925): DU]

boskiness drunkenness. See *have a touch of boskiness.* [Br., (1887): F&H]

bosky (also bosco absoluto, bosko absoluto) tipsy; almost drunk. Bosk = thicket. RS: *drunk.* [(1730): OED, FG: 1823, B&L: 1890, F&G: 1925, MHW: 1934; listed in PD: 1982]

bosom friend alcohol; an alcoholic drink. GEN: a good or close friend. RT: *booze.* [Br., late 1800s, F&H; listed in BVB: 1942]

boss having to do with the best quality drugs. GEN: excellent, knowledgeable. [U.S., M&V: 1967, RRL: 1969, EEL: 1971, M&V: 1973]

boss habit a very heavy addiction to heroin. *Cf. boss.* RT: *habit.* [U.S., M&V: 1967, H&C: 1975]

both barrels both nostrils used in the snorting of cocaine. Refers to the barrels of a double-barreled shotgun. *Cf. one and one.* [U.S., M&V: 1973]

both sheets in the wind alcohol intoxicated. Refers to a ship out of control because the lines securing the sails are free or both on the same side of the sail. This refers to a square rigged ship. *Cf. two sheets to the wind.* RT: *drunk.* [U.S., BVB: 1942]

bottle 1. a drunkard. RT: *sot.* [U.S., BVB: 1942] 2. a bottle of whiskey; a bottle of any hard liquor. See *the bottle.* Slightly euphemistic. [1900s and probably earlier, W&F: 1960] 3. amphetamines; a vial of methamphetamine. See *bottles.* RT: *amps.* [U.S., IGA: 1971, YKB: 1977, NIDA: 1980] 4. to drink liquor, probably to excess. RT: *guzzle.* [U.S., BVB: 1942]

bottleache a hangover; the delirium tremens. *Cf. wineache.* RT: *D.T.s, hangover.* [Br., B&L: 1890, F&H; listed in BVB: 1942]

bottle-a-day man a drunkard; an alcoholic. RT: *sot.* [U.S., AH: 1931, BVB: 1942]

bottle and stopper (also bottle stopper) a police officer. RT: *fuzz.* [U.S., (1928): DRS]

bottle baby a drunkard; an alcoholic. From the descriptive term given to a baby that takes milk from a bottle. RT: *sot.* [U.S., BVB: 1942, D&D: 1957, W&F: 1960, RDS: 1982]

bottle cracker a drunkard. Probably from the colloquial

expression *crack open a bottle*. RT: *sot*. [U.S., BVB: 1942]

bottled (also bottled up) alcohol intoxicated; tipsy. RT: *drunk*. [Br. and U.S., (1930): DSUE, BVB: 1942, W&F: 1960, PW: 1974]

bottled bellyache bad beer; cheap bottled beer. RS: *rotgut*. Hobo use. [1900s, DSUE]

bottle dealer a drug dealer selling pills in large volume, i.e., large bottles. *Cf. jar dealer*. RS: *dealer*. [U.S., IGA: 1971, RDS: 1982]

bottled earthquake whiskey. RT: *whiskey*. [Br., late 1800s, F&H; listed in BVB: 1942]

bottled in barn having to do with low-quality beverage alcohol especially whiskey. A play on *bottled in bond* (*q.v.*). RS: *rotgut*. [U.S., BVB: 1942]

bottled in bond having to do with high-quality beverage alcohol bottled before prohibition. Not necessarily bonded whiskey. [U.S., BVB: 1942]

bottled sunshine beer. *Cf. beer*. [Br. military, (1930): DSUE]

bottle fatigue a hangover; a depression from drinking. A play on *battle fatigue*. RT: *hangover*. [U.S., D&D: 1957]

bottle fever alcoholism. RS: *drunk*. [U.S., (1850-1900): RFA]

bottle heister a drunkard. The same as *booze heister*. RT: *sot*. [U.S., BVB: 1942]

bottle joint (also bottle factory) a place to purchase and drink liquor. RT: *bar*. [U.S., BVB: 1942]

bottle man a drinker; a drunkard; an alcoholic. RT: *sot*. [U.S., W&F: 1960]

bottle nose the swollen and reddened nose of a drinker. [U.S., BVB: 1942] See also *gin bud*.

bottles vials of injectable amphetamines. *Cf. jug*. See other senses at *bottle*. RT: *amps*. [U.S., C&H: 1974, NIDA: 1980]

bottle shop (also bottle store) a liquor store. RT: *L.I.Q*. [Br., (1929): OEDS; U.S., BVB: 1942, D&D: 1957; South African, JB: 1980]

bottle sucker a heavy drinker; a drunkard; an alcoholic. *Cf. bottle baby*. RT: *sot*. [Br., 1800s, F&H; listed in BVB: 1942]

bottle, the liquor; booze in general; a symbol of alcoholism or drinking. [(1709): OED, BVB: 1942, MW: 1983]

bounce Fruit flavored brandy; cherry brandy. RS: *brandy*. [Br. and U.S., (1800): DA, B&L: 1890, BWG: 1899, DSUE]

bounce the goof balls to smoke marijuana cigarettes. *Cf. goofball*. RT: *hit the hay*. [U.S., JES: 1959]

bouncing powder (also bounce powder) cocaine. RT: *cocaine*. [U.S., DU, A&T: 1953, RRL: 1969, EEL: 1971]

bourbon an American whiskey made from corn. Named for Bourbon County, Kentucky. RS: *whiskey*. Standard English.

[U.S., mid 1800s-p., (1851): DA, (1857): OEDS]

bout with John Barleycorn a drinking spree; a solitary drinking bout. RT: *spree*. [U.S., BVB: 1942]

bowing See *bending and bowing*.

bowl 1. to smoke opium. RT: *suck bamboo*. [U.S., (1925): DU] 2. marijuana or hashish smoking pipe; the bowl of a hashish pipe; a water pipe. [U.S., (1974): R&P: 1982, ADC: 1975] 3. an opium pipe; the bowl of an opium pipe. RT: *hop stick*. [U.S., (1887): RML: 1948, DU] 4. (also **bowl up**) to fill a hashish pipe with marijuana or hashish. [U.S., ADC: 1981] See also *lemon bowl, orange bowl, party bowl*.

bowler an opium smoker. Refers to the bowl of an opium pipe. RT: *campfire boy*. [U.S., GOL: 1950, A&T: 1953]

bowl up to fill a hashish pipe with marijuana or hashish. [U.S., ADC: 1975]

bow-sow narcotics; drugs. Chinese or mock-Chinese. West Coast (M&V: 1973). RS: *dope*. [U.S., DWM: 1938, VJM: 1949, A&T: 1953]

bowzed alcohol intoxicated. (BF: 1737: [He's] Bowz'd.) RT: *drunk*. [BF: 1737]

box a matchbox filled with marijuana. *Cf. bee*. RS: *load*. [U.S., IGA: 1971, ADC: 1981]

boxcar whiskey; beverage alcohol. RT: *booze*. From the prohibition era. [U.S., AH: 1931, MHW: 1934, W&F: 1960]

boxed (also **boxed up**) 1. alcohol intoxicated. RT: *drunk*. [U.S., (1950s): SBF: 1976, CM: 1970, EEL: 1971, W&F: 1975] 2. drug intoxicated. RT: *stoned*. [U.S., (1967): ELA: 1982, RRL: 1969, CM: 1970, EEL: 1971]

box fire a cigar; a cigarette. RT: *nail, seegar*. [U.S., DB: 1944, CM: 1970]

box of L a box of 100 *Methedrine* (TM; *q.v.*) ampules (injectable amphetamine). L = 100 in Roman numerals. RT: *speed*. Probably not a fixed term in drug slang. [U.S., M&V: 1967, SNP: 1977] See also *L.L.*

boy 1. heroin. *Cf. big boy*. RT: *heroin*. [U.S., HB: 1955, W&F: 1967, RRL: 1969, CM: 1970, EEL: 1971, MA: 1973, YKB: 1977, EAF: 1980, JWK: 1981] 2. cocaine. Compare to *girl*. RT: *cocaine*. [U.S., JWK: 1981] 3. (also **the boy**) champagne. *Cf. old boy*. RT: *cham*. [Br., B&L: 1890; listed in M&J: 1975]

boys in blue police officers. See *men in blue*.

bozo one ounce of heroin. Probably a play on *O.Z.* (*q.v.*). RS: *heroin*. [U.S., JES: 1959, H&C: 1975]

bracer a drink of an alcoholic beverage. From a term for any substance which braces the nerves (SOD, mid 1700s). RT: *nip*. [U.S., (1829): OEDS, DSUE, D&D: 1957, W&F: 1960]

brad a cigarette butt; a cigarette; a *smoke* (*q.v.*). [Br. and U.S., F&G: 1925, HNR: 1934, W&F: 1960] Terms for cigarette butts: *blind-pickings, blink, bonfire, brad, bumper, butsie, butt, butt-end, captain's butt, castaway, choker, cigarette end, clincher, corporal's butt, corpse, curbstones, dead soldier, dimp, dinch, dincher, dog, dog end, doggin, doofa, doofer, duck, dufer, dummy, dumper, durry, fag, fag end, grounder, hobo's delight, lip-burner, maggot, nicker, nub, nub end, old soldier, private's butt, Robinson Crusoe brand, scag, sergeant's butt, shavetail's butt, skag, snipe, stompie, stooper, stoop tobacco, straight, teaser, topper.*

brain burned incapacitated through chronic heavy smoking of marijuana. [U.S., ELA: 1982]

brain burners injected amphetamines, probably methamphetamine. RS: *amps.* [U.S., BR: 1972]

brain tablet a cigarette. RT: *nail.* [U.S., (1850-1900): RFA, MHW: 1934]

brain tickler any drug which affects the mind; an amphetamine; a barbiturate. [U.S., RRL: 1969, EEL: 1971, RDS: 1982]

brand X cannabis; marijuana cigarettes. RT: *joint.* [U.S., EAF: 1980]

brandy a beverage alcohol distilled from wine. Ultimately from the Dutch expression for *burned wine.* [since the early 1600s, (1622): OED] Synonyms and nicknames for brandy: *apple brandy, apple jack, avec, ball of fire, B. and S., binder, bingo, bounce, bumbo, Cape brandy, Cape smoke, Charley Randy, cherry bounce, cold tea, cool Nantz, fine, fine and dandy, French article, French cream, French elixir, grappa, jack-a-dandy, jackass brandy, Jack Dandy, Jersey lightning, kudu milk, liver destroyer, nantz, o-be-joyful, pale, red ribbin, red ribbon, red tape, smoke, snap-neck, sugar candy, the bane, upper cut, yadnarb.*

brandy blossom a red sore on the nose from drinking to excess. RT: *gin bud.* [Br., (1887): DSUE]

brandy face a heavy drinker; a drunkard; a sot with a red face. RS: *sot.* [(1687): F&H; listed in BVB: 1942, D&D: 1957]

brandy shunter a brandy drinker; a brandy tippler. *Cf. beer shunter.* RT: *sot.* [Br., JRW: 1909]

brannigan a riotous and possibly violent drinking bout. GEN: a riot, a brawl. RS: *spree.* [U.S., MHW: 1934, BVB: 1942]

brass rail a saloon. Named for the brass footrest at the base of the bar. Currently a popular name for a bar or tavern. RS: *bar.* [U.S., BVB: 1942]

brave maker whiskey; hard liquor. In the sense that drinking it is equivalent to an Amerindian initiation to the status of brave. Also a reference to *courage* (*q.v.*). RT: *whiskey.* [U.S., (c. 1900): DST: 1984, RFA]

brawl a riotous and sometimes violent drinking party. GEN: a mob fight. *Cf. brannigan.* RT: *spree.* [U.S., R&P: 1928, W&F: 1960]

break to terminate addiction to a drug. From *break the habit. Cf. kick.* [U.S., DWM: 1938, VJM: 1949]

break a stick to smoke a marijuana cigarette. *Cf. stick.* RT: *hit the hay.* [U.S., JES: 1959, H&C: 1975]

break o' day drum See *drum.*

break-out a drinking bout. RT: *spree.* [Aust., SJB: 1943]

break the habit (also **break**) to terminate one's drug addiction. RT: *kick.* [U.S., DWM: 1938, H&C: 1975]

break the needle 1. to inject a dose of a narcotic. RT: *shoot.* [U.S., BVB: 1942, DU] 2. to terminate one's drug addiction. *Cf. kick.* [U.S., JES: 1959, H&C: 1975]

breaky leg 1. whiskey; hard liquor. RT: *booze.* [Br., (1839): DSUE, B&L: 1890, F&H; listed in BVB: 1942] 2. a drinking bout. RT: *spree.* [U.S., MHW: 1934]

bream a half pint of liquor. An amount smaller than a *perch* (*q.v.*) or a *bass* (*q.v.*). [U.S., GU: 1975]

breath strong enough to carry coal with with a great amount of alcohol on the breath; alcohol intoxicated. RT: *drunk.* [JRW: 1909]

Breckenridge green a low grade of marijuana presumably from Breckenridge County, Kentucky, or some other Breckenridge. RT: *pot.* Probably local to Kentucky. [U.S., M&V: 1973, SNP: 1977]

breezer a marijuana cigarette. RT: *joint.* [U.S., BR: 1972]

breezy alcohol intoxicated. GEN: vigorous. RT: *drunk.* [U.S., (1850): W&F: 1960]

brew beer; a can, bottle, or glass of beer. *Cf. the amber brew.* RS: *beer.* [U.S., DCCU: 1972, W&F: 1975, ADC: 1981]

brewer's droop impotence due to heavy drinking. [Aust., BH: 1980]

brewer's fizzle beer; ale. This may also be a play on *brewer's fart. Cf. drunk as a brewer's fart.* [Br., (1714): DSUE]

brewer's horse a drunkard; an alcoholic. RT: *sot.* [late 15-1800s (Shakespeare), B&L: 1890, F&H, JOH: 1901]

brewery 1. the place where beer or ale is brewed. Not slang. [since the 1600s, (1658): OED] 2. a place to buy and smoke opium. RS: *opium den.* [U.S., JES: 1959, JTD: 1971, H&C: 1975]

brew-ha beer; a beer. RT: *beer.* [U.S., RAS: 1984]

brew house 1. a brewery. [U.S., 1700s, SBF: 1976] 2. a liquor store. RT: *L.I.Q.* [U.S., EAF: 1980]

brewski (also **brewsky**) a beer; a can of beer. RT: *beer.* [U.S., RAS: 1980, ADC: 1984]

brew with hocks an error for *brew with hops* (*q.v.*). [U.S., H&C: 1975, ELA: 1984]

brew with hops to inject opium into the median cephalic vein. RT: *shoot.* [U.S., JES: 1959]

Brian O'Linn (also **Brian O'Flinn, Brian O'Lynn**) gin. *Cf. quartern o' bry.* Rhyming slang. RT: *gin.* [Br., DA: 1857, B&L: 1890, F&H, DRS]

brick 1. (also **brick gum**) a brick of unprocessed opium. Compare to *leaf gum.* RS: *opium.* [U.S., BD: 1937, DWM: 1938, VJM: 1949, RRL: 1969, EAF: 1980] 2. a kilogram of compressed marijuana. RS: *load.* [U.S., GS: 1959, JBW: 1967, AHC: 1969, RRL: 1969, EEL: 1971, DCCU: 1972, W&F: 1975] 3. a bar of hashish. RS: *load.* [U.S., EEL: 1971, JWK: 1981]

bricked drug intoxicated. Possibly akin to *brick* (*q.v.*). Probably a synonym of *stoned* (*q.v.*). RT: *stoned.* [U.S., M&V: 1973]

brick gum a brick or cake of unprocessed opium. RS: *load.* [U.S., DWM: 1938, A&T: 1953]

bridge a holder for a marijuana cigarette butt. RT: *crutch.* [U.S., HB: 1955, IGA: 1971]

bridgey alcohol intoxicated. RT: *drunk.* [BF: 1737]

brifo marijuana. *Cf. grefa.* RT: *pot.* [U.S., (1937): ELA: 1982]

brightened drug intoxicated; high on marijuana. *Cf. on the beam.* RT: *wasted, stoned.* [U.S., JWK: 1981]

brightener a bit of hard liquor added to a soft drink. *Cf. lace.* [Br., (1922): DSUE]

bright in the eye alcohol intoxicated; tipsy. BVB also lists **bright-eyed**. RT: *drunk.* [Br., B&L: 1890, F&H; listed in BVB: 1942]

bring down 1. to terminate one's own or someone else's drug experience. GEN: to depress someone, (M&W: 1946). [U.S., (1930): RRL: 1969, EEL: 1971] 2. (usually **bring-down**) that which brings someone down, a drug etc. [U.S., M&W: 1946, D&B: 1978] 3. to sober someone up. Probably from sense one. [U.S., ADC: 1981] See also *come down.*

bring up (also **bring up a vein**) to tie off the arm so that the veins stand out for the purpose of injecting drugs. [U.S., DWM: 1938, BVB: 1942]

brink to make a drug purchase from a dealer. Origin unknown. RT: *score.* [U.S., JES: 1959, H&C: 1975]

brisket a small pack or *bindle* of narcotics. RS: *load.* [U.S., JES: 1959, H&C: 1975]

Bristol milk *sherry* (*q.v.*). Refers to Sherry imported to England via the port of Bristol. [(1662): OED, BE: 1690, FG: 1785, FG: 1823, B&L: 1890, F&H] See also *cold cream, cream, mother's milk.*

British champagne *porter* (*q.v.*), a low-quality alcoholic beverage. RT: *porter.* [FG: 1811, AAR: 1944]

broach it to inject drugs intravenously. From an old sense of *broach*: to stab. RS: *shoot.* [U.S., JES: 1959, H&C: 1975]

broccoli marijuana; a marijuana cigarette. RT: *pot, joint.* [U.S., (1969): ELA: 1982, H&C: 1975, YKB: 1977, NIDA: 1980; Br., M&J: 1975]

brody (also **brodie**) **1**. to go into a convincing but phony imitation of drug withdrawal symptoms in order to persuade a physician to prescribe drugs. See sense two. [U.S., DWM: 1936, RRL: 1969] **2**. a phony drug withdrawal spasm. See sense one. Named for Steve Brody who claimed he jumped off the Brooklyn Bridge around 1886. The expression is essentially an elaboration of *take a fall* (*q.v.*). [U.S., DWM: 1936, GOL: 1950, RRL: 1969] Terms and expressions related to phony drug withdrawal: *Arthur Duffy, brodie, brody, cartwheel, chuck a Charley, chuck a dummy, chuck a Willy, chuck a wingding, circus, Duffy, figure eight, frame a toss-out, frame a twister, inger, meter, put on a circus, shuck, take a Brody, take a Duffy, throw a Brody, throw a meter, throw a wing-ding, toss-out, turn a cartwheel, turn a wobbler, twister, whing-ding, wing-ding, wobbler, bagged, batted.*

broker 1. a dope pusher, seller, or connection. From the standard English term. RT: *dealer.* [U.S., GI: 1931, H&C: 1975, RDS: 1982] **2**. a ruined addict; a broken addict. RS: *junky.* [U.S., M&V: 1967]

Brompton cocktail (also **Brompton, Brompton mixture**) a powerful analgesic compound (liquid), typically composed of 60% morphine, 30% codeine, and 10% alcohol (gin, whiskey, or rum). An effective painkiller for persons with terminal diseases. Said to be named for the London hospital (Brompton Chest Hospital) where it was first used. [originally Br.; U.S. (1978): DNE: 1980 RAS: 1983]

brother heroin. *Cf. boy.* RT: *heroin.* [U.S., RRL: 1969, YKB: 1977, NIDA: 1980]

brother Ben an amphetamine, *Benzedrine* (TM; *q.v.*). *Cf. benny, copilot ben.* RT: *benz.* [U.S., MT: 1971]

brother bung a bartender. See *bung.*

Brother where art thou? a drunkard. RT: *sot.* [Br., 18-1900s, DSUE]

brought down depressed after a drug *high* (*q.v.*). *Cf. come down.* See *bring down.* [Br., BTD: 1968]

brown 1. whiskey. RT: *whiskey.* From the prohibition era. [U.S., GOL: 1950] **2**. (also **brown dope**) Mexican heroin. It is diluted with brown milk sugar. RT: *heroin.* [U.S., RRL: 1969, YKB: 1977, JWK: 1981] **3**. (also **brownie, browns**) a capsule of a specific amphetamine. Probably *Dexedrine* (TM; *q.v.*) capsules. See *brown and clears*. RT: *amps*. [U.S., RRL: 1969, IGA: 1971, YKB: 1977] 4. a hashish darker than that which comes from the Middle East, i.e., darker than *blond Lebanese* (*q.v.*). RS: *hash*. [U.S., JWK: 1981]

brown acid the hallucinogenic drug *L.S.D.* (*q.v.*). *Cf. acid*. RT: *L.S.D.* [Canadian, MMO: 1970]

brown and clears capsules of *Dexedrine* (TM; *q.v.*) amphetamine. One-half of the capsule is clear and the other half is brown. RT: *dex*. [U.S., RG: 1970]

brown bag to carry liquor concealed in a brown bag. GEN: to carry one's lunch in a brown paper bag. [U.S., (MW: 1976)]

brown bomber an amphetamine capsule, possibly *Durophet* (TM; *q.v.*). *Cf. black bombers*. RT: *amps*. [Br., BTD: 1968]

brown bottle beer; a bottle of beer. RT: *beer*. CB radio slang. [U.S., EE: 1976]

brown caps one or more brown capsules impregnated with L.S.D. RT: *L.S.D.* [U.S., S&R: 1972]

brown dope Mexican heroin. See *brown*. [U.S., MA: 1973]

brown dots the hallucinogenic drug *L.S.D.* (*q.v.*). *Cf. chocolate chips*. RT: *L.S.D.* [U.S., H&C: 1975, YKB: 1977]

brown food beer. May refer to brown beer bottles. RS: *beer*. [Br. military and nautical, WG: 1962]

brownies 1. small squares of chewy chocolate cake with marijuana included among the ingredients. *Cf. Alice B. Toklas*. [U.S., D&B: 1970c, EEL: 1971] 2. capsules of an amphetamine, probably *Dexedrine* (TM; *q.v.*). *Cf. brown*. RT: *amps*. [U.S., RRL: 1969, YKB: 1977]

brown one a marijuana cigarette. RT: *joint*. [U.S., BR: 1972]

brown plaid Scotch whiskey. *Cf. brown, waterbury watch*. RT: *whiskey*. [U.S., GOL: 1950]

brown rine heroin. As if it were pronounced *hair-o-rine*. *Cf. brown*. RT: *heroin*. [U.S., DU, A&T: 1953]

brown rock granules of diluted heroin for smoking. *Cf. brown*. RS: *heroin*. [U.S., RRL: 1969] See also *Mexican brown*.

brown shoes a nonuser of drugs; a square. RT: *square*. [U.S., JBW: 1967, IGA: 1971]

brown stone beer. *Cf. brown food*. RT: *beer*. [Br. and U.S., B&L: 1890, JSF: 1889, F&H, BVB: 1942]

brown stuff 1. opium. *Cf. black stuff*. RT: *opium*. [U.S., DU, RRL: 1969] 2. Mexican heroin. See *brown*. RT: *heroin*. [U.S., EEL: 1971, RDS: 1982]

brown sugar a grainy, low-potency heroin from the *golden triangle*. *Cf. brown, Mexican brown*. RT: *heroin*. [U.S., YKB: 1977, DNE: 1980, NIDA: 1980]

brown weed marijuana; a brown variety of marijuana. *Cf. weed.* RT: *pot.* [U.S., SNP: 1977]

bruised alcohol intoxicated. RT: *drunk.* [U.S., (1850): W&F: 1960]

brush an injection of narcotics. RT: *shot.* [U.S., JES: 1959, H&C: 1975]

brusher a full glass of liquor. *Cf. bumper.* [cant, FG: 1785, FG: 1823]

brush whiskey home-brewed whiskey. From the prohibition era. RT: *moonshine, whiskey.* [U.S., VR: 1929, AH: 1931, MHW: 1934]

brute an edible brown paste made from Coca leaves (the source of cocaine). From Colombia. [U.S., ELA: 1984]

bu marijuana. The same as *boo* (*q.v.*).

bub (also **bubb**) 1. beer; strong beer. RT: *beer.* [cant, (1671): OED; listed in BVB: 1953] 2. any beverage alcohol. RT: *booze.* [Br., BE: 1690] 3. to consume beverage alcohol, usually to excess. RT: *guzzle, mug oneself.* [cant, (1671): OED; listed in BVB: 1953]

bubbed alcohol intoxicated. *Cf. bub.* RT: *drunk.* [Br., 1800s, F&H; listed in BVB: 1942]

bubber 1. a large drinking bowl. [cant, BE: 1690] 2. a drunkard. A person with a large liquor capacity, like the drinking bowl. RT: *sot.* [cant, BE: 1690, FG: 1811, F&H; listed in BVB: 1942]

bubbery (also **bub factory, bub joint**) a tavern or other liquor dispensing establishment. RS: *bar.* [U.S., BVB: 1942]

bubble 1. a bubble of skin over an injection of a drug which has missed the vein. [U.S., D&B: 1970c] 2. to miss a vein in the injection of a drug and raise a bubble of skin with the drug. [U.S., D&B: 1970c]

bubbled alcohol intoxicated. RT: *drunk.* [PD: 1982]

bubblehead a heavy drinker of champagne. GEN: a giddy person. RS: *sot.* [U.S., RDS: 1982]

bubble water (also **bubbles**) champagne. RT: *cham.* [U.S., BVB: 1942, VJM: 1949, RDS: 1982]

bubbly 1. dark navy rum; rum grog. RT: *rum.* [Br. naval, 1900s, DSUE, WG: 1962] 2. (also **the bubbly**) champagne. RT: *cham.* [(1895): DSUE, (1920): OEDS, BVB: 1942, VJM: 1949, D&D: 1957, SSD]

bubby alcohol intoxicated. From *bub* (*q.v.*). RT: *drunk.* [late 1600s, DU]

bubster a drunkard; a tippler. *Cf. bubber.* RT: *sot.* [Br., 1800s, F&H]

buck illicitly-made prison alcohol. Usually made from water, sugar, yeast, raisins, etc. Probably from *canebuck* (*q.v.*). Prison use. [U.S., BL: 1982]

bucket a drink of liquor; liquor. RT: *booze.* See the following entry. [Br., (1870): DSUE; listed in BVB: 1942]

bucket of suds (also **bucket of beer**) a pail of beer. Draft beer was purchased in a container at a tavern and carried home to be drunk. [1900s, DSUE, (1904): SBF: 1976, MHW: 1934] See also ***rush the growler***.

bucket shop a liquor store; a liquor establishment. *Cf.* ***bucket, bucket of suds***. RS: ***bar***. [U.S., (1875): DA, BVB: 1942]

Buck's Hussar a cigar. Rhyming slang. RT: ***seegar***. Primarily music hall use. [Br., 18–1900s, DRS]

bud marijuana containing the dried flower tops; the buds of marijuana flowers. *Cf.* ***green bud, flower tops, mud-bud, redbud***. RS: ***pot***. Mentioned in passing in RPW: 1938. [U.S., (D&B: 1978), ADC: 1981]

Buddha stick a marijuana cigarette. *Cf.* ***Thaistick***. RT: ***joint***. [U.S., YKB: 1977]

budge 1. beverage alcohol. RT: ***booze***. [Br. and U.S., FG: 1823, (1874): W&F: 1960, JCH: 1887, BVB: 1942] 2. to drink liquor; to booze. RT: ***irrigate***. [cant, early 1800s, DU]

budger a heavy drinker; a drunkard. RT: ***sot***. [cant, B&L: 1890, F&H; listed in BVB: 1942]

budging-ken (also **budge ken**) a tavern; a pub. *Ken* (from ***kennel***) = a criminal hangout. RS: ***bar***. [cant, B&L: 1890, F&H]

budgy alcohol intoxicated. *Cf.* ***budge***. RT: ***drunk***. [Br., (1874): DSUE; listed in MHW: 1934]

budhead a beer drinker. From the Budweiser brand of beer. See the list at ***head***. RT: ***sot***. Black use. [U.S., DC: 1972]

buff to dilute a drug such as heroin or P.C.P. *Cf.* ***cut***. [U.S., FAB: 1979, JWK: 1981]

buffy alcohol intoxicated. *Cf.* ***biffy***. RT: ***drunk***. [Br., JCH: 1859, B&L: 1890, F&H; listed in BVB: 1942]

bug dust tobacco. May have some relationship to the use of nicotine as an insecticide. *Cf.* ***freckles***. RT: ***fogus***. [U.S., BVB: 1942]

bugged covered with sores from abscessed drug injections; covered with sores from "abscesses" self-inflicted in order to get drugs from a physician. *Cf.* ***loused***. See ***tracks***. [U.S., (DWM: 1936), JTD: 1971]

bug juice 1. (also **bug poison**) bad whiskey; strong whiskey. From a colloquial term for any insecticide. RT: ***rotgut***. [U.S., B&L: 1890, JSF: 1889, LWP: 1908, (FH: 1946), W&F: 1960] 2. narcotic knockout drops. RT: ***Mickey Finn***. [U.S., BVB: 1942, VJM: 1949]

build a smoke to roll a cigarette. Jocular cowboy talk. [U.S., 1900s or earlier, PW: 1977]

bulb the rubber bulb of a medicine dropper; the nipple of a baby's pacifier attached to a ***dropper*** (*q.v.*). [U.S., MA: 1973]

bull 1. Bull Durham (TM) tobacco. RS: *fogus*. [U.S., (1910): DST: 1984, BVB: 1942, GOL: 1950] 2. a police officer; a federal narcotics agent. RS: *fuzz*. [U.S., BVB: 1942, JBW: 1967, M&V: 1967, TRG: 1968]

bull dip a male narcotics addict. RS: *junky*. [U.S., JES: 1959]

bulldozed alcohol intoxicated. *Cf. ball-dozed*. RT: *drunk*. [Aust., (1935): DSUE]

bullet 1. a *Seconal* (TM; *q.v.*) capsule, a barbiturate capsule. RT: *sec*. [U.S., EAF: 1972] 2. (also **Bullet**) *butyl nitrite* (*q.v.*) sold as a room deodorizer. *Cf. Aroma*. [U.S., (1969): DNE: 1980, YKB: 1977] 3. a capsule of a drug. [Br., BTD: 1968]

bullethead a large *Seconal* (TM; *q.v.*) capsule. The same as *bullet*. RS: *barbs*. [U.S., EAF: 1972]

bulletproofed alcohol intoxicated. Akin to *Dutch courage* (*q.v.*). RT: *drunk*. [U.S., PD: 1982, N&S: 1983]

bullet Thai marijuana from Thailand. RT: *pot*. [U.S., ELA: 1984]

bull horrors 1. an addict's fear of the police. *Bull* (*q.v.*) = a police officer. [U.S., VJM: 1949, EEL: 1971] 2. the delirium experienced by heavy cocaine users. Senses one and two may actually refer to the same disability expressed from two different points of view. [U.S., BD: 1937, DWM: 1938, EEL: 1971]

bull jive diluted or adulterated marijuana; marijuana diluted with tea. *Jive* (*q.v.*) = marijuana. Bull = bogus. RS: *pot*. [U.S., M&V: 1973, RDS: 1982]

bullock's eye a drink of an alcoholic beverage. Something that hits the bull's eye. BVB: 1942 list **bull's eye** = a glass of port. RT: *nip*. [Br., 1800s, F&H]

bum a drinking bout. RT: *spree*. BVB: 1942 also lists a verb sense. [U.S., (1871): DAE, BVB: 1942]

bum bend a bad reaction to L.S.D.; a bad trip. *Cf. bent*. [U.S., RRL: 1969, EEL: 1971]

bumblebee dust snuff. *Cf. heifer dust, rest powder*. RT: *snoose*. [U.S., (1940): ADD]

bumblebees amphetamine tablets or capsules. RT: *amps*. [U.S., YKB: 1977, NIDA: 1980]

bumble whiskey strong whiskey; whiskey with a sting. RT: *rotgut, whiskey*. [U.S., (1850–1900): RFA]

bumbo rum or brandy mixed with water and sugar. [(1748): OED, (Smollett), FG: 1785, FG: 1811, B&L: 1890, DSUE; listed in BVB: 1942]

bum boozer a drunkard. RT: *sot*. Music hall use. [JRW: 1909]

bumclink 1. whiskey; inferior or poor-quality whiskey. [Br., 1800s, F&H] 2. (possibly also **bumchink**) inferior beer brewed for hired field hands. [Br., (1830): DSUE, JCH: 1887, F&H; listed in GWM: 1859, BVB: 1942, D&D: 1973]

bum kicks a bad L.S.D. experience; a bad trip. [U.S., RRL: 1969, EEL: 1971]

bummer (also **bum trip**) a bad L.S.D. experience; a bad trip. Now GEN: any disagreeable thing or person. [U.S., S&W: 1966, JBW: 1967, RRL: 1969, EEL: 1971, DNE: 1973, W&F: 1975]

bum out have a bad (drug) *trip* (*q.v.*). [U.S., D&B: 1978]

bump enough cocaine to form a *line* (*q.v.*). RS: *cocaine*. [U.S., ADC: 1981]

bumper 1. a cigarette butt. Possibly a portmanteau of *butt* and *stump* (DSUE). RT: *brad*. [Aust., (1910): GAW: 1978, SJB: 1943] 2. a full glass of wine or liquor for a toast. [Br., 16–1900s, (1676): OED, F&H, DSUE]

bumper sniping picking up cigar and cigarette butts for reuse. *Cf. guttersnipe*. [Aust. military, (1939): DSUE, SJB: 1943]

bumpsy (also **bumpsie**) alcohol intoxicated. *Cf. wallbanger*. RT: *drunk*. [(1611): OED, JOH: 1901; listed in BVB: 1942]

bum trip (also **bummer**) a bad experience with L.S.D.; a bad trip. Now GEN: any bad experience. [U.S., TRG: 1968, RRL: 1969, EEL: 1971, DNE: 1973, W&F: 1975]

bumy juice porter or beer. [GWM: 1859, JSF: 1889]

bun a load of liquor; the effects of alcohol. See *have a bun on*. RWB: 1912 indicates that this is short for *bundle*. [U.S., RWB: 1912, D&D: 1957]

bunch of grapes 1. a *wino* (*q.v.*). [Aust., SJB: 1966] See also *in the grip of the grape*. 2. a bar or a tavern. RT: *bar*. [U.S., EE: 1976]

bundle a package of drugs; 25 small packages of heroin. *Cf. bindle*. RS: *load*. [U.S., M&V: 1967, P&C: 1969, RRL: 1969, EEL: 1971, MA: 1973, W&F: 1975, RDS: 1982] See also *bun*.

bundler in the hierarchy of narcotics (usually heroin) distribution, the person who packs the diluted drugs into packets. [U.S., P&C: 1969, JWK: 1981]

bung 1. alcohol intoxicated. RT: *drunk*. [Br., 17–1800s, (1721): OED, DSUE] 2. (also **brother bung**) someone who sells and serves liquor at a bar. RT: *bartender*. [JRW: 1909, BVB: 1942, BH: 1980]

bunged alcohol intoxicated. RT: *drunk*. Not listed in JB: 1980. [South African, (c. 1935): DSUE]

bung eye a drunkard. RT: *sot*. [Br., 1800s, F&H; listed in BVB: 1942]

bung-eyed alcohol intoxicated. RT: *drunk*. [Br., 1800s, F&H; listed in BVB: 1942]

bunghole to inject narcotics. RT: *shoot*. Probably nonce. [U.S., JES: 1959]

bung it in gin. Rhyming slang. RT: *gin*. [Br., early 1900s, DRS]

bung juice beer; porter. RT: *beer.* [U.S., B&L: 1890, F&H, BVB: 1942]

bung starter 1. someone who sells and serves liquor at a bar. RT: *bartender.* [U.S., BVB: 1942] 2. a dealer in illicit liquor. RS: *bootlegger.* [U.S., AH: 1931]

bungy (also **bungey**) alcohol intoxicated. (BF: 1737: [He's] bungey.) RT: *drunk.* [BF: 1737]

bunk 1. bad liquor; synthetic liquor. From *buncomb*. GEN: nonsense. RT: *rotgut.* From the prohibition era. [U.S., MHW: 1934, VJM: 1949] 2. bogus heroin. RT: *blank.* [U.S., H&C: 1975] 3. low-quality marijuana. RS: *blank.* [U.S., ELA: 1982] 4. a pad to lie on while smoking opium. [U.S., (1887): RML: 1948] 5. opium. RT: *opium.* Probably early 1900s. [U.S., ELA: 1984]

bunker beer. Origin unknown. RT: *beer.* [Br., JCH: 1887, B&L: 1890, F&H; listed in BVB: 1942]

bunk fee the price of admission to an opium den. [U.S., JES: 1959, H&C: 1975]

bunk habit (also **bunk yen**) 1. a fascination with a bunk in an opium den which causes an addict to hang around the opium den hoping for a handout. [U.S., BD: 1937, DWM: 1938] 2. a passive addiction to opium achieved by being in the same room with opium vapors. Possibly used for other types of narcotics addiction. [U.S., DWM: 1936, DWM: 1938, RRL: 1969]

bunned alcohol intoxicated. *Cf. bun.* RT: *drunk.* [U.S., (1908): SBF: 1976, AH: 1931, MHW: 1934]

bun strangler a total abstainer. RT: *dry.* [Br., F&G: 1925, DSUE]

bun wallah a teetotaller. *Cf. bun strangler.* RT: *dry.* [Br. military, F&G: 1925] See also *wallah.*

buoyant (also **buoyed**) alcohol intoxicated. RT: *drunk.* [PD: 1982]

burdocked alcohol intoxicated. (BF: 1737: [He's] Burdock'd.) RT: *drunk.* [BF: 1737]

burese crystallized cocaine. See *Bernice.*

buried alcohol intoxicated. From the prohibition era. RT: *drunk.* [U.S., (1920s): SBF: 1976, MHW: 1934]

burn 1. a cigarette; a (tobacco) smoke. British: **have a burn**. RT: *nail.* [Aust. and U.S., SJB: 1943, DCCU: 1972, W&F: 1975] See also *burnie.* 2. to smoke tobacco. [Br. and elsewhere, late 18-1900s, DSUE, WG: 1962] 3. to smoke marijuana or hashish. RS: *hit the hay.* [U.S., HER: 1971, DC: 1972, RDS: 1982] 4. to cheat someone in a drug sale. In current use in general slang meaning to cheat or do harm to. GWM: 1859 lists **burning** = cheating. [U.S., JBW: 1967, (1967): DNE: 1973, RRL: 1969, EEL: 1971, MA: 1973] 5. to steal someone else's drugs. [Br., BTD: 1968] 6. a *rush* (*q.v.*) after an injection into a vein. RS: *rush.* [U.S., M&V: 1973] 7. an instance of cheating in a drug sale; an instance of being cheated in a drug sale. [U.S., MA: 1973,

ADC: 1981]

burn an Indian (also burn Indian hay) to smoke a marijuana cigarette. RT: *hit the hay*. [U.S., JES: 1959, H&C: 1975]

burn artist in the underworld or drug culture, someone who wrongs someone else, i.e., an addict who deceives another addict; a drug dealer who cheats his customers; a stool pigeon. [U.S., RRL: 1969, EEL: 1971, ADC: 1975]

burned cheated in a drug sale; cheated by a *burn artist*. [U.S., (1966): ELA: 1982, TRG: 1968, RRL: 1969, IGA: 1971, D&B: 1978]

burned by an Indian intoxicated with marijuana. Refers to *Indian hay* (*q.v.*). RT: *wasted*. [U.S., JES: 1959, H&C: 1975]

burned out (also burnt out) 1. having to do with veins which are so scarred by injections and abscesses that no further drug injection can be made. *Cf. vegged out*. [U.S., (1910): JES: 1959, DWM: 1938, A&T: 1953, RRL: 1969, D&B: 1970c, EEL: 1971] 2. having to do with a ruined addict; having to do with a broke and down-and-out addict; having to do with a teenager mentally or socially debilitated by devotion to marijuana. [U.S., JES: 1959, ADC: 1981] 3. having to do with an addict or drug user who is no longer affected by a particular drug. [U.S., RRL: 1969, EEL: 1971]

burner a drug habit. Short for *oil-burner* (*q.v.*). RT: *habit*. [U.S., RG: 1970]

Burnese crystallized cocaine. See *Bernice*.

burnie a partially smoked marijuana cigarette; a marijuana cigarette. RS: *joint*. [U.S., VJM: 1949, M&D: 1952, A&T: 1953, IGA: 1971]

burning smoking marijuana. *Cf. light up*. [U.S., RRL: 1969]

burnout 1. for an addict to voluntarily withdraw from drugs totally. RT: *kick*. [U.S., (W&F: 1975)] 2. a person whose mind or ambition has been destroyed by drugs. [U.S., ADC: 1975, H&C: 1975, FAB: 1979] 3. to destroy one's mind or ambition by the use of drugs. [U.S., ADC: 1975, FAB: 1979]

burn some bush to smoke marijuana. *Cf. bush*. RT: *hit the hay*. [U.S., BR: 1972]

burn the midnight oil to smoke opium. RT: *suck bamboo*. [U.S., BVB: 1942, VJM: 1949, GOL: 1950]

burn trip a bad *L.S.D.* (*q.v.*) trip. RT: *bad trip*. [U.S., JTD: 1971]

burn with a low blue flame to be very drunk. Refers to the blue flame of an alcohol fueled fire. RS: *drunk*. [U.S., MHW: 1934, D&D: 1957]

burps beverage alcohol. RT: *booze*. [U.S., BVB: 1942] See also *berps*.

burst a riotous drinking bout. *Cf. bust*. RT: *spree*. [Aust., (1852):

GAW: 1978; Br., (1881): OED; U.S., BVB: 1942]

burster a heavy drinker; a drunkard. *Cf. bust*. RT: *sot*. [Br., 1800s, F&H]

burst, on the on a drinking bout. *Cf. burst, burster*. RT: *spreeing*. [Aust., mid 1800s-p., GAW: 1978]

bush marijuana. *Cf. bo-bo bush*. RT: *pot*. [U.S., (M&W: 1946), W&F: 1967, RRL: 1969, EEL: 1971, DCCU: 1972, YKB: 1977, EAF: 1980, NIDA: 1980] See also *righteous bush*.

bushes home-grown marijuana. *Cf. domestic, mud-bud*. RS: *pot*. [U.S., JWK: 1981]

bush girlfriend gin. Meaning that liquor is a man's girlfriend in desolate country. *Cf. rainy-day woman*. RT: *gin*. [Aust., SJB: 1966]

bush tea tea brewed from marijuana. *Cf. bush*. [Br., BTD: 1968; U.S., ELA: 1982]

bushwhacker (also **bush smoker**) a marijuana smoker. *Cf. bush*. RT: *toker*. [U.S., (1930): JES: 1959, RDS: 1982]

business (also **the business**) **1**. equipment for preparing and administering addictive drugs. RT: *outfit*. [U.S., DWM: 1938, VJM: 1949, M&D: 1952, EEL: 1971] 2. the drug-selling business. [U.S., H&C: 1975]

businessman's trip (also **businessman's high, businessman's lunch time high, businessman's psychedelic martini, businessman's special, lunch hour trip**) the drug *D.M.T.* (*q.v.*). Similar to L.S.D. except that the *trip* can be completed during one's lunch hour. *Cf. forty-five minute psychosis*. [U.S., RRL: 1969, EEL: 1971, YKB: 1977, ADC: 1981]

busky (also **buskey**) alcohol intoxicated. (BF: 1737: [He's] Buskey.) RT: *drunk*. [BF: 1737] See also *bosky*.

bust 1. a riotous drinking bout. *Cf. burst*. RT: *spree*. [U.S., (1844): DAE, (1860): OED, JSF: 1889, MHW: 1934, GI: 1931, M&J: 1975] 2. a drunkard. See *busthead*. 3. a raid by the police; an arrest. [U.S., MB: 1938, M&H: 1959, ADC: 1981] **4**. to raid; to arrest. Said of the police or other law enforcement officers. [U.S., M&W: 1946, GS: 1959, S&W: 1966, JBW: 1967, RRL: 1969, EEL: 1971, MW: 1976, ADC: 1981] 5. arrested. A variant of *busted* (*q.v.*). 6. to inform the police about drug use or drug traffic, i.e., to provide information which will lead to a *bust*. [Br., BTD: 1968] 7. to smoke marijuana. RT: *hit the hay*. See *bust a joint*. [U.S., ELA: 1984]

bust a cap to take a drug in capsule form. *Cap* (*q.v.*) = capsule, pill. [U.S., W&F: 1967, EEL: 1971, DCCU: 1972, RDS: 1982] See also *cap out*.

bust a joint to smoke a marijuana cigarette. *Cf. joint*. RT: *hit the hay*. [U.S., (1956): ELA: 1982]

busted (also **bust**) **1**. arrested. [U.S., MB: 1938, GS: 1959, M&H:

1959, TRG: 1968, EEL: 1971, (DNE: 1973), M&V: 1973, (MW: 1976) JWK: 1981] (This entry continues after the following list.) Terms meaning arrested, raided, or detained: *batted out, been had, bust, busted, busted by the bobby in blue, clipped, clouted, collared, copped, crashed, dropped, flagged, gaffled, glomed, glued, guzzled, hit, jacked up, jammed, knocked in, nabbed, nailed, nicked, pinched, pinned, popped, rousted, sloughed, snapped, snapt, snatched, sneezed, sneezed down, tapped, wasted, yanked.* 2. alcohol intoxicated. RT: *drunk*. From the prohibition era. [U.S., 1920s, SBF: 1976]

busted by the bobby in blue arrested. RT: *busted*. [U.S., RAS: 1984]

buster 1. a riotous drinking bout. *Cf. bust*. RT: *spree*. [U.S., (1831): DA, BVB: 1942, M&J: 1975] 2. a man on a spree. *Cf. bust*. RS: *sot*. [U.S., BVB: 1942] 3. (usually **busters**) a barbiturate. The opposite of *thruster*: an amphetamine. *Cf. thrusters*. RT: *barbs*. [U.S., H&C: 1975, SNP: 1977] 4. a federal narcotics agent. RS: *fuzz*. [U.S., ELA: 1982]

busthead (also **bustskull**) 1. (also **bust**) a drunkard; a hobo drunkard. [U.S., W&F: 1960, RDS: 1982] 2. inferior liquor, especially whiskey; inferior wine; potent liquor. Named thus because it bursts one's skull open. *Cf. popskull*. RT: *rotgut*. [U.S., (1857): DA, (1863): DAE, JSF: 1889, VR: 1929, AH: 1931, MHW: 1934] See also *skull-buster*.

bust man a narcotics agent. *Cf. bust*. RT: *fuzz*. [U.S., ADC: 1981]

bust, on a on a spree. RT: *spreeing*. [U.S., MHW: 1934]

bust, on the on a spree. The same as *on the burst* (*q.v.*).

bust some suds to drink some beer. *Cf. suds*. [U.S., BR: 1972]

bust the mainline to inject a drug into a vein. RT: *shoot*. [U.S., DWM: 1938, A&T: 1953]

busy bee phencyclidine, *P.C.P.* (*q.v.*), an animal tranquilizer. Rhyming slang for *P.C.P.* RT: *P.C.P.* [U.S., (1970s): FAB: 1979, DNE: 1980, RDS: 1982]

butt 1. (also **butsie**) a tobacco cigarette or cigarette end; a cigar or cigar end. In the military there was a scheme for measuring "found" cigarette butts. The higher the rank, the longer the butt. *Cf. captain's butt, corporal's butt, private's butt, sergeant's butt, shavetail's butt*. RT: *brad*. [(1847): OEDS, JWC: 1905, (WWI): SBF: 1982, VWS: 1929, GI: 1931, MHW: 1934, GAS: 1941, ADC: 1981] 2. to smoke tobacco. Not common (W&F: 1960). [U.S., W&F: 1960] 3. a marijuana cigarette. *Cf. goof butt*. RT: *joint*. [U.S., H&C: 1975]

butt-end a cigar or cigarette butt. *Cf. brad*. [M&J: 1975]

butter flower marijuana. *Cf. puna butter*. *Butter* may refer to *resin*. RT: *pot*. [U.S., IGA: 1971, YKB: 1977]

buttlegging the transportation of untaxed or undertaxed cigarettes. Patterned on *bootlegging*. See *bootlegger*. [U.S., (1972): DNE: 1973]

button 1. a heroin capsule. RS: *dose*. [U.S., D&B: 1970c] 2. (also **buttons**) mescaline in the form of a small dried nodule of peyote cactus. RS: *peyote*. [U.S., RRL: 1969, D&B: 1970c, EEL: 1971, M&V: 1973, YKB: 1977, NIDA: 1980, ADC: 1981] 3. a medium size pellet of opium. *Cf. high hat*. RS: *load*. [U.S., DU, M&V: 1954, D&B: 1970c] 4. a police officer. RT: *fuzz*. [U.S., BVB: 1942]

butt-stooper a cigarette or cigar butt collector. Refers to a hobo or a low-ranking soldier. *Cf. butt-stooper, dumper-dasher, guttersnipe, sniper, snipe-shooter, topper-hunter*. [Aust., SJB: 1966]

butyl nitrite an inhalant almost identical to *amyl nitrite* (*q.v.*) in the effects it produces. See *Aroma, Bullet*.

buy 1. a purchase of drugs; a successful connection and purchase of drugs. [U.S., M&V: 1967, RRL: 1969, ADC: 1975] 2. a drug seller. *Cf. make a buy*. RT: *dealer*. [U.S., M&V: 1967, H&C: 1975]

buzz 1. the initial effects of drinking alcohol or the taking of certain drugs. *Cf. glow*. RS: *rush*. H&C: 1975 list **buz**. [U.S., BVB: 1942, M&D: 1952, A&T: 1953, RRL: 1969, CM: 1970, JWK: 1981] 2. euphoria or intoxication from alcohol. [U.S., M&D: 1952, RRL: 1969, EEL: 1971, GU: 1975] 3. to seek out and purchase drugs. RT: *score*. GWM: 1859 lists **buzzing** = searching for. [U.S., (VJM: 1949), (M&D: 1952), TRG: 1968, EEL: 1971] 4. *P.C.P.* (*q.v.*). See *heroin buzz*. RT: *P.C.P.* [U.S., (1970s): FAB: 1979]

buzzed 1. (also **buzzed up**) alcohol intoxicated. RT: *drunk*. [U.S., BF: 1737, BVB: 1942, D&D: 1957, ADC: 1984] 2. drug intoxicated; high on amphetamines, heroin, P.C.P., etc. RT: *stoned*. [U.S., BR: 1972, FAB: 1979, ADC: 1981]

buzzing attempting to find and buy drugs. See *buzz*. [U.S., VJM: 1949, M&D: 1952]

buzzy (also **buzzey**) alcohol intoxicated. (BF: 1737: [He's] Buzzey.) RT: *drunk*. [BF: 1737]

B.Y.O.B. (also B.Y.O.) "Bring your own (booze or bottle)." Pertaining to an informal type of entertaining where the guests are invited to bring with them their own alcohol supplies. [U.S., D&B: 1970c, EEL: 1971, DCCU: 1972, MW: 1976, DNE: 1980]

B.Y.O.G. (also B.Y.O.) "Bring your own grog." An Australian version of *B.Y.O.B.* (*q.v.*). [Aust., (1975): GAW: 1978]

B.Z. *S.T.P.* (*q.v.*). Possibly from *buzz*. [U.S., ELA: 1984]

C

C. 1. cocaine. *Cf. C-joint.* RT: *cocaine.* [U.S., PRB: 1930, GI: 1931, DWM: 1933, DWM: 1936, VJM: 1949, M&D: 1952, W&F: 1960, RRL: 1969, CM: 1970, EEL: 1971, MA: 1973] 2. heroin. From *Cadillac* (*q.v.*). Not widely known. RT: *heroin.* [U.S., W&F: 1960] 3. *Doriden* (TM; *q.v.*), a nonbarbiturate hypnotic. See *C.B.* From the first letter of the manufacturer's name: Ciba. RT: *dories.* [U.S., RRL: 1969] See also *big-C.* 4. a new drug user; a new heroin user. Probably from *cadet* (*q.v.*). Possibly an error for *C.A.* (*q.v.*). [U.S., H&C: 1975]

C.A. a cocaine addict. RT: *kokomo.* [U.S., JES: 1959]

caballo* 1. heroin. The Spanish word for *horse* (*q.v.*) = heroin. ELA: 1984 lists cabello (= cocaine), probably in error. *Cf. kabayo.* RT: *heroin.* [U.S., TRG: 1968, RRL: 1969, EEL: 1971, W&F: 1975, NIDA: 1980] 2. a person who smuggles drugs into jails. *Cf. mule.* Spanish for horse. [calo, RDS: 1982]

cabbage cheap tobacco; a cheap cigarette. RS: *fogus.* [U.S., MHW: 1934, D&D: 1957, W&F: 1960]

cabbagio perfumo a cheap and very bad-smelling cigar. In imitation of Spanish cigar names. *Cf. flor di cabaggio.* RT: *seegar.* [Br., late 18-1900s, DSUE]

caca (also **kaka**) inferior, bogus, or adulterated heroin or marijuana; any heroin or marijuana. LIT: dung. From Spanish. [U.S., RRL: 1969, EEL: 1971, JHF: 1971, YKB: 1977]

cache a (hidden) supply of drugs; a *stash* (*q.v.*). RT: *stash.* [U.S., (1976): ELA: 1982]

cached alcohol intoxicated. RT: *drunk.* [U.S., BVB: 1942]

cacil cocaine; morphine. Probably the same as or an error for *Cecil* (*q.v.*). [U.S., A&T: 1953, SNP: 1977]

cacko alcohol intoxicated; very drunk. Probably from *cack* = excrement. The -o is a typical Australian slang suffix. *Cf. shit-faced.* RT: *drunk.* [Aust., SJB: 1966] See also *caca.*

cactus (also **cactus buttons**) peyote cactus; mescaline found in peyote cactus. *Cf. button.* RS: *peyote.* [U.S., RRL: 1969, EEL: 1971, NIDA: 1980]

cactus juice liquor; Tequila. RT: *booze.* [U.S., EE: 1976, RDS:

1982]

cadet a new drug user; a new heroin user. *Cf. C.* RS: *user.* [U.S., BVB: 1942, VJM: 1949, A&T: 1953, EEL: 1971]

cadger (also **cager**) a drunkard. RT: *sot.* [U.S., W&F: 1960]

Cadillac 1. powerful, powdered drugs; a dose of a powdered drug. Named for the automobile because of the drug's power, cost, and quality. *Cf. C.* GEN: any superior thing. RT: *powder.* [U.S., JES: 1959, H&C: 1975] **2.** a one-ounce package of a powdered drug. RS: *load.* [U.S., MHW: 1934, GOL: 1950, W&F: 1960] **3.** one ounce of cocaine. Named thus because of the power of the drug and the shared initial C. RT: *cocaine.* [U.S., A&T: 1953, D&D: 1957] **4.** *P.C.P.* (*q.v.*), an animal tranquilizer. Named thus because of the power of P.C.P., and probably, an attempt to associate P.C.P. with other powerful drugs. RT: *P.C.P.* [U.S., YKB: 1977, FAB: 1979]

caffy avec coffee and rum. Eye-dialect for French *café avec.* [Br., late 18-1900s, DSUE] See also *coffee-and habit.*

caged alcohol intoxicated. See *cadger. Cf. boxed.* RT: *drunk.* [U.S., W&F: 1960]

cager See *cadger.*

cagrined alcohol intoxicated. Possibly from *chagrined.* RT: *drunk.* [BF: 1737]

cahoba See *cohoba.*

cake drugs smuggled into prison or a hospital. Alludes to the smuggling of a hacksaw in a cake into prison. RS: *load.* [U.S., JES: 1959]

California cornflakes cocaine. *Flake* (*q.v.*) = cocaine. RT: *cocaine.* [U.S., EE: 1976]

California sunshine the hallucinogenic drug *L.S.D.* (*q.v.*); L.S.D. combined with some other drug. *Cf. sunshine.* RT: *L.S.D.* [U.S., YKB: 1977, NIDA: 1980, KBH: 1982]

California turnarounds amphetamines. See *L.A. turnabouts.* RT: *amps.* CB radio slang. [U.S., EE: 1976]

call the early effects of a drug; the beginning of a rush; a rush. RS: *rush.* [U.S., M&V: 1967, D&B: 1970c]

calling card needle marks in one's arm. Viewed as proof of addiction. RT: *tracks.* [U.S., EEL: 1971]

cam *Cambodian red* (*q.v.*) marijuana. RS: *pot.* [U.S., M&V: 1973, ELA: 1982]

Cambodian red (also **cam red**) a reddish brown marijuana grown in Cambodian. RS: *pot.* [U.S., M&V: 1973, RDS: 1982]

Cambodian trip weed (also **cam trip**) high potency marijuana presumably from Cambodia. RS: *pot.* [U.S., M&V: 1973, RDS: 1982]

came cocaine. Possibly akin to or an error for *C-jame* (*q.v.* at

C-jam.) RT: *cocaine.* [U.S., A&T: 1953, SNP: 1977]

camel dung a cigarette manufactured in Egypt during wartime. RT: *nail.* [Aust., WWI, WHD: 1919, cited in SJB: 1966] See also *desert horse, hump.*

camioneros* amphetamines. Spanish for *truck drivers* (*q.v.*). RT: *amps.* [U.S., NIDA: 1980]

campfire boy an opium addict. Refers to the fire of the opium lamp, and is a play on *campfire girl.* Recurrent nonce (W&F: 1967). [U.S., W&F: 1967, RDS: 1982] Synonyms and nicknames for persons addicted to opium: ***bamboo, bamboo-puffer, barber's cat, black smoker, bowler, campfire boy, cooker, cookie, crock, ghost, gong beater, gonger, gong kicker, gowhead, gowster, habit smoker, hip-layer, hitter, hop, hop dog, hop fiend, hophead, hop hog, hop merchant, hopper, hoppie, hoppy, hopster, hop stiff, mud wiggler, opium kipper, piki, pill-cooker, pipe, pipe fiend, pipe-hitter, pipes, pipe-smoker, pipey, pipie, poppy-puffer, puff, puffer, smoker, smokey, stem artist, thin hips, three-tapper, viper, yen-chee-quay, yen-shee boy, yen-shee-kwoi, yen-shee-quay, yen-shee-quoy.***

can 1. (also **tin**) one ounce of marijuana. Possibly from *cannabis,* or it refers to a tin can used to carry it, at one time a can of Prince Albert (brand) of pipe tobacco. RS: *load.* [U.S., GS: 1959, S&W: 1966, JBW: 1967, RRL: 1969, EEL: 1971, MW: 1976, EAF: 1980, ADC: 1981] 2. one ounce of morphine or opium. RS: *load.* [U.S., BVB: 1942, GOL: 1950, EEL: 1971]

Canadian black a type of marijuana grown in Canada. RT: *pot.* [U.S., RRL: 1969, EEL: 1971]

Canadian bouncer low-potency *Seconal* (TM; *q.v.*) imported from Canada. RT: *sec.* [U.S., EEL: 1971, RDS: 1982]

Canadian quail methaqualone, specifically *Quaalude* (*q.v.*). *Quail* is from the *Quaal* in *Quaalude.* RT: *ludes.* [U.S., ELA: 1984]

cáñamo* hemp; marijuana. From the Spanish word for reed. RT: *pot.* [U.S., IGA: 1971, NIDA: 1980]

canappa* (also **canapa***) marijuana. Spanish. [U.S., RPW: 1938; listed in M&J: 1980]

canary a capsule of *Nembutal* (TM; *q.v.*), a barbiturate. The capsule is bright yellow. RT: *nemb.* [U.S., M&V: 1967, H&C: 1975]

cancelled stick a tobacco cigarette filled with marijuana; a marijuana cigarette. A play on *cancer stick* (*q.v.*). RT: *joint.* [U.S., G&B: 1969, RRL: 1969]

cancer stick a tobacco cigarette. From the notion that cigarette smoking is a major cause of lung cancer. RT: *nail.* [U.S., W&F: 1967, DCCU: 1972, DNE: 1973, ADC: 1984]

C. and H. (also **cold and hot, H. and C., hot and cold**) 1. a mixture of cocaine and heroin. RS: *set.* [U.S., RRL: 1969, CM: 1970, EEL: 1971] 2. heroin, cocaine, or both. A play on *C. and H.*

brand of *sugar* (*q.v.*). [U.S., EAF: 1980]

candied habituated to cocaine. *Cf. candy*. RS: *hooked*. [U.S., JES: 1959, H&C: 1975]

C. and M. cocaine and morphine. *Cf. M. and C.* RS: *set*. [U.S., GOL: 1950, RRL: 1969, CM: 1970, EEL: 1971]

candy 1. alcohol intoxicated. RT: *drunk*. [cant, FG: 1785, FG: 1811] 2. drugs in general; specific drugs: barbiturates, cocaine, hashish, the hallucinogenic drug *L.S.D.* (*q.v.*). Used specifically for cocaine in *nose candy* (*q.v.*). Used specifically for *L.S.D.* (*q.v.*) when referring to a sugar cube impregnated with a drop of the substance. The British attestation is for barbiturates only (BTD: 1968). Heroin only (EAF: 1980). *Cf. jelly beans*. [U.S., GM: 1931, MHW: 1934, W&F: 1960, RRL: 1969, EEL: 1971, DCCU: 1972, YKB: 1977, EAF: 1980, NIDA: 1980] See also *hard candy, needle candy, nose candy, sugar candy*.

candy a J. (also candy a joint) to lace a marijuana cigarette with another drug, often by placing a bit of the drug on the end of the cigarette. Heroin or opium was sometimes used. See *dust a joint* for a more modern practice. *Cf. joint*. [U.S., M&V: 1973]

candy bar 1. a place where cocaine is sold. *Cf. candy*. RS: *doperie*. [U.S., JES: 1959, H&C: 1975] 2. a bar of hashish. It looks like a chocolate covered candy bar. *Cf. chunks*. RS: *hash*. [U.S., JWK: 1981]

candy canes and gumdrops a good *L.S.D.* (*q.v.*) trip. [U.S., ADC: 1981]

candy cee cocaine. A respelling of *C.* (*q.v.*). *Cf. candy*. RT: *cocaine*. [U.S., JES: 1959, H&C: 1975]

candy fiend (also candyhead) a cocaine user. *Cf. candy*. Various writers have expressed doubt that any of the fiend terms are authentic drug argot. RT: *kokomo*. [U.S., JES: 1959, H&C: 1975]

candy man a drug seller, usually at the retail (street) level; a seller of hard drugs. *Cf. candy*. RT: *dealer*. [U.S., RRL: 1969, CM: 1970, EEL: 1971, M&V: 1973, W&F: 1975, ADC: 1981]

candy store a liquor store. *Candy* (*q.v.*) = drunk, liquor. RT: *L.I.Q.* [U.S., D&B: 1971]

canebuck potent liquor. *Cf. buck*. RT: *rotgut*. [U.S., (1940): ADD]

cane corn moonshine whiskey made from corn and sugar. *Cf. corn*. RT: *moonshine*. [U.S., D&D: 1957, W&F: 1960]

cane spirit (also cane) alcohol distilled from sugar cane. RT: *booze*. [South African, (1978): JB: 1980]

cannabinoids chemical compounds which have an effect on the mind similar to *cannabinol* (*q.v.*). Not drug argot. [U.S., RDS: 1982]

cannabinol 1. (also Cannabine) a chemical substance found in marijuana (hemp) plants. Usually refers to T.H.C.:

delta-9-tetrahydrocannabinol, the active principle in marijuana and hashish. [U.S., (c. 1896): MW: 1983, RPW: 1938] 2. phencyclidine, P.C.P.; P.C.P. sold on the streets as pure *T.H.C.* (sense one). [U.S., YKB: 1977, FAB: 1979]

cannabis a generic term for marijuana in any of its forms, usually the flowers or fruiting parts of the female hemp plant. From one of its botanical names: *Cannabis americana, Cannabis indica, Cannabis mexicana, Cannabis ruderalis, Cannabis sativa*. RT: *pot*. Standard English. [Latin, (1728): MW: 1983] See also *carmabis*.

cannabis tea tea leaves and marijuana leaves brewed together. [U.S., RDS: 1982]

canned (also **canned up**) alcohol intoxicated; tipsy. *Cf. tinned*. RT: *drunk*. [Br. and U.S., (1910): DSUE, HJS: 1922, F&G: 1925, WM: 1927, MP: 1928, MHW: 1934, BVB: 1942, B&P: 1965]

canned goods drugs sold in cans; marijuana sold in tobacco cans. RS: *dope*. [U.S., (1933): ELA: 1982]

canned heat 1. Sterno (TM); methyl alcohol derived from Sterno. This was drunk by hobo alcoholics and others. [U.S., HNR: 1934, BVB: 1942, VJM: 1949, GOL: 1950] 2. inferior whiskey; bad liquor in general. RT: *rotgut*. [U.S., SBF: 1982, BVB: 1942, VJM: 1949]

canned heater (also **heater**) a methyl alcohol drunkard; a user of canned heat. RT: *sot*. [U.S., BVB: 1942, VJM: 1949]

canned sativa hashish. A play on *Cannabis sativa*. RT: *hash*. [U.S., RRL: 1969, RDS: 1982]

canned stuff commercially canned opium. *Cf. stuff*. RT: *opium*. [U.S., BD: 1937, DWM: 1938]

cannon 1. (also **canon**) alcohol intoxicated. This probably relates in some way to *shot* (*q.v.*). RT: *drunk*. [Br., (1879): F&H, B&L: 1890, DSUE] 2. a hypodermic syringe. The same as *gun* (*q.v.*). RT: *monkey pump*. [U.S., JES: 1959, H&C: 1975]

cannonball an injection of mixed drugs. Similar to *speedball* (*q.v.*). RS: *set, shot*. [U.S., JES: 1959, H&C: 1975]

cant to drink a glass of liquor; to tilt the glass or one's arm while drinking. *Cf. bend*. RT: *irrigate*. [Br., FG: 1823]

canteen a club or meeting place for soldiers. Often the only place where soldiers can buy liquor. RS: *bar*. [since the 1700s, (1744): OED]

canteen stinker a cheap and bad-smelling cigar. *Cf. penny stinker, stinker*. RT: *seegar*. [Br. military, WWI, F&G: 1925, B&P: 1965]

canteen wallah a beer drinker; a drunkard. RS: *sot*. [Br. military, WWI, B&P: 1965] See other wallah terms at *bun wallah, char wallah, jake-wallah, lemonade wallah, pop-wallah, tack wallah*.

can't see a hole in a ladder (also **can't see, can't see through a ladder**) alcohol intoxicated. RT: *drunk*. [DA: 1857, (GWM: 1859),

F&H, MHW: 1934]

Can you do me good? "Can you sell me drugs?" One of a number of vague inquiries about the availability of drugs. See *How are you going to act?* [U.S., HB: 1955]

cap 1. a gelatin capsule used to package a dose of a powdered drug. This sense is much older in medical jargon. *Cf. H-caps.* [U.S., DWM: 1936, NAM: 1953, M&H: 1959, CM: 1970, EEL: 1971, MA: 1973, ADC: 1981] 2. (also **caps**) a capsule of a drug; a packet or *bindle* (*q.v.*) of a powdered drug. Originally referred to a dose of heroin, but now used for cocaine and the hallucinogenic drug *L.S.D.* (*q.v.*). [U.S., DWM: 1936, VJM: 1949, GOL: 1950, M&D: 1952, W&F: 1960, EEL: 1971, DCCU: 1972, DNE: 1973, M&V: 1973] 3. to make a purchase of drugs. See *cop.* [U.S., W&F: 1967] 4. to take a drug in pill form. [U.S., W&F: 1967] 5. (also **cap up**) to package a drug in gelatin capsules. *Cf. H-caps.* [U.S., M&V: 1967, D&B: 1970c]

capable alcohol intoxicated. RT: *drunk.* [BF: 1737]

caper a riotous drinking bout; a whiskey-drinking bout. GEN: a trick or prank; a robbery. RT: *spree.* [U.S., (1875): W&F: 1960, BVB: 1942]

caper juice whiskey; strong liquor. RS: *rotgut.* [U.S., JSF: 1889, BVB: 1942]

capernoited alcohol intoxicated. From a Scots word meaning muddle-headed. RT: *drunk.* [Br. (Scots), (1832): OED]

Cape smoke (also **Cape brandy**) a brandy made in the early days of South African settlement. It was cloudy or smoky and very powerful. [South African, (1848): DSUE, (1936): JB: 1980]

capital H. heroin. *Cf. big-H.* RT: *heroin.* [U.S., H&C: 1975]

capital H., on addicted to heroin. RS: *hooked.* [U.S., H&C: 1975]

cap out to pass out from marijuana or barbiturates. *Cf. bliss out.* [U.S., EAF: 1972]

Cappo (also **cappo**) a Capstan (TM) cigarette. RS: *nail.* [Aust., (1918): DSUE, SJB: 1943]

cap sick alcohol intoxicated. RT: *drunk.* [(1619): OED]

captain a high level drug distributor; a *kilo connection* (*q.v.*). RS: *dealer.* [U.S., P&C: 1969]

captain's butt a fairly long cigarette butt; a partially-smoked cigarette butt. See *butt* for related comments. RT: *brad.* [U.S. military, HS: 1933, HNR: 1934, D&D: 1957]

carbon tet a cleaning fluid used as an *inhalant* (*q.v.*). The term is short for carbon tetrachloride and is not limited to drug slang use. [U.S., RRL: 1969]

carburetor a marijuana smoking device which mixes the smoke with air. RS: *bong.* [U.S., (1966): ELA: 1982, YKB: 1977, (D&B: 1978), ADC: 1981]

carceleras* amphetamines. From Spanish for wardess, governess. RT: *amps*. [U.S., NIDA: 1980]

card 1. pieces of opium weighed out onto a card, usually a playing card. This is essentially a standard ration of prepared opium pellets for an opium smoking session. *Cf. paper*. RS: *load*. [U.S., (1933): OEDS, DWM: 1936] 2. a card containing drugs brought into a prison or a hospital. The card is carefully slit into two layers, the drug is added and the card is glued back together. The card may also be saturated with a solution of the drug and then dried before carrying into a prison or hospital. [U.S., JES: 1959]

cardenales* barbiturates; *Seconal* (TM; *q.v.*) capsules. A Spanish translation of *redbirds* (*q.v.*). RT: *sec*. [U.S., NIDA: 1980]

carga* a dose or ration of a drug: amphetamines, heroin, or marijuana. Spanish (calo) for charge. RS: *load*. [U.S., D&B: 1970c, IGA: 1971, EEL: 1971, NIDA: 1980]

cargador* a marijuana connection, carrier, or peddler. Spanish for shipper. RS: *dealer*. [U.S., EEL: 1971]

cargoed alcohol intoxicated. A play on *loaded* (*q.v.*). RT: *drunk*. [U.S., BVB: 1942]

carmabis allegedly marijuana. Possibly a portmanteau of *cannabis* and *Karma*. Probably an error for *cannabis* (*q.v.*). ELA: 1984 lists **carmabus**, possibly in error. RT: *pot*. [U.S., SNP: 1977]

carne* heroin. Spanish for meat. RT: *heroin*. [U.S., RDS: 1982]

carob chips hashish. *Cf. chocolate*. Compare to *chocolate chips*. RT: *hash*. [U.S., ADC: 1984]

carpet walker a drug addict. RT: *junky*. [U.S., early 1900s, DU, EEL: 1971]

Carrie (also **carrie**) cocaine. From the shared initial *C.* (*q.v.*). See *Carrie Nation*. RT: *cocaine*. [U.S., H&C: 1975, YKB: 1977]

Carrie Nation (also **Carry Nation**) cocaine. A further elaboration of *C.* (*q.v.*) and of *Carrie* (*q.v.*) = cocaine. From the name of the temperance crusader. RT: *cocaine*. [U.S., HB: 1955, IGA: 1971, NIDA: 1980]

carrier a narcotics seller; a *mule* (*q.v.*). Part of an organized drug distribution chain. RS: *dealer*. [U.S., DU, A&T: 1953, SH: 1972]

carry 1. to have drugs in one's immediate possession; to carry drugs on one's person. [U.S., BVB: 1942, RRL: 1969, EEL: 1971, ADC: 1981] 2. for a drug to last; for a drug to sustain its effect on the user; for a drug to carry the user through the day. [U.S., DWM: 1938, VJM: 1949] 3. drugs carried on the person to serve as an emergency supply in case of arrest or drug scarcity. *Cf. stash*. [U.S., M&V: 1967]

carry ballast to be drunk. to carry or hold one's liquor well. [Br. naval, WG: 1962]

carrying carrying drugs on one's person. See *carry, carry weights*. [U.S., RRL: 1969, CM: 1970, IGA: 1971]

carrying a heavy load (also **carrying a load, carrying something heavy**) alcohol intoxicated. RT: *drunk*. [U.S., MHW: 1934, DWH: 1947, D&D: 1957, RDS: 1982]

carrying the stick for an addict to be broke and out on the streets, living in a dump or an old car. Use not limited to the drug scene. [U.S., GG: 1981, JWK: 1981]

carrying too much sail alcohol intoxicated. (BF: 1737: He carries too much Sail.) RT: *drunk*. [BF: 1737]

carrying two red lights (also **carrying three red lights**) alcohol intoxicated. *Two red lights* refers to a ship showing the signal meaning not under command. *Three red lights* is a jocular exaggeration meaning really drunk. RT: *drunk*. [nautical, WG: 1962, DSUE]

Carry Nation See *Carrie Nation*.

carry weights to carry drugs on the person. *Cf. weight*. [U.S., (G&B: 1969)]

cartoon 1. a drug-induced hallucination. Associated with *L.S.D.* (*q.v.*) use. [U.S., EEL: 1971] 2. to have a drug-induced hallucination. [U.S., EEL: 1971, JH: 1979]

cartucho* a packet of marijuana cigarettes. Spanish for cartridge. RS: *load*. [U.S., HB: 1955]

cartwheel 1. a fake drug withdrawal spasm. See *turn a cartwheel*. RT: *brody*. [U.S., DWM: 1936, BVB: 1942] 2. a round, white cross-scored amphetamine tablet. The X of the scoring represents the spokes of this cartwheel. RT: *amps*. [U.S., JBW: 1967, RRL: 1969, EEL: 1971, YKB: 1977, ADC: 1981]

cascade to move from one drug to another, usually to a stronger and more dangerous substance. [Br., BTD: 1968]

cash bar a phrase signifying that one must pay for one's own drinks at a specified event. The phrase is often seen on invitations to, or announcements of an event. Compare to *open bar*. [U.S., (1972): MW: 1983]

cashed having to do with a pipe or other container of marijuana wherein the smokable contents have been exhausted. The same as *spent* (*q.v.*). LIT: cashed-in as with poker chips, finished. Now GEN: exhausted. [U.S., ADC: 1981]

cast alcohol intoxicated. As inert as cast metal. RT: *drunk*. [Br., (1935): DSUE]

castaway a discarded cigar or cigarette butt. *Cf. Robinson Crusoe brand*. RT: *brad*. [U.S., BVB: 1942]

casting up one's accounts alcohol intoxicated. (BF: 1737: He's casting up his accounts.) GEN: vomiting. RT: *drunk*. [BF: 1737]

cast-iron horrors the delirium tremens. *Cf. pig iron*. RT: *D.T.s*.

[Br. (Irish), early 1900s, DSUE]

castor oil artist a physician. RT: *croaker*. [U.S., D&D: 1957]

cat 1. alcohol intoxicated. (BF: 1737: He's Cat.) RT: *drunk*. [BF: 1737] 2. heroin. *Cf. boy, brother*. In the sense of a male or a dude, not the animal. RT: *heroin*. [U.S., RRL: 1969, NIDA: 1980, ADC: 1981]

catch a fox to get very drunk. Probably, to get stinking drunk. *Cf. foxed*. RT: *mug oneself*. [(BE: 1690), DSUE]

catch a hit to have a drink a liquor. *Cf. hit*. RT: *irrigate*. [Bahamas, JAH: 1982]

catched alcohol intoxicated. (BF: 1737: [He's] Catch'd.) RT: *drunk*. [BF: 1737]

catch up 1. to break the drug habit; to withdraw from drugs. RT: *kick*. [U.S., DWM: 1938, BVB: 1942, H&C: 1975] See also *caught*. 2. (also **catch-up**) beer. *Cf. ketchup*. RT: *beer*. [Aust., SJB: 1945]

cater to cook opium. *Cf. chef*. [early 1900s, DU]

caterpillar a drunkard; a pub-crawling drunkard. RT: *sot*. [Aust., SJB: 1945]

catgut inferior liquor. Akin to *rotgut* (*q.v.*). RT: *rotgut*. [U.S., D&D: 1957]

Catholic aspirin a cross-scored tablet of amphetamine. Catholic refers to the cross (X) of the cross-scoring on the tablet. RT: *amps*. [U.S., M&V: 1973, RDS: 1982]

catlap any inferior, thin, or weak drink. From a slang term for tea. *Cf. cat's water*. RS: *rotgut*. [Br., FG: 1785, B&L: 1890, JRW: 1909]

catnip fake or inferior marijuana; real catnip used to dilute marijuana; catnip smoked like marijuana. RS: *blank*. [U.S., RB: 1967, EEL: 1971, D&B: 1978, EAF: 1980]

Cat's Meow a "brand name" for *amyl nitrite* (*q.v.*). GEN: something very good. RS: *snapper*. [U.S., ELA: 1984]

catsood alcohol intoxicated. From French *quatre sous,* the price of getting drunk. RT: *drunk*. [Br., WWI, F&G: 1925, B&P: 1965]

catsous a drink of liquor. From French *quatre sous,* the price of getting drunk. RT: *nip*. [Br., WWI, F&G: 1925, B&P: 1965]

cat's water gin. Sometimes referred to as a women's drink, cat being a dysphemism for a woman. More likely a reference to cat urine. *Cf. panther piss, tiger piss*. See *old Tom, Tom*. RT: *gin*. [Br., JCH: 1859, F&H; listed in BVB: 1942]

cattail a marijuana cigarette. RT: *joint*. [U.S., ELA: 1982]

cattle-rustler an addict whose *hustle* (*q.v.*) is stealing meat from supermarkets for resale. The proceeds are used for the purchase of drugs. [U.S., RG: 1970, JWK: 1981]

caught 1. alcohol intoxicated. RT: *drunk*. [U.S., BVB: 1942] 2.

addicted to a drug, especially *caught in a snowstorm* (*q.v.*). RT: *hooked*. [Br., (1954): DUS]

caught in a snowstorm addicted to cocaine; under the effects of cocaine. A jocular evasion. RT: *hooked*. This was probably not uttered often by cocaine users, but this is the kind of expression that word collectors love. See *winter wonderland* for more terms on the snow theme. [U.S., HNR: 1934, VJM: 1949, GOL: 1950]

cauliflower the white foam head on a glass of beer. [Br., (1882): F&H]

caulker a drink; a stiff drink of brandy at the end of a drinking session. See *binder, settler*. RS: *nip*. [Br., (1808): F&H; Aust., SJB: 1943; U.S., D&D: 1973] See also *chaulkers*.

cave an abscess; a collapsed section of a vein. This is caused by an infection at the site of a drug injection. *Cf. crater*. [U.S., M&V: 1967, H&C: 1975]

cave digging searching with a needle for a suitable place in a well-used vein. *Cf. cave*. [U.S., M&V: 1967, H&C: 1975]

cavite allstars marijuana; marijuana cigarettes. Named for Cavite, a naval port in Manila Bay, and refers to Philippine marijuana. [U.S., SNP: 1977]

cawn corn whiskey; whiskey. The same as *corn* (*q.v.*). RT: *whiskey*. [U.S., BVB: 1942]

C.B. *Doriden* (TM; *q.v.*), a nonbarbiturate hypnotic drug, manufactured by Ciba. From the manufacturer's name. See *C*. RT: *dories*. [U.S., RRL: 1969]

C-duct (also **duct**) cocaine. Origin unknown. RT: *cocaine*.

Cecil 1. (also **Cecile**) morphine. Probably a play on *M. sul.* (*q.v.*). RT: *morphine*. [U.S., BVB: 1942, GOL: 1950, A&T: 1953] 2. cocaine. From the initial C. RT: *cocaine*. [U.S., DWM: 1938, VJM: 1949, M&D: 1952, W&F: 1960, YKB: 1977, NIDA: 1980]

ceciled addicted to morphine. RT: *hooked*. [U.S., JES: 1959, H&C: 1975]

Cecil Jones an addiction to morphine. *Cf. skag jones*. RT: *habit*. [U.S., JES: 1959, H&C: 1975]

cee cocaine. *Cf. C*. RT: *cocaine*. [U.S., BVB: 1942, W&F: 1960]

celebration water liquor. RT: *booze*. [U.S., BVB: 1942]

cellar-smeller 1. an avid prohibitionist; a federal prohibition agent. *Cf. leer-beer*. RT: *dry, fuzz*. [U.S., MHW: 1934, VJM: 1949] 2. a young (college) man who always shows up where free liquor is being served. [U.S., HJS: 1922]

cement 1. a large quantity of drugs; wholesale drugs. A disguise as in load of cement. RS: *dope*. [U.S., DWM: 1936, VJM: 1949] 2. codeine. Probably alludes to its constipating properties. RT: *codeine*. [U.S., (1942): HLM: 1982]

cement arm an addict's arm which is scarred from many injections and abscesses. [U.S., M&V: 1967]

cement water inferior whiskey. RT: *rotgut*. [U.S., early 1900s, DU]

cent in the drug trade, one dollar. [U.S., EEL: 1971]

central nervous system the brain and spinal cord. Abbreviated C.N.S., and CNS. Many of the drugs listed here are *central nervous system* stimulants. Standard English. [medical]

cets (also **sets**) *Darvocet* (TM; *q.v.*) tablets, a painkiller. *Cf. set*. [U.S., JWK: 1981]

C-game cocaine. See *C-jame*.

C-habit a cocaine habit. RS: *habit*. [U.S., D&D: 1957, HSD: 1984]

cha-cha opium pipe. RT: *hop stick*. [U.S., JES: 1959]

chain See *chain smoke*.

chain drink to take drink after drink. The person who does this is a chain-drinker. Patterned on *chain smoke*. [U.S., W&F: 1975, (RDS: 1982)]

chain lightning (also **chained lightning**) very strong whiskey; inferior whiskey; alcohol distilled from potatoes. *Cf. rotgut, whiskey*. [U.S., (1843): OEDS, JSF: 1889, JRW: 1909, BVB: 1942]

chain smoke (also **chain**) to smoke cigarette after cigarette. A backformation on *chain-smoker*. [Br. and U.S., BVB: 1953, DSUE, D&D: 1957, W&F: 1960]

chain-smoker someone who smokes cigarette after cigarette. [(1890): OEDS, D&D: 1957, W&F: 1960]

chalk 1. (also **choc**) beer; bad beer; home-brewed beer. Said to be bad beer made by Choctaw Indians (RFA). RS: *queer-beer*. [U.S., VR: 1929, VJM: 1949] 2. (also **choc**) liquor of any kind. From the prohibition era. [U.S., AH: 1931, MHW: 1934] 3. (also **chaulkers**) amphetamines; *Methedrine* (TM; *q.v.*). The white tablet looks like chalk. RT: *amps*. [U.S., S&W: 1966, RRL: 1969, EEL: 1971, YKB: 1977, EAF: 1980] 4. cocaine. So named for its whiteness. RT: *cocaine*. [U.S., IGA: 1971] 5. *methadone* (TM; *q.v.*), a synthetic narcotic analgesic. Possibly originated in confusion with sense three, both methamphetamine and methadone being called *meth* (*q.v.*). Also possibly an error. RT: *dolo*. [U.S., SNP: 1977]

chalked up under the effects of cocaine. Powdered cocaine is similar to chalk dust. [U.S., HB: 1955]

cham 1. (also **chammy, shammy**) champagne. [Br., (1871): F&H, B&L: 1890; listed in BVB: 1942] (This entry continues after the following list.) Nicknames and slang terms for champagne: *angel foam, berpwater, bitches' wine, boy, bubbles, bubble water, bubbly, cham, chammy, chamois, champers, dry, fiz, fizz, giggle juice, giggle soup, grape, grapes, Harry Champers, laughing soup, laughing water, Merry Widow, Minnehaha, pop, sham, shammy,* *shampers, shampoo, sparkle, squirt, the boy, the bubbly, the grapes, varnish, white fustian, whoopee, whoopee-water.* 2. to drink champagne. RT: *irrigate.* [Br., (1875): DSUE]

chamber pipe a pipe with a chamber to hold a large amount of marijuana. The resins of the smoke collect on the unsmoked marijuana producing a very potent smoke. RS: *bong.* [U.S., (D&B: 1978)]

chamois champagne. RT: *cham.* [U.S., BVB: 1942, VJM: 1949]

champ a (male) drug user who, when captured by the police, will not reveal his drug sources, even when under pressure. From *champion.* [U.S., JBW: 1967, EEL: 1971]

champers champagne. *Cf. Harry Champers.* RT: *cham.* Heard on M*A*S*H (U.S.), 1970s. [Br., (1821): DSUE, M&J: 1975]

chandoo (also **chandu**) Chinese opium prepared for smoking. RT: *opium.* RDS: 1982 lists it as a Malay word. [U.S., RDS: 1982]

channel 1. a source for drugs; a *connection* (*q.v.*). RS: *dealer.* [U.S., RRL: 1969] 2. a large vein into which injections are made. *Cf. ditch, gutter, home, line, mainline, pipe, pit, sewer.* [U.S., DWM: 1938, VJM: 1949, W&F: 1960, RRL: 1969, RDS: 1982]

channel swimmer an addict who takes drugs by injecting into a vein. A play on the name for a person who swims across the English Channel. *Cf. channel.* RS: *bangster.* [U.S., (1940): JES: 1959, H&C: 1975]

chap-fallen alcohol intoxicated. GEN: disappointed, showing disappointment. A spelling variant of *chop-fallen* referring to sagging jowls (cheeks) when a person is depressed. RT: *drunk.* [BF: 1737]

charas (also **chara, charash, charras**) 1. the pure resin (in cake form) of the Indian hemp usually from the top of the (marijuana) plant, possibly mixed with opium. RS: *hash.* [U.S., D&D: 1957, RRL: 1969, EEL: 1971, D&B: 1978, RDS: 1982; Br., (1875): OEDS, BTD: 1968, M&J: 1975] 2. marijuana. RT: *pot.* [U.S., EEL: 1971, JH: 1979]

charge 1. a dose or portion of a drug; an injection of a drug. *Cf. shot.* [U.S., PRB: 1930, GOL: 1950, RRL: 1969, ADC: 1981] 2. the *call* (*q.v.*) of a drug; the *rush* (*q.v.*) of a drug; drug euphoria. [U.S., DWM: 1938, M&D: 1952, RRL: 1969, CM: 1970, EEL: 1971, EAF: 1980] 3. marijuana; a marijuana cigarette. RT: *pot, joint.* [Br. and U.S., (1929): OEDS, (1943): DSUE, W&F: 1960, BTD: 1968, EEL: 1971, M&J: 1975, ADC: 1981]

charged 1. depressed or slightly overdosed with drugs; having taken a little more than is necessary for euphoria. [U.S., DWM: 1938, RRL: 1969] 2. drug intoxicated. *Cf. supercharged.* RT: *stoned.* [U.S., BVB: 1942, GOL: 1950, RRL: 1969]

charged up 1. alcohol intoxicated. GEN: excited. RT: *drunk.* [U.S., BVB: 1942] 2. drug intoxicated; high on heroin. RT:

stoned. [Br. and U.S., (1922): DU, GOL: 1950, TRG: 1968, EEL: 1971, BTD: 1968, W&F: 1975, ADC: 1981]

charged water weak or inferior liquor. RS: *rotgut*. [U.S., BVB: 1942]

Charley Coke (also **Charles, Charley, Charlie, Charlie Coke**) 1. cocaine; a personification of cocaine. *Cf. Cholly*. RT: *cocaine*. [U.S., (1920): DU, VJM: 1949, M&D: 1952, A&T: 1953, D&D: 1957, W&F: 1960, RRL: 1969, EEL: 1971] 2. a heavy user of cocaine. RT: *kokomo*. [U.S., DWM: 1936, BVB: 1942]

Charley Cotton (also **Charlie Cotton**) the *cotton* (*q.v.*) used to strain a drug before injection. Down-and-out addicts beg for and use this to maintain their habits. *Cf. ask for cotton, cotton brothers*. [U.S., DWM: 1938, VJM: 1949]

Charley Freer beer. Rhyming slang. RT: *beer*. [Br., JRW: 1909, DRS]

Charley Frisky (also **Charlie Frisky**) whiskey. Rhyming slang. RT: *whiskey*. [Br., mid 18-1900s, DSUE]

Charley goon a police officer. RT: *fuzz*. [U.S., CM: 1970]

Charley Randy (also **Charlie Randy**) brandy. Rhyming slang. RT: *brandy*. [Br., mid 18-1900s, DSUE]

Charlie cocaine. See *Charley Coke*.

char wallah a teetotaller. *Cf. wallah* for similarly formed expressions. RT: *dry*. [Br. military, early 1900s, DSUE]

chas (also **chez**) matches. A front-clipping. [U.S., ADC: 1981, ADC: 1984]

chaser an alcoholic drink taken after a non-alcoholic one; (or) beer, water, or some similar liquid drunk after a shot of hard liquor. [Br. and U.S., (1897): OEDS, MHW: 1934, W&F: 1960, SSD, K&M: 1968]

chase the dragon to inhale opium fumes through a straw. The opium pellet is heated on a piece of metal foil held over a flame. The vapors are drawn into the nostrils through a straw. The opium pellet (dragon) sputters across the foil and must be chased with the straw in order not to waste any of the fumes. M&V: 1973 label the expression "Hong Kong." [U.S., (RRL: 1969), IGA: 1971, M&V: 1973, DNE: 1980]

chase the duck to drink liquor heavily. See *duck*. RT: *guzzle*. [U.S., M&C: 1905, BVB: 1942]

chasing the bag addicted to heroin; trying to buy good heroin. RS: *hooked*. [U.S., RRL: 1969, ADC: 1981]

chasing the can See *rush the growler*.

chasing the nurse (also **chasing the white nurse**) addicted to morphine. RS: *hooked*. [U.S., JES: 1959, H&C: 1975]

chaulkers amphetamines. See *chalk*. The origin of the spelling is not known. RT: *amps*. [U.S., JH: 1979]

chaw (also **chaw tobacco**) a plug of chewing tobacco. From a dialect form of *chew,* (1530): SOD. RT: ***quid***. [U.S., (1837): DA, BVB: 1942]

C-head 1. a cocaine user. RT: ***kokomo***. [U.S., JH: 1979, RDS: 1982] See also ***A-head, B-head***. 2. an L.S.D. user who takes L.S.D. on sugar cubes. *Cf.* ***cubehead***. [U.S., RDS: 1982]

check a dose (usually one ounce) of a drug in a capsule or folded in a paper; a ***bindle*** (*q.v.*). RS: ***load***. [U.S., DWM: 1933, DWM: 1936, VJM: 1949]

cheeo marijuana seeds to be chewed. RS: ***pot***. [U.S., M&V: 1973, SNP: 1977]

cheer (also **cup of cheer**) beverage alcohol drunk to celebrate an event or a season. RT: ***booze***. [U.S., BVB: 1942] See also ***blue cheer***.

cheerer beverage alcohol; an alcoholic drink. RT: ***nip***. [Br., 1800s, JB: 1823, F&H; listed in BVB: 1942]

cheerer-upper beverage alcohol; a drink. RS: ***nip***. [U.S., BVB: 1942]

cheerio alcohol intoxicated. RT: ***drunk***. Not listed in JB: 1980. [South African, (1936): DSUE]

cheer the belly to drink alcohol; to drink to excess. RT: ***guzzle***. [U.S., BVB: 1942]

cheese cocaine ***free base*** (*q.v.*). RS: ***cocaine***. See ***bananas and cheese***. [U.S., ELA: 1984]

chef 1. an opium den attendant; someone who cooks and prepares opium for use in an opium den. [U.S., VFN: 1933, DWM: 1936, W&F: 1960] 2. to prepare and cook opium for use in an opium den. *Cf.* ***cater***. [U.S., BVB: 1942, VJM: 1949] 3. opium ashes; opium residue left from smoking. *Cf.* ***green ashes***. [U.S., BVB: 1942, VJM: 1949]

chemical dependence addiction to alcohol, drugs, or both. *Cf.* ***habit***. A polite euphemism. [U.S., RAS: 1980]

chemicals hallucinogenic drugs such as L.S.D. 25, M.D.A., T.H.C. Compare to ***plant***. RS: ***dope***. [U.S., ADC: 1975, FAB: 1979]

cherry bounce (also **cherry bouncer**) cherry brandy. *Cf.* ***bounce***. RS: ***brandy***. [late 16-1700s, DSUE]

cherry leb an alcohol extract of marijuana. From *Lebanese*. *Cf.* ***blond Lebanese***. RT: ***oil***. [U.S., (1976): ELA: 1982, DEM: 1981]

cherry-merry alcohol intoxicated. *Cf.* ***merry***. RT: ***drunk***. [BF: 1737, (1775): OED]

cherry ripe a tobacco pipe. RT: ***pipe***. [Br., JCH: 1887, DRS, SSD, B&P: 1965; U.S., M&B: 1944]

cherry top the hallucinogenic drug ***L.S.D.*** (*q.v.*). *Cf.* ***pink swirl***. RT: ***L.S.D.*** [U.S., YKB: 1977]

cherubimical alcohol intoxicated. RT: ***drunk***. [BF: 1737]

chew a hunk of tobacco. See *chaw*. RS: *quid*. [Br. and U.S., late 18–1900s, DU, DSUE]

chew-bacca chewing tobacco. Compare to *bacca chew*. RS: *fogus*. [Bahamas and Belize, JAH: 1982]

chewer a tobacco chewer. [U.S., (1850): DST: 1984]

chewing the gum using opium; addicted to opium. *Cf. mired in the mud, picking the poppies*. [U.S., JES: 1959, H&C: 1975]

chiba-chiba a potent variety of Colombian marijuana. RT: *pot*. [U.S., (1971): ELA: 1982]

Chicago black a dark marijuana grown in the Chicago area. RT: *pot*. [U.S., EEL: 1971, JH: 1979]

Chicago green a dark green marijuana grown in the Chicago area. RG: 1970 calls it marijuana cured in opium. *Cf. Illinois green*. RT: *pot*. [U.S., M&V: 1967, RG: 1970, EEL: 1971, EAF: 1972]

Chicago leprosy the scars of many abscesses on the arms of an addict. *Cf. Ab*. [U.S., M&V: 1967, RDS: 1982]

chice alcohol intoxicated. Probably from *shice* (*q.v.*). RT: *drunk*. [Br., JCH: 1887]

chicharra* (also **chicarra***) a large communal marijuana cigarette. From Spanish, meaning perhaps cicada, similar to *roach* (*q.v.*). RS: *joint*. [U.S., M&V: 1954, RRL: 1969, CG: 1980, NIDA: 1980]

chick heroin. See *girl*. RT: *heroin*. [U.S., RRL: 1969, NIDA: 1980]

chicken powder powdered amphetamine. RS: *amps*. [U.S., IGA: 1971, YKB: 1977, NIDA: 1980]

chicken shit habit (also **chick shit habit**) a small drug habit; a person with a small drug habit. *Cf. chipper*. [U.S., VJM: 1949, M&V: 1954, RRL: 1969]

chickory 1. (also **chickery**) alcohol intoxicated. (BF: 1737: [He's] Chickery.) *Cf. shicker, shickery*. RT: *drunk*. [BF: 1737] 2. low-quality opium. Possibly reprocessed opium. Chickory = cheap or inferior referring to chickory used as a substitute for coffee. *Cf. yen-chee*. RS: *opium*. [U.S., JES: 1959, H&C: 1975]

chied (also **tchied**) having to do with an opium pellet cooked (prepared) for smoking. [U.S., (1887): RML: 1948]

chief (also **the chief**) 1. mescaline. RS: *peyote*. [U.S., EEL: 1971, H&C: 1975] 2. the hallucinogenic drug *L.S.D.* (*q.v.*). RT: *L.S.D.* [U.S., JBW: 1967, EEL: 1971, W&F: 1975, YKB: 1977, KBH: 1982]

chill 1. to ignore someone suspected of being an informer; to refuse to sell drugs to a suspected informer. GEN: to reject someone. *Cf. freeze, ice*. [U.S., M&V: 1967, RRL: 1969, EEL: 1971, M&V: 1973, D&B: 1978] 2. a cold beer. *Cf. cold one*. RT: *beer*. [U.S., W&F: 1960]

chillum a device now used for the smoking of marijuana. RS: *bong*. [(1781): OED; RRL: 1969, D&B: 1978, ADC: 1981]

Chinaman on one's back (also **Chinaman on one's neck**) one's habit or addiction; withdrawal symptoms. See *have a monkey on one's back*. May have originally referred to opium addiction. RS: *habit*. [U.S., early 1900s, JES: 1959, M&V: 1967, RRL: 1969]

China white 1. (also **Chinese white**) pure or nearly pure heroin. *Cf. Chinese red*. RS: *heroin*. [U.S., RRL: 1969, EEL: 1971, ADC: 1981] 2. *fentanyl* (*q.v.*), a synthetic narcotic analgesic. *Cf. fen*. [U.S., JWK: 1981]

Chinese connection drug smuggling controlled by the Chinese. *Cf. connection*. [U.S., RDS: 1982]

Chinese cure gradual withdrawal from an addictive drug. Comparable to the Chinese water torture. RS: *kick*. [U.S., RRL: 1969]

Chinese molasses opium. Opium in its raw state is dark and gummy like molasses. RT: *opium*. [DU, A&T: 1953, SNP: 1977, RDS: 1982]

Chinese needlework 1. the drug trade; a code expression indicating drug trade. *Cf. embroidery*. See *tea accessories*. [U.S., DWM: 1938] 2. the injection of drugs. Does not necessarily refer to opium. [U.S., BVB: 1942, VJM: 1949] See *tracks*.

Chinese red heroin. *Cf. China white*. RT: *heroin*. [U.S., YKB: 1977, NIDA: 1980]

Chinese saxophone an opium pipe. RT: *hop stick*. [U.S., early 1900s, DU, RDS: 1982]

Chinese tobacco opium. RT: *opium*. [U.S., D&D: 1957, W&F: 1960, EEL: 1971]

Chinese white See *China white*.

chingadera* equipment used for injecting drugs. Probably from calo *chingar* (= to fuck). Mexican Spanish. RS: *outfit*. [U.S., M&V: 1967, H&C: 1975]

Chino a Chinese drug seller; a Chinese opium dealer. Chino = Chinese. RS: *dealer*. [U.S., DWM: 1936, BVB: 1942, A&T: 1953]

chip 1. to dabble in addictive drugs; to take an amount of an addictive drug small enough so as to avoid addiction. See *dip and dab, play around*. *Cf. joy pop*. [U.S., (M&V: 1954), (TRG: 1968), RRL: 1969, EEL: 1971, D&B: 1978, EAF: 1980, (RDS: 1982)] 2. to dilute drugs. See *cut*. Possibly similar to shaving a cube of morphine. *Cf. shave*. [U.S., JES: 1959, H&C: 1975] 3. heroin. Probably refers to cut heroin. See sense two. RS: *heroin*. [U.S., C&H: 1974, SNP: 1977]

chipper 1. alcohol intoxicated. In the sense of *merry* (*q.v.*). RT: *drunk*. [BF: 1737] 2. (also **chippie, chippy, chippy user**) an occasional user of an addictive drug. May refer to the use of highly-diluted heroin. *Cf. chip*. [U.S., DWM: 1938, VJM: 1949, GOL: 1950, RRL: 1969, CM: 1970, EEL: 1971] Nicknames and slang terms for persons who use drugs and who are not addicted:

chicken shit habit, chick shit habit, chipper, chippy, dabbler, fan, fortnighter, goofer, ice creamer, joy popper, joy rider, kick freak, light-weight chipper, lob, lobby gow, period hitter, pleasure smoker, pleasure user, Saturday nighter, Saturday night habit, skinner, skin-popper, skin-shooter, social junker, student, Sunday popper, undergrad, weekend doper, weekender, weekend tripper, weekend twister, weekend user, weekend warrior, youngblood.

chippy 1. (also **chipper, chippie**) an occasional user of an addictive drug. *Cf. chip.* GEN: someone who does something only occasionally, especially a part-time prostitute. [U.S., (1920s): JES: 1959, DWM: 1938, VJM: 1949, GOL: 1950, RRL: 1969, CM: 1970, EEL: 1971] 2. (also **chippy around**) to use addictive drugs infrequently. The same as *play around* (*q.v.*). See *chip.* [U.S., GOL: 1950, W&F: 1967, (RRL: 1969)]

chippy habit the occasional use of addictive drugs. Usually leads to addiction. *Cf. chip.* [U.S., DWM: 1938, BVB: 1942] Terms for a minor drug habit or for occasional use of drugs: *chicken shit habit, chick shit habit, chippy habit, coffee-and habit, cotton habit, hit-and-miss habit, ice cream habit, light-weight nothing, mickey mouse habit, Pepsi-Cola habit, Saturday night habit, skip and jump habit, spot habit, sugar habit, three-day habit, weekend habit.*

chiquita* a bit of a drug; a *taste* (*q.v.*). From the Spanish word meaning very little. RS: *load.* [U.S., EEL: 1971]

chira* shredded marijuana. *Cf. chicharra.* RS: *pot.* [U.S., IGA: 1971, NIDA: 1980] See also *charas.*

chirping merry alcohol intoxicated; tipsy; merry from liquor. RT: *drunk.* [BE: 1690, FG: 1823 F&H; listed in BVB: 1942]

chit-chat beverage alcohol; a drink. RT: *nip.* [Br., 1800s, F&H]

chiva* heroin. Spanish (calo). RT: *heroin.* [U.S., JBW: 1967, EEL: 1971, JBR: 1973, YKB: 1977, NIDA: 1980]

chlorals (also **corals**) chloral hydrate, a fast-acting sedative; knockout drops; the active ingredient in a *Mickey Finn.* RT: *Mickey Finn.* [U.S., SNP: 1977]

chloroform a volatile anesthetic occasionally inhaled for a high. Not argot. [since the early 1800s, (1838): OED]

choc See *chalk.*

chocolate 1. opium. From the consistency and color of raw opium. Both English and Spanish pronunciations. RT: *opium.* [calo, HB: 1955, JBR: 1973] 2. hashish. *Cf. candy bar, carob chips, chunks.* RT: *hash.* [U.S., D&B: 1978]

chocolate chips *L.S.D.* (*q.v.*); acid. *Cf. brown dots.* RT: *L.S.D.* [U.S., YKB: 1977, NIDA: 1980, KBH: 1982]

chocolate mesc mescaline. Possibly a particular variety of Peyote cactus. RS: *peyote.* [U.S., SNP: 1977]

choke to over-dilute drugs; to take a bit of drugs from the packet being sold. *Cf. chip, chop, cut.* [U.S., JWK: 1981]

choked having to do with over-diluted drugs; having to do with a short-weighted drug buy. RS: *cut*. [U.S., JWK: 1981]

choke dog raw whiskey; *moonshine* (*q.v.*). Because it is strong enough to choke a dog. RT: *rotgut*. [U.S., (1821): W&F: 1960]

choker 1. a cigarette; a cigarette butt. *Cf. gasper*. RT: *brad, nail*. [Br. and U.S., F&G: 1925, MHW: 1934] 2. a tobacco cigarette laced with cocaine. RS: *set*. [U.S., ELA: 1984]

Cholly (also **Cholley**) cocaine. A variant of *Charlie* (*q.v.*). RT: *cocaine*. [U.S., H&C: 1975, YKB: 1977]

chop to finely divide a drug; to process heroin; to cut or dilute heroin. *Cf. chip*. RT: *cut*. [U.S., D&B: 1970c, IGA: 1971]

christen to dilute or adulterate liquor. *Cf. baptized*. RT: *cut*. [Br., FG: 1785, FG: 1823]

Christian See *cristian*.

Christina *methamphetamine* (*q.v.*). See *cristina*.

Christmas cheer liquor; drinking. Seen in *BYTE* magazine, December, 1983. Surely much older. [U.S., RAS: 1983]

Christmas roll a mixture of different colored barbiturate capsules. RT: *barbs*. [U.S., M&V: 1967, H&C: 1975]

Christmas tree 1. a drunkard. Based on *lit up like a Christmas tree*, an elaboration of *lit* (*q.v.*). RT: *sot*. [U.S., BVB: 1942] 2. (also **Christmas trees**) any one (or more) of a variety of multi-colored tablets and capsules: a clear capsule filled with multi-colored pellets; *Dexamyl* (TM; *q.v.*); *Drinamyl* (TM; *q.v.*); *Tuinal* (TM; *q.v.*), red and blue capsules; etc. [U.S., RRL: 1969, D&B: 1970c, EEL: 1971, M&V: 1973, YKB: 1977, EAF: 1980, NIDA: 1980, ADC: 1981, HSD: 1984] 3. a variety of L.S.D. RT: *L.S.D.* [U.S., DEM: 1981]

chronic a drug addict or user. RT: *junky*. [U.S., (1920s): JES: 1959, BVB: 1942, VJM: 1949]

chuck 1. to eat voraciously while withdrawing from drugs. GEN: to eat (1876): DSUE. *Cf. Chuck habit*. [U.S., JTD: 1971] See also *chuckers*. 2. the food which is eaten voraciously when withdrawing from drugs. GEN: food (1850): OEDS. [U.S., IGA: 1971]

chuck a Charley (also **chuck a Willy**) to enact a false drug withdrawal spasm to get drugs from a medical practitioner. The same as *chuck a dummy* (*q.v.*). *Cf. brody*. [Aust., SJB: 1943]

chuck a dummy (also **chuck a wingding**) to enact a false drug withdrawal spasm to get drugs from a medical practitioner. From an earlier (late 1800s) expression for any kind of a staged fit. RS: *brody*. [Br. and U.S., F&G: 1925, GOL: 1950]

chucked tipsy; alcohol intoxicated. RT: *drunk*. [Br., (1889): F&H; listed in BVB: 1942]

chuckers (also **chucks, the chucks**) an enormous appetite after drug (heroin) withdrawal. *Cf. chuck*. From *chuck habit*. [U.S., M&V:

1967, RRL: 1969, EEL: 1971, JWK: 1981] See also *munchies*.

chuck habit an enormous appetite which follows drug withdrawal or abstinence. *Cf. chuckers, chuck horrors*. [U.S., DWM: 1936, BVB: 1942, RRL: 1969]

chuck horrors 1. *chuckers* (*q.v.*); craving for food while withdrawing. [U.S., VFN: 1933, DWM: 1936, VJM: 1949, A&T: 1953, W&F: 1960, RRL: 1969] 2. an intense aversion to food during drug withdrawal. (If one of these senses is an error, it is most likely this one.) [U.S., BVB: 1942, GOL: 1950]

chuck the habit to break a drug addiction. *Habit* (*q.v.*) = an addiction to a drug. RT: *kick*. [U.S., D&B: 1970c]

chug-a-lug (also **chug**) to drink down a whole beer (or other drink) without stopping. RS: *guzzle*. [U.S., D&D: 1957, W&F: 1960, DCCU: 1972, MW: 1976]

chunks (also **chunkies**) hashish. From the brand name of a chocolate candy. *Cf. candy bar*. RT: *hash*. [U.S., EEL: 1971, JH: 1979]

church key a beer can or bottle opener. [U.S., W&F: 1967, DCCU: 1972, MW: 1976]

churus (also **churrus**) marijuana. Listed as Spanish in NIDA: 1980. See *charas*. RT: *pot*. [U.S., JES: 1959, H&C: 1975, NIDA: 1980]

ciba (also **C.**, **C.B.**) *Doriden* (TM; *q.v.*) a non-barbiturate hypnotic. Ciba is a drug manufacturer's name. Doriden is a product of USV (P.R.) Development Corporation. RT: *dories*. [U.S., RRL: 1969, JHF: 1971]

ciclón* (also **ciclón de cristal***) phencyclidine, *P.C.P.* (*q.v.*), an animal tranquilizer. Spanish for *cyclone* (*q.v.*). RT: *P.C.P.* [U.S., NIDA: 1980]

cid (also **Sid**) the hallucinogenic drug *L.S.D.* (*q.v.*). From *acid*. RT: *L.S.D.* [U.S., ADC: 1981, JWK: 1981]

cig a cigarette; a cigar. *Cf. nail, seegar*. [Br. and U.S., DSUE, B&L: 1890, RB: 1915, BVB: 1942, SSD]

cigaboo (also **ciggaboo**) a cigarette. RT: *nail*. [Aust., (1948): DSUE]

cigar a thick or fat marijuana cigarette. RT: *joint*. [U.S., ELA: 1984]

cigareet (also **cigareete**) a cigarette. RT: *nail*. [U.S., BVB: 1942]

cigarette a marijuana cigarette. RT: *joint*. The tobacco cigarette dates from 1835 (MW: 1983). [U.S., IGA: 1971]

cigarette end a cigarette butt. RT: *brad*. Not slang. [Br., 1900s, (DSUE)]

cigarette paper 1. a small sheet of paper for rolling tobacco into a cigarette. RS: *paper*. Not slang. [(1860): OEDS] 2. a pack or *bindle* (*q.v.*) of heroin or some other drug. The paper is folded with the drug inside. RS: *load*. [U.S., DWM: 1936, VJM: 1949]

cigarette with no name (also **no brand cigarette, no name cigarette**) a marijuana cigarette. RT: *joint*. [U.S., EAF: 1980]

ciggy (also **ciggie**) a cigarette. *Cf. tiggy*. D&D: 1957 list **ciggie-break** and **ciggie-girl**. RT: *nail*. [Br. and U.S., RB: 1915, BVB: 1942, (D&D: 1957), (1962): OEDS, DNE: 1980]

cighead a heavy smoker of tobacco. [U.S., ADC: 1981]

cig-smug a smuggler of cigarettes, usually from a state with a low tobacco tax to a state with a higher tax. [U.S., RDS: 1982]

cinder a drink of liquor. RT: *nip*. [Br., JCH: 1864, F&H; listed in BVB: 1942] See also *clink*.

circus a feigned drug withdrawal reaction; a faker of withdrawal spasms. RT: *brody*. [U.S., DWM: 1936, VJM: 1949]

citizen a non-user of drugs; a *lame* (*q.v.*). RT: *square*. [U.S., JWK: 1981]

citroli* a potent variety of cannabis from Nepal. RT: *hash*. [U.S., ELA: 1984]

C.J. (also **K.J.**) phencyclidine, P.C.P.; a *crystal joint* (*q.v.*). A P.C.P. dose in crystalline form. RS: *P.C.P.* [U.S., YKB: 1977, FAB: 1979]

C-jam (also **C-game, C-jame**) cocaine. *Cf. jam Cecil*. RT: *cocaine*. [U.S., D&B: 1970c, IGA: 1971]

C-joint a place where cocaine is sold. From *coke joint* (*q.v.*). RT: *doperie*. [U.S., GOL: 1950]

C.K. cocaine. RT: *cocaine*. [U.S., EEL: 1971]

clanks the delirium tremens. *Cf. whips and jangles, triangles*. RT: *D.T.s*. [U.S., D&D: 1957, W&F: 1960, RDS: 1982]

clap of thunder a glass of gin. The same as *flash of lightning* (*q.v.*). RS: *gin*. [Br., early 1800s, DSUE]

clarabelle *T.H.C.* (*q.v.*). *Cf. clay, liquid grass, resin, synthetic grass, tea, tic*. [U.S., EEL: 1971, JH: 1979]

clay 1. *T.H.C.* (*q.v.*). [U.S., JH: 1979] 2. hashish; good hashish. See *brick*. RT: *hash*. [U.S., JWK: 1981] See also *mud*.

clean 1. (also **cleaned up, cleared up**) having to do with an addict who has ceased using drugs, temporarily or permanently; having to do with an addict's arm which is free of needle marks. [U.S., M&H: 1959, RRL: 1969, D&B: 1970c, EEL: 1971, EAF: 1972, W&F: 1975, MW: 1976] 2. having to do with someone who is not carrying drugs. The opposite of *dirty* (*q.v.*). [U.S., RRL: 1969, D&B: 1970c, EEL: 1971, DNE: 1973, MA: 1973, ADC: 1981, JWK: 1981] 3. having to do with marijuana which is free of seeds and stems. [U.S., RRL: 1969, EEL: 1971, ADC: 1981] 4. to clean and *manicure* (*q.v.*) marijuana. [U.S., (1961): ELA: 1982, JBW: 1967, RRL: 1969, ADC: 1981]

clean from the still having to do with undiluted liquor. Does not necessarily refer to *moonshine* (*q.v.*). RT: *neat*. [Br., 1800s, F&H]

clear 1. alcohol intoxicated; very drunk. RT: ***drunk***. [(1688): OED, BE: 1690, NCD: 1725, FG: 1785, FG: 1811, B&L: 1890; listed in BVB: 1942] 2. undiluted; ***neat*** (*q.v.*). RT: ***neat***. [U.S., BWG: 1899]

cleared up See *clean*.

clear light 1. high-quality ***L.S.D.*** (*q.v.*) in a gelatin capsule. *Cf.* ***windowpane***. RT: ***L.S.D.*** [U.S., YKB: 1977, RDS: 1982] 2. (also **white light**) an excellent high from the hallucinogenic drug L.S.D. RS: ***L.S.D.*** RRL: 1969 lists only **white light**. [U.S., RRL: 1969, JH: 1979]

clear liquid *L.S.D.* (*q.v.*) in liquid form. *Cf.* ***clear light***. RS: ***L.S.D.*** [U.S., RDS: 1982]

clear McCoy, the good-quality whiskey. *Cf.* ***the real McCoy***. RS: ***whiskey***. Known before U.S. prohibition. The term has also been applied to anything authentic or powerful, especially drugs. [U.S., early 1900s, SBF: 1976]

clear up to withdraw from drugs. RS: ***kick***. [U.S., JBW: 1967, RRL: 1969, EEL: 1971, W&F: 1975]

climb a marijuana cigarette; an assent to a ***high*** (*q.v.*) by the use of marijuana. RT: ***joint***. [U.S., (M&W: 1946)]

clinched alcohol intoxicated. RT: ***drunk***. [Br., 1800s, F&H; listed in BVB: 1942]

clincher a cigarette, pinched out for later use. *Cf.* ***dinch***. RS: ***brad***. [U.S., GOL: 1950]

clinic a pub. RS: ***bar***. [Br., (1955): DSUE]

clink inferior beer. See ***bumclink***. RT: ***queer-beer***. [Br., (1860): DSUE]

clip 1. a holder for a marijuana cigarette butt, a ***roach clip*** (*q.v.*). RT: ***crutch***. [U.S., EEL: 1971, ADC: 1981] 2. to dilute a drug; to shave bit off a cube of morphine. RS: ***cut***. [U.S., JES: 1959]

clip a butt to pinch out a cigarette for later smoking. *Cf.* ***dinch***. [U.S., GOL: 1950, D&D: 1957]

clipped arrested. Possibly from the expression to *clip someone's wings*. RT: ***busted***. [U.S., early 1900s, DU, (M&V: 1967)]

clipping the King's English alcohol intoxicated. RT: ***drunk***. [BF: 1737; Br., (1745): DSUE]

clobbered alcohol intoxicated. GEN: beaten, struck. RT: ***drunk***. [U.S., (1951): SBF: 1976, W&F: 1960]

clorofila* marijuana. From Spanish. RT: ***pot***. [calo, JBR: 1973]

closed said of a drug seller temporarily out of business because the police are suspicious. *Cf.* ***fold up***. [U.S., JWK: 1981]

cloud tobacco smoke; tobacco. RT: ***fogus***. [cant, (BE: 1690), FG: 1785, FG: 1823, DSUE]

clouted arrested for drug dealing or some other offense. RT:

busted. [U.S., M&V: 1967]

clove hunter a tippler; a drunkard. Because of the use of cloves to mask the smell of liquor. RT: *sot*. [JRW: 1909, MHW: 1934, BVB: 1942]

club 1. a drinking den; a *bar* (*q.v.*). RS: *bar*. [1900s, (1935): DSUE] 2. a place to use marijuana. *Cf. pad*. RS: *doperie*. [U.S., (1938): ELA: 1982]

C.N.S. (also **CNS**) the *central nervous system* (*q.v.*). [medical]

coach marijuana remaining after smoking. *Cf. cashed*. Perhaps this is a play on *roach* (*q.v.*). [U.S., D&B: 1970c]

coagulated alcohol intoxicated. RT: *drunk*. [U.S., PD: 1982]

coal tar wine; bad wine. RS: *wine*. [U.S., BVB: 1942]

coast to float in drug euphoria. [U.S., DWM: 1938, RRL: 1969, CM: 1970, EEL: 1971, W&F: 1975]

coasting experiencing euphoria from a slight overdose of cocaine; enjoying the effects of a drug; to be under the influence of drugs. See *coast*. RS: *stoned*. [U.S., DWM: 1936, VJM: 1949, TRG: 1968, (EEL: 1971), ADC: 1981]

coast-to-coasts amphetamines; long-lasting amphetamines. From their use by cross-country truck drivers. Possibly akin to *coast* (*q.v.*). *Cf. L. A. turnabouts*. RT: *amps*. [U.S., RG: 1970, SH: 1972, YKB: 1977]

cobics heroin. Either a local variant or an error (JWK: 1981). See *cobies*. RT: *heroin*. [U.S., YKB: 1977]

cobies morphine. The plural of *coby*. RT: *morphine*. [U.S., YKB: 1977]

coby morphine. See *cobies*.

coca* (also **coka***) cocaine. RT: *cocaine*. Spanish slang. Otherwise part of the scientific name. [U.S., RRL: 1969, EEL: 1971, CG: 1980]

cocaina* cocaine. *Cf. coca*. RT: *cocaine*. Spanish. [U.S., NIDA: 1980]

cocaine an alkaloid anesthetic derived from coca leaves. It was originally used as a local anesthetic in surgery. The drug is not addictive in the same way that heroin is, but it can cause psychic dependence with serious mental distress upon withdrawal. [(1874): OED] Terms for cocaine in various forms and strengths: *angel, angie, baking soda base, base, bernese, Bernice, Bernies, Bernies flake, big bloke, big-C., Billie Hoak, Billie Hoke, blinky, bloke, blow, blower, bounce powder, bouncing powder, boy, burese, Burnese, C., cacil, Cadillac, California cornflakes, came, C. and H., candy, candy cee, Carrie, Carrie Nation, Carry Nation, C-duct, Cecil, cee, C-game, chalk, Charles, Charley, Charley Coke, Charlie, cheese, Cholley, Cholly, C-jam, C-jame, C.K., coca, cocaina, cocanuts, coconut, coka, coke, cola, cookie, Corine, Corinne, Corrine, crystal,* *cube, cubes, Doctor White, dream, duct, dust, dynamite, evil powder, flake, free base, frisky, frisky powder, gin, girl, girlfriend, girli, girly, glad stuff, gold dust, golden girl, goofy dust, happy dust, happy flakes, happy powder, happy stuff, heaven dust, heaven flour, heavenly dust, her, H.M.C., hooter, ice, icicles, Inca message, incentive, initiative, jam, jam Cecil, joy dust, joy flakes, joy powder, lady, Lady Snow, Lady White, leaf, line, magic flake, Mama coca, mojo, mosquitoes, nieve, nose, nose candy, nose powder, nose stuff, number three, old lady White, old Madge, old Steve, paradise, perico, Peruvian flake, pimp dust, pogo pogo, polvito, powdered diamond, reindeer dust, rock, rock candy, rocks, schmack, sea, sister, sleighride, sniff, snow, snowball, snow-caine, snowflakes, snow stuff, sophisticated lady, stardust, star stuff, superblow, sweet stuff, talc, the leaf, the ultimate drug, toot, tootonium, tootuncommon, uptown, W.C., whiff, white, white cross, white drugs, white girl, white horse, white lady, white mosquitoes, white nurse, white stuff, white tornado, wings, witch, you know, 3.*

cocaine blues the depression suffered after a bout of cocaine use. [U.S., RAS: 1983, ELA: 1984]

cocaine cowboy a cocaine smuggler; a drug smuggler. RS: *mule*. Journalistic rather than argot. [U.S., RDS: 1982]

cocaine crash the severe anxiety or depression following a heavy bout of cocaine use. The crash may include a wide variety of additional physical symptoms. [U.S., S&F: 1984]

cocainized experiencing the effects of cocaine; habituated to cocaine use. [U.S., BVB: 1942, H&C: 1975] The following list of terms refers to someone who is high on cocaine: *candied, caught in a snowstorm, chalked up, cocainized, cocked up, coked, coked out, coked up, cooked up, dusted, flaky, frost, frosty, kicked out in the snow, loaded with coke, on the white scene, powdered, snowed, snowed under, snowed up, under the white cross, winged, wired, with a load of coke under the skin.*

cocainomania craving for cocaine. Not slang. [medical]

cocaroin a mixture of cocaine and heroin. RS: *set*. [U.S., JES: 1959, H&C: 1975]

cochornis* marijuana. RT: *pot*. Spanish. [U.S., NIDA: 1980]

cocked alcohol intoxicated. (BF: 1737: [He's] Cock'd.) A synonym of *bent* (*q.v.*). *Cf. full-cocked, half cocked, roostered*. RT: *drunk*. [BF: 1737, BVB: 1942, D&D: 1957]

cocked to the gills (also **cocked as a log**) alcohol intoxicated. Two cases of mixed metaphor. *Cf. cocked*. RT: *drunk*. [PD: 1982]

cocked up high on cocaine. See *coked*. [U.S., IGA: 1971, WCM: 1972]

cock-eyed (also **cock-eyed drunk**) alcohol intoxicated and not seeing straight. (BF: 1737: [He's] Cock Ey'd.) RT: *drunk*. [BF: 1737, (1933): DSUE, MHW: 1934, D&D: 1957]

cockle burrs amphetamines; amphetamine tablets and capsules. RT: *amps*. [U.S., EE: 1976]

cock pipe a penis-shaped device for smoking marijuana; a phallic *bong* (*q.v.*). *Cf. horn*. RS: *bong*. [U.S., (D&B: 1978)]

cocktail 1. an alcoholic drink compounded from a variety of components. [U.S., (1806): RHT: 1912, OED; now widespread] 2. a tobacco cigarette with a marijuana *roach* (*q.v.*) stuck into the tip; a cigarette containing a mixture of tobacco and marijuana; a tobacco cigarette with *hash oil* (*q.v.*) on the end. [U.S., JBW: 1967, EEL: 1971, W&F: 1975, ADC: 1981] 3. to smoke a *cocktail* (sense two). Black use. [U.S., CM: 1970, (D&B: 1978)]

cocktail lounge (also **lounge**) a bar; euphemistic for *saloon* (*q.v.*). RS: *bar*. [originally U.S., (1939): MW: 1983]

cocky's joy gin. *Cf. blackfellow's delight*. RT: *gin*. [Aust., SJB: 1945]

coconut (also **cocanuts, coconuts**) cocaine. An elaboration of *coke* (*q.v.*). RT: *cocaine*. ELA: 1984 lists **cocanuts**. [U.S., VJM: 1949, M&D: 1952, A&T: 1953, RRL: 1969, NIDA: 1980]

cod 1. a drunkard. RT: *sot*. [JRW: 1909] 2. (also **cods**) codeine. [U.S., JWK: 1981]

cod cock a codeine cocktail, made from cough syrup containing codeine. *Cod* (*q.v.*) = codeine. [U.S., IGA: 1971, WCM: 1972]

codeine an alkaloid of opium extracted from morphine. It has a weak painkilling effect and is often found in cough syrups. *Cf. denes*. [(1838): OED] Nicknames and slang terms for codeine: *cement, cod, cods, codys, deens, deines, denes, fours, schoolboy*.

cod, on the alcohol intoxicated. RT: *drunk*. [JRW: 1909]

codys (also **cods**) Codeine tablets. [U.S., JWK: 1981]

coffee the hallucinogenic drug L.S.D. RT: *L.S.D.* [U.S., YKB: 1977, NIDA: 1980, KBH: 1982] See also *cold coffee, corn coffee, white coffee*.

coffee-and habit a small drug habit; a chippy habit. From a phrase such as *coffee and doughnuts*, referring to refreshments RS: *habit*. ELA: 1984 lists **coffee habit**. [U.S., DWM: 1938, BVB: 1942]

coffin-dodger a heavy smoker. *Cf. coffin nail*. [U.S., EHB: 1900, MHW: 1934]

coffin nail 1. (also **coffin tack**) a cigarette; a cheap cigarette. RT: *nail*. [Br. and U.S., (1885): DSUE, (1890): W&F: 1960, F&G: 1925, MHW: 1934, D&D: 1957, B&P: 1965, SSD] 2. alcohol; a drink of liquor. RT: *nip*. [U.S., BVB: 1942, RRL: 1969, JH: 1979]

coffin varnish low-quality or very inferior hard liquor: moonshine, methyl alcohol. RT: *rotgut*. See the previous entry. Best known in the prohibition era. [U.S., (1845): SBF: 1982, DWM: 1935, (1945): DA, VJM: 1949, GOL: 1950]

cofradia* a communal marijuana-smoking party. From the Spanish term for a brotherhood or an association. Akin to *cofrade* = an accomplice (in calo). *Cf.* ***bonche.*** [U.S., M&V: 1954, H&C: 1975]

cogey (also **coguy**) alcohol intoxicated. (cogey from (1722); [He's] Coguy from (1737).) From *coque,* an old (16–1700s) term for a cup of strong liquor. RT: ***drunk.*** [BF: 1722; Br., JB: 1823]

cognacked alcohol intoxicated. *Cf.* ***incog.*** RT: ***drunk.*** [U.S., WWI, MPK: 1930, MHW: 1934, JL: 1972]

cohoba* (also **cahoba***) the pulverized seeds of a plant containing ***D.M.T.*** (*q.v.*). Possibly from Spanish *cohobar* = to distill. [U.S., RRL: 1969, IGA: 1971]

coiler a cigarette. *Cf.* ***quirley, twirlie.*** RT: ***nail.*** [Aust. naval, SJB: 1945]

coka* (also **coca***) cocaine. *Coca* is Spanish for cocaine. RT: ***cocaine.*** [U.S., NIDA: 1980]

coke cocaine. See the verb form at ***coke oneself.*** RT: ***cocaine.*** Widely known. [U.S., (1908): OEDS, (1910): DSUE, (1924): DU, VWS: 1929, GI: 1931, MHW: 1934, DWM: 1936, M&D: 1952, RRL: 1969, CM: 1970, EEL: 1971, YKB: 1977, NIDA: 1980, ADC: 1981, JWK: 1981; Br., SSD, BTD: 1968]

cokeaholic someone addicted to cocaine use. RS: ***junky.*** [U.S., S&F: 1984]

coke blower a cocaine user who sniffs (snorts) powdered cocaine. RT: ***kokomo.*** [U.S., early 1900s, DU]

coke break a period of time set aside for the use of cocaine to stimulate one in one's work. Patterned on *coffee break* and the expression referring to a work break to drink a *Coca-Cola* (TM). [U.S., S&F: 1984]

coke bugs See ***cokeroaches.***

coked (also **coked out, coked up**) high on cocaine. [U.S., (1924): OEDS, HS: 1933, GOL: 1950, W&F: 1960, EEL: 1971, RAS: 1984]

coke fiend a heavy user of cocaine. RT: ***kokomo.*** [U.S., BVB: 1942, DU]

coke freak a heavy user of cocaine. *Cf.* ***freak.*** RT: ***kokomo.*** [U.S., ADC: 1981]

cokehead a heavy cocaine user; any drug user. RT: ***kokomo.*** [U.S., EK: 1927, BVB: 1942, D&D: 1957, W&F: 1960, RRL: 1969, CM: 1970, EEL: 1971]

coke joint a place where cocaine is sold. *Cf.* ***C-joint.*** RS: ***doperie.*** [U.S., early 1900s, DU]

coke oneself to take a dose of cocaine. [U.S., early 1900s, DU]

coke oven a place where cocaine is sold or used. A play on the name of the furnaces which prepare coke (the nonvolatile residue of coal) for steelmaking. *Cf. doperie.* [U.S., BVB: 1942, VJM: 1949, H&C: 1975]

coke party 1. (also **coke time**) a gathering where the participants use cocaine. Both are from *coke* (*Coca-cola* TM) *break. Cf. kick party, pot party.* Probably recurrent nonce. [U.S., GI: 1931, VJM: 1949, M&V: 1973] 2. a party where illegal liquor is drunk. From *Coca-cola* (TM). From the prohibition era. [U.S., AH: 1931, MHW: 1934]

coke peddler a seller of cocaine. RS: *dealer.* [U.S., early 1900s, DU]

cokeroaches (also **cocaine bugs, coke bugs**) imaginary bugs crawling on or under the skin of someone who is deranged by a cocaine binge. A play on *cockroach.* [U.S., S&F: 1984]

coke-smoke a smoker of cocaine. RS: *kokomo.* [U.S., RDS: 1982]

cokespoon (also **flake spoon**) a small spoon with a bowl roughly the diameter of a human nostril. Used to carry powdered cocaine to the nostril where it can then be sniffed (snorted). [U.S., ADC: 1981] See also *quill.*

coke time See *coke party.*

coke whore a cocaine user who begs or borrows cocaine, or buys it with sexual acts. RS: *user.* [U.S., RAS: 1984, ELA: 1984]

cokey (also **cokie**) a cocaine user; a cocaine addict. RT: *kokomo.* [U.S., (1922): OEDS, DWM: 1931, DWM: 1933, MHW: 1934, VJM: 1949, GOL: 1950, W&F: 1960, RRL: 1969, EEL: 1971; RDS: 1982; Br., SSD, BTD: 1968]

cokomo a cocaine user. See *kokomo.*

cola cocaine. *Cf. coke.* RT: *cocaine.* [U.S., ADC: 1984] See also *colas.*

cola de borrego* marijuana. RT: *pot.* Spanish for lamb's tail. [calo, JBR: 1973]

cola de león* marijuana. RT: *pot.* Spanish for lion's tail. [calo, JBR: 1973]

cola de zorra* marijuana. RT: *pot.* Spanish for fox's tail. [calo, JBR: 1973]

colas* the flowering tops of marijuana plants. Spanish for tails. *Cf. flower tops, tops.* [U.S., RRL: 1969, D&B: 1978, RDS: 1982]

cold 1. sober. The opposite of *hot* (*q.v.*). *Cf. cold sober.* RT: *sober.* [U.S., BVB: 1942] 2. having to do with a sudden stop of an addict's drug use. From *cold turkey* (*q.v.*). RS: *kick.* [U.S., RRL: 1969, JWK: 1981]

cold and hot (also **C. and H., H. and C., hot and cold**) a mixture of cocaine and heroin. The same as *hot and cold* (*q.v.*). RS: *set.* Probably older than the attestations indicate. [U.S., EEL: 1971, RDS: 1982]

cold blood beer. *Cf. cold coffee.* RT: *beer.* [Br., 1800s, F&H; listed in BVB: 1942]

cold bust a drug arrest made during an arrest or an investigation of some other offense. Typically, finding drugs in an automobile stopped for a traffic offense. Compare to ***hot bust***. [U.S., RRL: 1969, (RDS: 1982)]

cold coffee beer. *Cf.* ***cold blood***. RT: ***beer***. The two attestations are unrelated. The second one is CB slang. [(1874): JRW: 1909, EE: 1976]

cold cream (also **golden cream**) gin. *Cf.* ***mother's milk***. RT: ***gin***. [Br., (1864): DSUE; listed in BVB: 1942]

cold one 1. an empty bottle. *Cf.* ***corpse***. RT: ***dead soldier***. [U.S., BVB: 1942] 2. a cold bottle, can, or glass of beer. RT: ***nip***. From U.S. beer advertising. [U.S., RAS: 1978, RAS: 1984]

cold shot a bogus dose of drugs. RS: ***blank***. The opposite of ***hot shot*** (*q.v.*). [U.S., H&C: 1975]

cold sober completely sober. *Cf.* ***dry, sober as a judge***. RS: ***sober***. [U.S., late 1800s–p., (1880s): SBF: 1976]

cold sody beer. *Cf.* ***cold one***. RT: ***beer***. [U.S., D&B: 1971]

cold tea brandy. Compare to ***cold coffee***. RT: ***brandy***. [BE: 1690, B&L: 1890, F&H; listed in BVB: 1942]

cold turkey 1. (also **cold**) having to do with a sudden and complete withdrawal from addictive drugs. May refer to the goose pimples one gets as a symptom of withdrawal. One is said to **go cold turkey**, **take the cold turkey**, or **take the cold turkey cure**. *Cf.* ***ice water cure, iron cure, quarry cure, rock pile cure, steel and concrete cure, sweat cure***. [U.S., DWM: 1936, GOL: 1950, M&D: 1952, W&F: 1960, RRL: 1969, EEL: 1971, DCCU: 1972, YKB: 1977, ADC: 1981, JWK: 1981, BW: 1984] 2. to stop an addiction suddenly and totally. RS: ***kick***. [U.S., (1974): DNE: 1980, ADC: 1981]

cold-water army a children's temperance group; abstainers; teetotallers. RS: ***dry***. *Cf.* ***blue-ribbon army***. [Br. and U.S., (1870): DSUE, F&H, DSUE, SBF: 1976, BVB: 1942]

cold-water man a teetotaller. RT: ***dry***. [Aust., 1800s, SJB: 1966]

coli marijuana. Possibly from ***broccoli*** (*q.v.*). See ***colly***. RT: ***pot***. [U.S., D&B: 1978]

coliflor tostao* marijuana. RT: ***pot***. [calo, JBR: 1973]

collar 1. paper, rubber, or other material used to hold a hypodermic needle onto a medicine dropper and to make the joint airtight. RT: ***gasket***. [U.S., M&V: 1954, RRL: 1969, D&B: 1970c, MA: 1973] 2. to arrest. See ***collared***.

collard greens marijuana. *Cf.* ***green***. RT: ***pot***. Black slang. [U.S., EAF: 1980]

collared arrested. From the image of a police officer grabbing a criminal by the collar. RT: ***busted***. [U.S., DWM: 1931, (BD:

1937), (RRL: 1969), (RDS: 1982)]

colly (also collie, colly-weed) marijuana; a marijuana cigarette. See *coli.* RT: *pot.* Jamaican (Rastafarian). [Bahamas, JAH: 1982]

Colombian connection the production and smuggling of marijuana and cocaine into the U.S. from Colombia. [U.S., RDS: 1982] See also *Chinese connection.*

Colombian gold (also Colombian, Colombo, Columbian, Columbian gold, Columbian pink, Columbian red) a potent marijuana from Colombia. The misspelling (Columbian) is seen frequently. *Cf. Acapulco gold.* RT: *pot.* [U.S., RRL: 1969, YKB: 1977, DNE: 1980, NIDA: 1980, ADC: 1981]

Colombian green a high-quality marijuana from Colombia. See *Colombian gold.* RT: *pot.* [U.S., JH: 1979]

Colombian roulette the smuggling of cocaine from Colombia. Played by someone serving as a *body-packer* (*q.v.*) in the smuggling of Colombian cocaine into the U.S. by swallowing packets of cocaine and excreting them in this country. If one of the packets should break, it means death to the smuggler. From Florida drug traffic. [U.S., RAS: 1982]

Colombo a kind of marijuana. See *Colombian gold.* RT: *pot.* [U.S., ADC: 1975, YKB: 1977]

colonial tangle (also colonial) beer. RT: *beer.* [Aust., SJB: 1945]

colorado* a *Seconal* (TM; *q.v.*) barbiturate capsule. Spanish for red. *Cf. red.* RT: *sec.* [U.S., EEL: 1971, RDS: 1982]

Colorado Kool-Aid beer, Coor's (TM) beer. *Cf. koolaid.* RT: *beer.* CB radio slang. [U.S., EE: 1976]

color, in alcohol intoxicated. *Cf. florid.* RT: *drunk.* [U.S., D&B: 1970c]

Columbian (also Columbia red, Columbian gold, Columbian pink, Columbian red) A frequently-seen misspelling of *Colombian.* See *Colombian gold.* [U.S., IGA: 1971, (1977): R&P: 1982 (at *nickel bag*)]

Columbus black marijuana said to be from Columbus, Ohio. See *black Columbus.* [U.S., ELA: 1982]

comb and brush a drunkard. Rhyming slang for *lush* (*q.v.*). RT: *sot.* [JRW: 1909]

comboozelated alcohol intoxicated. RT: *drunk.* College slang. [U.S., GU: 1975]

come down 1. (also come off) for a drug user to experience the waning of a drug's effects; to begin withdrawal from an addictive drug. Compare to *crash* (*q.v.*). [U.S., (1959): RSG: 1964, RB: 1967, (TRG: 1968), RRL: 1969, CM: 1970, M&V: 1973, W&F: 1975, ADC: 1981, (RDS: 1982)] 2. to begin to sober up from a drinking bout. From sense one. [U.S., ADC: 1981] 3. to feel the effects of a depressant drug. *Cf. downer.* [U.S., M&V: 1973] 4.

(also **come-down, comedown**) the return to reality from the effects of a drug or alcohol. Now GEN: any disappointment. [U.S., S&R: 1972, C&H: 1974, W&F: 1975, S&F: 1984]

come down hard to *crash* (*q.v.*); to come out of a drug trip (usually L.S.D.) badly. *Cf. come down*. [U.S., H&C: 1975]

come home to return to reality after an *L.S.D.* (*q.v.*) trip. [U.S., IGA: 1971, WCM: 1972]

come on to begin to feel the effects of a drug; for a drug to take effect. GEN: perform well (M&W: 1946). *Cf. org*. [U.S., RG: 1970, EEL: 1971, D&B: 1978]

comfort alcohol; liquor. *Cf. comfort station, creature comfort*. RT: *booze*. [Br., mid 1700s, DSUE; listed in BVB: 1942]

comfortable tipsy; mellow from drink. RS: *drunk*. [U.S., W&F: 1960, AP: 1980]

comfortable waters rum. RT: *rum*. [U.S., D&D: 1957]

comfort station an establishment which sells liquor. A playful reinterpretation of a euphemism for restroom. RS: *bar*. [U.S., BVB: 1942]

commode-hugging drunk very drunk; drunk and vomiting. Commode = toilet. *Cf. knee-walking drunk, snot-flinging drunk*. RT: *drunk*. College slang. [U.S., GU: 1975]

common sewer 1. a drink of liquor; a measure of liquor. Refers to the contents of a sewer. RT: *nip*. [Br., (1860): DSUE, JCH: 1887, F&H] 2. a drunkard. RT: *sot*. [Br., 1800s, F&H]

commune with the spirits to drink alcohol, probably to excess. A play on *spirits* = liquor. RT: *guzzle*. [U.S., BVB: 1942]

communist M. and M.s red pills; red pep pills. *Red* usually refers to capsules of *Seconal* (TM; *q.v.*) which are barbiturates, not pep pills. *Cf. turn communist*. [U.S., BR: 1972]

comp to buy drugs. Probably black urban dialect variant of *cop* (*q.v.*). RS: *score*. [U.S., ADC: 1975]

comp man a drug dealer. Probably black urban dialect variant of *cop man* (*q.v.*). RT: *dealer*. [U.S., ADC: 1975]

con to make contact with a drug seller. RS: *score*. [U.S., M&V: 1973]

concerned alcohol intoxicated. (BF: 1737: [He's] Concern'd.) RT: *drunk*. [(1686): F&H, BF: 1737; listed in BVB: 1942]

condensed corn whiskey; rotgut. RT: *whiskey*. [U.S. Army, (1860s): DST: 1984]

conductor an experienced guide during an L.S.D. trip. RT: *sitter*. [U.S., RAS: 1982]

confectionary a tavern, a barroom. RS: *bar*. [U.S., JRB: 1859, F&H, BVB: 1942]

conflummoxed alcohol intoxicated. RT: *drunk*. [U.S., BVB: 1942]

confoundedly cut alcohol intoxicated. *Cf. cut, half cut.* RT: *drunk.* [BF: 1722]

conga marijuana from central Africa, possibly with the addition of *Datura* (*q.v.*). *Cf. Congo dirt.* RS: *pot.* [Br., BTD: 1968; U.S., ELA: 1982]

Congo brown a brownish variety of marijuana from Africa. RT: *pot.* [U.S., ELA: 1982]

Congo dirt a good-quality marijuana, presumably from Africa. RS: *pot.* [U.S., JH: 1979]

Congo mataby marijuana. *Cf. African black.* RT: *pot.* [U.S., JTD: 1971, M&J: 1975]

conk-buster inferior liquor. *Cf. popskull.* RT: *rotgut.* Attested as black use. [U.S., W&F: 1960]

connect to find a drug source and make a drug purchase. RT: *score.* [U.S., BD: 1937, A&T: 1953, M&V: 1954, RRL: 1969, EEL: 1971, W&F: 1975]

connection (also connector) a drug seller; a drug distribution ring; a drug smuggling ring. RS: *dealer.* See *Chinese connection, Colombian connection.* [U.S., DWM: 1936, M&D: 1952, W&F: 1960, RRL: 1969, CM: 1970, EEL: 1971, ADC: 1981, JWK: 1981, MA: 1973]

constitutional 1. a drink of gin and bitters. [Aust., SJB: 1943] 2. an addict's first injection of the day. A play on a term for a morning walk. RS: *shot.* [U.S., JES: 1959, H&C: 1975]

consumption stick a tobacco cigarette. *Cf. cancer stick.* RT: *nail.* [Aust., WWI, WHD: 1919; listed in SJB: 1966]

contact a drug seller. *Cf. connection.* RT: *dealer.* [U.S., S&W: 1966, RRL: 1969, EEL: 1971, ADC: 1981]

contact high 1. drug euphoria gained from drug vapors in the immediate vicinity, such as from marijuana smoke. [U.S., M&V: 1967, RRL: 1969, DC: 1972] 2. euphoria obtained (without any drug intake) from one's immediate environment; a sympathetic high. This may be caused by the activities of marijuana smokers, L.S.D. users, or musicians. [U.S., S&W: 1966, TW: 1968, RRL: 1969, EEL: 1971, W&F: 1975]

contact lens *L.S.D.* (*q.v.*); L.S.D. combined with some other drug. *Cf. clear light, domes.* RT: *L.S.D.* [U.S., YKB: 1977, KBH: 1982]

contending with the Pharaoh drinking heavily; alcohol intoxicated. *Pharaoh* (*q.v.*) = strong ale. RT: *drunk.* [BF: 1737]

controlled substance one of a vast number of ethical drugs and abused substances regulated by the U.S. government. The expression includes *L.S.D.* (*q.v.*), marijuana, and mescaline. There are five categories (schedules) based on the harmful potential of the various drugs. This technical term is sometimes used euphemistically and in jest. The act establishing regulation was passed in 1970 and is revised periodically. Jargon, not slang.

[U.S., (1977): DNE: 1980] See also *substance counselor*.

conversation water (also conversation fluid) whiskey; liquor. *Cf. German conversation water*. RT: *whiskey*. [U.S., (1850–1900): RFA, BVB: 1942]

convert a recently *hooked* (*q.v.*) addict. From the term for a newly converted Christian. See *missionary*. RT: *junky*. [U.S., (c. 1920): JES: 1959, BVB: 1942, VJM: 1949]

coo-coo (also cuckoo, cuckooed) alcohol intoxicated. From a slang term meaning slightly crazy. RT: *drunk*. [U.S., BVB: 1942, D&D: 1957]

cook 1. an attendant in an opium den. *Cf. chef*. Part of the cook's duties involve preparing and heating opium pellets. [U.S., HNR: 1934, DWM: 1936, GOL: 1950, W&F: 1960] 2. (also **cook up**, **cook up a pill**) to prepare an opium pellet or pill for use in an opium den. *Cf. chef*. [U.S., (1887): RML: 1948, DWM: 1936, VJM: 1949, GS: 1959, CM: 1970] 3. to brew or distill beverage alcohol. [U.S., BVB: 1942] 4. to reclaim denatured alcohol. A complex procedure which is intended to recover the drinkable alcohol from various substances and leave the adulterants behind. [U.S., BVB: 1942, GOL: 1950] 5. (also **cook up**) to heat and dissolve a drug in water so that it can be injected, usually said of heroin. [U.S., W&F: 1967, RRL: 1969, D&B: 1970c, CM: 1970, EEL: 1971, ADC: 1981] 6. to smoke marijuana or hashish. RT: *hit the hay*. [U.S., ADC: 1981, RDS: 1982]

cooked 1. alcohol intoxicated. One of the many cooking terms meaning drunk. *Cf. baked, basted, boiled, fried, fried on both sides, parboiled, roasted, sauced, served up, souffled, stewed, toasted*. RT: *drunk*. [U.S., BVB: 1942, W&F: 1960] 2. high on marijuana. RT: *wasted*. [U.S., ADC: 1975] 3. having to do with marijuana which has been smoked and contains no more of the active principle. *Cf. cashed*. [U.S., ADC: 1981] 4. addicted to heroin. Possibly an error for *hooked* (*q.v.*). [U.S., JES: 1959, H&C: 1975]

cooked up under the effects of cocaine. Possibly an error for *coked up*. *Cf. cocainized*. [U.S., BVB: 1942, VJM: 1949, A&T: 1953]

cooker 1. an opium user or opium addict. An addict who "cooks" his dose and inhales the vapors rather than injecting it in solution. RS: *user*. [U.S., BVB: 1942, VJM: 1949] 2. a cocaine user. This may be an error for "coker" but there is no attestation for "coker." [U.S., BVB: 1942, VJM: 1949] 3. a moonshiner; a distiller of illegal liquor. *Cf. alki cooker*. [U.S., VJM: 1949] 4. any small heatable container in which to dissolve a drug for injection. Often an aluminum liquor bottle cap is used. *Cf. cooking spoon, spoon*. [U.S., DWM: 1936, BVB: 1942, RRL: 1969, EEL: 1971, MA: 1973, W&F: 1975, JWK: 1981] 5. a laboratory or refinery for making heroin from opium. [U.S., W&F: 1975]

cookie 1. (also cookee, cooky) an *opium den* (*q.v.*). Presumably a pronunciation influenced by the Chinese Language. [U.S., BVB: 1942, DU] 2. an opium addict or user. RT: *campfire boy*. [U.S., (1905): JES: 1959, DWM: 1933, DWM: 1936] 3. cocaine. Akin to *coke* (*q.v.*). RT: *cocaine*. [U.S., GM: 1931, MHW: 1934, GOL: 1950] 4. a tobacco cigarette. RT: *nail*. [U.S., EE: 1976]

cooking spoon a spoon or bottle cap heated to dissolve drugs in water. *Cf. cooker*. [U.S., DWM: 1938, DU, H&C: 1975]

cool in a mellow state analogous to drug euphoria. Compare to *uncool*. GEN: mellow, unabashed (1951): MW: 1983. [U.S., ADC: 1975]

cooler an alcoholic drink. Originally any cooling drink. *Cf. chill, cold one*. [(1821): DAE, (1840): DAE, JCH: 1887; listed in BVB: 1942]

coolie mud inferior opium; reclaimed opium, *yen-shee* (*q.v.*). *Cf. mud*. RS: *opium*. See *French article*. [U.S., BVB: 1942, VJM: 1949]

cool Nantz brandy. From the name of the city of Nantes, France. RT: *brandy*. [cant, BE: 1690, FG: 1785]

cool nod a mellow state induced by drugs. See *nod*. [U.S., ADC: 1975]

coozie stash (also **coosie stash**) a parcel (usually a condom) of drugs concealed in the vagina. Coozie = vagina. RS: *stash*. [U.S., M&V: 1967, H&C: 1975] See also *whammer*.

cop 1. to get drugs, usually heroin, or marijuana; to make a drug purchase. GEN: to pinch, to steal. RT: *score*. [U.S., (NAM: 1953), W&F: 1967, D&B: 1970c, EEL: 1971, ADC: 1981, JWK: 1981] 2. a police officer. See *copper*.

cop a buzz to smoke marijuana. *Buzz* (*q.v.*) = intoxication. RT: *hit the hay*. Prison use. [U.S., BL: 1982]

cop a drag to smoke a cigarette; to sneak a cigarette smoke. *Drag* (*q.v.*) = a smoke. [U.S., GOL: 1950]

cop a fix to obtain a dose of drugs. *Cf. cop*. RT: *score*. [U.S., M&V: 1967, H&C: 1975]

cop a head to get drunk; to get *stoned*. RT: *mug oneself*. [U.S., RAS: 1985]

cop a match to purchase a matchbox of marijuana. RS: *score*. [U.S., EAF: 1972]

cop and blow to make a drug purchase and leave quickly; to depart from anything quickly. [U.S., BD: 1937]

cop a pill to smoke an opium pellet. RT: *suck bamboo*. [U.S., M&V: 1954]

cop a reeler to get drunk; to get reeling drunk. *Cf. reeler*. RT: *mug oneself*. [early 1900s, DSUE]

copey alcohol intoxicated. RT: *drunk*. [BF: 1737]

copilot 1. (also copilots) a *Dexedrine* (TM; *q.v.*) amphetamine tablet; any amphetamines. From its use by long distance truckdrivers. The drug is a "co-driver" or *copilot*. RT: *dex*. [U.S., D&D: 1966, RRL: 1969, MT: 1971, W&F: 1975, YKB: 1977, DNE: 1980, NIDA: 1980, ADC: 1981] 2. one who helps another through an L.S.D. trip. RT: *sitter*. [U.S., G&B: 1969, EEL: 1971]

copilotas* amphetamines. Spanish. See *copilot*. RT: *amps*. [U.S., TRG: 1968, YKB: 1977, NIDA: 1980]

copilot ben *Benzedrine* (TM; *q.v.*) amphetamine tablets. RT: *benz*. [U.S., (MT: 1971)]

cop man a drug seller; the middle man in a drug sale; a drug runner. *Cf. comp man*. RT: *dealer*. [U.S., M&V: 1967, RRL: 1969]

copped arrested. RT: *busted*. [cant, GWM: 1859]

copper a police officer. From the old cant sense of cop, to pinch or nab. The name probably has nothing to do with copper stars, buttons, or belt buckles. RT: *fuzz*. [mid 1800s-p., GWM: 1859, BVB: 1942]

copper nose a drunkard; the red nose of a drunkard. BE: 1690 lists the adjective, copper-nosed. RT: *sot*. [BE: 1690, JCH: 1887, F&H; U.S., BVB: 1942, DB: 1944]

cop sickness the onset of involuntary narcotics withdrawal, a yearning to *cop a fix* (*q.v.*). [U.S., RRL: 1969]

cop the brewery to get drunk. *Cf. cop a head*. RT: *mug oneself*. [JRW: 1909]

cop the elephant to get drunk. Refers to *elephant's trunk* (*q.v.*) = drunk. RT: *mug oneself*. [early 1900s, JM: 1923]

corals chloral hydrate capsules; chloral hydrate. A variant of *chlorals* (*q.v.*). RT: *Mickey Finn*. [U.S., RG: 1970, IGA: 1971, SNP: 1977]

corazónes* amphetamines. RT: *amps*. [U.S., NIDA: 1980]

cord, on the taking *methadone* (*q.v.*) treatment for heroin addiction. The addict being treated must take a daily dose of methadone obtainable only from a clinic. This cord is like an umbilical cord which ties the addict to the clinic. [U.S., JWK: 1981]

corgy heroin. RT: *heroin*. [U.S., IGA: 1971, WCM: 1972]

Corine (also Corinne) cocaine; a personification of cocaine. RT: *cocaine*. [U.S., JBW: 1967, IGA: 1971, W&F: 1975, YKB: 1977]

corked 1. (also corkey, corky) pertaining to wine which tastes of the cork. [(1830): OED, JCH: 1887, K&M: 1968] 2. (also corked up, corky) alcohol intoxicated. RT: *drunk*. [Br., 18-1900s, F&H, DSUE; U.S., (1896): SBF: 1976, WM: 1927, AH: 1931, MHW: 1934]

corker beverage alcohol; a drink of liquor. RT: *nip*. [Br., 1800s, F&H; listed in BVB: 1942]

corkscrewed alcohol intoxicated. A clever elaboration of *screwed* (*q.v.*) = drunk. RT: *drunk*. [Br., 1800s, F&H; listed in BVB: 1942]

corkscrewed up courageous due to alcohol. Based on *screw up one's courage* = become brave. Other terms relating to alcohol-induced courage: *courage, Dutch courage, full of courage, Geneva courage, liquid courage, pot hardy, pot sure, pot valiant*. [Br., WWI, DSUE]

cork the air to sniff (snort) cocaine. RT: *snort*. [U.S., GOL: 1950, A&T: 1953]

corky alcohol intoxicated and smelling like a liquor bottle cork. See *corked*.

corn 1. corn mash whiskey; moonshine; illegal prohibition whiskey; inferior whiskey; strong whiskey. A popular term since prohibition. RT: *moonshine, whiskey*. [U.S., (1820): DA, VR: 1929, MHW: 1934, VJM: 1949, D&D: 1957] 2. to get drunk; to intoxicate. RS: *mug oneself*. [U.S., BWG: 1899; listed in BVB: 1942] 3. a lump or scar at the site of a narcotics injection. [U.S., EEL: 1971]

corn coffee moonshine; illegal whiskey. The same as *white coffee* (*q.v.*). Possibly akin to an earlier term for coffee made from parched corn (1844): DA. RT: *moonshine*. [U.S. dialect (Tennessee), early 1900s, ADD]

corned (also **corny**) alcohol intoxicated. *Corn* (*q.v.*) = whiskey. GEN: preserved (in salt). RT: *drunk*. [FG: 1785, FG: 1811, FG: 1823, JCH: 1887, BWG: 1899, MHW: 1934, DCCU: 1972]

corn husk some kind of liquor. RT: *booze*. [Bahamas, JAH: 1982]

corn juice whiskey made from corn mash. RS: *moonshine*. A popular term during prohibition. [U.S., (1845): W&F: 1960, JSF: 1889, (1904): ADD, VR: 1929, AH: 1931, MHW: 1934]

corn liquor (also **corn likker**) whiskey made from corn. RS: *whiskey*. [U.S., (1927): DA, BVB: 1942]

corn mule whiskey; hard liquor; moonshine; inferior liquor; illegal whiskey. It kicks like a mule. RS: *moonshine, whiskey*. [U.S., VR: 1929, MHW: 1934, D&D: 1957, W&F: 1960, RDS: 1982]

corn shucks tobacco. RT: *fogus*. [U.S., W&F: 1960] See also *corn husk*.

corn squeezings whiskey; moonshine. RT: *moonshine, whiskey*. [U.S., BVB: 1953] See also *silo drippings*.

corn whiskey (also **corn spirits**) whiskey made from corn mash. Corn spirits in 1764, (DA). *Cf. white whiskey*. RT: *whiskey*. [U.S., (1764): DA, (1840s): SBF: 1976, AH: 1931, BVB: 1942]

corn wine whiskey; rotgut. RT: *whiskey*. [U.S. Army, (1860s):

DST: 1984]

corny intoxicated with alcohol. See *corned.*

corporal's butt a fairly small cigarette butt. *Cf. captain's butt.* See comments at *butt.* RT: *brad.* [U.S., HS: 1933, MHW: 1934]

corpse 1. an empty liquor or beer bottle. See *cold one.* A play on *dead soldier* (*q.v.*). [U.S., BVB: 1942] 2. a cigarette butt. RT: *brad.* [U.S., military, BVB: 1942]

corpse reviver (also **reviver**) liquor; a drink of strong liquor which might wake the dead. RT: *nip.* [U.S., (1871): F&H, MHW: 1934, BVB: 1942; Br., SSD, M&J: 1975]

Corrine cocaine; a personification of cocaine. The same as *Corine* (*q.v.*). RT: *cocaine.* RRL: 1969 labels this obsolete. [U.S., A&T: 1953, RRL: 1969, EEL: 1971, W&F: 1975, YKB: 1977, NIDA: 1980]

corroboree a drinking bout. From a native Australian word. Erroneously said to be rhyming slang for *spree.* RT: *spree.* [Aust., (1859): GAW: 1978; Br., WWI, WWII, DRS]

corroboree water (also **corrobbery water**) cheap wine. RS: *wine.* *Cf. corroboree.* [Aust., SJB: 1943]

cortals *Mandrax* (TM; *q.v.*) *methaqualone* (*q.v.*), a hypnotic-sedative. RS: *ludes.* [U.S., SNP: 1977]

cosa* marijuana. Spanish for thing. RT: *pot.* [U.S., NIDA: 1980]

cosmos *P.C.P.* (*q.v.*). RT: *P.C.P.* [U.S., (1970s): FAB: 1979]

cotickery a place to buy narcotics. *Cf. cotics.* RT: *doperie.* A contrived term almost certainly not used by underworld addicts. [U.S., JES: 1959, H&C: 1975]

cotics (also **'cotics**) narcotics. RS: *dope.* [U.S., DWM: 1936, VJM: 1949, EEL: 1971, W&F: 1975, JWK: 1981]

cotton 1. a bit of cotton used to strain a dissolved narcotic when filling a syringe (or dropper) for an injection. These bits of drug-saturated cotton are saved up (for a shot) or given away as gifts. *Cf. satch cotton, tamp.* [U.S., VFN: 1933, DWM: 1936, RRL: 1969, MA: 1973, JWK: 1981] 2. a bit of cotton used to hold a liquid drug which is being sniffed (snorted); the amphetamine saturated paper from a Benzedrine (TM) inhaler. *Cf. glad rags.* [U.S., W&F: 1967, EEL: 1971] 3. a tip or gift of drugs in any form given to someone who does a favor such as procuring drugs. From sense one. *Cf. taste.* [U.S., JWK: 1981] See also *Charley Cotton, satch cotton, wet-cotton.*

cotton brothers 1. cocaine, heroin, and morphine, three drugs which require the use of a cotton strainer when injected; the cotton used with these drugs. [U.S., DWM: 1938, BVB: 1942] 2. addicts who use (possibly exclusively) used straining cotton as a source of narcotics. Possibly an error. See *cotton.* [U.S., H&C: 1975] 3. drug injection equipment: needle, syringe, heating devices, i.e., those things which go with *cotton.* [U.S., ELA: 1984]

cotton catcher (also cottonhead, cotton man, cotton picker, cotton shooter, cotton top, cotton woman) a down-and-out addict who must beg for used straining cotton or for other drugs. [U.S., (1920s): JES: 1959, DWM: 1936, BVB: 1942, RRL: 1969, EEL: 1971, JWK: 1981]

cotton fever an infection, allergic reaction, or other illness contracted through the use of used straining cotton as a source of narcotics. [U.S., H&C: 1975]

cotton freak a drug user who inhales a drug from cotton; someone with a *cotton habit* (*q.v.*). Originally referred to a person who inhaled *Benzedrine* (TM; *q.v.*). RS: *user.* [U.S., W&F: 1967, HSD: 1984]

cotton habit a small drug habit sustained by using the narcotics remaining in used straining cotton. RS: *habit.* [U.S., DWM: 1938, VJM: 1949, RRL: 1969]

cottonhead an addict or drug user who uses used straining cotton as a source of drugs. *Cf. cotton catcher.* See list at *head.* RS: *user.* [U.S., TRG: 1968, EEL: 1971]

cotton morphine the fibrous or cotton form of morphine. See *lint.*

cotton mouth a very dry mouth from smoking marijuana. Named for the cotton mouth water moccasin. [U.S., D&B: 1970c, (D&B: 1978)]

cotton shooter See *cotton catcher.*

cotton top See *cotton catcher.*

cougar milk strong liquor; *rotgut* (*q.v.*). See *milk.* RS: *whiskey.* [U.S., WFM: 1958]

count the quantity or weight of drugs agreed on in a drug purchase; the quality of a drug purchase. *Cf. weight.* RS: *load.* [U.S., RRL: 1969, IGA: 1971, JWK: 1981]

country drunk flamboyantly drunk; alcohol intoxicated; drunk and disorganized. *Cf. commode-hugging drunk, falling-down drunk, knee-walking drunk, snot-flinging drunk.* RT: *drunk.* [U.S., D&D: 1957]

courage liquor. *Cf. Dutch courage.* [U.S., BVB: 1942] See also *courage pill, Dutch courage, full of courage, full of Dutch courage, Geneva courage, liquid courage, pot hardy, pot sure, pot valiant.*

courage pill 1. a tablet of heroin. RS: *heroin.* [U.S., DWM: 1933, MHW: 1934, VJM: 1949] 2. a barbiturate capsule. RT: *barbs.* [U.S., RRL: 1969, YKB: 1977]

courier a small-time drug seller; a drug runner. *Cf. mule.* RS: *dealer.* [U.S., P&C: 1969, EEL: 1971]

courting Cecil addicted to morphine. *Cf. Cecil.* Probably never widely used. RS: *hooked.* [U.S., JES: 1959, H&C: 1975]

cowboy an independent drug seller. *Cf. cocaine cowboy.* RT: *dealer.* [U.S., RG: 1970, IGA: 1971]

cowboy cocktail a nip of straight whiskey. Cocktails were considered effeminate. [U.S., (1850–1900): RFA]

coxy-loxy alcohol intoxicated. RT: *drunk*. [Br. dialect (Norfolk), JCH: 1887]

cozmos phencyclidine, *P.C.P.* (*q.v.*). From *cosmos*. RT: *P.C.P.* [U.S., ELA: 1984]

C-pusher a cocaine pusher; a cocaine dealer. RS: *dealer*. [U.S., GOL: 1950, D&D: 1957]

cracked alcohol intoxicated. (BF: 1737: [He's] Crack'd.) RT: *drunk*. [BF: 1737]

cracker dry 1. sober. *Cf. bone dry*. RT: *sober*. From the prohibition era. [U.S., BVB: 1942] 2. a prohibitionist. RT: *dry*. [U.S., BVB: 1942]

crackers 1. the hallucinogenic drug *L.S.D.* (*q.v.*). Presumed to be an animal cracker containing a drop of the hallucinogenic drug *L.S.D.* (*q.v.*). RT: *L.S.D.* [U.S., JBW: 1967, IGA: 1971, KBH: 1982] 2. an ampule of *amyl nitrite* (*q.v.*); a *popper* (*q.v.*). RT: *snapper*. Attested as gay slang. [U.S., BR: 1972]

crack lip a prohibitionist. Refers to the parched and cracked lips of someone who has not had a drink in a long time. RT: *dry*. [U.S., BVB: 1942]

cramped alcohol intoxicated. (BF: 1737: [He's] Cramp'd.) RT: *drunk*. [BF: 1737]

cranberry eye a bloodshot eye from excessive drinking. [U.S., B&L: 1890, F&H, BVB: 1942, D&D: 1957]

crank 1. gin and water. RS: *gin*. [FG: 1785, FG: 1811, FG: 1823] 2. (also **cranks, crink**) an amphetamine; amphetamines. Because it cranks you up. RT: *amps*. [U.S., RRL: 1969, IGA: 1971, YKB: 1977, NIDA: 1980, ADC: 1981]

crank bugs the feeling or fear that insects are crawling under one's skin; formication; any drug induced hallucination. Due to over-use of cocaine, L.S.D., or amphetamines. See *acid mung, mungy*. *Cf. crank*. [U.S., RRL: 1969, YKB: 1977]

cranker a heavy user of amphetamines or other pills. A person who takes *cranks*. *Cf. crank*. RS: *user*. [U.S., JH: 1979]

crank freak (also **crank commando**) a drug user who alternates between stimulants (amphetamines) and depressants (barbiturates or tranquilizers). RS: *user*. [U.S., EEL: 1971, RDS: 1982, ELA: 1984]

crap heroin; bad heroin; diluted heroin; bogus heroin. A milder version of *shit* (*q.v.*). Can be used for any drug or, indeed, for anything at all. [U.S., BVB: 1942, RRL: 1969, EEL: 1971, YKB: 1977, NIDA: 1980]

crapper dick a police officer or detective who patrols public toilets looking for illicit sexual acts and drug sales. RS: *fuzz*. [U.S.,

RDS: 1982]

crapsick alcohol intoxicated. a spelling variant of *cropsick* (*q.v.*).

crapulous alcohol intoxicated. A playful use of a pompous technical term. From a Latin term meaning drunk. RT: *drunk*. [(1755): OED, BVB: 1942]

crash 1. (also **crash out**) to return abruptly from a drug trip; to go into a depression after a period of drug use; to fall asleep after a period of drug use. Now GEN: to spend the night at someone's *pad* (*q.v.*). [U.S., S&W: 1966, JBW: 1967, RRL: 1969, D&B: 1970c, EEL: 1971, DES: 1972, M&V: 1973, ADC: 1981, JWK: 1981] 2. to pass out from drinking alcohol to excess. Possibly from sense one. [U.S., W&F: 1967] 3. the act of returning from a drug *trip* (*q.v.*); to fall asleep at the end of a drug trip. [U.S., G&B: 1969]

crashed 1. alcohol intoxicated. *Cf. smashed*. RT: *drunk*. [U.S., W&F: 1967] 2. raided by the police in search of drugs. Probably from the expression *crash a party*. [Br., listed in BTD: 1968]

crash pad a place to recover from a drug trip. GEN: a place to stay and visit; a place to stay on out-of-town trips. [U.S., EEL: 1971, RDS: 1982]

crater 1. (also **the crater**) liquor; whiskey. A dialect pronunciation of *creature* (*q.v.*). [(1888): F&H, BVB: 1942] 2. a scar or a pit left from a healed abscess at the site of a drug injection. *Cf. cave*. [U.S., RRL: 1969, LVA: 1981]

crawrot strong and inferior alcohol, especially whiskey. A variant of *rotgut* (*q.v.*). [U.S., BVB: 1942]

crazy (also **crazed, crazy drunk**) intoxicated. *Cf. loony*. RT: *drunk*. [U.S., (1887): RML: 1950, GU: 1975]

crazy coke *P.C.P.* (*q.v.*). The *coke* is an allusion to cocaine. RT: *P.C.P.* [U.S., (1970): FAB: 1979]

crazy water alcohol; liquor. Mock-Amerindian. RT: *booze*. [U.S., BVB: 1942]

cream 1. whiskey. See the list at *milk*. RT: *whiskey*. [Aust., (1925): DSUE] See also *cold cream*. 2. to massage the skin of the arm in an effort to conceal the scars and marks left by drug injections. [U.S., EEL: 1971]

creamed alcohol intoxicated. In the sense of being beaten or mashed. GEN: beaten, overcome. RT: *drunk*. See *cream*. [U.S., ADC: 1975]

cream of the valley (also **cream of the wilderness**) gin. In playful opposition to *mountain dew* (*q.v.*) = whiskey. RT: *gin*. [Br., (1858): OED, JCH: 1887; listed in BVB: 1942]

creature (also **the creature**) wine; liquor; strong whiskey. *Cf. cup of the creature, good creature of God*. From *I Timothy IV*: "every creature of God is good." RT: *whiskey*. [(1570): OED, (1638): SOD, FG: 1811, GWM: 1859, F&H (at *taste*), BVB: 1942] See also ***the beast***.

creature comfort alcohol; liquor. Can be read as "a creature named comfort" or "the creature of comfort" or "comfort for creatures (humans)." RT: ***booze***. [U.S., BVB: 1942]

creeper slow-acting marijuana. RS: ***pot***. [U.S., ADC: 1981]

creeper joint a place where inferior marijuana is sold and used. People who go there stand a chance of getting robbed. Similar to ***creep joint***. [U.S., MB: 1938]

creep joint (also **creep dive**) a low drinking place. The kind of place where creeps (= jerks, bums) hang out. RT: ***dive***. [U.S., AH: 1931, MHW: 1934, D&D: 1957]

creeps, the the delirium tremens. GEN: the jitters; a case of nerves. RT: ***D.T.s***. [U.S., W&F: 1960]

cresta* (also **cresto***) the hallucinogenic drug ***L.S.D.*** (*q.v.*). Spanish for cock's comb. RT: ***L.S.D.*** [U.S., EEL: 1971, JH: 1979]

crib 1. a location where thieves gather to plot and drink liquor. ***Cf. booze crib, guzzle crib, lush crib, patter crib, suck crib***. [cant, (1812): OED; listed in BVB: 1942] 2. an addict's house or apartment; a dwelling where drugs are sold and used; any dwelling. Crib = a hangout (in cant). Currently used for any residence. RT: ***pad***. [U.S., M&V: 1967, RRL: 1969, MA: 1973, S&W: 1973, EAF: 1980, JWK: 1981]

Crimea beer. Rhyming slang for a British pronunciation of beer. RT: ***beer***. [Br., mid 1800s, DRS]

crimson dawn cheap red wine. Perhaps this describes the whites of one's eyes in the morning after a night spent drinking this wine. RS: ***wine***. [Br., early 1900s, DSUE]

crink amphetamines. See ***crank***. RT: ***amps***. [U.S., RG: 1970, IGA: 1971, NIDA: 1980]

cripple a marijuana cigarette, possibly a ***roach*** (*q.v.*). From ***crutch*** (*q.v.*), a name for a ***roach clip*** (*q.v.*). The ***crutch*** supports the ***cripple***. RT: ***joint***. [U.S., HB: 1955]

cris* amphetamines. From an English misspelling of *crystal* or from the correct Spanish spelling *cristal*. See ***cristal, crystal***. Also may refer to the cross-scoring on amphetamine tablets through a misspelling or the Spanish spelling of Christian. See ***cristian***. RT: ***amps***. [U.S., IGA: 1971, NIDA: 1980]

crisp drug intoxicated. In reference to the degree to which one is ***fried*** (*q.v.*) by marijuana. RT: ***stoned***. [U.S., ADC: 1975]

crispo (also **crispy**) a person who is mentally, socially, and physically burned out by marijuana use. [U.S., RAS: 1980]

crispy-critter a person under the effects of marijuana. A jocular reinterpretation of the brand name of a breakfast cereal. [U.S., ADC: 1975]

cristal* (also **cristales***) 1. amphetamines. The Spanish spelling of *crystal* (*q.v.*). RT: *amps*. [U.S., NIDA: 1980] 2. *P.C.P.* (*q.v.*), an animal tranquilizer. See *crystal*. RT: *P.C.P.* [U.S., NIDA: 1980]

cristian (also **Christian**) an amphetamine tablet; amphetamines. May refer to the cross-scoring on amphetamine tablets. It is a misspelling or the Spanish spelling of Christian. RT: *amps*. [U.S., IGA: 1971, NIDA: 1980]

cristina (also **Christina, Cristine**) amphetamines; methamphetamine. See *cristian*. RT: *speed*. [U.S., JHF: 1971, BR: 1972, RDS: 1982]

croaker a physician; a prison doctor. Because he causes his patients to croak = die. Not confined to drug addicts. [Br., JCH: 1859; U.S., GI: 1931, DWM: 1936, M&D: 1952, RRL: 1969, D&B: 1970c, EEL: 1971, MA: 1973, JWK: 1981] Nicknames and slang terms for a physician: *blood-sucker, bolus, castor oil artist, croaker, crocus, crooker, horse doctor, hungry croaker, ice tong, ice tong croaker, ice tong doctor, ice water doctor, ice water John, quack, right croaker, vet.*

crock 1. the bowl of an opium pipe; an opium pipe. RS: *hop stick*. [U.S., DWM: 1938, BVB: 1942] 2. a drunkard. RT: *sot*. [U.S., W&F: 1960, DCCU: 1972] 3. an opium addict. RT: *campfire boy*. [U.S., NAM: 1953]

crocked alcohol intoxicated. RT: *drunk*. [U.S., (1927): SBF: 1976, MHW: 1934, D&D: 1957, W&F: 1960, DCCU: 1972]

crocko alcohol intoxicated. RT: *drunk*. [U.S., BVB: 1942]

crocus 1. alcohol intoxicated. RT: *drunk*. [BF: 1737] 2. (also **crocus metallorum, crokus**) a doctor. Akin to *croaker* (*q.v.*). [FG: 1785, GWM: 1859; listed in BVB: 1942]

cronk alcohol intoxicated. From German *krank* = sick. RT: *drunk*. [U.S., (1850): W&F: 1960]

crooked whiskey illegal, untaxed whiskey. RT: *moonshine*. [U.S., JSF: 1889]

crooker 1. a drunkard; an alcoholic. RT: *sot*. From *elbow-crooker* (*q.v.*). [U.S., RDS: 1982] 2. a physician who is known to sell drugs to addicts illegally. A linguistic blend of *crook* and *croaker* (*q.v.*). RS: *croaker*. [U.S., IGA: 1971]

crook one's elbow (also **crook the elbow**) to drink liquor; to take a drink of liquor. The same as *bend one's elbow* (*q.v.*). RT: *irrigate*. [(1836): DAE, F&H, M&J: 1975]

cropsick drunk; sick from drinking alcohol; hungover. *Cf. crapsick*. [(1624): OED, FG: 1823]

cross-country hype an addict who drifts from one small town to another hoping to get drugs (probably morphine) from sympathetic small town doctors. *Cf. R.F.D. junker*. RS: *junky*. [probably early 1900s or before, M&V: 1967]

cross-drum See *drum*.

crosses cross-scored amphetamine tablets; *Benzedrine* (TM; *q.v.*)

tablets. *Cf. cris, crossroads*. RT: *amps*. [U.S., M&V: 1967, H&C: 1975]

cross-eyed (also **cross-eyed drunk**) alcohol intoxicated. RT: *drunk*. [U.S., MHW: 1934, BVB: 1942]

crossroads (also **cross tops**) cross-scored amphetamine tablets. RT: *amps*. [U.S., RRL: 1969, YKB: 1977, NIDA: 1980, ADC: 1981]

cross-tolerance a tolerance for one drug which also extends to related drugs. For instance, a heroin user develops cross-tolerance for methadone. [medical]

cross tops amphetamine tablets. RT: *amps*. [U.S., IGA: 1971, WCM: 1972, NIDA: 1980]

crown crap heroin. *Cf. crap*. RT: *heroin*. [U.S., H&C: 1975]

crown fire a hangover. From a logger's term for a raging fire that moves across the treetops. RT: *hangover*. [U.S., RM: 1942, W&F: 1960]

crumped out alcohol intoxicated. RT: *drunk*. [U.S., W&F: 1960]

crump-footed alcohol intoxicated. (BF: 1737: [He's] Crump Footed.) From an old term for club-footed. See *tanglefoot*. Refers to the drinker's awkward gate. RT: *drunk*. [BF: 1737]

crush a *crutch* (*q.v.*). [U.S., BR: 1972]

crusher a policeman. RT: *fuzz*. [GWM: 1859; listed in BVB: 1942]

crutch a device to hold a marijuana cigarette butt. Often a split twig or match stick. See *cripple*. Can be any type of *roach clip* (*q.v.*). [U.S., RPW: 1938, M&V: 1954, RRL: 1969, EEL: 1971, EAF: 1980, ADC: 1981] Terms for devices used to support the butt of a marijuana cigarette: *airplane, bridge, clip, crush, crutch, C.W.P., jefferson airplane, miser, potholder, roach clip, roach holder, roach pick, zooie*.

cruz* Mexican opium. Spanish. Possibly from the place name Veracruz. Braddy (HB: 1955) suggests "...possibly from *cruz de mayo*, red Mexican herb of the heath family." RT: *opium*. [U.S., HB: 1955]

cry a drink of liquor. *Cf. shout*. RT: *nip*. [1800s, F&H]

crying drunk alcohol intoxicated and weeping. The same as *maudlin drunk* (*q.v.*). RT: *drunk*. [cant, FG: 1785]

crying weed marijuana. *Cf. weed*. RT: *pot*. [U.S., A&T: 1953, SNP: 1977]

crystal 1. crystallized cocaine. RS: *cocaine*. [U.S., JWK: 1981] 2. *Methedrine* (*q.v.*) used for injection; amphetamines in general. RT: *amps*. [U.S., M&V: 1967, D&B: 1970c, EEL: 1971, YKB: 1977, NIDA: 1980, ADC: 1981] 3. (also **crystal flake**) phencyclidine, *P.C.P.* (*q.v.*), an animal tranquilizer. *Cf. crystal joint*. RT: *P.C.P.* [U.S., YKB: 1977, DNE: 1980, NIDA: 1980]

crystal joint (also **crystal points, krystal joint, crystal T.**)

phencyclidine, *P.C.P.* (*q.v.*), an animal tranquilizer; smokable P.C.P.; a marijuana cigarette with a bit of P.C.P. on the end. Essentially means marijuana in crystalline form. RT: *P.C.P.* ELA: 1984 lists **crystal points, crystal T., crystal weed.** [U.S., YKB: 1977, FAB: 1979]

crystal lady a homosexual male who uses amphetamines. *Cf. crystal.* Attested as gay slang. [U.S., BR: 1972]

crystallize for an injection of a dissolved powdered drug to re-crystallize in the vein. [U.S., EEL: 1971] See also *gravy.*

crystallized deeply under the effects of *Methedrine* (TM; *q.v.*). *Cf. crystal.* [U.S., M&V: 1967, H&C: 1975]

crystal palace a place where *Methedrine* (TM; *q.v.*) users gather. A contrived term never in wide use. GEN: a fancy brothel. RS: *pad.* [U.S., RRL: 1969]

crystal ship a syringe containing a dissolved crystalline drug. *Cf. rocket ship.* RS: *monkey pump.* [U.S., EEL: 1971]

C-stick a tobacco cigarette; a *cancer stick* (*q.v.*). RT: *nail.* [U.S., S&E: 1981]

Cuban candle a cigar. Refers to Cuban cigars. RT: *seegar.* [U.S., EE: 1976]

cube 1. (also **cubes**) morphine; a cube of morphine; a packet containing approximately one ounce of morphine. The term is also used for an ounce of hashish, cocaine, or opium. RS: *load.* [U.S., DWM: 1936, VJM: 1949, GOL: 1950, EEL: 1971, YKB: 1977, EAF: 1980] 2. (also **the cube**) *L.S.D.* (*q.v.*); a sugar cube impregnated with a dose of the hallucinogenic drug L.S.D. [U.S., JBW: 1967, W&F: 1967, RRL: 1969, EEL: 1971, YKB: 1977, NIDA: 1980] 3. opium. Possibly an error. [U.S., EEL: 1971, JH: 1979] 4. a person who does not use drugs. GEN: a real *square* (*q.v.*). RT: *square.* [U.S., TRG: 1968] 5. a gram of hashish. RS: *load.* [HSD: 1984]

cubehead an L.S.D. user who prefers to take the drug in the form of a sugar cube. See the list at *head.* RS: *user.* [U.S., RG: 1970, EEL: 1971, H&C: 1975]

cube juice morphine. Presumed to be morphine in an injectable solution. See *cube.* RT: *morphine.* [U.S., SNP: 1977, RDS: 1982]

cuckooed (also **cuckoo**) alcohol intoxicated and slightly crazy. GEN: giddy. *Cf. coo-coo.* RT: *drunk.* [U.S., HJS: 1922]

cud a chew of tobacco. Named for the cud that a cow chews. RT: *quid.* [U.S., NW: 1828, HK: 1917, BVB: 1942]

cues *Quaalude* (TM; *q.v.*) tablets. The term is a spelling-out of *Q.s* (*q.v.* at *Q.*). RT: *ludes.* [U.S., JWK: 1981]

cuff link a drink of liquor or beer. Rhyming slang for *drink.* RT: *nip.* [Aust., SJB: 1966]

culican* a potent variety of cannabis from Mexico. RT: *pot.*

[ELA: 1984]

Cum a "brand name" for *amyl nitrite* (*q.v.*). GEN: semen. See *amyl nitrite* for comments on the sexual uses of this substance. RS: *snapper.* [U.S., ELA: 1984]

cunt the area of a vein favored for an injection of drugs; the crease at the inside of the elbow. *Cf. valley.* [U.S., RG: 1970, JHF: 1971] See also *drunk as a cunt.*

cup a packet of heroin. Possibly an error for *cap* (*q.v.*). Possibly akin to *cop* (*q.v.*) [U.S., JTD: 1971]

cupcakes the hallucinogenic drug *L.S.D.* (*q.v.*). *Cf. orange cupcakes.* RT: *L.S.D.* [U.S., YKB: 1977, KBH: 1982]

cup of cheer See *cheer.*

cup of comfort a drink of alcohol. See *comfort.*

cup of the creature a drink of liquor. See *creature.* RT: *nip.* [BE: 1690, FG: 1785, FG: 1811, FG: 1823, DSUE]

cupped alcohol intoxicated. Disabled by the cup. RT: *drunk.* [PD: 1982]

cupshot alcohol intoxicated. RT: *drunk.* [cant, (1593): OED, BE: 1690, FG: 1785, FG: 1811, FG: 1823; U.S., GWM: 1859, BVB: 1942]

cups, in one's alcohol intoxicated. (BF: 1737: He's in his cups.) See *inter pocula.* RT: *drunk.* [(1593): F&H, BF: 1737, BVB: 1942, W&F: 1960, DCCU: 1972]

cup that cheers beverage alcohol; liquor. *Cf. cup of cheer* (at *cheer*). RT: *booze.* [U.S., MHW: 1934, BVB: 1942]

cura* an injection of heroin taken when it is most needed. *Cf. shot.* Spanish for cure. RT: *dose.* [U.S., RRL: 1969, EEL: 1971, JBR: 1973, CG: 1980]

curbstones cigarette butts picked up out of the gutter. See *kerbstone mixture.* RT: *brad.* Hobo use. [U.S., GI: 1931, MHW: 1934]

cure to make marijuana smoke milder by treating it with sugar or alcohol. This process also increases the weight of the marijuana. [U.S., M&V: 1967, RRL: 1969, EEL: 1971]

curse of Scotland Scotch whiskey. A playful dysphemism built on a nickname for the nine of diamonds in playing cards. RS: *whiskey.* [Br., 1800s, F&H]

curved alcohol intoxicated. (BF: 1737: [He's] Curv'd.) A variant of *bent* (*q.v.*). RT: *drunk.* [BF: 1737]

C-user a cocaine user. RT: *kokomo.* [U.S. GOL: 1950, D&D: 1957]

cushed alcohol intoxicated. RT: *drunk.* [U.S., BVB: 1942]

cushion a vein used for injecting heroin. [U.S., JES: 1959, H&C: 1975]

cut 1. alcohol intoxicated. RT: ***drunk***. [cant, (1673): OED, BE: 1690, BF: 1737, FG: 1785, FG: 1811, FG: 1823, GWM: 1859, WM: 1927, AH: 1931, MHW: 1934, W&F: 1960, RRL: 1969, EEL: 1971] 2. to dilute alcohol or drugs. [U.S., BD: 1937, DWM: 1938, GOL: 1950, M&D: 1952, GS: 1959, RRL: 1969, EEL: 1971, MA: 1973, YKB: 1977, ADC: 1981] (This entry continues after the following list.) Terms referring to the dilution or adulteration of drugs or alcohol: (The list includes adjective and verbs.) ***baptized, buff, chip, choke, chop, christen, clip, cut, cut up, hit it, lag, shave, step on, stepped on, stretch, sugar down, whack, whacked***. 3. (also **cut up**) having to do with adulterated or diluted drugs or alcohol. [(1938): OEDS, BVB: 1942, ADC: 1981]

cut alchy (also **cut alky**) diluted liquor; diluted whiskey. From the prohibition era. [U.S., VR: 1929, AH: 1931, MHW: 1934]

cut deck heroin or morphine diluted with powdered milk. *Cf.* ***deck***. [U.S., GOL: 1950]

cutered pill a prepared opium pellet made to give off inferior vapors by overheating. [U.S., BD: 1937, DWM: 1938]

cut in the back (also **cut in the leg**) alcohol intoxicated; very drunk. An explanation of why a drunkard staggers. RT: ***drunk***. [cant, (1673): OED, BE: 1690]

cut one's capers alcohol intoxicated. (BF: 1737: He cuts his Capers.) RT: ***drunk***. [BF: 1737]

cut one's leg (also **have cut one's leg**) to get drunk. RT: ***mug oneself***. [Br., (1767): F&H; listed in BVB: 1942]

cut one's wolf loose to go on a drinking bout; to get drunk. RT: ***mug oneself***. [U.S., PW: 1977]

cut the dust to take a drink of liquor. Such a drink is a dust-cutter. RT: ***irrigate***. [U.S., PW: 1977]

cutthroat strong liquor. RS: ***rotgut***. [U.S., BVB: 1942]

C.W.P. (also **CWP**) a device for holding a marijuana cigarette butt. RT: ***crutch***. [U.S., IGA: 1971, WCM: 1972]

cyc cyclazocine, a drug which reduces heroin dependence, a narcotic antagonist. [U.S., RRL: 1969, RDS: 1982]

cyclone (also **cyclones**) phencyclidine, ***P.C.P.*** (*q.v.*), an animal tranquilizer. Often plural. RT: ***P.C.P.*** [U.S., YKB: 1977, NIDA: 1980]

D

D. 1. *Dilaudid* (TM; *q.v.*), a potent painkiller. *Cf. big-D., little-D.* RT: *dids.* [U.S., M&V: 1954, YKB: 1977, JWK: 1981] 2. *Doriden* (TM; *q.v.*), a sedative. RT: *dories.* [U.S., RRL: 1969, SNP: 1977] 3. alcohol intoxicated. As in *D. and D.* (*q.v.*) = drunk and disorderly. RT: *drunk.* [U.S., D&B: 1971] 4. the hallucinogenic drug *L.S.D.* (*q.v.*). RT: *L.S.D.* [U.S., IGA: 1971, M&J: 1975] 5. *P.C.P.* (*q.v.*). *D.* = dust as in *angel dust* (*q.v.*). [U.S., FAB: 1979]

D.A. 1. a drug user or addict; an abbreviation of *drug addict. Cf. A.D.* RT: *user.* [U.S., BVB: 1942, GOL: 1950, A&T: 1953] 2. (also the D.A.) the drug *M.D.A.* (*q.v.*). [U.S., ADC: 1984]

dabble to use drugs occasionally and not become addicted. The same as *chippy* (*q.v.*). GEN: to play around, to *chippy* (*q.v.*). [U.S., DWM: 1938, VJM: 1949, RRL: 1969, CM: 1970, EEL: 1971, S&F: 1984]

dabbler an occasional drug user. GEN: a person who does just a little. RT: *chipper.* [U.S., EEL: 1971, RDS: 1982]

dad and mum rum. Rhyming slang. RT: *rum.* [Aust., SJB: 1966]

dagga (also **dacha, dagha**) marijuana of South African origin. The term refers to the marijuana grown and smoked there. It appears in many U.S. glossaries. Originally *dacha* or *dakka.* From Hottentot via Afrikaans. HB: 1955 claims that the word is of Spanish origin: "...probably from Spanish *daga,* a stove or furnace of a brick kiln." RT: *pot.* [South African and elsewhere, (1670): OEDS, (1834): JB: 1980, HB: 1955, BTD: 1968, EEL: 1971, ADC: 1981]

dagga rooker a marijuana smoker. See *dagga, roker.* RT: *toker.* [South African, early 1800s-p., DU, JB: 1980; listed in JES: 1959]

dagged alcohol intoxicated; tipsy. (BF: 1737: He's Dagg'd.) Possibly from the sense *to sprinkle and make wet* (1800s): OED. RT: *drunk.* [BF: 1737, F&H, DSUE, BVB: 1942, W&F: 1960]

dago red (also **dago**) cheap red wine; cheap Italian wine. Dago = Italian (derogatory). RS: *wine.* Hobo use (W&F: 1960). [U.S., (1888): SOD, EK: 1927, AH: 1931, GI: 1931, MHW: 1934, D&D: 1957, W&F: 1960]

dags cigarettes. RT: *nail.* See *do my dags.* Rhyming slang for *fags.*

Cf. fag. [Br., WWI, F&G: 1925]

daily mail ale. Rhyming slang. RT: *ale.* [Br., early 1900s, DRS]

dai-yen opium prepared for smoking. RT: *opium.* [U.S., M&V: 1954]

damaged (also **slightly damaged**) alcohol intoxicated. RT: *drunk.* [Br. and U.S., (1851): SBF: 1976, F&H, DSUE, BVB: 1942, W&F: 1960]

Dame DuPaw cannabis; marijuana. RT: *pot.* [U.S., JES: 1959]

damp 1. liquor; a drink of liquor. *Cf. wet.* RT: *booze, nip.* [Br, (1837): OED, DSUE; listed in BVB: 1942] 2. to take a drink of liquor. Short for *damp one's mug.* RT: *irrigate.* [U.S., MHW: 1934, BVB: 1942] 3. (also **slightly damp**) alcohol intoxicated. RT: *drunk.* [U.S., BVB: 1942] See also *damps.*

damper liquor; a drink of liquor. *Cf. wet one.* RT: *booze, nip.* [Br., 1800s, F&H; listed in BVB: 1942]

damp one's mug to drink liquor. Mug = face. RT: *irrigate.* [Br., (1860): DSUE, F&H]

damps barbiturates. The opposite of *amps* (*q.v.*). RT: *barbs.* [U.S., JH: 1979] See also *girl.*

dancing girl methyl alcohol used as beverage alcohol. RT: *methyl.* [Aust., SJB: 1966]

D. and D. alcohol intoxicated; drunk and disorderly. Originally a notation in police records. *Cf. disorderly.* RS: *drunk.* [(1870): SBF: 1976, (1889): F&H, DSUE, MHW: 1934, D&D: 1957, W&F: 1960]

dandy (also **dannie**) a small measure of liquor; a drink of liquor. RT: *nip.* [Br., (1838): OED, JCH: 1887; listed in BVB: 1942]

Darvocet part of the protected trade name, **Darvocet-N**. The drug is a mild analgesic (painkiller). See *N.s.* [in current use; consult a pharmaceutical reference for more information]

Darvon a protected trade name for propoxyphene hydrochloride (a mild analgesic) capsules, with or without additional ingredients. The drug is a painkiller. *Cf. vons.* [in current use; consult a pharmaceutical reference for more information]

Darvon-N a protected trade name for propoxyphene napsylate (a mild analgesic) available in a variety of forms and with or without additional ingredients. Similar to Darvocet-N (TM). *Cf. vons.* [in current use; consult a pharmaceutical reference for more information]

D.A.S. (also **DAS**) dextroamphetamine sulphate. The generic name of *Dexedrine* (TM; *q.v.*) amphetamine, and other brands. RT: *dex.* [U.S., RDS: 1982]

Datura a genus of poisonous plants of the deadly nightshade family. It is sometimes mixed with hemp resin of an African origin. [BTD: 1968, YKB: 1977]

day and night light ale; a drink of light ale. Rhyming slang for *light*. RS: *ale*. [Br., late 18-1900s, DRS]

D.D. a deadly dose, a fatal dose of drugs. *Cf. hot shot, O.D.* [U.S., TRG: 1968, RG: 1970]

dead 1. (also deado) alcohol intoxicated. Short for *dead drunk* (*q.v.*). RT: *drunk*. [U.S., BVB: 1942] 2. drug intoxicated; under the effects of marijuana. RT: *stoned*. [U.S., ADC: 1975] 3. out of money to buy drugs (said of a drug user); out of drugs (said of a dealer). [U.S., C&H: 1974, JWK: 1981]

dead bang a shot of bogus or over-diluted heroin. *Bang* (*q.v.*) = a dose of narcotics. RS: *blank*. [U.S., H&C: 1975]

dead drunk alcohol intoxicated; totally inebriated. *Cf. dead*. RT: *drunk*. [since the late 1500s, (1599): OED]

deadeye gin; Deady (TM) gin. Compare to *redeye*. RS: *gin*. [U.S., BVB: 1942]

deadfall a drinking den; a saloon. From the name of a kind of trap which catches an animal by dropping a weight on it. RS: *dive*. [U.S., OED, DU, PW: 1977]

deadhouse a drinking den; a saloon. RS: *dive*. [early 1900s, DU]

deadly nightshade belladonna. *Cf. beautiful lady, death's herb, horror drug*. The common name for the substance. [since the mid 1800s, SOD; drug culture use, RRL: 1969, YKB: 1977]

dead man See *dead soldier*.

dead man, be a to be drunk. (BF: 1737: He's a Dead Man.) RS: *drunk*. [BF: 1737]

dead marine See *dead soldier*.

dead-oh alcohol intoxicated. *Cf. dead drunk*. RT: *drunk*. [Br., B&L: 1890, F&H]

dead one an empty liquor bottle. See *dead soldier*.

dead, on the abstaining from alcohol. RS: *sober*. [Br. military, F&G: 1925, B&P: 1965]

deads alcohol intoxicated; dead drunk. *Cf. dead drunk*. RT: *drunk*. [Br. naval, (1920): DSUE]

dead soldier 1. (also dead man, dead marine, dead one) an empty liquor or beer bottle. *Cf. cold one, corpse*. BE: 1690 lists dead men. Wilkes lists only dead marine. The other forms became widespread during WWI. [GAW: 1978, F&G: 1925, MHW: 1934, WG: 1962, SSD, B&P: 1965] (This entry continues after the following list.) Nicknames and slang terms for empty bottles: *aras, Aristotle, arry, cold one, corpse, dead man, dead marine, dead one, dead soldier, dummy, em, long necker, marine, marine officer, marine recruit, M.T., old soldier, rabbit, soldier*. 2. a cigarette butt. RT: *brad*. [BVB: 1942, M&J: 1975]

dead to the world dead drunk; totally intoxicated with alcohol. GEN: fast asleep (1899): OEDS. RT: *drunk*. [(1926): SBF: 1976,

W&F: 1960, SSD, M&J: 1975]

deadwood an undercover federal agent or someone working as an agent to entrap someone in a drug sale. M&V: 1954 list the term but the meaning is not clear. RS: *fuzz*. [U.S., M&V: 1954, EEL: 1971]

deal 1. to traffic in drugs; to sell drugs on the retail (street) level. Both transitive and intransitive. *Cf. push*. [U.S., RB: 1967, RRL: 1969, EAF: 1980, ADC: 1981] 2. a small quantity of marijuana. Possibly akin to *deck*. RS: *load*. [Br., BTD: 1968]

dealer a drug seller or supplier. See *pusher*. [U.S., DWM: 1936, GS: 1959, S&W: 1966, MA: 1973, ADC: 1981] Terms for someone who sells drugs: *arreador, baggie, bag lady, bagman, bag woman, beat artist, big fish, bingle, bingle biff, bottle dealer, broker, bundler, buy, candy man, captain, cargador, carrier, channel, Chino, cocaine cowboy, coke peddler, comp man, connection, connector, contact, cop man, courier, cowboy, C-pusher, dealer, dope booster, dope daddy, dope man, dope peddler, doper, dope runner, do-right, drug booster, Dutchman, Egyptian driver, feed and grain man, fixer, flying Dutchman, frosty, Frosty the snowman, gage hustler, good time man, grog merchant, hawk, hop merchant, hop peddler, house connection, house dealer, hype, ice cream man, importer, jar dealer, juggler, junk connection, junk dealer, junker, junkie, junk man, junk peddler, junk pusher, kick man, kilo connection, kilo man, man, mooch pusher, mother, Mrs. White, my man, operator, ounce man, Oz man, panic man, paper boy, peddler, people, pin, pizza maker, player, powder monkey, pusher, quarter master, reefer hound, reefer man, reefing man, shovel, shover, snow drifter, snow eagle, source, stash man, street dealer, street pusher, sugar daddy, supplier, swing man, tambourine man, tea man, the big man, the man, the people, the source, ticket agent, trafficker, travel agent, turner, twirler, vendador, viper, weight dealer.*

dealing (also dealing drugs) currently supplied with dope or marijuana and offering it for sale. *Cf. dead, fold up*. [U.S., RRL: 1969]

deal with Lushington to drink alcohol to excess. *Lushington* (*q.v.*) = a personification of liquor. RT: *guzzle*. [JB: 1823]

DEARS (also DEERS) "Drug Enforcement Agency Rats"; federal narcotics agents. RS: *fuzz*. Probably not narcotics argot. [U.S., JWK: 1981]

death promoter liquor. RT: *booze*. [JRW: 1909, MHW: 1934, BVB: 1942]

death's head *Amanita muscaria* (*q.v.*), the death's head mushroom. See comments at *Amanita muscaria*. [U.S., YKB: 1977, RDS: 1982]

death's herb *belladonna* (*q.v.*). [U.S., YKB: 1977]

death trips L.S.D. mixed with Datura or some other drug. RS: *set*. [U.S., KBH: 1982]

death wish P.C.P., phencyclidine, an animal tranquilizer. RT: ***P.C.P.*** [U.S., AP: 1980]

deazingus the thing or gadget for injecting narcotics, a hypodermic syringe or medicine dropper with a needle attached. Narcotics ziph for ***dingus*** (*q.v.*) = gadget. RT: ***monkey pump.*** [U.S., M&V: 1954]

debris stems, seeds, and other matter cleaned out of a batch of marijuana. *Cf.* ***lumber, stem, timber.*** [U.S., EEL: 1971]

debs depressant pills, barbiturates or tranquilizers. [U.S., ADC: 1975]

decayed alcohol intoxicated. An elaboration of ***rotten*** (*q.v.*). RT: ***drunk.*** [U.S., DCCU: 1972]

deccy said to be ***Seconal*** (TM; *q.v.*). Almost certainly an error for ***seccy*** (*q.v.* at ***sec***). [U.S., SNP: 1977]

decent 1. having to do with good to very high-quality drugs. *Cf.* ***George smack, righteous bush.*** [U.S., MA: 1973, JWK: 1981] 2. having to do with a state of drug euphoria. Now also general slang for anything good. [U.S., JWK: 1981]

deck 1. a stack of packets of a powdered drug; a single packet (approximately 3 grains) of a narcotic; any measure of drugs. Now usually used for a packet of heroin. RS: ***load.*** [U.S., DWM: 1936, BD: 1937, VJM: 1949, GOL: 1950, M&D: 1952, W&F: 1967, RRL: 1969, DCCU: 1972, ADC: 1981] 2. a packet of tobacco cigarettes or marijuana cigarettes. *Cf.* ***stack.*** [U.S., BVB: 1942, VJM: 1949] 3. an injection of a drug. Probably from sense one. RS: ***shot.*** [Br., BTD: 1968]

decks awash alcohol intoxicated. RT: ***drunk.*** [U.S., SBF: 1976, MHW: 1934]

deck up to fill a packet or envelope with a dose of powdered drugs. *Cf.* ***cap, cap up.*** [U.S., RRL: 1969, EEL: 1971]

deeda the hallucinogenic drug ***L.S.D.*** (*q.v.*). *Cf.* ***D.*** RT: ***L.S.D.*** Black use. [U.S., JBW: 1967, RRL: 1969, IGA: 1971]

dee-horn denatured alcohol; reclaimed denatured alcohol; any beverage alcohol. See ***dehorn.***

deens codeine. See ***denes.***

deep cut alcohol intoxicated; very drunk. *Cf.* ***cut.*** RT: ***drunk.*** [BE: 1690]

deep noser (also **deep sinker**) a tall glass of beer. [Aust., (1920): DSUE, SJB: 1966, GAW: 1978] See also ***noser my knacker.***

dees ***Dilaudid*** (TM; *q.v.*) tablets, ampules, or suppositories. *Cf.* ***D.*** [U.S., JWK: 1981]

dehorn (also **dee-horn**) **1.** (also **dehorn alcohol**) reclaimed denatured alcohol. Probably dehorned in the sense that a bull or cow is dehorned, i.e., the danger is removed, or from a colloquial euphemism meaning castrated. From the prohibition era. [U.S.,

BVB: 1942] 2. any type of alcohol used as a substitute during prohibition: canned heat, bay rum, denatured alcohol, shoe polish, antifreeze; illegal or smuggled liquor. [U.S., BVB: 1942, W&F: 1960, K&M: 1968] 3. any alcohol; a dysphemism for whiskey or some other hard liquor. RS: *booze*. [RM: 1942, W&F: 1960] 4. to drink to excess; to get drunk. RT: *guzzle, mug oneself*. Probably early 1900s. [U.S., JLD: 1976] 5. a drunkard; a wino. RT: *sot, wino*. [AH: 1931, MHW: 1934, W&F: 1960, DCCU: 1972]

deines codeine. See *denes*.

delysid the hallucinogenic drug *L.S.D.* (*q.v.*). From the full chemical name D-lysergic acid diethylamide tartrate. An early trade name for this chemical substance. See *sid*.

Demerol a protected trade name for meperdine hydrochloride (a narcotic analgesic) available in a variety of forms. The drug is a central nervous system depressant and a smooth muscle relaxant. The painkilling action and dependence potential is similar to morphine. See *demis* for slang and jargon terms. [in current use; consult a pharmaceutical reference for more information]

demis (also **dems**) *Demerol* (TM; *q.v.*) sedative and painkiller in capsule or liquid form. *Cf. junk, shit, stuff, white stuff*. [U.S., YKB: 1977, JWK: 1981] Nicknames and slang terms for Demerol: *demies, demis, dems, junk, meperdine, meps, morals, shit, stuff, white stuff*.

demon rum (also **the demon rum**) rum; a personification of the evils of alcohol. Now used only in jest. RT: *rum*. [U.S., MHW: 1934, D&D: 1957]

demon vino cheap Italian wine; any wine. Based on *demon rum*. RS: *wine*. [Br., WWII, EP: 1948]

dems *Demerol* (TM; *q.v.*). See *demis*. [U.S., JWK: 1981]

den a truncation of *opium den* (*q.v.*). RT: *pad*. [U.S., GOL: 1950, JWK: 1981]

denatured having to do with (ethyl) alcohol rendered undrinkable by the addition of methyl alcohol. See *methyl*. Not slang. [since the late 1800s, (1878): OED]

denes (also **deens, deines**) *codeine* (*q.v.*). RT: *codeine*. [U.S., JWK: 1981]

Deprol a protected trade name for a combination of meprobamate (a tranquilizer) and benactyzine (antidepressant) tablets. The drug is a combination of a tranquilizer and an antidepressant, and is used in the treatment of depression. *Cf. sound*. [in current use; consult a pharmaceutical reference for more information]

derry-down-derry sherry. Rhyming slang. Music hall use. [Br., early 1900s, DRS]

descojonado* drug intoxicated; sick from drugs. From Spanish meaning castrated. [U.S., JWK: 1981]

desert horse a Camel (TM) cigarette; any cigarette. *Cf. hump*.

RT: *nail.* [U.S., MHW: 1934, BVB: 1942]

designer drug a type of *synthetic heroin* similar to and usually derived from *fen.* There are from 200 to 1000 varieties possible and most are technically legal to manufacture and sell. This type of drug can be permanently debilitating. See *Ecstasy, M.P.T.P.* [U.S., RAS: 1985]

Desoxyn a protected trade name for methamphetamine available in tablet form. The drug is a central nervous system stimulant. There are few slang terms specifically for this drug. It is covered by the generic *meth* (*q.v.*). [in current use; consult a pharmaceutical reference for more information]

dessicator a device used to smoke *free base* (*q.v.*). This is probably an error for *desiccator.* [U.S., ELA: 1984]

destroyed drug intoxicated; heavily stoned. RT: *stoned.* [U.S., G&B: 1969, EEL: 1971]

D.E.T. See *D.M.T.*

detox to detoxify (a person) from alcohol or drugs. Abbreviated as dtx. See *detoxed.* Not necessarily argot. [U.S., W&F: 1975]

detoxcen a center for the detoxification of alcoholics and drug addicts. Not necessarily drug argot. [U.S., RDS: 1982]

detoxed having been detoxified; sober; straight and free of drugs. RS: *sober.* [U.S., (1972): W&F: 1975]

Detroit pink a "trade name" for P.C.P. RT: *P.C.P.* [U.S., ELA: 1984]

deuce 1. a pair of marijuana cigarettes. *Cf. ace.* RS: *joint.* [U.S., MB: 1938] 2. (also **deuce bag**) a packet of heroin costing two dollars. *Cf. trey.* [U.S., IGA: 1971, H&C: 1975] 3. two amphetamine tablets; two barbiturate tablets. [U.S., EAF: 1980]

deuceways two dollars worth of drugs. RT: *load.* [U.S., JES: 1959]

developing paper rolling papers for marijuana cigarettes. From a theme based on the use of 35 mm film cans to carry marijuana or hashish. *Cf. paper.* [U.S., ADC: 1975]

developing room a place where communal marijuana smoking is done. *Cf. exposures, film can.* RS: *pad.* [U.S., ADC: 1975]

devil 1. a *Seconal* (TM; *q.v.*) capsule. A truncation of *red devils* (*q.v.*). *Cf. R.D., red.* RT: *sec.* [U.S., EEL: 1971, NIDA: 1980] 2. *S.T.P.* (*q.v.*). [U.S., EEL: 1971]

devil dust (also **devil's dust**) *P.C.P.* (*q.v.*). *Cf. dust.* RT: *P.C.P.* [U.S., FAB: 1979]

devil's apple (also **devil's trumpet, devil's weed**) *jimson weed* (*q.v.*). [U.S., YKB: 1977]

devil's eyewater whiskey; moonshine. RT: *whiskey.* [U.S., (Georgia), LP: 1977]

dew 1. whiskey; moonshine, usually in compound words. *Cf. Irish* *dew, honeydew, Kentucky dew, mountain dew, prairie dew, squirrel dew, swamp dew.* A dewdrop or dewhank is a single drink of *dew* (F&H). [(1826): OED, F&H; listed in W&F: 1960] 2. marijuana. RT: *pot.* [U.S., W&F: 1975] 3. hashish. Probably the same as sense two. Refers to the dewdrop-like beads of resin on the hemp plant. Hashish is often defined as resin. RS: *hash.* [U.S., RDS: 1982]

dex (also dexies, dexo) *Dexedrine* (TM; *q.v.*), a potent amphetamine. Also used for *Dexamyl* (TM; *q.v.*). [U.S., (c. 1956): MW: 1983, TRG: 1968, DCCU: 1972, DNE: 1980; Br., M&J: 1975; Aust., (1945): DSUE] Nicknames and slang terms for *Dexedrine: blues, brown, brown and clears, brownies, browns, Christmas tree, copilots, dex, dexie, dexo, dexy, green and clears, hearts, horse hearts, orange, peaches, purple hearts, purple passion.*

Dexamyl a protected trade name for a combination of dextroamphetamine and amobarbital available in tablets or capsules. The drug combines a central nervous stimulant and a sedative. Terms for Dexamyl (TM) usually can also refer to *Dexedrine* (TM), an amphetamine. Slang terms are totally unreliable in identifying this drug. [in current use; consult a pharmaceutical reference for more information]

dexed high on *Dexedrine* (TM; *q.v.*). *Cf. dex.* [U.S., (1972): DNE: 1980]

Dexedrine a protected trade name for dextroamphetamine sulfate (amphetamine) in a variety of forms. The drug is a central nervous system stimulant. Slang and jargon terms for *Dexedrine* (TM) may also apply to *Dexamyl* (TM; *q.v.*). Slang terms are totally unreliable in identifying this drug. See *dex* for a list of terms. [(1942): OEDS; in current use; consult a pharmaceutical reference for more information]

dexy (also dexie, dexies) *Dexedrine* (TM; *q.v.*). RT: *dex.* [U.S., (1956): MW: 1983, W&F: 1960, RRL: 1969, D&B: 1970c, DCCU: 1972, M&J: 1975, MW: 1976, YKB: 1977, DNE: 1980, NIDA: 1980, ADC: 1981]

D-free drug free; clean; detoxified. [U.S., JWK: 1981]

diablo rojas* a *Seconal* (TM; *q.v.*) capsule. RT: *sec.* Spanish for red devil. *Cf. red devils.* [U.S., NIDA: 1980]

diambista* marijuana. From Spanish. RT: *pot.* Cuban and Central American (M&V: 1954). [U.S., M&V: 1954, RDS: 1982]

dice tablets of *Desoxyn* (TM; *q.v.*), methamphetamine. From the first syllable of *Desoxyn.* RT: *speed.* [U.S., RG: 1970]

dick a detective; a police officer. From the word *detective.* RT: *fuzz.* [Canadian and U.S., 1900s, (1908): OEDS]

diddle 1. gin. RT: *gin.* Originally cant. [(1700): OED, (1724): DU, FG: 1785, FG: 1811, FG: 1823, BVB: 1942] 2. liquor; any alcoholic beverage including beer. From sense one. RT: *booze.*

[(1700): OED, GWM: 1859, MHW: 1934, BVB: 1942]

diddle can a bottle of whiskey. *Cf. diddle*. [U.S., (Boontling), late 18-1900s, CCA]

diddleums the delirium tremens. Based on *diddle* (*q.v.*). RT: *D.T.s.* [Aust., SJB: 1943]

didn't ought port wine. Rhyming slang. RT: *port*. [Br., late 18-1900s, DRS]

dido gin; rum; liquor in general. Possibly a variant of or punning on *diddle* (*q.v.*). RT: *booze*. [U.S., MHW: 1934, BVB: 1942, B&P: 1965]

Didrex a protected trade name for benzphetamine hydrochloride (amphetamine) tablets. The drug is a central nervous system stimulant used in the treatment of obesity. [in current use; consult a pharmaceutical reference for more information]

dids *Dilaudid* (TM; *q.v.*), a potent painkiller. [U.S., JWK: 1981] Nicknames and slang terms for Dilaudid: *big-D., D., dees, dids, dilies, dillies, dilly, drugstore stuff, D.s, footballs, hospital heroin, junk, little-D., shit, white stuff.*

dies (also **dis, dyes**) *Valium* (TM; *q.v.*), a tranquilizer. From the chemical name *diazepam*. RT: *vals*. [U.S., JWK: 1981]

diet pills amphetamines and other drugs used in weight loss. Medical and colloquial. [U.S., DES: 1972, DNE: 1973]

digatee a drug *rush* (*q.v.*) following an injection of a drug. RS: *rush*. [U.S., (1940): JES: 1959, H&C: 1975]

digester (also **patent digester**) liquor; a drink of liquor, a drink after a meal. RT: *nip, booze*. [Br., (1836): F&H]

digging the bowls smoking marijuana in a pipe. *Cf. bowl*. RS: *hit the hay*. [U.S., D&B: 1971]

Dilaudid a protected trade name for hydromorphone (narcotic analgesic) in a variety of forms. RT: *dids*. [in current use; consult a pharmaceutical reference for more information]

dill (also **dills, dyls**) *Placidyl* (TM; *q.v.*), a sedative and hypnotic drug. RT: *plass*. [U.S., ADC: 1981, JWK: 1981]

dillies (also **dilies, dilly**) *Dilaudid* (TM; *q.v.*), a potent painkiller available in a number of forms. RT: *dids*. [U.S., RRL: 1969, IGA: 1971, YKB: 1977, JWK: 1981]

dimba marijuana grown and smoked in West africa. This word is found in various forms in many West African Languages. See *djamba*. Its actual penetration into U.S. usage is not known. RT: *pot*. [U.S., RDS: 1982]

dime bag (also **dime, dime's worth**) a ten-dollar purchase of drugs. Usually attested in reference to heroin or marijuana. RS: *load*. [U.S., S&W: 1966, JBW: 1967, W&F: 1967, RRL: 1969, CM: 1970, EEL: 1971, DCCU: 1972, MA: 1973, EAF: 1980, JWK: 1981]

dime-dropper an informer; a former addict turned police informer. Dropping a dime on the sidewalk is a signal for the police to move in. From an earlier time when the dime was dropped into a public telephone to call the police. *Cf. drop a dime.* [U.S., JWK: 1981]

dimey a beer. Presumably a ten-cent beer. [U.S., D&B: 1970c]

dimp a cigarette butt. RT: *brad.* [Br., WWII, (1939): DSUE, M&J: 1975]

dinch 1. (also **dincher**) a cigarette butt; a presmoked cigarette; a cigarette crushed out to be smoked later. *Cf. clincher.* RT: *brad.* [U.S., EK: 1927, MHW: 1934, GOL: 1950] 2. (also **dinch a butt**) to crush out a cigarette or cigar. GOL: 1950 lists **dinch a butt.** [U.S., GOL: 1950, MW: 1976]

ding (also **dingbat**) marijuana. RT: *pot.* [U.S., M&V: 1954, H&C: 1975]

dingbats the delirium tremens. RT: *D.T.s.* [Aust., (1924): GAW: 1978, SJB: 1943]

dinged out alcohol intoxicated. RT: *drunk.* [U.S., DCCU: 1972]

dinghiyen probably an error for *dinghizen* (*q.v.*). [U.S., BVB: 1942, VJM: 1949]

dinghizen a hypodermic syringe or a medicine dropper with hypodermic needle attached. This word is a colloquial term for gadget. *Cf. deazingus.* RT: *monkey pump.* [U.S., DWM: 1938]

ding-swizzled alcohol intoxicated. RT: *drunk.* [PD: 1982]

dingus a medicine dropper with a hypodermic needle attached. Used for injecting narcotics. GEN: gadget (1876): OEDS. *Cf. deazingus, dinghizen.* [U.S., BD: 1937, DWM: 1938, VJM: 1949]

dingy (also **dinky**) alcohol intoxicated. RT: *drunk.* [U.S., BVB: 1942]

dinky dow marijuana; a marijuana cigarette. RT: *pot, joint.* [U.S., (1968): ELA: 1982, H&C: 1975, SNP: 1977]

dip 1. a pinch or helping of snuff. *Cf. pinch.* [U.S., LWP: 1908, DWM: 1931, HNR: 1934] 2. a drunkard. A truncation of *dipsomaniac* (*q.v.*). *Cf. dipso.* [DU, W&F: 1960] 3. a drug user or drug addict. RT: *user.* [U.S., BVB: 1942, A&T: 1953] 4. a dose of a drug. From sense one. RT: *dose.* [U.S., JES: 1959] 5. a wad of chewing tobacco. RT: *quid.* [U.S., ADC: 1984] 6. to chew tobacco. Recorded among baseball players. [U.S., ADC: 1984]

dip and dab to sample drugs or use them carefully in order to avoid addiction. *Dab* is from *dabble. Cf. chippy, dabble.* [U.S., RRL: 1969]

dipped addicted to narcotics. *Dip* (*q.v.*) = drug user. RT: *hooked.* [U.S., JES: 1959, H&C: 1975]

dipped his bill alcohol intoxicated. (BF: 1737: [He] has Dipp'd his Bill.) RT: *drunk.* [BF: 1737]

dipped too deep (also **dipped rather deep**) alcohol intoxicated. Akin to *dipsomaniac* (*q.v.*). RT: *drunk*. The entry appears to be a "translation" of British English into American English. The entry word is from BVB: 1942 and the *also* is F&H. [F&H, BVB: 1942]

dipper 1. an opium pipe. RT: *hop stick*. [U.S., VJM: 1949, A&T: 1953] 2. allegedly, a hypodermic syringe. Probably an error for *dripper* (*q.v.*). [U.S., H&C: 1975] 3. a snuff user. [U.S., LWP: 1908] 4. (also **double dipper**) phencyclidine, *P.C.P.* RT: *P.C.P.* [U.S., ELA: 1984]

dipso (also **dip, dips, dypso**) a drunkard. From *dipsomaniac* (*q.v.*) = a drunkard. RT: *sot*. [(1880): MW: 1983, (1925): DU, (1940s): SBF: 1976, W&F: 1967, SSD, DCCU: 1972, HSD: 1984]

dipsomaniac a person who has a craving for alcohol; an alcoholic. RS: *sot*. Often used euphemistically or in jest. [since the 1800s, (1858): OED]

dirt 1. a tobacco cigarette, as opposed to a marijuana cigarette. RT: *nail*. [U.S., EEL: 1971] 2. any drug, especially heroin or marijuana. *Dirt* is what one carries when one is *dirty* (*q.v.*). RS: *dope*. [U.S., M&V: 1973, ADC: 1975, JWK: 1981] See also *Congo dirt*.

dirt grass low-quality marijuana. RS: *pot*. [U.S., EEL: 1971, JH: 1979, RDS: 1982]

dirty 1. showing signs of being addicted to narcotics; having needle marks from injections. *Cf. greasy*. See *dirty arm*. [U.S., M&V: 1967] 2. carrying drugs on one's person. The opposite of *clean* (*q.v.*). [U.S., JBW: 1967, RRL: 1969, DNE: 1973, JWK: 1981] 3. under the influence of narcotics or marijuana; having drugs in one's system. [U.S., EEL: 1971, JHF: 1971, DNE: 1973] 4. having to do with marijuana containing stems and seeds. The opposite of *clean* (*q.v.*). [U.S., RRL: 1969, ADC: 1981, JWK: 1981]

dirty arm an arm showing much scarring and many needle marks from drug injections. *Cf. cement arm*. [U.S., M&V: 1973]

dirty drunk alcohol intoxicated; very drunk. RT: *drunk*. Anglo-Irish (DSUE). [Br., early 1900s, DSUE]

dis *Valium* (TM; *q.v.*). See *dies*. [U.S., JWK: 1981]

disco drug *butyl nitrite* (*q.v.*), the vapors of which are used by some disco dancers. [U.S., RAS: 1981]

discombobulated (also **discomboobulated**) alcohol intoxicated. GEN: confused. RT: *drunk*. [PD: 1982]

discouraged alcohol intoxicated. *Cf. chap-fallen*. RT: *drunk*. [U.S., D&D: 1957, W&F: 1960]

discumfuddled alcohol intoxicated. *Cf. fuddled*. RT: *drunk*. [U.S., BVB: 1942]

disguised (also **disguised in liquor**) alcohol intoxicated. (BF: 1737:

He's Disguiz'd.) *Cf. incog.* RT: ***drunk***. [(1607): OED, (1622): F&H, BE: 1690, BF: 1737, FG: 1785, FG: 1811, B&L: 1890, JRW: 1909, BVB: 1942, W&F: 1960]

dishwater inferior liquor. A dysphemism. RS: ***rotgut***. [Br. and U.S., BVB: 1942, M&J: 1975]

disorderly alcohol intoxicated; a euphemism for drunk. *Cf. D. and D.* RT: ***drunk***. [Br., 1800s, F&H; listed in BVB: 1942]

distillery stiff (also **distillery bum**) a hobo drunkard; any drunkard. Stiff = a hobo. RT: ***sot***. [U.S., EK: 1927, VJM: 1949]

ditch the inside of the elbow where the best vein for injection can be found. *Cf. **gutter, pit, sewer, valley***. [U.S., M&V: 1967, D&B: 1970c, IGA: 1971]

ditch weed marijuana; low-quality marijuana, especially low-quality Mexican marijuana. *Cf. **ragweed, railroad weed***. RS: ***pot***. [U.S., RDS: 1982]

dithered alcohol intoxicated. See ***dithers***. RT: ***drunk***. [Aust., (1932): OEDS, SJB: 1943]

dithers the delirium tremens. From an old term (mid 1600s) meaning to shake. [U.S., BVB: 1942]

dive a saloon; a low tavern; a pub. [U.S., (1882): OED, B&L: 1890, F&H, AH: 1931, MHW: 1934] The list contains terms for a low drinking establishment, probably patronized by criminals. See the list at ***bar*** for other types of drinking establishments. Various types of dives are: ***after-hours spot, barley bar, barrelhouse, benzinery, blue pig, boose-casa, boosing-ken, booze-casa, booze crib, boozing-ken, break o' day drum, budge ken, budging-ken, creep dive, creep joint, crib, cross-drum, deadfall, deadhouse, diving bell, doggery, drink den, drum, flash case, flash drum, flash ken, flash panny, gashouse, gin dive, gin mill, gin palace, groggery, grog mill, gut bucket, guzzle crib, hurdy-gurdy, joint, jook, jook house, juice-joint, juke-joint, lush crib, lush dive, lush drum, lushery, lushing crib, lushing ken, lush ken, lush panny, red nugget, red onion, rum hole, rummery, rum mill, shebang, shock joint, shoe polish shop, shypoo, shypoo joint, skee joint, smoke joint, suck casa, suck crib, Tom and Jerry shop, whiskey hole, whiskey mill.***

dive-keeper a bartender in a low saloon or dive. RT: ***bartender***. [U.S., (1890): OEDS, D&D: 1957]

divine weed tobacco. RT: ***fogus***. [U.S., BVB: 1942]

diving bell a basement saloon. *Cf. **dive***. RS: ***bar***. [U.S., GWM: 1859, F&H; listed in MHW: 1934]

dizzy alcohol intoxicated. GEN: giddy, disoriented. RT: ***drunk***. [since the late 1700s, DSUE, BVB: 1942]

dizzy as a coot (also **dizzy as a dame**) alcohol intoxicated. RT: ***drunk***. [U.S., BVB: 1942]

dizzy as a goose alcohol intoxicated. The expression survives with the meaning silly or giddy. RT: ***drunk***. [BF: 1737]

djamba (also dimba, djama, djoma) marijuana. Some form of this word occurs in many African languages, e.g., Mende *djamba*. The term is also used in South America. RT: ***pot***. [U.S., RPW: 1938, D&D: 1957, (1967): DNE: 1973]

D-man a federal drug enforcement officer. *Cf.* ***DEARS***. RS: ***fuzz***. [U.S., ADC: 1981]

D.M.T. (also D.E.T., dimethyltryptamine) a fast-acting chemical hallucinogen of short duration. *D.M.T.* = N,N-dimethyltryptamine; *D.E.T.* = N,N-diethyltryptamine. The substance is found naturally in the seeds of some South American plants, although most of it is now is synthesized. See ***businessman's trip***. [U.S., JBW: 1967, W&F: 1967, (TW: 1968), RRL: 1969, YKB: 1977, ADC: 1981]

D.O.A. "dead on arrival," phencyclidine, *P.C.P.* (*q.v.*), an animal tranquilizer. The term emphasizes the deadly nature of this drug. [U.S., EEL: 1971, YKB: 1977, NIDA: 1980]

do a doobie (also do a dooby) to smoke a marijuana cigarette. *Doobie* (*q.v.*) = a marijuana cigarette. See ***do drugs***. [U.S., BR: 1972]

do a drain (also do a beer, do a drink, do a smile, do a wet) to take a drink of liquor. *Cf.* ***smile, wet***. RT: ***irrigate***. [JCH: 1887, F&H, JRW: 1909, MHW: 1934]

do a joint to smoke a marijuana cigarette. *Cf. joint*. RT: ***hit the hay***. [U.S., (1967): ELA: 1982, RAS: 1980]

do a line snort a dose of a powdered drug, i.e., P.C.P., cocaine, etc. RS: ***snort***. [U.S., FAB: 1979]

do a number to smoke a marijuana cigarette. RT: ***hit the hay***. [U.S., RAS: 1980]

do a pub-crawl to go on a drinking bout, moving from pub to pub. *Cf. pub-crawl*. RS: ***mug oneself***. [Br., 1900s, DSUE, SSD]

doctor 1. a substance added to liquor by distillers to make the proof appear higher. [cant, FG: 1785, FG: 1823] 2. to add alcohol to homemade liquor to raise the proof. *Cf.* ***spike***. [U.S., MHW: 1934, BVB: 1942] 3. to give an injection of narcotics to an addict who is no longer able to care for his habit. *Cf.* ***pinch hitter***. RS: ***shoot***. [U.S., JWK: 1981] 4. a person hired to serve as a ***pinch hitter*** (*q.v.*). See sense three. [U.S., JWK: 1981]

Doctor Hall alcohol; a personification of alcohol. RT: ***booze***. The same as *Dr. Hall*. [U.S., early 1900s, DU]

Doctor White 1. cocaine. *Cf.* ***old lady White***. RT: ***cocaine***. [U.S., A&T: 1953] 2. narcotics addiction. RT: ***habit***. [U.S., early 1900s, DU]

dodo a drug addict. GEN: a stupid person. RT: ***junky***. [U.S., A&T: 1953]

do drugs (also **do dope**) to take drugs; to use drugs habitually. [U.S., RRL: 1969, RG: 1970, D&B: 1970c, EEL: 1971]

doe *methamphetamine* (*q.v.*). Origin unknown. Possibly akin to *D.O.A.* (*q.v.*). It is possibly an initialism. RRL: 1969 lists D.O.E. meaning taking drugs. RT: *speed.* [U.S., IGA: 1971, SNP: 1977]

dog 1. the weak, non-addictive residue of opium. *Cf. eng-shee, gee-fat, gee-yen, green ashes, green mud, suey-pow, yen-chee.* Compare to *old dog.* [U.S., BD: 1937, DU, D&B: 1970c] 2. weak heroin. RS: *blank.* [U.S., IGA: 1971] 3. a bottle of liquor. [U.S., BVB: 1942] 4. (also **dog end**) a cigarette butt. Compare to *old dog.* RT: *brad.* [Br., (1935): DSUE, SSD, M&J: 1975]

dog biscuits (also **biscuits**) peyote; peyote buttons. Named for their appearance. RS: *peyote.* [U.S., JWK: 1981]

dog drunk alcohol intoxicated; as drunk as a dog. Akin to *sick as a dog.* RT: *drunk.* [U.S., BVB: 1942]

dog end a cigarette butt. *Cf. dog.* RT: *brad.* Akin to **doggin** (New Zealand, early 1900s, DSUE). [Br., (1936): DSUE, DU, SSD, M&J: 1975]

dog food heroin. RT: *heroin.* Black use. [U.S., EAF: 1980]

doggery a low saloon. Possibly rhyming slang for *groggery* (*q.v.*). D&D: 1957 suggests that this is the type of a place where hot dogs are sold. More likely a place fit only for dogs. RT: *dive.* [U.S., (1835): RHT: 1912, (1843): OEDS, (1853): DA, B&L: 1890, BWG: 1899, AH: 1931, D&D: 1957]

doggin See *dog end.*

dogie heroin. *Cf. dojee.* RT: *heroin.* [U.S., RRL: 1969, EEL: 1971, NIDA: 1980]

dog's nose 1. (also **dognose**) a mixture of beer and gin. A dog's nose is cold and wet. [(1812): OED, F&H, DSUE, W&F: 1960, D&D: 1973] 2. a drunkard. A play on *wet* (*q.v.*). RT: *sot.* [Br., (1850): DSUE, B&L: 1890]

doing the lord (also **doing the emperor**) acting very drunk. See *drunk as a lord.* RS: *drunk.* [Br., 1800s, F&H]

do-it fluid liquor. RT: *booze.* [U.S., EAF: 1980]

dojee (also **dogie, dojie, doogie, doojee, doojer, doojes, dooji, dugee, dugie, dujer, duji, dujii**) heroin. RT: *heroin.* [U.S., TRG: 1968, RRL: 1969, W&F: 1975, YKB: 1977, NIDA: 1980, ADC: 1981, JWK: 1981]

dollar in underworld talk, one-hundred dollars. *Cf. dime bag, nickel bag, quarter bag.* [U.S., RRL: 1969, (JHF: 1971)]

dollies (also **dollys**) *Dolophine* (TM; *q.v.*) brand of methadone, a synthetic opiate. RT: *dolo.* [U.S., JBW: 1967, D&B: 1970c, RRL: 1969, M&V: 1973, YKB: 1977, DNE: 1980, ADC: 1981, JWK: 1981]

dolls pills; drugs in pill form. From the book and film title *Valley* *of the Dolls.* Refers primarily to amphetamines and barbiturates. *Cf. baby doll.* See *blue dolls, red dolls.* [U.S., RRL: 1969, W&F: 1975, DNE: 1980] See also *dollies.*

dolo *Dolophine* (TM; *q.v.*), a brand of *methadone* (*q.v.*). See *dollies.* [U.S., RDS: 1982] Nicknames and slang terms for Dolophine: *biscuits, chalk, dollies, dollys, dolo, done, medicine, meth, methadone, phy, wafer.*

Dolophine a protected trade name for methadone (synthetic narcotic analgesic) available in tablets for oral use and ampules for injection. The drug is a synthetic narcotic used in the treatment of heroin addiction. It is addictive itself. Created by German scientists during WWII to replace morphine which was in short supply. The drug name is from the *dol* in Adolph Hitler's first name. RT: *dolo.* [in current use; consult a pharmaceutical reference for more information]

D.O.M. *S.T.P.* (*q.v.*), 4-methyl-2,5-Dimethoxy-4-methyl-amphetamine, a hallucinogenic compound. [U.S., RRL: 1969, EEL: 1971]

domes (also **dome**) the hallucinogenic drug *L.S.D.* (*q.v.*). Each dose is dome shaped. *Cf. blue doubledomes, contact lens.* RT: *L.S.D.* [U.S., EEL: 1971, YKB: 1977, JH: 1979]

domestic having to do with marijuana grown in the U.S. *Cf. home-grown, mud-bud.* From the term for wine from one's own country. [U.S., RRL: 1969, DEM: 1981]

domino 1. (also **dominoes**) a black and white capsule containing an amphetamine and a barbiturate. Also used for *Biphetamine* (TM; *q.v.*) amphetamine capsules which are black and white, and for *Durophet* (TM; *q.v.*). *Cf. black and white.* RS: *set.* [BTD: 1968, EEL: 1971, M&J: 1975, ADC: 1981] 2. to complete a drug purchase. RT: *score.* General argot meaning to complete any action. Refers to a row of falling dominoes. [U.S., M&V: 1954, TRG: 1968, RG: 1970, IGA: 1971] 3. the receiver of smuggled drugs. RS: *mule.* Heard in the movie *$Dollars,* 1972. [U.S., RAS: 1984]

do my dags cigarettes. Rhyming slang for *fags. Cf. dags.* RT: *nail.* [Br., late 18-1900s, DRS]

Doña Juanita* (also **Doña Diabla***, **Doña Juana***) marijuana. Spanish (calo) for Lady Jane. RT: *pot.* [U.S., RPW: 1938, HB: 1955, JBR: 1973, NIDA: 1980]

done *methadone* (*q.v.*). Rhymes with *bone.* RT: *dolo.* [U.S., JWK: 1981]

done over alcohol intoxicated. RT: *drunk.* [Br., 18-1900s, F&H, DSUE; listed in BVB: 1942]

donjem hashish. See *djamba.* RT: *hash.* [U.S., JES: 1959, H&C: 1975]

donk illegal whiskey; moonshine. A truncation of *donkey* which suggests *mule* (*q.v.*). RT: *moonshine*. [U.S., MHW: 1934, D&D: 1957, W&F: 1960]

doobie (also dooby, dubee, duby) a marijuana cigarette; a fat marijuana cigarette. RT: *joint*. [U.S., JBW: 1967, RRL: 1969, EAF: 1972, RRL: 1974, W&F: 1975, ADC: 1981]

doofer (also doofa) a cigarette stub saved for smoking at another time. It will do for later. *Cf. dufer*. RT: *nail*. [Aust. and Br., (1937): OEDS, DSUE]

dooge heroin. See *dojee* for other spelling variants. RT: *heroin*. [U.S., ADC: 1975]

doojee See *dojee*.

dool a narcotics addict. RT: *junky*. Possibly from Greek *doulos* = a slave, JES: 1959. [U.S., JES: 1959, H&C: 1975]

doors (also dories, dors) *Doriden* (TM; *q.v.*) sedative in any form. RT: *dories*. [U.S., JWK: 1981]

dopatorium an opium den; a place where opium is sold. See *doperie*. RT: *opium den*. Contrived synthetic slang, not drug argot. [U.S., JES: 1959, H&C: 1975]

dope 1. any drug, narcotic, opiate, or chemical which produces sedation, euphoria, stimulation, analgesia or stupor. May include tobacco and alcohol, but currently in the U.S., it does not. The term has been used as slang even for *Coca-Cola* (TM). [U.S., (1895): DA, (1889): OEDS, GI: 1931, RRL: 1969, EEL: 1971, MA: 1973, ADC: 1981] (This entry continues after the following list.) This list includes the terms for drugs and narcotics: *A., abbot, A-bomb, Acapulco, Acapulco gold, Acapulco red, ace, acelerante, acid, acid cube, ácido, ad, Afghani, African black, African bush, ah-pen-yen, aimless Amy, A.I.P., alocados, alpha powder, amarilla, amies, amoeba, amphetamine, amphets, amps, A.M.T., amy, amy joy, amyl, amyl nitrite, amyls, amys, Amytal, anfetamina, angel, angel dust, angel hair, angel mist, angel puke, angie, Angola black, anhalonium, animal, animal crackers, animal tranquilizer, antifreeze, anything, apostle, apple, aprobarbs, Aroma, Aroma of Man, ashes, atom bomb, atshitshi, Augustus Owsley, Aunt Emma, Aunt Hazel, auntie, Aunt Mary, Aunt Nora, aurora borealis, avispa, ayahuasca, azulillos, B., baby, baby bhang, baby buds, baby doll, backwards, bad acid, bad grass, bad green, bador, bad seed, bag, baggage, baking soda base, bala, bale, balloon, balot, bam, bambalacha, bambalache, bambinos, bambita, bambs, bammies, bammy, bams, banana splits, banana with cheese, Ban Apple, banewort, banji, bank bandit pills, bank bandits, Barbidex, Barbie doll, barbies, barbitone, barbiturate, barbitúrico, barbs, barmecide, bar of soap, barrels, bars of soap, base, bash, basketballs, B.B., B-bomb, beaners, beans, beast, beautiful lady, belladonna, belt, belula, belyando sprue, benj, bennies, benny, benz, benzadrina, Benzedrine, benzies, bernese, Bernice, Bernies, Bernies flake, Bethesda gold, bhang, bhang ganjah, big boy, big-C., big chief, big-D., big daddy,* *big-H., big Harry, big-M., big-O., Big Three, big time, Billie Hoak, Billie Hoke, bingle, biphet, Biphetamine, birdie powder, birdie stuff, birdwood, biscuits, black, black acid, black and tan, black and white, black and white minstrel, black beauties, blackbirds, black bombers, black bottle, black Cadillac, black Columbus, black ganja, black gold, black gungeon, black gungi, black gunion, black gunnion, black gunny, black hash, blackjack, Black Jack, black mo, black moat, black mold, black mole, black mollies, black monte, black mota, black mote, black oil, black pills, black Russian, black shit, black silk, black smoke, black stuff, black tabs, black whack, black widow, blancas, blanco, blinky, block, blockbuster, bloke, blond, blond hash, blond hashish, blond Lebanese, blorphs, blotter, blotter acid, blow, blower, blue, blue acid, blue angel, blue angelfish, blue babies, blue barrel, bluebirds, blue bombers, blue bullets, blue caps, blue chair, blue cheer, blue cheese, blue clouds, blue de Hue, blue devils, blue dolls, blue dots, blue doubledomes, blue dragon, blue flag, blue flats, blue heavens, blue horse, blue jackets, blue jeans, blue jeans and T-shirts, blue mist, blue mornings, blue morphone, blue pyramids, blues, blue sage, blues and reds, blue sky blond, blue splash, blue star, blue tips, blue velvet, blue vials, blueys, bluies, blunt, B.M., bo, bo-bo, bo-bo bush, body, body drug, Bo Jimmy, Bolt, bomb, bomber, bombida, bombido, bombita, boo, boom, boo-reefer, booster, booster pills, booster stick, border, border red, bottle, bottles, bounce powder, bouncing powder, bow-sow, box of L, boy, bozo, brain burners, brain tickler, brand X, Breckenridge green, brick, brick gum, brifo, broccoli, brother, brother Ben, brown, brown acid, brown and clears, brown bomber, brown caps, brown dope, brown dots, brownies, brown rine, brown rock, browns, brown stuff, brown sugar, brown weed, brute, bu, bud, bug juice, bullet, bullethead, bullet Thai, bull jive, bumblebees, burese, Burnese, bush, bushes, bush tea, businessman's high, businessman's lunch time high, businessman's psychedelic martini, businessman's special, businessman's trip, busters, busy bee, butter flower, button, butyl nitrite, buzz, B.Z., C., caballo, caca, cacil, cactus, cactus buttons, Cadillac, cahoba, California cornflakes, California sunshine, California turnarounds, cam, Cambodian red, Cambodian trip weed, came, camioneros, cam red, cam trip, can, Canadian black, Canadian bouncer, Canadian quail, cáñamo, canapa, canappa, canary, C. and H., C. and M., candy, candy bar, candy cee, cannabinoids, cannabinol, cannabis, Cannabis americana, Cannabis indica, Cannabis mexicana, Cannabis ruderalis, Cannabis sativa, cannabis tea, canned goods, canned sativa, canned stuff, cannonball, cap, capital H., carbon tet, carceleras, card, cardenales, carga, carmabus, carne, carob chips, Carrie, Carrie Nation, Carry Nation, cartwheel, cat, Catholic aspirin, catnip, Cat's Meow, cavite allstars, C.B., C-duct, Cecil, Cecile, cee, cement, cets, C-game, chalk, chandoo, chandu, chara, charas, charash, charge, Charles, Charley, Charley Coke, Charlie, charras, chaulkers, cheeo, cheese, chef, chemicals, cherry leb, cherry top, chiba-chiba, Chicago black,*

Chicago green, chick, chicken powder, chickery, chickory, chief, China white, Chinese molasses, Chinese red, Chinese tobacco, Chinese white, chip, chira, chiva, chlorals, chloroform, chocolate, chocolate chips, chocolate mesc, Cholley, Cholly, Christian, Christina, Christmas roll, Christmas tree, chunkies, chunks, churrus, ciba, ciclón, ciclón de cristal, cid, citroli, C.J., C-jam, C-jame, C.K., clarabelle, clay, clear light, clear liquid, clorofila, coast-to-coasts, cobics, cobies, coby, coca, cocaina, cocaine, cocanuts, cocaroin, cochornis, cockle burrs, coconut, cod, codeine, cods, codys, coffee, cohoba, coka, coke, cola, cola de borrego, cola de león, cola de zorra, colas, cold and hot, coli, coliflor tostao, collard greens, collie, colly, colly-weed, Colombian, Colombian gold, Colombian green, Colombo, colorado, Columbian, Columbian gold, Columbian pink, Columbian red, Columbia red, Columbus black, communist M. and M.s, conga, Congo brown, Congo dirt, Congo mataby, contact lens, controlled substance, cookie, coolie mud, copilot, copilotas, copilot ben, copilots, corals, corazónes, corgy, Corine, Corinne, Corrine, cortals, cosa, cosmos, cotics, cotton morphine, courage pill, cozmos, crackers, crank, cranks, crap, crazy coke, creeper, cresta, crink, cris, cristal, cristales, cristian, cristina, Cristine, crosses, crossroads, cross tops, crown crap, cruz, crying weed, crystal, crystal flake, crystal joint, crystal points, crystal T., crystal weed, cube, cube juice, cubes, culican, Cum, cupcakes, cyclone, D., D.A., dacha, dagga, dagha, dai-yen, Dame DuPaw, damps, Darvocet, Darvon, Darvon-N, D.A.S., Datura, deadly nightshade, death's herb, death trips, death wish, debs, deeda, deens, dees, deines, delysid, Demerol, demies, demis, dems, denes, Deprol, designer drug, Desoxyn, D.E.T., Detroit pink, devil, devil dust, devil's apple, devil's trumpet, devil's weed, dew, dex, Dexamyl, Dexedrine, dexie, dexo, dexy, diablo rojas, diambista, dice, Didrex, dids, dies, diet pills, Dilaudid, dilies, dill, dillies, dills, dilly, dimba, ding, dingbat, dinky dow, dipper, dirt, dirt grass, dis, disco drug, ditch weed, djama, djamba, djoma, D.M.T., D.O.A., Doctor White, doe, dog biscuits, dog food, dogie, dojee, dojie, dollies, dolls, dollys, dolo, Dolophine, D.O.M., dome, domes, domino, dominoes, Doña Diabla, Doña Juana, Doña Juanita, done, donjem, dooge, doogie, doojee, doojer, doojes, dooji, doors, dope, dopium, doradilla, Doriden, dories, dors, dots, double-blue, double-crosses, double dipper, double-trouble, down, downer, downie, downs, downtown, D.P.T., dragon, drag weed, Dr. Bananas, dream, dream beads, dreamer, dream gum, dreams, dreamstick, dream stuff, dream wax, dreck, drin, Drinamyl, drivers, drug, drugstore stuff, Dr. White, dry booze, dry grog, dry high, dry whiskey, D.s, duct, dude, dugee, dugie, dujer, duji, dujii, dummy, dummy dust, duraznos, Durophet M, duros, dust, dust joint, dust of angels, dust of Morpheus, Dutch courage, dyes, dyls, dynamite, easing powder, easy powder, ea-tay, Ecstasy, eed-waggles, eed-way, eggs, eight, ekies, Elavil, electric koolaid, electric wine, elefante, elephant, elephant tranquilizer, elevator, eli lilly, el kif, els, em, embalming fluid, emm, Empirin, emsel, energizer, eng-shee, enns, erb, erth, esrar, estuffa, ether, ethical drug, evil powder, eye-opener, faggot, fairy dust, fairy powder, fake S.T.P., feed, feed bag, fees, fee-tops, fen, fender-benders, fennel, fentanyl, fe-ops, ferry dust, F-forties, fi-do-nie, fifty, fina-esmeralda, fine stuff, finger, fir, fire plug, first line, fives, flake, flake acid, flakes, flash, flat blues, flats, flea powder, Florida snow, flower of the virgin, flowers, flower tops, flying saucers, focus, foo-foo-dust, foolish powder, foon, footballs, foreign mud, foreign smoke, forties, forty-five minute psychosis, forwards, four-doors, fours, fours and doors, fourteen, four-way hit, four-ways, four-way star, four-way windowpane, fraho, frajo, freddy, free base, freebies, French blue, Frisco speedball, frisky, frisky powder, fruit salad, fu, fuel, full moons, fumo d'Angola, fun, fun medicine, funny stuff, gage, Gainesville green, galloping horse, gammon, gamot, gang, ganga, gange, ganger, gangster, gangster pills, ganja, ganjah, ganji, ganza, garbage, gas, gash, gato, gauge, G.B., gear, gee, gee-fat, geeser, gee-yen, geezer, gelatin, gem, George smack, geronimo, ghanja, gho, ghost, ghow, giggles, giggle smoke, giggle weed, G.I. gin, gin, girl, girlfriend, girli, girly, gizzy, glad stuff, glass, glory seeds, glue, goblet of jam, God's flesh, God's medicine, go-fasters, goies, gold, gold bud, gold Colombian, gold Columbian, gold dust, golden girl, golden grain, golden leaf, goldfinger, gold leaf special, golpe, G.O.M., goma, goma de moto, gong, gonga, gonger, gongerine, good giggles, goodies, good old M., goods, good stuff, goody, goofball, goofer, goofers, goofy dust, goon, goon dust, go-pills, goric, gorilla biscuits, gorilla pills, gorilla tabs, gow, goynik, goynk, goznik, grads, gram, gramma, grape parfait, grass, grass weed, gray dust, greafa, greapha, grease, great tobacco, Greece, greefa, greefo, green, green and blacks, green and clears, green angelfish, green ashes, green bud, green caps, green dot, green double domes, green dragon, green goddess, green griff, green hornets, greenies, green meanies, green moroccan, green mud, green pill, green rot, greens, green single domes, green snow, green swirls, green tea, green wedge, greese, greeta, grefa, greta, grief, griefo, grifa, griffa, griffo, grifo, guaza, gulf, gum, guma, gumdrop, gum hashish, gum opium, gumps, gunga, gungeon, gunja, gunjah, gunji, gunk, gunny, gunpowder, guy, gyve, H., hache, hachich, hairy, half moons, hallucinogen, halvah, H. and C., happy dust, happy flakes, happy gas, happy grass, happy medicine, happy pills, happy powder, happy stuff, happy-time weed, hard candy, hard-cutting mezz, hard drugs, hard narcotics, hard stuff, Hardware, Harry, has, haschí, hash, hasheesh, hashí, hashish, hashish oil, hash oil, hatch, Hawaiian, Hawaiian pods, Hawaiian sunshine, hawk, hawk-25, hay, haze, Hazel, H-caps, head drug, headfucker, Heart On, hearts, heaven and hell, heaven dust, heaven flour, heavenly blue, heavenly dust, heavenly sunshine, heavies, heavy drugs, heavy hash, heavy joint, heavy narcotics, heavy soul, heavy stuff, heeltap, heesh, Helen, hell dust, helpers, hemp, Henry, her, herb, herbs, hercules, herms, hero, hero-gin, heroin, heroina, heroin buzz, heron, hero of the underworld, hi-ball, Hi Baller, high-fi, high hat, hike, hikori, hikuli, him, H.M.C., hock-for, hocus, Hoffmann's bicycle, hog, hog foot, hog tranquilizer, hokus, hombrecitos, home-grown, honey oil, hong-yen, hooch, hook, hooter, hop, hops, horror drug, hors d'oeuvres, horse, horse heads, horse hearts, horseradish, horse trank, horse tranquilizer, hoska, hospital heroin, hot hay, hotstick, hot stuff, housewife's delight, H.R.N., huatari, hunk, Hycodan, hyke, ibogaine, ice, ice bag, iceberg, ice cream, ice pack, icicles, idiotic, idiot juice, idiot pills, Illinois green, inbetweens, Inca message, incense, incentive, India, Indian, Indian hay, Indian hemp, Indian oil, Indian rope, Indian weed, indico charras, inhalant, inhaler, initiative, instant Zen, isda, items, ixey, J., JacAroma, jack, jacket, jack-ups, jahooby, jaloney, jam, Jamaica ganga, Jamaica gold, Jamaican, Jamaican red, jam Cecil, Jane, jay, jazz, jeegee, jelly babies, jelly beans, jerez seco, Jersey green, Jersey hemp, jesca, jet, jet fuel, jimson weed, jingo, jive, jockey, jocky, johnson, Johnson grass, joint, jojee, jolly beans, jones, joy, joy dust, joy flakes, joy hemp, joy-juice, joy powder, joy root, joy smoke, joy weed, 'juana, Juana, juane, juanita, juanita weed, Juan Valdez, juice, juice and beans, ju-ju, juju, jungle drug, junk, K., kabayo, kaffir tobacco, kaif, kaka, Kansas grass, kaps, kat, Kaui, Kaui electric, K-blast, kee, keef, keeler, kef, keff, keif, Ken doll, ken-koy, Kentucky blue, ketamine, key, khat, khif, khutchu string, ki, kidstuff, kief, kif, killer weed, kingdom weed, King Kong pills, King Kong special, K.J., knockout drops, K.O., Kona coast gold, Kona gold, Kona Kona, kools, krystal joint, K.W., L., L.A., la amarilla, la cosa, La Dama Blanca, la duna, lady, lady in white, Lady Snow, Lady White, lakbay diwa, lambsbread, las mujercitas, lason sa daga, L.A. turnabouts, L.A. turnarounds, laudanum, laughing gas, laughing grass, laughing tobacco, laughing weed, lawn, lay-back, L.B.J., L.D.J., leaf, leaf gum, leaf hop, leaper, leather dew, leaves, Lebanese, Lebanese hash, Lebanese red, Lebanon red, leb hash, leeper, legume, lem-kee, leño, leños, lent, leper grass, let sunshine do, lettuce, lettuce opium, lhesca, Librium, lid-poppers, lid-proppers, lift pills, light green, lightning, lightning hashish, light stuff, lillys, limbo, lime acid, line, lint, Lipton's, Lipton's Tea, Lipton Tea, liquid bam, liquid grass, liquid hashish, little children, little-D., li-un, Li Young, li-yuen, L.L., llesca, lobo, Loc-A-Roma, Locker Popper, Locker Room, loco, locoweed, locus, locust, loo foo kee, lords, lorphs, los niños, love, love affair, love blow, love drug, love saves, love weed, love wood, lozerose, lozies, L.s, L.S.D., lubange, Lucy in the Sky with Diamonds, ludens, ludes, 'ludes, ludins, luds, luggage, lum, lumbo, Luminal, lums, lunch hour trip, lysergic acid, lysergide, M., mach, machinery, Machu Picchu, macoha, macon, maconha, MAD, M.A.D., maggie, magic, magic flake, magic mushrooms, magic pumpkin, maharishee, mahoska, ma-jen, majonda, majoon, majoun, mala hierba, male, Mama coca, M. and C., M and Ms, mandrakes, Mandrax, mandrix, Manhattan silver, Manhattan white, maní, manicure, manteca, manzoul, maran guango, marathons, marbles, margarita, margie-wanna, mari, mariahuana, Maria Johanna, marigold, mariguana, marihuana, Marijane, marijuana, mariweegee, Marjie, Marjorie, Marmon and Cadillac, marshmallow reds, Mary, Mary and Johnnie, Mary Ann, Mary Anner, Mary J., Mary Jane, Maryjane, Mary Johnas, Mary Jones, Mary Juanas, Mary Owsley, Mary Warmer, Mary Warner, Mary Weaver, Mary Werner, Mary Worner, mash Allah, matsakaw, Maud C., Maui, Maui Waui, Maui wowee, Maui wowie, mayo, ma-yo, mazra, M.C., McCoy, M.D.A., M.D.M.A., mean green, mecel, medicine, meg, Megg, meggs, mejambrea, mejorana, Mellow Drug of America, mellow-yellow, melter, meperdine, meprobamate, meps, merchandise, merck, merk, mesc, mescal, mescal bean, mescal button, mescalina, mescaline, mescalito, met, metanfetamina, meth, methadone, methamphetamine, methaqualone, Methedrine, Mex, Mexican, Mexican brown, Mexican bush, Mexican green, Mexican horse, Mexican jumping beans, Mexican locoweed, Mexican mud, Mexican mushrooms, Mexican red, Mexican tumbleweed, Mez, mezz, Michael, Michoacan, mickey, Mickey Finn, Mickey Flynn, mickey mouse, micky, microdot, midnight oil, mighty mezz, mighty Quinn, mike, Miltown, mind-bender, mind-blower, mind-detergent, mind-expander, mind-explorer, mind-opener, mind-spacer, mind-tripper, minibennies, Minnesota green, minstrels, mint leaf, mint weed, Mishwacan, Miss Emma, Miss Morph, mist, mister blue, M.J., mo, M.O., modams, moggles, mohasky, mohasty, mohoska, mojo, molly, monkey, monkey bait, monkey dust, monkey-medicine, monkey morphine, Monroe in a Cadillac, monster, monster weed, monte, moocah, mooch, mood altering drug, mood drug, moon, moon beams, mooster, moota, mootah, mooter, mootie, moragrifa, morals, more, morenas, morf, morfina, morning glory seeds, morotgara, morph, morphema, morphi, morphia, morphie, morphina, morphine, morphinum, morpho, morphy, morshtop, moscop, mosquitoes, mota, mother, motherdear, mother nature, mother nature's, mother nature's own tobacco, mother's little helper, M.P.T.P., M.S., M. sul., mu, mud, mud-bud, muggles, munsh, murder weed, muscle relaxer, mushrooms, musta, muta, mutah, mutha, muzzle, N., nalga angelical, nalga de angel, Nam black, Nam shit, Nam weed, narc, narco, narcotic, narky, nasties, neb, nebbies, needle candy, negrillos, nem, nemb, nembies, Nembutal, nemish, nemishes, nemmie, Nepalese hash, new acid, new magic, New York City Silver, New York City white, New York white, Nicotiana glauca, nicotine, niebla, nieve, nigger minstrels, nimbie, nimbles, nimby, nitrous, Nixon, njemu, noble princess of the waters, noble weed, nocks, noise, nose, nose candy, nose powder, nose stuff, N.s, nuggets, number eight, number thirteen, number three, nurse, O., Oaxacan, ogoy, oil, O.J., old lady White, old Madge, old Steve, old white lady, ololiuqui, one-hit grass, one on one, one-toke weed, one-way, op, ope, opiate, opiated hash, opium, opium of the poor, Optimil, orange, orange crystal, orange cube, orange cupcakes, orange micro, orange mushrooms, orange Owsley, orange sunshine, orange wafers, orange wedges, orégano, orégano chino, osley, outer, over and unders, Owsley, Owsley acid, Owsley blue dot, Owsley blues, Owsley power, Owsley purple, Owsleys, Owsley's stuff, oye, OZ, ozone, ozzy, P., pa'abajos, pa'arribas, paisley caps, pájaro azul, pakalolo, Pakistani hash, Panama, Panama gold, Panamanian gold, Panamanian red, Panama red, pangonadalot, pan-juice, Pantopon, pan-yen, paper acid, pap pills, paradise, paralyzing grass, Parest, Park Lane, Park Lane No. 2, parsley, pasto, pat, pato de gayina, paz, P.B.Z., P.C.P., PCPA, peace, peace pills, peace tab, peace tablet, peace weed, peaches, peanuts, pearls, pearly cakes, pearly gates, pearly whites, pee, peep, pekoe, pellet, pellicle, pen-yang, pen-yen, pen-yuen, pep-em-ups, peppermint swirl, pepper-uppers, pep pills, peps, Percodan, perico, perks, perls, Persian brown, Persian dust, Peruvian flake, peter, peter drops, petes, petrifying stuff, peyote, peyote button, peyotl, pfun, P.G., phencyclidine, phenies, phennies, phenobarb, phenobarbital, phenos, phy, piece, pig killer, pig tranquilizer, píldora de fuerza, píldora de paz, pill, pillow, pimp dust, pink, pink and greens, pink dots, pink ladies, pink Owsley, pink ozzy, pinks, pink swirl, pink wafers, pink wedges, pink witches, pins and needles, pin-yen, pinyon, pizza, plac, placidolls, Placidyl, plants, plass, Pleiku pink, P.O., pod, pogo pogo, poison, poison mushrooms, polboron, polillo, pol-pot, polvito, polvo, polvo de ángel, poor man's cocaine, pop, popo oro, poppy, poppy tea, poppy train, pot, potaguaya, potiguaya, pot likker, pot liquor, potted bush, powder, powdered diamond, powdered joy, pox, P.R., prels, Preludin, prescription reds, prescriptions, Proctor and Gamble, product IV, propper, P.S., psilocybin, P-stuff, psyl, puerco, puffy, pukalolo, pula, pumpkin seed, puna butter, punk, punk pills, punta roja, pure, pure love, purple, purple barrels, purple dot, purple dragon, purple flats, purple haze, purple hearts, purple microdots, purple Owsley, purple ozolin, purple ozoline, purple ozzy, purple passion, purple wedges, pushing Emma, puti, Pyribenzamine, Q., Q.s, quaal, Quaalude, quacks, quads, quarter moon, quartet, quas, quicksilver, racehorse Charley, Raggedy Ann, ragweed, railroad weed, rainbow roll, rainbows, rainy-day woman, rama, rangoon, R.D., red, red and blues, red angelfish, redbirds, redbud, red bullets, red chicken, red cross, red cross M., red devils, red dimple, red dirt marijuana, red dolls, red dot, red dragon, red gunyon, red jackets, red leb, red Lebanese, red lillys, red oil, red rock, reds, red-smoker, reef, reefer, reefer weed, reg, reindeer dust, resin, resting-powder, rhythms, Rice Krispies, righteous acid, righteous bush, rippers, Ritalin, rits, roach, road dope, robe, robin eggs, robo, Roche tens, rock, rock candy, rocket fuel, rocks, rojas, rojita, roll of reds, Rooster Brand, root, rope, Rosa Maria, rosas, roses, rough stuff, round head, royal blue, rubia de la costa, Rush, sacate, sacrament, sacred mushrooms, sage, salt, salt and pepper, saltos mortales, sam-lo, Sandoz, san-lo, San Pedro, Santa Marta gold, Santa Marta red, sassafrass, Satan's

Scent, sativa, sawi, scag, scar, scat, schlects, schlock, schmack, schmeck, schmecken, schmee, schmeek, schoolboy, scissors, score, scot, Scott, scours, scrubwoman's kick, scuffle, sea, sealed stuff, sealing wax, sec, seccies, seccy, secky, Seconal, secs, seeds, seggies, seggy, seni, sense, sense bud, serenity, Sernylan, sess, set, sets, seven-fourteens, sex, sex-juice, shake, sheets, sherm, sherman, shesha, shishi, shit, shmack, shmeck, shmee, shong-nie, Shotgun, shpleef, shrooms, shuzzit, sid, sidney, silk and satin, silly putty, silo, simple Simon, sin, sinse, sinsemilla, sister, sizzle, skag, skamas, skee, skid, skinny, skuffle, skunk, sky river, skyrockets, sleepers, sleeping pills, sleighride, slobbering shit, slobbering stuff, slum, slumber medicine, slumber party, smack, smak, smash, smeak, smears, smeck, smizz, smoke, snap, snapper, sniff, snop, snorts, snow, snowball, snow-caine, snowflakes, snow stuff, soap, soapers, soaps, softballs, soft drugs, soles, soma, something for one's head, soñadora, son-lo, son of one, sook-nie, sope, sophisticated lady, Sopor, sound, spangles, spansula, sparkle plenties, sparkler, speckled birds, speckled eggs, speed, speedball, speed demon, speeder, splash, splay, spleef, spliff, splim, splits, splivins, spores, squirrel, squirrel dew, Stanley's stuff, stardust, star stuff, stash, stinkweed, stoms, stone soup, stony bush, stoppers, S.T.P., straw, strawberries, strawberry, strawberry fields, strawberry flats, street drug, stud, stufa, stuka, stum, stumble-bumbles, stumblers, stumbles, stums, stupefying grass, subway silver, sucker weed, suckonal, suede, suey, sugar, sugar cube, sugar lump, sugar lump cubes, sugar weed, summer skies, sunflower seeds, sunshine, sunshine acid, sunshine pill, super, superblow, super-C., supergrass, superjoint, superpot, super-Quaalude, super-soaper, super-soper, superweed, super yerba, suprema verde de clorafila, suprema verde de mejorana, supremo, surfer, sweeties, sweet Jesus, sweet Lucy, sweet lunch, sweet Mary, sweet Morpheus, sweets, sweet stuff, Swiss purple, syndicate acid, synthetic grass, synthetic heroin, synthetic marijuana, synthetic T.H.C., syrup, T., tab, tac, talc, Talwin, tampi, tangerine, tar, T-buzz, té, tea, tecaba, tecata, Teddies and Betties, Teddy party, tee, tens, terp, Terpin Hydrate, tetrahydrocannabinol, Texas, Texas tea, Thai pot, Thaistick, Thai-weed, T.H.C., the animal, the beast, the chief, the cube, the D.A., The Dread Weed, the ghost, the gong, the hawk, the herb, the leaf, the Mezz, the mighty mezz, the needle, The One, the robe, the smoke, the ticket, the weed, thing, thirteen, threes, thrill-pills, thrusters, thrusts, thunder weed, tic, tich, tick, ticket, tic-tac, tinik, tish, titch, T.M.A., T.N.T., Toilet Water, toluene, tooeys, tooies, tooles, toolies, toot, tootonium, tootsie, tootuncommon, top, topi, tops, tops and bottoms, tosca, tostada, tragic-magic, trained nurse, trancs, tranks, tranquility, tranquilizer, tranx, travel agent, treacle, tree of knowledge, trees, triangle stuff, tric, tric acid, tricycles and bicycles, trip grass, triple line, trips, trip weed, truck drivers, truckers, trueno verde, trues, T.s, T.s and blues, T-stick, T-tabs, tuies, Tuinal, Turk dope, turnabouts, turnip greens, turps, tus, twang, twat teaser, twenty-five, twos, two-toke, two-way, Tylenol, uffi, uhffi, ums, Uncle Emil, uncut, unkie, upjohns, upper, uppers, uppies, up-pot, ups, uptown, utopiates, V., Valium, vals, vees, velocidad, verdosas, Vermont green, Veronal, viaje, vials, viper's weed, vodka acid, vonce, vongony, vons, wack, wacky-tabbacky, wacky-weed, wafer, wahegan, wake up, wakowi, wallbanger, wana, wangula, water, W.C., wedding bells, wedding bells acid, wedge, wedges, wedgies, weed, weed marijuana, weed tea, wen-chee, West-Coast turnarounds, whack, wheat, whiff, whiskey root, white, white angel, white birds, white cross, white domes, white double domes, white drugs, white dust, white girl, white goddess, white horse, white junk, white lady, white lightning, white merchandise, white mosquitoes, white nurse, white Owsley, white Owslies, white powder, whites, white Sandoz, white silk, white single domes, white stuff, white tornado, white whiskey, whities, whiz-bang, widow, wild geronimo, wildweed, windowpane, windowpane acid, wings, witch, witches brew, witch hazel, wobble weed, wokowi, wolf, worm, yage, yakenal, yam-yam, yanga, yedo, yellow, yellow angels, yellow bams, yellow birds, yellow bullets, yellow caps, yellow dimple, yellow dolls, yellow dots, yellow dust, yellow footballs, yellow jackets, yellows, yellow sunshine, yemtzem, yen, yen-chee, yen-pock, yen-pok, yen-pook, yen-pop, yen-shee, yerba, yerba buena, yerba del diablo, yerba del pasmo, yerba mala, yesca, yessa, yet-lo, yet-low, yocky-dock, yohimbe, you know, yukenal, zacate, Zacatecas purple, zacate ingles, zamal, Zen, zings, Z.N.A., zol, zoll, zombie buzz, zoom, zooms, 13, 25, 3, 40s, 50, 714s, 8. 2. to take drugs; to drug a horse. [(1868): MW: 1983, (1890): DSUE, JRW: 1909, BVB: 1942] 3. marijuana; heroin. A specialization of sense one. In some circles, *dope* is the word-of-choice for marijuana. [U.S., S&W: 1966, YKB: 1977, JH: 1979, NIDA: 1980]

dope addict a person addict to a drug. RT: *junky*. [(1933): OEDS]

dope booster (also **drug booster**) a dope seller; a drug pusher who creates addict-customers. RS: *dealer*. Not narcotics argot. [U.S., BVB: 1942, A&T: 1953] See also *booster*.

dope cigarette a marijuana cigarette. *Dope* (*q.v.*) = marijuana. RT: *joint*. [U.S., BR: 1972]

dope copper (also **dope arm, dope cop, dope bull**) a federal narcotics officer. RS: *fuzz*. [U.S., BVB: 1953, JES: 1959]

dope daddy (also **dope man**) a dope peddler, pusher, or seller. RS: *dealer*. [U.S., HB: 1955]

doped cigarette a marijuana cigarette; a tobacco cigarette with marijuana added to it. RS: *joint*. [U.S., (1939): ELA: 1982]

dope den an opium den; any place where any drug is consumed communally. RT: *opium den, pad*. Not narcotics argot. [U.S., BVB: 1942, VJM: 1949, D&D: 1957]

doped up (also **doped, dopey, dopie, dopy**) under the effects of narcotics, marijuana, or stimulants. Also used colloquially for being made groggy by any medication. Dopey since 1896 (OEDS). RT: *stoned.* [U.S., GI: 1931, BD: 1937, VJM: 1949, W&F: 1960, H&C: 1975]

dope fiend an addict who injects narcotics; a drug user; an addict who commits violent crimes to support a drug habit. Not originally narcotics argot although there is some use in the drug culture. See *fiend.* Maurer (DWM: 1938) stated that "dope" was almost taboo with narcotics addicts. He says further (M&V: 1973) that the term dope "...like dope fiend, tends to be taboo among addicts, though they use it pejoratively." DEM: 1981 claims of dope fiend: "often used by addicts to refer to themselves." [(1896): OEDS, BD: 1937, DWM: 1938, D&D: 1957, RRL: 1969, EEL: 1971, DES: 1972, MA: 1973]

dope fighter an addict trying to break a drug habit. *Cf. booze fighter.* [U.S., BVB: 1942, JES: 1959]

dope gun a hypodermic syringe; a medicine dropper with a hypodermic needle attached. RT: *monkey pump.* [U.S., BVB: 1942, JES: 1959]

dopehead (also **dopester, dopster**) a drug user or addict; a marijuana smoker. See list at *head.* GU: 1975 attests only *dopehead.* RT: *junky.* [U.S., (1938): OEDS, BVB: 1942, D&D: 1957, GU: 1975]

dopeheaded (also **dope hopped**) addicted to a narcotic. RT: *hooked.* [U.S., JES: 1959, H&C: 1975]

dope hop 1. a prison term for a drug related charge. [U.S., DWM: 1938] 2. a narcotics addict. RT: *junky.* [U.S., BVB: 1942] 3. a state of drug euphoria. [U.S., BVB: 1942, A&T: 1953]

dope jag (also **dope jagg**) a period of intoxication or euphoria induced by drugs. *Cf. jag.* [U.S., BVB: 1942, A&T: 1953]

dope man a drug seller. RT: *dealer.* [U.S., ADC: 1975]

dopenik a drug user or addict. RT: *junky, user.* Patterned on Russian *sputnik.* [U.S., W&F: 1975, RDS: 1982]

dope peddler a drug seller or pusher. *Cf. peddler.* RT: *dealer.* The term is widely known throughout the U.S. [U.S., (1923): OEDS, GI: 1931, BVB: 1942, D&D: 1957]

dope pimp a dope dealer who introduces people to drug use thereby creating new customers. *Cf. missionary.* RS: *dealer.* [U.S., JES: 1959, H&C: 1975]

dope pipe a pipe for smoking hashish or marijuana. RS: *bong.* [U.S., (1970): ELA: 1982]

dope-pop Possibly an error for *dope hop* (*q.v.*). [BD: 1937]

doper 1. a confirmed drug user; a drug addict; a marijuana smoker. RT: *junky, toker.* [U.S., (c. 1910): JES: 1959, GI: 1931, BVB: 1942, D&B: 1970c, EEL: 1971, W&F: 1975, ADC: 1981] 2. a drug seller; a drug runner. RS: *mule.* [U.S., MW: 1934]

dope racket the illegal narcotics business; drug trade. *Cf. connection.* [U.S., BVB: 1942, JES: 1959]

doperie a place where addicts can buy and use drugs. Contrived slang, not drug argot. See *pad.* [U.S., BVB: 1942, JES: 1959, HSD: 1984] Nicknames and slang terms for a place where one or more drugs can be bought and used: *black spot, candy bar, C-joint, club, coke joint, coke oven, cotickery, creeper joint, crib, doperie, dream boat, Dutch mill, feed store, freak house, gallery, gow cellar, grease pit, grogshop, hash house, hashish bar, hashish house, H-joint, hop joint, house, jab joint, joss house, locust point, marijuana bar, M-joint, mooch joint, opium den, pad, pad room, pill pad, poppy grove, powder room, psychedeli, psychedelicatessen, rifle range, scatter, setting, smoke joint, snowbank, splash house, splash parlor, Steve's mission, suey bowl, tea pad.*

dope ring an underworld organization involved in the wholesaling and retailing of drugs. *Cf. connection.* [U.S., (1929): OEDS, BVB: 1942, D&D: 1957]

dope run an excursion for the purchase of drugs. [U.S., RRL: 1974, RDS: 1982]

dope runner a drug seller. Patterned on *rum runner* (*q.v.*). RT: *dealer.* [U.S., (1933): OEDS, BVB: 1942, RDS: 1982]

dope smoke a marijuana smoke, a *dagga* (*q.v.*) smoke. RT: *toke.* Not listed in JB: 1980. [South African, late 18-1900s, DU]

dopester See *dopehead.*

dope stick 1. a tobacco cigarette. RT: *nail.* [(1918): OEDS, BVB: 1942, VJM: 1949, W&F: 1960] 2. a marijuana cigarette. Probably an error for sense one. [DUS] 3. a stick used to hold powdered narcotics being sniffed (snorted). *Cf. cokespoon.* [U.S., MHW: 1934, BVB: 1942]

dope up 1. to inject drugs; to take a dose of a narcotic; to use drugs habitually. [U.S., BVB: 1942, H&C: 1975] 2. to purchase a dose or a supply of drugs. RS: *score.* [U.S., JES: 1959, H&C: 1975]

dopey See *doped up.*

dopium opium. RT: *opium.* Not drug argot but "journalistic fantasy" (DU). [U.S., BVB: 1942, RDS: 1982]

dopster a drug user or addict. See *dopehead.*

doradilla* marijuana. A Spanish term for a type of fern. RT: *pot.* [calo, JBR: 1973]

Doriden a protected trade name for glutethimide (nonbarbiturate hypnotic) tablets and capsules. The drug is a central nervous system depressant. Slang and jargon terms for Doriden are usually based on the first syllable of the drug name. RT: *dories.* See *barbs* for a list of depressants. [in current use; consult a pharmaceutical reference for more information]

dories (also doors, dors) *Doriden* (TM; *q.v.*) sedative in any form.

[U.S., JWK: 1981] Nicknames and slang terms for Doriden: *C., C.B., ciba, D., doors, dories, dors.*

do-right a trustworthy drug seller. The term refers to anyone who treats people fairly. RS: *dealer.* [U.S., JH: 1979]

do-right Johns (also **do-right people**) nonaddicts. GEN: people who usually obey the law. [U.S., DWM: 1938, A&T: 1953]

dors *Doriden* (*q.v.*). See *doors, dories.*

dose a helping or portion of liquor or drugs. GEN: a specific quantity of a drug. Standard English. [since the mid 1800s, (1850): DSUE, JES: 1959] The following list includes terms for dose size measures of drugs. See *nip* for terms for individual drinks of alcohol. *ace, acid cube, am-dray, amps, ampule, autograph, back, bag, bang, bang in the arm, belt, bindle, bing, bingo, biz, block, blotter, blow, bolus, bomb, bombida, bombita, booster, boot shot, bop, brush, bullet, bump, button, Cadillac, can, cap, carga, charge, check, cold shot, constitutional, courage pill, cube, cup, cura, D.D., deck, deuce, deuceways, dip, dose, double-narky, dram, drop, eye-opener, feed bag, fix, fix-up, foil, front, fun, geeser, geez, geeze, geezer, get-up, glass, go, G-shot, half a tenth, hit, hocus, hunk, hype, hype shot, hype skin shot, hypo, items, jab, jab job, jab-off, jab-pop, jab-poppo, jack, jack off shot, jag, jell, jimmy, job, job off, joint, joke, jolly pop, jolt, joy pop, joy prick, jug, kick, kite, lay, line shot, load, mainline bang, make, morning glory, morning shot, muscle pop, needle, nose hit, paper, penitentiary shot, pen shot, pickup, piece, piggie, pill, pinch, ping in the wing, ping in wing, ping shot, ping-wing, pin shot, pleasure jolt, point shot, poke, pop, poppy pill, prod, prop, rack, rails, rare, rations, rip, shoot, shooter, shoot-up, short, short beer, short go, short order, short piece, short snort, shot, shot in the arm, shunt shot, skinner, skin pop, skin shot, snapper, sniff, snoodge, snooze, snort, snort of horse, speedball, S.S., strike, swallow hit, taste, toak, toat, toke, Tom, Tom Mix, toot, tote, twat teaser, twister, vein shot, verification shot, V.S., waker-upper, wake up, X., zoomar.*

do some stewing drink some beer. *Cf. stew.* RT: *irrigate.* [U.S., ADC: 1984]

dossing sleeping after narcotics use; sleeping off drugs. Doss = sleep. [U.S., CM: 1970, RDS: 1982]

dot to place a small (liquid) dose of L.S.D. on each unit of dosage medium, i.e., square of blotter, sheet of gelatin, tablet, sugar cube, animal, cracker, etc. See *dots* for a list of other doses. [U.S., (IGA: 1971), RDS: 1982]

do the honors to light up the communal cannabis pipe or cigarette. [U.S., D&B: 1978]

dots the hallucinogenic drug *L.S.D.* (*q.v.*) placed on paper or pills. From *microdots* (*q.v.*). *Cf. blue dot, brown dots, green dot, Owsley blue dot, purple dot, purple microdots.* RT: *L.S.D.*

[U.S., H&C: 1975, YKB: 1977, ADC: 1981]

dottle a burnt or half-burnt plug of tobacco in a pipe. Cf. *dottle, golleroy, old dog, topper*. [since the early 1800s, (1925): OED]

double an alcoholic drink with a double portion of liquor. RS: *nip*. [U.S., D&D: 1957, W&F: 1960]

double-blue a capsule of *Amytal* (TM; *q.v.*), a barbiturate. May also apply to other blue tablets or capsules. RT: *blue*. [Br., BTD: 1968, M&J: 1975]

double-crosses amphetamine tablets; cross-scored amphetamine tablets; amphetamines in general. *Cf. Catholic aspirin, cris, cristian* for the religious theme. *Cf. cartwheel, crossroads, cross tops* for the cross-marking theme. RT: *amps*. [U.S., IGA: 1971, YKB: 1977]

doubled up alcohol intoxicated. An elaboration of *bent* (*q.v.*). RT: *drunk*. [U.S., BVB: 1942]

double-headed alcohol intoxicated. RT: *drunk*. [U.S., BVB: 1942, H&C: 1975]

double-header two marijuana cigarettes smoked at once. [U.S., M&V: 1954]

double-narky a double dose of drugs. RS: *dose*. [U.S., D&D: 1957, JES: 1959]

double-tongued alcohol intoxicated. (BF: 1737: [He's] Double Tongu'd.) Refers to the slurred speech of the drinker. RT: *drunk*. [BF: 1737]

double-trouble *Tuinal* (TM; *q.v.*) barbiturate; any barbiturate. The drug is a combination of *Seconal* (TM; *q.v.*) and *Amytal* (TM; *q.v.*). RT: *tooies*. [U.S., TRG: 1968, RRL: 1969, EEL: 1971, YKB: 1977]

douche to inject a narcotic. Refers to a vaginal douche. RT: *shoot*. [U.S., JES: 1959, H&C: 1975]

douche, on the injecting drugs; accustomed to taking drugs by injection. [U.S., JES: 1959]

doup possibly an error for *do up* (*q.v.*). [JBW: 1967, IGA: 1971]

do up 1. to prepare one's arm for an injection by placing a tourniquet on it. [U.S., RRL: 1969, CM: 1970, EEL: 1971] 2. to inject a drug; to smoke a marijuana cigarette. [U.S., TRG: 1968, EEL: 1971, DCCU: 1972, W&F: 1975, ADC: 1981]

douse the lamp to ejaculate during a sexual dream in an opium stupor. As if to extinguish the opium lamp. [U.S., JES: 1959]

down 1. alcohol intoxicated. RT: *drunk*. [Br., 1800s, F&H] 2. (also down one) to drink down. GEN: to swallow food or drink. [(1922): OEDS, W&F: 1960, EE: 1976] 3. beer; inferior beer. RS: *beer, queer-beer*. [U.S., 1800s, F&H, BVB: 1942] 4. (also downer, downie, downs) a barbiturate or a tranquilizer. RT: *barbs, tranks*. [U.S., RB: 1967, RRL: 1969, D&B: 1970c, DCCU: 1972, DNE:

1973, W&F: 1975, MW: 1976, YKB: 1977, EAF: 1980, NIDA: 1980, ADC: 1981; Br. M&J: 1975] 5. to take drugs orally; to take barbiturates or tranquilizers. Akin to sense two. [U.S., D&B: 1970c, EEL: 1971, ADC: 1975, DNE: 1980] 6. depressed, suffering the after effects of drug-taking. [U.S., JES: 1959, G&B: 1969, H&C: 1975, D&B: 1978, ADC: 1981] 7. imitation whiskey. Probably from *hen down* = dung. RS: *rotgut*. [U.S., RDS: 1982]

down among the dead men alcohol intoxicated; dead drunk. *Cf. dead man*. RT: *drunk*. [Br., (1853): DSUE]

downer 1. (also **down, downie**) a barbiturate or a tranquilizer. From the depressant nature of these drugs. The same as *down* (sense four). RT: *barbs, tranks*. [RRL: 1969, D&B: 1970c, BR: 1972, DCCU: 1972, DNE: 1973, W&F: 1975, MW: 1976, YKB: 1977, EAF: 1980, NIDA: 1980, ADC: 1981, HSD: 1984] See also *upper*. 2. a bad drug experience, especially with *L.S.D.* (*q.v.*). Now generalized as a slang or colloquial expression for any unpleasant experience or state. RS: *bad trip*. [U.S., EEL: 1971, ADC: 1981]

downer freak a user of barbiturates, sedatives, and tranquilizers. *Cf. downer*. RS: *user*. [U.S., C&H: 1974]

down to the cotton having to do with a hard-up addict; an addict who cannot buy drugs and must rely on used straining cotton. *Cf. ask for cotton*. [U.S., VFN: 1933, MHW: 1934]

downtown heroin. The opposite of *uptown* = cocaine. RT: *heroin*. [U.S., ELA: 1984]

down trip a bad and depressing drug experience. *Cf. downer*. [U.S., RRL: 1969, D&B: 1970c, W&F: 1975]

down with barrel fever alcohol intoxicated. *Cf. barrel fever*. RT: *drunk*. [Br., 1800s, F&H]

down with the fish alcohol intoxicated; heavily saturated with alcohol. *Cf. fishy*. RT: *drunk*. [U.S., MHW: 1934, BVB: 1942]

Do you need a boy? "Do you have drugs for sale?" RT: *How are you going to act?* [U.S., M&D: 1952]

D.P.T. (also **DPT**) diphenyltryptamine, a hallucinogenic drug similar to *D.M.T.* (*q.v.*). [U.S., W&F: 1967, EEL: 1971]

drafty a draft beer; beer. RT: *beer*. [U.S., D&B: 1970c]

drag 1. a puff of a cigarette (tobacco or marijuana). RT: *toke*. [U.S., (1914): OEDS, WM: 1927, W&F: 1960, RRL: 1969, ADC: 1981] 2. a tobacco cigarette; a marijuana cigarette. RT: *nail, joint*. [U.S., BVB: 1942, W&F: 1960, ADC: 1981; listed in M&J: 1975] 3. to puff on a cigarette, tobacco or marijuana. [(1919): OEDS, D&B: 1978] 4. a bad drug experience; depression from barbiturates. GEN: anything dull or boring. RS: *bad trip*. [U.S., RRL: 1969, H&C: 1975]

dragged anxious or frightened after smoking marijuana. Compare to *wired*. See the fourth sense in the previous entry. *Cf. drug*.

[U.S., (1965): ELA: 1982, RRL: 1969, C&H: 1974]

dragon the hallucinogenic drug *L.S.D.* (*q.v.*). Probably from L.S.D. on small pieces of blotter stamped with the image of a dragon. *Cf. blue dragon, green dragon, purple dragon.* RT: *L.S.D.* [U.S., ADC: 1981]

drag weed marijuana. RT: *pot.* [U.S., VJM: 1949, A&T: 1953]

drain 1. beverage alcohol, especially gin because of its diuretic properties; a drink of liquor. RT: *gin, nip.* [FG: 1811, FG: 1823, (1835): F&H, JCH: 1887, B&L: 1890, BVB: 1942] 2. a drunkard. RT: *sot.* [U.S., BVB: 1942]

drain pipe (also **drainist**) a drunkard. RT: *sot.* [Br., 1800s, F&H; listed in BVB: 1942]

dram 1. liquor; a drink of liquor. RT: *nip.* [FG: 1785, FG: 1823, F&H, BWG: 1899] 2. whiskey. RT: *whiskey.* [U.S., LWP: 1908] 3. to ply with alcohol; to get someone drunk; to tipple. RS: *irrigate.* [U.S., BWG: 1899] 4. an eighth of an ounce of a drug. RS: *load.* [U.S., BD: 1937]

dramster (also **drammer**) a drunkard. *Cf. dram.* RT: *sot.* [Br., 1800s, F&H]

draped alcohol intoxicated. *Cf. ale draper.* RT: *drunk.* [Br., (1939): DSUE]

draper a bartender, an *ale draper* (*q.v.*). RT: *bartender.* [FG: 1785, FG: 1823]

draw a blank to get drunk; to be drunk. GEN: to get no answer; to come up with nothing. RS: *mug oneself.* [U.S., MHW: 1934, BVB: 1942] See also *blank.*

Dr. Bananas a "brand name" for *amyl nitrite* (*q.v.*). RT: *snapper.* [U.S., ELA: 1984]

Dread Weed, The marijuana. RT: *pot.* [U.S., (1972): R&P: 1982]

dream 1. (also **dreams, dream stuff**) opiates: opium, morphine, depressants; edible opium pellets. Refers to opium in *dream beads, dream gum, dreams, dream wax.* [U.S., PRB: 1930, MHW: 1934, GOL: 1950, EEL: 1971, JH: 1979] 2. cocaine. RT: *cocaine.* [U.S., YKB: 1977, NIDA: 1980]

dream beads (also **dream gum, dream wax**) opium; opium pellets. RT: *opium.* [U.S., PRB: 1930, VJM: 1949, GOL: 1950, W&F: 1967]

dream boat a drug dealer's establishment. Based on *dream* (*q.v.*). *Cf. candy bar, coke joint, doperie, hash house, powder room, rifle range, snowbank.* RS: *doperie.* [U.S., JES: 1959, H&C: 1975]

dream book a book of cigarette rolling papers. Refers only to tobacco use. RT: *paper.* [U.S., RFA]

dreamer 1. a depressant drug: opium, morphine, sedatives, barbiturates, or tranquilizers. *Cf. dream.* [U.S., RRL: 1969,

IGA: 1971] 2. an opium or morphine addict. RS: *junky*. [U.S., JES: 1959, EEL: 1971, RDS: 1982]

dream gum (also **dream wax**) opium. See *dream beads*. RT: *opium*. [U.S., HNR: 1934, VJM: 1949, GOL: 1950]

dream pipe an opium pipe. *Cf. dream*. RT: *hop stick*. [U.S., JES: 1959, H&C: 1975]

dreamstick 1. a tobacco cigarette. *Cf. dream book*. RT: *nail*. Not common (W&F: 1960). [U.S., BVB: 1953, W&F: 1960] 2. an opium pellet; opium. RT: *opium*. [U.S., W&F: 1960] 3. an opium pipe. RT: *hop stick*. [U.S., DWM: 1936, VJM: 1949] 4. marijuana; a marijuana cigarette. RT: *pot, joint*. [U.S., BVB: 1953, SNP: 1977] See also *stick*.

dream stuff narcotics. *Cf. stuff*. See *dream*. RS: *dope*. [U.S., JES: 1959, H&C: 1975]

dream wax See *dream beads*.

dreck dope; narcotics. *Cf. shit*. From German *dreck* = dregs, probably via Yiddish. RS: *dope*. [U.S., RAS: 1979]

drenched alcohol intoxicated. RT: *drunk*. [U.S., MHW: 1934, BVB: 1942]

drench the gizzard to drink to excess; to get drunk. RT: *irrigate, mug oneself*. [U.S., AH: 1931, MHW: 1934]

Dr. Hall (also **Doctor Hall**) liquor; a personification of alcohol. RT: *booze*. [U.S., BVB: 1942]

dried out (also **dried**) detoxified; no longer using drugs or alcohol. *Cf. clean, straight*. RT: *off*. [U.S., RRL: 1969, JTD: 1971, ADC: 1981]

drin *Benzedrine* (TM; *q.v.*). RT: *benz*. [HSD: 1984]

Drinamyl a British brand of an amphetamine and barbiturate compound. The same as U.S. *Dexamyl* (TM; *q.v.*). *Cf. purple hearts*. RS: *set*. [(1950): OEDS, BTD: 1968, RRL: 1969, ADC: 1981] Nicknames and slang terms for Drinamyl: *blueys, bluies, purple hearts, purple passion*.

drink 1. alcoholic drink; liquor. This has long been a standard English euphemism for alcohol. [since c. 1000, OED] 2. to tipple; to drink alcohol as a matter of habit or custom. RT: *irrigate*. Standard English. [since the 1400s, (1440): OED] 3. a drink. See *nip*. 4. to smoke tobacco. [since the late 1500s, (1598): OED; attested as U.S., early 1900s, ADD]

drinkative alcohol intoxicated. RT: *drunk*. [PD: 1982]

drinkatorium (also **drinkateria**) an establishment serving alcohol; a liquor store. RS: *bar, L.I.Q*. Contrived slang. [U.S., BVB: 1942]

drink den a bar; a drinking establishment. RT: *bar*. [U.S., M&W: 1946]

drinkery any drinking establishment. *Cf. imbibery*. RS: *bar*. [U.S., (1840): OED, BVB: 1942]

drink from the spigot to drink heavily; to go on a drinking bout; to drink liquor in quantity, directly from the barrel. RT: *guzzle*. [U.S., AH: 1931]

drink, in alcohol intoxicated. *Cf. in liquor*. RT: *drunk*. [since the 1500s (Shakespeare)]

drinkitite 1. an appetite for alcohol. [Br., (1864): DSUE, JRW: 1909] 2. a drunkard. RT: *sot*. This sense may be a misunderstanding of sense one, or simply an error. [U.S., MHW: 1934, BVB: 1942]

drink like a fish to drink heavily; to get drunk often. *Cf. down with the fish, fishy*. RT: *guzzle*. [(1640): OEDS, BVB: 1942]

drink like a funnel to drink heavily. RT: *guzzle*. [Br., 1800s, DSUE]

drink like a lord to drink heavily. *Cf. doing the lord, drunk as a lord*. RT: *guzzle*. [since the 1600s, DSUE]

drinkologist someone who sells and serves liquor at a bar. *Cf. mixologist*. RT: *bartender*. [U.S., D&D: 1957]

drink someone under the table to out-drink someone. The picture this expression paints is of two people engaged in drinking - drink for drink - until one person has had too much and slides beneath the table. RS: *guzzle*. [U.S., BVB: 1942]

drinkster a drunkard; a heavy drinker. RT: *sot*. [Br., 1800s, F&H; listed in BVB: 1942]

drink Texas tea to smoke marijuana. *Drink* (*q.v.*) = to smoke. *Texas tea* (*q.v.*) = marijuana. RT: *hit the hay*. [U.S., JES: 1959, H&C: 1975]

drinky alcohol intoxicated. RT: *drunk*. [Br., 18-1900s, (1846): OEDS]

drinkypoo a little drink of liquor. RT: *nip*. Mock-baby talk. [U.S., RAS: 1981]

dripper a medicine dropper with a hypodermic needle attached to the tip. This is often viewed as an improvised hypodermic syringe. It is often the preferred device for injecting drugs since it allows greater accuracy in controlling the input of the drug. See *back up*. *Cf. dingus, dropper, fake, fake-a-loo, spike and dripper*. RS: *monkey pump*. [U.S., (1926): ERH: 1982, BD: 1937, DWM: 1938, ADC: 1981]

dripping bummers the return from a cocaine experience. May refer to dripping sweat. See *bummer*. [U.S., ADC: 1981]

dripping tight alcohol intoxicated; very drunk. *Cf. tight*. RT: *drunk*. [Br., JM: 1923]

drive 1. the potency of the alcohol in liquor; the effect of potent alcohol. [U.S., BVB: 1942] See also *jolt* and *kick*. 2. the rush of euphoria after a narcotics injection. RS: *rush*. [U.S., GI: 1931, BD: 1937, DWM: 1938, BVB: 1942] 3. the power of a drug as pertains to the amount of time a given dose will sustain one's needs. *Cf. carry.* [U.S., M&V: 1967, H&C: 1975]

drivers amphetamine tablets or capsules. A truncation of *truck drivers* (*q.v.*). RT: *amps.* [U.S., EEL: 1971]

driving alki running liquor; bootlegging. From the prohibition era. [U.S., DWM: 1931, HNR: 1934]

dronkie (also **dronklap**) a drunkard; a heavy drinker. From Afrikaans. RT: *sot.* [South African, (1969): JB: 1980]

drop 1. (also **drops**) liquor, especially gin. In the sense of medicine drops. *Cf. took his drops.* RT: *booze.* [Br., (BE: 1690), DU] **2.** to take a drug dose orally; since c. 1962, to take the hallucinogenic drug *L.S.D.* (*q.v.*). *Cf. drop acid.* [U.S., GS: 1959, D&B: 1970c, DCCU: 1972, DNE: 1980, EAF: 1980, ADC: 1981] **3.** an oral dose of a drug. *Cf. hit.* RS: *dose.* [U.S., RDS: 1982] **4.** (also **drop-off, drop-off point**) a place to leave a purchase of drugs or liquor for pick-up by the purchaser; a place where drugs or liquor are hidden. *Cf. stash.* Not limited to drug argot. Ransom money or contraband of any type can be transferred at a **drop**. [U.S., (1931): DU, M&V: 1967, D&B: 1970c, RDS: 1982] **5.** to deliver drugs. [U.S., M&V: 1967]

drop a bop to take a drug in pill form. *Bop* (*q.v.*) = a dose or a pill. A synonym of *hit* (*q.v.*). [U.S., HER: 1971, DCCU: 1972]

drop acid to take a dose of the hallucinogenic drug *L.S.D.* (*q.v.*). *Acid* (*q.v.*) = L.S.D. This phrase has become known throughout the English speaking world. [U.S., D&B: 1970c, DCCU: 1972]

drop a dime to inform (the police) on someone. See explanation at *dime-dropper.* [U.S., RG: 1970, JHF: 1971, EAF: 1980, RDS: 1982]

drop a joint to smoke a marijuana cigarette. RT: *hit the hay.* [U.S., ELA: 1982]

drop a roll (also **drop a rack, pop a roll**) to take a variety of pills at one time, usually 3-5 pills. [U.S., EAF: 1980]

drop out to withdraw from conventional lifestyles and concentrate on introspection with drugs, especially the hallucinogenic drug *L.S.D.* (*q.v.*). [U.S., G&B: 1969, (1970): DNE: 1973, EEL: 1971]

dropped arrested on a drug related or other charge. RT: *busted.* [U.S., (DWM: 1935), M&H: 1959, TRG: 1968, S&W: 1973]

dropper 1. a medicine dropper with a hypodermic needle on its tip. See *dripper.* [U.S., DWM: 1936, RRL: 1969, D&B: 1970c, MA: 1973, ADC: 1981, JWK: 1981] **2.** a regular user of the hallucinogenic drug *L.S.D.* (*q.v.*). From *acid-dropper* (*q.v.*). *Cf. drop acid.* [U.S., RAS: 1981] **3.** a drunkard. RT: *sot.* [U.S., RDS: 1982]

drought a shortage of drugs in an area. Probably due to police suspicion or the arrest of a supplier. *Cf. dry spell, famine, panic.* [U.S., DCCU: 1972, (D&B: 1978)]

drowning the shamrock drinking to excess; *spreeing* (*q.v.*). Refers to Irish whisky. [(1888): F&H, (BVB: 1942)]

drown one's sorrows (also **drown one's troubles**) to drink; to drink to forget one's problems. RT: *guzzle, irrigate, mug oneself.* A widely known colloquial idiom. [U.S., MHW: 1934, BVB: 1942]

drudge whiskey; inferior whiskey. RS: *rotgut.* [U.S., JSF: 1889]

druffen alcohol intoxicated. RT: *drunk.* [Br., PW: 1974]

drug 1. a substance used in the diagnosis, treatment or prevention of disease; a substance used to produce a stupor or sleep; any substance, including L.S.D., marijuana, alcohol, nicotine, which is used primarily to produce stimulation, relaxation, hallucinations, or euphoria in the user. The first sense is standard English; the others are widely known colloquial. *Drug* replaced *narcotic* as the word-of-choice for substances abused by the underworld and drug culture. Whereas alcohol and nicotine are included under *drug*, they are seldom referred to individually as drugs. RT: *dope.* Standard English. [(1883): OEDS] 2. (also **drugg, drug out**) down, depressed, or doped. Probably a past tense or past participle of *drag.* There is no explanation for the form *drugg.* See *dragged.* [U.S., M&W: 1946, M&H: 1959, JWK: 1981] 3. to use drugs. [U.S., (1893): OEDS, BVB: 1942]

drug abuse criminal drug use; recreational drug use; use of drugs for a purpose other than what was intended by the manufacturer. Compare to *alcohol abuse.* Somewhat euphemistic. [(1970): OEDS, RDS: 1982]

drug booster a drug *pusher* (*q.v.*). *Cf. dope booster.* RT: *pusher.* [U.S., BVB: 1942, JES: 1959]

druggie (also **druggy**) a drug user; a drug experimenter; an addict. RT: *user.* [U.S., (1967): MW: 1983, (1968): DNE: 1973, RRL: 1969, W&F: 1975, ADC: 1981]

drugging taking drugs. Parallel to drinking. See *drug.* [U.S., 1900s, (BVB: 1942)]

drughead a heavy drug user. See list at *head.* RT: *user.* [U.S., W&F: 1975, RDS: 1982]

drug-of-choice the particular (or preferred) drug used by a drug addict or user. [U.S., (M&V: 1954), BW: 1984]

drug partisan a narcotic addict. RT: *junky.* Probably nonce. [U.S., JES: 1959]

drugs, on addicted; currently under the effects of a drug. RS: *hooked.* [U.S., DWM: 1936]

drugster a heavy drug user; a drug addict. RT: *user.* [U.S., (1970): DNE: 1973]

drugstore johnson an addiction to drugs normally used as medication; an addiction to a habit-forming medication such as codeine or morphine. Johnson = *jones* (*q.v.*), and both are slang terms for *thing.* [U.S., JWK: 1981]

drugstore man a male addict who steals narcotics from drugstores. [U.S., JWK: 1981]

drugstore stuff 1. drugs and narcotics which can be obtained at a drugstore; ethical drugs which are suitable for sustaining an addiction. [U.S., M&V: 1967, D&B: 1970c] 2. *Dilaudid* (TM; *q.v.*), probably Dilaudid (TM) cough syrup. RT: *dids*. [U.S., JWK: 1981]

drugstore whiskey alcohol bought by prescription during prohibition. RS: *whiskey*. [U.S., MHW: 1934]

drug up to take a large dose of drugs. [U.S., JES: 1959]

drum a low saloon, tavern, or pub. GWM: 1859 also lists break o' day drum, cross-drum, and flash drum (*q.v.*). RS: *bar*. [(1846): OEDS, GWM: 1859, F&H, DWM: 1935, VJM: 1949]

drunk 1. intoxicated with alcohol. Standard English. [(1340): OED] (This entry continues after the following list.) Terms for any degree of intoxication with alcohol: *a bit high, a bit lit, a bit on, a bit under, about drunk, about full, about gone, about had it, about half drunk, about right, about shot, about to cave in, about to go under, a-buzz, aced, activated, addled, adrip, afflicted, afloat, aglow, alcoholized, alecied, alight, alkeyed, alkeyed up, alkied, alkied up, alky-soaked, all at sea, all fucked up, all geezed up, all gone, all het up, all in, all keyhole, all mops and brooms, all out, all pink elephants, all schnozzled up, all there, all wet, almost froze, altogethery, among the Philistines, amuck, anchored in Sot's Bay, antifreezed, antiseptic, aped, a peg too low, arf arf an arf, arseholed, as good conditioned as a puppy, a sheet or two to the wind, at rest, awash, awry-eyed, Bacchi plenus, bagged, baked, ball-dozed, balmy, bamboozled, banged up to the eyes, banjaxed, baptized, barley sick, barmy, barreled, barreled up, barrelhouse drunk, bashed, basted, bats, batted, battered, batty, beargered, bearing the ensign, been among the Philippians, been among the Philistines, been at an Indian feast, been at a ploughing match, been at Barbadoes, been at Geneva, been before George, been bitten by a barn mouse, been crooking the elbow, been drowning the shamrock, been flying rather high, been having the eyes opened, been in the bibbing plot, been in the cellar, been in the sauce, been in the sun, been lapping in the gutter, been lifting the little finger, been looking through a glass, been making fun, been on sentry, been talking to Jamie Moore, been to a funeral, been to France, been to Jericho, been to Mexico, been too free with Sir John Strawberry, been too free with the creature, been to the salt water, been trying Taylor's best, been with Sir John Goa, beerified, beerily, beer-muddled, beer-soaked, beery, behind juice, behind the cork, belly up, below the mahogany, belted, bemused, bent, bent and broken, bent out of shape, besotted, bevvied, bewildered, bewitched, bewottled, bezzled, bibulous, biffy, biggy, biled, biled as an owl, binged, bingo'd, bingoed, bit by a barn weasel, blackjacked, blah, blanked, blank-ed, blasted, bleary-eyed, blewed, blimped, blind, blind as a bat, blind as* *a beetle, blind as a mole, blind as an owl, blind as Chloe, blind drunk, blinded, blinders, blindo, blindo-blotto, blissed out, blithered, blitzed, bloated, block and block, block and fall, blocked, blooey, blotted, blotto, blowed, blowed away, blown, blown away, blown up, blowzy, blue, blued, blue-eyed, boiled, boiled as an owl, boiling drunk, bokoo soused, bombed, bombed out, boned, bongo, bongo'd, bongoed, bonkers, boosed, boosy, boozeblind, boozed, boozed as the gage, boozed up, boozey, boozified, boozy, boozy-woozy, boraccho, bosco absoluto, boshy, bosko absoluto, bosky, both sheets in the wind, bottled, bottled up, bousy, bowzed, boxed, boxed up, breath strong enough to carry coal with, breezy, bridgey, bright-eyed, bright in the eye, bruised, bubbed, bubbled, bubby, budgy, buffy, bulldozed, bulletproofed, bumpsie, bumpsy, bung, bunged, bungey, bung-eyed, bungy, bunned, buoyant, buoyed, burdocked, buried, burn with a low blue flame, buskey, busky, busted, buzzed, buzzed up, buzzey, buzzy, cached, cacko, caged, cagrined, candy, canned, canned up, cannon, canon, can't see, can't see a hole in a ladder, can't see through a ladder, capable, capernoited, cap sick, cargoed, carry ballast, carrying a heavy load, carrying a load, carrying something heavy, carrying three red lights, carrying too much sail, carrying two red lights, cast, casting up one's accounts, cat, catched, catsood, caught, chap-fallen, charged up, cheerio, cherry-merry, cherubimical, chice, chickery, chickory, chipper, chirping merry, chucked, clear, clinched, clipping the King's English, clobbered, coagulated, cocked, cocked as a log, cocked to the gills, cock-eyed, cock-eyed drunk, cogey, cognacked, coguy, comboozelated, comfortable, commode-hugging drunk, concerned, conflummoxed, confoundedly cut, contending with the Pharaoh, coo-coo, cooked, copey, corked, corked up, corkscrewed, corkscrewed up, corky, corned, corny, country drunk, coxy-loxy, cracked, cramped, crapsick, crapulous, crashed, crazed, crazy, crazy drunk, creamed, crocked, crocko, crocus, cronk, cropsick, cross-eyed, cross-eyed drunk, crumped out, crump-footed, crying drunk, cuckoo, cuckooed, cupped, cupshot, curved, cushed, cut, cut in the back, cut in the leg, cut one's capers, D., dagged, damaged, damp, D. and D., dead, dead drunk, deado, dead-oh, deads, dead to the world, decayed, decks awash, deep cut, dinged out, ding-swizzled, dingy, dinky, dipped his bill, dipped rather deep, dipped too deep, dirty drunk, discombobulated, discomboobulated, discouraged, discumfuddled, disguised, disguised in liquor, disorderly, dithered, dizzy, dizzy as a coot, dizzy as a dame, dizzy as a goose, dog drunk, doing the emperor, doing the lord, done over, doubled up, double-headed, double-tongued, down, down among the dead men, down with barrel fever, down with the fish, draped, drenched, drinkative, drinky, dripping tight, druffen, drunk, drunk as a badger, drunk as a bastard, drunk as a bat, drunk as a beggar, drunk as a besom, drunk as a big owl, drunk as a biled owl, drunk as a boiled owl, drunk as a brewer's fart, drunk as a broom, drunk as a cook, drunk as a coon, drunk as a coot, drunk as a cooter, drunk as a cootie, drunk as a cunt, drunk as a dog, drunk as a Dutchman, drunk as a fiddle, drunk as a fiddler, drunk as a fiddler's bitch, drunk as a fish, drunk as a fly, drunk as a fool, drunk as a fowl, drunk as a goat, drunk as a Gosport fiddler, drunk as a hog, drunk as a kettlefish, drunk as a king, drunk as a kite, drunk as a little red wagon, drunk as a log, drunk as a loon, drunk as a lord, drunk as a monkey, drunk as a mouse, drunk as an earl, drunk as an emperor, drunk as a newt, drunk as an owl, drunk as a Perraner, drunk as a pig, drunk as a piper, drunk as a pissant, drunk as a poet, drunk as a prince, drunk as a rat, drunk as a rolling fart, drunk as a sailor, drunk as a skunk, drunk as a skunk in a trunk, drunk as a sow, drunk as a swine, drunk as a tapster, drunk as a tick, drunk as a top, drunk as a wheelbarrow, drunk as Bacchus, drunk as blazes, drunk as buggery, drunk as Chloe, drunk as Cooter Brown, drunk as David's sow, drunk as Davy's sow, drunk as Floey, drunk as hell, drunk as hoot, drunk as mice, drunk as muck, drunk as polony, drunk as the devil, drunk as Zeus, drunk back, drunker than whiskey, drunkulent, drunky, drunok, dry, dull-eyed, dull in the eye, eat a pudding bag, eaten a toad and a half for breakfast, eat opium, edged, electrified, elephants, elephant's, elephant's trunk, elevated, eliminated, embalmed, entered, exalted, extracted, faced, faint, falling-down drunk, farahead, far gone, far out, fears no man, featured, feavourish, feeling aces, feeling dizzy, feeling excellent, feeling frisky, feeling funny, feeling glorious, feeling good, feeling happy, feeling high, feeling his alcohol, feeling his booze, feeling his cheerios, feeling his drink, feeling his liquor, feeling his oats, feeling his onions, feeling it, feeling no pain, feeling pretty good, feeling real well, feeling right, feeling right royal, feeling the effect, feshnushkied, fettered, fettled, fiddled, fighting drunk, fighting tight, fired, fired up, fishy, fishy about the gills, fixed up, fizzed up, flabbergasted, flaked out, flako, flaky, flaring drunk, flaw'd, flawed, floating, flooded, flooey, floored, floppy, florid, fluffed, fluffy, flummoxed, flummuxed, flush, flushed, flustered, flusticated, flustrated, fly blown, fly-by-night, flying high, flying the ensign, fog bound, fogged, foggy, folded, foozlified, fortified, fossilized, fou, four sheets, four sheets in the wind, four sheets to the wind, fow, fox drunk, foxed, foxy, fractured, frazzled, fresh, freshish, fried, fried on both sides, fried to the eyebrows, fried to the eyes, fried to the gills, fried to the hat, froze his mouth, frozen, fucked out, fucked over, fucked up, fuddle, fuddled, full, full as a boot, full as a bull, full as a bull's bum, full as a fart, full as a fiddle, full as a goat, full as a goog, full as a goose, full as a lord, full as an egg, full as a piss-ant, full as a po, full as a tick, full as the family po, full-cocked, full-flavored, full of courage, full of Dutch courage, full of hops, full to the brim, full to the bung, full to the gills, full to the guards, full up, funky-drunk, funny, fuzzed, fuzzled, fuzzy, gaged, galvanized, gassed, gassed up, gauged, gay, gayed, geared up, geed up, geesed, geezed, geezed up, generous, giddy, giffed, giggled, giggled up, gilded, gingered up, ginned,*

ginned up, ginnified, ginny, gin soaked, glad, glassy-eyed, glazed, glazed drunk, glazed over, globular, glorious, glowing, glued, goat drunk, goggle-eyed, going to Jerusalem, gold-headed, gone, gone Borneo, gone under, goofy, googly-eyed, gordoned, gorey-eyed, gory-eyed, got a brass eye, got a bun on, got a drop in the eye, got a glow on, got by the head, got corns in his head, got his top gallant sails out, got kibbed heels, got on his little hat, got the back teeth well afloat, got the glanders, got the gout, got the gravel rash, got the hornson, got the Indian vapors, got the nightmare, got the pole evil, gowed, gowed up, grape shot, gravelled, greased, grilled, groatable, grogged, grogged up, groggified, groggy, guttered, guyed out, guzzled, had a few, had a kick in the guts, had a thump over the head with Samson's jawbone, had enough, had one or two, had one too many, had too much, half and half, half blind, half bulled, half canned, half cocked, half corned, half-crocked, half cut, half-doped, half gone, half-high, half hot, half in the bag, half in the boot, half in the tank, half lit, half-looped, half nelson, half on, half-out, half-pickled, half pissed, half rats, half rinsed, half screwed, half seas over, half seas under, half shaved, half shot, half-slammed, half slewed, half-slopped, half snapped, half-sober, half-soused, half sprung, half stewed, half-stiff, half-stoused, half-tanked, half the bay over, half there, half under, half up the pole, halfway over, halfway to Concord, hammered, hammerish, hanced, happy, hard up, hardy, Harry Flakers, Harry Honkers, Harry Screechers, harty, has been in the bibbing plot, has boozed the gage, has dipped his bill, has drunk more than he has bled, has heat his copper, has het his kettle, has scalt his head pan, has stolen a manchet out of the brewer's basket, has taken Hippocrates' grand elixir, has wet both eyes, haunted with evil spirits, have a brick in one's hat, have a bun on, have a cab, have a cup too much, have a cut leg, have a full cargo aboard, have a glow on, have a guest in the attic, have a jag on, have a keg aboard, have a load on, have an edge on, have a package on, have a pot in the pate, have a rosy glow on, have a skate on, have a skinful, have a slant on, have as much as one can carry, have a snootfull, have a swollen head, have a talking load, have a thick head, have a touch of boskiness, have a turkey on one's back, have been dipping rather deep, have been paid, have burnt one's shoulder, have cut one's leg, have eaten some Hull cheese, have got a dish, have got a skinfull, have grog on board, have had one over the eight, have knocked one's link out, have one over the eight, have one's back teeth afloat, have one's back teeth well afloat, have one's flag out, have one's nuff, have one's pots on, have punch aboard, have raised one's monuments, have sold one's senses, have swallowed a hair, have swallowed a hare, have the bighead, have the head full of bees, have the sun in one's eyes, have yellow fever, hazy, head is full of bees, hearty, heated, heated his copper, heeled, heeled over, helpless, hepped, hepped up, het up, hiccius-doccius, hickey, hickie, hicksius-doxius, hicky, hictius-doctius, hiddey, high, high as a cat's back, high as a fiddler's fist, high as a Georgia pine, high as a kite, high as a steeple, high as Lindbergh, high as the sky, higher than a kite, higher than Gilroy's kite, high in the saddle, hipped, hit under the wing, hoary-eyed, hockey, hocus, hocus-pocus, honked, honkers, hooched, hooched up, hoodman, hoodman blind, hooted, hopped, hopped up, horizontal, horseback, hot, hot as a red wagon, hotter than a biled owl, hotter than a boiled owl, hotter than a skunk, housed, How came you so?, howling, howling drunk, illuminated, impaired, impixlocated, in a bad way, in a fix, in a fuddle, in a heap, in a muddle, in armour, in a state of elevation, in a stew, in a trance, in bad shape, in beer, in booze, incog, incognitibus, incognito, in color, in drink, in fine fettle, in good fettle, injun drunk, inked, inky, inkypoo, in liquor, in one's airs, in one's altitudes, in one's armour, in one's cups, in one's element, in one's pots, in one's prosperity, in pots, in rare form, in soak, inspired, in the altitudes, in the bag, in the blues, in the grip of the grape, in the gun, in the gutter, in the ozone, in the pink, in the shakes, in the suds, in the sun, in the sunshine, in the wind, intox, intoxed, intoxicated, inundated, in very good humor, irrigated, ishkimmisk, It is a dark day with him., jagged, jagged up, jambled, jammed, jazzed, jazzed up, jiggered, jingled, jocular, jolly, jug-bitten, jugged, jugged up, jug-steamed, juiced, juiced to the gills, juiced up, juicy, jumbo's trunk, jungled, junked up, kanurd, kennurd, Kentucky fried, kenurd, kettled, keyed, keyed up, keyed up to the roof, keyholed, killed his dog, killed off, kisky, kissed black Betty, kited, knapped, knapt, knee-walking drunk, knocked out, knocked up, knows not the way home, laid back, laid out, laid to the bone, lapping in the gutter, lappy, lathered, leaping, leary, leery, legless, lifted, light, like a rat in trouble, likkered, likkered up, likkerish, likker soaked, limber, limp, lined, lion drunk, liquefied, liquored, liquored up, liquorish, liquor struck, lit, lit to the gills, lit to the guards, lit to the gunnels, lit up, lit up like a cathedral, lit up like a Catholic Church, lit up like a Christmas tree, lit up like a church, lit up like a church window, lit up like a high mass, lit up like a kite, lit up like a lighthouse, lit up like a skyscraper, lit up like a store window, lit up like Broadway, lit up like Main Street, lit up like the commonwealth, lit up like the sky, lit up like Times Square, loaded, loaded for bear, loaded his cart, loaded to the barrel, loaded to the gills, loaded to the guards, loaded to the gunnels, loaded to the gunwales, loaded to the muzzle, loaded to the Plimsoll mark, logged, looking lively, loony, looped, looped to the eyeballs, loop-legged, loopy, loose, loose in the hilts, lordly, lost his rudder, lubed, lubricated, lumpy, lush, lushed, lushed up, lushed up to the nuts, lushey, lushy, made an example, maggotty, makes Virginia fence, making Ms and Ws, making scallops, malted, malty, mashed, maudlin, maudlin drunk, maul'd, mauled, mawdlin, maxed out, mellow, melted, merry, merry as a Greek, messed up, Methodistconated, Mickey finished, middling, milled, miraculous, mixed, mixed up, mizzled, moccasoned, moist around the edges, mokus, molly, molo, mooney, moon-eyed, moonlit, moony, moored in Sot's Bay, mopped, moppy, mops and brooms, mortal, mortal drunk, mortallious, mortally drunk, mountous, muckibus, muddled, muddled up, muddy, mug blot, mug blotto, mug blotts, mugg blotts, mugged, mugged up, muggy, mulled, mulled up, muy tostado, muzzy, nappy, nase, nazy, nazzie, nazzy, need a reef taken in, Negro drunk, newted, nimptopsical, nipped, noddy-headed, noggy, nolo, non compos, non compos poopoo, nuts, nutty, N.Y.D., obfuscated, obfusticated, ocksecrotia, oddish, off, off at the nail, off one's nut, off the nail, oiled, on, on a jag, one over eight, one over the eight, on one's ass, on one's ear, on one's fourth, on sentry, on the batter, on the beer, on the bend, on the blink, on the fritz, on the fuddle, on the grog, on the kip, on the loose, on the muddle, on the rantan, on the ree-raw, on the re-raw, on the sauce, on the scoop, on the scoot, on the shicker, on the shikker, on the skyte, on the spree, oozy, organized, orie-eyed, orry-eyed, ossified, out, outasight, out cold, out like a light, out of funds, out of it, out of one's gourd, out of sight, out of the way, out on the fuddle, out on the roof, out to it, overboard, overcome, overseas, overseen, overserved, overset, overshot, over-sparred, overtaken, over the bar, over the bay, over the eight, over the mark, over-wined, owes no man a farthing, owled, owl-eyed, owly-eyed, oxycrocium, packaged, pafisticated, paid, palatic, palled, paralysed, paralytic, paralyzed, parboiled, passed out, passed out cold, passed out of the picture, pasted, peckish, pee'd, pee-eyed, peonied, pepped, pepped up, peppy, perked, petrificated, petrified, phfft, pickled, pied, pie-eyed, piffed, pifficated, piffled, pifflicated, pigeon-eyed, pilfered, pinked, pinko, piped, piped up, piper drunk, piper fou', piper merry, pipped, pipped up, pissed, pissed as a fiddler's bitch, pissed as a newt, pissed in the brook, pissed out of one's mind, pissed up, pissed up to the eyeballs, pissed up to the eyebrows, pissing drunk, pissing fou', pissy-arsed, pixilated, pixolated, pizz, pizzicato, plastered, pleasantly plastered, plonk, plonked, plonked up, plootered, ploughed, ploughed under, plowed, plowed under, poddy, podgy, poffered, pogey, poggled, pogy, polished, polished up, polite, polled off, polluted, pooped, pooped out, poopied, pop-eyed, popped, pot-eyed, pot shot, pot sick, potted, potted off, potted up, potulent, pot valiant, powdered, powdered up, preserved, pretty well enter'd, priddy, primed, primed to the barrel, primed to the ears, primed to the muzzle, primed to the nuts, primed to the trigger, Prince Eugene, pruned, psyched out, puggled, puggy drunk, pungey, pushed, pushed out, putrid, put to bed with a shovel, pye-eyed, quarrelsome, quartzed, queer, queered, quick-tempered, quisby, racked, racked up, raddled, ragged, raised, rammaged, ramping mad, rattled, ratty, raunchy, reeking, reeling, reeling ripe, reely, religious, rich, riffed, right before the wind with all his studding sail out, rigid, rileyed, ripe, ripped, ripped off, ripped to the tits, ripped up, roaring, roaring drunk, roaring fou', roasted, rocky, ronchie, roostered, rorty, rosey, rosie, rosined, rosy, rosy about the gills, rotten, rotten drunk, round the bend, royal, rum-dum, rummed, rummed up, rummy, salt, salted, salted down, salt junk, salubrious, sap happy, saturated, sauced, sawed, scammered, schice, schlockkered, schnockered, schnoggered, scooped, scorched, Scotch mist, scrambled, scranched, scratched, scraunched, screaming, screaming drunk, screechers, screeching, screeching drunk, screwed, screwed tight, screwy, scronched, scrooched, scrooched up, seafaring, seeing pink elephants, seeing pink spiders, seeing snakes, seeing-things drunk, seeing two moons, seen a flock of moons, seen the devil, seen the French king, seen the yellow star, sees the bears, sees the sun, sees two moons, sent, served up, sewed up, sewn up, S.F., shagged, shaking a cloth in the wind, shaking like cloth in the wind, shaky, shaved, shellacked, shice, shicer, shicery, shick, shicked, shickered, shickery, shikker, shikkered, shikkur, shined, shinny, shiny, shipwrecked, shise, shit-faced, shitty, shnockered, shot, shot-away, shot down, shot full of holes, shot in the neck, shot up, shredded, sizzled, skew-whiff, skimished, skimmished, skizzled, skunk-drunk, skunked, slathered, sleepy, slewed, slewy, slightly damaged, slightly damp, slightly elevated, slightly rattled, slightly-tightly, slopped, slopped over, slopped to the ears, slopped up, sloppy, sloppy drunk, sloshed, sloshed to the ears, sloughed, sloughed up, slued, slugged, slushed, slushed up, smashed, smeared, smeekit, smelling of the cork, smelt of an onion, smoked, snacked, snaped, snapped, snockered, snockered to the gills, snoggered, snooted, snoozamorooed, snot-flinging drunk, snotted, snozzled, snubbed, snuffy, snug, so, soaked, soapy-eyed, sodden, soft, soggy, somebody stole his rudder, sopping, sopping wet, soppy, sore-footed, soshed, so-so, sossled, sottish, souffled, soupy, soused, soused to the ears, soused to the gills, soust, southern-fried, sow drunk, sozzled, sozzly, speechless, spiffed, spifflicated, spifflo, spificated, spiflicated, spiked, spoke with his friend, spoony, spoony drunk, spreeish, sprung, squiffed, squiffy, staggerish, stale drunk, standing too long in the sun, starched, starchy, steady, steamed, steamed up, steeped, stepping high, stew, stewed, stewed to the ears, stewed to the gills, stewed up, stibbed, stiff, stiff as a board, stiff as a goat, stiff as a plank, stiff as a ring-bolt, stiffed, stiffo, stimulated, stinking, stinking drunk, stinko, stitched, stolled, stolling, stone blind, stoned, stoned to the tits, stonkered, stony blind, stove in, stozzled, stretched, striped, strong, stubbed, stuccoed, stung, stunned, sucked, suckey, sucky, supercharged, swacked, swacko, swallowed a tavern token, swamped, swampt, swatched, swattled, swazzled, swigged, swiggled, swilled, swilled up, swined, swine drunk, swinny, swiped, swipey, swipy, swivelly, swizzled, swoozled, swozzled, tacky, taken a chirriping glass, taken a cup too much, taking it easy, tangled, tangle-footed, tangle-legged, tanked, tanked up, tanned, tap shackled, taverned, tead up, tea'd up, teed, tee'd to the tits, teed up, teeth under, temulent, that way, thawed, there, there with both feet, the sun has shone on them, thirsty, three sheets, three sheets in the wind, three sheets to the wind, tiddled, tiddley, tiddly, tiffled, tight, tight as a boiled owl, tight as a brassiere, tight as a drum, tight as a fart, tight as a goat, tight as a lord, tight as a mink, tight as a newt, tight as an owl, tight as a ten-day drunk, tight as a tick, tight as the bark on a tree, tighter than a drum, tighter than a goat, tighter than a mink, tighter than a Scotchman, tighter than a tick, tighter than Dick's hatband, tin hats, tinned, tipium grove, tip merry, tipped, tippling, tipply, tipsey, tipsified, tipsy, tip-top, tired, tishy, tite, toasted, tongue-tied, took his drops, too many cloths in the wind, too numerous to mention, top heavy, topped, toppled, toppy, topsy-boosy, topsy-boozy, topsy-turvey, topy, tore, tore down, tore up, torn up, torrid, tossed, tosticated, tostificated, totalled, totty, touched, tough as a boiled owl, tow-row, toxed, toxicated, toxy, trammeled, translated, trashed, trimmed down, tripped, tubed, tumbling, tumbling drunk, tuned, tuned up, tuzzy, tweased, twisted, two sheets to the wind, unable to scratch himself, under, under the affluence of incohol, under the influence, under the table, under the weather, unk-dray, up a tree, upholstered, uppish, uppity, upsey, up the pole, up to the ears, up to the gills, valiant, varnished, vegetable, very weary, vulcanized, waa-zooed, walking on rocky socks, wall-eyed, wam-bazzled, wamble-cropped, wapsed-down, wasted, water logged, water soaked, weak-jointed, weary, well-away, well-bottled, well-fixed, well-heeled, well in for it, well-lit, well-lubricated, well-oiled, well-preserved, well-primed, well-soaked, well-sprung, well to live, well-under, wet, wet both eyes, wet-handed, whacked, what-nosed, whazood, whazooed, whiffled, whipped, whipsey, whiskey-frisky, whiskified, whistled, whistle drunk, whittled, whittled as a penguin, whooshed, whoozy, wigged, wigged out, wiggy, wilted, winey, wing'd, winged, wing heavy, wiped, wiped out, wiped over, wired, wired up, wise, with main brace well spliced, wobbly, womblety-cropt, woody, woofled, woozey, woozy, wrecked, yappish, yappy, yaupish, yaupy, zagged, zapped, zig-zag, zig-zagged, zissified, zoned, zonk, zonked, zonked out, zoobang, zooted, zorked, zounk. 2. stupefied by tobacco smoke. *Cf. drink.* [(1585): OED] 3. a spree; a drinking bout; a state of intoxication. [(1779): MW: 1983, (1839): OEDS, DSUE, BVB: 1942, MW: 1983] 4. a drunkard; a *sot* (*q.v.*). *Drunkard* dates from the early 1500s. Standard English. [(1852): OEDS, MW: 1983] 5. (also **drunken**) to make drunk. RS: *mug oneself.* [1300s, Wyclif Bible; Bahamas, JAH: 1982]

drunk as a badger alcohol intoxicated. These playful similes are quite common. Paul Dickson lists drunk as a bat, drunk as a besom, drunk as a big owl, drunk as a cook, drunk as a coon, drunk as a cootie, drunk as a dog, drunk as a hog, drunk as a king, drunk as a little red wagon, drunk as a log, drunk as a loon, drunk as a monkey, drunk as a Perraner, drunk as a pig, drunk as a poet, drunk as a sailor, drunk as a skunk in a trunk, drunk as a swine, drunk as a tapster, drunk as Cooter Brown, drunk as hoot, drunk as mice, drunk as muck, drunk as the devil, drunk as Zeus. Most of these are quite old. RT: *drunk*. [PD: 1982]

drunk as a bastard alcohol intoxicated. RT: *drunk*. [Aust., SJB: 1945]

drunk as a beggar alcohol intoxicated. (BF: 1737: [He's] As Drunk as a Beggar.) RT: *drunk*. [BF: 1737]

drunk as a boiled owl (also drunk as a biled owl) alcohol intoxicated. Possibly from the expression *tough as a boiled owl* (*q.v.*). RT: *drunk*. [F&H, JWC: 1905, JRW: 1909, MHW: 1934, SJB: 1945, D&D: 1957, M&J: 1975]

drunk as a brewer's fart alcohol intoxicated. *Cf. brewer's fizzle*. RT: *drunk*. [Br., 1800s or before, F&H (at *drunk*)]

drunk as a broom (also drunk as a besom) alcohol intoxicated. *Cf. all mops and brooms*. RT: *drunk*. [Br., (1830): DSUE]

drunk as a coot (also drunk as a cooter) alcohol intoxicated. *Cf. dizzy as a coot*. RT: *drunk*. [U.S., LWP: 1908, BVB: 1942; listed in M&J: 1975]

drunk as a cunt alcohol intoxicated. A mixed metaphor based on *black as a cunt*. RT: *drunk*. [Br., late 18-1900s, DSUE]

drunk as a Dutchman alcohol intoxicated. Probably originated as an insult to the Dutch. RT: *drunk*. [AAR: 1944]

drunk as a fiddler (also drunk as a fiddle) alcohol intoxicated. The British version is drunk as a Gosport fiddler (F&H). *Cf. rosined*. RT: *drunk*. [U.S., BVB: 1942, D&D: 1957, M&J: 1975]

drunk as a fiddler's bitch (also pissed as a fiddler's bitch) alcohol intoxicated. Probably an elaboration of *drunk as a fiddler*. RT: *drunk*. [Br., DSUE; U.S., BWG: 1899, LWP: 1908]

drunk as a fish alcohol intoxicated. *Cf. down with the fish, fishy*. RT: *drunk*. [U.S., BVB: 1942]

drunk as a fly alcohol intoxicated. RT: *drunk*. [Br., 1800s, F&H (at *drunk*)]

drunk as a fool alcohol intoxicated. RT: *drunk*. Probably recurrent nonce. [U.S., BWG: 1899]

drunk as a fowl alcohol intoxicated. RT: *drunk*. [Aust., SJB: 1943, DSUE]

drunk as a goat alcohol intoxicated. *Cf. full as a goat*. RT: *drunk*. [U.S., BVB: 1942]

drunk as a kettlefish alcohol intoxicated. Kettlefish = a small fish (OED). RT: *drunk*. [Br., 18-1900s, DSUE]

drunk as a kite alcohol intoxicated. This may also be from *high as a kite* (*q.v.*). RT: *drunk*. [M&J: 1975]

drunk as a lord (also drunk as an earl, drunk as a prince) alcohol intoxicated. RT: *drunk*. [since the mid 1600s, F&H, BWG: 1899, JRW: 1909, BVB: 1942, LDEI: 1979]

drunk as a mouse (also drunk as a rat) alcohol intoxicated.

Possibly a mixed metaphor based on *quiet as a mouse.* RT: *drunk.* [13-1900s, F&H, DSUE] See also *like a rat in trouble.*

drunk as an emperor alcohol intoxicated. RT: *drunk.* A royal degree of inebriation roughly "ten times as drunk as a lord" (FG: 1811). [Br., FG: 1785, FG: 1811, B&L: 1890]

drunk as a newt (also pissed as a newt) alcohol intoxicated. *Cf. newted.* RT: *drunk.* [Br., 1900s, DSUE, SSD, M&J: 1975]

drunk as an owl alcohol intoxicated. *Cf. drunk as a boiled owl.* RT: *drunk.* [U.S., D&D: 1957]

drunk as a piper (also fou' as a piper) alcohol intoxicated. *Cf. piper drunk.* RT: *drunk.* [Br., late 1700s, F&H; listed in BVB: 1942]

drunk as a pissant alcohol intoxicated. *Cf. pissed.* RT: *drunk.* [Aust., (1930): OEDS, SJB: 1945]

drunk as a rolling fart alcohol intoxicated. *Cf. drunk as a brewer's fart.* RT: *drunk.* [Br., mid 1800s, DSUE]

drunk as a skunk alcohol intoxicated. RT: *drunk.* Probably recurrent nonce. [Aust, SJB: 1966; U.S., BVB: 1942]

drunk as a tick alcohol intoxicated. Full of fluid like a tick. A mixed metaphor based on *full as a tick* (*q.v.*) or *tight as a tick* (*q.v.*). RT: *drunk.* [U.S., RAS: 1979]

drunk as a top alcohol intoxicated. Wobbling like a top running down. RT: *drunk.* [PD: 1982]

drunk as a wheelbarrow alcohol intoxicated. RT: *drunk.* [(1670): DSUE, BF: 1737, FG: 1811, BVB: 1942]

drunk as Bacchus alcohol intoxicated. *Cf. Bacchi plenus.* RT: *drunk.* [Br., 1800s, F&H (at *drunk*)]

drunk as blazes alcohol intoxicated. A euphemism for *drunk as hell* (*q.v.*). RT: *drunk.* [Br., (1860): DSUE; listed in BVB: 1942]

drunk as buggery alcohol intoxicated. RT: *drunk.* [Br., 1800s, F&H (at *drunk*)]

drunk as Chloe (also blind as Chloe) alcohol intoxicated. RT: *drunk.* [(1791): DSUE, (1892): GAW: 1978, BVB: 1942, SJB: 1945]

drunk as David's sow (also drunk as a sow, drunk as Davy's sow) alcohol intoxicated. (BF: 1737: [He's] As...) RT: *drunk.* [BF: 1737, FG: 1785, FG: 1811; listed in BVB: 1942]

drunk as Floey alcohol intoxicated. *Cf. drunk as Chloe.* RT: *drunk.* [JRW: 1909, SJB: 1945]

drunk as hell alcohol intoxicated; very drunk. *Cf. drunk as blazes.* Colloquial and recurrent nonce. [Br., 1800s, F&H (at *drunk*); listed in BVB: 1942]

drunk as polony alcohol intoxicated. RT: *drunk.* [JRW: 1909]

drunk back alcohol intoxicated; very drunk. Akin to *laid back* (*q.v.*). RT: ***drunk***. [U.S., ADC: 1981]

drunken 1. intoxicated with alcohol. RT: ***drunk***. [since c. 1000, OED] 2. to make drunk. See ***drunk***.

drunker a drunkard. RT: ***sot***. [(1538): OED; Bahamas, JAH: 1982]

drunker than whiskey alcohol intoxicated. RT: ***drunk***. [PD: 1982]

drunkery a drinking establishment. RS: ***bar***. [U.S., early 1800s, OED, B&L: 1890, K&M: 1968]

drunkok an error for ***drunok*** (*q.v.*). [PD: 1982]

drunk, on a (also **on the drunk**) on a prolonged drinking bout. RT: ***spreeing***. [since the late 1800s, (1871): F&H, DSUE]

drunk tank the cell in a police station into which the recently arrested drunks are placed. [U.S., D&D: 1957, W&F: 1960, K&M: 1968, EEL: 1971, MW: 1976]

drunkulent alcohol intoxicated. RT: ***drunk***. [PD: 1982]

drunk-up a drinking bout. *Cf.* ***beer-up, booze-up, gee-up, grog-up, jolly-up, swill-up, whooper-up***. RT: ***spree***. [Aust., SJB: 1943]

drunky alcohol intoxicated. RT: ***drunk***. [Br. dialect, early 1800s, OED] See also ***dronkie***.

drunok alcohol intoxicated. RT: ***drunk***. [Br., (1930): DSUE]

Dr. White 1. powdered, addictive drugs. A personification of powdered drugs. RS: ***powder***. [U.S., DWM: 1938] 2. narcotic addiction. RT: ***habit***. [U.S., DWM: 1938, BVB: 1942]

dry 1. champagne. RT: ***cham***. [Br., 1800s, F&H; listed in BVB: 1942] 2. alcohol intoxicated. *Cf.* ***wet***. RT: ***drunk***. [Br., 1800s, F&H] 3. a prohibitionist; an abstainer. *Cf.* ***wet***. [U.S., (1889): DA, AH: 1931] (This entry continues after the following list.) Terms for persons who do not drink or who are supporters of prohibition: ***aqua-duck, arid hound, balloon juice lowerer, bluenose, blue-ribbon army, blue ribboner, blue-ribbon faker, blue ribbonite, bone dry, bun strangler, bun wallah, cellar-smeller, char wallah, cold-water army, cold-water man, cracker dry, crack lip, dry, drymedaries, hydropot, lear-beer, leer-beer, lemonade wallah, likker pug, nondrinker, pop-wallah, pro, prohi, prohib, prohy, pump sucker, purger, pussyfoot, pussyfooter, sniffing squad, sobersides, spigot-bigot, tack wallah, teapot, teapot sucker, teeto, teetotalist, teetotaller, teetotalleress, tootootler, tote, T.T., T-totaler, Volsteadian, Volsteadite, wad scoffer, wagon rider, wassermucker, waterbag, water bottle, water-butt, water-drinker, whiffsniffer***. 4. having to do with a region where beverage alcohol cannot be purchased. The opposite of ***wet*** (*q.v.*). [(1870): DA, BVB: 1942] 5. sober, not inebriated. *Cf.* ***detoxed***. [U.S., BVB: 1942] 6. having to do with unsweetened wine, beverage alcohol, mixed drinks. Originally cant, but now standard English. [since the 1600s, BE: 1690] 7. having to do with an addict or drug user who is out of drugs and out of money to purchase them. *Cf.* ***dead***. [U.S., C&H: 1974, JWK: 1981] 8. off drugs; ***clean*** (*q.v.*). [U.S., RAS: 1984]

dry as a bone having to do with a prohibitionist; having to do with a sober person or an area where alcohol cannot be purchased. [U.S., 1920s, BVB: 1953]

dry era prohibition. Not slang. [U.S., early 1900s, SBF: 1976]

dry goods strong liquor; whiskey. RS: ***whiskey***. From the prohibition era. [U.S., early 1900s, DU]

dry grog (also **dry booze**) narcotics. *Cf.* ***grog***. RS: ***dope***. [U.S., BVB: 1942, VJM: 1949, A&T: 1953]

dry high marijuana. *Cf.* ***high***. RT: ***pot***. [U.S., YKB: 1977, NIDA: 1980]

drymedaries abstainers; prohibitionists. A play on the *dromedary* of the (dry) desert. RT: ***dry***. From the prohibition era. [U.S., MHW: 1934, BVB: 1942]

dry out (also **dry up**) to detoxify from drugs or alcohol. *Cf.* ***detox***. RS: ***kick***. [U.S., (1967): OEDS, RRL: 1969, EEL: 1971, MW: 1976, JWK: 1981]

dry spell a period of time when no drugs are available; a period of abstinence from drugs. Similar to ***drought*** (*q.v.*). [U.S., M&V: 1973, RAS: 1980]

dry whiskey *peyote* (*q.v.*) buttons. *Cf.* ***button***. RS: ***peyote***. [U.S., (1892): DA, K&M: 1968]

D.s tablets of *Dilaudid* (TM; *q.v.*) painkiller. See *D*. RT: ***dids***. [U.S., JWK: 1981]

D-T-ist a drunkard. *Cf.* ***D.T.s***. RT: ***sot***. [Br., 1800s, F&H]

D.T.s the delirium tremens. Sometimes called D.T. in the 1800s (British). [(1858): OEDS, B&L: 1890, MHW: 1934, K&M: 1968] Nicknames and slang terms for the delirium tremens: ***barrel fever, bats, B.J.s, black dog, blue devils, blue horrors, blue Johnnies, blues, bottleache, cast-iron horrors, clanks, diddleums, dingbats, dithers, D.T.s, gallon distemper, ginters, heebie-jeebies, horries, horrors, jams, jerks, jim-jams, jimmies, Joe Blakes, jumps, katzenjammer, ork-orks, pink elephants, pink spiders, quart-mania, rum fits, screaming abdabs, screaming hab-dabs, screaming-meemies, snakes, snakes in one's boots, snozzle-wobbles, staggers, stone wall horrors, the blues, the creeps, the jumps, the rams, the rats, the shakes, the staggers, the uglies, trembles, tremens, triangles, uglies, wet dog shakes, whips and jangles, whips and jingles, whoops and jingles, woolies, zings.***

dubber (also **dub**) a tobacco cigarette. Compare to ***doobie***. RT: ***nail***. [U.S., GU: 1975]

dubie (also **dubbe, dubee**) a marijuana cigarette. See ***doobie***.

duck 1. a cigarette butt. Probably from *dead duck*. *Cf.* ***dead soldier***. RT: ***brad***. [U.S., LWP: 1908, BVB: 1942] 2. a dealer in illicit liquor. Related in some way to ***wet*** (*q.v.*). See ***chase the duck***. From the prohibition era. [U.S., AH: 1931, BVB: 1942] 3. wine. Possibly akin to *cold duck*. RT: ***wine***. Black slang. [U.S.,

DC: 1972]

duct cocaine. See *C-duct.*

dude heroin, a personification of heroin. *Cf. brother, cat, him.* RT: *heroin.* [U.S., H&C: 1975]

dufer a borrowed cigarette; a cigarette stub saved for smoking later. This cigarette butt will *do for* later. *Cf. doofer.* RT: *brad.* [Aust., SJB: 1945]

Duffy a spasm feigned by an addict to get drugs. From *Arthur Duffy* (*q.v.*). RT: *brody.* [U.S., M&V: 1967, H&C: 1975]

dugee heroin. See *dojee.*

dugout 1. a burned-out addict. Refers to the veins of the arms which are pitted and dug out from many injections. RS: *junky.* [U.S., DWM: 1936, BVB: 1942, H&C: 1975] 2. a type of marijuana pipe. RS: *bong.* [U.S., RAS: 1980]

duji heroin. See *dojee.* [U.S., EEL: 1971, NIDA: 1980]

dull-eyed alcohol intoxicated. RT: *drunk.* [U.S., BVB: 1942]

dull in the eye alcohol intoxicated. *Cf. dull-eyed.* RT: *drunk.* [Br., 1800s, F&H; listed in BVB: 1942]

dummy 1. bogus heroin. A substance such as talcum, quinine, sugar, or powdered milk is substituted. RT: *blank.* [U.S., M&V: 1967, RRL: 1969] 2. a *Darvon* (TM; *q.v.*) painkiller capsule. *Cf. vons.* [U.S., SNP: 1977] 3. an empty liquor bottle. RT: *dead soldier.* [U.S., BVB: 1942] 4. a cigarette butt. RT: *brad.* [U.S., BVB: 1942]

dummy dust phencyclidine; *P.C.P.* (*q.v.*), an animal tranquilizer. Signifying that one has to be a dummy to use it, or that it is a bogus substitute for some other drug. *Cf. killer weed.* RT: *P.C.P.* [U.S., (1970s): FAB: 1979]

dumper a discarded cigarette butt. RT: *brad.* [Aust., SJB: 1943]

dumper-dasher someone who habitually picks up cigarette butts. *Cf. emu-bobbing.* [Aust., SJB: 1943]

duraznos* amphetamines. Spanish for *peaches* (*q.v.*). RT: *amps.* [U.S., NIDA: 1980]

durog said to be marijuana. Probably an error for *duros* (*q.v.*). [U.S., SNP: 1977]

Durophet a British brand name for a long-lasting amphetamine. Durophet M contains *methaqualone* (*q.v.*). Nicknames and slang terms for Durophet: *black and tan, black and white, black bombers, dominoes.*

duros* potent marijuana. Spanish for tough. RT: *pot.* [U.S., EEL: 1971, JH: 1979, HSD: 1984]

durry a cigarette; a cigarette butt. *Cf. brad, nail.* [Aust., (1910): DSUE, SJB: 1943]

dust 1. fine tobacco for rolling cigarettes. RS: *freckles.* Prison use.

[U.S., HS: 1933, BVB: 1942, GOL: 1950] 2. any powdered drug. Originally heroin, now including cocaine. [U.S., BVB: 1942, VJM: 1949, GOL: 1950, A&T: 1953, YKB: 1977, JWK: 1981] *Dust* occurs in a large number of drug terms: ***angel dust, bug dust, bumblebee dust, dummy dust, dust-cutter, dusted, duster, dust of angels, dust of Morpheus, fairy dust, foo-foo dust, gold dust, gold duster, gray dust, happy dust, happy duster, heaven dust, heifer dust, hell dust, joy dust, lay the dust, lung-duster, Persian dust, puff the dust, reindeer dust, sack of dust, star dust, white dust, yellow dust***. 3. phencyclidine, *P.C.P.* (*q.v.*), an animal tranquilizer. RT: *P.C.P.* [U.S., YKB: 1977, JWK: 1981] 4. marijuana. RT: *pot*. [U.S., GOL: 1950] 5. to add a powdered drug to the end of a tobacco cigarette. *Cf. lace*. [U.S., (RRL: 1969), EEL: 1971]

dust a joint to add P.C.P. to a cigarette (tobacco or marijuana). *Cf. crystal joint*. Probably applies to a number of different substances which can be put on a tobacco cigarette. The term is probably older than the attestation indicates. [U.S., NIDA: 1980]

dust-cutter a drink of whiskey. *Cf. phlegm-cutter*. RS: *nip*. [U.S., RFA]

dusted 1. drug intoxicated, especially with cocaine. *Cf. flaky, powdered*. RS: *stoned*. [U.S., JES: 1959, H&C: 1975] 2. having to do with a marijuana cigarette with *P.C.P.* (*q.v.*) added to it. [U.S., ADC: 1975] 3. taking P.C.P., an animal tranquilizer; ruined by *P.C.P.* (*q.v.*). [U.S., EEL: 1971, ADC: 1981]

duster 1. a tobacco cigarette with heroin or P.C.P. added to it. *Cf. dust*. [U.S., RRL: 1969, H&C: 1975, ELA: 1984] 2. a habitual P.C.P. user. RS: *user*. [U.S., FAB: 1979]

dusthead a user of *P.C.P.* (*q.v.*), an animal tranquilizer. From *angel dust*. See list at *head*. RS: *user*. [U.S., DNE: 1980]

dust joint a cigarette containing P.C.P. and mint, parsley, or marijuana. RS: *P.C.P.* [U.S., FAB: 1979]

dust of Morpheus powdered drugs; morphine. Morpheus = the god of sleep; a personification of sleep. Not narcotics argot. [U.S., JES: 1959, H&C: 1975]

Dutch courage 1. courage induced by drinking liquor. [since the late 1800s, F&H, W&F: 1960] 2. alcohol used to bolster one's courage. [U.S., BVB: 1942, D&D: 1957] 3. narcotics. From sense one. [U.S., BVB: 1942, VJM: 1949]

Dutchman (also **flying Dutchman**) a drug seller. RT: *dealer*. [U.S., JES: 1959, H&C: 1975]

Dutch milk (also **Dutch suds**) beer. See list at *milk*. RT: *beer*. [U.S., BVB: 1942]

Dutch mill a place where drugs are sold. *Cf. Dutchman*. RT: *doperie*. [U.S., JES: 1959, H&C: 1975]

dyes *Valium* (TM; *q.v.*) tranquilizers. See *dies*.

dyls *Placidyl* (TM; *q.v.*), a sedative-hypnotic drug. See *dill.* RT: *plass.* [U.S., JWK: 1981]

dyna having to do with a potent drug. See *dynamite.*

dynamite 1. cheap, strong whiskey. RT: *rotgut.* [U.S., BVB: 1942, RFA] 2. (also **dyna**, **dyno**) powerful powdered drugs or drugs in combination: highly purified heroin, heroin and cocaine, morphine and cocaine. [U.S., BD: 1937, DWM: 1938, GOL: 1950, W&F: 1967, RRL: 1969, CM: 1970, EEL: 1971, MA: 1973, YKB: 1977, ADC: 1981, JWK: 1981] 3. potent marijuana used for "blasting." *Cf. blast.* [U.S., (1951): M&D: 1952, W&F: 1960, EEL: 1971] 4. (also **dynamites**) amphetamines. RT: *amps.* [U.S., NIDA: 1980]

dynamiter 1. a cocaine addict or user. RT: *kokomo.* [U.S., GOL: 1950, A&T: 1953] 2. a potent marijuana cigarette. *Cf. dynamite.* RT: *joint.* [U.S., M&H: 1959]

dyno 1. liquor; inferior liquor. From *dynamite* (*q.v.*). RT: *rotgut.* [U.S., GI: 1931, MHW: 1934] 2. a drunkard. RT: *sot.* [U.S., BVB: 1942] 3. (also **dyna**) nearly pure heroin. An abbreviation of *dynamite* (*q.v.*). RS: *heroin.* [U.S., RRL: 1969, CM: 1970, JWK: 1981]

dypso a drunkard. Short for *dipsomaniac* (*q.v.*). See *dipso.* RT: *sot.* [U.S., DCCU: 1972, W&F: 1967]

E

ear, on one's alcohol intoxicated. A euphemism for *on one's ass* (*q.v.*). RT: *drunk*. [(1906): OEDS, (1910): DSUE, SJB: 1943]

ears, up to the alcohol intoxicated. RT: *drunk*. [U.S., BVB: 1942]

earth a marijuana cigarette. Compare to *erth*. RS: *joint*. [Bahamas (Nassau), JAH: 1982]

earthquake (also **earthquake protector**) liquor. RT: *booze*. [U.S., B&L: 1890, F&H]

easing powder 1. an opiate, probably morphine. RS: *powder*. Probably not argot. [U.S., HK: 1917, BVB: 1942] 2. (also **easy powder**) knockout drops. RT: *Mickey Finn*. [U.S., MHW: 1934, VJM: 1949]

eat a pudding bag alcohol intoxicated. (BF: 1737: [He's] Eat...) In modern English, "eaten a pudding bag." May refer to a drinker's belly shaped like a (British) pudding. The imagery is not clear. RT: *drunk*. [BF: 1737]

ea-tay marijuana. Pig Latin for *tea* (*q.v.*). = marijuana. RT: *pot*. [U.S., RPW: 1938]

eaten a toad and a half for breakfast alcohol intoxicated. (BF: 1737: He's eat a Toad...) Refers to a bad taste in the mouth after a night of drinking. RT: *drunk*. [BF: 1737]

eater a drug user or addict who takes drugs orally; a *pillhead* (*q.v.*). *Cf. belly habit, stomach habit*. See *opium eater*. [U.S., M&V: 1954, RRL: 1969, JWK: 1981]

eat opium alcohol intoxicated. In modern English, "eaten opium." The word drunk was used for the opium stupor as early as 1585 (OED). RT: *drunk*. [BF: 1737]

echoes repetitions of the effects of an L.S.D. trip after the immediate effects of the chemical have worn off. *Cf. cartoon, flashback, pattern, trail*. [U.S., C&H: 1974]

Ecstasy (also **ecstasy**) a relatively new drug similar to the hallucinogenic L.S.D. The chemical name is 3,4-methylenedioxymethamphetamine or *M.D.M.A*. The sale of this drug is highly restricted. The drug is currently thought to cause brain damage. It is made in private laboratories and easily altered into other drugs. See *M.D.M.A., designer drug*. [U.S., RAS: 1985]

edge 1. drunkenness; the early stage of intoxication from alcohol or drugs. [U.S., (1920): OEDS, GOL: 1950, W&F: 1960] 2. an addict's initial feelings of need for a dose of drugs. Widely known in *get the edge off*. [U.S., JWK: 1981]

Edge City the world of the drug user or addict, i.e., always being on the brink of withdrawing. *Cf. edge*. [U.S., E&R: 1971]

edged (also **have an edge on**) alcohol or drug intoxicated. *Cf. edge*. [U.S., AH: 1931, MHW: 1934, W&F: 1960]

eed-waggles marijuana. Possibly pig Latin for *weed muggles*. *Muggles* (*q.v.*) = marijuana cigarettes. RT: *pot*. [U.S., RPW: 1938]

eed-way marijuana. Pig Latin for *weed* (*q.v.*). RT: *pot*. [U.S., RPW: 1938]

eer-bay (also **er-bay**) beer. RT: *beer*. Pig Latin. [U.S., early 1900s, DU]

eggs pills. *Cf. dolls*. [U.S., JWK: 1981]

Egyptian driver a drug dealer. RT: *dealer*. Origin unknown. Heard on the West Coast. [U.S., RAS: 1980]

eight (also **8**) heroin. The eighth letter of the alphabet is H. RT: *heroin*. [U.S., EEL: 1971, JH: 1979, RDS: 1982]

eighteenth amusement the eighteenth amendment to the constitution which permitted national prohibition of alcohol sales (via the Volstead Act). [U.S., 1920s, BVB: 1942, D&D: 1957]

eighth piece (also **eighth**) one eighth of an ounce of morphine or heroin. Now usually the latter. *Cf. dram*. RS: *load*. [U.S., BD: 1937, DWM: 1938, RRL: 1969, EEL: 1971, JWK: 1981]

eight, over the alcohol intoxicated. *Cf. one over the eight*. RT: *drunk*. [Br. and U.S., F&G: 1925, D&D: 1957]

ekies tablets or capsules of *Mandrax* (TM; *q.v.*), a British brand of *methaqualone* (*q.v.*), a hypnotic-sedative. Probably from the *akes* of *mandrakes* (*q.v.*) = Mandrax. RT: *ludes*. [U.S., SNP: 1977]

Elavil a protected trade name for amitriptyline (antidepressant) available in tablet and injectable form. The drug is an antidepressant and a sedative. *Cf. els*. [in current use; consult a pharmaceutical reference for more information]

elbow a pound of marijuana. *Cf. arm*. RT: *load*. [U.S., (1976): ELA: 1982]

elbow-bending drinking; drinking to excess. RT: *spreeing*. [U.S., D&D: 1957, W&F: 1960

elbow-crooker (also **crooker**, **elbow-bender**) a drunkard; an alcoholic. *Cf. bend one's elbow*. RT: *sot*. [Br. and U.S., 18-1900s, F&H; listed in D&D: 1957]

Eleanor *Nalline* (TM; *q.v.*), a narcotic antagonist. From its chemical name N-allylnormorphine hydrobromide. [U.S., (M&V: 1954)]

electric having to do with L.S.D. or psychedelic matters. [U.S., RB: 1967, RRL: 1969, EEL: 1971]

electric butter marijuana leaves sauteed in butter. [U.S., (1970): ELA: 1982]

electric koolaid a soft drink or Kool-Aid (TM) fruit-flavored drink laced with the hallucinogenic drug *L.S.D.* (*q.v.*). This substance was served at the 1960s acid tests. Similar to *electric wine*. [U.S., RB: 1967, (TW: 1968), RRL: 1969]

electric wine L.S.D. combined with wine or a soft drink. RS: *set*. [U.S., D&B: 1971]

electrified alcohol intoxicated. RT: *drunk*. Curiously, this term has not been attested in reference to the hallucinogenic drug *L.S.D.* (*q.v.*). [Br. and U.S., B&L: 1890, F&H, BVB: 1942]

elefante* phencyclidine, *P.C.P.* (*q.v.*), an animal tranquilizer. Spanish for *elephant* (*q.v.*). RT: *P.C.P.* [U.S., NIDA: 1980]

element, in one's alcohol intoxicated. (BF: 1737: [He's] In his Element.) RT: *drunk*. [BF: 1737]

elephant (also elephant tranquilizer) phencyclidine, *P.C.P.* (*q.v.*), an animal tranquilizer. RT: *P.C.P.* [U.S., RRL: 1969, YKB: 1977, (DNE: 1980), NIDA: 1980] See also *pink elephants, seeing pink elephants*.

elephant's trunk (also elephant's, elephants, elephant trunk) alcohol intoxicated. Rhyming slang for *drunk*. RT: *drunk*. [JCH: 1859, B&L: 1890, JRW: 1909, BVB: 1942, DRS, SSD, PW: 1974]

elevated (also slightly elevated) alcohol intoxicated; tipsy. RT: *drunk*. [(1664): F&H, (1827): OEDS, B&L: 1890, AH: 1931, MHW: 1934, W&F: 1960]

elevator 1. a preparation of opium used regularly. RT: *opium*. ELA: 1984 lists elevation. [Br., JCH: 1887] 2. liquor. *Cf.* *elevated*. RT: *booze*. [U.S., BVB: 1942]

eli lilly morphine. Named for the drug manufacturer Eli Lilly and Company. *Cf.* *lillys*. RT: *morphine*. [U.S., HB: 1955]

eliminated alcohol intoxicated. RT: *drunk*. [U.S., ADC: 1975]

el kif See *kif*.

els *Elavil* (TM; *q.v.*) antidepressant tablets. [U.S., JWK: 1981]

em 1. an empty liquor bottle. RT: *dead soldier*. [U.S., BVB: 1942] 2. (also emm) morphine. A spelling out of the initial M. *Cf.* *emsel*. RT: *morphine*. Hobo use. [U.S., BVB: 1942, SNP: 1977]

embalmed alcohol intoxicated. *Cf.* *pickled*. RT: *drunk*. [U.S., MHW: 1934, D&D: 1957, W&F: 1960]

embalming fluid 1. strong liquor; bad whiskey. RT: *rotgut*. [U.S., BVB: 1942, W&F: 1960] 2. phencyclidine, *P.C.P.* RT: *P.C.P.* [U.S., ELA: 1984]

embroidery 1. a vague narcotics argot term referring to narcotics traffic and supplies. *Cf.* *Chinese needlework*. [U.S., DWM: 1938]

2. scars on the arms from many drug injections. RT: *tracks*. [U.S., RRL: 1969, RDS: 1982]

emergency gun an improvised means for getting a drug directly into the bloodstream. Typically a needle, sewing machine needle, or safety pin is used to open a vein and a medicine dropper is used to pump in the drug. RS: *monkey pump*. [U.S., DWM: 1936, BVB: 1942]

emperor a drunkard. Probably taken from *drunk as an emperor* (*q.v.*). RT: *sot*. [U.S., GWM: 1859, F&H, MHW: 1934, BVB: 1942]

Empirin a protected trade name for tablets of codeine phosphate (an analgesic) and additional ingredients. The drug reduces pain and lowers fevers. The drug is available in four different strengths based on the amount of codeine in each. The tablets are stamped 1, 2, 3, and 4, the latter being the strongest. *Cf. fours, threes*. [in current use; consult a pharmaceutical reference for more information]

empties empty gelatin capsules returned to a drug dealer for a discount on the next purchase. *Cf. cap*. [U.S., JWK: 1981]

emsel morphine. A respelling of *M. sul.* which is an abbreviation of morphine sulfate. RT: *morphine*. [U.S., M&V: 1954, YKB: 1977]

emu-bobbing (also **emuing**) collecting cigarette butts for reuse. [Aust., WWII, SJB: 1943]

ends money; money to be used for drugs. [U.S., TRG: 1968, M&V: 1973]

energizer phencyclidine, *P.C.P.* RT: *P.C.P.* [U.S., ELA: 1984]

enforcer a bully or strong-arm man for a drug dealer. [U.S., JWK: 1981]

en ganchos* addicted. LIT: hooked (in Spanish). RT: *hooked*. [U.S., EEL: 1971, RDS: 1982]

engine (also **the engine**) an opium smoking outfit. *Cf. lean against the engine*. RS: *outfit*. [U.S., BD: 1937, DWM: 1938, VJM: 1949, GOL: 1950, H&C: 1975]

English burgundy *porter* (*q.v.*), porter's ale. A sweet, low-proof beer drunk by (London) market porters. RT: *porter*. [cant, FG: 1785, GWM: 1859]

eng-shee an alcohol extraction of opium residue used for injections. *Cf. yen-shee*. [U.S., early 1900s, DU]

enhanced high on marijuana. RT: *wasted*. [U.S., JWK: 1981]

en juanado* marijuana intoxicated. Spanish: in a "juana-ed" state, *potted* (*q.v.*). RT: *wasted*. [U.S., EEL: 1971]

en leñado* intoxicated with marijuana. Spanish: in the bush. *Cf. bush*. RT: *wasted*. [U.S., EEL: 1971]

en motado* intoxicated with marijuana. Spanish for dusted. *Cf.*

dust, mota. RT: *stoned, wasted*. [U.S., EEL: 1971]

enns *Darvon-N* (TM; *q.v.*) or *Darvocet-N* (TM; *q.v.*) painkiller. The same as *N.s* (*q.v.*). *Cf. vons*. [U.S., JWK: 1981]

ensign-bearer a drunkard. See *flying the ensign*. The drunkard's red face is compared to a red flag (the ensign). RT: *sot*. [Br., FG: 1785, FG: 1811; listed in BVB: 1942]

entered alcohol intoxicated. (BF: 1737: [He's] Enter'd.) *Cf. pretty well enter'd*. RT: *drunk*. [BF: 1737]

enyedado* (also **enjedado***) intoxicated with marijuana. *Cf. yedo*. RT: *wasted*. Spanish. [U.S., EEL: 1971]

erb marijuana. See *herb*. RT: *pot*. [U.S., ADC: 1975]

erth phencyclidine, *P.C.P.* Probably eye-dialect for *earth*. RT: *P.C.P.* [U.S., ELA: 1984]

Ervine a police officer. See *Irvine*. RT: *fuzz*. [U.S., D&B: 1970c]

esar an error for *esrar* (*q.v.*). [ELA: 1982]

esrar a tobacco and hashish mixture; marijuana. From Turkish. ELA: 1982 lists **esar**. RT: *pot*. [U.S., (1926): RPW: 1938, D&D: 1957, RRL: 1969]

estuffa* heroin. From the Spanish word for *stuff*. RT: *heroin*. [U.S., ELA: 1984]

ether ethyl oxide, a highly volatile anesthetic gas. It has been drunk as a substitute for ethyl alcohol, injected into beer bottles, and inhaled for a high. [(1796): OEDS]

ethical drug a prescription drug; a drug which is dispensed only on the order of a physician. [(1952): OEDS]

ethyl alcohol drinkable alcohol. [(1896): MW: 1983]

evidence (also **the evidence**) liquor. GEN: contraband. RT: *booze*. Implying that the possession of liquor is illegal. From the prohibition era. [U.S., BVB: 1942]

evil powder cocaine; powdered cocaine. RT: *cocaine*. Probably not slang. [U.S., ADC: 1981]

exalted alcohol intoxicated. RT: *drunk*. [Br., (1836): F&H; listed in BVB: 1942]

experience an L.S.D. trip. Euphemistic. Not drug argot. [U.S., TRG: 1968, RG: 1970]

explorer's club *L.S.D.* (*q.v.*) users; a group of L.S.D. users. *Cf. Arctic explorer*. [U.S., JBW: 1967, EEL: 1971, IGA: 1971]

exposures marijuana cigarettes. See *developing room* for other terms on this theme. RT: *joint*. [U.S., ADC: 1975]

extracted drunk on flavoring extracts used in cooking. Flavoring extracts usually contain a fair amount of alcohol. RT: *drunk*. [U.S. Army, WWII, DST: 1984]

eyelid movies images seen during an L.S.D. experience. *Cf. cartoon*. RS: *hallucination*. [U.S., E&R: 1971]

eye-opener 1. a wake-up drink; the first drink of the day; a stiff drink any time. *Cf. morning rouser*. RS: *nip*. Probably recurrent nonce in this sense. [(1815): W&F: 1960, (1818): OEDS, BWG: 1899, (1916): DSUE, AH: 1931, GI: 1931, MHW: 1934, D&D: 1957] 2. the first narcotics injection of the day. From sense one. The same as *get-up* (*q.v.*). *Cf. constitutional, morning glory*. [U.S., DWM: 1938, RRL: 1969, W&F: 1975] 3. (also eye-openers) amphetamines; amphetamine tablets; *Methedrine* (*q.v.*). RT: *amps*. [U.S., RG: 1970, IGA: 1971, SH: 1972, YKB: 1977; Bahamas, JAH: 1982]

eyespeck See *bird's eye*.

eyewater (also eyewash) 1. gin. RT: *gin*. [Br., FG: 1823, JCH: 1887, B&L: 1890; listed in BVB: 1942] 2. cheap liquor. RS: *rotgut*. [U.S., BR: 1972]

F

faced alcohol intoxicated. A euphemism for *shit-faced* (*q.v.*). RT: *drunk*. [U.S., D&B: 1970c, N&S: 1983, RAS: 1985]

factory 1. a secret place where drugs are made, processed, packaged, and perhaps used; an *L.S.D.* (*q.v.*) manufacturing site. RS: *pad*. Probably not argot. [U.S., DWM: 1938, RRL: 1969] 2. the equipment for using drugs. *Cf. engine*. RT: *outfit*. [U.S., BD: 1937, DWM: 1938, VJM: 1949, TRG: 1968, EEL: 1971]

fag a cigarette butt; a cigarette. Short for *faggot* (*q.v.*) or *fag end* (*q.v.*). RT: *nail*. More popular in Britain than the U.S. [Br. and U.S., (1888): OEDS, DSUE, (1908): SBF: 1982, F&G: 1925, WM: 1927, VWS: 1929, GI: 1931, D&D: 1957, SSD, B&P: 1965, ADC: 1975]

fag drag a puff on a tobacco cigarette. [U.S., military, BVB: 1942]

fag end a cigar or cigarette butt. From a term for the frayed end of a nautical line (rope). GEN: the end piece of anything (FBL: 1898). RT: *brad*. [(1853): OED, B&P: 1965, M&J: 1975]

faggeroo a cigarette. RT: *nail*. [U.S., M&J: 1975]

faggot 1. a cigarette. *Cf. maggot*. RT: *nail*. [U.S., BVB: 1942, VJM: 1949] 2. a marijuana cigarette; cannabis. RT: *joint*. [U.S., JES: 1959, H&C: 1975]

faint alcohol intoxicated. RT: *drunk*. Never common (W&F: 1960). [U.S., mid 1800s, W&F: 1960]

fairy an opium smoker's lamp. These lamps burned peanut oil. The flame of the lamp comes in contact with the bowl of the lamp which passes the heat through to the opium pellets which are vaporized and drawn up the stem of the opium pipe by the smoker. GEN: a lamp containing a candle (1891): OEDS. [U.S., late 18–1900s, DU]

fairy dust phencyclidine, P.C.P., an animal tranquilizer. RT: *P.C.P.* [U.S., EEL: 1971, ADC: 1981] See also *ferry dust*.

fairy powder any powdered narcotic. RT: *powder*. [U.S., (c. 1930): JES: 1959, H&C: 1975]

fake (also **fake-a-loo, fake aloo**) a homemade substitute for a hypodermic syringe. *Cf. emergency gun*. RS: *monkey pump*. From a general slang term for any fake or substitute item. [U.S., DWM: 1938, VJM: 1949]

fake S.T.P. *P.C.P.* (*q.v.*). See *S.T.P.* RT: *P.C.P.* [U.S., FAB: 1979]

fall an injection of drugs. Probably from *lay* (*q.v.*). RT: *shot.* [U.S., S&W: 1973]

fall down the sink a drink. See *tumble.*

falling-down drunk 1. alcohol intoxicated; very drunk. *Cf. knee-walking drunk, snot-flinging drunk.* RT: *drunk.* [U.S., RAS: 1978] 2. a drunken person who falls down; a very drunken person. RT: *sot.* [U.S., RAS: 1984]

falling out nodding off into a nap while in a drug stupor. Possibly a sign of an overdose. *Cf. nodding, nodding out.* [U.S., (RRL: 1969), (EEL: 1971)]

fall in the thick to get drunk. *Thick* (*q.v.*) = *porter* (*q.v.*). *Cf. thick and thin.* [U.S., JRW: 1909]

fall off the wagon to resume drinking after having stopped. *Cf. on the wagon.* [U.S., BVB: 1942, DCCU: 1972]

fall out to overdose; to pass out from drugs. *Cf. falling out.* [U.S., D&B: 1978, JWK: 1981]

family disturbance whiskey. RT: *whiskey.* [U.S., B&L: 1890, F&H]

famine a lack of drugs; a period when one cannot locate or buy drugs. *Cf. drought, panic.* [U.S., JES: 1959, H&C: 1975]

fan a person who uses drugs only occasionally, perhaps an onlooker at drug parties. *Cf. panic.* GEN: a devotee. RS: *chipper.* [U.S., D&B: 1970c]

fancy smile a drink. *Cf. smile.* RT: *nip.* [Br., 1800s, F&H; listed in BVB: 1942]

fang (also **fang it**) to inject drugs rather than take them in some other fashion. Refers to the needle as a **fang**. RT: *shoot.* [U.S., JES: 1959, H&C: 1975]

farahead alcohol intoxicated. Pertaining to a person who has drunk more than anyone else. RT: *drunk.* [U.S., AH: 1931, MHW: 1934]

far and near beer; a glass of beer. Rhyming slang. RT: *beer.* [18-1900s, DRS, M&B: 1944]

far gone alcohol intoxicated. *Cf. gone.* GEN: in an extreme state. RT: *drunk.* [(1616): OEDS, F&H; listed in BVB: 1942]

farm a crop consume a fifth of liquor or wine. RT: *guzzle.* [U.S., GU: 1975]

farmer 1. someone who grows marijuana at home. [U.S., JWK: 1981] See also *domestic, home-grown.* 2. a *straight* (*q.v.*) or *square* (*q.v.*) person. RT: *square.* [U.S., ELA: 1982]

far out (also **far-fucking-out**) alcohol intoxicated; drug intoxicated;

in another world with or without the aid of drugs. GEN: extraordinary. *Cf. way out.* [U.S., S&W: 1966, EEL: 1971, N&S: 1983]

fat having to do with a drug user who has a large supply of drugs. GEN: with an overabundance. [U.S., IGA: 1971, D&B: 1978, RDS: 1982] See also *gee-fat.*

fat jay a thick marijuana cigarette. A fat *joint* (*q.v.*). RT: *joint.* [U.S., C&H: 1974]

fatty a thick marijuana cigarette. *Cf. bomber, rocket, sausage, submarine, torpedo.* RT: *joint.* [U.S., RRL: 1969, D&B: 1978, RDS: 1982]

favorite vice (also **vice**) liquor; drinking. RS: *booze.* [(1885): JRW: 1909]

fears no man alcohol intoxicated. *Cf. Dutch courage.* RT: *drunk.* [BF: 1737]

feathered under the influence of drugs and ready to fly. RT: *stoned.* [U.S., JES: 1959, H&C: 1975]

featured alcohol intoxicated. RT: *drunk.* [U.S., MHW: 1934, BVB: 1942]

feavourish alcohol intoxicated. The modern spelling is *feverish. Cf. barrel fever.* RT: *drunk.* [BF: 1722]

fed (also **the feds**) a federal narcotics agent; any federal agent. Now refers to a wide variety of federal enforcement and regulatory bodies. No longer argot. [U.S., M&W: 1946, VJM: 1949, M&H: 1959, RRL: 1969, EEL: 1971]

feeblo a drug addict. Possibly akin to *feeble.* RT: *junky.* [U.S., VJM: 1949, A&T: 1953]

feed 1. drugs. RS: *dope.* [U.S., BVB: 1942, H&C: 1975] 2. to use drugs; to take drugs. [U.S., (H&C: 1975)]

feed and grain man a drug seller. *Cf. feed.* Grain may refer to grains of heroin or morphine. RT: *dealer.* [U.S., JES: 1959, H&C: 1975]

feed bag narcotics; a pack of drugs; a dose of drugs. Used in the expression *put on the feed bag.* RS: *dope.* [U.S., JES: 1959, JTD: 1971]

feeder a hypodermic syringe. RT: *monkey pump.* [U.S., JES: 1959, H&C: 1975]

feeding candy taking cocaine. *Cf. candy.* [U.S., JES: 1959, H&C: 1975]

feed one's head to take drugs by mouth. *Cf. feed.* [U.S., M&V: 1973]

feed store a place to buy and use drugs. *Cf. feed.* RS: *doperie.* [U.S., JES: 1959, JTD: 1971]

feel a thing coming on (also **feel the habit coming on, feel the monkey coming on**) to experience the early symptom of narcotics withdrawal, i.e., craving for drugs. [U.S., DWM: 1938, (RRL: 1969)]

feeling aces alcohol intoxicated. Paul Dickson lists others along the same lines: feeling dizzy, feeling excellent, feeling frisky, feeling glorious, feeling happy, feeling his alcohol, feeling his booze, feeling his cheerios, feeling his drink, feeling his liquor, feeling his oats, feeling his onions, feeling it, feeling pretty good, feeling real well, feeling the effect. RT: *drunk*. [PD: 1982]

feeling funny alcohol intoxicated. RT: *drunk*. [Br., 1800s, F&H; listed in BVB: 1942]

feeling good alcohol intoxicated. RT: *drunk*. [U.S., (1850s): SBF: 1976, BVB: 1942, N&S: 1983]

feeling groovy drug intoxicated. *Cf. groovy*. RT: *stoned*. Now general slang for feeling good from any cause. [U.S., RRL: 1969]

feeling high (also feeling right) *mellow* (*q.v.*); alcohol or drug intoxicated. RT: *drunk, stoned*. [U.S., BVB: 1942]

feeling no pain alcohol intoxicated. RT: *drunk*. [U.S., (1940s): SBF: 1976, W&F: 1960]

feeling right royal alcohol intoxicated. Probably a play on *drunk as a lord, drunk as an earl, drunk as an emperor*. RT: *drunk*. [Br., 1800s, F&H; listed in BVB: 1942]

fee-tops (also fees, fe-ops) the female tops of marijuana plants. Compare to *male*. *Cf. tops*. RS: *pot*. [U.S., JWK: 1981]

feke methyl alcohol. Possibly from *fecal*. *Cf. jake*. RT: *methyl*. [Br., (1932): DSUE]

feke-drinker a drinker of *denatured* (*q.v.*) alcohol. RS: *sot*. [Br., (1932): DSUE, DU]

fen *fentanyl* (*q.v.*), a powerful painkiller now called Sublimaze (TM). See *designer drug* for more information about a class of drugs derived from this substance. [U.S., JWK: 1981]

fender-benders barbiturate tablets or capsules. RT: *barbs*. [U.S., IGA: 1971, EAF: 1972]

fennel marijuana. From the name of the herb fennel. *Cf. oregano*. RT: *pot*. [U.S., ELA: 1984]

fentanyl a narcotic analgesic now called Sublimaze (TM). See *fen*.

fermentarian a drunkard. *Cf. bartarian*. RT: *sot*. A contrived, jocular term. [U.S., BVB: 1942]

ferry dust heroin. See *fairy dust*. Possibly in error for *fairy dust*. RT: *heroin*. [U.S., ELA: 1984]

feshnushkied alcohol intoxicated. RT: *drunk*. [U.S., RAS: 1985]

fettered alcohol intoxicated. (BF: 1737: [He's] Fetter'd.) RT: *drunk*. [BF: 1737]

fettled (also in fine fettle, in good fettle) alcohol intoxicated. GEN: in good condition. RT: *drunk*. [Br., 1800s, F&H]

F-forties (also **F-40s**) *Seconal* (TM; *q.v.*) barbiturate capsules, specifically: 100 mg Puvules (capsules) of Seconal sodium bearing the Identi-Code symbol F40. Puvules, Seconal, and Identi-Code are registered trade names. RT: *sec.* [U.S., EAF: 1972, SNP: 1977, W&S: 1977]

fiddled alcohol intoxicated. *Cf. drunk as a fiddler's bitch.* RT: *drunk.* [U.S., AH: 1931, MHW: 1934]

fi-do-nie opium. RT: *opium.* [U.S., (M&V: 1954)]

fiend a drug addict. A truncation of *dope fiend* (*q.v.*). The OED attests to the use of fiend in the sense of *-buff,* or *-hound* as early as 1870. RT: *junky.* [U.S., (1887): RML: 1948, VWS: 1929, DWM: 1938, HB: 1955, RRL: 1969, EEL: 1971, ADC: 1981]

fiery snorter a drunkard's nose. *Cf. gin bud.* [U.S., BVB: 1942]

fifty (also **50**) the hallucinogenic drug L.S.D. RT: *L.S.D.* [U.S., YKB: 1977]

fighting drunk (also **fighting tight**) alcohol intoxicated and angry. [Br., B&L: 1890, F&H; U.S., BVB: 1942]

figure eight a feigned fit or spasm of an addict who is trying to get drugs. RT: *brody.* [U.S., DWM: 1936, VJM: 1949]

fill a blanket to roll a cigarette. *Blanket* (*q.v.*) = cigarette rolling paper. [U.S., PRB: 1930, VJM: 1949, GOL: 1950]

fillings (also **fillin's**) tobacco; tobacco for rolling cigarettes. *Cf. rollings.* RT: *freckles.* [U.S., HS: 1933, MHW: 1934, GOL: 1950]

filling station a tavern; a place to purchase liquor. Punning on the term for an automobile service station. RS: *bar, L.I.Q.* [U.S., BVB: 1942, EAF: 1980]

fillmill a bar; a tavern. RS: *bar.* Black slang. [U.S., M&W: 1946, BVB: 1953, W&F: 1960]

film can (also **film**) marijuana; a container for carrying marijuana. See *developing room* for other terms on this theme. [U.S., ADC: 1981]

filthy weed (also **the filthy weed**) tobacco. RT: *fogus.* Any current use is probably nonce. [U.S., BVB: 1942]

fina-esmeralda* marijuana. Spanish for fine emerald. RT: *pot.* [calo, JBR: 1973]

fine and dandy (also **fine**) brandy; a glass of brandy. Rhyming slang. RT: *brandy.* [18-1900s, DU, M&B: 1944, DRS]

fine stuff good-quality drugs or marijuana. In the case of marijuana, the stems and other *lumber* (*q.v.*) are removed before it is cut up. *Cf. manicure.* [U.S., HB: 1955, EEL: 1971]

finger 1. the height of liquor in a glass, equal to the width of a finger. Most common as **two fingers** or **three fingers**. [U.S., (1856): SBF: 1982, (1888): SOD, K&M: 1968] 2. (also **finger of stuff**) a condom or finger cot filled with drugs and swallowed or concealed in the rectum or vagina. *Cf. body-packer, internal,* *swallower*. [U.S., BD: 1937, DWM: 1938, VJM: 1949, RRL: 1969] 3. a bootlegger. RT: *bootlegger*. [U.S., AH: 1931] 4. (also **fingers**) Mediterranean hashish in stick form. RT: *hash*. [U.S., RRL: 1969]

finger and thumb rum. Rhyming slang. RT: *rum*. [Br., JCH: 1859, F&G: 1925, SSD, DRS; U.S., M&B: 1944]

finger of stuff a balloon or condom used to keep drugs dry while they are being transported. See *finger*.

finger wave a digital examination of the rectum for concealed drugs. Based on the slang term for the gesture called *the finger*. [U.S., H&C: 1975, RDS: 1982]

fir hashish. RT: *hash*. [U.S., ELA: 1984]

fire 1. the potency of the alcohol in liquor; the effect of potent alcohol. [U.S., BVB: 1942] 2. a tobacco cigarette. RT: *nail*. [U.S., DB: 1944] 3. to inject a dose of drugs. A synonym of *shoot* (*q.v.*). *Cf. gun*. RT: *shoot*. [U.S., DWM: 1936, VJM: 1949, JWK: 1981]

fire a line to sniff (snort) a *line* (*q.v.*) of cocaine. RS: *snort*. [U.S., RAS: 1980]

fire a slug to take a drink of liquor. *Slug* (*q.v.*) = a drink, a *shot* (*q.v.*) of liquor. RT: *irrigate*. [FG: 1785, FG: 1811, FG: 1823, MHW: 1934, K&M: 1968]

firecracker a fat marijuana cigarette. RT: *joint*. [U.S., JH: 1979]

fired 1. alcohol intoxicated. *Cf. fired up*. RT: *drunk*. [U.S., BVB: 1942] 2. having to do with marijuana ashes with no active ingredient remaining. *Cf. cashed*. [U.S., ADC: 1981]

fired up 1. alcohol intoxicated. *Cf. fired*. RT: *drunk*. [U.S., (c. 1850): W&F: 1960; listed in BVB: 1942] See also *fire up*. 2. high on marijuana. RT: *wasted*. [U.S., ADC: 1984].

fire plug a large pellet of opium. RS: *opium*. [U.S., BD: 1937, DWM: 1938, BVB: 1942]

fire up 1. to get high or hot with booze. RS: *irrigate*. [U.S., D&B: 1971] 2. to light a marijuana cigarette; to smoke marijuana; to take any drug. RT: *hit the hay*. [U.S., (1960): ELA: 1982, EEL: 1971, EAF: 1980]

firewater whiskey; hard liquor. Said to be an Amerindian term. One tale is that the liquor was thrown on a fire to test its proof. Another is that it burned one's insides like liquid fire. RT: *whiskey*. [U.S., (1817): OEDS, DSUE, (1826): RHT: 1912, JSF: 1889, AH: 1931, MHW: 1934, D&D: 1957, DCCU: 1972]

first line morphine. Refers to morphine as the highest quality line of merchandise. RT: *morphine*. [U.S., YKB: 1977]

fish a drunkard. *Cf. drunk as a fish*. RT: *sot*. [Br., 1800s, F&H]

fishy alcohol intoxicated. (BF: 1737: He's Fishey.) RT: *drunk*. [BF: 1737]

fishy about the gills alcohol intoxicated; appearing to be drunk. RT: *drunk*. [JRW: 1909]

fistaris (also **fisstaris, phystaris**) thing; gadget; any object related to drug use such as a needle or a cooking spoon. Essentially a *whatchamacallit*. [U.S., M&V: 1954]

fit equipment for injecting drugs. A truncation of *outfit* (*q.v.*). [U.S., GS: 1959, JBW: 1967, RRL: 1969, W&F: 1975, JWK: 1981]

five-cent bag (also **five-dollar bag**) a five-dollar bag of drugs. RS: *load*. [U.S., EEL: 1971, C&H: 1974]

five-cent paper five dollars worth of a powdered drug folded in a paper. *Cf. paper*. RS: *load*. [U.S., EEL: 1971]

fives 5 mg tablets of an amphetamine. *Cf. tens*. RT: *amps*. [U.S., RRL: 1969, YKB: 1977]

fix 1. (also **fix-up**) a ration of narcotics; an injection of narcotics. Now in general slang referring to a dose of substances such as soft drinks, nose spray, candy, and alcohol as well as insulin and painkillers. RS: *shot*. [U.S., (1934): OEDS, DWM: 1936, DWM: 1938, VJM: 1949, M&D: 1952, W&F: 1960, S&W: 1966, CM: 1970, EEL: 1971, ADC: 1981] 2. to buy a dose of drugs; to inject a dose of drugs. *Cf. re-fix*. RS: *shoot*. [U.S., BD: 1937, DWM: 1938, W&F: 1960, D&B: 1970c, RRL: 1969, MA: 1973, EAF: 1980, ADC: 1981]

fixed up 1. (also **fixed**) provided with a dose of drugs; high on drugs. *Cf. straight*. RT: *stoned*. [U.S., M&V: 1967, D&B: 1970c] 2. (also **in a fix**) alcohol intoxicated. RT: *drunk*. Rendered as "...in that fix..." (JRB: 1859). [U.S., BVB: 1942]

fixer a drug seller; a person who injects a dose of drugs. *Cf. fix*. RS: *dealer*. [U.S., NAM: 1953, AP: 1980]

Fix me! "Sell me a dose of drugs!" or "Give me an injection of drugs!" RT: *How are you going to act?* [U.S., M&D: 1952]

fizz (also **fiz**) champagne. RT: *cham*. [(1864): OED, JCH: 1887, B&L: 1890, JRW: 1909, D&D: 1957, SSD, M&J: 1975] See also *fizz water*.

fizzed up alcohol intoxicated; drunk or tipsy on champagne. RT: *drunk*. [U.S., BVB: 1942]

fizzical culturalist a bartender. A play on *physical culturist*. RT: *bartender*. [U.S., BVB: 1942, DB: 1944]

fizz water soda or seltzer water. *Cf. sizz water*. [U.S., (1889): OEDS, MHW: 1934]

flabbergasted alcohol intoxicated. GEN: surprised, baffled. RT: *drunk*. [PD: 1982]

flag blood which appears in a syringe or medicine dropper indicating that the needle has entered a vein. Pertains to the injection of drugs. *Cf. verification shot*. [U.S., JTD: 1971, MA:

1973, RDS: 1982]

flagged arrested. RT: *busted*. [U.S., (1971): ELA: 1982]

flag of defiance (also **flag of distress**) a drunkard; an angry drunkard. *Cf. ensign-bearer*. RS: *sot*. [nautical, (BE: 1690), FG: 1823, F&H]

flake 1. (also **Bernies flake**) cocaine; a medicinal form of crystallized cocaine. RT: *cocaine*. [U.S., (1922): DU, JBW: 1967, RRL: 1969, EEL: 1971, NIDA: 1980, ADC: 1984] 2. any drug which acts primarily on the mind rather than the body, one which makes you flaky. [U.S., H&C: 1975] 3. for the police to place drugs or traces of drugs on a person during an arrest. The person is then charged with possession of drugs. Underworld terminology. [U.S., JWK: 1981] **4**. (also **flake out**) to pass out from drugs or pills. Compare to *freak out*. [U.S., (1968): DNE: 1973, EEL: 1971] **5**. (also **flakes**) phencyclidine, *P.C.P.* (*q.v.*), an animal tranquilizer. RT: *P.C.P.* [U.S., FAB: 1979, ADC: 1981] 6. a person under the influence of cocaine. It is possible that the general slang expression *flaky* comes directly from sense one. This sense (six) may come either directly from sense one, from the general slang term meaning giddy, or from both. RS: *kokomo*. [U.S., RDS: 1982]

flake acid a diluted solution of L.S.D. placed on blotter paper and cut up into small servings. RT: *L.S.D.* [U.S., ELA: 1984]

flaked out 1. alcohol intoxicated. RT: *drunk*. [(1939): DSUE] 2. (also **flaked**) passed out due to the exertion of a drug experience. Now GEN: exhausted and disoriented. RS: *stoned*. [U.S., (EEL: 1971), (DNE: 1973)]

flakers See *Harry Flakers*.

flake spoon See cokespoon.

flako (also **flaky**) alcohol intoxicated. RT: *drunk*. [U.S., (1971): DNE: 1973]

flaky 1. habituated to the use of cocaine. *Cf. candied, caught in a snowstorm, dusted, powdered*. RS: *hooked*. [U.S., early 1900s, DU, RRL: 1969] 2. alcohol intoxicated. See *flako*.

flame up to light up a marijuana cigarette; to smoke a marijuana cigarette. RS: *hit the hay*. [U.S., BR: 1972]

flapper likker inferior liquor; prohibition era liquor, liquor from the flapper era. RS: *rotgut*. [U.S., BVB: 1942]

flare-up (also **flare**) a drinking bout. Akin to U.S. **flared up** (= alcohol intoxicated) and British **flaring drunk**. RT: *spree*. [1800s, F&H]

flash 1. a drink of liquor. *Cf. flash of lightning*. RT: *nip*. [Br., (1789): OED, F&H; listed in BVB: 1942] 2. a drug rush; a special kind of volatile drug *rush* (*q.v.*) from an injection. Various sources attribute it to the use of heroin or cocaine. [U.S., GS: 1959, M&V: 1967, W&F: 1967, MW: 1976, DNE: 1980, ADC:

1981] 3. to feel the initial effects of a drug; to feel a drug rush; to hallucinate, either initially or briefly upon taking a psychedelic drug, usually *L.S.D.* (*q.v.*) or an amphetamine. From sense one. [U.S., EEL: 1971, (DES: 1972), DNE: 1973] 4. a hallucination, especially if brief, caused by a psychedelic drug. From *flashback* (*q.v.*). *Cf. bean trip, cartoon, echoes, pattern, trail.* [U.S., D&B: 1971, EEL: 1971] 5. *L.S.D.* (*q.v.*) on a tablet. RT: *L.S.D.* [U.S., SNP: 1977] 6. to vomit after a heroin injection. From the phrase *flash the hash,* which has been underworld jargon for vomit (verb) since the 1700s. Its use is not limited to narcotics argot. [U.S., JBW: 1967, RRL: 1969, M&V: 1973] 7. to sniff glue to get high. *Cf. huffer.* [U.S., (RRL: 1969), IGA: 1971]

flashback (also **flashbacks**) a recurrent hallucination experienced (long) after an *L.S.D.* (*q.v.*) trip. Also said to occur after marijuana use in some people. *Cf. echoes, pattern, trail.* [U.S., RG: 1970, (1970): DNE: 1973, EEL: 1971, DES: 1972, S&R: 1972, W&F: 1975]

flash drum (also **flash case, flash ken, flash panny**) a tavern or pub for thieves. *Cf. drum.* RS: *dive.* [cant, BE: 1690, F&H; listed in GWM: 1859]

flash in the pan the brief rush caused by heroin which has been cut with quinine. GEN: something sudden and brief. *Cf. flash.* RS: *rush.* [U.S., JWK: 1981]

flash of lightning a glass of gin. *Cf. lightning.* RS: *gin.* [(1789): F&H, FG: 1823, JCH: 1887, B&L: 1890; listed in BVB: 1942]

flash out a momentary passing out from sniffing an *inhalant* (*q.v.*). Surely the verb sense is also used. [U.S., RG: 1970]

flask a flat bottle, usually made of metal, for carrying liquor. It is usually carried in the hip pocket. Standard English. [since the 1800s, (1814): OED] Additional terms and nicknames for liquor-carrying vessels: *hip flask, hip hooch, kid, life preserver, Michael, mickey, micky, monkey, pocket pistol, tickler.*

flatfoot (also **flat-arch, flathead, flatty**) a policeman; a *beat pounder* (*q.v.*). Refers to feet ruined by walking. Stereotypical underworld jargon. RS: *fuzz.* [U.S., (1913): OEDS, EK: 1927, BVB: 1942, D&D: 1957]

flats (also **blue flats, flat blues**) tablets of *L.S.D.* (*q.v.*); the hallucinogenic drug L.S.D. RT: *L.S.D.* [U.S., EEL: 1971, YKB: 1977]

flattened drug intoxicated; in a drug-induced stupor. RT: *stoned.* [U.S., JES: 1959, JTD: 1971] See also *mashed.*

flatten the poker to use narcotics to the point of impotence. Poker = penis. Probably nonce. [U.S., JES: 1959]

flawed (also **flaw'd**) alcohol intoxicated. RT: *drunk.* [cant, (1673): OED, BE: 1690, FG: 1785, FG: 1811, FG: 1823, GWM: 1859; listed in BVB: 1942]

flea powder bogus heroin; low-quality or bogus drugs of any type. RT: ***blank***. [U.S., HB: 1955, TRG: 1968, RRL: 1969, W&F: 1975]

flicker to drink liquor. RT: ***irrigate***. [cant, GWM: 1859, B&L: 1890, DU]

flick of tobacco a piece of tobacco. RS: ***quid***. [Bahamas, early 1900s, JAH: 1982]

flier (also **flyer**) a drug user or addict who is always high. RS: ***user***. [U.S., BVB: 1942, VJM: 1949, A&T: 1953]

flight, in high on drugs, especially amphetamines. RS: ***stoned***. [U.S., M&V: 1973, H&C: 1975]

fling a drinking bout; a ***spree*** (*q.v.*). A person who has frequent flings is a **flinger**. [U.S., BVB: 1942]

flip out (also **flip**) to lose control of oneself due to drugs; to become deranged due to an ***L.S.D.*** (*q.v.*) trip. GEN: to lose control. Probably from *flip one's wig*. [U.S., A&T: 1953, RRL: 1969, ADC: 1981]

flip over to go off drugs temporarily. RS: ***kick***. [U.S., M&V: 1967]

flipped stupefied by drugs; drug intoxicated. RT: ***stoned***. [U.S., JES: 1959]

floater a bit of congealed blood clogging a hypodermic needle. *Cf.* ***gravy***. [U.S., M&V: 1967]

floating 1. alcohol intoxicated. RT: ***drunk***. [U.S., BVB: 1942, W&F: 1960] 2. drug intoxicated; marijuana intoxicated. *Cf.* ***in flight, in orbit***. RT: ***stoned***. [U.S., DWM: 1936, RPW: 1938, W&F: 1960, RRL: 1969, CM: 1970, (EEL: 1971), ADC: 1975]

flogged drug intoxicated. RT: ***stoned***. [U.S., VJM: 1949, A&T: 1953]

flooded alcohol intoxicated. *Cf.* ***inundated***. RT: ***drunk***. [U.S., BVB: 1942]

flood one's sewers to get drunk. RT: ***mug oneself***. [U.S., BVB: 1942]

flooey alcohol intoxicated. GEN: kaput, destroyed. RT: ***drunk***. [U.S., AH: 1931, MHW: 1934, D&D: 1957, W&F: 1960]

floored alcohol intoxicated. GEN: surprised. LIT: having been knocked to the floor. RT: ***drunk***. [(1812): DSUE, F&H, (1850-1900): RFA]

flop to smoke opium at an opium den. This *flop* is from *flop house*. RT: ***suck bamboo***. [U.S., ELA: 1984]

floppy alcohol intoxicated; very drunk. *Cf.* ***limber, loose***. RT: ***drunk***. [JM: 1923]

flor di cabaggio* a cheap and bad-smelling cigar. Mock-Italian (or some other Romance language). *Cf.* ***cabbagio perfumo***. RT: ***seegar***. [Br., late 18-1900s, DSUE]

florid red with drink; alcohol intoxicated. GEN: flowery. *Cf.* ***in***

color. RT: ***drunk.*** [Br., 17-1800s, DSUE]

Florida snow a white powder anesthetic snorted like cocaine; cocaine. See more snow theme expressions at ***winter wonderland.*** [U.S., RAS: 1982, ELA: 1984]

flow to yield one's mind to the euphoria of a hallucinogenic drug. See ***go with the flow.*** [U.S., RRL: 1969, H&C: 1975]

flower children (also **flower people**) members of the youth culture of the 1960s and 1970s. Among other activities they used marijuana and other drugs. The term is synonymous with drug users for some people. [U.S., (1968): DNE: 1973, EEL: 1971, W&F: 1975]

flower of the virgin the hallucinogenic substance *ololiuqui* (*q.v.*). [U.S., YKB: 1977]

flower tops (also **flowers**) the resinous buds of marijuana plants. *Cf. fee-tops.* RS: ***pot.*** [U.S., RRL: 1969, ADC: 1981]

flowing bowl liquor. RT: ***booze.*** A stilted sobriquet; not slang. [U.S., MHW: 1934, BVB: 1942]

fluff to clean marijuana; to run powdered drugs (especially heroin) through a nylon stocking. *Cf.* ***clean.*** [U.S., RRL: 1969, H&C: 1975]

fluffed alcohol intoxicated. *Cf.* ***fluffy.*** RT: ***drunk.*** [Br., 1800s, F&H]

fluffer a drunkard; a drunken person. RS: ***sot.*** [Br., 1800s, F&H]

fluffiness drunkenness. [Br., (1886): OED]

fluffy alcohol intoxicated. RT: ***drunk.*** [Br., (1885): DSUE; listed in BVB: 1942]

flummoxed (also **flummuxed**) alcohol intoxicated. GEN: confused. *Cf. conflummoxed.* RT: ***drunk.*** [Br., mid 1800s, F&H; listed in BVB: 1942]

flunk out to begin to use strong drugs; to move from casual drug use to addiction. *Cf.* ***graduate.*** [U.S., IGA: 1971, WCM: 1972]

flunky an addict who is not competent enough to obtain drugs; in underworld drug slang, a *runner* (*q.v.*) = someone who delivers drugs. The flunky is usually paid in drugs. GEN: an errand runner. RS: ***mule.*** [U.S., RRL: 1969, EEL: 1971]

flush 1. alcohol intoxicated, full to the brim. GEN: with an abundance of something, i.e., full to (flush with) the brim. RT: ***drunk.*** [Br., B&L: 1890, F&H; listed in BVB: 1942] 2. a drug ***rush*** (*q.v.*). RT: ***rush.*** See ***flash.*** [U.S., RRL: 1969, H&C: 1975] 3. to flush one's entire drug supply down a toilet to prevent seizure by the police. See ***flush and mush.*** [U.S., EEL: 1971, ADC: 1981] 4. "cured," set ***straight*** (*q.v.*) after an injection of heroin. [U.S., RRL: 1969] 5. to ***boot*** (*q.v.*). See ***flushing.***

flush and mush a warning to flush drugs down the toilet or to swallow them to prevent detection. *Cf.* ***flush.*** [U.S., JH: 1979]

flushed alcohol intoxicated. (BF: 1737: [He's] Flush'd.) *Cf. florid.* RT: *drunk.* [BF: 1737, F&H, BVB: 1942]

flushing injecting and withdrawing a drug. The same as *booting* (*q.v.*). [U.S., ADC: 1975]

flusterate (also **flusticate**) to drink alcohol to excess; to get drunk. RT: *guzzle.* [U.S., BVB: 1942]

flustered alcohol intoxicated. GEN: confused. RT: *drunk.* [cant, (1673): OED, BE: 1690, FG: 1785, FG: 1811, FG: 1823, B&L: 1890, F&H; listed in MHW: 1934, BVB: 1942]

flustrated (also **flusticated**) alcohol intoxicated. GEN: confused (LWP: 1908). RT: *drunk.* [Br., mid 1800s, F&H; listed in BVB: 1942]

flutter a drinking bout. RT: *spree.* [U.S., M&J: 1975]

fly to take drugs; to be high on drugs. *Cf. floating.* [U.S., TRG: 1968, EEL: 1971, DCCU: 1972, W&F: 1975]

fly agaric a poisonous substance made from certain mushrooms. It has been used (undependably) as a medication and as a substance which can produce hallucinations. It gets its name from its use as the poison in fly paper. [drug culture use, RRL: 1969, YKB: 1977]

fly blown alcohol intoxicated. Related to a term having to do with an animal in whose skin flies have laid eggs. Probably an elaboration of *rotten* (*q.v.*). RT: *drunk.* [Aust. and Br., (1853): OEDS, F&H; listed in BVB: 1942]

fly-by-night alcohol intoxicated. Rhyming slang for *tight.* RT: *drunk.* [Br., WWI, DRS]

flyer See *flier.*

fly high 1. to get drunk. RT: *mug oneself.* [Br., (1860): DSUE; listed in BVB: 1942] 2. to experience the floating euphoria of drugs. *Cf. high.* [U.S., EEL: 1971]

flying Dutchman a drug seller. See *Dutchman.*

flying high (also **flying, flying in the clouds**) intoxicated with drugs or alcohol. RS: *drunk, stoned.* [U.S., BVB: 1942, VJM: 1949, M&D: 1952, RRL: 1969, ADC: 1981, BW: 1984]

flying jib a talkative drunkard. Jib = jaw. A flying jib is a type of sail. This pun refers to a rapidly moving jaw. RS: *sot.* [U.S., GI: 1931, VJM: 1949]

flying saucers a variety name of morning glory seeds. The seeds eaten for a high. RT: *seeds.* [U.S., RRL: 1969, EEL: 1971, YKB: 1977]

flying the ensign alcohol intoxicated. This probably refers to the red ensign or Baker signal flag. In addition to signaling B it indicated that a ship is carrying, loading, or unloading dangerous cargo. In this expression, the cargo is booze. *Cf. ensign-bearer.* RT: *drunk.* [U.S., MHW: 1934, BVB: 1942]

fly Mexican Airways (also **fly Mexican Airlines**) to smoke marijuana; to get high on marijuana. Alludes to Mexican marijuana such as *Acapulco gold* (*q.v.*). *Cf. hit the hay.* [U.S., BR: 1972]

fly swatter an *enforcer* (*q.v.*); a muscle man for a dealer. [U.S., JWK: 1981]

foam beer. *Cf. suds.* RT: *beer.* [U.S., M&W: 1946]

focus liquid narcotics for injecting. Compare to *hocus, locust, mokus.* [U.S., EEL: 1971, JHF: 1971]

fog bound alcohol intoxicated. RT: *drunk.* [Br., early 1900s, DSUE]

fog-cutter a drink of liquor, i.e., something to clear one's mind. The same as *fogmatic* (*q.v.*). *Cf. antifogmatic.* RT: *nip.* [U.S., (1833): OEDS, D&D: 1957]

fogged (also **foggy**) alcohol intoxicated. GEN: confused. RT: *drunk.* [Br., (1823): OED, JCH: 1887, F&H; U.S., MGH: 1915, BVB: 1942]

fogmatic a drink of liquor. The same as *fog-cutter* (*q.v.*) and *antifogmatic* (*q.v.*). RT: *nip.* [U.S., BHH: 1856; listed in D&D: 1957]

fogrum (also **fogram**) liquor; rum; inferior liquor. RT: *booze.* [Br., (1876): OED; listed in BVB: 1942, D&D: 1973]

fog up to smoke a pipe; to smoke tobacco. Compare to *fire up.* [U.S., JS: 1925]

fogus tobacco. Possibly from an old term meaning dried grass. Possibly mock-Latin for *fog.* [cant, (1673): OED, BE: 1690, FG: 1785, FG: 1823, GWM: 1859, JCH: 1887] Terms and nicknames for tobacco: *alfalfa, bacca, baccer, bacco, baccy, backa, backer, backey, backy, bit of leaf, bootlace, bug dust, bull, cabbage, chew-bacca, cloud, corn shucks, divine weed, dust, fillings, filthy weed, fogus, fragrant weed, gage, gold dust, hag's bush, Indian drug, jack, Lady Nicotine, leaf, mundungo, mundungus, Negro head, niggerhead, nose 'em, nose my, nose my knacker, noser my knacker, nosey me, nosey me knacker, occabot, old rope, piece of thick, pigtail, plug, rollings, sack of bull, sack of dust, screw, smash, snout, snuff, sot-weed, spit-quick-or-puke, state, state weed, stick of weed, tabacky, terbacker, the filthy weed, the weed, tib fo occabot, tobaccy, tobacker, tobarcoe, toffee, Tom Thacker, twak, weed.*

foil a small packet of drugs wrapped in foil. *Cf. paper.* RS: *load.* [U.S., TRG: 1968, EEL: 1971, W&F: 1975]

fold to collapse; to collapse from drinking. [U.S., JAS: 1932]

folded alcohol intoxicated. *Cf. bent.* RT: *drunk.* [U.S., MHW: 1934, D&D: 1957]

fold up to stop selling or taking drugs; to get out of the drug business. [U.S., DWM: 1938, VJM: 1949, RRL: 1969]

foo-foo-dust any powdered narcotic. RT: *powder.* [U.S., BVB: 1942, VJM: 1949, A&T: 1953]

foo-foo water barber's toilet water drunk for its alcoholic content. [U.S. Marines, (1930): DST: 1984]

foolish powder heroin; any powdered drug which effects one's mind. RT: *powder.* [U.S., GI: 1931, MHW: 1934, GOL: 1950, W&F: 1960, EEL: 1971]

foon (also **fun, pfun**) a pellet of prepared (roasted) opium. Rhymes with noon. RT: *opium.* [U.S., DWM: 1936, VJM: 1949, RRL: 1969]

footballs oval-shaped tablets. Usually refers to mescaline or amphetamines, but can be any oval tablet such as *Placidyl* (TM; *q.v.*) or *Dilaudid* (TM; *q.v.*). [U.S., TRG: 1968, RRL: 1969, M&V: 1973, YKB: 1977, NIDA: 1980, JWK: 1981] See also *softballs.*

foot juice cheap red wine; inferior liquor. Probably originated from the image of barefooted people stomping grapes. RT: *rotgut.* [U.S., early 1900s, DU]

foozlified alcohol intoxicated. GEN: bungled. RT: *drunk.* [Br. nautical, (1887): DSUE]

forbidden fruit fruit-flavored liqueurs. A play on the forbidden fruit of the Biblical Garden of Eden. [U.S., D&D: 1973]

foreign mud opium; prepared opium. *Mud* (*q.v.*) = opium. RT: *opium.* [U.S., HB: 1955]

foreign smoke opium; opium smoke. RT: *opium.* [Aust., (1910): DU, SJB: 1966]

formaldehyde inferior liquor. From the name of a chemical substance used as a preservative of animal tissue. *Cf. embalming fluid.* RT: *rotgut.* [U.S., BVB: 1942]

forties (also **40s, F-forties**) capsules of *Seconal* (TM; *q.v.*). RT: *sec.* [U.S., EAF: 1972]

fortified having to do with a person who has drunk alcohol; alcohol intoxicated. From the practice of fortifying wines or other drinks by adding alcohol to them. RS: *drunk.* [K&M: 1968]

fortnighter an occasional user of drugs. Fortnight = two weeks. ELA: 1984 lists **fortnightey**, probably in error. RT: *chipper.* [U.S., (1956): JES: 1959, H&C: 1975]

forty See *agur-forty.*

forty-five minute psychosis the hallucinogenic compound *D.M.T.* (*q.v.*). The substance is fast acting and of short duration. *Cf. businessman's trip.* [U.S., SNP: 1977]

forty-niner a cocaine user; a narcotics addict who uses cocaine. Related to *gold dust* (*q.v.*) and those who took part in the California gold rush of 1849. RT: *kokomo.* [U.S., JES: 1959, H&C: 1975]

forty-rod lightning (also **forty-rod, forty-rod whiskey**) whiskey;

potent whiskey; inferior whiskey. Whiskey so strong that it affects a person who is 500 feet away. RT: *rotgut, whiskey.* [(1858): SBF: 1982, (1869): ADD, JSF: 1889, B&L: 1890, VR: 1929, AH: 1931, MHW: 1934, D&D: 1957]

forty-two caliber potent whiskey. RT: *rotgut.* [U.S., MHW: 1934, BVB: 1942]

forty-weight beer. RT: *beer.* Attested as citizens band radio slang. [U.S., EE: 1976]

forwards amphetamines, i.e., stimulants. The opposite of *backwards* (*q.v.*). RT: *amps.* [U.S., S&W: 1966, W&F: 1967, RRL: 1969, DCCU: 1972, YKB: 1977, ADC: 1981]

fossilized alcohol intoxicated. *Cf. ossified.* RT: *drunk.* [PD: 1982]

fou See *full.*

four-bottle man a drunkard. A play on *four-letter man.* Probably refers to four bottles of wine per day. RT: *sot.* [U.S., BVB: 1942, D&D: 1957]

fours *Tylenol* (TM; *q.v.*) or *Empirin* (TM; *q.v.*) painkiller tablets or capsules with 60 mgs of codeine. Each tablet or capsule is marked with a 4. [U.S., RG: 1970, (H&C: 1975), JWK: 1981]

fours and doors (also fours and doors, four-doors) Tylenol No. 4 (with codeine) and *Doriden* (TM; *q.v.*). *Cf. doors, dors.* [U.S., RAS: 1984, ELA: 1984]

four sheets in the wind (also four sheets, four sheets to the wind) alcohol intoxicated, presumably much more severely than two or three sheets to the wind. See comments at *three sheets in the wind. Cf. two sheets to the wind.* RT: *drunk.* [F&H, MHW: 1934, D&D: 1957, AP: 1980]

fourteen (also **14**) narcotics. N is the fourteenth letter of the alphabet. RS: *dope.* [U.S., EEL: 1971, RDS: 1982]

fourth degree narcotics withdrawal sickness. In criminal and police jargon, the third degree refers to a severe and sometimes violent period of questioning. Sometimes narcotics addicts could be persuaded to talk by holding them prisoner until they began to suffer withdrawal sickness, i.e., the fourth degree. [U.S., JES: 1959]

fourth, on one's alcohol intoxicated; tipsy. Presumably drinking one's fourth drink. *Cf. farahead.* RT: *drunk.* [Br., 1800s, F&H]

four-way hit a cross-scored amphetamine tablet. It breaks into four pieces providing four hits or doses. *Hit* (*q.v.*) = dose. *Cf. double-crosses.* RS: *amps.* [U.S., ADC: 1975]

four-way star (also four-ways, four-way windowpane) the hallucinogenic drug *L.S.D.* (*q.v.*). *Four-way* implies that the L.S.D. is combined with three other substances. May also refer to an L.S.D. impregnated amphetamine tablet. See *crossroads.* RS: *L.S.D.* [U.S., RG: 1970, ADC: 1981]

fow See *full.*

fox to become alcohol intoxicated. RT: ***mug oneself.*** [Br., (1611): OED, F&H; U.S., BWG: 1899]

foxed (also **fox drunk, foxy**) alcohol intoxicated. The oldest form (15–1600s) is **fox drunk**. RT: ***drunk.*** [(1592): OED, (1611): F&H, BE: 1690, BF: 1722, FG: 1811, FG: 1823, BWG: 1899, MP: 1928, AH: 1931, MHW: 1934]

fox head illicit whiskey; ***moonshine*** (*q.v.*). RT: ***moonshine.*** [U.S., early 1900s, ADD, MHW: 1934]

foxy 1. high on marijuana. RT: ***wasted.*** [U.S., RPW: 1938] **2**. drunk. See *foxed.*

fractured alcohol intoxicated. RT: ***drunk.*** [U.S., BVB: 1953, D&D: 1957, W&F: 1960, EEL: 1971]

fragrant weed tobacco. RT: ***fogus.*** [U.S., MHW: 1934, BVB: 1942]

frajo* (also **fraho***) a tobacco or marijuana cigarette; cannabis. RT: ***nail, joint.*** From Spanish. [calo, M&D: 1952, A&T: 1953, EEL: 1971, JBR: 1973, NIDA: 1980]

frame a twister (also **frame a toss-out**) to fake a drug withdrawal spasm in order to get drugs from a physician. *Cf.* ***twister.*** See *brody.* [U.S., DWM: 1938, VJM: 1949]

frantic desperately in need of drugs. HB: 1955 lists **frantic character** = a frantic addict. [U.S., JBW: 1967, EEL: 1971, IGA: 1971]

frazzled alcohol intoxicated. GEN: unraveled, worn out. RT: ***drunk.*** [U.S., (1870s): SBF: 1976, MP: 1928, AH: 1931, MHW: 1934, W&F: 1960, DCCU: 1972]

freak 1. one's drug specialty. *Cf.* ***acid freak, barb freak, booze freak, kick freak, meth freak, needle freak, pill freak*** (at ***pillhead***), ***speed freak.*** The term is extended in general slang to cover all types of interests becoming synonymous with *one's bag* and *one's thing.* [U.S., (TW: 1968), RRL: 1969, EEL: 1971] **2**. a truncation of ***needle freak*** (*q.v.*). This may be the only sense of freak which is argot. [U.S., M&V: 1967] **3**. a hippie; a drug user or someone who looks like one. [U.S., (S&W: 1966), D&B: 1970c, DNE: 1973, ADC: 1981] **4**. (also **freak out**) to hallucinate; to have a superb L.S.D. trip; to have a very bad L.S.D. trip; to surprise or disorient someone Essentially, to do or experience something very strange. [U.S., (1965): OEDS, RRL: 1969, EEL: 1971, D&B: 1978, S&F: 1984]

freaked out (also **freaked**) **1**. to be disturbed by something strange such as a bad L.S.D. trip. *Cf.* ***freak.*** Also in general slang meaning to be spent. [U.S., ADC: 1981] **2**. under the effects of marijuana or some other drug; panicked by drugs. RT: ***wasted.*** [U.S., D&B: 1971]

freak house a place for the communal use of ***speed*** =

methamphetamine. RT: *doperie.* [U.S., ELA: 1984]

freaking freely experiencing an L.S.D. trip without using the drug. *Cf. echoes.* [U.S., RRL: 1969, RG: 1970, EEL: 1971]

freak out 1. (also **freak**) to panic and lose control under the effects of a drug, especially the hallucinogenic drug *L.S.D.* (*q.v.*). Now in general slang meaning to panic. [U.S., JBW: 1967, RRL: 1969, (1970): DNE: 1973, EEL: 1971, W&F: 1975, ADC: 1981] 2. (usually **freak-out**) a bad drug experience; a psychotic reaction to the hallucinogenic drug *L.S.D.* (*q.v.*). [U.S., (1966): OEDS, D&B: 1970c, DCCU: 1972, DNE: 1973, W&F: 1975, ADC: 1981] 3. (usually **freak-out**) a drug party; a wild party of any type. [Br. and U.S., EEL: 1971, PW: 1974]

freckles tobacco for rolling cigarettes. [U.S., D&D: 1957, W&F: 1960] For general terms for tobacco, see *fogus.* Terms for cut or chopped tobacco for cigarette rolling: *bashings, bug dust, dust, fillings, freckles, gold dust, jack, makings, rollings, sack of bull, sack of dust.*

freddy a tablet of ephedrine, a stimulant. [Br., BTD: 1968]

free base (also **base, freebase**) 1. a smokable, pure extract of cocaine. [U.S., RAS: 1980, RDS: 1982] 2. to use free base. [U.S., RAS: 1980, BW: 1984]

free base party a gathering where free base is used. [U.S., RDS: 1982]

freebaser a user of free base. RT: *kokomo.* [U.S., S&F: 1984]

free basing (also **baseballing, basing**) using an ether extract of cocaine as a recreational drug. [U.S., RAS: 1980, BW: 1984]

freebies 1. drug samples given by dope pushers for the purpose of creating new addicts. GEN: something given away free of charge (1928): RSG: 1964. *Cf. pusher.* See *monkey bait.* [U.S., M&V: 1973, JWK: 1981] 2. nonaddicts, i.e., persons who are free of drugs. RS: *square.* [U.S., M&V: 1973]

Freemans free cigarettes. See *Harry Freemans.*

free trip an echo or a *flashback* of an L.S.D. experience. This may happen some days or weeks after the drug has been taken. [U.S., ELA: 1984]

freeze 1. to refuse to sell drugs to someone. See *chill.* [U.S., M&V: 1967, RRL: 1969, MA: 1973] 2. a period of time when no drugs are available. [U.S., (1966): ELA: 1982, S&W: 1973]

freeze on a joint to hang onto a communal marijuana cigarette longer than necessary for a single *hit* (*q.v.*). *Cf. Bogart.* [U.S., BR: 1972]

freight smuggled liquor. RS: *moonshine.* [U.S., MHW: 1934]

French article (also **French cream, French elixir**) brandy. A euphemism. RT: *brandy.* [cant, FG: 1811, FG: 1823, GWM: 1859, JCH: 1887, B&L: 1890; listed in BVB: 1942, AAR: 1944]

French blue 1. a *Drinamyl* (TM; *q.v.*) tablet; an amphetamine tablet. From the manufacturer's name, Smith, Klein, and French. [U.S., RRL: 1969, JTD: 1971] 2. an injection of amphetamines and barbiturates. RS: *set*. [U.S., EEL: 1971]

French fried under the influence of marijuana. *Cf. fried*. RT: *wasted*. [U.S., ADC: 1975]

French fry one's brains to use drugs, especially *L.S.D.* (*q.v.*). [U.S., D&B: 1971]

French inhale the act of exhaling smoke (originally tobacco smoke) through the mouth while inhaling it through the nostrils. [U.S., D&D: 1957, W&F: 1960]

freon freak (also **frost freak**) a person who uses freon gas (from pressurized spray cans) as an inhalant. RS: *user*. [U.S., ELA: 1984]

fresh (also **freshish**) alcohol intoxicated; tipsy. RT: *drunk*. [Br., (1812): OED, FG: 1823; listed in BVB: 1942]

fresh and sweet just out of jail. In drug argot, this usually means withdrawn from drugs. Said of a prostitute (W&F: 1975). [U.S., JBW: 1967, EEL: 1971, S&W: 1973, W&F: 1975]

freshen to start taking drugs in an addictive manner. Akin to a heifer freshening and giving milk. [U.S., JES: 1959, H&C: 1975]

freshman a new drug addict or new drug user. *Cf. graduate*. [U.S., (1927): JES: 1959]

fried 1. alcohol intoxicated. RT: *drunk*. [U.S., (1920s): SBF: 1976, MHW: 1934, W&F: 1960, ADC: 1981] 2. drug intoxicated. RT: *stoned*. [U.S., ADC: 1975, ADC: 1981]

fried egg a drunkard. RT: *sot*. [U.S., BVB: 1942]

fried on both sides alcohol intoxicated; really drunk. An elaboration of *fried* (*q.v.*) = drunk. [U.S., BVB: 1942]

fried to the gills (also **fried to the hat**) alcohol intoxicated. A mixed metaphor consisting of *fried* and *full to the gills*. Akin to **fried to the eyebrows**, **fried to the eyes**, and **fried to the hat**. These are meant to indicate the level to which the body is filled with alcohol. *Cf. heaped to the gills*. [U.S., SBF: 1976, MHW: 1934, D&D: 1957]

Frisco speedball a mixture of heroin, cocaine, and *L.S.D.* (*q.v.*). The same as *San Francisco bomb* (*q.v.*). RS: *set*. [U.S., RRL: 1969, H&C: 1975]

frisky (also **frisky powder**) cocaine. RT: *cocaine*. [U.S., HB: 1955, IGA: 1971, NIDA: 1980] See also *highland frisky*.

frisky!, I'm so whiskey. See *highland frisky*.

frisky whiskey 100 proof alcohol. RT: *booze*. [U.S., EE: 1976]

fritz, on the alcohol intoxicated. From an expression meaning *out of order*. *Cf. under the weather*. [U.S., BVB: 1942]

frog an addict who hops from city to city. *Cf. globetrotter*. RS:

junky. [U.S., JWK: 1981]

frog's wine gin. Frog = Dutchman. Currently *frog* is better known as a term for a Frenchman. RT: *gin*. [Br., FG: 1811, FG: 1823, F&H]

front 1. to pay out money for drugs before receiving them; to pay up front. This term has expanded from underworld use to the general jargon of business and finance. [U.S., RRL: 1969, RG: 1970, ADC: 1981] 2. one drug taken before a dose of a different drug. Compare to *back*. [Br., BTD: 1968]

frosty 1. a beer; a cold beer. *Cf. chill, cold one*. RT: *beer*. [U.S., GU: 1975, ADC: 1984] 2. (also **frost, frosted**) under the influence of cocaine. *Cf. caught in a snowstorm, kicked out in the snow, snowed, snowed up, snowed under*. RT: *cocainized*. [U.S., JES: 1959, H&C: 1975] 3. (also **Frosty the snowman**) a cocaine seller. From the Christmas song *Frosty the Snowman*. See more snow terms at *winter wonderland*. RS: *dealer*. Probably recurrent nonce. [U.S., RAS: 1981]

froth beer. *Cf. suds*. RT: *beer*. [U.S., BVB: 1942]

frozen 1. (also **froze his mouth**) alcohol intoxicated. RT: *drunk*. [BF: 1737] 2. drug intoxicated. RT: *stoned*. [U.S., ELA: 1984]

fruit salad a collection of pills said to be taken by teenagers. The salad consists of a pooling of the various pills from family medicine chests, with each teenage child taking a mixed helping. This term is widely quoted, but there is little evidence for its widespread use. [U.S., RRL: 1969, IGA: 1971, W&F: 1975]

fry one's brains to get high on marijuana. RT: *hit the hay*. [U.S., (D&B: 1978)]

fu marijuana; marijuana seed pods. See *fee-tops*. RT: *pot*. [U.S., (1936): ELA: 1982, DWM: 1938, D&D: 1957, W&F: 1960, ADC: 1981]

fucked up 1. (also **fucked out, fucked over**) alcohol intoxicated. RT: *drunk*. [PD: 1982] 2. (also **fucked**) heavily drug intoxicated. RT: *stoned*. [U.S., EEL: 1971, ADC: 1975, JWK: 1981]

fuck the hop to have sexual fantasies while high on drugs. [U.S., JES: 1959, H&C: 1975]

fuddle 1. alcohol; liquor. RT: *booze*. [(1680): OED, F&H, FG: 1785, F&H, BVB: 1942] 2. (also **fuddle one's nose**) to drink liquor; to get drunk; to confuse someone with liquor. *Cf. befuddle*. RT: *mug oneself*. [(1588): OED, F&H, BWG: 1899, BVB: 1942] 3. (also **fuddled**) alcohol intoxicated. See *fuddled*. RT: *drunk*. [FG: 1811, FG: 1823] 4. a drinking bout. RT: *spree*. One who goes on fuddles often is a **fuddle cap** (16–1700s), a **fuddler**, or a **fuddling fellow** (1800s). [Br., early 1800s, DSUE, listed in BVB: 1942]

fuddled (also **in a fuddle, on the fuddle, out on the fuddle**) alcohol intoxicated; on a drinking bout. RT: *drunk*. [(1656): OED,

(1661): F&H, BF: 1737, FG: 1785, BVB: 1942, PW: 1974]

fuddle factory a saloon. RS: *bar.* [U.S., BVB: 1942]

fudge chocolate fudge with marijuana cooked into it. *Cf. brownies.* [U.S., EEL: 1971]

fuel 1. liquor. RT: *booze.* [U.S., 1900s, N&S: 1983] 2. phencyclidine, *P.C.P.* RT: *P.C.P.* [U.S., ELA: 1984]

fuete* a hypodermic needle. Cuban Spanish for whip. RT: *needle.* [U.S., M&V: 1973] See also *whip.*

full (also **full up**) alcohol intoxicated. Older versions include **fou, fou', fow.** RT: *drunk.* [(1840): SBF: 1976, F&H, BWG: 1899, (1911): GAW: 1978, MP: 1928, AH: 1931, W&F: 1960, SSD]

full as a boot alcohol intoxicated. As full of liquor as a tight boot is full of foot. RT: *drunk.* [Aust., (1925): DSUE, (1955): GAW: 1978, SJB: 1966]

full as a bull (also **full as a bull's bum**) alcohol intoxicated. Implying that the drinker is full of dung. Probably akin to *full as a fart.* Akin to the Australian *full as a po* and *full as the family po* where *po* = chamber pot. RT: *drunk.* [Aust. and New Zealand, 1900s, DSUE, SJB: 1966]

full as a fiddle alcohol intoxicated. *Cf. drunk as a fiddler's bitch, fiddled.* RT: *drunk.* [U.S., (1905): SBF: 1976, MHW: 1934]

full as a goat alcohol intoxicated. RT: *drunk.* [17-1800s, DSUE, (1882): SBF: 1976; LWP: 1908, BVB: 1942]

full as a goose alcohol intoxicated. RT: *drunk.* [U.S., (1883): SBF: 1976]

full as a lord alcohol intoxicated. A variant of *drunk as a lord* (*q.v.*). RT: *drunk.* [U.S., (1822): SBF: 1976; listed in MHW: 1934, BVB: 1942]

full as an egg (also **full as a goog**) alcohol intoxicated. Completely filled with liquor. **Full as a goog** is Australian (early 1900s). Goog = egg. [(1887): RML: 1950, DSUE, (1914): GAW: 1978, SJB: 1943, D&D: 1957, W&F: 1960]

full as a piss-ant alcohol intoxicated. Probably an elaboration of *pissed* (*q.v.*). RT: *drunk.* [Aust., (1961): GAW: 1978]

full as a tick alcohol intoxicated. See *tight as a tick.* RT: *drunk.* [(1822): SBF: 1976, (1890): DSUE, LWP: 1908, (1911): GAW: 1978, MHW: 1934, SJB: 1943]

full-blown angel a drunkard. See *angel altogether.* [Br., late 1800s, F&H]

full-cocked alcohol intoxicated; very drunk. An elaboration of *cocked* and *half cocked.* RT: *drunk.* [U.S., BVB: 1942]

full-flavored alcohol intoxicated. RT: *drunk.* [U.S., BVB: 1942]

full moons 1. a large chunk of peyote cactus; the entire top of a peyote cactus. *Cf. moon.* RS: *peyote.* [U.S., RRL: 1969, IGA: 1971, H&C: 1975] 2. hashish sold in a round shape. *Cf. half* *moons.* RT: ***hash.*** [U.S., H&C: 1975]

full of Dutch courage (also **full of courage**) alcohol intoxicated and brave. *Cf.* ***Dutch courage, Geneva courage.*** Probably since the early 1800s. [U.S., BVB: 1942]

full of hops alcohol intoxicated. Also said of a boasting drunkard, a play on *full of bull.* RT: ***drunk.*** [U.S., BVB: 1942]

full of junk (also **full of poison**) drug intoxicated. ***Junk*** (*q.v.*) = drugs. The *also* is from BD: 1937. *Cf.* ***stoned.*** [U.S., BVB: 1942, VJM: 1949]

full to the brim (also **full to the bung, full to the guards, full to the gills, up to the gills**) alcohol intoxicated; full of liquor. RT: ***drunk.*** [Br., 18-1900s, F&H, (1930): DSUE, M&J: 1975; U.S., BVB: 1942]

fu manchu a marijuana smoker. *Cf.* ***fu.*** From the name *Dr. Fu Manchu,* a character created by mystery writer Sax Rohmer. RT: ***toker.*** [U.S., JES: 1959, H&C: 1975]

fumo d'Angola* marijuana, presumed to be from Brazil. Portuguese meaning the smoke from Angola. RT: ***pot.*** [U.S., RRL: 1969, RDS: 1982]

fun (also **fong, foong, phun**) opium; a dose of opium. Rhymes with *noon.* See ***foon.***

funds, out of alcohol intoxicated. A play on *liquidated.* *Cf.* ***liquefied.*** RT: ***drunk.*** [U.S., BVB: 1942]

fun joint an opium den. See ***fun.*** *Cf.* ***hop joint, lay down, joint, pipe joint, smoke joint.*** RT: ***opium den.*** [U.S., early 1900s, DU, A&T: 1953]

funk 1. tobacco smoke. GEN: a bad odor. [cant, BE: 1690] 2. to smoke tobacco. [cant, BE: 1690, FG: 1785; listed in BVB: 1942]

funked out drug intoxicated; alcohol intoxicated. RT: ***drunk, stoned.*** [U.S., EEL: 1971, RDS: 1982]

funker a tobacco pipe. *Cf.* ***funk.*** [1800s, DSUE]

funky-drunk alcohol intoxicated; very drunk, stinking drunk. RT: ***drunk.*** [U.S., ADC: 1981]

fun medicine narcotics. RS: ***dope.*** [U.S., JES: 1959, H&C: 1975]

fun milk liquor. *Cf.* ***silly milk.*** RT: ***booze.*** [U.S., BVB: 1942]

funnel a heavy drinker; a drunkard. Attested in reference to college students. RT: ***sot.*** [U.S., WM: 1927, AH: 1931, JAS: 1932, MHW: 1934]

funny alcohol intoxicated. RT: ***drunk.*** [(1756): OED, DSUE; listed in BVB: 1942]

funny brownies brownies made with marijuana. See ***Alice B. Toklas.*** *Cf.* ***fudge.*** [U.S., ADC: 1981]

funny paper marijuana; a batch of marijuana concealed in a folded newspaper. *Cf.* ***funny stuff.*** RS: ***pot.*** [U.S., (1960s): BR: 1972]

funny stuff (also **funny cigarettes**) marijuana; marijuana cigarettes. RT: *pot*. [U.S., YKB: 1977]

fun water liquor; beverage alcohol. *Cf. firewater, fun milk*. RT: *booze*. [U.S., BVB: 1942]

fur the police; the narcotics squad. A play on *fuzz* (*q.v.*). RT: *fuzz*. [U.S., M&V: 1973]

fusel oil any inferior or adulterated liquor. Sometimes seen as fusil oil. From the standard term for oily, amyl alcohol which results from improper distillation. Slang when applied to beverage alcohol. RS: *rotgut*. [U.S., BVB: 1942]

fustian wine; red wine; port wine. *Cf. red fustian, white fustian*. Fustian = a coarse cotton cloth. RT: *wine*. [cant, FG: 1785, GWM: 1859, B&L: 1890, DSUE]

fuzz 1. (also **fuzzle**) to make drunk; to *fuddle* (*q.v.*). RS: *mug oneself*. [(1685): OED, (1770): SBF: 1976, DSUE, BVB: 1942] 2. a drug *high* (*q.v.*), a *buzz* (*q.v.*). [U.S., IGA: 1971] 3. (also **fuzz man, fuzzy, fuzzy tail**) the police; narcotics agents. Also in general slang for any kind of police. This fuzz is a play on *whiskers* (*q.v.*), an older term for a federal agent, referring to Uncle Sam's beard. [U.S., (1929): OEDS, GI: 1931, D&D: 1957, M&V: 1967, RRL: 1969, CM: 1970, EEL: 1971, EAF: 1980, JWK: 1981] Terms and nicknames for police officers and drug agents: *agent, alba de narco, arm, arm of the law, azul, bacon, beat pounder, big John, bim, black and white, blue, blue boys, blue coats, blue fascists, bottle and stopper, bottle stopper, boys in blue, bull, buster, bust man, button, cellar-smeller, Charley goon, cop, copper, crapper dick, crusher, deadwood, DEARS, DEERS, dick, D-man, dope arm, dope bull, dope cop, dope copper, Ervine, fed, flat-arch, flatfoot, flathead, flatty, fur, fuzz, fuzz man, fuzzy, fuzzy tail, G., gazer, gestapo, gimpy, harness boys, harness bulls, harness rollers, headache man, heat, hog, hudda, Irv, Irvine, jackal, J. Edgar, J. Edgar Hoover, John Law, Johnny-be-good, Johnny Law, junk squad, juvies, lard, law, little boy blue, long arm of the law, long limb of the law, mallet, man, men in blue, metros, mickey mouse, monkey, Mr. Whiskers, nab, nail-em-and-jail-em, nailer, narc, narco, narco fuzz, narcopper, narcotic bull, narcotic copper, nark, narko, oink, ossifer, owl, paddy, people, Peter Jay, pig, pork, pounder, pro, prohi, prohy, revenooer, roach, roller, Rover Boys, salt and pepper, Sam, Sam and Dave, Sherlock Holmes, skull-buster, snatcher, sniffing squad, sponge, T., the feds, the heat, the law, the man, T-man, tombo, U.C., uncle, Uncle nab, Uncle Sam, Uncle Whiskers, uzz-fay, whiskers, whiskers man.*

fuzzed (also **fuzzled, fuzzy**) alcohol intoxicated. (BF: 1737: [He's] fuzl'd.) F&H list **fuzd**. RT: *drunk*. [(1685): F&H, BF: 1737, F&H, MHW: 1934, M&J: 1975, AP: 1980]

G

G. 1. a piece of a dollar bill used to seal a hypodermic needle onto a medicine dropper. The paper is wrapped around the tip of the syringe and the needle is pressed on. RT: ***gasket***. The same as ***gee*** (*q.v.*). See ***gee rag***. ***Cf. dropper***. ELA: 1984 defines this as a paper funnel used when pouring heroin into an eyedropper. [U.S., MA: 1973, JWK: 1981] 2. a rolled-up dollar bill used for sniffing (snorting) cocaine. From sense one. [U.S., JWK: 1981] 3. the government; the federal government. This is probably extracted from *G-man*. RS: ***fuzz***. [U.S., BD: 1937]

gaffled arrested. RT: ***busted***. [U.S., M&V: 1967]

gaffus a hypodermic syringe; an improvised hypodermic syringe. ***Cf. dingus***. RT: ***monkey pump***. This is a slang term for a gadget. [U.S., M&V: 1967]

gage (also **gauge, guage**) 1. whiskey; liquor; inferior liquor. Probably akin to an old sense of the word meaning cask, quart, or pint (15–1800s). [U.S., MHW: 1934, GOL: 1950, W&F: 1960] 2. tobacco; cigarettes. RT: ***fogus***. [U.S., D&D: 1957, W&F: 1960] 3. marijuana; a marijuana cigarette. RT: ***pot***. [primarily U.S., DB: 1944, M&W: 1946, GOL: 1950, A&T: 1953, M&D: 1952, RRL: 1969, EEL: 1971, DCCU: 1972, M&J: 1975, NIDA: 1980]

gagebutt (also **gaugebutt**) a marijuana cigarette. RT: ***joint***. [U.S., MB: 1938, A&T: 1953, D&D: 1957, W&F: 1960]

gaged (also **gauged**) alcohol intoxicated. ***Gage*** (*q.v.*) = liquor. RT: ***drunk***. [U.S., MHW: 1934, BVB: 1942]

gage hustler a marijuana seller. RS: ***dealer***. [U.S., GOL: 1950]

Gainesville green a variety of marijuana presumably from Gainesville, Florida. See the list at ***green***. RT: ***pot***. [U.S., (1976): R&P: 1982, YKB: 1977]

gal a gallon of liquor. From ***gallon***. [U.S., BVB: 1942] See also ***guy***.

galhead a drug addict. Possibly a variant of or an error for ***gowhead*** (*q.v.*). RT: ***junky***. [U.S., C&H: 1974]

gallery an establishment which sells drugs and provides equipment for their use. From ***shooting gallery*** (*q.v.*). RS: ***doperie***. [U.S., MA: 1973, JWK: 1981]

gallon distemper a hangover; the delirium tremens. *Cf. barrel fever.* RS: *D.T.s.* [cant, B&L: 1890, DSUE, MHW: 1934, VJM: 1949]

galloping horse heroin. An elaboration of *horse* (*q.v.*). RT: *heroin.* [U.S., JES: 1959, H&C: 1975]

galvanized alcohol intoxicated. RT: *drunk.* [PD: 1982]

gammon one microgram of *L.S.D.* (*q.v.*). RS: *load.* [U.S., RRL: 1969, LVA: 1981]

gamot (also **gammot**) morphine; heroin. RT: *morphine, heroin.* [U.S., SNP: 1977]

ganga (also **gange**) marijuana. From Hindi. There are numerous spellings and pronunciations such as **ganja, ganjah, ganji, ganza, ghanja, gunga, gungeon, gunja, gunjah, gunjeh, gunny.** RT: *pot.* The entry word is widely used in Jamaica and other Caribbean Islands. Attested as *gang* in Nassau (JAH: 1982). [(1957): OEDS, RRL: 1969, M&J: 1975, NIDA: 1980, ADC: 1984]

ganger narcotics. Possibly akin to *ganga* (*q.v.*). Probably a spelling variant of *gonger* (*q.v.*). RS: *dope.* [U.S., H&C: 1975, SNP: 1977]

gangster 1. marijuana; a marijuana cigarette; a marijuana smoker. Akin to *ganga* (*q.v.*). [U.S., (1960): ELA: 1982, W&F: 1967, RRL: 1969, CM: 1970, EEL: 1971, EAF: 1980] **2.** a tobacco cigarette. RT: *nail.* Black use (DC: 1972). [U.S., DC: 1972]

gangster pills barbiturates. *Cf. gangster.* RT: *barbs.* [U.S., RRL: 1969, YKB: 1977]

gangster stick a marijuana cigarette. RT: *joint.* [U.S., EAF: 1980]

ganja (also **ganjah**) marijuana. This term is associated with the marijuana of Jamaica. It is known worldwide and is the slang word-of-choice in many of the Caribbean islands. *Cf. ganga.* See *gunja.* In English since about 1800 (SOD). [U.S., D&D: 1957, W&F: 1975, NIDA: 1980, ADC: 1981]

gap (also **gape**) to yawn and drool as an early sign of drug need; to show the early signs of drug craving. *Cf. call.* See *gapper.* [U.S., DWM: 1938, RRL: 1969]

gapper a drug addict in the early stages of withdrawal; an addict in need of a dose of drugs. LIT: one who yawns. *Cf. gap.* [U.S., DWM: 1938, VJM: 1949, A&T: 1953]

garbage 1. low-quality drugs; bogus or adulterated heroin. *Cf. junk.* RS: *blank.* Probably should be considered recurring nonce. [U.S., (1962): ELA: 1982, M&V: 1967, RRL: 1969, MA: 1973, ADC: 1981, JWK: 1981] **2.** amphetamines. RT: *amps.* [U.S., EEL: 1971]

garbage freak 1. (also **garbagehead**) an addict who will take any drug. RS: *junky.* [U.S., RRL: 1969, JH: 1979] **2.** an addict with a ravenous appetite due to withdrawal. This person will eat anything. *Cf. chuckers.* [U.S., M&V: 1967, H&C: 1975]

gargle 1. to drink liquor, presumably to excess. RT: *guzzle.* [(1859): DSUE, (1889): OED, MHW: 1934, VJM: 1949, SSD] 2. liquor; a drink of liquor. *Cf. neck oil.* RT: *booze.* [B&L: 1890, F&H, MHW: 1934, VJM: 1949, SSD]

gargle factory a pub or saloon. *Cf. gargle.* RS: *bar.* [Br., 1800s, F&H; U.S., BVB: 1942, W&F: 1960]

gargler a drinker; a drunkard. *Cf. gargle.* RT: *sot.* [Br., 1800s, F&H; U.S., BVB: 1942]

gargoyle an addict; a drug user. *Cf. fiend, monkey, zombie.* RS: *junky.* [U.S., (1930s): JES: 1959, H&C: 1975]

gas 1. methyl alcohol; ether; any intoxicating liquid substance which can ease the alcoholic need. Usually associated with denatured alcohol. *Cf. methyl.* Hobo use. [U.S., CS: 1927, VWS: 1929, GI: 1931, W&F: 1960] 2. booze; inferior, prohibition liquor. From the prohibition era. [U.S., AH: 1931, MHW: 1934] 3. (also **gas up**) to drink excessively; to get drunk. RT: *mug oneself.* [U.S., BVB: 1942, W&F: 1960] 4. to sniff gasoline fumes in an attempt to get high. [U.S., (TRG: 1968), EEL: 1971] 5. nitrous oxide, laughing gas. [U.S., (JBW: 1967), EEL: 1971, IGA: 1971, ADC: 1975, ADC: 1981]

gash marijuana. RT: *pot.* [U.S., (1968): ELA: 1982]

gashound a tramp who drinks only methyl alcohol, ether, or the like. *Cf. gas.* RS: *sot.* [U.S., CS: 1927, VWS: 1929, AH: 1931, GI: 1931, MHW: 1934, VJM: 1949, W&F: 1960]

gashouse a beer hall; a low saloon. From a term meaning gasworks. *Cf. gas.* RT: *dive.* [U.S., WWII, BVB: 1953, D&D: 1957, W&F: 1960]

gasket something used to seal a hypodermic needle onto a syringe. See comments at *G.* RT: *gasket.* [U.S., D&B: 1970c, IGA: 1971, JHF: 1971] Terms for material used to seal a hypodermic needle to a syringe: *boo-gee, boot, collar, G., gasket, gee, gee bag, geep, gee rag, G-rag, granny, jacket, jeep, shoulder.*

gasp a drink of liquor. *Cf. cry, shout.* RT: *nip.* [Br., late 1800s, F&H; listed in BVB: 1942]

gasper 1. (also **gasser**) a tobacco cigarette; a cheap cigarette. Gasser is an Australian version. RT: *nail.* [(1914): OEDS, F&G: 1925, WM: 1927, MHW: 1934, D&D: 1957, W&F: 1960, SSD, B&P: 1965, CM: 1970] 2. a marijuana cigarette. RT: *joint.* [U.S., ELA: 1984]

gass allegedly ampules of *Methedrine* (*q.v.*). Probably an error for *glass* (*q.v.*). [U.S., H&C: 1975, SNP: 1977]

gassed (also **gassed up**) 1. alcohol intoxicated. Usually refers to intoxication with ethyl alcohol. *Cf. gas.* RT: *drunk.* [primarily U.S., (1915): SBF: 1976, F&G: 1925, MHW: 1934, W&F: 1960] 2. drug intoxicated; high. From sense one. RT: *stoned.* [U.S., JES:

1959, M&V: 1967, RDS: 1982]

gasser a cigarette. See ***gasper***.

gassing using a drug-saturated cloth to administer an *inhalant* (*q.v.*); sniffing gasoline fumes. [U.S., TRG: 1968, RG: 1970]

gate 1. the vein into which drugs are injected. *Cf. channel, ditch, gutter, home, line, mainline, pipe, sewer*. [U.S., JES: 1959, H&C: 1975] 2. a marijuana cigarette. Akin to or an error for ***gage*** (*q.v.*). RT: *joint*. [U.S., (1968): ELA: 1982, H&C: 1975, SNP: 1977]

gate-keeper a person who helps another through an *L.S.D.* (*q.v.*) trip. RT: *sitter*. [U.S., JBW: 1967, IGA: 1971, LVA: 1981]

gato* heroin. Spanish for *cat* (*q.v.*). RT: *heroin*. [U.S., NIDA: 1980]

gatter *porter* (*q.v.*) and later beer; *stout* (*q.v.*); liquor. See ***shant***. Compare to ***gutter***. RT: *beer*. [U.S., (1818): F&H, GWM: 1859]

gauge See ***gage***.

gay alcohol intoxicated. *Cf. glad, happy, merry*. RT: *drunk*. [F&H; listed in BVB: 1942]

gay and frisky whiskey. Rhyming slang. *Cf. highland frisky*. RT: *whiskey*. [Br., (1928): DRS, M&B: 1944, SSD]

gayed alcohol intoxicated. *Cf. gay*. RT: *drunk*. [U.S., N&S: 1983]

gazer a federal narcotics agent. RS: *fuzz*. [U.S., GM: 1931, DWM: 1933, DWM: 1936, VJM: 1949, M&H: 1959]

gazoonie a drug seller's strong-arm man. Possibly narcotics ziph for *goon*. [U.S., JWK: 1981]

G.B. a *goofball* (*q.v.*). This has been used to refer to amphetamines, barbiturates, or a mixture of these or of other drugs. RS: *set*. [U.S., W&F: 1967, RRL: 1969, CM: 1970, EEL: 1971]

G.B.'ed drug intoxicated, "goofballed." *Cf. goofball*. RT: *stoned*. [U.S., RDS: 1982]

gear 1. equipment for injecting drugs. RT: *outfit*. [Br. and U.S., BTD: 1968, EEL: 1971, M&J: 1975, ADC: 1981] 2. marijuana; drugs in general. *Cf. junk, stuff*. [U.S., (1954): ELA: 1982, LVA: 1981; Br., (1940s): DSUE, M&J: 1980]

geared up alcohol intoxicated. *Gear* (*q.v.*) = drugs. RT: *drunk*. [U.S., W&F: 1960]

gee 1. liquor; a gallon of liquor; a drink of liquor. From the prohibition era. Probably widespread use. See ***gee-up***. [U.S., AH: 1931, GI: 1931, MHW: 1934] 2. opium; opiates; any narcotic. The G of **gee** may be pronounced hard or soft. David Maurer (DWM: 1938) speculates that the term is a respelling of G which could be the initial letter of *geezer, guy, gow, grease, gonger, gum*, or the Hindi word *ghee* (butter) via Chinese. Most uses of **gee** or *ghee* in argot stand for "guy" and this is the most likely source of this *gee*. M&W: 1946 list **Buddy ghee** = pal. GEN: person (MHW: 1934). See *cat, dude, him*. RT: *opium*. [U.S., BD: 1937, DWM: 1938, VJM: 1949] 3. (also **G.**, **gee bag**) bits of paper, thread, or other material used to seal a hypodermic needle onto the tip of a medicine dropper. See comments at *G*. RT: *gasket*. [U.S., DWM: 1936, IGA: 1971, JWK: 1981] See also *gee rag*.

geed up 1. (also **gheed up**) high on opium; drug intoxicated. Originally referred only to opium. *Cf. gee*. RT: *stoned*. [U.S., BD: 1937, DWM: 1938, GOL: 1950, M&D: 1952, W&F: 1960, EEL: 1971] 2. alcohol intoxicated. *Cf. gee*. RT: *drunk*. [U.S., BVB: 1942, GOL: 1950, D&D: 1957] 3. having to do with a ruined drug addict. [U.S., DWM: 1936]

gee-fat 1. the residue of a smoked opium pellet which lines the opium pipe bowl. *Gee* (*q.v.*) = opium. [U.S., BD: 1937, DWM: 1938] (This entry continues after the following list.) Other terms and nicknames for opium residue: *chef, coolie mud, dog, eng-shee, gee-yen, green ashes, green mud, greens, Rooster Brand, sam-lo, san-lo, suede, suey, yen-shee*. 2. narcotics; drugs in general. [U.S., BVB: 1942, VJM: 1949]

gee-gee an opium pipe. See *gee*. RT: *hop stick*. [U.S., JES: 1959, H&C: 1975]

geehead a drug addict who takes paregoric for its narcotic content. From *P.G.* (*q.v.*), an abbreviation of paregoric, or from *goric-head*. *Cf. gheid*. RS: *user*. See the list at *head*. [U.S., JBW: 1967, RRL: 1969]

geek a drunkard. RT: *sot*. A special use of a general term of approbation. Most current use is as a derogatory term for an Oriental. [U.S., W&F: 1960]

geep (also **jeep**) See *gee rag*.

gee rag (also **G.**, **geep**, **jeep**, **G-rag**) material used to hold the parts of an opium pipe together. String, thread, cigarette papers, or other materials could be used. See *G*. RT: *gasket*. [U.S., BD: 1937, DWM: 1938, VJM: 1949, D&B: 1970c]

geeser See *geezer*.

gee stick an opium pipe. *Cf. gee*. RT: *hop stick*. [U.S., DWM: 1938, VJM: 1949]

gee-up a drinking bout. *Cf. gee*. See *drunk-up* for other spree terms of this type. RT: *spree*. [Aust., (1920): DSUE]

gee-yen precipitated opium vapors in an opium pipe. Also defined as opium residue. *Cf. gee-fat*. Chinese or mock-Chinese. [U.S., DWM: 1936, VJM: 1949]

geez (also **geeze**) 1. to inject a drug. RT: *shoot*. This may be much older than the attestations indicate. [U.S., M&V: 1967, D&B: 1970c, M&V: 1973, EAF: 1980] 2. an injection of a drug. RT: *shot*. [U.S., M&V: 1967, JH: 1979]

geezed (also **geesed**, **geezed up**) 1. alcohol intoxicated. RT: *drunk*.

[U.S., MP: 1928, AH: 1931, MHW: 1934, GOL: 1950, W&F: 1960] 2. drug intoxicated. *Cf. geez.* RT: *stoned.* [U.S., MHW: 1934, W&F: 1960]

geezer (also **geeser**) a *snort* (*q.v.*) of a powdered drug; a *shot* (*q.v.*) of drugs; a drink of alcohol. *Cf. geez.* [U.S., GM: 1931, VFN: 1933, DWM: 1936, GOL: 1950, W&F: 1960, EEL: 1971]

geezy addict an addict who will take anything. *Cf. garbage freak.* This *geesy* may be a variant of or an error for *greasy* (*q.v.*). RS: *user.* [U.S., W&F: 1975] See also *greasy junkie.*

gelatin blotter paper soaked in a dilute solution of L.S.D., dried and cut into salable doses. RT: *L.S.D.* [U.S., ELA: 1984]

gem a narcotic. Perhaps from the colloquial *little gem.* Possibly akin to *donjem* (*q.v.*). RS: *dope.* [U.S., JES: 1959, H&C: 1975]

generous alcohol intoxicated. RT: *drunk.* [BF: 1737]

Geneva (also **Geneva liquor**) gin. A play on a Dutch word *genever* = juniper. Gin is flavored with juniper berries. RT: *gin.* [(1706): SOD, FG: 1811, D&D: 1957, W&F: 1960]

Geneva courage gin; bravado from drinking gin or other liquor. *Cf. Dutch courage.* [U.S., D&D: 1973]

George smack potent heroin. George = good. *Cf. righteous bush.* RT: *heroin.* [U.S., M&V: 1967, H&C: 1975]

German conversation water beer. A jocular and contrived expression. To talk German = to break wind. RT: *beer.* Hobo use. [U.S., EK: 1927, MHW: 1934, AAR: 1944]

German goiter (also **Milwaukee goiter**) a beer belly. Refers to the beer brewing skills of the Germans, including the German brewers of Milwaukee, Wisconsin. [U.S., AAR: 1944, D&D: 1957, W&F: 1960]

geronimo a combination of alcohol and barbiturates. From the name of an (Apache) Amerindian chief. RS: *set.* [U.S., RRL: 1969, IGA: 1971, W&S: 1977]

gestapo the police; police officers. From the name of the German secret state police during the Nazi era. RS: *fuzz.* Also in general slang for any oppressive person or group. [U.S., EAF: 1980]

get a bun on (also **get a can on**) to get drunk; to go on a drinking bout. *Cf. bun.* RS: *mug oneself.* [AH: 1931, BVB: 1942, DSUE]

get a fix (also **get a gift**) to buy drugs; to take a dose of drugs. *Cf. fix.* RS: *score.* [U.S., M&D: 1952, RDS: 1982]

get a load of pig iron to purchase liquor. *Pig iron* (*q.v.*) = liquor. This pig may be akin to the *blind pig* (*q.v.*). From the prohibition era. [U.S., AH: 1931]

get behind it to enjoy a drug and its effect; to appreciate a drug. Especially in **get behind some acid**, referring to *L.S.D.* (*q.v.*). *Cf. behind acid.* GEN: to enjoy something. [U.S., EEL: 1971, ADC: 1981]

get cannon (also **get canon**) to get drunk. May have something to do with a *shot* (*q.v.*) = a drink. *Cf. cannon*. RT: *mug oneself.* [U.S., BVB: 1942, VJM: 1949]

get down to inject heroin; to smoke cannabis; to take a drug. Probably from *get down to business*. Currently used in general slang (especially black slang) to mean get down to sex, dancing, etc. RT: *shoot*. [U.S., RRL: 1969, IGA: 1971, MA: 1973, JWK: 1981]

get high to smoke marijuana. Can be used in reference to any drug use, but is very specific among some marijuana users. *Cf. high*. RT: *hit the hay*. [U.S., TRG: 1968, EEL: 1971, EAF: 1980]

get in the groove to take on a drug habit; to take drugs. *Cf. feeling groovy*. GEN: to become attuned (to something). [U.S., H&C: 1975]

get it on (also **get on**) to take drugs; to smoke marijuana. Similar to *get down*. Now used in reference to sex, dancing, etc. Black use: to begin some activity (EAF: 1980). *Cf. get down*. [U.S., EEL: 1971, JWK: 1981]

get narkied to purchase drugs; to inject drugs; to become addicted. *Cf. narky*. [U.S., JES: 1959, H&C: 1975]

get off 1. to inject heroin and experience an orgasmic drug rush; to use any drug. GEN: reach an understanding (M&W: 1946). This term has moved into general slang meaning to copulate or to ejaculate. RS: *shoot*. [U.S., W&F: 1967, RRL: 1969, CM: 1970, MA: 1973 MW: 1976, EAF: 1980, ADC: 1981, JWK: 1981] 2. to come down or recover from a drug *trip* (*q.v.*). [U.S., IGA: 1971, GU: 1975]

get off on to achieve the desired level of euphoria from a drug, especially marijuana. Now also in general slang meaning to become stimulated by anything including academic subjects. [U.S., M&V: 1954]

get on a jag (also **get a jag on**) to get drunk. Jag = load. RT: *mug oneself.* [U.S., (1850–1900): RFA]

get one's biler loaded (also **get one's tank filled**) to get drunk. Biler = boiler. *Cf. tank up*. RT: *mug oneself.* [U.S., (1887): RML: 1950]

get one's gage up to get intoxicated on alcohol or drugs. This is probably the equivalent of getting *steamed up* (*q.v.*). *Cf. gage*. [U.S., MHW: 1934, GOL: 1950]

get one's nose cold to *snort* (*q.v.*) cocaine. RS: *snort*. [U.S., EAF: 1980]

get one's wings to succeed in becoming an addict, a qualified *flier* (*q.v.*). *Cf. wings*. See *give someone wings*. [U.S., JWK: 1981]

get one's yen off 1. (also **get the habit off**) to end one's craving for drugs by taking a dose of some drug. *Cf. yen*. [U.S., DWM: 1936, BD: 1937, RRL: 1969] 2. to end drug craving by giving up drugs. *Cf. kick.* [U.S., BVB: 1942, DU]

get on the pole to get drunk. *Cf. up the pole.* RT: *mug oneself.* [JRW: 1909]

get straight (also **get right**) to take a dose of a drug to end drug craving. See *straight.* [U.S., (M&W: 1946), M&V: 1967, EEL: 1971]

get the bighead to get drunk and have a hangover. *Cf. bighead.* [since the 1800s, F&H]

get there to get drunk. RT: *mug oneself.* [Br., late 18–1900s, DSUE]

get the sting to get addicted to a drug. *Cf. stinger.* [U.S., JES: 1959, H&C: 1975] See also *sting, stung.*

get through to purchase drugs. RT: *score.* [U.S., JTD: 1971]

get-up an addict's first dose of the day. See *eye-opener.* [U.S., M&V: 1967, H&C: 1975]

get wasted to get high on liquor, marijuana, or other drugs. [U.S., EEL: 1971, FAB: 1979, ADC: 1981]

get with it to inject a drug. *Cf. get down, get it on.* RT: *shoot.* Now GEN: hurry up, work with the group, get with the times. [U.S., M&V: 1967, H&C: 1975]

ghanja marijuana. See *ganga.*

gheed up See *geed up.*

gheid a paregoric user. See *gee, geehead.* Possibly a dialect pronunciation of *geehead* (*q.v.*), in which case the entry word would be written better as *G-heid.* RS: *user.* [U.S., EEL: 1971, IGA: 1971]

gho opium. Akin to *gow* (*q.v.*). RT: *opium.* [U.S., SNP: 1977]

ghost 1. an opium addict. *Cf. spook, zombie.* RS: *junky.* [U.S., DU, A&T: 1953] 2. (also **the ghost**) the hallucinogenic drug *L.S.D.* (*q.v.*). *Cf. the beast.* RT: *L.S.D.* [U.S., JBW: 1967, IGA: 1971, ADC: 1981]

ghow opium. See *gow.*

giant killer whiskey; potent whiskey. Possibly akin to the expression *Jack the giant killer* and *jack* (= denatured alcohol). RT: *whiskey.* [Br., (1910): DSUE]

giddy tipsy; alcohol intoxicated. GEN: silly. RT: *drunk.* [U.S., BVB: 1942]

giddy water liquor. *Cf. giddy.* RT: *booze.* [U.S., BVB: 1942]

giffed alcohol intoxicated. From *T.G.I.F* = Thank God it's Friday. RT: *drunk.* [U.S., N&S: 1983]

gig a drug *high* (*q.v.*); a high from pills. Possibly from *giggle.* [U.S., M&V: 1967]

giggle and titter ale; a bitter ale. Rhyming slang for *bitter.* RS: *ale.* Music hall use. [Br., early 1900s, DRS]

giggled (also **giggled up**) alcohol intoxicated. *Cf. giggle water.* RT: *drunk.* [U.S., BVB: 1942]

giggle goo liquor. *Cf. silly milk.* RT: *booze.* [U.S., BVB: 1942] See also *giggle water.*

giggle smoke (also **giggles**, **giggle weed**) marijuana; a marijuana cigarette. RT: *pot.* [U.S., (1937): ELA: 1982, RPW: 1938, D&D: 1957, W&F: 1960, RRL: 1969, EEL: 1971, DNE: 1973]

giggle water (also **giggle goo**, **giggle juice**, **giggle soup**) whiskey; liquor; champagne. *Cf. silly milk.* RT: *booze, cham.* [U.S., (1910): DSUE, VR: 1929, AH: 1931, JAS: 1932, MHW: 1934, BVB: 1942, VJM: 1949, W&F: 1960; Br., WG: 1962]

giggle weed marijuana; marijuana combined with wine. Marijuana makes some people giggle and laugh. RT: *pot.* [U.S., M&D: 1952, A&T: 1953, RRL: 1969]

giggle week allegedly marijuana. Almost certainly an error for *giggle weed* (*q.v.*). [U.S., SNP: 1977]

G.I. gin *Terpin Hydrate* (TM; *q.v.*) cough medicine containing alcohol. The *G.I.* refers to military use of this substance. G.I. is often used colloquially to refer to something which is a low-quality substitute for the genuine article. [U.S., H&C: 1975, DST: 1984]

gilded alcohol intoxicated. May be akin to an old (early 1600s, SOD) use of *gild* = to bring a flush to the face by drinking heavily. RT: *drunk.* [Br., 1800s, F&H; U.S., MHW: 1934, BVB: 1942]

gills, up to the alcohol intoxicated. A mixed metaphor based on *full to the gills. Cf. fishy about the gills, fried to the gills, heaped to the gills, lit to the gills, loaded to the gills, rosy about the gills, soused to the gills, to the gills.* RT: *drunk.* [U.S., AH: 1931, MHW: 1934]

gimmicks equipment for preparing and injecting drugs. *Cf. tools, toys.* RT: *outfit.* [U.S., JBW: 1967, RRL: 1969, MA: 1973]

gimpy a police officer. Gimp = a lame or crippled person (in slang). See *lame.* RT: *fuzz.* [U.S., M&H: 1959]

gin 1. gin; any kind of liquor. From *Geneva* (*q.v.*). [since the early 1700s, (1714): OED, K&M: 1968] (This entry continues after the following list.) Nicknames and synonyms for gin: *bathtub gin, blue ribband, blue ribbon, blue ruin, blue stone, blue tape, bob, Brian O'Flinn, Brian O'Linn, Brian O'Lynn, bung it in, bush girlfriend, cat's water, clap of thunder, cocky's joy, cold cream, crank, cream of the valley, cream of the wilderness, deadeye, diddle, dido, drain, eyewash, eyewater, flash of lightning, frog's wine, Geneva, Geneva courage, Geneva liquor, golden cream, Gordon, Gordon water, Gunga Din, gunpowder, heart's ease, Holland tape, Huckleberry Finn, in-jay, jackey, jacky, Jersey lightning, jinny, jump-steady, juniper, juniper-juice, kill-cobbler, Lady Dacre's wine, light blue,* *lightning, light wet, Lincoln's Inn, London Milk, max, mecks, misery, mother's milk, mother's ruin, needle, needle and pin, nig, nigger gin, old Tom, ould Tom, panther, panther piss, quartern o' bry, rag water, ribbon, right sort, royal poverty, ruin, satin, sky blue, sloe gin, snaps, snops, snopsy, staff naked, stark naked, stinkious, strip-me-naked, strong and thin, tape, the creature, thick and thin, tittery, Tom, twankay, unsweetened, water of life, wet-thee-through, whip, white, white face, white lace, white lady, white ribbin, white ribbon, white satin, white tape, white velvet, white wine, white wool, yard of satin.* 2. cocaine. RT: *cocaine.* [U.S., IGA: 1971, SH: 1972] See also *Geneva.*

gin and it gin and Italian vermouth; a martini. [Br., (1932): OEDS, DSUE, SSD]

gin bud a facial pimple due to drinking gin to excess. *Cf. rum blossom.* [JB: 1823] Terms for such pimples: *ale pock, bottle nose, brandy blossom, gin bud, grog blossom, ruby, rum blossom, rum bud, strawberry, toddy blossom.*

gin-crawl a pub-crawl; a gin-drinking visit to a number of pubs; an area of low saloons patronized by gin drinkers. RS: *spree.* [(1883): JRW: 1909]

gin-crawler a drunkard; a gin drinker. *Cf. pub-crawl.* RT: *sot.* [Br., 1800s, F&H]

gin disposal unit a heavy drinker of gin; a gin drunkard. RS: *sot.* Nonce. [Br., S&E: 1981]

gin dive See *gin mill.*

gin flat a speakeasy where *bathtub gin* (*q.v.*) could be obtained. RT: *speak.* From the prohibition era. [U.S., D&D: 1957]

ginger the potency of the alcohol in liquor; the effect of potent alcohol. [U.S., BVB: 1942]

ginger beer (also **ginger pop**) a slightly fermented drink made of Jamaican ginger, lemon, and sugar. Ginger ale is a nonalcoholic version of this drink. *Cf. jake.* [(1809): OED, (1827): OED]

gingered up alcohol intoxicated. GEN: stimulated. RT: *drunk.* [U.S., WFM: 1958]

ginhead (also **gin hound**) a drunkard; an alcoholic. Not necessarily a gin drinker. See the list at *head.* RT: *sot.* [U.S., BVB: 1942, D&D: 1957, W&F: 1960]

gin lane (also **gin trap**) 1. a drinker's mouth; the mouth; the throat. *Cf. beer street.* [Br., 1800s, DSUE] 2. the path of drunkenness. From the temperance movement. [Br., 1800s, F&H, DSUE]

gin-liver (also **gin-drinker's liver**) cirrhosis of the liver from excessive drinking. *Cf. hob-nailed liver.* [since the early 1800s, OED]

gin ma a female drunkard. *Cf. ginnums.* RT: *sot.* [U.S., early 1900s, D&D: 1973]

gin mill (also **gin dive, gin palace**) a saloon; a low liquor establishment. Probably based on ***gin spinner*** (*q.v.*). SBF: 1982 dates **gin palace** 1846. RT: ***dive***. [U.S., (1865): DA, (1872): F&H, B&L: 1890, JSF: 1889, (1922): W&F: 1960, GI: 1931, MHW: 1934, D&D: 1957, DCCU: 1972]

gin miller someone who sells and serves liquor at a bar. RT: ***bartender***. [U.S., (1888): DA, BVB: 1942, D&D: 1957]

ginned (also **ginned up**) alcohol intoxicated. RT: ***drunk***. [(1900): DA, GI: 1931, D&D: 1957, W&F: 1960]

ginnery a liquor establishment. *Cf.* ***gin flat***. RS: ***bar***. [U.S., BVB: 1942]

ginnified alcohol intoxicated; ***ginned*** (*q.v.*). RT: ***drunk***. [Br., 18-1900s, F&H; listed in BVB: 1942]

ginnums a gin-drinking old lady. *Cf.* ***gin ma***. RS: ***sot***. [Br., (1893): DSUE, F&H]

ginny alcohol intoxicated. GEN: physically damaged by gin-drinking. RT: ***drunk***. [Br. and U.S., 1900s, DSUE, BVB: 1942]

gin palace a saloon. See ***gin mill***. [U.S., (1846): DA, BVB: 1942]

gin rooster tail a gin cocktail. A jocular avoidance for *cock*. [U.S., JSF: 1889]

gin slinger a gin drinker; a drunkard. Possibly akin to a mixed drink called a *gin sling*. RT: ***sot***. [Br. and U.S., (1887): DA, JSF: 1889, F&H]

gin soaked alcohol intoxicated, not necessarily with gin. *Cf.* ***soaked***. RT: ***drunk***. [U.S., BVB: 1942]

gin spinner a distiller. *Cf.* ***draper, gin mill***. [Br., FG: 1785, JCH: 1887, F&H]

ginters the delirium tremens, jitters from drinking gin. RS: ***D.T.s***. [U.S., BVB: 1942]

gin trap See ***gin lane***.

gippy an Egyptian cigarette. RT: ***nail***. [Br., (1905): DSUE]

girl 1. (also **girli, girly**) cocaine. *Cf.* ***boy, her, lady, white girl***. RT: ***cocaine***. [U.S., A&T: 1953, HB: 1955, W&F: 1967, D&B: 1970c, CM: 1970, EEL: 1971, MA: 1973, EAF: 1980, NIDA: 1980, JWK: 1981] 2. heroin. *Cf.* ***boy, brother, him***. RT: ***heroin***. [U.S., JWK: 1981]

girlfriend cocaine. See ***girl***. RT: ***cocaine***. [U.S., JH: 1979]

give birth (also **give birth to a duster**) to defecate very hard feces after a constipating period of opium use. *Cf.* ***blockbuster, yen-shee baby***. [U.S., M&V: 1967]

give someone the go-by to refuse to recognize or sell drugs to an untrustworthy or undesirable buyer. See ***chill***. [U.S., DWM: 1936, A&T: 1953]

give someone wings to introduce someone to heroin by injection; to teach someone to *fly* (*q.v.*). [U.S., RDS: 1982]

give the needle to to spike with alcohol. See *needle beer*. From the prohibition era. [U.S., BVB: 1942]

gizzy marijuana. RT: *pot*. [U.S., RAS: 1985]

glad alcohol intoxicated. *Cf. gay, happy, merry*. RT: *drunk*. [BF: 1737]

glad rags 1. handkerchiefs or other cloths saturated with drugs for sniffing (snorting) glue or other inhalants. [U.S., JBW: 1967, RG: 1970, EEL: 1971] 2. a sniffer of inhalants. RS: *user*. [U.S., JTD: 1971]

glad stuff hard drugs such as heroin, morphine, opium, and cocaine. [U.S., A&T: 1953, IGA: 1971, SNP: 1977]

glass 1. a drunkard. Similar to *pot* (*q.v.*). RT: *sot*. Never common (W&F: 1960). [U.S., W&F: 1960] 2. a hypodermic syringe. *Cf. glass gun*. RT: *monkey pump*. [U.S., BVB: 1942, JWK: 1981] 3. an ampule of *Methedrine* (TM; *q.v.*). *Cf. jug*. RS: *speed*. [U.S., M&V: 1967, H&C: 1975] See also *gas*. 4. (always **a glass** or **the glass**) liquor; a glass or portion of liquor. Similar to *bottle* (*q.v.*). RT: *booze*. [U.S., BVB: 1942]

glass eyes (also **glass eye**) a drug user or addict. RT: *junky*. [U.S., BVB: 1942, VJM: 1949, A&T: 1953]

glass gun a hypodermic syringe. *Cf. glass*. RT: *monkey pump*. [U.S., VJM: 1949, A&T: 1953]

glassy-eyed (also **glass-eyed**) drug intoxicated or alcohol intoxicated, usually the later. GEN: detached; with glazed eyes. [U.S., MHW: 1934, W&F: 1960]

glazed (also **glazed drunk, glazed over**) alcohol intoxicated. (BF: 1737: [He's] Glaiz'd.) RT: *drunk*. [BF: 1737; U.S., BVB: 1942, W&F: 1967, DCCU: 1972]

globetrotter an addict who moves around looking for the highest quality heroin. *Cf. frog*. RS: *junky*. [U.S., M&V: 1967, RRL: 1969, CM: 1970, JWK: 1981]

globular alcohol intoxicated. *Cf. blimped*. RT: *drunk*. [BF: 1737]

glom to steal drugs; to snatch more than one's share of drugs; to take drugs. Essentially, to cop or pinch. [U.S., M&V: 1967, H&C: 1975]

glomed arrested; arrested on a drug charge. GEN: copped, nabbed. RT: *busted*. [U.S., M&V: 1954, H&C: 1975]

glooch a drug *burnout* (*q.v.*); a drug addict whose senses have been degraded by drugs. RS: *junky*. [U.S., JES: 1959, H&C: 1975]

glorious alcohol intoxicated; very drunk. RT: *drunk*. [Br., (1790): OED (Robert Burns); listed in BVB: 1942]

glory seeds morning glory seeds. Large numbers of these are chewed to produce a high. RT: *seeds*. [U.S., YKB: 1977]

glow a mild state of drug or alcohol intoxication. *Cf. buzz, got a glow on.* [U.S., BVB: 1942, RRL: 1969, EEL: 1971]

glowing alcohol intoxicated; tipsy. RS: *drunk.* [U.S., BVB: 1942]

glow worm a drunkard; an alcoholic. This drunkard, like the worm, is *lit* (*q.v.*). RT: *sot.* [U.S., BVB: 1942]

glue 1. model airplane cement containing toluene or a similar volatile substance. This glue is sniffed to produce a high. Not slang. [U.S., EEL: 1971] 2. the waste product of heroin processing. [U.S., JWK: 1981]

glued 1. arrested. RT: *busted.* [U.S., M&V: 1954, RDS: 1982] 2. alcohol intoxicated. *Cf. pasted.* RT: *drunk.* [U.S., W&F: 1960]

glue sniffer someone, presumably a teenager, who sniffs glue containing toluene for a high. *Cf. huffer.* RT: *user.* [HSD: 1984]

gluey (also **gluer**) a person, usually teenage or younger, who sniffs glue. *Cf. huffer.* RS: *user.* [U.S., JBW: 1967, IGA: 1971, JHF: 1971]

go 1. a drink of liquor. *Cf. go-down.* RT: *nip.* [Br., 1800s, F&H; listed in BVB: 1942] 2. a dose of drugs; an injection of drugs. RS: *shot.* [U.S., BD: 1937, DWM: 1938, BVB: 1942]

goat drunk alcohol intoxicated; drunk and lascivious. *Cf. drunk as a goat.* RT: *drunk.* [U.S., BVB: 1942]

goat hair illegal liquor. *Cf. hair of the dog.* RT: *moonshine.* [U.S., CM: 1970]

goblet of jam a translation of Arabic *m'juni akbar,* the name of a confection containing hashish. *Cf. brownies.* See *majoon.* It is doubtful that this expression has had wide use in the U.S. underworld or drug culture [U.S., RRL: 1969, RDS: 1982] See also *jam.*

go-by See *give someone the go-by.*

go-down a drink of liquor that goes down the throat. See *go.* RT: *nip.* [16-1700s, (1614): OED, F&H, DSUE]

go down the line to *snort* (*q.v.*) a *line* (*q.v.*) of cocaine. RS: *snort.* [U.S., JWK: 1981]

God's flesh mushrooms containing *psilocybin* (*q.v.*). *Cf. magic mushrooms.* RT: *psilocybin.* [U.S., ADC: 1981]

God's medicine (also **God's own medicine, G.O.M.**) morphine. Originally a medical expression. D&D: 1957 gloss it narcotics. RDS: 1982 glosses it opium. [U.S., DWM: 1936, D&D: 1957, RRL: 1969]

go-fasters (also **goies**) amphetamines. *Cf. speed.* RT: *amps.* ELA: 1984 (U.S.) lists **goies**. [Aust., SJB: 1966]

go for a sleighride (also **go on a sleighride, take a sleighride**) to take cocaine. *Cf. sleighride.* See *winter wonderland* for more expressions on the snow theme. [U.S., GOL: 1950, M&V: 1954]

go for veg to get drunk; to become drunk and unconscious. *Cf.*

vegetable. RT: *mug oneself.* [U.S., GU: 1975]

goggle-eyed (also **googly-eyed**) alcohol intoxicated. Refers to the staring eyes of someone who is very drunk. RT: *drunk.* [U.S., BVB: 1942]

going high a long-lasting type of drug high. It goes and goes. *Cf. high.* [U.S., RRL: 1969, CM: 1970]

going to Jerusalem alcohol intoxicated. RT: *drunk.* [BF: 1737]

go in the skin to miss the vein and inject into the skin. *Cf. blow a shot.* [U.S., BD: 1937, DWM: 1938, VJM: 1949]

go into the sewer (also **go in the sewer**) to inject drugs directly into to a vein; to hit a vein when injecting. *Cf. sewer.* RT: *shoot.* [U.S., BD: 1937, DWM: 1938]

gold any golden marijuana; any tan marijuana rich in resin. Usually refers to *Acapulco gold* (*q.v.*). *Cf. Acapulco gold, Colombian gold, gold leaf special, gold bud, golden leaf, Kona gold, Panama gold, Panamanian gold, Santa Marta gold.* RT: *pot.* [U.S., RRL: 1969, RRL: 1974, W&F: 1975, JWK: 1981]

gold bud a gold marijuana presumably from Colombia. See *Colombian gold. Cf. bud.* RT: *pot.* [U.S., ADC: 1981]

gold Colombian (also **gold Columbian**) a golden marijuana presumably from Colombia. See *Colombian gold.* RT: *pot.* [U.S., YKB: 1977]

gold dust 1. tobacco, especially when it is hard to get. *Cf. freckles.* RT: *fogus.* [Br. nautical, 18–1900s, DSUE] 2. cocaine. See *forty-niner.* RT: *cocaine.* [U.S., GI: 1931, MHW: 1934, VJM: 1949, RRL: 1969, EEL: 1971, NIDA: 1980] 3. heroin. RT: *heroin.* College use. [U.S., GU: 1975]

gold duster (also **golden duster**) a cocaine user. RT: *kokomo.* [U.S., D&D: 1957, RRL: 1969]

golden cream gin. *Cf. cold cream.* RT: *gin.* [Br., (1889): F&H]

golden crescent the heroin producing area in the countries Pakistan, Iran, and Afghanistan. See *golden triangle.* [U.S., RAS: 1983]

golden girl high-quality cocaine. An elaboration of *girl* (*q.v.*). RS: *cocaine.* [U.S., EAF: 1980]

golden grain Lebanese hashish. RT: *hash.* [U.S., RDS: 1982]

golden leaf high-quality marijuana; *Acapulco gold.* RT: *pot.* [U.S., M&W: 1946, G&B: 1969, CM: 1970, EEL: 1971]

golden spike a hypodermic syringe. *Cf. spike.* RT: *needle.* [U.S., HB: 1955]

golden triangle a 60,000 square mile area at the boundaries of Burma, Laos, and Thailand where opium is grown for export. Sometime this area is identified as being at the boundaries of Laos, Cambodia, and Vietnam. See *A.I.D.* [U.S., (1973): DNE: 1973, RDS: 1982]

goldfinger synthetic heroin. [U.S., RDS: 1982]

gold-headed alcohol intoxicated. RT: *drunk*. [BF: 1737]

gold leaf special a potent marijuana cigarette. *Cf. golden leaf.* RT: *joint*. [U.S., RPW: 1938, M&V: 1954]

golleroy a plug of burnt tobacco in a pipe; pipe dottle. RT: *dottle*. [U.S., early 1900s, ADD]

go loco to smoke marijuana. *Cf. locoweed.* RT: *hit the hay*. [U.S., BVB: 1942, H&C: 1975]

golpe* heroin. Spanish for jolt or blow. RT: *heroin*. [U.S., NIDA: 1980]

G.O.M. morphine, "God's own medicine" or "good old morphine." *Cf. God's medicine.* RT: *morphine*. Not originally drug slang. H&C: 1975 also define it as good old marijuana. [U.S., DWM: 1938, A&T: 1953]

goma (also **guma**) opium. *Cf. gum.* Possible akin to *G.O.M.* RT: *opium*. [U.S., W&F: 1967]

goma de moto hashish. From the Spanish for gum of dust. RT: *hash*. [U.S., ELA: 1984]

gone 1. (also **gone under**) alcohol intoxicated. *Cf. about gone, half gone.* RT: *drunk*. [U.S., MHW: 1934, W&F: 1960] 2. drug intoxicated. RT: *stoned*. [U.S., H&C: 1975]

gone Borneo alcohol intoxicated. RT: *drunk*. [U.S., N&S: 1983]

gone down arrested. RT: *busted*. [U.S., JWK: 1981]

gong 1. (also **the gong**) opium. Probably from an old (since about 1000 AD) term for dung. RT: *opium*. [U.S., DWM: 1936, BVB: 1942] 2. marijuana. RT: *pot*. See *ganga*. [U.S., SNP: 1977] 3. an opium pipe. RT: *hop stick*. [U.S., (1915): OEDS, DWM: 1933, DWM: 1938, D&D: 1957, EEL: 1971; Br. BTD: 1968]

gonga (also **gong**) marijuana. See *ganga*. [U.S., GOL: 1950] See also *gonger*.

gonga smudge a marijuana cigarette. RT: *joint*. [U.S., (1939): ELA: 1982]

gong beater (also **gong kicker**) an opium smoker. RT: *campfire boy*. Also attested as meaning a marijuana smoker (GOL: 1950). [U.S., VJM: 1949, GOL: 1950, HB: 1955, EEL: 1971]

gonger 1. (also **gongerine**) opium; an opium pipe. *Cf. on the gonger.* RT: *hop stick*. [U.S., (1914): OEDS, GI: 1931, DWM: 1931, DWM: 1933, GOL: 1950] 2. an opium addict. RT: *junky*. [U.S., BVB: 1942, H&C: 1975]

gonger den an opium den. RT: *opium den*. [U.S., JES: 1959]

gonger, on the (also **up against the gonger**) addicted to opium. *Cf. gonger.* RS: *hooked*. [U.S., GOL: 1950, D&D: 1957]

gongola an opium pipe. *Cf. gong.* RT: *hop stick*. [U.S., DWM: 1938, VJM: 1949]

goober a marijuana cigarette. RT: *joint*. [U.S., ELA: 1982]

good butt a marijuana cigarette. See *goof butt*. RT: *joint*. [U.S., W&F: 1960]

good creature of God (also **creature, good creature**) liquor. *Creature* (*q.v.*) = liquor. From the Bible, *I Timothy IV*. Not slang. [in various forms since the 1600s, (1624): OED]

good fettle, in (also **fettled, in fine fettle**) alcohol intoxicated. RT: *drunk*. [since the late 1800s, F&H]

good giggles marijuana; marijuana cigarettes. *Cf. giggle smoke*. RT: *pot*. [U.S., H&C: 1975, SNP: 1977]

good go good drugs for the amount paid. [U.S., HB: 1955, EEL: 1971, IGA: 1971]

goodies drugs in general. A specialized sense of the colloquial term meaning candy or snacks. *Cf. hard candy, needle candy, nose candy*. RS: *dope*. [U.S., D&B: 1970c]

good-natured alk (also **good-natured, good-natured alcohol**) grain alcohol, ethyl alcohol. In contrast to wood alcohol (methyl alcohol) which is ill-natured because it is undrinkable. *Cf. ill-natured alcohol*. From the prohibition era. [U.S., MHW: 1934, BVB: 1942]

good old M. (also **G.O.M., goody**) morphine, good old morphine. RT: *morphine*. [U.S., JES: 1959, H&C: 1975]

goods (also **good stuff**) heroin; narcotics; hard drugs. Used as a disguise in public communications. RS: *dope*. [U.S., BD: 1937, DWM: 1938, TRG: 1968, RRL: 1969, EEL: 1971, YKB: 1977]

good sick nausea and vomiting at the onset of heroin euphoria. [U.S., RRL: 1969, CM: 1970]

good stuff high-quality heroin; any potent drug including marijuana. *Cf. bad, decent*. GEN: anything good. [U.S., RRL: 1969, D&B: 1970c, ADC: 1981, EEL: 1971]

good time man a drug seller, i.e., a man who sells good times. RT: *dealer*. [U.S., E&R: 1971]

good trip a satisfactory or excellent session with a drug, especially *L.S.D.* (*q.v.*). The opposite of *bad trip* (*q.v.*). [U.S., RDS: 1982]

goody morphine. See *good old M.*

goof 1. a marijuana smoker. RT: *toker*. [U.S., GOL: 1950, A&T: 1953] 2. to take drugs; to take strange drugs or substances. See *goofing*. [U.S., EEL: 1971] 3. a drug buyer; a drug user; a pusher's customer. RS: *user*. [U.S., M&H: 1959, EEL: 1971]

goof artist a person who takes offbeat drugs; someone who plays around with drugs and other substances such as cough syrup with codeine, glue, barbiturates. RS: *user*. [U.S., M&V: 1967, H&C: 1975]

goofball 1. (also **goofer**) marijuana; a marijuana cigarette. RT: *pot*. [U.S., MB: 1938, D&D: 1957, W&F: 1960] 2. (also **goofballer**) a marijuana smoker. RT: *toker*. [U.S., DU, D&D: 1957] 3. (also **goofballs**) barbiturate tablets or capsules; tranquilizers. RT: *barbs, tranks*. [U.S., (1950): OEDS, M&D: 1952, M&V: 1954, W&F: 1960, RRL: 1969, MA: 1973, NIDA: 1980] 4. a mixture of cocaine and heroin; a mixture of amphetamines and barbiturates. RS: *set*. [U.S., RRL: 1969, EEL: 1971] 5. pills made from marijuana *resin* (*q.v.*). Possibly the same as sense one. [Br., BTD: 1968] 6. amphetamines; *Benzedrine* (TM; *q.v.*). RRL: 1969 indicates that this use is rare and erroneous. RT: *amps*. [U.S., EEL: 1971]

goof burner a marijuana smoker. RT: *toker*. [U.S. Army, early 1900s, DST: 1984]

goof butt (also **goofy butt**) a marijuana cigarette. RT: *joint*. [U.S., MB: 1938, GOL: 1950, D&D: 1957, W&F: 1960, YKB: 1977]

goofed up (also **goofed**) under the effects of marijuana; under the effects of a goofball. GEN: confused, bewildered. RT: *stoned*. [U.S., (1930): DU, A&T: 1953, M&V: 1954, W&F: 1960, TRG: 1968]

goofer 2. (also **goofers**) barbiturates. RT: *barbs*. [U.S., RRL: 1969, YKB: 1977] 2. a person who takes pills such as barbiturates or amphetamines; someone who just goofs around and plays around with drugs. See *goof artist*. [U.S., M&V: 1954, JBW: 1967, RRL: 1969]

go off the habit to stop using drugs; to break an addiction. RT: *kick*. [U.S., M&D: 1952]

goofing 1. the use of heroin before one becomes addicted to it. *Cf. chip*. [U.S., JWK: 1981] 2. scratching, nodding, and slobbering after an injection of heroin. *Cf. nod*. [U.S., M&V: 1954, JWK: 1981] 3. taking strange combinations of drugs. [U.S., M&V: 1973, H&C: 1975] See also *goof, goofball*.

goof, on the drug intoxicated. The same as *on the nod* (*q.v.*). [U.S., M&H: 1959]

goofy 1. alcohol intoxicated. *Cf. loony*. RT: *drunk*. [U.S., BVB: 1942] 2. craving drugs; withdrawing from drugs involuntarily. [U.S., early 1900s, DU, A&T: 1953]

goofy butt a marijuana cigarette. See *goof butt*.

goofy dust cocaine. RT: *cocaine*. [U.S., ELA: 1984]

goog beer; a glass of beer. RT: *beer*. [U.S., ADC: 1984]

googly-eyed See *goggle-eyed*.

goon (also **goon dust**) phencyclidine, P.C.P., an animal tranquilizer. RT: *P.C.P.* [U.S., YKB: 1977, FAB: 1979]

go on the boot to inject drugs in a manner which allows the user to control and prolong the *rush* (*q.v.*). See *boot*. [U.S., M&H: 1959]

go on the bottle to take up drinking. The opposite of being *on* *the wagon* (*q.v.*). [U.S., D&D: 1957]

go on the cousin sis to get drunk; to go on a drinking bout. Rhyming slang for *go on the piss* (*q.v.*). RT: *mug oneself.* [Br. military, (1925): DSUE]

go on the lap to get drunk. *Lap* (*q.v.*) = liquor. RT: *mug oneself.* [Br., late 1800s, DSUE]

go on the nod to become drowsy or depressed from drugs. *Cf. nodding out.* [U.S., M&D: 1952]

go on the piss to get drunk; to go on a drinking bout. See *pissed.* RT: *mug oneself.* [Br., EP: 1948]

go on the wagon to stop drinking alcohol, to get on the water wagon. [U.S., BVB: 1942]

go over the cognac trail to get drunk. RT: *mug oneself.* [U.S. military, WWI, MHW: 1934, BVB: 1942]

go-pills (also **"Go" pills**) amphetamine tablets or capsules. RT: *amps.* [U.S., early 1900s, D&D: 1957]

gordoned alcohol intoxicated; drunk on gin. See *Gordon water.* RT: *drunk.* [U.S., BVB: 1942]

Gordon water (also **Gordon**) gin. From the brand name *Gordon's Gin.* RT: *gin.* [U.S., VR: 1929, AH: 1931, MHW: 1934, W&F: 1960]

goric *paregoric* (*q.v.*). *Cf. P.G., Proctor and Gamble.* [U.S., YKB: 1977] Nicknames and slang terms for paregoric: *blackjack, black stuff, goric, paregoric, P.G., P.O., Proctor and Gamble.*

gorilla a very powerful addiction. *Cf. King Kong, Mighty Joe Young, monkey, tang* which are all names for a drug habit or for drug craving. All are based on *monkey on one's back.* [U.S., JWK: 1981]

gorilla biscuits amphetamines. RT: *amps.* [U.S., SH: 1972]

gorilla pills barbiturate tablets or capsules; *Tuinal* (TM; *q.v.*) barbiturates. RT: *barbs.* [U.S., RRL: 1969, W&S: 1977, YKB: 1977]

gorilla tabs phencyclidine, P.C.P. RT: *P.C.P.* [U.S., ELA: 1984]

gory-eyed (also **gorey-eyed**) alcohol intoxicated. *Cf. hoary-eyed.* Possibly a play on *gore* and *orie-eyed.* RT: *drunk.* [U.S., MHW: 1934, BVB: 1942]

go see a man about a dog (also **go give the Chinaman a music lesson**) to go out for a drink. Both are obvious, jocular contrivances, and both also mean to retire to the toilet. RT: *irrigate.* [U.S., BVB: 1942]

go straight to get off drugs. *Cf. straight.* RS: *kick.* [U.S., EEL: 1971]

got a brass eye (also **have a brass eye**) alcohol intoxicated. RT: *drunk.* [BF: 1737]

got a drop in the eye (also **have a drop in the eye**) alcohol intoxicated. *Cf. drop.* RT: *drunk.* [late 16-1700s, BE: 1690]

got a glow on drug intoxicated; alcohol intoxicated. *Cf. glow.* RT: *drunk, stoned.* [U.S., (EEL: 1971)]

go talk to Herbie and Al to smoke marijuana and drink liquor. Herbie = marijuana. Al = alcohol. *Cf. herb.* [U.S., ADC: 1981]

Got any zings? "Do you have any stimulants for sale?" *Zings* (*q.v.*) = amphetamines. See *How are you going to act?* for a list of similar inquiries. [U.S., JWK: 1981]

got by the head (also **got corns in his head**) alcohol intoxicated. RT: *drunk.* [BF: 1737]

got his top gallant sails out alcohol intoxicated. Refers to the top gallant sails of a square-rigged sailing ship. RT: *drunk.* [BF: 1737]

got kibbed heels (also **got the gout**) alcohol intoxicated. Kibbed heels is an old (1500s, OED) term for an affliction wherein one has chilblains on the heels and therefore must walk carefully. The gout also makes walking difficult or impossible. RT: *drunk.* [BF: 1737]

got on his little hat alcohol intoxicated. RT: *drunk.* [BF: 1737]

go to the cathedral to smoke hashish. [U.S., BR: 1972]

go to the vein to inject drugs into the median cephalic vein. This implies moving from subcutaneous injections to mainlining. RT: *shoot.* [U.S., BR: 1972]

got the glanders alcohol intoxicated. Glanders is a disease of horses. RT: *drunk.* [BF: 1737]

got the gravel rash alcohol intoxicated. Refers to scrapes and abrasions from falling in the gravel. RT: *drunk.* [Br., 1800s, F&H]

got the hornson alcohol intoxicated. This is probably "got the horns on." See *drunk as a goat, goat drunk.* RT: *drunk.* [BF: 1737]

got the Indian vapors (also **have the Indian vapors**) alcohol intoxicated. Vapors = mental depression. RT: *drunk.* [BF: 1737]

got the nightmare (also **got the pole evil**) alcohol intoxicated. RT: *drunk.* [BF: 1737]

gouch off to pass out under the influence of drugs. [U.S., JHF: 1971]

gouger a marijuana smoker. Perhaps a dialect pronunciation of *gauger,* or an error. RT: *toker.* [U.S., JES: 1959, H&C: 1975, ELA: 1984]

go under to become intoxicated. *Cf. under, under the influence.* RS: *mug oneself.* [U.S., DCCU: 1972]

go up to start to feel the effects of a drug; to become high on drugs, especially marijuana. *Cf. up.* [U.S., RB: 1967, W&F: 1967, EEL: 1971, M&V: 1973]

gourd, out of one's drug intoxicated; alcohol intoxicated. GEN: crazy, silly. [U.S., JWK: 1981]

gow 1. (also **ghow**) opium. Chinese or mock-Chinese. RT: *opium*. [U.S., WHW: 1922, GI: 1931, W&F: 1960] 2. (also **gow out**) to collect opium residue from an opium pipe; to use the *yen-shee-gow* (*q.v.*) to scrape the *yen-shee* (*q.v.*) from the bowl of an opium pipe. [U.S., (BD: 1937), DWM: 1938, BVB: 1942] 3. narcotics; drugs, including marijuana. RS: *dope*. [U.S., DWM: 1933, DWM: 1936, MHW: 1934] 4. the rush or euphoria obtained from drugs. *Cf. glow*. RT: *rush*. [U.S., W&F: 1960] See also *lobby gow, yen-gow, yen-shee-gow*.

gow cellar a place to buy opium; a drug seller's place of business. Probably based on *wine cellar*. *Cf. gow*. [U.S., JES: 1959, H&C: 1975]

gow crust opium residue, *yen-shee* (*q.v.*). Probably from the early 1900s. [U.S., ELA: 1984]

gowed up (also **gowed**) stupefied by alcohol or drugs. Originally, stupefied by opium. *Cf. gow*. RT: *drunk, stoned*. [U.S., GI: 1931, DWM: 1936, MHW: 1934, W&F: 1960, D&D: 1973]

gowhead an opium addict or user; any drug addict or user. *Cf. gheid*. Compare to *galhead*. RT: *campfire boy*. [U.S., BD: 1937, DWM: 1938, VJM: 1949, TRG: 1968]

go with the flow (also **go with it**) an expression of encouragement said to a person on an *L.S.D.* (*q.v.*) trip. Also a general slang expression encouraging someone to cope with adversity. [U.S., (TW: 1968)]

gow, on the (also **on gow**) 1. drug intoxicated. RT: *stoned*. [U.S., DWM: 1936] 2. using opium; addicted to opium. *Cf. chewing the gum, hit by the hop, in the smoke, mired in the mud, picking the poppies, poppy-headed, shoveling the black stuff, stung by the hop, up against the stem*. RS: *hooked*. [U.S., DWM: 1933, HNR: 1934]

gow out the lemon bowl to smoke opium. Probably an error. This should mean something like "scrape out the lemon bowl." *Cf. gow, lemon bowl*. [U.S., early 1900s, DU, JES: 1959]

gowster 1. (also **gowhead**) an opium addict; any addict. RT: *campfire boy*. [U.S., DWM: 1936, VJM: 1949, D&D: 1957] 2. a marijuana smoker. RT: *toker*. [U.S., W&F: 1960]

goznik (also **goynik, goynk**) opium; narcotics in general. A&T: 1953 list **goynk**. RS: *dope*. [U.S., DWM: 1938, VJM: 1949, A&T: 1953, SNP: 1977]

G.Q. having to do with good-quality drugs or anything of good quality. *Cf. Q. and Q*. [U.S., RAS: 1980]

grads amphetamine tablets. Possibly akin to *undergrad* (*q.v.*). RT: *amps*. [U.S., SNP: 1977]

graduate to move from casual drug use to addiction. *Cf. flunk out*. [U.S., IGA: 1971, WCM: 1972]

G-rag See *gee rag.*

grain alcohol ethyl alcohol of high proof; drinkable alcohol. As opposed to *wood alcohol* (*q.v.*). Not argot.

gram 1. hashish. May refer to a specific amount of hashish. Probably akin to *gramma* (*q.v.*). RS: *hash.* [U.S., SNP: 1977] 2. a gram of heroin. RS: *load.* [U.S., JBW: 1967, IGA: 1971] 3. a gram of cocaine; a typical purchase of cocaine. RS: *load.* [U.S., BW: 1984, S&F: 1984]

gramma* marijuana. Spanish. RT: *pot.* [calo, CG: 1980]

granny material used to hold the parts of an opium pipe together. A play on *granny rag,* an old country term for a menstrual cloth or napkin. See *gee rag.* [U.S., GOL: 1950]

grape cat (also **grape chick**) a wino. The cat is the male; the chick is the female. RS: *sot.* U.S. Black use. [U.S., DB: 1944, CM: 1970]

grape monger a wino. RT: *wino.* [(1606): OED; listed in BVB: 1942]

grape parfait the hallucinogenic drug *L.S.D.* (*q.v.*); L.S.D. and some other drug. Based on the purple color of the substance. *Cf. Owsley purple, purple, purple Owsley, purple dot, purple dragon, purple flats, purple haze, purple microdots, purple ozzy, purple wedges.* [U.S., SNP: 1977, KBH: 1982, RDS: 1982]

grapes (also **grape, the grape, the grapes**) champagne; wine. RT: *cham, wine.* [U.S., VJM: 1949, RG: 1970, IGA: 1971, DC: 1972]

grape shot alcohol intoxicated; drunk on wine. Based on *cup shot* or *half shot.* RT: *drunk.* [Br., late 1800s, F&H; listed in BVB: 1942]

grapes of wrath wine; overindulgence in wine; the result of over indulgence in wine. Refers to the resulting hangover or other problems. RT: *wine.* [U.S., early 1900s, CM: 1970]

grappa brandy distilled from wine or mash. From Italian. *Cf. grappo.* RT: *brandy.* [U.S., WWII, DST: 1984, VJM: 1949, K&M: 1968]

grapple the rails whiskey. RT: *whiskey.* [cant, FG: 1785, F&H]

grappo wine. From *grape. Cf. grappa.* RT: *wine.* Hobo use. [U.S., W&F: 1960]

grass marijuana. RT: *pot.* A very common term for marijuana. *Cf. bad grass, dirt grass, grass eater, grasshead, grasshopper, grass mask, grass weed, Johnson grass, Kansas grass, laughing grass, liquid grass, live in grass huts, paralyzing grass, stupefying grass, supergrass, synthetic grass.* [U.S., RPW: 1938, M&D: 1952, S&W: 1966, W&F: 1967, D&B: 1970c, CM: 1970, EEL: 1971, DCCU: 1972, ADC: 1975, MW: 1976, YKB: 1977, JB: 1980, NIDA: 1980, JWK: 1981]

grass brownies brownies with marijuana baked into them. *Grass* (*q.v.*) = marijuana. See *Alice B. Toklas, brownies*. [U.S., RRL: 1969, IGA: 1971]

grass cleaner a device for removing seeds and stems from marijuana. [U.S., YKB: 1977]

grass eater a marijuana smoker. *Grass* (*q.v.*) = marijuana. Possibly based on *opium eater* (*q.v.*). RT: *toker*. [U.S., JES: 1959, H&C: 1975]

grasser a marijuana smoker. RT: *toker*. [U.S., EE: 1976]

grasshopper (also **grasshead**) a marijuana smoker. See the list at *head*. W&F: 1975 lists only **grasshopper**. RT: *toker*. [U.S., (1948): ELA: 1982, M&V: 1954, (1968): DNE: 1980, D&B: 1970c, EEL: 1971, BR: 1972, W&F: 1975]

grass mask a face mask with a hose attached to a pipe for smoking cannabis. None of the smoke is lost. A play on *gas mask*. *Grass* (*q.v.*) = marijuana. See *grass cleaner*. [U.S., (1976): DNE: 1980, D&B: 1978]

grass party a marijuana-smoking party. [U.S., (1946): ELA: 1982]

grass pipe a pipe for smoking hashish or marijuana. RS: *bong*. [U.S., (1968): ELA: 1982]

grass reefer a marijuana cigarette. RT: *joint*. [U.S., DB: 1944]

grass trip a period of smoking marijuana; being high on marijuana (as opposed to L.S.D.). *Cf. get off, trip*. [U.S., RAS: 1981]

grass weed marijuana. *Cf. weed*. RT: *pot*. [U.S., M&D: 1952, W&F: 1960]

gravedigger liquor; strong liquor. RT: *booze*. [JRW: 1909]

gravel-grinder a drunkard who falls down a lot. *Cf. got the gravel rash*. RT: *sot*. [Br., (1860): DSUE, B&L: 1890, F&H]

gravelled alcohol intoxicated. From an old (late 1500s, OED) sense of the word meaning confused. See also *got the gravel rash*. RT: *drunk*. [Br., 18–1900s, F&H, DSUE; listed in BVB: 1942]

gravel rash See *got the gravel rash*.

gravy a mixture of coagulated blood and heroin solution in a hypodermic syringe or a *dripper* (*q.v.*). When an addict is *booting* (*q.v.*), the heroin may crystallize in the syringe or medicine dropper. If this happens the syringe or dropper is heated (with a match) to dissolve it again, and the blood is cooked. The entire mass is injected. The resulting **gravy** can clog the needle. *Cf. floater*. See *shoot gravy*. [U.S., RRL: 1969, EEL: 1971, MA: 1973]

gray dust old or stale phencyclidine powder. RS: *P.C.P.* [U.S., ADC: 1981]

greafa (also **greapha**) marijuana. See *grefa*.

grease 1. (also **greese**) prepared opium; raw opium. From the physical characteristics of raw opium. *Cf. gum*. See *Greece*. RT: *opium*. [U.S., BD: 1937, DWM: 1938] 2. to smoke opium. RT:

suck bamboo. [U.S., DU, A&T: 1953] 3. to eat ravenously after withdrawal from drugs. [U.S., M&V: 1967] 4. amphetamines. RT: *amps*. [U.S., RG: 1970]

greased alcohol intoxicated. *Cf. lubricated, oiled*. RT: *drunk*. [U.S., AH: 1931, MHW: 1934, W&F: 1960]

greased lightning strong liquor. From a colloquial expression having to do with anything fast or powerful. RS: *rotgut*. [U.S., BVB: 1942]

grease pit a narcotics seller's place of business. Possibly also means opium den. From the name of the trench in the floor of a commercial garage where cars can be serviced from below. *Cf. grease*. RS: *doperie*. [U.S., JES: 1959, H&C: 1975]

greasy having to do with an obvious drug addict or a down-and-out addict. Much worse than *dirty* (*q.v.*). *Cf. greasy junkie*. [U.S., JWK: 1981]

greasy bag a bag in which heroin is carried or sold. *Cf. skid bag*. Prison use. [U.S., TH: 1976]

greasy junkie (also **greasy junky**) a drug addict who get drugs by begging, running errands, or acting as a prostitute. RS: *junky*. [U.S., RRL: 1969, CM: 1970]

great Scott an opium pipe. Origin unknown. RT: *hop stick*. [U.S., JES: 1959]

great tobacco opium. *Cf. foreign smoke*. RT: *opium*. [U.S., DU, A&T: 1953, SNP: 1977]

Greece opium. A misunderstanding of, or a deliberate disguise of *grease* (*q.v.*). RT: *opium*. [U.S., SNP: 1977]

greefa (also **greefo**) marijuana. See *grefa* and *greefo*. [U.S., JES: 1959]

greefer (also **griefer**) a marijuana smoker. RT: *toker*. [U.S., H&C: 1975]

greefo 1. marijuana. See *grefa*. 2. an addict. [U.S., HB: 1955]

Greek fire inferior whiskey; strong whiskey. From the name of a combustible compound used by the Byzantine Greeks. The burning material was thrown at the enemy. RT: *rotgut*. [Br., (1889): F&H]

green 1. (also **greens**) marijuana with a low resin content. *Cf. Breckenridge green, Chicago green, Gainesville green, green moroccan, Illinois green, Jersey green, light green, Mexican green, Vermont green*. See *greens*. RS: *pot*. [U.S., JK: 1957, RRL: 1969] 2. ketamine hydrochloride, an anesthetic used as a hallucinogen. See *ketamine*. [U.S., YKB: 1977]

green and blacks *Librium* (TM; *q.v.*) tranquilizer capsules. The 10 mg capsules of Librium are black and green. RS: *tranks*. [Br., BTD: 1968]

green and clears *Dexamyl* (*q.v.*). RT: *set*. [U.S., RG: 1970]

green angelfish *L.S.D.* (*q.v.*) on a bit of blotter stamped with a green angelfish. RT: *L.S.D.* [U.S., ADC: 1981]

green ashes (also **green mud**) usable opium residue left in an opium pipe. *Cf. yen-shee.* [U.S., DWM: 1936, BVB: 1942]

green bud (also **mud-bud**) home-grown marijuana. *Cf. domestic, home-grown.* RS: *pot.* [U.S., ADC: 1981]

green caps one or more green capsules of *L.S.D.* (*q.v.*). RT: *L.S.D.* [U.S., S&R: 1972]

green dot an *L.S.D.* (*q.v.*) tablet. RT: *L.S.D.* [U.S., ADC: 1981]

green double domes (also **green single domes**) L.S.D. *Cf. white domes.* RT: *L.S.D.* [U.S., RG: 1970]

green dragon (also **green dragons**) **1**. an amphetamine tablet. RT: *amps.* [U.S., EEL: 1971, JH: 1979] 2. a barbiturate tablet. RT: *barbs.* [U.S., H&C: 1975, YKB: 1977, NIDA: 1980] 3. a bit of blotter containing *L.S.D.* (*q.v.*) and stamped with a green dragon; L.S.D. combined with some other drug. RT: *L.S.D.* [U.S., ADC: 1981, KBH: 1982]

green goddess marijuana; the effect of marijuana; the personification of the pleasure of marijuana smoking. *Cf. green.* RT: *pot.* [U.S., (RPW: 1938), D&D: 1957]

green griff marijuana. RT: *pot.* [U.S., ELA: 1982]

green hornets *Dexamyl* (TM; *q.v.*) capsules or tablets of dextroamphetamine and amobarbital. RS: *set.* [U.S., (1944): HLM: 1982, H&C: 1975, SNP: 1977]

green hype a newly addicted person. *Cf. hype.* RS: *junky.* [U.S., M&V: 1967, H&C: 1975]

greenies See *greens.*

green meanies amphetamines; *Dexamyl* (TM; *q.v.*) amphetamine and barbiturate capsules or tablets. *Cf. green dragon.* RS: *set.* [U.S., ADC: 1981]

green moroccan a variety of marijuana from Morocco. RT: *pot.* [U.S., ELA: 1982]

green mud usable opium residue found in an opium pipe. *Mud* (*q.v.*) = opium. See *green ashes.* [U.S., DWM: 1936, BVB: 1942]

green pill a poorly prepared opium pellet; a bad dose of opium smoke; the same as *cutered pill* (*q.v.*). *Cf. green ashes, green mud* for similar negative senses of green. [U.S., DWM: 1938, DU]

green rot very low grade opium. RT: *opium.* [U.S., JES: 1959]

greens 1. the greenish residue of smoked opium. The same as *green ashes. Cf. yen-shee.* [U.S., JES: 1959] 2. (also **greenies**) *Dexamyl* (TM; *q.v.*) tablets or capsules of dextroamphetamine and amobarbital. *Cf. green dragon, verdosas.* RS: *set.* [U.S., JBW: 1967, W&F: 1975, YKB: 1977, NIDA: 1980] 3. marijuana. Compare to *green.* RT: *pot.* [U.S., EAF: 1980]

green swirls L.S.D.; L.S.D. combined with some other drug. RS:

L.S.D. [U.S., KBH: 1982]

green tea (also **green snow**) phencyclidine, *P.C.P.* (*q.v.*), an animal tranquilizer. Possibly an attempt to associate the effects of P.C.P. with that of other drugs, i.e., *snow* (*q.v.*) = cocaine; *tea* (*q.v.*) = marijuana. RT: *P.C.P.* [U.S., (1978): DNE: 1980]

green wedge the hallucinogenic drug *L.S.D.* (*q.v.*). *Cf.* *wedges.* RT: *L.S.D.* [U.S., H&C: 1975]

grefa (also **greafa, greapha, greefa, greefo, griefo, grifa, griffa, griffas, griffo, grifo**) marijuana. From Spanish cant (calo). RT: *pot.* [U.S., GM: 1931, DWM: 1936, RPW: 1938, VJM: 1949, GOL: 1950, M&D: 1952, HB: 1955, W&F: 1960, RRL: 1969, JBR: 1973, EEL: 1971, YKB: 1977, NIDA: 1980] See also *moragrifa.*

gret 1. (also **grette, grit**) a tobacco cigarette. A front-clipping of *cigarette.* See *greta.* RT: *nail.* [U.S., DCCU: 1972, ADC: 1981] 2. to provide someone with a cigarette. [U.S., DCCU: 1972]

greta (also **greeta**) a marijuana cigarette; marijuana. Akin to *grefa* (*q.v.*) or *gret* (*q.v.*). Possibly a misprint for *grefa* (*q.v.*). RT: *joint.* [U.S., M&D: 1952, A&T: 1953, RRL: 1969, NIDA: 1980]

grief marijuana. A play on *grefa* (*q.v.*) or one of its variant forms. RT: *pot.* Attested as gay slang. [U.S., BR: 1972]

griefer 1. a marijuana smoker. RT: *toker.* [U.S., A&T: 1953] 2. a down-and-out drug addict. From *grief.* RS: *junky.* [U.S., M&H: 1959] See also *grefa.*

grifado* high on drugs. Spanish. RT: *stoned.* [U.S., D&B: 1970a]

griffas marijuana. See *grefa.*

grilled alcohol intoxicated. RT: *drunk.* [HSD: 1984]

grip of the grape, in the alcohol intoxicated. RT: *drunk.* [Aust., SJB: 1966]

grit See *gret.*

groatable alcohol intoxicated. Groats are cracked grain probably referring to the grains used to make beer or ale. RT: *drunk.* [BF: 1722]

groceries liquor. RT: *booze.* [U.S., BVB: 1942]

grocery a saloon or pub. RS: *bar.* [U.S., (1806): OEDS, (1847): F&H, (1853): DA]

grocery boy an addict who wants food; an addict with the *chuckers* (*q.v.*). From a colloquial term for a man or boy who delivers groceries. [U.S., DWM: 1938, BVB: 1942]

grog 1. rum diluted with water. From (British) Admiral Vernon's nickname "old Grog," referring to his grogram coat. He ordered the ship's rum to be diluted with water allegedly to prevent scurvy. The dilution was actually to prevent intoxication. [since the 1700s, (1770): OED] 2. any strong liquor; any common or available beverage alcohol including beer. *Cf.* *booze.* [since the late 1800s, DSUE, (1938): GAW: 1978, DC: 1972] 3. a drinking party; a drinking bout. *Cf. grog-up.* RT: *spree.* [late 1800s, OED] 4. (also **grog up**) to drink to excess; to booze. RT: *guzzle.* [(1833): OED; listed in BVB: 1942]

grog-bibber a drunkard. RT: *sot.* [Br., (1824): OED]

grog blossom 1. a pimple or a swollen red nose from drinking grog or some other liquor. The same as *rum blossom* (*q.v.*). RT: *gin bud.* [cant, FG: 1796, FG: 1811, B&L: 1890, BWG: 1899, EP: 1948, WG: 1962, RDS: 1982] 2. a drunkard; a drinker with a grog blossom. RT: *sot.* [Br., 1800s, F&H]

grog fight a drinking party; a drinking bout. *Grog* (*q.v.*) = liquor. RT: *spree.* [Br., (1865): OED, JCH: 1887, B&L: 1890]

grogged (also **grogged up**) alcohol intoxicated. RT: *drunk.* [(1770): SBF: 1976, FG: 1796, BVB: 1942, W&F: 1960, SJB: 1966]

groggery a low saloon; a grogshop. *Cf. rummery.* RS: *dive.* [Br. and U.S., (1822): OEDS, B&L: 1890, F&H, BWG: 1899]

groggy (also **groggified**) alcohol intoxicated. GEN: (groggy only) tired, dull witted. RT: *drunk.* Also colloquial for *in a stupor.* [Br. and U.S., FG: 1785, (1818): SBF: 1976, FG: 1823, B&L: 1890, BWG: 1899, BVB: 1942, K&M: 1968]

grog hound a heavy drinker. RT: *sot.* [U.S., W&F: 1960, RDS: 1982]

grog men the drinking sailors aboard ship as opposed to the teetotallers. [Br., WG: 1962]

grog merchant a drug seller; a drug pusher. RT: *dealer.* [U.S., H&C: 1975]

grog mill a tavern or bar. *Cf. gin mill.* RT: *dive.* [U.S., D&D: 1957, W&F: 1960]

grog on 1. to drink and drink some more. *Cf. grog.* RS: *irrigate.* [Aust., (1945): DSUE, (1965): GAW: 1978, SJB: 1966] 2. (spelled **grog-on**) a drinking party; a drinking bout. RT: *spree.* [Aust., 1900s, DSUE]

grog, on the alcohol intoxicated. *Grog* (*q.v.*) = liquor. RT: *drunk.* [Br., FG: 1823; Aust., BH: 1980]

grogshop 1. a place where liquor is sold. RS: *bar.* [since the late 1700s, (1790): OED] 2. a place where drugs are sold. Refers to *dry grog* (*q.v.*) = drugs. *Cf. coke joint, feed store, hash house, powder room, rifle range.* RS: *doperie.* [U.S., JES: 1959, H&C: 1975] 3. the mouth. *Cf. gin lane, gin trap.* [Br., (1843): F&H]

grog-up (also **grog-on**) 1. a drinking party; a drinking bout. RT: *spree.* [Aust., (1976): GAW: 1978] 2. (spelled **grog up**) to drink heavily. See *grog.*

groover a drug user; a teenage drug user. RS: *user.* [U.S., RRL: 1969, EEL: 1971, JH: 1979]

grooving becoming high on a drug; drug intoxicated. RS: *stoned.* Also in general slang for getting to like someone or something.

[U.S., M&V: 1967, RRL: 1969, H&C: 1975]

groovy drug intoxicated; enjoying a high. RS: *stoned*. GEN: anything stylish or captivating, especially music (1937): MW: 1983. [U.S., S&W: 1966, RRL: 1969, EEL: 1971]

ground control (also **controller, ground man**) a person who tends someone who is on an *L.S.D.* (*q.v.*) trip. RT: *sitter*. [U.S., JBW: 1967, RRL: 1969, IGA: 1971, KBH: 1982]

grounder a cigarette butt picked up from the ground for reuse. *Cf. curbstones, stooper*. RT: *brad*. Hobo use. [U.S., JAR: 1930, W&F: 1960]

grower a grower of marijuana. In contrast to a seller. *Cf. farmer*. [U.S., RRL: 1974]

growler 1. (also **growler of suds**) a can for carrying beer home from a saloon. See *rush the growler*. [U.S., JSF: 1889] 2. a can for carrying illicit liquor; a whiskey flask. [U.S., (1893): W&F: 1960, MHW: 1934, GOL: 1950]

G-shot a small injection of a drug to fix up the addict until a larger dose can be injected. *Cf. booster*. RT: *shot*. [U.S., JTD: 1971]

guage an error for *gauge* (*q.v.*). [U.S., M&V: 1967]

guagebutt an error for *gaugebutt* (*q.v.* at *gagebutt*) = a marijuana cigarette. [U.S., RDS: 1982]

guaza marijuana; a form of marijuana. RS: *pot*. [U.S., RPW: 1938, BTD: 1968]

guide an experienced *L.S.D.* (*q.v.*) user who sits with and coaches a person through an L.S.D. trip. See *ground control*. RT: *sitter*. [U.S., (TW: 1968), RRL: 1969, M&V: 1973]

gulf heroin from the Persian Gulf region. RT: *heroin*. [U.S., JWK: 1981]

gullet wash (also **belly wash**) liquor. RT: *booze*. [U.S., BVB: 1942]

gum 1. (also **gum opium**) opium; refined opium. The term has seen use as a generic for opium and for little bits of opium which can be carried around like chewing gum. These bits can be chewed or eaten to stave off withdrawal symptoms. Opium vapors are so powerful that it is not always possible to smoke it without detection. RT: *opium*. [U.S., DWM: 1936, VJM: 1949, D&D: 1957, RRL: 1969] 2. (also **gum hashish**) hashish; good-quality hashish of a chewy consistency. RS: *hash*. [U.S., JWK: 1981] 3. heroin. RT: *heroin*. [U.S., IGA: 1971]

guma opium. See *goma*.

gumdrop a *Seconal* (TM; *q.v.*) capsule; any tablet or capsule. RT: *sec*. [U.S., EAF: 1980]

gumdrop cocktail alcohol recovered from shellac by straining it through cheesecloth. The gummy shellac is then discarded. *Cf.*

buck. U.S. prison use. [U.S., GOL: 1950]

gum hashish good-quality hashish. *Cf. gum*. RT: *hash*. [U.S., M&V: 1973]

gum opium refined opium. *Cf. gum*. RT: *opium*. [U.S., RRL: 1969]

gumps a drug of some type. Probably heroin. [U.S., JES: 1959]

gum tickler a drink of liquor. RT: *nip*. [(1814): DSUE, (1864): F&H]

gun a hypodermic syringe (or a substitute) and needle for injecting drugs. RT: *monkey pump*. [U.S., (1904): OEDS, DWM: 1933, MHW: 1934, DWM: 1936, D&B: 1970c, RRL: 1969, MA: 1973, JWK: 1981]

gunga marijuana. See *ganga*.

Gunga Din gin. Rhyming slang. RT: *gin*. [Aust., early 1900s, DRS]

gungeon 1. a potent marijuana from Africa or Jamaica. *Cf. black gungeon*. RS: *pot*. [U.S., RRL: 1969, CM: 1970, IGA: 1971, SNP: 1977] 2. a marijuana cigarette made from *gungeon* (sense one). RT: *joint*. [U.S., RRL: 1969]

gun, in the alcohol intoxicated. *Cf. cannon*. RT: *drunk*. [cant, BE: 1690, FG: 1785, FG: 1823] See also *gun*.

gunja (also **ganjah**, **gunjah**) marijuana; Jamaican marijuana. See *ganga*. RT: *pot*. [U.S., M&W: 1946, RRL: 1969, EEL: 1971, D&B: 1978]

gunji 1. opium. RT: *opium*. [U.S., EEL: 1971] 2. marijuana. RT: *pot*. [HSD: 1984]

gunk 1. morphine. GEN: any sticky substance. RT: *morphine*. [U.S., M&V: 1954, H&C: 1975; Br. BTD: 1968] 2. glue or other solvents sniffed to get a high. From a colloquial expression for any gooey substance. [U.S., YKB: 1977, RDS: 1982]

gunny a potent marijuana from Jamaica or Africa. Possibly akin to the *gunny* of the hemp *gunny sack*. Probably from *gungeon* or *ganja*. RT: *pot*. Black use. [U.S., D&B: 1970c, EEL: 1971, EAF: 1972]

gunpowder 1. raw opium. RS: *opium*. [U.S., H&C: 1975] 2. gin. *Cf. lightning*. RT: *gin*. [U.S., CM: 1970]

gups an error for *gumps* (*q.v.*). [U.S., H&C: 1975]

gurgle liquor. *Cf. gargle*. RT: *booze*. [U.S., BVB: 1942]

guru an experienced *L.S.D.* (*q.v.*) user who coaches someone through an L.S.D. trip. This guru may also act as a spiritual guide as in the standard sense of the term. RT: *sitter*. [U.S., JBW: 1967, RB: 1967, (TW: 1968), AHC: 1969, RRL: 1969, W&F: 1975, KBH: 1982]

gussey a drunkard. RT: *sot*. [U.S., AH: 1931, BVB: 1942]

gusto 1. beer. RT: *beer*. Black use. [U.S., DC: 1972] 2. to drink beer; to beer. From an advertising slogan. RS: *guzzle*. Black use. [U.S., DC: 1972]

gut bucket a cheap saloon. RT: *dive*. The term is a general slang dysphemism used for a toilet, battleship, or anything else one would call a vessel or a bucket. [U.S., W&F: 1960, DCCU: 1972]

gut rot inferior liquor. The British version of *rotgut* (*q.v.*). [Br., EP: 1948; Aust., SJB: 1943]

guts the potency of the alcohol in liquor; the effect of potent alcohol. [U.S., BVB: 1942]

gutter 1. *porter* (*q.v.*); a dysphemism for *gatter* (*q.v.*) or an error for *gatter* (*q.v.*). RT: *porter*. [listed in GWM: 1859] 2. the vein inside the elbow which is the favorite place for injecting drugs. *Cf. sewer*. Probably older than the attestations indicate. [U.S., RRL: 1969, H&C: 1975] 3. an addict who injects into a main vein. [U.S., (1934): OEDS, DWM: 1936, BVB: 1942] 4. a ruined addict. See *gutter hype*. See also *lapping in the gutter*.

guttered alcohol intoxicated. RT: *drunk*. [PD: 1982]

gutter hype (also **gutter, gutter junky**) a down-and-out addict. One reduced to using inferior drugs or living in the gutter. Probably a play on *guttersnipe* (*q.v.*). RS: *junky*. [U.S., DWM: 1936, VJM: 1949, GOL: 1950]

gutter, in the alcohol intoxicated; decimated by alcohol or alcoholism; hopeless. RS: *drunk*. [U.S., D&D: 1957 W&F: 1960]

gutter junky the same as *gutter hype* (*q.v.*). [U.S., JWK: 1981]

guttersnipe a tramp who collects cigarette butts for reuse. GEN: a child of the slums who inhabits the streets. *Snipe* (*q.v.*) = cigarette butt. [U.S., VJM: 1949]

gut warmer whiskey. RT: *whiskey*. [U.S., (1850-1900): RFA]

guy marijuana. RT: *pot*. [U.S., ADC: 1981] See also *gal*.

guyed out alcohol intoxicated. A guy wire is stretched or guyed out *tight* (*q.v.*). Of nautical origin. RT: *drunk*. [U.S., MHW: 1934, W&F: 1960]

guzzery a bar; a liquor establishment. RS: *bar*. [U.S., D&D: 1957, W&F: 1960] See also *guzzlery*.

guzzle 1. to drink heavily and greedily. [since the 1500s, (1583): OED] (This entry continues after the following list.) See *irrigate* for terms meaning to take a drink. See *mug oneself* for terms meaning to get drunk. These terms mean to drink heavily: *absorb, alki up, barrel, beer, beer up, beezzle, belt the grape, binge, booze, booze the jib, booze up, boozify, bottle, bowze, bub, chase the duck, cheer the belly, chug, chug-a-lug, commune with the spirits, crook one's elbow, deal with Lushington, dehorn, drench the gizzard, drink from the spigot, drink like a fish, drink like a funnel, drink like a lord, drink someone under the table, drown one's sorrows, drown one's troubles, farm a crop, gargle, gas up, go on* *the cousin sis, grog, grog on, grog up, guzzle, hit the bottle, hit the pot, hit the sauce, inhale, jug, jug up, juice, juice back, likker up, liquor, liquor up, lush, lush it, lush it up, mop up, muzz, muzzle, pack, paint the tiger, paint the town red, party, play camels, play the Greek, pot, raise one's elbow, rinse, shicker, siphon, slam some beers, slosh, sluice one's bolt, sluice one's dominoes, sluice one's gob, sluice the worries, soak, soak one's face, souse, sozzle, sponge, spunge, swamp, swamp down, swig, swill, swipe, tank, tank up, toot, tope, whip, whip down, whip off.* 2. liquor; booze. RT: *booze.* [since the 1700s, (1704): OED, BVB: 1942] 3. a drinking bout. RT: *spree.* [(1836): OED; listed in BVB: 1942]

guzzle crib a low drinking establishment. See *booze crib.*

guzzled 1. arrested. RT: *busted.* [U.S., DWM: 1936, W&F: 1960, EEL: 1971] 2. alcohol intoxicated. RT: *drunk.* [U.S., W&F: 1960]

guzzle guts a drunkard; a heavy drinker. RT: *sot.* [Br., FG: 1788, FG: 1811, FG: 1823; listed in BVB: 1942]

guzzler a heavy drinker. RT: *sot.* [(1704): OED, F&H, BWG: 1899, BVB: 1942, ADC: 1975]

guzzlery (also **guzzle factory, guzzle shop, guzzle crib**) a place to purchase liquor. *Cf. guzzery.* RS: *L.I.Q.* [U.S., BVB: 1942, W&F: 1960]

guzzle the grape to drink champagne. Grape = wine, in this case, champagne. RS: *irrigate.* [U.S., early 1900s, DU]

gyve marijuana; a marijuana cigarette. *Cf. jive.* RT: *pot.* [U.S., MB: 1938, A&T: 1953, W&F: 1960]

gyvestick a marijuana cigarette. The same as *jivestick* (*q.v.*).

H

H. heroin. *Cf. big-H., hache.* RT: *heroin.* [U.S., PRB: 1930, DWM: 1933, GOL: 1950, M&D: 1952, W&F: 1960, RRL: 1969, EEL: 1971, DCCU: 1972, ADC: 1975, NIDA: 1980; Br., BTD: 1968, M&J: 1975]

habit the feeling of need or craving for drugs; the "demon" of drug addiction; narcotic addiction; one's own addiction. Now usually refers to heroin addiction. *Cf. monkey, yen.* [U.S., (1887): RML: 1948, VWS: 1929, GI: 1931, HS: 1933, DWM: 1936, M&D: 1952, W&F: 1960, RRL: 1969, EEL: 1971, DCCU: 1972, MA: 1973, ADC: 1975, BW: 1984] Nicknames and slang terms for drug addiction: *army disease, baby, backwards, bee, bee that stings, belly habit, big time, boss habit, bunk habit, bunk yen, burner, Cecil Jones, C-habit, chemical dependence, chicken shit habit, chick shit habit, Chinaman on one's back, Chinaman on one's neck, chippy habit, cotton habit, Doctor White, drugstore johnson, Dr. White, gorilla, habit, H-habit, high hat, hit-and-miss habit, ice cream habit, jag, jones, King Kong, lamp habit, mickey mouse habit, Mighty Joe Young, Miss Emma Jones, monkey, monkey on one's back, monkey wagon, mouth habit, needle, needle habit, nose habit, oil-burner, oil-burning habit, Pepsi-Cola habit, righteous jones, Saturday night habit, scag jones, skag jones, stomach habit, sugar habit, sweet tooth, tang, thang, theng, three-day habit, two-arm habit, weekend habit.*

habit, off the not using drugs; cured of an addiction. RS: *off.* [U.S., W&F: 1960]

habit, on the addicted to narcotics. RT: *hooked.* [U.S., HNR: 1934]

habit smoker an addicted opium smoker as opposed to a *pleasure smoker* (*q.v.*). RS: *campfire boy.* [U.S., GOL: 1950, A&T: 1953]

hache* heroin. The Spanish name for the letter *H.* (*q.v.*). See *hashí*. RT: *heroin.* [U.S., HB: 1955]

hachich* hashish. RT: *hash.* Spanish. [U.S., NIDA: 1980]

had a thump over the head with Samson's jawbone (also **had a kick in the guts**) alcohol intoxicated. Refers to the jawbone of an ass that Samson used against the Philistines. RT: *drunk.* [BF: 1737]

H-addict a heroin addict. *Cf. H.* RT: *junky*. [U.S., D&D: 1957]

had one too many (also had a few, had enough, had one or two, had too much) tipsy; alcohol intoxicated. RT: *drunk*. [late 18-1900s, DSUE, BVB: 1942, AP: 1980]

hag's bush tobacco. RT: *fogus*. Prison camp use. [Aust., SJB: 1966]

Haight-Ashbury See *Hashbury*.

hail fellow all wet a drunkard; a drinker. A play on *hail fellow well met*. *Wet* (*q.v.*) = *drunk*. RT: *sot*. [U.S., BVB: 1942]

hair curler strong liquor. RT: *rotgut*. [M&J: 1975]

hair of the dog (also hair of the dog that bit one) a drink of liquor; a drink of liquor taken to cure a hangover. RS: *nip*. [(1546): F&H, (1842): SBF: 1982, BVB: 1942, W&F: 1960]

hairy heroin. A misunderstanding or a deliberate spelling disguise of *Harry* (*q.v.*). RT: *heroin*. [U.S., M&V: 1954, IGA: 1971]

half one-half of an ounce of a narcotic. A truncation of *half piece* (*q.v.*). RS: *load*. [U.S., M&V: 1954, MA: 1973, H&C: 1975]

half a cup of tea a cup of tea and whiskey mixed. [Br., early 1900s, DSUE]

half and half 1. a mixture of porter and ale. *Cf. arf an arf.* [17-1800s, (1715): OED] 2. alcohol intoxicated; half drunk. RT: *drunk*. [BF: 1737, DSUE, BVB: 1942]

half a tenth 1/20th of a gram of a powdered drug such as cocaine. RT: *load*. [U.S., BW: 1984]

half bag (also half a load) a measurement of drugs. RS: *load*. See *bag*.

half blind alcohol intoxicated; half *blind drunk* (*q.v.*). RT: *drunk*. [U.S., BVB: 1942]

half bulled alcohol intoxicated; half *bulldozed* (*q.v.*). RT: *drunk*. [Aust. military, SJB: 1945]

half can one half of a tobacco can of marijuana. *Cf. can*. RS: *load*. [U.S., EEL: 1971]

half canned alcohol intoxicated; tipsy. *Cf. canned*. RT: *drunk*. [Br., (1925): DSUE]

half cocked tipsy; alcohol intoxicated. *Cf. cocked*. GEN: unprepared. RT: *drunk*. [(1830): OEDS, (1887): F&H, MHW: 1934, SJB: 1943, D&D: 1957, W&F: 1960]

half corned alcohol intoxicated. *Corned* (*q.v.*) = preserved, as in corned beef, thus, drunk. RT: *drunk*. [U.S., W&F: 1960, RDS: 1982]

half-crocked alcohol intoxicated. Paul Dickson lists a number of similar half-drunk terms: half-doped, half-high, half in the boot, half in the tank, half-looped, half-out, half-pickled, half-slammed, half-slopped, half-sober, half-soused, half-stiff, half-stoused, half-tanked, half the bay over, halfway over. RT: *drunk*. [PD: 1982]

half cut alcohol intoxicated; tipsy. *Cf. cut*. RT: *drunk*. [(1860): DSUE, F&H, BVB: 1942, SJB: 1943]

half gone alcohol intoxicated; tipsy. *Cf. about gone*. RT: *drunk*. [18–1900s, F&G: 1925, DSUE]

half hot alcohol intoxicated; almost drunk. *Cf. hot*. RT: *drunk*. [Bahamas, JAH: 1982]

half in the bag alcohol intoxicated; tipsy. *Cf. in the bag*. RT: *drunk*. [U.S., D&B: 1970c]

half lit alcohol intoxicated; tipsy. *Cf. lit*. RT: *drunk*. [U.S., BVB: 1942]

half load in the drug trade, fifteen $3.00 bags of heroin handled by a street dealer. This price is no doubt out of date. RS: *load*. [U.S., P&C: 1969, MA: 1973]

half moons 1. hashish molded in the shape of a half moon. *Cf. full moons*. RT: *hash*. [U.S., H&C: 1975, SNP: 1977] 2. peyote; a piece of peyote cactus. RS: *peyote*. [U.S., RG: 1970, IGA: 1971, SNP: 1977]

half nelson alcohol intoxicated; tipsy. May allude to the body of Admiral Lord Nelson which was said to have been preserved in rum or brandy for passage back to England from Trafalgar. To *tap the admiral* (*q.v.*) was to drink from the cask. See also *Nelson's blood*. The term may also be a pun on the name of a wrestling hold. RT: *drunk*. [Br., JM: 1923, DSUE]

half on alcohol intoxicated; tipsy. *Cf. on*. RT: *drunk*. [U.S., BVB: 1942]

half piece (also **half bag**) one-half ounce of a powdered drug, usually heroin. RS: *load*. [U.S., DWM: 1938, EEL: 1971]

half pissed alcohol intoxicated; almost *pissed* (*q.v.*). RT: *drunk*. [Br., 1900s, DSUE, PW: 1974] See also *Scotch mist*.

half rats alcohol intoxicated; tipsy. RT: *drunk*. [JRW: 1909]

half rinsed alcohol intoxicated; tipsy. *Rinsed* is a modern synonym of *soused* (*q.v.*). RT: *drunk*. [New Zealand, (1912): DSUE; Aust., SJB: 1943, DSUE]

half screwed alcohol intoxicated; tipsy. *Cf. screwed*. RT: *drunk*. [(1835): DSUE, (1839): F&H, MHW: 1934, W&F: 1960, DCCU: 1972]

half seas over (also **half seas under, half the bay over**) alcohol intoxicated; tipsy. *Cf. overseas, over the bay*. Alludes to a ship which is halfway to its destination. From an old (1500s) term of nautical origin referring to the half-way point of anything. Also attested (Br., PW: 1974) as **half seas under**. [BE: 1690, BF: 1737, FG: 1785, FG: 1811, FG: 1823, JCH: 1887, B&L: 1890, MP: 1928, AH: 1931, W&F: 1960, WG: 1962, SSD]

half shaved alcohol intoxicated; tipsy. *Cf. shaved*. RT: *drunk*.

[(1818): OEDS, (F&H), W&F: 1960]

half shot alcohol intoxicated; almost *shot* (*q.v.*). RT: *drunk*. An old expression revived during WWI. [(1838): OEDS, DSUE, MHW: 1934, W&F: 1960, WG: 1962]

half slewed alcohol intoxicated; almost *slewed* (*q.v.*). RT: *drunk*. [(1860): W&F: 1960, F&H]

half snapped alcohol intoxicated; almost *snapped* (*q.v.*). RT: *drunk*. [U.S., (1850): W&F: 1960]

half spoon one half gram of cocaine. *Cf. spoon*. RS: *load*. [U.S., H&C: 1975]

half sprung tipsy; alcohol intoxicated; almost *sprung* (*q.v.*). RT: *drunk*. [U.S., mid 1800s, W&F: 1960]

half stewed tipsy; alcohol intoxicated; almost *stewed* (*q.v.*). RT: *drunk*. [U.S., W&F: 1960, DCCU: 1972]

half there alcohol intoxicated; tipsy. Almost *there* (*q.v.*). *Cf. half seas over*. RT: *drunk*. [U.S., BVB: 1942]

half under alcohol intoxicated; tipsy. *Cf. under*. RT: *drunk*. [U.S., W&F: 1960, RDS: 1982]

half up the pole alcohol intoxicated; tipsy. *Cf. up the pole*. RT: *drunk*. [JRW: 1909]

halfway house 1. a place where illicit liquor is sold. RS: *bar*. From the prohibition era. [U.S., AH: 1931, MHW: 1934] 2. a residential center for persons undergoing drug or alcohol addiction treatment. Such a center provides controlled re-entry to society. [U.S., RAS: 1975]

halfway to Concord alcohol intoxicated; tipsy. May refer to Concord grapes. RT: *drunk*. [BF: 1737]

hall alcohol, *booze* (*q.v.*). *Cf. Al K. Hall*. From the prohibition era. [U.S., BVB: 1942, W&F: 1960]

hallucination a false perception with a sense of absolute reality. Experienced with certain types of drugs. Recently the term has been used casually for any type of strong auditory, visual, etc. response to a drug. *Cf. head drug*. Standard English. [since the 1600s, (1646): OED] Nicknames and slang terms for hallucination: *bean trip, cartoon, echoes, eyelid movies, flash, flashback, hallucination, pattern, stevie, trail, trip*.

hallucinogen a drug or other chemical substance which causes hallucinations. Hallucinogens are not considered to be physically addictive. Marijuana and L.S.D. are hallucinogens. *Cf. head drug*. [(1954): OEDS, JF: 1972]

halvah narcotics; drugs. From the Turkish word for a kind of sweet. In English via Yiddish. RS: *dope*. [U.S., JES: 1959, H&C: 1975]

halvahed drug intoxicated. *Cf. halvah*. RT: *stoned*. [U.S., JES: 1959, H&C: 1975]

halves one-half ounce of heroin. *Cf. half bag, half piece.* RS: *load.* [U.S., H&C: 1975]

hammered alcohol intoxicated. RT: *drunk.* [U.S., W&F: 1960, N&S: 1983, ADC: 1984]

hammerhead a drunkard or a drug user. *Cf. hammered.* RT: *sot, user.* [U.S., ADC: 1984]

hammerish alcohol intoxicated. RT: *drunk.* [BF: 1737]

hanced alcohol intoxicated. See *enhanced.* RT: *drunk.* [(1630): OED, F&H]

H. and C. (also C. and H., cold and hot, hot and cold) a mixture of heroin and cocaine. RS: *set.* [U.S., EEL: 1971, W&F: 1975]

H. and R. "hit and run," making a purchase of narcotics and leaving the area immediately. RS: *score.* [U.S., M&V: 1973]

hand-to-hand having to do with a drug sale where the merchandise is delivered by hand to the customer. [U.S., HB: 1955, RRL: 1969, RG: 1970]

hang a few on (also hang on a few) to take a few drinks or have a few beers. RT: *irrigate.* [U.S., W&F: 1960, AP: 1980] See also *tie one on.*

hang bluff (also Harry Bluff) snuff. Rhyming slang. RT: *snoose.* [DA: 1857, GWM: 1859, JCH: 1859, DRS]

hanger (also hangar) a nonaddict follower of street addicts, a *hanger-on.* [U.S., JWK: 1981]

hang it up break the habit. RT: *kick.* [U.S., M&V: 1967, H&C: 1975]

hang one on to drink heavily; to make oneself drunk. *Cf. tie one on.* RT: *mug oneself.* The DSUE attestation is for Canadian (from the U.S.) use. [(1935): DSUE, DCCU: 1972, RDS: 1982]

hangover the effects of heavy drinking. From a term meaning residue. [(1904): OEDS, (1912): DA] Nicknames and slang terms for a hangover: *a head, a mouth, barrel fever, beezy-weezies, bighead, Bob, Harry, and Dick, body hangover, booze blues, Bordeaux hammer, bottleache, bottle fatigue, crown fire, gallon distemper, hooch-humps, horries, hot coppers, jim-jams, katzenjammer, long stale drunk, Monday blues, morning after, shakes, snozzle-wobbles, sore head, the moaning after, the morning after the night before, the shakes, the zings, touch of the brewer, whoofits, wineache, woefits, woofits.*

happy 1. alcohol intoxicated; tipsy and light-hearted. *Cf. glad, jocular, merry.* RT: *drunk.* Probably recurrent nonce. [(1770): OED, F&H, MHW: 1934, BVB: 1942] 2. drug intoxicated. RT: *stoned.* [U.S., early 1900s, DU]

happy cigarette (also funny cigarette, happy gas) a marijuana cigarette. RT: *joint.* [U.S., ELA: 1982]

happy dust (also happy flakes, happy powder, happy stuff) **1.**

cocaine; any powdered drug. RT: *powder*. [U.S., (1922): OEDS, EK: 1927, VWS: 1929, GI: 1931, DWM: 1933, VJM: 1949, GOL: 1950, M&D: 1952, W&F: 1960, EEL: 1971, YKB: 1977] 2. chloral hydrate. *Cf. chlorals*. [U.S., BVB: 1942]

happy duster a user of powdered cocaine; a cocaine sniffer. RS: *kokomo*. [U.S., DU, A&T: 1953]

happy grass (also **happy gas**) marijuana. *Cf. grass*. RT: *pot*. Black use. [U.S., EAF: 1980]

happy hour cocktail time; a special drinking time at a bar or cocktail lounge. [U.S., (1971): DNE: 1980, DCCU: 1972, MW: 1976]

happy juice liquor. RT: *booze*. [U.S., W&F: 1960]

happy medicine morphine. *Cf. medicine*. RT: *morphine*. [U.S., JES: 1959, H&C: 1975]

happy pills tranquilizers. RT: *tranks*. [(1956): OEDS]

happy powder powdered drugs, such as cocaine, heroin, or morphine. RT: *powder*. [U.S., BVB: 1942, VJM: 1949, A&T: 1953]

happy sale strong ale. Rhyming slang. Not listed in DRS. RS: *ale*. [Br., early 1900s, DU]

happy shop a liquor store. RT: *L.I.Q*. [U.S., HER: 1971, DCCU: 1972]

happy sticks marijuana cigarettes dusted with *P.C.P.* (*q.v.*). RS: *set*. [U.S., RAS: 1984]

happy-time weed marijuana. RT: *pot*. [U.S., (1971): R&P: 1982]

hard 1. having to do with ale or cider which is fermented or souring. [since the 1700s, FG: 1785, FG: 1823] 2. having to do with potent or intoxicating beverages. [BE: 1690, FG: 1785, (1890): SBF: 1982, SSD] 3. having to do with addictive drugs. [U.S., AHC: 1969, (EEL: 1971)]

hard candy heroin. *Cf. hard drugs*. Named for a hard sugar candy. RT: *heroin*. [U.S., RG: 1970]. See also *nose candy, needle candy*.

hard case a case of liquor. *Cf. hard*. [U.S., BVB: 1942]

hard cider cider (apple juice) which has fermented, sometimes producing a drink with moderately high alcohol content. [U.S., (1789): MW: 1983]

hard-cutting mezz the highest quality marijuana. *Cf. mezz*. RT: *pot*. [U.S., M&W: 1946]

hard drugs (also **hard narcotics**) addictive drugs: heroin, morphine, cocaine, opium. *Cf. hard*. Compare to *soft drugs*. RS: *dope*. [U.S., RB: 1967, RRL: 1969, DCCU: 1972, DNE: 1973, W&F: 1975]

hard-liner a person addicted to hard drugs. RS: *junky*. [HSD: 1984]

hard liquor corn liquor; potent liquor such as whiskey, gin, rum etc. *Cf. hard.* RT: *booze.* [U.S., (1890): SBF: 1982, W&F: 1960, RDS: 1982]

hard nail a hypodermic needle. RT: *needle.* [U.S., HB: 1955, H&C: 1975]

hardroll a factory made cigarette. RS: *nail.* [U.S., military, early 1900s, DST: 1984]

hard stuff 1. (also **hard liquor**) potent liquor, especially as compared to beer and wine. *Cf. hard.* RS: *booze.* [(1879): DSUE, B&L: 1890, BVB: 1942, W&F: 1960] 2. (also **hard dope, hard drugs**) addictive drugs such as morphine, heroin, and opium. [U.S., HB: 1955, S&W: 1966, RRL: 1969, DCCU: 1972, DNE: 1973, GU: 1975, YKB: 1977]

hardstuff party a gathering where hard drugs are used. Compared to a party where only soft drugs are used. [U.S., (1968): DNE: 1973]

hard up 1. alcohol intoxicated. RT: *drunk.* [Br., 1800s, F&H; listed in BVB: 1942] 2. in need of drugs or alcohol. Usually said of someone addicted to either or both. [U.S., 1900s, RAS: 1978]

hardware 1. whiskey; potent liquor. An elaboration or disguise of *hard stuff* (*q.v.*). RT: *whiskey.* From the prohibition era. [(1830): OEDS, (1850): W&F: 1960, HNR: 1934, GOL: 1950, D&D: 1957] 2. (usually **Hardware**) a "brand name" for *amyl nitrite* (*q.v.*). *Hard* refers to penile erections. See also *Heart On.* See *amyl nitrite* for an explanation of the sexual aspects of this chemical. RS: *snapper.* [U.S., ELA: 1984]

hard water potent liquor; hard liquor. *Cf. hard.* RS: *booze.* [U.S., BVB: 1942, W&F: 1960]

hardy alcohol intoxicated. RT: *drunk.* [BF: 1737]

harness bulls (also **harness boys, harness rollers**) police officers in uniform. RT: *fuzz.* [U.S., TRG: 1968, RG: 1970, EEL: 1971, JWK: 1981]

harpoon a hypodermic syringe and needle. RS: *monkey pump.* [U.S., DWM: 1938, VJM: 1949, IGA: 1971]

Harry heroin. A reinterpretation of *H.* (*q.v.*). *Cf. big Harry.* RT: *heroin.* [U.S., M&V: 1954, RRL: 1969, DCCU: 1972, NIDA: 1980]

Harry Bluff snuff. See *hang bluff.*

Harry Champers champagne. *Cf. champers.* RT: *cham.* [Br., mid 1900s, DSUE]

Harry Flakers (also **flakers**) alcohol intoxicated. *Cf. flakers.* RT: *drunk.* [Aust., (1945): DSUE]

Harry Freemans (also **Freemans, freemans**) free cigarettes. Possibly cigarette butts. [Br., 1900s, SSD]

Harry Honkers alcohol intoxicated. An elaboration of *honkers* (*q.v.* at *honked*). RT: *drunk.* [HSD: 1984]

Harry Screechers alcohol intoxicated; screeching drunk; screaming drunk. *Cf. screechers.* RT: *drunk.* Not common (DSUE). [Br., (1950s): DSUE]

Harry Wragg a cigarette. Rhyming slang for *fag* (*q.v.*). Named for a famous (horse) jockey. RT: *nail.* [Br., early 1900s, SSD, DRS]

harsh toke a bad or burning puff of a marijuana cigarette. Now GEN: anything unpleasant. [U.S., ADC: 1984]

harty alcohol intoxicated. See *hearty.*

has marijuana. From *hashish.* RT: *pot.* [U.S., IGA: 1971, YKB: 1977]

has been in the bibbing plot alcohol intoxicated; tipsy. RT: *drunk.* [BF: 1737]

has boozed the gage (also **boozed as the gage**) alcohol intoxicated. (BF: 1737: [He's] Booz'd the Gage.) *Cf. gage.* RT: *drunk.* [BF: 1737]

haschí* (also **hashí***, **hashís***) hashish. Spanish. RT: *hash.* [U.S., NIDA: 1980]

has dipped his bill alcohol intoxicated. (BF: 1737: [He] Has Dipp'd his Bill.) *Cf. dipped too deep.* RT: *drunk.* [BF: 1737]

has drunk more than he has bled alcohol intoxicated. (BF: 1737: [He] Has drank more...) *Bled* is probably a replacement for *pissed.* RT: *drunk.* [BF: 1737]

hash 1. (also **hatch**) hashish. [U.S., BVB: 1942, D&D: 1957, W&F: 1967, D&B: 1970c, DSUE, RRL: 1969, CM: 1970, EEL: 1971, DNE: 1973, MW: 1976, NIDA: 1980, ADC: 1981, JWK: 1981, ADC: 1984] (This entry continues after the following list.) Nicknames and slang terms for hashish: *African bush, black, black hash, black Russian, block, blond, blond hash, blond hashish, blond Lebanese, blue cheese, blue sage, bo-bo, bo-bo bush, brick, brown, candy, candy bar, canned sativa, carob chips, chara, charas, chocolate, chunkies, chunks, citroli, clay, cube, dew, donjem, finger, fir, full moons, golden grain, goma de moto, gram, gum, gum hashish, hachich, half moons, haschí, hasheesh, hashí, hatch, heavy hash, heesh, hunk, Indian rope, keef, kef, keff, keif, khif, kief, kif, Lebanese, Lebanese hash, leb hash, lightning hashish, love wood, lubange, moon, mud, Nepalese hash, opium of the poor, Pakistani hash, potted bush, quarter moon, red gunyon, red leb, red Lebanese, sawi, sealing wax, shesha, shishi, shit, soles, supremo, wangula, yellow, zamal.* 2. *cannabis* (*q.v.*) in general. RT: *pot.* [U.S., D&B: 1970c, DCCU: 1972, DNE: 1973, M&J: 1975] 3. any drug. RS: *dope.* [U.S., D&B: 1970c]

hashaholic a heavy hashish user. Patterned on *alcoholic.* RS: *user.* *Cf. mariholic.* Not underworld argot. [U.S., (1972): DNE: 1980]

hash brownies brownies with marijuana (or hashish) baked inside. See *Alice B. Toklas.* [U.S., ADC: 1975]

Hashbury (also **the Haight**, **the Hashbury**) the Haight-Ashbury district in San Francisco. A center for flower children and drug use in the 1960s. The term is a play on *hash* (*q.v.*). [U.S., RB: 1967, (1967): R&P: 1982, RRL: 1969, EEL: 1971, W&F: 1975]

hash cannon a device used in the smoking of cannabis. Like the *shotgun* (*q.v.*), it is used to force the smoke deep into the lungs. RS: *bong*. [U.S., (1970): ELA: 1982]

has heat his copper (also has het his kettle, has scalt his head pan) alcohol intoxicated. RT: *drunk*. [BF: 1737]

hasheesh See *hashish*.

hashhead a smoker of hashish or marijuana. See list at *head*. RS: *toker*. [U.S., (1969): DNE: 1973, W&F: 1975]

hash house a place where hashish is sold or used. See *hashish house*.

hashí* hashish. See *haschí*.

hashish (also hasheesh) gum hashish, the resin of the female marijuana plant; marijuana with a very high resin content. The Arabic word for dried herb. Sometimes used to mean any marijuana. RT: *hash*. [since the late 1500s, (1598): OED]

hashish house (also hash house, hashish bar) a bar which sells hashish as well as liquor; a place where hashish is sold and used. *Cf. marijuana bar*. RS: *pad*. Probably earlier than the attestations indicate. [U.S., YKB: 1977, RDS: 1982]

hash oil (also hashish oil) an extract of *Cannabis sativa*, rich in *T.H.C.* (*q.v.*). RPW: 1938 mentions hashish oil in passing. RT: *oil*. [U.S., RPW: 1938, (1972): DNE: 1980, ADC: 1975, D&B: 1978, ADC: 1981]

hash pipe a small pipe for smoking hashish. RS: *bong*. [U.S., (1970): R&P: 1982, E&R: 1971, ADC: 1981]

has stolen a manchet out of the brewer's basket alcohol intoxicated. (BF: 1737: [He] Has stole...) A *manchet* (= loaf) is associated with bakers. Figuratively: *has stolen a portion of the brewer's product*. RT: *drunk*. [BF: 1737]

has taken Hippocrates' grand elixir alcohol intoxicated. *Grand elixir* = liquor. RT: *drunk*. [BF: 1737]

has wet both eyes alcohol intoxicated. A reference to the height of the fluid level in a drunkard. *Cf. up to the ears, up to the gills*. RT: *drunk*. [BF: 1737]

hatch hashish. See *hash*.

haunted with evil spirits alcohol intoxicated. A play on *spirits of alcohol*. RT: *drunk*. [BF: 1737]

have a brick in one's hat to be alcohol intoxicated. RS: *drunk*. [U.S., JSF: 1889, MGH: 1915, BVB: 1942]

have a bun on (also got a bun on) to be alcohol intoxicated. RWB: 1912 states that *bun* is short for *bundle*. RS: *drunk*. [U.S., early 1900s, (c. 1900): SBF: 1976, MHW: 1934, VJM: 1949, W&F:

1960]

have a cab to be alcohol intoxicated. Origin unknown. RS: ***drunk***. [JRW: 1909]

have a Chinaman on one's back for an addict's habit to demand drugs; to experience withdrawal symptoms. May have referred originally to opium. *Cf. **have a monkey on one's back***. RS: ***hooked***. [U.S., DWM: 1938, BVB: 1942]

have a crooked elbow to be a tippler or a sot. *Cf. **bending an elbow, elbow-crooker***. [M&J: 1975]

have a cup too much to be alcohol intoxicated. RS: ***drunk***. [(1678): DSUE, F&H]

have a cut leg (also **have cut one's leg**) to be alcohol intoxicated. *Cf. **legless***. RS: ***drunk***. [listed in F&H (at *screwed*)]

have a full cargo aboard (also **have a keg aboard, have grog on board**) to be alcohol intoxicated. Refers to a heavily loaded ship. See ***loaded to the Plimsoll mark*** and similar nautical expressions at ***loaded to the gills***. RS: ***drunk***. [Br., 1800s, F&H; listed in BVB: 1942]

have a glow on (also **have a rosy glow on**) to be alcohol intoxicated. *Cf. **glow***. RS: ***drunk***. [U.S., JAS: 1932, D&D: 1957]

have a guest in the attic to be alcohol intoxicated. *Attic* = head, brain. The *guest* is liquor. RS: ***drunk***. [Br., 1800s, F&H; listed in BVB: 1942]

have a habit to be addicted to drugs. *Cf. **habit***. RS: ***hooked***. [U.S., DWM: 1938, JES: 1959]

have a hanger to get or smoke a tobacco cigarette. Refers to a cigarette which hangs from the mouth. [U.S., D&B: 1970c]

have a hollow leg to have a great capacity for liquor. Also used for a large appetite of any kind. [K&M: 1968]

have a jag on to be alcohol intoxicated. *Jag* = load. *Cf. **have a load on***. [Br., 1800s, F&H; listed in BVB: 1942, D&D: 1957]

have a jug fuck to get drunk. *Cf. **fuck the hop***. RT: ***mug oneself***. [U.S., DST: 1984]

have a load on to be alcohol intoxicated. RS: ***drunk***. [B&L: 1890, BVB: 1942, GOL: 1950]

have a monkey on one's back to be addicted to drugs; to suffer from drug withdrawal. *Cf. **have a Chinaman on one's back***. *Monkey* is an old term for a cask of liquor. JCH: 1887 records the phrase (which he labels as old) as meaning to be out of temper. JRW: 1909 records *have a monkey on the house*, meaning to have a mortgage. RS: ***hooked***. [U.S., DWM: 1938, D&D: 1957, W&F: 1960, DCCU: 1972] See also ***have an orangutan on one's back***.

have an edge on (also **edged**) to be intoxicated by alcohol or drugs. *Cf. **edge***. [U.S., early 1900s, DU, W&F: 1960]

have an orangutan on one's back (also **have a tang on one's back**) to be addicted to a drug; to experience drug withdrawal symptoms. *Cf. King Kong, Mighty Joe Young, tang* which are all large apes. RS: *hooked*. [U.S., JWK: 1981]

have a package on to be alcohol intoxicated. RS: *drunk*. [U.S., (RWB: 1912), W&F: 1960]

have a pot in the pate to be alcohol intoxicated. RS: *drunk*. [K&M: 1968]

have a run to go on a drinking bout. *Cf. irrigate, mug oneself*. [Aust., WWII, DSUE]

have a skate on to be alcohol intoxicated. Refers to unstable walking. RS: *drunk*. [U.S., AH: 1931, MHW: 1934]

have a skinful (also **have got a skinful**) to be alcohol intoxicated. RS: *drunk*. [since the 1600s, F&H, (1922): W&F: 1960, M&J: 1975]

have a slant on to be alcohol intoxicated. Refers to an inability to stand up. *Cf. leanaway*. RS: *drunk*. [U.S., M&C: 1905, MHW: 1934]

have as much as one can carry to be alcohol intoxicated. RS: *drunk*. [M&J: 1975]

have a snake in one's boots (also **have snakes in one's boots**) to have the delirium tremens. *Cf. D.T.s*. [U.S., MHW: 1934]

have a snootfull to be alcohol intoxicated. RS: *drunk*. [U.S., (1918): SBF: 1976, BVB: 1942, AP: 1980; Canadian, early 1900s, DSUE]

have a sparkin' in the throat (also **have a spark in the throat**) to be thirsty for a drink of liquor. The sparks are from dryness. [U.S., MHW: 1934, BVB: 1942]

have a swollen head (also **have a thick head, have the bighead**) to be alcohol intoxicated; in an alcoholic stupor; hungover. *Bighead* (*q.v.*) = hangover. [late 18-1900s, DSUE, BVB: 1942]

have a talking load to be alcohol intoxicated and talkative. *Cf. load*. RS: *drunk*. [U.S., MHW: 1934]

have a toot to have a drink of liquor. *Toot* = a drink. RT: *irrigate*. [Br., (1930): DSUE]

have a touch of boskiness to be alcohol intoxicated. *Cf. bosky*. RS: *drunk*. [Br., 1800s, F&H]

have a turkey on one's back to be alcohol intoxicated. RS: *drunk*. Early college slang. [U.S., BHH: 1856, JRB: 1859] See also *turkey*.

have a yen on (also **have a yen**) to crave a dose of drugs. *Cf. yen*. [U.S., PRB: 1930, MHW: 1934, DWM: 1938]

have barrel fever to be or go drinking or spreeing. *Cf. barrel fever* for an entirely different sense. [U.S., AH: 1931]

have been dipping rather deep to be alcohol intoxicated. *Cf. has* *dipped his bill.* RS: *drunk.* [Br., 1800s, F&H]

have been paid to be alcohol intoxicated. *Paid* (*q.v.*) = made drunk; drunk. Perhaps in the sense of one's being paid for one's sins. RS: *drunk.* [Br., 1800s, F&H]

have burnt one's shoulder to be alcohol intoxicated. (BF: 1737: He's burnt his Shoulder.) A play on *been in the sun* (*q.v.*). RS: *drunk.* [BF: 1737]

have cut one's leg alcohol intoxicated. See *cut one's leg.*

have eaten some Hull cheese to be alcohol intoxicated. RS: *drunk.* Yorkshire dialect. [Br., FG: 1811]

have got a dish to be alcohol intoxicated. (BF: 1737: [He's] got a Dish.) RS: *drunk.* [BF: 1737, DSUE]

have had one over the eight (also have one over the eight) alcohol intoxicated. *Cf. over the eight.* RS: *drunk.* [M&J: 1975]

have knocked one's link out to be alcohol intoxicated. RS: *drunk.* [early 1700s, DSUE]

have one for the worms to take an early morning drink. This could be a drink to the worms that early birds will get, or a strong drink to rid oneself of worms. RS: *irrigate.* [Br., (1880): DSUE]

have one's back teeth afloat (also got the back teeth well afloat, have one's back teeth well afloat, have one's back teeth well awash) to be alcohol intoxicated. *Cf. teeth under.* RS: *drunk.* [BE: 1690, JSF: 1889, WG: 1962]

have one's flag out to be alcohol intoxicated. (BF: 1737: His Flag is out.) *Cf. flying the ensign.* RS: *drunk.* [BF: 1737]

have one's nose wide open to be high on cocaine. Refers to sniffing cocaine into the nose. RS: *stoned.* [U.S., EAF: 1972]

have one's nuff to be alcohol intoxicated; to have had enough. RS: *drunk.* [Br., 1800s, F&H]

have one's pots on to be alcohol intoxicated. RS: *drunk.* [U.S., early 1900s, (Runyon), W&F: 1960]

have punch aboard to be alcohol intoxicated. *Cf. have a full cargo aboard.* RS: *drunk.* [U.S., (1887): RML: 1950]

have raised one's monuments to be alcohol intoxicated. (BF: 1737: [He's] Rais'd his Monuments.) RS: *drunk.* [BF: 1737]

have sold one's senses to be alcohol intoxicated. (BF: 1737: [He] Has Sold his Senses.) RS: *drunk.* [BF: 1737]

have swallowed a hare (also have swallowed a hair) to be alcohol intoxicated. RS: *drunk.* [Br., FG: 1823]

have the bighead See *have a swollen head.*

have the head full of bees to be alcohol intoxicated. (BF: 1737: His Head is full of Bees.) RS: *drunk.* [BF: 1737]

have the sun in one's eyes to be alcohol intoxicated. RS: *drunk.*

[Br., 1800s, F&H]

have yellow fever to be alcohol intoxicated. From the practice (at Greenwich Hospital) of making sailors wear (partly) yellow coats as punishment for drunkenness. RS: *drunk*. [Br., (1867): OED, (F&H)]

Have you got a thing? (also **Have you got anything?**) "Do you have any drugs to sell?" RT: *How are you going to act?* [U.S., M&D: 1952]

Hawaiian (also **Hawaiian sunshine**) marijuana, presumably grown in Hawaii. *Cf. Kaui, Maui*. RT: *pot*. [U.S., SNP: 1977, YKB: 1977, DEM: 1981]

Hawaiian pipe a small pipe for smoking potent Hawaiian marijuana. RS: *bong*. [U.S., ADC: 1981]

Hawaiian pods a hallucinogen allegedly stronger than L.S.D. This probably refers to potent Hawaiian marijuana. [U.S., EEL: 1971]

Hawaiian sunshine 1. marijuana. See *Hawaiian*. [U.S., SNP: 1977] 2. the hallucinogenic drug L.S.D; L.S.D. combined with some other drug. RT: *L.S.D*. [U.S., KBH: 1982, RDS: 1982]

hawk 1. (also **hawk-25, the hawk**) the hallucinogenic drug L.S.D. RT: *L.S.D*. [U.S., JBW: 1967, RRL: 1969, IGA: 1971, ADC: 1975, NIDA: 1980, KBH: 1982] 2. an L.S.D. user. RS: *user*. [U.S., EEL: 1971] 3. an L.S.D. seller. RS: *dealer*. [U.S., EEL: 1971]

hay marijuana; low-grade marijuana. *Cf. bale, straw*. RT: *pot*. [U.S., (1920): DU, M&W: 1946, VJM: 1949, M&D: 1952, W&F: 1960, TRG: 1968, RRL: 1969, D&B: 1978]

hay-burner a marijuana smoker. *Cf. hay*. A reinterpretation of a slang term for a useless horse. RT: *toker*. [U.S., BVB: 1942, VJM: 1949]

hay butt a marijuana cigarette. *Cf. hay*. RT: *joint*. [U.S., BVB: 1942, VJM: 1949]

hayhead a marijuana smoker. *Cf. hay*. See the list at *head*. RT: *toker*. [U.S., BVB: 1942, HB: 1955, TRG: 1968, EEL: 1971]

hay puffer a marijuana smoker. *Cf. hay*. RT: *toker*. [U.S., early 1900s, DU]

haywire disoriented from drugs. Can refer to marijuana or other drugs. GEN: out of order. *Hay* (*q.v.*) = marijuana. *Cf. wired*. Probably nonce. [U.S., RAS: 1982] See also *on the fritz*.

haze the hallucinogenic drug *L.S.D.* (*q.v.*). From *purple haze* (*q.v.*). RT: *L.S.D*. [U.S., YKB: 1977]

Hazel heroin. From *witch hazel* (*q.v.*). An elaboration of *H.* (*q.v.*). RT: *heroin*. [U.S., VJM: 1949, A&T: 1953, SNP: 1977]

hazy alcohol intoxicated. GEN: confused, uncertain. RT: *drunk*. [(1824): DSUE, JCH: 1887, F&H, MGH: 1915]

H-caps powdered heroin packed into gelatin capsules; gelatin capsules for heroin. *Cf. cap*. [U.S., RRL: 1969, SNP: 1977]

head 1. a drug user with a special fondness or compulsion for a particular drug. Often appears in compounds. See narcotics heads at: *A-head, acidhead, beanhead, candyhead, cokehead, cottonhead, cubehead, dopehead, drughead, dusthead, garbagehead, geehead, gowhead, grasshead, hashhead, hayhead, hophead, methhead, mugglehead, P-head, pillhead, pinhead, poppyhead, pothead, shithead, smackhead, speedhead, syrup head, teahead, terphead, weedhead.* See alcohol heads at: *bubblehead, budhead, busthead, farahead, ginhead, jickhead, juicehead, largehead, liquorhead, lush head, oilhead, pisshead, pothead, rumhead, swellhead.* [in various forms since early 1900s] 2. a drug addict or drug user. RT: *user.* [U.S., (1937): ELA: 1982, A&T: 1953, W&F: 1967, (TW: 1968), RRL: 1969, CM: 1970, EEL: 1971, DCCU: 1972, DNE: 1973, ADC: 1975, JWK: 1981] 3. a member of the drug culture; a hippie or a person who drops out of mainstream society due to drug use. In the 1960s head was sometimes assumed to refer to long unkempt hair or to Afro-style hairdos. Currently the term has some slang use for a fan or devotee of something. [U.S., JBW: 1967, (TW: 1968), JWK: 1981]

head, a a hangover. See *have the bighead* at *have a swollen head.* [(1869): OEDS, AP: 1980]

headache liquor. Named for the hangover it produces. GEN: any annoyance. RT: *booze.* [U.S., BVB: 1942]

headache department (also **headache house**) a liquor store or counter. A specialized use of a general colloquial expression for any chronic source of problems. This refers specifically to a hangover headache. RT: *L.I.Q.* [U.S., RDS: 1982]

headache man a (male) federal narcotics agent. RS: *fuzz.* [U.S., DU, A&T: 1953]

head and body trip a drug experience which affects both the mind and the body. *Cf. body drug, head drug.* [U.S., M&V: 1973]

head drug a drug which affects the brain creating hallucinations but not causing physical addiction, for example, L.S.D. [U.S., RB: 1967, RRL: 1969, EEL: 1971] See also *body drug.*

headfucker a potent head drug. Used often for *L.S.D.* (*q.v.*). [U.S., ADC: 1975]

head is full of bees alcohol intoxicated. RT: *drunk.* [BF: 1737]

head kit (also **head gear**) equipment for smoking or injecting drugs. *Cf. head.* RT: *outfit.* [U.S., W&F: 1975, RDS: 1982]

head, out of one's alcohol intoxicated; drug intoxicated. GEN: crazy, senseless. RT: *drunk, stoned.* This sense is probably recurrent nonce. [U.S., RAS: 1978]

headpiece a drug user or addict; an alcoholic. An elaboration of *head* (*q.v.*). RT: *sot, user.* [U.S., RDS: 1982]

head shop (also **head store**) a shop which sells drug-use equipment in addition to other youth-oriented goods such as incense, records, tapes, posters, etc. [U.S., (RB: 1967), D&B: 1970c, (1970): DNE: 1973, EEL: 1971, W&F: 1975, RDS: 1982]

heaped to the gills (also **heaped**) drug intoxicated. RT: *stoned*. [U.S., HNR: 1934, JES: 1959]

heap, in a alcohol intoxicated. RT: *drunk*. [U.S., BVB: 1942]

hear the owl hoot to go on a drinking bout. *Cf. hooted*. RS: *spreeing*. Probably from the late 1800s. [U.S., JLD: 1976]

Heart On a "brand name" for *amy nitrite*. Based on *hard-on* = a penile erection. See comments at *Hardware*. RT: *snapper*. [U.S., ELA: 1984]

hearts *Dexamyl* (TM; *q.v.*) tablets of dextroamphetamine and amobarbital; *Dexedrine* (TM; *q.v.*) amphetamine; *Benzedrine* (TM; *q.v.*) amphetamine. Refers to heart-shaped tablets of these drugs. RS: *dex*. [U.S., JBW: 1967, D&B: 1970c, ADC: 1975, YKB: 1977, NIDA: 1980] See also *horse hearts, purple hearts*.

heart's ease (also **heartsease**) gin. RT: *gin*. [BE: 1690, BVB: 1942]

hearty (also **harty**) alcohol intoxicated. RT: *drunk*. [Br., mid 1800s, F&H; listed in BVB: 1942]

heat (also **the heat**) the police; pressure from the police or from drug enforcement officers. This term has been in U.S. criminal jargon, and to some extent general slang, for decades. RS: *fuzz*. The citations show when it was recorded in drug argot. [U.S., JBW: 1967, M&V: 1967, (1969): DNE: 1973, RRL: 1969, EEL: 1971, MA: 1973, MW: 1976, EAF: 1980, JWK: 1981]

heated alcohol intoxicated. RT: *drunk* [U.S., RAS: 1985]

heated his copper alcohol intoxicated. (BF: 1737: He's heat his Copper.) RT: *drunk*. [BF: 1737]

heater (also **canned heater**) a drunkard who is inebriated with Sterno (TM) canned heating alcohol. RS: *sot*. [U.S., BVB: 1942]

heaven and hell (also **heaven 'n' hell**) phencyclidine, *P.C.P.* (*q.v.*), an animal tranquilizer. RT: *P.C.P.* [U.S., RDS: 1982]

heaven dust 1. (also **heavenly dust, heaven flour**) cocaine; any powdered drug. RT: *cocaine*. [U.S., DWM: 1933, MHW: 1934, DWM: 1936, VJM: 1949, D&D: 1957, RRL: 1969, YKB: 1977, NIDA: 1980] 2. phencyclidine, *P.C.P.* (*q.v.*), an animal tranquilizer. RT: *P.C.P.* [U.S., ADC: 1975]

heavenly blue 1. (also **heavenly sunshine**) the hallucinogenic drug *L.S.D.* (*q.v.*). *Cf. blue, blue acid*. RT: *L.S.D.* [U.S., SNP: 1977, YKB: 1977] 2. (usually **heavenly blues**) a color variety of morning glory seeds. The seeds are eaten in great quantity to produce a high. RT: *seeds*. [U.S., RRL: 1969, W&F: 1975, YKB: 1977]

heavies hard drugs; addictive drugs. [U.S., D&B: 1970c]

heavy 1. a drug user. *Cf. heavy man*. RT: *user*. [U.S., GU: 1975]

2. *porter* (*q.v.*). See ***heavy brown***. 3. powerful; potent, referring to drug strength. See ***heavy drugs***.

heavy artillery equipment for preparing and injecting drugs. The opposite of ***light artillery*** (*q.v.*). RT: ***outfit***. [U.S., JH: 1979]

heavy brown (also **heavy**) porter. *Cf.* ***heavy wet***. RT: ***porter***. [Br., JB: 1823, DU]

heavy drugs (also **heavy narcotics, heavy stuff**) addictive drugs. The same as ***hard drugs*** (*q.v.*). *Cf.* ***stuff***. [U.S., RRL: 1969, EEL: 1971]

heavy hash potent hashish. RS: ***hash***. [U.S., ELA: 1982]

heavy jag a heavy drinking bout. *Cf.* ***jag***. RT: ***spree***. [U.S., BVB: 1942]

heavy joint a marijuana cigarette tipped with ***P.C.P.*** (*q.v.*), an animal tranquilizer. *Cf.* ***joint***. [U.S., S&E: 1981]

heavy man a man with a large drug ***stash*** (*q.v.*). *Cf.* ***fat***. [U.S., RDS: 1982]

heavy soul heroin. RT: ***heroin***. Black use. [U.S., CM: 1970]

heavy stuff See ***heavy drugs***.

heavy wet 1. beer; malt liquor; porter; stout. *Cf.* ***heavy brown***. RS: ***beer***. [Br., FG: 1823, JCH: 1887] 2. a heavy drinking bout. RT: ***spree***. [Br., mid 18-1900s, DSUE]

He drank till he gave up his half-penny "He got drunk." [BF: 1737]

heebie-jeebies (also **heeby-jeebies**) 1. the delirium tremens. GEN: an extreme case of anxiety. RT: ***D.T.s***. [U.S., (1910): SBF: 1976, MHW: 1934, D&D: 1957] 2. the discomfort of a person who has experienced a bad ***L.S.D.*** (*q.v.*) trip. [U.S., ADC: 1981]

heeled 1. (also **heeled over**) alcohol intoxicated. *Cf.* ***well-heeled*** (at ***well-fixed***). RT: ***drunk***. [U.S., BVB: 1942, GOL: 1950] 2. carrying drugs on one's person; having drugs (or the money to buy them) at one's disposal. *Cf.* ***carrying***. [U.S., TRG: 1968, RRL: 1969, EEL: 1971]

heeltap 1. a drink of liquor. RT: ***nip***. [Br., 1800s, F&H] 2. chloral hydrate. RS: ***Mickey Finn***. Compare to sense one. Probably older than the dating indicates. [ELA: 1984]

heesh hashish. RT: ***hash***. [U.S., early 1900s, DU, A&T: 1953, W&F: 1960]

heifer dust snuff. RT: ***snoose***. [U.S., MHW: 1934, VJM: 1949, W&F: 1960]

heister a drunkard. See ***hister***.

Helen heroin. An elaboration of ***H.*** (*q.v.*). RT: ***heroin***. [U.S., IGA: 1971, WCM: 1972, SNP: 1977]

hellbender 1. a drinking bout. *Cf.* ***bender***. RT: ***spree***. [U.S., JSF: 1889, D&D: 1957, W&F: 1960] 2. a heavy drinker; a drunkard.

RT: *sot*. [U.S., BVB: 1942]

hell broth inferior liquor. RT: *rotgut*. [Br., 1800s, F&H]

hell dust powdered drugs such as heroin or morphine. RT: *powder*. [U.S., early 1900s, DU, A&T: 1953, SNP: 1977] See also *heaven dust*.

heller (also **hell raiser**) a rowdy person on a drunken spree. GEN: a rowdy person (1895): OEDS. From *hellbender* (*q.v.*). [U.S., BVB: 1942]

helpers stimulants; amphetamines. RS: *amps*. [U.S., MT: 1971]

helpless alcohol intoxicated. RT: *drunk*. [since the mid 1800s, F&H, BVB: 1942, DSUE, M&J: 1975]

He makes indentures with his legs "He is drunk." [BF: 1737]

hemp 1. a cigar; a bad cigar. *Cf. rope*. RT: *seegar*. [U.S., W&F: 1960] 2. marijuana; cannabis. This is the common name for the marijuana plant. *Cf. rope*. RT: *pot*. [U.S., in drug argot, (1931): ELA: 1982, DB: 1944, M&W: 1946, BVB: 1953, M&V: 1954, W&F: 1960, RRL: 1969, EEL: 1971, ADC: 1975, NIDA: 1980, ADC: 1984; Br., (1955): DSUE, M&J: 1975]

hemp-humper a marijuana smoker; a marijuana user. *Cf. hump the sage*. RT: *toker*. Attested as gay slang. [U.S., BR: 1972]

hemp-roller a marijuana cigarette smoker. Refers to the rolling of marijuana cigarettes. RT: *joint*. [U.S., JES: 1959, H&C: 1975]

Henry heroin. An elaboration of *H*. (*q.v.*). RT: *heroin*. [U.S., RRL: 1969, EEL: 1971, ADC: 1975]

hen wine inferior wine. So-called because it makes one lay (lie) right there. RS: *wine*. [Aust., SJB: 1966]

hepped (also **hepped up**) alcohol intoxicated. RT: *drunk*. [U.S., BVB: 1942]

her cocaine. *Cf. girl, lady*. RT: *cocaine*. [U.S., RRL: 1969, EEL: 1971] See also *him*.

herb (also **erb**, **herbs**, **the herb**) marijuana. RT: *pot*. [U.S., RRL: 1969, D&B: 1970b, DCCU: 1972, W&F: 1975, DNE: 1980, EAF: 1980, NIDA: 1980, JWK: 1981; Br., BTD: 1968, M&J: 1975; Bahamas, JAH: 1982]

Herb and Al marijuana and alcohol. See *go talk to Herbie and Al*.

hercules high-quality phencyclidine, *P.C.P.* (*q.v.*), an animal tranquilizer. RT: *P.C.P.* [U.S., ADC: 1981]

herion heroin. *Cf. heron*. Regarded as a pronunciation error. RT: *heroin*. Black use. [U.S., RDS: 1982]

herms phencyclidine, P.C.P. RT: *P.C.P.* [U.S., ELA: 1984]

hero (also **hero of the underworld**) heroin. Spanish, according to EEL: 1971. RT: *heroin*. [U.S., DU, A&T: 1953, EEL: 1971, IGA: 1971]

hero-gin a drink of gin with a pinch of powdered heroin in it.

[U.S., early 1900s, DU]

heroin a highly addictive derivative of morphine. The name is derived from the Greek *Hero*. It was originally developed as a cure for morphine addiction. Standard English. [since (1898): OEDS] Nicknames and slang terms for various types of heroin: *A-bomb, A.I.P., antifreeze, Aunt Hazel, balloon, balot, big boy, big daddy, big-H., big Harry, big time, black stuff, blanca, blanco, bomb, boy, bozo, brother, brown, brown dope, brown rine, brown rock, brown stuff, brown sugar, button, C., caballo, caca, C. and H., candy, cap, capital H., carga, carne, cat, chick, China white, Chinese red, Chinese white, chip, chiva, cobics, corgy, courage pill, crap, crown crap, deck, dirt, dog, dog food, dogie, dojee, dojie, dooge, doogie, doojee, doojer, doojes, dooji, dope, downtown, dude, dugee, dugie, dujer, duji, dujii, dust, dynamite, dyno, eight, estuffa, ferry dust, foolish powder, galloping horse, gamot, gato, George smack, girl, glad stuff, gold dust, golpe, goods, good stuff, gulf, gum, H., hache, hairy, hard candy, hard stuff, Harry, Hazel, H-caps, heavy soul, Helen, hell dust, Henry, hero, heroina, heron, hero of the underworld, him, hong-yen, hook, horse, horseradish, H.R.N., isda, jack, jazz, jeegee, joint, jojee, jones, joy dust, joy powder, junk, kabayo, kaka, ken-koy, la cosa, La Dama Blanca, la duna, lady in white, Lady White, manteca, matsakaw, mejambrea, Mexican brown, Mexican horse, Mexican mud, mojo, morotgara, muzzle, nieve, noise, nose, nose candy, nose powder, nose stuff, number eight, ogoy, old lady White, old Steve, P., pangonadalot, pee, Persian brown, Persian dust, poison, polboron, pure, racehorse Charley, red chicken, red rock, rock, rocks, salt, scag, scar, scat, schmack, schmeck, schmecken, schmee, schmeek, scot, Scott, shit, shmack, shmeck, shmee, skag, skid, smack, smak, smeck, smizz, snow, snowball, stufa, stuff, sugar, syrup, tecaba, tecata, thing, tinik, T.N.T., top, tragic-magic, triangle stuff, Turk dope, uncut, white, white junk, white lady, white nurse, white stuff, witch, witch hazel, yen-shee, 8.*

heroina* heroin. Spanish. RT: *heroin*. [U.S., NIDA: 1980]

heroin buzz phencyclidine, potent P.C.P. RT: *P.C.P.* [U.S., ELA: 1984]

heron heroin. Possibly a dialect pronunciation. *Cf. herion*. Black use (BR: 1972). Regarded as a pronunciation error. RT: *heroin*. [U.S., BR: 1972]

He's a king (also **The king is his cousin**) "He is drunk." [BF: 1737]

He's in. "He is addicted to drugs." *Cf. in*. RS: *hooked*. [U.S., M&V: 1973]

het up alcohol intoxicated. LIT: heated up. RT: *drunk*. [U.S., AH: 1931, MHW: 1934]

H-habit a case of heroin addiction. *Cf. H*. See the list at *habit*. [U.S., GOL: 1950, D&D: 1957]

hi-ball 1. a *Benzedrine* (TM; *q.v.*) amphetamine tablet. From a term for a tall drink of diluted liquor. *Cf. highball.* RT: *benz.* [U.S., EEL: 1971] 2. See *highball.*

Hi Baller a "brand name" for *amyl nitrite.* There is a sexual reference to the involuntary raising of the testicles during sexual excitement. RS: *snapper.* [U.S., ELA: 1984]

hiccius-doccius (also **hicksius-doxius, hictius-doctius**) alcohol intoxicated. RT: *drunk.* [FG: 1785, F&H; listed in BVB: 1942]

hickey (also **hickie, hicky**) alcohol intoxicated. Probably from *hiccius-doccius.* RT: *drunk.* [cant, FG: 1788, FG: 1823, GWM: 1859, JSF: 1889; listed in BVB: 1942] See also *hockey.*

hiddey alcohol intoxicated. RT: *drunk.* [BF: 1737]

high 1. alcohol intoxicated; tipsy; mellow. Akin to an older sense *tainted,* referring to meat (OED). A synonym of *rotten* (*q.v.*). RT: *drunk.* [(1627): OED, F&H, BWG: 1899, MP: 1928, MHW: 1934, EEL: 1971, DC: 1972, W&F: 1960, CM: 1970] 2. drug intoxicated; under the effects of drugs. RT: *stoned.* Also extended into general slang meaning enthusiastic. DWM: 1936 lists in **high.** Still current in general slang. [U.S., (1932): OEDS, MHW: 1934, DWM: 1938, M&D: 1952, W&F: 1960, RRL: 1969, CM: 1970, ADC: 1975, EAF: 1980] 3. (also **a high**) a state of drug intoxication or euphoria. [U.S., (1953): OEDS, EEL: 1971, W&F: 1975]

high and light drug intoxicated. *Cf. high, light.* RT: *stoned.* [U.S., M&D: 1952, A&T: 1953]

high as a cat's back alcohol intoxicated. Dickson lists similar forms: **high as a fiddler's fist, high as a Georgia pine, high as Lindberg, high in the saddle.** RT: *drunk.* [PD: 1982]

high as a kite (also **high as a steeple, high as the sky**) alcohol intoxicated; drug intoxicated; heavily intoxicated with drugs or alcohol. The DRS claims this is rhyming slang for *tight* (*q.v.*). RT: *drunk, stoned.* [U.S., (1939): OEDS, BVB: 1942, GOL: 1950, W&F: 1960; Br., DRS]

highball (also **hi-ball**) a drink of whiskey or other hard liquor diluted and served in a tall glass. [(1898): DAE, MHW: 1934, D&D: 1957, W&F: 1960] See also *hi-ball.*

higher than a Georgia pine heavily drug intoxicated. See list at *high as a cat's back.* RS: *stoned.* [U.S., BD: 1937, (M&W: 1946)]

higher than a kite (also **higher than Gilroy's kite**) alcohol intoxicated; extremely drunk. Compare to *high as a kite.* RT: *drunk.* [U.S., D&D: 1957, W&F: 1960]

high-fi a mixture of morphine and cocaine. From the term *high fidelity* as it pertains to high-quality sound reproduction. RS: *set.* [U.S., JES: 1959, H&C: 1975]

high-goer a heavy drinker; a person on a spree; a drunkard. RT: *sot.* [Br., 1800s, F&H; listed in BVB: 1942]

high hat 1. a large pellet of prepared opium. RT: *opium.* [U.S.,

DWM: 1938, VJM: 1949] 2. a specific type of tall *opium lamp* (*q.v.*). Akin to sense one. [U.S., DWM: 1938] 3. a serious addiction to opium. RS: *habit*. [U.S., DWM: 1938, H&C: 1975]

high, in drug intoxicated; at the peak of a drug high. Based on *high* (*q.v.*) and possibly *in high gear*. RT: *stoned*. [U.S., DWM: 1936, BVB: 1942]

high kick a drug high; a drug rush. RS: *rush*. [(1940): DSUE] See also *kick*.

highland frisky whiskey, probably Scotch whiskey. Highland = Scotland. See *I'm so frisky!* Rhyming slang. RT: *whiskey*. [Br., (1870): DSUE, (1891): DRS; listed in BVB: 1942]

high lonesome a drinking bout. From a movie title (1950). RS: *spree*. [U.S., D&D: 1957, PW: 1977] See also *lonesome*.

high octane (also **high voltage**) potent liquor; having to do with potent liquor. GEN: potent, powerful. RS: *rotgut*. [U.S., BVB: 1942]

high tea 1. a marijuana smoking party. A play on British *high tea*. See *high tea*. [U.S., BR: 1972] 2. a tea brewed from the waste parts of marijuana plants. *Cf. pot likker*. [U.S., BR: 1972]

high-toned tonic liquor; potent alcohol. RT: *booze*. [U.S., BVB: 1942]

high wine a soft drink laced with grain alcohol. From a standard term referring to high-proof distilled spirits. Hobo use. [U.S., CS: 1927, BVB: 1942, W&F: 1960, K&M: 1968]

hike See *hyke*.

hikori* (also **hikuli***) *peyote* (*q.v.*); *mescaline* (*q.v.*). Probably from an Amerindian language. RS: *peyote*. Probably since the late 1800s. [U.S., IGA: 1971, YKB: 1977]

him heroin. RT: *heroin*. [U.S., RRL: 1969, EEL: 1971, ADC: 1975] See also *her*.

hip disease the practice of carrying a liquor flask on the hip. The disease may be alcoholism. [Aust., SJB: 1943]

hipe a hypodermic needle. See *hype*.

hip flask a liquor flask, usually metal, of a size and shape to fit in a man's trouser pocket. RT: *flask*. [1900s, (1923): OEDS]

hip hooch alcohol carried in a hip flask; a hip flask. [U.S., BVB: 1942]

hip-layer an opium smoker; an opium addict. From the practice of lying on one's side while smoking opium. RT: *campfire boy*. [U.S., early 1900s, DU, A&T: 1953]

hipped 1. with one hip slightly atrophied from being addicted to opium. From the practice of lying on one's hip while smoking opium. RS: *hooked*. [U.S., DWM: 1936, BVB: 1942] 2. alcohol intoxicated. Refers to the frequent use of a hip flask. RT: *drunk*. [U.S., EKM: 1926, MHW: 1934, BVB: 1942]

hippy (also **hippie**) the long haired, drug using, flower child youth of the 1960s–70s. Best known for the use of marijuana and L.S.D. See *flower children*. Widespread by the 1970s. [U.S., M&V: 1967, (1968): DNE: 1973, RRL: 1969]

His shoe pinches him "He is drunk." [BF: 1737]

His skin is full "He is drunk." [BF: 1737]

His tang is hongry. "He is craving drugs."; he is withdrawing. *Hongry* is dialect (black) for hungry; the *tang* (*q.v.*) is short for *orangutan*, one of the forms of ape as found in *have a monkey on one's back* (*q.v.*). [U.S., JWK: 1981]

hister (also **heister**, **hyster**) a drunkard; one who hoists many drinks to his mouth. RT: *sot*. [U.S., BVB: 1942, VJM: 1949]

hit 1. a successful insertion of a hypodermic needle into a vein. GEN: a success. This is the opposite of a *miss* (*q.v.*). RS: *shot*. [U.S., M&V: 1954, (1962): OEDS, RRL: 1969, MA: 1973, JWK: 1981] 2. a dose of a drug in any form: injection, pill, inhalation. In drug culture contexts this refers most often to a puff (toke) of a marijuana cigarette or to a dose of the hallucinogenic drug *L.S.D.* (*q.v.*). RT: *dose*. GU: 1975 defines it only as a tablet or pill dose. *Cf. strike*. [U.S., (1952): ELA: 1982, (1962): OEDS, JBW: 1967, D&B: 1970c, RRL: 1969, DC: 1972, DNE: 1973, ADC: 1975, GU: 1975, W&F: 1975, MW: 1976, EAF: 1980, JWK: 1981, BW: 1984, ADC: 1984] 3. to meet a seller and purchase drugs. *Cf. hit on*. See *H. and R.* RT: *score*. [U.S., DWM: 1936, M&D: 1952, TRG: 1968, RG: 1970, EEL: 1971] 4. (also **hit up**) to give a person (including oneself) a dose of drugs or a puff of a marijuana cigarette. Akin to the *Hit me!* of poker playing. Black use. [U.S., RRL: 1969, CM: 1970, DC: 1972, ADC: 1975, JWK: 1981] See also *four-way hit, nose hit, one-hit grass*. 5. for a dose or injection of drugs to be felt, i.e., the drug hits the user. [U.S., DWM: 1936, BVB: 1942] 6. arrested. RT: *busted*. [U.S., TRG: 1968, RDS: 1982] 7. a successful drug purchase. [(1951): OEDS]

hit-and-miss habit an amateurish (and nonaddictive) use of drugs. May refer to the hitting and missing of a vein in injecting. RS: *habit*. *Cf. chippy habit*. [U.S., DWM: 1938, BVB: 1942]

hit, be to feel the effects of a drug injection; to feel a rush. *Cf. hit*. [U.S., DWM: 1938]

hit by the hop addicted to opium. This expression like many others for opium addiction seems contrived. *Cf. chewing the gum, in the smoke, mired in the mud, on the gow, picking the poppies, poppy-headed, shoveling the black stuff, stung by the hop, up against the stem*. Probably not narcotics argot. [U.S., JES: 1959, H&C: 1975]

hitch up the reindeer (also **hook up the reindeer**) to prepare for a cocaine injection or inhalation; to take cocaine. See other terms on the snow theme at *winter wonderland*. [U.S., BD: 1937, DWM: 1938, GOL: 1950]

hit it 1. to take a dose of drugs; to inject a dose of drugs. *Cf. hit the flute, hit the gonger, hit the gow, hit the hay, hit the hop, hit the mainline, hit the needle, hit the pipe, hit the sewer, hit the stem.* See *hit.* [U.S., DU, A&T: 1953, RRL: 1969] 2. to dilute heroin to half its original strength. RS: *cut.* [U.S., P&C: 1969, RG: 1970]

hit man a man hired by a helpless addict to inject drugs. Often payment is made in drugs. See *hit.* From the underworld slang term for a man who does the dirty work, a hired killer. [U.S., JWK: 1981]

hit on to make a purchase of drugs. Usually: **hit on grass, hit on acid.** RS: *score.* [U.S., TRG: 1968, RG: 1970, IGA: 1971]

hit spike a substitute for a hypodermic needle. *Spike* (*q.v.*) = needle. RS: *needle.* [U.S., M&V: 1973]

hitter an opium addict. *Cf. hit.* RT: *campfire boy.* [U.S., BVB: 1942]

hit the bottle (also **hit the booze**) to go on a drinking bout; to get drunk. RT: *irrigate, mug oneself.* [U.S., (1889): DA, (1906): SBF: 1976, BVB: 1942, W&F: 1960]

hit the ceiling to smoke marijuana; to get high on marijuana. A reinterpretation of an expression meaning to become very angry suddenly. RS: *hit the hay.* [U.S., GOL: 1950, A&T: 1953]

hit the dope to take drugs. [early 1900s, DU]

hit the flute to smoke opium. The flute is the opium pipe. RT: *suck bamboo.* [U.S., late 18-1900s, DU]

hit the gonger 1. (also **hit the gong**) to smoke opium; to smoke an opium pipe. *Cf. gong, gonger.* RT: *suck bamboo.* [U.S., DWM: 1931, MHW: 1934, DWM: 1936, VJM: 1949] 2. to smoke marijuana. RT: *hit the hay.* [U.S., M&V: 1954]

hit the gow (also **hit the grease, hit the hop, hit the mud**) to smoke opium; to be addicted to opium or another drug. *Cf. gow, hop.* RT: *suck bamboo.* [U.S., DWM: 1933, VJM: 1949, A&T: 1953]

hit the hay to smoke marijuana. *Hay* (*q.v.*) = marijuana. [U.S., BVB: 1942, JES: 1959] Slang expressions meaning to light up and smoke marijuana: *airplane, bang a reefer, beat a weed, beat the weeds, bite one's lips, blast, blast a joint, blast a stick, blast Mary Jane to kingdom, blast the roach, blast the weed, blow, blow a stick, blow gage, blow grass, blow hay, blow it, blow jive, blow one's roof, blow one's top, blow pot, blow smoke, blow tea, blow weed, bong, boot the gong around, bounce the goof balls, break a stick, burn, burn an Indian, burn Indian hay, burn some bush, bust, bust a joint, cook, cop a buzz, cop a head, do a doobie, do a dooby, do a joint, do a number, do the honors, do up, drink Texas tea, drop a joint, fire up, flame up, fly Mexican Airlines, fly Mexican Airways, fry one's brains, get high, get it on, get wasted, go loco, go talk to Herbie and Al, hit the ceiling, hit the gonger, hit the hay,* *hit the pipe, hump the sage, kick the gong, kick the gong around, kick the gonger, kiss Mari, kiss Mary, kiss Maryjane, kiss the fish, lie in state with the girls, light up, live in grass huts, party, pot out, puff, puff the dust, read the tea leaves, send, shlook, sip, sip tea, smoke, smoke some bongs, snork, suck up some dope, take off, take up, toke, toke a number, toke up, torch up, turkey, turn a few hits, turn on, twist a giraffe's tail, vipe, weed out.*

hit the hot bozel to get drunk; to go on a drinking bout. See *hot bozel*. RT: *mug oneself*. [U.S., AH: 1931, MHW: 1934]

hit the jug to drink often and heavily; to drink alcoholically. *Cf. jug*. RT: *irrigate*. [U.S., M&W: 1946]

hit the mainline to inject drugs into a vein. *Cf. hit*. RS: *shoot*. [U.S., GOL: 1950, A&T: 1953]

hit the moon to reach the peak of a drug experience. *Cf. peak*. [U.S., EEL: 1971]

hit the needle to inject a drug. *Cf. needle*. RT: *shoot*. [U.S., GOL: 1950, A&T: 1953]

hit the pipe 1. to smoke opium. RT: *suck bamboo*. [U.S., (1886): OEDS, (1902): DA, VJM: 1949, GOL: 1950] 2. to smoke marijuana; to smoke any smokable drug. RS: *hit the hay*. [U.S., W&F: 1960]

hit the pot to drink excessively. *Cf. pot*. RT: *guzzle*. [U.S., DWM: 1935, GOL: 1950]

hit the sauce to drink heavily; to get drunk. *Cf. hit the bottle*. RT: *guzzle, mug oneself*. [U.S., W&F: 1960, DCCU: 1972]

hit the sewer to inject drugs into a major vein. *Sewer* (*q.v.*) = the median cephalic vein. RT: *shoot*. [U.S., GOL: 1950, M&V: 1967, H&C: 1975]

hit the steam to smoke opium. Possibly an error for *hit the stem* (*q.v.*). *Cf. suck bamboo*. [U.S., RDS: 1982]

hit the stem to smoke opium. *Cf. stem*. RT: *suck bamboo*. [U.S., VJM: 1949]

hit the stuff (also hit the dope) to use drugs. *Cf. stuff, dope, gow*. [U.S., DWM: 1936, BVB: 1942, A&T: 1953]

hit under the wing alcohol intoxicated. Probably an elaboration of *shot* (*q.v.*). *Cf. winged*. RT: *drunk*. [(1844): OED]

hit up to inject drugs. See *hit*.

H-joint a place where heroin is sold. *Cf. C-joint, H., M-joint, mooch joint*. RS: *doperie*. [U.S., GOL: 1950]

H.M.C. 1. heroin, morphine, and cocaine. These were the major narcotics of the early 1900s. RT: *heroin, morphine, cocaine*. [U.S., BVB: 1942, DU] 2. "Her Majesty Cocaine." RT: *cocaine*. Probably nonce. [U.S., JES: 1959]

hoary-eyed alcohol intoxicated. See *orie-eyed* for which this is a pun or a misspelling. *Cf. gory-eyed*. RT: *drunk*. [U.S., MHW:

1934, D&D: 1957, W&F: 1960]

hob-nailed liver a liver diseased with cirrhosis. The medical term is *hob-nail liver* (1854): OED. *Cf.* ***gin-drinker's liver*** (at ***gin-liver***). [(1847): OED]

hobo cocktail water. *Cf.* ***Adam's ale***. Black use. [U.S., CM: 1970]

hobo's delight a cigarette butt. RT: ***brad***. [U.S., BVB: 1942, VJM: 1949]

hobster almost certainly an error (or pronunciation variant) for ***hopster*** (*q.v.*). [U.S., H&C: 1975, ELA: 1984]

hockey alcohol intoxicated; drunk on stale beer. RT: ***drunk***. [FG: 1796, FG: 1811, FG: 1823, GWM: 1859, F&H, MHW: 1934]

hock-for opium. RT: ***opium***. [U.S., M&V: 1954]

hocus 1. (also **hocus-pocus**) alcohol intoxicated. RT: ***drunk***. [cant, NCD: 1725; listed in BVB: 1942] 2. (also **hocus-pocus**) drugged liquor. [Br., JB: 1823] 3. morphine in solution. RS: ***morphine***. [U.S., DWM: 1938, RG: 1970, YKB: 1977] See also ***hokus***. 4. a dose of narcotics in solution. RS: ***dose***. [U.S., DWM: 1938] See also ***hokus***. 5. to put a drug into liquor. [Br., (1836): F&H]

hod of mortar ***porter*** (*q.v.*). Rhyming slang. RT: ***porter***. [Br., JCH: 1887, B&L: 1890]

Hoffmann's bicycle the hallucinogenic drug ***L.S.D.*** (*q.v.*). From the name of the man who invented the procedure for making L.S.D. at Sandoz Laboratories in Switzerland. Refers to the bicycle ride Dr. Albert Hoffmann reported taking to his home while under the influence of his first experimental dose of L.S.D. The exact significance is obscure. [U.S., RRL: 1969]

hog 1. an addict who requires very large doses to sustain the habit; a person who takes more of a drug than is needed. RS: ***junky***. [U.S., M&D: 1952, A&T: 1953, JBW: 1967, EEL: 1971] 2. (also **hog tranquilizer**) phencyclidine, ***P.C.P.*** (*q.v.*), an animal tranquilizer. The drug was developed as a veterinary tranquilizer (***Sernylan*** TM; *q.v.*) for use on animals such as hogs. RT: ***P.C.P.*** [U.S., (1967): FAB: 1979, W&F: 1975, DNE: 1980, NIDA: 1980] 3. chloral hydrate. *Cf.* ***chlorals***. RT: ***Mickey Finn***. [U.S., SNP: 1977] 4. a policeman. A play on ***pig*** (*q.v.*). RT: ***fuzz***. [U.S., EAF: 1980]

hogwash inferior liquor; bad beer; diluted liquor; bad beer; moonshine. From the name for matter fed to hogs (c. 1400). RT: ***rotgut, moonshine***. [(1712): OED, FG: 1785, FG: 1811, F&H, BVB: 1942, W&F: 1960]

hoister a drunkard; an alcoholic. *Cf.* ***heister***. RT: ***sot***. [Br., 1800s, F&H; listed in BVB: 1942]

hoist one to have a drink. RS: ***irrigate***. [U.S., MHW: 1934, BVB: 1942]

hokus narcotics including opium. SNP: 1977 glosses this as opium. This is probably the same as ***hocus*** (*q.v.*). [U.S., VFN: 1933,

MHW: 1934, VJM: 1949, W&F: 1960]

hold 1. to sustain or maintain a drug habit. The same as *carry* (*q.v.*). [U.S., DWM: 1938] 2. to possess drugs; to have drugs in one's immediate possession. The term can be used intransitively. *Cf. Are you holding?* [U.S., (1935): OEDS, DWM: 1938, VJM: 1949, GOL: 1950, S&W: 1966, (TRG: 1968), RRL: 1969, (CM: 1970), EEL: 1971, ADC: 1975, W&F: 1975, JWK: 1981]

Holding any eggs? "Do you have any drugs?" *Eggs* (*q.v.*) = pills. RS: *How are you going to act?* [U.S., JWK: 1981]

hold one's high to behave reasonably well under the influence of drugs. Akin to *hold one's liquor* (*q.v.*). [U.S., EAF: 1980]

hold one's liquor to be able to handle alcohol in quantity without passing out, vomiting, or becoming violent. [U.S., BVB: 1942]

hole a tobacco cigarette. RT: *nail.* [U.S., EEL: 1971]

Holland tape gin. See *tape*. RT: *gin.* [(1755): F&H]

Hollywood cocktail a drink made of gin mixed with *Benzedrine* (TM; *q.v.*). RS: *set.* [U.S., SNP: 1977]

hombrecitos* mushrooms containing *psilocybin* (*q.v.*). Mexican Spanish for little men. RT: *psilocybin*. [U.S., YKB: 1977]

home 1. the vein in the arm which is a target for in injection. *Cf. send it home.* [U.S., M&V: 1967, H&C: 1975] 2. ether as used in the preparation of *free base*. A play on the *home base* of baseball. [U.S., ELA: 1984]

home-brew homemade liquor or beer. RS: *moonshine*. Became well-known during prohibition. [(1754): SOD, AH: 1931, MHW: 1934]

home-grown marijuana grown domestically or locally. *Cf. domestic, mud-bud*. RS: *pot.* [U.S., RRL: 1974, ADC: 1975, ADC: 1981]

homespun homemade liquor or beer. From the name of homemade cloth. RS: *moonshine*. [U.S., VR: 1929, MHW: 1934]

honey beer as in *honey wagon* (*q.v.*). See also *nectar*.

honeydew whiskey. *Cf. mountain dew*. RT: *whiskey*. Logger's use. [U.S., RFA]

honey dip liquor; whiskey. RT: *booze, whiskey*. Logger's use. [U.S., HNR: 1934, BVB: 1942]

honeymoon (also **honeymoon period, honeymoon stage**) an early stage in drug use before the severe craving of addiction. [U.S., M&D: 1952, (A&T: 1953), EEL: 1971]

honey oil an extract of hashish. RT: *oil*. [U.S., (1976): ELA: 1982, YKB: 1977]

honey wagon a beer truck. GEN: a septic tank pumping truck. Citizens band radio slang. [U.S., EE: 1976]

hongry having to do with an addict who craves drugs. *Cf. His* *tang is hongry*. Black use. [U.S., JWK: 1981]

hong-yen heroin in the form of red pills. *Cf. yen*. RT: *heroin*. [U.S., VJM: 1949] See also *red chicken*.

honk a drinking spree; a *toot* (*q.v.*). RT: *spree*. [Br., (1945): DSUE]

honked (also **honkers**) alcohol intoxicated. *Cf. Harry Honkers*. RT: *drunk*. [Br. military, (1950): DSUE; PD: 1982, RDS: 1982]

honky-tonk (also **honka-tonk**) a saloon; a bar. RS: *bar*. [U.S., (1894): DA, W&F: 1960]

hooch 1. (also **hootchenoo, hoochinoo, hootch**) hard liquor; any alcoholic beverage. Used much during prohibition for illegal liquor, inferior liquor, and moonshine. The DA dates **hoochinoo** as 1877. RT: *booze*. Said to be of Amerindian (Tlingit) origin. [U.S., (1898): SBF: 1976, (1902): SOD, F&G: 1925, VR: 1929, AH: 1931, GI: 1931, MHW: 1934, GOL: 1950, W&F: 1960, SSD, CM: 1970, DCCU: 1972] 2. marijuana. Probably in the sense of contraband material. RT: *pot*. [U.S., YKB: 1977, ADC: 1984]

hooched (also **hooched up**) alcohol intoxicated. RT: *drunk*. Not listed in JB: 1980. [U.S., BVB: 1942; South African, (1939): DSUE]

hoocher (also **hootcher**) 1. a dealer in illegal liquor; a *bootlegger* (*q.v.*). RT: *bootlegger*. [U.S., BVB: 1942] 2. a drunkard. RT: *sot*. [U.S., S&E: 1981]

hoochfest a drinking bout; a drinking party. *Cf. hooch*. RT: *spree*. [U.S., BVB: 1942]

hooch hound (also **hooch head, hooch hister, hooch hitter, hooch hoister**) a drunkard; a heavy drinker. RT: *sot*. [U.S., BVB: 1942, M&W: 1946, D&D: 1957, RDS: 1982]

hooch house (also **hoocherie**) a place where liquor is sold; a place where illegal liquor is sold. RS: *bar*. [U.S., BVB: 1942]

hooch-humps a hangover. *Cf. hooch*. RT: *hangover*. [U.S., BVB: 1942]

hoodman blind (also **hoodman**) alcohol intoxicated. The hoodman is the blindfolded person in the children's game called blindman's bluff. RT: *drunk*. [Br., B&L: 1890, F&H]

hook 1. an improvised drug injection device; a needle or pin used to open a vein for the injection of drugs. RS: *needle*. [U.S., W&F: 1960] 2. to addict someone. Said of a drug pusher or of an addictive drug. *Cf. hooked*. [U.S., M&D: 1952, W&F: 1960] 3. addictive drugs; an addictive drug; heroin. RS: *dope*. [U.S., W&F: 1960] 4. (also **hook down**) to swallow some type of drug. Attested in reference to *L.S.D.* (*q.v.*). [U.S., (TW: 1968)] 5. the same as *yen-hok* (*q.v.*).

hookah (also **hooka, hukka**) an eastern water pipe used in the smoking of tobacco, hashish, opium, or marijuana. It cools the smoke. *Cf. hubble-bubble, narghile*. RS: *bong*. [(1763): OED,

RRL: 1969, EEL: 1971, ADC: 1975, ADC: 1981]

hook down to swallow a drug. See *hook*.

hooked physically dependent on alcohol, tobacco, drugs, or other substances; addicted. Some glossaries indicate that being hooked is a mild or early stage of addiction. Also means habituated to anything: cola soft drinks, nasal spray, small cars, a certain author, etc. [(1925): OEDS, DWM: 1936, (1945): DSUE, VJM: 1949, W&F: 1960, RRL: 1969, CM: 1970, EEL: 1971, DCCU: 1972, H&C: 1975, JWK: 1981] Nicknames and slang terms meaning addicted: *atop Mt. Shasta, bamboozled, behind stuff, behind the stuff, belong, betting on a horse, billied, bindle stiffened, bitten by white mosquitoes, candied, caught, caught in a snowstorm, ceciled, chasing the bag, chasing the nurse, chewing the gum, cooked, courting Cecil, dipped, dopeheaded, dope hopped, en ganchos, flaky, from Mt. Shasta, have a Chinaman on one's back, have a monkey on one's back, have an orangutan on one's back, have a tang on one's back, He's in., hipped, hit by the hop, hooked, hopheaded, hung up, kicked by a horse, mired in the mud, mosquito bit, narkied, on, on capital H., on drugs, on the gonger, on the habit, on the hop, on the horse, on the hype, on the junk, on the mojo, on the mooch, on the needle, on the nod, on the pipe, on the prod, on the schmeck, on the spike, on the stuff, picking the dream wax, picking the poppies, poppy-headed, pushed, pushing Emma, riding the witch's broom, rumping, scagged, shoveling the black stuff, strung, strung out, strung up, stung by the hop, stung by the white nurse, stung by white mosquitoes, tarred and feathered, up against it, up against the gonger, up against the stem, using, viper mad, wired, zunked.*

hooker 1. a drink of whiskey. RT: *nip*. [U.S., (1833): OEDS, (1887): RML: 1950, W&F: 1960] 2. a drug seller who uses sales tactics which encourage new customers to become addicted easily and cheaply. *Cf. pusher*. [U.S., DCCU: 1972, H&C: 1975]

hook up the reindeer prepare to use cocaine. See *hitch up the reindeer*.

hoosier fiend (also hoosier) an addicted yokel; a nonunderworld addict; a novice addict. See *square*. RS: *junky*. Possibly nonce. [U.S., DWM: 1938, VJM: 1949, A&T: 1953]

hootawater beer. RT: *beer*. [U.S., ADC: 1981]

hootch liquor. See *hooch*.

hootchenoo home-brewed liquor; moonshine. See *hooch*.

hooted alcohol intoxicated. *Cf. hear the owl hoot*. Possibly akin to *hootch* (*q.v.*). RT: *drunk*. Not common (W&F: 1960). [U.S., (1915): SBF: 1976, MHW: 1934, D&D: 1957, W&F: 1960]

hooter 1. a drink of liquor. Possibly something like a *shout* (*q.v.*). RT: *nip*. [U.S., BWG: 1899] 2. cocaine. A slang synonym of *nose*. RT: *cocaine*. [U.S.,. JH: 1979] 3. a marijuana cigarette. RT: *joint*. [U.S., RAS: 1984]

hoozle a drink of liquor. RT: *nip*. Attested in Kentucky. [U.S., (1919): ADD]

hop 1. (also **hops**) opium. Possibly from a Chinese word. RT: *opium*. [U.S., (1887): RML: 1948, GI: 1931, HS: 1933, MHW: 1934, DWM: 1936, D&D: 1957, W&F: 1960, RRL: 1969] 2. (also **hops**) any opiate or smokable drug (used in underworld contexts in the early 1900s); any drug. This includes opium and marijuana, and the term is still in use for the latter. RS: *dope*. [U.S., (1898): W&F: 1960, EK: 1927, GI: 1931, DWM: 1935] 3. a drug user; an addict; an opium addict. *Cf. hophead*. RT: *junky*. Used primarily for opium users. [U.S., HS: 1933, W&F: 1960, H&C: 1975] 4. the state of euphoria induced by opium. [U.S., BVB: 1942]

hop dog an opium user; an opium addict. RT: *campfire boy*. [U.S., (M&W: 1946), RRL: 1969]

hop dream a dream or vision experienced while under the influence of opium. *Cf. hop*. [U.S., BVB: 1942]

hope allegedly opium. Probably an error for *hop* (*q.v.*). [U.S., JH: 1979]

hope city a state of drug induced euphoria. [U.S., EEL: 1971]

hopfest 1. (also **hop party**) a communal opium (or marijuana) session. Probably not in underworld use. [U.S., BVB: 1942, VJM: 1949] 2. a beer drinking party. Refers to the hops in beer. RS: *spree*. [U.S., BVB: 1942, D&D: 1957]

hop fiend an opium user or addict. *Cf. fiend*. RT: *campfire boy*. [U.S., (1898): OEDS, D&D: 1957, W&F: 1960]

hop gun a hypodermic syringe. Probably does not refer to opium use. *Cf. gun*. RT: *monkey pump*. [U.S., BVB: 1942, VJM: 1949, H&C: 1975]

hophead an opium addict; an addict of any opiate: heroin, morphine, etc. RS: *junky*. [U.S., (1911): OEDS, EK: 1927, VWS: 1929, DWM: 1931, DWM: 1933, HS: 1933, MHW: 1934, DWM: 1936, GOL: 1950, RRL: 1969, DCCU: 1972]

hopheaded addicted to opiates. *Cf. hophead*. [U.S., BVB: 1942]

hop hog an opium addict. RT: *campfire boy*. [U.S., GI: 1931, MHW: 1934, D&D: 1957, RRL: 1969]

hop joint 1. an *opium den* (*q.v.*). *Hop* (*q.v.*) = opium. [U.S., (1887): RML: 1948, DWM: 1933, MHW: 1934, DWM: 1936, VJM: 1949, W&F: 1960] 2. a saloon. RS: *bar*. [U.S., HER: 1915]

hop layout the equipment used in the preparation and smoking of opium. *Cf. hop*. RS: *outfit*. [U.S., DWM: 1938, BVB: 1942]

hop merchant 1. an opium addict; a narcotics addict. RT: *campfire boy*. [U.S., (1912): JES: 1959, H&C: 1975] 2. (also **hop peddler**) a narcotics dealer; a dope pusher. RT: *dealer*. [U.S., (1914): JES: 1959, GI: 1931, MHW: 1934]

hop, on the addicted to opium; addicted to opiates; under the influence of opiates. RS: ***stoned***. [U.S., BVB: 1942, H&C: 1975] See also ***on the hop***.

hop party See ***hopfest***.

hopped (also **hopped up**) **1**. under the influence of opium; under the influence of any drug. RT: ***stoned***. [U.S., (1924): OEDS, VWS: 1929, GI: 1931, GOL: 1950, W&F: 1960, TRG: 1968] **2**. alcohol intoxicated. Refers to the hops in beer. *Cf.* ***hopfest***. RT: ***drunk***. [U.S., BVB: 1942]

hop peddler a drug seller. See ***hop merchant***.

hopper See ***hoppy***.

hop pipe an opium pipe. RT: ***hop stick***. [U.S., (1887): RML: 1948]

hoppy 1. (also **hopper**, **hoppie**) a narcotics addict; an opium smoker. RT: ***junky***. [(1922): OEDS, VJM: 1949] **2**. drug intoxicated; smelling of drugs. Probably refers to opium. RS: ***stoned***. [U.S., BVB: 1942]

hoppy dust Probably an error for ***happy dust***. [U.S., ELA: 1984]

hops 1. opium; opiates; narcotics. See ***hop***. **2**. parts of a vining plant (Humulus lupulus) used to give a bitter flavor to malt liquors. Standard English. **3**. beer. *Cf.* ***berps***. RT: ***beer***. [(1929): OEDS, BVB: 1942, W&F: 1960, DC: 1972]

hops, on the on a drinking bout; on a ***beer-bust*** (*q.v.*). Refers to the hops in beer. *Cf.* ***hopped***. RS: ***spreeing***. [Br., (1920): DSUE] See also ***on the hop***.

hopster an opium user; an opium addict. *Cf.* ***gowster***. RT: ***campfire boy***. [U.S., BVB: 1942, JES: 1959]

hop stick 1. a marijuana cigarette. RT: ***joint***. [U.S., ADC: 1975] **2**. (also **hop pipe**) an opium pipe. *Cf.* ***stick***. [U.S., DWM: 1938, BVB: 1942, W&F: 1960] Nicknames and slang terms for an opium pipe: ***alter, bamboo, bowl, cha-cha, Chinese saxophone, crock, dipper, dream pipe, dreamstick, engine, gee-gee, gee stick, gong, gonger, gongerine, gongola, great Scott, hop pipe, hop stick, humming gee bowl, joystick, lemon bowl, log, orange bowl, pipe, pipsky, poppy pipe, popstick, saxophone, stem, stick, straw, yen-cheung, yen-chiang, yen-chung, yen-hank***.

hop stiff a narcotics addict; an opium addict. RT: ***campfire boy***. Probably hobo use. [U.S., early 1900s, DU]

hop toad a drink of liquor. *Cf.* ***hop***. RT: ***nip***. [U.S., MHW: 1934]

hop toy (also **toy**) a container for opium which is ready to be smoked, a small tin (can) or an English Walnut shell. A ***toy*** holds about 25 ***fun*** (*q.v.*) of opium pellets (M&V: 1973). [U.S., (1887): RML: 1948, BD: 1937, DWM: 1938]

hop up to use narcotics; to drug a person or a horse. *Cf.* ***hopped, hopped up***. [U.S., BVB: 1942, NAM: 1953, W&F: 1960]

horizontal alcohol intoxicated. *Cf.* ***laid out***. RT: ***drunk***. [Br.

military, (1935): DSUE, EP: 1948]

horn 1. to take a drink of liquor; to partake of the drinking horn. RT: *irrigate*. [U.S., (Boontling), late 18–1900s, CCA] 2. to inhale drugs; to snort a powdered drug. Horn = nose. RS: *snort*. Currently used in reference to snorting cocaine. [U.S., JBW: 1967, RRL: 1969, D&B: 1970c, (H&C: 1975)] 3. a pipe or other device for smoking marijuana. *Cf. cock pipe*. RS: *bong*. [U.S., JWK: 1981]

horner 1. a heavy drinker; a drunkard. RT: *sot*. [U.S., (Boontling), late 18–1900s, CCA] 2. a cocaine user (sniffer). RT: *kokomo*. [U.S., W&F: 1975, YKB: 1977]

horries the ill-effects of drugs or drinking. See *horrors*. From Afrikaans. RT: *D.T.s*. [South African, (1971): JB: 1980]

horror drug 1. *belladonna* (*q.v.*). [U.S., RRL: 1969] 2. L.S.D. combined with *belladonna* (*q.v.*), or *Datura*. RS: *set*. [U.S., KBH: 1982]

horrors 1. the delirium tremens. *Cf. uglies*. RT: *D.T.s*. [Br. and U.S., (1860): SBF: 1976, JCH: 1887, BWG: 1899, MHW: 1934, SSD] 2. bad or frightening hallucinations from a bad L.S.D. trip. *Cf. panic trip*. [U.S., RRL: 1969, JTD: 1971] 3. a psychotic seizure from an overdose of amphetamines. [BTD: 1968, EEL: 1971] 4. a depression during drug withdrawal. [Br., BTD: 1968] See also *chuck horrors*.

hors d'oeuvres* capsules of *Seconal* (TM; *q.v.*) barbiturate capsules. From French. RT: *sec*. [U.S., EAF: 1972]

horse 1. heroin. A reinterpretation of the initial letter H. RT: *heroin*. [Br. and U.S., M&D: 1952, A&T: 1953, M&V: 1954, M&H: 1959, W&F: 1960, BTD: 1968, RRL: 1969, CM: 1970, EEL: 1971, M&J: 1975, EAF: 1980, NIDA: 1980, JWK: 1981] 2. P.C.P., an animal tranquilizer. Short for *horse tranquilizer* (*q.v.*). RT: *P.C.P.* [U.S., ADC: 1981]

horse and buggy (also **horse and wagon**) a hypodermic needle and medicine dropper for injecting heroin. *Cf. horse*. Perhaps indicating that this type of drug use is old-fashioned, that the two items go together like horse and buggy, or perhaps akin to *bugged* (*q.v.*). Most likely an elaboration of *bugged* (*q.v.*). ELA: 1984 lists **horse and wagon**. [U.S., EEL: 1971]

horseback alcohol intoxicated. Possibly a play on *bent* (*q.v.*). RT: *drunk*. [U.S., MHW: 1934, BVB: 1942]

horse brine synthetic whiskey; inferior whiskey. Almost certainly a euphemism for *horse piss*. RS: *rotgut*. [U.S., RDS: 1982]

horsed (also **on the horse**) under the effects of heroin; addicted to heroin. *Cf. horse*. RS: *stoned*. [Br., (1950): DSUE]

horse doctor a physician; a derogatory term for a hospital or prison doctor. *Cf. vet*. GEN: a quack doctor. Relevant to drug argot in so far as doctors are viewed as a source of drugs. [U.S.,

BVB: 1942, RDS: 1982]

horse heads amphetamine tablets. RT: *amps*. [U.S., IGA: 1971, WCM: 1972]

horse hearts (also **hearts**) *Dexedrine* (TM; *q.v.*) tablets in the shape of hearts. Possibly akin to *horse* (*q.v.*). RT: *dex*. [U.S., RG: 1970, JTD: 1971]

horse liniment strong liquor. RT: *rotgut*. [U.S., BVB: 1942]

horseradish heroin. An elaboration of *horse* (*q.v.*). Conceivably because powdered heroin has some resemblance to grated horseradish. RT: *heroin*. [U.S., JES: 1959, H&C: 1975]

horse tranquilizer (also **horse trank**) phencyclidine, *P.C.P.* (*q.v.*), an animal tranquilizer. RT: *P.C.P.* [U.S., (1970s): FAB: 1979, YKB: 1977, RDS: 1982]

hoska marijuana. A truncation of *mahoska* (*q.v.*) RT: *pot*. East coast (M&V: 1973). [U.S., M&V: 1973]

hospital heroin *Dilaudid* (TM; *q.v.*). RT: *dids*. [U.S., ELA: 1984]

hot 1. alcohol intoxicated. See the list at *cooked*. *Cf. all het up, hot as a red wagon, hotter than a skunk, half hot*. RT: *drunk*. [U.S., BHH: 1856, BWG: 1899] 2. carrying drugs and subject to arrest. GEN: wanted by the police. *Cf. sizzle*. [U.S., TRG: 1968, MA: 1973, JBW: 1967]

hot and cold a mixture of heroin and cocaine. A reinterpretation of *H. and C.* (*q.v.*). The same as *cold and hot* (*q.v.*). RS: *set*. [U.S., EEL: 1971, ADC: 1975, W&F: 1975]

hot as a red wagon alcohol intoxicated. *Cf. hot*. RT: *drunk*. [U.S., MHW: 1934, D&D: 1957]

hot bozel (also **hot bottle, hot bozzle, the hot bozzle**) liquor; a bottle of liquor. *Cf. hit the hot bozel*. RS: *booze*. [U.S., BVB: 1942]

hot bust a drug bust and arrest made on a tip from an informer. Compare to *cold bust*. *Cf. sizzle*. [U.S., RRL: 1974]

hot coppers a hangover; great thirst after drinking. RT: *hangover*. [Br., 1800s, F&H]

hot dream possibly an error for *hop dream* (*q.v.*). But see *fuck the hop*. [A&T: 1953]

hotel a hotel bar; an inn; a *pub* (*q.v.*). RS: *bar*. [Aust., 18–1900s, SJB: 1966, AD: 1982]

hot hay marijuana. *Hay* (*q.v.*) = marijuana. RT: *pot*. [U.S., (1951): M&D: 1952]

hot shot a poisonous injection given to an informer or other such person. The substance may be cyanide, heroin and cyanide, or pure heroin. *Cf. ten-cent pistol*. [Br. and U.S., DWM: 1936, W&F: 1967, BTD: 1968, RRL: 1969, CM: 1970, EEL: 1971]

hotstick a marijuana cigarette. *Cf. stick*. RT: *joint*. Compare to *hop stick*. [U.S., D&D: 1957, RDS: 1982]

hot stuff 1. liquor; potent liquor. RT: *booze*. [U.S., BVB: 1942] 2. inferior drugs. [U.S., M&V: 1967]

hotter than a boiled owl (also hotter than a biled owl) alcohol intoxicated; very drunk. A mixed metaphor based on *drunk as a boiled owl* and *hot*. RT: *drunk*. [U.S., MHW: 1934, BVB: 1942]

hotter than a skunk alcohol intoxicated; very drunk. A mixed metaphor based on *drunk as a skunk* and *hot*. [U.S., MHW: 1934, BVB: 1942]

hot turkey an act of igniting an entire marijuana cigarette or *roach*. Based on *cold turkey* (*q.v.*). *Cf. turkey*. [U.S., EEL: 1971, JH: 1979]

house a place where drugs can be bought. RS: *doperie*. [U.S., ADC: 1975] See also *barrelhouse, barrelhouse bum, barrelhouse drunk, barrelhouse stiff, bawdy-house-bottle, deadhouse, gashouse, halfway house, hedge alehouse, hooch house, house connection, house dealer, housewife's delight, hush-house, jook house, joss house, mug house, public house, roadhouse, rum house, sluice house, tippling house.*

housed alcohol intoxicated. Probably short for *shit-housed,* akin to *shit-faced* (*q.v.*). RT: *drunk*. [U.S., ADC: 1984]

house dealer 1. a drug dealer who is superior to the street dealer in the drug hierarchy. RS: *dealer*. [U.S., JWK: 1981] 2. (also house connection) a drug seller who lives in and sells in an apartment building, private home, or other multiunit dwelling. RS: *dealer*. [U.S., MA: 1973, RDS: 1982]

house, on the having to do with a drink (and now anything else) which is provided free by the management. [originally U.S., since the late 1800s, (1889): OEDS]

housewife's delight tranquilizers. *Cf. mama's mellow*. RT: *tranks*. Probably not drug argot. [U.S., JH: 1979]

How are you going to act? "Do you have any drugs for sale?" All of the coded inquiries for seeking drugs are meant to find out how the questioned person is going to respond to the question. [U.S., M&D: 1952] Expressions indicating that the speaker is seeking drugs: *Anyone out?, Are you anywhere?, Are you holding?, Can you do me good?, Do you need a boy?, Fix me!, Got any zings?, Have you got anything?, Have you got a thing?, Holding any eggs?, How are you going to act?, I'm looking., I'm way down., Is you anywhere?, Let me go!, Let me hold something!, Put me straight!, Set me straight!, Throw me out!, What is it?, What's happening?, What street are you on?, Where's Mary?, Who's dealing?, You got any of them thangs on you?*.

How came you so? alcohol intoxicated. See comments at *so*. RT: *drunk*. [(1816): OEDS; U.S. Civil War, DST: 1984]

howling (also howling drunk) alcohol intoxicated; wildly and loudly drunk. RT: *drunk*. [(1899): OEDS]

H.R.N. heroin. This is *heroin* with the vowels left out. RT: *heroin*. [U.S., JES: 1959, H&C: 1975] See also *C.K.*

huatari* *peyote* (*q.v.*); *mescaline* (*q.v.*). Probably from an Amerindian language. RS: *peyote*. [U.S., IGA: 1971, YKB: 1977]

hubble-bubble (also **hubbly-bubbly**) a *hookah* (*q.v.*), a water pipe. Any current use refers to hashish or marijuana smoking. RS: *bong*. [(1634): OED, JCH: 1887, B&L: 1890, RRL: 1969, RG: 1970, RDS: 1982]

Huckleberry Finn gin. From the novel by Mark Twain. Rhyming slang. RT: *gin*. [Aust., SJB: 1966]

hudda a police officer. Mexican-American use (M&V: 1973). RT: *fuzz*. [U.S., M&V: 1967]

huffer a person (usually a teenager) who inhales glue vapors or some other solvent. *Cf. sniff*. [U.S., RRL: 1969, D&B: 1970c, IGA: 1971, (NIDA: 1980)]

hum cap (also **hum, humming bub, humming liquor, humming October, October**) very strong beer or ale. It makes one's head hum. RT: *beer*. [cant, (1616): OED, BE: 1690, FG: 1785, FG: 1811, JB: 1823]

humming (also **hummin'**) drug intoxicated. GEN: running smoothly like a well-oiled machine. RT: *stoned*. [U.S., JWK: 1981]

humming gee bowl an opium pipe bowl made from a human skull. *Humming* may be a corruption of a Chinese name. Possibly *humming* = human and *gee* = guy (in U.S. cant). RS: *hop stick*. ELA: 1984 lists **humming gay**. [U.S., BD: 1937, DWM: 1938]

hump a Camel (TM) tobacco cigarette. From the camel's hump. *Cf. desert horse*. RT: *nail*. [U.S., WM: 1927 MHW: 1934]

Humphrey to monopolize a marijuana cigarette. The same as *Bogart* (*q.v.*). [U.S., BR: 1972]

hump, on the addicted. RT: *hooked*. [U.S., H&C: 1975]

hump, over the past the worst point in drug withdrawal. GEN: past the worst part. [U.S., DWM: 1938, BVB: 1942]

hump the sage to smoke marijuana. *Cf. hemp-humper*. RT: *hit the hay*. [U.S., H&C: 1975]

hundred proof very potent whiskey. One hundred proof liquor contains 50 percent alcohol. RS: *booze*. [U.S., DU, W&F: 1960]

hung (also **hungover**) afflicted with a *hangover* (*q.v.*). In the movie *Auntie Mame*, (1958). [U.S., (1950): OEDS, D&B: 1970c, DCCU: 1972]

hungries, the (also **hungry horrors**) the need to eat after using marijuana, the same as *munchies* (*q.v.*). ELA: 1984 lists **hungry horrors**. [U.S., IGA: 1971]

hungry croaker a physician who can be bribed to prescribe narcotics for an addict. *Croaker* (*q.v.*) = physician (in criminal argot). [U.S., RRL: 1969, EEL: 1971]

hung up addicted to a drug; having a hang-up about a drug. GEN: troubled (JRW: 1909). RT: *hooked*. [U.S., M&V: 1954, H&C: 1975]

hunk a small amount of hashish. RT: *load*. [U.S., E&R: 1971]

hunt a tavern fox to drink heavily; to get drunk. *Cf. foxed*. RT: *mug oneself*. [1600s, DSUE]

hunting seeking a drug supplier; seeking a new drug supplier. *Cf. looking*. [U.S., JWK: 1981]

hurdy-gurdy a low saloon. A hurdy-gurdy is a medieval music instrument. The term is also used for a barrel organ. See *barrelhouse*. RT: *dive*. [U.S., RFA]

hurting (also **hurtin'**) seriously in need of a dose of drugs. [U.S., M&V: 1967, JWK: 1981]

H-user a heroin addict. RT: *junky*. [U.S., D&D: 1957]

hush-house (also **hushie, hush joint**) a speakeasy. RT: *speak*. From the prohibition era. [U.S., BVB: 1942]

hustle 1. an addict's own special way of getting money for drugs. Most hustles involve theft or the provision of sexual services. M&W: 1946 list **hustler**. *Cf. scam*. [U.S., JWK: 1981] **2**. to get money for the purpose of buying drugs. [U.S., RG: 1970, MA: 1973, JWK: 1981, RDS: 1982; Br., RG: 1970, MA: 1973, BTD: 1968] 3. to sell drugs. RT: *push*. [U.S., (1967): ELA: 1982]

Hycodan a protected trade name for a cough syrup containing hydrocodone (a semisynthetic narcotic) and homatropine. The drug is used as a cough suppressant. *Cf. hyke*. [in current use; consult a pharmaceutical reference for more information]

hydropot a teetotaller. LIT: a water drinker. RT: *dry*. [(1727): OED]

hygelo an addict; a morphine addict. [U.S., VJM: 1949, A&T: 1953, HB: 1955]

hyke (also **hike**) *Hycodan* (TM; *q.v.*), a cough syrup containing a derivative of codeine. [U.S., RG: 1970, JHF: 1971]

hype 1. a narcotics addict who injects drugs. From hypodermic needle. BD: 1937 spells it **hyp**. [U.S., BD: 1937, DWM: 1938, VJM: 1949, GOL: 1950, M&D: 1952, D&B: 1970c, MA: 1973, ADC: 1975, W&F: 1975] **2**. (also **hyp**) an injection of drugs. RT: *shot*. [U.S., (1924): OEDS, HS: 1933, PRB: 1930, MHW: 1934, BVB: 1942, VJM: 1949, W&F: 1960] 3. a drug dealer. RT: *dealer*. This almost certainly refers to an addict who is trying to hook new customers for the pusher. [U.S., W&F: 1960, RDS: 1982] **4**. (also **hipe, hyp**) a hypodermic syringe; a hypodermic syringe and needle. RS: *monkey pump, needle*. [U.S., (1913): W&F: 1960, HS: 1933, MHW: 1934, DWM: 1936, VJM: 1949, GOL: 1950, M&D: 1952, DCCU: 1972, JWK: 1981]

hyped (also **hyped up**) drug intoxicated. RT: *stoned*. GEN: excited, stimulated. [U.S., ADC: 1975, HSD: 1984]

hype, on the injecting drugs; addicted to injectable drugs. *Hype* (*q.v.*) = hypodermic syringe and needle. *Cf. on the needle*. RS: *hooked*. [U.S., GOL: 1950]

hype shoot to inject drugs. RS: *shoot*. Such an injection is a **hype shot** or a **hype skin shot**. [U.S., JES: 1959, H&C: 1975]

hypestick a hypodermic syringe and needle. *Cf. stick*. RT: *monkey pump*. [U.S., HS: 1933, MHW: 1934, VJM: 1949, GOL: 1950, D&D: 1957, W&F: 1960]

hypnotic a drug which induces sleep. Akin to *Hypnos,* the name of the Greek god of sleep. [(1681): OED]

hypo 1. a hypodermic syringe and needle. From medical usage. RT: *monkey pump*. [(1925): OEDS, MHW: 1934, D&D: 1957, H&C: 1975] **2.** an injection carried out with a hypodermic syringe. Usually refers to the injection of a sedative. From medical usage. RT: *shot*. [in U.S. drug argot: BVB: 1942, RDS: 1982] **3.** a drug addict who injects drug doses. RS: *junky*. [U.S., (1904): OEDS, VWS: 1929, GI: 1931, MHW: 1934, W&F: 1960; Br., (1904): OEDS, BTD: 1968] **4.** to inject drugs. RT: *shoot*. [(1925): OEDS]

hypo juggler an addict who injects drugs. RS: *junky*. [U.S., (1930s): JES: 1959, H&C: 1975]

hypo smecker an addict who injects drugs. *Cf. smeck*. RS: *bangster*. [U.S., BD: 1937, DWM: 1938]

hyster a heavy drinker. See *hister*. [U.S, RFA]

I

I. and I. "intoxication and intercourse," a play on *R. and R.*, "rest and recuperation." [U.S. military, since the 1950s, DST: 1984]

ibogaine* a stimulant compound from a central African shrub *Tabernanthe iboga*. This substance received attention during the peak of the drug culture. See YKB: 1977, for instance. [(1902): OEDS]

ice 1. cocaine. Refers to a crystalline form of cocaine. *Cf. icicles*. RT: *cocaine*. [U.S., C&H: 1974, SNP: 1977] 2. to kill someone; to kill an informer. *Cf. chill, freeze*. Not limited to drug argot. [U.S., JWK: 1981]

ice bag See *ice pack*.

iceberg marijuana smuggled into Los Angeles with iceberg lettuce. *Cf. ice pack*. RT: *pot*. [U.S., EEL: 1971, JH: 1979]

ice cream opium, and perhaps other hard drugs. RT: *opium*. [U.S., EEL: 1971, JH: 1979]

ice creamer an occasional user of narcotics; a *chipper* (*q.v.*). See *ice cream habit*. [U.S., RDS: 1982]

ice cream habit a moderate and nonaddictive habit leading to addiction. *Cf. chippy habit*. RS: *habit*. [U.S., DWM: 1938, VJM: 1949, RRL: 1969, W&F: 1975]

ice cream man a (male) seller of opium. *Cf. ice cream*. RS: *dealer*. [U.S., M&D: 1952, EEL: 1971]

ice pack (also **ice bag**) a potent variety of marijuana treated with dry ice to increase its potency. The carbon dioxide is said to combine with the active ingredient in cannabis making it more potent. *Cf. iceberg*. RT: *pot*. [U.S., (1969): ELA: 1982, EEL: 1971, ADC: 1975]

icer an *isomerizer* (*q.v.*) for increasing the potency of marijuana. RS: *bong*. [U.S., JWK: 1981]

ice tong doctor (also **ice tong, ice tong croaker**) a physician who is willing to sell or prescribe drugs illegally to addicts. *Ice tong* refers to the tools of the abortion trade. *Cf. hungry croaker*. [U.S., MHW: 1934, DWM: 1936, D&D: 1957, EEL: 1971] See also *ice water doctor*.

ice tray to smoke marijuana using an ice tray covered with foil.

The smoke is cooled and thought to sink to the depths of the lungs where it displaces the warmer air and is better absorbed. See *ice pack*. [U.S., EEL: 1971]

ice water cure terminating drug addiction by ceasing drug intake completely and suffering through the withdrawal period. *Cf. cold turkey*. [U.S., M&V: 1967, H&C: 1975]

ice water doctor (also **ice water John**) a doctor who refuses to give drugs to a suffering addict. Probably a play on *ice tong doctor*. *Cf. ice water cure*. [U.S., M&V: 1967, RDS: 1982]

icicles pure cocaine in its crystallized form. *Cf. ice*. See list at *winter wonderland*. RT: *cocaine*. [U.S., JWK: 1981]

idiot juice (also **idiotic**) a mixture of ground nutmeg and water. Used in prisons for its hallucinogenic effects. *Cf. buck, jail house high*. Prison use. [U.S., M&V: 1967, H&C: 1975]

idiot oil (also **ignant, ignant oil, ignorant oil**) alcohol. From the point of view of drug users who think that alcohol is bad because of its debilitating effects. RS: *booze*. [U.S., JWK: 1981]

idiot pills barbiturates. RT: *barbs*. [U.S., RRL: 1969, M&V: 1973]

igaret-say a tobacco cigarette. Pig Latin. RT: *nail*. [U.S. and Aust., (1940s): DSUE]

ignite oil liquor. A variant of or an error for *ignorant oil* (*q.v.*). RT: *booze*. [U.S., EAF: 1980]

ignorant oil (also **ignant, ignant oil**) wine; whiskey; liquor; alcohol. See *idiot oil*. RS: *booze*. [U.S., DC: 1972, JWK: 1981]

ike-spay a hypodermic needle. Pig Latin for *spike* (*q.v.*). RT: *needle*. [U.S., M&V: 1973]

Illinois green a type of marijuana, presumably grown in Illinois. See list at *green*. RT: *pot*. [U.S., EEL: 1971]

ill-natured alcohol (also **ill-natured**) denatured alcohol, methylated alcohol. The opposite of *good-natured alcohol* (*q.v.* at *good-natured alk*). RS: *methyl*. [U.S., BVB: 1942]

illuminated alcohol intoxicated. *Cf. lit* of which this is an elaboration. RT: *drunk*. [U.S., (1926): OEDS, AH: 1931, MHW: 1934]

I.M. having to do with an intramuscular injection; an intramuscular injection. *Cf. I.V.* [1900s; drug use, EEL: 1971, JWK: 1981]

imbibery a liquor establishment. *Cf. drinkery*. RS: *bar*. [U.S., BVB: 1942]

I'm in trouble. (also **I'm hurting, I'm sick**) LIT: I am withdrawing; I need drugs. [U.S., DWM: 1938, RAS: 1980]

I'm looking. a coded expression meaning "I want to buy drugs." RS: *How are you going to act?* [U.S., RAS: 1980]

impaired alcohol intoxicated. RT: *drunk*. [(1951): OEDS, PD: 1982]

impaired physician a physician addicted to alcohol, drugs, or both. A polite euphemism. RS: *junky, sot*. [U.S., RAS: 1979, RDS: 1982]

impixlocated alcohol intoxicated. *Cf. pixilated*. RT: *drunk*. [Br., (1932): DSUE]

impixocated drunk. Possibly an error for *impixlocated* (*q.v.*). [PD: 1982]

importer a drug seller who smuggles drugs into the U.S. Probably used as a euphemism as well as argot. RS: *mule*. [U.S., P&C: 1969, RDS: 1982]

I'm sick. See *I'm in trouble*.

I'm so frisky! (also **I'm so**) whiskey. Rhyming slang. See *highland frisky*. [1900s, DRS, DSUE, SSD]

I'm way down. "I need drugs.; I need marijuana." RS: *How are you going to act?* [U.S., EEL: 1971]

in 1. high on marijuana. RT: *wasted*. [U.S., (1938): ELA: 1982] 2. involved with drugs; addicted to drugs; accepted in the drug-using community. A specialized use of a widespread colloquial expression. [U.S., JTD: 1971]

in and out rhyming slang for *stout* (*q.v.*). A play on the drink's entrance into and exit from of the body. RT: *stout*. [Br., 18-1900s, DRS, SSD]

inbetweens a mixture of amphetamines and barbiturates. RS: *set*. [U.S., H&C: 1975]

Inca message cocaine. Alludes to Peru, the home of the Incas and the site of much cocaine growth and use. RT: *cocaine*. [U.S., ADC: 1984]

incense marijuana. RT: *pot*. [U.S., (1969): ELA: 1982]

incentive cocaine. The drug is a stimulant and can provide energy and apparent motivation. *Cf. initiative*. RT: *cocaine*. [U.S., RRL: 1974, NIDA: 1980]

incog (also **incognito**) alcohol intoxicated. *Cf. disguised*. RT: *drunk*. [Br., JB: 1823; listed in BVB: 1942]

incognitibus alcohol intoxicated. *Cf. incog*. RT: *drunk*. [PD: 1982]

India marijuana, *Cannabis indica* (*q.v.* at *cannabis*). RT: *pot*. [Br., BTD: 1968, M&J: 1975]

Indian Bay allegedly marijuana. Almost certainly an error for *Indian hay* (*q.v.*). [U.S., SNP: 1977, ELA: 1984]

Indian drug tobacco. Refers to the cigar store Indian. RT: *fogus*. [U.S., BVB: 1942]

Indian hat an error for *Indian hay* (*q.v.*). [RG: 1970]

Indian hay (also **India**, **Indian**, **Indian hemp**, **Indian rope**, **Indian weed**) marijuana. Refers to East Indian hemp, *Cannabis indica*. RT: *pot*. [originally U.S., (1936): ELA: 1982, RPW: 1938, VJM:

1949, D&D: 1957, RRL: 1969, M&J: 1975]

Indian liquor (also **Indian whiskey**) trade whiskey, a sometimes horrible mixture of alcohol, water, and other substances. Also a dysphemism for any strong or inferior liquor. Refers to Amerindians. RS: *rotgut*. [U.S., (1858): JRB: 1859, (1907): PW: 1977]

Indian oil an extract of hashish. Based on *Indian hay* (*q.v.*) or one of its variants. Refers to the Indians of India. RT: *oil*. [U.S., YKB: 1977, ELA: 1982]

indico charras* marijuana, *Cannabis indica*. RT: *pot*. Spanish. [U.S., NIDA: 1980]

indulge to take a drink of an alcoholic beverage; to drink any amount of alcohol. RS: *irrigate*. [since the late 1800s, DSUE]

infernal compound whiskey. RT: *whiskey*. Probably not slang. [Br., (Scots), 1800s, F&H]

influence to *spike* (*q.v.*) a drink with alcohol. [U.S., (1970): DNE: 1973]

influence, under the alcohol intoxicated. A truncation of under the influence of alcohol. More colloquial and euphemistic than slang. RT: *drunk*. [Br. and U.S., 18–1900s, F&H, BVB: 1942]

inger a feigned spasm. RT: *brody*. [U.S., JES: 1959]

inhalant gas or vapors which are inhaled to produce a high. *Cf. gluey, huffer, sniff, glad rags, glue, snifter*. [(c. 1890): MW: 1976; drug culture, 1900s]

inhale to guzzle liquor, especially beer. Also means to gobble down food. RT: *guzzle*. [U.S., (BVB: 1942), W&F: 1960]

inhaler 1. an *inhalant* (*q.v.*). [U.S., EEL: 1971] **2**. a person who inhales volatile vapors to get high. RS: *user*. [U.S., RRL: 1969, RDS: 1982]

initiative cocaine. *Cf. incentive*. RT: *cocaine*. [U.S., JH: 1979]

in-jay gin. RT: *gin*. Pig Latin. [U.S., BVB: 1942]

injun drunk alcohol intoxicated. RT: *drunk*. [PD: 1982]

ink cheap red wine. *Cf. red ink*. RS: *wine*. [U.S., (1917): JL: 1972, GI: 1931, W&F: 1960, CM: 1970; Aust., SJB: 1943]

inked alcohol intoxicated. *Cf. ink*. RT: *drunk*. [Aust., (1898): GAW: 1978, (1920): DSUE, SJB: 1943]

inkpot a liquor establishment. *Cf. ink*. RS: *bar*. [U.S., GOL: 1950]

inky (also **inkypoo**) alcohol intoxicated. *Cf. ink*. RT: *drunk*. [Aust. and Br. wartime, F&G: 1925, SJB: 1945]

inside dope liquor. A play on an expression meaning privileged information. RT: *booze*. [U.S., BVB: 1942]

inspired alcohol intoxicated. RT: *drunk*. [Br., 18–1900s, F&H; listed in BVB: 1942]

instant Zen the hallucinogenic drug *L.S.D.* (*q.v.*). *Cf. Zen*. Refers to Zen Buddhism in which meditation is a central feature. RT: *L.S.D.* [U.S., DCCU: 1972, YKB: 1977, KBH: 1982]

intense having to do with a potent drug. *Cf. decent.* [U.S., ADC: 1975]

internal a drug smuggler who swallows numerous small, rubber packages of a powdered drug. The same as *body-packer* (*q.v.*). Attested in reference to Florida cocaine smuggling. RS: *mule.* [U.S., RAS: 1982]

inter pocula* between drinks; alcohol intoxicated. LIT: between drinks, while drinking. RT: *drunk.* Literary use. Not slang or argot. [Latin]

into, be involved with. In the context of drugs: taking, using. *Cf. do drugs.* The expressions: into drugs, into pot, into coke, etc. are being replaced by doing drugs, doing pot, doing coke etc. [U.S., RRL: 1969, H&C: 1975]

intoxed (also **intox**) intoxicated with alcohol or drugs, especially marijuana. RS: *drunk, stoned.* [U.S., RDS: 1982]

intoxicated alcohol intoxicated. RT: *drunk.* Now standard English. [BF: 1737]

inundated alcohol intoxicated. *Cf. flooded.* RT: *drunk.* [U.S., BVB: 1942]

invigorator a drink of liquor. *Cf. eye-opener, livener, pick-me-up, shot in the arm.* RT: *nip.* [Br., early 1800s, F&H; listed in BVB: 1942]

Irish (also **Irish aqua vitae, Irish dew**) Irish whiskey. RS: *whiskey.* [Br., (1893): F&H; U.S., RDS: 1982]

Irish jigs cigarettes. Rhyming slang for *cigs. Cf. cig.* RT: *nail.* [Br., PW: 1974]

Irish pot whiskey homebrewed (Irish) whiskey. See *poteen, potsheen.*

iron cure (also **iron bound cure**) total withdrawal from addictive drugs. This is done without tapering off and the addict suffers through the withdrawal agonies without the aid of drugs. Usually the result of imprisonment. The iron refers to prison bars. See *cold turkey, ice water cure.* [U.S., DWM: 1938, RRL: 1969]

irrigate to take a drink of liquor; to drink liquor to excess. The greatest use of this term dates from the late 1800s. [early 17–1800s, F&H; U.S., (1856): OEDS, JSF: 1889, EHB: 1900] Terms and expressions meaning to take a drink of liquor: *absorb, alcoholize, alki up, bang a pitcher, barrel, bash the turps, beer, beezzle, belt, belt down, belt the grape, bend, bend one's elbow, bend the elbow, bevie, bevvy, bezzle, bibble, binge, bite into the brute, bite one's name in, bite the brute, blink, booze, booze it, booze it up, boozify, bottle, bowse, bub, bubb, budge, bust some suds, cant, catch a hit, chain drink, cham, cheer the belly, commune with the spirits, cop a head, cop a reeler, cop the* *brewery, cop the elephant, crook the elbow, cut one's leg, cut the dust, damp, damp one's mug, do a beer, do a drain, do a drink, do a smile, do a wet, do some stewing, down, down one, dram, draw a blank, drench the gizzard, drink, drink like a fish, drown one's sorrows, drown one's troubles, fire a slug, fire up, flicker, flood one's sewers, flusterate, flusticate, fly high, fuddle, gargle, gas, get a bun on, get a can on, get a jag on, get cannon, get canon, get on a jag, get one's biler loaded, get one's gage up, get one's tank filled, get there, go on the cousin sis, go over the cognac trail, go see a man about a dog, go talk to Herbie and Al, grog, grog on, gusto, guzzle, guzzle the grape, hang a few on, hang on a few, hang one on, have a run, have a toot, have one for the worms, hit the hot bozel, hit the jug, hit the pot, hoist one, horn, hunt a tavern fox, indulge, irrigate, jug, jug up, juice, juice back, kiss the babe, knock back a drink, knock down, knock over, lage, lay the dust, lift one's elbow, likker up, liquor, lower, lower a drink, lower liquor, lubricate, lug, lush up, moisten, moisten one's chafer, moisten one's clay, mop up, oil one's whistle, oil one's wig, oil the wig, pack, paddle, paint, peg, play the Greek, pong, pound a beer, puddle, pull, pull jive, raise one's elbow, rinse, scupper up, see a man, see a man about a dog, shanty, shed a tear, shicker, shift, sink, siphon, six-pack, skimish, slam some beers, slop up, slosh, sluice, sluice one's bolt, sluice one's dominoes, sluice one's gob, sluice the worries, slum, slush up, smile, soak, sop, splice the main brace, stoll, stozzle, suck, suck suds, suck up, swizzle, tap the admiral, tickle one's innards, tiff, tip, tip off, tip one, tip one's elbow, tipple, tip the finger, tip the little finger, toss, wash one's ivories, wattle, wet, wet an eye, wet one's eye, wet one's goozle, wet one's neck, wet one's throat, wet one's throttle, wet one's whistle, whip, wipe one's eye.*

irrigated alcohol intoxicated. *Cf. irrigate.* RT: *drunk.* [U.S., BVB: 1942]

Irvine (also **Irv**) the police; a policeman. *Cf. Ervine.* RT: *fuzz.* [U.S., EEL: 1971, EAF: 1980]

isda heroin. Origin unknown. Possibly Pig Latin. RT: *heroin.* [U.S., SNP: 1977]

ishkimmisk alcohol intoxicated. From Shelta, a tinker's jargon. RT: *drunk.* [17-1900s, B&L: 1890, DSUE]

isomerizer a device used to increase the potency of marijuana. *Cf. icer.* [U.S., (D&B: 1978), JWK: 1981]

Is you anywhere? "Do you have drugs for sale?" See *Are you anywhere?* [U.S., M&W: 1946]

it Italian vermouth in *gin and it* (*q.v.*). RT: *wine.* [Br., 1900s, (DSUE)]

itchy habituated to the drinking of *Terpin Hydrate* (TM; *q.v.*) cough medicine. *Cf. schoolboy.* [U.S., ADC: 1981]

items drugs; portions of a drug. RS: *dose.* [U.S., NAM: 1953]

It is a dark day with him. (also **It is star-light with him.**) "He is drunk." RS: *drunk.* [BF: 1737]

I.V. intravenous; having to do with an intravenous injection of drugs. *Cf.* *I.M.* [medical, 1900s; drug culture use, EEL: 1971, RDS: 1982]

ixey morphine. Origin unknown. RT: *morphine.* [U.S., RDS: 1982]

J

J. (also **jay**) a marijuana cigarette; marijuana. From the initial letter of *joint*. RT: *joint*. [U.S., RRL: 1969, D&B: 1970c, DCCU: 1972, ADC: 1975, W&F: 1975, DNE: 1980, EAF: 1980, ADC: 1981, JWK: 1981] See also *J-smoke*.

jab 1. (also **jab a vein**) to inject drugs. See comment at *jab artist*. RT: *shoot*. [(1926): OEDS, DWM: 1938, RRL: 1969] 2. an injection of drugs. RT: *shot*. [(1914): OEDS, GI: 1931, M&V: 1954]

jab artist an addict who takes drugs by injection as opposed to one who smokes or takes pills. This may also apply to addicts who must jab around (in places other than the arm) in order to find a suitable vein. This may also imply either skill or incompetence at finding veins by jabbing. RT: *bangster*. This is also a term for a tatoo artist (D&D: 1957). [U.S., M&V: 1967, H&C: 1975]

jabber 1. a hypodermic needle; a hypodermic needle and syringe. RT: *monkey pump*. Probably recurrent nonce. [U.S., (1918): W&F: 1960, HS: 1933, VJM: 1949] 2. (also **jab-popper**) an addict who injects drugs; an addict who must jab around to find a vein. RT: *bangster*. [U.S., DWM: 1938, GOL: 1950]

jab job an injection of narcotics. RT: *shot*. [U.S., JES: 1959, H&C: 1975]

jab joint a place to buy and use drugs. *Cf. rifle range, shooting gallery*. RS: *doperie*. [U.S., BVB: 1942, JES: 1959]

jab-off an injection of drugs and the rush which follows. RS: *rush*. [U.S., DWM: 1933, DWM: 1938, GOL: 1950, D&D: 1957, W&F: 1960]

jab-pop (also **jab-poppo**) a dose of drugs to be injected; an injection of drugs. *Cf. jab*. Compare to *job-pop*. BD: 1937 actually lists japbopp. The *pop* may refer to the rush. RT: *shot*. [U.S., (BD: 1937), DWM: 1938, BVB: 1942]

jab-popper an addict who injects drugs. RT: *bangster*. [U.S., H&C: 1975]

jab stick a hypodermic syringe and needle. *Cf. jabber*. RT: *monkey pump*. [U.S., JES: 1959, H&C: 1975]

JacAroma (also Aroma) a brand of ***butyl nitrite*** (*q.v.*) room deodorizer. This product is sniffed for a high. See ***butyl nitrite***. *Cf.* ***Locker Room***. [U.S., YKB: 1977]

jack 1. tobacco for rolling cigarettes. RT: ***freckles***. Jack = money. Tobacco serves as money in prisons. [U.S., HS: 1933, GOL: 1950, W&F: 1960] 2. methyl alcohol, denatured alcohol. *Cf.* ***jake***. RS: ***methyl***. [Br., (1930): DSUE] 3. heroin; 1/16 gram of heroin; a heroin tablet. Possibly rhyming slang: Jack and Jill = pill. RS: ***load***. [Br. and U.S., (1967): OEDS, BTD: 1968, S&W: 1973, M&J: 1975] 4. (also jack a fix) to inject and withdraw a small amount of a drug (and blood) repeatedly. This prolongs the ***rush*** (*q.v.*). From ***jack off*** (*q.v.*). See ***boot***. [U.S., M&V: 1967, EEL: 1971, MA: 1973]

jack-a-dandy (also Jack Dandy) brandy. RT: ***brandy***. Primarily British rhyming slang. [Br., DA: 1857, F&H, JRW: 1909, DRS; U.S., M&B: 1944]

jack a fix See ***jack***.

jackal a narcotics agent disguised as a buyer of drugs. GEN: a low and sneaky person. *Cf.* ***deadwood***. JES: 1959, the probable source for this entry, lists "to jackal[:] for a narcotics agent to buy drugs undercover." RS: ***fuzz***. [U.S., H&C: 1975]

jack and wrappers tobacco and cigarette rolling papers. RT: ***freckles, paper***. See ***jack, wrapper***.

jackass (also jackass brandy) raw corn whiskey; any strong whiskey. Named (like ***mule*** *q.v.*) for its kick. RS: ***rotgut***. [U.S., BHL: 1920, MHW: 1934, BVB: 1942]

Jack Dandy See ***jack-a-dandy***.

jacked up 1. having to do with an addict who needs drugs. [U.S., JES: 1959, H&C: 1975] 2. high on drugs, including cannabis; under the effects of amphetamines; overdosed with amphetamines. GEN: excited. RS: ***stoned***. [U.S., AJP: 1935, EEL: 1971] 3. arrested. RT: ***busted***. [U.S., JBW: 1967, IGA: 1971]

jacket 1. material used to seal a hypodermic needle onto a medicine dropper. RT: ***gasket***. [U.S., M&V: 1967, H&C: 1975] 2. (also jackets) a ***Nembutal*** (TM; *q.v.*) barbiturate capsule. Refers to yellow capsules and is a truncation of ***yellow jackets*** (*q.v.*). RT: ***nemb***. [U.S., M&D: 1952]

jackey gin. See ***jacky***.

jack off (also jack, jerk off) to ***boot*** (*q.v.*); to manipulate drug injection equipment so that the drug enters the blood stream slowly, thereby prolonging the rush. From a slang term meaning to masturbate. [U.S., M&V: 1967, RRL: 1969, M&V: 1973]

jack off shot an injection of drugs where the ***rush*** (*q.v.*) is deliberately prolonged. See ***jack off***.

Jack Surpass a glass of liquor. Rhyming slang for *glass*. [Br., mid 1800s, DRS]

Jack Tar a pub or saloon. Rhyming slang for *bar* (*q.v.*). [Br., early 1900s, DRS]

jack up to inject a drug. RT: *shoot*. [U.S., W&F: 1975]

jack-ups capsules of *Amytal* (TM; *q.v.*) barbiturate. Possibly as a bracer or temporary drug *fix* (*q.v.*). RS: *barbs*. *Cf. eye-opener, get-up, go-pills, lift pills*. [U.S., M&V: 1967, SNP: 1977]

jacky (also **jackey**) gin. RT: *gin*. [Br., FG: 1811, F&H]

jag 1. a drinking bout. RT: *spree*. [primarily U.S., (1887): RML: 1950, (1895): OEDS, BVB: 1942, SSD, B&P: 1965, DCCU: 1972] 2. a party where drugs are used. [U.S., BVB: 1942] 3. a load of drink; a state of alcohol or drug intoxication; later, a prolonged state of drug intoxication. [(1678): OEDS; U.S., BVB: 1942, RRL: 1969, EEL: 1971; Br., BTD: 1968] See also *benny jag*. **4**. a drinker or a drunkard. RT: *sot*. [U.S., F&H, BVB: 1942, W&F: 1960] 5. a dose of drugs; an inhalation or injection of drugs. RS: *dose*. [Aust. and Br., (1945): DSUE, BTD: 1968] 6. a drug rush; a drug kick. RT: *rush*. [U.S., (1928): ELA: 1982, H&C: 1975] 7. a drug habit. RT: *habit*. [U.S., RDS: 1982]

jagged (also **jagged up**) intoxicated with drugs or alcohol. (BF: 1737: [He's] Jagg'd - referring only to alcohol.) RT: *drunk, stoned*. Originally referred to alcohol intoxication. Refers to drug intoxication since c. 1900. [U.S., BF: 1737, F&H, (1904): OEDS, BVB: 1942, A&T: 1953, AP: 1980]

jag, on a alcohol intoxicated. *Cf. jag*. GEN: on any drug. RT: *drunk*. [U.S., MP: 1928, MHW: 1934]

jag party a group of addicts gathered to use drugs. *Cf. jag*. [mid 1900s, DU]

jagster a person on a spree; a heavy drinker. RS: *sot*. [U.S., BVB: 1942]

jahooby marijuana. RT: *pot*. [U.S., (1956): ELA: 1982]

jail an overdose of drugs. *Cf. jam, O.D.* [U.S., H&C: 1975]

jail house high a high from drinking an infusion of nutmeg or mace. *Cf. buck, idiot juice*. Prison use. [U.S., C&H: 1974]

jake 1. (also **jakey, jamake**) Jamaica ginger extract. See *ginger beer*. [U.S., CS: 1927, DWM: 1931, GI: 1931] 2. liquor made from Jamaica ginger; denatured alcohol and Jamaica ginger. RS: *methyl*. [(1926): OEDS, (1932): OEDS] 3. illegal liquor. RS: *moonshine*. From the prohibition era. [U.S., AH: 1931, MHW: 1934]

jake-drinker (also **jake-wallah**) an alcoholic addicted to wood alcohol. Jake = dung. *Wallah* (*q.v.*) = merchant. *Cf. feke-drinker*. RS: *sot*. [Br., early 1900s, DSUE]

jake hound a drinker of *jake* (*q.v.*). *Cf. booze hound, gashound, gin hound, grog hound, hooch hound, lush hound, rum hound, rummy hound*. RS: *sot*. [U.S., AH: 1931, MHW: 1934]

jake-leg a physical disability afflicting men addicted to *jake* (*q.v.*). [U.S., (1933): DA, D&D: 1957]

jaloney bogus narcotics. Probably a portmanteau of *junk* and *baloney*. RS: *blank*. [U.S., M&V: 1967]

jam 1. cocaine. Because it gets you in a jam. *Cf. C-jam, jam Cecil.* [U.S., RRL: 1969, NIDA: 1980, RAS: 1981, ADC: 1984] 2. an overdose of drugs. Possibly from *in a jam*. *Cf. jammed up.* [U.S., DWM: 1936, M&V: 1973] See also *jams*. 3. amphetamines. This may be the original form of *C-jam* (*q.v.*) being *cocaine jam*, and *jam* (sense one) being a truncation of *C-jam*. RT: *amps*. [U.S., A&T: 1953, SNP: 1977] See also *goblet of jam*.

Jamaican (also **Jamaica ganga, Jamaica gold**) a potent marijuana grown in Jamaica. RT: *pot*. [U.S., (1974): ELA: 1982, ADC: 1975, RDS: 1982]

Jamaican red a reddish-brown marijuana said to be from Jamaica. RT: *pot*. [U.S., EAF: 1980]

jamake See *jake*.

jambled alcohol intoxicated. RT: *drunk*. [BF: 1737]

jamboree a drinking bout; a *spree* (*q.v.*). GEN: any relatively informal celebration. An Australian version is **jamberoo**. [U.S., (1872): OED, BVB: 1942]

jam Cecil 1. cocaine. *Cf. Cecil, C-jam, jam.* See *jam*. RT: *cocaine*. [U.S., H&C: 1975] 2. amphetamines. See *jam*. RT: *amps*. [U.S., SNP: 1977] See also *goblet of jam*.

jam gorg an error for *jam grog* (*q.v.*) [U.S., SNP: 1977]

jam grog powdered drugs; powdered narcotics. Because it gets one in a jam. *Cf. dry grog*. RT: *powder*. [U.S., JES: 1959, H&C: 1975]

jammed 1. arrested. GEN: in trouble. RT: *busted*. [U.S., JWK: 1981] 2. alcohol intoxicated. *Cf. jams*. RT: *drunk*. [U.S., HJS: 1922, BVB: 1942]

jammed up having taken an overdose of drugs. *Cf. jam*. [U.S., M&V: 1967, RRL: 1969]

jams the delirium tremens. From *jim-jams*. *Cf. jammed*. RT: *D.T.s*. [U.S., JSF: 1889]

Jane marijuana. From the *juana* of *marijuana*. RT: *pot*. [U.S., DCCU: 1972]

Jane's better half a marijuana smoker. *Cf. Jane*. RT: *toker*. [U.S., JES: 1959, H&C: 1975]

jango liquor; booze. RT: *booze*. [(1721): F&H]

Japanese dogs whiskey. a code name used where liquor was locally prohibited. RT: *whiskey*. [U.S., JRW: 1909] See also *Chinese needlework*.

japbopp an error for *jab-pop* (*q.v.*). [BD: 1937]

jar a large quantity of pills. RS: *load*. [U.S., EEL: 1971, EAF: 1980]

jar dealer the same as *bottle dealer* (*q.v.*). [U.S., IGA: 1971]

jay a marijuana cigarette; marijuana; a *J.* (*q.v.*). From the initial letter of *joint*. RT: *joint*. [U.S., (1968): ELA: 1982, IGA: 1971, D&B: 1971, ADC: 1975, (1976): DNE: 1980]

jay-pipe See *J-pipe*.

jay smoke a marijuana cigarette. *Cf. J., jay*. RT: *joint*. [U.S., RRL: 1969, W&F: 1975]

jazz heroin. RT: *heroin*. Identified as Canadian. [ADC: 1975]

jazzed 1. (also **jazzed up**) alcohol intoxicated. RT: *drunk*. [U.S., MHW: 1934, W&F: 1960] 2. drug intoxicated; wrecked. LIT: *fucked* (*q.v.*). From the original sense of the word *to copulate with a woman* (said of a man). RT: *stoned*. [U.S., EEL: 1971]

J.C.L. a new drug addict. The initials of *Johnnie-come-lately* (*q.v.*). A special use of an old hobo and carnival term for a newcomer, c. 1900. RS: *junky*. [U.S., M&V: 1967]

J.D. "Jack Daniels" (TM) whiskey. RS: *whiskey*. [U.S., ADC: 1981]

J. Edgar Hoover (also **J. Edgar**) the police; federal officers. RT: *fuzz*. Black use. [U.S., EAF: 1980]

jeegee (also **jee gee**) heroin. See *jojee*. [U.S., IGA: 1971, WCM: 1972]

jeep (also **geep**) packing for a hypodermic needle. See *gee rag*. [U.S., M&V: 1967, D&B: 1970c]

jefferson airplane match used to hold the butt of a marijuana cigarette while smoking it. RT: *crutch*. [U.S., (1967): ELA: 1982, EEL: 1971, DCCU: 1972, ADC: 1975] 2. to sniff (snort) marijuana cigarette smoke or a powdered drug such as cocaine. RS: *snort*. [U.S., D&B: 1970c, EEL: 1971]

jell a bad dose of heroin which gels rather than dissolves when heated in water. Possibly from *Jello* (TM). A verb form is not recorded. RS: *blank*. [U.S., JWK: 1981]

jelly beans (also **jelly babies**) 1. amphetamine tablets or capsules. RT: *amps*. [U.S., EEL: 1971, YKB: 1977] 2. capsules of chloral hydrate. RS: *Mickey Finn*. [U.S., SNP: 1977]

jerez seco* marijuana. LIT: dry sherry. *Cf. dry grog*. Spanish (calo). [JBR: 1973]

jerker 1. a drunkard; an alcoholic. From jerky movements as with the D.T.s or from repeatedly jerking a glass to the mouth. *Cf. jerks*. RT: *sot*. [Br., 1800s, DSUE] 2. a heavy user of cocaine; someone under the effects of a large dose of cocaine. The same as *leaper* (*q.v.*). RT: *kokomo*. [U.S., M&V: 1967, H&C: 1975]

jerk off to *boot* (*q.v.*). See *jack off*.

jerks the delirium tremens. RT: *D.T.s*. [Br., 1800s, F&H]

Jersey green marijuana presumably grown in New Jersey. *Cf. green*. RT: *pot*. [U.S., W&F: 1967, EEL: 1971, DCCU: 1972]

Jersey hemp a poor grade of marijuana, presumably from New Jersey. *Cf. hemp*. RS: *pot*. [U.S., JH: 1979]

Jersey lightning 1. gin. RT: *gin*. [U.S., (1827): DU] 2. apple brandy. RS: *brandy*. [U.S., (1780): SBF: 1982, (1852): DA, JSF: 1889, B&L: 1890] 3. strong liquor; inferior liquor. RS: *rotgut*. [U.S., BVB: 1942, VJM: 1949]

jesca* marijuana. The same as *yesca* (*q.v.*). RT: *pot*. [U.S., JWK: 1981]

jet *ketamine* (*q.v.*) hydrochloride, a hallucinogenic drug like L.S.D. [U.S., ELA: 1984]

jet fuel phencyclidine, P.C.P. RT: *P.C.P.* [U.S., ELA: 1984]

jickhead a drunkard. RT: *sot*. Black slang. [U.S., CM: 1970]

jigger 1. whiskey; a drink of whiskey. RS: *nip*. [U.S., (1882): RHT: 1912, OED; listed in BVB: 1942] 2. a device for measuring out 1 and 1/2 ounces of liquor. Standard English. There is no other term for this device. Probably from an old (1800s) term for a gadget. 3. a cigarette. RT: *nail*. [U.S., BVB: 1942]

jigger boy someone who sells and serves liquor at a bar. *Cf. jigger*. [U.S., BVB: 1942]

jiggered alcohol intoxicated. Akin to *jigger*. RT: *drunk*. [U.S., AH: 1931, MHW: 1934]

jig-juice (also **jig-water**) whiskey; inferior liquor. *Cf. nigger pot*. RS: *rotgut, whiskey*. [U.S., JSF: 1889, MHW: 1934]

jim-jams (also **jams**) the delirium tremens; a hangover. GEN: a nervous fit; the blues. RT: *D.T.s*. [primarily U.S., (1852): SBF: 1976, JSF: 1889, BWG: 1899, LWP: 1908, D&D: 1957, DCCU: 1972]

Jim Johnson equipment for preparing and injecting drugs. An elaboration of the slang term johnson = thing, gadget. RT: *outfit*. [U.S., EEL: 1971]

jimmies the delirium tremens. *Cf. jams, jim-jams*. GEN: a case of nerves. The Australian attestation is probably from *Jimmy Britts* = fits. RT: *D.T.s*. [(1900): OEDS, LWP: 1908, (1941): GAW: 1978, D&D: 1957]

jimmy 1. an illegal saloon. RT: *sly grogshop*. [U.S., MHW: 1934] 2. a subcutaneous injection of narcotics. RT: *shot*. [U.S., M&D: 1952] See also *Jim Johnson*.

jimson weed *Datura stramonium*. See *Datura*. A common plant containing hallucinogenic substances. [U.S., EEL: 1971, YKB: 1977]

jingle 1. a buzz or tingle from alcohol. In Jack London's *John Barleycorn*. [U.S., late 18–1900s] 2. a drinking bout. In Jack London's *John Barleycorn*. RT: *spree*. [U.S., late 18–1900s]

jingled alcohol intoxicated. *Cf. jingle.* RT: *drunk.* [U.S., (1908): OEDS, DSUE, (WWI): W&F: 1960, AH: 1931, MHW: 1934, D&D: 1957]

jingler a drunkard; an alcoholic; a person who gets *jingled* (*q.v.*) frequently. *Cf. jingle.* RT: *sot.* [U.S., RDS: 1982]

jingo marijuana. Origin unknown. RT: *pot.* [U.S., (1968): ELA: 1982, RDS: 1982]

jinny 1. synthetic gin; gin. RS: *gin.* From the prohibition era. [U.S., early 1900s, DU] 2. a speakeasy. *Cf. jimmy.* RT: *speak.* [U.S., HNR: 1934, BVB: 1942]

jive marijuana; a marijuana cigarette. GEN: deception. RT: *pot.* [U.S., (1938): OEDS, VJM: 1949, M&D: 1952, A&T: 1953, W&F: 1960, TRG: 1968, EEL: 1971, D&B: 1978]

jivestick (also **gyvestick**) a marijuana cigarette. *Cf. jive.* RT: *joint.* [U.S., (1945): DUS, HB: 1955, EEL: 1971, W&F: 1975]

job 1. a drunkard. RT: *sot.* [Aust., (1939): DSUE, SJB: 1943] 2. an injection of drugs; a batch of drugs. *Cf. jab.* RT: *shot.* [Br., and U.S., BTD: 1968, EEL: 1971, S&W: 1973] 3. to inject a drug. Possibly akin to *jab* (*q.v.*). RT: *shoot.* [U.S., JBW: 1967, JTD: 1971]

jober as a sudge sober. A deliberate spoonerism on *sober as a judge* (*q.v.*). *Cf. bone dry, cold sober, cracker dry, detoxed, dry, dry as a bone.* RT: *sober.* [U.S., 1900s, RAS]

Jobes a hypodermic syringe. See *Job's antidote.* RT: *monkey pump.* [U.S., H&C: 1975]

job off 1. an injection of drugs. The same as *jab-off. Cf. job.* RT: *shot.* [U.S., EEL: 1971] 2. a rush from an injection of drugs. RT: *rush.* [U.S., EEL: 1971]

job-pop to inject drugs. *Cf. job.* Akin to *jab-pop.* RT: *shoot.* [U.S., W&F: 1960]

Job's antidote a hypodermic syringe. This may refer to the Jobes brand of hypodermic syringe or to the miseries of the Biblical Job. RT: *monkey pump.* [U.S., JES: 1959]

jockey (also **jocky**) an addictive drug. Because it rides you and controls you. *Cf. have a monkey on one's back.* [U.S., JES: 1959, H&C: 1975]

jocular 1. alcohol intoxicated. *Cf. glad, happy, merry.* RT: *drunk.* [BF: 1737] 2. high on marijuana. RT: *wasted.* [U.S., ELA: 1984]

jodido* sickness from drug use. From a Spanish word for *fucked.* [U.S., JBR: 1973, JWK: 1981]

Joe Blakes the delirium tremens. Rhyming slang for *shakes* (*q.v.*) or *snakes* (Partridge). RT: *D.T.s.* [Aust., (1910): DSUE]

Joe Roke tobacco smoke. Rhyming slang. [U.S., Chicago, (1928): DRS]

John Barleycorn (also Sir John Barleycorn) whiskey; booze; the personification of the evils of alcohol. The term was used often in the British and U.S. temperance movements. RS: *booze*. [(1620): OED, (1791): F&H, BWG: 1899, MHW: 1934, D&D: 1957]

John Hall (also Jon Hall) alcohol; liquor; a personification of alcohol. *Cf. Al K. Hall*. RT: *booze*. Hobo use. [U.S., MHW: 1934, BVB: 1942, W&F: 1960]

johnnie a drink of whiskey. Probably based on *John Barleycorn* (*q.v.*). RT: *nip*. [Br., JCH: 1887, F&H]

Johnnie-come-lately Someone new to drug use or addiction. See *J.C.L.* [U.S., (M&W: 1946)]

Johnny-be-good a police officer. RT: *fuzz*. [U.S., EAF: 1980]

Johnny Law (also John Law) a police officer. RT: *fuzz*. [U.S., BVB: 1942, (M&W: 1946), GOL: 1950, D&D: 1957]

johnson marijuana; drugs; any contraband. An underworld term meaning thing. Compare to *jones*. *Cf. Johnson grass, Jim Johnson*. [U.S., D&B: 1970b, JWK: 1981]

Johnson grass (also johnson) marijuana; low-grade marijuana. Possibly an elaboration of *johnson* (*q.v.*) and the name of former president Lyndon B. Johnson. *Cf. Nixon*. RT: *pot*. [U.S., EEL: 1971, RRL: 1974, JWK: 1981]

joint 1. an opium smoker's equipment. RS: *outfit*. [U.S., DWM: 1936, BD: 1937, M&D: 1952] 2. an opium den. [U.S., (1883): OED, (1887): RML: 1948, VJM: 1949] 3. a saloon; a speakeasy (in the prohibition era). Now any low drinking establishment. RT: *speak*. [(1899): OED, HNR: 1934, BVB: 1942, DC: 1972] 4. equipment for preparing and injecting drugs especially the hypodermic syringe (or medicine dropper) and needle. This sense essentially means thing, the same as *johnson* (*q.v.*). RT: *outfit*. [U.S., DWM: 1938, VJM: 1949, M&D: 1952, W&F: 1960, JWK: 1981] 5. a tobacco cigarette. RT: *nail*. [U.S., BVB: 1942] 6. prison. General underworld slang used in reference to imprisonment for narcotics or other offenses. [U.S., RRL: 1969, JWK: 1981] 7. a capsule of heroin. RT: *heroin*. [U.S., JWK: 1981] 8. a *stash* (*q.v.*); concealed drugs and drug equipment. [U.S., H&C: 1975] 9. a marijuana cigarette; marijuana. *Cf. blast a joint*. RT: *joint*. General slang in the last decade. [Br. and U.S., (1945): DU, M&D: 1952, W&F: 1960, S&W: 1966, CM: 1970, EEL: 1971, M&J: 1975, EAF: 1980, JWK: 1981, BW: 1984] Nicknames and slang terms for a marijuana cigarette: *A-bomb, ace, African Woodbines, atom bomb, bammies, bammy, bams, bat, belt, bhang, blue sage, bomb, bomber, bone, boo, boo-reefer, brand X, breezer, broccoli, brown one, Buddha stick, burnie, butt, cancelled stick, cattail, cavite allstars, charge, chicarra, chicharra, cigar, cigarette, cigarette with no name, climb, cocktail, cripple, deuce, dinky dow, doobie, dooby, dope cigarette, doped cigarette, double-header, drag, dreamstick, dubbe, dubee, dubie, duby,* *dynamiter, earth, exposures, faggot, fat jay, fatty, firecracker, fraho, frajo, gage, gagebutt, gangster, gangster stick, gasper, gaugebutt, giggles, giggle smoke, gonga smudge, goober, good butt, good giggles, goofball, goof butt, goofy butt, grass reefer, greeta, greta, gungeon, gyve, gyvestick, happy cigarette, happy gas, happy sticks, hay butt, heavy joint, hooter, hop stick, hotstick, J., jay, jay smoke, jive, jivestick, joint, jointstick, jolt, jones, joy hemp, joy root, joy smoke, joystick, J-smoke, J-stick, juju, kaya, kickstick, killers, killersticks, kilters, ladyfinger, leño, loco, locoweed, log, loose joint, mari, Mary and Johnnie, meg, Megg, meggs, meserole, Mez, mezz, mezzroll, Mezz's roll, mig, miggles, mighty mezz, ming, moggles, moota, mootah, mooter, mootie, muggles, muta, mutah, mutha, nail, no brand cigarette, no name brand cigarette, number, off-brand cigarette, pack of rockets, panatela, panatella, Park Lane, Park Lane No. 2, pee-wee, pill, pin, pinhead, pin J., pin joint, pinner, rainy-day woman, reaper, reef, reefdogger, reefer, reefer weed, rocket, root, rope, sausage, seeds, sherm, sherman, skoofer, skoofus, skrufer, skrufus, slow boat, smoke, solid, spleef, spliff, splim, splint, sploff, stencil, stick, stick of gage, stick of T., stick of tea, stogie, submarine, tamale, tea bag, teastick, Thaistick, thing, thriller, thumb, thunder-cookie, Tijuana 12, toke, toothpick, tootsie roll, torch, torpedo, trigger, T-stick, tube, tuskee, twig, twist, twister, viper butt, weed, wee-wee, zol, zoll.*

join the stream to inject narcotics intravenously. RS: *shoot*. [U.S., JES: 1959, H&C: 1975]

joint-roller a cannabis smoker who rolls cigarettes made from the drug. Compared to a user who consumes cannabis in some other manner. RT: *toker*. [U.S., (D&B: 1978)]

jointstick a marijuana cigarette. *Cf. stick*. RT: *joint*. [U.S., SNP: 1977]

join up to become addicted to a drug. *Cf. cadet, convert, green hype, lame, lame hype, lane, shirt tail hype, student, undergrad.* [U.S., JES: 1959, H&C: 1975]

jojee (also **jeegee**) heroin. RT: *heroin*. [U.S., IGA: 1971, WCM: 1972]

joker 1. a speakeasy. RT: *speak*. [U.S., 1920s, MHW: 1934, BVB: 1942] 2. (also **joke**) an injection of morphine. RS: *shot*. [U.S., (1925): DU, A&T: 1953] 3. a hypodermic syringe. RT: *monkey pump*. [U.S., (1925): DU, A&T: 1953]

jollo a drinking party. Possibly short for jollification = *spree* (*q.v.*). [Aust., SJB: 1945]

jollop a drink of liquor; whiskey; strong liquor. Possibly akin to *dollop*; conceivably based on *jolly-up* (*q.v.*) or *julep*. RT: *whiskey*. [(1920): OEDS, SJB: 1943]

jolly happily tipsy; alcohol intoxicated. *Cf. gay, glad, happy, jocular, merry*. RS: *drunk*. Probably recurrent nonce. [(1652): OEDS, BF: 1737, F&H, BVB: 1942]

jolly beans amphetamine tablets or capsules. A play on *jelly beans* (*q.v.*). RT: *amps*. [U.S., EEL: 1971, SH: 1972, YKB: 1977]

jolly nose a man whose nose is red with excessive drinking; a drunkard. RT: *sot*. [Br., JCH: 1887]

jolly pop a dose or portion of heroin. RT: *dose*. [U.S., ELA: 1984]

jolly-up a drinking party; a drinking bout. RT: *spree*. [Br., early 1900s, DSUE]

jolt 1. a drink of strong liquor. RT: *nip*. [Aust. and U.S., (1904): OEDS, (1920): DSUE, (1920): W&F: 1960, GI: 1931, RDS: 1982] 2. the potency of the alcohol in liquor; the effect of potent alcohol. [U.S., BVB: 1942] 3. an injection of drugs; a measure of drugs. Obviously, this refers to the effect of the drug. RT: *shot*. [(1916): OEDS, BVB: 1942, VJM: 1949, A&T: 1953, M&V: 1954, W&F: 1960, TRG: 1968, EEL: 1971] 4. the *rush* (*q.v.*) from an injection of drugs. RT: *rush*. [U.S., DWM: 1936, M&D: 1952, W&F: 1960, TRG: 1968, EEL: 1971] 5. a dose of cocaine. RS: *dose*. [U.S., early 1900s, DU] 6. a marijuana cigarette. RT: *joint*. [U.S., W&F: 1960. HSD: 1984] 7. to inject drugs; to inject heroin. RT: *shoot*. [U.S., A&T: 1953, W&F: 1960, JH: 1979]

jones 1. a drug habit; drug addiction. From a term meaning thing. *Cf. johnson*. RT: *habit*. Extended (in narcotics argot) to refer to an intense interest in anything. [U.S., M&V: 1967, RRL: 1969, CM: 1970, EEL: 1971, (1972): DNE: 1980, MA: 1973, ADC: 1975, W&F: 1975, EAF: 1980] 2. to crave drugs; to suffer from drug need while beginning to withdraw. Attested as jonesing. [U.S., (ADC: 1975)] 3. a drug addict. RT: *junky*. [U.S., TRG: 1968, JWK: 1981] 4. narcotics, especially heroin; drugs in general. RT: *dope*. [U.S., (1970): DNE: 1980, MA: 1973, RDS: 1982] 5. a marijuana cigarette. RT: *joint*. Black slang. [U.S., EAF: 1980]

jones-man a male drug addict; a man with a heroin *habit* (*q.v.*). *Cf. jones*. [U.S., (1974): OEDS]

Jon Hall liquor. See *John Hall*.

jook house (also jook) a saloon; a brothel serving liquor. See *juke-joint*.

joss house an opium den. Based on the Pidgin English term for a Chinese temple. RT: *opium den*. [U.S., (1925): DU, GOL: 1950, D&D: 1957]

joy 1. the state of euphoria from drug use. This is the usual sense of the word in the context of drug use. [U.S., DU, A&T: 1953] 2. marijuana. RT: *pot*. Black slang. [U.S., EAF: 1980]

joy-boy a (male) drug addict. RT: *junky*. [U.S., early 1900s, DU]

joy dust 1. Vietnamese heroin. RS: *heroin*. [U.S., S&W: 1973] 2. cocaine. See *joy flakes*. RT: *cocaine*. [U.S., A&T: 1953, SNP: 1977]

joy flakes (also joy dust) powdered or crystallized cocaine; any powdered narcotic. RS: *powder*. [U.S., BVB: 1942, VJM: 1949, A&T: 1953]

joy-juice 1. a solution of chloral hydrate, knockout drops. *Cf. chlorals*. RT: *Mickey Finn*. [U.S., RRL: 1969, EEL: 1971] 2. liquor; wine; whiskey; beer. RT: *booze*. [U.S., (1940): CM: 1970, W&F: 1960, DC: 1972, GU: 1975] 3. liquid *amyl nitrite* (*q.v.*). RT: *snapper*. [U.S., BR: 1972]

joy pop 1. to inject heroin subcutaneously, occasionally. Applies to occasional users who avoid addiction. See *skin pop*. *Cf. chipper*. [U.S., JBW: 1967, M&V: 1967, RRL: 1969, ADC: 1975, W&F: 1975] 2. a subcutaneous injection of drugs. *Cf. chip*. [U.S., BVB: 1942, M&D: 1952, M&H: 1959, JH: 1979] 3. a bout of opium smoking. [U.S., early 1900s, DU]

joy popper (also **joy rider**) Someone who takes narcotics only occasionally; a non-addicted user; a *chipper* (*q.v.*). [U.S., VFN: 1933, MHW: 1934, DWM: 1936, GOL: 1950, M&D: 1952, D&D: 1957, W&F: 1960, TRG: 1968]

joy powder powdered drugs: cocaine, heroin, morphine. RS: *powder*. Some of the following citations are for specific powdered drugs. [U.S., WHW: 1922, GI: 1931, MHW: 1934, D&D: 1957, W&F: 1960, TRG: 1968, EEL: 1971]

joy prick an injection of drugs. *Cf. prick*. RT: *shot*. [U.S., JES: 1959, H&C: 1975]

joy ride 1. a drinking bout or party. RT: *spree*. [U.S., MHW: 1934] 2. a state of euphoria from drug use. [U.S., BVB: 1942, H&C: 1975]

joy rider an occasional user of drugs. See *joy popper*.

joy smoke (also **joy hemp**, **joy root**) marijuana; a marijuana cigarette. RT: *pot, joint*. [U.S., RPW: 1938, BVB: 1953, M&V: 1954, EEL: 1971]

joystick 1. an opium pipe. RT: *hop stick*. [U.S., (1910): DU, DWM: 1936] 2. a marijuana cigarette. RT: *joint*. [U.S., M&V: 1967, EEL: 1971] 3. a marijuana pipe. RS: *bong*. [U.S., AP: 1980]

joy water liquor; strong liquor. RT: *booze*. [U.S., VR: 1929, MHW: 1934, D&D: 1957]

joy weed marijuana. *Cf. weed*. RT: *pot*. [U.S., early 1900s, DU]

J-pipe (also **jay-pipe**) a pipe for smoking marijuana. *J.* (*q.v.*) = *joint* (*q.v.*). RS: *bong*. [U.S., M&V: 1973, RDS: 1982]

J-smoke (also **J-stick**) a marijuana cigarette. Based on *joint* (*q.v.*) or joy. *Cf. J*. RT: *joint*. [U.S., EEL: 1971, W&F: 1975]

juju marijuana. RT: *pot*. [U.S., ELA: 1984]

juane (also **juana**, **Juana**, **'juana**) marijuana. *Cf. Jane*. RT: *pot*. [U.S., (1934): W&F: 1960, EAF: 1980]

Juan Valdez* marijuana. Spanish. RT: *pot*. [U.S., ELA: 1984]

juanita (also **juanita weed**) marijuana. From Spanish for little John. RT: *pot*. [U.S., (1917): ELA: 1982, RPW: 1938, RRL: 1969]

jug 1. (also **the jug**) liquor; a container or jug of liquor, especially illicit liquor; a jug of *moonshine* (*q.v.*); wine. Akin to *little brown jug* (*q.v.*). [U.S., 1900s and probably earlier, DB: 1944, W&F: 1960] 2. a liquor container; a can of beer. [Br. military, (1930): DSUE] 3. (also **jug up**) to drink heavily. RT: *guzzle*. [Br. Royal Air Force, (1930): DSUE, EP: 1948; U.S., BVB: 1942] 4. (also **jugs**) a glass vial of *Methedrine* (*q.v.*). [U.S., M&V: 1967, EEL: 1971, NIDA: 1980] 5. the jugular vein used for an injection of narcotics. [U.S., JWK: 1981]

jug-bitten alcohol intoxicated. *Jug* (*q.v.*) = liquor. RT: *drunk*. [(1630): OED, F&H; listed in BVB: 1942]

jugged (also **jugged up**) alcohol intoxicated. *Jug* (*q.v.*) = to drink heavily. RT: *drunk*. From the prohibition era. [U.S., (1919): SBF: 1976, BVB: 1942]

jugger an alcoholic. RT: *sot*. [U.S., RDS: 1982]

juggler a drug addict who also sells drugs; a drug seller; a street drug dealer. RT: *dealer*. [U.S., P&C: 1969, RG: 1970, RDS: 1982]

jughead an alcoholic; a drunkard. From a general slang term for an oaf. *Jug* (*q.v.*) = liquor. RT: *sot*. [U.S., LP: 1971a, RDS: 1982]

jug-man (also **jug-broad**) an addict who has no remaining veins suitable for injection except the jugular vein. *Jug* (*q.v.*) = jugular vein. [U.S., JWK: 1981]

jug, on the having to do with an addict who is reduced to injecting into the jugular vein. *Cf. jug, jug-man*. [U.S., JWK: 1981]

jug-steamed alcohol intoxicated. *Jug* (*q.v.*) = liquor. *Cf. steamed up*. RT: *drunk*. [U.S., mid 1800s, W&F: 1960]

juice 1. liquor; whiskey. In drug usage, liquor as opposed to drugs. See *juice freak*. RT: *booze*. [U.S., LWP: 1908, (1920): SBF: 1982, MHW: 1934, M&W: 1946, W&F: 1960, RRL: 1969, CM: 1970, EEL: 1971, DCCU: 1972, DNE: 1973, MW: 1976] 2. (also **juice back**) to drink heavily. RT: *guzzle*. [U.S., M&W: 1946, D&B: 1970c, CM: 1970] 3. liquid amphetamine for injecting; drugs for injection. RS: *amps*. [U.S., HER: 1971, JWK: 1981] 4. wine; wine with marijuana. RS: *wine*. [U.S., SNP: 1977] 5. cough syrup containing codeine. *Cf. juice and beans*. [U.S., RAS: 1984] A number of other terms for drugs and alcohol are based on ***juice***. See *A-bomb juice, alley juice, balloon juice, bamboo juice, barley juice, bug juice, bumy juice, bung juice, cactus juice, caper juice, corn juice, giggle juice, idiot juice, jig-juice, joy-juice, jungle-juice, juniper-juice, panther juice, prune juice, rookus juice, scamper juice, snake juice, stagger juice,* *tarantula juice, tiger juice, tornado juice, torpedo juice, wolf juice.*

juice and beans a narcotic cough syrup taken with *Doriden* (TM; *q.v.*). Beans = pills. Typically about six ounces of syrup and three pills. [U.S., RAS: 1983]

juiced (also **juiced to the gills, juiced up**) alcohol intoxicated. *Cf. juice.* RT: *drunk.* [U.S., (1920): SBF: 1976, M&W: 1946, D&D: 1957, W&F: 1960, EEL: 1971, CM: 1970, DNE: 1973]

juice freak someone who prefers alcohol use to drug use; someone who uses alcohol to boost the effect of drugs. *Juice* (*q.v.*) = liquor. [U.S., D&B: 1971, M&V: 1973, GU: 1975]

juicehead a heavy drinker; a drunkard. RT: *sot.* [U.S., (1955): OEDS, W&F: 1967, (1967): DNE: 1973, RRL: 1969, CM: 1970, EEL: 1971, DCCU: 1972, MW: 1976]

juice house a liquor store. RT: *L.I.Q.* Black use. [U.S., EAF: 1980] See also *jickhead.*

juice-joint a saloon; a speakeasy. *Juice* (*q.v.*) = liquor. RT: *speak.* From the prohibition era. [U.S., (1927): OEDS, MHW: 1934, GOL: 1950, D&D: 1957, W&F: 1960, CM: 1970]

juice, on the drinking heavily; on a drinking bout. *Cf. juice.* RT: *spreeing.* [1900s, DSUE]

juicer 1. a person who habitually chews tobacco. From the tobacco spittle, i.e., juice. [U.S., (archaic): W&F: 1960] 2. a heavy drinker; a drunkard. *Juice* (*q.v.*) = to drink heavily. RT: *sot.* [U.S., (1967): DNE: 1973, RDS: 1982]

juicery a bar; a place to buy liquor. RT: *bar.* [U.S., (1853): DA]

juicy alcohol intoxicated. *Juice* (*q.v.*) = liquor. RT: *drunk.* [BF: 1737]

juju 1. marijuana; a marijuana cigarette. Possibly from *juane* (*q.v.*). RT: *pot.* [U.S., (1940): W&F: 1960, A&T: 1953] 2. (also **ju-ju**) a cap of *Seconal* (TM; *q.v.*); a capsule or tablet of any drug. RT: *sec.* [U.S., EAF: 1980]

juke-joint a low saloon; a saloon and brothel combined. The same as *jook house* (*q.v.*). RS: *dive.* [U.S., GOL: 1950]

jumbo's trunk alcohol intoxicated. Rhyming slang for *drunk.* A synonym of *elephant's trunk.* RT: *drunk.* [Br., late 1800s, DRS]

jumps (also **the jumps**) the delirium tremens. GEN: nervousness. RT: *D.T.s.* [(1879): F&H, MHW: 1934, D&D: 1957]

jump-steady a glass of gin; a drink to stave off alcohol withdrawal symptoms. See *jumps. Cf. bracer, reposer, settler.* RS: *nip.* [U.S., GOL: 1950, EAF: 1980]

jumpy Stevie a person who is jumpy from the use of cocaine. See *stevie.* RS: *kokomo.* [U.S., M&V: 1967] See also *old Steve, Steve's mission.*

jungled alcohol intoxicated; affected by *jungle-juice* (*q.v.*). Possibly a play on or an error for *jingled* (*q.v.*) = drunk. RT: *drunk.*

[U.S., MHW: 1934]

jungle drug a form of *yage* (*q.v.*). [U.S., RRL: 1969, YKB: 1977]

jungle-juice 1. African rum. RT: *rum*. [Br., (1920): DSUE] 2. any homemade liquor made from materials at hand such as raisins, potatoes, fruit, coconuts, and various forms of alcohol; any strong liquor. *Cf. buck*. RS: *moonshine*. Said to have originated in New Zealand or the jungles of the Pacific. [WWII, (1939): DSUE, SJB: 1945, DWH: 1947, EP: 1948, D&D: 1957, W&F: 1960]

juniper gin. See *juniper-juice*. RT: *gin*. [Br., JB: 1823, JCH: 1887, F&H]

juniper-juice 1. gin. From the use of juniper berries to flavor gin. RT: *gin*. [U.S., VR: 1929, MHW: 1934, D&D: 1957, W&F: 1960] 2. strong alcohol; illicit alcohol. RS: *moonshine*. From the prohibition era. [U.S., BVB: 1942]

junk 1. liquor; inferior liquor. RT: *booze*. [U.S., BVB: 1942] 2. hard drugs; addictive drugs; heroin; any kind of drugs. Has been used at various times for *Demerol* (TM; *q.v.*), *Dilaudid* (TM; *q.v.*), heroin, opium, and morphine. It is frequently used to refer to any drug which is injected. Possibly akin to the Chinese sailing boat of the same name, hinting at (Chinese) opium and opium use. *Cf. on the junk*. The word is widely known outside the underworld and drug culture. [U.S., (1925): OEDS, EK: 1927, GI: 1931, GM: 1931, DWM: 1933, HS: 1933, DWM: 1936, (1945): DSUE, GOL: 1950, D&D: 1957, W&F: 1960, BTD: 1968, RRL: 1969, D&B: 1970c, CM: 1970, EEL: 1971, DCCU: 1972, ADC: 1975, NIDA: 1980, ADC: 1981]

junk connection someone who knows how and where to get drugs. *Junk* (*q.v.*) = any kind of drugs. *Cf. connection*. [U.S., GOL: 1950]

junk dealer (also **junk man**, **junk peddler**) a drug seller; a seller of morphine and cocaine. A reinterpretation of the term for someone who deals in junk (unwanted articles). RS: *dealer*. [U.S., (1925): DU, GI: 1931, BVB: 1942]

junked (also **junked up**) drug intoxicated; drug addicted. *Junk* (*q.v.*) = drugs. RT: *stoned*. [U.S., BVB: 1942, W&F: 1967, DCCU: 1972]

junker 1. a drug addict. See *junky*. [U.S., (1922): OEDS, DWM: 1931, GI: 1931, DWM: 1933, MHW: 1934, DWM: 1936, D&D: 1957, W&F: 1975] 2. a drug seller. RT: *dealer*. [U.S., (1930): OEDS, RRL: 1969, EEL: 1971]

junker man a marijuana smoker. RT: *toker*. [U.S., (1945): ELA: 1982]

junk graft narcotics traffic. Graft = *hustle* (*q.v.*). [U.S., BVB: 1942, JES: 1959]

junk hound (also **junk hog**) a drug user or addict; an addict with a big drug appetite. RT: *junky*. [U.S., (c. 1910): JES: 1959, GI:

1931, DWM: 1938, MHW: 1934, VJM: 1949, D&D: 1957, M&H: 1959]

junkie See *junky*.

junkie pro a prostitute who is addicted to drugs or who sells drugs. Pro = prostitute. RS: *junky*. [U.S., RDS: 1982]

junk, on the addicted to opium; addicted to any narcotic. Possibly akin the Chinese sailing boat of the same name. *Cf. junk*. RT: *hooked*. [U.S., BVB: 1942, GOL: 1950, D&D: 1957, W&F: 1960]

junk peddler (also junk man) a dope dealer. See *junk dealer*. RT: *dealer*. [U.S., GI: 1931, BVB: 1942]

junk pusher a dope seller who promotes his product and seeks to get people addicted. See *pusher*. *Cf. missionary*. [U.S., DU, D&D: 1957, RDS: 1982]

junk simple crazy due to drug intoxication. [U.S., BD: 1937]

junk squad police who enforce the narcotics laws. RS: *fuzz*. [U.S., D&D: 1957]

junk tank a jail cell where addicts are kept. Based on *drunk tank*, the name of the cell where drunks are kept. [U.S., EEL: 1971, RDS: 1982]

junky (also junker, junkey, junkie) 1. a drug seller. RT: *dealer*. Probably older than 1951. [(1951): OEDS] 2. a drug addict. [U.S., (1923): OEDS, GM: 1931, MHW: 1934, BD: 1937, M&D: 1952, D&D: 1957, W&F: 1960, RRL: 1969, D&B: 1970c, CM: 1970, EEL: 1971, DCCU: 1972, MA: 1973, PW: 1974, ADC: 1975, ADC: 1981] Nicknames and slang terms for a person addicted to a drug: *A.D., Add., addict, ad-it, Arctic explorer, attic, backdoor artist, bamboo, bangster, barber's cat, beat artist, bindle bum, Bindle Kate, bindle stiff, birdcage hype, birdhouse hype, black smoker, boomer, boost and shoot, booster, booster shooter, boot and shoe, boot and shoe dope fiend, boot and shoer, booter, boots and shoes, booze fighter, bowler, broker, bull dip, burn artist, cadet, campfire boy, carpet walker, cattle-rustler, champ, channel swimmer, Charlie, Charlie Coke, chronic, cokeaholic, cokomo, convert, cooker, cookie, cotton catcher, cottonhead, cotton picker, cotton shooter, crock, cross-country hype, D.A., dip, dodo, dool, dope addict, dope fiend, dope fighter, dopehead, dope hop, dopenik, doper, dopester, dopster, dreamer, drug partisan, drugstore man, dugout, dynamiter, eater, feeblo, fiend, flier, flunky, flyer, forty-niner, frog, galhead, gapper, garbage freak, garbagehead, gargoyle, geehead, geezy addict, ghost, glass eyes, globetrotter, glooch, gold duster, golden duster, gong beater, gonger, gowhead, gowster, greasy junkie, greasy junky, greefo, green hype, grocery boy, gutter, gutter hype, gutter junky, habit smoker, H-addict, hard-liner, head, hip-layer, hitter, hog, hoosier, hoosier fiend, hop, hop dog, hop fiend, hophead, hop hog, hop merchant, hopper, hoppie, hoppy, hopster, hop stiff, H-user, hygelo, hype, hypo, hypo juggler, hypo smecker, impaired physician, jab artist, jabber,* *jab-popper, J.C.L., jones, jones-man, joy-boy, jug-broad, juggler, jug-man, junker, junk hog, junk hound, junkie, junkie pro, junky, kokomo, Kokomo Joe, leaper, leech, lifer, lighter, low rider, maggot, mainliner, mainline shooter, medical addict, medical hype, Miss Emma, mojo, monkey, monkey-meat, mooch, moocher, morfiend, mud wiggler, M-user, narco, needle fiend, needle freak, needle jabber, needle knight, needle man, needle nipper, needle pusher, oil-burner, oiler, opium kipper, panic man, panic woman, pasty face, pill-cooker, pinhead, pipe, pipe fiend, pipe-hitter, pipes, pipe-smoker, pipey, pipie, poison people, poppyhead, poppy-puffer, pricked-arm, prodder, puff, puffer, pug, racehorse Charley, railroader, R.F.D., R.F.D. dopehead, R.F.D. gowster, R.F.D. junker, roller, safety pin mechanic, schmecker, schnozzler, scratcher, sharp shooter, shirt tail hype, shithead, shmecker, shooter, slag, slave, sleepwalker, slim, smackhead, smeaker, smecker, smokey, spook, station worker, stone addict, straight shooter, street addict, streeter, student, syrup head, takeoff artist, tecate, tecato, thin hips, three-tapper, twitcher, under-the-influencer, vegetable, vein-shooter, V.S., wallbanger, witch hazel man, yen-chee-quay, yen-shee boy, yen-shee-kwoi, yen-shee-quay, yen-shee-quoy, zombie.*

just what the doctor ordered a drink of liquor; a catch phrase said upon seeing, receiving, or drinking liquor. GEN: just what is needed. RT: *nip*. [1900s, DSUE]

juvies a police officer concerned with juveniles. Not limited to drug argot. RS: *fuzz*. [U.S., TRG: 1968, RG: 1970]

K

K. 1. a kilo of marijuana. *Cf. kee.* RS: *load.* [U.S., RDS: 1982] 2. *ketamine (q.v.)* hydrochloride, a hallucinogenic drugs similar to L.S.D. [U.S., ELA: 1984]

kabayo heroin. An incorrect (but phonetically accurate) spelling of Spanish *caballo* (*q.v.*) = *horse* (= heroin). RT: *heroin.* [U.S., SNP: 1977]

kaffir tobacco marijuana; *dagga* (*q.v.*). RT: *pot.* [South African, (1971): JB: 1980]

kaif marijuana. One of many spellings of this word. See *kif.* RT: *pot.* [U.S., YKB: 1977]

kaka heroin; bogus heroin. The same as *caca* (*q.v.*) = dung, *shit* (*q.v.*). RS: *blank.* [U.S., YKB: 1977]

kanger (also **kangeroo**) a quid of chewing tobacco. Rhyming slang for *chew.* RT: *quid.* [Br., early 1900s, DU]

Kansas grass low-quality marijuana. May refer to *wheat* (*q.v.*) = marijuana. RT: *pot.* [U.S., RG: 1970]

kaps phencyclidine, P.C.P. RT: *P.C.P.* [U.S., ELA: 1984]

K-blast phencyclidine, P.C.P. RT: *P.C.P.* [U.S., ELA: 1984]

kat See *khat.*

katzenjammer (also **katzenjammers**) a severe hangover; the delirium tremens. RT: *D.T.s.* A German word meaning cats' yammering. [U.S., (1849): DA, BVB: 1942]

Kaui (also **Kaui electric**) a potent grade of marijuana supposedly grown on the island of Kaui, Hawaii. *Cf. Maui.* RT: *pot.* [U.S., YKB: 1977, RAS: 1981]

kaya a marijuana cigarette. RT: *joint.* The term is probably from Jamaica. JAH: 1982 implies that it is currently used. [Bahamas, JAH: 1982]

kee (also **K.**, **ki**, **key**) a kilogram (of marijuana). RS: *load.* [U.S., S&W: 1966, JBW: 1967, RRL: 1969, D&B: 1970c, DCCU: 1972, DNE: 1973, ADC: 1975, W&F: 1975, EAF: 1980] See also *lem-kee.*

keef marijuana; hashish. RT: *hash, pot.* See *kif.* [(1938): DU, D&D: 1957, W&F: 1960]

keek an addict who injects drugs (rather than take them in some other form). GEN: strange person. RT: ***bangster***. [U.S., ELA: 1984]

keeler chloral hydrate knockout drops. RS: ***Mickey Finn***. [U.S., ELA: 1984]

kef (also **keff**) See ***kif***.

keg 1. a keg of beer. [Aust., N.Z., and U.S., 1900s, (1945): OEDS] 2. a kilogram of marijuana; five pounds of marijuana. RS: ***load***. [U.S., IGA: 1971]

kegger 1. a beer-blast where beer is served from a keg. RS: ***spree***. [U.S., DCCU: 1972, ADC: 1981] 2. (usually **keggers**) a keg of beer. [U.S., RAS: 1981, C&W: 1982]

keg party a drinking party; a party where illicit liquor is served. RS: ***spree***. From the prohibition era. [U.S., AH: 1931, MHW: 1934, FAB: 1979]

keif hashish. See ***kif***.

keister plant drugs concealed in the rectum. See ***keyster plant***. RT: ***stash***. [U.S., VJM: 1949, EEL: 1971]

Ken doll a barbiturate tablet or capsule. A mate for ***Barbie doll*** (*q.v.*). RT: ***barbs***. [U.S., JH: 1979]

kenird a drink. This is drink spelled backwards (backslang) with an *e* added to make it pronounceable. RT: ***nip***. [Br. backslang, (1887): DSUE]

ken-koy narcotics; heroin. Origin unknown, probably Chinese or mock-Chinese. RS: ***dope***. [U.S., SNP: 1977]

Kennedy rot a drunkard. Rhyming slang for ***sot*** (*q.v.*). Recorded in the U.S. (M&B: 1944), but of Australian origin. [M&B: 1944, DRS]

kennurd (also **kanurd, kenurd**) backslang for drunk meaning alcohol intoxicated or a drunkard. See ***kenird***. [Br., (1851): DSUE, JCH: 1859, F&H]

ken-ten a lamp used in the smoking of opium. *Cf.* ***high hat***. See explanation at ***opium lamp***. Probably from Chinese. [U.S., (1951): W&F: 1960, RDS: 1982]

Kentucky blue marijuana. Named for the ***grass*** (*q.v.*) in *Kentucky bluegrass*. RT: ***pot***. [U.S., (RRL: 1969), RAS: 1975]

Kentucky corn (also **Kentucky horn**) corn whiskey; moonshine. Julian Franklyn lists **Kentucky horn** as rhyming slang. RT: ***whiskey***. [U.S., BVB: 1942, DRS]

Kentucky dew (also **Kentucky fire**) whiskey; moonshine. Based on ***mountain dew*** (*q.v.*). RT: ***whiskey***. [U.S., BVB: 1942, D&D: 1957]

Kentucky fried alcohol intoxicated. An elaboration of ***fried*** (*q.v.*) based on the trade name *Kentucky Fried Chicken*. RT: ***drunk***. [U.S., PD: 1982]

kerbstone mixture cigar and cigarette butts found at the curb of the street, mixed for resale. A mock-brand name. See *curbstones*. [Br., 1900s, DSUE]

kero beer. From *kerosene*. RT: *beer*. [Aust., (1930): DSUE, SJB: 1966]

ketamine an anesthetic, ketamine hydrochloride, widely used in the Vietnamese War. It is used in pills, powders, and cigarettes and has an effect something like L.S.D. The drug is green. *Cf. green*. [U.S., YKB: 1977]

ketchup beer. Akin to *catch up* (*q.v.*) = beer. RT: *beer*. [Aust., SJB: 1943]

kettled alcohol intoxicated. A play on *potted* (*q.v.*). *Cf. drunk as a kettlefish*. RT: *drunk*. [Br., PW: 1974]

key a kilogram of marijuana. See *kee*.

key club a speakeasy where all of the members have a door key. RT: *speak*. From the prohibition era, and still used for some private clubs. RT: *bar*. [U.S., early 1900s, SBF: 1976]

keyed 1. (also **keyed up, keyed up to the roof**) alcohol intoxicated. From a colloquial term meaning excited. RT: *drunk*. [U.S., RWB: 1912, MHW: 1934, BVB: 1942] 2. drug intoxicated. From sense one. Possibly akin to a *kee* (*q.v.*) of marijuana. [U.S., EAF: 1972]

keyholed alcohol intoxicated. *Cf. keyed*. RT: *drunk*. [Br., (1860): DSUE]

keyster plant (also **keister plant, kiester plant, kiester stash**) a cache of narcotics concealed in the rectum or vagina. *Keyster* = the anus or buttocks, from a term meaning case or suitcase. *Cf. coozie stash, turd, U-boat*. RS: *stash*. See a list of drug smugglers at *mule*. [U.S., DWM: 1938, VJM: 1949, D&B: 1970c, EEL: 1971, H&C: 1975]

khat (also **kat**) a leaf of the plant *Catha edulis* which is chewed or brewed into a tea for its stimulating effects. In African and Arabic-speaking cultures. From Arabic *qat*. [Br. and U.S., (1858): OEDS, BTD: 1968, RRL: 1969]

khutchu string marijuana. Origin unknown. RT: *pot*. [U.S., JES: 1959, H&C: 1975]

ki a kilogram of marijuana. See *kee*.

kick 1. (also **kick it**) to voluntarily stop taking drugs completely; to go *cold turkey* (*q.v.*). From *kick the habit* (*q.v.*). [U.S., BD: 1937, DWM: 1938, BVB: 1942, TRG: 1968, EEL: 1971, DCCU: 1972, ADC: 1975, JWK: 1981] (This entry continues after the following list.) Terms and expressions having to do with breaking a drug habit: *bend the habit, bend the needle, boil out, boot the habit, break, break the habit, break the needle, catch up, chuck the habit, clear up, dry out, dry up, flip over, fold up, get one's yen off, go off the habit, go straight, hang it up, kick, kick cold, kick cold turkey, kick it, kick the habit, kick the tip, knock the habit, put it down,*

slack off, sneeze it out, sweat it out, take a boil-out, take the boil-out, take the cure, taper off, turn around, turn over, unhemp, wash up. 2. the potency of the alcohol in liquor; the effect of potent alcohol. [(1844): OEDS, BVB: 1942] 3. (also **kicks**) a jolt or rush from a drug injection, or from alcohol. GEN: a good feeling from something; a change from something. *Cf. **high kick***. RT: ***rush***. [U.S., DWM: 1938, NAM: 1953, RRL: 1969, DCCU: 1972] 4. two tablets of heroin. RS: ***dose***. [Br., BTD: 1968] 5. (also **kicks**) any pleasure from drug use. GEN: any kind of pleasure or enjoyment. [U.S., M&H: 1959, W&F: 1960, RRL: 1969]

kickapoo joy-juice whiskey; distilled wine. *Kickapoo* is the name of a (U.S.) Amerindian tribe. From the name of a horrible brew in Al Capp's comic strip *Li'l Abner*. RT: ***whiskey***. [U.S. WWII, DST: 1984]

kick back for a person to return to addiction after having been detoxified and withdrawn. *Cf. **re-wired***. [U.S., DWM: 1936, GOL: 1950, RRL: 1969]

kick cold (also **kick cold turkey, take the cold turkey, take the cold turkey cure**) to stop taking drugs without tapering off. RT: ***kick***. [U.S., M&V: 1967, RRL: 1969, M&V: 1973]

kicked by a horse addicted to heroin. *Cf. **horse***. RT: ***hooked***. [U.S., JES: 1959, H&C: 1975]

kicked out in the snow drug intoxicated. Probably refers to powdered drugs. *Cf. **snow***. RT: ***stoned***. [U.S., M&V: 1973] See also ***winter wonderland***.

kick freak a nonaddictive drug user; a ***chipper*** (*q.v.*). RT: ***chipper***. [U.S., M&V: 1967, H&C: 1975]

kick in the guts a drink of liquor. RT: ***nip***. [(FG: 1785), DSUE; listed in BVB: 1942]

kick in the wrist a drink of liquor. Refers to rotating the wrist while drinking. RT: ***nip***. [U.S., RB: 1915, MHW: 1934, BVB: 1942] See also ***shot in the neck***.

kick man a (male) drug seller. RT: ***dealer***. [HSD: 1984]

kick off to sleep off (the effects of drugs). [U.S., M&D: 1952, A&T: 1953]

kick party an ***L.S.D.*** (*q.v.*) party. ***Kick*** (*q.v.*) = pleasure from drug use. [U.S., TRG: 1968, EEL: 1971, W&F: 1975]

kickstick a marijuana cigarette. *Cf. **stick***. RT: ***joint***. [U.S., (1967): ELA: 1982, RRL: 1969, W&F: 1975]

kick the clouds to be intoxicated with drugs; to be high. RS: ***stoned***. [U.S., JES: 1959, H&C: 1975]

kick the engine around to smoke opium. ***Engine*** (*q.v.*) = opium pipe. RT: ***suck bamboo***. [U.S., GOL: 1950]

kick the gong (also **kick the gong around, kick the gonger**) 1. to smoke opium. *Cf.* ***boot the gong around***. See ***gong***. RT: ***suck bamboo***. [U.S., (GM: 1931), MHW: 1934, DWM: 1936, VJM: 1949, GOL: 1950, W&F: 1960, EEL: 1971, JWK: 1981] 2. to smoke marijuana. RT: ***hit the hay***. [U.S., GOL: 1950, M&V: 1954, (1956): W&F: 1960, D&D: 1957, M&V: 1973]

kick the habit to break one's addiction. The same as ***boot the habit*** (*q.v.*). RT: ***kick***. GEN: to voluntarily end any habit or custom. [U.S., MHW: 1934, DWM: 1936, GOL: 1950, RRL: 1969, EEL: 1971]

kick the mooch around to smoke opium. ***Mooch*** (*q.v.*) = narcotics. RT: ***suck bamboo***. [U.S., GOL: 1950, A&T: 1953]

kick the tip to break a heroin habit. The meaning of *tip* is not clear. RT: ***kick***. [U.S., H&C: 1975]

kid a liquor flask. RT: ***flask***. [U.S., MHW: 1934, BVB: 1942]

kidstuff marijuana. Something for beginners. *Cf.* ***chicken powder, schoolboy***. RT: ***pot***. [U.S., D&D: 1957]

kiester plant See ***keyster plant***.

kif (also el kif, kaif, keef, kef, keif, khif, kief, kiff) marijuana; hashish. Arabic for tranquility. RT: ***pot***. BTD: 1968 list keff, kif, keif. [in various spelling, (1878): OEDS, RPW: 1938, D&D: 1957, W&F: 1960, (1967): DNE: 1973, BTD: 1968, RRL: 1969, EEL: 1971, M&J: 1975, NIDA: 1980]

kill-cobbler gin. *Cf.* ***kill-priest***. RT: ***gin***. [(1728): DSUE]

kill-devil rum. *Cf.* ***kill-grief***. GWM: 1859 defines it as new rum. RT: ***rum***. [West Indian, 1600s, (1639): OEDS; BE: 1690, FG: 1785, FG: 1811, GWM: 1859, JSF: 1889, D&D: 1957]

killed drug intoxicated; marijuana intoxicated. RT: ***wasted, stoned***. [U.S., JWK: 1981]

killed his dog alcohol intoxicated. (BF: 1737: [He's] Kill'd his Dog.) RT: ***drunk***. [BF: 1737]

killed off drunk and on the floor; alcohol intoxicated. *Cf.* ***dead***. RT: ***drunk***. [Br., JB: 1823]

killersticks (also killers) marijuana cigarettes. *Cf.* ***kilters***. RT: ***joint***. [U.S., (1943): ELA: 1982, A&T: 1953, JES: 1959]

killer weed 1. very potent marijuana. This is probably parsley laced with P.C.P. sold as potent marijuana. *Cf.* ***weed***. RT: ***pot***. [U.S., (1967): ELA: 1982, RRL: 1969, SNP: 1977] 2. phencyclidine, ***P.C.P.*** (*q.v.*), an animal tranquilizer. It is mixed with dried parsley, mint, or dill and then smoked. One of the effects of this drug is to make one feel dead. *Cf.* ***mint weed, weed***. [U.S., (1970s): FAB: 1979, DNE: 1980, NIDA: 1980]

kill-grief strong liquor; rum. *Cf.* ***kill-devil***. RT: ***rum***. [early 1700s, DSUE]

killmequick (also killemquick) a type of rotgut whiskey or other strong and debilitating hard liquor. *Cf.* ***moonshine***. RS: ***rotgut***.

[U.S. military, (Philippines), (1898): DST: 1984]

kill one's dog to become alcohol intoxicated. [BF: 1737]

kill-priest port wine. RS: *port*. [cant, FG: 1785, FG: 1811, FG: 1823]

kill-the-beggar whiskey; inferior whiskey. RS: *whiskey*. [Br., mid 1800s, F&H]

kilo a kilogram of a drug, usually marijuana, sometimes heroin. *Cf. kee.* A specialized use of a standard English term. [U.S., GS: 1959, JBW: 1967, RRL: 1969, ADC: 1981]

kilo brick a brick-shaped block of marijuana weighing approximately one kilogram. *Cf. brick, kilo.* RS: *load*. [U.S., RDS: 1982]

kilo connection (also **kilo man**) a drug seller who starts with larger volumes of drugs and dilutes it before selling it to the dealer at the next level. Compare to *ounce man*. RS: *dealer*. [U.S., P&C: 1969, RRL: 1969, W&F: 1975]

kilters marijuana cigarettes. Probably from *killers* (*q.v.*) at *killersticks*. Possibly an error for *killers*. RT: *joint*. [U.S., RRL: 1969, SNP: 1977]

King Alky liquor. Probably patterned on *King Cotton*, the personification of cotton in the Old South. Refers to the liquor racket during prohibition. RT: *booze*. [U.S., BVB: 1942]

kingdom come rum. Rhyming slang. RT: *rum*. Not listed in DRS. [Br., 1900s, DSUE]

kingdom weed marijuana; good-quality marijuana. RS: *pot*. [U.S., BR: 1972]

King Kong 1. denatured alcohol; any potent, illicit alcohol; RS: *rotgut*. [U.S., M&W: 1946, GOL: 1950, (1956): W&F: 1960, D&D: 1957, M&V: 1967] 2. a large and demanding heroin addiction. *Cf. Mighty Joe Young, tang.* RS: *habit*. [U.S., RRL: 1969, RDS: 1982] See also *King Kong pills*.

King Kong pills (also **King Kong special**) barbiturate tablets or capsules. An elaboration of *gorilla pills* (*q.v.*). RT: *barbs*. [U.S., RRL: 1969, YKB: 1977]

kip, on the sleeping off drug intoxication; passed out from drugs or alcohol use; alcohol intoxicated; drug intoxicated. Kip = sleep, nap, bed. [U.S., GOL: 1950]

Kipper Lane an urban opium district. See *poppy alley*. Kip = to lie down, to sleep. [U.S., JES: 1959, H&C: 1975]

kisky alcohol intoxicated; tipsy. Probably rhyming slang on *whiskey*. RT: *drunk*. [Br., B&L: 1890, F&H]

kissed black Betty alcohol intoxicated. (BF: 1737: He's kiss'd...) RT: *drunk*. [BF: 1737]

kiss Mary (also **kiss Mari, kiss Maryjane**) to smoke marijuana. *Mary* (*q.v.*) = marijuana. The *kiss* may refer to blowing smoke into someone else's mouth. RT: *hit the hay*. [U.S., JES: 1959, D&B: 1970c, H&C: 1975]

kiss the babe (also **kiss the baby**) to take a drink of liquor. RT: *irrigate*. [Br., (1913): DSUE; listed in BVB: 1942]

kiss the fish to smoke marijuana or hashish. The significance of *fish* is unclear. RS: *hit the hay*. [U.S., EEL: 1971]

kit equipment for preparing and injecting drugs. RT: *outfit*. [U.S., GS: 1959, TRG: 1968, RRL: 1969]

kite 1. one ounce of drugs. RS: *load*. [U.S., VJM: 1949, IGA: 1971, EEL: 1971] 2. a drug user who is always as *high as a kite* (*q.v.*). RT: *user*. [U.S., GU: 1975]

kited alcohol intoxicated. Made higher than a kite. *Cf. high, high as a kite*. RT: *drunk*. Not common (W&F: 1960). [U.S., W&F: 1960]

K.J. (also **C.J.**) phencyclidine, *P.C.P.* (*q.v.*), an animal tranquilizer. From *krystal joint* (*q.v.*). *Cf. crystal joint*. RT: *P.C.P.* [U.S., (1970s): FAB: 1979, YKB: 1977, DEM: 1981]

knapt (also **knapped**) alcohol intoxicated. (BF: 1737: [He's] Knapt.) LIT: broken off. RT: *drunk*. [BF: 1737]

knee-walking drunk alcohol intoxicated; very drunk. *Cf. snot-flinging drunk*. RT: *drunk*. [U.S., RAS: 1979, PD: 1982]

knock back a drink to take a drink of liquor; to drink a beer; to have a quick drink of liquor. RT: *irrigate*. [(1931): OED; U.S., D&D: 1957; Aust., (1962): GAW: 1978]

knock down 1. (also **knock-me-down**) beer; strong ale. GWM: 1859 lists **knock-me-down**. RT: *ale, beer*. [BE: 1690, (1756): OED, GWM: 1859, F&H, BVB: 1942, D&D: 1957] 2. to drink. See *knock over*.

knocked in arrested on a drug charge. RS: *busted*. [U.S., EEL: 1971, IGA: 1971]

knocked out drug intoxicated; alcohol intoxicated. RT: *drunk, stoned*. Also means unconscious or exhausted from any cause. [U.S., AH: 1931, MHW: 1934, TRG: 1968, EEL: 1971, DCCU: 1972, W&F: 1975]

knocked up alcohol intoxicated. GEN: battered, screwed. RT: *drunk*. [Br., 1800s, F&H]

knockout drops 1. liquor. RT: *booze*. [U.S., AH: 1931, MHW: 1934] 2. (also **K.O.**, **K.O. drops**) a chemical such as chloral hydrate used to drug liquor. *Cf. chlorals*. RT: *Mickey Finn*. [Aust., (1910): DSUE; Br., (1904): SSD; U.S., (1896): DA, MHW: 1934, D&D: 1957, W&F: 1960, RRL: 1969] 3. drugs in general. RS: *dope*. [U.S., BVB: 1942]

knock over (also **knock back, knock down**) to take a drink of liquor. RT: *irrigate*. [Aust. and U.S., MHW: 1934, BVB: 1942, DSUE]

knock the habit to stop using drugs; to break a drug addiction.

Cf. kick. [U.S., BVB: 1942, JES: 1959]

knock up to inject drugs. Compare to *knocked up*. GEN: batter, copulate with. *Cf. fucked up*. RT: *shoot.* [U.S., JES: 1959, H&C: 1975]

knose allegedly tobacco. Probably an error for *noser my knacker* (DU). [GWM: 1859]

knows not the way home alcohol intoxicated. RT: *drunk.* [BF: 1737]

K.O. (also **K.O. drops**) opiates used as *knockout drops* (*q.v.*). From the initials of *knock out,* originally from boxing. RT: *Mickey Finn.* [U.S., BVB: 1942, H&C: 1975]

K.O.ed knocked out from drugs; overdosed; drug intoxicated. RT: *stoned.* [U.S., BVB: 1942, JES: 1959]

kokomo (also **cokomo, Kokomo Joe**) a cocaine user; a cocaine addict. [U.S., DWM: 1938, BVB: 1942, GOL: 1950, D&D: 1957, EEL: 1971] Nicknames and slang terms for a cocaine user or a cocaine addict: *Arctic explorer, bloker, blower, C.A., candy fiend, candyhead, Charley, Charley Coke, Charlie, Charlie Coke, C-head, coke blower, coke fiend, coke freak, cokehead, coke-smoke, cokey, cokie, cokomo, cooker, C-user, dynamiter, flake, forty-niner, freebaser, gold duster, golden duster, happy duster, horner, jerker, jumpy Stevie, kokomo, Kokomo Joe, leaper, schnozzler, schoolboy, sleighrider, sniffer, sniffler, snifter, snowbird, snow flier, snow flower, social sniffer, wing captain.*

Kona gold (also **Kona coast gold, Kona Kona**) a potent form of marijuana from Hawaii, probably *sinsemilla* (*q.v.*). RT: *pot.* [U.S., (1976): ELA: 1982, RDS: 1982]

kong strong whiskey; illicit whiskey. Probably from *King Kong,* the giant movie ape. RT: *moonshine.* Black use (W&F: 1960). [U.S., DB: 1944, D&D: 1957, W&F: 1960]

koolaid beer. From the brand name of a powdered drink mix. See *Colorado Kool-Aid.* RT: *beer.* [U.S., EE: 1976]

kools phencyclidine, P.C.P. RT: *P.C.P.* [U.S., ELA: 1984]

kosher having to do with undiluted alcohol. RT: *neat.* [U.S., (BVB: 1942)]

krystal joint phencyclidine, *P.C.P.* (*q.v.*), an animal tranquilizer. *Cf. K.J.* RT: *P.C.P.* See *crystal joint.*

K.T. a cocktail. [U.S., D&D: 1957]

kudu milk brandy; strong liquor. Similar to *moose milk, tiger milk* (*q.v.*). RT: *brandy.* The kudu is a South African antelope. [South African, (1971): JB: 1980]

K.W. phencyclidine, P.C.P. Origin unknown. RT: *P.C.P.* [U.S., ELA: 1984]

L

L. (also **L.s**) 1. the hallucinogenic drug *L.S.D.* (*q.v.*). RT: *L.S.D.* [U.S., RRL: 1969, EEL: 1971] 2. (usually **L.s**) an *Elavil* (TM; *q.v.*) antidepressant tablet. [U.S., JWK: 1981]

L.A. amphetamines. Short for *long-acting* or for *Los Angeles*. See *L.A. turnabouts*. [U.S., RG: 1970]

lace 1. to add alcohol to coffee or tea; to add alcohol to any food or drink. [since the 1600s, (1677): OED] 2. to add a bit of one drug to another; to add drugs to any food or drink. From sense one. *Cf. dust*. [U.S., (ADC: 1975), GU: 1975, (D&B: 1978)] 3. a beer. See *lace curtain*. 4. money; money for drugs. From general underworld jargon. [U.S., TRG: 1968]

lace curtain (also **lace**) a beer; a Burton (TM) beer. Rhyming slang for *Burton*. RS: *beer*. [Br., early 1900s, DRS, DSUE]

la cosa* heroin. Spanish for the thing. *Cf. things*. RT: *heroin*. [U.S., NIDA: 1980] See also *cosa*.

La Dama Blanca* heroin. See *blanco, white lady*.

la duna* heroin. Spanish for the dune. May refer to granular brown Mexican heroin. *Cf. Mexican brown*. RT: *heroin*. [U.S., NIDA: 1980]

lady cocaine. RT: *cocaine*. [U.S., YKB: 1977, JH: 1979, ADC: 1984] See also *beautiful lady, crystal lady, old lady White, white lady*.

Lady Dacre's wine gin. RT: *gin*. [cant, FG: 1811, FG: 1823]

ladyfinger a marijuana cigarette; a large marijuana cigarette. RT: *joint*. [U.S., BR: 1972]

lady in white heroin. May refer to a nurse dressed in white, or may refer to a bride. Some addicts claim to be married to their drug. RT: *heroin*. [U.S., JHF: 1971]

Lady May a gallon of liquor. *Cf. gal*. [U.S., BVB: 1942]

Lady Nicotine tobacco; a personification of tobacco. RT: *fogus*. [U.S., BVB: 1942, VJM: 1949]

Lady Snow (also **lady**) cocaine. *Snow* (*q.v.*) = cocaine. RT: *cocaine*. [U.S., RRL: 1969, ADC: 1975, NIDA: 1980]

Lady White (also **old Lady White**) powdered narcotics: heroin, cocaine, morphine. RT: *powder*. [U.S., (BVB: 1942)]

lag 1. wine. RT: *wine*. [cant, 15–1800s, TH: 1567, DSUE] 2. to dilute liquor. RS: *cut*. [cant, TH: 1567, DSUE]

lage 1. to drink liquor; to wash down liquor. RT: *irrigate*. [cant, TH: 1567] 2. weak liquor. RT: *rotgut*. [16–1700s, DSUE, B&L: 1890]

laid back drug intoxicated; alcohol intoxicated; *mellow* (*q.v.*). GEN: relaxed. RS: *drunk, stoned*. [U.S., ADC: 1975, JWK: 1981]

laid out alcohol intoxicated; drug intoxicated. RT: *drunk, stoned*. [U.S., MP: 1928, AH: 1931, MHW: 1934, W&F: 1960]

laid to the bone alcohol intoxicated. A mixed metaphor consisting of *cut to the bone* and *laid out* (*q.v.*), or possibly *laid*. RT: *drunk*. Black use. [U.S., DC: 1972]

laine a hick; a sucker. The same as *lane* (*q.v.*). The nature of this spelling is not known. RT: *square*. [U.S., M&W: 1946]

lakbay diwa marijuana. Origin unknown. RT: *pot*. [U.S., SNP: 1977]

lambsbread marijuana; Jamaican marijuana. Possibly from a local plant name. RT: *pot*. [U.S., ADC: 1981]

lame (also lane, lame duck) a square; someone who does not use drugs; a new and inexperienced addict. Lame is being replaced by *lane* (*q.v.*). RT: *square*. Only ELA: 1984 lists lame duck [U.S., (c. 1950): RSG: 1964, (1967): DNE: 1973, W&F: 1967, (TW: 1968), RRL: 1969, MA: 1973, MW: 1976, JWK: 1981, ELA: 1984]

lame hype a new addict; an inexperienced addict. *Cf. join up, lame*. RT: *user*. [U.S., M&V: 1973]

lamp habit 1. an addiction to opium; a serious and debilitating addiction to opium. RS: *habit*. [U.S., DWM: 1938, BVB: 1942] 2. opium addiction (or habituation) from breathing opium vapor in an opium den. RS: *habit*. [U.S., DWM: 1938, VJM: 1949] 3. an opium habit wherein the addict desires to see the opium lamp burning continuously. It is said that this addict is more addicted to the lamp than to the opium. [U.S., BD: 1937, DWM: 1938]

lamp oil whiskey. *Cf. kero*. RT: *whiskey*. [U.S., (1850–1900): RFA]

lane square. The same as *lame* (*q.v.*) and *laine* (*q.v.*). Probably in use since the 1920s. RT: *square*. [U.S., M&W: 1946, JWK: 1981]

lap 1. liquor; inferior liquor. From an old term meaning any weak or watered drink. RT: *booze*. [cant, (1618): OED, GWM: 1859, JCH: 1887, B&L: 1890, HNR: 1934] 2. a swallow of whiskey or other liquor. RS: *nip*. [U.S., W&F: 1960]

lapper 1. liquor. RT: *booze*. [Br., B&L: 1890, F&H] 2. a drunkard. RT: *sot*. [Br., B&L: 1890, F&H; listed in BVB: 1942]

lapping in the gutter alcohol intoxicated; very drunk. *Cf. in the gutter*. RT: *drunk*. [(1850): DSUE, BVB: 1942] See also *gutter, gutter hype*.

lappy alcohol intoxicated. *Lap* (*q.v.*) = liquor. RT: *drunk*. [(1718): DU, BF: 1737]

lappy cull a drunkard. Cull = man (in cant). *Cf. lappy*. RT: *sot*. [cant, 17-1800s, DSUE]

lard the police. *Cf. bacon, pig, pork*. RT: *fuzz*. [U.S., IGA: 1971, ELA: 1982]

largehead a drunkard. Compare to *bighead*. RT: *sot*. [JRW: 1909, MHW: 1934]

las mujercitas* mushrooms containing *psilocybin* (*q.v.*). Mexican Spanish for little women. RT: *psilocybin*. [U.S., YKB: 1977]

lason sa daga* the hallucinogenic drug *L.S.D.* (*q.v.*). Origin unknown. RT: *L.S.D.* [U.S., SNP: 1977]

lathered alcohol intoxicated. *Cf. soapy-eyed*. RT: *drunk*. [U.S., MHW: 1934, W&F: 1960]

L. A. turnabouts (also **L.A., L. A. turnarounds**) amphetamines. Alludes to the alleged use of amphetamines by truck drivers. Probably refers to long-acting (L.A.) amphetamine capsules. *Cf. California turnarounds, L.A., truck drivers, turnabouts*. RT: *amps*. [U.S., IGA: 1971, MT: 1971, YKB: 1977]

laudanum a tincture of opium. Compare to *paregoric* (*q.v.*) which is a camphorated tincture of opium. Used primarily before the twentieth century. [(1602): OED] Other terms for *laudanum*: *black stuff, locus, locust*.

laugh and joke a (tobacco) smoke. Rhyming slang for *smoke*. [Br., (1934): DRS]

laugh and scratch to inject narcotics. The injection of drugs causes itching and laughter in some people (M&V: 1973). RT: *shoot*. [U.S., DWM: 1938, VJM: 1949]

laughing gas nitrous oxide. Use as an *inhalant* (*q.v.*) drug for recreational purposes since it was discovered. This substance is used as an anesthetic. [(1842): OED; drug culture use, RRL: 1969, ADC: 1975]

laughing grass marijuana. A play on *laughing gas* (*q.v.*). See *giggle smoke*. *Cf. grass*. RT: *pot*. [U.S., M&V: 1954, SNP: 1977]

laughing soup (also **laughing water**) liquor; champagne. RT: *booze, cham*. [U.S., MHW: 1934, D&D: 1957, W&F: 1960]

laughing weed (also **laughing tobacco**) marijuana. *Cf. laughing grass, weed*. RT: *pot*. [U.S., early 1900s, DU, SNP: 1977, ELA: 1982]

launching pad (also **launch pad**) a place to use drugs and get high; a place to use L.S.D. An elaboration of *pad* (*q.v.*) and the rocketry theme in drug culture use. RS: *pad*. [U.S., EEL: 1971, W&F: 1975] For other terms on the rocketry theme see: *blast, bum trip, come down, copilot, crash, down trip, ground control, ground man, hit the moon, pack of rockets, rocket, rocket fuel,* *rocket ship, skyrockets, trip.*

lawn poor quality marijuana. The type of grass one might find in one's own yard. RS: *pot.* [U.S., BR: 1972]

law, the (also **law**) the police. Often glossed without *the.* RT: *fuzz.* [Br. and U.S., (1929): OEDS, BVB: 1942, BTD: 1968]

lay 1. a lay (standard English lying) on one's hip for the purpose of smoking opium; an act of smoking opium; a dose of opium. [U.S., DWM: 1936, BVB: 1942] 2. an opium den; a place to smoke opium. RT: *opium den.* [U.S., DWM: 1936, BVB: 1942] 3. an injection or other dose of any *hard* (*q.v.*) drug. RS: *shot.* [U.S., DWM: 1938, H&C: 1975]

lay a hip (also **lay on one's hip, lay the hip, lie on the hip**) to lay down one's hip or lie on one's hip to smoke opium in an opium den. The posture for smoking opium is reclining on one's hip. *Cf. hipped, suck bamboo.* [U.S., DWM: 1936, BD: 1937, VJM: 1949]

lay-back a barbiturate. *Cf. laid back.* RT: *barbs.* [U.S., RG: 1970]

lay down 1. (also **lay down joint**) an opium den; any drug *pad* (*q.v.*). *Cf. lay.* [U.S., BD: 1937, DWM: 1938, VJM: 1949] 2. the fee for a session in an opium den. [U.S., DWM: 1936, BVB: 1942] 3. (usually **lay-down**) an act of smoking opium; an opium smoking session. [U.S., M&V: 1954] 4. (also **lay the hip**) to lie down to smoke opium. This is done to prevent (or control) nausea. RT: *suck bamboo.* [U.S., BVB: 1942, M&W: 1946, VJM: 1949, RRL: 1969]

layed drug intoxicated. Possibly a variant of *fucked* (*q.v.*). *Lay* (*q.v.*) = a dose of a drug. RT: *stoned.* [U.S., S&E: 1981]

lay one on to get drunk. The same as *tie one on* (*q.v.*).

layout (also **layette**) equipment for smoking opium; equipment for preparing and injecting narcotics, especially heroin and cocaine. A specialized use of the general colloquial term for an assemblage of equipment or apparatus. RT: *outfit.* [U.S., (1882): OEDS, (1887): RML: 1948, GI: 1931, DWM: 1936, VJM: 1949, JES: 1959]

lay the dust to take a drink of liquor; to drink heavily. To settle the dust. RT: *irrigate.* [early 1900s, (1910): DSUE, JLD: 1976]

lay the hypo to inject narcotics. *Hypo* (*q.v.*) = hypodermic syringe and needle. RT: *shoot.* [U.S., RDS: 1982]

L.B. (also **lb.**) a pound of marijuana. This is the standard abbreviation for *pound. Cf. kee.* RS: *load.* [U.S., RRL: 1969, ADC: 1975]

L.B.J. *L.S.D.* (*q.v.*) combined with some other drug. RS: *set.* [U.S., KBH: 1982]

L.D.J. the hallucinogenic drug *L.S.D.* (*q.v.*). Possibly an error for *L.B.J.* (*q.v.*). RT: *L.S.D.* [U.S., H&C: 1975, SNP: 1977]

leach someone who begs drugs. A misspelling of *leech* (*q.v.*). *Cf. mooch*. [U.S., IGA: 1971]

leaf 1. tobacco. Short for *tobacco leaf*. RT: *fogus*. [U.S., (1853): OED] 2. (also **leaf gum**) narcotics; drugs in general. RS: *dope*. [U.S., DWM: 1938, VJM: 1949] See also *leaf gum*. 3. (also **the leaf**) cocaine. RT: *cocaine*. [U.S., JES: 1959, RG: 1970, EEL: 1971, W&F: 1975, YKB: 1977] **4**. marijuana. RT: *pot*. See *leaves*. [U.S., BR: 1972; Br., (1972): OEDS]

leaf gum (also **leaf**, **leaf hop**) gum opium wrapped in a poppy leaf. This is the form it comes in from the poppy fields. RS: *opium*. [U.S., BD: 1937, DWM: 1938, VJM: 1949]

lean against the engine to smoke opium; to use an opium pipe. *Engine* (*q.v.*) = opium pipe. RT: *suck bamboo*. [U.S., BVB: 1942, A&T: 1953]

leanaway a drunkard; a drunken person. This drinker cannot stand up straight. RT: *sot*. [Aust., late 18-1900s, DSUE, SJB: 1943]

leaper 1. a cocaine user; an advanced cocaine user suffering from tremors. The same as *jerker* (*q.v.*). *Cf. leaps*. RT: *kokomo*. [U.S., DU, A&T: 1953, M&V: 1967] 2. (also **leeper**) an amphetamine tablet or capsule. Because of its stimulant effect. Compare to *sleepers*. RT: *amps*. [U.S., RRL: 1969, ADC: 1975]

leaping 1. alcohol intoxicated. RT: *drunk*. [U.S., MHW: 1934, BVB: 1942] 2. drug intoxicated. RT: *stoned*. [U.S., BD: 1937, VJM: 1949]

leaping and stinking drug intoxicated and in need of drugs. *Cf. bending and bowing*. RT: *stoned*. [U.S., DWM: 1938, BVB: 1942]

leaps intense overactivity from cocaine overuse; hallucinations from habitual cocaine use. *Cf. leaper*. [U.S., DWM: 1938, BVB: 1942]

leary (also **leery**) alcohol intoxicated. RT: *drunk*. [U.S., F&H, MHW: 1934, BVB: 1942]

leather dew inferior drugs. Origin unknown. Compare to *mountain dew*. RS: *blank*. [U.S., JES: 1959, H&C: 1975]

leaves marijuana. *Cf. leaf*. RT: *pot*. [U.S., IGA: 1971, WCM: 1972]

Lebanese hash (also **Lebanese**, **leb hash**) a reddish-brown hashish from Lebanon. RT: *hash*. [U.S., RRL: 1969, (1970): DNE: 1973, ADC: 1981]

Lebanese red (also **Lebanon red**, **red leb**, **red Lebanese**) Lebanese marijuana. RS: *pot*. [U.S., YKB: 1977, ELA: 1982]

leech a ruined heroin addict; a heroin addict who must beg for drugs. See *leach*. GEN: an acquaintance who always begs or borrows. RS: *junky*. [U.S., JWK: 1981]

leeky store a liquor store. Probably a corruption of liquor store. RT: *L.I.Q*. Black use. [U.S., EAF: 1980]

leeper See *leaper*.

leer-beer (also **lear-beer**) a prohibitionist. Someone who leers at beer or other liquor. Contrived and jocular. *Cf. cellar-smeller*. RT: *dry*. From the prohibition era. [U.S., 1920s, BVB: 1942]

leg to *bootleg* (*q.v.*); to smuggle liquor. From the prohibition era. [U.S., BVB: 1942]

legger a bootlegger; a liquor smuggler. RT: *bootlegger*. From the prohibition era. [U.S., (1926): OEDS, AH: 1931, BVB: 1942]

leggery (also **leg joint**) an illicit bar; a speakeasy. RT: *speak*. From the prohibition era. [U.S., BVB: 1942]

legless alcohol intoxicated. RT: *drunk*. [Br., RAS: 1980, HSD: 1984] See also *all arms and legs, legs and arms*.

leg-opener a drink to soften up a woman for seduction. Based on *eye-opener* (*q.v.*). RT: *nip*. [Aust., (1959): GAW: 1978, SJB: 1966]

legs and arms weak, bodiless beer. RT: *queer-beer*. See *all arms and legs*.

legume a *button* (*q.v.*) or piece of peyote cactus. Refers to the vegetable origin of peyote. *Cf. plant*. RS: *peyote*. [U.S., RDS: 1982]

lem-kee (also **Lem Kee**) a brand of commercially prepared opium. RS: *opium*. [U.S., BD: 1937, DWM: 1938, VJM: 1949]

lemo lemon extract drunk for its alcohol content. Prison and military use. [U.S., HS: 1933, BVB: 1942, VJM: 1949, W&F: 1960]

lemonade (also **lemon**) bogus drugs; inferior heroin. Lemon = something which is defective in manufacture. Lemonade is an elaboration of lemon. RS: *blank*. [U.S., M&V: 1967, RRL: 1969, ADC: 1975, W&F: 1975]

lemonade wallah a teetotaller, a lemonade drinker. *Cf. wallah*. RT: *dry*. [Br. military, late 18-1900s, DSUE]

lemon bowl an opium pipe with a lemon rind covering its bowl. The lemon rind is formed into a hood over the bowl to contain the vapors and aid in inhaling them. The rind also imparts some flavor to the vapors. *Cf. orange bowl*. RS: *hop stick*. [U.S., DWM: 1938, VJM: 1949]

leño* marijuana; a marijuana cigarette. The Spanish word for faggot = a stick of wood. RT: *pot, joint*. [U.S., HB: 1955, EEL: 1971, CG: 1980]

leños* phencyclidine, P.C.P. Probably related to *leño*. Spanish. RT: *P.C.P.* [U.S., ELA: 1984]

lent See *lint*.

leper grass a potent variety of marijuana from Colombia. RT: *pot*. [U.S., ELA: 1982]

leth bringer liquor. Leth is an obsolete Anglo-Saxon word meaning ill-will. RT: *booze*. From the prohibition era. [U.S., AH: 1931, MHW: 1934]

Let me hold something! (also **Let me go!**) "Do you have drugs for sale?" *Cf. hold*. RT: *How are you going to act?* [U.S., M&D: 1952]

let sunshine do *L.S.D.* (*q.v.*) combined with some other drug. An elaboration of the initials L.S.D. RS: *set*. [U.S., KBH: 1982]

lettuce opium (also **lettuce**) an opium substitute made from the common lettuce plant. [(1816): OED; U.S., RB: 1967, EEL: 1971, YKB: 1977]

level to buy drugs. Possibly also to use the drugs to get *straight* (*q.v.*). RT: *score*. Black use. [U.S., ADC: 1975]

lhesca See *llesca*.

Librium a protected trade name for chlordiazepoxide capsules. The drug is used to relieve anxiety and related states. [in current use; consult a pharmaceutical reference for more information]

lick papers cigarette rolling papers. RT: *paper*. [U.S. military, BVB: 1942]

lick up a tab to take (swallow) a tablet. *Cf. tab*. [U.S., M&V: 1973]

lid (also **lids**) 1/2 to one ounce of marijuana. The amount which will fill the lid of a Prince Albert tobacco can lid. See *can*. RS: *load*. [U.S., S&W: 1966, JBW: 1967, (1967): DNE: 1973, RRL: 1969, D&B: 1970c, DCCU: 1972, ADC: 1975, W&F: 1975, MW: 1976, EAF: 1980, JWK: 1981]

lid-poppers (also **lid-proppers**) amphetamine tablets or capsules. Refers to the eyelids. *Cf. eye-opener*. RT: *amps*. [U.S., JBW: 1967, RRL: 1969, IGA: 1971, YKB: 1977]

lie down Standard English for *lay down* (*q.v.*) = to smoke opium.

lie in state with the girls to smoke marijuana. The girls are Mary and Jane. RT: *hit the hay*. [U.S., JES: 1959, H&C: 1975] See also *rainy-day woman*.

lie on the hip (also **lie on the side**) to smoke opium. Standard English for *lay a hip* and related forms. RT: *suck bamboo*. [U.S., MHW: 1934, DWM: 1936]

life preserver a drinking flask. RT: *flask*. [U.S., BVB: 1942]

lifer a lifetime drug addict. From the prison term for a convict serving a lifetime sentence. RT: *junky*. [U.S., EEL: 1971]

Life, The the life of a heroin addict. [U.S., MA: 1973]

lift 1. the potency of the alcohol in liquor; the effect of potent alcohol. [U.S., BVB: 1942] 2. (also **lift-up**) drug euphoria; a rush; a high. GEN: a brief, spirit-lifting occurrence. RS: *rush*. [U.S., BVB: 1942, EEL: 1971]

lifted alcohol intoxicated. *Cf. elevated*. RT: *drunk*. [U.S., BVB: 1942]

lift one's elbow to take a drink of alcohol. See *bend one's elbow.* RT: *irrigate.* [U.S., BVB: 1942, D&D: 1957, SSD, M&J: 1975]

lift pills amphetamine capsules or tablets. *Cf. go-pills.* RT: *amps.* [U.S., EEL: 1971]

light alcohol intoxicated. RT: *drunk.* [BF: 1737] See also *walking in the air.*

light artillery 1. equipment for preparing and injecting drugs. *Cf. artillery.* RS: *outfit.* [U.S., BVB: 1942, VJM: 1949, GOL: 1950, D&D: 1957] 2. equipment for using soft drugs, i.e., rolling paper, pipes, roach clips. The opposite of *heavy artillery* (*q.v.*). [U.S., JH: 1979]

light blue gin. *Cf. sky blue.* RT: *gin.* [Br., FG: 1823]

lighter a drug addict. RT: *junky.* [U.S., A&T: 1953]

light food chewing tobacco; a quid of chewing tobacco. RT: *quid.* [JRW: 1909]

light green marijuana; a low-grade of marijuana. *Cf. green.* RS: *pot.* [U.S., M&V: 1967, H&C: 1975]

lightning 1. gin. RT: *gin.* [(1781): OED, FG: 1823, JCH: 1887, B&L: 1890, (1891): SBF: 1982] 2. (also **lightning flash**) inferior whiskey; moonshine; rotgut. RT: *rotgut, whiskey.* [U.S., (1858): DA, F&H, GOL: 1950] 3. amphetamines. RT: *amps.* [U.S., YKB: 1977, NIDA: 1980]

lightning hashish potent hashish. RT: *hash.* [U.S., ELA: 1982]

light somebody up to introduce someone to marijuana. [U.S., (M&W: 1946)]

light stuff 1. low-proof liquor. [U.S., early 1900s, DU] 2. marijuana and nonaddictive drugs. The opposite of heavy drugs. [U.S., RRL: 1969, EEL: 1971]

light up (also **fire up, flame up, torch up**) to smoke a marijuana cigarette; to indulge in marijuana smoking. GEN: to light tobacco. *Cf. fire up, flame up, toke up, torch up.* RT: *hit the hay.* [U.S., M&W: 1946, RRL: 1969, M&V: 1973, ADC: 1975, D&B: 1978]

light-weight having to do with a minimal addiction. An infrequent user is a **light-weight chipper** and a small habit is a **light-weight nothing**. GEN: insignificant. [U.S., M&V: 1967]

light wet gin. The opposite of *heavy wet* (*q.v.*) = *porter* (*q.v.*) or *stout* (*q.v.*). RT: *gin.* [cant, FG: 1823; listed in BVB: 1942]

like a rat in trouble alcohol intoxicated. RT: *drunk.* [BF: 1737]

likker liquor. Eye-dialect. RT: *booze.* [U.S., BVB: 1942, D&D: 1957]

likkered up (also **likkered, likkerish, likker soaked**) alcohol intoxicated. Eye-dialect for *liquored up* (*q.v.*). *Likkerish* may be a play on *licorice.* RT: *drunk.* [U.S., BVB: 1942, D&D: 1957]

likker pug an abstainer; a teetotaller. Compare to *liquor pug.* RT:

dry. From the prohibition era. [U.S., BVB: 1942]

Likkersham Commission (also **Liquorsham Commission**) a play on *Wickersham Commission*, See explanation at *wickedsham commission*. From the prohibition era. [U.S., MHW: 1934]

likker up to drink heavily; to spree. Eye-dialect for *liquor up* (*q.v.*). RT: *guzzle*. [U.S., BVB: 1942]

lillys (also **lilies, lillies**) *Seconal* (TM; *q.v.*) barbiturate capsules. From the name of the manufacturer *Eli Lilly*. RT: *sec*. [U.S., EEL: 1971, EAF: 1972]

limber alcohol intoxicated. *Cf. loose*. RT: *drunk*. [BF: 1737]

limbo Colombian marijuana. See *lumbo*. RS: *pot*. [U.S., ADC: 1981]

lime acid the hallucinogenic drug *L.S.D.* (*q.v.*). Origin unknown. *Cf. acid*. RT: *L.S.D.* [U.S., RG: 1970]

limp alcohol intoxicated. *Cf. limber*. RT: *drunk*. [U.S., JAS: 1932, MHW: 1934, W&F: 1960]

Lincoln's Inn gin. Rhyming slang. RT: *gin*. [Br., late 18-1900s, DRS]

line 1. the mainline (vein) in the arm; the median cephalic vein. An injection into this vein is called a **line shot**. [U.S., DWM: 1938, BVB: 1942, RRL: 1969] 2. to inject into the mainline (vein). RS: *shoot*. [U.S., RRL: 1969, EEL: 1971] 3. (also **lines**) a dose of chopped cocaine ready to be snorted. The cocaine is chopped fine on a mirror or a record album cover. The term can be used for any powdered drug which can be snorted. RS: *cocaine*. [U.S., JH: 1979, ADC: 1981, JWK: 1981, BW: 1984]

lined alcohol intoxicated. RT: *drunk*. [U.S., MP: 1928, AH: 1931, MHW: 1934, W&F: 1960]

line of the old author a drink of brandy. RS: *nip*. No longer used as slang. [since the late 1600s, BE: 1690]

liner an addict who shoots into the mainline. See *line*. *Cf. mainliner*. RS: *bangster*. [U.S., (c. 1917): JES: 1959, H&C: 1975]

line shot an injection of drugs into the median cephalic vein. *Cf. line*. RT: *shot*. [U.S., M&V: 1954, H&C: 1975]

lint (also **lent**) morphine in fibrous or cotton form. *Cf. cotton morphine*. Imported from Japan, it saw little use in the U.S. [U.S., DWM: 1936, BVB: 1942]

lion drunk roaring drunk; very drunk and angry. RT: *drunk*. [(1592): OED, PD: 1982]

lip 1. to suck the air out of drug apparatus to test its airtightness. Especially in **lip the dripper** meaning to test the airtightness of the contact of the rubber bulb of a medicine dropper. The bulb is depressed and the glass tip of the dropper is touched to the inside of the upper lip. The bulb is released and if the dropper holds on to the lip, it is considered airtight. [U.S., (BD: 1937), (DWM:

1938)] 2. a drink of liquor. RT: *nip.* [Br., 1800s, F&H]

lip-burner a very short tobacco cigarette butt. RT: *brad.* [U.S., HS: 1933, VJM: 1949, GOL: 1950]

lip the dripper See *lip.*

Lipton's Tea (also **Lipton's, Lipton Tea**) 1. weak heroin; inferior narcotics. From a tea brand name. RS: *blank.* [U.S., M&V: 1967, CM: 1970, ADC: 1975] 2. tea used to cut (dilute) marijuana. [U.S., H&C: 1975] 3. low-quality marijuana; much-diluted marijuana. [U.S., (c. 1940): RSG: 1964, CM: 1970, ADC: 1975] 4. chloral hydrate or some other drug added to an alcoholic drink to knock someone out or cause urgent diarrhea. RT: *Mickey Finn.* [U.S., M&V: 1967, H&C: 1975]

lip-trap liquor. *Cf. lip.* RT: *booze.* [U.S., BVB: 1942, DU]

L.I.Q. a liquor store. Black use. [U.S., D&B: 1970b, EAF: 1972] Nicknames and slang terms for a place where liquor can be bought by the bottle: *bottle factory, bottle joint, bottle shop, bottle store, brew house, bucket shop, candy store, drinkateria, drinkatorium, filling station, grogshop, guzzle factory, guzzlery, guzzle shop, happy shop, headache department, headache house, juice house, leeky store, L.I.Q., liquorama, liquor factory, liquorium, malt shop, package store, thirst-aid station.*

liquefied alcohol intoxicated. RT: *drunk.* [U.S., BVB: 1942]

liquid amber, the beer. *Cf. the amber brew.* RT: *beer.* [Aust., BH: 1980]

liquid bam injectable amphetamines. *Cf. bam.* RS: *amps.* [U.S., JWK: 1981]

liquid bread beer. Refers to the grain used in its manufacture. RT: *beer.* [U.S., RDS: 1982]

liquid courage liquor. *Cf. courage, Dutch courage, Geneva courage.* RS: *booze.* [U.S., BVB: 1942]

liquid fire (also **liquid lightning**) inferior liquor; strong whiskey. RT: *whiskey.* [(1858): OEDS, (1873): OEDS, BVB: 1942]

liquid fuel (also **liquid joy**) liquor. RT: *booze.* [U.S., BVB: 1942]

liquid grass T.H.C., the active principle of marijuana; hashish oil. See *T.H.C. Grass* (*q.v.*) = marijuana. [U.S., E&R: 1971, JWK: 1981]

liquid hashish (also **liquid hash**) hashish oil. RT: *oil.* [U.S., (D&B: 1978), RDS: 1982]

liquor 1. beverage alcohol. Originally, any sauce or juice. Standard English. RT: *booze.* [1700s (or before) to the present, OED] 2. (also **liquor up**) to take a drink; to drink to excess. RT: *guzzle.* [(1560): OED; U.S., (1831): DA, (1850): SBF: 1976, JSF: 1889, DCCU: 1972]

liquorama (also **liquor factory, liquorium**) a liquor store. *Cf. L.I.Q.* [U.S., BVB: 1942, D&D: 1957]

liquored alcohol intoxicated. *Cf. liquored up.* RT: *drunk.* [(1667): DSUE, BVB: 1942, W&F: 1960]

liquored up alcohol intoxicated. *Cf. likkered up.* RT: *drunk.* [U.S., (1830): SBF: 1976, MP: 1928, MHW: 1934, D&D: 1957, W&F: 1960, DCCU: 1972]

liquorhead a drunkard; an alcoholic. A British version is liquorer. RT: *sot.* [U.S., M&W: 1946, LP: 1971a]

liquor, in alcohol intoxicated. RT: *drunk.* Still occasionally used. [BF: 1737, JCH: 1887, F&H, BWG: 1899, BVB: 1942]

liquorish (also likkerish) fond of liquor; alcohol intoxicated. RT: *drunk.* [(1894): OED; listed in BVB: 1942]

liquor one's boots to take a drink before leaving on a journey. RS: *irrigate.* [cant, (1702): OED, FG: 1785] See also *one for the road.*

liquor plug a drunkard. Possibly an error for *liquor pug* (*q.v.*). RT: *sot.* [VJM: 1949]

liquor pug a drunkard; a hobo drunkard. Compare to *likker pug.* RT: *sot.* [U.S., BVB: 1942]

liquor struck alcohol intoxicated. RT: *drunk.* [Br. dialect, 1800s, EDD]

liquor up to drink heavily; to get drunk. RT: *guzzle, mug oneself.* [U.S., JRB: 1859, JSF: 1889, M&C: 1905, DCCU: 1972]

lit (also lit up) 1. alcohol intoxicated. RT: *drunk.* [U.S., (1900): SBF: 1976, (1922): OEDS, MP: 1928, GI: 1931, JAS: 1932, MHW: 1934; Br., EP: 1948 SSD, M&J: 1975] 2. drug intoxicated. RT: *stoned.* [U.S., DWM: 1938, BVB: 1942, D&D: 1957, TRG: 1968, EEL: 1971]

lit the dripper an error for *lip the dripper.* See *lip.* [DU]

little boy blue the police; a (male) police officer. *Cf. men in blue.* RT: *fuzz.* Black use. [U.S., EAF: 1980]

little brown jug liquor. Refers to the crockery jug in which *moonshine* (*q.v.*) was kept. From an old Song. *Cf. jug.* RT: *booze.* [U.S., BVB: 1942]

little children the hallucinogenic compound *ololiuqui* (*q.v.*). [U.S., YKB: 1977] See also *los niños.*

little church round the corner a pub or saloon. *Cf. church key.* RS: *bar.* [Br., 1800s, F&H; U.S., BVB: 1942] See also *one of the faithful.*

little-D. a tablet of *Dilaudid* (TM; *q.v.*) hydromorphone painkiller. Dilaudid tablets are relatively small. *Cf. D.s.* See *big-D.* RT: *dids.* [U.S., SNP: 1977]

little whack a small drink of liquor. RT: *nip.* [JRW: 1909]

lit to the gills (also lit to the guards, lit to the gunnels) alcohol intoxicated. These are mixed metaphors based on *lit and loaded to the gills, guards,* or *gunnels.* The *alsos* refer to an overloaded ship whose hull is deeply submerged. RT: *drunk*. [U.S., MP: 1928, AH: 1931, D&D: 1957, W&F: 1960]

lit up See *lit*.

lit up like a church (also lit up like a cathedral, lit up like a Catholic Church, lit up like a church window, lit up like a high mass) alcohol intoxicated; very drunk; under the influence of narcotics. Additional forms not on the church theme are: lit up like a Christmas tree, a lighthouse, a skyscraper, a store window, Broadway, Main Street, the commonwealth, the sky, Times Square. These expressions can be created at will and there are surely many more. RT: *drunk*. [U.S., SBF: 1976, MHW: 1934, D&D: 1957, W&F: 1960]

lit up like a kite alcohol intoxicated. A mixed metaphor based on *lit up* and *high as a kite*. RT: *drunk*. [U.S., BVB: 1942]

live in grass huts to smoke marijuana. *Grass* (*q.v.*) = marijuana. Attested as gay slang. [U.S., BR: 1972]

live in the suburbs to use drugs occasionally; to *chippy* (*q.v.*). Probably nonce. [U.S., JES: 1959]

livener (also livvener) an early morning drink. RS: *nip*. [Br., B&L: 1890, F&H; listed in BVB: 1942]

liver destroyer brandy. Refers to cirrhosis of the liver. RT: *brandy*. [Br., late 18–1900s, DU]

live soldier (also live marine) a bottle of beer or liquor. The jocular opposite of *dead soldier* (*q.v.*) and *dead marine* (*q.v.*). [U.S., BVB: 1942]

li-yuen (also li-un, Li Young) high-quality opium for smoking. RT: *opium*. Chinese or mock-Chinese. [U.S., DWM: 1936, BD: 1937, VJM: 1949, JES: 1959]

L.L. marijuana. Origin unknown. RT: *pot*. [U.S., IGA: 1971, WCM: 1972]

llesca (also lhesca) marijuana. Lhesca is Portuguese for tinder. See *yesca*. [U.S., RG: 1970, IGA: 1971, JHF: 1971]

load 1. as much liquor as one can carry. [since the late 1500s, OED, (1893): W&F: 1960] 2. a drink of liquor. RT: *nip*. [U.S., (1880s): RML: 1950] 3. a dose of drugs; an injection of drugs. RS: *shot*. [U.S., PRB: 1930, MHW: 1934, VJM: 1949, M&V: 1954, EEL: 1971] 4. a drug supply; a *stash* (*q.v.*). [U.S., RRL: 1974] 5. a large purchase of heroin; a $25.00 purchase of heroin. RS: *load*. [U.S., RRL: 1969, JTD: 1971, SNP: 1977] Terms for a saleable volume of drugs or a parcel of drugs: *Abe, am-dray, amp, ampule, arm, arsenal, asskash, B., bag, baggie, bale, bale of hay, balloon, bar, bee, big bag, bindle, bing, bird's eye, biz, block, bolsa, bombita, book, bottle, box, bozo, brick, brick gum, brisket, bump, bundle, button, buy, Cadillac, cake, can, candy bar, cap, card, carga, cartucho, check, chiquita, cigarette paper, count, cube, cup, deal, deck, deuce, deuceways, dime, dime bag, dime's worth, dram,* *eighth, eighth piece, elbow, feed bag, finger, finger of stuff, fire plug, five-cent bag, five-cent paper, five-dollar bag, fives, foil, foon, full moons, fun, funny paper, gammon, gram, half, half a load, half a tenth, half bag, half can, half load, half piece, half spoon, halves, hunk, jar, jug, K., kee, keg, key, ki, kilo, kilo brick, kite, lay, L.B., lid, lids, load, match, matchbox, mic, mike, moon, nickel, nickel bag, nickel deck, O., Oz., O.Z., o-zee, ozee, pack, packet, paper, pfun, piece, pillow, pinch, pin-yen toy, poco, pound, quarter bag, quarter piece, quarters, rack, rations, roll, sealed stuff, shell, shell of hop, short, short buy, short can, short count, short piece, short toy, shorty, skid bag, smudge, spoon, spur, stack, street ounce, tad, taste, ten-cent bag, ten-cent pistol, test, tin, toy, trey, weight, Z., zee.*

loaded 1. alcohol intoxicated. *Cf. load.* RT: *drunk.* [U.S., (1880s): RML: 1950, (1886): W&F: 1960, (1890): OED, MP: 1928, MHW: 1934, D&D: 1957, RRL: 1969, CM: 1970, DCCU: 1972; Br., (1958): DSUE] 2. drug intoxicated. *Cf. load.* [U.S., (1923): OEDS, BD: 1937, DWM: 1938, M&D: 1952, D&D: 1957, RRL: 1969, CM: 1970, EEL: 1971] 3. spiked with liquor; containing much alcohol. [U.S., W&F: 1960, DCCU: 1972]

loaded for bear alcohol intoxicated. From an expression meaning very angry. This sense is an elaboration of *loaded* (*q.v.*). RT: *drunk.* [U.S., B&L: 1890, (1896): SBF: 1976, MHW: 1934]

loaded his cart alcohol intoxicated. RS: *drunk.* [BF: 1737]

loaded to the barrel (also loaded to the muzzle) alcohol intoxicated. Refers to the size of the drinker's load in comparison to a loaded gun. RT: *drunk.* [U.S., MHW: 1934, BVB: 1942]

loaded to the gills (also loaded to the guards, loaded to the gunnels, loaded to the gunwales, loaded to the Plimsoll mark) alcohol intoxicated. All are elaborations of *loaded* (*q.v.*). *Cf. over the mark.* RT: *drunk.* Loaded to the gunwales is from the late 1800s (B&L: 1890). [U.S., MHW: 1934, BVB: 1942]

loaded to the Plimsoll mark See *loaded to the gills.*

loaded with coke intoxicated with cocaine. *Coke* (*q.v.*) = cocaine. Possibly in the same way that a blast furnace is loaded with coke and iron. [U.S., JES: 1959, H&C: 1975]

loaded with hop drug intoxicated. *Cf. hop.* RT: *stoned.* [U.S., BVB: 1942]

lobby gow (also lob) someone who hangs around an opium den; an opium smoker. An occasional user or a bum hoping for a free smoke or a high from the ambient vapors. GEN: an errand boy working for the Chinese in Chinatown (1906): OEDS; a hanger-on (in underworld jargon). *Cf. gow.* [U.S., BD: 1937, DWM: 1938, VJM: 1949, D&D: 1957, W&F: 1960]

lobo cannabis; marijuana. RT: *pot.* [U.S., ELA: 1984]

Locker Room (also Loc-A-Roma, Locker Popper) the brand name of a *butyl nitrite* (*q.v.*) room deodorizer which is sniffed for a high. *Cf. JacAroma.* [U.S., (1978): DNE: 1980, ELA: 1984]

locoweed (also **loco**) 1. marijuana; a marijuana cigarette. From the name of a plant which affects livestock when eaten. Also refers to any smokable substitute for marijuana. RT: *pot.* [U.S., (1931): ELA: 1982, RPW: 1938, M&D: 1952, D&D: 1957, TRG: 1968, RRL: 1969, DCCU: 1972, ADC: 1975, YKB: 1977, NIDA: 1980] 2. *jimson weed* (*q.v.*). [U.S., YKB: 1977, RDS: 1982]

locust (also **locus**) 1. knockout drops; laudanum. From the name for a policeman's club made out of locust wood. *Cf. hocus.* RS: *Mickey Finn.* [(1851): OED, BVB: 1942, SNP: 1977] 2. to drug and rob (or otherwise harm) someone. [U.S., (1831): OED, JCH: 1887] 3. drugs in general. From sense one. [U.S., BVB: 1942, VJM: 1949, A&T: 1953]

locust point a place where drugs are sold. *Cf. locust.* RT: *doperie.* Probably a specific location. [U.S., JES: 1959, H&C: 1975]

log 1. an opium pipe. RS: *hop stick.* [U.S., BD: 1937, DWM: 1938, VJM: 1949] 2. a marijuana cigarette. RT: *joint.* [U.S., SNP: 1977, RDS: 1982]

logged alcohol intoxicated. From *water logged* (*q.v.*). RT: *drunk.* [Br. (1920): DSUE]

London Milk gin. RT: *gin.* [Br., B&L: 1890] See also *milk.*

lonesome a drink taken alone. RS: *nip.* [U.S., 1900s and perhaps before, PW: 1977] See also *high lonesome.*

long arm of the law (also **long limb of the law**) See *arm of the law.*

long draw a long hard pull on an opium pipe. The prepared pellet of opium is to be completely vaporized and inhaled in this single draw. The pipe is then passed to another smoker and another pellet of opium is inserted. GEN: a deep pull on any smoking device. [U.S., (1887): RML: 1948]

long drink a drink of hard liquor diluted with water and served in a tall glass. [U.S., BVB: 1942, D&D: 1957]

long hitter a heavy drinker. RS: *sot.* [U.S., W&F: 1967, RDS: 1982]

long necker a liquor bottle. RT: *dead soldier.* [U.S., MHW: 1934, BVB: 1942]

long pull (also **long one**) a large drink of liquor. RS: *nip.* [JRW: 1909, MHW: 1934, BVB: 1942]

long sleever a large drink; a tall glass of beer. RS: *nip.* [Aust. and U.S., MHW: 1934, BVB: 1942, SJB: 1943, (1877): GAW: 1978]

long stale drunk a long and depressing hangover combined with continued drinking. RT: *hangover.* [JRW: 1909]

long white roll a tobacco cigarette. RT: *nail.* [U.S., DB: 1944]

long wine potent wine. RS: *wine.* [U.S., BR: 1972]

loo foo kee second quality smoking opium sold in a can. *Cf.*

li-yuen. RS: *opium*. [U.S., M&V: 1973]

loogan beer; a beer. RT: *beer*. [U.S., AP: 1980]

looking seeking a drug dealer. See *I'm looking*. *Cf.* *hunting*, *scratching*. [U.S., EEL: 1971, S&W: 1973, JWK: 1981]

looking lively alcohol intoxicated. RT: *drunk*. [Br., 1800s, F&H]

look through a glass to get drunk. Refers to seeing through the bottom of a drinking glass. RT: *mug oneself*. [Br., (1840): DSUE, F&H; listed in BVB: 1942]

loony alcohol intoxicated. *Cf.* *crazy*. RT: *drunk*. [U.S., BVB: 1942]

loop to drink liquor to excess; to intoxicate oneself. RS: *mug oneself*. [U.S., D&D: 1957]

looped alcohol intoxicated. Also the elaboration **looped to the eyeballs**. RT: *drunk*. [U.S., MHW: 1934, (1940): SBF: 1976, BVB: 1942, D&D: 1957, W&F: 1960]

loop-legged alcohol intoxicated. *Cf.* *limber*, *loose*. RT: *drunk*. [U.S., D&D: 1957, W&F: 1960]

loopy alcohol intoxicated; tipsy. *Cf.* *looped*. RT: *drunk*. [U.S., (1890s): SBF: 1976, W&F: 1960]

loose alcohol intoxicated. *Cf.* *limber*. RT: *drunk*. [Br., 1800s, F&H]

loose in the hilts (also **loose in the hilt**) alcohol intoxicated. Refers to a loose knife blade. An elaboration of *loose* (*q.v.*). RT: *drunk*. [BF: 1737]

loose joint a single marijuana cigarette as opposed to several. *Cf.* *ace*. RT: *joint*. [U.S., (D&B: 1978)]

loose, on the alcohol intoxicated; drinking heavily. *Cf.* *loose*. RT: *drunk*. [Br., F&H; U.S., MHW: 1934]

loose price the price of a drug (including marijuana) bought by the dose rather than by the *deck* (*q.v.*). [U.S., MA: 1973, RDS: 1982]

lordly alcohol intoxicated. From *drunk as a lord* (*q.v.*). RT: *drunk*. [BF: 1737]

lords hydromorphone painkiller. Probably *Dilaudid* (TM; *q.v.*). Possibly akin to *lorphs* (*q.v.*). [U.S., IGA: 1971, SNP: 1977]

lorphs *blue morphone* (*q.v.*); hydromorphone, a painkiller. Possibly also a blue elixir or morphine sulfate. *Cf.* *blorphs*, *lords*. [U.S., JWK: 1981]

lose one's legs to get drunk. *Cf.* *legless*. RS: *mug oneself*. [late 1700s, DSUE]

lose one's shit to become deranged after taking drugs. Perhaps the reverse of U.S. 1960–70s slang *get one's shit together*. [U.S., ADC: 1981]

los niños* mushrooms containing *psilocybin* (*q.v.*). Mexican Spanish for *little children* (*q.v.*). RT: *psilocybin*. [U.S., YKB: 1977]

lost his rudder alcohol intoxicated. RT: ***drunk***. [BF: 1737]

lotion liquor; a drink of liquor. RT: ***booze, nip***. [Br., (1876): DSUE, B&L: 1890, F&H; U.S., MHW: 1934, BVB: 1942]

lounge short for ***cocktail lounge*** (*q.v.*).

loused covered with scars from injection abscesses. *Cf.* ***bugged***. See ***tracks***. [U.S., JTD: 1971]

love See ***love saves***.

love affair a mixture of heroin and cocaine. *Cf.* ***girl, boy***. RS: ***set***. [U.S., ADC: 1975]

love blow marijuana. *Cf.* ***love weed***. RS: ***pot***. [U.S., JH: 1979]

love drug a drug acting as an aphrodisiac; a drug which increases sexual pleasure. It has been defined as ***M.D.A.*** (*q.v.*), ***Methedrine*** (TM; *q.v.*), and ***methaqualone*** (*q.v.*), a hypnotic-sedative. The most widely-known reference is to ***methaqualone*** (*q.v.*). *Cf.* ***love weed***. [U.S., M&V: 1973, ADC: 1975, W&F: 1975, YKB: 1977] See also ***sex-juice***.

love pot a drunkard; a heavy drinker, one who loves a pot of booze. RT: ***sot***. The OED has also **love-pot woman** = a drunken woman, (early 1600s). [JF: 1598, 1800s, DSUE; listed in BVB: 1942]

lover a marijuana smoker. *Cf.* ***mezzanine lover***. RT: ***toker***. [U.S., JES: 1959, H&C: 1975]

love saves (also **love**) ***L.S.D.*** (*q.v.*) combined with some other drug. RS: ***set***. [U.S., KBH: 1982]

love weed marijuana; hashish. *Cf.* ***love drug***. RT: ***pot***. [U.S., RPW: 1938, BVB: 1953, M&V: 1954, D&D: 1957, EEL: 1971, M&V: 1973, YKB: 1977]

low a bad drug trip. From a colloquial expression for a depressed state from any cause. *Cf.* ***bum bend, bum kicks, bummer, bum trip, downer, down trip, drag, freak out, horrors, negative, panic trip***. RT: ***bad trip***. [U.S., EEL: 1971, W&F: 1975]

lowerer a heavy drinker; a drunkard. *Cf.* ***lower liquor***. RT: ***sot***. [Br., 1800s, F&H]

lower liquor (also **lower, lower a drink**) to take and swallow a drink of liquor. *Cf.* ***lowerer***. RT: ***irrigate***. [(1895): OEDS, MHW: 1934, SSD]

low rider a ruined drug addict. Probably akin to riding ***high*** or to riding a ***low*** (*q.v.*). [U.S., M&V: 1967, H&C: 1975]

low talk a speakeasy; an illegal liquor establishment. RT: ***speak***. From the prohibition era. [U.S., BVB: 1942]

lozerose (also **lozies**) a nickname for the marijuana sold by Mezz Mezzrow in the 1920s in Harlem. RT: ***pot***. [U.S., M&W: 1946]

L.s See ***L***.

L.S.D. (also **LSD**) D-lysergic acid diethylamide 25, a hallucinogenic chemical (drug). From the German chemical name Lyserg-säure-diethylamid. Accidentally discovered by Dr. Albert Hoffmann at Sandoz Laboratories, Basel, Switzerland in 1943. *Cf. let sunshine do, Lucy in the Sky with Diamonds.* [U.S., (1950): OEDS, S&W: 1966, S&R: 1972, BW: 1984] Nicknames and slang terms for various types of L.S.D.: *A., acid, acid cube, ácido, animal, animal crackers, Augustus Owsley, barrel, barrels, beast, big chief, big-D., black acid, black tabs, blotter, blotter acid, blue, blue acid, blue angelfish, blue babies, blue barrel, blue caps, blue chair, blue cheer, blue dot, blue doubledomes, blue dragon, blue flag, blue flats, blue heavens, blue jeans, blue mist, blue pyramids, blue splash, blue vials, brown acid, brown caps, brown dots, California sunshine, candy, cap, chemicals, cherry top, chief, chocolate chips, Christmas tree, cid, clear light, clear liquid, coffee, contact lens, crackers, cresta, cube, cupcakes, D., death trips, deeda, delysid, dome, domes, dots, dragon, electric koolaid, electric wine, fifty, flake acid, flash, flat blues, flats, four-ways, four-way star, four-way windowpane, gammon, gelatin, ghost, grape parfait, green angelfish, green caps, green dot, green double domes, green dragon, green single domes, green swirls, green wedge, hawk, hawk-25, haze, heavenly blue, heavenly sunshine, Hoffmann's bicycle, horror drug, instant Zen, L., lason sa daga, L.B.J., L.D.J., let sunshine do, lime acid, love, love saves, L.s, L.S.D., Lucy in the Sky with Diamonds, luggage, lysergic acid, lysergide, Mary Owsley, mellow-yellow, mickey mouse, microdot, mighty Quinn, mike, mind-bender, mind-blower, mind-detergent, mind-expander, mind-explorer, mind-opener, mind-spacer, mind-tripper, one-way, orange, orange crystal, orange cube, orange cupcakes, orange micro, orange mushrooms, orange Owsley, orange sunshine, orange wafers, orange wedges, osley, outer, Owsley, Owsley acid, Owsley blue dot, Owsley blues, Owsley power, Owsley purple, Owsleys, Owsley's stuff, ozzy, paisley caps, paper acid, peace, peace tablet, pearly gates, pellet, peppermint swirl, pink, pink dots, pink Owsley, pink ozzy, pink swirl, pink wafers, pink wedges, pink witches, product IV, pure love, purple, purple barrels, purple dot, purple dragon, purple flats, purple haze, purple microdots, purple Owsley, purple ozolin, purple ozoline, purple ozzy, purple wedges, quicksilver, Raggedy Ann, red angelfish, red dimple, red dot, red dragon, righteous acid, robin eggs, royal blue, sacrament, Sandoz, serenity, sid, sidney, sky river, smears, squirrel, squirrel dew, Stanley's stuff, strawberries, strawberry, strawberry fields, strawberry flats, sugar, sugar cube, sugar lump, sunshine, sunshine acid, sunshine pill, Swiss purple, T., tab, the animal, the beast, the chief, the cube, the ghost, the hawk, the ticket, ticket, topi, travel agent, tric, tric acid, trips, twenty-five, two-way, viaje, vials, wafer, wedding bells, wedding bells acid, wedge, wedges, wedgies, white domes, white double domes, white lightning, white Owsley, white Owslies, white Sandoz, white single domes, windowpane, windowpane acid, witches brew, yellow, yellow caps, yellow dimple, yellow dots, yellows, yellow sunshine, Zen, 25, 50.*

lubange hashish; marijuana. An East African version of *banji* (*q.v.*). The lu- is a prefix. The language involved is not Swahili. RT: *hash, pot.* [U.S., RDS: 1982]

lube a drink of liquor; a beer. *Cf. oil.* RT: *nip.* [Aust., SJB: 1943, DSUE]

lubricate to drink liquor. RT: *irrigate.* [since the late 1800s, F&H; listed in BVB: 1942]

lubricated (also **lubed**) alcohol intoxicated. *Cf. lube, lubricate, well-oiled.* RT: *drunk.* [U.S., MP: 1928, MHW: 1934, VJM: 1949, D&D: 1957, W&F: 1960, RDS: 1982; Br., DSUE, M&J: 1975]

lubrication alcohol; booze. RT: *booze.* [HSD: 1984]

Lucy in the Sky with Diamonds the hallucinogenic drug *L.S.D.* (*q.v.*). An elaboration of the initials L.S.D. RT: *L.S.D.* [U.S., H&C: 1975, YKB: 1977] See also *sweet Lucy.*

luded out intoxicated with *Quaalude* (TM; *q.v.*) *methaqualone* (*q.v.*), a sedative-hypnotic. May also refer to Quaalude taken with liquor. *Cf. ludes.* RT: *stoned.* [U.S., (RRL: 1969), (YKB: 1977), ADC: 1981, (RDS: 1982)]

ludens See *ludins.*

ludes (also **lude, 'ludes, luds**) *Quaalude* (TM; *q.v.*) *methaqualone* (*q.v.*), a sedative and hypnotic. *Cf. luded out.* RS: *dope.* [U.S., RRL: 1969, ADC: 1975, W&F: 1975, YKB: 1977, DNE: 1980, ADC: 1981, JWK: 1981] See also *soaper.* Nicknames and slang terms for *Quaalude*: *Canadian quail, cortals, cues, ekies, ludes, luds, mandrakes, Mandrax, mandrix, methaqualone, Optimil, Parest, pillow, puti, Q., Q.s, quaal, quacks, quads, quas, seven-fourteens, soap, soapers, soaps, sope, Sopor, super-Quaalude, super-soaper, super-soper, wallbanger, white birds, yanga, 714s.*

ludins (also **ludens**) *Preludin* (TM; *q.v.*) central nervous system stimulant. Named for Luden's (TM) cough drops. *Cf. prels, sweeties.* RS: *dope.* [U.S., JWK: 1981]

luds allegedly methamphetamine. Almost certainly an error for *ludes* (*q.v.*) which is *methaqualone* (*q.v.*). Probably due to the confusing use of *meth* as an abbreviation. [U.S., SNP: 1977]

Luer a hypodermic syringe. From the Luer brand hypodermic syringes. RT: *monkey pump.* [U.S., DWM: 1936, VJM: 1949]

lug to drink liquor. RT: *irrigate.* [(1577): OED, JCH: 1887]

luggage the hallucinogenic drug *L.S.D.* (*q.v.*). Because you cannot go on a *trip* without it. RT: *L.S.D.* [U.S., RAS: 1981] See also *baggage.*

lug pot a drinker; a drunkard. *Cf. lug.* [Br., 1800s and perhaps before, F&H]

lum (also **lums**) *Cannabis indica* from Colombia. See *lumbo.* [U.S., JWK: 1981, ADC: 1984]

lumber stems and hard chunks in a portion of marijuana. *Cf. debris, timber.* [U.S., RRL: 1974, D&B: 1978, JH: 1979]

lumbo (also **lum**) Colombian marijuana. See *Colombian gold.* RS: *pot.* [U.S., ADC: 1981, JWK: 1981]

Luminal a protected trade name for *phenobarbital* (*q.v.*) a *barbiturate* (*q.v.*). RT: *barbs.* [in current use; consult a pharmaceutical reference for more information]

lumpy alcohol intoxicated. RT: *drunk.* [Br., (1810): DSUE, JCH: 1887, F&H; U.S., (1810): DSUE, MHW: 1934]

lunatic soup (also **lunatic broth**) brandy; cheap red wine; red wine laced with denatured alcohol; booze in general. *Cf. ignorant oil.* [Aust., Br., and New Zealand, (1933): OEDS, SJB: 1943, DU; listed in RDS: 1982]

lunch hour trip the drug *D.M.T.* (*q.v.*). See *businessman's trip.*

lung-disturber a cigarette. RT: *nail.* [U.S., VJM: 1949]

lung-duster (also **lung-fogger**) a tobacco cigarette. RT: *nail.* [U.S., BVB: 1942, D&D: 1957, W&F: 1960]

lush 1. liquor; beer; ale. RT: *booze.* [FG: 1823, (1840): SBF: 1976, GWM: 1859, JCH: 1887, F&H, EK: 1927, WG: 1962, W&F: 1960, RRL: 1969] 2. (also **lush it, lush it up, lush up**) to drink liquor; to get drunk; to provide liquor for. RS: *guzzle, mug oneself.* [since the early 1800s, JCH: 1887, BVB: 1942, M&W: 1946] 3. a heavy drinker; a drunkard; an alcoholic. RS: *sot.* [(1890): SBF: 1976, GI: 1931, GM: 1931, GOL: 1950, D&D: 1957, W&F: 1960, RRL: 1969, CM: 1970, EEL: 1971] 4. alcohol intoxicated. RT: *drunk.* [FG: 1811, (1880s): SBF: 1976, GI: 1931, MHW: 1934, BVB: 1942] 5. a drinking bout. RT: *spree.* [Br., early 1800s, OED]

lush cove (also **lushing cove, lushing man, lushy cove**) a (male) drunkard. A female drunkard is a **lush blowen**. Cove = a man. Blowen = a young woman. RS: *sot.* [cant, (1810): DSUE]

lush crib (also **lushing crib, lushing ken, lush ken, lush panny**) a low pub. RT: *dive. Crib, ken,* and *panny* all refer to a criminal hangout. [cant, (1790): DSUE, FG: 1823, GWM: 1859, F&H]

lush dive (also **lush drum**) a low saloon. Drum = a criminal hangout. RT: *dive.* [U.S., late 18–1900s, DU, GOL: 1950]

lushed (also **lushed up**) 1. alcohol intoxicated. *Cf. lush.* RT: *drunk.* [U.S., (1880s): SBF: 1976, MP: 1928, MHW: 1934, D&D: 1957, W&F: 1960, DCCU: 1972, RDS: 1982] 2. drug intoxicated. RT: *stoned.* [U.S., W&F: 1960]

lushed up to the nuts alcohol intoxicated. Full of alcohol from the feet up to the testicles. *Cf. lushed.* RT: *drunk.* [U.S., GOL: 1950]

lusher 1. a heavy drinker; a drunkard; an alcoholic. RT: *sot.* [U.S., (1848): W&F: 1960, HB: 1955] 2. a sot who mixes marijuana with wine. [U.S., HB: 1955]

lushery a low tavern or saloon. RT: *dive.* [Br., late 1800s, F&H]

lush head a heavy drinker; and alcoholic. RT: ***sot***. [U.S., DB: 1944, (1945): OEDS, (M&W: 1946)]

lush hound a drunkard. RT: ***sot***. [(1935): OEDS, RM: 1942, M&W: 1946, CM: 1970]

lush house a pub or tavern. RS: ***bar***. [cant, late 1800s, F&H; listed in BVB: 1942]

lushington a drunkard. From ***lush*** and *Lushington*, a brewer's name. *Cf.* ***Alderman Lushington, boozington, swipington, thirstington***. RT: ***sot***. [cant, FG: 1823, GWM: 1859, B&L: 1890, F&H]

lush merchant a drunkard. Cf lush. RT: ***sot***. [Aust., SJB: 1943]

lush-out a drinking bout. RT: ***spree***. [Br., JB: 1823]

lush stash a saloon or bar. Compare to ***stash***. RT: ***bar***. [U.S., DB: 1944]

lushy (also **lushey, lushie**) **1**. a drunkard. RT: ***sot***. [U.S., (1944): OEDS, M&W: 1946, CM: 1970] **2**. alcohol intoxicated. RT: ***drunk***. [FG: 1811, (1840): SBF: 1976, GWM: 1859, JCH: 1887, B&L: 1890, F&H, MHW: 1934, D&D: 1957]

lysergic acid (also **lysergide**) the hallucinogenic drug ***L.S.D.*** (*q.v.*). a truncation of D-lysergic acid diethylamide 25, a hallucinogenic chemical (drug). See ***L.S.D.*** [U.S., (1952): OEDS, RRL: 1969]

M

M. 1. (also **M.s**) morphine. RT: ***morphine***. [U.S., (1914): OEDS, WHW: 1922, PRB: 1930, GI: 1931, DWM: 1933, VJM: 1949, GOL: 1950, M&D: 1952, (D&D: 1957), W&F: 1960, RRL: 1969, CM: 1970, YKB: 1977] 2. marijuana. RT: ***pot***. [U.S., (1956): ELA: 1982, D&B: 1970c, EEL: 1971]

mach marijuana. From ***machinery*** (*q.v.*) or ***maconha*** (*q.v.*). RT: ***pot***. [U.S., YKB: 1977]

machinery 1. (also **machine**) equipment used for preparing and injecting drugs. RT: ***outfit***. [U.S., BD: 1937, DWM: 1938, VJM: 1949, EEL: 1971] 2. marijuana. *Cf.* ***mach***. RT: ***pot***. [U.S., SNP: 1977]

Machu Picchu notably strong marijuana from Peru. Named for the ancient Peruvian city, Machu Picchu. *Cf.* ***Peruvian flake***. RT: ***pot***. [U.S., ELA: 1982]

maconha (also **mach, machona, macoha, macon**) marijuana, presumably from Brazil. RT: ***pot***. Said to be from an African language via Brazilian Portuguese. [U.S., RPW: 1938, D&D: 1957, (1967): DNE: 1973, RRL: 1969]

MAD (also **M.A.D.**) "mind-altering drug." Probably from M.D.A., a drug related to L.S.D. See ***M.D.A., M.D.M.A***. [U.S., RDS: 1982]

mad dog 1. strong ale. RS: ***ale***. [late 15-1600s, DSUE] 2. Mogen David (TM) wine. A reinterpretation of the initials M.D. RT: ***wine***. [U.S., RAS: 1982]

made an example alcohol intoxicated. (BF: 1737: [He's] made an Example.) RT: ***drunk***. [BF: 1737]

madman's broth cheap wine. See ***idiot oil, lunatic soup***. RT: ***wine***. [Aust., SJB: 1966]

maggie (also **Maggie**) marijuana. *Cf.* ***Megg***. RT: ***pot***. [U.S., JES: 1959, H&C: 1975]

maggot 1. a cigarette butt. Probably rhyming slang for ***faggot*** (*q.v.*). RT: ***brad***. [U.S., W&F: 1967] 2. an addict whose typical means of getting money to buy drugs is through assault and theft. *Cf.* ***beat artist***. [U.S., JWK: 1981]

maggotty (also **maggoty**) alcohol intoxicated; very drunk. An elaboration of ***rotten*** (*q.v.*). RT: ***drunk***. [Br. (Anglo-Irish), 1900s,

DSUE; Newfoundland, GAE: 1925]

magic 1. illicit liquor. RS: *moonshine*. From the prohibition era. [U.S., GOL: 1950] 2. See *magic dust*.

magic dust (also **magic, magic mist**) phencyclidine, P.C.P. RT: *P.C.P.* [U.S., ELA: 1984]

magic flake high-quality cocaine. RS: *cocaine*. [U.S., S&F: 1984]

magic mushrooms (also **sacred mushrooms**) mushrooms of the genus *Psilocybe* which cause hallucinations when eaten. This is sometimes used to refer to *peyote* which is a cactus, not a mushroom. *Cf. poison mushrooms*. [U.S., RRL: 1969, D&B: 1971, WCM: 1972, ADC: 1975, (1978): DNE: 1980, ADC: 1981] See also *shrooms*.

magic pumpkin mescaline. RS: *peyote*. [U.S., IGA: 1971, WCM: 1972]

maharishee marijuana. RT: *pot*. Black use. [U.S., EAF: 1980]

mahoska (also **hoska**) narcotics; any contraband. Akin to *mohasky* (*q.v.*). RS: *dope*. [U.S., GOL: 1950, A&T: 1953, M&V: 1967]

mainline (also **main**) 1. the median cephalic vein (in the forearm), the favored site for intravenous injections. *Cf. channel, gutter, home, line, sewer*. Widely known outside drug slang. [U.S., (1925): DU, DWM: 1936, GOL: 1950, RRL: 1969, ADC: 1975] 2. to inject into the median cephalic vein. RT: *shoot*. [U.S., DWM: 1938, RRL: 1969, (1970): DNE: 1973, EEL: 1971, W&F: 1975]

mainline bang an injection into the median cephalic vein. RT: *shot*. [U.S., GOL: 1950]

mainliner (also **mainline shooter**) a drug addict who injects into the *mainline* (*q.v.*). RT: *bangster*. [U.S., (1934): OEDS, DWM: 1936, BVB: 1942, M&D: 1952, W&F: 1960, D&B: 1970c, EEL: 1971]

mainstash one's home; the home of a drug user described in terms of where one's major store of drugs is kept. [U.S., M&W: 1946, LVA: 1981]

maintain to take an addictive drug in sufficient strength to maintain an addiction or to ward off withdrawal symptoms. Used as an intransitive verb in this sense. [U.S., IGA: 1971, RDS: 1982]

ma-jen marijuana. RT: *pot*. From Chinese (BTD: 1968). But see *majoon*. [Br., BTD: 1968]

majonda drugs. *Cf. maconha*. RS: *dope*. [U.S., GOL: 1950, A&T: 1953, SNP: 1977]

majoon* (also **majoun***) a Middle East confection containing marijuana or hashish. Arabic for jam. See *goblet of jam*. RS: *hash, pot*. Not slang. [U.S., RRL: 1969, RDS: 1982]

Major Loder whiskey and soda. *Cf. Rosy Loader*. Rhyming slang on *soder* = soda. [early 1900s, DRS]

make 1. a *shot* (*q.v.*) or dose of a drug. RS: *dose*. [U.S., EEL:

1971, JH: 1979] 2. to purchase drugs. See *make a buy*.

make a buy (also **make, make a connection, make a contact, make a hit, make a meet, make a strike, make it, make the man**) to locate a drug dealer and purchase drugs. RT: *score*. [U.S., BD: 1937, VJM: 1949, M&D: 1952, TRG: 1968, EEL: 1971, BW: 1984]

make a croaker for a reader (also **make a reader**) to get a prescription from a physician. *Reader* (*q.v.*) = prescription. *Croaker* = physician. [U.S., DWM: 1936, BVB: 1942, RRL: 1969]

make a spread to set up equipment for drug use. [U.S., DWM: 1938, BVB: 1942, VJM: 1949]

makes Virginia fence to be alcohol intoxicated. The drunkard makes a zigzag pattern when walking. *Cf. making Ms and Ws*. RS: *drunk*. [BF: 1737]

make tracks to inject drugs and leave a series of needle marks. *Cf. tracks*. [U.S., EEL: 1971]

making Ms and Ws walking in a drunken fashion; being drunk. *Cf. makes Virginia fence*. RS: *drunk*. Partridge (DSUE) identifies this as printer's slang. [Br., (1860): DSUE, B&L: 1890; listed in BVB: 1942]

makings (also **makin's**) tobacco and rolling papers for rolling cigarettes. *Cf. rollings*. RS: *freckles, freckles*. [(1905): OEDS, GI: 1931, HS: 1933, BVB: 1942, GOL: 1950, WG: 1962]

making scallops alcohol intoxicated. Refers to zigzag walking. RT: *drunk*. [U.S., BVB: 1942]

mala hierba* bad marijuana. Spanish for bad grass. RS: *pot*. [U.S., RRL: 1969]

male male marijuana. In contrast to the female flower tops. The male plants are less desirable because they have less resin. *Cf. fee-tops*. [U.S., JWK: 1981]

mallet a police officer. RT: *fuzz*. Black use. [U.S., EAF: 1980]

malt beer; malt liquor. RT: *beer*. [(1718): OED, B&L: 1890, MHW: 1934]

malted alcohol intoxicated. *Cf. hopped, malty*. RT: *drunk*. [18–1900s, F&H, BVB: 1942, D&D: 1957]

maltimillionaire someone made wealthy in the liquor business. Contrived word play. [U.S., BVB: 1942, D&D: 1957]

malt is above the water (also **malt is above the meal, malt is above the beer, malt is above the wheat**) having to do with a drunken person. (BF: 1737: The malt is above the water.) [(1546): OED, BF: 1737]

malt liquor any mild alcoholic beverage made by fermenting grain. Beer and ale are *malt liquor*. Very strong beer is sold as *malt liquor* in the U.S. [since the late 1600s, OED]

malt shop a liquor store. Probably refers to the use of malt in beer. From a mid 1900s term for an ice cream parlor catering to young people. RT: *L.I.Q.* [U.S., D&B: 1970b]

malt worm (also malt bug) a drunkard. RT: *sot.* [(1550): OED, PW: 1974]

malty alcohol intoxicated. *Cf. malted.* RT: *drunk.* [Br., JB: 1823; listed in BVB: 1942]

malty cove a drunkard. Cove = a man (in cant). RT: *sot.* [cant, mid 1800s, DSUE]

Mama coca cocaine. *Cf. coca.* RT: *cocaine.* [U.S., RAS: 1983]

mama's mellow the sedative effects of *Seconal* (TM; *q.v.*). *Cf. housewife's delight.* [U.S., EEL: 1971, JWK: 1981]

man (also the man) **1.** a drug seller or pusher. RT: *dealer.* [U.S., BVB: 1942, RRL: 1969, MA: 1973] 2. the police; a narcotics agent. RS: *fuzz.* [U.S., MB: 1938, BVB: 1942, (1967): DNE: 1973, M&V: 1967, MA: 1973, ADC: 1975, MW: 1976, ADC: 1981, JWK: 1981] See also *my man.*

M. and C. (also M. C.) a mixture of morphine and cocaine injected. *Cf. speedball.* RS: *set.* [U.S., GI: 1931, BVB: 1942, A&T: 1953, RRL: 1969]

M and Ms capsules of *Seconal* (TM; *q.v.*) barbiturate. From the brand name of some brightly-colored candy pellets. This expression probably applies to any brightly-colored capsules. *Cf. communist M. and M.s.* RT: *sec.* [U.S., IGA: 1971, BR: 1972, EAF: 1980]

mandrakes (also mandrix) pills of a British brand of *methaqualone* (*q.v.*), a hypnotic-sedative, *Mandrax* (TM; *q.v.*). RT: *ludes.* [U.S., SNP: 1977, YKB: 1977]

Mandrax a British brand of *methaqualone* (*q.v.*) used as a sleeping pill. *Cf. mandrakes.* [(1963): OEDS; in current use; consult a pharmaceutical reference for more information]

mandrix *Mandrax* (TM; *q.v.*). See *mandrakes.*

Manhattan white (also Manhattan silver) a jocular term for an imaginary, high-potency white (from lack of sunlight) marijuana which grows from seeds flushed down the New York City sewer system. RS: *pot.* [U.S., (1976): ELA: 1982, R&P: 1982]

maní* a barbiturate tablet or capsule. Spanish for peanut. See *peanuts.* RT: *barbs.* [U.S., NIDA: 1980]

manicure 1. to trim, clean, and dress marijuana for smoking. [U.S., RPW: 1938, M&V: 1954, RRL: 1969, RG: 1970] 2. good-quality, cleaned marijuana. *Cf. fine stuff.* RS: *pot.* [U.S., TRG: 1968]

manita milk sugar used to dilute heroin. From the Spanish word for *mannitol* (*q.v.*). [U.S., M&V: 1967, RRL: 1969]

mannitol (also mannite) a crystalline form of laxative used to dilute drugs. [U.S., RRL: 1969, JWK: 1981, S&F: 1984]

manteca* 1. heroin; bad heroin. Spanish for grease. *Cf. grease.*

RT: *heroin*. [U.S., CG: 1980, NIDA: 1980] 2. marijuana. RT: *pot*. [U.S., IGA: 1971]

man, the See *man*.

manzoul marijuana. From Arabic. RT: *pot*. [U.S., RPW: 1938, D&D: 1957]

maran guango* marijuana. Said to be from Portuguese. Possibly the source of Mexican Spanish *mariguana* (*q.v.*). [1900s, RRL: 1969]

marathons amphetamines. Because they greatly increase a person's energy and endurance. See *run*. RT: *amps*. [U.S., IGA: 1971, WCM: 1972, M&V: 1973, NIDA: 1980]

marbles round, red capsules of *Placidyl* (TM; *q.v.*) hypnotic sedative. RT: *plass*. [U.S., JWK: 1981]

marcia a water-pipe used for smoking marijuana. RS: *bong*. [U.S., POW: 1949, M&V: 1954]

margarita marijuana. RT: *pot*. [U.S., EEL: 1971, JH: 1979]

margie-wanna marijuana. *Cf. Marjorie*. RT: *pot*. [U.S., (1971): R&P: 1982]

margin man a dope runner or smuggler who does not own the drugs which he delivers. RS: *mule*. [U.S., BD: 1937, DWM: 1938]

mari marijuana; a marijuana cigarette. From *marijuana*. *Cf. Mary*. RT: *pot, joint*. [U.S., (1933): ELA: 1982, VJM: 1949, M&D: 1952]

Maria Johanna marijuana. Spanish. RT: *pot*. [U.S., RPW: 1938]

marigold marijuana; golden marijuana. A portmanteau of *marijuana* and *Acapulco gold*. RS: *pot*. [U.S., BR: 1972]

mariguana marijuana. Possibly from Portuguese *maran guango* = intoxication. Probably the source of the word *marijuana* (*q.v.*). RT: *pot*. [U.S., YKB: 1977]

mariholic a person psychically addicted to marijuana. A portmanteau (blend) of *marijuana* and *holic* from *alcoholic*. *Cf. hashaholic, marijuanaholic*. RS: *toker*. Not argot. Probably journalistic. [U.S., RDS: 1982]

Marijane marijuana. RT: *pot*. [U.S., H&C: 1975]

marijuana (also **mariahuana, mariguana, marihuana**) chopped cannabis; products of the cannabis plant. RT: *pot*. The most common standard American English term for this subject. Standard English. The spelling *marihuana* was common until the sixties. New dictionaries list *marijuana* as an entry with *marihuana* as an alternate. Probably from Mexican Spanish. [(1894, 1918): OEDS]

marijuana bar a bar where marijuana is sold in addition to alcohol. *Cf. hashish bar* (at *hashish house*). RS: *doperie*. [U.S., RDS: 1982]

marijuanaful having to do with wonderful marijuana. A play on *wonnerful* = wonderful. [U.S., BR: 1972]

marijuanaholic a person who is totally habituated to marijuana. *Cf. mariholic.* RS: *toker.* [U.S., (1981): R&P: 1982]

marijuana munchies (also **munchies**) a craving for food sometimes brought on by the use of marijuana. *Cf. M.M.s.* [U.S., D&B: 1970b]

marine (also **marine recruit, marine officer**) an empty beer or liquor bottle. The expression is built on the supposed worthlessness of both the empty bottle and the marine. RT: *dead soldier.* [FG: 1823, JCH: 1887, BVB: 1942]

mariweegee marijuana. RT: *pot.* Black use. [U.S., EAF: 1980]

Marjorie (also **Marje, Marjie**) marijuana. RT: *pot.* Marjie is Australian (DU). [U.S. EEL: 1971, JH: 1979, HSD: 1984] See also *mejorana.*

marks needle marks at the sites of drug injections. RT: *tracks.* Black use. [U.S., D&B: 1970c, EEL: 1971, EAF: 1980]

Marmon and Cadillac a mixture of morphine and cocaine. From the name of a business firm. A reinterpretation of *M. and C.* (*q.v.*). RT: *set.* [U.S., BVB: 1942, (A&T: 1953)]

marshmallow reds capsules of *Seconal* (TM; *q.v.*) barbiturate. RT: *sec.* [U.S., YKB: 1977]

martooni the *martini* gin-based mixed drink as if pronounced by a drunk person. [U.S., W&F: 1960]

Mary 1. morphine. A reinterpretation of *M.* (*q.v.*). RT: *morphine.* [U.S., VJM: 1949, M&D: 1952, EEL: 1971] 2. (also **mari**) marijuana. See *Mary Warner.* Spanish (calo). RT: *pot.* [U.S., M&D: 1952, JBR: 1973, RRL: 1969, YKB: 1977]

Mary and Johnnie marijuana; a marijuana cigarette. M&B: 1944 claim this is rhyming slang. DRS disagrees. RT: *pot.* See *Mary Warner.* [U.S., AJP: 1935, M&B: 1944, DRS, SNP: 1977]

Mary Jane (also **Mary Ann, Mary Anner, Mary J., Maryjane**) marijuana. EEL: 1971 also defines **Mary Ann** as morphine. RT: *pot.* [U.S., (1928): OEDS, RPW: 1938, M&D: 1952, W&F: 1960, (1967): DNE: 1973, RRL: 1969, CM: 1970, EEL: 1971, DCCU: 1972, MW: 1976, EAF: 1980, NIDA: 1980, ADC: 1981, JWK: 1981; Br., BTD: 1968, M&J: 1975]

Mary Jones marijuana. RT: *pot.* [U.S., H&C: 1975]

Mary Juanas* (also **Mary Johnas***) marijuana. See *Mary Jane.*

Mary Owsley the hallucinogenic drug *L.S.D.* (*q.v.*). *Cf. Owsley.* RT: *L.S.D.* [U.S., SNP: 1977]

Mary Warner (also **Mary Warmer, Mary Weaver, Mary Werner, Mary Worner**) marijuana. RT: *pot.* [U.S., DWM: 1938, RPW: 1938, VJM: 1949, D&D: 1957, W&F: 1960, RRL: 1969, EEL: 1971, DCCU: 1972, YKB: 1977] Other drug personifications are: *Aunt Emma, Aunt Hazel, Aunt Mary, Aunt Nora, Bernice, big Harry, Billy Hoke, Carrie, Carrie Nation, Cecil, Charles, Charley,*

Cholly, Corine, Doctor White, Doña Juanita, Harry, Hazel, Henry, Jane, Lady Snow, Maggie, Maryjane, Marjie, Marjorie, Mary, Mary Ann, Mary Jane, Mary Jones, Mary Owsley, Mary Weaver, Mary Werner, Mary Worner, Maud C., McCoy, Miss Emma, Megg, Owsley, Sid, Sidney.

mash Allah opium. Arabic: the gift of God. RS: *opium*. [U.S., RRL: 1969, JH: 1979]

mashed alcohol intoxicated. Probably from the mash used in distilling whiskey. RT: *drunk*. [Br., 1800s, F&H; listed in BVB: 1942]

matchbox (also **match**) a small matchbox full of marijuana. *Cf. B.* RS: *load*. [U.S., S&W: 1966, JBW: 1967, RRL: 1969, GU: 1975, EAF: 1980]

matsakaw* heroin. Origin unknown. RT: *heroin*. [U.S., SNP: 1977]

Maud C. Said to be a mixture of morphine and cocaine. Almost certainly a misprint for *M. and C.* (*q.v.*). [U.S., MHW: 1934, BVB: 1942, ELA: 1984]

maudlin drunk (also **maudlin**, **mawdlin**) alcohol intoxicated; drunk and weeping. (BF: 1737: [He's] Maudlin.) From the proper name *(Mary) Magdalene*. RS: *drunk*. [(1509): OED, BF: 1737, FG: 1785, FG: 1823; listed in BVB: 1942]

Maui Waui (also **Maui**, **Maui wowee**, **Maui wowie**) a potent variety of marijuana supposedly grown on the island of Maui, Hawaii. RT: *pot*. [U.S., YKB: 1977, ADC: 1981]

mauled (also **maul'd**) alcohol intoxicated. RT: *drunk*. [cant, BE: 1690, FG: 1785, FG: 1811, GWM: 1859, JSF: 1889, B&L: 1890, F&H]

max gin; any liquor. Also in a dialect (or eye-dialect) version, **mecks**. RT: *gin*. [FG: 1811, (1812): DU, FG: 1823, GWM: 1859, JCH: 1887, B&L: 1890]

maxed out alcohol intoxicated. GEN: done-in, exhausted. RT: *drunk*. [U.S., PD: 1982]

mayo powdered drugs: cocaine, heroin, morphine. Possibly an error for *ma-yo* (*q.v.*). RT: *powder*. [U.S., VJM: 1949, A&T: 1953, SNP: 1977]

ma-yo hemp, marijuana. Said to be Chinese. RT: *pot*. [U.S., IGA: 1971]

mazra marijuana. RT: *pot*. [U.S., MB: 1938]

M.C. See *M. and C.*

McCoy pure drugs or alcohol; chemically pure narcotics; medical narcotics as opposed to diluted contraband; genuine distiller's liquor as opposed to bootlegged liquor. *Cf. the real McCoy*. [U.S., DWM: 1938, VJM: 1949]

M.D. Mogen David wine. A reinterpretation of the initials *M.D.*

See *mad dog*. RS: *wine*. [U.S., RAS: 1982]

M.D.A. (also **mellow drug of America**) a drug acting much like L.S.D. 25, 3,4-methylenedioxyamphetamine. Can be injected, inhaled, or taken in pills. [U.S., RRL: 1969, ADC: 1975, W&F: 1975, YKB: 1977, ADC: 1981]

M.D.M.A. the drug *Ecstasy*, 3,4-methylenedioxymethamphetamine. This substance may be different from *M.D.A.*, but the formula is the same. This term is more recent than *M.D.A.* [U.S., RAS: 1985]

mean having to do with very good drugs or very bad drugs. *Cf. decent, intense*. [U.S., JWK: 1981]

mean green phencyclidine, P.C.P. RT: *P.C.P.* [U.S., ELA: 1984]

mecel morphine. Akin to or an error for *emsel* (*q.v.*) = *M. sul.* = morphine sulfate. [U.S., H&C: 1975]

mecks See *max*.

medical hype (also **medical addict**) someone who has become addicted to a drug as part of legal and recognized medical treatment. RS: *junky*. [U.S., RRL: 1969, EEL: 1971]

medicine 1. alcohol; liquor. RT: *booze*. [Br., (1850): DSUE; U.S., BVB: 1942] 2. morphine; narcotics; any drug which will sustain an addiction. Includes anything which can be used for a fix. RS: *dope*. [U.S., DWM: 1936, VJM: 1949] 3. *methadone* (*q.v.*). Because methadone is used in the clinical treatment of heroin addiction as a substitute for heroin. RT: *dolo*. [U.S., YKB: 1977, DEM: 1981]

meet a meeting or an appointment with a drug dealer to buy drugs. RS: *score*. [U.S., DWM: 1938, BVB: 1942, RRL: 1969, EEL: 1971, ADC: 1981]

Megg (also **meg, meggs**) marijuana; a marijuana cigarette. *Cf. maggie*. RT: *pot, joint*. [U.S., BVB: 1942, VJM: 1949, A&T: 1953]

mejambrea* heroin. Spanish (calo). RT: *heroin*. [calo, JBR: 1973]

mejorana* marijuana. The Spanish word for marjoram, an *herb* (*q.v.*). RT: *pot*. [calo, JBR: 1973]

mellow 1. slightly alcohol intoxicated. RS: *drunk*. GEN: calm, relaxed. [BE: 1690, BF: 1722, NCD: 1725, FG: 1785, FG: 1811, FG: 1823, F&H, BWG: 1899, MP: 1928, AH: 1931, D&B: 1970c, DCCU: 1972, ADC: 1981] 2. drug intoxicated; experiencing drug euphoria. RS: *stoned*. [U.S., EEL: 1971, ADC: 1981] 3. the early part of a drug trip when everything seems fine. [U.S., E&R: 1971]

Mellow Drug of America See *M.D.A.*

mellow dude a habitual drug user who is usually *mellow* (*q.v.*). RT: *user*. [U.S., (1966): ELA: 1982, EEL: 1971]

mellow out to relax by taking a drug or smoking marijuana.

GEN: to relax; to turn cool (W&F: 1975). *Cf. mellow.* [U.S., AP: 1980]

mellow-yellow 1. the inside of banana peels which were said to be scraped and smoked for a high. Said to be practiced by the young who thought that it made them high. The whole idea of smoking banana peels probably had its origin in the phrase "to *trip* (*q.v.*) on a banana peel." [U.S., RB: 1967, D&B: 1970c, EEL: 1971] 2. the hallucinogenic drug *L.S.D.* (*q.v.*). *Cf. yellows, yellow sunshine.* RT: *L.S.D.* [U.S., EEL: 1971, YKB: 1977, NIDA: 1980]

melted alcohol intoxicated. RT: *drunk.* [U.S., MHW: 1934, D&D: 1957, W&F: 1960]

melter morphine. May refer to a particular form of morphine or the dilution of morphine for injection. RT: *morphine.* [U.S., IGA: 1971, SNP: 1977]

melt wax to smoke opium. RT: *suck bamboo.* [U.S., ELA: 1984]

men in blue (also **boys in blue**) the police, including narcotics officers. RS: *fuzz.* [(1882): F&H; listed in BVB: 1942]

meperdine a synthetic narcotic analgesic. Best known as *Demerol* (TM; *q.v.*). RT: *demis.* [U.S., (1947): OEDS]

meprobamate a tranquilizer sold under various brand names such as *Miltown* (TM; *q.v.*). RT: *tranks.* [(1955): OEDS]

meps (also **mep**) merperdine, probably *Demerol* (TM; *q.v.*) painkiller. [U.S., JWK: 1981]

merchandise drugs; any contraband. *Cf. goods.* RS: *dope.* [U.S., BD: 1937, DWM: 1938, JWK: 1981]

merck (also **merk**) ethical drugs; the medicinal form of a drug such as cocaine. From the name of the drug manual and the drug company: *Merck. Cf. mean.* [U.S., RRL: 1969, JH: 1979, S&F: 1984]

meridian a drink of liquor taken at noon. *Cf. nooner.* RT: *nip.* [Br., EDD, (1815): DSUE; listed in MHW: 1934]

merry alcohol intoxicated. *Cf. gay, glad, happy, jolly.* RT: *drunk.* [BF: 1722, BF: 1737]

merry as a Greek alcohol intoxicated. Akin to an earlier term for drunkard, **merry Greek** (F&H, 1800s). RT: *drunk.* [U.S., BVB: 1942, D&D: 1957]

merry-go-down ale; strong ale. RT: *ale.* [(1500): OED, DSUE]

merry-go-up snuff. An obvious play on *merry-go-down.* RT: *snoose.* [Br., FG: 1823]

Merry Widow champagne. RT: *cham.* [Br., (1906): DSUE]

mesc (also **mescal**) mescaline, usually in the form of pills. RS: *peyote.* [U.S., RRL: 1969, (1971): DNE: 1980, DCCU: 1972, W&F: 1975, YKB: 1977, NIDA: 1980, ADC: 1981]

mesca marijuana. See *yesca.* Possibly a pronunciation error or variant of *yesca.* [U.S., ELA: 1984]

mescal *mescaline* (*q.v.*). Also an alcoholic beverage made by Mexicans from the fermented juice of the agave plant. The drink is sometimes confused with *mescaline* (*q.v.*). [(1702): MW: 1983, (1885): OEDS; U.S., drug culture, RRL: 1969, YKB: 1977, NIDA: 1980]

mescal button (also button) mescaline in the form of a small dried nodule of peyote cactus. *Cf. mesc.* RS: *peyote.* [U.S., (1888): OEDS, RPW: 1938, D&D: 1957, YKB: 1977, NIDA: 1980]

mescalina* (also mescalito*) *mescaline* (*q.v.*). Spanish. See *mesc.* RS: *peyote.* [U.S., NIDA: 1980, DEM: 1981]

mescaline an alkaloid hallucinogen derived from the tops of the peyote cactus, *Lophorophora williamsii.* It can also be synthesized in the laboratory and is similar in effect to L.S.D. The term refers to the mescaline found in the peyote cactus or that which has been synthesized. RS: *peyote.* [U.S., (1896): OEDS, RPW: 1938, D&D: 1957, RRL: 1969, YKB: 1977]

mescaline eyes red eyes from mescaline use. [U.S., ADC: 1975]

meserole* a marijuana cigarette. "[A] corruption of mezzroll" (Mezz Mezzrow in M&W: 1946). RT: *joint.* [U.S., RRL: 1969, IGA: 1971, NIDA: 1980]

messed up 1. alcohol intoxicated; drug intoxicated. RT: *drunk, stoned.* [U.S., EEL: 1971, GU: 1975] 2. addicted; debilitated physically and mentally by drug use. RT: *hooked.* [U.S., EEL: 1971, E&R: 1971]

met* (also metanfetamina*) *methamphetamine* (*q.v.*). Mexican-American. *Cf. meth.* RT: *speed.* [U.S., NIDA: 1980]

meter a violent and fake display of drug withdrawal distress to win the sympathies of a physician who might prescribe narcotics. See *throw a meter* at *throw a Brody.* RT: *brody.* [U.S., JES: 1959]

meth 1. denatured alcohol; methyl alcohol. RT: *methyl.* Hobo use. [Br., (1933): DSUE] 2. *Methedrine* (TM; *q.v.*) methamphetamine. RT: *speed.* [U.S., S&W: 1966, (1967): DNE: 1973, AHC: 1969, W&F: 1975, YKB: 1977, NIDA: 1980; Br. BTD: 1968] 3. *methadone* (*q.v.*). RT: *dolo.* [U.S., JWK: 1981]

methadone the chemical name of a synthetic narcotic analgesic. The drug is used in the treatment of heroin addiction. It is addictive itself. Many of the slang terms are based on the trade name *Dolophine* (TM; *q.v.*). RT: *dolo.* Not slang. [(1947): OEDS, in current use; consult a pharmaceutical reference for more information]

methadone maintenance a type of treatment for heroin addiction where the patient is switched from heroin to daily doses of methadone. The methadone satisfies the heroin craving but does not make the patient high. It is dispensed free at clinics so that the patient need not beg or steal to satisfy the craving. As the patient makes social adjustment, the dosage can be reduced.

[U.S., (1972): DNE: 1980]

methamphetamine a central nervous system stimulant, more potent than the amphetamines. Best known as *Methedrine* (TM; *q.v.*). RT: *speed*. [(1949): OEDS]

methaqualone a nonbarbiturate hypnotic-sedative. Best known as *Quaalude* (TM; *q.v.*) and *Sopor* (TM; *q.v.*). The British brand is *Mandrax* (TM; *q.v.*). See slang terms at *ludes*. [(1961): OEDS]

Methedrine a protected trade name for *methamphetamine* (*q.v.*) hydrochloride (amphetamine). The drug is a potent central nervous system stimulant. There is a list of slang and jargon synonyms at *speed*. Amphetamine terms are listed at *amps*. [(1939): OEDS, in current use; consult a pharmaceutical reference for more information]

meth freak (also methhead, meth monster) a habitual user of *Methedrine* (TM; *q.v.*). *Cf. speed demon, speed freak*. [U.S., S&W: 1966, RG: 1970, IGA: 1971, SH: 1972]

meth maintenance *methadone* (*q.v.*) maintenance of a heroin habit with daily doses of methadone. *Cf. maintain*. [U.S., JWK: 1981]

metho 1. (also meths) denatured alcohol; methyl alcohol. From the (British) term *methylated (denatured) spirits*. [(1933): OEDS, (1935): DSUE] 2. (also metho artist, metho drinker) a methyl-drinking alcoholic. RS: *sot*. [Aust., (1933): OEDS, (1935): GAW: 1978, SJB: 1943]

Methodistconated alcohol intoxicated. A play on the Methodist denomination and its views on alcohol in the early 1900s. RT: *drunk*. From the prohibition era. [U.S., AH: 1931, BVB: 1942]

Methodist hellinium the prohibition era. A play on *millennium*, with reference to the Methodist's condemnation of drinking. RT: *prohibition*. [U.S., BVB: 1942]

methyl (also meths) denatured alcohol; methyl alcohol. Methyl alcohol dates from 1847 (MW: 1983). Meths is British. See *metho*. [Br. and N.Z., BTD: 1968, DSUE, (1968): DNE: 1973] Nicknames and other terms for methyl alcohol: *alley juice, bidgee, canned heat, dancing girl, dee-horn, dehorn, feke, gas, ill-natured, ill-natured alcohol, jack, jake, meth, metho, meths, pink-eye, pinkie, pinky, red biddy, rub-a-dub, rubbydub, smoke, steam, Sterno, Sterno Club, yakky-dak.*

metros the police; the metropolitan police. RT: *fuzz*. [U.S., EAF: 1980]

Mex (also Mexican) marijuana, presumably grown in Mexico. RT: *pot*. [U.S., ADC: 1975, (D&B: 1978), ADC: 1981]

Mexican brown 1. a brownish Mexican marijuana. A higher grade of marijuana than *Mexican green* (*q.v.*). RT: *pot*. [U.S., RRL: 1969, EEL: 1971, JH: 1979] 2. weak heroin form Mexico; heroin. *Cf. Mexican horse, Mexican mud*. RT: *heroin*. [U.S., JHF: 1971, (1975): DNE: 1980]

Mexican bush marijuana from Mexico, possibly low-quality marijuana. RT: *pot.* [U.S., (M&W: 1946)]

Mexican commercial the standard grade of Mexican marijuana. RT: *pot.* [U.S., (D&B: 1978)]

Mexican green a common variety of marijuana from Mexico. *Cf. green.* RT: *pot.* [U.S., (1961): ELA: 1982, RRL: 1969, EEL: 1971, EAF: 1980, NIDA: 1980]

Mexican horse brown Mexican heroin. *Cf. la duna, Mexican brown.* RT: *heroin.* [U.S., SNP: 1977, RDS: 1982]

Mexican jumping beans capsules of *Seconal* (TM; *q.v.*) barbiturates manufactured in Mexico. *Cf. beans.* RT: *sec.* [U.S., EEL: 1971, BR: 1972]

Mexican locoweed (also **Mexican tumbleweed**) Mexican marijuana. From a common name for the *jimson weed* (*q.v.*). *Cf. Mex.* RT: *pot.* [U.S., RRL: 1969, SNP: 1977]

Mexican milk tequila. RS: *booze.* [U.S., EE: 1976]

Mexican mud brown Mexican heroin. *Cf. mud.* RT: *heroin.* [U.S., YKB: 1977, NIDA: 1980]

Mexican mushrooms a hallucinogenic mushroom of the genus *Psilocybe* which grows in Mexico. *Cf. magic mushrooms.* RT: *psilocybin.* [U.S., RRL: 1969, RDS: 1982]

Mexican red 1. a capsule of *Seconal* (TM; *q.v.*) barbiturates manufactured in Mexico. The same as *Mexican jumping beans.* RT: *sec.* [U.S., RRL: 1969, YKB: 1977, NIDA: 1980] 2. (also **Mexican**) a potent reddish-brown marijuana from Mexico. RT: *pot.* [U.S., EEL: 1971, DCCU: 1972, W&F: 1960]

mezz (also **mez, Mez, Mezz, the Mezz**) the best quality marijuana; marijuana; a marijuana cigarette. From the proper name *Mezz Mezzrow* a jazz musician known for his marijuana as well as his music. RT: *joint, pot.* [U.S., (1936): ELA: 1982, M&W: 1946, D&D: 1957, W&F: 1960, YKB: 1977]

mezzanine lover a marijuana smoker. From a colloquial expression for someone who necks in a movie theater mezzanine and from *mezz* (*q.v.*). *Cf. lover.* RT: *toker.* [U.S., JES: 1959, H&C: 1975]

mezzroll (also **Mezz's roll**) a marijuana cigarette; a fat marijuana cigarette. From *mezz* (*q.v.*). *Cf. meserole.* RT: *joint.* [U.S., M&W: 1946, BVB: 1953, CM: 1970, D&B: 1978, RDS: 1982]

mic See *mike.*

Michael 1. a hip flask for carrying liquor. RT: *flask.* [U.S., MHW: 1934, BVB: 1942] 2. (also **Michael Finn**) knockout drops; chloral hydrate. *Cf. chlorals.* RT: *Mickey Finn.* [U.S., BVB: 1942, DU]

Michoacan (also **Mishwacan**) a potent marijuana presumably grown in the Mexican State, Michoacan. *Cf. Mex.* RT: *pot.* [U.S., EEL: 1971, ADC: 1975]

mick to slip (or give) a *Mickey Finn* (*q.v.*) to someone; to drug someone. *Cf. mike.* [U.S., M&V: 1954, H&C: 1975]

mickey (also **micky**) 1. a hip flask for carrying liquor; a *Michael* (*q.v.*). RT: *flask.* [Canadian and U.S., (1914): OEDS, BVB: 1942, DU] 2. a *Mickey Finn* (*q.v.*). [U.S., BVB: 1942, RRL: 1969] 3. a small bottle of wine. [U.S., EAF: 1980] 4. a tranquilizer. RT: *tranks.* [U.S., GU: 1975]

Mickey finished alcohol intoxicated; totally drunk. A pun on *Mickey Finn. Cf. totalled.* RT: *drunk.* [U.S., BVB: 1953, D&D: 1957]

Mickey Finn (also **mickey, Mickey, Mickey Flynn, micky**) a drink containing chloral hydrate; chloral hydrate knockout drops; a drink containing a fast-acting laxative; any drugged drink. *Cf. chlorals.* [U.S., (1904): DU, (1928): OEDS, DWM: 1936, BVB: 1942, D&D: 1957, RRL: 1969, DCCU: 1972, H&C: 1975] Nicknames and slang expressions for knock-out drinks: *bug juice, chlorals, corals, easing powder, easy powder, heeltap, hog, jelly babies, jelly beans, joy-juice, keeler, knockout drops, K.O., K.O. drops, Lipton's, Lipton's Tea, Lipton Tea, locus, locust, Michael, mickey, Mickey Finn, Mickey Flynn, micky, peter, peter drops, petes, pillow, torpedo.*

mickey mouse 1. a bit of blotter impregnated with *L.S.D.* (*q.v.*) and stamped with the image of Mickey Mouse as the Sorcerer's Apprentice. RT: *L.S.D.* [U.S., ADC: 1981] 2. a police officer. RT: *fuzz.* [U.S., EEL: 1971]

mickey mouse habit a small drug habit; a minor case of drug addiction. RT: *chippy habit.* [U.S., ELA: 1984]

micky See *mickey.*

microdot (also **microdots**) a small portion (microgram) of *L.S.D.* (*q.v.*) on a tablet or on blotting paper. See *dot.* RT: *L.S.D.* [Br., Canadian, and U.S., (1971): OEDS, (1972): DNE: 1973, YKB: 1977, ADC: 1981]

middling alcohol intoxicated. Possibly in the sense *not very well (healthy)* as in *fair to middling.* RT: *drunk.* [BF: 1737]

midget a very young child used as a drug runner. Such children do not draw suspicion. RS: *mule.* [U.S., M&H: 1959, NAM: 1953]

midnight oil opium in the expression burning the midnight oil. RT: *opium.* [U.S., BVB: 1942, VJM: 1949, A&T: 1953]

mig a marijuana cigarette; a miggle. Possibly akin to *Megg* (*q.v.*). See *miggles.* RT: *joint.* [U.S., W&F: 1960]

miggles marijuana; marijuana cigarettes. See *muggles.* RT: *pot.* [U.S., BVB: 1942, VJM: 1949, A&T: 1953]

Mighty Joe Young a powerful addiction to drugs, a big *monkey* (*q.v.*) on one's back. *Cf. have a monkey on one's back, have an orangutan on one's back, King Kong, tang* for other expressions on the ape theme. RT: *habit.* [U.S., RRL: 1969, JH: 1979]

mighty mezz (also **the mighty mezz**) marijuana; a fat marijuana cigarette. From *mezz* (*q.v.*). RT: *pot, joint.* [U.S., M&W: 1946, W&F: 1960, EEL: 1971, JH: 1979]

mighty Quinn the hallucinogenic drug *L.S.D.* (*q.v.*). RT: *L.S.D.* [U.S., H&C: 1975, SNP: 1977] See also *quin* at *quill.*

mike (also mic) L.S.D.; a microgram (one millionth of a gram) of *L.S.D.* (*q.v.*). RS: *load.* [U.S., G&B: 1969, S&R: 1972, ADC: 1975, W&F: 1975]

milk 1. beer; liquor. From or akin to *mother's milk* (*q.v.*). RT: *beer, booze.* [U.S., D&B: 1970c, ADC: 1975] 2. See *milk a rush.*

milk a rush (also milk) to inject a drug and draw blood back into the syringe to dilute it. This can be repeated in order to delay or control the *peak* (*q.v.*) of the rush. The same as *boot* (*q.v.*). *Rush* (*q.v.*) = the initial burst of euphoria after an injection of drugs. [U.S., RG: 1970, MA: 1973]

milled alcohol intoxicated. Probably a variant of *cut* (*q.v.*). RT: *drunk.* [Br., JOH: 1901]

Miltown a protected trade name for *meprobamate* (*q.v.*), a mild tranquilizer. RT: *tranks.*

Milwaukee goiter (also German goiter) a beer belly. Refers to Milwaukee, Wisconsin, a major beer-brewing center. [U.S., D&D: 1957, W&F: 1960]

mind-bender (also mind-blower, mind-detergent, mind-expander, mind-explorer, mind-opener, mind-spacer, mind-tripper) a hallucinogenic drug, typically *L.S.D.* (*q.v.*). Each term except mind-detergent can also mean a user of a hallucinogenic drug. RS: *L.S.D.* [U.S., (1967): DNE: 1973, TW: 1968, ADC: 1975, W&F: 1975, MW: 1976]

mind-fuck to give someone L.S.D. (possibly secretively) and watch the results. To fuck-up someone's mind. [U.S., (EEL: 1971)]

mind-spacer a psychedelic drug, i.e., L.S.D. or S.T.P. *Cf. spaced out.* RS: *dope.* [U.S., DCCU: 1972, AP: 1980]

ming a marijuana cigarette made from a collection of butts or roaches. *Cf. roach.* RS: *joint.* [U.S., ELA: 1982]

minibennies amphetamines; *Benzedrine* (*q.v.*). *Cf. bennies, benz.* RT: *amps.* [U.S., YKB: 1977]

Minnehaha champagne. From Longfellow's *Song of Hiawatha.* Minnehaha = laughing waters. *Cf. laughing water* (at *laughing soup*). RT: *cham.* [U.S., BVB: 1942]

Minnesota green homegrown (Minnesota-grown) marijuana. *Cf. Chicago green, Vermont green.* RT: *pot.* Probably limited to Minnesota. [U.S., D&B: 1971]

minstrels an amphetamine and barbiturate capsule. Probably a capsule of *Biphetamine* (TM; *q.v.*) or *Durophet* (TM; *q.v.*) because they come in black and white capsules. *Cf. black and tan, black and white minstrel.* RS: *set.* [U.S., EEL: 1971; Br., (1967): OEDS,

BTD: 1968]

mint weed (also **mint leaf**) mint leaves or perhaps dried parsley impregnated with P.C.P. and smoked. *Cf. peace weed.* RT: *P.C.P.* [U.S., (1970s): FAB: 1979, JHF: 1971]

miraculous alcohol intoxicated. RT: *drunk.* [Br., listed in F&H (at *screwed*); listed in BVB: 1942]

mired in the mud addicted to opium. Mud = opium. RS: *hooked.* [U.S., JES: 1959, H&C: 1975]

misc allegedly mescaline. Probably an error for *mesc* (*q.v.*). [SH: 1972]

miser a device for holding a marijuana cigarette butt. The resin accumulates in the butt and can be released only by smoking it clear to the end. Miser = stingy. This may allude to gold as *Acapulco gold* (*q.v.*). RT: *crutch.* [U.S., BR: 1972]

misery gin. Synonymous with *ruin* (*q.v.*) = gin. RT: *gin.* [Br., (1820): DSUE, F&H]

Mishwacan See *Michoacan.*

miss 1. (also **miss the channel**) to miss a vein when injecting drugs and release the substance subcutaneously or intramuscularly. [U.S., HB: 1955, EEL: 1971, JWK: 1981] 2. an instance of missing the vein when injecting a drug. [U.S., EEL: 1971, JWK: 1981]

Miss Carrie a stash of drugs carried on the person. Because it is carried on the person and can carry one through withdrawal if arrested. *Cf. carry.* RS: *stash.* [U.S., M&V: 1967]

Miss Emma 1. morphine. An elaboration of *M.* (*q.v.*). *Cf. Miss Morph.* RT: *morphine.* [U.S., DWM: 1938, BVB: 1942, VJM: 1949, TRG: 1968, EEL: 1971, DCCU: 1972, YKB: 1977] 2. a morphine addict. See *Miss Emma Jones.* Possibly an error. [U.S., early 1900s, DU]

Miss Emma Jones an addiction to morphine. *Cf. Miss Emma, jones. Jones* (*q.v.*) = addiction. RS: *habit.* [U.S., JES: 1959, H&C: 1975]

Miss Freeze someone who monopolizes a communal marijuana cigarette. *Cf. Bogart, Humphrey.* Attested as gay slang. [U.S., BR: 1972]

missionary a drug pusher who attempts to create new addicts (customers). See *convert. Cf. drug booster.* RS: *pusher.* [U.S., BVB: 1942, DU]

Miss Morph morphine. *Cf. Miss Emma.* RT: *morphine.* [U.S., M&V: 1967, SNP: 1977]

Missouri meerschaum a simple corncob pipe. This is the kind of pipe symbolic of the hillbilly of the Missouri Ozark mountains. *Cf. pipe.* A contrived sobriquet. [U.S., BVB: 1942, D&D: 1973]

mist (also **magic mist**) phencyclidine, *P.C.P.* (*q.v.*), an animal tranquilizer. RT: *P.C.P.* [U.S., (1970s): FAB: 1979, YKB: 1977, DEM: 1981] See also *Scotch mist.*

mister blue the compound hydromorphone found in *Dilaudid* (TM; *q.v.*) cough syrup. Possibly a blue elixir of morphine sulfate. [U.S., RG: 1970]

mix 1. to inject a drug, probably heroin. RS: *shoot.* See *Tom Mix.* [U.S., JH: 1979] 2. juices and other liquids used in mixing drinks. See *mixer.* [U.S., MW: 1976]

mixed (also **mixed up**) alcohol intoxicated. GEN: confused. *Cf. half and half.* RT: *drunk.* **Mixed up** is not attested as British. [Br., late 1800s, F&H; listed in BVB: 1942]

mixer 1. someone who sells and serves liquor at a bar. RS: *bartender.* [U.S., (1858, 1919): OEDS, BVB: 1942] 2. (also **mix**) fruit juices, soda water, etc. for use in mixed drinks. [U.S., mid 1900s-p., W&F: 1960] 3. a person hired to cut (dilute) large quantities of a drug, usually heroin. [U.S., JWK: 1981]

mixologist someone who sells and serves liquor at a bar. *Cf. mixer.* [U.S., (1856): OEDS, JRW: 1909, BVB: 1942]

mizake the mizan *make the man* = meet a seller (to purchase drugs). Narcotics ziph. RS: *score.* [U.S., DWM: 1936, BVB: 1942]

mizzled alcohol intoxicated; tipsy. From a term meaning *drizzled on.* RT: *drunk.* [Br., JM: 1923]

M.J. marijuana. From the initials of *Mary Jane.* RT: *pot.* [U.S., RRL: 1969, EEL: 1971, W&F: 1975]

M-joint a place where morphine can be bought. RS: *doperie.* [U.S., GOL: 1950, D&D: 1957]

M.M.s the marijuana *munchies* (*q.v.*), hunger following marijuana use. [U.S., E&R: 1971] See also *M and Ms.*

mo (also **M.O.**) marijuana. Akin to *mohasky* (*q.v.*). *Cf. black mo.* RT: *pot.* [U.S., SNP: 1977]

moaning after, the a hangover. Punning on *the morning after.* RT: *hangover.* [U.S., BVB: 1942, D&D: 1957]

moccasoned alcohol intoxicated. Probably from *water moccasin,* implying snakebite poisoning. RT: *drunk.* [U.S., JRB: 1859]

modams marijuana. Origin unknown. RT: *pot.* [U.S., SNP: 1977]

moggles marijuana cigarettes; marijuana. See *muggles.*

mohaska, on the addicted to narcotics. RT: *hooked.* [U.S., GOL: 1950]

mohasky 1. (also **mohasty, mohoska, moshky**) marijuana. *Cf. mahoska.* RT: *pot.* [U.S., RPW: 1938, W&F: 1960, YKB: 1977] 2. under the effects of marijuana. RT: *wasted.* [U.S., W&F: 1960]

moist around the edges alcohol intoxicated. *Cf. damp, mizzled, wet.* RT: *drunk.* [Br., early 1900s, DSUE]

moisten one's clay (also moisten, moisten one's chafer) to take a drink of liquor. RT: *irrigate.* [Br., (1830): DSUE, JCH: 1887; listed in BVB: 1942]

moisture liquor. RT: *booze.* [U.S., BVB: 1942]

mojo 1. hard drugs; the powdered narcotics: cocaine, heroin, morphine. HB: 1955 defines it as morphine. Possibly akin to *mojo* = magic spell or charm. RT: *powder.* [U.S., (1935): OEDS, DWM: 1936, BVB: 1942, VJM: 1949, GOL: 1950, M&D: 1952, HB: 1955, W&F: 1960, RRL: 1969, ADC: 1975] 2. a narcotics addict. Possibly an error. [U.S., RDS: 1982]

mojo, on the addicted to morphine; using morphine. RT: *hooked.* Black use (M&V: 1973). [U.S., DWM: 1936]

mokus 1. liquor. RT: *booze.* Hobo use. [U.S., early 1900s, W&F: 1960] 2. alcohol intoxicated. RT: *drunk.* Hobo use. [U.S., early 1900s, W&F: 1960] See also *moocah.*

molly 1. (also molo) alcohol intoxicated. RT: *drunk.* [F&G: 1925, SJB: 1966] 2. an amphetamine capsule. See *black mollies.* RT: *amps.* [U.S., EE: 1976]

molo alcohol intoxicated. Assumed to be an error for *nolo* (*q.v.*). Possibly from *molotov cocktail.* RT: *drunk.* [Br., F&G: 1925]

Monday blues a Monday morning hangover. RT: *hangover.* [U.S., BVB: 1942]

monkey 1. a flask; a liquor flask used on hunting expeditions. Probably akin to the use of the term for a globular jug with an upright neck (OED, early 1800s). RT: *flask.* [(1834): OED] 2. a shipboard cask for serving the sailors' allowances of grog. [(1822): OED] See also *suck the monkey.* 3. a drug habit or an addiction. See *have a monkey on one's back.* RT: *habit.* [U.S., BD: 1937, JBW: 1967, RRL: 1969, DCCU: 1972, ADC: 1975] 4. a prohibition agent. RS: *fuzz.* [U.S., GM: 1931, MHW: 1934, GOL: 1950] 5. morphine; an addictive drug. Possibly akin to sense three. See *monkey-medicine.* RT: *morphine.* [U.S., JTD: 1971, SNP: 1977] 6. an addict. RT: *junky.* Black use. [U.S., HER: 1971, DC: 1972]

monkey bait free samples of an addictive drug. This leads to having a monkey on one's back. *Cf. freebies.* [U.S., JES: 1959, H&C: 1975]

monkey drill a hypodermic syringe. RT: *monkey pump.* [U.S., JES: 1959]

monkey dust a brownish form of *P.C.P.* (*q.v.*). RT: *P.C.P.* [U.S., (1970s): FAB: 1979]

monkey jumps a drug addict's disoriented motions and staggering. [U.S., JES: 1959, H&C: 1975]

monkey-meat a heavily drug intoxicated person; a narcotics addict. RS: *junky.* [U.S., JES: 1959, H&C: 1975]

monkey-medicine (also monkey morphine) morphine. *Cf. medicine.*

RT: *morphine*. [U.S., JES: 1959, H&C: 1975]

monkey on one's back an addiction. *Monkey* (*q.v.*) = drug addiction. See *have a monkey on one's back*. [U.S., GS: 1959, M&V: 1967, RRL: 1969]

monkey pump 1. a straw or quill for sucking liquor out of a cask. *Monkey* (*q.v.*) = a flask. [nautical, 1800s and perhaps before, BVB: 1942, PKK: 1976] 2. a hypodermic syringe. *Monkey* (*q.v.*) = an addictive drug. [U.S., JES: 1959, H&C: 1975] Nicknames and slang terms for a hypodermic syringe: *antidote, arm squirt, artillery, Banette, banger, bayonet, Bay State, biz, blunt, business, cannon, crystal ship, deazingus, dinghizen, dingus, dope gun, dripper, dropper, emergency gun, factory, fake, fake-a-loo, feeder, gaffus, glass, glass gun, golden spike, gun, harpoon, hop gun, hype, hypestick, hypo, jabber, jab stick, Jobes, Job's antidote, joint, joker, layout, light artillery, Luer, machine, machinery, monkey drill, monkey pump, nail, needle, oint-jay, pacifier, pin, pin gun, pistola, prick, rig, rocket ship, serpent, silver, silver bike, silver serpent, sky-the-wipe, spike, spike and dripper, stinger, the biz, tube.*

monkey swill liquor; inferior liquor; strong liquor. RS: *rotgut*. From the prohibition era. [U.S., VR: 1929, AH: 1931, MHW: 1934, BVB: 1942]

monkey talk distorted speech as uttered while drug intoxicated. *Cf. monkey*. [U.S., H&C: 1975]

monkey wagon drug addiction. *Cf. monkey*. RT: *habit*. [U.S., JES: 1959, H&C: 1975]

monolithic heavily drug intoxicated. A play on *stoned* (*q.v.*). RT: *stoned*. [U.S., EEL: 1971]

Monroe in a Cadillac a mixture of morphine and cocaine. Akin to *Marmon and Cadillac* (*q.v.*). RS: *set*. [U.S., JES: 1959, H&C: 1975]

monster any powerful drug effecting the central nervous system. See *the beast*. *Cf. hard drugs*. [U.S., W&F: 1975, JWK: 1981]

monster weed marijuana; powerful, marijuana. RT: *pot*. [U.S., BR: 1972]

monte* marijuana. Spanish for thicket = *bush* (*q.v.*). RT: *pot*. [U.S., NIDA: 1980]

moocah marijuana. RT: *pot*. [U.S., (1926): RPW: 1938, D&D: 1957, W&F: 1960, RRL: 1969, EEL: 1971, JH: 1979]

mooch 1. drugs. To be addicted is to be on the mooch. *Cf. moocher*. RS: *dope*. [U.S., GOL: 1950] See also *hooch*. 2. to beg for money for drugs; to beg drugs. GEN: to beg in public (1914): OEDS. *Cf. leech*. [U.S., BD: 1937, WCM: 1972] 3. a drug addict. RT: *junky*. [U.S., GOL: 1950]

moocher 1. someone who hangs around a saloon. GEN: a beggar. [U.S., MGH: 1915] 2. a drug addict. [U.S., GOL: 1950, D&D: 1957]

mooch joint a place where narcotics are sold; a bar where narcotics as well as booze can be bought; an opium den. RS: *doperie*. [U.S., GOL: 1950, D&D: 1957]

mooch pusher a drug seller. *Mooch* (*q.v.*) = drugs. RT: *pusher*. [U.S., GOL: 1950, D&D: 1957]

mood altering drug (also **mood drug**) a drug affecting a person's moods: a stimulant or a depressant. DNE: 1973 attests **mood drug**. *Cf. downer, upper*. From medical terminology. [U.S., (1970): DNE: 1973]

moon 1. illicit liquor; any liquor. From *moonshine* (*q.v.*). RT: *booze*. From the prohibition era. [U.S., (1928): DA, MHW: 1934, BVB: 1942] 2. (also **moons**) a portion of peyote cactus eaten for its *mescaline* (*q.v.*) content. *Cf. full moons, half moons*. RS: *peyote*. [U.S., RRL: 1969, YKB: 1977, NIDA: 1980] 3. a cake of hashish. RS: *load*. [U.S., RRL: 1969]

moon beams P.C.P., phencyclidine. RT: *P.C.P.* [U.S., JH: 1979]

mooner a heavy drinker; a drunkard; a drinker of *moonshine* (*q.v.*). GEN: an idler. RT: *sot*. [listed in F&H (at *Lushington*)]

mooney (also **moony**) **1**. illicit whiskey. RT: *moonshine*. [U.S., VR: 1929, MHW: 1934] 2. alcohol intoxicated; tipsy. *Cf. moonshine*. [(1854): OED, JCH: 1887, B&L: 1890; listed in MHW: 1934]

moon-eyed alcohol intoxicated. (BF: 1737: [He's] Moon-ey'd.) RT: *drunk*. [BF: 1737, MHW: 1934, BVB: 1942]

moonlight 1. to traffic in illicit liquor. Because this is done best under the cover of darkness. [U.S., BVB: 1942, D&D: 1973] 2. illicit liquor. The same as *moonshine* (*q.v.*). [U.S., (1809): OED, F&H, BVB: 1942]

moonlighter a bootlegger; a moonshiner. From *moonlight* (*q.v.*). From the prohibition era. RT: *bootlegger*. [U.S., BVB: 1942]

moonlight inn an illicit saloon; a speakeasy. *Cf. moonlight*. RT: *speak*. From the prohibition era. [U.S., AH: 1931, MHW: 1934]

moonlit alcohol intoxicated. *Lit* (*q.v.*) by *moonshine* (*q.v.*). RT: *drunk*. [U.S., BVB: 1942]

moonshine 1. illicit liquor. This term has referred to smuggled gin, brandy, or whiskey, and to illicitly distilled whiskey during prohibition, or to adulterated liquor. [FG: 1785, FG: 1811, (1877): SBF: 1976, F&H, MP: 1928, VR: 1929, AH: 1931, GI: 1931, MHW: 1934, D&D: 1957, W&F: 1960] (This entry continues after the following list.) See terms for strong liquor at *rotgut*. See terms for bad beer at *queer-beer*. Nicknames and slang terms for illicit liquor or homemade liquor: *A-bomb juice, alkali, bald face, bald-face whiskey, balm, balm of Gilead, barrel goods, bead, blackstrap alchy, boilermaker's delight, bootleg, brush whiskey, buck, busthead, bustskull, canebuck, cane corn, cawn, choke dog, coffin varnish, condensed corn, corn, corn coffee, corn juice, corn likker, corn liquor, corn mule, corn spirits, corn* *squeezings, corn whiskey, corn wine, crooked whiskey, devil's eyewater, dew, donk, fox head, freight, goat hair, hard liquor, hardware, hogwash, home-brew, homespun, hooch, hoochinoo, hootch, hootchenoo, jake, jungle-juice, juniper-juice, Kentucky corn, Kentucky dew, Kentucky fire, Kentucky horn, kickapoo joy-juice, King Kong, kong, lightning, magic, moon, mooney, moonlight, moonshine, moony, mountain dew, mule, nigger pot, nockum stiff, oil of gladness, panther, panther juice, panther piss, panther pizen, panther's breath, panther's piss, panther's pizen, panther sweat, pig iron, pink-eye, pizen, popskull, pot, potato water, poteen, potheen, potsheen, prairie dew, queer, raisinjack, rerun, rerun alky, roasting-ear wine, rye sap, scrap iron, seafood, shine, shine liquor, shinny, silo drippings, sly grog, snakebite medicine, snakebite remedy, snakehead whiskey, snake juice, snake medicine, snake poison, snake water, squirrel, squirrel dew, squirrel whiskey, stuff, stump, stump likker, stump rum, stump water, swamp dew, swamp root, swipe, the sma' still, third rail, tiger eye, tiger juice, tiger milk, tiger's milk, tiger sweat, torpedo juice, two and over, wet goods, white coffee, white lightning, white liquor, white mule, white stuff, Who shot John?* 2. to distill or traffic in illicit liquor. The perpetrator of this act is a *bootlegger* or a *moonshiner*. [U.S., (1883): OEDS, BVB: 1942]

moonshiner a manufacturer of *moonshine* (*q.v.*). RS: *bootlegger*. [U.S., (1860): OED, B&L: 1890, LWP: 1908, AH: 1931, VJM: 1949, D&D: 1957]

moonshiner's gopher a bootlegger; a seller of illicit liquor. *Cf. moonshine*. Gopher = go for. RS: *bootlegger*. From the prohibition era. [U.S., MHW: 1934, BVB: 1942]

moonshinery an illicit saloon; a speakeasy. RT: *speak*. From the prohibition era. [U.S., BVB: 1942]

moonshine victim an alcoholic. RT: *sot*. [U.S., RDS: 1982]

moony See *mooney*.

moored in Sot's Bay alcohol intoxicated. RT: *drunk*. [Br., 18-1900s, DSUE]

moose milk whiskey; strong liquor. *Cf. kudu milk*. RT: *whiskey*. [U.S. and Canadian, W&F: 1960]

mooster marijuana. Possibly an error. *Cf. mooter*. RT: *pot*. [U.S., H&C: 1975]

mooter (also **moota, mootah, mootie, musta, muta, mutah, mutha**) marijuana; a marijuana cigarette. Possibly akin to *mother* (*q.v.*). *Mutha* could be from black speech, (= mother), but may also be an error. RT: *pot*. [U.S., (1926): RPW: 1938, DWM: 1938, DU, D&D: 1957, W&F: 1960, RRL: 1969, EEL: 1971, YKB: 1977]

mop 1. a drinking bout. RT: *spree*. [Br. and U.S., JCH: 1887, F&H, MHW: 1934, BVB: 1942] 2. (also **mopper-up**) a heavy drinker; a drunkard. *Cf. sponge*. RT: *sot*. [Br., (1860): DSUE, JCH: 1887, F&H; listed in BVB: 1942]

mopped (also moppy) alcohol intoxicated. *Cf. mop*. RT: *drunk*. [Br., FG: 1823; listed in MHW: 1934, BVB: 1942]

mops and brooms alcohol intoxicated; tipsy. Possibly a bit less drunk than *all mops and brooms* (*q.v.*). RT: *drunk*. [Br., (1814): OED, JCH: 1887, JRW: 1909; listed in MHW: 1934]

mop up 1. to drink up; to drink heartily. RT: *guzzle*. [cant FG: 1811, FG: 1823; listed in BVB: 1942] 2. (usually mop-up) a tavern; a pub. RS: *bar*. [Br., 1800s, F&H]

moragrifa* (also mor a grifa) marijuana. *Cf. grefa*. From Spanish. RT: *pot*. [U.S., (1966): ELA: 1982, JBW: 1967, IGA: 1971, SNP: 1977]

morals tablets of *Demerol* (TM; *q.v.*) brand of meperdine painkiller. From the last two syllables of *Demerol*. *Cf. meps*. RT: *demis*. [U.S., JWK: 1981]

more phencyclidine, P.C.P. RT: *P.C.P.* [U.S., ELA: 1984]

morenas* amphetamines. From the Spanish word for mulattos. *Cf. brown and clears, black and white*. RT: *amps*. [U.S., NIDA: 1980]

morf (also morph, morphi, morphie, morpho, morphy) morphine. See *morphine*. [U.S., HS: 1933, GOL: 1950, W&F: 1960, RRL: 1969, EEL: 1971, YKB: 1977]

morfiend a morphine addict. RS: *junky*. Probably not narcotics argot. [U.S., BVB: 1942, DU]

morfina* (also morphema*) morphine. Spanish. RT: *morphine*. [U.S., NIDA: 1980]

morning after (also the morning after the night before) a hangover; having to do with a hangover. RT: *hangover*. [since the early 1900s, BVB: 1942]

morning glory (also morning shot) an addict's first injection of the day. *Cf. constitutional, eye-opener, get-up*. RS: *shot*. [U.S., M&V: 1954, RRL: 1969]

morning glory seeds flower (morning glory) seeds which are ingested for a high. RT: *seeds*. [U.S., RB: 1967, ADC: 1981]

morning rouser the first drink of the day; a drink with which to begin the day. *Cf. eye-opener*. RT: *nip*. [Br., 1800s, F&H; listed in BVB: 1942]

morning shot See *morning glory*.

morotgara* heroin. Origin unknown. RT: *heroin*. [U.S., SNP: 1977]

morph morphine. See *morf*. [U.S., (1914): OEDS, HS: 1933, GOL: 1950, W&F: 1960, RRL: 1969, YKB: 1977, EAF: 1980]

morphia (also morphina, morphinum) morphine. The entry and the *alsos* are Latinized forms of *morphine*. [since the early 1800s; drug culture use, H&C: 1975, YKB: 1977]

morphine an addictive narcotic derivative of opium. Named for

Morpheus, the god of dreams (shapes). [(1828): MW: 1983] Nicknames and other terms for morphine: *Aunt Emma, barmecide, big-M., block, cacil, Cecil, Cecile, cobies, coby, cotton morphine, cube, cube juice, cubes, dope, dream, dreamer, eli lilly, em, emm, emsel, first line, gamot, glad stuff, God's medicine, G.O.M., good old M., goody, gunk, happy medicine, happy powder, hard stuff, hell dust, hocus, ixey, joy powder, junk, Lady White, lent, lint, M., Mary, mecel, medicine, melter, Miss Emma, Miss Morph, mojo, monkey, monkey-medicine, monkey morf, morfina, morph, morphema, morphi, morphia, morphie, morphina, morphine, morphinum, morpho, morphy, morshtop, M.S., M. sul., nose powder, nose stuff, number thirteen, old lady White, old Steve, pink, pins and needles, racehorse Charley, red cross, red cross M., sister, slumber medicine, slumber party, snow, snowball, stuff, sugar lump cubes, sweet Jesus, sweet Morpheus, uffi, uhffi, unkie, white, white angel, white goddess, white merchandise, white nurse, white silk, witch.*

morpho morphine. RT: *morphine.* [U.S., RG: 1970]

morshtop morphine. Origin unknown. *Cf. moscop.* RT: *morphine.* [U.S., H&C: 1975, SNP: 1977]

mortallious (also **mortal, mortal drunk, mortally drunk**) alcohol intoxicated; dead drunk. Only BVB: 1942 (U.S.) lists **mortally drunk**. RT: *drunk.* [Br., (1808): DSUE, (1844): OED; U.S., BVB: 1942]

moscop a mixture of morphine and scopolamine. RS: *set.* [U.S., H&C: 1975, SNP: 1977]

moshky a marijuana smoker. RT: *toker.* [U.S., EEL: 1971]

mosquito bit addicted to cocaine; high on cocaine. *Cf. cocainized.* [U.S., JES: 1959, H&C: 1975]

mosquitoes cocaine. This may refer to marks left by hypodermic injections rather than the drug itself. RT: *cocaine.* [U.S., VJM: 1949, A&T: 1953]

mota marijuana. Probably akin to *mooter* (*q.v.*). From the Spanish (calo) for *mote* = dust. *Cf. en motado.* RT: *pot.* [U.S., GOL: 1950, RRL: 1969, EEL: 1971, PW: 1974, YKB: 1977, NIDA: 1980]

mother 1. marijuana. Possibly akin to *mutha* (*q.v.*) at *muta.* RT: *pot.* [U.S., RRL: 1969] 2. a drug dealer; one's own drug dealer upon whom one depends. Possibly from motherfucker. RT: *dealer.* [U.S., RRL: 1969, CM: 1970, EEL: 1971]

motherdear *Methedrine* (TM; *q.v.*), a brand of methamphetamine, a stimulant. RT: *speed.* [U.S., D&B: 1970c]

mother nature (also **mother nature's, mother nature's own tobacco**) marijuana. RT: *pot.* [U.S., EAF: 1980]

mother's little helper *Miltown* (TM; *q.v.*), a tranquilizer. RT: *tranks.* [U.S., W&S: 1977]

mother's milk (also **mother's ruin**) gin; any liquor. *Mother's ruin* is rhyming slang (DRS). RT: *booze, gin*. Heard on the M*A*S*H television program (1970s). [Br., (1821): OEDS, (1823): F&H, DRS]

motter a marijuana smoker. *Cf. mota*. RT: *toker*. [U.S., EEL: 1971]

mountain dew (also **dew**) 1. whiskey (Scotch). RT: *whiskey*. [Br., (1816): OED, JCH: 1887; listed in BVB: 1942] 2. illicit liquor; any liquor. RT: *moonshine*. Well known during prohibition. [(1816): SBF: 1976, JB: 1823, VR: 1929, AH: 1931, MHW: 1934, D&D: 1957, W&F: 1960, SJB: 1966]

mountous alcohol intoxicated. Possibly akin to *elevated* (*q.v.*). RT: *drunk*. [BF: 1737]

mouth, a a hangover. Refers to a dry mouth or a bad taste in the mouth. *Cf. a head*. RT: *hangover*. [Br., 1800s, F&H]

mouth habit an addiction to drugs taken orally. *Cf. belly habit*. RS: *habit*. [U.S., BD: 1937, DWM: 1938, VJM: 1949, H&C: 1975]

mouthwash liquor; a drink of liquor. RT: *booze*. [Br. and U.S., (1930): DSUE, BVB: 1942]

mouth worker a drug user who takes drugs orally. *Cf. mouth habit*. RS: *user*. [U.S., D&D: 1957, RDS: 1982]

move to traffic in marijuana; to sell drugs. *Cf. push*. [U.S., RRL: 1974, S&F: 1984]

M.P.T.P. a type of *designer drug* similar to or derived from *Demerol* (TM). The substance is addictive and considered extremely dangerous. Found on the West Coast. [U.S., RAS: 1985]

Mrs. White a general nickname for a drug seller. Refers to white powder. *Cf. Dr. White, old lady White*. RT: *dealer*. [early 1900s, DU, A&T: 1953]

Mr. Twenty-six a hypodermic needle. Refers to its size, 26 gauge. RT: *needle*. [U.S., M&V: 1967, H&C: 1975]

Mr. Warner a marijuana smoker. *Cf. Mary Warner*. RT: *toker*. [U.S., JES: 1959, H&C: 1975]

Mr. Whiskers (also **whiskers, whiskers man**) a federal agent; a federal narcotics agent. Named for the bewhiskered Uncle Sam, the personification of the U.S. Heard in the film *How to Marry a Millionaire* (1953). RS: *fuzz*. [U.S., DSUE, D&D: 1957]

M. sul. (also **M.S.**) "morphine sulfate." *Cf. M., emsel*. RT: *morphine*. [U.S., RRL: 1969, RG: 1970, SNP: 1977]

M.T. an empty bottle. RT: *dead soldier*. [U.S., BVB: 1942]

Mt. Shasta, from (also **atop Mt. Shasta**) addicted; having to do with an addict. Mt. Shasta is an extinct volcano in Northern California. RT: *hooked*. [U.S., DWM: 1933, BVB: 1942, JES: 1959]

M.U. a marijuana user. RS: *toker, user*. See *mu*. [U.S., EEL: 1971] See also *M.J.*

mu marijuana. *Cf. mooter*. RT: *pot*. [U.S., (1936): ELA: 1982, RPW: 1938, A&T: 1953, W&F: 1960, RRL: 1969, CM: 1970, YKB: 1977]

muckibus alcohol intoxicated. RT: *drunk*. [nonce, (1756): OED]

mud 1. unprocessed opium; opium in general. YKB: 1977 define it as morphine. *Cf. green mud*. RT: *opium*. [U.S., WHW: 1922, (1926): ERH: 1982, GI: 1931, DWM: 1933, D&D: 1957, W&F: 1960, D&B: 1970c, EEL: 1971] 2. the leftovers of heroin or morphine processing. [U.S., JWK: 1981] See also *coolie mud, foreign mud, green mud, Mexican mud*. 3. hashish. RT: *hash*. [U.S., (1939): ELA: 1982]

mud-bud home-grown marijuana. *Cf. green bud*. RS: *pot*. [U.S., ADC: 1981]

muddled (also **in a muddle, muddled up, on the muddle**) alcohol intoxicated. RT: *drunk*. [BF: 1737, (1791): DSUE, F&H, MHW: 1934, D&D: 1957]

muddler liquor. *Cf. muddled*. RT: *booze*. [U.S., BVB: 1942]

muddy alcohol intoxicated. *Cf. dirty drunk*. RT: *drunk*. [BF: 1737]

muddy water bad beer. GEN: any inferior drink. RT: *queer-beer*. [U.S., MHW: 1934]

mud wiggler an opium addict. *Mud* = opium. From the common name of an insect. RT: *campfire boy*. [U.S., H&C: 1975]

mug blotts (also **mug blot, mug blotto, mugg blotto, mugg blotts**) alcohol intoxicated. RT: *drunk*. [U.S., WM: 1927, MHW: 1934]

mugged (also **mugged up**) alcohol intoxicated. From the overuse of a drinking mug. *Cf. potted*. RT: *drunk*. [Br., 1800s, F&H; U.S., listed in BVB: 1942, D&D: 1957]

muggled (also **muggled up**) under the effects of marijuana. RT: *wasted*. [U.S., (1934): ELA: 1982, M&V: 1954, H&C: 1975]

mugglehead a marijuana smoker. *Cf. muggles*. RT: *toker*. [U.S., (1926): RPW: 1938, VJM: 1949, M&D: 1952, TRG: 1968, EEL: 1971]

muggles 1. (also **moggles, muggle**) marijuana leaves; marijuana; a marijuana cigarette. See *miggles*. RT: *joint, pot*. [U.S., (1926): RPW: 1938, DWM: 1936, VJM: 1949, GOL: 1950, M&D: 1952, D&D: 1957, W&F: 1960, RRL: 1969, CM: 1970, EEL: 1971, YKB: 1977] 2. marijuana smokers. RT: *toker*. [U.S., EEL: 1971]

muggy alcohol intoxicated. *Cf. mugged*. Muggy = damp. RT: *drunk*. [Br., JCH: 1859, F&H; U.S., MHW: 1934]

mug house a tavern or saloon. The *mug* is a drinking mug. RS: *bar*. [(1685): OED; listed in BVB: 1942]

mug oneself to get oneself drunk; to drink excessively. [Br., 1800s, F&H] Terms meaning to get drunk: *alcoholize, bash the* *turps, beer, befuddle, belt the grape, bemuse, bite into the brute, bite the brute, bub, catch a fox, cop a reeler, cop the brewery, cop the elephant, corn, cut one's leg, cut one's wolf loose, dehorn, do a pub-crawl, draw a blank, drench the gizzard, drink from the spigot, drink like a fish, drown one's sorrows, drown one's troubles, drunk, drunken, fall in the thick, flood one's sewers, flusterate, flusticate, fly high, fox, fuddle, fuddle one's nose, fuzz, fuzzle, gas, get a bun on, get a can on, get a jag on, get cannon, get canon, get on a jag, get one's biler loaded, get one's gage up, get one's tank filled, get on the pole, get the bighead, get there, go for veg, go on the cousin sis, go on the lap, go on the piss, go over the cognac trail, go under, hang one on, have a jug fuck, have a run, hit the booze, hit the hot bozel, hit the pot, hit the sauce, hunt a tavern fox, lay one on, liquor up, look through a glass, loop, lose one's legs, lush, lush up, mug oneself, oil one's wig, oil the wig, paint the town red, play camels, powder up, puff, pull a Daniel Boone, pull a shut-eye, rack up, raise hell, shicker, skate, slew, slop up, slush up, souse, splice the main brace, steam up, swack, take in cargo, take on cargo, take on fuel, tie it on, tie one on.*

mule 1. raw corn whiskey. *Cf. corn mule, jackass, white mule.* So named because of its kick. Some hobo use. RS: *rotgut.* [U.S., NK: 1926, EK: 1927, GI: 1931, MHW: 1934, D&D: 1957] 2. any illicit liquor. So named for its kick. RS: *moonshine.* From the prohibition era. Essentially the same as sense one. [U.S., (c. 1900): SBF: 1976, VR: 1929, AH: 1931, BVB: 1942] 3. marijuana soaked in whiskey. [U.S., HB: 1955] 4. someone who delivers or smuggles drugs for a dealer. Refers to a mere runner, not a manager or supplier. [U.S., (1935): OEDS, M&D: 1952, A&T: 1953, W&F: 1975, EEL: 1971, MW: 1976, JWK: 1981, RDS: 1982] Nicknames and slang terms for a drug runner: *bingle biff, body carrier, body-packer, caballo, carrier, cocaine cowboy, connection, connector, cop man, courier, domino, doper, dope runner, flunky, importer, internal, margin man, midget, mule, runner, stash man, swallower, trojan horse.*

mule skinner in drug running or smuggling, the person who recruits and watches over the mules or runners. *Cf. mule.* [U.S., RAS: 1983]

mulled (also **mulled up**) alcohol intoxicated. Mulled is a variant of *muddled* (*q.v.*). Never common (W&F: 1960). RT: *drunk.* [U.S., D&D: 1957, W&F: 1960]

munchies (also **blind munchies, marijuana munchies**) 1. a craving for food induced by the use of marijuana. Now used in slang outside the drug context. [U.S., RG: 1970, D&B: 1971, (1971): DNE: 1980, ADC: 1975, ADC: 1981] 2. snacks eaten to satisfy the craving described in sense one. Now general slang. [U.S., EEL: 1971, W&F: 1975, D&B: 1978, ADC: 1981]

munch out to eat ravenously after marijuana use. A blend of *munchies* (*q.v.*) and the slang expression *pig out* or some similar expression. [U.S., ADC: 1975]

mundungus (also mundungo) nasty, foul tobacco. Based on Spanish *mondongo* = entrails. Partridge (DU) suggests that it is based on *dung*. RT: *fogus*. [(1641): OED, FG: 1785, FG: 1823]

mung an uncomfortable feeling after taking *L.S.D.* (*q.v.*). See *acid mung*.

mungy having to do with an oily feeling of the face of a person taking an *L.S.D.* (*q.v.*) trip. *Cf. acid mung*. [U.S., EEL: 1971]

munsh opium. Origin unknown. RT: *opium*. [U.S., JES: 1959]

mur rum. This is *rum* spelled backwards (backslang). RT: *rum*. [Br., JCH: 1859, F&H, F&G: 1925, SSD]

murder weed cannabis. Marijuana was said to be responsible for driving people to crimes of passion including murder. RT: *pot*. [U.S., AJP: 1935]

muscateer a wino who favors muscatel wine. A play on *musketeer*. RS: *wino*. [Aust., (1930): DSUE, SJB: 1943]

muscle to inject a drug in to a muscle rather than into the skin or a vein. See *skin*. RS: *shoot*. [U.S., RG: 1970, IGA: 1971, RDS: 1982]

muscle pop a drug injection into a muscle. Usually because there are no suitable veins. RS: *shot*. [U.S., JHF: 1971]

muscle relaxant (also muscle relaxer) barbiturates. RT: *barbs*. Compare to *diet pills*. Not slang. [U.S., M&V: 1973, SNP: 1977]

M-user a morphine user. RT: *user*. [U.S., D&D: 1957]

mushrooms mushrooms of the genus Psilocybe containing psilocybin. *Cf. magic mushrooms, sacred mushrooms*. RT: *psilocybin*. [U.S., JHF: 1971, SH: 1972, ADC: 1975, YKB: 1977, ADC: 1981, BW: 1984] See also *shrooms*.

musta marijuana. See *muta*. RT: *pot*. [U.S., W&F: 1960, RDS: 1982]

mustika liquor. RT: *booze*. From the prohibition era. [U.S., AH: 1931, MHW: 1934]

muta (also mutah, mutha) marijuana. Possibly Spanish meaning pack of hounds. *Mutha*, which has only one attestation (EEL: 1971) may be an error or it may be from *mother* (*q.v.*). See *mooter*. RT: *pot*. [U.S., DWM: 1938, M&W: 1946, D&D: 1957, W&F: 1960, EEL: 1971, YKB: 1977, JH: 1979]

mutiny rum; grog. On shipboard, too much rum might lead to mutiny. RT: *rum*. [Br. nautical, late 18-1900s, DSUE]

muy tostado* alcohol intoxicated. Spanish for toasted. RT: *drunk*. High school use. [U.S., RAS: 1985]

muzzle 1. (also muzz) to drink to excess. RT: *guzzle*. [Br., (1828): OED, F&H] 2. heroin. Origin unknown. RT: *heroin*. [U.S., JES: 1959, H&C: 1975]

muzzler a drink of liquor; liquor. *Cf. muzzle.* RT: *nip.* [Br., 1800s, F&H; listed in BVB: 1942]

muzzy alcohol intoxicated. *Cf. muzzle.* RT: *drunk.* [Br., (1775): OED, JCH: 1887, B&L: 1890, F&H, (WWI): B&P: 1965, M&J: 1975; U.S., MHW: 1934, BVB: 1942]

my man an addict's drug supplier. *Cf. mother, sugar daddy.* RT: *dealer.* [U.S., ADC: 1975]

myrrh rum. See *mur.* [U.S., W&F: 1960]

N

N. 1. narcotics. RS: *dope.* [U.S., RDS: 1982] 2. a *Darvocet-N* (TM; *q.v.*) painkiller capsule. *Cf. N.s.* [U.S., JWK: 1981]

nab (also **nabber**) a police officer; a cop. **Nab** is a synonym of *pinch* and *cop*. *Cf. Uncle nab.* RS: *fuzz.* [Br., (1813): OED; U.S., BVB: 1942, S&W: 1966, RRL: 1969, EEL: 1971]

nabbed caught by the police; arrested. RT: *busted.* [U.S., since the 1800s, GWM: 1859]

nail 1. a tobacco cigarette. From *coffin nail* (*q.v.*). **Nail-rod** is given as Australian and New Zealand for a stick of tobacco. [(1910): DSUE, (WWI): B&P: 1965, F&G: 1925, BVB: 1942, W&F: 1960, SSD] (This entry continues after the following list.) Nicknames and slang terms for a tobacco cigarette: *aspirin smoke, birdwood, blinder, blower, bonfire, box fire, brad, brain tablet, burn, butt, camel dung, cancer stick, canteen stinker, cappo, choker, cig, cigaboo, cigareet, cigareete, ciggie, ciggy, coffin nail, coffin tack, coiler, consumption stick, cookie, C-stick, dags, desert horse, dirt, do my dags, dope stick, drag, dreamstick, dub, dubber, durry, duster, fag, faggeroo, faggot, fire, frajo, Freemans, gage, gangster, gasper, gasser, gippy, gret, grit, hardroll, Harry Freemans, Harry Wragg, hole, hump, igaret-say, Irish jigs, jigger, joint, long white roll, lung-disturber, lung-duster, lung-fogger, nail, needle, oil rag, oily rag, old nag, pill, pimpstick, pito, poison sausage, Q.B., quirley, quirlie, quirly, racehorse, ready-mades, ready-rolls, reefer, ret, roller, rollie, roll-your-own, root, scag, shuck, skag, slim, smoke, smokestick, snart, snout, soldier, solid, sparkle, spit, spit and drag, square, square joint, stick of weed, straight, sweet Marguerite, tab, tailor-mades, tailors, tiggy, T.M., toke, touch, tube, tuffler, twirlie, twirly, virgin.* 2. a hypodermic syringe and needle; a hypodermic needle; a makeshift hypodermic needle. *Cf. needle.* [U.S., DWM: 1936, VJM: 1949, RRL: 1969, EEL: 1971, ADC: 1975, W&F: 1975, JWK: 1981] 3. a drink of liquor. RT: *nip.* [U.S., BVB: 1942] 4. a marijuana cigarette. RT: *joint.* [U.S., D&B: 1978]

nailed 1. arrested. RT: *busted.* [U.S., (1889): OEDS, BD: 1937, M&V: 1967] 2. having had one's opiate use detected by the use of *Nalline* (TM; *q.v.*). See *pinned* for an explanation. [U.S., EEL: 1971]

nail-em-and-jail-em (also **nailer**) the police in general; a police officer. RT: *fuzz*. Black use. [U.S., EAF: 1980]

nail in one's coffin a drink of liquor; another drink of liquor. See *another nail in one's coffin*. Compare to *coffin nail*. RS: *nip*. [Br., (1821): DSUE, FG: 1823; listed in BVB: 1942]

nail, off the (also **off at the nail**) alcohol intoxicated. RT: *drunk*. [Br., F&H, (1922): DSUE]

nail-rod a stick of tobacco. See *nail*.

naked raw; having to do with neat liquor, especially gin. *Cf. strip-me-naked*. RT: *neat*. [Br., B&L: 1890, F&H]

nalga de angel* (also **nalga angelical***) marijuana. Spanish for angel's ass. RT: *pot*. [U.S., JBR: 1973, RDS: 1982]

Nalline the protected trade name for a narcotics antagonist derived from morphine. The drug reverses the effects of morphine and related opiates. Nalline brings on withdrawal symptoms in drug users and can be used to detect the use of morphine and its derivatives. See *nailed*.

Nam black (also **Nam shit, Nam weed**) potent black marijuana, allegedly from Vietnam or Southeast Asia. RT: *pot*. Black use. [U.S., EAF: 1980]

nanny goat sweat illicit or inferior liquor. *Cf. panther sweat, tiger sweat*. RS: *moonshine, rotgut*. [U.S., D&D: 1957, W&F: 1960]

nantz brandy. Refers to the French city Nantes. RT: *brandy*. [late 16-1800s, (1691): F&H]

nappy 1. (also **nap, nappy ale**) beer; strong ale. RT: *beer*. [(1529): OED, BE: 1690, (1743): OED, FG: 1785, FG: 1811, FG: 1823] 2. having to do with potent alcoholic beverages. [late 15-1700s, F&H] 3. alcohol intoxicated. RT: *drunk*. [Br., 17-1800s, F&H; listed in BVB: 1942]

narc (also **narco**) **1.** narcotic; a narcotic. [(1958): OEDS, SNP: 1977] 2. (also **narco fuzz, nark, narko**) a federal narcotics agent; any narcotics enforcement officer. RS: *fuzz*. [U.S., (1960): OEDS, (1967): DNE: 1973, M&V: 1967, W&F: 1967, D&B: 1970c, RRL: 1969, DCCU: 1972, ADC: 1975, MW: 1976, EAF: 1980] See also *nocks*.

Narcan a protected trade name for naloxone hydrochloride, a narcotics antagonist. The drug reverses the effects of narcotics and will bring on withdrawal symptoms where there is physical addiction. The drug is used in the treatment of a narcotics overdose.

narco 1. a narcotics addict. RT: *junky*. [U.S., JES: 1959] 2. a narcotics agent. See *narc*.

narco card a registration card carried by addicts. This allows the addict to receive *methadone* (*q.v.*). [U.S., MA: 1973, RDS: 1982]

narcoland the world of narcotics users. *Cf. narkiland*. Probably not drug argot. [U.S., JES: 1959, JTD: 1971]

narcopper an officer in the narcotics squad. RT: *fuzz*. Probably not narcotics argot. [U.S., JES: 1959]

narcotic an opiate; a sleep inducing, pain-relieving substance; any illegal or addictive drug substance. All of these senses are now standard English. The term, through police and underworld use, became generic and now includes L.S.D., marijuana, amphetamines, and other drugs regardless of their painkilling, sleep-inducing, or addictive properties. *Narcotic* was the word-of-choice in the early 1900s and has been replaced to a great extent by *drug* or *dope* both of which have become similarly generic. RS: *dope*. The term, which is very old, referred originally only to sleep inducing drugs like the opiates. Not slang. [since the 1300s, (1385): OED, (Chaucer)]

narcotic antagonist a drug which blocks or reverses the effects of a narcotic. *Cf. Nalline, Narcan* (TM). [DEM: 1981]

narcotic bull (also **narcotic copper**) a federal narcotics agent. RS: *fuzz*. [U.S., BD: 1937, DWM: 1938, VJM: 1949]

narghile (also **nargile**) a Turkish water pipe used in the smoking of tobacco or hashish. *Cf. hookah*. RS: *bong*. Standard English (obsolete). [(1830): OED; listed in RRL: 1969, RDS: 1982]

nark 1. a federal narcotics agent. The same as *narc* (*q.v.*). 2. to tell a law enforcement agency about illegal narcotics activity. [U.S., ADC: 1975]

narkied addicted to narcotics. RT: *hooked*. [U.S., JES: 1959]

narkiland the world of drug use and of drug addicts. *Cf. narcoland*. Not drug argot. [U.S., D&D: 1957, JES: 1959]

narky a narcotic drug. RT: *dope*. [U.S., D&D: 1957]

nasties drugs. RS: *dope*. [HSD: 1984]

natch (also **on the natch**) *clean* (*q.v.*); free of drugs. From *natural*. *Cf. burned out, clean, cleaned up, cleared up, dried, dried out, straight, turned off, washed up*. RS: *off*. [U.S., RRL: 1969, EEL: 1971, JH: 1979]

natch trip (also **natural high, natural trip**) a high from legal substances such as nutmeg. GEN: any positive emotional feeling from everyday living. [U.S., RRL: 1969, EEL: 1971, JWK: 1981]

naturalized alky drinkable alcohol reclaimed from denatured alcohol. A play on *denatured*. *Cf. good-natured alk, ill-natured alcohol*. From the prohibition era. [U.S., BVB: 1942]

nazy (also **nace, nase, nazzie, nazzy**) alcohol intoxicated. A drunken man was a **nazy cove** or a **nazy nab** and a drunken woman was a **nazy mort**. RT: *drunk*. [cant, (1550): OED, BE: 1690, FG: 1785, FG: 1811, GWM: 1859, B&L: 1890, JSF: 1889]

near and far a saloon. Rhyming slang for *bar* (*q.v.*). Akin to *far and near* (*q.v.*) = beer. RS: *bar*. [U.S., M&B: 1944, DRS]

near-beer beer with less than 1/2 percent alcohol content. This was legal during national prohibition. RS: *queer-beer*. [U.S., (1909): OEDS, GI: 1931, K&M: 1968]

neat having to do with pure or undiluted liquor. [(1579): SOD, JCH: 1887, B&L: 1890, F&H, BWG: 1899, W&F: 1960] Terms meaning undiluted: *aboriginal, as it came from its mother, baldfaced, bare-footed, clean from the still, clear, in a state of nature, in puris naturalibus, kosher, naked, neat, plain, primitive, pure, raw, reverend, reverent, short, stark naked, straight, stripped, unalloyed, uncorrupted, unmarried, unsophisticated, untempered, virgin, without a shirt.*

neaters undiluted naval rum, as opposed to *grog* (*q.v.*). Based on *neat* (*q.v.*). RS: *rum*. [Br. naval, F&G: 1925, SSD]

nebbies (also **neb**) *Nembutal* (TM; *q.v.*) barbiturate capsules. RT: *nemb*. [U.S., RRL: 1969, EEL: 1971, BR: 1972, YKB: 1977, NIDA: 1980]

nebo a drunkard. The *neb* is from *inebriate*. The o is a popular Australian slang suffix. RT: *sot*. [Aust., SJB: 1966]

necessities drug supplies: rolling papers, pipes, spoons, etc. A (well-known) code word for this equipment when it is offered for sale in record shops, tobacco stands, and novelty shops. *Cf. accessories, supplies*. [U.S., RAS: 1979]

neck-basting drinking liquor, perhaps to excess. *Cf. neck oil*. RS: *spreeing*. [Br., (1887): DSUE]

neck oil liquor, especially beer. RT: *beer*. [Br. and U.S., (1830): DSUE, JCH: 1887, B&L: 1890, JRW: 1909, MHW: 1934, RDS: 1982]

nectar (also **nectar of the gods**) liquor. In Greek mythology, nectar is the drink of the gods. Used in Standard English meaning excellent wine since the 1600s. RT: *booze*. [Br., 1800s, F&H; listed in BVB: 1942]

ned red wine in *red ned* (*q.v.*).

need a reef taken in alcohol intoxicated. From a nautical expression indicating that a ship has too much sail for the weather and is thus moves erratically. RT: *drunk*. [Br., late 1800s, DSUE; listed in BVB: 1942]

needle 1. a hypodermic needle; a hypodermic syringe and needle. [U.S., DWM: 1936, GOL: 1950, W&F: 1960, RRL: 1969, EEL: 1971] (This entry continues after the following list.) Nicknames and slang terms for a hypodermic needle: *artillery, barb, fuete, golden spike, hard nail, hipe, hit spike, hook, hype, ike-spay, jabber, joint, Mr. Twenty-six, nail, needle, point, prick, prod, prod of joy, safety, serpent, sharp, silver, silver serpent, sky-the-wipe, smackse, spear, spike, thorn, tom cat, toy, Yale*. 2. to inject drugs. RT: *shoot*. [U.S., BVB: 1942] 3. an injection of a drug with a hypodermic syringe and needle. RT: *shot*. [Aust., (1918): DSUE; Br., (1910): DU; U.S., BVB: 1942] 4. to inject alcohol or ether into a bottle of liquor or beer by using a hypodermic needle to penetrate the cork. *Near-beer* (*q.v.*) could be strongly fortified in this fashion and still appear to be legal. From the prohibition era. [U.S., (1929): OEDS, GI: 1931, MHW: 1934] 5. to lace any food or drink with alcohol. Said especially of punch which is not considered as essentially alcoholic in the U.S. *Spike* (*q.v.*) is more common. [U.S., BVB: 1942, W&F: 1960, DCCU: 1972] 6. a thin tobacco cigarette. RT: *nail.* Prison use. [Br., early 1900s, DU] 7. (also **the needle**) a drug addiction. *Cf. on the needle.* RS: *habit.* [U.S., M&V: 1954, (1968): DNE: 1973, ADC: 1975] 8. gin. See *needle and pin.*

needle and pin (also **needle**) gin. Rhyming slang. RT: *gin.* [Br., late 18-1900s, DSUE, DRS] See also *pins and needles.*

needle beer (also **needled beer**) *beer* (*q.v.*) or *near-beer* (*q.v.*) which has been injected with alcohol or ether to make it more potent. From the prohibition era. [U.S., (1928): OEDS, VR: 1929, DWM: 1931, GI: 1931, MHW: 1934, D&D: 1957]

needle candy narcotics which are taken by injection. See *nose candy. Cf. candy man.* [U.S., EEL: 1971, D&D: 1957]

needle flash a brief tingle when the needle is inserted, before the drug is injected. [U.S., RG: 1970, IGA: 1971, JHF: 1971]

needle freak (also **needle fiend, needle jabber**) 1. an addict whose habit is based on injectable drugs. [U.S., BD: 1937, DWM: 1938, VJM: 1949, GU: 1975] 2. an addict or drug user who will inject almost any substance. [U.S., RRL: 1969, JHF: 1971] 3. a person (not necessarily an addict) who has a needle fetish which can be relieved by playing with hypodermic syringe and needle, often giving injections of (and booting) any substance. This addict may get a sexual *rush* (*q.v.*) from sticking the needle into anything. *Cf. needle habit, needle yen.* [U.S., DWM: 1938, RRL: 1969, JWK: 1981]

needle habit (also **needle yen**) 1. a drug addiction based on injected drugs. RS: *habit.* [U.S., DWM: 1938, VJM: 1949] 2. a fetish or obsession with hypodermic needles. A person with a needle habit derives great pleasure from injecting and *booting* (*q.v.*). *Cf. needle freak.* A form of masochism rather than a form of addiction. See *sugar habit.* RS: *habit.* [U.S., DWM: 1938, JWK: 1981]

needle jabber See *needle freak.*

needle knight (also **needle nipper, needle pusher**) an addict who injects drugs. *Cf. bangster.* [U.S., BVB: 1942, GOL: 1950]

needle man 1. an addict who injects drugs. RT: *bangster.* [U.S., DU, EEL: 1971] 2. a man who adds alcohol or ether to beer as in *needle* (sense four). See *needle.* From the prohibition era. [U.S., JLK: 1934, MHW: 1934, GOL: 1950]

needle, on the addicted to injectable drugs; on injectable narcotics. *Cf. needle.* RT: *hooked.* [U.S., BVB: 1942, D&D: 1957, W&F:

1960, (1963): DNE: 1973, RRL: 1969, EEL: 1971]

needles, the 1. tremens induced by cocaine abstinence. [early 1900s, DU] 2. a sensation of an electric shock passing through the body after a drug injection. Possibly a *rush* (*q.v.*). [U.S., NAM: 1953]

needle yen See *needle habit.*

negative a bad drug trip. *Cf. bum bend, bum kicks, bummer, bum trip, downer, down trip, drag, freak out, horrors, low, panic trip.* Compare to *positive.* [U.S., RRL: 1969]

negrillos* amphetamine capsules, probably *Biphetamine* (TM; *q.v.*). From Spanish for blacks. *Cf. black and white, black beauties, blackbirds, black Cadillac, black mollies, black widow, minstrels.* RT: *amps.* [U.S., NIDA: 1980]

Negro drunk alcohol intoxicated; very drunk. Primarily a slur on blacks. RS: *drunk.* [U.S., RHT: 1912] See also *jig-juice.*

Negro head (also **niggerhead**) a particular kind of black tobacco. RS: *fogus.* [U.S., (1809, 1843): OEDS]

Nelly's death (also **Nelly**) cheap red wine. If this is rhyming slang, the rhyme is not clear, unless it is on *meth* = methyl alcohol. RS: *wine.* [Aust., (1930): DSUE, SJB: 1943]

Nelson's blood dark (British) naval rum. From the tale that the body of Admiral Lord Nelson was returned to England (from the Battle of Trafalgar) preserved in rum or brandy. *Cf. tap the admiral.* RS: *rum.* [Br., (1806): F&G: 1925, DSUE, EP: 1948]

nemb (also **nem, nembies, nemmie, nimbie, nimbles, nimby**) a capsule of *Nembutal* (TM; *q.v.*) barbiturate. RS: *barbs.* [U.S., (1950): OEDS, M&V: 1954, RRL: 1969, ADC: 1975, W&F: 1975, YKB: 1977, NIDA: 1980, JWK: 1981] Nicknames and slang terms for Nembutal: *abbot, amarilla, blockbuster, canary, jacket, neb, nebbies, nem, nemb, nembies, nemishes, nemishes, nemmie, nimbie, nimbles, nimby, yakenal, yellow, yellow angels, yellow bams, yellow birds, yellow bullets, yellow dolls.*

Nembutal a protected trade name for phenobarbital (barbiturate) in a variety of forms. The drug is a central nervous system depressant. Most slang terms refer to yellow capsules of Nembutal (TM) sodium, although other capsule colors exist. See *nemb* for a list of terms. See *barbs* for a list of terms for barbiturates. [(1930): OEDS, in current use; consult a pharmaceutical reference for more information]

nemish (also **nemishes**) *Nembutal* (TM; *q.v.*) barbiturate. See *nemb.* [U.S., RRL: 1969, EEL: 1971]

Nepalese hash a potent variety of hashish from Nepal. RT: *hash.* [U.S., ELA: 1982]

never fear a beer; beer. Rhyming slang. RT: *beer.* [Br., JCH: 1859, F&H, DRS]

new acid *P.C.P.* (*q.v.*). The old acid is *L.S.D.* (*q.v.*). RT: *P.C.P.*

[U.S., (1970s): FAB: 1979]

newer freedom, the the end of prohibition. Based on *the new freedom*. [U.S., 1930s, BVB: 1942]

newted alcohol intoxicated. From *pissed as a newt* (*q.v.*). RT: *drunk*. [PD: 1982]

New York City Silver (also Subway Silver) a mythological albino marijuana. The same as *Manhattan white* (*q.v.*). RS: *pot*. [U.S., (1981): R&P: 1982]

New York City white (also New York white) The same as *New York City Silver* (*q.v.*). [U.S., (1975): R&P: 1982]

nic fit (also nicotine fit) This is older than the attestation indicates. [U.S., E&R: 1971]

nicked arrested. RT: *busted*. [U.S., EEL: 1971]

nickel bag (also nickel) a five-dollar bag of marijuana, heroin, or other drugs. RS: *load*. [U.S., S&W: 1966, JBW: 1967, M&V: 1967, W&F: 1967, D&B: 1970c, RRL: 1969, EEL: 1971, MA: 1973, ADC: 1975, ADC: 1981, JWK: 1981]

nickel deck a five-dollar portion of heroin. RS: *load*. [U.S., H&C: 1975]

nicker a tobacco cigarette butt. RT: *brad*. [Br., (1930): DSUE, M&J: 1975]

Nicotiana glauca* marijuana, literally: green nicotine. An imitation scientific name. RS: *pot*. [U.S., RDS: 1982]

nicotine a poisonous substance found in tobacco; the active principle of tobacco smoke. From Latin *nicotiana*. Standard English. [since the early 1800s, (1819): OED]

nieve* one of the white, powdered drugs: heroin or cocaine. Spanish for *snow* (*q.v.*). RS: *powder*. [calo, JBR: 1973, NIDA: 1980]

niebla* phencyclidine, P.C.P. Spanish for *mist* (*q.v.*). RT: *P.C.P.* [U.S., ELA: 1984]

nig gin. This is *gin* spelled backwards (backslang). RT: *gin*. [Br., 1800s, F&H]

nigger gin inferior gin; synthetic gin. *Cf. nigger pot*. RS: *rotgut*. From the prohibition era. [U.S., VR: 1929, MHW: 1934, AAR: 1944, VJM: 1949, D&D: 1957]

nigger minstrels amphetamines, probably *Biphetamine* (TM; *q.v.*). See *black and white minstrel*. RT: *amps*. [Br., M&J: 1975]

nigger pot home-brewed whiskey. *Cf. jig-juice*. RT: *moonshine*. [U.S., dialect (Southern), W&F: 1967]

nightcap a drink of liquor taken before retiring. RS: *nip*. [(1818): OED, JSF: 1889, F&H, BWG: 1899, W&F: 1960]

night on the rainbow a night spent under the influence of drugs. [U.S., GOL: 1950]

nimbies *Nembutal* (TM; *q.v.*). See *nemb.*

nimbles *Nembutal* (TM; *q.v.*) barbiturate capsules. Possibly an error for *nimbies* (*q.v.* at *nemb*). RT: *nemb.* [U.S., SNP: 1977]

nimptopsical alcohol intoxicated. RT: *drunk.* [BF: 1737]

nineteenth hole a drink of an alcoholic beverage after a golf game; a bar likely to be frequented by golfers who have played eighteen holes of golf. Often seen as the name of such a bar. RS: *bar.* [U.S., (1928): OEDS, D&D: 1957, W&F: 1960]

ninety-weight liquor. Possibly ninety proof alcohol. *Cf. forty-weight.* RT: *booze.* [U.S., EE: 1976]

nip (also **nipper**) a small drink of liquor or beer. [FG: 1796, F&H, (1891): SBF: 1976, BVB: 1942] Nicknames for a single drink of liquor: *alleviator, anotherie, another nail in one's coffin, ante-lunch, antifogmatic, appetizer, ball, ball of fire, base burner, belt, bender, big reposer, binder, bit of blink, blob, boilermaker, bracer, bucket, bullock's eye, catsous, caulker, chaser, cheerer, cheerer-upper, chit-chat, cinder, clap of thunder, cocktail, coffin nail, cold one, common sewer, cooler, corker, cowboy cocktail, cry, cuff link, cup of cheer, cup of comfort, cup of the creature, cup that cheers, damp, damper, dandy, dannie, deep noser, deep sinker, dewdrop, dewhank, digester, double, drain, dram, drink, drinkypoo, dust-cutter, eye-opener, fall down the sink, fancy smile, flash, fog-cutter, fogmatic, gasp, geeser, geezer, go, go-down, gum tickler, hair of the dog, hair of the dog that bit one, heeltap, hi-ball, highball, hooker, hooter, hoozle, hop toad, Jack Surpass, jigger, johnnie, jolt, jump-steady, just what the doctor ordered, kenird, kick in the guts, kick in the wrist, K.T., lap, leg-opener, line of the old author, lip, little whack, livener, livvener, load, lonesome, long drink, long one, long pull, long sleever, lotion, lube, meridian, morning rouser, mouthwash, muzzler, nail, nail in one's coffin, nightcap, nip, nipper, nobbler, nooner, nut, old crow, one for the bitumen, one for the road, out, patent digester, peg, pepper-upper, pick-me-up, pill, pistol shot, plug, pony, powder, pull, quencher, quickie, quick one, quicky, raw recruit, refresher, reposer, revelation, reviver, rinse, rosiner, rosner, rouser, rozener, rub of the relic, scoop, screw, sensation, settler, shant, shanty, short, short one, short snort, shot, shot in the arm, shot in the neck, slash, slight sensation, slosh, slug, smile, smiler, sniff, snifter, snoozer, snort, snorter, something, something cool, something damp, something short, something wet, soother, sparkler, spot, squail, squirrel load, stick, stinger, streak of lightning, sundowner, swap of the mop, swig, swill, tall one, taste, taste of the creature, tiddle-a-wink, tiddledy wink, tiddly, tiddlywink, tiff, tift, tillywink, tip, titley, tod, tonic, tonsil bath, toot, top o' reeb, toss, tot, touch, tumble, tumble down, tumble down the sink, Vera Lynn, wad, warmer, waxer, wet, whack, wheep, yell.*

NIP (also **N.I.P.**) not in possession of drugs, including marijuana. A law enforcement notation. *Cf. clean.* [U.S., RDS: 1982]

nipped alcohol intoxicated. Probably akin to *nip*. RT: *drunk*. [U.S., BVB: 1942]

nippitate (also **nippitato, nippitati, nippitatum, nippitaty**) liquor. The term appears to have been revived in the U.S. during prohibition. [(1575): OED, F&H, MHW: 1934]

nipster a tippler; a drunkard. RT: *sot*. [Br., 1800s, F&H]

nitrous nitrous oxide, laughing gas. Sometimes inhaled for a high. [U.S., (RRL: 1969), ADC: 1975, ADC: 1981]

Nixon low-potency marijuana; low-quality marijuana sold as high-quality marijuana. Based on the name of a former U.S. President. *Cf. Johnson grass*. RS: *pot*. [U.S., RRL: 1969, SNP: 1977]

njemu* an East African name for marijuana. RT: *pot*. [U.S., RDS: 1982]

nobbler a small drink of liquor. RT: *nip*. [Aust., (1759): F&H, (1851): GAW: 1978, (1852): OEDS, SJB: 1943]

noble princess of the waters *psilocybin* (*q.v.*) from mushrooms. See *magic mushrooms*. [U.S., YKB: 1977]

noble weed marijuana. *Cf. weed*. RT: *pot*. [U.S., D&B: 1970c]

no brand cigarette (also **no name brand cigarette**) a marijuana cigarette. See *cigarette with no name*. RT: *joint*. [U.S., EAF: 1980]

nocks narcotics. Possibly an eye-dialect spelling for a dialect pronunciation of *narks*. *Cf. narc*. RS: *dope*. [U.S., BVB: 1942, VJM: 1949, A&T: 1953]

nockskeller a place where drugs can be bought and used. RT: *doperie*. [U.S., JES: 1959]

nockum stiff moonshine; strong rotgut whiskey. RT: *rotgut*. [U.S. Civil War, DST: 1984]

nod 1. the relaxed, undulating euphoria caused by certain drugs. Probably referred originally to opium. [U.S., RRL: 1969, MA: 1973, JWK: 1981] 2. (also **nod off, play the nod**) to experience drug euphoria; to fall asleep under the effects of a drug. [U.S., BD: 1937, DWM: 1938, (RRL: 1969), IGA: 1971, MA: 1973] 3. a session of heroin use. The same as a *snooze* (*q.v.*). See *on the nod*.

nodded out in heroin euphoria; under the influence of heroin. RS: *stoned*. [U.S., RAS: 1980]

nodding out (also **nodding**) drug intoxicated; experiencing a *nod* (*q.v.*). *Cf. wag out*. RS: *stoned*. Black use. [U.S., M&V: 1967, RRL: 1969, DC: 1972]

noddy-headed alcohol intoxicated. RT: *drunk*. [Br., 1800s, F&H]

nod, on the 1. in an opium stupor. RS: *stoned*. [U.S. GOL: 1950] 2. drug intoxicated. The drug is probably heroin. From sense one. RT: *stoned*. [U.S., NAM: 1953, HB: 1955, M&H: 1959,

RRL: 1969, EEL: 1971] 3. addicted to a drug. RT: *hooked*. [U.S., JWK: 1981]

noggy alcohol intoxicated. RT: *drunk*. [Br., 18-1900s, DSUE; listed in BVB: 1942]

noise heroin. RT: *heroin*. [U.S., BVB: 1942, GOL: 1950, A&T: 1953, SNP: 1977]

nolo alcohol intoxicated. RT: *drunk*. Possibly an error for *molo* (*q.v.*). [S&E: 1981, PD: 1982]

nonaddict someone who uses drugs but is not addicted to them. This refers also to persons who do not use drugs at all. [U.S., (1970): DNE: 1973]

non compos alcohol intoxicated. RT: *drunk*. [BF: 1737]

non compos poopoo alcohol intoxicated. From *non compos* (*q.v.*). RT: *drunk*. [PD: 1982]

nondrinker a person who does not drink alcohol. RT: *dry*. Standard English. [U.S., MW: 1976]

nooner a noontime drink of liquor; the day's first drink taken at noon. *Cf. meridian*. RT: *nip*. [Br., WG: 1962]

NORMAL "National Organization for the Reform of Marijuana Laws." [U.S., (D&B: 1978)]

nose a powdered drug which can be inhaled: heroin or cocaine. *Cf. hooter, nose candy*. RS: *powder*. [U.S., YKB: 1977] See also *noser my knacker*.

nose-burner (also **nose-warmer**) a marijuana cigarette stub, a *roach* (*q.v.*). [U.S., M&V: 1967, SNP: 1977] See also *lip-burner*.

nose candy (also **nose**) powdered drugs which are inhaled, primarily cocaine, sometimes heroin. See *needle candy*. RS: *powder*. [U.S., MHW: 1934, D&D: 1957, W&F: 1960, YKB: 1977, NIDA: 1980]

nose 'em tobacco. See *noser my knacker*.

nose habit an addiction to sniffed (snorted) drugs, usually heroin or cocaine. RS: *habit*. [U.S., D&B: 1970c, IGA: 1971]

nose hit a puff of marijuana smoke taken through the nose from the burning end of the cigarette. *Cf. hit*. RT: *toke*. [U.S., ADC: 1975, GU: 1975]

nose paint liquor; strong whiskey. From the drinker's red nose. *Cf. tonsil paint*. RT: *booze, rotgut*. [U.S., (1881): DA, VR: 1929, MHW: 1934, D&D: 1957]

nose powder (also **nose stuff**) powdered drugs used for inhaling: cocaine, heroin, morphine. Cocaine in current use. See *nose candy*. RT: *powder*. [U.S., VJM: 1949, D&D: 1957, YKB: 1977]

noser my knacker (also **nose 'em, nose my, nose my knacker, nosey me, nosey me knacker**) tobacco. Rhyming slang for *terbacker*. GWM: 1859 lists **nosemy** and the erroneous *knose* (*q.v.*). *Knacker* usually means testicle. RT: *fogus*. [cant, DA: 1857, F&H, DRS]

nose-warmer 1. a short tobacco pipe. *Cf. pipe.* [Br., late 1800s, F&H; U.S., MHW: 1934, BVB: 1942] 2. (also **nose-burner**) the stub of a marijuana cigarette. RT: *roach.* [U.S., M&V: 1973]

N.s capsules of *Darvocet-N* (TM; *q.v.*) painkiller. *Cf. N.* [U.S., JWK: 1981]

nub (also **nub end**) a tobacco cigarette butt. RT: *brad.* [M&J: 1975]

nuff a sufficiency of alcohol in *have one's nuff* (*q.v.*); alcohol intoxicated. [Br., B&L: 1890, JM: 1923]

nuggets amphetamine capsules or tablets. RT: *amps.* [U.S., YKB: 1977, NIDA: 1980]

numbed out nearly paralyzed by P.C.P. RS: *stoned.* [U.S., ELA: 1984]

number a marijuana cigarette. May refer to number *thirteen* (*q.v.*). GEN: a deed, a thing. RT: *joint.* [U.S., (1963): ELA: 1982, JBW: 1967, EEL: 1971, RRL: 1974, ADC: 1975, GU: 1975, W&F: 1975]

number eight (also **eight**, 8) heroin. H is the eighth letter of the alphabet. RT: *heroin.* [U.S., DU, A&T: 1953, D&D: 1957]

number thirteen (also **thirteen**, 13) morphine. M is the thirteenth letter of the alphabet. RT: *morphine.* [U.S., DU, A&T: 1953, D&D: 1957]

number three (also **three**, 3) cocaine. C is the third letter of the alphabet. RT: *cocaine.* [U.S., DU, A&T: 1953, D&D: 1957]

nurse powdered drugs. See *white nurse.*

nut 1. a drink of liquor. RT: *nip.* [Br., late 1800s, F&H] 2. a mixture of water and (much) nutmeg used in prisons to get high. *Cf. buck, idiot juice, jail house high.* [U.S., M&V: 1967, H&C: 1975]

nut, off one's alcohol intoxicated. GEN: slightly crazy. Nut = head. RT: *drunk.* [Br., 1800s, F&H]

nuts (also **nutty**) alcohol intoxicated. *Cf. off one's nut.* RT: *drunk.* [U.S., BVB: 1942]

N.Y.D. alcohol intoxicated. The notation "not yet diagnosed" used in (British) military hospitals. RS: *drunk.* [Br., JRW: 1909]

O

O. 1. opium. RT: *opium*. [U.S., DWM: 1933, MHW: 1934, VJM: 1949, M&D: 1952, D&D: 1957, W&F: 1960, RRL: 1969, CM: 1970, EEL: 1971, RDS: 1982] 2. an portion of drugs; an ounce of drugs. *Cf. O.Z.* RS: *load*. [U.S., BD: 1937, DWM: 1936]

O.A. 1. an overdose of *Methedrine* (TM; *q.v.*). 2. to take an overdose of *Methedrine* (TM). From *overamp* (*q.v.*). [U.S., JH: 1979]

oasis a liquor establishment. *Cf. watering hole*. RS: *bar*. [U.S., BVB: 1942]

Oaxacan Mexican marijuana from the state of Oaxaca. RT: *pot*. [U.S., (1976): ELA: 1982, D&B: 1978]

o-be-joyful liquor; brandy; rum. One who sells rum in an o-be-joyful works was called an o-be-joyful merchant. One who overuses it was an o-be-joyfuller. RT: *booze*. [Br., FG: 1823; U.S., FBL: 1898]

obfuscated alcohol intoxicated. From *obfuscate* = to stupefy, to bewilder (late 1500s): SOD. RT: *drunk*. [(1855): DSUE, JCH: 1887, B&L: 1890, M&J: 1975, MHW: 1934, BVB: 1942]

obfusticated alcohol intoxicated. A play on *obfuscated* (*q.v.*). GEN: excited (LWP: 1908). RT: *drunk*. [Br., mid 1800s, DSUE]

ob sale a sale of narcotics observed by the police. From *observation sale*. [U.S., JWK: 1981]

occabot tobacco. *Tobacco* spelled backwards (backslang). RT: *fogus*. [Br., (1851): DSUE, JCH: 1887, F&H]

ocksecrotia alcohol intoxicated. See *oxycrocium*.

October strong ale. See *hum cap*.

O.D. 1. an overdose of drugs. Used for fatal and non-fatal overdoses. The term has become part of medical (emergency room) jargon and is widely known in general slang or colloquial U.S. English. *Cf. jail*. [U.S., JBW: 1967, M&V: 1967, W&F: 1967, D&B: 1970c, RRL: 1969, MA: 1973, ADC: 1975, ADC: 1981] 2. to purposely or accidentally give oneself a dangerous dose of one or more drugs. Can refer to fatal or non-fatal overdosing. The past tense, O.D.-ed or O.D.eed, is widely known. [U.S., D&B: 1970b, DCCU: 1972, ADC: 1975, JWK: 1981] 3. to die from an overdose of drugs. From sense one. [U.S., (1971): DNE: 1973, ADC: 1975, W&F: 1975] 4. a person who has taken an overdose. [U.S., (1970): DNE: 1973, MW: 1976]

oddish alcohol intoxicated. RT: *drunk*. [Br., mid 1800s, F&H]

O.D. man a heroin user; a careless heroin user. See *O.D.* RS: *user*. [U.S., ADC: 1975]

off 1. alcohol intoxicated. *Cf. off one's nut*. RT: *drunk*. [Br., 1800s, F&H; listed in BVB: 1942] 2. drug intoxicated. Probably from sense one. *Cf. get off*. RT: *stoned*. [U.S., RRL: 1969] 3. (also **off drugs**) free from drugs; withdrawn from an addictive drug. *Cf. clean*. [U.S., (1910): DU, BD: 1937, DWM: 1938, TRG: 1968] (This entry continues after the following list.) Nicknames and slang terms for the state of being off drugs: *away, away from the habit, burned out, clean, cleaned up, cleared up, D-free, dried, dried out, natch, off, off drugs, off the habit, on the natch, squared up, straight, turned off*. 4. (as a transitive verb: **off someone, off something**) to do away with; to kill someone; to sell something; to steal something. An **off-artist** is a thief. Also used in underworld contexts other than drug traffic. [U.S., (1968): OEDS, RRL: 1969, C&H: 1974, JWK: 1981]

off-brand cigarette a marijuana cigarette. *Cf. cigarette with no name*. RT: *joint*. Black use. [U.S., EAF: 1980]

officer's brand papers cigarette rolling papers. RT: *paper*. [U.S., military, BVB: 1942]

ogoy heroin. *Cf. oye*. RT: *heroin*. [U.S., SNP: 1977]

Oh my dear! (also **Oh my!**) 1. beer. Rhyming slang. *Cf. pot of O*. RT: *beer*. [(1868): JRW: 1909, (1928): DRS, M&B: 1944] 2. *near-beer* (*q.v.*). RS: *queer-beer*. From the prohibition era. [U.S., HNR: 1934, MHW: 1934]

oil 1. chewing tobacco. RS: *quid*. [U.S. nautical, HB: 1928, MHW: 1934, W&F: 1960] 2. liquor. *Cf. neck oil, tongue oil*. RT: *booze*. [U.S., DC: 1972] 3. an alcohol extract of hashish. [U.S., RRL: 1969, YKB: 1977] (This entry continues after the following list.) Nicknames and slang terms for hashish oil: *Afghani, black oil, cherry leb, hash oil, honey oil, Indian oil, liquid hashish, oil, red oil, smash, son of one, The One*. 4. to inject (oneself) with a drugs, usually heroin. RT: *shoot*. [U.S., JWK: 1981]

oil-burner 1. a user of chewing tobacco. *Cf. oil*. [U.S. nautical, HB: 1928, MHW: 1934, W&F: 1960] 2. (also **oil-burning habit**) a large and expensive heroin (or other drug) addiction. A habit this size may cost hundreds of dollars per day. RS: *habit*. [U.S., DWM: 1938, M&H: 1959, JWK: 1981] 3. an addict with a large and expensive habit. RT: *junky*. Prison use. [U.S., TH: 1976] See also *burn the midnight oil*.

oiled 1. alcohol intoxicated; tipsy. *Cf. oil*. RT: *drunk*. [BF: 1737, (1916): OEDS, F&G: 1925, MP: 1928, GI: 1931, MHW: 1934, VJM: 1949, D&D: 1957, W&F: 1960, SSD, DCCU: 1972] 2. drug intoxicated; injected with drugs. RT: *oil*. [U.S., JWK: 1981]

oiler 1. a drunkard. *Cf. oil*. RT: *sot*. [Br., (1916): DSUE] 2. a smoker of hashish oil. *Cf. oil*. [U.S., D&B: 1978] 3. an addict who injects drugs. *Cf. oil*. RT: *bangster*. [U.S., JWK: 1981]

oilhead a drunkard; an alcoholic. *Cf. oil*. RT: *sot*. [U.S., M&V: 1973, RDS: 1982]

oil of barley (also **oyl of barley**) beer; strong beer. RT: *beer*. [cant, BE: 1690, FG: 1785, GWM: 1859, F&H; listed in BVB: 1942]

oil of gladness moonshine; strong rotgut liquor. RT: *rotgut*. [U.S. Civil War, DST: 1984]

oil of joy liquor. *Cf. oil*. RT: *booze*. [U.S., GI: 1931, MHW: 1934]

oil one's whistle (also **wet one's whistle**) to take a drink of liquor. RT: *irrigate*. [U.S., MHW: 1934]

oil one's wig (also **oil the wig**) to drink liquor; to get slightly drunk. RT: *guzzle*. [17-1800s, F&H]

oil, on the on a drinking bout. *Oil* (*q.v.*) = liquor. RT: *spreeing*. [Br., 1900s, DSUE]

oily rag (also **oil rag**) a cigarette. Rhyming slang for *fag*. RT: *nail*. [Br., (1932): DSUE, DRS]

oink a police officer. A play on *pig* (*q.v.*). RT: *fuzz*. [U.S., CM: 1970]

oint-jay a hypodermic syringe and needle. Pig Latin for *joint* (*q.v.*). RT: *monkey pump*. [U.S., (1935): OEDS]

O.J. 1. marijuana; a marijuana cigarette dipped in opium. From *opium joint*. *Cf. joint*. Also a play on the well-known abbreviation of orange juice. RT: *pot*. [U.S., Vietnamese War, (1970): ELA: 1982, SNP: 1977] 2. an overdose of a hard drug. From *overjolt* (*q.v.*). [U.S., JH: 1979]

old boy strong ale. Possibly from the use of this term as a nickname for the devil. *Cf. boy*. See *old Tom*. RT: *ale*. [early 1700s, DSUE]

old crow a drink of liquor. Also an American brand of whiskey. RT: *nip*. [(c. 1860): F&H]

old dog a plug of burnt or half-burnt tobacco remaining in a tobacco pipe. See *dog*. RT: *dottle*. [mid 1800s, DSUE]

old lady White (also **old white lady**) powdered drugs: cocaine, heroin, morphine. *Cf. Dr. White, white nurse*. RT: *powder*. [U.S., BVB: 1942, VJM: 1949, A&T: 1953]

old Madge cocaine. RT: *cocaine*. Probably from the early 1900s. [U.S., ELA: 1984]

old man whiskey. *Cf. old boy, old man's milk*. RT: *whiskey*. Hobo use. [U.S., early 1900s, DU]

old man's milk whiskey. Borrowed from a term for a milk dish prepared for a toothless, old man. See also *bottle baby*. RT:

whiskey. [Br., 1800s, F&H]

old nag a tobacco cigarette. Rhyming slang for *fag* (*q.v.*). RT: *nail*. [Br., WWI, DSUE, B&P: 1965, DRS]

old redeye (also **redeye**) whiskey; raw whiskey; moonshine. Because its use reddens the eyes. RT: *rotgut*. [U.S., since the 1800s, F&H]

old red goofy cheap rotgut liquor, especially wine. RT: *rotgut*. [U.S., BR: 1972]

old rope strong, bad-smelling tobacco. *Cf. rope*. RT: *fogus*. [Br. military, (1925): DSUE]

old shoes rum. *Cf. shoe polish*. Possibly rhyming slang for *booze*. RT: *rum*. [JRW: 1909]

old soaker (also **soaker**) a drunkard. *Cf. soak*. RT: *sot*. [cant, FG: 1811]

old soldier 1. a cigarette or cigar butt; a quid of tobacco. *Cf. old dog*. [Br. and U.S., (1850s): W&F: 1960, (1892): OED, BVB: 1942, D&D: 1957, M&J: 1975] 2. an empty liquor or beer bottle (or can). RT: *dead soldier*. [U.S., BVB: 1942]

old Steve powdered narcotics: heroin, morphine, or cocaine. RT: *powder*. [U.S., DWM: 1936, BVB: 1942, A&T: 1953] See also *Steve's mission*.

old Tom (also Tom, ould Tom) gin. A play on (a Tom) *cat's water* (*q.v.*) = cat urine. Attested as lower-class usage. RT: *gin*. [Br., JB: 1823, JCH: 1887, F&H]

olive a bit of *cotton* (*q.v.*) used to strain a drug solution as it is pulled into a syringe or a medicine dropper. Like an olive in a martini in the sense that it contains some of the liquid. [U.S., JES: 1959, H&C: 1975]

ololiuqui the seeds of a vine, *Rivea corymbosa*, which are eaten to produce a high. The effect is similar to that of *morning glory seeds* (*q.v.*). From the Nahuatl language. Also (mis)spelled ololuiqui (YKB: 1977). [(1915): OEDS, BTD: 1968, RRL: 1969, YKB: 1977]

on 1. alcohol intoxicated. RT: *drunk*. [Br., B&L: 1890, F&H; U.S., BVB: 1942, W&F: 1960] 2. drug intoxicated; using drugs habitually. RS: *stoned*. [U.S., M&V: 1954, RRL: 1969, EEL: 1971]

one and one having to do with the use of both nostrils in snorting a drug, usually cocaine. *Cf. both barrels*. [U.S., RRL: 1969] See also *one on one*.

one for the road (also one for the bitumen) a drink; a drink before a journey. One for the bitumen is an Australian version and may refer specifically to the road between Darwin and Alice Springs. RT: *nip*. [Aust., (1945): DSUE, GAW: 1978; Br., SSD; U.S., D&D: 1957, W&F: 1960]

one-hit grass *D.M.T.* (*q.v.*) smoked with tobacco, marijuana, or parsley. This combination is said to be so strong that only one puff will produce a high. [U.S., YKB: 1977] See also *one-toke weed*.

one-hitter (also **one-hit bowl**) a marijuana pipe which is only big enough for one use. *Cf. four-way hit*. RS: *bong*. [U.S., ADC: 1981]

one of the faithful a drunkard. RT: *sot*. [since the early 1600s, (1609): OED]

one on one a tablet of *Talwin* (TM; *q.v.*) painkiller and a tablet of *Pyribenzamine* (TM; *q.v.*), antihistamine. From the buzz-word expression meaning one to one. *Cf. tricycles and bicycles, T.s and blues*. RS: *set*. [U.S., RAS: 1981] See also *one and one*.

one over the eight (also **one over eight, over the eight**) alcohol intoxicated. RT: *drunk*. [BVB: 1942, SSD]

One, The an alcohol extract of hashish. RT: *oil*. [U.S., (1971): ELA: 1982, YKB: 1977, D&B: 1978]

one-toke weed very potent marijuana. A single puff makes one high. RS: *pot*. [U.S., ELA: 1982]

one-way *L.S.D.*, (*q.v.*). *Cf. four-ways* (at *four-way star*). RT: *L.S.D.* [U.S., RG: 1970]

oof the potency of the alcohol in liquor; the effect of potent alcohol. GEN: onomatopoetic for the sound a person utters when struck in the stomach. [U.S., BVB: 1953]

ooze, on the on a drinking bout. Rhyming slang on *booze* (*q.v.*). *Cf. River Ooze*. RT: *spreeing*. [Br., (1920): DSUE, (WWI): DRS]

oozy alcohol intoxicated. *Cf. River Ooze*. RT: *drunk*. [PD: 1982]

ope (also **op**) opium. RT: *opium*. [U.S., PRB: 1930, MHW: 1934, RRL: 1969, EEL: 1971]

open bar a bar operating in connection with a meeting or social event where guests are able to order free drinks. Compare to *cash bar*. [U.S., MW: 1976]

operating selling drugs; *in action* (*q.v.*). *Cf. move, shove*. [U.S., M&V: 1973, (RDS: 1982)]

operator a drug seller. RT: *dealer*. [U.S., M&D: 1952, H&C: 1975]

opiate a derivative of opium; a narcotic. Standard English. [since the 1600s, (1603): OED]

opiated hash hashish loaded with opium. RS: *set*. [U.S., ELA: 1984]

opium a narcotic made from the dried juice of the opium poppy. Standard English. [since the 1300s, (1398): OED] Nicknames and slang terms for opium: *ah-pen-yen, apostle, auntie, balot, big-O., black, black pills, black shit, black silk, black smoke, black stuff, block, brick, brick gum, brown stuff, bunk, button, can, canned stuff, card, chandoo, chandu, chef, chickery, chickory, Chinese* *molasses, Chinese tobacco, chocolate, coolie mud, cruz, cube, dai-yen, dog, dope, dopium, dream, dream beads, dreamer, dream gum, dreams, dreamstick, dream wax, elevator, eng-shee, fi-do-nie, fire plug, foon, foreign mud, foreign smoke, fun, gee, gee-fat, gee-yen, gho, ghow, glad stuff, goma, gong, gonger, gongerine, gow, goynik, goynk, goznik, grease, great tobacco, Greece, green ashes, green mud, green pill, green rot, greese, gum, guma, gum opium, gunji, gunpowder, hard stuff, high hat, hock-for, hokus, hop, hops, ice cream, junk, leaf gum, leaf hop, lem-kee, li-un, Li Young, li-yuen, loo foo kee, mash Allah, midnight oil, mud, munsh, O., op, ope, oye, pan-juice, Pantopon, pan-yen, pekoe, pellicle, pen-yang, pen-yen, pen-yuen, pfun, pill, pillow, pin-yen, pinyon, pop, poppy, poppy pill, poppy train, pox, P.S., red-smoker, Rooster Brand, sam-lo, san-lo, scours, sealed stuff, sealing wax, shong-nie, skamas, skee, soñadora, son-lo, sook-nie, tar, the gong, the smoke, treacle, twang, wen-chee, yam-yam, yemtzem, yen, yen-chee, yen-pock, yen-pok, yen-pook, yen-shee.*

opium den (also opium joint) a place where opium is sold and consumed, usually by smoking. [since the late 1800s, (1882): OEDS] Nicknames and slang terms for a place where opium is sold and smoked: *black spot, brewery, cookee, cookie, cooky, den, dopatorium, dope den, fun joint, gonger den, gow cellar, hop, joint, joint, joss house, lay, lay down, lay down joint, opium joint, opium pad, pad room, pill pad, pipe joint, pop joint, poppy grove, slum dump, smoke joint, suey bowl, three-tap joint.*

opium eater a person who eats opium for its effects; an opium user; a *laudanum* (*q.v.*) user. RS: *user*. [(1821): OED] See also *smoke eater*.

opium kipper an opium addict who is smoked on opium vapors in the way that a kipper is smoked over wood smoke. RT: *campfire boy*. Possibly an error. [U.S., JES: 1959]

opium lamp a small, open-flame lamp which burns peanut oil and provides heat for opium preparation and smoking. [since the 1800s, (1897): OED]

opium of the poor marijuana; hashish. RT: *hash, pot*. Probably not drug argot. [U.S., RDS: 1982]

opium pad an *opium den* (*q.v.*). *Cf. pad*. [U.S., (M&W: 1946)]

Optimil a protected trade name for *methaqualone* (*q.v.*).

orange 1. (also orangies) a *Dexedrine* (TM; *q.v.*) amphetamine tablet. From its orange color. RT: *dex*. [U.S., JBW: 1967, EEL: 1971, YKB: 1977, NIDA: 1980] 2. an orange tablet impregnated with *L.S.D.* (*q.v.*). RS: *L.S.D.* [U.S., EEL: 1971]

orange bowl an opium pipe fitted with an orange rind which contains the smoke and allows it to be inhaled more easily. See comments at *lemon bowl*. BVB: 1942 says that the rind is used to shade the opium lamp. RT: *hop stick*. [U.S., DWM: 1938, VJM: 1949]

orange cube (also **orange cubes**) a sugar cube impregnated with an orange dot of *L.S.D.* (*q.v.*). *Cf. cube.* RT: *L.S.D.* [U.S., H&C: 1975, SNP: 1977]

orange cupcakes the hallucinogenic drug *L.S.D.* (*q.v.*), usually with other drugs added. *Cf. cupcakes.* RS: *L.S.D.* [U.S., RG: 1970]

orange mushrooms (also **orange crystal, orange micro, orange wafers, orange wedges**) a tablet or bit of blotter impregnated with *L.S.D.* (*q.v.*). The entry word describes a bit of blotter stamped with the image of a mushroom. The tablet may be a *Dexedrine* (TM; *q.v.*) amphetamine tablet. Terms such as these served as L.S.D. "brand name's." [MMO: 1970, RG: 1970, EEL: 1971, S&R: 1972, ADC: 1975, YKB: 1977, NIDA: 1980, ADC: 1981]

orange Owsley the hallucinogenic drug *L.S.D.* (*q.v.*). *Cf. Owsley.* RT: *L.S.D.* [U.S., C&H: 1974]

orange sunshine a "brand" of L.S.D. See *orange mushrooms.* RT: *L.S.D.* [U.S., ADC: 1975, W&F: 1975, YKB: 1977]

orbit, in high on a drug; peaking in drug euphoria. RS: *stoned.* [U.S., M&V: 1973, H&C: 1975]

orégano* (also **orégano chino***) marijuana. Spanish for oregano, i.e., (pseudo) Chinese oregano. RT: *pot.* [calo, JBR: 1973]

org the rush caused by potent drugs. From *orgasm.* RS: *rush.* [U.S., JWK: 1981]

organ a tobacco pipe. From *pipe organ.* [cant, FG: 1785; listed in GWM: 1859]

organized alcohol intoxicated. And the phrase **getting organized** means getting drunk. RT: *drunk.* [U.S., JCR: 1914, MP: 1928, AH: 1931, MHW: 1934]

orie-eyed (also **awry-eyed, orry-eyed**) alcohol intoxicated. *Cf. hoary-eyed, oryide.* RT: *drunk.* [U.S., (1910): SBF: 1976, MP: 1928, AH: 1931, MHW: 1934]

ork-orks the delirium tremens. RT: *D.T.s.* [U.S., BVB: 1942]

oryide a drunkard. *Cf. orie-eyed.* RT: *sot.* [U.S., late 1800s, W&F: 1960]

osley See *Owsley.*

oscar charlie Old Crow (brand) whiskey. The entry words are the *O* and *C* of the military "phonetic alphabet." [U.S., DST: 1984]

ossifer a police officer. Originally in imitation of drunken speech. Also used for a military officer (DST: 1984). RT: *fuzz.* [U.S., BVB: 1942, RAS: 1975]

ossified 1. alcohol intoxicated. *Cf. stoned.* RT: *drunk.* [U.S., (1901): SBF: 1976, MP: 1928, AH: 1931, MHW: 1934, BVB: 1942, DCCU: 1972] 2. drug intoxicated; very high. RT: *stoned.* Black use. [U.S., EAF: 1980]

ounce man (also **Oz man**) a drug seller who deals in small amounts of a drug. *Cf. kilo man* (at *kilo connection*). RT: *dealer.* [U.S.,

RRL: 1969, P&C: 1969, W&F: 1975, HSD: 1984]

out 1. a drink of liquor; a glass for liquor. RT: *nip*. [Br., 1800s, F&H] 2. (also **passed out**) alcohol intoxicated. RT: *drunk*. [since the late 1700s, SBF: 1976] 3. drug intoxicated. RT: *stoned*. [U.S., RAS: 1978] 4. recovered from drug intoxication; recovered from a marijuana high. [U.S., ELA: 1984]

out and out a drinking bout. Possibly rhyming slang. Not listed in DRS. RT: *spree*. [U.S., GWM: 1859]

out cold (also **out on the roof**) alcohol intoxicated. RT: *drunk*. [BVB: 1942, W&F: 1960, DSUE]

outer 1. L.S.D. Possible from *outer limits*. RT: *L.S.D.* [U.S., ELA: 1984] 2. *mescaline (q.v.)*. RT: *peyote*. [U.S., ELA: 1984]

outfit equipment for preparing and injecting drugs. [U.S., BD: 1937, M&D: 1952, D&B: 1970c, RRL: 1969, EEL: 1971, MA: 1973, JWK: 1981] Various terms and expressions for drug using equipment: *accessories, apps, arm squirt, artillery, Banette, banger, biz, biz stuff, bizz, business, chingadera, engine, factory, fit, gear, gimmicks, head gear, head kit, heavy artillery, hop layout, horse and buggy, Jim Johnson, joint, kit, layette, layout, light artillery, machine, machinery, oint-jay, outfit, paraphernalia, rig, rocket ship, saddle and bridle, set of works, supplies, the business, the engine, the works, tools, toys, trigger, unit, works, Z-kit*.

out like a light alcohol intoxicated. Refers to a light which has been turned out. Also means unconscious or sleeping soundly. RT: *drunk*. [Br. and U.S., DSUE, HJS: 1922, BVB: 1942]

out of it (also **outasight, out of sight, out to it**) drug intoxicated; drunk; not in touch with the real world due to drug use. **Outasight** (= **out of touch**) dates from 1893 (OEDS). Not limited to drug culture use. The Australian version is **out to it** (1880): DSUE. RS: *stoned*. [U.S., S&W: 1966, M&V: 1967, RG: 1970, EEL: 1971, ADC: 1975, JWK: 1981]

out of the way alcohol intoxicated. RT: *drunk*. [BF: 1737]

overamp 1. an overdose of *Methedrine* (TM; *q.v.*) or some other amphetamine. [U.S., EEL: 1971, JH: 1979] 2. to take an overdose of an amphetamine. [U.S., H&C: 1975, YKB: 1977]

overamped high on amphetamines; overdosed with amphetamines, especially *Methedrine* (TM; *q.v.*). RS: *stoned*. [U.S., M&V: 1967, JHF: 1971, RDS: 1982]

over and unders amphetamines and barbiturates. *Cf. downer, upper*. RS: *set*. [U.S., M&V: 1973]

overboard alcohol intoxicated. RT: *drunk*. [U.S., W&F: 1960]

over-charged overdosed; drowsy from too much of a drug; drug intoxicated. RS: *stoned*. [U.S., DWM: 1936, RRL: 1969, A&T: 1953,

overcome alcohol intoxicated. RT: *drunk*. [Br., 1800s F&H; listed in BVB: 1942]

overdose 1. a dose larger than required or safe. [(1700): OEDS; U.S. drug culture, (1953): OEDS, (1973): DNE: 1980] 2. (also O.D.) to take a dose larger than required; to take a lethal dose. [U.S., (1973): OEDS, D&B: 1978] 3. to become seriously ill or die from taking a large dose of drugs. See *O.D.* [U.S., (1973): DNE: 1973, (1974): OEDS]

overjolt (also O.J.) an overdose of drugs, especially heroin. See *O.D.* [U.S., M&V: 1967, RRL: 1969]

overseas alcohol intoxicated. *Cf. half seas over.* RT: ***drunk.*** [Br., (1930): DSUE]

overseen alcohol intoxicated. RT: ***drunk.*** [(1475): OED; Br. dialect, 18-1900s, DSUE; listed in PD: 1982]

overserved having to do with a drunk person in a bar; alcohol intoxicated. Euphemistic. *Cf. served up.* RS: ***drunk.*** [U.S., RAS: 1981]

overset alcohol intoxicated. From the literal sense: to capsize, to throw into confusion. RT: ***drunk.*** [BF: 1737]

overshot alcohol intoxicated. *Cf. shot.* RT: ***drunk.*** [(1605): OED, B&L: 1890, F&H, DSUE, MHW: 1934]

over-sparred alcohol intoxicated; unsteady from liquor. From a nautical expression meaning unsteady. The term describes a ship rigged with too much weight aloft in spars, yards, masts, etc. RT: ***drunk.*** [probably nonce, (1890): OED]

overtaken alcohol intoxicated, overtaken with drink. RT: ***drunk.*** [(1587): OED, EDD; listed in BVB: 1942]

over the bay (also over the bar) alcohol intoxicated. Over the bar may refer to a sand bar (nautical) or a saloon bar. RT: ***drunk.*** [Br. and U.S., (1587): SOD, (1655): F&H, (1810): DSUE, (1830): SBF: 1976, MHW: 1934, BVB: 1942]

over-the-counter (also O.T.C.) having to do with drugs which are sold without prescription. Now GEN: anything sold casually or directly. [U.S., JF: 1972]

over the eight alcohol intoxicated. See ***have had one over the eight.***

over the hump drug intoxicated. RT: ***stoned.*** [U.S., BVB: 1942, A&T: 1953, M&V: 1954]

over the mark alcohol intoxicated. See ***loaded to the Plimsoll mark.*** RT: ***drunk.*** [Br., mid 1800s, DSUE]

over-wined alcohol intoxicated. RT: ***drunk.*** [PD: 1982]

owes no man a farthing alcohol intoxicated. RT: ***drunk.*** [BF: 1737]

owl a narcotics agent who works at night. GEN: anyone who works at night. RS: ***fuzz.*** [U.S., JWK: 1981]

owled (also owl-eyed, owly-eyed) alcohol intoxicated. *Cf. boiled as an owl, boiled owl.* RT: ***drunk.*** [U.S., EHB: 1900, MHW: 1934,

W&F: 1960]

Owsley (also **osley, Owsley acid, Owsley blue dot, Owsley blues, Owsley power, Owsley purple, Owsleys, Owsley's stuff, pink Owsley, purple Owsley, white Owsley**) *L.S.D.* (*q.v.*); very pure L.S.D. From the name of one of the early L.S.D. makers *Augustus Owsley Stanley III*. Osley is a spelling error. Owsley acid was thought to be top quality. RT: *L.S.D.* Some extended use in drug slang for anything excellent. [U.S., JBW: 1967, RB: 1967, (TW: 1968), EEL: 1971, ADC: 1975, W&F: 1975, YKB: 1977, ADC: 1981]

oxycrocium alcohol intoxicated. *Cf. ocksecrotia*. From *oxycroceum*, a healing plaster. RT: *drunk*. [BF: 1737]

oye opium. *Cf. ogoy*. RT: *opium*. [U.S., JH: 1979]

oyl of barley See *oil of barley*.

OZ a "brand name" for *amyl nitrite*. RS: *snapper*. [U.S., ELA: 1984]

O.Z. (also **Oz., o-zee, ozee**) an ounce of a drug, now usually marijuana. [U.S., HNR: 1934, DWM: 1936, GOL: 1950, RRL: 1969, CM: 1970, EEL: 1971, JWK: 1981]

Oz man a drug seller or distributor. RT: *dealer*. See *ounce man*. [U.S., JH: 1979]

ozone *P.C.P.* (*q.v.*). RT: *P.C.P.* [U.S., (1970s): FAB: 1979]

ozoned *high* (*q.v.*) on *P.C.P.* (*q.v.*). RS: *stoned*. [U.S., FAB: 1979]

ozone, in the alcohol intoxicated; drug intoxicated; very high. RT: *drunk, stoned*. [U.S., ADC: 1975]

ozzy the hallucinogenic drug *L.S.D.* (*q.v.*), especially in compound words. From *Owsley* (*q.v.*).

P

P. 1. *peyote* (*q.v.*) cactus. RS: *peyote*. [U.S., RRL: 1969, RG: 1970, IGA: 1971] 2. heroin; pure or nearly pure heroin. *Cf. pee*. The P is from *pure*. RS: *heroin*. [U.S., GG: 1981] 3. P.C.P. Probably from *peace*. RT: *P.C.P.* [U.S., FAB: 1979]

pa'abajos* barbiturates. From Spanish *par abajos* = downers. *Cf. downer*. RT: *barbs*. [U.S., NIDA: 1980]

pa'arribas* amphetamines. From Spanish *par arribas* = uppers. *Cf. upper*. RT: *amps*. [U.S., NIDA: 1980]

pacifier a homemade hypodermic syringe; a *dripper* (*q.v.*) using the rubber nipple of a baby pacifier. *Cf. bulb*. RS: *monkey pump*. [U.S., RG: 1970, IGA: 1971]

pack 1. alcohol made from molasses; liquor. From the name *Packenham*, an English general (W&F: 1960). Compare to *grog*. RS: *booze*. [U.S., MHW: 1934, W&F: 1960] 2. (also **packet**) a packet of heroin; a packet of drug capsules. RS: *load*. [U.S., M&D: 1952, TRG: 1968, EEL: 1971] 3. to drink liquor; to pack liquor in. Possibly akin to sense one. RT: *guzzle*. [U.S., (1847): F&H] 4. to carry or *hold* (*q.v.*) drugs. [U.S., MA: 1973]

packaged alcohol intoxicated. *Cf. boxed, canned*. RT: *drunk*. [U.S., (1890): SBF: 1976]

package store a place where liquor can be bought in bottles and cans. It cannot be consumed on the premises. RT: *L.I.Q.* [U.S., D&D: 1957, K&M: 1968]

packed up drug intoxicated. Probably packed up for a *trip* (*q.v.*). *Cf. pack*. RT: *stoned*. [U.S., RRL: 1969]

packet See *pack*.

pack of rockets a pack of marijuana cigarettes. *Cf. rocket*. A&T: 1953 list pack of rocks, probably in error. [U.S., BVB: 1942, JES: 1959] See also *skyrockets*.

pack one's coozie to place a small parcel of drugs into the vagina and attempt to smuggle it into or out of a country or into prison. *Cf. whammer*. [U.S., H&C: 1975]

pack one's keyster to conceal one or more small containers of drugs within the rectum or vagina. *Keyster* (which is spelled a great number of ways) means both rectum and suitcase. *Cf.*

keyster plant, pack. See *body-packer.* [U.S., M&V: 1967]

pack one's nose to use (snort) cocaine. RT: *snort.* [U.S., ADC: 1984]

pad (also pad room) a place to use drugs; a residence where one can buy and use drugs; a drug user or addict's place of residence. Originally named for the pad reclined on in an opium den. Now refers to a place where marijuana is used communally. *Cf. tea pad.* [U.S., (1938): DU, M&D: 1952, W&F: 1960, M&V: 1967, RRL: 1969, MA: 1973, JWK: 1981] See also *doperie* and *opium den.* Terms for a residence where drugs can be bought and used: *acid pad, balloon room, bang room, beat pad, bing room, club, coke oven, creeper joint, crib, crystal palace, den, developing room, dopatorium, dope den, factory, gallery, launching pad, launch pad, lay down, lay down joint, opium den, pad, pad room, pill pad, shooting gallery.*

padded having drugs (or other contraband) taped to one's body for international smuggling. *Cf. body-packing.* [U.S., GOL: 1950]

paddle to drink liquor. RT: *irrigate.* [Br., mid 1800s, F&H]

paddy a police officer; an Irish cop. RS: *fuzz.* [U.S., M&W: 1946]

pad money 1. the cost of admission to an opium den. Customers recline on pads to smoke opium. *Cf. pad.* [U.S., BVB: 1942, VJM: 1949] 2. money to purchase marijuana. *Cf. tea pad.* [U.S., JES: 1959, H&C: 1975]

pafisticated alcohol intoxicated. Possibly akin to *sophisticated.* RT: *drunk.* [PD: 1982]

paid alcohol intoxicated. Probably from the obsolete sense of *paid* = pleased. RT: *drunk.* [(1638): OED; listed in BVB: 1942]

painkiller liquor. *Cf. feeling no pain.* RT: *booze.* [U.S., BVB: 1942]

paint 1. cheap wine. RS: *wine.* [Aust., SJB: 1945] 2. to drink liquor. *Cf. nose paint, paint the town red.* RT: *irrigate.* [Br., (1853): DSUE]

paint remover inferior whiskey; strong liquor. *Cf. varnish remover.* RT: *rotgut.* [U.S., W&F: 1960, RDS: 1982]

paint the tiger to go on a drinking bout. RT: *guzzle.* [PW: 1977]

paint the town red (also paint the town) to go on a drinking bout; to get drunk. RT: *guzzle, mug oneself.* [U.S., (1889): F&H, JRW: 1909, BVB: 1942, W&F: 1960, DCCU: 1972; Br., SSD]

paisley caps capsules or pills impregnated with *L.S.D.* (*q.v.*), probably in a design similar to paisley. RT: *L.S.D.* [U.S., S&R: 1972]

pájaro azul* capsules of *Amytal* (TM; *q.v.*) barbiturate. Spanish for *bluebirds* (*q.v.*). RT: *barbs.* [U.S., NIDA: 1980]

pakalolo marijuana. From the Hawaiian Language. *Cf. pukalolo.* RT: *pot.* [U.S., AD: 1981]

Pakistani hash a potent variety of cannabis (marijuana or hashish) from Pakistan. RT: *hash*. [U.S., (1972): ELA: 1982]

palatic alcohol intoxicated. RT: *drunk*. [Br., (1885): F&H, PW: 1974]

palatio an error for *palatic* (*q.v.*). [PD: 1982]

pale 1. pale brandy. RS: *brandy*. [Br, (1861): DSUE, (Mayhew)] 2. *near-beer* (*q.v.*). Possibly from *pale ale*. *Cf. queer-beer*. [U.S., MHW: 1934, BVB: 1942]

paleface whiskey; inferior whiskey. Probably akin to *pale* (*q.v.*). RS: *rotgut*. [U.S., (1846): DA]

palled alcohol intoxicated; dead drunk. From a term meaning weak or impaired. RT: *drunk*. [BE: 1690]

Panama red (also **Panama, Panama gold, Panamanian gold, Panamanian red, P.R.**) a potent red-topped marijuana presumably grown in Panama. RT: *pot*. [U.S., W&F: 1967, RRL: 1969, (1970): DNE: 1973, EEL: 1971, DCCU: 1972, ADC: 1975, EAF: 1980, NIDA: 1980, ADC: 1981]

panatela (also **panatella**) a cigar-shaped marijuana cigarette. Borrowed from the term for a particular shape of a cigar. From Spanish for *long, thin loaf of bread*. RS: *joint*. [U.S., (1944): ELA: 1982, (M&W: 1946), RRL: 1969, NIDA: 1980]

pangonadalot heroin. Origin unknown. RT: *heroin*. [U.S., SNP: 1977]

panic 1. a scarcity of narcotics; a period of time when drug dealers are not selling because of police suspicion or the arrest of a major supplier. BD: 1937 lists **panic on**. *Cf. drought, famine*. [U.S., (BD: 1937), DWM: 1938, RRL: 1969, MA: 1973, JWK: 1981] 2. the state of an addict who cannot get narcotics. This is probably just colloquial English. [U.S., M&V: 1954]

panic man an addict who needs drugs desperately but cannot obtain them. *Cf. panic*. RS: *junky*. RDS: 1982 also lists **panic woman**. H&C: 1975 list **panicked man**. BVB: 1942 also define this as a dope peddler. [U.S., DWM: 1936, VJM: 1949, RRL: 1969]

panic trip a very bad experience with *L.S.D.* (*q.v.*) or another hallucinogen. *Cf. bum bend, bum kicks, bummer, bum trip, downer, down trip, drag, freak out, horrors, low, negative*. RT: *bad trip*. [U.S., D&B: 1970c]

pan-juice crude (unprocessed) opium. RS: *opium*. [U.S., JES: 1959]

panther piss (also **panther, panther juice, panther pizen, panther's breath, panther's piss, panther's pizen, panther sweat**) gin; inferior whiskey; hard liquor; moonshine. The *also* entries are euphemistic in some cases. *Cf. rotgut* for similar terms. **Panther's piss** is Australian. RT: *rotgut*. [U.S., JAS: 1932, BVB: 1942, D&D: 1957, W&F: 1960, EAF: 1980; Aust., SJB: 1943]

Pantopon the protected trade name for an opium derivative. [U.S., (1909): OEDS]

pan up to heat and dissolve a drug for injection. *Cf. cook.* [U.S., EEL: 1971]

pan-yen opium. See *pen-yen.*

paper 1. a folded paper containing a dose of drugs; a glassine envelope of drugs; a ration of drugs. BD: 1937 lists paper of stuff. HB: 1955 lists papel (Spanish). RS: *load.* [U.S., DWM: 1936, M&H: 1959, RRL: 1969, EEL: 1971] 2. a prescription for drugs. *Cf. reader, per, script.* [U.S., TRG: 1968, RG: 1970, C&H: 1974] 3. a postcard or other paper product saturated with drugs or containing drugs between layers of paper. Drugs are smuggled into prison in this fashion. [U.S., DWM: 1936, BVB: 1942] 4. cigarette rolling paper. Usually in the plural. Since the 1960s, most frequently known in the making of marijuana cigarettes. [U.S., DWM: 1935, BVB: 1942, RRL: 1969, ADC: 1975, EAF: 1980, ADC: 1981, TH: 1976] Nicknames and slang terms for cigarette rolling paper: *Acapulco gold paper, Bambu, Banana, Bible, blanco y negro, blanket, cigarette paper, developing paper, dream book, lick papers, makings, officer's brand papers, paper, papes, prayer book, Rizla, roll, rolling papers, sheets, skin, snow papers, Stella, straw, tissue, Top, Wheaties, wrapper, Zigzag.*

paper acid *L.S.D.* (*q.v.*), especially when consumed on a bit of blotter; L.S.D. combined with some other drug. *Cf. blotter, blotter acid.* RT: *L.S.D.* [U.S., YKB: 1977, NIDA: 1980, KBH: 1982]

paper boy a heroin dealer. See *paper.* RT: *dealer.* [U.S., RG: 1970]

paper fiend a drug user who uses amphetamine saturated paper strips from an amphetamine inhaler. Probably from the 1940s. [U.S., M&V: 1967]

papes tobacco rolling papers. See *paper.* This term is attested only for the use of such papers in making marijuana cigarettes. RT: *paper.* [U.S., JWK: 1981]

pap pills amphetamines. In error for, or a play on *pep pills* (*q.v.*). RT: *amps.* [U.S., SNP: 1977] See also *suckonal.*

parackie *paraldehyde* (*q.v.*). [U.S., RRL: 1969, SNP: 1977]

paradise cocaine. RT: *cocaine.* [U.S., IGA: 1971, SH: 1972, SNP: 1977]

paral (also paraldy) *paraldehyde* (*q.v.*). [U.S., SNP: 1977]

paraldehyde a nonbarbiturate hypnotic in liquid form. The drug acts as a central nervous system depressant. It has been used in the treatment of the delirium tremens and is similar in effect to the barbiturates. It is addictive. *Cf. parackie.* Widely known among older alcoholics and addicts. [(1857): OED]

paralytic alcohol intoxicated; dead drunk. RT: *drunk.* [(1921): OEDS, BVB: 1942, SJB: 1943, M&J: 1975]

paralyzed (also paralysed) alcohol intoxicated; dead drunk. The Australian version is paralytic. RT: *drunk.* [U.S., (1888): SBF:

1976, MP: 1928, GI: 1931, GOL: 1950, W&F: 1960, RDS: 1982; listed in F&H]

paralyzing grass marijuana. RT: *pot.* [U.S., BR: 1972]

paraphernalia drug use accessories; marijuana smoking *accessories* (*q.v.*). RT: *outfit.* More euphemistic than slangy. [U.S., ADC: 1975]

parboiled alcohol intoxicated. Probably from *boiled* or *boiled as an owl.* See the list at *cooked.* RT: *drunk.* [U.S., W&F: 1960, RDS: 1982]

paregoric a camphorated tincture of opium. Once used in the treatment of colic and other aches and pains of children. Also used by addicts who managed to extract the opium (about 10%) from the drug. RT: *goric.* [since the mid 1700s, (1751): OED]

Parest a protected trade name for *methaqualone* (*q.v.*). RT: *ludes.* See *methaqualone.*

Park Lane No. 2. (also **Park Lane, Parklane**) a variety of marijuana (and marijuana cigarettes) sold and used during the Vietnamese war. RT: *pot.* [U.S. military, (1970s): ELA: 1982]

parsley *P.C.P.* (*q.v.*). From the use of parsley as a base for smoking P.C.P. RT: *P.C.P.* [U.S., (1970s): FAB: 1979]

party 1. a gathering of L.S.D. users. [U.S., M&V: 1973] 2. to use L.S.D., marijuana, heroin, or alcohol socially. The term has numerous other slang meanings. [U.S., M&V: 1973, ADC: 1975, ADC: 1981]

party bowl a marijuana pipe with a bowl large enough to serve a number of smokers. RS: *bong.* [U.S., ADC: 1975, ADC: 1981]

pass a successful drug transfer; a successful drug purchase or sale. RS: *score.* [U.S., RRL: 1969, RG: 1970, LVA: 1981]

passed out (also **passed out cold, passed out of the picture**) alcohol intoxicated. RT: *drunk.* [U.S., WM: 1927, AH: 1931, MHW: 1934]

pass-go to complete a drug purchase or sale without going to jail. From *pass go and collect $200.00* in the game Monopoly (TM). RS: *score.* [U.S., JH: 1979]

pass whiskey whiskey from El Paso, Texas. RT: *whiskey.* [U.S. Mexican War, (c. 1848): DST: 1984]

pasted alcohol intoxicated; drug intoxicated. *Cf. glued.* RT: *drunk, stoned.* [U.S., JES: 1959, H&C: 1975]

pasto* marijuana. The Spanish word meaning pasture. RT: *pot.* [U.S., CG: 1980, NIDA: 1980]

pasty face a drug addict; a sickly and debilitated narcotics addict. RT: *junky.* [U.S., BVB: 1942, VJM: 1949, A&T: 1953]

pat marijuana. Possibly an error for *pot* (*q.v.*). [RG: 1970]

pato de gayina* cannabis; *sinsemilla* (*q.v.*). Spanish for chicken feet. RT: *pot.* [U.S., ELA: 1984]

patent digester See *digester*.

patter crib a tavern or saloon. See *crib*. *Cf. booze crib, guzzle crib, lush crib, suck crib*. RS: *bar*. [cant, 1800s, F&H]

pattern a particular type of drug-induced hallucination. *Cf. cartoon, echoes, flashback, trail*. RT: *hallucination*. [U.S., EEL: 1971]

paz* phencyclidine, P.C.P. Spanish for peace. RT: *P.C.P.* [U.S., ELA: 1984]

pay street having to do with drugs which must be bought rather than stolen or obtained free; having to do with an expensive drug habit. Compare to *freebies*. [U.S., JWK: 1981]

P.B.Z. *Pyribenzamine* (TM; *q.v.*), an antihistamine. It is used in combination with other drugs and heightens their effect. See *T.s and blues*. [medical]

P.C.P. (also **PCE, PCP, PCPA**) phencyclidine, a veterinary anesthetic. The initials are from *peace pill*. This drug, sold under the trade name Sernylan, has been sold on the street as *T.H.C.* (*q.v.*), L.S.D., mescaline, psilocybin, and other substances. [U.S., RRL: 1969, (1970): DNE: 1980] Nicknames and slang terms for phencyclidine: *ace, ad, amoeba, angel dust, angel hair, angel mist, angel puke, animal tranquilizer, aurora borealis, bad grass, black whack, busy bee, buzz, Cadillac, cannabinol, ciclón, ciclón de cristal, C.J., cosmos, cozmos, crazy coke, cristal, cristales, crystal, crystal flake, crystal joint, crystal points, crystal T., crystal weed, cyclone, D., death wish, Detroit pink, devil dust, dipper, D.O.A., double dipper, dummy dust, dust, dust joint, dust of angels, elefante, elephant, elephant tranquilizer, embalming fluid, energizer, erth, fairy dust, fake S.T.P., flake, flakes, fuel, goon, goon dust, gorilla tabs, gray dust, green snow, green tea, heaven and hell, heaven dust, hercules, herms, heroin buzz, hog, hog tranquilizer, horse, horse trank, horse tranquilizer, jet fuel, kaps, K-blast, killer weed, K.J., kools, krystal joint, K.W., leños, magic, mean green, mint leaf, mint weed, mist, monkey dust, moon beams, more, new acid, new magic, niebla, ozone, P., parsley, paz, P.C.P., PCPA, peace pills, peace weed, peep, pig killer, pig tranquilizer, píldora de paz, polvito, polvo, polvo de ángel, P-stuff, puerco, puffy, rocket fuel, scuffle, Sernylan, sheets, skuffle, snorts, soma, spores, stardust, super, supergrass, superjoint, superweed, super yerba, surfer, synthetic grass, synthetic marijuana, synthetic T.H.C., T., tac, T-buzz, tea, T.H.C., tic, tich, tick, tic-tac, tish, titch, toot, trank, tranks, T-tabs, wack, water, weed, whack, white dust, wobble weed, wolf, worm, yellow dust, yerba mala, zombie buzz.*

PDR (also **P.D.R.**) the Physicians' Desk Reference, a book containing information about ethical drugs manufactured in the United States. Published annually by Medical Economics Company.

peace 1. *S.T.P.* (*q.v.*), "serenity, tranquility, and peace." [U.S.,

IGA: 1971, SNP: 1977] See also *P*. 2. the hallucinogenic drug *L.S.D.* (*q.v.*). *Cf. peace pills*. RT: *L.S.D.* [U.S., KBH: 1982, RDS: 1982]

peace pills 1. a mixture of L.S.D. and *Methedrine* (TM; *q.v.*). RS: *set*. [U.S., EEL: 1971, KBH: 1982] 2. *P.C.P.* (*q.v.*), an animal tranquilizer. Said to be the source of P.C.P., i.e., *PeaCe Pills*. RT: *P.C.P.* [U.S., RRL: 1969, DES: 1972, ADC: 1975, (DNE: 1980), NIDA: 1980] 3. (also **peace tab**) *psilocybin* (*q.v.*). [U.S., EEL: 1971] See also *peace tablet*.

peace tablet 1. (also **peace tab**) *psilocybin* (*q.v.*). [U.S., EEL: 1971] 2. a tablet with a drop of *L.S.D.* (*q.v.*) on it. *Cf. peace, peace pills*. RT: *L.S.D.* [U.S., RDS: 1982]

peace weed a form of *P.C.P.* (*q.v.*), the same as *mint weed* (*q.v.*). RT: *P.C.P.* [U.S., JHF: 1971]

peaches orange or peach-colored amphetamine tablets, either *Dexedrine* (TM; *q.v.*) or *Benzedrine* (TM; *q.v.*). RT: *amps*. [U.S., JBW: 1967, RRL: 1969, D&B: 1970c, NIDA: 1980] See also *duraznos*.

peak 1. to hit the highest point of an L.S.D. trip. [U.S., (RRL: 1969), EEL: 1971, ADC: 1975, (ADC: 1981)] 2. the highest point of an *L.S.D.* (*q.v.*) trip. [U.S., EEL: 1971]

peanuts barbiturate capsules. *Cf. maní*. RT: *barbs*. [U.S., JBW: 1967, EEL: 1971, NIDA: 1980]

pearls (also **perls**) ampules of *amyl nitrite* (*q.v.*). These are broken to release the volatile drug. RT: *snapper*. From medical slang. [U.S., RRL: 1969, BR: 1972, ADC: 1975]

pearly gates 1. (also **pearly cakes, pearly whites**) morning glory seeds of a specific color variety. These seeds are eaten in great numbers to produce a high. RT: *seeds*. [U.S., EEL: 1971, YKB: 1977] 2. the hallucinogenic drug *L.S.D.* (*q.v.*). RT: *L.S.D.* [U.S., IGA: 1971, YKB: 1977, KBH: 1982]

peckish alcohol intoxicated. A colloquial term meaning hungry. RT: *drunk*. [Br., 1800s, F&H, (at *screwed*)]

peddler a drug seller; a drug pusher. *Cf. dope peddler*. RS: *dealer*. [U.S., GI: 1931, DWM: 1936, RPW: 1938, EEL: 1971]

pee pure heroin. See *P*. This is probably an intentional reference to pee = piss. *Cf. shit*. RS: *heroin*. [U.S., SNP: 1977]

pee'd alcohol intoxicated. Euphemistic for *pissed* (*q.v.*). RT: *drunk*. [U.S., BR: 1972]

pee-eyed alcohol intoxicated. A spelling-out of first two letters of *pissed* (*q.v.*). RT: *drunk*. [U.S., VJM: 1949]

peep *P.C.P.* (*q.v.*). *Cf. pee*. RT: *P.C.P.* [U.S., FAB: 1979]

pee-wee a thin marijuana cigarette. *Cf. wee-wee*. RS: *joint*. Black use. [U.S., early 1900s, CM: 1970]

peg 1. a drink of liquor or beer. From the pegs once used to mark the amount drunk from a tankard. RT: *nip*. [Br., B&L: 1890, SSD; listed in BVB: 1942] 2. to drink liquor. RT: *irrigate*. [Br., (1873): OED; listed in BVB: 1942]

pegger a tippler; a drunkard. A person who takes a peg too many. RT: *sot*. [Br., (1873): OED]

peg too low, a alcohol intoxicated. *Cf. peg*. RT: *drunk*. [Br., late 18-1900s, (1930): DSUE; listed in BVB: 1942]

pekoe good-quality opium. From the name of a high-quality, black Chinese tea. RS: *opium*. [U.S., JES: 1959, H&C: 1975]

pellet (also **pellets**) capsules of the hallucinogenic drug *L.S.D.* (*q.v.*). Currently a very popular form of the drug. RT: *L.S.D.* [U.S., RRL: 1969, EEL: 1971, JH: 1979]

pellicle high-quality opium. From Latin *pellis* skin, possibly referring to the processing of opium from poppy juice. RS: *opium*. [U.S., JES: 1959]

penitentiary highball an alcoholic drink made from strained shellac and milk. Prison use. [U.S., GOL: 1950]

penitentiary shot (also **penn shot, pen shot**) an injection of drugs accomplished by using a pin and a medicine dropper. May refer to the type or strength of injection that one can get in prison. See comment at *pin shot*. RS: *shot*. Prison use. [U.S., DWM: 1938, VJM: 1949]

penny stinker a foul-smelling cigar. *Cf. canteen stinker, stinker*. RT: *seegar*. [Br. (Cockney), (1880): DSUE]

pen shot an injection of drugs. Short for *penitentiary shot* (*q.v.*). See *pin shot*.

pen-yen (also **ah-pen-yen, pan-yen, pen-yang, pen-yuen, pin-yen, pinyon**) opium. Said to be the Chinese word for opium (WHW: 1922). RT: *opium*. [U.S., (1915): DU, (1920): W&F: 1960, WHW: 1922, GI: 1931, DWM: 1936, BVB: 1942, VJM: 1949, D&D: 1957, EEL: 1971]

peonied alcohol intoxicated. Probably a play on *pee'd* (*q.v.*) from *pissed* (*q.v.*). RT: *drunk*. [PD: 1982]

people 1. narcotics agents. RS: *fuzz*. Black use. [U.S., CM: 1970] 2. (also **the people**) high-level drug distributors. RS: *dealer*. [U.S., P&C: 1969, DEM: 1981]

pepped up (also **pepped, peppy**) alcohol intoxicated. RT: *drunk*. [U.S., BVB: 1942]

peppermint swirl *L.S.D.* (*q.v.*) or L.S.D. combined with some other drug. RS: *set*. [U.S., KBH: 1982]

pepper-upper 1. liquor; a drink of liquor. RS: *booze*. [U.S., (1938): OEDS, BVB: 1942, D&D: 1957] 2. (also **pepper-uppers**) an amphetamine tablet or capsule. RT: *amps*. [U.S., D&D: 1966] See also *jack-ups*.

pep pills (also **pep-em-ups, peps**) stimulant pills; amphetamines, particularly the brands *Dexedrine* (TM; *q.v.*) and *Benzedrine* (TM; *q.v.*). RT: *amps*. Now also in general slang. [U.S., (1937): OEDS, M&V: 1954, W&F: 1967, RRL: 1969, DCCU: 1972, ADC: 1975, EAF: 1980, NIDA: 1980]

Pepsi-Cola habit a small or inexpensive drug habit. RT: *chippy habit*. [U.S., ELA: 1984]

per a prescription (for drugs). *Cf. paper, reader, script*. [U.S., RRL: 1969, RG: 1970, EEL: 1971]

perch a pint of liquor. Smaller than the *bass* (*q.v.*) and larger than the *bream* (*q.v.*). [U.S., GU: 1975]

Percodan a protected trade name for tablets containing oxycodone hydrochloride, oxycodone terephthalate, and additional ingredients. The drug is a painkiller and a sedative. *Cf. perks*. [in current use; consult a pharmaceutical reference for more information]

perico* cocaine. Spanish for Pete. RT: *cocaine*. [U.S., CG: 1980, NIDA: 1980]

period hitter one who takes drugs only occasionally; a *chipper* (*q.v.*). *Cf. fortnighter, weekender, weekend warrior*. RT: *chipper*. [U.S., M&V: 1967]

perisher a drinking bout. LIT: a killer. RT: *spree*. [Aust., SJB: 1943]

perked alcohol intoxicated. From *perked up* = stimulated. RT: *drunk*. [Br. military, F&G: 1925]

perks tablets of *Percodan* (TM; *q.v.*) painkiller. [U.S., IGA: 1971, YKB: 1977]

perls See *pearls*.

Persian brown (also **Persian dust**) a brownish heroin from Iran or elsewhere in the middle east. [U.S., (1977): BW: 1984]

Peruvian flake high-quality cocaine from Peru. *Cf. flake*. RT: *cocaine*. [U.S., S&F: 1984]

peter (also **peter drops, petes**) knockout drops; dope in general. This is the same *peter* that is found in *peter man* = safe-cracker, and refers to a drug derived from nitro-glycerin. RS: *Mickey Finn*. [U.S., DWM: 1933, MHW: 1934, VJM: 1949, RRL: 1969, EEL: 1971]

Peter Jay a police officer. RT: *fuzz*. Black use. [U.S., EAF: 1980]

petrificated alcohol intoxicated. A play on *petrified* (*q.v.*). RT: *drunk*. [PD: 1982]

petrified 1. alcohol intoxicated. LIT: *stoned* (*q.v.*). *Cf. ossified*. RT: *drunk*. The current meaning: frozen with fear. [U.S., (1903): SBF: 1976, BVB: 1942, D&D: 1957] 2. drug intoxicated. RT: *stoned*. [U.S., NAM: 1953]

petrifying stuff potent marijuana. RS: *pot*. [U.S., BR: 1972]

peyote (also **peyotl**) a species of cactus, *Lophophora williamsii*;

mescaline, a hallucinogenic drug found in the peyote cactus. The young cactus are gathered as they emerge from the sand and eaten for a hallucinogenic effect. This substance is frequently confused with mushrooms. The term is from *peyotl*, a Nahuatl word, and came into English via Mexican Spanish. RS: *peyote*. [U.S., (1849): OEDS, D&D: 1957, RRL: 1969, ADC: 1975, NIDA: 1980] The following list includes terms for the cactus and for both natural and synthesized mescaline. *anhalonium, bad seed, beans, big chief, biscuits, button, cactus, cactus buttons, chief, chocolate mesc, dog biscuits, dry whiskey, footballs, full moons, half moons, hikori, hikuli, huatari, legume, magic mushrooms, magic pumpkin, mesc, mescal, mescal bean, mescal button, mescalina, mescaline, mescalito, moon, outer, P., peyote, peyote button, peyotl, plants, pumpkin seed, seni, shrooms, strawberry, top, topi, tops, wakowi, whiskey root, white whiskey, wokowi, yellow footballs.*

peyote button the emergent tip of the *peyote* (*q.v.*) cactus, a source of mescaline. RS: *peyote*. [U.S., (1921): OEDS, (1930): DA, D&D: 1957]

pfun a dose of prepared opium. *Cf. foon, fun*. [early 1900s, DU]

P.G. (also **P.O.**) paregoric. Paregoric is a camphorated tincture of opium from which the opium can be recovered. RT: *goric*. [U.S., DWM: 1936, BVB: 1942, RRL: 1969, W&F: 1975]

P.G.A. "pure grain alcohol." [U.S., D&B: 1970c]

pharaoh (also **pharo**) a strong ale or beer. *Cf. contending with the Pharaoh*. RS: *ale, beer*. GWM: 1859 lists **pharo**. [cant, BE: 1690, FG: 1785, FG: 1811, FG: 1823, GWM: 1859]

phased (also **phazed**) drug intoxicated; under the effects of marijuana. RT: *stoned, wasted*. [U.S., ADC: 1975]

P-head a user of *phenobarbital* (*q.v.*). RT: *user*. See list at *head*. [U.S., RDS: 1982]

phencyclidine a tranquilizer and anesthetic drug with uses in veterinary medicine. The trade name is Sernylan (TM). The drug is used to *lace* (*q.v.*) or *doctor* (*q.v.*) marijuana cigarettes or is mixed with other drugs. It is sold on the street under many names and often substituted for other substances. It is commonly known as P.C.P., and it has caused many deaths. See *P.C.P.* for a list of slang terms. [(1959): OEDS]

phennies (also **phenies, phenos**) *phenobarbital* (*q.v.*) tablets, capsules, or elixir. RT: *barbs*. [U.S., RG: 1970, EEL: 1971, ADC: 1975, M&J: 1975, NIDA: 1980]

pheno 1. (also **phenobarb**) a *phenobarbital* (*q.v.*) tablet. RT: *barbs*. Not necessarily drug argot. [(1950): OEDS, RRL: 1969, EEL: 1971] 2. a habitual user of *phenobarbital* (*q.v.*). RS: *user*. [U.S., RDS: 1982]

phenobarbital (also **phenobarb**) a barbiturate compound used as a sedative-hypnotic. *Cf. phennies, pheno.* See a list of other barbiturates at *barbs.* [(1919): OEDS]

phfft alcohol intoxicated. GEN: finished, kaput. RT: *drunk.* [U.S., BVB: 1942]

philistine a drunkard. *Cf. been among the Philistines.* GEN: a despised person. RT: *sot.* [cant, BE: 1690, (1708): F&H, FG: 1785]

phlegm-cutter (also **phlegm-disperser**) liquor. *Cf. dust-cutter.* RT: *booze.* [U.S., (1806): DA, JSF: 1889, MHW: 1934]

phumfed drug intoxicated. RT: *stoned.* [U.S., JES: 1959, H&C: 1975]

phy *methadone* (*q.v.*). From the British form of the drug, Physeptone (TM), a brand of methadone. RT: *dolo.* [Br., BTD: 1968, (1971): OEDS]

physic liquor; strong liquor. GEN: a laxative. RS: *rotgut.* [Br., 1800s, F&H; listed in MHW: 1934, BVB: 1942]

phystaris See *fistaris.*

pick and choose liquor. Rhyming slang for *booze.* RT: *booze.* British music hall use. [early 1900s, DRS]

picked up drug intoxicated. RT: *stoned.* [U.S., DWM: 1936, BVB: 1942]

picking the poppies (also **picking the dream wax**) addicted to opium. Refers to the opium poppy. *Cf. chewing the gum, hit by the hop, mired in the mud, shoveling the black stuff, stung by the hop.* Neither the entry word nor the cross-references sound like criminal narcotics argot. [U.S., JES: 1959, H&C: 1975]

pickled 1. alcohol intoxicated. *Cf. corned, salted, soused.* RT: *drunk.* [F&H, (1890s): SBF: 1976, MP: 1928, (1938): W&F: 1960, HSD: 1984] drug intoxicated. RT: *stoned.* [U.S., NAM: 1953]

pickler a drunkard; an alcoholic. One who gets *pickled* often. RT: *sot.* [U.S., RDS: 1982]

pick-me-up a drink of liquor. RT: *nip.* Now common for any food or drink that boosts energy. It is now common colloquial English. [Br. and U.S., (1867): OED, (1867): SBF: 1982, AH: 1931, MHW: 1934, SSD, K&M: 1968]

pickup 1. to meet a seller or *mule* (*q.v.*) and take delivery of drugs. Standard English used in the drug context. *Cf. mule skinner.* RT: *score.* [U.S., EEL: 1971, RAS: 1983] 2. a successful act of taking delivery of drugs, as in *make a pickup.* This term implies some sort of scheme to avoid detection. This must be much older than the attestations indicates. [U.S., RAS: 1981] 3. a dose or shot of drugs. Similar to *pick-me-up* (*q.v.*). *Cf. fix, get-up.* RT: *dose.* [U.S., BD: 1937, DWM: 1938] See also *jack-ups.* 4. a sudden burst of drug euphoria. RT: *rush.* [U.S., DWM: 1936, BVB: 1942]

piece one ounce of drugs; one ounce of heroin; a dose of drugs. *Cf. half piece.* RS: *load.* [U.S., DWM: 1936, BD: 1937, GOL: 1950, M&D: 1952, W&F: 1967, D&B: 1970c, RRL: 1969, CM: 1970, EEL: 1971, MA: 1973]

piece of thick a plug of tobacco. RS: *quid.* [Br., B&L: 1890]

pied alcohol intoxicated. Possibly from *pie-eyed* (*q.v.*). RT: *drunk.* [U.S., BVB: 1942]

pie-eyed (also pye-eyed) alcohol intoxicated. Meaning wide-eyed. *Cf. owled.* RT: *drunk.* From the prohibition era. [U.S., (1880): SBF: 1976, (WWI): W&F: 1960, MP: 1928, GI: 1931, HNR: 1934, MHW: 1934, VJM: 1949, D&D: 1957]

piffed (also pifficated, piffled, pifflicated) alcohol intoxicated. RT: *drunk.* Attested as piflicated, Bahamas (JAH: 1982). [U.S., EHB: 1900, (1905): OEDS, MP: 1928, AH: 1931, MHW: 1934, D&D: 1957, W&F: 1960, JAH: 1982]

pig 1. an illicit liquor establishment. From *blind pig* (*q.v.*). *Cf. blue pig.* RT: *speak.* From the prohibition era. [U.S., MHW: 1934, BVB: 1942] 2. a policeman; a narcotics agent. *Cf. pork.* RS: *fuzz.* Not limited to drug argot. [U.S., BVB: 1942, RG: 1970, EEL: 1971, ADC: 1975, MW: 1976, ADC: 1981] 3. an addict or a drug user who will use any and every drug available. The same as *hog* (*q.v.*). RS: *user.* [U.S., JBW: 1967, IGA: 1971] See also *pig tranquilizer.* 4. a container for opium. RS: *stash.* [U.S., JES: 1959]

pigeon-eyed alcohol intoxicated. (BF: 1737: [He's] Pidgeon Ey'd.) RT: *drunk.* [BF: 1737]

pig foot marijuana. RT: *pot.* [U.S., ELA: 1984]

piggie a dose of opium made into pellets for smoking. RT: *dose.* [U.S., JES: 1959]

pig iron moonshine; bad liquor; liquor in general. From *pig* (*q.v.*). RS: *rotgut.* From the prohibition era. [U.S., R&P: 1928, W&F: 1960]

pig killer phencyclidine, P.C.P. A play on *hog tranquilizer* (*q.v.* at *hog*). RT: *P.C.P.* [U.S., ELA: 1984]

pig outfit the laboratory equipment required to produce phencyclidine, i.e., *P.C.P.* *Cf. outfit.* See *hog, pig tranquilizer.* [U.S., RDS: 1982]

pig's ear (also pig's) beer. Rhyming slang. RT: *beer.* [Br., late 18–1900s, DRS, (WWI): B&P: 1965, SSD, PW: 1974]

pig sweat beer. Probably not from *pig's ear.* From *pig* (*q.v.*) and the various euphemisms for urine: *nanny goat sweat, panther sweat, tiger sweat.* [U.S., W&F: 1960]

pigtail a coil of twisted, coarse tobacco. RS: *quid.* [(1688): OED, DSUE, EP: 1948; U.S., BWG: 1899, BVB: 1942]

pig tranquilizer the drug phencyclidine, *P.C.P.* (*q.v.*), an animal tranquilizer. *Cf. hog.* See *pig killer, pig outfit.* RT: *P.C.P.* [U.S., (1970s): FAB: 1979, YKB: 1977, DEM: 1981]

piki an opium smoker. Origin unknown. RT: *campfire boy.* [U.S., RDS: 1982]

píldora de fuerza* an amphetamine tablet or capsule. Spanish for power pill. *Cf. pep pills.* RT: *amps.* [U.S., NIDA: 1980]

píldora de paz* phencyclidine, *P.C.P.* (*q.v.*), an animal tranquilizer. Spanish for peace pill. *Cf. peace pills, peace tablet.* RT: *P.C.P.* [U.S., NIDA: 1980]

pilfered alcohol intoxicated. RT: *drunk.* [U.S., (1916): ADD, AP: 1980]

pill 1. a drink of liquor. RT: *nip.* [Br., late 1800s, F&H; listed in BVB: 1942] 2. (also **poppy pill**) an opium pellet prepared for smoking. *Cf. pfun.* [U.S., (1887): RML: 1948, DWM: 1936, MHW: 1934, VJM: 1949, GOL: 1950, W&F: 1960, (1946): RRL: 1969] 3. a cigarette doped with a drug, possibly opium. [U.S., (1914): OEDS, DU] 4. a tobacco cigarette. *Cf. tab.* Akin to sense three. RS: *nail.* Prison use. [U.S., BTH: 1914, (1927): W&F: 1960, BVB: 1942, GOL: 1950] 5. a marijuana cigarette; a puff of a marijuana cigarette. RT: *joint.* Probably from sense four. [(c. 1910): JES: 1959, (1929): DU; South African, (1974): JB: 1980] 6. any tablet or capsule of a drug; an amphetamine or barbiturate tablet or capsule. *Cf. bolus.* This is standard English. [drug culture use, (1963): OEDS, RRL: 1969, EEL: 1971, MA: 1973]

pill-cooker an opium user or addict. RT: *campfire boy.* [U.S., (1929): OEDS, BVB: 1942, VJM: 1949]

pillhead (also **pill freak, pill-gulper, pill-guzzler, pill-popper**) a heavy user of drugs in pill form; a drug user partial to amphetamines and barbiturates. RS: *user.* [U.S., (1965): DNE: 1973, JBW: 1967, RRL: 1969, D&B: 1970c, EEL: 1971, W&F: 1975, MW: 1976]

pillow 1. knockout drops. Refers to lying down on a pillow. RT: *Mickey Finn.* [U.S., BVB: 1942, VJM: 1949] 2. opium. RT: *opium.* [U.S., JES: 1959] 3. a plastic bag containing pills. [U.S., LVA: 1981, RDS: 1982] 4. *methaqualone (q.v.).* RT: *ludes.* [U.S., ELA: 1984]

pill pad a place to smoke opium (early 1900s) or use other drugs (mid 1900s). *Pad* (*q.v.*) = a place to use drugs. RS: *opium den.* [U.S., W&F: 1960, HSD: 1984]

pill-popper (also **pill-dropper**) a drug user who prefers pills such as amphetamines and barbiturates. RS: *user.* Now also in general colloquial use for someone who takes pills for therapeutic purposes. [U.S., (1963): OEDS, RDS: 1982]

pillster a drug user who takes drugs in pill form. RT: *user.* [U.S., D&D: 1957]

pilly a user of pills, especially amphetamines and barbiturates. *Cf.*

pillhead. RT: ***user***. [U.S., JBW: 1967, RG: 1970, IGA: 1971]

pimp dust cocaine. Compare to ***pimpstick***. RT: ***cocaine***. Black slang. [U.S., EAF: 1980]

pimple and blotch Scotch whiskey. Rhyming slang for *Scotch*. May also refer to blemishes caused by heavy drinking. *Cf.* ***gin bud***. RS: ***whiskey***. [early 1900s, DRS, SSD]

pimple and wart 1. a quart of liquor. Rhyming slang for *quart*. [early 1900s, DRS] 2. port wine. Rhyming slang for *port*. RT: ***port***. [early 1900s, DRS]

pimpstick a cigarette; a machine-made cigarette, the kind that fancy pimps smoke as opposed to the rugged, roll-your-own type. RS: ***nail***. RFA attests it as loggers' use. All others are criminal use. [U.S., JS: 1925, GI: 1931, D&D: 1957]

pin 1. (also **pin gun**) a hypodermic syringe and needle; a pin (sewing needle, safety pin, etc.) and medicine dropper used to inject drugs. *Cf.* ***pin shot***. RS: ***monkey pump***. [U.S., MA: 1973, RDS: 1982] 2. (also **pin J., pin joint, pinner**) a very thin marijuana cigarette. RT: ***joint***. [U.S., (1967): ELA: 1982, RRL: 1969, ADC: 1975, W&F: 1975, D&B: 1978] 3. a drug seller. Probably from *kingpin*. RT: ***dealer***. [U.S., RAS: 1983]

pinch 1. to arrest. See ***pinched***. [U.S., (GWM: 1859), RWB: 1912] 2. a small amount of marijuana or snuff. This is standard English in the context of tobacco or marijuana use. RS: ***load***. Standard English. Black use. [U.S., (1968): EAF: 1980]

pinched arrested. RT: ***busted***. [(1837): OEDS, GWM: 1859, (RWB: 1912), (BD: 1937), D&B: 1970c]

pinch-gut vengeance inferior or weak liquor. See ***belly vengeance***. RS: ***rotgut***. [Br., 1800s, DSUE]

pinch hitter someone who is hired by a debilitated addict to inject drugs. GEN: a substitute (person). From the baseball expression. *Cf.* ***hit man***. RS: ***bangster***. [U.S., JWK: 1981]

pine top cheap, raw whiskey; whiskey; hard liquor. RT: ***rotgut***. [U.S., (1858): OEDS, JSF: 1889, BWG: 1899, MHW: 1934]

ping a pill to scrape or shave off a bit of a drug for a small dose. *Cf.* ***chip***. [U.S., IGA: 1971, WCM: 1972]

ping in the wing (also **ping in wing, ping shot, ping-wing**) an injection of drugs in the arm; a drug injection given with a ***pin*** (*q.v.*). RT: ***shot***. [U.S., VJM: 1949, M&D: 1952, A&T: 1953, W&F: 1960]

ping-pong ***Pantopon*** (TM; *q.v.*). [U.S., (1944): HLM: 1982]

pin gun equipment for injecting drugs made from a pin (sewing needle, safety pin, etc.) and a medicine dropper. RS: ***monkey pump***. [U.S., JES: 1959, H&C: 1975]

pinhead 1. a narcotics addict who injects narcotics with the aid of a ***pin*** (*q.v.*). See list at ***head***. RT: ***junky***. [U.S., (c. 1920): JES:

1959, MHW: 1934, VJM: 1949] 2. an amphetamine user. RS: *user.* [U.S., EEL: 1971] 3. a very thin marijuana cigarette. RS: *joint.* [U.S., RRL: 1969, JH: 1979]

pin joint (also pin J.) a very thin marijuana cigarette. *Cf. pin.* RS: *joint.* [U.S., ADC: 1981]

pink 1. *L.S.D.* (*q.v.*). *Cf. pink swirl.* [U.S., EEL: 1971] 2. a *Seconal* (TM; *q.v.*) capsule. See *pinks.* [U.S., JBW: 1967, EEL: 1971] 3. morphine. *Cf. pinks.* RT: *morphine.* [U.S., SNP: 1977]

pink and greens amphetamines. May refer to *Benzedrine* (TM; *q.v.*) and *Dexamyl* (TM; *q.v.*) tablets which are rose and green respectively. RT: *amps.* [U.S., YKB: 1977]

pink dots See *pink swirl.*

pinked alcohol intoxicated; tipsy. RS: *drunk.* Not common (W&F: 1960). [U.S., W&F: 1960]

pink elephants the delirium tremens; hallucinatory creatures seen during the delirium tremens. *Cf. seeing pink elephants.* RT: *D.T.s.* [(1940): OEDS, D&D: 1957, K&M: 1968]

pink-eye 1. inferior whiskey; *moonshine* (*q.v.*). *Cf. redeye.* RT: *rotgut.* [U.S., D&D: 1957] 2. (also pinkie, pinky) methyl alcohol; cheap red wine. RT: *methyl, wine.* [Aust., (1897): OEDS, (1935): GAW: 1978, DSUE, SJB: 1966] 3. a methyl alcohol drunkard. RT: *sot.* [Aust., SJB: 1966, GAW: 1978]

pink, in the alcohol intoxicated. GEN: feeling on top of the world. *Cf. pinked.* RT: *drunk.* [U.S., JAS: 1932, MHW: 1934]

pink ladies 1. (usually pink lady) *torpedo juice* (*q.v.*), a drink made from the alcohol fuel used to power American torpedoes. RT: *rotgut.* [U.S. Navy, (1930s): DST: 1984] 2. (also pinks) barbiturates, especially *Seconal* (TM; *q.v.*) capsules. RS: *barbs.* [U.S., D&B: 1970c, IGA: 1971, SH: 1972, YKB: 1977, NIDA: 1980] 3. (also pinks) capsules of *Darvon* (TM; *q.v.*). Black slang. [U.S., EAF: 1980]

pinko alcohol intoxicated; drunk on methylated spirits. *Cf. pinked.* RT: *drunk.* [primarily Aust., (1910): DU, F&G: 1925, SJB: 1943, M&J: 1975]

pink Owsley *L.S.D.* (*q.v.*). See *Owsley.* [U.S., C&H: 1974, SNP: 1977]

pinks 1. *Seconal* (TM; *q.v.*) barbiturates. See *pink ladies.* [U.S., TRG: 1968, RRL: 1969, EEL: 1971, YKB: 1977] See also *pink swirl.* 2. Darvon (TM). See *pink ladies.*

pink spiders the delirium tremens; hallucinations experienced as part of the delirium tremens. *Cf. pink elephants.* RT: *D.T.s.* [Br., 18-1900s, DSUE]

pink swirl (also pink dots, pink ozzy, pink wafers) the hallucinogenic drug *L.S.D.* (*q.v.*). *Cf. pink, pink Owsley.* RT: *L.S.D.* [U.S., EEL: 1971, S&R: 1972, ADC: 1981]

pink tea whiskey. *Cf. pink-eye.* RT: *whiskey.* [U.S., JSF: 1889]

pink witches (also **pink wedges**) the hallucinogenic drug *L.S.D.* (*q.v.*). *Cf. orange mushrooms.* RT: *L.S.D.* [U.S., RG: 1970, H&C: 1975, SNP: 1977]

pinky See *pink-eye.*

pinned 1. arrested. RT: *busted.* [GWM: 1859] 2. having to do with the pin point-sized pupils of a heroin addict. The drug *Nalline* (TM; *q.v.*) notably dilates the pupils allowing detection of an addict. A play on sense one. *Cf. nailed.* [U.S., M&V: 1967, RRL: 1969, EEL: 1971, W&F: 1975]

pinner a thin marijuana cigarette. See *pin.*

pins and needles morphine. From the expression *on pins and needles.* RT: *morphine.* [U.S., EEL: 1971, JH: 1979] See also *needle and pin.*

pin shot an injection of drugs performed using a pin (sewing-machine needle, safety pin, etc.) to open a vein and a medicine dropper to squirt in the drug solution. The dropper is slipped over the pin and may be pushed into the open vein itself. This is an underworld term recorded in prisons. Pin shot may be from the *pen* of penitentiary. RT: *shot.* [U.S., (1922): DU, HS: 1933, VFN: 1933, BD: 1937, DWM: 1938, VJM: 1949, M&D: 1952, W&F: 1960]

pint peddler a bootlegger; a liquor smuggler. He sells only small amounts. RT: *bootlegger.* From the prohibition era. [U.S., BVB: 1942]

pint pot 1. a beer seller. [(1563): OED] 2. a drunkard. Rhyming slang for *sot* (*q.v.*). [U.S., M&B: 1944, DRS]

pin-yen opium. See *pen-yen.* [U.S., SNP: 1977]

pin-yen toy a container for prepared opium. See *toy.* [U.S., VJM: 1949]

pinyon opium. A variation of *pen-yen* (*q.v.*). [U.S., (c. 1930): DU, A&T: 1953, SNP: 1977]

pipe 1. a tobacco pipe. *Cf. artichoke ripe, bowl, cherry ripe, funker, hay-burner, Missouri meerschaum, nose-warmer, organ, raw and ripe, steamer, stove.* [standard English since the late 1500s, (1594): OED] 2. to smoke a pipe to pass the time. [U.S., BWG: 1899; listed in BVB: 1942] 3. a cigar. RT: *seegar.* [U.S., (1848): W&F: 1960] 4. an opium smoker. RT: *campfire boy.* [U.S., M&V: 1954, M&H: 1959] 5. an opium pipe. RT: *hop stick.* [U.S., (1887): RML: 1948, RDS: 1982] 6. a smoker of marijuana. Possibly from sense four. RT: *toker.* [U.S., EEL: 1971] 7. a pipe for smoking marijuana or hashish. RS: *bong.* [U.S., EEL: 1971, ADC: 1975] 8. a large vein into which drugs can be injected easily, the median cephalic vein. *Cf. line, mainline, sewer.* [U.S., RRL: 1969, IGA: 1971] 9. someone who is alcohol intoxicated or drug intoxicated. *Cf. sewer pipe.* [U.S., VJM: 1949] 10. a glass water pipe used for *free basing* (*q.v.*). [U.S., S&F: 1984]

piped (also **piped up**) alcohol intoxicated; drug intoxicated. RT: *drunk, stoned*. [(1912): OEDS, SBF: 1976, DSUE, BVB: 1942, VJM: 1949] See also *pipped up*.

pipe dream a dream had while under the effects of opium. GEN: a dream; a fantasy. [(1901): OEDS, BVB: 1942, H&C: 1975]

pipe fiend an opium smoker. RT: *campfire boy*. [U.S., (1913): OEDS, BD: 1937, DWM: 1938, VJM: 1949]

pipe-hitter 1. (also **pipe-smoker**) an opium smoker. RT: *campfire boy*. [U.S., DWM: 1936, BVB: 1942] 2. a marijuana smoker. RT: *toker*. [U.S., S&E: 1981]

pipe joint an *opium den* (*q.v.*). [U.S., early 1900s, DU]

pipe, on the addicted to opium. *Cf. pipe*. RS: *hooked*. [U.S., DU, GOL: 1950]

piper drunk (also **piper fou'**, **piper merry**) alcohol intoxicated. *Cf. drunk as a piper*. RT: *drunk*. [Br., 1800s, F&H]

pipes an opium smoker; an opium addict. *Cf. pipe*. [U.S., M&H: 1959]

pipe-smoker See *pipe-hitter*.

pipie (also **pipey**) 1. high on opium. [U.S., BVB: 1942, VJM: 1949] 2. (also **pipy**) an opium user or addict. BD: 1937 lists **pipies**. RS: *user, junky*. [U.S., BD: 1937, DWM: 1938, BVB: 1942, GOL: 1950]

pipped up (also **pipped**) alcohol intoxicated. *Cf. piped*. RT: *drunk*. [U.S., (1911): OEDS, RDS: 1982]

pippy (also **pipy**) drug intoxicated. Possibly a misspelling of *pipie* (*q.v.*). [U.S., JES: 1959, H&C: 1975]

pipsky an opium pipe. RT: *hop stick*. [U.S., early 1900s (M&V: 1954)]

pirate a bootlegger; a liquor smuggler. From the prohibition era. RT: *bootlegger*. [U.S., BVB: 1942]

pish liquor; inferior liquor or beer. Probably a disguise for *piss* (*q.v.*). RT: *queer-beer, rotgut*. [Br., F&G: 1925]

piss beer; weak beer; inferior liquor. RS: *rotgut*. [(1914): DSUE; U.S., BVB: 1942] See also *drunk as a pissant, full as a piss-ant, go on the piss, half pissed, panther piss, panther's piss, piss factory, pissed, pissed as a fiddler's bitch, pissed as a newt, pissed in the brook, pissed up, pissed up to the eyebrows, pisshead, pissing drunk, pissing fou', piss-maker, pisso, piss-up, pissy-arsed, squaw piss, tiger piss, witch piss*.

pissed (also **pissed up**) alcohol intoxicated. RT: *drunk*. See *piss*. Probably very old. [Br. and U.S., (1929): OEDS, PW: 1974, M&J: 1975, ADC: 1984]

pissed as a fiddler's bitch (also **pissed as a newt**) alcohol intoxicated. *Cf. drunk as a fiddler's bitch, drunk as a newt*. RT:

drunk. **Pissed as a newt** is current and popular in Britain. [Br., 1900s, DSUE]

pissed in the brook alcohol intoxicated. (BF: 1737: [He's] Piss'd in the Brook.) An elaboration of *pissed* (*q.v.*). RT: *drunk*. [BF: 1737]

pissed out of one's mind alcohol intoxicated; dead drunk. RT: *drunk*. [1900s, LDEI: 1979]

pissed up to the eyebrows (also **pissed up to the eyeballs**) alcohol intoxicated. RT: *drunk*. [Br., (1930): DSUE]

piss factory a saloon or tavern. *Cf. piss, piss-maker*. RS: *bar*. [Br., late 18-1900s, F&H; listed in BVB: 1942]

pisshead a drunkard. *Cf. piss*. RT: *sot*. [N.Z. and elsewhere, (1930): DSUE]

pissing drunk (also **pissing fou'**) alcohol intoxicated. RT: *drunk*. [Br., 1800s or earlier, F&H (at *drunk*)]

piss-maker 1. liquor; beer. From the urination it causes. RT: *booze*. [U.S., early 1900s and perhaps before, BVB: 1942] 2. a drunkard. RT: *sot*. [FG: 1823, F&H]

pisso a drunkard. RT: *sot*. The final o is characteristic of Australian slang. *Cf. pinko*. [Aust., (1930): DSUE]

pissticide cheap, rotgut wine. A play on *pesticide*. RT: *rotgut*. [U.S., BR: 1972]

piss-up a drinking bout. *Cf. piss*. RT: *spree*. [Br., 1900s, (1952): OEDS]

pissy-arsed alcohol intoxicated. *Cf. pissed*. RT: *drunk*. [Br., 1900s, DSUE]

pistola* a hypodermic syringe and needle. Spanish for pistol, i.e., *gun* (*q.v.*). RT: *monkey pump*. [U.S., HB: 1955]

pistol shot a drink of liquor. An elaboration of *shot* (*q.v.*) = a drink. *Cf. pistol shot*. RT: *nip*. [Br., late 1800s, F&H; listed in BVB: 1942]

pit the crease on the inside of the elbow; the median cephalic vein in the forearm. *Cf. valley*. [U.S., M&V: 1967, RRL: 1969, EEL: 1971]

pitch to sell drugs; to *push* (*q.v.*) drugs. *Cf. pitching jive*. RT: *push*. [U.S., BVB: 1942, A&T: 1953, M&H: 1959]

pitching jive selling drugs. *Cf. jive*. [U.S., TH: 1976]

pito* a cigarette. Spanish for straw. RT: *nail*. [calo, JBR: 1973, CG: 1980, NIDA: 1980]

pixilated (also **pixolated**) alcohol intoxicated. *Cf. impixlocated*. GEN: bewildered. RT: *drunk*. The early attestations probably refer to the generic sense. [Br. and U.S., (1848): DA, (1930): DSUE, SSD, (1955): OEDS, RDS: 1982]

pizen liquor; strong or inferior liquor; whiskey. A dialect pronunciation of *poison*. *Cf. panther pizen*. RT: *rotgut*. [U.S., (1875): JRW: 1909, F&H, MHW: 1934, D&D: 1957]

pizz alcohol intoxicated. Possibly from *pissed* (*q.v.*). See *pizzicato*. RT: *drunk*. [Br., early 1900s, DSUE]

pizza marijuana. *Cf. orégano*. RT: *pot*. [U.S., (1965): BR: 1972]

pizzacato an error for *pizzicato* (*q.v.*). [PD: 1982]

pizza maker a marijuana seller. RS: *dealer*. [U.S., BR: 1972]

pizzicato alcohol intoxicated. Probably a disguise and elaboration for *pissed*. *Cf. pizz*. RT: *drunk*. [Br., (1935): DSUE]

plac See *plass*.

placidolls *Placidyl* (TM; *q.v.*) sedative capsules. *Dolls* (*q.v.*) = pills. RT: *plass*. [U.S., ADC: 1981]

Placidyl a protected trade name for ethchlorvynol capsules. The drug is a hypnotic. See *plass* for a list of terms. [in current use; consult a pharmaceutical reference for more information]

plain having to do with undiluted liquor. RT: *neat*. Colloquial. [since the mid 1800s, F&H, DSUE]

plant 1. a place where liquor is made illicitly. From the prohibition era. [U.S., HNR: 1934, BVB: 1942] See also *factory*. 2. a place where opium is prepared or where opium equipment is kept. *Cf. stash*. [U.S., HNR: 1934, DWM: 1936, BD: 1937] 3. to conceal narcotics on an unsuspecting person for the purpose of smuggling; to conceal contraband on someone who will later be arrested for possessing the contraband. [U.S., (1933): OEDS, DWM: 1936, RRL: 1969, EEL: 1971] 4. a secret cache of drugs or drug equipment. This can be on (in) the person or elsewhere. GEN: a hiding place. RT: *stash*. [U.S., (1926): OEDS, DWM: 1936, M&H: 1959, RRL: 1969] 5. (also **plants**) peyote cactus, a source of mescaline. Compare to *chemicals*. RS: *peyote*. [U.S., YKB: 1977]

plant manager in illicit drug traffic, the supervisor of a drug processing factory or plant. Probably from *plant* sense four. [U.S., M&H: 1959]

plass (also plac) *Placidyl* (TM; *q.v.*) a sedative. [U.S., JWK: 1981] Nicknames and slang terms for Placidyl: *basketballs, dill, dills, dyls, footballs, marbles, plac, placidolls, plass.*

plastered alcohol intoxicated. RT: *drunk*. [U.S., RWB: 1912, MP: 1928, MHW: 1934, VJM: 1949, D&D: 1957, W&F: 1960, DCCU: 1972; Br., F&G: 1925]

play around to experiment with drugs; to use addictive drugs infrequently in an attempt to avoid addiction. This is a common colloquial expression used in the drug culture context. The same as *chippy* (*q.v.*). [U.S., DWM: 1938, BVB: 1942]

play camels to drink heavily; to see how much liquor one can hold; to get drunk. RT: *mug oneself*. [JRW: 1909]

played having to do with a portion of marijuana (cigarette or other) which has had all of the active principle smoked out of it. Short for **played out**. *Cf. cashed.* [U.S., D&B: 1978, ADC: 1984]

player 1. a drug user. RT: *user.* [U.S., EEL: 1971, JWK: 1981] **2.** a drug seller. RT: *dealer.* [U.S., EEL: 1971]

play the Greek to drink to excess. Refers to Bacchus, the god of wine and merrymaking. RT: *guzzle.* [U.S., BVB: 1942, AAR: 1944] See also *merry as a Greek.*

play the nod See *nod.*

pleasantly plastered alcohol intoxicated; mellow with drink. *Plastered* (*q.v.*) = drunk. RS: *drunk.* [U.S., BVB: 1942]

pleasure jolt a (small) dose of drugs taken by a nonaddict. This is in contrast to a dose taken because of an addiction. *Jolt* (*q.v.*) = a *rush* (*q.v.*), a drug charge. [U.S., DWM: 1936, A&T: 1953]

pleasure smoker 1. a nonaddict who smokes opium for pleasure only. RS: *chipper.* [U.S., BD: 1937, DWM: 1938, VJM: 1949, GOL: 1950] **2.** an occasional marijuana smoker. RS: *toker.* [U.S., EEL: 1971]

pleasure user (also **pleasure shooter**) a nonaddict who uses narcotics (including opium) for pleasure only. RS: *chipper.* [U.S., DWM: 1938, BVB: 1942]

Pleiku pink a variety of marijuana sold and used during the Vietnamese war. RT: *pot.* [U.S. military, (1970s): ELA: 1982]

plonk (also **plink, plinkety-plonk, plink-plonk, plunk**) white wine; wine; cheap wine; inferior liquor; liquor adulterated with methyl alcohol. All are based on French *vin blanc.* RS: *wine.* These terms are originally Australian and became known more widely during WWI. [Aust., (1919): OEDS, (1941): GAW: 1978, SJB: 1943, EP: 1948, SJB: 1966, DSUE, DRS, B&P: 1965, SSD]

plonk artist (also **plonk dot, plonk fiend, plonk merchant, plonko**) a derelict wine drunkard. Based on *plonk* which is from French *vin blanc.* RT: *wino.* [Aust., (1930): DSUE, (1963): OEDS, SJB: 1966]

plonked alcohol intoxicated. From *plonk.* RT: *drunk.* [U.S., (1943): OEDS, W&F: 1960, DCCU: 1972]

plonked up alcohol intoxicated. RT: *drunk.* [Aust., SJB: 1966]

plonko a drunkard. RT: *sot.* [Aust., HSD: 1984]

plootered alcohol intoxicated. RT: *drunk.* [Br. (Anglo-Irish), (1920): DSUE]

plowed 1. (also **ploughed, ploughed under, plowed under**) alcohol intoxicated. RT: *drunk.* [Br., JCH: 1887, B&L: 1890, F&H; U.S., MHW: 1934, DCCU: 1972] **2.** drug intoxicated. RT: *stoned.* [U.S., ADC: 1981]

pluck wine; cheap wine. RT: *wine.* Black use. CM: 1970 suggests that this is from *plug.* DC: 1972 suggests that the *pluck* is from *pluck grapes.* [U.S., (1964): OEDS, CM: 1970, DC: 1972, EAF:

1972, C&H: 1974]

plug 1. a bite-sized, pressed mass of chewing tobacco. RT: *quid*. [(1728): OED, (1818): SBF: 1976, BWG: 1899] 2. a drink of beer. RS: *nip*. [(1816): OED] 3. wine; cheap wine. The same as *pluck*. [U.S., CM: 1970 (at *pluck*)]

plugged in excited by drugs; a member of the drug culture. The same as *turned on* (*q.v.*). [U.S., W&F: 1975]

P.O. paregoric. See *P.G.*

pocket pistol a hip flask for liquor. Because one can take a *shot* (*q.v.*) with it. *Cf. pistol shot*. RT: *flask*. [U.S., BWG: 1899, MHW: 1934]

poco a small packet of narcotics. Spanish for small. RT: *load*. [U.S., JES: 1959]

pod the seed pods of marijuana plants which contain the most *resin* (*q.v.*). *Cf. bud*. RT: *pot*. [U.S., (1952): W&F: 1960, EEL: 1971, M&V: 1973, YKB: 1977, D&B: 1978, RDS: 1982]

poddy (also **podgy**) alcohol intoxicated. *Cf. pogy*. RT: *drunk*. [Br., JCH: 1887, F&H; U.S., MHW: 1934]

poffered alcohol intoxicated. RT: *drunk*. [U.S., BVB: 1942]

poggled alcohol intoxicated. *Cf. puggled*. RT: *drunk*. [Br., (1933): OEDS, DSUE]

pogo pogo cocaine. RT: *cocaine*. [U.S., ELA: 1984]

pogy (also **pogey**) alcohol intoxicated. RT: *drunk*. [cant, FG: 1785, FG: 1811, FG: 1823]

point a hypodermic needle; a sewing machine needle or other needle or pin used for opening a vein for drug injections. RS: *needle*. [U.S., BD: 1937, DWM: 1938, W&F: 1967, D&B: 1970c, EEL: 1971, EAF: 1980, AD: 1981, ADC: 1981, JWK: 1981]

point blank wine; white wine. From the French *vin blanc* and the expression describing a bullet shot from a short distance. RT: *wine*. [Br., WWI, F&G: 1925, B&P: 1965]

point shot an injection of drugs given with a pin or a broken hypodermic needle and a medicine dropper. The broken needle or pin is first inserted into a vein and worked around to open the skin and wall of the vein. A medicine dropper is then slipped over the metal, pushed down into the vein, and the drug is injected. Also reported is the use of a pin or needle to open the skin and a vein. Then the end of the syringe or medicine dropper is inserted. Almost the same as *pin shot* (*q.v.*). RS: *shot*. [U.S., BVB: 1942, JES: 1959]

poison 1. liquor; beverage alcohol. *Cf. pizen*. RT: *booze*. [Br., (1805): OEDS, F&H, SSD; listed in BVB: 1942] 2. pure heroin; heroin; any powdered drug. Pure heroin (which is never sold on the U.S. streets) is fatal even in small amounts. RT: *heroin*. [U.S., M&V: 1954, RRL: 1969, EEL: 1971] 3. any drug. [U.S.,

JWK: 1981]

poison mushrooms mushrooms of the genus *Psilocybe* which are sometimes eaten for hallucinogenic effects. These mushrooms are often confused with those of the genus *Amanita* which are deadly poison. See ***magic mushrooms***. [U.S., ADC: 1981]

poison people heroin addicts; ***methadone*** (*q.v.*) addicts. RT: ***junky***. [U.S., RRL: 1969, EEL: 1971]

poison sausage a tobacco cigarette. RT: ***nail***. [U.S., BVB: 1942] See also ***sausage***.

poke a puff of a marijuana cigarette or pipe. The same as ***toke*** (*q.v.*). [U.S., (1955): ELA: 1982, RRL: 1969, IGA: 1971, S&W: 1973, JWK: 1981]

polboron heroin. From Spanish for big powder. *Cf.* ***pulboron***. RT: ***heroin***. [U.S., SNP: 1977]

pole, up the alcohol intoxicated. RT: ***drunk***. [(1896): JRW: 1909, BVB: 1942, SSD]

polillo* marijuana. RT: ***pot***. Spanish. [U.S., NIDA: 1980]

polished (also **polished up**) alcohol intoxicated. RT: ***drunk***. [U.S., MP: 1928, AH: 1931, MHW: 1934, W&F: 1960]

polite alcohol intoxicated. *Cf.* ***wise***. RT: ***drunk***. [BF: 1737]

polled off alcohol intoxicated. **Poll off** = get drunk. RT: ***drunk***. [Br., 1800s, (F&H)]

polluted 1. alcohol intoxicated. RT: ***drunk***. [U.S., RWB: 1912, R&P: 1928, MHW: 1934, D&D: 1957, DCCU: 1972, ADC: 1981] 2. drug intoxicated. RT: ***stoned***. [U.S., BD: 1937, DWM: 1938, DU]

pol-pot marijuana with female flowers and much pollen showing. Based on ***pollen*** and ***pot*** (*q.v.*), and probably patterned on the name of the Cambodian leader. RS: ***pot***. [U.S., JWK: 1981]

polvito* powdered drugs: cocaine, ***P.C.P.*** (*q.v.*). Spanish for ***powder*** (*q.v.*). [U.S., NIDA: 1980]

polvo de ángel* (also **polvo***) phencyclidine, ***P.C.P.*** (*q.v.*), an animal tranquilizer. Spanish for ***angel dust*** (*q.v.*) = P.C.P. RT: ***P.C.P.*** [U.S., NIDA: 1980]

pong 1. (also **ponge**) beer. See ***pongelow***. RT: ***beer***. [Br., JCH: 1887, F&H] 2. to drink beer. RS: ***irrigate***. [Br., (1870): DU]

pongelow (also **pongellorum, pongelo, pongelorum, ponjello**) beer. RT: ***beer***. [Br., JCH: 1864, B&L: 1890, F&H, JRW: 1909, F&G: 1925; listed in GWM: 1859]

pony a small drink of beer or liquor. Usually refers to the glass as well as its contents. RS: ***nip***. [18–1900s, F&H, (1895): GAW: 1978, MHW: 1934, K&M: 1968]

pooped (also **pooped out**) alcohol intoxicated. Possibly from the nautical expression describing a ship over whose stern a large wave has broken. GEN: tired out. RT: ***drunk***. [U.S., BVB: 1942]

poopied alcohol intoxicated. Probably a euphemism for *shit-faced* (*q.v.*). *Cf. pooped.* RT: *drunk.* [U.S., D&B: 1970c]

poopkie a pipe for smoking marijuana. RS: *bong.* [U.S., EEL: 1971]

poor man's cocaine isobutyl nitrite, a drug similar to *amyl nitrite* (*q.v.*). *Cf. opium of the poor.* See *snapper.* [U.S., RDS: 1982]

pop 1. champagne. From the sound of the cork being withdrawn. This nickname has become common for any carbonated beverage. RT: *cham.* [(1870): DSUE] 2. opium. This *pop* is from (opium) *poppy.* *Cf. pop joint.* RT: *opium.* [U.S., GOL: 1950] 3. an injection of narcotics; a subcutaneous injection of narcotics. GEN: a try; a "go" at something (1904): OEDS. RT: *shot.* [U.S., (1935): OEDS, DWM: 1936, BD: 1937, VJM: 1949, M&D: 1952, GS: 1959, RRL: 1969, JH: 1979] 4. to inject narcotics; to inject narcotics subcutaneously. The same as *skin pop* (*q.v.*). RT: *shoot.* [U.S., (1956): OEDS, M&V: 1967, RRL: 1969, ADC: 1975, W&F: 1975] 5. (also **pop a cap, pop a pill**) to take a pill or pills. This is widely known outside the drug culture. [U.S., (1968): DNE: 1973, RRL: 1969, D&B: 1970c, ADC: 1975, GU: 1975, W&F: 1975, MW: 1976]

pop a roll to take some pills. The same as *drop a roll* (*q.v.*).

pop-eyed alcohol intoxicated. GEN: with bulging eyes. RT: *drunk.* [U.S., BVB: 1942]

pop joint an opium den. *Pop* (*q.v.*) = opium (from poppy). RT: *opium den.* [U.S., GOL: 1950]

popo oro* a potential variety of marijuana from Mexico. Probably Spanish. RT: *pot.* ELA: 1984 lists popo ore. [U.S., ELA: 1982]

pop party a gathering where drugs are injected. *Pop* (*q.v.*) = to inject. Akin to *coke party* (*q.v.*). [U.S., EEL: 1971, W&F: 1975]

popped 1. arrested with drugs. A synonym of *busted* (*q.v.*). RT: *busted.* [U.S., (1906): OEDS, RRL: 1969, D&B: 1970c, M&V: 1973, JWK: 1981] 2. alcohol intoxicated; drug intoxicated. RT: *drunk, stoned.* [U.S., RDS: 1982]

popper 1. (also **popsie**) a vial or ampule of amyl nitrite. The glass vial is broken (popped) and the drug is inhaled. RT: *snapper.* [U.S., RRL: 1969, BR: 1972, ADC: 1975, YKB: 1977, DNE: 1980, NIDA: 1980] 2. a pill taker; a *pill-popper* (*q.v.*). *Cf. pop.* [U.S., ADC: 1975]

poppied under the influence of opium; in an opium stupor. Based on *opium poppy.* RS: *stoned.* [U.S., JES: 1959, H&C: 1975]

poppy (also **pop**) opium. See *pop.* RT: *opium.* [U.S., (1935): OEDS, VJM: 1949, GOL: 1950, RDS: 1982]

poppy alley a district where opium dens are located; any city's Chinatown. [U.S., BVB: 1942, VJM: 1949, D&D: 1957]

poppy grove an opium den; a place where opium is sold. RT: *doperie.* [U.S., JES: 1959]

poppyhead an opium addict. *Cf. poppy.* RS: *junky.* [U.S., BVB: 1942, VJM: 1949, D&D: 1957]

poppy-headed addicted to opium. *Cf. picking the poppies, poppied.* See *poppy.* RS: *hooked.* [U.S., JES: 1959, H&C: 1975]

poppy pill an opium pellet. *Cf. pfun.* See *pill.*

poppy pipe an opium pipe. *Cf. poppy.* RT: *hop stick.* [U.S., GOL: 1950]

poppy-puffer an opium smoker; an opium addict. *Poppy* (*q.v.*) = opium. RT: *campfire boy.* [U.S., D&D: 1957]

poppy rain allegedly the juice of an opium poppy. Probably an error for *poppy train* (*q.v.*). [U.S., JES: 1959, H&C: 1975]

poppy straw the dried stems and seed capsules remaining after a poppy field has been mowed. Morphine can be extracted from poppy straw. [U.S., BTD: 1968]

poppy tea a tea brewed from the waste parts of the marijuana plant. Not related to *poppy* (*q.v.*) = opium. [U.S., JH: 1979]

poppy train opium; opium smoking in *ride the poppy train* (*q.v.*). [U.S., BVB: 1942, VJM: 1949]

popsie See *popper.*

popskull strong liquor; inferior whiskey; moonshine. *Cf. conk-buster.* RT: *rotgut.* [U.S., (1867): OEDS, (1904): ADD, VR: 1929, MHW: 1934, D&D: 1957]

popstick an opium pipe. *Pop* (*q.v.*) = opium. RT: *hop stick.* [U.S., M&V: 1967]

pop-wallah a teetotaller. *Wallah* (*q.v.*) = merchant. This *pop* is soda pop. RT: *dry.* [Br. military, late 18-1900s, F&G: 1925]

pop wine a cheap, sparkling, fruit-flavored wine. It was popular in the sixties and seventies was often used as a vehicle for drugs. [U.S., (1971): DNE: 1980, W&F: 1975, MW: 1976]

pork the police in general. A variation of *pig* (*q.v.*). *Cf. bacon, hog, oink.* If caught by the **pork** one is put in the **pork barrel**, i.e., jail. RS: *fuzz.* [U.S., JWK: 1981]

port port wine, a dark red wine from Portugal. [standard English since the late 1600s, (1691): OED] Nicknames and slang terms for port wine: *blackstrap, bone-clother, didn't ought, fustian, kill-priest, pimple and wart, port, red fustian, red ribbin, red ribbon, treacle.*

porter (also **porter's ale, porter's beer, porter's booze**) a dark brown, bitter beer, high in alcohol content. A favorite drink of London's laborers, served at a porterhouse. Not related to *port* (*q.v.*). [since the early 1700s, (1727): OED] Nicknames and slang terms for porter's ale: *British champagne, English burgundy, gatter, gutter, heavy, heavy brown, heavy wet, hod of mortar, porter, porter's beer, porter's booze, red fustian, red ribbin, red ribbon, stout, thick.*

positive a good state of mind before or after taking drugs. *Cf. set, up*. Compare to ***negative***. [U.S., RRL: 1969]

possession a truncation of ***possession of drugs***. *Cf. hold*. [U.S., (1970): OEDS]

pot 1. a drinking container for beer, liquor, or the liquor itself. [since the 1400s, (1440): OED] 2. to drink heavily. RT: ***guzzle***. [early 1600s, (Shakespeare)] 3. inferior whiskey; homemade whiskey; moonshine. From *pot whiskey* = *poteen* (*q.v.*). RT: *moonshine*. [U.S., W&F: 1960] 4. a drunkard. Probably from *rum pot* (*q.v.*) or something similar. RT: *sot*. [U.S., W&F: 1960] 5. marijuana. Possibly a truncation of the Mexican Indian word *potaguaya* (*q.v.*). Possibly refers to the pot (pipe) in which it is smoked. The term is widely known and is one of the slang words-of-choice for marijuana. [(1938): OEDS, (1951): M&D: 1952, A&T: 1953, M&V: 1954, RRL: 1969, CM: 1970, EEL: 1971, DCCU: 1972, ADC: 1975, NIDA: 1980, ADC: 1981, BW: 1984; elsewhere, (1954): DSUE, M&J: 1975, JB: 1980] Nicknames, technical, and slang terms for various types and grades of marijuana: *Acapulco, Acapulco gold, Acapulco red, African black, amarilla, angel dust, Angola black, ashes, atshitshi, Aunt Mary, baby, baby bhang, baby buds, bad green, bale, bambalacha, bambalache, bammies, bammy, bang, banji, bash, belt, belula, belyando sprue, Bethesda gold, bhang, bhang ganjah, birdwood, black Columbus, black ganja, black gold, black gungeon, black gungi, black gunion, black gunnion, black gunny, black mo, black moat, black mold, black mole, black monte, black mota, black mote, block, blond, blue de Hue, blue sage, blue sky blond, bo, bo-bo, bo-bo bush, Bo Jimmy, bomber, boo, boom, boo-reefer, brand X, Breckenridge green, brick, brifo, broccoli, brown weed, bu, bud, bullet Thai, bull jive, bush, bushes, butter flower, cam, Cambodian red, Cambodian trip weed, cam red, cam trip, Canadian black, cáñamo, canapa, canappa, cannabis, Cannabis americana, Cannabis indica, Cannabis mexicana, Cannabis ruderalis, Cannabis sativa, carga, carmabus, cavite allstars, chara, charas, charash, charge, charras, cheeo, chiba-chiba, Chicago black, Chicago green, chira, churrus, cigarette with no name, clorofila, cochornis, cola de borrego, cola de león, cola de zorra, colas, coli, coliflor tostao, collard greens, collie, colly, colly-weed, Colombian, Colombian gold, Colombian green, Colombo, Columbian, Columbian gold, Columbian pink, Columbian red, Columbia red, Columbus black, conga, Congo brown, Congo dirt, Congo mataby, cosa, creeper, crying weed, culican, dacha, dagga, dagha, Dame DuPaw, dew, diambista, dimba, ding, dingbat, dinky dow, dirt, dirt grass, ditch weed, djama, djamba, djoma, Doña Diabla, Doña Juana, Doña Juanita, dope, doradilla, drag weed, dreamstick, dry high, duros, dust, dynamite, ea-tay, eed-waggles, eed-way, electric butter, el kif, erb, esrar, fees, fee-tops, fennel, fe-ops, film, film can, fina-esmeralda, fine stuff, flowers, flower tops, fu, fumo d'Angola, funny stuff, gage, Gainesville green, gang, ganga, gange, gangster, ganja, ganjah,* *ganji, ganza, gash, gauge, gear, ghanja, giggles, giggle smoke, giggle weed, gizzy, gold, gold bud, gold Colombian, gold Columbian, golden leaf, gold leaf special, gong, gonga, good giggles, goofball, gow, gramma, grass, grass weed, greafa, greapha, greefa, greefo, green, green bud, green goddess, green griff, green moroccan, greens, greeta, grefa, greta, grief, griefo, grifa, griffa, griffo, grifo, guaza, gunga, gungeon, gunja, gunjah, gunjeh, gunji, gunny, guy, happy gas, happy grass, happy-time weed, hard-cutting mezz, has, hash, Hawaiian, Hawaiian sunshine, hay, hemp, herb, herbs, hog foot, home-grown, hooch, hop, hoska, hot hay, hotstick, ice bag, iceberg, ice pack, Illinois green, incense, India, Indian, Indian hay, Indian hemp, Indian rope, Indian weed, indico charras, J., jahooby, Jamaica ganga, Jamaica gold, Jamaican, Jamaican red, Jane, jay, jerez seco, Jersey green, Jersey hemp, jesca, jingo, jive, johnson, Johnson grass, joy, joy hemp, joy root, joy smoke, joy weed, 'juana, Juana, juane, juanita, juanita weed, Juan Valdez, juju, kaffir tobacco, kaif, Kansas grass, Kaui, Kaui electric, kee, keef, kef, keff, keg, Kentucky blue, key, khutchu string, ki, kidstuff, kief, kif, killer weed, kingdom weed, Kona coast gold, Kona gold, Kona Kona, la amarilla, lakbay diwa, lambsbread, laughing grass, laughing tobacco, laughing weed, lawn, leaf, leaves, Lebanese red, Lebanon red, leño, leper grass, lhesca, lid, light green, light stuff, limbo, Lipton's, Lipton's Tea, Lipton Tea, L.L., llesca, lobo, loco, locoweed, love blow, love weed, lozerose, lozies, lubange, lum, lumbo, lums, M., mach, machinery, Machu Picchu, macoha, macon, maconha, maggie, maharishee, ma-jen, majoon, majoun, mala hierba, male, Manhattan silver, Manhattan white, manicure, manteca, manzoul, maran guango, margarita, margie-wanna, mari, mariahuana, Maria Johanna, marigold, mariguana, marihuana, Marijane, marijuana, mariweegee, Marjie, Marjorie, Mary, Mary and Johnnie, Mary Ann, Mary Anner, Mary J., Mary Jane, Maryjane, Mary Johnas, Mary Jones, Mary Juanas, Mary Warmer, Mary Warner, Mary Weaver, Mary Werner, Mary Worner, Maui, Maui Waui, Maui wowee, Maui wowie, ma-yo, mazra, meg, Megg, meggs, mejorana, Mex, Mexican, Mexican brown, Mexican bush, Mexican green, Mexican locoweed, Mexican red, Mexican tumbleweed, Mez, mezz, Michoacan, mighty mezz, Minnesota green, Mishwacan, M.J., mo, M.O., modams, moggles, mohasky, mohasty, mohoska, monster weed, monte, moocah, mooster, moota, mootah, mooter, mootie, moragrifa, mota, mother, mother nature, mother nature's, mother nature's own tobacco, mu, mud-bud, muggles, mule, murder weed, musta, muta, mutah, mutha, nalga angelical, nalga de angel, Nam black, Nam shit, Nam weed, New York City Silver, New York City white, New York white, Nicotiana glauca, Nixon, njemu, noble weed, Oaxacan, O.J., one-toke weed, opium of the poor, orégano, orégano chino, pakalolo, Panama, Panama gold, Panamanian gold, Panamanian red, Panama red, paralyzing grass, Park Lane, Park Lane No. 2, pasto, pat, pato de gayina, petrifying stuff, pizza, Pleiku pink, pod, polillo, pol-pot, popo oro, pot, potaguaya, potiguaya, powder, P.R., pukalolo, puna butter, punk, punta roja, purple, ragweed, railroad weed, rama, rangoon, red, redbud, red dirt marijuana, red gunyon, red leb, red Lebanese, reef, reefer, reefer weed, reg, righteous bush, rope, Rosa Maria, rough stuff, rubia de la costa, sacate, sage, salt and pepper, Santa Marta gold, Santa Marta red, sassafrass, sativa, scissors, seeds, sense, sense bud, sess, shake, shishi, shit, shpleef, shuzzit, sinse, sinsemilla, skinny, skunk, smoke, snop, soma, soñadora, splay, spleef, spliff, splim, stash, stinkweed, stony bush, straw, stuff, stum, stupefying grass, subway silver, sucker weed, sugar weed, supergrass, superweed, suprema verde de clorafila, suprema verde de mejorana, supremo, sweet Lucy, sweet lunch, sweet Mary, T., tampi, té, tea, Teddy party, Texas, Texas tea, Thai pot, Thaistick, Thai-weed, The Dread Weed, the herb, the Mezz, the mighty mezz, the weed, thirteen, thunder weed, tops, tosca, tostada, tree of knowledge, trip grass, triple line, trip weed, trueno verde, T-stick, turnip greens, two-toke, up-pot, V., Vermont green, viper's weed, vonce, vongony, wacky-tabbacky, wacky-weed, wahegan, wana, wangula, weed, weed marijuana, weed tea, wheat, wildweed, yedo, yen-pop, yerba, yerba buena, yesca, yessa, zacate, Zacatecas purple, zacate inglés, zol, zoll, 13.*

potaguaya (also potiguaya) marijuana; crude marijuana; marijuana seed pods. A Mexican Indian word. See *pot*. Neither *pot* nor *potaguaya* was listed in the large vocabulary given in RPW: 1938. [U.S., DWM: 1938, RRL: 1969]

potato soup vodka. A colorless (originally Russian) spirit distilled from rye. See *spud*. [U.S., MG: 1970]

potato water alcohol made by fermenting potato peelings. RS: *moonshine*. Prison use. [U.S., GOL: 1950, RDS: 1982]

pot bust the capture and arrest of a group of marijuana users. [U.S., (1970): R&P: 1982]

pot culture the marijuana-centered faction of the drug culture. Based on the expression describing plants grown in pots rather than in the ground. This is essentially a pun. [U.S., (1970): DNE: 1973]

poteen (also potheen, potsheen) the *moonshine* (*q.v.*) of Ireland. RS: *moonshine*. VJM: 1949 lists the spelling poteen. [(1812): SOD, JCH: 1887, F&H, VJM: 1949]

pot-eyed alcohol intoxicated. *Cf. pot*. RT: *drunk*. [U.S., (1901): SBF: 1976]

pot fury 1. a drunkard. *Cf. pot*. RT: *sot*. [late 1500s, F&H] 2. drunkenness; a drunken rage. [listed in F&H, K&M: 1968]

pot hardy courageous from drinking liquor. *Cf. Dutch courage, full of courage, Geneva courage, pot valiant*. [mid 1600s, F&H]

pothead 1. a drunkard. *Cf. pot*. RT: *sot*. [mid 1800s, F&H] 2. a marijuana smoker. *Cf. pot*. RT: *toker*. [U.S., (1959): OEDS, (1966): R&P: 1982, JBW: 1967, W&F: 1967, (1968): DNE: 1973, D&B: 1970c, EEL: 1971, DCCU: 1972, ADC: 1975, MW: 1976]

potheen See *poteen*.

potholder a device for holding the butt of a marijuana cigarette; a *roach clip*. A pun on name for a cloth pad used to handle hot pans. RT: *crutch*. [U.S., BR: 1972]

pot hound a dog trained to sniff out marijuana. See *pot sniffer*. [U.S., (1974): R&P: 1982]

potiguaya See *potaguaya*.

pot knight a drunkard, especially one who is *pot valiant* (*q.v.*). *Cf.* *pot*. RT: *sot*. [late 1500s, F&H, K&M: 1968]

pot likker (also **pot liquor**) a tea brewed from marijuana waste. From a southern term for the fluids in which meat and vegetables have been cooked. [U.S., (1967): DNE: 1973, RRL: 1969, CM: 1970, BR: 1972]

pot lush a heavy smoker of marijuana; a *mariholic* (*q.v.*). RS: *toker*. [U.S., (1969): ELA: 1982]

pot of O. a beer; a pot or pint of beer. Based on *Oh my dear!* (*q.v.*) which is rhyming slang for *beer*. See *top o' reeb*. RT: *beer*. [Br., (1868): JRW: 1909]

pot o' reeb. See *top o' reeb*.

pot out to smoke marijuana; to abandon everything and turn to marijuana use. *Cf.* *pot culture*. RS: *hit the hay*. [U.S., D&B: 1970c]

pot party a communal marijuana smoking session. *Cf.* *kick party*. [U.S., (1967): OEDS, RRL: 1969, D&B: 1970c, W&F: 1975]

potsheen See *poteen*.

pot shot alcohol intoxicated. *Pot* (*q.v.*) = liquor. Shot = exhausted. RT: *drunk*. [1800s, F&H]

pot sick alcohol intoxicated. *Cf.* *pot*. RT: *drunk*. [JF: 1598, F&H; listed in K&M: 1968]

pots, in one's (also **in pots**) alcohol intoxicated. *Cf.* *in one's cups*. RT: *drunk*. [U.S., BVB: 1942, K&M: 1968]

pot sniffer a dog trained to sniff out marijuana. The same as *pot hound* (*q.v.*). See *whiffsniffer*. [U.S., (1970): R&P: 1982]

potster a drunkard. *Cf.* *pot*. RT: *sot*. [listed in F&H]

pot-struck intoxicated with marijuana. RT: *wasted*. [U.S., (1973): R&P: 1982]

potsville under the influence of marijuana. *Cf.* *pot*. RT: *wasted*. [U.S., EEL: 1971, LVA: 1981]

potted 1. (also **potted off, potted up**) alcohol intoxicated. *Pot* (*q.v.*) = to drink heavily. Probably punning on *pot shot* (*q.v.*). RT: *drunk*. Potted off is British (1800s) F&H. [U.S., HJS: 1922, MP: 1928, AH: 1931, MHW: 1934, DCCU: 1972] 2. under the influence of marijuana; drug intoxicated. *Cf.* *pot*. RT: *wasted*. [U.S., (1955): ELA: 1982, W&F: 1960, D&B: 1970c, DCCU: 1972; Br.,

(1956): DSUE]

potted bush hashish. *Bush* = marijuana. *Potted* is used here as in *potted meat,* i.e., preserved in a closed vessel. RT: *hash.* [U.S., JES: 1959, H&C: 1975]

potten bush allegedly hashish. Probably an error for *potted bush* (*q.v.*). [U.S., SNP: 1977]

potulent alcohol intoxicated. *Cf. drunkulent.* RT: *drunk.* [PD: 1982]

pot vague intoxicated with marijuana; disoriented by marijuana. RT: *wasted.* [U.S., (1970): R&P: 1982]

pot valiant (also **pot sure, valiant**) alcohol intoxicated; drunk and fearless. *Cf. pot hardy.* See *courage.* RT: *drunk.* [BE: 1690, F&H, D&D: 1957]

pot walloper a heavy drinker; a drunkard. *Pot* (*q.v.*) = a drinking vessel. LIT: someone who hits the pot hard. RT: *sot.* [Br., 18–1900s, F&H, SSD; listed in BVB: 1942]

pound 1. a pound of marijuana. *Cf. kee.* RS: *load.* [U.S., M&V: 1967, EEL: 1971, ADC: 1975] 2. five-dollars worth of heroin. [U.S., MA: 1973, RDS: 1982]

pound a beer to drink a beer. RS: *irrigate.* [U.S., ADC: 1981]

pound cotton to extract drugs from *cotton* (*q.v.*). [U.S., EEL: 1971]

pounder a police officer. See *beat pounder.* RT: *fuzz.* [U.S., MB: 1938, M&W: 1946, M&H: 1959, CM: 1970]

pour man (also **pour-out man**) a bartender. RT: *bartender.* [U.S., BVB: 1942, DB: 1944]

poverty liquor. RT: *booze.* [mid 1700s, DSUE] See also *royal poverty.*

powder 1. a drink of liquor. From the practice of drinking powdered medicine dissolved in water, as in *take a powder.* RS: *nip.* [U.S., (1921): W&F: 1960, GI: 1931, MHW: 1934] 2. (also **powdered joy**) powdered narcotics; cocaine, heroin, morphine. [U.S., (1920): DU, BVB: 1942, A&T: 1953, NIDA: 1980] (This entry continues after the following list.) Nicknames and slang terms for various kinds of powdered drugs: *alpha powder, Aunt Nora, birdie powder, birdie stuff, Cadillac, chicken powder, deck, Dr. White, dry grog, dust, dust of Morpheus, easing powder, evil powder, fairy powder, flea powder, Florida snow, foo-foo-dust, foolish powder, frisky powder, happy dust, happy flakes, happy powder, heaven dust, heaven flour, heavenly dust, hell dust, joy dust, joy flakes, joy powder, Lady White, mayo, mojo, nieve, nose, nose candy, nose powder, nose stuff, nurse, old lady White, old Steve, old white lady, poison, polvito, powder, powdered joy, racehorse Charley, reindeer dust, resting-powder, salt, snow, snowball, snowflakes, snow stuff, sugar, sweet stuff, white, white merchandise, white mosquitoes, white nurse, white powder, white*

stuff, white tape, wings, witch. 3. finely-textured marijuana. RS: ***pot.*** [U.S., (1954): ELA: 1982, ADC: 1975]

powdered (also **powdered up**) alcohol intoxicated. From ***powder*** (*q.v.*). RT: ***drunk.*** [U.S., GI: 1931, BVB: 1942]

powdered diamond cocaine. So-named, in part, because of its high cost. SNP: 1977 lists **powder diamonds**. RT: ***cocaine.*** [U.S., JES: 1959, M&V: 1973]

powdered joy powdered narcotics of any type. RT: ***powder.*** [U.S., JES: 1959]

powder monkey a drug seller. RT: ***dealer.*** [HSD: 1984]

powder room a place to buy and use powdered narcotics. A play on the name of a small bathroom or a restroom. RS: ***doperie.*** [U.S., JES: 1959, H&C: 1975] See also ***pad.***

powder up to drink heavily; to get drunk. RT: ***mug oneself.*** [U.S., MHW: 1934, BVB: 1942, DU]

power hitter 1. a device for concentrating marijuana smoke. *Cf.* ***pinch hitter.*** RS: ***bong.*** [U.S., ADC: 1981] 2. a person who blows marijuana smoke into someone else's mouth. [U.S., ELA: 1984]

power, in (also **in the power**) having to do with a person who has heroin for sale. RS: ***dealer.*** [U.S., EEL: 1971, JH: 1979]

pox an opium pellet prepared for smoking. A dysphemism based on ***yen-pok*** (*q.v.*). This may represent the plural of ***pok.*** *Cf.* ***pfun.*** RS: ***opium.*** [U.S., BVB: 1942, VJM: 1949, GOL: 1950, A&T: 1953]

P.R. ***Panama red*** (*q.v.*) marijuana. RT: ***pot.*** [U.S., RRL: 1969, EEL: 1971]

prairie dew inferior whiskey; illicit whiskey. *Cf.* ***moonshine, rotgut.*** [U.S., (1848): F&H, (1850-1900): RFA; listed in BVB: 1942]

prayer book a pack or book of cigarette rolling papers. *Cf.* ***Bible.*** RS: ***paper.*** [U.S., BVB: 1942, (1850-1900): RFA]

prels ***Preludin*** (TM; *q.v.*), a central nervous system stimulant. *Cf.* ***ludens, ludins, sweeties.*** [Br., (1963): DSUE]

Preludin a protected trade name for phenmetrazine hydrochloride tablets. The drug is a central nervous system stimulant used in weight-loss therapy. *Cf.* ***ludens, ludins, prels, sweeties.*** [in current use; consult a pharmaceutical reference for more information]

pre-prohi having to do with liquor produced and bottled before national (U.S.) prohibition. *Cf.* ***pre-war stuff.*** From the prohibition era. [U.S., BVB: 1942]

prescription reds ***Seconal*** (TM; *q.v.*) capsules. RT: ***sec.*** Black use. [U.S., EAF: 1980]

prescriptions ethical drugs available only on prescription. Compare to ***over-the-counter.*** Black slang. [U.S., EAF: 1980]

prescription whiskey (also **prescription**) grain alcohol which is available only on prescription during prohibition; whiskey bottled in bond; any liquor. *Cf. medicine.* [U.S., VR: 1929, BVB: 1942]

preserved alcohol intoxicated. *Cf. corned, pickled.* RT: *drunk.* [U.S., MP: 1928, MHW: 1934, W&F: 1960]

pretty well enter'd alcohol intoxicated; entered by much alcohol. *Cf. entered.* RT: *drunk.* [BF: 1722]

pre-war stuff liquor bottled before prohibition; *pre-prohi* (*q.v.*) liquor. From the prohibition era. [U.S., MP: 1928, AH: 1931, MHW: 1934]

prick 1. a hypodermic needle; a hypodermic syringe and needle. An addict is said to be on **pricks**. RT: *monkey pump, needle.* [U.S., JES: 1959, H&C: 1975] 2. to inject drugs. *Cf. shoot.* [U.S., JES: 1959, H&C: 1975] See also *joy prick.* 3. a scar from a hypodermic injection. RT: *tracks.* [U.S., BR: 1972]

pricked-arm a morphine addict. Named for the marks at the sites of injection. RS: *junky.* [U.S., early 1900s, DU]

priddy alcohol intoxicated. Probably akin to *pretty.* RT: *drunk.* [BF: 1737]

primed 1. alcohol intoxicated. *Cf. well-primed.* RT: *drunk.* [Br. and U.S., (1858): SBF: 1976, JCH: 1887, B&L: 1890, MP: 1928, AH: 1931, MHW: 1934, GOL: 1950] 2. drug intoxicated. RT: *stoned.* [U.S., GOL: 1950]

primed to the ears (also **primed to the barrel, primed to the muzzle, primed to the nuts, primed to the trigger**) alcohol intoxicated; drug intoxicated. RT: *drunk, stoned.* [U.S., BVB: 1942, VJM: 1949, GOL: 1950]

primitive having to do with undiluted liquor. RT: *neat.* [Br., B&L: 1890, F&H]

primo (also **el primo**) having to do with top-quality drugs. *Cf. bad, decent, intense, wicked.* [U.S., (1971): ELA: 1982, RRL: 1974, D&B: 1978, (1979): R&P: 1982]

Prince Albert cannabis in general, especially marijuana sold or transported in a Prince Albert (TM) pipe smoking tobacco can. [U.S., 1960s, D&B: 1978]

Prince Eugene alcohol intoxicated. RT: *drunk.* [BF: 1737]

private's butt a very small cigarette butt. See comment at *butt.* RT: *brad.* [U.S., HS: 1933, MHW: 1934]

pro (also **prohi, prohy**) a federal liquor enforcement agent; any supporter of prohibition. From *prohibition agent.* RS: *dry, fuzz.* [U.S., DWM: 1931, MHW: 1934, VJM: 1949, GOL: 1950, W&F: 1960] See also *junkie pro.*

problem drinker an alcoholic. A polite euphemism. RS: *sot.* [U.S., K&M: 1968, RDS: 1982]

Proctor and Gamble paregoric. A reinterpretation of *P.G.* (*q.v.*) = paregoric. RT: *goric.* [U.S., M&V: 1967, H&C: 1975]

prod 1. a hypodermic needle. RT: *needle*. [U.S., BVB: 1942, H&C: 1975] 2. an injection of narcotics. *Cf. prodder*. JES: 1959 also lists prod of joy. RT: *shot*. [U.S., BD: 1937, DWM: 1938, A&T: 1953]

prodder an addict who injects drugs. *Cf. prod*. RT: *bangster*. [U.S., early 1900s, DU, H&C: 1975]

prod, on the injecting narcotics; addicted to narcotics administered by injection. RS: *hooked*. [U.S., BVB: 1942, H&C: 1975]

product IV L.S.D. combined with some other drug, perhaps P.C.P. RS: *set*. [U.S., SNP: 1977, KBH: 1982]

prohi 1. a prohibition agent. See *pro*. [U.S., BVB: 1942] 2. a supporter of prohibition. RT: *dry*. [U.S. (Boontling), (1880–1920): CCA]

prohib a person in favor of prohibition. RS: *dry*. [U.S., BVB: 1942]

prohibition the national prohibition of the sale of alcoholic beverages. National prohibition was established by the passage of the 18th amendment to the U.S. Constitution in 1919, becoming effective in 1920. The amendment was repealed in 1933. Nicknames and slang terms for U.S. national prohibition: *age of pain, alcoholiday, dry era, eighteenth amusement, Methodist hellinium, Prohibition Error*.

Prohibition Error a play on *Prohibition Era*. [U.S., BVB: 1942]

prohy See *pro*.

prop an injection of drugs; a fix. RT: *shot*. [U.S., DWM: 1938, BVB: 1942, A&T: 1953]

propper an amphetamine tablet. From *lid-proppers* (*q.v.* at *lid-poppers*).

prosperity, in one's alcohol intoxicated. RT: *drunk*. [BF: 1737]

pruned alcohol intoxicated. RT: *drunk*. [Br., 1800s, F&H; listed in BVB: 1942]

prune juice hard liquor. Possibly from the disturbance it might cause in one's bowels. See the list at *juice*. RS: *rotgut*. [Br., (1935): DSUE]

pruno a home-brewed wine made of fermented prune juice. *Cf. buck, potato water*. Prison use. [U.S., HS: 1933, MHW: 1934, GOL: 1950, W&F: 1960]

P.S. opium, *Papaver somniferum*, the botanical name for the opium poppy. Probably not argot. RT: *opium*. [U.S., JES: 1959]

psilocybin the hallucinogenic substance contained in the mushroom of the genus *Psilocybe* which contains the hallucinogen psilocybin. The chemical name is Standard English. Its use for the mushroom is drug jargon. [(1958): OEDS, BW: 1984] Nicknames and slang terms for psilocybin and the Psilocybe mushroom: *God's flesh, hombrecitos, las mujercitas, los niños, magic mushrooms, Mexican mushrooms, mushrooms, noble* *princess of the waters, peace pills, peace tab, peace tablet, poison mushrooms, psyl, sacred mushrooms, silly putty, silo, simple Simon, spores.*

P-stuff phencyclidine, *P.C.P.* (*q.v.*), an animal tranquilizer. *Cf. stuff.* RT: *P.C.P.* [U.S., RDS: 1982]

psychedelicatessen (also **psychedeli**) a place where drug supplies are sold, a *head shop* (*q.v.*). Refers to a specific shop in New York City. [U.S., RB: 1967, (1967): DNE: 1973]

psyched out drug intoxicated; alcohol intoxicated. This term is derived from *psychedelic* and is supported by *psycho*. GEN: excited. [U.S., GU: 1975]

psychoactive having to do with a drug which effects perception. *Cf. head drug.* [(1961): OEDS, (1970): DNE: 1973]

psyl *psilocybin* (*q.v.*). RT: *psilocybin*. [U.S., (1971): DNE: 1973]

pub 1. a tavern; a bar; a lounge. A truncation of *public house*. See *public*. RS: *bar*. [Br., JCH: 1859, F&H; Aust., SJB: 1966] 2. to wander from pub to pub; to *pub-crawl* (*q.v.*). [Br., (1889): OED]

pubbing doing a *pub-crawl* (*q.v.*). [HSD: 1984]

pub-crawl 1. to go from tavern to tavern. This is done by a pub-crawler. [Br., 1900s, DSUE; listed in D&D: 1957] 2. an evening spent visiting a large number of pubs. RS: *spree*. [Br., M&J: 1975]

public a tavern; a pub. A truncation of *public house*. [Br., (1709): OED, JCH: 1887, SSD]

publican an alehouse keeper; a keeper of a public house. Currently used (jocularly) for a bartender. RT: *bartender*. [(1728): OED, K&M: 1968]

public bar the lower-class bar in a drinking establishment. In contrast to the fancier saloon bar. RS: *bar*. [Br., 18-1900s, K&M: 1968]

public house a licensed tavern or bar. *Cf. pub.* RS: *bar*. [Br., 17-1900s, (1768): OED, JCH: 1887, F&H]

pub-ornament a tippler; a *bar-fly* (*q.v.*). RT: *sot*. [Br., early 1800s, F&H]

puddle to drink liquor; to tipple. RS: *irrigate*. [Br., 1800s, F&H]

puerco* phencyclidine, *P.C.P.* (*q.v.*), an animal tranquilizer. Spanish for *hog* (*q.v.*). RT: *P.C.P.* [U.S., NIDA: 1980]

puff 1. an opium user or addict. RT: *campfire boy*. [U.S., BVB: 1942, A&T: 1953] 2. (also **puff the dust, puff bamboo**) to smoke opium, marijuana, or hashish. *Cf. dust.* RS: *hit the hay, suck bamboo*. [U.S., BD: 1937, DWM: 1938, RRL: 1969] 3. to get drunk. RT: *mug oneself*. [U.S. Marines, (1930s): DST: 1984]

puffer 1. a cigar. RT: *seegar*. [U.S., (1887): RML: 1950] 2. an opium smoker. RT: *campfire boy*. [U.S., RDS: 1982]

puff the dust to smoke cannabis cigarettes. RT: *hit the hay*. [U.S.,

JES: 1959]

puffy phencyclidine, P.C.P. RT: *P.C.P.* [U.S., ELA: 1984]

pug an addict who fights his own addiction. RS: *junky*. [U.S., BVB: 1942, DU] See also *booze fighter*.

puggled alcohol intoxicated; crazy drunk. *Cf. poggled*. GEN: crazy, exhausted. RT: *drunk*. [Br., F&G: 1925, EP: 1948]

puggy drunk alcohol intoxicated; very drunk. Possibly from *puggy*, the nickname for a fox (DSUE). *Cf. puggled*. RT: *drunk*. [Br., 18-1900s, DSUE]

pukalolo marijuana. Either a misprint or a dysphemism for *pakalolo* (*q.v.*), or a blend of *pakalolo* and *puke* = vomit. RT: *pot*. [U.S., RAS: 1981]

pula a *Seconal* (TM; *q.v.*) barbiturate capsule. Language origin unknown. RT: *sec*. [U.S., SNP: 1977]

pulaski a marijuana smoker. JES: 1959 says this is rhyming slang for *mohasky* (*q.v.*). RT: *toker*. [U.S., JES: 1959, H&C: 1975]

pulboron an error for *polboron* (*q.v.*). [U.S., SNP: 1977]

pull 1. a drink; a swig; a drink from a flask. RT: *nip*. [U.S., BWG: 1899, MHW: 1934] 2. to take a drink or a mouthful of liquor from a bottle or other container. *Cf. suck*. RT: *irrigate*. [1800s, JCH: 1887] See also *pull jive*. 3. a drawing of smoke from a (tobacco or marijuana) cigarette; a drag on a cigarette. [U.S., BVB: 1942, DEM: 1981] 4. to smoke a (tobacco or marijuana) cigarette. [U.S., (1926): W&F: 1960, DEM: 1981]

pull a Daniel Boone (also **pull a shut-eye**) to get drunk. RT: *mug oneself*. [U.S., MHW: 1934, BVB: 1942]

puller 1. a liquor smuggler; a bootlegger. RT: *bootlegger*. [U.S., HNR: 1934] 2. a marijuana smoker. RT: *toker*. [U.S., W&F: 1960]

pull jive to drink liquor. *Cf. pull*. RT: *irrigate*. Black use. [U.S., RDS: 1982] See also *jive*.

pumpkin seed a yellow, football-shaped pill of mescaline. RS: *peyote*. [U.S., EEL: 1971]

pump sucker a teetotaller. Refers to a water pump. RT: *dry*. [Br., (1870): DSUE]

pump up to *bring up* a vein for injection by making a fist repeatedly. [U.S., RG: 1970, EEL: 1971]

puna butter a potent variety of Hawaiian marijuana. *Cf. butter flower*. RS: *pot*. [U.S., RAS: 1981]

pungey alcohol intoxicated. *Cf. sponge, spunge*. RT: *drunk*. [BF: 1737]

punk inferior marijuana. From the name of the stick of soft tinder now used to light fireworks. RS: *pot*. [U.S., D&B: 1978]

punk pills tranquilizers, or possibly *Seconal* (*q.v.*). RT: *tranks*.

[U.S., D&B: 1970c]

punk stuff inferior liquor. RS: ***booze***. [U.S., BVB: 1942]

punta roja* a potent variety of marijuana from Colombia. RT: ***pot***. Spanish for *red point*. [U.S., (1978): ELA: 1982]

pure 1. having to do with undiluted liquor. RT: ***neat***. [Br., 1800s, F&H] 2. pure or nearly pure heroin; very potent narcotics. *Cf.* ***P***. RS: ***heroin***. [U.S., JBW: 1967, RRL: 1969, RG: 1970]

pure love the hallucinogenic drug ***L.S.D.*** (*q.v.*). *Cf.* ***wedding bells acid***. RT: ***L.S.D.*** [U.S., SNP: 1977]

purge beer; bad beer. Named for what it does to the bowels. RT: ***queer-beer***. [Br., late 1800s, F&H]

purger a teetotaller. RT: ***dry***. [Br., (c. 1864): F&H]

puris naturalibus, in having to do with undiluted liquor. LIT: naked. RT: ***neat***. [Br., B&L: 1890, F&H]

purple 1. ***Zacatecas purple*** (*q.v.*) marijuana. RT: ***pot***. [U.S., RRL: 1969] 2. the hallucinogenic drug ***L.S.D.*** (*q.v.*). See ***purple Owsley***. RT: ***L.S.D.*** [U.S., RRL: 1969, EEL: 1971]

purple haze See ***purple Owsley***.

purple hearts tablets of ***Luminal*** (TM; *q.v.*) or ***Drinamyl*** (TM; *q.v.*) amphetamines and barbiturates; various amphetamines. DSUE says it is ***Dexedrine*** (TM; *q.v.*). Probably akin to the military award of the same name or to drug use during WWII. RT: ***amps, barbs***. [U.S., W&F: 1967, RRL: 1969, DNE: 1973, RDS: 1982; Br., (1960): DSUE, BTD: 1968, M&J: 1975]

purple Owsley (also **purple, purple barrels, purple dot, purple dragon, purple flats, purple haze, purple microdots, purple ozolin, purple ozoline, purple ozzy, purple wedges**) ***L.S.D.*** (*q.v.*); a purplish variety of pure and powerful L.S.D.; a mixture of L.S.D. and ***Methedrine*** (TM; *q.v.*). RT: ***L.S.D.*** [U.S., RG: 1970, EEL: 1971, E&R: 1971, DES: 1972, S&R: 1972, ADC: 1975, SNP: 1977, ADC: 1981, JWK: 1981, KBH: 1982; Canadian, MMO: 1970]

purple passion pills combining a stimulant and a depressant. Probably the same as ***purple hearts*** (*q.v.*). RS: ***set***. [U.S., H&C: 1975, SNP: 1977]

purring (also **purring like a cat**) having to do with a drug user who has taken just enough of a drug for a state of euphoria. *Cf.* ***coasting, floating***. Borrowed from colloquial use. [U.S., DWM: 1936, BVB: 1942]

push to recruit new drug users and sell drugs to them; to deal in drugs. *Cf.* ***move, pitch, shove***. [U.S., DWM: 1938, BVB: 1942, (1949): W&F: 1960, RRL: 1969, CM: 1970, EEL: 1971] Terms meaning to actively recruit drug users and sell them drugs: ***deal, hustle, move, pitch, push, shove, shove shorts, swing, twirl***.

pushed 1. alcohol intoxicated. A current U.S. version is pushed out (EEL: 1971). RT: ***drunk***. [Br., 1800s, F&H] 2. addicted to a drug. RT: *hooked*. [U.S., JES: 1959]

pusher a drug dealer who works hard to establish new addicts and customers. Now widely known outside drug argot. [U.S., (1935): OEDS, BD: 1937, (1951): M&D: 1952, A&T: 1953, M&H: 1959, RRL: 1969, CM: 1970, EEL: 1971, DCCU: 1972, ADC: 1975, JH: 1979; Br., (1955): DSUE, PW: 1974] Nicknames and slang terms for someone who attempts to recruit drug users as customers: *arreador, broker, candy man, cop man, C-pusher, dope booster, dope pimp, drug booster, good time man, grog merchant, hooker, junker, junk peddler, junk pusher, junky, missionary, mooch pusher, pusher, quarter master, shover, snowbird, street pusher, the man, turner, vendador.*

pushing Emma addicted to morphine. Compare to *push*. *Cf. Aunt Emma*. RS: *hooked*. [U.S., H&C: 1975]

push muggles to sell or peddle marijuana. *Muggles* (*q.v.*) = marijuana. *Cf. push*. [U.S., GOL: 1950]

push powder (also **push schmeck**) to sell powdered narcotics. *Powder* (*q.v.*) = powdered narcotics. *Schmeck* (*q.v.*) = heroin. [U.S., DU, GOL: 1950; Br. (1955): DSUE]

push shorts to sell drugs in small amounts, presumably at the retail level; to sell less drugs than specified, i.e., to cheat someone in a drug sale. [U.S., BD: 1937, DWM: 1938, BVB: 1942]

pussyfoot (also **pussyfooter**) a prohibitionist. Implies weakness or effeminacy on the part of non-drinkers. RT: *dry*. [U.S., BVB: 1942]

puti* *methaqualone* (*q.v.*), a hypnotic-sedative. RT: *ludes*. Origin unknown. [U.S., SNP: 1977]

put it down to break a drug addiction. RT: *kick*. [U.S., H&C: 1975, M&V: 1973]

put it on paper (also **put it in writing**) to saturate a postcard with drugs in order to smuggle drugs into a prison or a hospital. *Cf. paper*. [U.S., M&V: 1967, RRL: 1969]

Put me straight! "Sell me drugs!" RT: *How are you going to act?* [U.S., BVB: 1953, JES: 1959]

put on a circus to fake a drug withdrawal spasm. RS: *brody*. [U.S., (1920): DU, JES: 1959]

put oneself straight to take a needed dose of drugs. *Cf. straight*. [U.S., (M&D: 1952), (BVB: 1953)]

putrid alcohol intoxicated. A play on *rotten* (*q.v.*). RT: *drunk*. [PD: 1982]

put somebody on to introduce someone to cannabis use, usually smoking. *Cf. turn someone*. [U.S., M&W: 1946]

put to bed with a shovel alcohol intoxicated. GEN: to be buried (at death) FG: 1785. RT: *drunk*. [U.S., W&F: 1960, AP: 1980]

put to the mouth to eat or drink narcotics which could otherwise be used as evidence. *Cf. scarf a joint, scoff.* [U.S., HB: 1955]

pye-eyed alcohol intoxicated. The same as *pie-eyed* (*q.v.*). RT: *drunk.* [U.S., MHW: 1934]

Pyribenzamine a protected trade name for tripelennamine (antihistamine) available in a variety of forms. The drug is used in the treatment of allergy and a variety of other conditions. It is currently taken mixed with *Talwin* (TM; *q.v.*). Slang and jargon terms for this drug are usually found to include Talwin (TM). See *T.s and blues* for a list. [(1946): OEDS; in current use; consult a pharmaceutical reference for more information]

Q

Q. 1. a quart bottle of liquor. A disguise for *quart*. *Cf. gal.* [U.S., BVB: 1942] 2. (also Q.s) *Quaalude* (TM; *q.v.*) brand of *methaqualone* (*q.v.*), a hypnotic-sedative. RT: *ludes*. [U.S., SNP: 1977, JWK: 1981] 3. the quality of a drug. [U.S., JH: 1979]

Q. and Q. (also Q. & Q.) the quality and quantity of a drug. [U.S., JH: 1979]

Q.B. a cigarette; a "quick butt." RT: *nail*. High school use. [U.S., RAS: 1985]

Q.T. an illicit liquor establishment. From *quiet* and the expression *on the Q.T.* A play on *speakeasy*. RT: *speak*. From the prohibition era. [U.S., BVB: 1942]

quaal See *quads*.

Quaalude a protected trade name for *methaqualone* (*q.v.*) nonbarbiturate sedative-hypnotic tablets. The full trademarked logo includes macrons over the "aa" indicating the pronunciation kway-lood. The drug is a central nervous system depressant. Slang and jargon terms are usually based on the first or second syllable of the drug name. But see *seven-fourteens*. Slang and jargon terms for methaqualone are also based on another trade name Sopor (TM), or the name methaqualone itself. See *ludes* for a list of methaqualone terms, including Sopor (TM) and Quaalude (TM) terms. [(1966): OEDS; in current use; consult a pharmaceutical reference for more information]

quack a physician; a fake physician. RS: *croaker*. [1900s, (1919): OEDS]

quacks *Quaalude* (TM; *q.v.*) *methaqualone* (*q.v.*), a hypnotic-sedative. RT: *ludes*. [U.S., YKB: 1977, DEM: 1981]

quads (also quaal) *Quaalude* (TM; *q.v.*) *methaqualone* (*q.v.*), hypnotic-sedative tablets. RT: *ludes*. [U.S., (1973): DNE: 1980, YKB: 1977]

quaffer a drunkard; an alcoholic. From *quaff* = to drink. RT: *sot*. [U.S., RDS: 1982]

quality Joe a nonaddict. JES: 1959 also lists quality folks. RT: *square*. [U.S., JES: 1959, H&C: 1975]

quarrelsome alcohol intoxicated and in a bad humor. *Cf.*

quick-tempered. RT: *drunk*. [BF: 1737]

quarry cure See *rock pile cure*.

quarter bag (also **quarters**) a twenty-five dollar bag of drugs; one-quarter ounce of heroin or morphine. RS: *load*. [U.S., RB: 1967, RRL: 1969, D&B: 1970c, EAF: 1980, JWK: 1981]

quarter master a drug pusher; a master of the *quarter bag* (*q.v.*). RS: *dealer*. [U.S., JES: 1959, H&C: 1975]

quarter moon hashish. *Cf. half moons, moon*. RT: *hash*. [U.S., YKB: 1977, NIDA: 1980]

quartern o' bry gin; a quart of gin. From *Brian O'Linn* (*q.v.*) which is rhyming slang for *gin*. RT: *gin*. [Br., (1868): JRW: 1909]

quartern o' finger rum; a quart of rum. From *finger and thumb* which is rhyming slang for *rum*. RT: *rum*. [Br., (1868): JRW: 1909]

quarter piece a portion of drugs, one quarter of an ounce of powdered drugs. See *quarter bag*. RS: *load*. [U.S., DWM: 1938, JES: 1959]

quarter pot a drunkard. RT: *sot*. [U.S., M&B: 1944]

quarters See *quarter bag*.

quartet the four drugs morphine, cocaine, heroin, and opium. RS: *set*. [U.S., JES: 1959]

quart-mania the delirium tremens; sickness from drink. RT: *D.T.s*. [Br., B&L: 1890, F&H]

quartzed alcohol intoxicated. Probably a play on *quarts* or a play on *stoned* (*q.v.*). RT: *drunk*. [PD: 1982]

quas *Quaalude* (TM; *q.v.*) brand of *methaqualone* (*q.v.*) tablets. RT: *ludes*. [U.S., YKB: 1977, RDS: 1982]

Queen of Scotch a (male) homosexual drunkard. A play on *Mary Queen of Scots*. RS: *sot*. Attested as gay slang. [U.S., BR: 1972]

queer 1. illicit liquor, especially whiskey. RS: *moonshine*. From the prohibition era. [U.S., BVB: 1942] 2. alcohol intoxicated. RT: *drunk*. [Br. and U.S., SSD, BVB: 1942] 3. bogus or inferior drugs. GEN: counterfeit (1740): OEDS. RS: *blank*. [U.S., H&C: 1975]

queer-beer bad beer; beer of low alcohol content. *Cf. near-beer*. [U.S., EE: 1976] Nicknames and slang terms for bad beer: *army brew, beer-a-bumble, belch, belly vengeance, bilge water, bumclink, chalk, choc, clink, down, hogwash, legs and arms, muddy water, near-beer, Oh my!, Oh my dear!, pish, piss, purge, queer-beer, queer belch, queer bub, queer lap, rot, rotgut, sheep-dip, sheep-wash, shypoo, sissy beer, slip-slop, slop, slops, small beer, squaw piss, squirt, strike-me-dead, swipes, tanglefoot, tangleleg, three-two, tiger piss, water-bewitched, whip-belly, whip-belly vengeance, whistle-belly vengeance, wish-wash, witch piss.*

queer belch bad beer; sour beer. *Cf. berps*. RT: *queer-beer*. [Br., (1848): DSUE]

queer booze bad beverage alcohol. RS: *queer-beer, rotgut.* [TH: 1567, DSUE]

queer bub (also **queer lap**) inferior beverage alcohol. RS: *rotgut, queer-beer.* [17-1800s, DU]

queered alcohol intoxicated. *Cf. queer.* RT: *drunk.* [Br., (1822): DSUE; listed in BVB: 1942]

quencher a drink of liquor. RT: *nip.* [Br., (1840): DSUE, (1901): F&H; MHW: 1934, BVB: 1942]

quick one (also **quickie, quicky**) a quick drink of liquor; a small drink of liquor; a single beer consumed rapidly. RT: *nip.* [(1910): DSUE, EP: 1948, SSD, SJB: 1966, DCCU: 1972]

quicksilver *L.S.D.* (*q.v.*) combined with some other drug. RS: *set.* [U.S., KBH: 1982]

quick-tempered alcohol intoxicated. *Cf. quarrelsome.* RT: *drunk.* [Br., 1800s, F&H]

quid a mouthful or *cud* of tobacco. [Br., FG: 1823, JCH: 1887, EP: 1948] See *fogus* for general terms for tobacco. Nicknames and slang terms for a hunk of tobacco: *bacca chew, bit o' beef, bootlace, chaw, chaw tobacco, chew, cud, dip, flick of tobacco, kanger, kangeroo, light food, oil, old soldier, piece of thick, pigtail, plug, quid, screw, spit-quick-or-puke, twist, wing.*

quill 1. (also **quin**) genuine whiskey; pre-prohibition whiskey. RS: *whiskey.* From the prohibition era. [U.S., 1920s, BVB: 1942, VJM: 1949] 2. a folded matchbook cover used to inhale (snort) drugs, usually cocaine. [U.S., JBW: 1967, RRL: 1969, CM: 1970, EEL: 1971, ADC: 1975, W&F: 1975]

quirley (also **quirlie, quirly**) a tobacco cigarette. *Cf. twirlie.* RT: *nail.* [Aust., (1930): DSUE, SJB: 1966; U.S., (1932): OEDS, (1940): ADD]

quisby alcohol intoxicated. GEN: strange, queer. RT: *drunk.* [1800s, F&H]

quitter a person who has quit drug use. GEN: someone who gives up easy. [U.S., H&C: 1975]

R

rabbit a bottle of beer; a container of (or for) liquor. [Aust., (1895): OEDS, SJB: 1945]

racehorse a long, thin tobacco cigarette. RS: *nail*. [Aust., (1930): DSUE] See *thoroughbred*.

racehorse Charley 1. heroin; any powdered drug. *Cf. horse* of which this is an elaboration. JES: 1959 defines this as morphine. RT: *heroin*. [U.S., DWM: 1936, BVB: 1942, A&T: 1953] 2. a morphine user. RS: *junky*. [U.S., JES: 1959, H&C: 1975]

rack a group of 3–5 pills which are to be taken at once. Probably from billiards. *Cf. drop a rack* (at *drop a roll*). RS: *load*. Black use. [U.S., EAF: 1980]

racked (also **racked up**) 1. alcohol intoxicated. RT: *drunk*. [U.S., ADC: 1975] 2. under the effects of marijuana. RT: *wasted*. [U.S., ADC: 1975]

rack up to get drunk. *Cf. racked*. RT: *mug oneself*. [U.S., D&B: 1970c]

raddled alcohol intoxicated. **Raddled** = reddened. RT: *drunk*. [BF: 1737, F&H; listed in BVB: 1942]

ragged alcohol intoxicated. RT: *drunk*. [BF: 1737]

Raggedy Ann L.S.D. solution on blotter paper stamped with the image of the character Raggedy Ann. RT: *L.S.D.* [U.S., ELA: 1984]

rag water gin; liquor, possibly inferior liquor. Because it will reduce you to rags. *Cf. ragged*. RS: *booze*. [cant, BE: 1690, FG: 1785, FG: 1788, FG: 1811, FG: 1823, GWM: 1859]

ragweed inferior marijuana; marijuana. RT: *pot*. [U.S., RRL: 1969, BR: 1972, ADC: 1975]

railroad 1. whiskey; Scotch whiskey. RT: *whiskey*. [U.S., 1800s, F&H] See also *railroad whiskey*. 2. *railroad tracks* (*q.v.*).

railroader a drug user who injects intravenously. *Cf. railroad tracks*. RT: *bangster*. [U.S., BR: 1972]

railroad tracks (also **railroad**) rows of needle scars along the median cephalic veins of the arms. A sign of drug addiction through hypodermic injection. RT: *tracks*. [U.S., JWK: 1981]

railroad weed inferior marijuana. Refers to weeds which grow along railroad tracks. RS: *pot.* [U.S., C&H: 1974, SNP: 1977]

railroad whiskey cheap wine; Santa Fe brand wine. RS: *wine.* Black use. [U.S., EAF: 1980]

rails lines of cocaine. See *line.* RS: *dose.* [U.S., ADC: 1984, S&F: 1984]

rainbow roll a mixture of various colored barbiturates. Probably the same as *rainbows* (*q.v.*), i.e., Tuinal (TM). [U.S., M&V: 1967, H&C: 1975]

rainbows *Tuinal* (TM; *q.v.*) barbiturate capsules. The tops are red, the bottoms are blue, and the overlap of top and bottom is purple. RS: *barbs.* [U.S., JBW: 1967, RRL: 1969, D&B: 1970c, ADC: 1975, MW: 1976, EAF: 1980]

rain in Spain tequila. [U.S., EE: 1976]

rainy-day woman marijuana. RT: *pot.* [U.S., RRL: 1969, RG: 1970, ADC: 1975, JH: 1979]

raised alcohol intoxicated. (BF: 1737: [He's] Rais'd.) *Cf. elevated.* RT: *drunk.* [BF: 1737]

raise hell to go on a drinking spree and get drunk. GEN: to act in a wild manner; to make trouble. RT: *mug oneself.* [U.S., BVB: 1942, W&F: 1960]

raise one's elbow to take a drink of liquor. *Cf. bend one's elbow.* RT: *irrigate.* [Br., SSD, M&J: 1975]

raisinjack alcohol made from fermented raisins. *Cf. buck, potato water, pruno.* RS: *moonshine.* Prison use. [U.S., RDS: 1982]

rally 1. a party; a drinking party. RS: *spree.* [U.S., D&B: 1970c] 2. to hold a drinking party. [U.S., D&B: 1970c]

rama* marijuana. The Spanish word for branch. RT: *pot.* [U.S., EEL: 1971, JH: 1979]

rammaged alcohol intoxicated. RT: *drunk.* [17-1800s, F&H]

ramping mad alcohol intoxicated; wildly drunk. RT: *drunk.* [U.S., B&L: 1890, F&H]

rams, the the delirium tremens. RT: *D.T.s.* [Br., 1800s, F&H]

rangoon "bush cannabis" (BTD: 1968), probably wild marijuana. RT: *pot.* [Br., BTD: 1968, HSD: 1984]

rantan a drinking bout. RT: *spree.* [(1853): OED, JCH: 1887, BVB: 1942, D&D: 1957]

rantan, on the on a drinking bout; drunk. *Cf. rantan.* RT: *spreeing.* [(1853): OED, B&L: 1890, F&H, BVB: 1942, SSD]

rare 1. a drinking bout. RT: *spree.* [Aust., SJB: 1966] 2. to sniff (snort) heroin or cocaine. IGA: 1971 says "inhale through the mouth." The example found in M&D: 1952 is "Take it rare..." indicating adverbial usage. This *rare* may refer to uncooked (see *cook*) powdered narcotics which are snorted rather than injected.

RT: *snort*. [U.S., VJM: 1949, M&D: 1952, EEL: 1971, JH: 1979] See also *rear of snoose*. 3. a dose of cocaine or other powdered drug taken nasally. *Cf. snort*. [U.S., VJM: 1949]

rare form, in alcohol intoxicated. GEN: in a special or unusual state. RT: *drunk*. [U.S., RAS: 1985]

rare lapper a drunkard. *Cf. rare*. RT: *sot*. [Br., JCH: 1887, F&H]

raspberry an abscessed injection site. *Cf. Ab*. [U.S., M&V: 1967, H&C: 1975] See also *strawberry*.

rations (also **ration**) a dose of drugs; a stash of drugs; an injection of drugs. RS: *dope*. [U.S., DWM: 1933, MHW: 1934, VJM: 1949]

rat poison inferior liquor. *Cf. poison*. RS: *rotgut*. [U.S., BVB: 1942]

rats, the the delirium tremens. RT: *D.T.s*. [Br., mid 18-1900s, F&H, SSD]

rat-tail cure ending addiction to a drug by tapering off. Refers to a (tapered) rat-tail file. [U.S., JES: 1959, H&C: 1975]

rattle-belly pop (also **rattle-blank pop**) a mixture of whiskey and lemonade (a soft drink). The *also* is a jocular parody of the main entry, avoiding the *belly*. [JRW: 1909, MHW: 1934, BVB: 1942]

rattled (also **slightly rattled**) alcohol intoxicated. GEN: confused (1905): OEDS. Compare to *raddled*. RT: *drunk*. [Br., 18-1900s, F&H, DSUE; listed in BVB: 1942]

rat-track whiskey very potent whiskey. Rat-track = rat dung. RS: *rotgut*. [U.S., VR: 1929]

ratty alcohol intoxicated. RT: *drunk*. [U.S., BVB: 1942] See also *like a rat in trouble*.

raunchy (also **ronchie**) alcohol intoxicated; rude and drunk. GEN: rude, loud. RT: *drunk*. Student use (W&F: 1960). [U.S., W&F: 1960]

raw 1. having to do with undiluted liquor. RT: *neat*. [Br., OED, B&L: 1890, F&H] 2. having to do with unaged whiskey, straight from the still. [18-1900s, NW: 1828, (1830): OED]

raw and ripe a tobacco pipe. Rhyming slang for *pipe*. [U.S., M&B: 1944, DRS]

raw recruit a drink of undiluted liquor. *Raw* (*q.v.*) = undiluted. RT: *nip*. [Br., late 1800s, F&H]

razee (also **razzee**) a drinking bout; a wild party. RT: *spree*. [U.S., LWP: 1908, BVB: 1942]

razors inferior liquor. Perhaps something with which to get *cut* (*q.v.*) = drunk. RS: *rotgut*. [Br. army, late 18-1900s, DSUE; listed in BVB: 1942]

razzle-dazzle a drinking bout. GEN: glitter, excitement. RT: *spree*. [Br. and U.S., MHW: 1934, SSD]

razzle, on the on a drinking bout. See the previous entry. RT:

spreeing. [Br., (1915): OEDS, SSD]

R.D. (also **R.D.s**) a capsule of *Seconal* (TM; *q.v.*) barbiturate, a "red devil." *Cf. red devils*. RT: *sec*. [U.S., EEL: 1971, H&C: 1975, RDS: 1982]

reader a prescription for narcotics. *Cf. paper, per, script*. GEN: a written document or a piece of paper (in cant). [U.S., DWM: 1936, BVB: 1942, RRL: 1969, W&F: 1975, JH: 1979]

read the tea leaves to smoke marijuana. RT: *hit the hay*. [U.S., BR: 1972]

ready-mades (also **ready-rolls**) factory-made cigarettes (as opposed to do-it-yourself cigarettes). *Cf. tailor-mades*. RS: *nail*. [U.S., since the late 1800s, PW: 1977]

real A.V. (also **real goods**) genuine liquor made before the days of prohibition. The A.V. is "ante-Volstead" (act). From the prohibition era. [U.S., MP: 1928, MHW: 1934]

real McCoy, the (also **real mokoy, real stuff, McCoy, the real thing**) genuine whiskey; pre-prohibition whiskey or other liquor. *Cf. real A.V., the clear McCoy*. From the prohibition era except *the real thing* which is from the 1800s, F&H. Can now refer to anything which is authentic. [U.S., MHW: 1934, BVB: 1942]

reaper a marijuana cigarette. From *reefer* (*q.v.*). RT: *joint*. [U.S., D&B: 1970c]

rear of snoose a pinch of *snuff* (*q.v.*). *Cf. rare*. [U.S., JS: 1925, BVB: 1942]

red 1. cheap red wine. *Cf. red ned*. RS: *wine*. [Aust., SJB: 1943; listed in BVB: 1942] 2. rye whiskey. *Cf. redeye*. RS: *whiskey*. [U.S., BVB: 1942] 3. Panama red marijuana; any red marijuana. *Cf. Acapulco red, Cambodian red, Colombian red, Jamaican red, Lebanese red, Lebanon red, Panama red, Panamanian red, red dirt marijuana, redbud, red gunyon*. Others are listed at *pot*. [U.S., RRL: 1969, EEL: 1971, ADC: 1975] 4. (also **reds**) *Seconal* (TM; *q.v.*) barbiturate capsules; Seconal (TM) in general. From the color of the capsule. RT: *sec*. [U.S., (1966): DNE: 1980, RRL: 1969, DCCU: 1972, ADC: 1975, NIDA: 1980, JWK: 1981]

red and blues (also **blue and reds, reds and blues**) *Tuinal* (TM; *q.v.*) barbiturate capsules. From their red and blue colors. RS: *barbs*. [U.S., RRL: 1969, EEL: 1971, YKB: 1977]

red angelfish a bit of blotter impregnated with *L.S.D.* (*q.v.*) and stamped with the image of a red angelfish. RT: *L.S.D.* [U.S., ADC: 1981]

red biddy 1. (also **redders**) cheap red wine. RS: *wine*. *Cf. red*. [Br. (1920): DSUE, K&M: 1968] 2. methyl alcohol; red wine mixed with methyl alcohol. Methyl alcohol was dyed pink to distinguish it from drinkable (ethyl) alcohol. *Cf. pinky*. RT: *methyl*. [Br., (1910): DSUE, K&M: 1968]

redbirds *Seconal* (TM; *q.v.*) barbiturate capsules. RT: *sec*. [U.S.,

M&V: 1954, RRL: 1969, DCCU: 1972, ADC: 1975, YKB: 1977] See also *blackbirds, bluebirds, speckled birds.*

red bread the blood of a drug addict, a wino, or an alcoholic sold (to a blood bank) to obtain money for drugs or booze. Bread = money. The practice is older than the term. [U.S., EEL: 1971]

redbud potent red marijuana; marijuana with the red hairs of the flower buds. *Cf. red.* RS: *pot.* [U.S., ADC: 1975, ADC: 1981]

red bullets *Seconal* (TM; *q.v.*) barbiturate capsules. *Cf. red.* RT: *sec.* [U.S., IGA: 1971, NIDA: 1980]

red chicken Chinese heroin. *Cf. red rock.* RS: *heroin.* [U.S., RRL: 1969, (1970): DNE: 1980]

red cross (also **red cross M.**) morphine. Compare to *white cross* = cocaine. RT: *morphine.* [U.S., WHW: 1922, GI: 1931, MHW: 1934, VJM: 1949, A&T: 1953; Br., DSUE]

redders See *red biddy.*

red devils (also **R.D.**) capsules of *Seconal* (TM; *q.v.*) barbiturate. RT: *sec.* [U.S., GS: 1959, JBW: 1967, RRL: 1969, DCCU: 1972, ADC: 1975, W&F: 1975, MW: 1976, EAF: 1980]

red dimple *L.S.D.* (*q.v.*) combined with some other drug. RS: *set.* [U.S., KBH: 1982]

red dirt marijuana marijuana growing in the wild. *Cf. mud-bud.* RS: *pot.* [U.S., (1960): ELA: 1982, RRL: 1969, EEL: 1971, D&B: 1978]

red disturbance whiskey; inferior whiskey. *Cf. red.* RT: *whiskey.* [U.S., (1850–1900): RFA, (c. 1900): DST: 1984]

red dolls *Seconal* (TM; *q.v.*) barbiturate capsules. *Cf. dolls.* RT: *sec.* [U.S., SNP: 1977, W&S: 1977]

red dot a tablet of L.S.D. with a red dot; a red tablet of *L.S.D.* *Cf. blue dot, brown dots, dots, green dot, microdot.* RS: *L.S.D.* [U.S., ADC: 1981]

red dragon a bit of white blotter impregnated with *L.S.D.* (*q.v.*) and stamped with the image of a red dragon. RT: *L.S.D.* [U.S., ADC: 1981]

redeye (also **redhead, red liquor**) whiskey; strong whiskey; inferior whiskey. A nickname for any whiskey during prohibition. *Cf. old redeye.* F&H also list **redhead**. RT: *rotgut, whiskey.* [U.S., (1819): DA, JSF: 1889, BWG: 1899, EK: 1927, MP: 1928, VR: 1929, AH: 1931, GI: 1931, D&D: 1957, K&M: 1968]

red fustian red wine: port, claret, etc.; porter. LIT: red cloth. *Cf. fustian.* RS: *wine.* [cant, BE: 1690, FG: 1785, FG: 1811, FG: 1823, GWM: 1859, B&L: 1890, F&H]

red gunyon a particular type of (reddish) marijuana or hashish which is smoked in a water pipe. The term is akin to *black gungeon, black gungi, black gunion, black gunnion, black gunny.* *Cf. ganjah.* See *red* for a list of the various types of red marijuana. RS: *pot*. [U.S., M&V: 1973, ELA: 1982]

red ink cheap red wine; homemade red wine. *Ink* (*q.v.*) = cheap red wine. RS: *wine*. [Br. and U.S., (1918): JL: 1972, (WWI): F&G: 1925, EK: 1927, MHW: 1934, VJM: 1949, D&D: 1957, W&F: 1960]

red jackets (also **red lillys**) Capsules of *Seconal* (TM; *q.v.*) barbiturate. *Lillys* (*q.v.*) = Seconal (TM). *Cf. yellow jackets*. RT: *sec*. [U.S., EEL: 1971, ADC: 1975]

red leb (also **red Lebanese**) a potent variety of cannabis from Lebanon. The same as *Lebanese red* (*q.v.*). RT: *hash*. [U.S., ELA: 1982]

red ned (also **red**) cheap red wine. RT: *wine*. [Aust. and New Zealand, SJB: 1943]

red nugget (also **red onion**) an illicit saloon. RS: *dive*. From the prohibition era. [U.S., MHW: 1934, BVB: 1942]

red oil an alcohol extract of hashish. *Cf. red*. RT: *oil*. [U.S., EEL: 1971, YKB: 1977, RDS: 1982]

red ribbon (also **red ribbin**) brandy; port; porter. *Cf. red tape*. Compare to *blue ribbon*. [cant, FG: 1811, FG: 1823, GWM: 1859, B&L: 1890, JSF: 1889; listed in BVB: 1942]

red rock (also **rock**) a granular form of heroin from China. *Cf. red chicken*. RS: *heroin*. [U.S., RRL: 1969, SNP: 1977]

red ruin strong liquor. Probably a play on *blue ruin* (*q.v.*). *Cf. red, redeye, red ribbon*. RS: *rotgut*. [U.S., BVB: 1942, DST: 1984]

reds and blues See *blues and reds*.

red-smoker opium. RT: *opium*. [U.S., (M&V: 1954)]

red steer a beer. Rhyming slang for *beer*. RT: *beer*. [U.S., M&B: 1944, DRS]

red tape brandy; strong liquor. [cant, FG: 1785, B&L: 1890]

red tea liquor. *Cf. pink tea*. RT: *booze*. [U.S., (1887): RML: 1950, W&F: 1960]

reeb beer. This is *beer* spelled backwards. See *top o' reeb*. RT: *beer*. [Br., JCH: 1859; U.S., MHW: 1934]

reef marijuana; a marijuana cigarette. Perhaps a back formation of *reefer* (*q.v.*). RT: *pot*. [U.S., ADC: 1975, JWK: 1981]

reefdogger a marijuana cigarette. *Cf. dog, dog end*. RT: *joint*. [U.S., BR: 1972]

reefer 1. cannabis; a marijuana cigarette; a cigarette made completely of marijuana. Akin to *grefa* (*q.v.*). [U.S., (1931): OEDS, DWM: 1936, RPW: 1938, M&D: 1952, M&H: 1959, W&F: 1960, TRG: 1968, RRL: 1969, CM: 1970, EEL: 1971, DCCU: 1972, ADC: 1975, ADC: 1981] 2. a smoker of marijuana. RT: *toker*. Not common. [U.S., W&F: 1960] 3. a drug; a narcotic. RT: *dope*. [U.S., DB: 1944] 4. a cigarette. RT: *nail*. [U.S., DB: 1944]

reefer butt a marijuana cigarette butt, a *roach* (*q.v.*). RT: *roach*. [U.S., RDS: 1982]

reefer man (also **reefer hound, reefing man**) a marijuana smoker; a marijuana seller. RT: *dealer*. [U.S., (1932): OEDS, DWM: 1936, (1948): ELA: 1982]

reefer weed marijuana; a marijuana cigarette. *Reefer* (*q.v.*) = marijuana cigarette. RT: *pot*. [U.S., D&D: 1957, W&F: 1960]

reeking alcohol intoxicated; *stinking drunk* (*q.v.*). RT: *drunk*. [U.S., S&E: 1981]

reeler 1. a drinking bout. RT: *spree*. [Br., (1937): OEDS, DSUE; U.S., W&F: 1960] 2. a drunkard. To reel = to stagger. RT: *sot*. [Br., late 1800s, DU]

reeling ripe (also **reeling, reely**) alcohol intoxicated. This seems to be, but is not, rhyming slang. Reeling = staggering. *Ripe* (*q.v.*) = drunk. RT: *drunk*. [Br., late 1800s, F&H, (1933): DSUE; U.S., BVB: 1942]

re-entry the return from a drug trip. *Cf. come down*. [U.S., EEL: 1971, W&F: 1975]

ree-raw, on the (also **on the re-raw**) alcohol intoxicated. *Ree-raw* = *spree* (*q.v.*). RT: *drunk*. [Br., (1854): F&H, (Dickens)]

re-fix (also **re-up**) to get (another) dose of drugs; to take a *fix* (*q.v.*) when one needs one badly. [U.S., JWK: 1981]

refresher a drink of liquor. RT: *nip*. [(1822): OED; listed in BVB: 1942]

refreshery a bar; a place to buy a drink of liquor. RS: *bar*. [U.S., BVB: 1942]

reg regular quality marijuana. *Cf. Mexican commercial*. RS: *pot*. [U.S., S&W: 1973]

register in injecting drugs, to verify that the needle tip is in a vein by pulling a bit of blood back into the syringe or medicine dropper. *Cf. back up, home, score*. [U.S., DWM: 1938, BVB: 1942, D&B: 1970c, EEL: 1971]

rehash to reuse the cotton used in straining drugs for injection. The drug is later extracted from the cotton and injected. Straining cotton is saved up for this purpose. See *ask for cotton*. [U.S., M&V: 1954]

reindeer dust powdered narcotics: cocaine, heroin, morphine, especially cocaine. A play on *snow* (*q.v.*) = cocaine. RT: *powder*. [U.S., BVB: 1942, VJM: 1949, GOL: 1950, A&T: 1953]

religious alcohol intoxicated. RT: *drunk*. [BF: 1737]

repealer a person in favor of the repeal of prohibition. Compare to *dry*. [U.S., AH: 1931]

repeal milk liquor; liquor available after the repeal of prohibition. RT: *booze*. From the prohibition era. [U.S., BVB: 1942]

reposer a drink of liquor taken before retiring; a *nightcap* (*q.v.*).

RS: *nip*. [Br., (1870): DSUE]

rerun alky (also **rerun**) redistilled denatured alcohol. Most of the adulterants are left behind in a careful distillation. RS: *moonshine, rotgut*. From the prohibition era. [U.S., BVB: 1942, GOL: 1950]

resin 1. liquor given to musicians playing at parties. (The word is **rosin** in the U.S.) Based on the string players' need to rosin their bows in order to play. See *rosin*. RS: *booze*. [Aust., 1900s, DSUE] 2. (also **resins**) the sticky substance found predominately in female cannabis plants. It is sought because it contains more of the active principle of marijuana. See sense three. [U.S., ADC: 1975, JWK: 1981] 3. *T.H.C.* (*q.v.*), tetrahydrocannabinol, a name for the active ingredient in marijuana. While resin is not pure T.H.C., it is rich in it. Since *P.C.P.* (*q.v.*) and other dangerous drugs have been sold on the street as T.H.C., the term is rarely used in this sense. [U.S., RDS: 1982] 4. the residue left in a pipe after smoking marijuana. This is an erroneous term if it refers to marijuana ash which has been thoroughly burned. *Cf. cashed*. [U.S., ADC: 1981]

resinator a device for catching *resin* (sense two) bled from marijuana while it is being smoked. A play on *resonator*. RS: *bong*. [U.S., ADC: 1975]

rest, at alcohol intoxicated. RT: *drunk*. [Br., 1800s, F&H; listed in BVB]

resting-powder (also **restin'-powder**) an opiate given to relieve pain, probably morphine. RS: *powder*. [U.S., HK: 1917, ADD]

rest powder snuff; *snoose* (*q.v.*). Because one uses it during rest periods. [U.S., MHW: 1934, VJM: 1949]

ret a tobacco cigarette. A front-clipping of *cigarette*. *Cf. cig*. RT: *nail*. [U.S., D&B: 1971, ADC: 1981]

re-up to take a needed dose of drugs. Also means to reenlist in the Army (DST: 1984). The same as *re-fix* (*q.v.*). *Cf. get-up*. [U.S., JWK: 1981]

revelation a drink of liquor. A play on *out-pouring of the spirit*. RT: *nip*. [U.S., 1800s, F&H]

revenooer a federal revenue agent; a T (treasury) man. The term is eye-dialect for revenuer, a federal agent who went about the country seeking untaxed liquor distillers, i.e., moonshiners. RS: *fuzz*. [U.S., D&D: 1957]

reverend (also **reverent**) having to do with undiluted liquor; having to do with strong liquor. RT: *neat*. [U.S., B&L: 1890, JSF: 1889, BWG: 1899]

reviver a drink of strong liquor. From *corpse reviver* (*q.v.*). The OED lists less certain examples from 1592. [Br., (1876): F&H, SSD, M&J: 1975; listed in MHW: 1934]

re-wired having to do with an addict who returns to drug use or addiction after having broken the habit. *Cf. kick back*. From an electronics expression. See *wired*. [U.S., JWK: 1981]

R.F.D. junker (also **R.F.D., R.F.D. dopehead, R.F.D. gowster**) an addict who wanders from small town to small town hoping to get narcotics (usually morphine) from sympathetic country doctors. The earliest attestation is for **R.F.D. dopehead**. The same as *cross-country hype* (*q.v.*). [U.S., DWM: 1938, BVB: 1942]

rhythms amphetamines. Compare to *blues* which are depressants. RT: *amps*. [U.S., RG: 1970, YKB: 1977]

ribbon liquor, especially gin. *Cf. blue ribbon, red ribbon*. RT: *booze*. [cant, GWM: 1859, JCH: 1887, B&L: 1890, F&H]

Rice Krispies ampules of *amyl nitrite* (*q.v.*). Based on *Snap, Crackle, and Pop* from the Rice Krispies advertising jingle. RT: *snapper*. [U.S., BR: 1972]

rich alcohol intoxicated. RT: *drunk*. [BF: 1737]

ride shotgun to travel with and covertly guard a dope smuggler or runner. See *shotgun*. [U.S., JHF: 1971]

ride the poppy train (also **ride the pipe**) to smoke opium. *Cf. poppy*. This is probably the source of *poppy train* and the erroneous *poppy rain*. RT: *suck bamboo*. [U.S., JES: 1959, H&C: 1975]

riding a thorn injecting drugs. *Thorn* (*q.v.*) = hypodermic needle. [U.S., JES: 1959, H&C: 1975]

riding the waves (also **riding a wave**) drug intoxicated. RT: *stoned*. [U.S., PRB: 1930, MHW: 1934, GOL: 1950]

riding the white horse addicted to heroin; in a heroin stupor. Refers to heroin as a white powder and *horse* (*q.v.*) from the initial *H*. RT: *hooked*. [U.S., HB: 1955]

riding the witch's broom addicted to heroin. *Witch hazel* (*q.v.*) = heroin. RT: *hooked*. [U.S., JES: 1959, H&C: 1975]

riffed alcohol intoxicated; drug intoxicated. RT: *drunk, stoned*. [U.S., BR: 1972]

rifle range 1. a place to buy and inject narcotics. *Cf. gallery, shooting gallery*. RT: *doperie*. [U.S., H&C: 1975] 2. an ironic nickname for the detoxification and withdrawal ward of a narcotics addiction treatment hospital. [U.S., M&V: 1967, RRL: 1969]

rig equipment for preparing and injecting drugs; a hypodermic syringe. RT: *outfit, monkey pump*. [U.S., RRL: 1969, RG: 1970, GU: 1975]

right before the wind with all his studding sails out alcohol intoxicated. In a square-rigged ship studding sails were lateral extensions of the square sails of the ship. These sails extended overboard and, when sailing before the wind, could greatly increase the speed of a ship. RT: *drunk*. [BF: 1737]

right croaker a physician who gives drugs to addicts, or who will give or sell drug prescriptions to addicts. RS: *croaker*. [U.S., DWM: 1938, BVB: 1942, A&T: 1953]

righteous having to do with something (in this case, drugs) of good quality or high potency. GEN: right, satisfying. This is an elaboration of *right* as in *right croaker* (*q.v.*). The term has nothing to do with the standard virtues. *Cf. decent*. [U.S., RPW: 1938, DB: 1944, M&W: 1946, W&F: 1960, RRL: 1969, S&R: 1972, EAF: 1980, RDS: 1982]

righteous acid L.S.D. of high quality and purity. RS: *L.S.D.* [U.S., (TW: 1968)]

righteous bush potent marijuana. *Bush* (*q.v.*) = marijuana. RS: *pot*. [U.S., M&W: 1946, BVB: 1953, RRL: 1969, H&C: 1975, JH: 1979]

righteous jones a genuine addiction; a real drug habit. *Jones* (*q.v.*) = a drug addiction. [U.S., RG: 1970]

righteous scoffer a drug user who craves food after drug use; someone with a severe case of the munchies. *Cf. righteous*. *Scoffer* is a variant of *scarfer*, a slang term meaning one who eats. [U.S., M&V: 1967] See also *scarfing*.

right sort gin. Possibly rhyming slang for *quart* as in *quartern o' bry* (*q.v.*). RT: *gin*. [Br., mid 1800s, F&H]

rigid alcohol intoxicated. RT: *drunk*. [U.S., W&F: 1960, DCCU: 1972]

rileyed alcohol intoxicated. RT: *drunk*. [U.S., MP: 1928, AH: 1931, MHW: 1934, W&F: 1960]

rinse 1. a drink of liquor. RT: *nip*. [Br., 1800s, F&H; listed in BVB: 1942] 2. to drink liquor or beer, probably excessively. *Cf. souse*. RT: *irrigate, guzzle*. [Br., B&L: 1890, F&H; listed in BVB: 1942]

rinsings a residue of drugs left on the *cotton* (*q.v.*) used for straining a drug solution before injecting. [U.S., DWM: 1938, VJM: 1949]

rip 1. a drinking bout. RT: *spree*. [U.S., BVB: 1942] 2. a puff of a marijuana cigarette. *Cf. toke*. [U.S., ADC: 1975] 3. a drug session; an L.S.D. *trip* (*q.v.*). See *on a rip*.

ripe alcohol intoxicated. *Cf. reeling ripe*. RT: *drunk*. [early 1600s, (Shakespeare); Br., JB: 1823; U.S., BVB: 1942, W&F: 1960]

rip, on a high on *L.S.D.* (*q.v.*). Compare to *ripped*. RS: *stoned*. [U.S., TRG: 1968, RG: 1970]

ripped (also **ripped up, ripped off**) 1. alcohol intoxicated. RT: *drunk*. [U.S., MG: 1970, E&R: 1971, AP: 1980] 2. drug intoxicated; under the effects of marijuana. *Cf. rip*. RT: *wasted, stoned*. [U.S., S&W: 1966, M&V: 1967, RRL: 1969, ADC: 1975, EAF: 1980]

ripped to the tits alcohol intoxicated. RT: ***drunk***. *Cf.* ***stoned to the tits***. [PD: 1982]

rippers amphetamines. Because one can get ***ripped*** (*q.v.*) on them. RT: ***amps***. [U.S., RRL: 1969, SNP: 1977]

ripping and running supporting an addiction; doing whatever is necessary (i.e., stealing) to maintain a heroin addiction. Used as the title of a book (MA: 1973). [U.S., RG: 1970]

rise and shine wine. Rhyming slang. RT: ***wine***. [Br., late 18–1900s, DRS]

Ritalin a protected trade name for methylphenidate hydrochloride (stimulant) tablets. The drug is a central nervous system stimulant. *Cf.* ***rits***. [(1919): OEDS; in current use; consult a pharmaceutical reference for more information]

rits tablets of ***Ritalin*** (TM; *q.v.*) stimulant. [U.S., JWK: 1981]

River Ooze (also **River Ouse, The River**) liquor; booze. Rhyming slang for ***booze***. RT: ***booze***. [Br., late 18–1900s, DRS, (1910): DSUE]

Rizla a brand of marijuana cigarette rolling paper. RT: ***paper***. [U.S., (1969): ELA: 1982]

roach 1. a police officer. Derogatory. From *cockroach*. RT: ***fuzz***. [U.S., (1932): OEDS, BVB: 1942, D&D: 1957] 2. the butt end of a marijuana cigarette. The ***resin*** (*q.v.*) tends to concentrate in the unsmoked portion of the cigarette and the butts are usually smoked down to nothing. Named for its similarity to a cockroach. The term is widely known outside the drug culture. [U.S., RPW: 1938, M&D: 1952, W&F: 1960, D&B: 1970c, CM: 1970, EEL: 1971, DCCU: 1972, ADC: 1975, EAF: 1980, ADC: 1981, JWK: 1981, ADC: 1984] Nicknames and slang terms for a marijuana cigarette butt: ***burnie, nose-burner, nose-warmer, reefer butt, roach, seeds, snipe, stub, vonce***. 3. a drug; a narcotic. RT: ***dope***. [U.S., DB: 1944] 4. a ***Librium*** (TM; *q.v.*) capsule. [U.S., LVA: 1981]

roach bender a marijuana smoker. See ***roach***. *Cf.* ***elbow-bender*** (at ***elbow-crooker***). RT: ***toker***. [U.S., BVB: 1942, DU]

roach clip (also **roach holder, roach pick**) a device designed to hold a marijuana cigarette butt in a manner which will allow it to be totally smoked. The clip is often an (electrical) alligator clip. The pick may be improvised or elaborately carved from ivory or custom made from metal. Other improvisations include a split match stick and an unfolded paper clip. RT: ***crutch***. [U.S., (1967): DNE: 1980, RRL: 1969, D&B: 1970c, DCCU: 1972, ADC: 1975, W&F: 1975, ADC: 1981]

roached hungover. GEN: exhausted. As if one were burned down to a ***roach*** (*q.v.*). [U.S., ADC: 1984]

roach pipe a small pipe used for smoking collected butts of marijuana cigarettes. See ***roach***. RS: ***bong***. [U.S., (D&B: 1978)]

road dope amphetamines. Refers to the alleged use of amphetamines by cross-country truckdrivers. See *L.A. turnabouts*. RT: *amps*. [U.S., ELA: 1984]

roadhouse a tavern or saloon, particularly one outside a town on a highway. RS: *bar*. [U.S., (1857): MW: 1983, D&D: 1957]

roaring drunk (also **roaring, roaring fou'**) alcohol intoxicated. *Cf. lion drunk*. RT: *drunk*. [Br., 1800s, F&H; U.S., BVB: 1942]

roasted alcohol intoxicated. See the list at *cooked*. RT: *drunk*. Recent black use. [U.S., BVB: 1942, ADC: 1984]

roasting-ear wine whiskey; illicit whiskey; corn whiskey; moonshine. Roasting-ear = corn. RT: *moonshine, whiskey*. [U.S., VR: 1929, MHW: 1934, (1941): ADD, W&F: 1960]

robe See *robo*.

robin eggs *L.S.D.* (*q.v.*) in blue capsules. RT: *L.S.D.* [U.S., ADC: 1981]

Robinson Crusoe brand a cigarette or cigar butt, a castaway. RT: *brad*. [Aust., SJB: 1966; U.S., BVB: 1942]

robo (also **robe, the robe**) Robitussin (TM) cough syrup with *codeine* (*q.v.*). [U.S., RG: 1970, M&V: 1973]

Roche tens 10 mg capsules of *Librium* (TM; *q.v.*) tranquilizer. RT: *tranks*. Roche Products Inc. is the manufacturer. Not necessarily drug argot. [U.S., SNP: 1977]

rock (also **rocks**) 1. (also **rock candy**) a crystallized form of cocaine. RS: *cocaine*. [U.S., S&W: 1973, NIDA: 1980, JWK: 1981, S&F: 1984] 2. a crystallized form of heroin used for smoking. *Cf. red rock*. RS: *heroin*. [U.S., RRL: 1969] See also *brown rock*.

rocket a marijuana cigarette. RT: *joint*. [U.S., BVB: 1942, VJM: 1949, A&T: 1953] See also *skyrockets*.

rocket fuel phencyclidine, *P.C.P.* (*q.v.*), an animal tranquilizer. RT: *P.C.P.* [U.S., (1970s): FAB: 1979, YKB: 1977, DEM: 1981]

rocket ship a hypodermic syringe and needle. RT: *monkey pump*. [U.S., ADC: 1981]

rock out to pass out from the use of marijuana or pills. *Cf. bliss out, cap out*. [U.S., EAF: 1972]

rock pile cure to break a drug habit by being deprived of drugs and performing hard labor in a rock quarry. *Cf. quarry cure*. RS: *kick*. [U.S., DU, A&T: 1953, M&V: 1973]

rocks, on the having to do with liquor served with ice. The *rocks* are the ice cubes. [1900s, (1945): DSUE, SSD, K&M: 1968]

rocky alcohol intoxicated. RT: *drunk*. This now means feeling ill. [BF: 1737; Br., F&H]

roger rum. Possibly akin to *jolly roger*, the name given to the alleged pirate flag. RT: *rum*. [Br., F&G: 1925]

rojas* capsules of *Seconal* (TM; *q.v.*) barbiturate. Spanish for reds. *Cf. red.* RT: *sec.* [U.S., NIDA: 1980]

rojita* a capsule of *Seconal* (TM; *q.v.*) barbiturate. Spanish for little red one. *Cf. red.* RT: *sec.* [U.S., EEL: 1971]

roker (also **rooker**) a marijuana smoker; a *dagga rooker* (*q.v.*). From Dutch *roken* = to smoke, via Afrikaans. RS: *toker.* [South African, (1838, 1967): JB: 1980]

roll 1. in **roll a drunk**, to rob a drunken person. [(1810): DSUE, (1873): W&F: 1960, GI: 1931, ADC: 1975] 2. a drug *high* (*q.v.*). [U.S., RRL: 1969] 3. a roll of *Benzedrine* (TM; *q.v.*) tablets; a roll of any drug. RS: *load.* [U.S., (1962): OEDS, RRL: 1969, IGA: 1971, BR: 1972, EAF: 1980] 4. (usually plural) a cigarette rolling paper. Used for rolling marijuana cigarettes. RT: *paper.* [U.S., ADC: 1981] 5. (also **roll up**) to roll a marijuana cigarette. [U.S., ADC: 1975, ADC: 1981] 6. to roll an opium pellet. *Cf. chef.* See *roll a pill.* [U.S., (1887): RML: 1948]

roll a pill 1. to prepare a pellet of opium for smoking. *Cf. chef.* [U.S., MHW: 1934, DWM: 1936, VJM: 1949] 2. to roll a tobacco cigarette. *Pill* (*q.v.*) = tobacco cigarette. [U.S., BVB: 1942, GOL: 1950] 3. to roll a marijuana cigarette. [U.S., M&V: 1967]

roll a pusher to attack a drug seller and steal the drugs. As in **roll a drunk.** *Cf. roll.* [U.S., H&C: 1975]

roll a stick to roll a marijuana cigarette. *Cf. stick.* [U.S., M&V: 1967, H&C: 1975]

roller 1. a person who rolls gum opium into smokable pellets; a *chef* (*q.v.*). [U.S., (1887): RML: 1948] 2. someone who rolls drunks. *Cf. roll.* [U.S., (1935): OEDS, BVB: 1942] 3. (also **rollie**) a tobacco cigarette. RT: *nail.* [U.S., BVB: 1942] 4. a drug user or addict. May refer to pills or to opium pellets. RT: *user.* [U.S., (1930): DU, BVB: 1942] 5. a police officer in a police car; any police officer. Refers to the rolling wheels of a police car. *Cf. harness rollers* (at *harness bulls*). RS: *fuzz.* [U.S., (1964): DNE: 1980, D&B: 1970b, MA: 1973, EAF: 1980, JWK: 1981] 6. a vein which rolls aside when one tries to insert a needle. [U.S., RG: 1970, EEL: 1971, JWK: 1981]

rollie a tobacco cigarette. See *roller.* RT: *nail.* [U.S., 1982]

rolling buzz a moderate, long-lasting drug high. *Cf. buzz.* [U.S., (1966): ELA: 1982, RRL: 1969, EEL: 1971]

rolling papers cigarette rolling papers used for making marijuana cigarette rollings. RT: *paper.* [U.S., DEM: 1981]

rollings (also **rollin's**) fine tobacco for rolling one's own cigarettes. *Cf. fillings.* RT: *freckles.* [U.S., HNR: 1934, GAS: 1941, BVB: 1942, GOL: 1950]

roll of reds a roll of *Seconal* (TM; *q.v.*) barbiturate capsules. See *red, roll.* RT: *sec.* [U.S., M&V: 1967, H&C: 1975]

roll the boy to smoke opium. RT: *suck bamboo.* [U.S., VJM: 1949, A&T: 1953]

roll the log to smoke opium; to smoke an opium pipe. *Cf. log.* From the expression *log-rolling.* RT: *suck bamboo.* [U.S., BD: 1937, DWM: 1938]

roll-your-own a homemade cigarette, at first a tobacco cigarette and by the 1960s, a marijuana cigarette. RS: *nail.* [U.S., (1860s): SBF: 1982, BVB: 1942, EEL: 1971]

ronchie alcohol intoxicated. The same as *raunchy* (*q.v.*).

roof, out on the alcohol intoxicated. *Cf. on the tiles.* RT: *drunk.* [U.S., D&D: 1957, W&F: 1960]

rooje See *rouge.*

rooker a (marijuana) smoker. See *roker.* [South African, 1900s, DSUE]

rookus juice potent whiskey; powerful liquor. From *ruckus.* See list at *juice.* RT: *rotgut, whiskey.* [U.S., VR: 1929, MHW: 1934, PW: 1977]

Rooster Brand cheap, bootlegged opium made from the smoked residue of opium. *Cf. dog, eng-shee, gee-fat, gee-yen, green ashes, green mud, suey-pow, yen-chee, yen-shee.* [U.S., DWM: 1936, BVB: 1942]

roostered alcohol intoxicated. A play on *cocked* (*q.v.*) = drunk, and a parody on the taboo against the word *cock.* RT: *drunk.* [U.S., (1850–1900): RFA]

root 1. a cigarette or a cigar. Probably a truncation of *cheroot.* RT: *nail, seegar.* [U.S., EHB: 1900, BVB: 1942] 2. a marijuana cigarette. RT: *joint.* [U.S., JES: 1959, (1965): ELA: 1982, RRL: 1969, ADC: 1975, W&F: 1975, D&B: 1978] 3. an amphetamine pill. RT: *amps.* [U.S., EEL: 1971] 4. to be very hungry after drug use and to eat food like a pig. *Cf. munchies.* [U.S., M&V: 1967]

rope 1. a cigar; a very bad-smelling cigar. *Cf. old rope.* RT: *seegar.* [U.S., (1934): OEDS, BVB: 1942, W&F: 1960] 2. marijuana. *Cf. hemp.* Cannabis (marijuana) is known as the hemp plant. Possibly rhyming slang for *dope.* RT: *pot.* [U.S., DB: 1944, JBW: 1967, RRL: 1969, YKB: 1977] 3. a marijuana cigarette. RT: *joint.* [U.S., CM: 1970] 4. a vein used for injecting a drug. [U.S., (1940s): CM: 1970, MA: 1973]

rort a drinking bout; a bash. RT: *spree.* [Aust., SJB: 1966]

rorty alcohol intoxicated. *Cf. rort.* [Br., mid 18–1900s, (1864): SOD, DSUE]

Rosa Maria* marijuana. Mexican Spanish. RT: *pot.* [U.S., RPW: 1938]

rosas* amphetamines. Spanish for reds *Cf. red.* RT: *amps.* [U.S., ELA: 1984]

rosebud (also **rosenbloom**) an inflamed and swollen rectum after passing a *blockbuster* (*q.v.*) = a hard fecal mass. This is a frequent result of extended opium use. [U.S., M&V: 1973]

roses tablets of *Benzedrine* (TM; *q.v.*) amphetamine. From their rose color. RT: *benz*. [U.S., JBW: 1967, RRL: 1969, ADC: 1975, NIDA: 1980]

rosin drinks given to musicians; liquor or beer in general. See comments at *resin*. [(1729): OED, SJB: 1945, GAW: 1978; listed in BVB: 1942]

rosined alcohol intoxicated. *Cf. resin*. RT: *drunk*. [U.S., MHW: 1934, BVB: 1942]

rosiner (also rosner, rozener) a drink of liquor. RT: *nip*. [Aust., (1932): OEDS, SJB: 1966, BH: 1980]

rosy (also rosey, rosie) 1. (also rosy about the gills) alcohol intoxicated. RT: *drunk*. [U.S., M&C: 1905, MHW: 1934] 2. red wine; rosé wine. [(1854): F&H, B&L: 1890, SSD, SNP: 1977]

Rosy Loader whiskey and soda. British rhyming slang. *Cf. Major Loder*. [1900s, DRS]

rotgut 1. weak or otherwise inferior beer. RT: *queer-beer*. [cant, (1633): OED, BE: 1690, FG: 1785, FG: 1811, FG: 1823, JCH: 1887, F&H] 2. (also rot) strong liquor; inferior liquor; fiery liquor; any beverage alcohol which might cause gastric distress. [U.S., (1819): DA, JSF: 1889, BWG: 1899, MP: 1928, VWS: 1929, GI: 1931, DCCU: 1972] Terms for bad beer are at queer-beer. Nicknames and slang terms for potent or inferior liquor: *A-bomb juice, Africa speaks, agur-forty, alkali, bagman's blood, balderdash, bald face, bald-face whiskey, barbed wire, barbwire, belly wash, benzine, blinder, blind tiger, blotto, blue pig, blue ruin, blue stone, boilermaker's delight, bootleg, bottled bellyache, bug juice, bug poison, bumble whiskey, bumclink, bunk, busthead, bustskull, canebuck, canned heat, caper juice, Cape smoke, catgut, catlap, cement water, chained lightning, chain lightning, chalk, charged water, Charley Frisky, choke dog, coal tar, coffin varnish, condensed corn, conk-buster, corn, corn mule, corn wine, cougar milk, cowboy cocktail, crawrot, cutthroat, death promoter, dehorn, dishwater, down, drudge, dry goods, dynamite, dyno, embalming fluid, eyewash, eyewater, family disturbance, firewater, flapper likker, fogram, fogrum, foot juice, formaldehyde, forty-rod, forty-rod lightning, forty-rod whiskey, forty-two caliber, fox head, fusel oil, gage, gas, gay and frisky, giant killer, gravedigger, greased lightning, Greek fire, grog, gut rot, hair curler, hard stuff, hardware, hell broth, highland frisky, high octane, high-toned tonic, high voltage, hogwash, hootch, horse brine, horse liniment, hundred proof, Indian liquor, Indian whiskey, Jersey lightning, jig-juice, jig-water, John Barleycorn, jollop, jungle-juice, killemquick, killmequick, kill-the-beggar, King Kong, lage, lap, lightning, lightning flash, liquid fire, liquid lightning, madman's broth, monkey swill, nanny goat sweat, nigger gin, nockum stiff, nose paint, oil of gladness, old redeye, old red goofy, oyl of barley, paint remover, paleface,* *panther, panther juice, panther piss, panther pizen, panther's breath, panther's piss, panther's pizen, panther sweat, physic, pig iron, pinch-gut vengeance, pine top, pink-eye, pink lady, pish, piss, pissticide, pizen, plink, plonk, plunk, popskull, pot, prairie dew, prune juice, punk stuff, queer booze, queer bub, queer lap, rag water, rat poison, rat-track whiskey, razors, red disturbance, redeye, redhead, red liquor, red ruin, rerun, rerun alky, rookus juice, rot, rotgut, rotto, rub-a-dub, rubbydub, sagebrush whiskey, scamper juice, scat, scorching fluid, scorpion Bible, scrap iron, screech, shake-up, sheep-dip, sheepherder's delight, sheep-wash, shellac, shoe polish, shorty, Sir John Barleycorn, skilly, skink, slip-slop, slop, slops, slumgullion, smoke, snake, snakebite medicine, snakebite remedy, snakehead whiskey, snake juice, snake medicine, snake poison, snake water, sneaky Pete, steam, Sterno, sting, stingo, stinkibus, stupor juice, suck, swipe, Taos, Taos lightning, tarantula juice, third rail, throat gag, tickle brain, tiger eye, tiger juice, tiger milk, tiger sweat, torn thumb, trade whiskey, turpentine, varnish, varnish remover, vitriol, wanks, white eye, white lightning, white line, white mule, wibble, wild mare's milk, wish-wash, witch piss, woozle water.* 3. having to do with strong or inferior liquor. [since the 1700s, (1706): OED]

rotten (also rotten drunk) alcohol intoxicated. *Cf. decayed.* RT: *drunk.* [Aust. and Br., (WWII): SJB: 1966, (1934): DSUE, GAW: 1978]

rotto bad liquor; *rotgut* (*q.v.*). [U.S., B&L: 1890]

rouge (also rooje) red wine. Rooje is eye-dialect. RS: *wine.* [U.S., EK: 1927, BVB: 1942]

rough stuff marijuana containing much debris. *Cf. debris, lumber, timber.* [U.S., EEL: 1971, JH: 1979]

round head a *Seconal* (TM; *q.v.*) capsule; any rounded capsule. RS: *sec.* Black use. [U.S., EAF: 1980]

round the bend alcohol intoxicated. GEN: far gone; too far gone. RT: *drunk.* [U.S., RAS: 1979]

rouser a drink of liquor. *Cf. corpse reviver, reviver.* RT: *nip.* [Br., 1800s, F&H; listed in BVB: 1942]

rousted arrested. RT: *busted.* [U.S., (JBW: 1967), JWK: 1981]

Rover Boys the police. RT: *fuzz.* [U.S., (1945): DUS]

royal alcohol intoxicated. This is attested only in BVB: 1942, and probably is akin to *feeling right royal* (*q.v.*) which was recorded by F&H. RT: *drunk.* [Br., early 1800s, DSUE; U.S., BVB: 1942]

royal blue a bluish type of *L.S.D.* (*q.v.*). *Cf. blue, blue acid, blue angelfish, blue babies, blue barrel, blue cheer, blue dragon, blue flag, blue heaven, blue mist, blue pyramids, blue vials.* RT: *drunk.* [U.S., IGA: 1971, YKB: 1977]

royal poverty gin. *Cf. poverty.* RT: *gin.* [listed in F&H]

rub-a-dub 1. (also rub-a, rub-a-dub-dub, rubbedy, rubbity) a pub.

Rhyming slang for *pub*. RS: *bar*. [Br., late 18-1900s, DSUE, DRS; Aust., (1926): OEDS, BH: 1980] 2. denatured alcohol, rubbing alcohol drunk as liquor. See *rubbydub*. [U.S., GOL: 1950]

rub-a-dub bum a drinker of denatured alcohol. RS: *sot*. [U.S., GOL: 1950]

rubber drink a drink of liquor which is vomited; a drink that bounces up from a sick or a full stomach. [U.S., BVB: 1942, D&D: 1957, W&F: 1960]

rubber pill a condom or the finger of a rubber glove used to store or transport powdered drugs. [U.S., JES: 1959, H&C: 1975]

rubbydub 1. (also **rub-a-dub, rubby-dubby**) any alcohol-rich substance other than liquor: bay rum, sterno, paint thinner, methyl alcohol, rubbing alcohol. RS: *rotgut*. [1900s, K&M: 1968] 2. a person who drinks *rubbydub* (sense one). RS: *sot*. [Br., (1920): DSUE, K&M: 1968]

rubia de la costa* a special, light-colored Colombian marijuana. Spanish for blond from the coast. RT: *pot*. [U.S., (1976): R&P: 1982]

rub of the relic a drink of liquor. RT: *nip*. [U.S., N&S: 1983]

ruby 1. red wine; claret. RS: *wine*. [Br., (1820): OED, B&L: 1890; U.S., BVB: 1942, D&D: 1957, W&F: 1960] 2. a fiery pimple on the nose from drinking too much liquor. Named for the gemstone. RT: *gin bud*. [Br., (1558): OED, F&H]

ruin gin. From *blue ruin* (*q.v.*). RT: *gin*. [Br., B&L: 1890; listed in BVB: 1942] See also *red ruin*.

rum a liquor distilled from sugar or molasses. Standard English. [since the 1600s, (1654): OED] Nicknames and slang terms for rum: *avec, blackfellow's delight, blue rum, bubbly, bumbo, comfortable waters, dad and mum, demon rum, dido, finger and thumb, fogram, fogrum, grog, jungle-juice, kill-devil, kill-grief, kingdom come, mur, mutiny, myrrh, neaters, Nelson's blood, o-be-joyful, old shoes, quartern o' finger, roger, scooch, slim, the demon rum, thimble and thumb, Tom Thumb, torn thumb, toth, whip, white eye, white face, wine.*

rum bag a drunkard, not necessarily a rum drinker. RT: *sot*. [U.S., W&F: 1960, RDS: 1982]

rum blossom (also **rum bud**) a fiery red pimple caused by drinking too much liquor. *Cf. brandy blossom, grog blossom, toddy blossom*. RT: *gin bud*. [U.S., (1848): OED, JSF: 1889, BVB: 1942]

rum boy an itinerant alcoholic; a hobo drunkard. RS: *sot*. [Bahamas (Nassau), listed in JAH: 1982]

rum-dum (also **rum-dumb**) 1. alcohol intoxicated. RT: *drunk*. [U.S., EK: 1927, (1931): SBF: 1976, BVB: 1942] 2. a drunkard; an alcoholic; a ruined alcoholic. RT: *sot*. [U.S., (1940s): SBF: 1976, GOL: 1950, D&D: 1957]

rum fits the delirium tremens, not necessarily from rum. *Cf.*

woofits. RT: *D.T.s*. [(1955): K&M: 1968]

rum fleet (also **rum row**) during prohibition, the boats of liquor smugglers standing 30 miles offshore waiting for a chance to run it to the shore undetected. See *rum runner*. From the prohibition era. [U.S., (1923): OEDS, D&D: 1957]

rumhead (also **rum hound**) a rum drinker; a drunkard. RT: *rum*. [U.S., (1914): SBF: 1976, BVB: 1942]

rum hole a low drinking establishment. RT: *dive*. [U.S., (1834): DA, JRB: 1859]

rum house (also **rum shop**) a tavern or shop where rum is sold. [U.S., (1730): SBF: 1982]

rummed (also **rummed up**) alcohol intoxicated. RT: *drunk*. [U.S., MP: 1928, MHW: 1934]

rummery a place where liquor is sold. *Cf. groggery*. RS: *dive*. [K&M: 1968]

rum mill a tavern or saloon. Compare to *gin mill*. RS: *bar*. [U.S., (c. 1849): DA, B&L: 1890, JSF: 1889, BVB: 1942]

rummy 1. (also **rummy hound, rummy stiff**) a drunkard; an alcoholic; an alcoholic hobo. RT: *sot*. [U.S., (1851): DA, (1860): DAE, (1884): SBF: 1976, MHW: 1934, W&F: 1960, EEL: 1971] 2. alcohol intoxicated. *Cf. beery, winey*. RT: *drunk*. [U.S., BVB: 1942] 3. habitually confused and inept while (or as if) under the effects of alcohol or drugs. [U.S., GI: 1931] 4. a liquor dealer; a wine maker; a small-time bootlegger. *Cf. bootlegger*. [U.S., BVB: 1942]

rum nose a red nose, perhaps with one or more fiery red pimples, from drinking too much rum or other liquor. *Cf. rum blossom*. [(1891): OED, K&M: 1968]

rumpet a drunkard or an alcoholic. Probably a variant of *rum pot* (*q.v.*). RS: *sot*. [U.S., AP: 1980]

rumping using heroin. RS: *hooked*. [U.S., EEL: 1971]

rum pot (also **rumpot, rum soak**) a drunkard; an alcoholic. RT: *sot*. [U.S., BVB: 1942, D&D: 1957, W&F: 1960]

rum runner a liquor smuggler during prohibition; a bootlegger. RT: *bootlegger*. From the prohibition era. [U.S., (1920): OEDS, BVB: 1942, GOL: 1950, D&D: 1957]

rum sucker a drunkard; a tippler. RT: *sot*. [U.S., (1844): DA, (1858): DAE, JSF: 1889, K&M: 1968]

run 1. to transport contraband, alcohol or drugs. Since the prohibition era. [U.S., 1920s-p., D&D: 1957, ADC: 1975] 2. an instance of transporting contraband. [U.S., EEL: 1971, ADC: 1975] 3. a period of time (at least three days) spent high on amphetamines, especially methamphetamine. [U.S., RB: 1967, RRL: 1969, EEL: 1971, YKB: 1977] 4. for a marijuana cigarette to burn overly fast for a short time. [U.S., ADC: 1981]

run a railroad to be addicted to heroin. *Railroad* (*q.v.*) = injection sites. *Cf. railroad tracks, tracks.* [U.S., BR: 1972]

runner a person who transports contraband, now usually drugs. Originally referred to alcohol smugglers and bootleggers. RT: *mule.* [U.S., GI: 1931, BVB: 1942, M&D: 1952, M&H: 1959, EEL: 1971]

run up to inject drugs. RT: *shoot.* [U.S., ADC: 1975]

rush the initial, orgasmic-like jolt following an injection of drugs; the sudden onset of exhilaration or euphoria from a drug dose. It has been called an abdominal orgasm. The rush precedes the high. Now GEN: any pleasure. [U.S., M&V: 1967, RRL: 1969, MA: 1973, W&F: 1975, DNE: 1980, EAF: 1980, ADC: 1981, JWK: 1981] Nicknames and slang terms for rush: *bang, belt, bing, blast, boot, burn, buzz, call, charge, digatee, drive, flash, flash in the pan, flush, gow, high kick, jab-off, jag, job off, jolt, kick, kicks, lift, lift-up, org, pickup, splash, tag, tingle, Xmas.*

Rush a brand of *butyl nitrite* (*q.v.*) sold as a room deodorizer. It is now also sold as a sexual stimulant. See *amyl nitrite. Cf. Locker Room.* [U.S., YKB: 1977, (1978): DNE: 1980]

rush the growler (also **rush the can**) to carry beer (rapidly) in a bucket from a saloon to a residence. [U.S., (1880s): DWH: 1947, (1887): RML: 1950, BVB: 1942, D&D: 1957]

rye whiskey made from rye. RS: *whiskey.* [since the early 1800s, (1835): OEDS, JSF: 1889, BWG: 1899]

rye sap whiskey; illicit whiskey. RS: *moonshine.* From the prohibition era. [U.S., VR: 1929, AH: 1931, MHW: 1934, D&D: 1957, W&F: 1960]

S

sacate* marijuana. Spanish for grass, hay. RT: ***pot***. [U.S., NIDA: 1980]

sach (also **sacht**) See ***satch***.

sack of bull (also **sack of dust**) a sack of Bull Durham (TM) cigarette tobacco. Some attestations refer to it as a prison tobacco ration. RS: ***freckles***. [U.S., HS: 1933, VJM: 1949, D&D: 1957]

sacrament ***L.S.D.*** (*q.v.*) in tablet or blotter form. Because it is a wafer placed on the tongue as is the communion wafer. RT: ***L.S.D.*** [U.S., RRL: 1969, SNP: 1977]

sacred mushrooms mushrooms of the genus *Psilocybe* which contain the hallucinogenic compound ***psilocybin***. *Cf.* ***magic mushrooms***. RT: ***psilocybin***. [U.S., (1930): MW: 1983, RRL: 1969, MW: 1976]

saddle and bridle an opium smoker's outfit. *Saddle* is defined as a brass ring on an opium pipe (1887): RML: 1948. RS: ***outfit***. [U.S., DWM: 1938, VJM: 1949]

safety a safety pin used to open a vein for the injection of drugs. RS: ***needle***. [U.S., M&D: 1952, A&T: 1953]

safety pin mechanic a drug addict who injects using a ***safety*** (*q.v.*) and a medicine dropper. RS: ***bangster***. [U.S., JES: 1959, H&C: 1975]

sage marijuana in ***hump the sage*** (*q.v.*). See also ***blue sage***.

sagebrush whacker a marijuana smoker. Patterned on *bush whacker*. *Cf.* ***sage***. RT: ***toker***. [U.S., JES: 1959, H&C: 1975]

sagebrush whiskey inferior whiskey said to be made from sagebrush. RT: ***rotgut***. [U.S., late 1800s, PW: 1977]

sailor's champagne beer. RT: ***beer***. [U.S., JRW: 1909]

salmon and trout stout, a type of malt liquor or a type of ***porter*** (*q.v.*). Rhyming slang. RT: ***stout***. [Br., 1900s, DRS, SSD]

saloon a drinking establishment; a low or rowdy bar; a frontier bar. RT: ***bar***. [U.S., (1841): OEDS]

saloonist 1. someone who sells and serves liquor at a bar. RT: ***bartender***. [U.S., (1870): OEDS, D&D: 1957, K&M: 1968] 2.

someone who is against prohibition and for saloons. From the prohibition era. [U.S., 1920s, K&M: 1968]

salt 1. alcohol intoxicated. From *salt junk* (*q.v.*). RT: *drunk*. [U.S., JRW: 1909] 2. powdered heroin. RT: *heroin*. [U.S., EEL: 1971, W&F: 1975, SNP: 1977]

salt and pepper 1. inferior or impure marijuana. *Cf. ditch weed*. RS: *pot*. [U.S., M&W: 1946, BVB: 1953, M&H: 1959, W&F: 1975] 2. a Negro and a Caucasian working together in some sort of *hustle* (*q.v.*) to earn money to buy drugs. [U.S., JWK: 1981] 3. a black and white police squad car; the police; a police squad car carrying a Negro and a Caucasian officer. An elaboration of *black and white* (*q.v.*). RT: *fuzz*. Black use. [U.S., EAF: 1980, RDS: 1982]

salted (also **salted down**) alcohol intoxicated. *Cf. salt, salt junk*. RT: *drunk*. [U.S., (c. 1850): W&F: 1960; Br., early 1900s, DSUE]

salt junk alcohol intoxicated. *Cf. salt*. Rhyming slang for *drunk*. RT: *drunk*. [U.S., JRW: 1909]

saltos mortales* amphetamine tablets or capsules. Spanish for somersaults. RT: *amps*. [U.S., NIDA: 1980]

salt shot an injection of saline solution given in the treatment of drug overdose. [U.S., SH: 1972, LVA: 1981]

salubrious alcohol intoxicated. RT: *drunk*. [Br., 1800s, F&H; listed in BVB: 1942]

Sam federal agents; federal narcotics agents. From *Uncle Sam*. RS: *fuzz*. [U.S., JBW: 1967, M&V: 1967, EEL: 1971, W&F: 1975]

Sam and Dave the police; police officers. RT: *fuzz*. Black slang. [U.S., EAF: 1980]

Sandoz (also **Sandoz's**) *L.S.D.* (*q.v.*); authentic L.S.D. 25 produced in the Sandoz Laboratories, Basel, Switzerland. RT: *L.S.D.* [U.S., ADC: 1975, H&C: 1975]

San Francisco bomb a mixture of heroin, cocaine, and *L.S.D.* (*q.v.*). The same as *Frisco speedball*. RS: *set*. [U.S., M&V: 1973, RDS: 1982]

sangaree 1. a spiced red wine. Ultimately from Latin *sanguis* = blood. RS: *wine*. [(1736): OED, FG: 1785, JSF: 1889, BWG: 1899] 2. a drinking bout. Rhyming slang for *spree*. RT: *spree*. [Br., JOH: 1901]

san-lo (also **sam-lo, Sam Low, son-lo**) the cheap, refined residue of opium. Chinese or mock-Chinese. *Cf. yet-low*. [U.S., DWM: 1936, VJM: 1949]

San Pedro a South American cactus producing *mescaline* (*q.v.*). [U.S., YKB: 1977]

Santa Marta gold (also **Santa Marta red**) a potent grade of marijuana from Colombia. *Cf. gold, red*. RT: *pot*. [U.S., (1979): DNE: 1980, ELA: 1982]

sap happy alcohol intoxicated. A play on *slap happy*. Sap = liquor. *Cf. rye sap*. RT: *drunk*. [U.S., W&F: 1960]

sapper a drunkard. *Cf. rye sap*. RT: *sot*. [Br., 1800s, F&H]

sassafrass (also sas-fras) marijuana. RT: *pot*. [U.S., (1944): ELA: 1982, IGA: 1971, WCM: 1972]

Satan's Scent a "brand name" for *amyl nitrite*. RS: *snapper*. [U.S., ELA: 1984]

satch 1. (also sach, sacht, satch) paper (especially a postcard or a letter) saturated with a drug and then mailed or smuggled into prison; clothing saturated with a drug and worn or smuggled into prison. DWM: 1936 lists sach. BD: 1937 lists sacht. M&V: 1954 list satch. [U.S., DWM: 1936, BD: 1937, GOL: 1950, RRL: 1969, RDS: 1982] 2. *satch cotton* (*q.v.*).

satch cotton (also satch) cotton used to filter a drug before injecting it. The residual drugs may be used later. *Cf. cotton*. [U.S., JBW: 1967, RG: 1970, EEL: 1971]

satin gin. *Cf. white satin, yard of satin*. RT: *gin*. [Br., JCH: 1887, B&L: 1890, F&H; listed in BVB: 1942]

sativa marijuana. From the botanical name *Cannabis sativa*. RT: *pot*. [U.S., SNP: 1977, YKB: 1977]

saturated alcohol intoxicated. RT: *drunk*. [Br. and U.S., (1902): SBF: 1976, DSUE, MHW: 1934, D&D: 1957, W&F: 1960]

Saturday night habit 1. occasional drug use; a *chippy habit* (*q.v.*). [U.S., DWM: 1938, BVB: 1942, DU] 2. a person with a small habit; a person who uses drugs too infrequently to become addicted. Possibly an error. JES: 1959 lists Saturday nighter with this meaning. RT: *chipper*. [U.S., early 1900s, DU]

sauce liquor, beer, or wine. RT: *booze*. [U.S., (1920s): SBF: 1982, W&F: 1960, DCCU: 1972]

sauced alcohol intoxicated. *Cf. sauce*. RT: *drunk*. [U.S., S&E: 1981]

sauce, off the no longer drinking; sober. RS: *sober*. Older than the attestation. [U.S., AP: 1980]

sauce, on the on a drinking bout; alcohol intoxicated. [U.S., W&F: 1960, DCCU: 1972]

sausage a fat marijuana cigarette. *Cf. bomber, fat jay, submarine, tamale, thumb, torpedo*. RT: *joint*. [Br., BTD: 1968, M&J: 1975] See also *poison sausage*.

sawed alcohol intoxicated. Perhaps an elaboration of *cut* (*q.v.*). RT: *drunk*. [U.S., (1833): DA]

sawi* hashish made from an Indian variety of hemp. From (colloquial) Arabic. RT: *hash*. [U.S., RDS: 1982]

saxophone an opium pipe. RT: *hop stick*. [U.S., BVB: 1942, VJM: 1949, A&T: 1953]

scabbed cheated in a drug deal; having been sold bogus or inferior drugs. [U.S., EEL: 1971]

scag 1. a cigarette or cigar; a cigarette or cigar butt. [U.S., RB: 1915, JAR: 1930, MHW: 1934] 2. heroin. See *skag*. [U.S., RB: 1967, EEL: 1971, DNE: 1973, MA: 1973, W&F: 1975, MW: 1976, NIDA: 1980]

scagged addicted to heroin. *Cf. scag, skag*. RS: *hooked*. [U.S., RDS: 1982]

scag jones See *skag jones*.

scam a *hustle;* the (illicit) activity an addict employs in order to get money for drugs. *Cf. hustle*. GEN: a swindle or a racket (1963): OEDS. [U.S., JWK: 1981]

scammered alcohol intoxicated. RT: *drunk*. [Br., DA: 1857, JCH: 1887, (1891): F&H; listed in MHW: 1934, BVB: 1942]

scamper juice inferior liquor; strong liquor. This may refer to scampering away to a toilet. RT: *rotgut*. [U.S., RFA]

Scandihoovian dynamite snuff. RT: *snoose*. [U.S., RFA]

scar 1. a needle scar from a heroin injection or an abscessed heroin injection. Usually plural. RT: *tracks*. [U.S., RRL: 1969, EEL: 1971] 2. heroin. Probably refers to needle scars left from injections and abscesses. Possibly an error for *scag*. RT: *heroin*. [U.S., YKB: 1977]

scarf a joint to swallow a marijuana cigarette to avoid detection. *Scarf* = eat (in cant). *Joint* (*q.v.*) = marijuana cigarette. [U.S., EEL: 1971]

scarfing (also **scoffing**) taking opium or other drugs orally. *Cf. belly habit, mouth habit*. From an old cant term meaning to eat. See *scoff*.

scat 1. inferior whiskey. LIT: shit. *Cf. skat*. RT: *rotgut*. [U.S., (1940): OEDS, DU, GOL: 1950] 2. heroin. (also **scatt**) *Cf. scag, scar, skag*. LIT: shit. RT: *heroin*. [U.S., VJM: 1949, A&T: 1953, EEL: 1971, NIDA: 1980] See also *Scott*.

scatter a saloon; a dope den; a speakeasy. A place where *scat* (*q.v.*) can be bought and used. *Cf. doperie, sly grogshop*. [U.S., (1916): W&F: 1960, DWM: 1931, HNR: 1934]

scattered drug intoxicated; confused by drug use. Possibly akin to *scat* (*q.v.*). RS: *stoned*. [Canadian, MMO: 1970]

scene the drug-use environment, the drug scene. See *acid scene*. [U.S., (1957): ELA: 1982, S&W: 1966, M&V: 1967, RRL: 1969, JWK: 1981; Br., S&W: 1966, BTD: 1968]

schice (also **chice**) alcohol intoxicated. See *shicker*. RT: *drunk*. [Br., JCH: 1887]

schicker alcohol intoxicated. See *shikker*.

schlects narcotics. From German *schlect* = bad (plus the English plural -s) via Yiddish. RS: *dope*. [U.S., JES: 1959, H&C: 1975]

schlock narcotics; drugs. From Yiddish for junky merchandise.

According to Leo Rosten, from the German *schlag* = a blow, a punch. Possibly from German sense of *beat* referring to the punch packed by narcotics. It is more probable that the word is from German *Schlacke* = slag, cinders, sediment, via Yiddish. RS: ***dope***. [U.S., (1920): DU, BVB: 1942, H&C: 1975]

schlockkered alcohol intoxicated. RT: ***drunk***. [PD: 1982]

schmack (also **shmack**) A variant of ***schmeck*** (*q.v.*).

schmeck (also **schmack, schmecken, schmee, schmeek, shmack, shmeck, shmee, smeck**) heroin; narcotics in general. From German *schmecken* = a taste (via Yiddish). Maurer (DWM: 1938) defines **shmeck** as a card = portion of opium. **Schmeck** may also be a distortion of *smoke*. RT: ***heroin***. [U.S., (1932): OEDS, DWM: 1938, RRL: 1969, ADC: 1975, JWK: 1981]

schmeck biz the business of trafficking in narcotics. [U.S., JES: 1959, H&C: 1975]

schmecken a variant of ***schmeck*** (*q.v.*).

schmecker (also **shmecker, smeaker, smecker**) a heroin addict. From ***schmeck*** (*q.v.*). RS: ***junky***. [U.S., GOL: 1950, RRL: 1969, EEL: 1971]

schmeck, on the under the effects of heroin; addicted to heroin. RS: ***hooked***. [U.S., GOL: 1950]

schmee heroin. A variant of ***schmeck*** (*q.v.*). RT: ***heroin***. [U.S., ADC: 1975]

schnockered (also **shnockered**) alcohol or drug intoxicated. *Cf.* ***snockered***. RT: ***drunk, stoned***. [U.S., BR: 1972, PD: 1982, HSD: 1984]

schnoggered alcohol intoxicated. See ***snockered***.

schnozzler a user of cocaine; a snorter of cocaine. LIT: a noser, a sniffer. From German *Schnautze* = nose (via Yiddish). *Cf.* ***snort***. RT: ***kokomo***. [U.S., (1929): DU]

schoolboy 1. a cocaine user. RT: ***kokomo***. [U.S., EEL: 1971] **2.** codeine; codeine cough syrup. A beginner's drug. *Cf.* ***baby, kidstuff***. [U.S., RRL: 1969, RG: 1970, ADC: 1975, YKB: 1977]

schoolboy Scotch wine. RT: ***wine***. Black use. [U.S., EAF: 1980]

schooner 1. a beer glass. [U.S., (1877): DA, BVB: 1942; Aust., (1939): GAW: 1978, BH: 1980] **2.** an illicit saloon. [U.S., AH: 1931, MHW: 1934]

scissors marijuana. Origin unknown. RT: ***pot***. [U.S., SNP: 1977]

scoff 1. to take drugs orally (rather than inject them). GEN: to eat (in cant). [U.S., BD: 1937, VJM: 1949] **2.** to dispose of drugs when arrested by swallowing them. *Cf.* ***scarf a joint***. [U.S., DWM: 1938]

scooch liquor; rum. RT: ***booze***. [Br., F&G: 1925, DSUE]

scoop 1. liquor in ***on the scoop*** (*q.v.*). This *scoop* is a dipper used for serving liquor. RT: ***booze***. [(1884): OED] **2.** a glass of beer.

[U.S., (1887): RML: 1950] 3. a folded matchbook cover used to snort cocaine or heroin. *Cf. quill.* [U.S., RRL: 1969] 4. to *snort* (*q.v.*) cocaine or heroin using a folded matchbook cover. RT: *snort.* [U.S., RRL: 1969, LVA: 1981] 5. a narcotics bust or round-up of dealers and users. [U.S., JWK: 1981]

scooped alcohol intoxicated. *Cf. scoop.* RT: *drunk.* [Br., 1800s, F&H; listed in BVB: 1942]

scoop, on the on a drinking bout; alcohol intoxicated. *Cf. scoop.* An Australian version is on the scoot (early 1900s). RS: *drunk.* [(1884): OED, B&L: 1890]

scorched alcohol intoxicated; drug intoxicated. RT: *drunk, stoned.* [U.S., ADC: 1975, PD: 1982]

scorching fluid liquor; strong or inferior liquor. RS: *rotgut.* [U.S., BVB: 1942]

score 1. to penetrate a vein and *register* (*q.v.*) when injecting. *Cf. hit, hit the sewer, home.* RS: *shoot.* [U.S., RG: 1970, H&C: 1975] 2. to find and purchase drugs. [U.S., (1926): ERH: 1982, DWM: 1936, BVB: 1942, D&B: 1970c, RRL: 1969, MA: 1973, ADC: 1975] (This entry continues after the following list.) Terms meaning to buy or to find and buy drugs: *bag, brink, buzz, cap, comp, con, connect, cop, cop a fix, cop a match, domino, dope up, get a fix, get a gift, get narkied, get through, H. and R., hit, hit on, level, make, make a buy, make a connection, make a contact, make a hit, make a meet, make a strike, make it, make the man, mizake the mizan, pass, pass-go, pickup, score, score a connection, ziv.* 3. to obtain money for drugs; to obtain money for any purpose. GEN: to obtain something. [U.S., VJM: 1949] 4. money to purchase drugs; a purchase of marijuana or other drugs. [U.S., DU, A&T: 1953, GS: 1959] 5. any drugs. RT: *dope.* [U.S., ADC: 1975]

score a connection to buy drugs. *Cf. score.* [U.S., DWM: 1936, BVB: 1942]

score dough money to be used in buying drugs. *Cf. score.* [U.S., BD: 1937, DWM: 1938]

score weight to sell drugs. It should be noted that the literal interpretation of this phrase is to buy drugs. *Cf. weight.* [Bahamas, JAH: 1982]

scorpion Bible inferior whiskey. RT: *rotgut, whiskey.* [U.S., RFA]

Scotch whiskey made in Scotland from malted barley. RS: *whiskey.* Standard English. [since the 1800s, (1886): OED]

Scotch mist alcohol intoxicated. Rhyming slang for *pissed* (*q.v.*). RT: *drunk.* [Br., (1920): DSUE, DRS]

Scotch tea (Scotch) whiskey. RS: *whiskey.* [late 1800s, OED]

Scott (also scot) heroin. Probably akin to *scat* (*q.v.*). RT: *heroin.* [U.S., IGA: 1971, WCM: 1972]

scours opium; crude opium. Possibly in reference to the severely constipating nature of opium. RT: *opium*. [U.S., JES: 1959, H&C: 1975]

scrambled alcohol intoxicated. RT: *drunk*. [U.S., BVB: 1942]

scrambled egg a drunkard. *Cf. scrambled*. RT: *sot*. [U.S., BVB: 1942]

scranched See *scraunched*.

scrap iron homemade whiskey. It may contain, antifreeze, mothballs, or bleach. Akin to *pig iron* (*q.v.*). RT: *moonshine, rotgut*. Prison use. [U.S., D&D: 1957, W&F: 1960, CM: 1970]

scratched alcohol intoxicated. RT: *drunk*. [(1622): OED; listed in BVB: 1942]

scratcher a down-and-out addict. Refers to having to scratch around for drugs or perhaps to scratching fleas. RS: *junky*. [U.S., M&V: 1967, (RRL: 1969)]

scratching looking for drugs to purchase. *Cf. hunting, looking*. [U.S., (EEL: 1971), JTD: 1971, ADC: 1975]

scraunched (also **scranched, scronched**) alcohol intoxicated. RT: *drunk*. [U.S., D&D: 1957, W&F: 1960]

screaming abdabs (also **screaming hab-dabs**) the delirium tremens. RT: *D.T.s*. [Br., early 1900s, DSUE, (1962): OEDS]

screaming drunk (also **screaming**) alcohol intoxicated. *Cf. screeching drunk*. [U.S., BVB: 1942]

screaming-meemies (also **screaming-meamies**) the delirium tremens. RT: *D.T.s*. [U.S., (1927): W&F: 1960, MHW: 1934, (1941): SBF: 1976, D&D: 1957, DCCU: 1972]

screech whiskey; *rotgut* (*q.v.*); liquor. RT: *whiskey*. [Br. and U.S., F&H, (1880): DSUE, D&D: 1957, W&F: 1967]

screechers alcohol intoxicated; very drunk. Short for *Harry Screechers* (*q.v.*). *Cf. screech*. RT: *drunk*. [Br., (1950s): DSUE]

screeching drunk (also **screeching**) alcohol intoxicated; very drunk. *Cf. screech*. RT: *drunk*. [U.S., MHW: 1934, D&D: 1957, W&F: 1960]

screw 1. a twisted hank of tobacco. *Cf. pigtail*. RS: *fogus*. [Br., JCH: 1887] 2. a drink of liquor. Possibly a backformation based on *screwed* (*q.v.*). RT: *nip*. [Br., 1800s, DSUE; listed in BVB: 1942]

screwed alcohol intoxicated. *Cf. screwed tight*. RT: *drunk*. [Br. and U.S., (1837): OEDS, MHW: 1934, SDD]

screwed, blued, and tatooed alcohol intoxicated. GEN: badly mistreated; badly screwed. RT: *drunk*. An elaboration of *screwed*. Probably nonce. [U.S., 1970s, S&E: 1981]

screwed tight alcohol intoxicated. An elaboration of *screwed* (*q.v.*) and *tight* (*q.v.*). RT: *drunk*. [listed in S&E: 1981]

screwy alcohol intoxicated. *Cf. screwed*. GEN: crazy, silly. RT:

drunk. [(1820): OED; listed in BVB: 1942]

scribe a drug addict known to be able to write acceptable prescriptions. The same as *author*. [U.S., JWK: 1981]

scridgin snuff. This probably refers to a small amount of snuff, i.e., just a scridgin. RT: *snoose*. [U.S., (1939): ADD]

script (also **scrip**) a prescription for drugs. *Cf. paper, reader*. FG: 1785 defines *script* as any scrap of paper with something written on it. [U.S., DWM: 1936, A&T: 1953, RRL: 1969, D&B: 1970c, ADC: 1975, W&F: 1975; Br., BTD: 1968]

scronched See *scraunched*.

scrooched up (also **scrooched**) alcohol intoxicated. RT: *drunk*. [U.S., (c. 1925): W&F: 1960, MHW: 1934, D&D: 1957]

scrubwoman's kick naptha inhaled for a high. *Cf. inhalant*. [U.S., RRL: 1969, JH: 1979, LVA: 1981]

scuffle (also **scaffle, skuffle**) phencyclidine, *P.C.P.* (*q.v.*), an animal tranquilizer. RT: *P.C.P.* [U.S., YKB: 1977, ELA: 1984]

scupper up to drink liquor, especially beer. RT: *irrigate*. [Br., DSUE]

scuttle, on the on a drinking bout. RT: *spreeing*. [Br., 1800s, DSUE]

sea cocaine. A spelling-out (in error or as a disguise) of *C.* (*q.v.*). RT: *cocaine*. [U.S., EEL: 1971]

seafaring alcohol intoxicated. RT: *drunk*. [BF: 1737]

seafood illicit whiskey. Refers to the whiskey which was smuggled into the U.S. by sea during prohibition. RS: *moonshine*. [U.S., 1920s, D&D: 1957, W&F: 1960]

sealed stuff a can or bottle of opium. *Cf. stuff*. RS: *opium*. [early 1900s, DU]

sealing wax hashish; opium. From the gummy consistency of these two substances. RT: *hash, opium*. Probably nonce. [U.S., (1939): ELA: 1982]

sec (also **seccies, seccy, secky, secs**) a *Seconal* (TM; *q.v.*) barbiturate capsule. Sometimes used for any barbiturates. RS: *barbs*. [U.S., M&V: 1967, RRL: 1969, JHF: 1971, NIDA: 1980, JWK: 1981] Nicknames and slang terms for Seconal: *apple, bala, blunt, border, border red, bullet, bullethead, Canadian bouncer, cardenales, colorado, devil, diablo rojas, dolls, F-forties, forties, gumdrop, hors d'oeuvres, ju-ju, juju, lillys, M and Ms, marshmallow reds, Mexican jumping beans, Mexican red, pink ladies, pinks, prescription reds, pula, R.D., red, redbirds, red bullets, red devils, red dolls, red jackets, red lillys, reds, rojas, rojita, roll of reds, round head, sec, seccies, seccy, secky, secs, seggies, seggy, sex, suckonal, 40s*.

Seconal a protected trade name for secobarbital (barbiturate) in a variety of forms. The drug is a central nervous system depressant. Many of the slang and jargon terms refer to bright red capsules of Seconal (TM). RT: *sec*. [in current use; consult a pharmaceutical reference for more information]

sedative a drug which soothes, calms, and brings on sleep. Not slang or jargon. [(1797): OED]

see a man about a dog (also **see a man**) to have a drink; to go out to have a drink; to go out to buy liquor. Also used to mean go to the bathroom. [B&L: 1890, AH: 1931]

see double to be drunk. *Cf. seeing two moons*. GEN: to be disoriented. RS: *drunk*. [U.S., BVB: 1942]

seeds 1. (also **seed**) marijuana; marijuana cigarettes; marijuana cigarette butts, roaches. Usually singular. *Cf. roach*. RT: *pot, joint*. [U.S., G&B: 1969, EEL: 1971, ADC: 1975, W&F: 1975] 2. the hemp seeds found in uncleaned marijuana. [U.S., JBW: 1967, ADC: 1975] 3. (also **glory seeds**) *morning glory seeds* (*q.v.*). These are eaten to produce a high. [U.S., YKB: 1977, RDS: 1982] Nicknames and slang terms for morning glory seeds: *blue mornings, blue star, flying saucers, glory seeds, heavenly blue, pearly cakes, pearly gates, pearly whites, seeds, summer skies, wedding bells*.

seegar a cigar. This is eye-dialect used by Mark Twain, late 1800s. The stress is on the first syllable. It is slang when used outside the dialects of which it is a part. This pronunciation, but not this spelling is recorded in JWC: 1905. [U.S., (1884): ADD, BVB: 1942] Nicknames and slang terms for a cigar: *blinder, box fire, Buck's Hussar, cabbagio perfumo, cig, Cuban candle, flor di cabbagio, hemp, penny stinker, pipe, puffer, root, rope, seegar, Spanish guitar, stinker, stogie, sweet Marguerite, weed, zeppelin*.

seeing pink elephants (also **seeing pink spiders, seeing snakes**) alcohol intoxicated; recovering from a drinking bout; having the delirium tremens. RS: *drunk*. [U.S., (1890s): SBF: 1976, AH: 1931, MHW: 1934, SSD]

seeing Steve using cocaine to the point of having hallucinations. [U.S., VJM: 1949, M&D: 1952] See also *old Steve, Steve's mission*.

seeing-things drunk alcohol intoxicated; drunk enough to have hallucinations. RT: *drunk*. [U.S., RAS: 1979]

seeing two moons (also **sees two moons, seen a flock of moons**) alcohol intoxicated. And along the same theme: **seen the French king, sees the bears**, (referring to the constellations, Ursa Major and Ursa Minor), *sees the sun, seen the yellow star*. *Sees the sun* and *sees two moons* are BF: 1722. RT: *drunk*. [BF: 1737; some also listed in BVB: 1942]

seen the devil alcohol intoxicated. RT: *drunk*. [BF: 1737]

seggies (also **seggy**) capsules of *Seconal* (TM; *q.v.*) barbiturate. RT: *sec*. [U.S., JBW: 1967]

selling selling drugs. An ellipsis resulting in an intransitive verb. [U.S., 1900s, (M&W: 1946)]

send to smoke marijuana. RT: *hit the hay*. Akin to the musician's expression *That really sends me!* = It moves me. See *sent*. [U.S., (1936): ELA: 1982, DWM: 1938, BVB: 1942]

send it home to inject into a vein. *Cf. home*. [U.S., M&V: 1967, C&H: 1974]

seni *mescaline* (*q.v.*); *peyote* (*q.v.*). Language origin not known. RS: *peyote*. [U.S., SNP: 1977, YKB: 1977]

sensation (also **slight sensation**) a drink of liquor; gin. RS: *nip*. [Aust., (1859): OED, B&L: 1890; listed in BVB: 1942]

sense See *sinse*.

sent alcohol intoxicated; drug intoxicated. *Cf. send*. [U.S., (1935): W&F: 1960, MB: 1938, H&C: 1975]

sentimental water liquor. *Cf. crying drunk, maudlin drunk*. RT: *booze*. [U.S., BVB: 1942]

sentry, on alcohol intoxicated. From the immobility of a sentry on guard. RT: *drunk*. [Br., late 18-1900s, DSUE]

serenity 1. *L.S.D.* (*q.v.*). RS: *L.S.D.* [U.S., KBH: 1982] 2. *S.T.P.* (*q.v.*). [U.S., IGA: 1971]

serenity, tranquility, and peace *S.T.P.* (*q.v.*). [U.S., (IGA: 1971)]

sergeant's butt a small cigarette butt. RT: *brad*. [U.S., HS: 1933]

Sernylan a protected brand name of the drug phencyclidine, an animal tranquilizer. See slang terms at *P.C.P.*

serpent a hypodermic syringe and needle. See *silver serpent*. RT: *monkey pump*. [U.S., H&C: 1975]

serum liquor, including beer. RT: *booze*. [U.S., WWII, W&F: 1960, AP: 1980]

served up alcohol intoxicated. *Cf. overserved*. RT: *drunk*. [U.S., MHW: 1934, BVB: 1942]

service stripes needle marks from injections. RT: *tracks*. [U.S., M&V: 1967, H&C: 1975]

sess seedless marijuana, *sinsemilla* (*q.v.*). RT: *pot*. [U.S., ELA: 1982]

session 1. a drinking bout. RT: *spree*. [Aust., SJB: 1966] 2. a marijuana smoking session; time spent on a drug high. *Cf. run*. [U.S., RB: 1967, EEL: 1971, W&F: 1975, ADC: 1984]

set 1. a combination of amphetamine and barbiturate capsules. Many of the sets come with paired terms: *thrusters* and *busters*, *ups* and *downs*, *amps* and *damps*, etc. [U.S., EEL: 1971, W&F: 1975] (This entry continues after the following list.) Terms for combinations of drugs: *A-bomb, angel dust, atom bomb, bam, bams, banana with cheese, Barbidex, birdie powder, birdie stuff, black and tan, black and white, black and white minstrel, black* *beauties, black bombers, black hash, blue jeans and T-shirts, blue velvet, bluies, bombida, bombido, bombita, bombito, booster stick, California sunshine, C. and H., C. and M., cannonball, charas, cocaroin, cod cock, cold and hot, conga, contact lens, cupcakes, death trips, dominoes, double-trouble, Drinamyl, Durophet, Durophet M, dynamite, electric wine, esrar, four-doors, fours and doors, French blue, Frisco speedball, fruit salad, G.B., geronimo, goofball, grape parfait, green dragon, green hornets, green meanies, greens, green swirls, H. and C., happy sticks, heavy joint, high-fi, H.M.C., Hollywood cocktail, horror drug, hot and cold, inbetweens, L.B.J., let sunshine do, love, love affair, love saves, M. and C., Marmon and Cadillac, Maud C., M.C., minstrels, Monroe in a Cadillac, moscop, nigger minstrels, one on one, opiated hash, over and unders, paper acid, peace pills, peppermint swirl, product IV, purple hearts, purple passion, quartet, quicksilver, red dimple, San Francisco bomb, set, silk and satin, sky river, spansula, speedball, squirrel, squirrel dew, superpot, synthetic heroin, Teddies and Betties, tops and bottoms, tricycles and bicycles, trip grass, triple line, T.s and blues, two-way, white lightning, whiz-bang, wild geronimo, witches brew, yellow dimple, zoom.* 2. (usually sets) a *Darvocet-N* (TM; *q.v.*). See *cets.* [U.S., JWK: 1981] 3. the state of mind of a person about to begin an *L.S.D.* (*q.v.*) trip. Akin to *mindset. Cf. setting.* [U.S., RRL: 1969, S&R: 1972, S&F: 1984] 4. a party, especially one where drugs are used. GEN: musician's term for pieces of music played back-to-back before a break. [U.S., ADC: 1975]

Set me straight! "Can you sell me drugs or tell me where I can get them?" *Cf. straight.* RT: *How are you going to act?* [U.S., M&D: 1952]

set of works equipment for injecting drugs. RT: *outfit.* [U.S., M&V: 1967, H&C: 1975]

sets See *cets, set.*

setting 1. a place to obtain drugs. RT: *doperie.* [U.S., NAM: 1953] 2. the environment of an *L.S.D.* (*q.v.*) or other drug trip. A good *set* (*q.v.*) and setting are important in L.S.D. use. *Cf. bad scene.* [U.S., RRL: 1969, EEL: 1971, S&F: 1984]

settler a drink of liquor; a parting drink. *Cf. binder, caulker.* RS: *nip.* [U.S., JSF: 1889; listed in BVB: 1942]

seven-fourteens (also **714s**) 300 mg tablets of *Quaalude* (TM; *q.v.*) brand of *methaqualone* (*q.v.*). RS: *ludes.* [U.S., YKB: 1977, DEM: 1981]

sewed up (also **sewn up**) alcohol intoxicated. **Sewn up** is chiefly British. RT: *drunk.* [Br. and U.S., (1818): DSUE, B&L: 1890, BWG: 1899, F&G: 1925, MP: 1928, AH: 1931, EP: 1948]

sewer the median cephalic vein in the forearm. In reference to its use as a channel for heroin or *shit* (*q.v.*). *Cf. go into the sewer, hit the sewer.* [U.S., BVB: 1942, VJM: 1949, M&V: 1967]

sewer pipe a drunkard. *Cf. pipe.* RT: *sot.* [U.S., BVB: 1942]

sex *Seconal* (TM; *q.v.*) barbiturate capsules. The same as *secs.* RT: *sec.* [U.S., JWK: 1981]

sex-juice a drug, presumably a liquid, used to stimulate a person sexually. *Cf. love drug.* [U.S., RAS: 1980]

S.F. alcohol intoxicated. From *shit-faced* (*q.v.*). RT: *drunk.* [PD: 1982]

shagged alcohol intoxicated. RT: *drunk.* [U.S., MHW: 1934, BVB: 1942]

shake bits of granular marijuana, usually of low quality. RS: *pot.* [U.S., D&B: 1978, ELA: 1982]

shaker a drunkard; a drunk with the delirium tremens. RT: *sot.* [U.S., RAS: 1978]

shakes (also the shakes) a hangover; the delirium tremens; the beginning of drug withdrawal. RT: *D.T.s.* [(1850s): SBF: 1976, F&H, MHW: 1934, K&M: 1968]

shakes, in the alcohol intoxicated. RT: *drunk.* [Br., (1884): F&H]

shake-up imitation liquor made from water, coloring, and alcohol shaken up together. RT: *rotgut.* [U.S., (Harlem), MB: 1938]

shaking like a cloth in the wind (also shaking a cloth in the wind) alcohol intoxicated; shaking from alcohol withdrawal. Also used to mean shaking from fright or illness. RT: *drunk.* [Br., (1826): DSUE, B&L: 1890]

shaky alcohol intoxicated. RT: *drunk.* [Br., 1800s, F&H; listed in BVB: 1942]

sham (also cham) champagne. RT: *cham.* [Br., (1849): OED, M&J: 1975; U.S., BVB: 1942]

shammy (also chammy) champagne. RT: *cham.* [U.S., BVB: 1942; Br., M&J: 1975]

shampers champagne. The same as *champers* (*q.v.*). [M&J: 1980]

shampoo champagne. RT: *cham.* [U.S., W&F: 1960, RDS: 1982]

shandy beer; beer and ginger-ale. From *shandygaff.* RT: *beer.* [Br., mid 1800s-p., (1853): SOD; Aust., (1918): GAW: 1978]

shant a tankard for booze. A pot of beer is a shant of bivvy or a shant of gatter. [Br., (1851): F&H, SSD]

shanty 1. a drink of liquor; a pot of beer; a tankard of booze. RS: *nip.* [Br., late 18-1900s, DSUE] 2. to drink liquor including beer; to tipple. RT: *irrigate.* [Br. and Aust., late 18-1900s, DSUE, SJB: 1943] 3. a tavern or pub; an illicit liquor establishment. RS: *bar, sly grogshop.* [Aust., 18-1900s, F&H, SJB: 1943]

sharp 1. drug intoxicated. RT: *stoned.* [U.S., M&D: 1952, A&T: 1953] 2. a hypodermic needle. RT: *needle.* [U.S., RDS: 1982]

sharp shooter a drug injector who never (or seldom) fails to hit the vein. RS: *bangster.* [U.S., M&V: 1967]

shave to cut (shave) down a cube of morphine. This is a way of stealing a bit of drugs. It is usually done along the line in drug distribution. *Cf. chip*. [U.S., DWM: 1938, BVB: 1942]

shaved alcohol intoxicated. *Cf. half shaved*. RT: *drunk*. [late 1500s, (Shakespeare); U.S., (1851): SBF: 1976]

shavetail's butt a small cigarette butt, about 1/3 of a cigarette. See a list of similar forms at *butt*. RT: *brad*. [U.S., HS: 1933, MHW: 1934]

shebang a saloon or other rendezvous for criminals. *Cf. shebeen*. RT: *dive*. [U.S., GOL: 1950]

shebeen an unlicensed *public house* (*q.v.*) in Scotland or Ireland. RT: *sly grogshop*. [17-1900s, (1787): OED, JCH: 1887, F&H]

shed a tear to take a drink of liquor. RT: *irrigate*. [Br., JCH: 1887, JRW: 1909]

sheep-dip inferior liquor; bad beer. *Cf. sheep-wash*. RS: *rotgut*. [U.S., (1865): SBF: 1982, W&F: 1967, DCCU: 1972]

sheepherder's delight inferior whiskey. Based in part on the cowboy's disdain for sheepherders. RT: *rotgut*. [U.S., RFA]

sheep-wash inferior liquor; bad beer. The Australian version of *sheep-dip*. RT: *queer-beer, rotgut*. [Aust. and New Zealand, SJB: 1943]

sheet or two to the wind, a alcohol intoxicated. See similar expressions at *two sheets to the wind*. RT: *drunk*. [Br., (1832): DSUE]

sheets 1. tobacco rolling papers. RT: *paper*. [U.S., (1925): DU, DWM: 1935, VJM: 1949] 2. papers for rolling marijuana cigarettes. This refers to the same material as sense one, and differs only in date of use. RT: *paper*. Black use. [U.S., ADC: 1975] 3. phencyclidine, *P.C.P.* (*q.v.*), an animal tranquilizer. RT: *P.C.P.* [U.S., (1970s): FAB: 1979, YKB: 1977, DEM: 1981]

shell See *shell of hop*.

shellac inferior liquor. *Cf. gumdrop cocktail*. RT: *rotgut*. [U.S., BVB: 1942]

shellacked alcohol intoxicated; overcome by booze. *Cf. varnished*. GEN: beaten, overcome. RT: *drunk*. [U.S., (1905): SBF: 1976, MHW: 1934, D&D: 1957]

shell, by the having to do with opium sold in small amounts. The *shell* may refer to a half walnut shell. See *toy*. [U.S., (1887): RML: 1948]

shell of hop (also **shell**) a can of prepared opium. This may refer to one half of a walnut shell which could serve as an opium *toy* (*q.v.*). Opium packaged in this way was said to be sold by the shell. *Cf. toy*. RT: *load*. [U.S., (1887): RML: 1948, DU]

Sherlock Holmes a police officer; a police detective. RS: *fuzz*. Black use. [U.S., EAF: 1980]

sherman (also **sherm, Sherman**) 1. a device for smoking marijuana. RS: ***bong***. [U.S., ADC: 1981] 2. a tobacco or marijuana cigarette soaked in a solution of phencyclidine, (P.C.P.). Named for a brand of cigarettes. [U.S., RDS: 1982]

sherry a fortified wine from Spain. *Cf.* ***Bristol milk, derry-down-derry***. From the Spanish town of Jerez, formerly spelled *Xerez*, with the X pronounced as *sh*. Standard English. [since the early 1600s, (1608): OED]

shesha a type of hashish grown in Israel. RS: ***hash***. [U.S., RDS: 1982]

shice (also **chice, schice**) alcohol intoxicated. Possibly akin to ***shikker*** via ***shicer***. Possibly akin to German *scheiss* = shit. RT: ***drunk***. [Br., 18–1900s, DSUE]

shicer alcohol intoxicated. A variant of ***shikker*** (*q.v.*).

shicery alcohol intoxicated. A variant of ***shickery*** (*q.v.*).

shick 1. (also **shicked**) alcohol intoxicated. A spelling variant or pronunciation variant of ***shicker***. RT: ***drunk***. [Aust., (1898): GAW: 1978, SJB: 1943] 2. a drunkard. RT: ***sot***. [Aust., (1920): DSUE, SJB: 1943]

shicker 1. (also **shikker**) alcohol intoxicated. From Hebrew *shiqor*, probably via Yiddish. RT: ***drunk***. [Br. and U.S., (1890s): SBF: 1976, F&G: 1925, BVB: 1942, DSUE, SSD] 2. liquor, including beer. Rhymes with ***liquor***. RT: ***booze***. [Aust. and U.S., (1916): GAW: 1978, MHW: 1934, BVB: 1942, SJB: 1943] 3. to tipple; to get drunk, to take in ***shicker***. RT: ***irrigate, mug oneself***. [(1913): GAW: 1978, MHW: 1934, DSUE, SSD, M&J: 1975]

shickered (also **on the shikker, shikkered**) alcohol intoxicated. From Hebrew *shiqor* plus the English *-ed* past participle suffix. An Australian and New Zealand variant is **on the shicker**. The *alsos* are U.S. *Cf.* ***shicker***. RT: ***drunk***. [(1890s): SBF: 1976, (1911): GAW: 1978, W&F: 1960, DSUE, SSD, SJB: 1966]

shickery (also **shicery**) alcohol intoxicated. *Cf.* ***shicker***. RT: ***drunk***. [Aust. and Br., (1878): GAW: 1978, F&H, DSUE]

shift to drink liquor. RT: ***irrigate***. [Br., 1800s, F&H]

shifter a drunkard. *Cf.* ***shift***. RT: ***sot***. [Br., 1800s, F&H]

shikker (also **on the shikker, shikkered, shikkur**) alcohol intoxicated. An American spelling of ***shicker***. From Yiddish. RT: ***drunk***. [U.S., (1890s): SBF: 1976, W&F: 1960, AP: 1980]

shine (also **shine liquor**) illicit whiskey; ***moonshine*** (*q.v.*). Much use during the prohibition era. [U.S., MP: 1928, VR: 1929, GI: 1931, MHW: 1934, D&D: 1957, W&F: 1960, DCCU: 1972]

shined alcohol intoxicated; done in by ***shine*** (*q.v.*). *Cf.* ***polished***. RT: ***drunk***. [U.S., MHW: 1934, W&F: 1960]

shiner a bootlegger; a liquor smuggler; a ***moonshiner*** (*q.v.*). From ***moonshine*** (*q.v.*). A prohibition term. [U.S., 1920s, AH: 1931,

BVB: 1942]

shinery an illicit liquor establishment. RT: *speak*. From the prohibition era. [U.S., BVB: 1942]

shinny 1. (also **shinney**) liquor; illicit liquor. Probably from *moonshine* (*q.v.*). [U.S., MHW: 1934] 2. (also **shiny**) alcohol intoxicated. Probably from *moonshine* via *shine*. RT: *drunk*. [U.S., JSF: 1889]

ship in full sail (also **ship in sail**) ale. RT: *ale*. The American version is **ship in sail** (M&B: 1944). Rhyming slang. [DA: 1857, M&B: 1944, DRS]

shipwrecked alcohol intoxicated. RT: *drunk*. [JRW: 1909]

shirt tail hype a newly addicted person. *Cf. cadet, convert, green hype, J.C.L., lame hype*. RS: *junky*. [U.S., M&V: 1967]

shise (also **chice, shice**) alcohol intoxicated. See *shicker*.

shishi hashish; marijuana. A front-clipping of *hashish*. RT: *hash*. [U.S., JES: 1959, H&C: 1975]

shit drugs in general; a specific drug: *Demerol* (TM; *q.v.*), *Dilaudid* (TM; *q.v.*), hashish, heroin, or marijuana. *Cf. black shit* = opium. BTD: 1968 define it only as *marijuana*. See *shuzzit*. RS: *dope*. [(1946): ELA: 1982, BTD: 1968, RRL: 1969, CM: 1970, EEL: 1971, PW: 1974, ADC: 1975, M&J: 1975, YKB: 1977, EAF: 1980, JWK: 1981]

shit-faced (also **shitty**) alcohol intoxicated. *Cf. cacko, S.F.* RT: *drunk*. [U.S., (1940s): SBF: 1976, W&F: 1967, ADC: 1984]

shithead a heroin user; a drug user. *Cf. shit*. RT: *user*. [U.S., EEL: 1971, JH: 1979]

shlook 1. a puff of a marijuana cigarette. *Cf. hit*. RT: *toke*. [U.S., RRL: 1969; ELA: 1982] 2. to puff a marijuana cigarette. RS: *hit the hay*. [U.S., RRL: 1969]

shmack (also **shmeck**) heroin. Both are variants of *schmeck* (*q.v.*).

shmecker a heroin addict. A variant of *schmecker* (*q.v.*).

shmee heroin. A variant of, or akin to *schmeck* (*q.v.*).

shnockered alcohol intoxicated. See *schnockered*.

shock to take a dose of drugs. *Cf. jolt*. Possibly akin to *schlock* (*q.v.*). [early 1900s, DU]

shock joint a cheap saloon. Possibly based on, akin to, or an error for *schlock joint*. RT: *dive*. [U.S., (1922): DU, GI: 1931, MHW: 1934]

shoe polish liquor; whiskey; inferior whiskey. A term of disguise for *whiskey* (JWC: 1905). RT: *rotgut*. [U.S., JWC: 1905, BVB: 1942]

shoe polish shop an illicit saloon. RT: *sly grogshop*. [U.S., JWC: 1905, BVB: 1942]

shoestring cheap red wine. RT: *wine*. [U.S., MHW: 1934, W&F:

1960]

shong-nie opium. RT: *opium*. Probably much older than the attestation suggests. [U.S., (M&V: 1954)]

shoot 1. (also **shoot up**) to inject a specific drug into the bloodstream; to take a dose of drugs by injection. Reflexive, transitive, and intransitive use. [U.S., (1914): DU, DWM: 1938, BVB: 1942, M&D: 1952, (1970): DNE: 1973, EEL: 1971, ADC: 1975, MW: 1976, BW: 1984] (This entry continues after the following list.) Terms meaning to inject a drug: *bang, bang up, blast, boot, break the needle, brew with hops, broach it, bunghole, bust the mainline, doctor, dope up, douche, do up, fang, fang it, fire, fix, geez, geeze, get down, get it on, get narkied, get off, get one's yen off, get the habit off, get with it, go in the skin, go into the sewer, go on the boot, go to the vein, hit, hit it, hit the mainline, hit the needle, hit the sewer, hit up, hype shoot, hypo, jab, jab a vein, jack a fix, jack off, jack up, jerk off, job, job-pop, join the stream, jolt, joy pop, knock up, laugh and scratch, lay the hypo, line, main, mainline, make tracks, milk, milk a rush, mix, muscle, needle, oil, pop, prick, re-fix, re-up, run up, score, send it home, shoot, shoot below the belt, shoot shit, shoot skin, shoot the pin, shoot up, shoot yancey, shoot yen-shee, skin, skin pop, splash, straddle the spike, syringe, syringe it, take it in line, take it in the line, take it main, take it straight, take off, take the needle, take the works, take to the needle, Tom Mix, tongue, tough, turn on, tweak, use the needle*. 2. (also **shoot-up**) an injection of heroin. RT: *shot*. [U.S., VJM: 1949, A&T: 1953, (1970): DNE: 1973, W&F: 1975] 3. to spike with liquor. See *spike*. *Cf. needle beer*. From the prohibition era. [U.S., BVB: 1942]

shoot a snipe to pick up a discarded tobacco cigarette butt. *Cf. guttersnipe, snipe*. [U.S., JWC: 1905, GOL: 1950]

shoot below the belt to administer an injection of drugs into a vein in the lower part of the body. Addicts do this when the veins of the arm are no longer usable. The expression refers to shots in the legs, although any accessible veins, including those in the genitals have been used. A play on *hit below the belt*. RS: *shoot*. [U.S., HB: 1955] See also *belt*.

shooter 1. an injection of a drug. Based on *shoot* (*q.v.*). RT: *shot*. [U.S., H&C: 1975] 2. a drug user (or addict) who injects heroin. In contrast to a smoker or a pill-popper. RS: *bangster*. [U.S., IGA: 1971, ADC: 1975]

shoot gravy to inject a mixture of cooked blood and a dissolved drug. See explanations at *boot* and *gravy*. [U.S., M&V: 1967, (RRL: 1969), EEL: 1971]

shooting gallery 1. a place where addicts can go to inject drugs. *Cf. rifle range*. From the name for a place where firearms training is conducted. [U.S., M&D: 1952, M&H: 1959, W&F: 1960, M&V: 1967, RRL: 1969, MA: 1973] 2. an ironic nickname for a ward in a narcotics treatment hospital. [U.S., M&H: 1959, M&V: 1967, RRL: 1969]

shoot shit to inject heroin. *Shit* (*q.v.*) = heroin. RS: *shoot*. [U.S., RDS: 1982]

shoot skin to miss the vein and inject into the skin. *Cf. skin shot*. [U.S., D&B: 1970c]

shoot the pin to inject drugs. *Cf. pin*. RT: *shoot*. [U.S., GOL: 1950]

shoot up 1. to inject drugs. See *shoot*. [U.S., (1926): DU, (M&D: 1952), M&V: 1967, RRL: 1969, D&B: 1970c, EEL: 1971, MA: 1973, ADC: 1975, W&F: 1975, MA: 1973, JWK: 1981] 2. (usually **shoot-up**) an injection of drugs. RT: *shot*. [U.S., W&F: 1960]

shoot yancey to inject opium. *Yancey* is an accidental or deliberate mispronunciation (or misspelling) of *yen-shee* (*q.v.*). RS: *shoot*. [U.S., (1955): JES: 1959, H&C: 1975]

shoot yen-shee to inject opium extracted from opium ashes. Done by morphine addicts when nothing else is available. *Cf. shoot yancey*. See *yen-shee*. RS: *shoot*. [U.S., DWM: 1938, BVB: 1942, DU]

short 1. a small drink of hard liquor or of beer. RT: *nip*. [U.S., EE: 1976] 2. having to do with undiluted liquor. In contrast to long or tall, referring to diluted drinks. RT: *neat*. [Br., FG: 1823] 3. a purchase of drugs which counts or weighs out less than the amount agreed upon. *Cf. short buy*. RS: *load*. [U.S., JES: 1959, (1967): ELA: 1982, H&C: 1975, JWK: 1981] 4. to deliver less drugs than agreed upon and paid for. An underworld use of a widely known slang or colloquial term. [U.S., JWK: 1981] 5. to sniff (snort) cocaine. Possibly an error for *snort* (*q.v.*). Possibly from *short snort* (*q.v.*). [U.S., W&F: 1967, AP: 1980] 6. a single-dose purchase of drugs; a retail order of drugs. *Cf. shove shorts*. RS: *dose*. [U.S., DWM: 1938]

short beer a small shot of heroin. RS: *shot*. [U.S., JES: 1959, H&C: 1975]

short but an error for *short buy* (*q.v.*). [U.S., EEL: 1971]

short buy (also **short count**, **short go**, **short weight**) 1. a small purchase of drugs. RS: *load*. [U.S., HB: 1955, RRL: 1969] 2. a purchase of bogus drugs; a short-weight purchase of drugs. See *short*. [U.S., (EEL: 1971), JH: 1979]

short can (also **short toy**) a short-weighted can of prepared opium. *Cf. short, toy*. RS: *load*. [U.S., M&V: 1954]

short count a smaller amount of marijuana (or some other drug) than paid for. See *short buy*. [U.S., RG: 1970, MA: 1973]

short dog cheap wine; a small bottle of cheap wine. *Cf. mad dog*. RS: *wine*. [U.S., D&B: 1970c, EAF: 1972]

short go 1. (also **short beer**, **short order**, **short piece**) a small amount of drug for the money paid; a small or weak injection of heroin. RS: *shot*. [U.S., BD: 1937, DWM: 1938, VJM: 1949, H&C: 1975] 2. a *short buy* (*q.v.*).

short one (also **short beer**) a small or quickly drunk drink of liquor including beer. Compare to *tall one*. RT: *nip*. [U.S., MHW: 1934, AP: 1980]

short piece a small amount of a drug, usually heroin; a weak injection of heroin. [U.S., (1930): DU, DWM: 1938, BVB: 1942, RRL: 1969, H&C: 1975]

short snort 1. a quick drink from a bottle, flask, or jug of liquor, especially a drink of whiskey. RT: *nip*. [U.S., BVB: 1953, D&D: 1957] 2. an inhalation (snort) of powdered (crystallized) drugs. Extended from sense one. Possibly nonce. *Cf. snort*. [U.S., S&E: 1981]

shorts, on the short of drugs; short of money to buy drugs. Said of a drug addict. [U.S., M&V: 1967]

shorty 1. a short-weighted can of prepared opium. The same as *short can, short toy*. *Cf. short, toy*. RS: *load*. [U.S., M&V: 1954] 2. strong, inferior liquor. RT: *rotgut*. From the prohibition era. [U.S., AH: 1931, MHW: 1934, VJM: 1949]

shot 1. a small or quickly drunk drink of liquor, usually whiskey. *Cf. pistol shot*. RT: *nip*. [(1676): OED, (1906): SBF: 1982, W&F: 1960, DSUE, SSD, RDS: 1982] 2. an injection of drugs. [(1922): DU, (1929): OEDS, DWM: 1936, BD: 1937, EEL: 1971, MA: 1973] (This entry continues after the following list.) General terms for a dose of drugs are listed at *dose*. Terms for an injected dose of a drugs: *autograph, bang, bang in the arm, belt, bing, bingo, boot, boot shot, brush, cannonball, charge, Chinese needlework, constitutional, cura, deck, fall, fix, fix-up, geez, geeze, geezer, go, G-shot, hit, hype, hype shot, hype skin shot, hypo, jab, jab job, jab-off, jab-pop, jab-poppo, jack, jack off shot, jag, jimmy, job, job off, joke, jolly pop, jolt, joy pop, joy prick, lay, line shot, load, mainline bang, make, morning glory, morning shot, muscle pop, needle, penitentiary shot, pen shot, ping in the wing, ping in wing, ping shot, ping-wing, pin shot, point shot, pop, prod, prop, rations, shoot, shooter, shoot-up, short beer, short go, short order, short piece, shot, shot in the arm, shunt shot, skinner, skin pop, skin shot, speedball, S.S., Tom, Tom Mix, twister, vein shot, verification shot, V.S., waker-upper, wake up, X*. 3. alcohol intoxicated. See *cupshot, grape shot, half shot, overshot, pot shot, shot full of holes, shot in the neck, shot up, shot-away*. RT: *drunk*. [(1864): DA, B&L: 1890, MP: 1928, D&D: 1957, W&F: 1960]

shot-away alcohol intoxicated. *Cf. blowed away*. RT: *drunk*. [Br., late 18-1900s, DSUE]

shot beer bottled beer into which alcohol or ether has been injected through the cork. *Cf. needle beer*. RS: *beer*. From the prohibition era. [U.S., VR: 1929, MHW: 1934]

shot down drug intoxicated. RT: *stoned*. [U.S., RDS: 1982]

shot full of holes alcohol intoxicated. An elaboration of *shot* (*q.v.*). RT: *drunk*. [Aust., N.Z., and elsewhere, (1915): DSUE, SJB: 1943]

shotgun 1. a pipe designed to aid a person in blowing marijuana smoke into someone else's mouth. *Cf. hash cannon*. RS: *bong*. [U.S., ADC: 1975] 2. to blow a puff of marijuana smoke into someone else's mouth. [U.S., EEL: 1971, ADC: 1975, ADC: 1981] 3. someone who accompanies a drug smuggler or runner - a *mule* (*q.v.*) - and observes the success or failure of the act of smuggling or transfer. From the practice of a man riding shotgun as an armed guard for a overland shipment in the old West. From Florida cocaine smuggling traffic. *Cf. mule skinner*. [U.S., RAS: 1981] 4. a "brand name" for *amyl nitrite* RS: *snapper*. [U.S., ELA: 1984]

shot in the arm 1. a drink of liquor. RT: *nip*. [U.S., RB: 1915, MHW: 1934, W&F: 1960] 2. an injection of narcotics. A *booster* (*q.v.*). RS: *shot*. Colloquial for a boost or act of encouragement in any form. [U.S., DWM: 1936, BVB: 1942, W&F: 1960, RDS: 1982]

shot in the neck 1. a drink of straight whiskey. A play on *shot in the arm* (*q.v.*). RT: *nip*. [U.S., (c. 1850): W&F: 1960, BVB: 1942, D&D: 1957] 2. alcohol intoxicated. An elaboration of *shot* (*q.v.*). RT: *drunk*. [U.S., (1830): DA, (1833): DAE, JSF: 1889, B&L: 1890]

shot up 1. alcohol intoxicated. *Cf. shot-away*. RT: *drunk*. [(1924): DU, EP: 1948] 2. drug intoxicated. RT: *stoned*. [U.S., DWM: 1938, A&T: 1953] 3. having to do with an addict covered with scars or *tracks* (*q.v.*). [U.S., M&V: 1967]

shoulder the cloth or paper sealing a hypodermic needle onto a medicine dropper. RT: *gasket*. [U.S., DWM: 1938, BVB: 1942]

shout a call for a drink of liquor; an announcement such as "I'm buying the next round"; a drink of liquor. *Cf. cry*. [Aust., (1860): GAW: 1978, JCH: 1887, SJB: 1943, BH: 1980; listed in BVB: 1942]

shove to sell drug; to *push* (*q.v.*) drugs. [U.S., (1920): DU, DWM: 1938, RRL: 1969, H&C: 1975]

shovel a drug pusher. The same as *shover* (*q.v.*) and possibly an error for it. *Cf. shove*. [U.S., H&C: 1975]

shoveling the black stuff addicted to opium. RS: *hooked*. [U.S., JES: 1959, H&C: 1975]

shovel snow to snort cocaine. See a list of terms on the same theme at *winter wonderland*. *Cf. snow*. [U.S., BR: 1972]

shover a drug pusher. *Cf. shovel*. RT: *pusher*. [U.S., BD: 1937, VJM: 1949, GOL: 1950, A&T: 1953]

shove shorts to sell small (retail) portions of drugs; to sell drugs one dose at a time. [U.S., (1925): DU, BD: 1937, DWM: 1938]

show drink (also **show one's drink**) to be drunk; to appear to be (inappropriately) drunk. [JRW: 1909, BVB: 1942]

shpleef a marijuana cigarette. See *spleef*.

shredded alcohol intoxicated. RT: *drunk*. [Br., RAS: 1985]

shroom to use a hallucinogenic substance; to use *shrooms* (*q.v.*). [U.S., ADC: 1984]

shrooms tips of the peyote cactus containing *mescaline* (*q.v.*). This is a cactus not a mushroom. May also be used to refer to any hallucinogenic substance, specifically *psilocybin*. RS: *peyote*. [U.S., ADC: 1981, ADC: 1984]

shuck 1. a tobacco cigarette with a corn husk wrapper. RS: *nail*. [U.S., BVB: 1942] 2. to fake a drug withdrawal spasm in order to get drugs from a sympathetic physician. Probably from an old dialect form of the past tense of *shake*. This sense is slang or argot. *Cf. brody*. [U.S., M&V: 1967]

shuffler a drunkard; a tippler. RT: *sot*. [(1642): OED]

shunt shot a heroin injection. RS: *shoot*. [U.S., JES: 1959, H&C: 1975]

shuzzit cannabis. Narcotics ziph for *shit* (*q.v.*). RT: *pot*. [U.S., (1971): ELA: 1982]

shy to prepare opium pellets. The same as *tchi* (*q.v.*). [U.S., (M&W: 1946), BVB: 1953, M&V: 1954, (RRL: 1969)]

shypoo 1. beer; inferior beer. RT: *beer, queer-beer*. [Aust., (1901): GAW: 1978, (1920): DSUE, SJB: 1943] 2. (also **shypoo joint, shypook, shypoo shop**) a low beer house; a *sly grogshop* (*q.v.*); any pub. RS: *bar*. [Aust., (1925): DSUE, (1936): GAW: 1978, SJB: 1943]

sick experiencing serious withdrawal symptoms and badly in need of drugs. Said of an addict who craves drugs. *Cf. call*. [U.S., DWM: 1938, BVB: 1942, M&D: 1952, RRL: 1969, DCCU: 1972, MA: 1973, W&F: 1975, JWK: 1981]

sid (also **delysid, Sid**) the hallucinogenic drug *L.S.D.* (*q.v.*). From the second syllable of *acid*. RT: *L.S.D.* [U.S., ADC: 1981, JWK: 1981]

sidney (also **Sidney**) the hallucinogenic drug *L.S.D.* (*q.v.*). An elaboration of *sid* (*q.v.*) from *acid* (*q.v.*). *Cf. delysid*. RT: *L.S.D.* [U.S., ADC: 1981]

sight, out of (also **oudasight, outasight**) drug intoxicated; very high. LIT: so high as to be invisible. The *alsos* are eye-dialect. RT: *stoned*. The expression has become a catch phrase outside the drug culture. [U.S., IGA: 1971]

silk and satin amphetamines and barbiturates; an amphetamines and a barbiturate taken together, usually in pill form. RS: *set*. Black slang. [U.S., EAF: 1980]

silk and twine wine. *Cf. string and twine*. RT: *wine*. [U.S., M&B:

1944, DRS]

silken twine (also **silken**) wine. Clearly akin to *silk and twine,* and more widely attested. RT: *wine.* [U.S., BVB: 1942, VJM: 1949]

silly milk liquor. *Cf. giggle goo.* RT: *booze.* [U.S., MHW: 1934, BVB: 1942]

silly putty psilocybin. RT: *psilocybin.* [U.S., M&V: 1973, SNP: 1977]

silo *psilocybin* (*q.v.*). RT: *psilocybin.* [U.S., M&V: 1973]

silo drippings liquor, especially (homemade) corn liquor. *Cf. roasting-ear wine.* RS: *whiskey.* [U.S., 1900s, M&M: 1976]

silver bike a chrome-plated hypodermic syringe. Possibly an error for *silver spike.* RS: *monkey pump.* [U.S., RG: 1970]

silver serpent (also **silver**) a hypodermic needle; a hypodermic needle and syringe. *Cf. serpent.* RT: *needle.* [U.S., M&V: 1967, C&H: 1974]

Simon Pure (also **Simon**) good whiskey; genuine, pre-prohibition whiskey. RS: *whiskey.* The British use is attested before U.S. prohibition. [Br., 1800s, F&H; listed in BVB: 1942]

simple Simon 1. a non-addict. RS: *square.* [U.S., (1954): JES: 1959, H&C: 1975] 2. *psilocybin* (*q.v.*), a hallucinogenic substance. RT: *psilocybin.* [U.S., RG: 1970, IGA: 1971 JHF: 1971]

simpy drug intoxicated. RT: *stoned.* [U.S., M&W: 1946]

sin synthetic marijuana; *T.H.C.* (*q.v.*). Sometimes confused with *sinse* (*q.v.*). *Cf. synthetic grass.* [U.S., JH: 1979]

singles price the price of a single unit of a drug, such as one marijuana cigarette. RPW: 1938 lists **single** defined as one marijuana cigarette. *Cf. loose price.* [U.S., MA: 1973]

sink 1. to down a small drink of liquor. RT: *irrigate.* [Br., early 1900s, DSUE, SSD] 2. a drunkard. *Cf. drain.* RT: *sot.* [Br., 18-1900s, DSUE]

sinse (also **sense, sense bud**) seedless marijuana. A truncation of *sinsemilla* (*q.v.*). RS: *pot.* [U.S., ADC: 1981, JWK: 1981]

sinsemilla seedless marijuana; the (seedless) female flower tops of marijuana. Female marijuana plants are grown with no male plants in the vicinity so that no seeds are produced. RS: *pot.* From the Spanish expression for seedless. [U.S., (1977): DNE: 1980, D&B: 1978, ADC: 1981, JWK: 1981]

sip 1. a puff or toke of a marijuana cigarette. *Cf. toke.* See *sip tea.* [U.S., (M&W: 1946), (1950): ELA: 1982] 2. to take a puff of a marijuana cigarette. See *sip tea.*

siphon to drink liquor; to drink liquor to excess. RT: *guzzle.* [U.S., BVB: 1942]

sipster a tippler; a drunkard. RT: *sot.* [Br., 1800s, F&H]

sip tea to draw a puff of marijuana smoke. *Cf. sip.* [U.S., (M&W:

1946), M&H: 1959]

Sir John Barleycorn strong beer; strong whiskey; liquor. A personification of beverage alcohol. Essentially the same as *John Barleycorn* (*q.v.*). [cant, FG: 1785, FG: 1811]

Sir Richard has taken off his considering cap. "He is drunk." RS: *drunk*. [BF: 1737]

Sir Walter Scott a tankard of beer. Rhyming slang for *pot* (of beer). It is possible that the M&B: 1944 attestation is only for *chamber pot*. [Br., DA: 1857; U.S., M&B: 1944]

sissy beer beer with a low alcohol content: near-beer, three-two beer. RS: *queer-beer*. From the prohibition era. [U.S., MHW: 1934, D&D: 1957]

sissy cure the breaking of a drug habit by tapering off. RS: *kick*. [U.S., JES: 1959, H&C: 1975]

sister 1. morphine. Sister = nurse. *Cf. white nurse*. RT: *morphine*. [U.S., YKB: 1977] 2. cocaine. *Cf. girl, her*. RT: *cocaine*. [U.S., S&W: 1973]

sitter a person who attends another person during an L.S.D. trip. Short for *baby sitter* (*q.v.*). [U.S., TRG: 1968, EEL: 1971, KBH: 1982] Terms for an L.S.D. trip attendant: *baby sitter, conductor, controller, copilot, gate-keeper, ground control, ground man, guide, guru, sitter, tour guide, travel agent*.

sitting well drug intoxicated. RT: *stoned*. [U.S., H&C: 1975]

six-pack 1. a package (or group) of six cans of beer. Now colloquial for any product sold in packages of six. [U.S., (1952): MW: 1983] 2. to while away a specified period of time drinking a six-pack of beer. RS: *irrigate*. [U.S., RAS: 1970]

sizzle to be hot, i.e., carrying drugs. Perhaps akin to *hot bust* and *cold bust*, types of arrests for drug possession. This sizzle makes the carrier *hot*, or subject to arrest for drug possession. RS: *dope*. [U.S., (M&V: 1967), RRL: 1969, CM: 1970]

sizzled alcohol intoxicated. Akin to *fried*. RT: *drunk*. [U.S., BVB: 1942]

sizz water seltzer water; soda water. [U.S., D&D: 1957]

skag (also scag) 1. a tobacco cigarette; a tobacco cigarette butt. RT: *brad, nail*. Military and then general slang. [U.S., (1915): W&F: 1960, HB: 1928, MHW: 1934] 2. to smoke a tobacco cigarette. [U.S., HB: 1928, MHW: 1934] 3. heroin. RT: *heroin*. See other attestations at *scag*. [U.S., RG: 1970, DCCU: 1972, ADC: 1975, MW: 1976, DNE: 1980, EAF: 1980] 4. hard liquor. [U.S., DCCU: 1972] 5. any hard drug. RS: *dope*. [U.S., Chicago, GG: 1981]

skagged out drug intoxicated; very high. *Skag* (*q.v.*) = a hard drug. RT: *stoned*. [U.S., RAS: 1980]

skag jones (also scag jones) a heroin habit; heroin addiction. The *jones* is not a personification, but an example of a thing or gadget term used when a name is not known or the speaker does not wish to say it. *Jones* (*q.v.*) is essentially a personification of *whatchamacallit*. *Cf. johnson*. RS: *habit*. [U.S., W&F: 1975, RDS: 1982] See also *Cecil Jones*.

skagtown a neighborhood of the city inhabited by drug addicts. *Cf. narkiland*. See *skag*. [U.S., RDS: 1982]

skamas opium. Some writers have speculated that this word is Yiddish. RT: *opium*. [U.S., BD: 1937, DWM: 1938, A&T: 1953]

skat beer. Skat = dung. See *skit*. RT: *beer*. [U.S., early 1900s, DU]

skate 1. a drinking bout. RT: *spree*. [U.S., BVB: 1942] 2. a drunkard; a person on a spree. RS: *sot*. [U.S., BVB: 1942] 3. to get drunk. RT: *mug oneself*. [U.S., EHB: 1900, BVB: 1942] 4. to use morphine. [U.S., early 1900s, DU, A&T: 1953]

skating drug intoxicated. RT: *stoned*. Probably nonce. [Br., (1955): DSUE]

skee 1. whiskey. A respelling of the *skey* of *whiskey*. This is attested in Boontling (CCA) which was used in Boonville, California between 1880 and 1920. This type of front-clipping is quite prevalent in Boontling. [U.S., late 18-1900s, CCA, (1914): DU, VR: 1929, MHW: 1934, GOL: 1950, W&F: 1960] 2. opium. From sense one or perhaps akin to *skamas*. RT: *opium*. [U.S., (1930): W&F: 1960, A&T: 1953]

skee joint a saloon; a low saloon. RS: *dive*. [U.S., GOL: 1950, D&D: 1957]

skew-whiff alcohol intoxicated. RT: *drunk*. [Br., M&J: 1975]

skid heroin; heroin in the phrase *skid bag* (*q.v.*). See *skid bag*. RT: *heroin*. [U.S., SNP: 1977, RDS: 1982]

skid bag a bag of highly diluted heroin. *Cf. skid*. See *greasy bag*. RS: *load*. [U.S., RRL: 1969]

skilly inferior or weak liquor. From a slang term (British, 1800s, JCH: 1887), *skilligalee*, = thin, watery porridge served in work houses. [Br., M&J: 1975]

skimish liquor. *Cf. skimmished*. RT: *booze*. [Br., early 1900s, DSUE]

skimmished (also **skimished**) alcohol intoxicated. From Romany. See *ishkimmisk*. Related terms include **skimmisher** = a sot, and **skimmish** = booze, to booze. [cant, (1908): DU, POS: 1979]

skin 1. a rolling paper used for tobacco and marijuana cigarettes. RT: *paper*. [U.S., G&B: 1969, ADC: 1975, LVA: 1981] 2. to *skin pop* (*q.v.*), either by accident or on purpose. Compare to *muscle*. RS: *shoot*. [U.S., (RRL: 1969), (1970): DNE: 1973, W&F: 1975, (RDS: 1982)]

skinful an intoxicating quantity of liquor; enough liquor. Widely known in the context have a skinful (*q.v.*). [U.S., MHW: 1934, EP: 1948, GOL: 1950]

skink weak or inferior liquor. [1800s, OED]

skinker a bartender who fills glasses full with booze. RS: *bartender*. [cant, BE: 1690]

skinner 1. a subcutaneous injection of drugs. *Cf. skin pop*. RS: *shot*. [U.S., M&V: 1954, H&C: 1975] 2. a drug user who prefers subcutaneous injections to intravenous injections. Compare to *artillery man, hype, hypo, hypo juggler, hypo smecker, mainliner, mainline popper, vein shooter*. RS: *bangster*. [U.S., M&V: 1967, H&C: 1975]

skinning taking drugs (usually heroin) by subcutaneous injection. See *skin*.

skinny marijuana. Possibly in reference to a thin marijuana cigarette. *Cf. pin, pin joint*. RT: *pot*. [U.S., YKB: 1977]

skin pop 1. a subcutaneous or intramuscular injection of drugs, usually heroin. This may be done in the early stages of heroin use before vein shots are attempted or in the latter stages when readily accessible veins have been ruined. *Cf. skin shot*. RS: *shot*. [U.S., M&D: 1952, A&T: 1953, RRL: 1969] 2. to inject drugs subcutaneously or intramuscularly. One who uses heroin in this fashion is a **skin-popper** and is considered a *chipper* (*q.v.*). RS: *shoot*. [U.S., M&H: 1959, W&F: 1967, (RRL: 1969), (CM: 1970), EEL: 1971, MW: 1976, (RDS: 1982)]

skin pumping taking skin pops. A variant of *skin pop* (*q.v.*). [U.S., M&D: 1952]

skin-search a *strip-search* (*q.v.*) conducted on a suspected drug user. The skin is examined for needle marks (tracks) and the body orifices are examined for concealed drugs. [U.S., W&F: 1975]

skin-shooter (also **skin-popper**) a drug user who injects subcutaneously rather than into the vein. The implication is that this user is not yet addicted. RS: *bangster*. [U.S., BD: 1937]

skin shot a subcutaneous injection of a drug. The same as *skin pop* (*q.v.*). RS: *shot*. [U.S., DWM: 1936, M&D: 1952, A&T: 1953, D&B: 1970c]

skin the punk to miss a vein when attempting an intravenous injection of drugs. Perhaps punk = punch. [U.S., M&V: 1967]

skin yen a craving for an injection of a drug (rather than an oral dose). Said of addicts. *Cf. yen*. [U.S., (1910): DU, DWM: 1936, BVB: 1942]

skip and jump habit the use of drugs on an occasional basis; a *chippy habit* (*q.v.*). [U.S., JES: 1959, H&C: 1975]

skit beer. Possibly a dysphemism based on the old term *skit* meaning watery excrement. See *skat*. RT: *beer*. [Br., late 18–1900s, DSUE, F&G: 1925]

skizzled alcohol intoxicated. RT: *drunk*. [U.S., RAS: 1982]

skoofer (also **skoofus, skrufer, skrufus**) a marijuana cigarette. RT: *joint*. Black use. [U.S., EAF: 1972]

skuffle *P.C.P.* (*q.v.*). The same as *scuffle* (*q.v.*). RT: *P.C.P.* [U.S., (1970s): FAB: 1979]

skull-buster a police officer. RT: *fuzz*. [U.S., BVB: 1942, D&D: 1957]

skull drag to beg for drinks at a saloon. Said of a hobo. [U.S., EK: 1927, GI: 1931, MHW: 1934]

skunk a potent variety of marijuana. Said to be grown in California. RS: *pot*. [U.S., RDS: 1982]

skunk-drunk (also **skunked**) alcohol intoxicated. *Cf. drunk as a skunk*. RT: *drunk*. [PD: 1982]

sky whiskey. A front-clipping of the alternate (British) spelling of *whiskey: whisky*. *Cf. skee*. RT: *whiskey*. [Aust., (1950): DSUE; U.S., (1950): BVB: 1942]

sky blue gin. *Cf. blue ribband, blue ribbon, blue ruin, blue stone, blue tape, light blue*. RT: *gin*. [cant, (1755): F&H, FG: 1785, FG: 1788, FG: 1811, GWM: 1859, B&L: 1890; listed in MHW: 1934, BVB: 1942]

sky river *L.S.D.* (*q.v.*) mixed with some other drug. RS: *set*. [U.S., KBH: 1982]

skyrockets amphetamine tablets or capsules. RT: *amps*. [U.S., YKB: 1977] See also *pack of rockets, rocket fuel, rocket ship*.

skyte, on the alcohol intoxicated. This *skyte* is probably akin to *skit* and *shit* (*q.v.*). RT: *drunk*. [Br. (Scots), late 1800s, F&H]

sky-the-wipe a hypodermic needle; a hypodermic syringe and needle. Rhyming slang for *hype*. RT: *monkey pump, needle*. [U.S., M&B: 1944, DRS, A&T: 1953]

sky-wannocking a drinking bout; a drinking party. RT: *spree*. [Br., 1800s, F&H]

slack off cure (also **slack off**) an attempt to break a drug habit by tapering off. *Cf. sissy cure*. RS: *kick*. [U.S., (1920): DU, BVB: 1942]

slag a drug addict. RT: *junky*. [U.S., JHF: 1971]

slam some beers to drink beer; to drink a number of beers. RT: *irrigate*. [U.S., ADC: 1984]

slash a drink of liquor. GEN: an act of urination. *Cf. slash*. RT: *nip*. [Br., (1930): DSUE]

slathered alcohol intoxicated. Possibly akin to *slithered*. RT: *drunk*. [Aust., (1920): DSUE]

slave a drug addict. RT: *junky*. Probably not argot. [U.S., RDS: 1982]

slave master a specific model of water pipe. RS: *bong*. [U.S.,

(1972): ELA: 1982]

slave of the beast a drunkard. RT: *sot*. [U.S., BVB: 1942] See also *the beast*.

sleepers (also **sleeping pills**) tablets or capsules of barbiturate. Refers to their medical use as a sedative. RT: *barbs*. *Sleeping pill* is standard English. [Br., (c. 1926): DSUE; U.S., M&V: 1967, RRL: 1969, D&B: 1970c, ADC: 1975, W&F: 1975, MW: 1976, W&S: 1977]

sleep it off to sleep while the effects of drugs or alcohol wear off. [U.S., 1900s, AP: 1980, RDS: 1982]

sleepwalker a heroin addict. RS: *junky*. [U.S., RRL: 1969, RDS: 1982]

sleepy alcohol intoxicated. *Cf. tired, weary*. RT: *drunk*. [U.S., mid 1800s, W&F: 1960]

sleighride 1. cocaine. RT: *cocaine*. [U.S., IGA: 1971, EEL: 1971] 2. a cocaine spree; a cocaine party; a period of cocaine use. *Cf. go for a sleighride*. [U.S., (1908): DU, BVB: 1942, VJM: 1949, A&T: 1953] 3. to take cocaine. Probably earlier than attestations suggest. [U.S., EEL: 1971, W&F: 1975]

sleighride, on a on a cocaine binge; under the influence of cocaine. See other snow terms at *winter wonderland*. RS: *cocainized*. [U.S., BVB: 1942, JES: 1959]

sleighrider a cocaine user. *Cf. kokomo*. [U.S., (1910): W&F: 1960, (1915): DU, BVB: 1942, D&D: 1957]

slew to drink to intoxication. RT: *mug oneself*. Attested as **slough** in the U.S. by EK: 1927. [(1888): OED]

slewed (also **slewy, slued, sloughed, sloughed up**) alcohol intoxicated. *Cf. half slewed*. RT: *drunk*. [Br. and U.S., (1801): OEDS, (1834): OED, JCH: 1887, B&L: 1890, BWG: 1899, MHW: 1934, VJM: 1949]

slightly damaged alcohol intoxicated. See *damaged*.

slightly damp alcohol intoxicated. See *damp*.

slightly elevated alcohol intoxicated. See *elevated*.

slightly rattled alcohol intoxicated. See *rattled*.

slightly-tightly a bit tipsy; alcohol intoxicated. *Cf. tight*. RS: *drunk*. [JRW: 1909]

slight sensation a drink of liquor. See *sensation*.

slim 1. rum. RT: *rum*. [possibly nonce, (1789): DSUE] 2. a tobacco cigarette. Possibly for a long (100 mm) cigarette. The same as *straight* (*q.v.*). RT: *nail*. Jazz musician use. [U.S., W&F: 1967] 3. a drug user or addict. RT: *user*. [U.S., (c. 1930): JES: 1959, BVB: 1942]

slip-slop very weak liquor. *Cf. slop*. RS: *queer-beer, rotgut*. [U.S., BVB: 1942, D&D: 1957]

slip someone a Mickey to secretly put a *Mickey Finn* (*q.v.*) in someone's alcoholic drink. *Cf. mick.* [U.S., 1900s, PE: 1980]

slobbering shit (also **slobbering stuff**) potent hard drugs. Strong enough to make one nod and slobber. Here *stuff* is a euphemism for *shit* (*q.v.*). [U.S., JWK: 1981]

sloe gin Gin flavored with sloe berries. [18–1900s, (1895): OED]

sloosh beer. Possibly a variant of *slosh*. RT: *beer*. [Br. naval, early 1900s, WG: 1962]

slop inferior liquor; bad beer. GEN: any undesirable material, particularly edible material. It is clearly a variant of *slops* (*q.v.*). RT: *queer-beer, rotgut*. [U.S., (1904): DU, AH: 1931, MHW: 1934]

slopped (also **slopped over, slopped to the ears, slopped up, sloppy, sloppy drunk**) alcohol intoxicated; heavily intoxicated. *Slopped to the ears* is a blend of *slopped* and an expression such as *primed to the ears, soused to the ears, stewed to the ears, up to the ears. Sloppy* and *sloppy drunk* are from 1896 (SBF: 1976). RT: *drunk*. [U.S., (1907): SBF: 1976, MP: 1928, AH: 1931, MHW: 1934, GOL: 1950, D&D: 1957]

slops weak beer; beer; inferior liquor. This is assumed to come directly from the term for used wash-bowl water, chamber pot contents, and liquid material fed to hogs. See *slop*. RT: *queer-beer, rotgut*. [JCH: 1887, (1920): DSUE, EK: 1927, GI: 1931, BVB: 1942, BH: 1980]

slop up to drink heavily; to get drunk. RT: *guzzle, mug oneself.* DSUE lists **slopping-up** = a *binge* (late 1800s). [U.S., (1899): DU, EK: 1927, GI: 1931, VJM: 1949, GOL: 1950]

slosh 1. beer; liquor. RT: *beer, booze*. [Br. and U.S., (1819): OED, MHW: 1934, D&D: 1957] 2. to drink liquor, including beer; to drink to excess. RT: *irrigate, guzzle*. [Br., B&L: 1890, DU]

sloshed (also **sloshed to the ears**) alcohol intoxicated. See *slopped* for comments. [Br., late 18–1900s, DSUE, M&J: 1975; U.S., (1950s): SBF: 1976, D&D: 1957, DCCU: 1972]

slough See *slew*.

sloughed 1. (also **sloughed up**) alcohol intoxicated. See *slewed*. [U.S., JCR: 1914] 2. arrested. RT: *busted*. [U.S., EK: 1927]

slow boat a marijuana cigarette; a *dagga* (*q.v.*) cigarette. RT: *joint*. [South African, (1967): JB: 1980] See also *steamboat*.

sludge beer. RT: *beer*. [Br., (1955): DSUE]

slued alcohol intoxicated. See *slewed*.

slug a drink of liquor; a shot of whiskey. RT: *nip*. [(1756): OED, (1762): F&H, FG: 1823, LWP: 1908, VJM: 1949, DCCU: 1972] See also *fire a slug*.

slugged alcohol intoxicated. *Cf. slug*. RT: *drunk*. [U.S., (1951): W&F: 1960]

sluice to drink liquor. RT: *irrigate.* [cant, FG: 1796, GWM: 1859]

sluice house a drinking establishment. RS: *bar.* [Br., B&L: 1890]

sluice one's gob (also **sluice one's bolt, sluice one's dominoes, sluice the worries**) to drink liquor, perhaps to excess. **Sluice the worries** is from D&D: 1957. RT: *irrigate, guzzle.* [cant, FG: 1788, FG: 1811, FG: 1823, (1846): DU, GWM: 1859]

sluicery a pub; a gin shop. *Cf. sluice.* RS: *bar.* [Br., FG: 1823, JCH: 1859, F&H]

slum 1. narcotics. RT: *dope.* [U.S., (1925): DU] **2.** to use cocaine or morphine. [U.S., (1925): DU] **3.** to drink liquor. RT: *irrigate.* [U.S., early 1900s, DU]

slumber party (also **slumber medicine**) morphine. RT: *morphine.* [U.S., DWM: 1933, MHW: 1934, VJM: 1949]

slum dump an opium den. *Cf. slum.* RT: *opium den.* [U.S., A&T: 1953]

slumgullion weak or inferior liquor. From a term for a humble (meat) stew. RS: *rotgut.* [Br., 1800s, F&H; listed in BVB: 1942]

slush (also **slusher**) a drunkard. *Cf. lush, slosh.* RT: *sot.* [U.S., BVB: 1942]

slushed (also **slushed up**) alcohol intoxicated. RT: *drunk.* [U.S., BVB: 1942, VJM: 1949]

slush up to drink liquor; to get drunk. RT: *irrigate, mug oneself.* [U.S., BVB: 1942, DU]

sly grog illicit liquor. RS: *moonshine.* [(1844): OED; Aust. and New Zealand, GAW: 1978, SJB: 1943]

sly grogshop (also **sly groggery, sly grog joint**) a secret or illicit liquor establishment. [Aust., (1829): GAW: 1978, (1920): DSUE, SJB: 1943, K&M: 1968] Nicknames and slang terms for secret or illicit liquor-selling establishments: *barbecue, barrelhouse, beer flat, blind pig, blind pigger, blind tiger, blue pig, booze foundry, boozery, club, creep joint, dive, doggery, halfway house, hush-house, hushie, hush joint, jimmy, leggery, leg joint, low talk, moonlight inn, moonshinery, pig, Q.T., red nugget, red onion, schooner, shanty, shebeen, shinery, shoe polish shop, shypook, shypoo shop, sly groggery, sly grog joint, sly grogshop, spun joint.*

smack 1. (also **smak**) heroin. Originally, a *card* (*q.v.*) of opium, and later, heroin. From *schmeck* or *schmack.* Probably reinforced semantically by the jolt of heroin. RT: *heroin.* Possibly black slang originally, or possibly Yiddish. [U.S., DWM: 1938, W&F: 1967, RRL: 1969, D&B: 1970c, CM: 1970, EEL: 1971, DC: 1972, DCCU: 1972, DNE: 1973, MA: 1973, ADC: 1975, EAF: 1980, NIDA: 1980, JWK: 1981, ADC: 1984] **2.** the punch or jolt from liquor. [U.S., BVB: 1942]

smackhead a heroin addict. See *head* for a list of similar terms. RS: *junky.* [U.S., (1972): DNE: 1980]

smackse a hypodermic needle used in the injection of heroin. RT: *needle*. [U.S., EEL: 1971]

small beer weak beer; diluted beer. *Cf. thin drink*. RS: *queer-beer*. Now primarily British. In the U.S., this means *nothing* or *next to nothing*. [since the 1500s, (1568): OED]

smash 1. tobacco. RT: *fogus*. Prison use. [Br., B&L: 1890, F&H] **2.** liquor in general. RT: *booze*. [U.S., MHW: 1934, BVB: 1942] **3.** wine. Refers to the crushed grapes from which wine is made. RT: *wine*. Possibly a backformation of *smashed*. Black use. [U.S., HER: 1971, DC: 1972, W&F: 1975, EAF: 1980] **4.** hashish oil. RT: *oil*. [U.S., YKB: 1977, ELA: 1982]

smashed heavily intoxicated with drugs or alcohol. RT: *drunk, stoned*. [U.S., W&F: 1960, M&V: 1967, RRL: 1969, D&B: 1970c, EEL: 1971, MW: 1976; Br., (1960): DSUE, PW: 1974]

sma' still, the whiskey. Refers to illicit whiskey from *the small still*. From Scots English in the 1800s or before, and still seen occasionally even in the U.S. RT: *whiskey*. [18–1900s, F&H]

smeak drugs. A variant of, or an error for *smeck* (*q.v.*). *Cf. smeaker* (at *smecker*). RT: *dope*. [U.S., VJM: 1949]

smeared alcohol intoxicated; drug intoxicated. RT: *drunk, stoned*. [U.S., mid 1900s, S&E: 1981]

smears *L.S.D.* (*q.v.*), probably in a specific form. Probably L.S.D. smeared on tablets or blotting paper. RT: *L.S.D.* [U.S., SNP: 1977, RDS: 1982]

smeck heroin. A variant of *schmeck* (*q.v.*). RT: *heroin*. [U.S., (1920): DU, MHW: 1934, DWM: 1938, DU, RRL: 1969, YKB: 1977]

smecker (also **smeaker**) a heroin addict. A variant of *schmecker* (*q.v.*). RT: *junky*. [U.S., (1920): DU, BD: 1937, DWM: 1938, VJM: 1949]

smeekit alcohol intoxicated. From Scots English for *smoked* (*q.v.*). RT: *drunk*. [Br., 1800s, F&H]

smelling of the cork alcohol intoxicated. *Cf. corked*. RT: *drunk*. [Br., 1800s, F&H; listed in BVB: 1942]

smell it up to sniff or *snort* (*q.v.*) powdered drugs. RT: *snort*. [U.S., M&V: 1973]

smell the reindeer dust to take cocaine nasally. RT: *snort*. [U.S., JES: 1959]

smell the stuff to *snort* (*q.v.*) cocaine. *Cf. smell it up*. [U.S., D&D: 1957]

smelt of an onion alcohol intoxicated. (BF: 1737: [He's] Smelt...) RT: *drunk*. [BF: 1737]

smile 1. (also **smiler, smiley**) a drink of liquor; liquor. RT: *nip*. Smiley was heard in Chicago in 1983. An old term revived during prohibition. [U.S., (1855): JRB: 1859, GWM: 1859,

DSUE, M&C: 1905, EK: 1927, GI: 1931, AH: 1931, MHW: 1934] 2. to drink liquor; to have a drink of liquor. RT: *irrigate*. [GWM: 1859; M&C: 1905, BVB: 1942]

smizz heroin. RT: *heroin*. [HSD: 1984]

smokatorium a place to smoke tobacco. A contrived and jocular expression patterned on auditorium. [U.S., MHW: 1934]

smoke 1. a tobacco cigarette; a pipe; a cigar; the act of smoking anything smokable, including smokable drugs. The earliest attestation is for tobacco and the later ones are for marijuana. [(1830): SBF: 1976, (1882): OED, BVB: 1942, W&F: 1960, (WWI): B&P: 1965, M&J: 1975, PW: 1977, ADC: 1981] 2. marijuana; a marijuana cigarette. [U.S., (1946): ELA: 1982, W&F: 1960, RRL: 1969, ADC: 1975, DNE: 1980, EAF: 1980, ADC: 1981, JWK: 1981, ADC: 1984] 3. to smoke a marijuana cigarette; to smoke marijuana. RT: *hit the hay*. [U.S., D&B: 1970a, EEL: 1971, IGA: 1971, DC: 1972, ADC: 1975, DNE: 1980, JWK: 1981, ADC: 1984] 4. methyl alcohol; antifreeze, bad liquor; any liquor. Usually refers to some (dangerous) substitute for liquor during prohibition or to a liquor substitute used in prison or by hobos. A hobo using smoke was called a smoke-bum. *Cf. alky bum*. The term is said to be from the cloudy appearance of denatured alcohol diluted in water and shaken. It is probably akin to the word *wood* in wood alcohol. The SOD dates smoke as 1849 referring to a strong South African brandy. See *Cape smoke*. [U.S., (1904): OEDS, (1928): DU, VR: 1929, AH: 1931, GI: 1931, MHW: 1934, GOL: 1950, W&F: 1960, K&M: 1968, EEL: 1971]

smoke a bowl to smoke a (pipe) bowl of hashish or opium. *Cf. bowl*. RS: *suck bamboo*. [U.S., RDS: 1982]

smoke bum (also smokehound) a hobo drinker of denatured alcohol or other liquor substitutes. RS: *sot*. [U.S., GOL: 1950, D&D: 1957]

smoked alcohol intoxicated. *Cf. smeekit*. "Preserved" as in *corned* (*q.v.*). RT: *drunk*. [U.S., (c. 1850): W&F: 1960]

smoke eater a heavy smoker. Patterned on *opium eater* (*q.v.*). [U.S., MHW: 1934, BVB: 1942]

smoke-in a young peoples' public event of the 1960s where marijuana was smoked in open defiance of the law in a public gathering. Patterned on *sit-in, teach-in,* and *love-in*. [U.S., (1970): DNE: 1973]

smoke, in the using opium; addicted to opium. [U.S., early 1900s, DU]

smoke joint 1. a place to buy or smoke opium. RT: *opium den*. [Br., early 1900s, DU] 2. a low saloon selling inferior liquor or *smoke* (*q.v.*). RS: *dive*. [U.S., (1922): DU, GOL: 1950, D&D: 1957]

smoker 1. a gathering of men where tobacco is smoked. The same term is used to refer to the hall, room, or railway car where tobacco can be smoked. Not argot. [U.S., MHW: 1934] 2. a person who smokes opium. RT: *campfire boy*. [U.S., (1887): RML: 1948, BD: 1937] 3. a marijuana smoker. RT: *toker*. [U.S., JWK: 1981]

smoke some bongs to smoke marijuana in a water pipe. Refers to more than one filling of the *bong* (*q.v.*). RS: *hit the hay*. [U.S., ADC: 1981]

smokestick a tobacco cigarette. Patterned on smokestack. *Cf. stick*. RT: *nail*. [U.S., MHW: 1934, BVB: 1942]

smoke, the opium. See *smoke*.

smokey an opium smoker. *Cf. smoker*. RT: *campfire boy*. [U.S., BVB: 1942, DU]

smudge a small amount of heroin. RS: *load*. [U.S., EEL: 1971]

snacked alcohol intoxicated. RT: *drunk*. [U.S. (Southern), JSF: 1889]

snake 1. inferior or strong whiskey. A truncation of *snake poison* (*q.v.*) or *snakebite medicine* (*q.v.*). RT: *rotgut*. [U.S., MHW: 1934, W&F: 1960] 2. a marijuana smoker. The same as *viper* (*q.v.*). RT: *toker*. [U.S., GOL: 1950, A&T: 1953]

snakebite medicine (also **snakebite remedy, snakehead whiskey, snake juice, snake medicine, snake poison, snake water**) inferior whiskey; strong whiskey; homemade whiskey. *Cf. medicine*. The various expressions allude to snake venom or whiskey used as a cure for snakebite. **Snake juice** is Australian (early 1900s), all others are U.S. A few of these expressions are still occasionally used. RT: *rotgut*. [Aust. and U.S., (1865): DA, (1889): DAE, (1904): GAW: 1978, LWP: 1908, BVB: 1942, SJB: 1943, PW: 1977]

snakes (also **seeing snakes, snakes in one's boots**) the delirium tremens. *Cf. snake*. RT: *D.T.s*. [Br. and U.S., (1865): DA, F&H, JRW: 1909, MHW: 1934, D&D: 1957]

snap See *snapper*.

snap-neck apple brandy. RT: *brandy*. [U.S., BVB: 1942]

snapped 1. (also **snaped**) alcohol intoxicated. RT: *drunk*. [U.S., (1844): F&H, JRB: 1859, B&L: 1890, BVB: 1942] 2. (also **snapt**) arrested. RT: *busted*. [GWM: 1859]

snapped up stimulated by a drug; drug intoxicated. RT: *stoned*. [U.S., D&D: 1957]

snapper (also **snap**) a vial or ampule of *amyl nitrite* (*q.v.*). *Cf. popper*. Snap is British (1962): DSUE. [U.S., RRL: 1969, BR: 1972, ADC: 1975, NIDA: 1980, ADC: 1981] Nicknames and slang terms for a vial of amyl nitrite: *aimless Amy, amy, amy joy, amyl, amyl nitrite, amyls, amys, Aroma of Man, banana splits, Ban Apple, Black Jack, Bolt, Cat's Meow, crackers, Cum, Dr. Bananas,*

Hardware, Heart On, Hi Baller, joy-juice, Loc-A-Roma, Locker Popper, OZ, pearls, perls, popper, popsie, Rice Krispies, Satan's Scent, Shotgun, snap, snapper, sniff, Toilet Water, Uncle Emil.

snaps (also snapps, snops) gin; liquor. A variant of *schnapps*. RT: *booze*. [JCH: 1887, F&H]

snart a tobacco cigarette. RT: *nail*. [Br. army, (1925): DSUE]

snatched arrested. RT: *busted*. [U.S., M&V: 1967]

snatcher a policeman; a detective. RT: *fuzz*. [U.S., DB: 1944]

snaved in drug intoxicated. RT: *stoned*. [U.S., MHW: 1934, A&T: 1953]

sneakeasy (also sneaker, sneakery, sneakie) an illicit liquor establishment; possibly an illegal distillery. The entry word (at least) is patterned on *speakeasy*. RS: *speak*. From the prohibition era. [U.S., BVB: 1942, GOL: 1950]

sneaky Pete 1. cheap red wine; inferior fortified wine. RS: *wine*. [Aust. and U.S., (1920s): DST: 1984, M&D: 1952, D&D: 1957, W&F: 1960, SJB: 1966, K&M: 1968] 2. marijuana and wine. ELA: 1984 lists Sneaky Peat. *Cf. lusher*. [U.S., HB: 1955]

sneezed down (also sneezed) having to do with an addict who has been arrested and is held without drugs as a means of getting information. Sneezing is one of the early symptoms of drug withdrawal. See *Miss Carrie*. [U.S., DWM: 1936, BD: 1937, BVB: 1942]

sneeze it out to attempt to break a drug habit by withdrawing from drugs completely. See *sneezed down*. [U.S., DWM: 1938, BVB: 1942, A&T: 1953, EEL: 1971]

snerf to sniff or snort cocaine. A variant of *sniff*. RT: *snort*. Black use. [U.S., Chicago, GG: 1981]

sniff 1. a drink of liquor. Based on *snort* (*q.v.*). *Cf. whiff*. RT: *nip*. [U.S., MHW: 1934, BVB: 1942] 2. to take cocaine nasally; to snort cocaine. Most attestations are for sniffing. RT: *snort*. [U.S., (1925): DU, (DWM: 1936), (BD: 1937), (M&D: 1952), W&F: 1960, (RRL: 1969), ADC: 1975, JWK: 1981; Br., BTD: 1968] 3. cocaine; a snort of cocaine; a nasal dose of cocaine. RT: *dose*. It is not clear what evidence the DU date is based on. [U.S., (1934): DU, RRL: 1974, NIDA: 1980] 4. to inhale glue vapors or other gasses in an attempt to get high. *Cf. huffer*. [U.S., DCCU: 1972, H&C: 1975] 5. *amyl nitrite* (*q.v.*). RT: *snapper*. [U.S., BR: 1972]

sniffer (also sniffler) a drug user who habitually takes cocaine or heroin nasally. *Cf. snifter*. RS: *kokomo*. [U.S., EK: 1927, GI: 1931, MHW: 1934, DWM: 1936, GOL: 1950, D&D: 1957, W&F: 1960]

sniffing squad federal officers enforcing prohibition; people who attempted to locate illicit alcohol use by sniffing for it. Contrived and jocular. *Cf. cellar-smeller, whiffsniffer*. RS: *dry, fuzz*. From the prohibition era. [U.S., early 1900s, DU]

snifter 1. a drink of liquor. *Cf. sniff.* RT: *nip.* [U.S., (1848): DA, F&H, AH: 1931, GI: 1931, D&D: 1957, W&F: 1960] 2. a cocaine user. RT: *kokomo.* See *sniffer.* [U.S., (1925): DU, EK: 1927, DWM: 1933, MHW: 1934, DWM: 1936, D&D: 1957, W&F: 1960]

snipe a cigarette butt. Originally a tobacco cigarette or a cigar butt, now primarily known as a marijuana cigarette butt. *Cf. roach.* RT: *brad.* Originally hobo usage. [U.S., JWC: 1905, EK: 1927, VWS: 1929, VJM: 1949, GOL: 1950, D&D: 1957, H&C: 1975; Br. M&J: 1975]

snipe-shooter (also **sniper**) a cigarette or cigar butt collector. *Cf. butt-stooper, dumper-dasher, guttersnipe, topper-hunter.* Originally hobo usage. [U.S., (1891): DU, GI: 1931, GOL: 1950, D&D: 1957]

snockered (also **schnoggered, snoggered, snockered to the gills**) alcohol intoxicated. RT: *drunk.* [Aust., SJB: 1966; U.S., GU: 1975, PD: 1982]

snoodge a dose of a drug. See *snooze.* RT: *dose.* [U.S., early 1900s, DU]

snoose (also **snus**) snuff. Snoose is a brand of *snuff.* Akin to *snooser* = a Scandinavian. Attested as loggers' use and underworld use. [U.S., JS: 1925, DWM: 1931, (1934): ADD, GOL: 1950] Nicknames and slang terms for snuff: *bumblebee dust, dip, hang bluff, Harry Bluff, heifer dust, merry-go-up, rest powder, Scandihoovian dynamite, scridgin, snoose, snuff, snus, Swedish condition powder.*

snooted alcohol intoxicated. *Cf. have a snootfull.* RT: *drunk.* [U.S., BVB: 1942]

snoozamorooed alcohol intoxicated. RT: *drunk.* [PD: 1982]

snooze a dose of drugs. Probably refers to the period of lethargy following narcotics use. RT: *dose. Cf. nod.* [U.S., HNR: 1934, DU]

snoozer a drink of strong liquor. RS: *nip.* [U.S., early 1900s, DU]

snop marijuana. RT: *pot.* [U.S., RRL: 1969, W&F: 1975, YKB: 1977]

snops (also **snopsy**) gin. Probably akin to *schnapps.* RT: *gin.* [U.S., B&L: 1890, F&H]

snork to smoke marijuana or hashish. Possibly akin to *snorkel.* RT: *hit the hay.* [U.S., JTD: 1971]

snort 1. a drink of strong liquor; a glass of beer. *Cf. snorter.* RS: *nip.* [Br. and U.S., (1889): SBF: 1982, (1920s): DSUE, MHW: 1934, W&F: 1960, SSD, DCCU: 1972] 2. to take cocaine (or other powdered drugs) nasally as one takes snuff. Although this is sometimes defined as inhaling, the goal is to coat the nasal passages with the crystalline drug, not to inhale the drug into the lungs. Although glue vapors and other gasses are occasionally snorted, the goal is to take those substances into the bloodstream by way of the lungs. [U.S., DWM: 1938, M&H: 1959, W&F: 1967, RRL: 1969, CM: 1970, EEL: 1971, MA: 1973, MW: 1976, DNE: 1980, ADC: 1981, JWK: 1981] (This entry continues after the following list.) Terms meaning to sniff up cocaine: ***bang, blow, blow Charlie, blow coke, blow dust, blow horse, blow snow, blow the coke, cork the air, do a line, fire a line, get one's nose cold, go down the line, horn, jefferson airplane, pack one's nose, rare, scoop, short, short snort, shovel snow, smell it up, smell the reindeer dust, smell the stuff, snerf, sniff, snort, snozzle, snuff the stuff, soot the chimney, sweep, take a sweep, take it through the nose, thwip, tickle one's smokestack, toot, wake up***. 3. a nasal dose of cocaine or other powdered drugs, especially heroin. RS: ***dose***. [U.S., A&T: 1953, RRL: 1969, (1973): DNE: 1980, ADC: 1975] See also ***snorts***.

snorter 1. a drink of undiluted whiskey. *Cf.* ***snort***. RT: ***nip***. [U.S., (1891): SBF: 1976] 2. a drunkard. *Cf.* ***snort***. RT: ***sot***. [U.S., BVB: 1942] 3. a drug user who typically takes drugs nasally. RS: ***user***. [U.S., RAS: 1982] 4. a device for snorting cocaine. [U.S., ELA: 1984]

snort of horse a nasal dose of heroin. See ***horse***. *Cf.* ***snort***. [U.S., M&D: 1952]

snorts phencyclidine, ***P.C.P.*** (*q.v.*), an animal tranquilizer. The term has many possible sources. The terms for P.C.P. indicate that it is sold on the street as a variety of other drug substances. This term may be an effort to disguise P.C.P. as cocaine. See ***snort***. It may be akin to ***hog*** (*q.v.*) or ***horse*** (*q.v.*) (the latter from ***horse tranquilizer***) in imitation of sounds made by those animals. It may also simply reflect the fact that the crystals can be snorted. RS: ***P.C.P.*** [U.S., (1970s): FAB: 1979, YKB: 1977]

snot-flinging drunk alcohol intoxicated. Similar to commode-hugging drunk, knee-walking drunk. RT: ***drunk***. [U.S., BR: 1972]

snotted alcohol intoxicated. RT: ***drunk***. [U.S., B&L: 1890, AH: 1931, MHW: 1934]

snout tobacco; a tobacco cigarette; a cigar. *Cf.* ***nose 'em, noser my knacker***. RT: ***fogus, nail***. Prison and hobo use (F&H). [Br. and U.S., 18-1900s, F&H, VJM: 1949, PW: 1977, M&J: 1975]

snow (also **snowball, snowflakes, snow stuff**) a powdered or crystalline narcotic: morphine, heroin, or cocaine. Currently the term refers primarily to cocaine. RT: ***powder***. [U.S., (1921): OEDS, VWS: 1929, GI: 1931, DWM: 1933, DWM: 1936, GOL: 1950, D&D: 1957, W&F: 1960, RRL: 1969, DCCU: 1972, MW: 1976, EE: 1976, EAF: 1980] See ***winter wonderland*** for a list of terms on the snow theme.

snowbank a place to buy (and use) powdered drugs. Based on ***snow*** (*q.v.*). See the list at ***winter wonderland***. RS: ***doperie***. [U.S., (1927): DU, BVB: 1942, GOL: 1950]

snowbird 1. (also **snow flier**) a user of powdered narcotics; a cocaine user. *Cf. snow.* RT: ***kokomo.*** [U.S., BHL: 1920, (1922): OEDS, EK: 1927, VWS: 1929, DWM: 1931, GI: 1931, DWM: 1933, MHW: 1934, DWM: 1936, VJM: 1949, GOL: 1950, D&D: 1957, W&F: 1960, EEL: 1971] 2. a female cocaine pusher. From *bird* = woman, girl. Attested only by Partridge. Probably a misunderstanding of sense one. [Br., (1938): DSUE, DU] 3. cocaine. Probably an error. [U.S., YKB: 1977]

snow-caine cocaine. RT: *cocaine.* [U.S., BVB: 1942, VJM: 1949]

snow drifter a cocaine seller. RS: *dealer.* [U.S., (1938): DU]

snow eagle a major figure in a drug ring. From the name of a species of eagle. Bigger than a *snowbird. Cf. snow.* RS: *dealer.* [U.S., early 1900s, DU]

snowed (also **snowed in, snowed under, snowed up**) under the effects of cocaine; drug intoxicated. *Cf. snow.* RS: *stoned.* [U.S., HNR: 1934, VJM: 1949, D&D: 1957, W&F: 1960]

snowfall a spree of powdered cocaine or heroin use. *Cf. snow.* [U.S., DU, A&T: 1953]

snow flower a female cocaine user. *Cf. snowbird.* RT: ***kokomo.*** [U.S., DU, A&T: 1953]

snowmobiling using cocaine. *Cf. winter wonderland.* [U.S., D&B: 1971]

snow papers small sheets of paper used in the packaging and transporting of doses of cocaine. RS: *paper.* [U.S., RAS: 1983]

snow shed a *stash* for cocaine or other drugs. RT: *stash.* [U.S., ELA: 1984]

snowstorm a large quantity of cocaine; a wild cocaine party. *Cf. caught in a snowstorm.* See a list of snow terms at *winter wonderland.* [U.S., DU, D&D: 1957]

snozzled to snort a powdered drug such as cocaine or heroin. RT: *snort.* [U.S., ELA: 1984]

snozzled alcohol intoxicated. *Cf. sozzled.* RT: *drunk.* [U.S., MP: 1928, AH: 1931, MHW: 1934, W&F: 1960, D&D: 1957]

snozzle-wobbles a hangover; the delirium tremens. RT: *hangover, D.T.s.* [U.S., BVB: 1942, D&D: 1973]

snubbed alcohol intoxicated. RT: *drunk.* [U.S., (obsolete): W&F: 1960; listed in PD: 1982]

snuff finely powdered tobacco which is usually consumed by sniffing it up the nose. RT: *snoose.* Standard English. [since the late 1600s, (1671): MW: 1983]

snuff brush (also **snuffstick**) a brush or stick (perhaps a chewed twig) for dipping powdered snuff. [U.S., (1882): DA]

snuff spoon a small spoon used for snorting *snuff* (*q.v.*) or cocaine. The heavy cocaine use of the 1970s–80s has brought this term (and the spoon) into current use. [U.S., RDS: 1982]

snuff the stuff to *snort* (*q.v.*) a powdered drug. *Cf. stuff.* RT: *snort.* [U.S., JES: 1959, H&C: 1975]

snuffy 1. alcohol intoxicated. RT: *drunk.* [(1820): SBF: 1976, FG: 1823, JB: 1823, JCH: 1887, B&L: 1890, F&H, BVB: 1942] 2. one who snorts powdered drugs. RS: *user.* [U.S., DU, A&T: 1953]

snug alcohol intoxicated. *Cf. comfortable.* RT: *drunk.* [Br., 18–1900s, F&H, DSUE; listed in BVB: 1942]

snus snuff. See *snoose.*

so alcohol intoxicated. *Cf. How came you so?* A general term of disguise meaning pregnant, homosexual, or menstruating. See *so-so.* RT: *drunk.* [Br., 18–1900s, F&H; listed in BVB: 1942]

soak 1. to drink heavily; to go on a drinking bout; to get drunk. RT: *guzzle, mug oneself.* [(1766): F&H, (1851): SOD, EHB: 1900, BVB: 1942, W&F: 1960] 2. a drinking bout. RT: *spree.* [(1851): OED, BVB: 1942] 3. a drunkard. RT: *sot.* [Br. and U.S., FG: 1785, (1820): OED, F&H, (1910): DSUE, BWG: 1899, EHB: 1900, BVB: 1942, K&M: 1968]

soaked alcohol intoxicated. (BF: 1737: [He's] soak'd.) *Cf. soak.* RT: *drunk.* [BF: 1737, F&H, MP: 1928, MHW: 1934, BVB: 1942, DSUE, RDS: 1982]

soaker a drunkard; a tippler. *Cf. old soaker.* In an earlier (BE: 1690) spelling, **soker**. RT: *sot.* [(1589): SOD, FG: 1811, FG: 1823, JCH: 1887, B&L: 1890, BVB: 1942, K&M: 1968]

soak, in alcohol intoxicated. *Cf. soaked.* RT: *drunk.* [Br., late 1800s, DSUE; listed in BVB: 1942]

soak one's face to drink heavily. *Cf. soak.* RT: *guzzle.* [18–1900s, DSUE, OED]

soaper (also **soap, soapers, soaps, sope**) a *methaqualone* (*q.v.*) hypnotic-sedative tablet. From the drug name *Sopor* (TM; *q.v.*). *Cf. super-soaper.* RT: *ludes.* [U.S., RRL: 1969, (1973): DNE: 1980, ADC: 1975, H&C: 1975]

soapy-eyed alcohol intoxicated. From the redness of one's eyes from contact with soap or from drinking liquor. *Cf. lathered.* RT: *drunk.* [U.S., MP: 1928, MHW: 1934, D&D: 1957, W&F: 1960]

sober not under the effects of alcohol; not under the effects of either alcohol or drugs; never under the effects of alcohol or drugs. Standard English. [since the 1300s, (1387): OED] Other terms for sober: *bone dry, cold, cold sober, cracker dry, detoxed, dried, dried out, dry, dry as a bone, jober as a sudge, off the sauce, on the dead, sober as a buck shad, sober as a church, sober as a deacon, sober as a judge, sober as a powderhorn, sober as a shoemaker, stone sober.*

sober as a judge as sober as one can be. *Cf. jober as a sudge.* [U.S., (1835–1949): JW: 1954, BVB: 1942]

sober as a powderhorn (also **sober as a buck shad, sober as a church, sober as a deacon, sober as a shoemaker**) sober, as dry as a powderhorn. *Cf. dry as a bone.* [(1835–1949): JW: 1954]

sobersides a prohibitionist. Based on an old term for a prig. RT: *dry.* [U.S., BVB: 1942]

sober up to recover from drunkenness or drug intoxication. *Cf. detox.* [U.S., IGA: 1971, WCM: 1972]

social drinker someone who drinks alcohol in the company of others in a non-obsessive manner. Standard English. [U.S., 1940s–p., K&M: 1968]

social junker a chipper; someone who uses drugs only occasionally and in social settings. As opposed to an addicted drug user. Jargon, not argot. RT: *chipper.* [U.S., RAS: 1983]

social sniffer a casual or "recreational" user of cocaine. RT: *kokomo.* [U.S., S&F: 1984]

sod a drunkard; a sodden sot. From *sodden* or from confusion with *sot* (*q.v.*). Also possible confusion with British *sod* which is short for *sodomist.* RT: *sot.* [U.S., EK: 1927, GI: 1931, MHW: 1934, GU: 1975]

soda-pop wine a carbonated, sweet, fruit-flavored wine. The same as *pop wine* (*q.v.*) RS: *wine.* [U.S., (1972): DNE: 1980]

sodden alcohol intoxicated. RT: *drunk.* [U.S., BVB: 1942]

sodden bum a drunken tramp; a drunkard. RT: *sot.* [U.S., BVB: 1942, VJM: 1949]

soft 1. alcohol intoxicated. RT: *drunk.* [BF: 1737] 2. the same as *soft drugs* (*q.v.*). [U.S., AHC: 1969]

softballs barbiturates. RT: *barbs.* [U.S., IGA: 1971, W&S: 1977, NIDA: 1980] See also *footballs.*

soft drugs (also **soft**) nonaddictive drugs such as marijuana, hashish, amphetamines, barbiturates, mescaline. Users may become dependent or habituated, but soft drugs are not considered physically addictive. Compare to *hard drugs.* RS: *dope.* [U.S., RB: 1967, AHC: 1969, (1970): DNE: 1973, EEL: 1971, W&F: 1975, MW: 1976]

soggy alcohol intoxicated. RT: *drunk.* [U.S., BVB: 1942]

soker a drunkard. See *soaker.*

soldier 1. a liquor bottle; an empty liquor bottle. RT: *dead soldier.* [U.S., BVB: 1942, W&F: 1960] 2. a whole tobacco cigarette. Compare to *dead soldier.* RT: *nail.* [U.S. military, BVB: 1942]

soles hashish. Alludes to the smuggling of hashish in the soles of shoes. RT: *hash.* [U.S., YKB: 1977, NIDA: 1980]

solid a cigarette made form tobacco and marijuana. GEN: (adjective) good. RS: *nail, joint.* [U.S., EEL: 1971, ADC: 1975]

soma phencyclidine, *P.C.P.* (*q.v.*), an animal tranquilizer; marijuana or any hallucinogenic. One of the many misleading names given to this substance. Originally the name of an intoxicating drink used in Vedic rituals. RT: *P.C.P.* [U.S.,

(1970s): FAB: 1979, YKB: 1977]

somebody stole his rudder having to do with a drunk man. RS: *drunk*. Clearly a nautical allusion, but attested as cowboy use. [U.S., RFA]

something cool (also **something, something damp, something short, something wet**) liquor; a drink of liquor. RT: *booze, nip*. [JCH: 1887, F&H, BVB: 1942, SSD]

something for one's head a hallucinogenic drug; a *head drug* (*q.v.*). [U.S., M&V: 1973]

soñadora* smokable drugs: marijuana; opium. The Spanish word for dreams. RT: *opium*. [calo, JBR: 1973]

son-lo See *san-lo*.

son of one an alcohol extract of hashish. RT: *oil*. [U.S., (1971): ELA: 1982, YKB: 1977]

sook-nie opium. *Cf. shong-nie*. RT: *opium*. [U.S., (M&V: 1954)]

soother (also **soothing syrup**) liquor; a drink of liquor. RT: *booze*. [Br., 1800s, F&H; listed in BVB: 1942]

soot the chimney to snort cocaine. *Cf. snort*. [U.S., JES: 1959, H&C: 1975]

sop 1. a drunkard; an alcoholic. RT: *sot*. [U.S., BVB: 1942, W&F: 1960, DCCU: 1972] 2. to *guzzle* (*q.v.*) liquor; to sop up liquor. RT: *irrigate*. [U.S., W&F: 1967]

sope *methaqualone* (*q.v.*). The same as *soaper* (*q.v.*). RT: *ludes*. [U.S., RDS: 1982]

sophisticated lady cocaine. RT: *cocaine*. Black use. [U.S., EAF: 1980]

Sopor a protected trade name for *methaqualone* (*q.v.*), a hypnotic sedative. The drug is a sedative and a hypnotic. RT: *ludes*. [in current use; consult a pharmaceutical reference for more information]

sopping (also **sopping wet, soppy**) alcohol intoxicated. An elaboration of *wet* (*q.v.*) = drunk. RT: *drunk*. [U.S., BVB: 1942]

sore-footed alcohol intoxicated. RT: *drunk*. [BF: 1737]

sore head a hangover. RT: *hangover*. Scots (F&H). [since the 1800s, F&H]

soshed alcohol intoxicated. From *sloshed* or *soused* (*q.v.*). RT: *drunk*. [U.S., (1928): W&F: 1960, D&D: 1957]

so-so (also **so**) alcohol intoxicated. See *so*. RT: *drunk*. [Br., (1809): F&H, DSUE; listed in BVB: 1942]

sossled alcohol intoxicated. The same as *sozzled* (*q.v.*).

sot a heavy drinker; a person who is drunk often; an alcoholic. [since the 1500s, (1592): OED] Nicknames and slang terms for heavy drinkers and alcoholics: *admiral of the red, after-dinner man, afternoon man, alchy, alcoholic, alcoholist, alkee stiff, alki* *bum, alkie, alki stiff, alky, alky bum, angel altogether, artillery man, bar-bug, bar-fly, bar-polisher, barrel, barrel bum, barrel dosser, barrelhouse bum, barrelhouse stiff, barrel stiff, bat, batster, beeraholic, beer barrel, beer belly, beer-bibber, beer bottle, beer-eater, beer freak, beer heister, beer jerker, beeroholic, beer shunter, beer slinger, beer swiper, belcher, belch-guts, bencher, bench-whistler, bender, berper, bevvy-merchant, bezzle, bezzler, bib-all-night, bibber, bibbler, biled owl, billiard drinker, Billie-born-drunk, bimmy, bingo boy, bingo mort, bloak, bloat, bloater, bloke, blossom nose, blot, blotter, bluey, boiled owl, bombo, bombo-basher, booze artist, booze bum, booze fighter, booze freak, booze gob, booze guzzler, booze heister, booze hister, booze hitter, booze hound, booze king, booze mopper, boozer, booze shunter, booze stiff, boozician, boozington, borachio, boracho, borrachio, bottle, bottle-a-day man, bottle baby, bottle cracker, bottle heister, bottle man, bottle sucker, brandy face, brandy shunter, brewer's horse, Brother where art thou?, bubber, bubblehead, bubster, budger, budhead, bum boozer, bunch of grapes, bung eye, burster, bust, buster, busthead, bustskull, cadger, cager, canned heater, canteen wallah, caterpillar, chain-drinker, Christmas tree, clove hunter, cod, comb and brush, common sewer, copper nose, crock, crooker, dead one, dehorn, dip, dips, dipso, dipsomaniac, distillery bum, distillery stiff, dog's nose, drain, drainist, drain pipe, drammer, dramster, drinkster, dronkie, dronklap, dropper, drunk, drunker, D-T-ist, dyno, dypso, elbow-bender, elbow-crooker, emperor, ensign-bearer, falling-down drunk, feke-drinker, fermentarian, fish, flag of defiance, flag of distress, flinger, fluffer, flying jib, four-bottle man, fried egg, fuddle cap, fuddler, fuddling fellow, full-blown angel, funnel, gargler, gashound, geek, gin-crawler, gin disposal unit, ginhead, gin hound, gin ma, ginnums, gin slinger, glass, glow worm, grape cat, grape chick, grape monger, gravel-grinder, grog-bibber, grog blossom, grog hound, gussey, guzzle guts, guzzler, hail fellow all wet, hammerhead, headpiece, heater, heister, hellbender, heller, hell raiser, high-goer, hister, hoister, hoocher, hooch head, hooch hister, hooch hitter, hooch hoister, hooch hound, hootcher, horner, hyster, impaired physician, jag, jagster, jake-drinker, jake hound, jake-wallah, jerker, jickhead, jingler, job, jolly nose, jugger, jughead, juice freak, juicehead, juicer, kanurd, Kennedy rot, kennurd, kenurd, lapper, lappy cull, largehead, leanaway, liquorer, liquorhead, liquor plug, liquor pug, long hitter, love pot, lowerer, lug pot, lush, lush cove, lusher, lush head, lush hound, lushie, lushing cove, lushing man, lushington, lush merchant, lushy, lushy cove, malt bug, malt worm, malty cove, merry Greek, metho, metho artist, metho drinker, mooner, moonshine victim, mop, mopper-up, muscateer, nazy cove, nazy mort, nazy nab, nebo, nipster, o-be-joyfuller, o-be-joyful merchant, oiler, oilhead, old soaker, one of the faithful, oryide, pegger, philistine, pickler, pink-eye, pint pot, pipe, pisshead, piss-maker, pisso, plonk artist, plonk dot, plonk fiend, plonk merchant, plonko, pot, pot fury, pothead, pot knight, potster, pot walloper, problem drinker, pub-crawler, pub-ornament, quaffer, quarter pot, Queen of Scotch, rare lapper, reeler, rub-a-dub bum, rubbydub, rum bag, rum boy, rum-dum, rumhead, rum hound, rummy, rummy hound, rummy stiff, rumpet, rum pot, rum soak, rum sucker, sapper, schicker, scrambled egg, sewer pipe, shaker, shick, shifter, shikker, shuffler, sink, sipster, skate, skimmisher, slave of the beast, slush, slusher, smoke bum, smokehound, snorter, soak, soaker, sod, sodden bum, soker, sop, sot, souse, sozzler, spigot-sucker, sponge, spreester, spud, spunge, squiff, steady lapper, stew, stew bum, stewed fruit, stewie, stewy, stick, stiff, stinko, suck bottle, suck can, sucker, sucking cull, suck pint, suck pot, suck spigot, swallower, swellhead, swigsby, swigster, swill belly, swill bowl, swiller, swillocks, swill pot, swill tub, swipington, swipster, swizzle guts, swizzle nick, tank, tanker, tank-up, thirstington, thirsty soul, tid, tight skirt, tipple-arse, tippler, toast, toddycask, tooter, toper, toss pot, tote, tun, tussey, two-bottle man, two-bottler, two-fisted drinker, under-the-influencer, walking whiskey vat, wallbanger, wassailer, wet hand, wet one, wet-Quaker, wet smack, wetster, wet subject, whale, whipcan, whiskey bloat, white liner, white line stiff, winebag, wineeo, wine jockey, wine-o, winer, wino, yeaster, zonker.*

sottish alcohol intoxicated. GEN: self-indulgent. *Cf. sot.* RS: *drunk.* [16-1900s, OED]

sotto voce parlor a low-voice parlor, a speakeasy. RT: *speak.* From the prohibition era. [U.S., BVB: 1942]

sot-weed tobacco. RT: *fogus.* [cant, (1702): DSUE, FG: 1785, FG: 1823, GWM: 1859]

souffled alcohol intoxicated. *Cf. baked.* See list at *cooked.* RT: *drunk.* [U.S., BR: 1972]

soul destroyer whiskey. RT: *whiskey.* [Br., 1800s, F&H]

soul searching looking for a vein suitable for the injection of drugs. *Cf. jabber.* [U.S., M&V: 1967]

sound *Deprol* (TM; *q.v.*) tranquilizer. Derivation unknown. RS: *tranks.* [U.S., SNP: 1977]

soupy alcohol intoxicated; drunk and vomiting. RS: *drunk.* [JRW: 1909]

source (also **the source**) a drug supplier; a drug wholesaler. RS: *dealer.* [U.S., RRL: 1969, EEL: 1971, ADC: 1975]

souse 1. to drink excessively; to go on a drinking bout; to get drunk. From the original sense: to soak, to pickle. RT: *guzzle.* [Br., (1923): SOD, SSD; U.S., BVB: 1942, D&D: 1957] 2. a drinking bout. RT: *spree.* [Br. and U.S., (1905): W&F: 1960, DSUE, DCCU: 1972, SSD] 3. (also **souse pot**) a drunkard. RT: *sot.* [Aust., (1925): DSUE, SJB: 1943; U.S., (1890): SBF: 1976, GI: 1931, BVB: 1942, RDS: 1982]

soused (also **soust**) alcohol intoxicated. LIT: soaked or pickled. The verb *souse* has the basic meaning to soak and pickle meat. RT: ***drunk***. [(1613): OED; U.S., (1902): OEDS, MP: 1928, GI: 1931, MHW: 1934, W&F: 1960, DCCU: 1972]

soused to the gills (also **soused to the ears**) alcohol intoxicated. *Cf. soused*. RT: ***drunk***. [U.S., (1890s): SBF: 1982, BVB: 1942, D&D: 1957]

southern-fried alcohol intoxicated. An elaboration of *fried* (*q.v.*). RT: ***drunk***. [PD: 1982]

sow drunk alcohol intoxicated. *Cf.* ***drunk as a sow, drunk as David's sow***. RT: ***drunk***. [Br., (1857): F&H; listed in BVB: 1942]

sozzle to drink to excess. The same as ***guzzle*** (*q.v.*).

sozzled (also **sossled**) alcohol intoxicated. RT: ***drunk***. [Br. and U.S., (1880): W&F: 1960, (1897): F&H, (1921): OEDS, D&D: 1957, SSD, PW: 1977, M&J: 1975]

sozzler a drunkard. RT: ***sot***. [HSD: 1984]

sozzly alcohol intoxicated. From ***sozzled***. RT: ***drunk***. [U.S., BVB: 1942, D&D: 1957]

space cadet a person who is always high on drugs. RS: ***user***. [U.S., FAB: 1979, ADC: 1981] See also ***cadet***.

spaced out (also **spaced**, **spacey**) drug intoxicated, especially from marijuana smoking. RT: ***stoned***. This term quickly became a slang, fad expression. [U.S., RB: 1967, (1969): DNE: 1973, RRL: 1969, DCCU: 1972, ADC: 1975, W&F: 1975, MW: 1976, JWK: 1981]

space out 1. a spaced-out person. *Cf.* ***space cadet***. [U.S., ADC: 1975] 2. to become euphoric under the influence of a drug. [U.S., D&B: 1970c, ADC: 1975]

spangles capsules of ***Librium*** (TM; *q.v.*). [Br., listed in BTD: 1968]

Spanish guitar a cigar. Rhyming slang. RT: ***seegar***. This word, according to the attestations, is from musical comedy, in both British and American slang. [Br. and U.S., HNR: 1934, M&B: 1944, VJM: 1949, WG: 1952, DRS]

spansula a mixture of amphetamines and barbiturates. Probably from the trademarked "Spansule," a type of medicinal capsule. RS: ***set***. [U.S., EEL: 1971]

sparkle 1. champagne. RT: ***cham***. [U.S., BVB: 1942] 2. a cigarette or a match. RT: ***nail***. [U.S., early 1900s, CM: 1970]

sparkle plenties amphetamine capsules and tablets. From a character in the Dick Tracy comic strip. *Cf.* ***sparkler***. RT: ***amps***. [U.S., RRL: 1969, EEL: 1971, NIDA: 1980]

sparkler 1. a drink of liquor. RT: ***nip***. [Br., 1800s, F&H] 2. an amphetamine capsule. From the name of a type of fireworks. RT: ***amps***. [U.S., SNP: 1977]

speak (also **speaker**, **speakie**) an illicit liquor establishment; a speakeasy. A truncation of ***speakeasy*** (*q.v.*). From the prohibition era. [U.S., HNR: 1934, D&D: 1957] Nicknames and slang terms for drinking establishments during U.S. national prohibition: ***blind pig, blind pigger, blind tiger, blue pig, booze benderie, booze foundry, booze joint, gin flat, hush-house, hushie, hush joint, jinny, joint, joker, juice-joint, key club, leggery, leg joint, low talk, moonlight inn, moonshinery, pig, Q.T., scatter, shinery, sneakeasy, sneaker, sneakery, sneakie, sotto voce parlor, speak, speakeasy, speaker, speaketeria, speakie, spot, tiger, whisper joint, whisper low, whisper parlor.***

speakeasy an illicit liquor establishment. The term became widely known in the U.S. during prohibition although it is much older. It refers to the practice of speaking softly when discussing contraband, and is similar to a *speak softly shop*, = the house of a smuggler (JB: 1823). RT: ***speak***. [U.S., (1889): OED, AH: 1931, GI: 1931, MHW: 1934]

speaketeria a speakeasy; a cafeteria speakeasy. RT: ***speak***. Contrived and jocular. [U.S., BVB: 1942]

spear a hypodermic needle. RT: ***needle***. [U.S., ELA: 1984]

speckled birds (also **speckled eggs**) amphetamine capsules. Probably refers to multicolored time release capsules. RT: ***amps***. [U.S., YKB: 1977, DEM: 1981]

speechless alcohol intoxicated. RT: ***drunk***. [Br., (1881): OED, M&J: 1975]

speed 1. methamphetamine; sometimes, amphetamine in general. A widely-known slang term. [U.S., S&W: 1966, (1968): DNE: 1973, RRL: 1969, DCCU: 1972, ADC: 1975, W&F: 1975, MW: 1976, NIDA: 1980; Br. M&J: 1975] (This entry continues after the following list.) Nicknames and other terms for methamphetamine: ***acelerante, bambita, beans, box of L, brain burners, chalk, Christina, cristina, Cristine, crystal, dice, doe, glass, met, metanfetamina, meth, Methedrine, motherdear, speed, speedball, speed demon, speeder, splash, stuka, tab, tangerine, velocidad, water***. 2. to use methamphetamine; to be high on methamphetamine or amphetamine. [U.S., RRL: 1969, ADC: 1975, EAF: 1980]

speedball 1. liquor. RT: ***booze***. Probably from sports terminology. From the prohibition era. [U.S., AH: 1931, MHW: 1934] 2. a glass of wine fortified with alcohol or ether to increase its intoxicating power. Hobo use. [U.S., NK: 1926, VWS: 1929, GI: 1931, BVB: 1942] 3. sherry wine. RT: ***sherry***. [early 1900s, DU] 4. a dose of narcotics; an injection of narcotics. RS: ***dose***. [U.S., (1931): DU, GM: 1931, MHW: 1934, GOL: 1950] 5. a mixture of two drugs injected together. The two drugs may be heroin and cocaine, cocaine and amphetamine, heroin and amphetamine, cocaine and morphine, morphine and heroin. *Cf.* ***whiz-bang***. RS:

sot. [U.S., DWM: 1936, BVB: 1942, VJM: 1949, M&D: 1952, M&H: 1959, RRL: 1969, CM: 1970, EEL: 1971, DCCU: 1972, YKB: 1977; Br., BTD: 1968] 6. methamphetamine. RT: *speed*. [U.S., EEL: 1971, SNP: 1977]

speed demon 1. amphetamine; methamphetamine. RS: *speed*. [U.S., IGA: 1971, EE: 1976] 2. a habitual user of methamphetamine. RS: *user*. [U.S., RG: 1970, IGA: 1971, M&V: 1973]

speeder 1. an amphetamine or methamphetamine tablet, capsule, or ampule. *Cf. speed*. [U.S., ADC: 1981] 2. a user of amphetamine or methamphetamine; someone who is hyperactive from frequent amphetamine use. RS: *user*. [U.S., EEL: 1971, C&H: 1974]

speed freak (also **speedhead**) a drug user who injects methamphetamine; an amphetamine user. *Cf. speed*. RS: *user*. A widely known, popular slang term. [U.S., (1967): OEDS, RRL: 1969, D&B: 1970c, DES: 1972, GU: 1975, W&F: 1975, MW: 1976]

Speed kills! a slogan which encourages young people not to use *Methedrine* (TM; *q.v.*). *Cf. speed*. [U.S., EEL: 1971, YKB: 1977]

speed lab a place where amphetamine or methamphetamine is processed illegally. *Cf. speed*. [U.S., YKB: 1977]

speedster a methamphetamine user. See *speed*. RT: *user*. [U.S., RG: 1970]

spent 1. having to do with a person who is burned out on drugs. *Cf. wasted*. [U.S., ADC: 1975] 2. having to do with marijuana from which the active principle has been completely burned off. *Cf. cashed, played*. [U.S., ADC: 1981]

spiders and snakes descriptive of a good *L.S.D.* (*q.v.*) trip with fascinating hallucinations. *Cf. trip*. [U.S., ADC: 1981]

spiffed alcohol intoxicated. RT: *drunk*. [(1860): SBF: 1976, JCH: 1887, B&L: 1890, F&H, BVB: 1942]

spifflicated (also **spifflo, spificated, spiflicated**) alcohol intoxicated. From a verb meaning to crush or destroy, (1785, SOD). RT: *drunk*. [U.S., (1906): SBF: 1976, MHW: 1934, AP: 1980]

spigot-bigot a prohibitionist. RT: *dry*. From the prohibition era. [U.S., BVB: 1942]

spigot-sucker a drunkard; a tippler. RT: *sot*. [(1611): F&H]

spike 1. a hypodermic needle. RT: *needle*. [U.S., DWM: 1936, VJM: 1949, D&B: 1970c, EEL: 1971, DC: 1972, MA: 1973, EAF: 1980, JWK: 1981] 2. a hypodermic syringe and needle; a medicine dropper and needle. RT: *monkey pump*. [U.S., BVB: 1942, W&F: 1967, JWK: 1981] 3. to add ether or alcohol to beer or other liquor by injecting it through the cork with a hypodermic needle. *Cf. needle beer*. The practice appears to have started in the late 1800s. See sense four. Made popular during prohibition. [U.S., 1920s, BVB: 1942, DU] 4. to add alcohol or liquor to a drink; to fortify a drink with alcohol. Not necessarily done with a hypodermic needle. [U.S., BWG: 1899, R&P: 1928, W&F: 1960, DCCU: 1972]

spike and dripper a hypodermic needle and syringe; a hypodermic needle attached to a medicine dropper. *Cf. dripper, dropper.* [U.S., M&D: 1952]

spiked 1. having to do with a drink with alcohol added; having to do with a punch with an alcoholic content. [(1899): DU, EEL: 1971] 2. having to do with a tobacco cigarette with dope added. [U.S., (1937): ELA: 1982, DU] 3. alcohol intoxicated; drug intoxicated. RT: *drunk.* [U.S., EEL: 1971]

spiked beer 1. beer aged artificially by passing electricity through it. [U.S., W&F: 1960] 2. beer with alcohol, whiskey, or ether added. *Cf. needle beer.* From the prohibition era. [U.S., 1920s, VR: 1929, MHW: 1934, W&F: 1960]

spike, on the on narcotics; injecting narcotics addictively. RT: *hooked.* [U.S., BVB: 1942, H&C: 1975]

spirits alcoholic spirits. Euphemistic and vague. *Cf. ardent spirits, commune with the spirits, haunted with evil spirits.* RS: *booze.* [since the late 1600s, OED]

spit and drag (also **spit**) a tobacco cigarette. Rhyming slang for *fag* (*q.v.*). RT: *nail.* [Br., DRS, (1958): DSUE, M&J: 1975]

spit ball a mouthfull of *free base* vapor puffed into someone else's mouth. This is a play on the *spitball* of baseball. [U.S., ELA: 1984]

spit-quick-or-puke chewing tobacco. GEN: anything bad tasting. [U.S. military, BVB: 1942]

splash 1. liquor. RT: *booze.* [U.S., MHW: 1934, BVB: 1942] 2. amphetamine; methamphetamine. Refers to liquid amphetamine sold in glass ampules. RT: *amps, speed.* ELA: 1984 also lists **splach**. [U.S., S&W: 1966, RRL: 1969, IGA: 1971, S&W: 1973, NIDA: 1980] 3. a sexual rush at the beginning of a methamphetamine injection. This is described as an orgasmic rush, and the *splash* may refer to ejaculation. RS: *rush.* [U.S., IGA: 1971, WCM: 1972] 4. to inject methamphetamine. RS: *shoot.* ELA: 1984 also lists **splach**. [U.S., RG: 1970]

splash house (also **splash parlor**) a place where methamphetamine is sold and used. RS: *doperie.* [U.S., RG: 1970]

splay marijuana. RT: *pot.* [U.S., W&F: 1967]

spleef (also **shpleef**) marijuana; a marijuana cigarette. The same as *spliff* (*q.v.*). RT: *joint.* [U.S., ADC: 1984]

splice the main brace to take a drink; to get drunk. This is an elaboration of make (something) tight. May also refer to *grog* as the main brace. See *bracer.* RT: *mug oneself.* [Br., JCH: 1887; U.S., mid 1800s, (Melville), BVB: 1942] See also *with main brace well spliced.*

spliff (also **shpleef, spleef, splim**) a Jamaican marijuana cigarette wrapped in newspaper; marijuana; a marijuana cigarette; hashish. See *sploff*. RT: *pot*. [U.S., (1967): ELA: 1982, EEL: 1971, IGA: 1971, W&F: 1975, (D&B: 1978)]

splint a marijuana cigarette. RT: *joint*. [U.S., IGA: 1971, WCM: 1972]

splits tranquilizer tablets or capsules. RT: *tranks*. [U.S., RRL: 1969, RDS: 1982]

splivins amphetamines. RT: *amps*. [U.S., RG: 1970, SNP: 1977, RDS: 1982]

sploff a marijuana cigarette; a puff of a marijuana cigarette. Probably akin to *spliff*. RT: *joint*. [M&J: 1975]

spodiodi a mixture of cheap port and whiskey. In Jack Kerouac's *On The Road*. [U.S., JK: 1957; Br., (1959): DSUE]

spoke with his friend alcohol intoxicated. RS: *drunk*. [BF: 1737]

sponge 1. to drink heavily. RT: *guzzle*. See *spunge*. [U.S., BVB: 1942] 2. a drunkard; a tippler. A person who just soaks up liquor. See *spunge*. RT: *sot*. [(1596): SOD, F&H; U.S., WM: 1927, JAS: 1932, MHW: 1934, W&F: 1960] 3. a liquor law enforcement officer; a prohibition enforcement officer. RS: *fuzz*. [U.S., BVB: 1942, VJM: 1949]

spook a narcotics addict. From the ghost-like appearance of an advanced addict. *Cf. ghost*. RS: *junky*. [Br., early 1900s, DU]

spoon 1. two grams of heroin. Approximately a teaspoonful. RS: *load*. [U.S., RRL: 1969, D&B: 1970c, EEL: 1971, MA: 1973] 2. a spoon used in heating and dissolving narcotics for injection. See *cooker*. [U.S., (1920): DU, DWM: 1938, BVB: 1942, RRL: 1969, JWK: 1981] 3. a spoon used in the snorting of cocaine. *Cf. cokespoon*. [U.S., ADC: 1975]

spoony drunk (also **spoony**) alcohol intoxicated; drunk and sentimental. RT: *drunk*. [Br., 1800s, F&H]

spores 1. the mushroom containing the hallucinogenic compound *psilocybin* (*q.v.*). [U.S., S&W: 1973] 2. phencyclidine, P.C.P. RT: *P.C.P.* [U.S., ELA: 1984]

sport of the gods cocaine use. [U.S., IGA: 1971, WCM: 1972]

spot 1. a small drink of liquor. RT: *nip*. [Br., late 18-1900s, F&H; SSD U.S., BVB: 1942, W&F: 1960] 2. a speakeasy; a nightspot. RS: *speak*. [U.S., HNR: 1934, MHW: 1934]

spot habit a small drug habit; the practice of using drugs when one can get them. [U.S., C&H: 1974]

sprang liquor. RT: *booze*. [Br. and U.S., F&G: 1925, MHW: 1934]

spread the good news to share a marijuana cigarette. RS: *hit the hay*. [U.S., ELA: 1984]

spread the joint to lay out opium-smoking equipment in preparation for smoking opium. See the first sense of *joint*.

[U.S., BD: 1937, DWM: 1938, BVB: 1942]

spree a bout of drinking; a fit of drunkenness; a wild party. [FG: 1811, FG: 1823, BWG: 1899, M&C: 1905] Now standard English. Nicknames and slang terms for a drinking bouts: *alcoholiday, ball, bash, bass attack, bat, batch, batter, beano, beerathon, beer-blast, beerburst, beer-bust, beer-drink, beer fest, beer-up, bender, binge, bingle, blast, blindo, blow, blow-out, booze bout, boozefest, booze fight, boozeroo, booze-up, bout with John Barleycorn, brannigan, brawl, break-out, breaky leg, bum, bun, burst, bust, buster, caper, corroboree, drunk, drunk-up, flare, flare-up, fling, flutter, fuddle, gee-up, gin-crawl, grog, grog fight, grog-on, grog-up, guzzle, heavy jag, heavy wet, hellbender, high lonesome, honk, hoochfest, hopfest, jag, jamberoo, jamboree, jingle, jollification, jollo, jolly-up, joy ride, kegger, keg party, lush, lush-out, mop, out and out, perisher, piss-up, pub-crawl, rally, rantan, rare, razee, razzee, razzle-dazzle, reeler, rip, rort, sangaree, session, skate, sky-wannocking, slopping-up, soak, souse, spree, stew, swill-up, tank-up, tea party, tear, tipple, toot, whing-ding, whinger, whooper-up, whooper-upper.*

spreeing drinking heavily; getting drunk. *Cf. irrigate, mug oneself.* Standard English. [(1890): OED] Nicknames and slang terms for an act of drinking heavily: *bending an elbow, drowning the shamrock, elbow-bending, hear the owl hoot, neck-basting, on a bat, on a bend, on a bender, on a bust, on a drunk, on a spree, on a tank, on a toot, on the beer, on the blink, on the booze, on the burst, on the bust, on the cod, on the drunk, on the hops, on the juice, on the loose, on the oil, on the ooze, on the razzle, on the ree-raw, on the sauce, on the scoop, on the scoot, on the scuttle, on the squiff, on the stun, on the tank, on the tiger, on the tiles, on the turps, spreeing.*

spreeish alcohol intoxicated; fond of going on sprees. RS: *drunk.* [Br., (1825): OED]

spree, on a (also **on the spree**) alcohol intoxicated; on a drinking bout. The main entry is U.S., the *also* is British. RS: *drunk.* [Br., (1852): F&H; U.S., AH: 1931, MHW: 1934]

spreester a drunkard. RT: *sot.* [U.S., BVB: 1942]

sprung alcohol intoxicated. Meaning sprung out of shape. RT: *drunk.* [Br. and U.S., (1833): OEDS, JCH: 1887, B&L: 1890, BWG: 1899, MHW: 1934, BVB: 1942]

spud 1. vodka. Refers to vodka made from potatoes. [U.S., Marines and Navy, DST: 1984] 2. a vodka drunkard. RS: *sot.* [U.S. Marines and Navy, DST: 1984]

spunge 1. to drink heavily; to drink when someone else is paying. See *sponge.* RS: *guzzle.* [cant, BE: 1690] 2. a heavy drinker; a drunkard. See *sponge.* RS: *sot.* [cant, FG: 1785, FG: 1811]

spun joint a place where illicit liquor is sold. From *homespun* (*q.v.*), a prohibition term for illicit liquor. RS: *sly grogshop.* [U.S., 1920s, VR: 1929, AH: 1931, BVB: 1942]

spur one gram of a powdered drug. RS: *load*. [U.S., H&C: 1975]

squail a drink of liquor. RT: *nip*. [GWM: 1859]

square 1. a person who does not use drugs. *Cf. square John*. Square means *right* as in a square or right angle, and has had this meaning since the 1500s (SOD). GEN: any person who behaves "properly". [U.S., DB: 1944, VJM: 1949, M&D: 1952, M&H: 1959, W&F: 1967, RRL: 1969, EEL: 1971, MA: 1973] (This entry continues after the following list.) Nicknames and slang terms for someone who does not use drugs: *apple, brown shoes, citizen, cube, do-right Johns, do-right people, farmer, freebies, laine, lame, lame duck, lane, nonaddict, quality folks, quality Joe, simple Simon, square, square apple, square John, straight*. 2. (also square joint) a tobacco cigarette. As compared to a marijuana cigarette. RT: *nail*. Black use. [U.S., W&F: 1967, G&B: 1969, DC: 1972]

squared up no longer taking drugs. *Cf. square*. RT: *off*. [U.S., M&V: 1967]

square John (also square apple) a person who does not use drugs; a *square* (*q.v.*). RT: *square*. [U.S., (1920s): JES: 1959, DWM: 1936, DWM: 1938, VJM: 1949]

squaw piss inferior beer; weak beer. *Cf. witch piss*. RT: *queer-beer*. [U.S., D&B: 1970c]

squeeze liquor. RT: *booze*. Black use. [U.S., D&B: 1970b]

squiff a drunkard. RT: *sot*. [Aust., (1920): DSUE]

squiffed alcohol intoxicated. RT: *drunk*. [Br. and U.S., (1880s): SBF: 1976, B&L: 1890, DSUE, MP: 1928, AH: 1931, MHW: 1934]

squiff, on the on a drinking bout. RS: *spreeing*. [Aust., (1925): DSUE, SJB: 1943]

squiffy alcohol intoxicated. RT: *drunk*. [Br. and U.S., (1874): OED, (WWI): B&P: 1965, MHW: 1934, SSD, M&J: 1975]

squirrel 1. (also squirrel dew) illicit liquor: *moonshine* (*q.v.*). See *squirrel dew*. RT: *moonshine*. [U.S., 1920s, VR: 1929, MHW: 1934, D&D: 1957] 2. (also squirrels) *L.S.D.* (*q.v.*); L.S.D. combined with some other drug. RT: *L.S.D.* [U.S., SNP: 1977, KBH: 1982]

squirrel dew (also squirrel, squirrel whiskey) moonshine; illicit whiskey. Based on *mountain dew* (*q.v.*). RT: *moonshine*. [U.S., VR: 1929, MHW: 1934]

squirrel load a small drink of liquor. RT: *nip*. [U.S., BWG: 1899]

squirt 1. beer; inferior beer which causes diarrhea. RS: *queer-beer*. [Aust. and Br., early 1900s, DSUE, SJB: 1943] 2. champagne. RT: *cham*. [(1870): JRW: 1909]

S.S. a skin shot; a hypodermic injection which misses the vein. RS: *shot*. [U.S., DWM: 1938, BVB: 1942]

stack a pack of marijuana cigarettes. *Cf. deck*. RS: *load*. [U.S., HB: 1955, TRG: 1968, EEL: 1971, IGA: 1971]

staff naked gin. See *stark naked*. RT: *gin*. [cant, DA: 1857]

staggerish alcohol intoxicated. RT: *drunk*. [BF: 1737]

stagger juice (also **staggering juice, stagger soup, stagger water**) liquor. RT: *booze*. [JSF: 1889, (1907): F&G: 1925, MHW: 1934, SJB: 1943, D&D: 1957, WG: 1962, RDS: 1982]

staggers 1. liquor. RT: *booze*. [U.S., MHW: 1934, BVB: 1942] 2. (also **the staggers**) drunkenness; the delirium tremens. RT: *D.T.s*. [18-1900s, F&H; listed in BVB: 1942]

stale drunk a long-standing and frequently renewed drunken state; drunk for a very long time. *Cf. long stale drunk*. RS: *drunk*. [Br., JCH: 1887, F&H, B&L: 1890; listed in BVB: 1942]

stall a finger stall or condom used to package powdered drug for transporting or smuggling. *Cf. rubber pill*. [U.S., M&V: 1967]

standing too long in the sun alcohol intoxicated. See *been in the sun*.

Stanley's stuff *L.S.D.* (*q.v.*). Refers to Augustus Owsley Stanley III. See *Owsley*. RT: *L.S.D.* [U.S., IGA: 1971]

starched (also **starchy**) alcohol intoxicated. A synonym of *stiff* (*q.v.*). Also means dead = stiff. RT: *drunk*. F&H list only **starchy**. [Br., 1800s, F&H; listed in BVB: 1942]

stardust 1. cocaine. See *star stuff*. RT: *cocaine*. [U.S., M&V: 1954, RRL: 1969, EEL: 1971, NIDA: 1980] 2. phencyclidine, P.C.P. RT: *P.C.P.* [U.S., ELA: 1984]

stark naked 1. (**staff naked**) gin; undiluted gin; undiluted liquor. RT: *gin*. [Br., (1820): OED, FG: 1823, DA: 1857, JCH: 1887, B&L: 1890] 2. having to do with undiluted liquor, especially undiluted gin. RT: *neat*. [Br., B&L: 1890, F&H]

star stuff cocaine. Because one gets as high as the stars, both celestial and Hollywood. RT: *cocaine*. [U.S., JH: 1979]

start cooking (also **start pasting**) to start injecting drugs addictively. Refers to ending a period of injecting a drug subcutaneously. [U.S., JES: 1959, H&C: 1975]

stash 1. (also **stasch**) a supply of drugs; a concealed supply of drugs especially marijuana; drugs and equipment to use them stored in a secret place. Only BD: 1937 and DWM: 1938 list **stasch**. [U.S., (1930): DU, BD: 1937, DWM: 1938, RRL: 1969, MA: 1973, ADC: 1975, W&F: 1975, EAF: 1980, ADC: 1981, JWK: 1981, S&F: 1984] (This entry continues after the following list.) Nicknames and slang terms for a supply of drugs: *arsenal, asscache, asskash, cache, carry, coosie stash, coozie stash, finger, joint, keister plant, keyster plant, kiester plant, kiester stash, load, Miss Carrie, pig, plant, rations, snow shed, stasch, stash, stash bag, stash box, stash container, stuff bag, teat, trap, turd, U-boat*. 2. to store drugs in a secret place. GEN: to hide. [U.S., CM: 1970, MA: 1973, ADC: 1975, ADC: 1981, JWK: 1981] 3. marijuana; any drugs. RT: *dope*. [U.S., GU: 1975]

stash bag (also **stash box, stash container, stuff bag**) a container for marijuana and smoking supplies. The same as ***stuff bag*** (*q.v.*). *Cf.* ***stash***. RS: ***load***. [U.S., DCCU: 1972, ELA: 1982]

stash man a drug dealer; a drug runner. RT: ***dealer, mule***. [HSD: 1984]

stash-sitter someone who guards a ***stash*** (*q.v.*) of drugs. [U.S., M&H: 1959]

state prison tobacco, the same as ***state weed*** (*q.v.*). [U.S., BVB: 1942, VJM: 1949]

state of elevation, in a alcohol intoxicated. *Cf.* ***elevated***. RT: ***drunk***. [(1749): F&H, (Smollett)]

state of nature, in a having to do with undiluted liquor. *Cf.* ***stark naked***. RT: ***neat***. [Br., 1800s, F&H]

state weed prison tobacco. RS: ***fogus***. Prison use. [U.S., TH: 1976]

station worker an addict who uses both arms and legs for injection sites. *Cf.* ***mouth worker***. RS: ***junky***. [U.S., RDS: 1982]

steady alcohol intoxicated. RT: ***drunk***. [BF: 1737]

steady lapper a drunkard. RT: ***sot***. [Aust., (1919): Downing]

steam 1. cheap wine; wine spiked with methyl alcohol. RS: ***methyl***. [Aust., SJB: 1943] 2. liquor; beer; inferior liquor. RT: ***booze***. [U.S., (1920s), W&F: 1967, DC: 1972]

steamboat 1. a toilet paper roll tube used as a chamber which cools marijuana smoke and mixes it with air. *Cf.* ***steamroller***. RS: ***bong***. [U.S., (1967): ELA: 1982, G&B: 1969, C&H: 1974, ADC: 1975] 2. to use a toilet paper roll tube in the smoking of marijuana. [U.S., RRL: 1969, EEL: 1971, LVA: 1981] See also ***slow boat***.

steamed up (also **steamed**) alcohol intoxicated; drug intoxicated. *Cf.* ***jug-steamed***. RT: ***drunk, stoned***. [chiefly U.S., (1920): DU, AH: 1931, HS: 1933, MHW: 1934, DSUE]

steamer a tobacco pipe. [cant, FG: 1823, GWM: 1859; listed in BVB: 1942]

steamroller a ***steamboat*** (*q.v.*) for smoking marijuana. From the toilet paper roll used. RS: ***bong***. [U.S., (RG: 1970), C&H: 1974]

steam up 1. to drink heavily; to get drunk. RS: ***mug oneself***. [U.S., EK: 1927, GI: 1931, MHW: 1934] 2. (also **steam someone up**) to excite someone with drugs or alcohol. [U.S., early 1900s, DU]

steel and concrete cure (also **steel and concrete, steel cure**) a cure for addiction consisting of total abstinence from drugs. *Cf.* ***cold turkey***. [U.S., DWM: 1938, D&D: 1957]

steeped alcohol intoxicated. *Cf.* ***stewed***. RT: ***drunk***. [U.S., MHW: 1934, BVB: 1942]

Stella a brand of marijuana cigarette rolling paper. RT: ***paper***. [U.S., ELA: 1982]

stem 1. an opium pipe; the bamboo stem of an opium pipe. Used by a **stem artist**. RT: *hop stick*. [U.S., (1887): RML: 1948, DWM: 1933, DWM: 1936, MHW: 1934, VJM: 1949] 2. (in the plural) marijuana stems, especially those considered as debris. *Cf. timber*. [U.S., ADC: 1975]

stencil a long, thin marijuana cigarette. RS: *joint*. Black use. [U.S., EAF: 1972]

step on to dilute powdered drugs by one half. This can be repeated a number of times. See *cut*. [U.S., (IGA: 1971), JWK: 1981]

stepped on having to do with diluted drugs; having to do with overly-diluted drugs. *Cf. cut*. [U.S., RRL: 1974, JWK: 1981, S&F: 1984]

stepping high alcohol intoxicated; drug intoxicated. An elaboration of *high* (*q.v.*). RT: *drunk*. [U.S., (1930): DU, DWM: 1938, BVB: 1942]

Sterno Club (also **Sterno**) alcohol from the canned heat product Sterno (TM). Based on Canadian Club (TM) or a similarly named brand. [U.S., early 1900s, DU]

Steve's mission a place to buy drugs. *old Steve* (*q.v.*) = powdered drugs. RS: *doperie*. [U.S., JES: 1959, H&C: 1975]

stevie a hallucination from smoking marijuana. Probably refers to any drug induced hallucination. Compare to *old Steve, Steve's mission*. [U.S., M&V: 1967]

stew 1. a state of drunkenness. *Cf. in a stew*. [U.S., GI: 1931, BVB: 1942, DU] 2. alcohol intoxicated. A variant of *stewed* (*q.v.*). 3. a drinking bout. RT: *spree*. [U.S., W&F: 1960] 4. a drunkard. The same as *stew bum* (*q.v.*). RT: *sot*. [U.S., (1908): SBF: 1976, BVB: 1942, D&D: 1957, W&F: 1960]

stew bum a drunkard; an alcoholic. *Cf. stewie*. RS: *sot*. [U.S., (1918): SBF: 1976, VWS: 1929, GI: 1931, MHW: 1934, D&D: 1957]

stewed alcohol intoxicated. (BF: 1737: [He's] Stew'd.) *Cf. stew*. See list at *cooked*. RT: *drunk*. [BF: 1737, (1874): DSUE, MP: 1928, MHW: 1934, D&D: 1957, SSD]

stewed fruit a drunkard. RT: *sot*. [U.S., BVB: 1942]

stewed to the gills (also **stewed to the ears**) alcohol intoxicated. RT: *drunk*. [U.S., (1925): SBF: 1976, R&P: 1928, MHW: 1934, D&D: 1957, W&F: 1960]

stewed up alcohol intoxicated. From *stewed*, but more recent. RT: *drunk*. [U.S., AH: 1931, BVB: 1942]

stewie (also **stewy**) a drunkard. An elaboration of *stew* (*q.v.*). *Cf. stew bum*. RT: *sot*. [U.S., BVB: 1942, DB: 1944]

stew, in a alcohol intoxicated. The expression can refers to being in any type of difficulty or to being resentful. RT: *drunk*. [U.S.,

BVB: 1942]

stewy See *stewie.*

stibbed alcohol intoxicated. RT: *drunk.* [U.S., BVB: 1942]

stick 1. an opium pipe; a homemade opium pipe. RS: *hop stick.* [U.S., DWM: 1936, VJM: 1949, GOL: 1950] 2. a handler of illicit liquor. From the prohibition era. RS: *bootlegger.* [U.S., AH: 1931] 3. a small glass of beer. [Br., (1925): DSUE] 4. a drunkard. RT: *sot.* [U.S., DB: 1944, DU] 5. a marijuana cigarette. See *sticks. Cf. Thaistick.* RT: *joint.* [U.S., MB: 1938, DB: 1944, (M&W: 1946), M&D: 1952, M&V: 1954, RRL: 1969, DC: 1972, EAF: 1980, JWK: 1981; Br., BTD: 1968] 6. phencyclidine, P.C.P. RT: *P.C.P.* [U.S., ELA: 1984]

stick man a smoker of marijuana. In contrast to other types of drug users. *Cf. stick.* RT: *toker.* [U.S., M&V: 1967, H&C: 1975]

sticko an error for *stick* (*q.v.*). [U.S., (M&V: 1954)]

stick of tea (also **stick of gage, stick of T.**) a marijuana cigarette. RT: *joint.* [U.S., M&W: 1946, BVB: 1953, D&D: 1957, W&F: 1960, H&C: 1975]

stick of weed a tobacco cigarette; enough tobacco to roll a cigarette. *Cf. weed.* RS: *nail.* Prison use. [Aust., SJB: 1966]

sticks marijuana waste. *Cf. stem, timber.* See *stick.* [U.S., RRL: 1969]

stiff 1. alcohol intoxicated; dead drunk. RT: *drunk.* [U.S., BF: 1737, AH: 1931, GI: 1931, BVB: 1942, W&F: 1960] 2. a drunkard. RT: *sot.* [U.S., (1870s): SBF: 1976, AH: 1931, MHW: 1934, RDS: 1982]

stiff as a goat alcohol intoxicated. RT: *drunk.* [U.S., (1937): SBF: 1976]

stiff as a plank (also **stiff as a board**) alcohol intoxicated. GEN: rigid. RT: *drunk.* [U.S., (1932): SBF: 1976]

stiff as a ring-bolt alcohol intoxicated. (BF: 1737: [He's] As Stiff...) RT: *drunk.* [BF: 1737]

stiffed alcohol intoxicated. *Cf. stiff.* RT: *drunk.* [U.S., EEL: 1971]

stiffo alcohol intoxicated. *Cf. stiff.* RT: *drunk.* [U.S., BVB: 1942, D&D: 1957]

stim liquor. From *stimulant.* RT: *booze.* [Br., late 1800s, DSUE; listed in BVB: 1942]

stimulated alcohol intoxicated. RT: *drunk.* [U.S., BVB: 1942]

sting strong liquor. *Cf. stung.* RS: *rotgut.* [Aust., (1920): DSUE, (1929): GAW: 1978]

stinger 1. a small drink of liquor. *Cf. sting.* RT: *nip.* [Br., (1890): DSUE] 2. a hypodermic syringe and needle. RT: *monkey pump.* [U.S., JES: 1959, H&C: 1975]

stingo very strong liquor; strong beer or ale. RS: *rotgut.* [cant,

(1635): OED, BE: 1690, FG: 1785, FG: 1811, FG: 1823, JCH: 1887, B&L: 1890; listed in BVB: 1942]

stinker a foul-smelling cigar. *Cf. canteen stinker, penny stinker.* RT: *seegar.* [(1899): DSUE, BVB: 1942, D&D: 1957]

stinkibus inferior liquor. RS: *rotgut.* [(1706): OED]

stinking alcohol intoxicated. Akin to *rotten* (*q.v.*). RT: *drunk.* [U.S., (1837): SBF: 1976, (1887): RML: 1950, BVB: 1942, D&D: 1957, W&F: 1960, RDS: 1982; Br., (1934): DSUE, EP: 1948, SSD, M&J: 1975]

stinking drunk (also **stinking**) alcohol intoxicated. RT: *drunk.* [U.S., (1926): SBF: 1976, BVB: 1942; Br., M&J: 1975]

stinkious gin. RT: *gin.* [(1700s): F&H, B&L: 1890]

stinko 1. liquor; wine. RT: *booze.* [Aust., early 1900s, DSUE] 2. alcohol intoxicated. RT: *drunk.* [(1927): SBF: 1976, MP: 1928, MHW: 1934, SJB: 1943, GOL: 1950, D&D: 1957, W&F: 1960, DSUE, SSD] 3. a drunken tramp who drinks the alcohol from canned heat. A play on Sterno (TM). *Cf. Sterno Club.* RS: *wino.* [U.S., GOL: 1950]

stinkweed 1. *jimson weed* (*q.v.*). [U.S., JRB: 1859, YKB: 1977] 2. marijuana. RT: *pot.* [U.S., GOL: 1950, A&T: 1953, YKB: 1977]

stitched alcohol intoxicated. (BF: 1737: He's Stitch'd.) RT: *drunk.* [BF: 1737; Br., (1925): DSUE, EP: 1948, WG: 1962]

stogie (also **stogy**) 1. a fat cigar. From the Conestoga cigar, manufactured in Conestoga, Pennsylvania. RT: *seegar.* [U.S., (1892): OED, D&D: 1957] 2. a marijuana cigarette. From sense one. RT: *joint.* [U.S., ADC: 1975, RAS: 1980]

stoll to tipple. RT: *irrigate.* [Br., 1800s, F&H]

stolled (also **stolling**) alcohol intoxicated. RT: *drunk.* [Br., 1800s, F&H]

stomach habit an addiction satisfied by eating a drug, especially opium, or by taking it in pill form. RS: *habit.* [U.S., M&V: 1954, D&B: 1970c, IGA: 1971]

stompie a cigarette butt. Akin to *stump.* RT: *brad.* [South African, late 18-1900s, DU, (1973): JB: 1980]

stoms barbiturate capsules. See *stumblers.*

stone addict a completely addicted person. RT: *junky.* [U.S., RRL: 1969, EEL: 1971]

stone blind alcohol intoxicated; very drunk. *Cf. stony blind.* RT: *drunk.* [U.S., W&F: 1960, DCCU: 1972]

stoned 1. alcohol intoxicated; dead drunk; stone drunk. Stone = total. RT: *drunk.* [U.S., D&D: 1957, W&F: 1960, CM: 1970, DCCU: 1972, ADC: 1984; Br., (1950): DSUE] 2. drug intoxicated; under the effects of marijuana. [U.S., A&T: 1953, M&H: 1959, S&W: 1966, D&B: 1970c, CM: 1970, EEL: 1971, ADC: 1975, ADC: 1981, JWK: 1981, RDS: 1982, ADC: 1984; Br., (1960):

DSUE] Slang terms meaning drug intoxicated: *all geezed up, all lit up, amped, around the bend, backed up, baked, basted, beaming, beaned up, belted, bending and bowing, bennied up, bent, bent out, bent out of shape, besotted, blasted, blind, blissed out, blitzed, blixed, blocked, blowed, blowed away, blown away, blown out, boggy, bombed, bombed out, boxed, boxed up, bricked, brightened, buzzed, caught in a snowstorm, chalked up, charged, charged up, coasting, cocainized, cocked up, coked, coked out, coked up, cooked, cooked up, crazy, crisp, crystallized, dead, descojonado, destroyed, dexed, dirty, doped, doped up, dopey, dopie, dopy, dusted, elevated, en ganchos, enhanced, enjedado, en juanado, en leñado, en motado, enyedado, far-fucking-out, far out, feathered, feeling groovy, fired up, fixed, fixed up, flaked, flaked out, flattened, flipped, floating, flogged, flying, flying in the clouds, foxy, freaked, freaked out, French fried, fried, frost, frosty, frozen, fucked, fucked up, full of junk, full of poison, funked out, gassed, gassed up, G.B.'ed, geed up, geezed, geezed up, gheed up, glassy-eyed, gone, goofed, goofed up, goofing, got a glow on, gowed, gowed up, grifado, grooving, groovy, halvahed, happy, have one's nose wide open, haywire, heaped, heaped to the gills, high, high and light, high as a kite, higher than a Georgia pine, hopped, hopped up, hoppie, hoppy, horsed, humming, hyped, hyped up, in, in flight, in high, in orbit, in the ozone, in the wind, intox, intoxed, in transit, jacked up, jagged, jagged up, jazzed, jocular, junked, junk simple, keyed, kicked out in the snow, kick the clouds, killed, knocked out, K.O.ed, laid back, laid out, layed, leaping, leaping and stinking, lit, lit up, loaded, loaded with coke, loaded with hop, luded out, lushed, lushed up, mellow, messed up, mohasky, monolithic, muggled, muggled up, nodded out, nodding, nodding out, numbed out, off, oiled, on, on a rip, on the beam, on the goof, on the gow, on the hump, on the kip, on the nod, on the stuff, ossified, out, out of it, out of one's gourd, out of sight, out of the world, out of this world, out to it, overamped, over-charged, over the hump, ozoned, packed up, pasted, petrified, phased, phazed, phumfed, picked up, pickled, piped, piped up, pipes, pipey, pipie, pippy, pipy, plowed, polluted, popped, poppied, pot-struck, potsville, potted, pot vague, primed, primed to the barrel, primed to the ears, primed to the nuts, psyched out, purring, purring like a cat, racked, racked up, riding the waves, riding the white horse, riffed, ripped, ripped off, ripped up, rummy, scattered, schnockered, scorched, sent, sharp, shot up, simpy, sitting well, skagged out, skating, smashed, smeared, snapped up, snaved in, snowed, snowed in, snowed under, snowed up, spaced, spaced out, spacey, steamed, steamed up, stepping high, stoned, stoned out of one's head, strung, strung out, stung by a viper, supercharged, switched on, syrupped up, taken, tall, tea'd up, tead up, teed up, tipping, tore, tore down, tore up, torn, torn up, totalled, trashed, tribed up, tripped out, tripping heavy, trippy, turned on, twisted, under, under the white cross, up, walking in the air, warped, wasted, way out, weirded out, whacked, whacked out, wide, wigged, wigged out, wiggy, winged, wiped, wiped out, wiped over, wired, wired on whites, wired up, with a load of coke under the skin, wrecked, zapped, zerked, zerked out, zig-zag, zipped, zoned, zonk, zonked, zonked out, zounk, zunked.*

stoned out of one's head (also stoned out of one's gourd) under the effects of marijuana. Gourd = head. RT: *wasted.* [U.S., JWK: 1981]

stoned out of one's squash marijuana intoxicated. RT: *wasted.* [U.S., BR: 1972]

stoned to the tits alcohol intoxicated. *Cf. ripped to the tits.* RT: *drunk.* [U.S., BR: 1972]

stoner a person who is stoned frequently; a teenager who prefers smoking marijuana to anything else. *Cf. burnout.* RS: *user.* [U.S., EEL: 1971, ADC: 1981]

stone sober completely sober. See *sober as a judge.* [U.S., (1880s): SBF: 1976]

stone soup a tea brewed from the waste parts of the marijuana plant. From *stoned* (*q.v.*). *Cf. pot likker.* [U.S., BR: 1972]

stone wall horrors the delirium tremens. RT: *D.T.s.* [Br. (Anglo-Irish), early 1900s, DSUE]

stonkered alcohol intoxicated. GEN: out of action (1914): DSUE. RT: *drunk.* [New Zealand, JAWB: 1943; Aust., listed in BH: 1980]

stony blind drunk, a variant of *stone blind* (*q.v.*). RT: *drunk.* [Aust., (1920): DSUE]

stony bush marijuana. *Cf. bush, stoned.* RT: *pot.* [U.S., BR: 1972]

stooper (also stoop tobacco) a cigar or cigarette butt picked up from the ground. RT: *brad.* [Br. and U.S., EK: 1927, (1930): DSUE, GI: 1931, MHW: 1934, D&D: 1957]

stoppers barbiturates. *Cf. downer.* RT: *barbs.* [U.S., SNP: 1977, RDS: 1982]

stout originally a type of malt liquor, now a variety of *porter* (*q.v.*). *Cf. black varnish, salmon and trout.* Originally cant. [since the late 1600s, (1677): OED] Nicknames and slang terms for stout: *black varnish, black velvet, gatter, heavy wet, in and out, salmon and trout, stout, swizzle.*

stove a tobacco pipe. [U.S., RB: 1915, MHW: 1934]

stove in alcohol intoxicated. From the nautical sense, i.e., *crushed in.* RT: *drunk.* [U.S., BVB: 1942]

stozzle to drink liquor, perhaps to excess. RT: *irrigate.* [U.S., late 1800s, F&H]

stozzled alcohol intoxicated. RT: *drunk.* [U.S., late 1800s, F&H]

S.T.P. a hallucinogenic chemical produced by the Dow Chemical Company. The initials are said to represent "serenity, tranquility, and peace" or "scientifically treated petroleum," (the name of a gasoline additive). *Cf.* ***D.O.M.*** [U.S., RB: 1967, AHC: 1969, ADC: 1975, W&F: 1975, ADC: 1981, RDS: 1982; Br., BTD: 1968]

straddle the spike to inject drugs. *Cf.* ***spike.*** RT: ***shoot.*** [U.S., H&C: 1975]

straight 1. a tobacco cigarette; a tobacco cigarette butt. In its early years this term referred to a cigarette made solely of one type of tobacco (JM: 1923). In more recent use, it refers to tobacco cigarettes in contrast to marijuana cigarettes. RT: ***nail.*** [U.S., RRL: 1969, EEL: 1971, TH: 1976, JWK: 1981] **2**. having to do with undiluted liquor. RT: ***neat.*** [(1867): RHT: 1912, B&L: 1890, F&H, BWG: 1899, M&C: 1905, RRL: 1969, D&D: 1957, DCCU: 1972] **3**. relieved and satisfied by a dose of drugs; straightened out by drugs, i.e., not ***sick*** (*q.v.*). Said of an addict. *Cf.* ***Set me straight!*** [U.S., JBW: 1967, M&V: 1967, W&F: 1967, RRL: 1969, D&B: 1970c, CM: 1970, JWK: 1981] **4**. off drugs; no longer addicted to drugs. [U.S., (1944): ELA: 1982, RRL: 1969, EEL: 1971, ADC: 1975, JWK: 1981] **5**. not currently under the influence of a drug; temporarily ***straight*** (*q.v.*). This is more likely to be said of a marijuana or pill user than a narcotics addict. [U.S., RRL: 1969, DCCU: 1972, ADC: 1975, JWK: 1981] **6**. not addicted to drugs; not using drugs; square. Said of persons who are not actively involved in drug use. [U.S., S&W: 1966, D&B: 1970c, DCCU: 1972] **7**. a person who does not use drugs; a square. RT: ***square.*** [U.S., G&B: 1969, MA: 1973, ADC: 1975, RDS: 1982]

straight shooter an addict who injects drugs. RT: ***bangster.*** [U.S., D&B: 1970c]

straight up having to do with liquor served without ice. *Cf.* ***straight.*** [U.S., W&F: 1975, AP: 1980]

straw 1. an opium smoking pipe. RT: ***hop stick.*** [U.S., JES: 1959] **2**. marijuana. *Cf.* ***hay.*** RT: ***pot.*** [U.S., IGA: 1971, YKB: 1977] **3**. papers for rolling marijuana cigarettes. RT: ***paper.*** [U.S., JWK: 1981] **4**. a length of common drinking straw used for snorting cocaine. [U.S., JWK: 1981]

strawberry 1. a pimple from drinking excessively. RT: ***gin bud.*** [Br., (1887): DSUE] **2**. (also **strawberry tablets**) a pink tablet of mescaline. RS: ***peyote.*** [U.S., IGA: 1971, WCM: 1972] **3**. ***L.S.D.*** (*q.v.*). See ***strawberry fields.*** [U.S., C&H: 1974, SNP: 1977] **4**. an amphetamine tablet. RT: ***amps.*** [U.S., ELA: 1984]

strawberry fields (also **strawberry flats, strawberries**) the hallucinogenic drug ***L.S.D.*** (*q.v.*). The entry word is also the name of a female character in the movie *Sergeant Pepper's Lonely Hearts Club Band* and in the song *Strawberry Fields Forever*. RT: ***L.S.D.*** [U.S., RG: 1970, H&C: 1975, YKB: 1977]

streak of lightning a glass of gin. *Cf.* ***flash of lightning.*** RS: ***nip.*** [Br., 18-1900s, DSUE]

street dealer a person who sells drugs retail to anyone who will buy. RS: *dealer.* [U.S., MA: 1973, JWK: 1981]

street drug any drug (usually diluted) sold casually on the retail level, usually on urban streets. Such drugs may be diluted, adulterated, bogus, or otherwise misrepresented. The term is widely known outside the underworld. [U.S., (RG: 1970), RAS: 1980]

streeter (also **street addict**) an urban "street person" addict. An addict who is wise to the way of the street drug dealer and the city police. [U.S., M&V: 1973, JWK: 1981]

street, on the using drugs; selling drugs; looking for drugs. Also means engaged in prostitution. [U.S., TRG: 1968, RRL: 1969, EEL: 1971, RDS: 1982]

street ounce an ounce of heroin diluted for sale on the streets. RS: *load.* [U.S., P&C: 1969]

street pusher a drug dealer who works at the retail level on the streets. RT: *dealer.* [U.S., DEM: 1981]

street value the final retail price of drugs sold illegally, i.e., on the street. This expression is not argot. It appears in reports of drug seizures as an estimation of value. [U.S., RDS: 1982]

stretch to cut or dilute a drug. RS: *cut.* [U.S., RAS: 1983]

stretched alcohol intoxicated. RT: *drunk.* [U.S., N&S: 1983]

stretcher something used to dilute or *stretch* a drug. [U.S., ELA: 1984]

stretchies one of the early symptoms of drug withdrawal. One feels like stretching all of the time. *Cf. gap.* [U.S., JWK: 1981]

strike 1. a dose of drugs in any form. A synonym of *hit* (*q.v.*). RT: *dose.* [U.S., EEL: 1971] 2. to go barhopping; to move from bar to bar. *Cf. pub-crawl.* [U.S., DST: 1984]

strike-me-dead inferior beer; weak beer. *Cf. kill-grief, kill-priest, kill-the-beggar.* RS: *queer-beer.* [Br., early 1800s, DSUE; listed in BVB: 1942]

string and twine wine. See *silk and twine.* Rhyming slang. RT: *wine.* [U.S., M&B: 1944, DRS]

striped alcohol intoxicated. RT: *drunk.* [U.S., W&F: 1960]

strip-me-naked gin; raw gin. *Cf. staff naked, stark naked.* RT: *gin.* [cant, (1751): OED, FG: 1811, FG: 1823, B&L: 1890, F&H]

stripped having to do with undiluted liquor. RT: *neat.* [Br., 1800s, F&H]

strip-search a search of the body and its orifices for drugs or other contraband. The same as *skin-search* (*q.v.*). [U.S., W&F: 1975]

strong alcohol intoxicated. RT: *drunk.* [BF: 1737]

strong and thin gin. RT: *gin.* [U.S., M&B: 1944, DRS]

strong out Possibly an error for *strung out* (*q.v.*). This may reflect a (Black) dialect pronunciation. [U.S., TRG: 1968]

strong stuff (also **strong drink, strong water, strong waters**) hard liquor; distilled spirits, compared to beer and wine. RS: *booze*. [U.S., BWG: 1899, GI: 1931, BVB: 1942, D&D: 1957]

strung out (also **strung, strung up**) 1. drug intoxicated and bewildered. RT: *stoned*. Some use in general slang for nervous or exhausted. [U.S., (1965): W&F: 1975, CM: 1970, (1970): DNE: 1973, EEL: 1971, DCCU: 1972, MW: 1976] 2. badly addicted to heroin; dissipated by heroin. RS: *hooked*. [U.S., W&F: 1967, RRL: 1969, D&B: 1970c, MA: 1973, ADC: 1975, MW: 1976, JWK: 1981]

stub a marijuana cigarette butt. RT: *roach*. [U.S., JWK: 1981]

stubbed alcohol intoxicated. (BF: 1737: [He's] Stubb'd.) RT: *drunk*. [BF: 1737]

stuccoed alcohol intoxicated. A play on *plastered* (*q.v.*). RT: *drunk*. [U.S., MP: 1928, AH: 1931, MHW: 1934, D&D: 1957]

stud dope. *Cf. cat, dude*. RT: *dope*. [U.S., S&W: 1973]

student a novice addict; a newly addicted person. *Cf. cadet, freshman, green hype*. Compare to *graduate*. RS: *user*. [U.S., DWM: 1936, VJM: 1949, M&D: 1952]

stufa* heroin. Spanish for *stuff* (*q.v.*). RT: *heroin*. [U.S., NIDA: 1980]

stuff illegal intoxicants: bootlegged whiskey, *Demerol* (TM; *q.v.*), heroin, marijuana, opium, morphine, etc. Sometimes **stuff** is euphemistic for *shit*. RS: *dope*. Expressions including the word stuff are: *birdie stuff, black stuff, brown stuff, canned stuff, dream stuff, drugstore stuff, fine stuff, glad stuff, good stuff, happy stuff, hard stuff, heavy stuff, kidstuff, nose stuff, snow stuff, sweet stuff, triangle stuff, white stuff*. [U.S., VWS: 1929, DWM: 1936, BD: 1937, GOL: 1950, M&H: 1959, S&W: 1966, (1969): DNE: 1973, RRL: 1969, CM: 1970, D&B: 1970c, EEL: 1971, DCCU: 1972, EAF: 1972, MA: 1973, ADC: 1975, NIDA: 1980, JWK: 1981, BW: 1984; Br., DSUE, M&J: 1975]

stuff bag a bag containing marijuana and the supplies needed for using it. *Cf. stash bag*. RS: *stash*. [U.S., DCCU: 1972]

stuff, on the drug intoxicated; addicted to a drug. Refers primarily to opium. RT: *stoned, hooked*. [U.S., DWM: 1936, GOL: 1950, TRG: 1968, H&C: 1975]

stuka *Methedrine* (TM; *q.v.*). From the name of a German WWII dive bomber. RT: *speed*. [U.S., SNP: 1977]

stum 1. marijuana. Because it makes one stumble. RT: *pot*. [U.S., EEL: 1971, JH: 1979] 2. a barbiturate. *Cf. stoms, stumbles, stumblers*. RT: *barbs*. [U.S., EEL: 1971, EAF: 1972] 3. to get high. [U.S., EAF: 1980]

stumblers (also **stoms, stum, stums**) barbiturate capsules or tablets. RT: *barbs*. [U.S., RRL: 1969, D&B: 1970c, IGA: 1971,

EAF: 1972, S&W: 1973, ADC: 1975]

stumbles 1. (also **stumble-bumbles**) barbiturates; sedatives; tranquilizers; alcohol. *Cf. barbs.* [U.S., D&B: 1970c, YKB: 1977, EAF: 1980] 2. the inability to stand up and walk straight. A symptom of advanced drug debilitation. [U.S., EEL: 1971]

stump water (also **stump, stump likker, stump liquor, stump rum**) home-brewed whiskey; illicit liquor. Named for the way it was procured. Money was left on a stump as payment for the bottle of moonshine which would be found there some time later. RT: *moonshine.* [U.S., MHW: 1934, BVB: 1942, D&D: 1957, LP: 1977]

stung alcohol intoxicated. *Cf. sting.* RT: *drunk.* [Aust., (1919): GAW: 1978, (1920): DSUE]

stung by a viper intoxicated with marijuana; addicted to marijuana. *Cf. viper.* RT: *wasted.* [U.S., JES: 1959, H&C: 1975]

stung by the hop addicted to opium. *Cf. hop.* RS: *hooked.* [U.S., JES: 1959, H&C: 1975]

stung by the white nurse addicted to morphine. RS: *hooked.* [U.S., JES: 1959, H&C: 1975]

stung by white mosquitoes addicted to cocaine. RS: *hooked.* [U.S., JES: 1959]

stunned alcohol intoxicated. RT: *drunk.* [New Zealand, (1910): DSUE, JAWB: 1943; Aust., SJB: 1943; U.S., W&F: 1960, RDS: 1982]

stun, on the on a drinking bout. RT: *spreeing.* [Aust., (1920): DSUE, SJB: 1943]

stupefying grass marijuana. RT: *pot.* [U.S., BR: 1972]

stupor juice powerful, high proof liquor of some kind. Recorded in Normandy, France. RS: *rotgut.* [U.S., WWII, DST: 1984]

submarine a large marijuana cigarette. *Cf. torpedo.* RT: *joint.* [South African, early 1900s, DU]

substance abuse in general, drug abuse; taking too much alcohol or drugs. In most usage, the expression is jargon or euphemism. [U.S., RAS: 1981] See also *substance counselor.*

substance counselor a counselor for people with drug problems. The *substance* is from *controlled substance* (*q.v.*). [U.S., RAS: 1981]

subway silver See *New York City Silver.*

suck 1. (also **suction**) liquor; wine; beer; strong drink. RT: *booze.* [cant, BE: 1690, FG: 1785, FG: 1811, FG: 1823, GWM: 1859] 2. (also **suck up**) to drink liquids, i.e., beer or liquor. RT: *irrigate.* [17–1800s, (1774): OED]

suck a butt (also **suck a fag**) to smoke a tobacco cigarette. [U.S., BVB: 1942]

suck bamboo (also **suck the bamboo**) to smoke opium in an opium pipe. [U.S., EK: 1927, MHW: 1934] Terms meaning to smoke opium: *beat the gong, blow a pill, boot the gong around, bowl, burn the midnight oil, cop a pill, flop, gow out the lemon bowl, grease, hit the flute, hit the gong, hit the gonger, hit the gow, hit the grease, hit the hop, hit the mud, hit the pipe, hit the steam, hit the stem, kick the engine around, kick the gong, kick the gong around, kick the gonger, kick the mooch around, lay a hip, lay down, lay on one's hip, lay the hip, lean against the engine, lie down, lie on the hip, lie on the side, melt wax, puff, puff bamboo, ride the pipe, ride the poppy train, roll the boy, roll the log, smoke a bowl, suck bamboo, suck the bamboo, whiff the yen-shee.*

suck bottle (also **suck can, sucking cull, suck pint, suck pot, suck spigot**) a drunkard; a tippler. RT: *sot.* [primarily Br., 16–1700s, F&H]

suck crib (also **suck casa**) a tavern; a low drinking establishment. *Cf. suck.* RS: *bar, dive.* [cant, JCH: 1859, B&L: 1890, F&H, DU]

sucked alcohol intoxicated. *Cf. suck.* RT: *drunk.* [cant, 1800s, DU]

sucker a drunkard. From *spigot-sucker* (*q.v.*). RT: *sot.* [Br., 1800s, F&H; listed in BVB: 1942]

sucker weed (also **sugar weed**) fake or inferior marijuana. RT: *blank.* Black use. [U.S., EAF: 1980]

suckey (also **sucky**) alcohol intoxicated. *Cf. suck.* RT: *drunk.* [cant, BE: 1690, FG: 1785, FG: 1823, F&H]

suckonal *Seconal* (TM; *q.v.*) barbiturates. RT: *sec.* Attested as gay slang. [U.S., BR: 1972]

suck suds to drink beer. *Cf. suds.* RS: *irrigate.* [U.S., D&B: 1970c]

suck the monkey (also **sup the monkey**) 1. to drink from a fermented coconut; to drink from a spiked coconut. Monkey = a coconut. This may be nonce. [late 1700s, OED, (1837): F&H, BVB: 1942, PKK: 1976] 2. (also **bleed the monkey**) to steal rum from a cask by sucking it through a straw or a quill. See *monkey pump.* [Br., FG: 1785, FG: 1823, JCH: 1887, F&H, WG: 1962, K&M: 1968]

suck up some dope to smoke marijuana. RT: *hit the hay.* [U.S., BR: 1972]

sucky alcohol intoxicated. See *suckey.*

suction See *suck.*

suds beer; a head of foam on a beer. *Cf. froth.* Originally referred to any alcoholic drink (W&F: 1960). RT: *beer.* [(1907): OEDS, (1915): W&F: 1960, JAS: 1932, MHW: 1934, VJM: 1949, D&D: 1957, DC: 1972, DCCU: 1972, EE: 1976, ADC: 1984]

sudsery (also **suds joint**) a beer hall; a beer joint. RS: *bar.* [U.S., BVB: 1942, D&D: 1957]

suds factory a brewery. [U.S., BVB: 1942]

suds, in the alcohol intoxicated. (BF: 1737: [He's] In the Sudds.)

RT: ***drunk***. [BF: 1737, (1770): OED]

suede a liquid solution of opium residue. *Cf.* ***suey***. [U.S., EEL: 1971] See also ***blue velvet***.

suet liquor. RS: ***booze***. [GWM: 1859]

suey a liquid solution of opium pipe residue. *Cf.* ***suede***. [U.S., EEL: 1971, IGA: 1971]

suey bowl an opium den. Chinese. RT: ***opium den***. [U.S., BVB: 1942, VJM: 1949]

suey-pow a rag, powder puff, or sponge for cooling and cleaning an opium pipe. The *pow* may be from *powder puff*. [U.S., (1914): DU, DWM: 1936, BD: 1937, GOL: 1950]

sugar 1. powdered drugs in general. Because their consistency is similar to powdered sugar. RT: ***powder***. [U.S., DWM: 1936, VJM: 1949, TRG: 1968, IGA: 1971] 2. heroin. Because it is a white powder and because it is sometimes diluted with sugar. In addition, **sugar** is a euphemism for ***shit*** (*q.v.*), a popular name for heroin. RT: ***heroin***. [U.S., YKB: 1977] 3. inferior or bogus heroin which is overly-diluted with sugar. RS: ***blank***. [U.S., M&V: 1967] 4. the hallucinogenic drug ***L.S.D.*** (*q.v.*). From ***sugar cube*** (*q.v.*). RT: ***L.S.D.*** [U.S., EEL: 1971, IGA: 1971, DCCU: 1972, ADC: 1975, W&F: 1975, NIDA: 1980; Br., BTD: 1968, M&J: 1975]

sugar candy brandy. Rhyming slang. RT: ***brandy***. [Br., JCH: 1859, F&H, DRS]

sugar cube (also **sugar lump**) the hallucinogenic drug ***L.S.D.*** (*q.v.*). Refers to taking L.S.D. impregnated sugar cubes. RT: ***L.S.D.*** [U.S., M&V: 1967, EEL: 1971, YKB: 1977]

sugar daddy a doctor who sells drugs to addicts; one's drug seller or supplier. Similar to ***mother*** (*q.v.*). GEN: an older man who takes care of a younger person. *Cf.* ***sugar***. RT: ***dealer***. [U.S., JES: 1959, H&C: 1975]

sugar down to dilute powdered drugs with sugar. *Cf.* ***sugar***. RS: ***cut***. [U.S., RG: 1970, EEL: 1971]

sugar habit a light drug addiction. The implication is that the user is more addicted to the sugar used for dilution than to the drug. Compare to ***needle habit***. *Cf.* ***chippy habit***. [U.S., M&V: 1967, H&C: 1975]

sugar lump cubes cubes of morphine the size of sugar lumps. Morphine was once sold in cubes. *Cf.* ***cube***. Compare to ***sugar cube***. RT: ***morphine***. [U.S., M&V: 1954]

sugar weed 1. marijuana which has been compressed into a brick with sugar or honey. This process increases the weight, i.e., the purchaser gets less actual cannabis per ounce. *Cf.* ***brick***. RS: ***pot***. [U.S., RRL: 1969, EAF: 1980] 2. the same as ***sucker weed*** (*q.v.*).

summer skies morning glory seeds. From the name of a color variety. RT: ***seeds***. [U.S., YKB: 1977]

Sunday popper a person who takes drugs infrequently. *Cf. Saturday night habit.* RT: *chipper.* [U.S., M&V: 1967]

sundowner a drink of liquor at sundown. RS: *nip.* [Aust., late 18-1900s, DSUE; U.S., BVB: 1942; South African, (1937): JB: 1980]

sunflower seeds amphetamine capsules. RT: *amps.* [U.S., BR: 1972]

sun, in the (also **in the sunshine, the sun has shone on them**) alcohol intoxicated. See the full BF: 1737 entry at *been in the sun.* RT: *drunk.* [BF: 1737, B&L: 1890, F&H, F&G: 1925, (WWI): B&P: 1965, MHW: 1934]

sunshine (also **sunshine acid, sunshine pill**) an orange or yellow tablet of *L.S.D.* (*q.v.*). RS: *L.S.D.* [U.S., RRL: 1969, (1970): DNE: 1973, EEL: 1971, IGA: 1971, W&F: 1975, YKB: 1977]

superblow cocaine. *Cf. blow.* RT: *cocaine.* [U.S., YKB: 1977]

supercharged alcohol or (later) drug intoxicated. *Cf. charged.* RT: *drunk, stoned.* [Br. military, (1936): DSUE; U.S., S&E: 1981]

supergrass 1. high-quality marijuana. *Cf. superweed.* RS: *pot.* [U.S., RG: 1970, DEM: 1981] 2. (also **super, super cools, superjoint**) phencyclidine, *P.C.P.* (*q.v.*), an animal tranquilizer. Probably refers to some type of smokable vegetable matter doctored with P.C.P. One of many misleading terms for P.C.P. *Cf. superweed, super yerba.* RT: *P.C.P.* [U.S., YKB: 1977, NIDA: 1980]

super C. *ketamine* (*q.v.*) hydrochloride. [U.S., ELA: 1984]

superpot marijuana mixed with alcohol and smoked as a cigarette or drunk as a tea; tobacco cigarettes impregnated with alcohol. [U.S., RB: 1967, EEL: 1971, SNP: 1977, D&B: 1978]

super-soaper (also **super-Quaalude, super-soper**) *methaqualone* (*q.v.*), a hypnotic-sedative. From the brand name *Sopor* (TM; *q.v.*). RT: *ludes.* [U.S., YKB: 1977, DEM: 1981]

super-suds beer; Coor's (TM) beer. From the brand name of a laundry powder. RT: *beer.* [U.S., EE: 1976]

superweed 1. marijuana; powerful marijuana. RT: *pot.* [U.S., DEM: 1981] 2. (also **superjoint**) phencyclidine, *P.C.P.* (*q.v.*), an animal tranquilizer. See *supergrass.* RT: *P.C.P.* [U.S., (1970s): FAB: 1979, YKB: 1977]

super yerba *P.C.P.* (*q.v.*), an animal tranquilizer. Spanish for *supergrass* (*q.v.*). RT: *P.C.P.* [U.S., NIDA: 1980]

supplier a seller of drugs, usually at a high level in the chain of distribution. RT: *dealer.* [U.S., RG: 1970, IGA: 1971, TRG: 1968, BW: 1984]

supplies drugs and the equipment used to inject or smoke them. Often seen in advertising as a code word for drug equipment. *Cf. tea accessories.* [U.S., EEL: 1971]

suprema verde de clorafila* (also **suprema verde de mejorana***) marijuana. Spanish. RT: *pot.* [calo, JBR: 1973]

supremo top-quality cannabis. RT: *pot.* [U.S., ELA: 1982]

sup the monkey See *suck the monkey.*

surfer phencyclidine, *P.C.P.* (*q.v.*), an animal tranquilizer. RT: *P.C.P.* [U.S., (1970s): FAB: 1979, YKB: 1977]

swack to drink liquor to excess; to get drunk. RT: *mug oneself.* [U.S., BHL: 1920, MHW: 1934]

swacked (also **swacko**) alcohol intoxicated. RT: *drunk.* [U.S., JAS: 1932, MHW: 1934, (1941): SBF: 1976]

swag liquor. RT: *booze.* [U.S., EAF: 1980]

swallow a puff of cigarette smoke. [Br. and U.S., 1900s, DSUE] See also *swallow hit.*

swallowed a tavern token has become alcohol intoxicated. (BF: 1737: [He] Has...) Tavern tokens were given as change by tavern keepers. [(1596): F&H, BF: 1737, F&H]

swallower 1. a drunkard; a tippler. RT: *sot.* [Br., 1800s, F&H] 2. a person who is hired to smuggle drugs by swallowing rubber packages of powdered drugs and retrieving the packages from excreted stools. See *body-packer, internal.* RS: *mule.* [U.S., RAS: 1983]

swallow hit a puff of marijuana smoke which is swallowed. *Cf. hit, toke.* [U.S., RAS: 1979]

swamp dew moonshine; illicit corn whiskey. RT: *moonshine.* [U.S., (1940): ADD]

swamp down (also **swamp**) to drink heavily; to gulp down a drink. RT: *guzzle.* [Aust., (1910): DSUE, SJB: 1943]

swamped (also **swampt**) alcohol intoxicated. (BF: 1737: [He's] Swampt.) RT: *drunk.* [BF: 1737; Br., (1920): DSUE, EP: 1948]

swamp root illicit whiskey. *Cf. swamp dew.* RT: *moonshine.* [U.S., (1918): ADD, VR: 1929]

swap of the mop a drink of liquor. RT: *nip.* [U.S., N&S: 1983]

swatched alcohol intoxicated. RT: *drunk.* [Br., (1950): DSUE]

swattled alcohol intoxicated. RT: *drunk.* [Br., (1785): OED; listed in BVB: 1942]

swazzled alcohol intoxicated. See *swozzled* at *swoozled.* RT: *drunk.* [U.S., W&F: 1960, RDS: 1982]

sweat liquor. A generic term, probably euphemistic for *piss* (*q.v.*), found in *nanny goat sweat, panther sweat, pig sweat, tiger sweat.*

sweat cure an attempt to cure drug addiction by total abstinence from drugs. [U.S., BVB: 1942, DU]

sweat it out to attempt to cure a drug addiction by total abstinence from drugs. RS: *kick.* From general slang. [U.S., BVB: 1942, VJM: 1949]

sweat room a room (or cell) used to detoxify drug or alcohol intoxicated persons. [U.S., JES: 1959, H&C: 1975]

Swedish condition powder snuff. *Cf. Scandihoovian dynamite.* RT: *snoose.* Loggers' use. [U.S., RFA]

sweep (also **sweep with both barrels**) to snort a line of cocaine. RS: *snort.* [U.S., RAS: 1982, ELA: 1984]

sweeties capsules of *Preludin* (TM; *q.v.*) stimulant. *Cf. prels.* [U.S., EEL: 1971, IGA: 1971]

sweet Jesus morphine. RT: *morphine.* This must be older than the attestations indicate. [U.S., M&V: 1967, SNP: 1977]

sweet Lucy 1. marijuana. RT: *pot.* [U.S., RRL: 1969, ADC: 1975, YKB: 1977, NIDA: 1980] 2. muscatel wine (as drunk by winos) and barbiturates. RS: *wine.* [U.S., M&V: 1967] 3. marijuana resin dissolved in wine. [U.S., (1948): ELA: 1982, M&V: 1954, SNP: 1977]

sweet lunch marijuana. RT: *pot.* [U.S., (1967): ELA: 1982, YKB: 1977]

sweet Marguerite (also **sweet Margaret**) a cigarette or a cigar. Rhyming slang for *cigareet* or *cigarette.* [U.S., M&B: 1944, DRS]

sweet Mary cannabis. RT: *pot.* [U.S. military, (1968): ELA: 1982]

sweet Morpheus morphine. RT: *morphine.* [U.S., M&V: 1973, SNP: 1977]

sweets amphetamine capsules or tablets. *Cf. sweeties.* RT: *amps.* [U.S., EEL: 1971, IGA: 1971, ADC: 1975, YKB: 1977, JH: 1979; Br., BTD: 1968]

sweet stuff powdered narcotics, especially morphine and cocaine. *Cf. sugar.* RT: *powder.* [U.S., DWM: 1936, VJM: 1949]

sweet tooth addiction to narcotics. *Cf. sugar, sweet stuff.* RS: *habit.* [U.S., W&F: 1967, DCCU: 1972]

swellhead a drunkard. *Cf. got on his little hat.* RT: *sot.* [Br., late 18-1900s, DSUE; U.S., GI: 1931]

swicky whiskey. RT: *whiskey.* [U.S., RWB: 1912, MHW: 1934, (1939): ADD, BVB: 1942]

swig 1. a deep drink of liquor; a swallow of liquor. RT: *nip.* [(1621): OED, FG: 1823, MHW: 1934, AP: 1980] 2. to drink liquor deeply. RT: *guzzle.* [(1654): OED, JCH: 1887, BWG: 1899, BVB: 1942, SSD, M&J: 1975, AP: 1980] 3. liquor. RT: *booze.* [(1635): OED, GWM: 1859, DSUE]

swigged (also **swiggled**) alcohol intoxicated; tipsy. RT: *drunk.* [Br., 18-1900s, DSUE; listed in BVB: 1942]

swigsby (also **swigster**) a drinker; a drunkard. *Cf. swig.* RT: *sot.* [Br., 1800s, F&H]

swill 1. to drink liquor deeply; to swig down booze. RT: *guzzle.* [FG: 1811, FG: 1823, JCH: 1887, F&H, BWG: 1899, BVB: 1942, M&J: 1975] 2. a drink of liquor. RT: *nip.*

[(1602): SOD] 3. liquor. RT: *booze*. [U.S., BVB: 1942]

swilled (also **swilled up**) alcohol intoxicated. RT: *drunk*. [Br., 1800s, F&H; listed in BVB: 1942]

swiller (also **swill belly, swill bowl, swillocks, swill pot, swill tub**) a drinker; a drunkard. *Cf. swill*. RT: *sot*. [JF: 1598, FG: 1785, FG: 1811, F&H, BWG: 1899, BVB: 1942]

swill-up a drinking bout. RT: *spree*. [U.S., BVB: 1942]

swined (also **swinny**) alcohol intoxicated. *Cf. drunk as David's sow*. RT: *drunk*. [Br., 1800s, F&H]

swine drunk alcohol intoxicated. *Cf. drunk as a sow, drunk as David's sow, swine drunk*. The pig image alludes to the fullness of a greedy hog. RT: *drunk*. [(1592): F&H; listed in BVB: 1942]

swing to sell drugs. *Cf. deal*. [U.S., M&V: 1967, IGA: 1971]

swinger one who uses all forms of drugs. RS: *user*. [U.S., (RG: 1970), EEL: 1971]

swing into high gear to get high on a drug. *Cf. high*. [U.S., HB: 1955]

swing man a drug seller; a drug connection. A man who can swing a drug deal. RS: *dealer*. [U.S., A&T: 1953, JBW: 1967, RRL: 1969, W&F: 1975]

swinny alcohol intoxicated. See *swined*.

swipe 1. to drink rapidly and to excess; to bolt a drink of liquor. See *swipes*. RS: *guzzle*. [Br., FG: 1823, (1829): SOD, JCH: 1887, F&H] 2. *moonshine* (*q.v.*); inferior liquor. RT: *rotgut*. [U.S., (1962): W&F: 1975]

swiped (also **swipey, swipy**) alcohol intoxicated. *Cf. swipe, swipes*. RT: *drunk*. [Br., JCH: 1887, B&L: 1890, F&H, DSUE]

swiper a drunkard; a heavy drinker. RT: *sot*. [Br. and U.S., 1800s, OED, BWG: 1899]

swipes inferior beer; thin, weak, sour, or stale beer. Often used as a dysphemism for beer in general. RS: *queer-beer*. [FG: 1785, (1796): OED, JCH: 1887, B&L: 1890, F&H, BVB: 1942, EP: 1948, WG: 1962, SSD] See also *swipe*.

swipey alcohol intoxicated. See *swiped*. RT: *drunk*. [Br., (1821): DSUE]

swipington (also **swippington**) a drunkard. *Cf. boozington, lushington, thirstington*. RT: *sot*. [Aust., SJB: 1943]

swipster a drunkard. RT: *sot*. [Br., 1800s, F&H]

Swiss purple a type of high-quality L.S.D. Refers to Sandoz Laboratories in Switzerland where the substance was developed. RT: *L.S.D.* [U.S., ELA: 1984]

switched on 1. introduced to drug use; awakened to the pleasures of L.S.D. and other hallucinogenic drugs. Akin to the switching on of electricity as with *electric koolaid* (*q.v.*). [U.S., MW: 1976]

2. drug intoxicated. *Cf. turned on*. RT: *stoned*. [U.S., DCCU: 1972]

switch on to get high on drugs; to begin taking L.S.D. or other hallucinogens. See *turn on*. [U.S., (1966): DNE: 1973]

swivelly alcohol intoxicated. RT: *drunk*. [Br., 1800s, F&H; listed in BVB: 1942]

swizzle 1. to drink liquor, probably to excess; to tipple. RT: *irrigate*. [(1847): OED, BWG: 1899, JOH: 1901, BVB: 1942, D&D: 1957, M&J: 1975] 2. liquor; beer or *stout* (*q.v.*). RT: *booze*. [(1791): DSUE, FG: 1811, JCH: 1887, B&L: 1890, JSF: 1889, BVB: 1942, D&D: 1957]

swizzled alcohol intoxicated. RT: *drunk*. [Br. and U.S., (1843): OEDS, (1850s): SBF: 1976, F&H, BVB: 1942, D&D: 1957]

swizzle guts a drunkard. RT: *sot*. [Br., 1800s, F&H; listed in BVB: 1942]

swizzle nick a drunkard. RT: *sot*. [U.S., BVB: 1942]

swizzle stick a stick for stirring an alcoholic mixed drink. [since the late 1800s, (1885): OED, BWG: 1899]

swoozled (also **swozzled**) alcohol intoxicated. RT: *drunk*. [U.S., (archaic): W&F: 1960; listed in PD: 1982]

syndicate acid *S.T.P.* (*q.v.*) sold as *L.S.D.* (*q.v.*), presumably by the crime syndicate. [U.S., IGA: 1971, SNP: 1977]

synthetic grass (also **synthetic marijuana**) 1. a real or imagined chemical synthesis of T.H.C., the active principle of marijuana. *Cf. sin*. [U.S., EEL: 1971, ELA: 1982] 2. (also **synthetic T.H.C.**) phencyclidine, *P.C.P.* (*q.v.*), an animal tranquilizer. One of the many appealing nicknames under which this drug is sold. *Cf. T.H.C., tic*. RT: *P.C.P.* [U.S., H&C: 1975, YKB: 1977]

synthetic heroin the drug *Talwin* (TM; *q.v.*), a painkiller mixed with *Pyribenzamine* (TM; *q.v.*) antihistamine. *Cf. one on one, tricycles and bicycles, T.s and blues*. RS: *set*. [U.S., RAS: 1981]

syringe (also **syringe it**) to inject a drug. RT: *shoot*. [U.S., JES: 1959]

syrup dark brown Mexican heroin, probably in liquid form. This heroin is *brown sugar* (*q.v.*) in powdered form. RS: *heroin*. [U.S., M&V: 1967, H&C: 1975]

syrup head a drug user or addict who takes cough syrup (with codeine) and a depressant. See *head*. RS: *user*. [U.S., RAS: 1984]

syrupped up intoxicated on cough syrup. RS: *stoned*. [U.S., D&B: 1970b]

T

T. 1. (also **T-man**) a federal agent. T-man = treasury man. RS: *fuzz*. [U.S., M&V: 1954, H&C: 1975] 2. marijuana. From *tea* (*q.v.*). RT: *pot*. [U.S., M&D: 1952, EEL: 1971, W&F: 1960, ADC: 1975] 3. *Tuinal* (TM; *q.v.*), a barbiturate. See *T.s and blues*. [U.S., RAS: 1981] 4. (also **tee**) *T.H.C.* (*q.v.*). RT: *T.H.C.* [U.S., FAB: 1979] 5. a tablet of some sort (i.e, saccharine) with a dot of L.S.D. on it. Short for *tablet*. RT: *L.S.D.* [U.S., IGA: 1971] 6. P.C.P., i.e., T.H.C. RT: *P.C.P.* [U.S., FAB: 1979]

tab 1. a tobacco cigarette. Possibly a play on *pill* (*q.v.*), i.e., tablet. Probably akin to *tabacky* (*q.v.*) or some similar word. RT: *nail*. [Br. military, EP: 1948, DU, M&J: 1975] 2. any tablet or pill form of a drug. From *tablet*. [U.S., RG: 1970, EEL: 1971, DCCU: 1972, ADC: 1975] 3. (also **tabs**) a portion of L.S.D.; L.S.D. on a tablet of sugar or saccharine. RT: *L.S.D.* [U.S., RRL: 1969, D&B: 1970c, IGA: 1971, W&F: 1975, LVA: 1981] 4. a stimulant drug; a *Methedrine* (*q.v.*) tablet. [U.S., M&V: 1967; Bahamas, JAH: 1982] 5. to dot a piece of blotter paper with L.S.D. [U.S., ELA: 1984]

tabacky (also **tobaccer, tobacker, tobacky**) tobacco. There are many pronunciation and spelling variants. All are regarded as dialect. See *bacca* for other variants. RT: *fogus*. [U.S., BVB: 1942]

table, under the alcohol intoxicated. See *under the table*.

tabs the hallucinogenic drug *L.S.D.* (*q.v.*). See *tab*.

tac P.C.P., a variant of *tic* (*q.v.*). RT: *P.C.P.* [U.S., (1970s): FAB: 1979]

tack wallah a total abstainer. *Wallah* (*q.v.*) = merchant. RT: *dry*. [Br., (WWI): B&P: 1965]

tacky alcohol intoxicated. *Cf. wet*. RT: *drunk*. Attested at numerous U.S. colleges and universities. [U.S., EHB: 1900]

tad just a bit of a drug. The same as *taste* (*q.v.*). RS: *load*. [U.S., JWK: 1981]

tag the euphoria from a dose of drugs; a drug rush. RT: *rush*. [U.S., JES: 1959, H&C: 1975]

tailor-mades mass-produced, machine-made tobacco cigarettes.

RS: *nail.* Originally military slang. [Br. and U.S., (1910): DSUE, GI: 1931, BVB: 1942, WG: 1962, SSD]

tailors tailor-made cigarettes. An Australian version of *tailor-mades* (*q.v.*). [Aust., (1920): DSUE]

take a band to take drugs. The band may refer to the tourniquet used while injecting drugs. [U.S., TRG: 1968, IGA: 1971]

take a boil-out (also **take the boil-out**) to withdraw from drugs completely. *Cf. sweat cure.* [U.S., BVB: 1942, VJM: 1949]

take a Brody 1. (also **take a Brodie, throw a Brody**) to fake a drug withdrawal spasm; to fall down. See *brody* for an explanation. [U.S., GOL: 1950] 2. to be arrested. *Cf. busted.* [U.S., GOL: 1950]

take a Duffy to fake a drug withdrawal spasm. *Cf. Arthur Duffy, Duffy.* RS: *brody.* [U.S., M&V: 1967]

take a fall to get arrested on a drug charge. *Cf. take a Brody.* [U.S., GOL: 1950, JWK: 1981]

take a sleighride (also **go for a sleighride**) to take cocaine. *Cf. sleighride.* See *winter wonderland* for other expressions on the snow theme. [U.S., BVB: 1942, JES: 1959]

take a sweep (also **take a sweep with both barrels, sweep**) to sniff (snort) cocaine. *Cf. one and one.* RT: *snort.* [U.S., DWM: 1938, A&T: 1953]

take a trip to take a dose of *L.S.D.* (*q.v.*). *Cf. trip.* [U.S., M&V: 1967, ADC: 1975]

take in cargo (also **take on cargo, take on fuel**) to get drunk. *Cf. flying the ensign.* RT: *mug oneself.* Of nautical origin. [cant, (1815): DSUE, FG: 1823]

take it in line (also **take a main, take it in the line, take it main, take it straight**) to inject drugs into the median cephalic vein of the forearm. RS: *shoot.* [U.S., DWM: 1938, BVB: 1942]

take it through the nose to sniff (snort) cocaine. A play on *take it on the nose.* RT: *snort.* [U.S., JES: 1959, H&C: 1975]

taken drug intoxicated; unconscious from drugs. RT: *stoned.* [U.S., DWM: 1936, BVB: 1942]

taken a cup too much (also **taken a chirriping glass**) alcohol intoxicated. *Cf. had one too many.* RT: *drunk.* [BF: 1737]

take off 1. to use opium pellets; to take opium pellets off of the card on which they are served. [U.S., M&V: 1954] 2. to begin a drug high by taking pills, injecting a drug, or lighting up marijuana. [U.S., M&V: 1954, M&H: 1959, RRL: 1969, MA: 1973, JWK: 1981]

takeoff artist an addict who supports his habit by stealing other addict's drugs. RS: *junky.* [U.S., RRL: 1969, EEL: 1971]

take off on to get a high from a particular drug, as in **take off on pot.** [U.S., RG: 1970, EEL: 1971]

take the cure (also take the boil-out) to stop taking addictive substances, i.e., drugs or alcohol; to enter a treatment center. RS: *kick*. [U.S., BVB: 1942, VJM: 1949, EEL: 1971]

take the needle (also take to the needle) to inject drugs. RT: *shoot*. [U.S., BVB: 1942, JES: 1959]

take the pipe to kill oneself with an overdose of drugs. *Cf. O.D.* Not limited to drug culture use. [U.S., EEL: 1971]

take the pledge to pledge abstinence from beverage alcohol. [1900s if not earlier, K&M: 1968]

take the works to inject narcotics. *Cf. works*. RT: *shoot*. [U.S., BVB: 1942]

take up to *light up* (*q.v.*) a marijuana cigarette. This is possibly an error for *toke up* (*q.v.*). [U.S., TRG: 1968, RG: 1970]

taking it easy alcohol intoxicated. RT: *drunk*. Euphemistic and probably recurrent nonce. [18-1900s, F&H, DSUE]

taking on a number smoking marijuana. Probably an error for *toking on a number*. *Cf. toke*. May refer to *thirteen* (*q.v.*) = marijuana. [U.S., RRL: 1969]

talc cocaine. RT: *cocaine*. [HSD: 1984]

talcum powder bogus powdered drugs. This may refer to pure talcum powder being sold as a drug, an adulterated drug, or a weak and ineffective drug. *Cf. flea powder*. RS: *blank*. [U.S., M&V: 1967, RDS: 1982]

tall 1. high on drugs; intoxicated with marijuana. A variant of *high* (*q.v.*). RT: *stoned*. [U.S., M&W: 1946, BVB: 1953, RRL: 1969] 2. having to do with high-quality drugs; having to do with anything of a high quality. [U.S., EEL: 1971, JHF: 1971]

tall one a large drink; a long drink. Compare to *short one*. [U.S., MHW: 1934]

Talwin a protected trade name for pentazocine (analgesic) available in a variety of forms. The drug is a potent painkiller. Most of the slang terms including Talwin (TM) refer to Talwin (TM) in combination with Pyribenzamine (TM) (an antihistamine). See *T.s and blues* for a list. [in current use; consult a pharmaceutical reference for more information]

tamale a badly rolled marijuana cigarette. From the size and structure of the Mexican tamale. RS: *joint*. [U.S., BR: 1972]

tambourine man a drug seller. RT: *dealer*. [U.S., EEL: 1971, JH: 1979]

tamp cotton used to filter drugs before injection. Probably from *tampon*. The same as *olive* (*q.v.*). *Cf. cotton*. [U.S., JES: 1959, H&C: 1975]

tampi marijuana. RT: *pot*. [M&J: 1975]

tang drug addiction; one's drug habit. From *orangutan*. RT: *habit*. *Cf. have a monkey on one's back, have an orangutan on one's back,*

King Kong, for other entries on the ape theme. [U.S. JWK: 1981]

tangerine *Methedrine* (TM; *q.v.*). Possibly a corruption of *Methedrine*. RT: *speed*. [U.S., BR: 1972]

tanglefoot (also **tangleleg**) beer; bad beer; whiskey; liquor. Because it tangles one's feet so that one stumbles. RS: *booze*. [U.S., JRB: 1859, B&L: 1890, JSF: 1889, BWG: 1899, JRW: 1909; Aust., SJB: 1943]

tangle-footed (also **tangled, tangle-legged**) alcohol intoxicated. RT: *drunk*. [GWM: 1859, B&L: 1890, BVB: 1942, D&D: 1957]

tank 1. (also **tank up**) to drink much beer; to drink to excess. RT: *guzzle*. [U.S., EHB: 1900, (1912): DU, F&G: 1925, (1925): W&F: 1960, EEL: 1971, GU: 1975] 2. a drunkard. *Cf. barrel, tanker*. RT: *sot*. [U.S., EHB: 1900, WM: 1927, AH: 1931, JAS: 1932, DWM: 1935, D&D: 1957] 3. one's capacity or need for drugs. Addicts need to fill their tanks periodically. [U.S., JWK: 1981]

tanked (also **tanked up**) alcohol intoxicated. *Cf. tank*. RT: *drunk*. [Br. and U.S., (1897): DA, (1906): OEDS, (1917): DSUE, F&G: 1925, MP: 1928, AH: 1931, GI: 1931, W&F: 1960, DCCU: 1972]

tanker a drinker; a drunkard. RS: *sot*. [Canadian, listed in DSUE]

tank, on the (also **on a tank**) on a drinking bout. RT: *spreeing*. [Br, (1890): DSUE; Aust., SJB: 1943]

tank up 1. to consume much beer or other liquor. See *tank*. RT: *guzzle*. [EHB: 1900, (1912): DU, F&G: 1925, (1925): W&F: 1960, EEL: 1971, GU: 1975] 2. (usually **tank-up**) a drinking spree. RT: *spree*. [U.S., BVB: 1942] 3. (usually **tank-up**) a drunkard. *Cf. tank, tanker*. RT: *sot*. [Br., F&G: 1925]

tanned alcohol intoxicated. (BF: 1737: [He's] Tann'd.) Probably refers to tanning hides as a means of preserving them. RT: *drunk*. [BF: 1737]

Taos lightning (also **Taos**) inferior whiskey; strong whiskey; whiskey from Taos, New Mexico. RS: *rotgut*. [U.S., (1846): DA, (1901): DA, PW: 1977]

tap See *tap room*.

tape gin; liquor. RT: *gin*. [cant, NCD: 1725, FG: 1785, FG: 1823, GWM: 1859, JCH: 1887, B&L: 1890; listed in BVB: 1942] See also *bit of tape, blue tape, Holland tape, red tape, white tape, yard of satin*.

taper off to attempt to end addiction to drugs or alcohol by reducing the dosage over a period of time. RS: *kick*. [U.S., (1920): DU, BVB: 1942, VJM: 1949]

tapita* a bottle cap used to heat drugs for injection. Spanish meaning little cap. [U.S., RRL: 1969]

tapped arrested. RT: *busted*. [GWM: 1859]

tappeteria a *tap room* (*q.v.*); a *beer hall* (*q.v.*); a self-serve beer hall. A play on *cafeteria*. RS: *bar*. [U.S., BVB: 1942]

tap room (also tap) a room where liquor, including beer, is on tap and ready to be sold and consumed. RS: *bar*. [(1807): OED, BVB: 1942]

taps beer. Refers to beer on tap. RT: *beer*. [U.S., BVB: 1942]

tap shackled alcohol intoxicated. LIT: shackled to the ale spigot. RT: *drunk*. [(1604): OED; listed in BVB: 1942, K&M: 1968]

tapster a bartender. The feminine is tapstress. RS: *bartender*. [(1385): OED; listed in BVB: 1942, K&M: 1968]

tap the admiral to drink on the sly. From the tradition that the body of Admiral Lord Nelson was preserved in rum on shipboard as it was brought back to England from the Battle of Trafalgar. *Cf. bleed the monkey, half nelson*. [Br., JCH: 1887, F&H]

tap the bag for drug dealers to take a small amount of drugs from a *bag* or *bindle* before it is sold. [U.S., (P&C: 1969), RRL: 1969]

tar opium; gum opium. Refers to the black gummy nature of raw opium. RT: *opium*. [U.S., DWM: 1936, BD: 1937, VJM: 1949, M&D: 1952, RRL: 1969, JH: 1979]

tarantula juice rotgut whiskey; strong whiskey. Presumably it had a kick like the bite of a tarantula. RT: *rotgut*. [U.S., (1850–1900): RFA, (1861): DA, BVB: 1942]

tarred and feathered addicted to opium. An elaboration of *tar* (*q.v.*). *Feathered* may refer to flying. RS: *hooked*. [U.S., JES: 1959, H&C: 1975]

taste 1. a short drink of liquor. RT: *nip*. [since the 1800s, F&H, W&F: 1967, EEL: 1971] 2. a sample portion of a drug; a bit of heroin. [U.S., M&V: 1967, RRL: 1969, MA: 1973, ADC: 1975, D&B: 1978, JWK: 1981] 3. to test a sample of a drug. [U.S., (1968): ELA: 1982, ADC: 1975, D&B: 1978] See also *test, tester*. 4. whiskey; wine. RT: *whiskey, wine*. Black use. [U.S., HER: 1971, DC: 1972, HLF: 1974]

taste blood to use drugs for the first time. GEN: to experience something exciting for the first time. [U.S., JES: 1959, H&C: 1975]

taste of the creature a drink of liquor. *Cf. been too free with the creature, creature, creature comfort, cup of the creature, good creature of God*. RT: *nip*. [(1694): F&H]

tattoos marks or scars at the sites of drug injections. RT: *tracks*. [U.S., BR: 1972]

taverned alcohol intoxicated. RT: *drunk*. [Br., 1800s, F&H]

T-buzz P.C.P., an animal tranquilizer. *Cf. T*. RT: *P.C.P.* [U.S., (1970s): FAB: 1979]

tchi to roll an opium pellet for smoking. Also spelled *shy* (*q.v.*). *Cf. tchied*. Probably Chinese. [U.S., DWM: 1936, VJM: 1949]

tchied having to do with a prepared opium pellet. From *tchi* (*q.v.*). *Cf. chied*. [U.S., (1887): RML: 1948]

té* marijuana. Spanish for *tea* (*q.v.*). RT: *pot*. [U.S., NIDA: 1980]

tea 1. any liquor. RT: *booze*. Used in combinations since the 1600s. See *cold tea*. [(1902): OED] 2. marijuana. RT: *pot*. Because tea leaves and marijuana leaves look much the same. Widely known outside the drug culture. [U.S., (1930): ELA: 1982, RPW: 1938, M&H: 1959, W&F: 1960, RRL: 1969, EEL: 1971, ADC: 1975, EAF: 1980, NIDA: 1980; BR., BTD: 1968, M&J: 1975] 3. phencyclidine, P.C.P. RT: *P.C.P.* [U.S., ELA: 1984]

tea accessories a code word meaning apparatus for marijuana use. *Tea* (*q.v.*) = marijuana. *Cf. necessities, supplies*. Seen in an advertisement. [U.S., RAS: 1980]

tea bag a marijuana cigarette. An elaboration of the tea theme. RT: *joint*. Probably from the 1930s. [U.S., ELA: 1982]

tea bag, in the smoking marijuana. An elaboration of *in the bag*. *Cf. bag*. [U.S., RRL: 1969, (EEL: 1971)]

tea blower a marijuana smoker. *Cf. tea*. RT: *toker*. [U.S., (1938): DU, M&D: 1952, EEL: 1971]

tea'd up (also **tead up, teaed up, teed, teed up**) 1. alcohol intoxicated. *Cf. tea*. RT: *drunk*. [U.S., (1887): RML: 1950, (RWB: 1912), MHW: 1934, GOL: 1950] 2. high on marijuana. RT: *wasted*. [U.S., DU, GOL: 1950, RDS: 1982]

teahead (also **tea hound**) a marijuana smoker. Braddy (HB: 1955, possibly in error): "... an addict of drugs in liquid form." RT: *toker*. [U.S., BVB: 1942, DWM: 1946, VJM: 1949, GOL: 1950, HB: 1955, W&F: 1960, RRL: 1969, RDS: 1982]

tea man 1. a seller of marijuana. RS: *dealer*. [U.S., GOL: 1950, D&D: 1957] 2. a marijuana smoker. RT: *toker*. [U.S., DWM: 1938, GOL: 1950]

team meeting a gathering (perhaps after a game) to smoke marijuana. [U.S., ADC: 1984]

tea pad a place where marijuana is bought and smoked. GOL: 1950 indicates that opium was used in tea pads also. *Cf. tea*. RS: *doperie*. [U.S., MB: 1938, M&W: 1946, BVB: 1953, GOL: 1950, A&T: 1953, RRL: 1969, CM: 1970]

tea party 1. an occasion of communal marijuana use. See *Texas tea party* which is older. [U.S., (1945): ELA: 1982, (1948): W&F: 1960, TRG: 1968, IGA: 1971, SH: 1972] 2. a wild drinking party. RT: *spree*. [U.S. Army, DST: 1984]

teapot sucker (also **teapot**) a total abstainer from alcohol. RT: *dry*. [JRW: 1909]

tear a wild drinking bout. The same as *rip* (*q.v.*). RT: *spree*. [U.S., MHW: 1934, DCCU: 1972]

teaser a cigarette butt. RT: *brad*. [U.S., BVB: 1942, VJM: 1949]

tea-sipper a marijuana smoker. *Tea* (*q.v.*) = marijuana. *Cf. sip tea*. RT: *toker*. [U.S., BR: 1972]

teastick a marijuana cigarette. RT: *joint*. [U.S., W&F: 1960, AP: 1980]

teat a finger cut off of a rubber glove and used to conceal drugs in the rectum or stomach (by swallowing). RS: *stash*. [U.S., JES: 1959, H&C: 1975]

tecata* (also **tecaba***) heroin. From Spanish. RT: *heroin*. [U.S., RRL: 1969, CG: 1980, NIDA: 1980, RDS: 1982]

tecato* (also **tecate***) a heavy user of marijuana; a morphine or heroin addict. Mexican Spanish. RS: *user*. [U.S., D&B: 1970c, EEL: 1971, JHF: 1971, CG: 1980]

Teddies and Betties a mixture of *Talwin* (TM; *q.v.*) and *Pyribenzamine* (TM; *q.v.*). See *T.s and blues*. RS: *set*. [U.S., ELA: 1984]

Teddy party marijuana. Origin unknown. RT: *pot*. [U.S., ELA: 1984]

tee (also **T.**) *T.H.C.* (*q.v.*). RT: *T.H.C.* [U.S., ADC: 1981]

teed (also **teed up**) alcohol or drug intoxicated. *Cf. tea*. See *tea'd up*. RT: *drunk*. [(1930): DU, VJM: 1949, GOL: 1950, W&F: 1960, CM: 1970]

tee'd to the tits alcohol intoxicated. *Cf. stoned to the tits*. RT: *drunk*. [U.S., BR: 1972]

teeth under alcohol intoxicated. An expression indicating the depth of accumulated liquor, in this instance, up to the teeth. See *have one's back teeth afloat*. RT: *drunk*. [Br., 1800s, F&H; listed in BVB: 1942]

teeto a person who abstains from the drinking of alcohol; a teetotaler. See *teetotalist*. RT: *dry*. [U.S., RDS: 1982]

teetotal (also **T-total**) **1**. having to do with total abstinence from alcohol. Based on a stylistic device for emphasizing the importance of a word by prefixing the name of the initial letter. The *tee* is from the initial T of the word *total*. [(1834): OED] 2. to practice total abstinence from alcohol. [since the early 1800s, (1834): OED]

teetotaler (also **teetotaller**) someone who practices *teetotalism*, the total abstinence from alcohol. See *teetotalist*.

teetotalism (also **T-totalism**) the practice of abstaining totally from alcohol. [(1834): OED]

teetotalist (also **teeto, teetotaler, teetotaller, teetotalleress, T-totaler**) someone who practices *teetotalism*. RT: *dry*. [(1834): OED, BVB: 1942, RDS: 1982]

temperance 1. the practice of total abstention from alcohol. A misnomer from the beginning. Much older in the sense of moderation. Standard English. [since the early 1800s, (1826):

OED] 2. having to do with a person or establishment observing total abstinence from alcohol. Typically **temperance bar, temperance hotel, temperance inn, temperance lady, temperance man, temperance sailor.** [since the early 1800s, (1836): OED]

temulent alcohol intoxicated. *Cf. drunkulent.* RT: *drunk.* [(1628): OED; listed in PD: 1982]

ten-cent bag a ten-dollar purchase of narcotics. *Cf. bag.* RS: *load.* [U.S., EEL: 1971]

ten-cent pistol a ten-dollar bag of poisoned heroin, sold to an informer. *Cf. hot shot.* [U.S., C&H: 1974, JH: 1979]

tens 10 mg amphetamine tablets. *Cf. fives.* RS: *amps.* [U.S., RRL: 1969, YKB: 1977]

teo a marijuana smoker. RT: *toker.* [U.S., ELA: 1984]

terbacker tobacco. RT: *fogus.* [U.S., (1873): ADD]

terp See *turps.*

terphead a person who tries to get high from drinking *Terpin Hydrate* (TM; *q.v.*) cough syrup. See list at *head.* [U.S., ADC: 1981]

Terpin Hydrate a brand name of a cough syrup. In the context of drug abuse, the term usually refers to *Terpin Hydrate And Codeine Elixir.* The cough syrup is an expectorant available with or without codeine. See *turps.* [in current use; consult a pharmaceutical reference for more information]

test a small quantity of a drug. *Cf. taste.* [U.S., SNP: 1977]

tester a person heavily addicted to heroin who can judge the strength of diluted heroin for a dealer. [U.S., JWK: 1981]

test-smoke 1. to try out a batch of marijuana before purchasing it. [U.S., (D&B: 1978)] 2. an act of test-smoking marijuana before purchase. [U.S., (D&B: 1978)]

tetrahydrocannabinol the active principle of marijuana. Abbreviated as T.H.C. Not argot. [U.S., RRL: 1969, DES: 1972]

Texas leaguer a marijuana smoker. From *Texas tea* (*q.v.*). RT: *toker.* [U.S., JES: 1959, H&C: 1975]

Texas tea (also **Texas**) marijuana. *Cf. tea, tea party.* Probably borrowed from a slang term for crude oil. RT: *pot.* [U.S., DWM: 1938, VJM: 1949, D&D: 1957, RRL: 1969, NIDA: 1980]

Texas tea party a occasion of communal marijuana use. Also the title of a popular song in the early 1900s. [U.S., DWM: 1938]

Thaistick (also **T-stick**) 1. a marijuana cigarette made of very potent marijuana wrapped around a bamboo twig. [U.S., ADC: 1975, DNE: 1980, ADC: 1981, RDS: 1982] 2. a wooden stick wrapped with potent Thai marijuana or hashish and tied in 3-5 places with animal hairs which have been soaked in opium. RS: *joint.* [U.S., JWK: 1981]

Thai-weed (also **Thai pot**) a potent variety of marijuana. *Cf.*

weed. RT: *pot*. [U.S., D&B: 1978, ADC: 1981]

thang (also **theng**) a drug addiction. Southern (black) pronunciation of *thing*. Possibly a play on *tang* (*q.v.*). Essentially the same as *jones* and *johnson* (*q.v.*). RT: *habit*. [U.S., JWK: 1981] See also *thing*.

that way alcohol intoxicated. *Cf. so*. RT: *drunk*. [U.S., BVB: 1942]

thawed alcohol intoxicated. (BF: 1737: [He's] Thaw'd.) RT: *drunk*. [BF: 1737]

T.H.C. 1. (also **THC**) tetrahydrocannabinol, the active principle of marijuana. Street sales of what is claimed to be T.H.C. are usually of P.C.P. or some other substance. [U.S., RRL: 1969, (1970): DNE: 1973, EEL: 1971, DES: 1972, ADC: 1975, W&F: 1975, MW: 1976, EAF: 1980, ADC: 1981, JWK: 1981] Nicknames and other terms for T.H.C.: *cannabinol, clarabelle, clay, liquid grass, resin, sin, synthetic grass, synthetic marijuana, T., tee, tetrahydrocannabinol, tic, tich, tick*. 2. (also **T.H.C. tabs**) *P.C.P.* (*q.v.*), an animal tranquilizer. RT: *P.C.P.* [U.S., (c. 1968): FAB: 1979]

the animal *L.S.D.* (*q.v.*). See *animal*.

the bad seed peyote cactus. See *bad seed*.

there 1. (also **there with both feet**) alcohol intoxicated. *Cf. get there*. RT: *drunk*. [U.S., BVB: 1942] 2. at the peak of a drug high. [U.S., EEL: 1971, ELA: 1982]

there you are a *bar* (*q.v.*). Rhyming slang. RT: *bar*. [Br., 18–1900s, DRS]

thick black beer; *porter* (*q.v.*). RT: *beer, porter*. [Br., JRW: 1909]

thick and thin gin. RT: *gin*. [U.S., Chicago, (1928): DRS]

thimble and thumb rum. Rhyming slang. RT: *rum*. [Br., (1946): DSUE, DRS]

thin drink See *small beer*.

thing 1. a marijuana cigarette. *Cf. number*. RT: *joint*. [U.S., (1967): ELA: 1982] 2. heroin. RT: *heroin*. [U.S., IGA: 1971, NIDA: 1980] See also *la cosa, thang*.

things drugs; pills; doses of drugs. Essentially euphemistic. [U.S., TRG: 1968, JWK: 1981]

thin hips a nickname for a long-time opium addict. In such addicts one hip is atrophied from lying on it while smoking opium. *Cf. hipped*. [U.S., (c. 1920): JES: 1959, DWM: 1936]

third eye an inward-looking, all-seeing eye through which drug users gain insight about themselves. Primarily associated with the L.S.D. cult. [U.S., RRL: 1969]

third rail very potent whiskey; raw whiskey; illicit whiskey; moonshine. Named for the current-carrying, third rail in electric railways. So named because it will, like the electrified rail, give someone a jolt. (The third rail of an electric railway carries sufficient power to cause death.) RT: *rotgut*. From the prohibition era. [U.S., VR: 1929, MHW: 1934, GOL: 1950, D&D: 1957]

thirst-aid station a place to purchase liquor. RS: *L.I.Q.* [U.S., BVB: 1942]

thirstington a drunkard. *Cf. boozington, lushington, swipington*. RT: *sot*. [Br., 1800s, F&H]

thirsty alcohol intoxicated. RT: *drunk*. [Br., 1800s, F&H]

thirsty soul a drunkard; a person in need of a drink. RS: *sot*. [U.S., BVB: 1942]

thirteen marijuana. From the initial M which is the thirteenth letter of the alphabet. RT: *pot*. [U.S., D&B: 1970c, EEL: 1971]

thorn a hypodermic needle. *Cf. riding a thorn*. RT: *needle*. [U.S., RG: 1970]

thoroughbred (also **thorough**) an underworld person who is loyal and trustworthy to the underworld. *Cf. champ*. Said of drug sellers, drug users, prostitutes, and fellow prisoners. [U.S., JBW: 1967, EEL: 1971, MA: 1973, JWK: 1981] See also *racehorse*.

three-day habit 1. a drug addiction which has been causing craving for three days. RS: *habit*. [U.S., DWM: 1938, BVB: 1942] 2. a weak drugs habit which one can recover from in three days; a *chippy habit* (*q.v.*). RS: *habit*. [U.S., DWM: 1938, BVB: 1942]

three fingers (also **three of**) a measurement of liquor in a glass. Refers to the width of the fingers. *Cf. two fingers*. [Br., (1907): OEDS; U.S., (BVB: 1942)]

three point two a kind of weak beer. See *three-two*.

threes 1. *Empirin* (TM; *q.v.*) painkiller containing 30 mgs of codeine. A 3 is stamped on each capsule. [U.S., JWK: 1981] 2. *Tylenol* (TM; *q.v.*) painkiller containing 30 mgs of codeine. [U.S., JWK: 1981]

three sheets in the wind (also **three sheets, three sheets to the wind, two sheets to the wind**) alcohol intoxicated; unsteady from liquor. *Sheets* are the lines used to manage a ship's sails. Clearly this expression (and the alsos) are nautical in origin. The expressions refer to square-rigged ships and refer to having too many lines attached to the wrong places to control a sail properly. The drunkard's lack of control is compared to the ship's lack of control. RT: *drunk*. [Br. and U.S., (1821): SBF: 1976, FG: 1823, (1857): DSUE, JCH: 1887, B&L: 1890, F&H, MP: 1928, AH: 1931, WG: 1962, RDS: 1982]

three-tap joint an opium den. Refers to three taps one must make on the door to gain entry. RT: *opium den*. [U.S., GOL: 1950]

three-tapper an opium smoker. See *three-tap joint*. RT: *campfire boy*. [U.S., GOL: 1950]

three-two (also **three point two, three-two beer**) a weak beer containing 3.2 percent alcohol. RS: *queer-beer*. [U.S., since 1933, BVB: 1942, SBF: 1976]

thriller a marijuana cigarette. RT: *joint*. [U.S., (1938): ELA: 1982]

thrill-pills barbiturate. Probably used for many different tablets and capsules. RS: *dope*. [U.S., (1940s): YKB: 1977]

throat gag liquor; strong liquor. RT: *rotgut*. [U.S., BVB: 1942]

throw a Brody (also **take a Brody, throw a meter, throw a wing-ding**) to fake a drug withdrawal spasm in order to get drugs from a sympathetic physician. *Cf. brody, take a Duffy*. **Brody** is attested in 1936 (DWM: 1936). **Throw a meter** is attested in 1938. Mostly prison use. [U.S., DWM: 1938, GOL: 1950]

Throw me out! "Give or sell me some drugs!" RS: *How are you going to act?* [U.S., EEL: 1971, JH: 1979]

thrusters (also **thrust, thrusts**) amphetamines. RT: *amps*. [U.S., RRL: 1969, ADC: 1975, NIDA: 1980]

thumb a marijuana cigarette; a fat marijuana cigarette. Because one sucks it (W&F: 1960). RT: *joint*. [U.S., RRL: 1969, ADC: 1975, W&F: 1975, D&B: 1978] See also *thimble and thumb, Tom Thumb*.

thunder-cookie a marijuana cigarette. *Cf. cookie*. RT: *joint*. [U.S., EE: 1976]

thunder weed marijuana. RT: *pot*. [U.S., AJP: 1935]

thwip onomatopoetic for the sound of snorting cocaine. RS: *snort*. [U.S., ADC: 1984]

tib fo occabot tobacco. Backslang for *bit of tobacco*. RS: *fogus*. [Br., JCH: 1887]

tic (also **tich, tick**) **1.** tetrahydrocannabinol, *T.H.C.* (*q.v.*). A spelling pronunciation of T.H.C. RT: *T.H.C.* [U.S., (1974): ELA: 1982, ADC: 1975] **2.** (also **tic-tac**) phencyclidine, *P.C.P.* (*q.v.*), an animal tranquilizer. See comment at *synthetic grass*. RT: *P.C.P.* [U.S., (1970s): FAB: 1979, ADC: 1975]

ticket 1. (also **the ticket**) L.S.D.; L.S.D. on a piece of paper (a "ticket"); a dose of L.S.D. considered as a ticket for a ride into a *high* (*q.v.*). Probably a play on *just the ticket* = exactly the thing needed. RT: *L.S.D.* [U.S., RRL: 1969, EEL: 1971] **2.** money paid in advance for an *L.S.D.* (*q.v.*) session. [Br., BTD: 1968]

ticket agent a drug seller. *Cf. ticket*. RT: *dealer*. [U.S., RG: 1970, IGA: 1971]

tickle brain liquor; strong liquor. RT: *booze*. [(1596): OED, (Shakespeare)] See also *brain tickler*.

tickle one's innards to take a drink of liquor. RT: *irrigate*. [Br. and U.S., (1885): JRW: 1909]

tickle one's smokestack to snort powdered drugs. Smokestack = nose. RT: *snort*. [U.S., H&C: 1975]

tickler a small flask of whiskey. RT: *flask*. [U.S., (1840): F&H, BWG: 1899; listed in BVB: 1942]

tid a drunken person; a drunkard. Akin to *tiddly* (*q.v.*). RT: *sot*. [Aust., (1925): DSUE, SJB: 1943]

tiddled alcohol intoxicated. *Cf.* *tiddly*. RT: *drunk*. [Br., (1920): DSUE]

tiddledy wink 1. an unlicensed drinking shop. [(1844): OED] 2. (also **tiddle-a-wink, tiddlywink**) a drink of liquor. Rhyming slang for *drink*. RT: *nip*. [Br. and U.S., F&H, (1895): DRS, JRW: 1909, M&B: 1944, VJM: 1949, D&D: 1957, SSD, K&M: 1968, VJM: 1949]

tiddley See *titley*.

tiddly 1. (also **titley**) a drink of liquor. RT: *nip*. [Br., JCH: 1859, SSD, M&J: 1975] 2. alcohol intoxicated. RT: *drunk*. [Br. and U.S., 18-1900s, DSUE, D&D: 1957, W&F: 1960, SSD, M&J: 1975]

tiddlywink a drink of liquor. See *tiddledy wink*.

tie 1. a belt or stocking used as a tourniquet for drug injection. *Cf.* *take a band*. [U.S., RRL: 1969, IGA: 1971, MA: 1973, JWK: 1981] 2. (also **tie off, tie up**) to use a tourniquet to bind the arm or leg to bring up a vein for an injection of drugs. [U.S., GS: 1959, M&V: 1967, RRL: 1969, JWK: 1981]

tie one on (also **lay one on, tie it on**) to get drunk. RT: *mug oneself*. [U.S., BVB: 1942, W&F: 1960, EEL: 1971, DCCU: 1972]

tiff 1. (also **tift**) a small drink of liquor or beer; liquor; inferior liquor. [(1635): OED, FG: 1785] 2. to tipple. RT: *irrigate*. [(1769): OED]

tiffled alcohol intoxicated. *Cf.* *tiff*. RT: *drunk*. [U.S., D&D: 1957]

tiger a *blind tiger* (*q.v.*).

tiger beer a brand of beer brewed in Indochina. There is an image of a tiger on the label. This may bear some relation to *tiger piss* (*q.v.*). RS: *beer*. [U.S., Vietnam War, DST: 1984]

tiger drug a form of *yage* (*q.v.*). [U.S., YKB: 1977]

tiger milk (also **tiger's milk**) raw whiskey; moonshine. See *tiger sweat*.

tiger, on the on a drinking bout. See *tiger piss*. RT: *spreeing*. [Aust., (1910): DSUE, SJB: 1943]

tiger piss inferior beer. From the picture of a tiger on the labels of bottles of a certain brand of beer. RT: *queer-beer*. [Br. naval, (1930): DSUE, EP: 1948, WG: 1962; listed in RDS: 1982]

tiger sweat (also **tiger eye, tiger juice, tiger milk, tiger's milk, tiger's sweat**) bad liquor; raw whiskey; moonshine; any beer or liquor. Euphemistic for *tiger piss* (*q.v.*). Tiger's milk is also attested as South African, early 1900s (JB: 1980). RS: *rotgut*. [(1929): DU, JAS: 1932, MHW: 1934, D&D: 1957, W&F: 1960,

SJB: 1966, RDS: 1982]

tiggy a tobacco cigarette. *Cf. ciggy*. RT: *nail*. [M&J: 1975]

tight (also **tite**) alcohol intoxicated. RT: *drunk*. [Br. and U.S., (1843): OEDS, B&L: 1890, BWG: 1899, MP: 1928, JAS: 1932, MHW: 1934, EEL: 1971, DC: 1972, DCCU: 1972, PW: 1974]

tight as a tick (also **tight as a boiled owl, tight as a brassiere, tight as a drum, tight as a fart, tight as a goat, tight as a lord, tight as a mink, tight as a newt, tight as a ten-day drunk, tight as an owl, tight as the bark on a tree**) alcohol intoxicated. The *alsos* are variants of the "full as a... " and "drunk as a..." expressions. RT: *drunk*. [JRW: 1909, DSUE, MHW: 1934, D&D: 1957, W&F: 1960]

tighten (also **tighten up**) to give a dose of drugs to someone; to take a dose of drugs. [U.S., RRL: 1969, IGA: 1971, D&B: 1978, JWK: 1981]

tighten someone's wig to introduce someone to marijuana smoking. [U.S., (1930s): ELA: 1982, M&W: 1946]

tighter than a tick (also **tighter than a drum, tighter than a goat, tighter than a mink, tighter than a Scotchman, tighter than Dick's hatband**) alcohol intoxicated; very drunk. *Cf. tight as a tick*. RT: *drunk*. [U.S., BVB: 1942]

tight skirt a female drunkard; a drunken woman. *Cf. tight*. RS: *sot*. [U.S., BVB: 1942]

Tijuana 12 a tobacco and marijuana cigarette. RS: *joint*. [U.S., RDS: 1982]

tiles, on the on a drinking bout. A variant of *out on the roof* (*q.v.*). RT: *spreeing*. [Br., DA: 1857]

tillywink a drink of liquor. Rhyming slang for *drink*. See *tiddledy wink*.

timber stems and stalks of the hemp plant in a batch of marijuana. *Cf. debris, lumber*. [U.S., ADC: 1975]

tin a can of marijuana. See *can*. RS: *load*. [U.S., M&W: 1946]

tinge probably an error for *tingle* (*q.v.*). [C&H: 1974]

tingle the beginning of a heroin rush. RS: *rush*. Probably not slang. [U.S., RRL: 1969, IGA: 1971, WCM: 1972]

tin hats (also **tin hat**) alcohol intoxicated. RT: *drunk*. [Br., JRW: 1909, F&G: 1925, WG: 1962]

tinik heroin. RT: *heroin*. Origin unknown. [U.S., SNP: 1977]

tinned alcohol intoxicated. The British version of *canned* (*q.v.*). RT: *drunk*. [Br., (1946): DSUE]

tinny a can of beer. Tin (British) = can (American). [Aust., BH: 1980]

tip 1. liquor; a drink of liquor. From the tip or tilt required to empty a drinking vessel. RS: *nip*. [cant, BE: 1690] **2.** (also **tip off**) to drink a drink; to drink something up. See *tip one*. [Br.,

BE: 1690, DSUE; U.S., GU: 1975] See also *kick the tip*.

tipium grove alcohol intoxicated. (BF: 1737: [He's] Tipium Grove.) *Tipium* is probably a play on *tip* (*q.v.*). RT: *drunk*. [BF: 1737]

tip merry alcohol intoxicated. *Cf. merry, tip*. RT: *drunk*. [(1612): OED; listed in PD: 1982]

tip one to take a drink of liquor; to tip (and drink) a glass of liquor. See *tip*. RT: *irrigate*. [U.S., MHW: 1934, BVB: 1942]

tip one's elbow to drink alcohol; to take a drink. *Cf. bend one's elbow*. RT: *irrigate*. [U.S., W&F: 1960, AP: 1980]

tipped (also tip-top) alcohol intoxicated. *Cf. tip*. RT: *drunk*. [U.S., BVB: 1942]

tipping drug intoxicated. RT: *stoned*. [U.S., M&D: 1952]

tipple 1. liquor; strong liquor. RT: *booze*. [(1581): OED, FG: 1785, FG: 1811, D&D: 1957, SSD] 2. to drink liquor; to sip at a vessel of liquor. RT: *irrigate*. [(1560): OED, JSF: 1889, (MHW: 1934), (BVB: 1942)] 3. a drinking bout; a drink of liquor. RT: *spree*. [since the 1700s, DSUE, BVB: 1942]

tipple-arse a drunkard. RT: *sot*. [Br., 1800s, F&H]

tippler 1. a tavern keeper. RS: *bartender*. [(1396): OED] 2. a drunkard; a constant drinker. RT: *sot*. [(1580): OED, (1700): SBF: 1976, FG: 1811, FG: 1823, D&D: 1957, RDS: 1982]

tippling alcohol intoxicated. RT: *drunk*. Defined by Noah Webster (1828) as a session of drinking to excess. [U.S., DWM: 1931, MHW: 1934]

tipply alcohol intoxicated. RT: *drunk*. [early 1900s, DSUE]

tipsey alcohol intoxicated. The same as *tipsy* (*q.v.*), a modern spelling. RT: *drunk*. [BF: 1722, FG: 1811]

tipsified alcohol intoxicated. RT: *drunk*. [Br., (1837): OED]

tipsify to make drunk. *Cf. tipsy*. RS: *mug oneself*. [(1830): OED, K&M: 1968]

tipsy (also tipsey) alcohol intoxicated; nearly drunk. RT: *drunk*. [(1577): OED, FG: 1823, F&H, MP: 1928, MHW: 1934]

tip the little finger (also tip the finger) to have a drink. Refers to raising the little finger when drinking. RT: *irrigate*. [Aust., SJB: 1943, DSUE]

tip-top alcohol intoxicated. *Cf. tip*. RT: *drunk*. [U.S., BVB: 1942]

tired alcohol intoxicated. Euphemistic. *Cf. sleepy, weary*. RT: *drunk*. [U.S., (c. 1850): W&F: 1960, N&S: 1983]

tish (also titch) *P.C.P.* (*q.v.*). A variant of *tic* (*q.v.*). RT: *P.C.P.* [U.S., FAB: 1979]

tishy alcohol intoxicated; *tipsy* (*q.v.*). A mispronunciation of *tipsy*. RS: *drunk*. [Br., (1910): DSUE]

tissue paper for rolling cigarettes. RT: *paper*. [Aust., SJB: 1966]

titch P.C.P. See *tish*.

tite alcohol intoxicated. A respelling of *tight* (*q.v.*).

titley (also **tiddley**) liquor; a drink of liquor. RT: *nip*. [Br., JCH: 1859, DSUE]

tittery gin. RT: *gin*. [NCD: 1725; listed in BVB: 1942]

tittey (also **titty**) liquor. RT: *booze*. [Br., 1800s, F&H; listed in BVB: 1942]

T.J. allegedly marijuana. Probably an error. See *Tijuana 12*. [U.S., SNP: 1977]

T.M. machine-made tobacco cigarettes. An abbreviation of *tailor-mades*. RS: *nail*. [Aust., SJB: 1966]

T.M.A. a chemical hallucinogen: 3,4,5-trimethoxyphenyl-B-aminopropane. Not widely known. [U.S., RRL: 1969, JHF: 1971]

T-man 1. a federal narcotics agent; a treasury agent. RS: *fuzz*. [U.S., M&V: 1954] 2. a marijuana smoker. RT: *toker*. [U.S., (1936): ELA: 1982]

T.N.T. heroin. From the name of a powerful explosive, trinitrotoluene. GEN: anything powerful. RT: *heroin*. [U.S., SNP: 1977]

toak (also **toat**) a puff of marijuana smoke. See *toke*. [U.S., S&W: 1966, JHF: 1971]

toast a drunkard. *Cf. toasted*. RT: *sot*. [cant, (1670): OED, BE: 1690, DSUE]

toasted alcohol intoxicated. *Cf. baked, basted, boiled, fried, fried on both sides, sauced, served up, stewed*. See *cooked* for a full list. RT: *drunk*. [U.S., ADC: 1981, ADC: 1984]

tobaccy tobacco. RT: *fogus*. [late 1800s, DSUE]

tobacker tobacco. RT: *fogus*. [U.S., (1915): ADD]

tobarcoe tobacco. RT: *fogus*. [U.S., BWG: 1899]

tod a drink of liquor; a toddy. Possibly akin to *tot* (*q.v.*), but clearly akin to *toddy*. RS: *nip*. [(1861): F&H, BWG: 1899]

toddy 1. liquor; rum, sugar, and hot water. A corruption of a Hindi term (*tari*) for palm wine. [since the 1600s, (1609): Y&B, FG: 1823, F&H] 2. to drink liquor; to get drunk; to make drunk. RS: *mug oneself*. [(1849): OED]

toddy blossom a pimple from excessive drinking. RT: *gin bud*. [Br., 18-1900s, DSUE; listed in BVB: 1942]

toddycask a drunkard. *Cf. barrel, tank*. RT: *sot*. [Br., 1800s, F&H]

toffee chewing tobacco. Because like toffee, it is brown and sticky. RS: *fogus*. Probably nonce. [Br., (1932): DSUE]

together having to do with an addict or drug user who has enough drugs. GEN: organized. Refers to having one's shit together. [U.S., JWK: 1981]

toilet water 1. draft beer. A play on *piss* (*q.v.*). RS: *beer*. [U.S., BR: 1972] 2. (usually **Toilet Water**) a "brand name" for *amyl nitrate*. RS: *snapper*. [U.S., ELA: 1984]

toke 1. (also **toak, toat**) a puff of a marijuana cigarette. *Cf. joint*. Probably akin to *toke*, a portion or piece, especially of food (Br., JCH: 1887). [U.S., S&W: 1966, (1968): DNE: 1973, RRL: 1969, D&B: 1970c, DCCU: 1972, WCM: 1972, ADC: 1975, GU: 1975, MW: 1976, ADC: 1981, JWK: 1981] 2. to take a draw of a marijuana cigarette; to take a draw of any cigarette. M&D: 1952 refers to any cigarette. [U.S., M&D: 1952, D&D: 1957, RRL: 1969, DCCU: 1972, ADC: 1975, DNE: 1980, ADC: 1981, RDS: 1982] (This entry continues after the following list.) Terms meaning to draw on a marijuana cigarette: *bang, blast, bong, dope smoke, drag, harsh toke, hit, nose hit, pill, poke, rip, shlook, sip, sploff, swallow hit, toak, toat, toke, toque*. 3. a marijuana cigarette; a pipeful of marijuana. RT: *joint*. [U.S., D&B: 1970c, GU: 1975, EAF: 1980] 4. a tobacco cigarette. RT: *nail*. [U.S., GU: 1975] 5. a puff of freebase. [U.S., S&F: 1984] 6. to freebase. [U.S., S&F: 1984]

toke a number to smoke a marijuana cigarette. The number is probably *thirteen* (*q.v.*). *Cf. number*. RT: *hit the hay*. [U.S., RAS: 1979]

toke pipe a small clay pipe suitable for smoking a *hit* (*q.v.*) of marijuana. RS: *bong*. [U.S., RRL: 1969, EEL: 1971]

toker 1. a smoker of marijuana. [U.S., RAS: 1975, ELA: 1982] (This entry continues after the following list.) Nicknames and slang terms for a marijuana smoker: *bambalacha rambler, bato marijuano, bender, blowtop, bo-bo jockey, boom boy, boredom beater, bush smoker, bushwhacker, crispo, crispy, crispy-critter, dagga rooker, doper, fu manchu, gangster, gong kicker, goof, goofball, goofballer, goof burner, gouger, gowster, grass eater, grasser, grasshead, grasshopper, greefer, griefer, hashhead, hay-burner, hayhead, hay puffer, hemp-humper, hemp-roller, Jane's better half, joint-roller, junker man, lover, mariholic, marijuanaholic, mezzanine lover, moshky, motter, Mr. Warner, M.U., mugglehead, muggles, pipe, pipe-hitter, pleasure smoker, pothead, pot lush, pulaski, puller, reefer, reefer hound, reefer man, reefing man, roach bender, roker, rooker, sagebrush whacker, smoker, snake, stick man, stoner, tea blower, teahead, tea hound, tea man, tea-sipper, teo, Texas leaguer, T-man, toker, twister, vegetarian, vipe, viper, weed eater, weedhead, weed hound, weedly, weed twister, zol rooker, zonker*. 2. a water pipe for smoking marijuana. RS: *bong*. [U.S., H&C: 1975, ELA: 1982]

toke up to light up a marijuana cigarette. The same as *light up*. *Cf. toke*. RT: *hit the hay*. [U.S., GS: 1959, RRL: 1969, EEL: 1971, LVA: 1981]

toll *mannitol* (*q.v.*) used in diluting heroin. [U.S., JWK: 1981]

toluene a solvent found in model airplane glue (and in other substances) which is inhaled for a high. [U.S., (1871): MW: 1983, drug culture use, 1960s]

Tom 1. (also tom) gin. Possibly from rhyming slang *Tom Thumb* (*q.v.*). See *old Tom*. It is this Tom which means *gin* in the U.S. mixed drink Tom Collins. RT: *gin*. [Br., JB: 1823] 2. an injection of a drug. See *tom cat*. Probably rhyming slang; *Tom Mix* = *fix* (*q.v.*). RT: *shot*. [U.S., EEL: 1971]

Tom and Jerry shop a low drinking establishment. This *Tom* may mean *gin*. RS: *dive*. [Br., JCH: 1887, F&H, K&M: 1968]

tombo* a police officer. Spanish (calo). RT: *fuzz*. [U.S., EEL: 1971, JBR: 1973]

tom cat a (stolen) sewing machine needle used to open a vein for drug use (in prison). *Cf. needle*. [U.S., BD: 1937, DWM: 1938, VJM: 1949]

Tom Mix 1. an injection of drugs. Rhyming slang for *fix* (*q.v.*). RT: *shot*. [U.S., EEL: 1971, JH: 1979] 2. (also mix) to inject a drug, probably heroin. From sense one. RT: *shoot*. [U.S., JH: 1979]

Tom, old gin. See *old Tom*.

Tom Thacker tobacco. Rhyming slang for *terbacker* or something similar. RT: *fogus*. [Br., 18-1900s, DRS, SSD]

Tom Thumb rum. See *Tom*. *Cf. finger and thumb*. Rhyming slang. RT: *rum*. [Br., F&G: 1925, DSUE, SSD, DRS, PW: 1974]

tongue to inject a drug into a vein under the tongue. This is done when other suitable sites cannot be found. *Cf. shoot*. [U.S., EEL: 1971] See also *jug-man*.

tongue oil (also **tongue loosener**) whiskey; liquor. RT: *booze*. [U.S., (1850-1900): RFA, BVB: 1942]

tongue-tied alcohol intoxicated. (BF: 1737: [He's] Tongue-ty'd.) RT: *drunk*. [BF: 1737]

tonic a drink of liquor; liquor. RT: *nip, booze*. [Br., FG: 1823, F&H; U.S., MHW: 1934]

tonsil bath liquor; a drink of liquor. RT: *booze*. From the prohibition era. [U.S., EK: 1927, AH: 1931, MHW: 1934]

tonsil paint (also **tonsil oil, tonsil varnish, tonsil wash**) liquor; whiskey. *Cf. nose paint*. RT: *booze*. [U.S., (1850-1900): RFA, BVB: 1942, D&D: 1957]

tooies (also **tooeys, tooles, toolies, tuies, tuis**) capsules of *Tuinal* (TM; *q.v.*) barbiturate. RS: *barbs*. [U.S., JBW: 1967, RRL: 1969, ADC: 1975, ADC: 1981] Nicknames and slang terms for Tuinal: *blues and reds, Christmas tree, double-trouble, rainbows, red and blues, T., tooeys, tooies, tooles, toolies, tootsie, trues, T.s, tuies, tus, twos*.

took his drops alcohol intoxicated. (BF: 1737: [He] Took...) *Cf.*

drop. RS: *drunk*. [BF: 1737]

tools equipment for injecting drugs. RS: *outfit*. [U.S., M&V: 1967, RRL: 1969, JWK: 1981]

too many cloths in the wind (also **too many cloths on the wind**) alcohol intoxicated. Compare to *three sheets to the wind*. These cloths may be sails, although finished sails are not usually referred to as cloths. This is probably synonymous with *carrying too much sail* (*q.v.*). This may also be a parody or a misunderstanding of *sheets*. RT: *drunk*. [Br., 18-1900s, DSUE]

too numerous to mention alcohol intoxicated; drunk and angry. A play on a common cliche. RT: *drunk*. [(1882): JRW: 1909]

toot 1. to drink heavily. RT: *guzzle*. [Br., WWII, (1939): DSUE, EP: 1948, WG: 1962, SSD] 2. a spree; a binge. *Cf. honk*. RT: *spree*. [U.S., (1891): DA, EHB: 1900, HNR: 1934] 3. a drink or swallow of liquor in *have a toot* (*q.v.*). RT: *nip*. [Br., (1939): DSUE] 4. to inhale (snort) cocaine. RS: *snort*. [U.S., ADC: 1975, (1977): DNE: 1980, ADC: 1984] 5. a dose of crystallized cocaine for snorting. RT: *cocaine, dose*. [U.S., ADC: 1975, (1977): DNE: 1980, NIDA: 1980] 6. a sample of a drug; a sample of P.C.P. *Cf. taste*. [U.S., FAB: 1979]

tooter 1. a person on a spree. Usually refers to a male. [U.S., BVB: 1942] 2. a heavy drinker; a drunkard. RT: *sot*. [Br., WWII, (1930): DSUE, WG: 1962] 3. a tube to aid in the snorting of cocaine. *Cf. snort*. [U.S., ADC: 1981]

toothpick a long thin marijuana cigarette. RT: *joint*. Black use. [U.S., EAF: 1980]

toot, on a on a drinking binge. *Cf. toot*. RT: *spreeing*. [U.S., (1877): SBF: 1976, JSF: 1889]

tootonium a fabled, potent type of cocaine. A play on *titanium*. *Cf. tootuncommon*. RT: *cocaine*. [U.S., ELA: 1984]

tootootler a non-drinker; a *teetotaler* (*q.v.*). *Cf. teetotalist*. RS: *dry*. [Newfoundland, GAE: 1925]

tootsie a capsule of *Tuinal* (TM; *q.v.*) barbiturate. RT: *tooies*. [U.S., EEL: 1971, W&S: 1977]

tootsie roll a marijuana cigarette; a marijuana cigarette rolled in brown paper. *Cf. tamale*. RS: *joint*. [U.S., BR: 1972]

tootuncommon very high-quality cocaine. A play on (King) *Tutankhamun*. *Cf. toot*. RT: *cocaine*. [U.S., RAS: 1982]

top 1. heroin. RT: *heroin*. [Br., early 1900s, DU] 2. (usually **Top**) a brand of flavored cigarette rolling papers. This is *pot* (*q.v.*) spelled backwards. RT: *paper*. [U.S., RRL: 1969, LVA: 1981] 3. the top of the *peyote* (*q.v.*) cactus. See *tops*. [U.S., EEL: 1971]

tope to drink liquor to excess; to drink liquor constantly. RT: *guzzle*. [(1654): OED, BE: 1690, F&H]

toper a drunkard; a heavy drinker. RT: *sot*. [(1673): OED, BE:

1690, FG: 1785, FG: 1811; listed in VJM: 1949]

top heavy alcohol intoxicated. Refers to the feeling in a drinker's head. RT: *drunk*. [(1687): OED, BE: 1690, BF: 1737, FG: 1785, FG: 1811, JCH: 1887, B&L: 1890; listed in MHW: 1934, BVB: 1942]

topi 1. peyote cactus. Possibly akin to *tops* (*q.v.*). RS: *peyote*. [U.S., RRL: 1969, H&C: 1975] 2. the hallucinogenic drug L.S.D. Possibly an error. RT: *L.S.D.* [U.S., NIDA: 1980]

top o' reeb (also pot o' reeb) a pot of beer. *Cf. reeb*. Backslang. [Br., JCH: 1859, B&L: 1890, F&H]

topped alcohol intoxicated. (BF: 1737: He's top'd.) RT: *drunk*. [BF: 1737]

topper 1. the tobacco left at the bottom of a pipe bowl. RT: *dottle*. [Br., JCH: 1887] 2. a cigar butt. RS: *brad*. [Br., late 18–1900s, F&H, DSUE]

topper-hunter a collector of, and dealer in cigar butts. *Cf. butt-stooper, dumper-dasher, guttersnipe, sniper, snipe-shooter*. [Br., JCH: 1887]

toppled alcohol intoxicated. Possibly a play on *tipple* (*q.v.*) and *topple*. RT: *drunk*. [U.S., BVB: 1942]

toppy (also topy) alcohol intoxicated; tipsy. RS: *drunk*. [Br., (1885): OED]

tops 1. *peyote* (*q.v.*) cactus buttons; the tops of peyote cactus. *Cf. topi*. RS: *peyote*. [U.S., RG: 1970, EEL: 1971, IGA: 1971] 2. the female tops of marijuana plants. *Cf. fee-tops*. Mentioned in a technical (not slang or argot) sense in RPW: 1938. [U.S., JWK: 1981]

tops and bottoms a mixture of *Talwin* (TM; *q.v.*) painkiller and *Pyribenzamine* (TM; *q.v.*). *Cf. one on one, synthetic heroin, tricycles and bicycles, T.s and blues*. An elaboration or disguise of *T.s and Blues*. RS: *set*. [U.S., RAS: 1982]

topsy-boozy (also topsy-boosy) alcohol intoxicated. RT: *drunk*. [Br., B&L: 1890; listed in BVB: 1942]

topsy-turvey alcohol intoxicated. RT: *drunk*. [BF: 1737; recurrent nonce]

toque* a puff of marijuana smoke. Spanish for *toke* (*q.v.*). [calo, CG: 1980]

torch a marijuana cigarette. RT: *joint*. [U.S., (1977): ELA: 1982, LVA: 1981]

torch up to light up and smoke a marijuana cigarette. *Cf. light up, toke up*. RT: *hit the hay*. [U.S., HB: 1955, TRG: 1968, EEL: 1971, BR: 1972]

tore up (also tore, tore down, torn, torn up) alcohol intoxicated; drug intoxicated; torn between the effects of amphetamines and barbiturates taken together. GEN: distraught. RT: *drunk*, *stoned*. [U.S., HB: 1955, RRL: 1969, D&B: 1970c, CM: 1970, EEL: 1971, DC: 1972, ADC: 1975, ADC: 1981]

tornado juice whiskey; strong whiskey. RT: *whiskey*. [U.S., (1850–1900): RFA]

torn thumb rum; inferior rum. Rhyming slang. *Cf. finger and thumb, thimble and thumb*. RS: *rum, rotgut*. [Br., early 1900s, DRS]

torn up (also **torn**) alcohol intoxicated; drug intoxicated. See *tore up*. [U.S., S&W: 1966, IGA: 1971, D&B: 1978] See also *tear*.

torpedo 1. a drink containing chloral hydrate; a knockout drink. RT: *Mickey Finn*. [U.S., M&V: 1954, RRL: 1969] 2. a marijuana cigarette; a fat marijuana cigarette. *Cf. bomber*. RT: *joint*. [U.S., (1943): ELA: 1982; South African, (1946): DSUE]

torpedo juice alcohol extracted from torpedo fuel; raw, homemade liquor; an alcoholic beverage made from whatever is available. *Cf. pink ladies*. RT: *rotgut*. [U.S. military, WWII, D&D: 1957 W&F: 1960]

torrid alcohol intoxicated; tipsy. RS: *drunk*. [late 17-1800s, DSUE]

torture chamber a nickname for a jail or prison where prisoners cannot buy drugs. [U.S., DWM: 1936, BVB: 1942, RRL: 1969]

tosca* marijuana. Spanish for rough. RT: *pot*. [U.S., EEL: 1971, JH: 1979]

toss 1. to drink liquor; to take a drink of liquor. RT: *irrigate*. [(1599): F&H; listed in BVB: 1942] 2. a drink of liquor. RT: *nip*. [U.S., BVB: 1942] 3. to search a person for concealed drugs. Akin to *shake down*. [U.S., TRG: 1968, (RRL: 1969), IGA: 1971, (1973): DNE: 1980]

tossed 1. alcohol intoxicated. RT: *drunk*. [Br., 18-1900s, DSUE] 2. bodily searched for drugs by the police. *Cf. yanked*. [U.S., RRL: 1969, EEL: 1971]

toss-out a fake drug withdraw spasm. See *frame a toss-out* (at *frame a twister*). RT: *brody*. [U.S., DWM: 1938, RRL: 1969]

toss pot a drunkard; a heavy drinker. RT: *sot*. [(1568): OED, FG: 1785, FG: 1823, F&H; listed in D&D: 1957]

tostada* marijuana. Spanish for toast. RT: *pot*. [calo, JBR: 1973] See also *muy tostado*.

tosticated (also **tostificated**) alcohol intoxicated. Probably a mispronunciation of *intoxicated*. RT: *drunk*. [Br., F&H, (1811): OED; listed in BVB: 1942]

tot a small drink of liquor; a cup for drinking liquor; the official naval ration of rum: 1/64th of a gallon. Akin to the dialect meaning of *tot*, a small child's (tot's) drinking mug. Conceivably much older. See *totty*. RS: *nip*. [Br., 1800s, F&H, (1828): OED; U.S., BWG: 1899]

totalled (also **totaled**) 1. alcohol intoxicated. From a colloquial expression for a totally wrecked automobile. RT: *drunk*. [U.S., ADC: 1981] 2. under the effects of marijuana; heavily intoxicated with marijuana. RT: *wasted*. [U.S., DCCU: 1972, ADC: 1981]

tote 1. a heavy drinker. This is probably sense two uttered in sarcasm. RT: *sot*. [Br., late 1800s, DSUE] 2. an abstainer from beverage alcohol, a *teetotaller*. RT: *dry*. [Br., (1870): F&H, DSUE] 3. a small dose of marijuana. Possibly akin to *toke* (*q.v.*). RT: *dose*. [U.S., M&V: 1973] 4. a small marijuana pipe. RS: *bong*. [U.S., M&V: 1973]

toth rum. Possibly akin to *tot* (*q.v.*). Possibly an error (DU). RT: *rum*. [GWM: 1859]

totty alcohol intoxicated; tipsy. GEN: tottery. *Cf. toddy, tot*. RS: *drunk*. [13-1800s, (1592): OED]

touch 1. a small drink of liquor. The same as *taste*. RT: *nip*. From the prohibition era. [U.S., JAR: 1930, AH: 1931, MHW: 1934] 2. a tobacco cigarette. Probably refers to a cigarette which has been begged from someone. *Touch* or *put the touch on* means to beg or borrow. RT: *nail*. [U.S., BVB: 1942]

touched alcohol intoxicated. From a slang or colloquial expression meaning slightly crazy. RT: *drunk*. [U.S., BVB: 1942]

touch of the brewer a *hangover* (*q.v.*). [Br., 1800s, F&H]

tough to inject a drug in a vein on the underside of the tongue. This is done when other veins have been ruined. Akin to *tough it* = do it the hard way. *Cf. tongue*. RS: *shoot*. [U.S., EEL: 1971]

tough as a boiled owl alcohol intoxicated. This may be the original phrase from which *drunk as a boiled owl* was derived. RT: *drunk*. [U.S., MHW: 1934, BVB: 1942]

tour guide a person who guides another through an *L.S.D.* (*q.v.*) trip. *Cf. guide*. RT: *sitter*. [U.S., RG: 1970, EEL: 1971]

touse liquor. RT: *booze*. [U.S., (1850): ADD]

tow-row alcohol intoxicated. RT: *drunk*. [(1709): OED]

toxed alcohol intoxicated. RT: *drunk*. [(1635): OED, DWO]

toxicated alcohol intoxicated. RT: *drunk*. [U.S., BVB: 1942]

toxy 1. alcohol intoxicated. RT: *drunk*. [Br. and U.S., (1905): DSUE, MHW: 1934] 2. a small container of opium. A variant of, or an error for, *toy* (*q.v.*). [U.S., TRG: 1968, RG: 1970, EEL: 1971, IGA: 1971]

toy 1. a small (one inch in diameter) tin box for prepared opium. SNP: 1977 also lists toye and toyce. One half of a walnut shell was also used. RDS: 1982 lists toye. [U.S., (1934): DSUE, DWM: 1936, BD: 1937, VJM: 1949, GOL: 1950, M&D: 1952, RRL: 1969] 2. a hypodermic needle. Probably the same as *toys* (*q.v.*). RT: *needle*. [U.S., RRL: 1969]

toys equipment for injecting drugs. *Cf. toy*. RT: *outfit*. Black use. [U.S., DC: 1972]

tracked up covered with scars caused by hypodermic scar and abscesses. *Cf. tracks.* [U.S., JBW: 1967, RRL: 1969, IGA: 1971]

tracking repeating a drug hallucination; repeating words or phrases as if under the effects of drugs. [U.S., (YKB: 1977)]

tracks scars and collapsed veins from numerous drug injections. [U.S., GS: 1959, M&V: 1967, RRL: 1969, CM: 1970, EEL: 1971, MA: 1973, W&F: 1975, JWK: 1981] Nicknames and slang terms for needle marks: *bee bites, calling card, embroidery, marks, prick, railroad, railroad tracks, scar, service stripes, tattoos, tracks, trail, turkey-trots, whore scars.*

trade whiskey cheap whiskey for trading with Amerindians; any inferior whiskey regardless of its use. RS: *rotgut.* [U.S., (1850–1900): RFA]

trafficker a drug seller or pusher. More of a journalist's term than drug argot. RT: *dealer.* [U.S., EEL: 1971]

tragic-magic heroin. RT: *heroin.* Probably not drug argot. [U.S., W&F: 1975, RDS: 1982]

trail 1. needle marks in the skin. RT: *tracks.* [U.S., EEL: 1971] 2. a component of a drug hallucination. See *tracking.* [U.S., EEL: 1971]

trained nurse narcotics smuggled into jail or prison. This describes a private nurse who will "take care of" an addicted person. *Cf. white nurse.* [U.S., DWM: 1936, VJM: 1949]

trammeled alcohol intoxicated. (BF: 1737: [He's] Trammel'd.) From a verb meaning to hobble, to impede. RT: *drunk.* [BF: 1737]

trance, in a alcohol intoxicated. RT: *drunk.* [BF: 1737]

tranks 1. (also **trancs, trank, tranx**) tablets or capsules of a tranquilizing drug. [U.S., W&F: 1967, (1972): DNE: 1980, ADC: 1975, JWK: 1981, RDS: 1982] Nicknames and other terms for tranquilizers: *backwards, barbitone, blues, dies, dis, down, downer, downie, downs, dyes, goofballs, green and blacks, happy pills, housewife's delight, meprobamate, mickey, Miltown, mother's little helper, muscle relaxer, punk pills, Roche tens, sound, splits, trancs, tranks, tranx, ums, V., Valium, vals, Veronal, yellow.* 2. (also **trank**) phencyclidine, P.C.P. RT: *P.C.P.* [U.S., ELA: 1984]

tranquility *S.T.P.* (*q.v.*); a hallucinogenic drug. [U.S., IGA: 1971, SNP: 1977]

tranquilizer a drug which induces calm and relieves anxiety. Standard English. See *tranks.*

transit, in on an L.S.D. trip. *Cf. high.* RS: *stoned.* [U.S., RRL: 1969, EEL: 1971, LVA: 1981]

translated alcohol intoxicated. RT: *drunk.* [(1880): JRW: 1909]

tranx tranquilizers. See *tranks.*

trap a hiding place for one's supply of drugs. RT: *stash.* [U.S.,

RB: 1967, RRL: 1969, EEL: 1971]

trashed 1. heavily intoxicated with drugs. RT: *stoned.* [U.S., DCCU: 1972, ADC: 1981] 2. alcohol intoxicated. RT: *drunk.* [U.S., ADC: 1984]

travel agent 1. the hallucinogenic drug *L.S.D.* (*q.v.*). RT: *L.S.D.* [U.S., RRL: 1969] 2. a seller of the hallucinogenic drug *L.S.D.* (*q.v.*). RS: *dealer.* [U.S., JBW: 1967, RB: 1967, RRL: 1969, IGA: 1971] 3. an experienced person who guides another during an L.S.D. experience. RT: *sitter.* [U.S., TRG: 1968, RG: 1970, KBH: 1982]

treacle 1. opium. RT: *opium.* [Aust., DU, HSD: 1984] 2. inferior port wine. RT: *port.* [late 1700s, DSUE]

treated one drug laced with a stronger drug; a tobacco or marijuana cigarette laced with a drug. *Cf. doctor.* [U.S., ADC: 1975]

tree of knowledge marijuana; *dagga* (*q.v.*). *Cf. boom.* RT: *pot.* [South African, early 1900s, DU]

trees multicolored pills and capsules of drugs. See *Christmas tree.* RT: *dope.* Black use. [U.S., W&S: 1977, GG: 1981]

tree, up a alcohol intoxicated. RT: *drunk.* [Br., 1800s, F&H]

trembles (also **tremens**) the delirium tremens. RT: *D.T.s.* [1800s, F&H]

trey a three-dollar bag of narcotics, usually heroin. RS: *load.* [U.S., W&F: 1967, RRL: 1969, MA: 1973]

triangles the delirium tremens. May refer to a ringing in the ears like the sound of triangles. RT: *D.T.s.* [Br., JCH: 1887, F&H]

triangle stuff heroin from the *golden triangle* (*q.v.*): Burma, Laos, Thailand. RS: *heroin.* [U.S., JWK: 1981]

tribed up drug intoxicated. Origin unknown. RT: *stoned.* [U.S., ELA: 1984]

tric acid (also **tric**) high-quality *L.S.D.* (*q.v.*). From *electric acid.* [U.S., EEL: 1971, JH: 1979]

tricycles and bicycles a mixture of *Talwin* (TM; *q.v.*) painkiller and *Pyribenzamine* (TM; *q.v.*). *Cf. one on one, T.s and blues.* RS: *set.* [U.S., RAS: 1982]

trigger 1. equipment used for injecting drugs. This trigger enables one to *shoot* (*q.v.*) drugs. RS: *outfit.* [U.S., JWK: 1981] 2. a marijuana cigarette smoked after taking L.S.D., presumably to trigger the effects of the drug and improve one's state of mind. ELA: 1982 lists the verb form. [U.S., IGA: 1971]

trimmed down alcohol intoxicated. From submariner's jargon meaning with submergence tanks full. RT: *drunk.* [Br. naval, WG: 1962]

trip 1. a high from a hallucinogenic drug, L.S.D. [U.S., (1957): PT: 1981, S&W: 1966, (1967): DNE: 1973, W&F: 1967, D&B:

1970c, RRL: 1969, DCCU: 1972, MW: 1976] 2. a bad drug experience. Short for *bad trip, down trip, panic trip*. Used now to mean any bad experience. [U.S., ADC: 1975] 3. to experience a L.S.D. high; to take a hallucinogenic drug. [U.S., JBW: 1967, M&V: 1967, RRL: 1969, (1970): DNE: 1973, EEL: 1971, ADC: 1975, MW: 1976, ADC: 1981]

trip grass marijuana doctored with amphetamine. RS: *set*. [U.S., ELA: 1982]

triple line high-quality marijuana laced with heroin. May refer to the "lines" of opium-saturated hair on a *Thaistick* (*q.v.*). [U.S., SNP: 1977] See also *first line*.

trip out to take a psychedelic drug trip; to become heavily intoxicated with any drug. [U.S., S&W: 1966, CM: 1970, (1970): DNE: 1973, EEL: 1971, DCCU: 1972]

tripped alcohol intoxicated. RT: *drunk*. [U.S., RAS: 1985]

tripped out drug intoxicated. RT: *stoned*. [U.S., RB: 1967, EEL: 1971, DCCU: 1972, W&F: 1975]

tripper an L.S.D. user; a drug user. RS: *user*. [U.S., M&V: 1967, E&R: 1971, EEL: 1971]

tripping heavy drug intoxicated and very emotional. RS: *stoned*. [U.S., D&B: 1970c]

tripping without luggage fantasizing or having hallucinations without having taken drugs. Possibly nonce. [U.S., RAS: 1981]

trippy having to do with a person who is silly or disoriented with or without drugs. [U.S., (1975): DNE: 1980]

trips the hallucinogenic drug *L.S.D.* (*q.v.*). RT: *L.S.D.* [U.S., RRL: 1969, ADC: 1975, NIDA: 1980] See also *trip*.

tripsville a nickname for San Francisco referring to the drugs used there. *Cf. trip*. [U.S., RRL: 1969]

trip weed marijuana; potent marijuana. RT: *pot*. [U.S., ADC: 1975]

trojan horse a nurse or guard who smuggles drugs to prisoners or patients. *Cf. white horse*. RT: *mule*. [U.S., JES: 1959, H&C: 1975]

trophy one half gallon of liquor. This may refer to a trophy-sized fish. See *bass, bream, perch*. [U.S., GU: 1975]

truck drivers (also **truckers**) amphetamines. Because they are said to be used frequently by long distance truck drivers. *Cf. L.A. turnabouts, turnabouts, West-Coast turnarounds*. RT: *amps*. [U.S., JBW: 1967, EEL: 1971, W&F: 1975]

trueno verde* marijuana. Spanish for green bombshell. RT: *pot*. [calo, JBR: 1973]

trues *Tuinal* (TM; *q.v.*). RT: *tooies*. [U.S., BR: 1972]

T.s See T.

T.s and blues a mixture of *Talwin* (TM; *q.v.*) painkiller and *Pyribenzamine* (TM; *q.v.*). This combination is usually injected. See *blue velvet*. *Cf. one on one, synthetic heroin, Teddies and Betties, tops and bottoms, tricycles and bicycles.* [U.S., DEM: 1981, RAS: 1981]

T-stick See *Thaistick*.

T.T. a total abstainer from alcohol. From *teetotaller* (*q.v.*). RT: *dry*. [U.S., BVB: 1942]

T-tabs *P.C.P.* (*q.v.*), an animal tranquilizer. RT: *P.C.P.* [U.S., (c. 1968): FAB: 1979]

T-Total See *teetotal*.

tube 1. a tobacco cigarette. RT: *nail*. [Br. (Cambridge University), (1925): DSUE] 2. a marijuana cigarette. RT: *joint*. [U.S., (1937): ELA: 1982] 3. a hypodermic syringe. RT: *monkey pump*. [U.S., H&C: 1975] 4. a can of beer. *Cf. tinny*. [Aust., BH: 1980]

tubed alcohol intoxicated. From *down the tubes*. RT: *drunk*. [U.S., ADC: 1975]

tuffler a tobacco cigarette. RT: *nail*. [cant (Lincolnshire), POS: 1979]

tuies See *tooies*.

Tuinal a protected trade name for a mixture of secobarbital and amobarbital (barbiturates) in capsule form. The drug is a central nervous system depressant containing Amytal (TM) and Seconal (TM) in equal amounts. Slang and jargon terms are based on the first syllable of *Tuinal*. *Cf. tooies*. [in current use; consult a pharmaceutical reference for more information]

tumble (also **tumble down, tumble down the sink**) a drink of liquor. Rhyming slang for *drink*. *Cf. fall down the sink*. RT: *nip*. [late 18-1900s, DRS, DSUE, MHW: 1934, SJB: 1943]

tumbling drunk (also **tumbling**) alcohol intoxicated. RT: *drunk*. [Br., 1800s, F&H; listed in BVB: 1942]

tumblings and blankets (also **tumblings and sheets**) tobacco and papers for making cigarettes. *Cf. blanket*. Hobo and military use. [U.S., EK: 1927, GI: 1931, MHW: 1934, BVB: 1942]

tun a heavy drinker; a drunkard. Tun = cask. *Cf. barrel, tank*. RT: *sot*. [Br., 18-1900s, DSUE; listed in BVB: 1942]

tuned (also **tuned up**) alcohol intoxicated. Not related to *tun*. RT: *drunk*. [U.S., MP: 1928, AH: 1931, MHW: 1934, W&F: 1960]

tuning in beginning to experience the effects of a dose of the hallucinogenic drug *L.S.D.* (*q.v.*). [U.S., TRG: 1968, RG: 1970, IGA: 1971]

turd 1. bad drugs; a purchase of bogus or weak drugs. RS: *blank*. [U.S., G&B: 1969] 2. a supply of narcotics contained in a condom (or similar device) and concealed in the rectum. *Cf. U-boat*. RS: *stash*. [U.S., JES: 1959, H&C: 1975]

Turk dope heroin derived from Turkish-grown opium poppies. RS: *heroin*. [U.S., RDS: 1982]

turkey 1. a purchase of bogus dope; a bogus drug capsule. GEN: a dud; a sham. RS: *blank*. [U.S., DWM: 1936, A&T: 1953, EEL: 1971, W&F: 1975] 2. to breathe in marijuana smoke through the nose. [U.S., D&B: 1970c] See also *turn someone*.

turkey-trots needle marks on the arms of an addict. Caused by drug (heroin) injections. From the name of the old dance: the turkey trot. RT: *tracks*. [U.S., LVA: 1981, RDS: 1982]

turn for an addict to become a police informer or spy. [U.S., JWK: 1981] See also *turn someone*.

turnabouts amphetamines. Akin to the term *cartwheel* (*q.v.*) or *L.A. turnabouts* (*q.v.*). RT: *amps*. [U.S., RG: 1970, IGA: 1971, YKB: 1977, NIDA: 1980]

turn a cartwheel (also **turn a wobbler**) to fake a drug withdrawal spasm in order to get drugs from a sympathetic physician. RS: *brody*. [U.S., JES: 1959, H&C: 1975]

turn a few hits to smoke marijuana. Probably based on *turn a trick*. *Cf. hit*. RT: *hit the hay*. [U.S., BR: 1972]

turn around (also **turn over**) to get off drugs; to break a narcotics addiction. GEN: to undergo a major, dynamic change. RS: *kick*. [U.S., M&V: 1967]

turn a trick to earn enough money for one's immediate drug needs. Tricks include theft and prostitution. [U.S., H&C: 1975]

turn communist to take a *Seconal* (TM; *q.v.*) capsule. Refers to (red) Seconal capsules as *communist M. and M.s* (*q.v.*). [U.S., BR: 1972]

turned off withdrawn from drugs; not on drugs or carrying drugs. *Cf. clean, cleared up, dried, dried out, on the natch, straight*. [U.S., (S&W: 1966), JBW: 1967, IGA: 1971, W&F: 1975]

turned on drug intoxicated; under the influence of marijuana. *Cf. wasted, stoned*. [U.S., (S&W: 1966), JBW: 1967, (M&V: 1967), (RRL: 1969), EEL: 1971, ADC: 1975, W&F: 1975; Br., (1960s): DSUE]

turned on to made aware of the pleasures of using a particular drug or drugs in general. GEN: made interested in. [U.S., EEL: 1971]

turned out made aware of the pleasures of drug use or of the drug culture. [U.S., RRL: 1969, (CM: 1970), EEL: 1971]

turner a drug seller. A person who turns people on or who turns someone astray. *Cf. twirl*. RT: *pusher*. [U.S., ADC: 1975]

turnip greens marijuana. *Cf. collard greens, greens*. RT: *pot*. Black use. [U.S., EAF: 1980]

Turn me on! "Sell me some drugs!" RS: *How are you going to act?* [U.S., (1930s): DUS]

turn on 1. to inject drugs. RT: *shoot*. [U.S., M&V: 1967] 2. (also **switch on**) to smoke marijuana; to take a dose of drugs; to get high. [U.S., HB: 1955, (1966): DNE: 1973, W&F: 1967, RRL: 1969, MW: 1976, ADC: 1981] 3. (also **turn someone on**) to introduce someone to drug use. [U.S., GS: 1959, JBW: 1967, M&V: 1967, W&F: 1967, RRL: 1969, CM: 1970, EEL: 1971, MA: 1973, EAF: 1980]

turn on, tune in, drop out a slogan promoting the use of L.S.D. among young people. Attributed to Timothy Leary. It suggests that one start using L.S.D. and drop out of society. [U.S., IGA: 1971]

turn out (also **turn someone out**) to introduce someone to drugs, prostitution, homosexuality, etc. *Cf. turned out*. [U.S., CM: 1970, TH: 1976]

turn over to get off of drugs. RS: *kick*. [U.S., M&V: 1967]

turn someone (also **turn**) to sell drugs to a person. *Cf. turner*. Possibly akin to *turn on* (*q.v.*). Probably akin to colloquial *turn a deal* or *turn a trick*. [U.S., MA: 1973]

turps (also **turp**) 1. (also **turpentine**) liquor; beer, inferior liquor, especially whiskey. RT: *booze*. [Aust. and U.S., (1935): DSUE, D&D: 1957, (1962): GAW: 1978, SJB: 1966] 2. (also **terp, terps**) Terpin Hydrate and *Codeine* (TM; *q.v.*) cough syrup. [U.S., RRL: 1969, EEL: 1971, ADC: 1981]

turps, on the on a drinking spree. *Cf. turps*. RT: *spreeing*. [Aust., SJB: 1966]

tus (also **twos**) Capsules of *Tuinal* (TM; *q.v.*) barbiturate. Pronounced *twos*. RT: *tooies*. [U.S., JWK: 1981]

tuskee a very large marijuana cigarette. RT: *joint*. Black use. [U.S., EAF: 1980]

tussey a drunkard; a slovenly drunk. RS: *sot*. [Br., 1800s, F&H]

tuzzy alcohol intoxicated. RT: *drunk*. [Br., probably 1800s, EDD]

T.V. action a drug high. [U.S., M&V: 1967, H&C: 1975]

twak tobacco. RT: *fogus*. [South African, (1963): JB: 1980]

twang opium. RT: *opium*. [Aust., (1898): GAW: 1978, SJB: 1943]

twankay gin. RT: *gin*. [Br., DSUE, (1900): OED]

twat teaser a small dose of a narcotic. Possibly related to seduction. Twat = vagina. *Cf. leg-opener*. RS: *dope*. [U.S., JES: 1959]

tweak to inject heroin. RT: *shoot*. Attested as motorcycle gang slang. [U.S., RDS: 1982]

tweased alcohol intoxicated. RT: *drunk*. [U.S., ADC: 1984]

tweeds, in smoking marijuana. Possibly akin to *weed* (*q.v.*) or *the weeds*. [U.S., JES: 1959, H&C: 1975]

tween the knees having to do with potent drugs or the use of very potent drugs. Said of heroin so strong that one's nodding has one virtually bent over. *Cf. nodding out.* [U.S., JWK: 1981]

twenty-five (also 25) the hallucinogenic drug *L.S.D.* (*q.v.*). RT: *L.S.D.* [U.S., JBW: 1967, RRL: 1969, IGA: 1971, W&F: 1975, KBH: 1982]

twig a marijuana cigarette. RT: *joint.* [U.S., (1970): ELA: 1982]

twine wine. Probably from a rhyming slang couplet such as *silk and twine, silken twine, string and twine.* RT: *wine.* [U.S., VJM: 1949]

twirl to sell drugs, especially heroin. *Cf. turner.* RT: *push.* [U.S., JWK: 1981]

twirler a drug seller; a seller of heroin. See *twirl.* This twirler can get you *twisted* (*q.v.*). *Cf. turner.* RT: *dealer.* [U.S., JWK: 1981]

twirlie (also **twirly**) a tobacco cigarette. Possibly a play on *quirley* (*q.v.*). Possibly *twirl* refers to rolling a cigarette. RT: *nail.* [Aust. naval, (1920): DSUE, SJB: 1966]

twist 1. a twisted roll of tobacco for chewing. RT: *quid.* [U.S., since the early 1700s, SBF: 1976] 2. a marijuana cigarette. Because of the twisted ends of these homemade cigarettes. RT: *joint.* [U.S., (1920): DSUE, DWM: 1936, M&D: 1952, RRL: 1969, EEL: 1971, ADC: 1975, RDS: 1982]

twist a burn to roll a cigarette. *Cf. burn, twist one.* [Aust. naval, (1918): DSUE]

twist a dream to roll a tobacco or marijuana cigarette. Hobo use (DU). [U.S., BVB: 1942, VJM: 1949]

twist a giraffe's tail to smoke a marijuana cigarette; to roll and smoke a marijuana cigarette. *Cf. hit the hay.* [U.S., JES: 1959, H&C: 1975]

twisted 1. intoxicated with drugs or alcohol. *Cf. bent.* GEN: confused (EHB: 1900). RT: *drunk, stoned.* [U.S., (1950s): CM: 1970, M&V: 1967, RRL: 1969, DC: 1972, DCCU: 1972, W&F: 1975, ADC: 1984] 2. suffering severe withdrawal symptoms. Perhaps meaning twisted in agony. [U.S., RRL: 1969, RDS: 1982]

twister 1. an injection of heroin (or morphine) and cocaine. *Cf. speedball.* [U.S., BVB: 1942] 2. a marijuana cigarette. *Cf. twist.* RT: *joint.* [U.S., VJM: 1949] 3. a marijuana smoker or user. One who twists marijuana cigarettes. *Cf. twist.* RT: *toker.* [U.S., DWM: 1936, VJM: 1949] 4. a faked or authentic withdrawal symptom. *Cf. frame a twister.* RT: *brody.* [U.S., DWM: 1936, VJM: 1949]

twist one to roll a cigarette. [U.S., GOL: 1950, D&D: 1957]

twist up a few to prepare and smoke a few pellets of opium. ELA: 1984 lists twisting a few. [U.S., DSUE, A&T: 1953]

twitcher a drug addict. RT: *junky.* [U.S., DSUE, A&T: 1953]

two and over whiskey; illicit liquor. The *two* probably refers to the percentage of alcohol. RS: ***moonshine***. From the prohibition era. [U.S., GOL: 1950]

two-arm habit an addiction where both arms are used for injections. RS: ***habit***. [U.S., HB: 1955]

two-bottle man (also **two-bottler**) a man who drinks two bottles of wine at one sitting. RS: ***sot***. [(1876): K&M: 1968]

two fingers a measurement of liquor in a glass. See comment at ***three fingers***. [U.S., (1886): OEDS]

two-fisted drinker someone who drinks heavily; someone who sips from a drink in each hand. Two-fisted = virile. RS: ***sot***. [U.S., K&M: 1968]

twos capsules of ***Tuinal*** (TM; *q.v.*) barbiturate. The same as ***tus*** (*q.v.*). RT: ***tooies***. [U.S., JWK: 1981]

two sheets to the wind alcohol intoxicated. See ***three sheets in the wind***.

two-toke a potent batch of marijuana which produces results after only two puffs. Compare to ***one-hit grass***. RS: ***pot***. [U.S., ELA: 1984]

two-way a mixture of the hallucinogenic drug ***L.S.D.*** (*q.v.*) and S.T.P. See other drug combinations at ***set***. [U.S., RG: 1970]

Tylenol a protected trade name for acetaminophen (analgesic) tablets. The drug is a painkiller and lowers fevers. ***Cf. fours***. [in current use; consult a pharmaceutical reference for more information]

U

U-boat a length of sealed rubber tubing, filled with drugs and concealed in the rectum. Named for the WWII submarine. *Cf. turd*. RS: *stash*. [U.S., JES: 1959, H&C: 1975]

U.C. an undercover agent. May be an officer of the law or an informer. RS: *fuzz*. [U.S., RRL: 1969]

uffi (also **uhffi**) morphine. RT: *morphine*. [U.S., M&V: 1954, SNP: 1977]

uglies (also **the uglies**) the delirium tremens. *Cf. horrors*. RT: *D.T.s*. [Br., late 1800s, F&H; listed in MHW: 1934]

ultimate drug, the cocaine. Because of its power and because it is not addictive in the same way that heroin is. RT: *cocaine*. [U.S., RDS: 1982]

umbilical cord methadone treatment for heroin addiction. If a daily dose of *methadone* (*q.v.*) is taken, there will be no heroin craving. Methadone is addictive and it can enter drug traffic by being sold by the addicts it is supposed to help. It is therefore dispensed, on a daily basis, at clinics. The addict under treatment is attached to the clinic by a metaphorical umbilical cord. [U.S., JWK: 1981]

ums *Valium* (TM; *q.v.*) tablets. RT: *vals*. [U.S., JWK: 1981]

unable to scratch himself alcohol intoxicated. RT: *drunk*. [Aust., SJB: 1966]

unalloyed having to do with undiluted liquor. RT: *neat*. [Br., B&L: 1890, F&H]

uncle (also **Uncle Sam, Uncle Whiskers**) a federal agent; a person who is an informer to federal agents. From *Uncle Sam*. H&C: 1975 spell this *unkle*. RS: *fuzz*. [U.S., DWM: 1933, MHW: 1934, DWM: 1936, A&T: 1953, M&H: 1959, RRL: 1969, ADC: 1975]

Uncle Emil *amyl nitrite* (*q.v.*); a personification of amyl nitrite. See *amy*. RT: *snapper*. [U.S., JH: 1979]

Uncle nab a policeman. *Cf. nab*. RT: *fuzz*. Black use. [U.S., EAF: 1980]

uncool having to do with a person who does not use drugs or who does not move in drug circles. *Cf. cool*. [U.S., ADC: 1975]

uncorrupted having to do with undiluted liquor. RT: *neat*. [Br.,

B&L: 1890, F&H]

uncut 1. having to do with any undiluted drug including marijuana. Compare to *cut*. [U.S., EEL: 1971, EAF: 1980, JWK: 1981] 2. pure or very high quality heroin. RS: *heroin*. [U.S., JWK: 1981, HSD: 1984]

under alcohol intoxicated; drug intoxicated; anesthetized. A truncation of *under the influence*. GEN: unconscious. RT: *drunk, stoned*. [(1934): DSUE, BVB: 1942, H&C: 1975]

undergrad a non-addicted drug user; a drug user who is not yet addicted. Compare to *cadet, convert, green hype, lame, lame hype, lane, shirt tail hype, student, youngblood*. [U.S., JES: 1959, H&C: 1975]

under the affluence of incohol alcohol intoxicated. A deliberate spoonerism based on *under the influence of alcohol*. [DSUE, PD: 1982, N&S: 1983]

under the influence alcohol intoxicated. A truncation of *under the influence of alcohol*. RS: *drunk*. [BVB: 1942, DSUE, SSD, RDS: 1982]

under-the-influencer an alcoholic; a drug addict. RT: *sot, junky*. [U.S., RDS: 1982]

under the table alcohol intoxicated; very drunk. Probably a reapplication of the expression *sub rosa,* meaning under the table, i.e., surreptitiously. Here it implies that the drinker has passed out and slipped under the table. [U.S., BVB: 1942, D&D: 1957, RDS: 1982]

under the weather alcohol intoxicated; hungover. GEN: slightly ill. RS: *drunk*. *Cf. hangover*. Of nautical origin. [(c. 1850): DSUE, BVB: 1942, SJB: 1943, W&F: 1960, SSD]

under the white cross under the effects of cocaine. *Cf. white cross*. RS: *stoned*. [U.S., JES: 1959, H&C: 1975]

unhemp to cease using marijuana. *Cf. hemp*. RS: *kick*. [U.S., JES: 1959, H&C: 1975]

unit equipment for injecting drugs; a hypodermic syringe and needle. RT: *outfit*. [U.S., S&W: 1973]

unk-dray alcohol intoxicated. Pig Latin for *drunk*. RT: *drunk*. [U.S., BVB: 1942]

unkie (also **unkle**) morphine. RT: *morphine*. YKB: 1977 list **uunkie**. [U.S., M&V: 1954, IGA: 1971, C&H: 1974]

unkle See *uncle* and *unkie*.

unmarried 1. having to do with undiluted alcohol. *Cf. unalloyed*. RT: *neat*. [Br., B&L: 1890, F&H; listed in BVB: 1942] 2. addicted to narcotics but not having a regular or dependable pusher. [U.S., JES: 1959, H&C: 1975]

unsophisticated having to do with undiluted alcohol. RT: *neat*. [Br., B&L: 1890, F&H]

unsweetened gin; unsweetened gin. RT: *gin*. [Br., B&L: 1890, F&H]

untempered having to do with undiluted liquor. RT: *neat*. [Br., B&L: 1890, F&H]

up 1. drug intoxicated; high on drugs; high on amphetamines; high on cocaine. *Cf. upper*. RS: *stoned*. [U.S., S&W: 1966, W&F: 1967, RRL: 1969, DCCU: 1972, ADC: 1975, H&C: 1975, RDS: 1982] 2. having to do with the state of mind of a person who has used drugs. Now in general slang for any positive state of mind. This *up* seems to have taken over *upbeat* which was originally from music. *Cf. positive*. [U.S., DCCU: 1972] 3. a suffix found in terms meaning a spree, usually British or Australian. *Cf. beer-up, booze-up, drunk-up, flare-up, gee-up, grog-up, jolly-up, piss-up, slopping-up, swill-up, tank-up, whooper-up*. 4. to take a stimulant drug. *Cf. re-up*. [U.S., (1972): DNE: 1980] 5. an amphetamine. *Cf. upper*. See *ups*.

up high a stimulating rather than a relaxing *high* (*q.v.*). *Up* is an adjective here. [U.S., JWK: 1981]

upholstered alcohol intoxicated. RT: *drunk*. [U.S., BVB: 1942]

upjohns stimulant tablets manufactured by The Upjohn Company. Probably refers to *Didrex* (TM; *q.v.*), an appetite suppressant similar to the amphetamines. [U.S., MT: 1971, ADC: 1981]

upper (also **uppers, uppies, ups**) a tablet or capsule of amphetamine. RT: *amps*. [U.S., RRL: 1969, D&B: 1970c, CM: 1970, (1970): DNE: 1973, EEL: 1971, DCCU: 1972, ADC: 1975, W&F: 1975, MW: 1976, EAF: 1980, NIDA: 1980, ADC: 1981, JWK: 1981] See also *downer*.

upper cut brandy. Probably analogous to *upper cut* meaning a high cut (of better quality) on a loin of meat. Possibly based on *upper cut* meaning an upward blow struck with the fist. RT: *brandy*. [U.S., BVB: 1942, VJM: 1949]

uppish alcohol intoxicated. RT: *drunk*. [(1728): OED; listed in BVB: 1942]

uppity (also **upsey**) alcohol intoxicated. RT: *drunk*. [U.S., BVB: 1942]

up-pot stimulating marijuana. In contrast to marijuana which sedates. *Cf. up*. RS: *pot*. [U.S., JWK: 1981]

up-Quaalude *free base* (*q.v.*). [U.S., ELA: 1984]

ups amphetamines. *Cf. upper*. See *up*. RT: *amps*. [U.S., RB: 1967, AHC: 1969, CM: 1970, (1970): DNE: 1973, EEL: 1971, ADC: 1975, YKB: 1977]

up tight out of drugs; high strung and in need of drugs. [U.S., M&V: 1967]

uptown cocaine. The term uptown generally refers to the better part of town. Cocaine is thought of as the drug of the wealthy. RT: *cocaine*. [U.S., NIDA: 1980]

use to take drugs; to take drugs habitually. [U.S., (BVB: 1942), W&F: 1967, RRL: 1969, EAF: 1980]

user a smoker of marijuana; a user of drugs who is not necessarily addicted; an addict. [U.S., BVB: 1942, GOL: 1950, W&F: 1960, DC: 1972, DCCU: 1972, EAF: 1980, ADC: 1981] See terms for drug addicts at *junky*. Nicknames and slang terms for a drug user: *acid-dropper, acid freak, acidhead, addict, ad-it, A-head, Arctic explorer, aspirin hound, attic, bambalacha rambler, bamboo, bamboo-puffer, bangster, barber's cat, barb freak, baseman, bato marijuano, bato narco, beanhead, beanup, bender, benzadrina, B-head, Bindle Kate, blaster, bloker, blower, bo-bo jockey, bonche, boom boy, booster shooter, boredom beater, bowler, bull dip, bushwhacker, C., C.A., cadet, candy fiend, candyhead, champ, Charlie Coke, C-head, chipper, chippy, chippy user, chronic, cokeaholic, coke blower, coke fiend, coke freak, cokehead, coke-smoke, coke whore, cokey, cokie, cokomo, cooker, cookie, cotton brothers, cotton freak, cotton man, cotton top, cotton woman, crank commando, cranker, crank freak, crispo, crispy, crispy-critter, cross-country hype, crystal lady, cubehead, C-user, D.A., dabbler, dagga rooker, dip, dopehead, dope hop, dopenik, doper, dopester, dopster, downer freak, dropper, druggie, druggy, drughead, drug partisan, drugster, duster, dusthead, dynamiter, eater, fan, first baseman, flake, flier, flyer, fortnighter, forty-niner, freak, freebaser, freon freak, frost freak, fu manchu, gangster, garbage freak, garbagehead, gargoyle, geehead, geezy addict, gheid, ghost, glad rags, glass eyes, glooch, gluer, glue sniffer, gluey, gold duster, golden duster, gong beater, gong kicker, goof, goof artist, goofball, goofballer, goof burner, goofer, gowhead, gowster, grass eater, grasser, grasshead, grasshopper, greefer, griefer, groover, habit smoker, hammerhead, hangar, hanger, hard-liner, hashaholic, hashhead, hawk, hay-burner, hayhead, hay puffer, head, headpiece, heavy, heavy man, hemp-humper, hemp-roller, hip-layer, hippy, hophead, horner, huffer, H-user, ice creamer, impaired physician, inhaler, Jane's better half, J.C.L., jerker, joint-roller, joy popper, joy rider, jumpy Stevie, junker man, keek, kick freak, kite, kokomo, Kokomo Joe, lame hype, leaper, light-weight chipper, lob, lobby gow, lover, mariholic, marijuanaholic, medical addict, medical hype, mellow dude, meth freak, methhead, meth monster, mezzanine lover, mind-explorer, mind-opener, mig-tripper, mojo, moshky, motter, mouth worker, Mr. Warner, M.U., mugglehead, muggles, M-user, narco, nonaddict, O.D. man, oiler, opium eater, opium kipper, panic man, panic woman, paper fiend, period hitter, P-head, pheno, pig, piki, pill-cooker, pill-dropper, pill freak, pill-gulper, pill-guzzler, pillhead, pill-popper, pillster, pilly, pinhead, pipe, pipe-hitter, pipey, player, pleasure shooter, pleasure smoker, pleasure user, popper, pothead, pot lush, pulaski, puller, reefer, reefer hound, reefer man, reefing man, righteous scoffer, roach bender, roker, roller, rooker, sagebrush whacker, schnozzler, second baseman, sharp shooter, shithead, skinner, skin-popper,* *skin-shooter, sleighrider, slim, smoker, snake, sniffer, sniffler, snifter, snorter, snowbird, snow flier, snow flower, snuffy, social junker, social sniffer, space cadet, space out, speed demon, speeder, speed freak, speedhead, speedster, stem artist, stick man, stoner, student, Sunday popper, swinger, syrup head, tea blower, teahead, tea hound, tea man, tea-sipper, tecate, tecato, teo, terphead, Texas leaguer, T-man, toker, tripper, undergrad, user, vegetarian, vipe, viper, voyager, wad, weed eater, weedhead, weed hound, weedly, weed twister, weekend doper, weekender, weekend tripper, weekend twister, weekend warrior, Western Union Man, wing captain, youngblood, zol rooker, zonker.*

use the needle to be addicted to drugs; to take a dose of an addictive drug. RT: *shoot.* [U.S., D&D: 1957, W&F: 1960]

using addicted; currently taking addictive drugs. [U.S., BVB: 1942, RRL: 1969]

usquebaugh (also **usquabae**) whiskey. Irish Gaelic for *the water of life.* See *aqua vitae.* [Irish, Scots and other varieties of English, (1581): OED]

utopiates hallucinogenic drugs. A portmanteau of *utopia* and *opiates.* Not drug argot. [U.S., RG: 1970]

uzz-fay federal narcotics officers; any law enforcement agent. *Fuzz* is a synonym of *whiskers* (*q.v.*). Pig Latin for *fuzz* (*q.v.*). [U.S., HB: 1955]

V

V. 1. ***Valium*** (TM; *q.v.*), a muscle relaxant. The victory sign made with the fingers also indicates Valium. RT: ***vals***. [U.S., JWK: 1981] 2. marijuana, the ***viper's weed*** (*q.v.*). RT: ***pot***. See ***viper***. [U.S., RRL: 1969]

valiant alcohol intoxicated. *Cf.* ***pot valiant***. RT: ***drunk***. [BF: 1737]

Valium a protected trade name for diazepam (tranquilizer) tablets. The drug is a tranquilizer. See ***vals*** for a list of slang terms. [in current use; consult a pharmaceutical reference for more information]

valley the crease inside the elbow, favored for injections. *Cf.* ***pit***. [U.S., RG: 1970, IGA: 1971, JHF: 1971]

vals ***Valium*** (TM; *q.v.*) tranquilizers. [U.S., JWK: 1981] See also ***tranks***. Nicknames and slang terms for valium: ***B.B.***, ***blue***, ***blue bombers***, ***blues***, ***dies***, ***dis***, ***dyes***, ***ums***, ***V.***, ***vals***, ***vees***, ***yellows***.

van blank (also **van blonk**) white wine. An Anglecized spelling of French *vin blanc*. RS: ***wine***. [Br. military, F&G: 1925, B&P: 1965]

van blank Anglais (also **van blonk Anglee**) whiskey, (Scotch whiskey). This implies that the English drink whiskey the way that the French drink white wine. See also ***English burgundy***. See comment at ***van blank***. RS: ***whiskey***. [Br. military, WWI, F&G: 1925, B&P: 1965]

van rooge See ***vin ruge***.

varnish inferior champagne; inferior liquor. See ***varnish remover***. RS: ***rotgut***. Possibly nonce. [(1860): JRW: 1909; listed in BVB: 1942]

varnished alcohol intoxicated. *Cf.* ***shellacked***. RT: ***drunk***. [U.S., ADC: 1975, PD: 1982]

varnish remover inferior liquor; inferior whiskey. *Cf.* ***paint remover***. RS: ***rotgut***. [U.S., D&D: 1957, W&F: 1960]

veeno wine. A respelling of Italian *vino*. *Cf.* ***weeno***. RT: ***wine***. Hobo use. [U.S., CS: 1927, MHW: 1934]

vees ***Valium*** (TM; *q.v.*) tranquilizer tablets. A spelling-out of *V.s*. See ***V***. RT: ***vals***. [U.S., JWK: 1981]

vegetable 1. alcohol intoxicated. *Cf.* ***go for veg***. RT: ***drunk***. [U.S., GU: 1975] 2. a person almost totally destroyed by drugs. *Cf.*

burnout. [U.S., C&H: 1974]

vegetarian a marijuana smoker. Based on *herb* (*q.v.*). In contrast to a person who prefers other types of drugs. RT: *toker*. [U.S., JES: 1959, H&C: 1975]

vegged out (also **veg'ed out**) debilitated by marijuana, alcohol, or other drugs. *Cf. vegetable, vegetarian*. See *burned out*. [U.S., RDS: 1982]

vein-shooter a person who injects drugs directly into a vein. In contrast to a person who shoots into the skin or the muscle. RS: *bangster*. [U.S., DWM: 1936, BD: 1937]

vein shot (also **V.S.**) an injection of drugs directly into a vein. RS: *shot*. [U.S., DWM: 1936, BVB: 1942]

velocidad* methamphetamine. Spanish for *speed* (*q.v.*). RT: *speed*. [U.S., NIDA: 1980]

velvet mallet "the effect of coke [?] with a marijuana cigarette." This could refer to cocaine or to a cola drink. [U.S., BR: 1972]

vendador* a drug seller or pusher. Spanish for seller. RT: *dealer*. [U.S., RRL: 1969]

Vera Lynn gin; a drink of gin. Rhyming slang for *gin*. RT: *gin*. Gay slang (BR: 1972). Music Hall rhyming slang (WG: 1952). [Br., (1940): DSUE, WG: 1952, DRS; U.S., (1940): DSUE, BR: 1972]

verdosas* amphetamine tablets, probably *Dexedrine* (TM; *q.v.*) amphetamines. Spanish for *greens* (*q.v.*). RT: *amps*. [U.S., NIDA: 1980]

verification shot 1. an injection, during which the syringe is pulled back to make certain that the needle is in the vein, and so that the addict can observe the mixing of the drug and the blood. *Cf. flag*. RS: *shot*. [U.S., DWM: 1936, BVB: 1942] 2. an injection of a drug taken to judge the strength of the drug; a test injection of a drug. *Cf. taste*. [U.S., M&V: 1954]

Vermont green a type of green marijuana presumably grown in Vermont. See comments at *green*. RT: *pot*. [U.S., E&R: 1971]

Veronal a trade name for *barbitone* (*q.v.*), a barbiturate. RS: *barbs*. [(1903): RRL: 1969]

very good humor, in alcohol intoxicated. *Cf. merry*. RT: *drunk*. [BF: 1722]

very weary alcohol intoxicated. See *weary*. RT: *drunk*. [BF: 1737]

vet a jocular term for a physician. The same as *horse doctor* (*q.v.*). RT: *croaker*. [U.S., M&V: 1967]

viaje* the hallucinogenic drug *L.S.D.* (*q.v.*). Spanish for *trip* (*q.v.*). RT: *L.S.D.* [calo, CG: 1980, NIDA: 1980]

vials *L.S.D.* (*q.v.*); a glass container of doses of L.S.D. RS: *L.S.D.* [U.S., H&C: 1975]

vic a victim of a *hot shot* (*q.v.*); someone who has been given a very potent or poisoned dose of drugs. [U.S., TRG: 1968, RG: 1970, RDS: 1982]

vice liquor. See *favorite vice*.

vin blink white wine; French white wine. A play on French *vin blanc*. RS: *wine*. [New Zealand, (1916): DSUE; U.S., (WWI): MPK: 1930, HNR: 1934]

vinegar blink (also **vinegar-de-blink**) white wine; French white wine. A dysphemism based on French *vin blanc*. RS: *wine*. [U.S., WWI, JL: 1972, MPK: 1930, MHW: 1934, W&F: 1960]

vine, the wine. RT: *wine*. [U.S., EAF: 1980]

ving blong white wine; French white wine. A spelling-out of an Anglecization of French *vin blanc*. RS: *wine*. [Br., WWI, (1933): DSUE]

vino 1. (also **wino**) wine; Italian wine. From Italian. RS: *wine*. [Br. and U.S., DSUE, BVB: 1942] 2. a *wino* (*q.v.*). [U.S., RDS: 1982]

vin ruge (also **van rooge**) red wine. A play on French *vin rouge*. The *also* is British, WWI. RT: *wine*. [U.S., (WWI): MPK: 1930, MHW: 1934]

vin sisters white wine and red wine. Probably similar to the *rhea sisters*, (*dia*, *pyo*, *gono*, etc.) from the same period. RT: *wine*. [U.S., (WWI): JL: 1972]

vipe 1. to smoke marijuana. RT: *hit the hay*. [U.S., DWM: 1938, RRL: 1969] 2. to crave marijuana. [U.S., DWM: 1938] 3. (also **viper**) a marijuana smoker. RT: *toker*. Possibly an error. JES: 1959 defines it: "To be on the drawing end of a hashishi cigarette." Probably early 1900s. [U.S., H&C: 1975]

viper 1. (also **vipe**) a marijuana smoker. See *snake*. RT: *toker*. GOL: 1950 and M&H: 1959 also attest the term for an opium user. EEL: 1971 found the term still used for long-time smokers of marijuana. [U.S., (1935): W&F: 1960, DWM: 1938, VJM: 1949, GOL: 1950] 2. a drug seller. Probably not akin to sense one. RT: *dealer*. Black use. Probably early 1900s. [U.S., CM: 1970]

viper butt a marijuana cigarette. RT: *joint*. Probably early 1900s. [U.S., JES: 1959, H&C: 1975]

viper mad hooked on marijuana; habitually craving marijuana. RS: *hooked*. [Canadian and U.S., early 1900s, DU]

viper's weed (also **viper weed**) marijuana. *Cf. vipe*. RT: *pot*. [U.S., (1920): DSUE, DWM: 1938, VJM: 1949, YKB: 1977]

virgin 1. a tobacco cigarette made of Virginia tobacco. RS: *nail*. [Br., JM: 1923] 2. having to do with undiluted liquor. RT: *neat*. [Br., B&L: 1890, F&H] 3. gin and vermouth, a martini. A portmanteau of *vir-* (the *ver* of vermouth) plus *gin*. [Br., JM: 1923]

virgin state having to do with a drug user who is not yet addicted. [U.S., IGA: 1971, WCM: 1972] See also *chip*.

vitriol inferior liquor. See the explanation at *blue stone*. RS: *rotgut*. From the prohibition era. [U.S., MHW: 1934, BVB: 1942]

vivor a survivor; a drug-using street person who manages to survive. Compare to *vic*. [U.S., JWK: 1981]

vodka acid vodka containing *L.S.D.* (*q.v.*). *Cf. electric koolaid*. [U.S., RG: 1970, EEL: 1971, IGA: 1971]

Volstead exile genuine, pre-prohibition liquor. Refers to the Volstead Act, the legislation which established national prohibition in 1919. This expression refers to smuggled or otherwise illegally obtained liquor. From the prohibition era. [U.S., BVB: 1942]

Volsteadian (also **Volsteadite**) a prohibitionist. RT: *dry*. From the prohibition era. [U.S., BVB: 1942]

volunteer (also **vol**) an addict who submits willingly to treatment or enters a hospital voluntarily. [U.S., (1952): JES: 1959, RRL: 1969]

vonce marijuana; a marijuana cigarette; a *roach*. From the Yiddish word for bedbug, and used in this expression to mean *roach*. RT: *roach*. [U.S., (1959): RSG: 1964, JHF: 1971]

vongony marijuana grown and used on the island of Madagascar. Possibly akin the Indian place name, Vangani. RT: *pot*. [U.S., IGA: 1971, RDS: 1982]

vons capsules of *Darvon* (TM; *q.v.*), a painkiller. [U.S., JWK: 1981]

voyager a person on an L.S.D. *trip* (*q.v.*). RS: *user*. [U.S., RRL: 1969, EEL: 1971]

V.S. **1.** a vein shot. RT: *shot*. [U.S., DWM: 1938, RDS: 1982] **2.** a drug user who injects into a vein; a vein-shooter. RS: *bangster*. [U.S., JES: 1959, H&C: 1975] See also *V*.

vulcanized alcohol intoxicated. RT: *drunk*. [U.S., (1925): W&F: 1960, MP: 1928, AH: 1931, MHW: 1934, DCCU: 1972, N&S: 1983]

W

waa-zooed See *whazood.*

wack See *whack.*

wacky-tabbacky (also **wacky-weed**) marijuana. RT: *pot.* [U.S., ADC: 1975, ELA: 1982]

wad 1. a drink of liquor. RT: *nip.* [Br., (1910): DSUE] 2. a cloth which is used to breathe an *inhalant* (*q.v.*), usually a sock. [U.S., JBW: 1967, RG: 1970, IGA: 1971] 3. a person who uses inhalants habitually. [U.S., JTD: 1971]

wad scoffer a *teetotaller* (*q.v.*). Scoffer = eater. RS: *dry.* [Br. military, F&G: 1925]

wafer 1. a cookie (usually a vanilla wafer) containing a dose of *L.S.D.* (*q.v.*). RS: *L.S.D.* [U.S., RG: 1970, EEL: 1971] 2. (usually **wafers**) *methadone* (*q.v.*). RT: *dolo.* [U.S., ELA: 1984]

wagon, off the 1. drinking liquor after a period of abstinence. [U.S., D&D: 1957, DCCU: 1972, RDS: 1982] 2. back on drugs. [U.S., JWK: 1981]

wagon, on the abstaining from alcohol. The *wagon* is the water wagon. This usually implies abstinence after a long period of drinking. RS: *sober.* [U.S., (1905): SBF: 1976, RDS: 1982]

wagon rider a person who abstains from alcohol, someone who is on the wagon. RS: *dry.* [U.S., BVB: 1942]

wag out to take a drug to get high. Probably akin to *nod* (*q.v.*). See *wig out.* [U.S., EEL: 1971]

wahegan a potent variety of marijuana from Hawaii. RT: *pot.* [U.S., ELA: 1982]

wake up 1. (also **waker-upper**) an addict's first injection or dose of the day. RS: *shot.* [U.S., M&V: 1954, RRL: 1969, MA: 1973, NIDA: 1980] 2. an amphetamine tablet or capsule. Usually plural. *Cf. eye-opener.* RT: *amps.* [U.S., JBW: 1967, RG: 1970, EEL: 1971] 3. a snort of cocaine for energy or for help in waking up. RS: *snort.* [U.S., S&F: 1984]

wakowi peyote cactus containing *mescaline* (*q.v.*). Presumably an Amerindian name. The same as *wokowi* (*q.v.*). RS: *peyote.* [U.S., YKB: 1977]

walking in the air drug intoxicated; high on drugs. RT: *stoned.*

[U.S., BVB: 1942, JES: 1959]

walking on rocky socks alcohol intoxicated. RT: *drunk*. [U.S., N&S: 1983]

walking whiskey vat a drunkard. RT: *sot*. [U.S., (1850–1900): RFA]

wallah an owner, merchant, agent, or keeper. A Hindi word. Used only in British slang, it dates to the British Empire in India. *Cf. bun wallah, canteen wallah, char wallah, lemonade wallah, pop-wallah, tack wallah*. Other terms are based on the consumer or the seller of intoxicants. See also *bevvy-merchant, grog merchant, hop merchant, lush merchant*. [Br., (1785): Y&B: 1902]

wallbanger 1. a narcotics addict; a drunkard. Because this person bumps into things. RS: *junky*. [U.S., (YKB: 1977), LVA: 1981] 2. *Mandrax* (TM; *q.v.*), *methaqualone* (*q.v.*), a hypnotic-sedative. *Cf. stumblers*. RT: *ludes*. [Br., RRL: 1969, YKB: 1977]

wall-eyed alcohol intoxicated. RT: *drunk*. [U.S., (1927): SBF: 1976, MHW: 1934, W&F: 1960, DCCU: 1972]

wallop beer. RT: *beer*. [Br., (1930): DSUE, EP: 1948, WG: 1962, K&M: 1968]

walloper a pub. *Cf. wallop*. RS: *bar*. [Br., early 1900s, DSUE]

wam-bazzled alcohol intoxicated. RT: *drunk*. [PD: 1982]

wamble-cropped alcohol intoxicated. (BF: 1737: [He's] Wamble Crop'd.) The same as *womblety-cropt* (*q.v.*). GEN: crest-fallen. RT: *drunk*. [BF: 1737]

wampo liquor; *booze* (*q.v.*). [Br. Royal Air Force, (1930): DSUE]

wana marijuana. *Cf. juana* (at *juane*). RT: *pot*. Black use. [U.S., EAF: 1980]

wangula marijuana and hashish. RT: *pot, hash*. Language origin unknown. [U.S., RDS: 1982]

wanks liquor. RT: *booze*. [Br. Royal Air force, (1930): DSUE]

wapsed-down alcohol intoxicated. RT: *drunk*. Rural use. [U.S., MHW: 1934, W&F: 1960]

warmer a drink of liquor. RT: *nip*. [Br., F&H; listed in BVB: 1942] See also *nose-burner*.

warped drug intoxicated. A variant of *bent* (*q.v.*). RT: *stoned*. [U.S., M&V: 1973]

washed up off drugs; withdrawn from drug addiction. GEN: finished, ruined. A pun on *clean* (*q.v.*) and finished. *Cf. clean*. RT: *off*. [U.S., DWM: 1938, (TRG: 1968), EEL: 1971, BTD: 1968]

wash one's ivories to drink liquor; to take a drink of liquor. Ivories = teeth. RT: *irrigate*. [Br., JCH: 1887]

wash up to withdraw from drugs. LIT: to get *clean* (*q.v.*). RS: *kick*. [U.S., VJM: 1949, A&T: 1953, (M&V: 1954), (TRG: 1968)]

wassailer a drunkard; a heavy drinker. RS: *sot*. The term experienced some use during prohibition. [(1634): OED; U.S., MHW: 1934, BVB: 1942]

wassermucker a prohibitionist. RT: *dry*. Seen in a Kansas newspaper. Probably nonce. [U.S., (1908): JCR: 1914]

waste to kill. *Cf. off.* Not limited to narcotics argot. [U.S., RRL: 1969]

wasted 1. alcohol intoxicated. GEN: exhausted, beat up (1956): RSG: 1964. RT: *drunk*. [U.S., D&B: 1970c, EEL: 1971, DC: 1972, ADC: 1984] 2. high on marijuana or some other drug. [U.S., JBW: 1967, RRL: 1969, ADC: 1975, ADC: 1981] (This entry continues after the following list.) Terms meaning marijuana intoxicated: *baked, beaming, bent, blind, blixed, blown away, brain burned, brightened, buzzed, cooked, crisp, dead, enhanced, enjedado, en juanado, en leñado, en motado, enyedado, fired up, foxy, freaked, freaked out, French fried, fucked up, goofed, goofed up, grifado, in, in the ozone, intox, intoxed, jocular, killed, mohasky, muggled, muggled up, on the beam, phased, phazed, pot-struck, potsville, potted, pot vague, racked, racked up, ripped, ripped off, ripped up, sent, stoned, stoned out of one's gourd, stoned out of one's head, stoned out of one's squash, stung by a viper, tea'd up, tead up, teed up, totalled, turned on, twisted, wasted, whacked, wrecked, zerked, zerked out*. 3. arrested. Probably from the general slang sense: killed. RT: *busted*. [U.S., M&V: 1967]

wasted his paunch he is drunk. *Cf. wasted*. [BF: 1737]

water 1. injectable amphetamines; methamphetamines. *Cf. splash*. RT: *speed*. [U.S., RRL: 1969, RG: 1970, YKB: 1977] 2. phencyclidine, P.C.P. RT: *P.C.P.* [U.S., ELA: 1984]

waterbag a total abstainer from alcohol. *Cf. water bottle, water-butt*. RT: *dry*. [Aust., (1920): DSUE, SJB: 1943]

water-bewitched week beer or punch; very dilute rum grog. Also used to mean weak tea (British military, early 1900s, Partridge). [(1672): F&H, FG: 1785, FG: 1811, FG: 1823, JCH: 1887]

water bottle a total abstainer from alcohol. *Cf. waterbag, water-butt*. RT: *dry*. [JRW: 1909]

waterbury watch Scotch. Rhyming slang. RS: *whiskey*. Never popular (Franklyn). [Br., late 18-1900s, DRS]

water-butt a total abstainer from alcohol. *Butt* = cask, keg. RT: *dry*. [(1898): OED]

water cart, on the abstaining from alcohol. The same as U.S. *on the wagon* (*q.v.*) which is short for *on the water wagon*. [Br., F&G: 1925]

water damaged having to do with alcohol, punch, or other liquor which is too dilute. A play on the literal sense. *Cf. water-bewitched*. [Br., 1900s, DSUE]

water-drinker a total abstainer from alcohol. A polite euphemism.

RT: *dry*. [late 1800s, OED]

watering hole (also **water hole, watering place**) a place to drink alcohol. *Cf. oasis*. RS: *bar*. [U.S., W&F: 1975]

watering out withdrawing suddenly and totally from drugs. *Cf. kick*. [U.S., RRL: 1969]

water logged alcohol intoxicated. *Cf. logged*. RT: *drunk*. [JM: 1923]

water of life gin. In later times the term is used for any alcoholic beverage. RT: *gin*. [Br., FG: 1823, JCH: 1887]

water pipe a pipe or *hookah* (*q.v.*) for smoking opium, hashish, or marijuana. An early English term for the *hookah* (*q.v.*). RS: *bong*. [Br. and U.S., (1824): SOD, EEL: 1971, ADC: 1981]

water soaked alcohol intoxicated. (BF: 1737: He's Water-soaken.) *Cf. water damaged*. RT: *drunk*. [BF: 1737, BVB: 1942]

water wagon, on the abstaining from alcohol. *Cf. on the wagon, off the wagon*. [Br. and U.S., F&G: 1925, MHW: 1934]

wattle to drink alcohol. From *What'll you have?* (DSUE). RT: *irrigate*. [Br., early 1900s, DSUE]

waxer a drink of liquor. RT: *nip*. [Br., 18-1900s, F&H, DSUE; listed in BVB: 1942]

way down depressed from taking drugs; depressed by the need for drugs. *Cf. down*. Probably older than the 1950s. [U.S., HB: 1955]

way out drug intoxicated. *Cf. far out*. RT: *stoned*. The expression moved quickly into general slang as a general expression of approbation. [U.S., RG: 1970, IGA: 1971]

way, out of the alcohol intoxicated. RT: *drunk*. [BF: 1737]

W.C. cocaine, i.e., *white cross* (*q.v.*). RT: *cocaine*. [U.S., GI: 1931]

weak-jointed alcohol intoxicated. *Cf. falling-down drunk*. RT: *drunk*. [U.S., W&F: 1960]

weary alcohol intoxicated. (BF: 1737: He's very weary.) *Cf. sleepy, tired*. RT: *drunk*. [BF: 1737; Br., late 18-1900s, F&H, DSUE]

weather, under the alcohol intoxicated. See *under the weather*.

wedding bells 1. a color variety of morning glory seeds. These are eaten as a hallucinogenic drug. RT: *seeds*. [U.S., SNP: 1977, YKB: 1977] 2. See *wedding bells acid*.

wedding bells acid (also **wedding bells**) the hallucinogenic drug *L.S.D.* (*q.v.*). RT: *L.S.D.* [U.S., IGA: 1971, YKB: 1977, KBH: 1982]

wedges (also **wedge, wedgies**) the hallucinogenic drug *L.S.D.* (*q.v.*). [U.S., RRL: 1969, IGA: 1971]

weed 1. (also **the weed**) tobacco. RT: *fogus*. [(1606): OED, JCH: 1887, F&H, M&C: 1905, VJM: 1949, D&D: 1957] 2. a cigar; a cheap cigar. RT: *seegar*. [Br. and U.S., (1858): DAE, JCH: 1887, SSD] 3. a cigarette. RT: *nail*. [U.S., (1904): SBF: 1982, BVB: 1942] 4. (also **the weed**) marijuana; a marijuana cigarette. Can refer to any quality of marijuana. RT: *pot*. [U.S., (1926): RPW: 1938, VWS: 1929, DWM: 1938, VJM: 1949, GOL: 1950, W&F: 1960, D&B: 1970c, DCCU: 1972, ADC: 1975, EAF: 1980, NIDA: 1980, ADC: 1981, JWK: 1981, RDS: 1982, ADC: 1984; South African, JB: 1980] 5. phencyclidine, *P.C.P.* (*q.v.*), an animal tranquilizer. From *killer weed* (*q.v.*). RT: *P.C.P.* [U.S., YKB: 1977]

weedhead (also **weed eater**) a smoker of marijuana. RT: *toker*. [U.S., (1933): ELA: 1982, M&D: 1952, M&V: 1954, W&F: 1960, D&B: 1970c, EEL: 1971, DCCU: 1972, D&B: 1978]

weed hound a smoker of marijuana. RT: *toker*. [U.S., (1920s): JES: 1959, BVB: 1942]

weedly a female marijuana smoker. RT: *toker*. [U.S., HB: 1955]

weed marijuana marijuana of low potency. RS: *pot*. [U.S., RRL: 1969]

weed, on the 1. smoking tobacco cigarettes. [U.S., D&D: 1957] 2. smoking marijuana. [U.S., D&D: 1957]

weed out to smoke marijuana and pass out; to escape from life into marijuana smoking. *Cf. weed*. RS: *hit the hay*. [U.S., (RRL: 1969), EEL: 1971, LVA: 1981]

weed tea marijuana. *Cf. tea*. Possibly marijuana brewed into a tea. RS: *pot*. [U.S., W&F: 1960, SNP: 1977]

weed twister a marijuana smoker; someone who makes marijuana cigarettes. Alludes to twisting the ends of roll-your-own marijuana cigarettes. RT: *toker*. [U.S., AJP: 1935]

weekender (also **weekend doper, weekend tripper, weekend twister, weekend user**) a person who uses drugs only occasionally or only on weekends. The same as *chipper* (*q.v.*). *Cf. weekend warrior*. [U.S., HB: 1955, SNP: 1977]

weekend habit a pattern of occasional drug use. A weekend habit is nonaddictive or preaddictive. *Cf. chippy habit*. RS: *habit*. [U.S., DWM: 1938, VJM: 1949, A&T: 1953, RRL: 1969]

weekend warrior a person who uses drugs only occasionally or on weekends. The same as *weekender*. *Cf. chipper*. [U.S., RRL: 1969, JWK: 1981]

weeno wine. An innovative spelling of *vino* (*q.v.*). *Cf. veeno*. RT: *wine*. [Aust. and Canadian, early 1900s, DSUE]

wee-wee a marijuana cigarette. Perhaps named for a child's penis. ELA: 1982 says the word is from Nigeria. *Cf. pee-wee*. RT: *joint*. [Br., BTD: 1968]

weight one ounce of a drug; a large amount of heroin or marijuana; a drug stash. RS: *load*. [U.S., W&F: 1967, RRL: 1969, MA: 1973, ADC: 1975, ADC: 1981, JWK: 1981]

weight dealer a drug seller above the retail level. *Cf. weight*. RS: *dealer*. [U.S., RDS: 1982]

weirded out disturbed or unnerved by drugs or by events which occur while one is under the effects of drugs. [U.S., ADC: 1975]

well-away alcohol intoxicated. See *well-under*. GEN: far along. RT: *drunk*. [Br., early 1900s, DSUE, M&J: 1975]

well-bottled alcohol intoxicated. RT: *drunk*. [Br. military, (1920): DSUE]

well-fixed (also **well-heeled**) alcohol intoxicated. Both are colloquial expressions meaning rich. **Well-heeled** is of nautical origin and refers to the tilting or leaning of a ship under sail. RT: *drunk*. [U.S., MHW: 1934]

well in for it alcohol intoxicated. (BF: 1737: [He's] Well in for't.) RT: *drunk*. [BF: 1737]

well-lit alcohol intoxicated. A variant of *lit* (*q.v.*). RT: *drunk*. [M&J: 1975]

well-oiled (also **well-lubricated**) alcohol intoxicated. Refers to a well-oiled machine, and may imply talkativeness. *Cf. lubricated*. RT: *drunk*. [Br. and U.S., F&G: 1925, BVB: 1942, W&F: 1960, SSD]

well-preserved alcohol intoxicated. *Cf. pickled*. RT: *drunk*. [U.S., BVB: 1942]

well-primed alcohol intoxicated. *Cf. primed*. RT: *drunk*. [M&J: 1975]

well-soaked alcohol intoxicated. *Cf. soaked, water soaked*. RT: *drunk*. [M&J: 1975]

well-sprung alcohol intoxicated. RT: *drunk*. [(1851): OEDS, (1870): F&H, (1910): DSUE; listed in BVB: 1942]

well to live alcohol intoxicated. RT: *drunk*. [BF: 1737]

well-under (also **well-away**) alcohol intoxicated. *Cf. under*. RT: *drunk*. [DSUE, BVB: 1942, SJB: 1943, SSD, M&J: 1975]

wen-chee gum opium. Possibly an error (pronunciation or spelling) for *yen-chee* (*q.v.*). SNP: 1977 lists **wen-shee**. [U.S., RDS: 1982]

West-Coast turnarounds amphetamines. Refers to their use by truck drivers. *Cf. L.A. turnabouts, truck drivers*. RT: *amps*. [U.S., IGA: 1971, EE: 1976]

Western Union Man a drug user who talks too much about his suppliers (connections). [U.S., JWK: 1981]

wet 1. alcohol intoxicated. RT: *drunk*. [U.S., (1704): SBF: 1976, BF: 1737, F&H, BVB: 1942, W&F: 1960] 2. a drink of liquor; a sip of liquor. RT: *nip*. [JCH: 1887, B&L: 1890, F&H, (WWII): MMO: 1970, DSUE, BVB: 1942, (obsolete): W&F: 1960] See also *wet one*. 3. to drink liquor; to take a drink of liquor. RT: *irrigate*. [Br., 1800s, F&H; listed in GWM: 1859] 4. a person who is against national prohibition. The opposite of *dry* (*q.v.*). [U.S., (1918): OEDS, MHW: 1934] 5. having to do with a political subdivision (a city, state, or county) which does not have laws against the selling of liquor. [U.S., (1870): SBF: 1976]

wet an eye to take a drink of liquor. RT: *irrigate*. [Br., 1800s, DSUE]

wet both eyes alcohol intoxicated. RT: *drunk*. [BF: 1737]

wet-cotton a bit of cotton still damp from use in straining drugs for injection. This cotton is still usable and is considered a handout for a down-and-out addict or a reward for a small favor. *Cf. cotton*. [U.S., JWK: 1981]

wet dog shakes violent tremors from the D.T.s or from drug withdrawal. RS: *D.T.s*. [U.S., (1973): DNE: 1980]

wet goods liquor; illicit liquor. A play on *dry goods*. *Cf. wet stuff*. RS: *moonshine*. From the prohibition era. [U.S., BVB: 1942, VJM: 1949]

wet hand a drunkard. Probably a nautical reference. RT: *sot*. [Br., F&H, JM: 1923]

wet-handed alcohol intoxicated. RT: *drunk*. [Br., 1800s, F&H; listed in BVB: 1942]

wet one 1. a cold beer. *Cf. cold one*. [U.S., RAS: 1976] 2. (also **wet 'un**) a drunkard; a *wet* (*q.v.*) person. RT: *sot*. [Br., 1800s, listed in F&H (at *wet*)]

wet one's goozle to take a drink of liquor. RT: *irrigate*. [U.S., MP: 1928, MHW: 1934, W&F: 1960]

wet one's whistle (also **wet one's eye, wet one's neck, wet one's throat, wet one's throttle**) to take a drink of liquor; to drink much liquor. *Cf. oil one's whistle*. RT: *irrigate*. The imagery is quite old. In Chaucer's *Canterbury Tales*, "The Reeve's Tale": "So was her jolly whistle well wet." [FG: 1823, B&L: 1890, (1924): DSUE, MHW: 1934, D&D: 1957, W&F: 1960, CM: 1970]

wet parson a parson or other cleric who drinks liquor. *Cf. wet*. [Br., 1900s, DSUE]

wet-Quaker a Quaker who drinks alcohol; any secret or closet drinker. *Cf. wet*. RS: *sot*. [BE: 1690, FG: 1785, FG: 1823, B&L: 1890, F&H]

wet smack a drunkard. RT: *sot*. [U.S., MHW: 1934, W&F: 1960]

wetster a drunkard. RT: *sot*. [Br., 1800s, F&H; listed in BVB: 1942]

wet stuff liquor. *Cf. wet goods*. RT: *booze*. [U.S., BVB: 1942]

wet subject a drunkard. Perhaps the punning opposite of a dry (dull) subject. RT: *sot*. [Br., 1800s, F&H; listed in BVB: 1942]

wet-thee-through gin. Possibly in reference to gin's diuretic qualities. RT: *gin*. [Br., FG: 1823]

whack (also **wack**) 1. a drink of liquor. RT: *nip*. [U.S., BVB:

1942] 2. to *cut* (*q.v.*) or dilute heroin or cocaine. RT: *cut*. [U.S., (1970s): FAB: 1979, W&F: 1975] 3. phencyclidine, P.C.P. RT: *P.C.P.* [U.S., ELA: 1984]

whacked 1. (also **whacked out**) drug intoxicated; under the effects of marijuana. RT: *stoned*. [U.S., JWK: 1981] 2. diluted; cut. Said of narcotics, especially heroin. [U.S., RRL: 1969, (W&F: 1975)] 3. alcohol intoxicated. RT: *drunk*. [Aust., BH: 1980]

whale a drunkard; a person with an enormous drinking capacity. Worse than a person who drinks like a fish. RT: *sot*. [U.S., MHW: 1934]

whammer a female drug smuggler who transports containers of drugs in her vagina. RT: *mule*. [U.S., RAS: 1982]

What is it? "Sell me some drugs!"; "What drugs do you have for sale?" See *How are you going to act?* for similar inquiries. [U.S., JWK: 1981]

what it takes liquor, what it takes to get drunk. From phrases such as *have what it takes*, i.e., *He's got what it takes*. RT: *booze*. [U.S., BVB: 1942]

what-nosed alcohol intoxicated. RT: *drunk*. [Br., 1800s, F&H; listed in BVB: 1942]

What's happening? "Where are there drugs for sale?"; "Where is the [drug] action?" See *How are you going to act?* [U.S., (1930): DUS, M&D: 1952, IGA: 1971]

What street are you on? a coded inquiry about the availability of drugs. If it is answered with "What street are you looking for?", drugs cannot be far away. RT: *How are you going to act?* [U.S., JWK: 1981]

What will you liq? (also **What will you have?**, **What's your liquor?**, **What's yours?**) "What do you want to drink?" *Liq* may be a play on *lick*. The entry is British. [18-1900s, DSUE, JRW: 1909]

whazood (also **waa-zooed**, **whazooed**) alcohol intoxicated. RT: *drunk*. [U.S., GU: 1975]

wheat marijuana. See *Kansas grass*. *Cf. hay, straw*. RT: *pot*. [U.S., RRL: 1969, SNP: 1977]

Wheaties marijuana cigarette rolling paper; wheat cigarette paper. A "brand name." RT: *paper*. [U.S., ELA: 1982]

wheep a small glass of beer. RS: *nip*. [U.S., W&F: 1960]

Where's Mary? "Can you tell me where I can buy marijuana?" RS: *How are you going to act?* [U.S., M&D: 1952]

whiff 1. a drink of liquor; a small drink of liquor. The same as *sniff* (*q.v.*). RT: *nip*. [1600s, OED; listed in BVB: 1942] 2. cocaine. Refers to the snorting of cocaine. *Cf. snort, toot*. RT: *cocaine*. [U.S. ADC: 1981]

whiffled alcohol intoxicated. RT: *drunk*. The OED dates **whiffle** (to drink) as 1693. [Br., (1930): DSUE]

whiffsniffer an enthusiastic prohibitionist; a person who is always alert to the slightest whiff of alcohol on someone's breath. *Cf. cellar-smeller.* RS: *dry.* From the prohibition era. [U.S., 1920s, BVB: 1942]

whiff the yen-shee to smoke opium. *Yen-shee* (*q.v.*) = opium. RT: *suck bamboo.* [U.S., BVB: 1942, JES: 1959]

whina white allegedly, pure heroin. Almost certainly an error for *China white* (*q.v.*). [U.S., SNP: 1977]

whing-ding (also **wing-ding**) 1. (also **whinger**) a wild drinking party. RT: *spree.* [U.S., BVB: 1942] 2. a simulated withdrawal convulsion enacted to get drugs from a sympathetic physician. RT: *brody.* [U.S., DWM: 1936]

whip 1. gin; rum. RT: *gin, rum.* [Aust., SJB: 1966, DSUE] 2. (also **whip off, whip down**) to take a drink of alcohol quickly. [Br., FG: 1823, DSUE; listed in BVB: 1942]

whip-belly vengeance (also **whip-belly, whistle-belly vengeance**) thin, weak, or sour beer; beer that is hard on one's digestive tract. *Cf. whip.* RT: *queer-beer.* [Br., (1709): F&H, FG: 1823, B&L: 1890]

whipcan (also **whipcat**) a drunkard who whips down many cans of liquor. *Cf. whip.* Whipcan may be an error for, or a variant of whipcat, or vice versa. RT: *sot.* [(1611): OED]

whip off to drink quickly. RT: *guzzle.* See *whip.*

whipped alcohol intoxicated. *Cf. whip.* RT: *drunk.* [U.S., (1851): SBF: 1976, JAS: 1932, MHW: 1934]

whippets nitrous oxide (for inhalation purposes) dispensed from a pressurized can of whipped cream. [U.S., ELA: 1984]

whips and jangles (also **whips and jingles**) symptoms of withdrawal from alcohol or narcotics. Essentially the same as *whoops and jingles* (*q.v.*). *Cf. D.T.s.* [U.S., M&V: 1954, RDS: 1982]

whipsey alcohol intoxicated. A portmanteau of *whipped* and *tipsy.* RT: *drunk.* [MP: 1928, AH: 1931]

whip the cat to get drunk. This is also a very old expression meaning to vomit. *Cf. whipcat* (at *whipcan*). RT: *mug oneself.* [(1622): OED]

whiskers (also **Mr. Whiskers, whiskers man, Uncle Whiskers**) a federal agent. This is a play on *Uncle Sam,* the bewhiskered personification of the U.S. RS: *fuzz.* [U.S., DWM: 1933, MHW: 1934, BVB: 1942, DWM: 1936, BD: 1937, VJM: 1949, A&T: 1953, M&H: 1959, TRG: 1968]

whiskey (also **whisky**) a strong liquor distilled from fermented grain. *Whisky* is the British spelling. Usually refers to Scotch whiskey in the (British) English-speaking world. The term is used generically in the U.S., although in a large part of the South it refers to *bourbon* (*q.v.*) whiskey. From Irish Gaelic *usquebaugh* (*q.v.*). Now standard English. [since the 1700s, (1715): OED]

Nicknames and slang terms for whiskey: *alkali, alky, angel teat, angel tit, bald face, bald-face whiskey, barbed wire, barbwire, barley-bree, benzine, blackjack, blind tiger, blockade, blockade whiskey, blue pig, blue stone, boiled corn, boilermaker's delight, bombo, bootleg, bottled earthquake, bourbon, boxcar, brave maker, breaky leg, brown, brown plaid, brush whiskey, bug juice, bug poison, bumble whiskey, bumclink, bun, busthead, bustskull, cane corn, canned heat, caper juice, cawn, cement water, chained lightning, chain lightning, Charley Frisky, choke dog, coffin varnish, condensed corn, conversation fluid, conversation water, corn, corn coffee, corn juice, corn likker, corn liquor, corn mule, corn spirits, corn squeezings, corn whiskey, corn wine, cowboy cocktail, crater, cream, creature, crooked whiskey, curse of Scotland, dehorn, devil's eyewater, dew, donk, dram, drudge, drugstore whiskey, dry goods, dust-cutter, dynamite, embalming fluid, family disturbance, firewater, forty-rod, forty-rod lightning, forty-rod whiskey, forty-two caliber, fox head, frisky whiskey, gage, gay and frisky, giant killer, giggle soup, giggle water, grapple the rails, Greek fire, gut warmer, hell broth, highland frisky, hogwash, honeydew, honey dip, ignorant oil, I'm so, I'm so frisky!, Indian liquor, Indian whiskey, infernal compound, Irish, Irish aqua vitae, Irish dew, jackass, Japanese dogs, J.D., Jersey lightning, jig-juice, jig-water, John Barleycorn, jollop, joy-juice, Kentucky corn, Kentucky dew, Kentucky fire, Kentucky horn, kickapoo joy-juice, kill-the-beggar, kong, lamp oil, lightning, lightning flash, liquid fire, liquid lightning, moon, mooney, moonlight, moonshine, moony, moose milk, mountain dew, mule, nanny goat sweat, nigger pot, nockum stiff, nose paint, old man, old man's milk, old redeye, paint remover, paleface, panther, panther juice, panther piss, panther pizen, panther's breath, panther's piss, panther's pizen, panther sweat, pass whiskey, pig iron, pimple and blotch, pine top, pink-eye, pink tea, pish, pizen, popskull, pot, poteen, potheen, potsheen, prairie dew, prescription, prescription whiskey, queer, quill, quin, railroad, rat-track whiskey, red, red disturbance, redeye, redhead, red ink, red liquor, roasting-ear wine, rookus juice, Rosy Loader, rye, rye sap, sagebrush whiskey, scamper juice, scat, scorpion Bible, Scotch, Scotch tea, scrap iron, screech, seafood, sheepherder's delight, shine, shine liquor, shoe polish, silo drippings, Simon, Simon Pure, Sir John Barleycorn, skee, sky, snake, snakebite medicine, snakebite remedy, snakehead whiskey, snake juice, snake medicine, snake poison, snake water, soul destroyer, squirrel, squirrel dew, squirrel whiskey, stump, stump likker, stump rum, stump water, swamp root, swicky, tanglefoot, tangleleg, Taos, Taos lightning, tarantula juice, taste, the clear McCoy, the real thing, the sma' still, third rail, tiger eye, tiger juice, tiger milk, tiger piss, tiger's milk, tiger sweat, tongue loosener, tongue oil, tonsil oil, tonsil paint, tonsil varnish, tonsil wash, tornado juice, trade whiskey, two and over, usquebaugh, van blank Anglais, varnish remover, waterbury watch, white coffee, white eye, white lightning, white line, white liquor, white mule, white whiskey, Who shot John?, wildcat, wildcat whiskey, wild mare's milk, woofle water, woozle water.*

whiskey bloat a drunkard. *Cf. bloat, bloater.* RT: *sot.* [U.S., JSF: 1889]

whiskey-frisky alcohol intoxicated; drunk on whiskey. RT: *drunk.* [Br., (1782): DSUE; U.S., BVB: 1942]

whiskey legger a bootlegger of whiskey. From the prohibition era. [U.S., BVB: 1942]

whiskey mill (also **whiskey joint, whiskey hole, whiskey house**) a bar where whiskey is sold; a saloon. Based on *gin mill* (*q.v.*). RS: *bar.* Whiskey house from 1835 (DA), the other terms are newer. [U.S., (1835): DA, (1870): F&H, BVB: 1942, D&D: 1957]

whiskey root *peyote* (*q.v.*). RS: *peyote.* [U.S., JRB: 1859]

whiskified alcohol intoxicated; drunk on whiskey. RT: *drunk.* [Br., (1802): OED, (1857): F&H; listed in BVB: 1942]

whisper low (also **whisper joint, whisper parlor**) a speakeasy. All of these terms are punning on the original *speakeasy* (*q.v.*). RT: *speak.* From the prohibition era. [U.S., 1920s, JAS: 1932, MHW: 1934, BVB: 1942, D&D: 1957]

whistle-belly vengeance low-quality beer. See *whip-belly vengeance.*

whistle drunk (also **whistled, whistled drunk**) alcohol intoxicated. Whistled drunk is probably an error (DSUE). RT: *drunk.* [(1749): F&H; listed in PD: 1982]

whistle wetter liquor. *Cf. wet one's whistle.* RT: *booze.* [U.S., BVB: 1942]

white 1. gin; a glass or bottle of gin. *Cf. white wine, white wool.* RT: *gin.* [Br., (1848): DSUE; U.S., MHW: 1934, GOL: 1950] 2. liquor; *booze* (*q.v.*). *Cf. white line.* [U.S., GI: 1931, HNR: 1934] 3. (also **white powder**) powdered drugs: heroin, cocaine, morphine. RT: *powder.* [U.S., (1914): DSUE, HNR: 1934, EEL: 1971, NIDA: 1980] 4. (also **whites, whitie**) *Benzedrine* (TM; *q.v.*); an amphetamine tablet. RT: *amps.* [U.S., JBW: 1967, M&V: 1967, RRL: 1969, D&B: 1970c, ADC: 1975, NIDA: 1980]

white angel 1. a hospital or prison nurse, or other white-clothed attendant who smuggles narcotics to addicts. RT: *mule.* [U.S., DWM: 1936, VJM: 1949] 2. (also **white nurse**) morphine. RT: *morphine.* [U.S., DWM: 1936]

white birds *methaqualone* (*q.v.*). RT: *ludes.* [U.S., SNP: 1977]

white coffee liquor; illicit liquor; moonshine. The same as *corn coffee* (*q.v.*). RT: *moonshine.* From the prohibition era. [U.S., EK: 1927, GI: 1931, MHW: 1934, VJM: 1949] See also *coffee.*

white cross 1. (also **W.C.**) cocaine. RT: *cocaine.* [U.S., WHW: 1922, GI: 1931, MHW: 1934] 2. amphetamine tablets. See *cartwheel.* RT: *amps.* [U.S., C&H: 1974, ADC: 1975, GU: 1975]

white domes (also **white double domes, white single domes**) the hallucinogenic drug *L.S.D.* (*q.v.*). *Cf. domes.* [U.S., RG: 1970]

white drugs cocaine. RT: *cocaine.* [U.S., EEL: 1971]

white dust high-quality *P.C.P.* (*q.v.*), an animal tranquilizer. *Cf. yellow dust.* Compare to *gray dust.* RT: *P.C.P.* [U.S., ADC: 1981]

white eye corn liquor; corn whiskey; inferior liquor; rum. As the story goes, this liquor is so powerful that if you drink it only the whites of your eyes will show. Probably a play on *redeye* (*q.v.*). RS: *rotgut.* [U.S., (1827): DA, JCH: 1887, B&L: 1890, F&H; listed in BVB: 1942]

white face 1. gin. RT: *gin.* [Aust., (1849): DSUE] 2. rum. RT: *rum.* [U.S., (1855): DA]

white fustian champagne; white wine. *Cf. red fustian.* RT: *wine.* [Br., (1834): DSUE]

white girl cocaine. *Cf. girl.* RT: *cocaine.* [U.S., IGA: 1971, YKB: 1977]

white goddess morphine. RT: *morphine.* Probably not narcotics argot. [U.S., M&V: 1973, SNP: 1977]

white horse 1. alcohol diluted for drinking. RT: *booze.* [U.S., JCR: 1914] 2. cocaine. In comparison to heroin which is sometimes brown or off-white. RT: *cocaine.* [U.S., SNP: 1977]

white junk heroin, possibly heroin of high purity; white heroin. RS: *heroin.* See *junk.* [U.S., SNP: 1977, RDS: 1982]

white lace gin. Akin to *white tape* (*q.v.*). RT: *gin.* [cant, (1700s): DSUE]

white lady 1. gin. RT: *gin.* [Br., 18-1900s, F&H, DSUE] 2. denatured alcohol; a drink prepared with methyl alcohol. RS: *methyl.* [Aust., (1920): DSUE, (1935): GAW: 1978] 3. heroin; cocaine. Probably used for other powdered drugs. [U.S., RRL: 1969, EEL: 1971, ADC: 1975, JWK: 1981]

white light See *clear light.*

white lightning 1. raw liquor; strong liquor; corn liquor; inferior liquor. Akin to *white mule* (*q.v.*). Refers to the lightning-like jolt of raw liquor. *Cf. moonshine, rotgut.* [U.S., (c. 1900): SBF: 1982, MP: 1928, VR: 1929, MHW: 1934, D&D: 1957, EAF: 1980] 2. *L.S.D.* (*q.v.*); L.S.D. mixed with some other drug such as methamphetamine. Often (mis)spelled *lightening* in this sense. RS: *L.S.D.* [U.S., RG: 1970, EEL: 1971, S&R: 1972, W&F: 1975, KBH: 1982, RDS: 1982; Canadian, (1969): MMO: 1970]

white lime liquor; grain alcohol. Probably akin to *white line* (*q.v.*). RS: *booze.* From the prohibition era. Hobo use. [U.S., CS: 1927, VR: 1929, AH: 1931]

white line alcohol mixed with water; inferior liquor; strong liquor; corn liquor. *Cf. white, white line.* RS: *rotgut.* From the prohibition era. [U.S., EK: 1927, NK: 1926, GI: 1931, GOL:

1950, D&D: 1957, W&F: 1960]

white liner 1. (also **white line stiff**) a drinker of rotgut booze. *Cf. white line.* RS: *sot.* From the prohibition era. [U.S., (1918): DSUE, GOL: 1950, D&D: 1957] 2. a dealer in illicit liquor or rotgut. From the prohibition era. RT: *bootlegger.* [U.S., GOL: 1950]

white liquor corn whiskey; homemade liquor; raw whiskey. RT: *moonshine.* [U.S., BVB: 1942]

white merchandise powdered narcotics: heroin, morphine, and cocaine. *Cf. merchandise.* RT: *powder.* [U.S., D&D: 1957, SNP: 1977]

white mosquitoes cocaine. VJM: 1949 defines this as any powdered drug. The expression probably refers to marks left on the skin after injecting drugs or perhaps to the sting of the injections. *Cf. bitten by white mosquitoes.* RT: *cocaine.* [U.S., BVB: 1942, VJM: 1949]

white mule raw liquor; corn liquor; grain alcohol; homemade liquor. Essentially the same as *white lightning* (*q.v.*). Refers to the kick of the mule. RT: *rotgut.* [U.S., (1889): DA, MP: 1928, VWS: 1929, GI: 1931, GOL: 1950, W&F: 1960]

white nurse powdered drugs: heroin, cocaine, and morphine. From the white of the white powdered drugs, or the aid rendered by nurses. *Cf. stung by the white nurse.* RT: *powder.* [U.S., DWM: 1936, BVB: 1942, D&D: 1957]

white Owsley (also **white Owslies**) a high grade of *L.S.D.* (*q.v.*). See *Owsley* for a list of similar terms. [U.S., C&H: 1974, SNP: 1977]

white powder powdered drugs. See *white.*

white ribbon (also **white ribbin**) gin. *Cf. white tape* for a list of ribbon words. RT: *gin.* [cant, FG: 1811, FG: 1823, F&H]

whites See *white.*

white Sandoz the hallucinogenic *L.S.D.* (*q.v.*). *Cf. Sandoz.* RT: *L.S.D.* [U.S., KBH: 1982]

white satin gin. RT: *gin.* [Br., DA: 1857, JCH: 1887, F&H, SSD]

white silk morphine crystals for dissolving and injecting. *Cf. cotton morphine, lint.* RT: *morphine.* [U.S., DU, A&T: 1953]

white stuff 1. illicit liquor. *Cf. white, white lightning, white lime, white line.* RS: *moonshine.* [U.S., (c. 1920): W&F: 1960, HNR: 1934, VJM: 1949, GOL: 1950] 2. powdered drugs in general; a specific powdered drug: heroin, morphine, or cocaine. RT: *powder.* [U.S., DWM: 1936, M&W: 1946, M&D: 1952, W&F: 1960, RRL: 1969, EEL: 1971] 3. *Demerol* (TM; *q.v.*) painkiller in its white crystalline form. *Cf. demis, junk, shit, stuff.* The drug also comes in a colored tablet to which this term does not apply. [U.S., YKB: 1977] 4. *Dilaudid* (TM; *q.v.*) painkiller in its white crystalline form. *Cf. D., dees, dilies, dillies, drugstore stuff, D.s,* *footballs, shit, stuff, white stuff.* The drug is also available in colored tablets to which this term does not apply. [U.S., YKB: 1977]

white tape 1. gin. RT: *gin.* Another term on the ribbon theme. *Cf. blue ribbon, blue ruin, blue tape, Holland tape, ribbon, satin, tape, white lace, white ribbon, white satin, white velvet.* RT: *gin.* [cant, (1725): DSUE, FG: 1785, FG: 1811, FG: 1823, GWM: 1859, JCH: 1887, B&L: 1890, F&H] 2. powdered drugs: cocaine, heroin, morphine. Possibly an error. RT: *powder.* [U.S., ELA: 1984]

white tornado *free base* (*q.v.*). RS: *cocaine.* [U.S., ELA: 1984]

white velvet gin. RT: *gin.* [GWM: 1859] See also *blue velvet.*

white whiskey 1. moonshine; *corn whiskey* (*q.v.*). [U.S., 1900s, LP: 1977] 2. peyote cactus berries chewed to release the mescaline. *Cf. peyote.* [U.S., RDS: 1982]

white wine gin. RT: *gin.* [Br., FG: 1823, JCH: 1887, B&L: 1890, F&H]

white wool gin. RT: *gin.* [cant, FG: 1785, FG: 1811, FG: 1823]

whities amphetamine tablets. See *white.*

whittled 1. alcohol intoxicated. Also elaborated as **whittled as a penguin**. RT: *drunk.* The word is from a verb *whittle,* meaning to ply with drink, (OED). It is also punning on *cut* (*q.v.*). [(1530): OED, JRB: 1859, B&L: 1890, F&H, BVB: 1942, SJB: 1966] 2. overdosed. [U.S., JES: 1959, H&C: 1975]

whiz-bang (also **whizz-bang**) an injected mixture of drugs: heroin and cocaine or cocaine and morphine. *Cf. speedball.* RS: *set.* [U.S., VFN: 1933, MHW: 1934, DWM: 1938, GOL: 1950, D&D: 1957]

whoofits a hangover. See *woofits.*

whoopee-water (also **whoopee**) liquor; champagne. RT: *booze.* [U.S., VR: 1929, MHW: 1934, D&D: 1957, W&F: 1960]

whooper-up (also **whooper-upper**) a drinking bout. RT: *spree.* [U.S., MHW: 1934, BVB: 1942]

whoops and jingles the delirium tremens. The same as *whips and jangles.* RT: *D.T.s.* [U.S., MHW: 1934, D&D: 1957, W&F: 1960]

whooshed alcohol intoxicated. RT: *drunk.* [U.S., D&D: 1957, W&F: 1960]

whoozy alcohol intoxicated. RT: *drunk.* [U.S., BVB: 1942]

whore scars needle marks from injecting narcotics. RT: *tracks.* Black use. [U.S., CM: 1970]

Who's dealing? "Who is the local dope dealer?"; "Where can I buy drugs?" See *How are you going to act?* for similar phrases. [U.S., RAS: 1980]

Who shot John? moonshine; illicit whiskey. From the prohibition era. RT: *moonshine.* [U.S., AH: 1931, MHW: 1934]

wibble inferior liquor. RS: *rotgut.* [cant, (1728): DSUE, FG: 1785, FG: 1811, FG: 1823, GWM: 1859]

wicked having to do with very good or very potent drugs. A synonym of *bad* (*q.v.*). *Cf. mean.* [U.S., JWK: 1981]

wickedsham commission the Wickersham commission set up by President Herbert Hoover to oversee study the enforcement of prohibition. The Wickersham Commission was the National Commission on Law Observance and Enforcement. Many U.S. citizens viewed national prohibition as a wicked sham. *Cf. Likkersham Commission.* [U.S., 1920s, MHW: 1934]

wide drug intoxicated. Perhaps this is a play on *far out* (*q.v.*). RT: *stoned.* Black use. [U.S., EAF: 1972]

widow an amphetamine capsule. May refer to a black *Biphetamine* (TM; *q.v.*) capsule. See *black widow.* RT: *amps.* [U.S., GU: 1975]

wiffsniffer a prohibitionist. See *whiffsniffer.*

wig to take an overdose of drugs. *Cf. wig out.* [U.S., RDS: 1982]

wigged out (also **wigged, wiggy**) alcohol intoxicated; drug intoxicated. Based on *flip one's wig.* RT: *drunk, stoned.* [U.S., HB: 1955, W&F: 1967, CM: 1970, EEL: 1971, DCCU: 1972, ADC: 1975]

wig out to have a psychotic episode due to drug use. Based on flip one's wig. [U.S. and Canadian, S&W: 1966, RRL: 1969, MMO: 1970, EEL: 1971]

wildcat (also **wildcat whiskey**) whiskey; illicit whiskey. *Cf. panther, panther juice.* RT: *moonshine, whiskey.* Wildcat = unauthorized. From the prohibition era. [U.S., (1881): DA, LWP: 1908, (1928): DA, BVB: 1942, D&D: 1957]

wildcat beer illicit beer during prohibition. See comments at *wildcat.* [U.S., 1920s, SBF: 1976]

wild geronimo barbiturates mixed with alcohol. See *geronimo.* RS: *set.* [U.S., IGA: 1971]

wild mare's milk raw whiskey; strong liquor; inferior liquor. RT: *rotgut.* Jocular Western (W&F: 1960). [U.S., (1850–1900): RFA, W&F: 1960]

wildweed wild marijuana. RT: *pot.* [U.S., (1976): ELA: 1982]

wilted alcohol intoxicated. RT: *drunk.* [U.S., W&F: 1960]

wind, in the alcohol intoxicated, later, also drug intoxicated. Probably a truncation of *three sheets in the wind.* RT: *drunk.* Of nautical origin. [Br., FG: 1823; U.S., (motorcycle gangs), RDS: 1982]

windowpane (also **windowpane acid**) a small sheet of gelatin impregnated with *L.S.D.* (*q.v.*). RS: *L.S.D.* [U.S., ADC: 1975, NIDA: 1980, ADC: 1981]

window-watcher an addict who covertly peers into car windows while walking down the street. Anything of value will be stolen to pay for drugs. [U.S., JWK: 1981]

wine 1. any kind of fermented fruit juice, usually the juice of grapes. Standard English. (The entry continues after this following list.) [since the 800s, OED] Nicknames and slang terms for wine: *Africa speaks, aristippus, atombombo, Bacchus, bagman's blood, bamboo juice, beverage wine, blink-blonk, bombo, bone-clother, coal tar, corroboree water, crimson dawn, dago, dago red, demon vino, didn't ought, duck, foot juice, fustian, grape, grapes, grapes of wrath, grappo, hen wine, ignorant oil, ink, it, joy-juice, juice, kill-priest, lag, long wine, lunatic broth, lunatic soup, mad dog, madman's broth, M.D., Nelly, Nelly's death, old red goofy, paint, pimple and wart, pink-eye, pinkie, pissticide, plink, plinkety-plonk, plink-plonk, plonk, pluck, plug, plunk, point blank, pop wine, port, pruno, railroad whiskey, red, red biddy, red fustian, red ink, red ned, red ribbin, red ribbon, rise and shine, rooje, rosie, rosy, rouge, ruby, sangaree, schoolboy Scotch, sherry, shoestring, short dog, silk and twine, silken, silken twine, smash, sneaky Pete, soda-pop wine, speedball, steam, stinko, string and twine, suck, sweet Lucy, taste, the berries, the grape, the grapes, the vine, treacle, twine, van blank, van blonk, van rooge, veeno, vin blink, vinegar blink, vinegar-de-blink, ving blong, vino, vin ruge, vin sisters, weeno, white fustian, wino*. 2. rum. RT: *rum*. [Br. (naval), WG: 1962; Bahamas, listed in JAH: 1982]

wineache a hangover from drinking cheap wine in great volumes. A wino's ailment. RS: *hangover*. Hobo and wino use. [U.S., JPS: 1970]

winebag a drunkard; a wino. RS: *wino*. [Br., late 18-1900s, DSUE]

wine-bibber See *bibber*.

wine jockey a *wino* (*q.v.*). [U.S., RAS: 1982]

winey alcohol intoxicated; drunk on wine. *Cf. beery, rummy*. RS: *drunk*. [Br., JCH: 1859, F&H; listed in MHW: 1934]

wing 1. a quid of tobacco. RS: *quid*. Prison use. [Br., (1882): DSUE] 2. to conceal shoplifted goods under one's arm; to conceal shoplifted goods on any part of the torso. In the context of drug argot, the proceeds from such thefts go for the purchase of drugs. [U.S., JWK: 1981] See also *wings*.

wing captain a nickname for a person who is under the effects of cocaine. See *wings*. [U.S., H&C: 1975]

wing-ding See *whing-ding*.

winged 1. (also **wing'd**) alcohol intoxicated. That is to say disabled from being hit in the wing, having to do with a fowl which has been shot. *Cf. hit under the wing*. Possibly akin to *pot shot* (*q.v.*). RT: *drunk*. [Br., 1800s, DSUE] 2. under the effects of cocaine; addicted to cocaine. Based on *wings* (*q.v.*). RT: *cocainized*. [U.S., JES: 1959, H&C: 1975]

wing heavy alcohol intoxicated. RT: *drunk*. Probably originated in aviation. [U.S. army, GAS: 1941, W&F: 1960]

wings 1. any of the powdered drugs, especially cocaine, morphine, heroin. Because they make a person fly. RT: *powder*. [U.S., A&T: 1953, SNP: 1977] 2. cocaine. RT: *cocaine*. [U.S., WHW: 1922, GI: 1931, MHW: 1934]

winky a device for smoking *free base*. The same as a *blinky*. [U.S., ELA: 1984]

wino 1. wine. Probably pronounced the same as *vino* (*q.v.*). RT: *wine*. [U.S., BVB: 1942] 2. (also **wineeo, wine-o, winer**) a wine drunkard; a derelict wine drunkard; any drunkard. *Cf. vino*. The entry word is originally U.S. but now widely known. **Wine-o** is attested as Australian (SJB: 1966). [(1920s): SBF: 1976, CS: 1927, DSUE, GI: 1931, D&D: 1957, W&F: 1960, DCCU: 1972] Nicknames and slang terms for a wine drunkard: *bombo, bombo-basher, booze bum, bunch of grapes, dehorn, grape cat, grape chick, grape monger, muscateer, plonk artist, plonk dot, plonk fiend, plonk merchant, plonko, stinko, vino, winebag, wineeo, wine jockey, wine-o, winer, wino*.

winter wonderland euphoria from cocaine use. [U.S., BR: 1972] Terms for cocaine or cocaine use on the snow or winter theme are: *arctic explorer, blow snow, caught in a snowstorm, Florida snow, Frosty the snowman, go for a sleighride, hitch up the reindeer, kicked out in the snow, Lady Snow, nieve, reindeer dust, shovel snow, sleighride, sleighrider, snow, snowball, snowbank, snowbird, snow-caine, snow drifter, snow eagle, snowed, snowfall, snowflakes, snow flowers, snowmobiling, snowstorm, snow stuff*.

wiped out (also **wiped, wiped over**) drug intoxicated; alcohol intoxicated. In current use meaning totally demolished by drugs. RT: *drunk, stoned*. There is also the colloquial meanings: tired, bushed. [Canadian and U.S., W&F: 1967, RRL: 1969, D&B: 1970c, MMO: 1970, EEL: 1971, ADC: 1975, JWK: 1981]

wipe one's eye (also **wipe the other eye**) to take a drink of liquor. The *also* is for all subsequent drinks. RS: *irrigate*. [Br., JCH: 1887]

wired 1. addicted to heroin. As if one were tied or wired to the habit. RT: *hooked*. [U.S., RRL: 1969, H&C: 1975] 2. (also **wired up**) under the effects of a powerful stimulant, amphetamines or cocaine. It takes a *run* (*q.v.*) of several days to get wired. This refers to electrical wiring; the wired person acts electrified. This is the most common current drug culture usage. Now GEN: alert. RS: *cocainized*. [U.S., RRL: 1969, EAF: 1980, ADC: 1975, JWK: 1981, BW: 1984] 3. (also **wired up**) drug intoxicated. A milder state than that of sense two. RT: *stoned*. [U.S., M&V: 1967, EEL: 1971, EAF: 1972, ADC: 1975, W&F: 1975, ADC: 1981, JWK: 1981] 4. (also **wired up**) alcohol intoxicated. RT: *drunk*. [U.S., W&F: 1975, ADC: 1981]

wired on whites under the effects of amphetamines. *Cf. white.* RS: *stoned.* [U.S., M&V: 1967, H&C: 1975]

wise alcohol intoxicated. Possibly a play on *owled* (*q.v.*). RT: *drunk.* [BF: 1737]

wisher allegedly the police. Probably an error for *whiskers* (*q.v.*). RS: *fuzz.* [U.S., IGA: 1971, JHF: 1971]

wish-wash inferior liquor. Possibly a portmanteau of *wishy-washy* and any of the *-wash* words meaning bad liquor. *Cf. belly wash, eyewash, hogwash, mouthwash, sheep-wash, tonsil wash, whitewash. RT: queer-beer, rotgut.* [M&J: 1975]

witch any of the powdered drugs: heroin, cocaine, and morphine. RT: *powder.* [U.S., VJM: 1949, SNP: 1977]

witches brew L.S.D. combined with *Datura* (*q.v.*). RS: *set.* [U.S., KBH: 1982]

witch hazel heroin. *Cf. Hazel, witch.* RT: *heroin.* [U.S., DWM: 1936, D&D: 1957]

witch hazel man a heroin addict. *Cf. witch hazel.* RT: *junky.* [U.S., early 1900s, DU]

witch piss inferior liquor; bad beer. *Cf. squaw piss.* RS: *rotgut.* [Br., Royal Air Force, WWII, DSUE]

with a load of coke under the skin under the influence of cocaine. RS: *stoned.* [early 1900s, DSUE, BVB: 1942]

withdrawal (also **withdrawal syndrome**) the process of ceasing using an addictive drug. The symptoms, beginning with anxiety and yawning, include nausea, cramps, and convulsions. Standard English. [1900s, (1938): M&V: 1954]

with main brace well spliced alcohol intoxicated. An elaboration of *tight* (*q.v.*). See comments on origin at *splice the main brace.* RT: *drunk.* [nautical, 1900s, DSUE]

without a shirt having to do with undiluted liquor. Punning on *naked* (*q.v.*). RT: *neat.* [Br., 1800s, F&H]

wobbler a simulated drug withdrawal convulsion enacted to get drugs from a sympathetic physician. RT: *brody.* [U.S., BVB: 1942, JES: 1959]

wobble weed phencyclidine, P.C.P. *Weed* refers to marijuana, a substance often used with P.C.P. RT: *P.C.P.* [U.S., ELA: 1984]

wobbly alcohol intoxicated. RT: *drunk.* [U.S., BVB: 1942]

woefits a hangover. See *woofits.*

wokowi (also **wakowi**) peyote; mescaline. RS: *peyote.* Known since the turn of the century. [U.S., IGA: 1971, YKB: 1977]

wolf *P.C.P.* (*q.v.*), an animal tranquilizer. RT: *P.C.P.* [U.S., (1970s): FAB: 1979]

womblety-cropt (also **wamble-cropped, womble-cropped, womble-ty-cropt**) alcohol intoxicated; drunk and hungover. RT: *drunk.*

[BF: 1737, FG: 1785]

wood 1. (also **woodie**) a Woodbine (TM) cigarette. RS: *nail*. [Br., M&J: 1975] See also *woody*. 2. a marijuana smoking device, a pipe or a bong. RS: *bong*. [U.S., JWK: 1981]

wood alcohol methanol. An alcohol not usually used for drinking. It is poisonous when drunk. Compare to *grain alcohol*. [since the 1800s, (1861): OED]

woodpecker of Mars the *Amanita muscaria* (*q.v.*) mushroom. Bits of this highly toxic fungus are eaten to produce hallucinations. Other mushrooms of the genus *Amanita* are deadly poison. [U.S., YKB: 1977]

woody deranged from drinking wood alcohol; alcohol intoxicated. [U.S., W&F: 1960] See also *wood*.

woofits (also **whoofits, woefits**) a hangover; sickness from liquor. RT: *hangover*. [U.S., MHW: 1934, BVB: 1942, D&D: 1957; Br., (1916): DSUE]

woofled alcohol intoxicated. RT: *drunk*. [U.S., BVB: 1942, D&D: 1957, W&F: 1960]

woofle water whiskey. RT: *whiskey*. [U.S., W&F: 1960]

woolies the D.T.s.; a severe hangover. RT: *D.T.s*. [U.S., RWB: 1912]

woozle water whiskey; inferior whiskey. RT: *rotgut, whiskey*. [U.S., D&D: 1957, W&F: 1960]

woozy (also **woozey**) alcohol intoxicated; tipsy. *Cf. boozy-woozy*. GEN: confused. RT: *drunk*. [Br. and U.S., (1897): DA, (1917): DSUE, MP: 1928, BVB: 1942, D&D: 1957, M&J: 1975, SSD, RDS: 1982]

works (also **the works**) equipment used for preparing and injecting drugs. RT: *outfit*. [U.S., BD: 1937, M&H: 1959, DSUE, M&D: 1952, M&H: 1959, W&F: 1967, RRL: 1969, DCCU: 1972, MA: 1973, JWK: 1981]

world, out of this (also **out of the world**) drug intoxicated. RT: *stoned*. [U.S., TRG: 1968]

worm phencyclidine, P.C.P. RT: *P.C.P.* [U.S., ELA: 1984]

wrapper a cigarette paper. RT: *paper*. [U.S., HS: 1933, VJM: 1949, GOL: 1950]

wrecked alcohol intoxicated; drug intoxicated; under the effects of marijuana. RT: *drunk, stoned*. [U.S., D&B: 1970c, IGA: 1971, DCCU: 1972, ADC: 1975, W&F: 1975, RAS: 1980]

wring-jaw hard cider. [U.S., (1775): ADD]

write script to forge a prescription for narcotics. *Cf. script*. [U.S., M&V: 1954, JES: 1959]

writing a prescription; a legal prescription for drugs. *Cf. paper, per, script*. [U.S., BVB: 1942, M&V: 1954]

X

X. an injection of drugs. RT: ***shot***. [U.S., JES: 1959, H&C: 1975]

Xmas drug euphoria; a drug rush. Possibly related to *Christmas rush*. RT: ***rush***. [U.S., JES: 1959, H&C: 1975]

Y

yadnarb (also **yardnab**, **yardnarb**) brandy. Backslang for *brandy*. RT: *brandy*. [Br., JCH: 1859, JRW: 1909]

yage* (also **yaje***, **yake***) a hallucinogen derived from a South American vine. The same as *ayahuasca* (*q.v.*). [U.S., RRL: 1969, YKB: 1977]

yakenal (also **yukenal**) *Nembutal* (TM; *q.v.*) barbiturate. Because it makes one talkative. RT: *nemb*. [U.S., BR: 1972, RDS: 1982]

yakky-dak (also **yocky-dock**) pills, drugs, booze; methyl alcohol or some other substitute for ethyl alcohol. [U.S., W&F: 1960, RAS: 1984]

Yale a hypodermic needle. The brand name of a hypodermic needle. RT: *needle*. [U.S., M&V: 1967, H&C: 1975]

yam-yam opium; unprocessed opium. RT: *opium*. [U.S., GOL: 1950]

yanga *methaqualone* (*q.v.*). RT: *ludes*. [U.S., SNP: 1977]

yanked arrested on drug charges; abused or pushed around generally. *Cf. tossed*. RT: *busted*. [U.S., JWK: 1981]

yappish (also **yaupish**) alcohol intoxicated. RT: *drunk*. [Br., 1800s, F&H]

yappy (also **yaupy**) alcohol intoxicated. RT: *drunk*. [Br., 1800s, F&H; listed in BVB: 1942]

yard a drink of liquor. A truncation of *yard of satin* (*q.v.*).

yard of satin gin; a glass of gin. RT: *gin*. [Br., (1828): DSUE, JRW: 1909]

yeaster a beer-drinking alcoholic; a *beeroholic* (*q.v.*). A play on *yeast* used in brewing beer. RS: *sot*. [U.S., RDS: 1982]

yedo* marijuana. Spanish for a smoke. RT: *pot*. [U.S., EEL: 1971, JH: 1979]

yell a drink; a beer. From its yellow color (DSUE). *Cf. cry, shout*. RS: *nip*. [Br., (1848): DSUE]

yellow 1. a capsule of *Nembutal* (TM; *q.v.*) barbiturate. Usually in the plural. RT: *nemb*. [U.S., RRL: 1969, D&B: 1970c, SH: 1972, JWK: 1981] 2. the hallucinogenic drug *L.S.D.* (*q.v.*). Often in the plural. *Cf. yellow sunshine*. RT: *L.S.D.* [U.S., YKB: 1977] 3. a mild form of Eastern hashish. *Cf. blond Lebanese.* RT: *hash.* [U.S., JWK: 1981] 4. (always plural) 10 mg tablets of *Valium* (*q.v.*). RT: *vals.* [U.S., JWK: 1981]

yellow angels (also **yellow bams, yellow birds, yellow bullets, yellow dolls, yellow jackets, yellows**) *Nembutal* (TM; *q.v.*) barbiturate capsules. RT: *nemb.* [U.S., (1944): HLM: 1982, M&D: 1952, EEL: 1971, IGA: 1971, DCCU: 1972, ADC: 1975, W&S: 1977, NIDA: 1980]

yellow dimple L.S.D. combined with some other drug. *Cf. red dimple.* RS: *set.* [U.S., KBH: 1982]

yellow dust strong phencyclidine, *P.C.P.* (*q.v.*), an animal tranquilizer. RT: *P.C.P.* [U.S., ADC: 1981] See also *gray dust, white dust.*

yellow footballs yellow pills or capsules of synthetic mescaline. See *footballs.* RS: *peyote.* [U.S., EEL: 1971]

yellow jackets (also **yellow jacks, yellows**) *Nembutal* (TM; *q.v.*) barbiturates. See *yellow angels.* RT: *nemb.* [U.S., M&D: 1952, M&V: 1954, RRL: 1969, D&B: 1970c, CM: 1970, EEL: 1971, DCCU: 1972, ADC: 1975, EAF: 1980, NIDA: 1980, RDS: 1982]

yellows See *yellow.*

yellow sunshine (also **yellow caps, yellow dots**) the hallucinogenic drug *L.S.D.* (*q.v.*). *Cf. yellows.* RT: *L.S.D.* [U.S., DCCU: 1972, S&R: 1972, W&F: 1975, ADC: 1981]

yemtzem opium. RT: *opium.* [U.S., JES: 1959]

yen 1. opium; opium smoke; opium addiction; opium craving. RT: *opium.* [U.S., GI: 1931, BVB: 1942] 2. a craving for opium, heroin, or other drugs; withdrawal from heroin or opium. [U.S., VFN: 1933, DWM: 1936, BD: 1937, BVB: 1942, TRG: 1968, (RRL: 1969), EEL: 1971, H&C: 1975]

yen-burn a craving for narcotics. *Cf. yen.* [U.S., JES: 1959]

yen-chee opium; pellets of prepared opium. Chinese or mock-Chinese. A spelling variant of *yen-shee* (*q.v.*). RT: *opium.* [U.S., BVB: 1942, VJM: 1949]

yen-chee-quay an opium addict. See *yen-shee-kwoi.* Chinese or mock-Chinese. [U.S., VJM: 1949]

yen-cheung (also **yen-chiang, yen-chung**) an opium pipe. RT: *hop stick.* Chinese or mock-Chinese. [U.S., VJM: 1949, H&C: 1975]

yen-gow an opium pipe cleaner. *Cf. gow.* Chinese or mock-Chinese. [U.S., GOL: 1950]

yen-hank an opium pipe. RT: *hop stick.* Chinese or mock-Chinese. [attested as U.S., early 1900s DSUE]

yen-hok (also **hook, yen-hock, yen-hoke, yen-hook**) a needle-like tool for transferring an opium pellet to the opium pipe. The tool is also used for roasting a pellet of opium. Chinese or mock-Chinese. [U.S., (1887): RML: 1948, VFN: 1933, DWM:

1936, BD: 1937, MHW: 1934, VJM: 1949, W&F: 1960, RRL: 1969, D&B: 1970c, EEL: 1971]

yen-pok (also yen-pock, yen-pook) a roasted pellet of prepared opium to be taken orally, away from an opium den. Chinese or mock-Chinese. *Cf. pox.* [U.S., (1934): DSUE, DWM: 1936, BD: 1937, VJM: 1949, GOL: 1950, RRL: 1969]

yen-pop marijuana. RT: *pot.* [U.S., GOL: 1950, A&T: 1953, IGA: 1971]

yen-shee (also yen-she) **1.** opium. RT: *opium.* Chinese or mock-Chinese. [U.S., GI: 1931, BVB: 1942] **2.** residue (from a smoked opium pellet) found in the opium pipe. It can be strained, dissolved in alcohol and drunk, or injected. The later will almost certainly produce an abscess. [U.S., (1891): DSUE, DWM: 1933, BD: 1937, DWM: 1938, VJM: 1949, GOL: 1950, EEL: 1971] **3.** heroin. In the early 1900s, all opiates and sometimes cocaine and marijuana were included under the term *opium.* See BD: 1937 for instance. RT: *heroin.* [U.S., W&F: 1960]

yen-shee baby impacted fecal matter due to constipation from opium use. *Cf. blockbuster.* [U.S., DWM: 1938, BVB: 1942]

yen-shee bowl the bowl of an opium pipe used to catch the residue from the roasted pellet of opium. [U.S., GOL: 1950]

yen-shee boy an opium addict or user who eats *yen-shee.* A&T: 1953 list yen-shee doy in error. RT: *campfire boy.* [U.S., DWM: 1938, BVB: 1942]

yen-shee-gow a tool for scraping the residue out of opium pipes. RML: 1948 records ynchi-gow and recognizes it as an error. [U.S., (1887): RML: 1948, DWM: 1936, BD: 1937, GOL: 1950, A&T: 1953]

yen-shee-kwoi (also yen-chee-quay, yen-shee-quay, yen-shee-quoy) an opium addict or opium user. RT: *campfire boy.* [U.S., DWM: 1936, BVB: 1942]

yen-shee no 1. (also yen-shee no 2.) the entry word means opium residue in its first re-use. The *also* means opium residue in its second re-use. [U.S., VJM: 1949]

yen-shee rag a cloth used for cleaning and cooling the opium pipe. [U.S., GOL: 1950]

yen-shee rasper a great breaking of wind by a constipated opium smoker. [U.S., JES: 1959]

yen-shee-suey (also yen-shee-suui) opium or opium residue dissolved in wine. *Cf. suey.* [U.S., VJM: 1949, A&T: 1953, M&V: 1954, TRG: 1968, EEL: 1971]

yen sleep a restless sleep in drug withdrawal. *Cf. yen.* [U.S., EEL: 1971, RDS: 1982]

yen-yen craving for drugs; craving for opium; a craving for more and more of a drug. *Cf. yen.* [U.S., (1918): DSUE, MHW: 1934, GOL: 1950, W&F: 1960]

yerba* 1. marijuana. Spanish for herb. RT: *pot*. [U.S., (1967): ELA: 1982, RRL: 1969, ADC: 1975, CG: 1980, NIDA: 1980] 2. *yohimbe* (*q.v.*). [U.S., SNP: 1977, YKB: 1977]

yerba buena* marijuana; good marijuana. Compare to *yerba mala*. RS: *pot*. [U.S., BR: 1972, CG: 1980]

yerba del diablo* *jimson weed* (*q.v.*). Spanish for devil's weed. [U.S., YKB: 1977]

yerba del pasmo* *yohimbe* (*q.v.*). [U.S., YKB: 1977]

yerba mala* phencyclidine, *P.C.P.* (*q.v.*), an animal tranquilizer. Spanish for bad herbs, i.e., bad *grass* (*q.v.*) = marijuana. RT: *P.C.P.* [U.S., NIDA: 1980]

yesca* (also **yessa***) marijuana. Spanish for tinder, fuel. Spelled **llesca**, **lhesca**, the latter being Portuguese. RT: *pot*. Also widely attested in the English-speaking drug culture. Originally Spanish (calo). [U.S., VJM: 1949, M&D: 1952, HB: 1955, D&D: 1957, W&F: 1960, EEL: 1971, JBR: 1973, M&V: 1973, NIDA: 1980, JWK: 1981]

yet-lo (also **yet-low**) second or third use opium. Chinese or mock-Chinese. *Cf. san-lo*. See *yen-shee no 1*. [U.S., M&V: 1954]

yocky-dock See *yakky-dak*.

yohimbe* a stimulant and aphrodisiac. Synthesized or made from the bark of the *Corynanthe yohimbe* tree of West Africa. Known since 1898 (OED). [U.S., YKB: 1977]

You got any of them thangs on you? "Do you have any drugs?" *Cf. thang*. See similar inquiries at *How are you going to act?* [U.S., JWK: 1981]

you know cocaine. Rhyming slang for *snow* (*q.v.*) or *blow* (*q.v.*). RT: *cocaine*. [U.S., (1910): DU, DWM: 1938, M&B: 1944, DRS]

youngblood a novice drug user. Compare to *cadet, convert, green hype, lame, lame hype, lane, shirt tail hype, student, undergrad*. RT: *user*. [U.S., TRG: 1968, JTD: 1971, IGA: 1971, D&B: 1978]

yukenal See *yakenal*.

Z

Z. (also **zee**) one ounce of a drug, especially marijuana. *Cf. O., O.Z.* RS: *load*. [U.S., W&F: 1975, D&B: 1978, JWK: 1981]

Zacatecas purple marijuana assumed to be grown in the vicinity of Zacatecas, Mexico. RT: *pot*. [U.S., RRL: 1974, NIDA: 1980]

zacate inglés* (also **zacate***) marijuana. Spanish for English hay. RT: *pot*. [calo, JBR: 1973]

zagged alcohol intoxicated. See *zig-zagged (*at *zig-zag*).

zamal* hashish on Madagascar and Reunion islands. From (colloquial) Arabic. RT: *hash*. [U.S., RDS: 1982]

zapped alcohol intoxicated; drug intoxicated. RT: *drunk, stoned*. [U.S., DCCU: 1972]

zee an ounce. See *Z*.

Zen the hallucinogenic drug *L.S.D.* (*q.v.*). *Cf. instant Zen*. RT: *L.S.D.* [Br. and U.S., BTD: 1968, EEL: 1971, YKB: 1977]

zeppelin a cigar packaging tube (aluminum) used to contain drugs which are concealed in the vagina or rectum. Named for the dirigible inventor, Zeppelin. RS: *stash*. [U.S., JES: 1959, H&C: 1975]

zerked (also **zerked out**) drug intoxicated; heavily drug intoxicated; very high on marijuana. RT: *stoned*. [U.S., JWK: 1981]

zig-zag 1. (also **zig-zagged**) alcohol intoxicated. From French. RT: *drunk*. [Br. and U.S., WWI, F&G: 1925, MPK: 1930, MHW: 1934, EP: 1948, B&P: 1965, JL: 1972] 2. drug intoxicated. From sense one. RT: *stoned*. [U.S., JES: 1959] 3. (usually **Zigzag**) a brand name of cigarette rolling papers. RS: *paper*. [U.S., (RB: 1967), RRL: 1969, D&B: 1970c, ADC: 1975, EAF: 1980]

zings 1. amphetamines. *Cf. Got any zings? RT: amps*. [U.S., JWK: 1981] 2. (also **the zings**) the delirium tremens; a hangover. RT: *D.T.s*. [U.S., MHW: 1934, W&F: 1960]

zipped drug intoxicated. LIT: zeroed. RT: *stoned*. [U.S., M&V: 1973]

zissified alcohol intoxicated. RT: *drunk*. [U.S., BVB: 1942]

ziv to make a drug purchase. RT: *score*. [U.S., JES: 1959]

Z-kit equipment and supplies used in marijuana smoking. RS:

outfit. [U.S., ELA: 1982]

Z.N.A. dill weed and monosodium glutamate smoked to get a high. [U.S., RRL: 1969, EEL: 1971]

zol (also **zoll**) a marijuana cigarette; marijuana. From Afrikaans or from Dutch *zoel* = mild. RT: *joint*. In spite of the early citations, the word is assumed to be South African. [U.S., HB: 1955, JES: 1959; South African, (1967): JB: 1980]

zol rooker a marijuana smoker. RT: *toker*. See *roker*.

zombie a drug addict; a drug or marijuana user who is debilitated from drug or marijuana use; someone who is always high on drugs. RT: *junky, user*. [U.S., JWK: 1981]

zombie buzz a potent variety of phencyclidine, P.C.P. RT: *P.C.P.* [U.S., ELA: 1984]

zoned alcohol intoxicated; drug intoxicated. RT: *drunk, stoned*. [U.S., HSD: 1984]

zonked (also **zonk, zonked out, zounk**) alcohol intoxicated; drug intoxicated. RT: *drunk*. [U.S., (1958): RSG: 1964, (1967): DNE: 1973, JBW: 1967, M&V: 1967, W&F: 1967, (TW: 1968), RRL: 1969, D&B: 1970c, (1969): MMO: 1970, CM: 1970, EEL: 1971, DCCU: 1972, ADC: 1975, GU: 1975, MW: 1976, JWK: 1981]

zonker 1. a drunkard. RT: *sot*. [U.S., RDS: 1982] 2. a marijuana smoker. RT: *toker*. [U.S., GU: 1975]

zoobang alcohol intoxicated. RT: *drunk*. [U.S., RAS: 1985]

zooie a device for holding the butt of a marijuana cigarette. See *roach*. RS: *crutch*. [U.S., G&B: 1969, ELA: 1982]

zoom 1. marijuana doctored with *P.C.P.* (*q.v.*). RS: *set*. [U.S., ELA: 1982] 2. to have a drug *rush* (*q.v.*). See *zoom off*.

zoomar a powerful narcotic; a large dose of a narcotic. RT: *dose*. [U.S., JES: 1959]

zoom off (also **zoom**) to experience a drug rush; to take drugs for the purpose of experiencing a drug rush. [U.S., M&V: 1973]

zooms amphetamines. RT: *amps*. [U.S., EEL: 1971, JH: 1979]

zooted alcohol intoxicated. RT: *drunk*. [U.S., RAS: 1985]

zorked alcohol intoxicated. RT: *drunk*. [PD: 1982]

zunked drug intoxicated; drug addicted. Probably a variant of *zonked* (*q.v.*). RT: *hooked, stoned*. [U.S., RG: 1970]

Source Index

A&T: 1953 Anslinger, Harry J., and Tompkins, William F. *The Traffic in Narcotics.* New York: Funk and Wagnalls.

AAR: 1944 Roback, A.A. *A Dictionary of International Slurs.* Cambridge, Mass.: Sci-Art Publishers.

AD: 1981 Douglas, Angela. Personal Communications.

AD: 1982 Delbridge, Arthur, ed. *The Macquarie Dictionary.* McMahons Point, Aust.: Macquarie Library.

ADC: 1975 Affluent Drug Culture. Various informants.

ADC: 1981 Affluent Drug Culture. Various informants.

ADC: 1984 Affluent Drug Culture. Various informants.

ADD Wentworth, Harold. *American Dialect Dictionary.* New York: Crowell. 1944.

AH: 1931 Hardin, Achsah. "Volstead English." *American Speech* 7: 81–88.

AHC: 1969 Cain, Arthur H. *Young People and Drugs.* New York: John Day.

AJP: 1935 Pollock, Alben J. *The Underworld Speaks.* San Francisco: The Prevent Crime Bureau.

AP: 1980 Pearl, Anita. *Dictionary of Popular Slang.* Middle Village, N.Y.: Jonathan David.

B&L: 1890 Barrère, Albert, and Leland, Charles G. *A Dictionary of Slang, Jargon, and Cant.* 2 vols. London: Ballantyne. 1889–1890.

B&L: 1972 Brill, Leon, and Lieberman, Louis. *Major Modalities in the Treatment of Drug Abuse.* New York: Behavioral Publications.

B&P: 1965 Brophy, John, and Partridge, Eric. *The Long Trail.* New York: London House and Maxwell.

BD: 1937 Dai, Bingham. *Opium Addiction in Chicago.* Shanghai, China: Commercial Press.

BE: 1690 B.E. *A New Dictionary of the Canting Crew.*

BF: 1722 Franklin, Benjamin. "Silence Dogwood."

BF: 1737 Franklin, Benjamin. "A Drinker's Dictionary." *Pennsylvania Gazette,* January 6, 1737.

BH: 1980 Hornadge, Bill. *The Australian Slanguage.* North Ryde,

NSW: Cassell Australia.

BHH: 1856 Hall, B.A. *A Collection of College Words and Customs.* Cambridge, Mass.: John Bartlett.

BHL: 1920 Lehman, B.H. "California Word List." *Dialect Notes* 5: 109-114.

BL: 1982 Little, Bert. "Prison Lingo: A Style of American English Slang." *Anthropological Linguistics* 24: 206-244.

BR: 1972 Rodgers, Bruce. *The Queen's Vernacular: A Gay Lexicon.* San Francisco: Straight Arrow Books.

BTD: 1968 Dawtry, Frank. ed. *Social Problems of Drug Abuse.* London: Butterworths.

BTH: 1914 Harvey, Bartle T. "Word List From the Northwest." *Dialect Notes* 4: 26-28, 162-164.

BVB: 1942 Berrey, Lester V., and Van den Bark, Melvin. *The American Thesaurus of Slang.* New York: Crowell.

BVB: 1953 Berrey, Lester V., and Van Den Bark, Melvin. *The American Thesaurus of Slang.* Second edition. New York: Crowell.

BW: 1984 Woodward, Bob. *Wired: The short Life and Fast Times of John Belushi.* New York: Simon and Schuster.

BWG: 1899 Green, B.W. *Word-Book of Virginia Folk-Speech.* Richmond, Virginia: Wm. Ellis Jones.

C&H: 1974 Cull, John G., and Hardy, Richard E. *Types of Drug Abusers and Their Abuses.* Springfield, Illinois: Thomas.

C&W: 1982 Carey, Mary, and Westermark, Victoria. *How to be a Valley Girl.* New York: Bantam Books.

CCA Adams, Charles C. *Boontling, An American Lingo.* Austin: Univ. of Texas Press. [1880-1920] 1971.

CG: 1980 Gallo, Cristino. *Language of the Puerto Rican Street.* Santurce, P.R.: Book Service of Puerto Rico.

CM: 1970 Major, Clarence. *Dictionary of Afro-American Slang.* New York: International Publishers.

CS: 1927 Samolar, Charlie. "The Argot of the Vagabond." *American Speech* 2: 385-392.

D&B: 1970a Dill, Stephen H., and Bebeau, Donald E. eds. *Current Slang* 5: No. 3.

D&B: 1970b Dill, Stephen H., and Bebeau, Donald E. eds. *Current Slang* 5: No 2.

D&B: 1970c Dill, Stephen H., and Bebeau, Donald E. eds. *Current Slang* 3 & 4.

D&B: 1971 Dill, Stephen H., and Bebeau, Donald E. eds. *Current Slang* 6.

D&B: 1978 Dennis, Paul, and Barry, Carolyn. *The Marijuana Catalogue*. Chicago: Playboy Press.

D&D: 1957 Deak, Etienne, and Deak, Simone. *Grand Dictionnaire d'Americanismes*. Second edition. Paris: Editions De Dauphin.

D&D: 1966 Deak, Etienne, and Deak, Simone. *Grand Dictionnaire d'Americanismes*. Fourth edition. Paris: Editions De Dauphin.

D&D: 1973 Deak, Etienne, and Deak, Simone. *Grand Dictionnaire d'Americanismes*. Fifth edition. Paris: Editions De Dauphin.

DA Mathews, Mitford. *A Dictionary of Americanisms on Historical Principles*. Chicago: Univ. of Chicago Press. 1951.

DA: 1857 Angelicus, Ducange. *The Vulgar Tongue*. London: Bernard Quaritch.

DA: 1970 Horman, Richard E., and Fox, Allan M. *Drug Awareness*. New York: Avon Books.

DA: 1975 Anderson, Dennis. *The Book of Slang*. Middle Village, N.Y.: Jonathan David.

DAE Craigie, W.L., and Hulbert, R.J. *Dictionary of American English*. Chicago: Univ. of Chicago Press. 1942.

DB: 1944 Burley, Dan. *Dan Burley's Original Handbook of Harlem Jive*. New York: Dan Burley.

DC: 1972 Claerbaut, David. *Black Jargon in White America*. Grand Rapids: Eerdmans.

DCCU: 1972 Dahlskog, Helen. ed. *A Dictionary of Contemporary and Colloquial Usage*. Chicago: English-Language Institute of America.

DEM: 1981 Miller, Don Ethan. *The Book of Jargon*. New York: Collier Books.

DES: 1972 Smith, David E. "The Trip - There and Back." [in Brill and Lieberman, B&L: 1972.]

DNE: 1973 Barnhart, Clarence L.; Steinmetz, Sol; and Barnhart, Robert. *The Barnhart Dictionary of New English Since 1963*. Bronxville, N.Y.: Barnhart/Harper & Row.

DNE: 1980 Barnhart, Clarence L.; Steinmetz, Sol; and Barnhart, Robert. *The Second Barnhart Dictionary of New English*. Bronxville, N.Y.: Barnhart/Harper & Row.

DRS Franklyn, Julian. *Dictionary of Rhyming Slang*. London: Routledge & Kegan Paul. 1961.

DST: 1984 Elting, John R., *et al*. *A Dictionary of Soldier Talk*. New York: Scribner.

DSUE Partridge, Eric. *A Dictionary of Slang and Unconventional English*. Seventh edition. New York: Macmillan. 1970.

DU Partridge, Eric. *A Dictionary of the Underworld.* London: Routledge & Kegan Paul. 1949.

DUS Partridge, Eric. *Dictionary of the Underworld.* Third edition. London: Routledge & Kegan Paul. 1968.

DWH: 1947 Hamilton, Delbert W. "Pacific War Language." *American Speech* 22: 54-56.

DWM: 1931 Maurer, David W. "The Argot of the Underworld." *American Speech* 7: 99-118.

DWM: 1933 Maurer, David W. "Junker Lingo, By-Product of Underworld Lingo." *American Speech* 8.2: 27-28.

DWM: 1935 Maurer, David W. "The Lingo of the Good-People." *American Speech* 10: 10-23.

DWM: 1936 Maurer, David W. "Argot of the Underworld Narcotics Addict, (Part One)." *American Speech* 11: 116-127.

DWM: 1938 Maurer, David W. "The Argot of the Underworld Narcotics Addict, (Part two)." *American Speech* 13: 179-192.

DWM: 1946 Maurer, David W. "Marijuana Users and Their Lingo." *American Mercury* 63: 571-576.

DWO Shipley, Joseph T. *Dictionary of Word Origins.* Totowa, New Jersey: Littlefield, Adams. 1945.

E&R: 1971 Eschholz, Paul A., Rosa, Alfred F. "Slang at the University of Vermont." *Current Slang* 5: 1-10.

EAF: 1972 Folb, Edith A. *A Comparative Study of Urban Black Argot.* Arlington, Virginia: ERIC Document ED-066-758.

EAF: 1980 Folb, Edith A. *Runnin' Down Some Lines.* Cambridge, Mass.: Harvard Univ. Press.

EDD Wright, Joseph. *The English Dialect Dictionary.* 6 vols. London: Henry Frowde. 1898-1905.

EE: 1976 Martin, Julian S., ed. *Dictionary of CB Lingo.* New York: Davis Publications.

EEL: 1971 Landy, Eugene E. *The Underground Dictionary.* New York: Simon and Schuster.

EHB: 1900 Babbit, Eugene H. "College Words and Phrases." *Dialect Notes* 2: 3-70.

EK: 1927 Kane, Elisha. "The Jargon of the Underworld." *Dialect Notes* 5: 433-467.

EKM: 1926 Maxfield, E.K. "Maine List." *Dialect Notes* 5: 385-390.

ELA: 1982 Abel, Ernest L. *A Marihuana Dictionary.* Westport, Conn.: Greenwood Press.

ELA: 1984 Abel, Ernest L. *A Dictionary of Drug Abuse Terms and*

Terminology. Westport, Conn.: Greenwood Press.

EP: 1948 Partridge, Eric. *Dictionary of Forces Slang*. London: Secker and Warburg.

ERH: 1982 Hageman, E.R. "A 1926 Glossary of Criminal Slang." *American Speech* 57: 260–263.

F&G: 1925 Fraser, Edward, and Gibbons, John. *Soldier and Sailor Words and Phrases*. London: George Routledge and Sons.

F&H Farmer, John S., and Henley, W.E. *Slang and Its Analogs*. 7 vols. Published for subscribers at London and Edinburgh. 1890–1904.

FAB: 1979 Feldman, H.W.; Agar, M.H.; and Beschner, G.M., eds. *Angel Dust*. Lexington, Mass.: Lexington Books.

FBL: 1898 Lee, Francis B. "Jerseyisms." *Dialect Notes* 1: 327–337.

FG: 1785 Grose, Francis. *A Classical Dictionary of the Vulgar Tongue*. London: S. Hooper.

FG: 1788 Grose, Francis. *A Classical Dictionary of The Vulgar Tongue*. Second edition. London: S. Hooper.

FG: 1796 Grose, Francis. *A Classical Dictionary of the Vulgar Tongue*. Third edition. London: Hooper and Widstead.

FG: 1811 Grose, Francis. [Clarke H., ed.] *Lexicon Balatronicum*. London: W.N. Jones.

FG: 1823 Grose, Francis. [Egan, Pierce, ed.] *A Classical Dictionary of the Vulgar Tongue*. London: Sherwood, Neely, and Jones.

FH: 1946 Hamann, Fred. "Stillers' Argot." *American Speech* 21: 193–195.

G&B: 1969 Geller, Allen, and Boas, Maxwell. *The Drug Beat*. New York: McGraw-Hill.

GAE: 1925 England, George Allan. "Newfoundland Dialect Terms." *Dialect Notes* 5: 322–346.

GAS: 1941 U.S. Army, Public Relations Division. "Glossary of Army Slang." *American Speech* 16: 163–169.

GAW: 1978 Wilkes, Gerald Alfred. *A Dictionary of Australian Colloquialisms*. London: Routledge & Kegan Paul.

GG: 1981 Gallup, Grant. Personal Communication.

GI: 1931 Irwin, Godfrey. *American Tramp and Underworld Slang*. London: Scholartis Press.

GM: 1931 Milburn, George. "Convicts Jargon." *American Speech* 6: 436–442.

GOL: 1950 Goldin, Hyman; O'Leary, Frank; and Lipsius, Morris. *Dictionary of American Underworld Lingo*. New York: Twayne.

GS: 1959 Sherman, Gene. "Mexican Monkey on Our Back." *Los Angeles Times*, July, 12–20.

GU: 1975 Underwood, Gary. "Razorback Slang." *American Speech* 50: 50–69.

GWM: 1859 Matsell, George W. *Vocabulum: or, The Rogue's Lexicon.* New York: George W. Matsell.

H&C: 1975 Hardy, Richard E., and Cull, John G. *Drug Language and Lore.* Springfield, Ill.: Thomas.

HB: 1928 Brackbill, Hervey. "Midshipman's Jargon." *American Speech* 3: 451–455.

HB: 1955 Braddy, Haldeen. "Narcotic Argot along the Mexican Border." *American Speech* 30: 84–90.

HER: 1915 Rollins, Hyder E. "A West Texas Word List." *Dialect Notes* 4: 224–230.

HER: 1971 Roberts, Hermese E. *The Third Ear: A Black Glossary.* Chicago: English-Language Institute of America.

HJS: 1922 Savage, Howard J. "College Slang." [Bryn Mawr] *Dialect Notes* 5: 139–148.

HK: 1917 Kephart, Horace. "A Word List From the Mountains of Western North Carolina." *Dialect Notes* 3: 279–391, 344–391.

HLF: 1974 Foster, Herbert L. *Ribbin', Jivin', and Playin' the Dozens.* Cambridge, Mass.: Ballinger Publishing.

HLM: 1982 Mencken, H.L. [Raven I. McDavid, ed.] *The American Language.* New York: Knopf. 1982.

HNR: 1934 Rose, Howard N. *A Thesaurus of Slang.* New York: Macmillan.

HS: 1933 Simons, Hi. "A Prison Dictionary (Expurgated)." *American Speech* 8.3: 22–33.

HSD: 1984 Pratt, Jane, ed. *Harrap's Slang Dictionary.* London: Harrap.

HY: 1927 Yenne, Herbert. "Prison Lingo." *American Speech* 2: 280–282.

IGA: 1971 Illinois Legislative Investigating Commission. *The Drug Crisis: Report on Drug Abuse in Illinois.* Chicago: Illinois Legislative Investigating Commission.

JAH: 1982 Holm, John A., with Shilling, Alison W. *Dictionary of Bahamian English.* Cold Spring, N.Y.: Lexik House.

JAR: 1930 Russell, Jason Almus. "Colgate University Slang." *American Speech* 5: 238–239.

JAS: 1932 Shidler, John Ashton. "More Stanford Expressions." *American Speech* 7: 434–437.

JAWB: 1943 Bennet, J.A.W. "English As It Is Spoken in New Zealand." *American Speech* 18: 81-95.

JB: 1823 Badcock, Jon [Jon Bee]. *Slang*. London: T. Hughes.

JB: 1980 Branford, Jean. *A Dictionary of South African English*. Cape Town: Oxford.

JBR: 1973 Rosensweig, Jay B. *Calo: Gutter Spanish*. New York: Dutton.

JBW: 1967 Williams, John B. ed. *Narcotics and Hallucinogens*. Beverly Hills, California: Glencoe Press.

JC: 1972 Carr, J. *The Second Oldest Profession*. Englewood Cliffs, N.J.: Prentice-Hall.

JCH: 1859 Hotten, John Camden. *The Slang Dictionary*. London: John Camden Hotten.

JCH: 1864 Hotten, John Camden. *The Slang Dictionary*. London: John Camden Hotten.

JCH: 1887 Hotten, John Camden. *The Slang Dictionary*. London: Chatto and Windus.

JCR: 1914 Ruppenthal, J.C. "A Word List From Kansas." *Dialect Notes* 4: 101-114.

JES: 1959 Schmidt, J. E. *Narcotics Lingo and Lore*. Springfield, Ill.: Thomas.

JF: 1598 Florio, John. *A Worlde of Words*.

JF: 1972 Fort, Joel. "The Treatment of Sedative, Stimulant, Marijuana, and LSD Abuse." [in Brill and Lieberman, B&L 1972.]

JH: 1979 Homer, Joel. *Jargon*. New York: Times Books.

JHF: 1971 Frykman, John H. *A New Connection*. San Francisco: Scrimshaw.

JK: 1957 Kerouac, Jack. *On the Road*. New York: Viking.

JL: 1972 Lighter, Jonathan. "The Slang of the American Expeditionary Forces in Europe." *American Speech* 47: 5-142.

JLD: 1976 Dillard, J.L. *American Talk*. New York: Random House.

JLD: 1977 Dillard, J.L. *Lexicon of Black English*. New York: Seabury.

JLK: 1934 Kuethe, J. Louis. "Prison Parlance." *American Speech* 9: 25-28.

JM: 1923 Manchon, Joseph. *Le Slang*. Paris.

JOH: 1901 Halliwell, James Orchard. *A Dictionary of Archaic and Provincial Words*. Fifth edition. London: Gibbings.

JPS: 1970 Spradley, James P. *You Owe Yourself a Drunk*. Boston:

Little, Brown.

JRB: 1859 Bartlett, John Russell. *Dictionary of Americanisms.* Second edition. Boston: Little, Brown.

JRW: 1909 Ware, J. Redding. *Passing English of the Victorian Era.* London: George Routledge & Sons.

JS: 1925 Stevens, James. "Logger Talk." *American Speech* 1: 135-140.

JSF: 1889 Farmer, John S. *Americanisms.* London: Thomas Poulter and Sons.

JTD: 1971 Dunigan, Jay T. *Drug Abuse: A Resource Guide for Educators.* Albany, N.Y.: Capital District RSEC.

JW: 1954 Weingarten, Joseph. *An American Dictionary of Slang and Colloquial Speech.* New York: Joseph Weingarten.

JWC: 1905 Carr, Joseph William. "Words From Northwestern Arkansas." *Dialect Notes* 3: 68-103, 124-165.

JWK: 1981 Kaiser, Jay Weadon. Personal Communications.

K&M: 1968 Keller, Mark, and McCormick, Mairi. *A Dictionary of Words About Alcohol.* New Brunswick, N.J.: Rutgers Center For Alcohol Studies.

KBH: 1982 Harder, Kelsie B. Review of *Language of the Underworld* by David W. Maurer. *American Speech* 57: 288-290.

LDEI: 1979 Long, Thomas Hill, ed. *Longman Dictionary of English Idioms.* London: Longman Group.

LP: 1971a Pederson, Lee. "An Approach to Urban Word Geography." *American Speech* 46: 73-86.

LP: 1971b Pederson, Lee. "Chicago Words: The Regional Vocabulary." *American Speech* 46: 163-192.

LP: 1977 Pederson, Lee. "The Randy Sons of Nancy Whisky." *American Speech* 52: 112-121.

LR: 1968 Rosten, Leo. *The Joys of Yiddish.* New York: McGraw-Hill.

LVA: 1981 Allen, Loyd V. *Drug Abuse.* Ventura, California: Regal Books.

LWP: 1908 Payne, L.W. "A Word-List From East Alabama." *Dialect Notes* 3: 279-328, 343-391.

M&B: 1944 Maurer, David W., with Baker, Sidney J. "Australian Rhyming Argot in the American Underworld." *American Speech* 19: 183-195.

M&C: 1905 Mead, William E., and Chase, George D. "A Central Connecticut Word-List." *Dialect Notes* 3: 1-24.

M&D: 1952 De Lannoy, William C., and Masterson, Elizabeth.

"Teen-Age Hophead Jargon." *American Speech* 27: 23-31.

M&H: 1959 Murtagh, John M., and Harris, Sara. *Who Live in Shadow.* New York: McGraw-Hill.

M&J: 1975 Marks, Georgette A., and Johnson, Charles B. *The New English-French Dictionary of Slang and Colloquialisms.* New York: Dutton.

M&J: 1980 Marks, Georgette A., and Johnson, Charles B. *Harrap's French and English Dictionary of Slang and Colloquialisms.* London: Harrap.

M&M: 1977 Morris, William, and Morris, Mary. *Morris Dictionary of Word and Phrase Origins.* New York: Harper and Row.

M&V: 1954 Maurer, David W., and Vogel, Victor H. *Narcotics and Narcotic Addiction.* Springfield, Ill.: Thomas.

M&V: 1967 Maurer, David W., and Vogel, Victor H. *Narcotics and Narcotic Addiction.* Third edition. Springfield, Ill.: Thomas.

M&V: 1973 Maurer, David W., and Vogel, Victor H. *Narcotics and Narcotic Addiction.* Fourth edition. Springfield, Ill.: Thomas.

M&W: 1946 Mezzrow, Mezz, and Wolfe, Bernard. *Really the Blues.* New York: Random House.

MA: 1973 Agar, Michael. *Ripping and Running.* New York: Seminar Press.

MB: 1938 Berger, Meyer. "Tea For a Viper." *New Yorker,* March 12.

MG: 1970 Goldsmith, Michael. "Slang Used by USAF Personnel: Vietnam and California." *Current Slang* 5: No. 1.

MGH: 1915 Hayden, Marie Gladys. "Terms of Disparagement." *Dialect Notes* 4: 194-223.

MHW: 1934 Weseen, Maurice H. *Dictionary of American Slang.* New York: Crowell.

MMO: 1970 Orkin, Mark M. *Speaking Canadian English.* Toronto: General Publishing.

MP: 1928 Prenner, Manuel. "Slang Synonyms for Drunk." *American Speech* 4: 102-103.

MPK: 1930 Keeley, Mary Paxton. "A.E.F. English." *American Speech* 5: 372-386.

MT: 1971 Tak, Monty. *Truck Talk.* Philadelphia: Chilton.

MW: 1934 Neilson, William A., ed. *Webster's New International Dictionary of the English Language.* Springfield, Mass.: G. & C. Merriam.

MW: 1961 Gove, Philip B., ed. *Webster's Third New International Dictionary of the English Language.* Springfield, Mass.: G. &

C. Merriam.

MW: 1976 Kay, Mairé Weir, *et al.* *6,000 Words.* Springfield, Mass.: G. & C. Merriam.

MW: 1983 Mish, Frederick C., ed. *Webster's Ninth New Collegiate Dictionary.* Springfield, Mass.: Merriam-Webster.

N&S: 1983 Neaman, Judith S., and Silver, Carole G. *Kind Words: A Thesaurus of Euphemisms.* New York: Facts On File.

NAM: 1953 New York Academy of Medicine. *Conference on Drug Addiction Among Adolescents.* New York: Blakiston.

NCD: 1725 *New Canting Dictionary.* London.

NIDA: 1980 National Institute on Drug Abuse. "Glossary of Drug Terms." Washington, D.C.

NK: 1926 Klein, Nicholas. "Hobo Lingo." *American Speech* 1: 650-653.

NW: 1828 Webster, Noah. *An American Dictionary of the English Language.* New York: S. Converse.

OED Murray, James A.H., *et al.* 12 vols. *Oxford English Dictionary.* Oxford: Clarendon Press. 1888-1928.

OEDS Burchfield, R.W., ed. *A Supplement to the Oxford English Dictionary.* Oxford: Clarendon Press. 1972-1982.

P&C: 1969 Preble, Edward A., and Casey, John R. Jr. "Taking Care of Business." *International Journal of the Addictions* 4: 1-24.

PD: 1982 Dickson, Paul. *Words.* New York: Dell.

PE: 1980 Urdang, Laurence, ed. *Picturesque Expressions: A Thematic Dictionary.* Detroit, Mich.: Gale Research.

PKK: 1976 Kemp, Peter K. *The Oxford Companion to Ships and the Sea.* London: Oxford.

POS: 1979 O'Shaughnessy, Patrick. *Market Trader's Slang.* Boston, Lincolnshire: Richard Kay.

POW: 1949 Wolff, Pablo Oswaldo. *Marihuana in Latin America.* Washington, D.C.: The Linacre Press.

PRB: 1930 Beath, Paul Robert. "More Crook Words." *American Speech* 4: 131-134.

PT: 1981 Tamony, Peter. "Tripping out From San Francisco." *American Speech* 56: 98-103.

PW: 1974 Wright, Peter. *The Language of British Industry.* London: Macmillan.

PW: 1977 Watts, Peter. *A Dictionary of the Old West, 1850-1900.* New York: Knopf.

R&P: 1928 Randolph, Vance, and Pingry, Carl. "Kansas University Slang." *American Speech* 3: 218-221.

R&P: 1982 Russell, I. Willis, and Porter, Mary Gray. "Among the New Words." *American Speech* 57: 270–276.

RAS: 19-- Spears, Richard A., Notebooks and word lists. 1974–1985.

RB: 1915 Bolwell, Robert. "College Slang at Western Reserve University." *Dialect Notes* 4: 231–238.

RB: 1967 Bronsteen, Ruth. *The Hippy's Handbook.* New York: Canyon Book Co.

RDS: 1982 De Sola, Ralph. *Crime Dictionary.* New York: Facts on File.

RFA Adams, Ramon F. *Western Words.* Second edition. Norman, Oklahoma: Univ. of Oklahoma Press. 1968.

RG: 1970 Gilmore, Robert. *Drug Education Handbook.* Denver, Colo.: Department of Health.

RHT: 1912 Thornton, Richard H. *An American Glossary.* Philadelphia: J.B. Lippincott.

RM: 1942 Mulvey, Ruth. "Pitchman's Cant." *American Speech* 17: 89–93.

RML: 1948 Lumiansky, R.M. "Opium Argot: New Orleans, 1887." *American Speech* 23: 245–247.

RML: 1950 Lumiansky, R.M. "New Orleans Slang in the 1880s." *American Speech* 25: 28–40.

RPW: 1938 Walton, Robert P. *Marijuana: America's New Drug Problem.* Philadelphia: Lippincott.

RRL: 1969 Lingeman, Richard R. *Drugs From A to Z: A Dictionary.* New York: McGraw-Hill.

RRL: 1974 Lingeman, Richard R. *Drugs From A to Z: A Dictionary.* Second edition. New York: McGraw-Hill.

RSG: 1964 Gold, Robert S. *A Jazz Lexicon.* New York: Knopf.

RWB: 1912 Brown, Rollo Walter. "A Word-List From Western Indiana." *Dialect Notes* 3: 570–593.

S&E: 1981 Spears, Richard A. *Slang and Euphemism.* Middle Village, New York: Jonathan David.

S&F: 1984 Stone, Nannette; Fromme, Marlene; and Kagan, Daniel. *Cocaine: Seduction and Solution.* New York: Clarkson N. Potter.

S&R: 1972 Smith, David E., and Rose, Allan J. "LSD, Its Use, Abuse, and Suggested Treatment." [in Brill and Lieberman, B&L: 1972.]

S&W: 1966 Simmons, J.L., and Winograd, Barry. *It's Happening.* Santa Barbara, California: Marc-Laird Publications.

S&W: 1973 Smith, David E., and Wesson, Donald R. *Uppers and*

Downers. Englewood Cliffs, N.J.: Prentice-Hall.

SBF: 1976 Flexner, Stuart Berg. *I Hear America Talking.* New York: Van Nostrand.

SBF: 1982 Flexner, Stuart Berg. *Listening to America.* New York: Simon and Schuster.

SH: 1972 Halpern, Susan. *Drug Abuse and Your Company.* New York: American Management Association.

SJB: 1943 Baker, Sidney J. *A Popular Dictionary of Australian Slang.* Melbourne: Robertson and Mullens.

SJB: 1945 Baker, Sidney J. *The Australian Language.* Sydney: Angus and Robertson.

SJB: 1966 Baker, Sidney J. *The Australian Language.* Second edition. Sydney: Currawong Publishing.

SND Grant, William, and Murison, David D., eds. *Scottish National Dictionary.* Edinburgh: The Scottish National Dictionary Association. 1976.

SNP: 1977 Pradhan, Sachindra N., ed. *Drug Abuse.* St. Louis, Missouri: C.V. Mosby.

SOD Onions, C.T., ed. *Shorter Oxford Dictionary.* Third edition. Oxford: Clarendon Press. 1947.

SSD Partridge, Eric. *Smaller Slang Dictionary.* London: Routledge & Kegan Paul. 1964.

TH: 1567 Harman, Thomas. *A Caveat.* London: William Gryffith.

TH: 1976 Hicks, Tom. Personal Communication.

TRG: 1968 "Teacher's Resource Guide on Drug Abuse." [in Horman and Fox, DA: 1970.]

TW: 1968 Wolfe, Tom. *The Electric Kool-aid Acid Test.* New York: Farrar, Straus and Giroux.

VFN: 1933 Nelson, Victor Folke. "Addenda to 'Junker Lingo'." *American Speech* 8.3: 2.

VJM: 1949 Monteleone, Vincent J. *Criminal Slang.* Revised edition. Boston: Christopher.

VR: 1929 Randolph, Vance. "Wet Words in Kansas." *American Speech* 4: 385-389.

VWS: 1929 Saul, Vernon W. "The Vocabulary of Bums." *American Speech* 4: 337-346.

W&F: 1960 Wentworth, Harold, and Flexner, Stuart Berg. *Dictionary of American Slang.* New York: Crowell.

W&F: 1967 Wentworth, Harold, and Flexner, Stuart Berg. *Dictionary of American Slang.* [with supplement] New York: Crowell.

W&F: 1975 Wentworth, Harold, and Flexner, Stuart Berg.

Dictionary of American Slang. Second edition. New York: Crowell.

W&S: 1977 Wesson, Donald R., and Smith, David E. *Barbiturates: Their Use, Misuse, and Abuse.* New York, N.Y.: Human Sciences Press.

WCM: 1972 Martin, William C., ed. *Operation Drug Prevention: A Curriculum Guide K-12.* Pensacola, Florida.: Univ. of West Florida.

WFM: 1958 McCulloch, Walter F. *Woods Words.* Portland, Oregon: Oregon Historical Society.

WG: 1952 Granville, Wilfred. *The Theatre Dictionary.* New York: Philosophical Library.

WG: 1962 Granville, Wilfred. *Dictionary of Sailor's Slang.* London: Andre Deutsch.

WHD: 1919 Downing, W.H. *Digger Dialect.* Melbourne, Aust.: Lothian.

WHW: 1922 Wells, Whitney Hastings. "Terms Used in the Drug Traffic." *Dialect Notes* 5: 181–182.

WM: 1927 Morse, William R. "Stanford Expressions." *American Speech* 2: 275–279.

WSB: 1953 Burroughs, W.S. *Junkie.* New York: Ace Books.

WSB: 1959 Burroughs, W.S. *Naked Lunch.* New York: Grove Press.

WT: 1976 Kay, Mairé Weir, ed. *Webster's Collegiate Thesaurus.* Springfield, Mass.: G. & C. Merriam.

Y&B: 1902 Yule, Henry, and Burnell, A.C. *Hobson-Jobson.* Second edition. London: John Murray.

YKB: 1977 Young, Lawrence A., *et al. Recreational Drugs.* New York: Collier Books.

Authors Cited

The authors of printed material cited in the dictionary are listed alphabetically followed by the title of the work or works cited. Following each work is the source code for the work in question. Additional bibliographical information can be found by consulting the appropriate source code in the Source Index which begins on page 563.

Abel, E.L. *A Marihuana Dictionary.* ELA: 1982; *A Dictionary of Drug Abuse Terms and Terminology.* ELA: 1984.

Adams, C.C. *Boontling.* CCA.

Adams, R.F. *Western Words.* RFA.

Agar, M. *Ripping and Running.* MA: 1973.

Allen, L.V. *Drug Abuse.* LVA: 1981.

Anderson, D. *The Book of Slang.* DA: 1975.

Angelicus, Ducange. *The Vulgar Tongue.* DA: 1857.

Anslinger, H.J. *The Traffic in Narcotics.* A&T: 1953.

B.E. *A New Dictionary of the Canting Crew.* BE: 1690.

Babbit, E.H. "College Words and Phrases." EHB: 1900.

Badcock, Jon [Jon Bee]. *Slang.* JB: 1823.

Baker, S.J. *A Popular Dictionary of Australian Slang.* SJB: 1943; *The Australian Language.* SJB: 1945, SJB: 1966.

Barnhart, C.L. *et al. The Barnhart Dictionary of New English Since 1963. DNE: 1973; The Second Barnhart Dictionary of New English.* DNE: 1980.

Barrère, A., and Leland, C.G. *A Dictionary of Slang, Jargon, and Cant.* B&L: 1890.

Bartlett, J.R. *Dictionary of Americanisms.* JRB: 1859.

Beath, P.R. "More Crook Words." PRB: 1930.

Bee, Jon. See Jon Badcock.

Bennet, J.A.W. "English As It Is Spoken in New Zealand." JAWB: 1943.

Berger, M. "Tea For a Viper." MB: 1938.

Berrey, L.V., and Van den Bark, M. *The American Thesaurus of*

Slang. BVB: 1942, BVB: 1953.

Bolwell, R. "College Slang at Western Reserve University." RB: 1915.

Brackbill, H. "Midshipman's Jargon." HB: 1928.

Braddy, H. "Narcotic Argot along the Mexican Border." HB: 1955.

Branford, J. *A Dictionary of South African English*. JB: 1980.

Brill, L., and Lieberman, L. *Major Modalities in the Treatment of Drug Abuse*. B&L: 1972.

Bronsteen, R. *The Hippy's Handbook*. RB: 1967.

Brophy, J., and Partridge, E. *The Long Trail*. B&P: 1965.

Brown, R.W. "A Word-List From Western Indiana." RWB: 1912.

Burchfield, R.W. *A Supplement to the Oxford English Dictionary*. OEDS.

Burley, D. *Dan Burley's Original Handbook of Harlem Jive*. DB: 1944.

Burns, Robert. Various works cited in F&H, OED.

Burroughs, W.S. *Junkie*. WSB: 1953; *Naked Lunch*. WSB: 1959.

Cain, A.H. *Young People and Drugs*. AHC: 1969.

Carey, M. *How to be a Valley Girl*. C&W: 1982.

Carr, J. *The Second Oldest Profession*. JC: 1972.

Carr, J. "Words From Northwestern Arkansas." JWC: 1905.

Chaucer, G. Various works cited in F&H, OED.

Claerbaut, D. *Black Jargon in White America*. DC: 1972.

Craigie, W.L., and Hulbert, R.J. *Dictionary of American English*. DAE.

Cull, J.G.. and Hardy, R.E. *Types of Drug Abusers and Their Abuses*. C&H: 1974.

Dahlskog, H. *A Dictionary of Contemporary and Colloquial Usage*. DCCU: 1972.

Dai, B. *Opium Addiction in Chicago*. BD: 1937.

Dawtry, F. *Social Problems of Drug Abuse*. BTD: 1968.

De Lannoy, W.C., and Masterson, E. "Teen-Age Hophead Jargon." M&D: 1952.

De Sola, R. *Crime Dictionary*. RDS: 1982.

Deak, E., and Deak, S. *Grand Dictionnaire d'Americanismes*. D&D: 1957, D&D: 1966, D&D: 1973.

Delbridge, A. *The Macquarie Dictionary*. AD: 1982.

Dennis, P., and Barry, C. *The Marijuana Catalogue*. D&B: 1978.

Dickens, Charles. Various novels cited in F&H, OED.

Dickson, P. *Words.* PD: 1982.

Dill, S., and Bebeau, D., D&B: 1970c, D&B: 1970b, D&B: 1970a, D&B: 1971.

Dillard, J.L. *American Talk.* JLD: 1976; *Lexicon of Black English.* JLD: 1977.

Downing, W.H. *Digger Dialect.* WHD: 1919.

Dunigan, J.T. *Drug Abuse.* JTD: 1971.

Egan, P. See FG: 1823.

Elting, J.R. *A Dictionary of Soldier Talk.* DST: 1984.

England, G.A. "Newfoundland Dialect Terms." GAE: 1925.

Eschholz, P.A., Rosa, A.F. "Slang at the University of Vermont." E&R: 1971.

Farmer, J.S. *Americanisms.* JSF: 1889.

Farmer, J.S., and Henley, W.E. *Slang and Its Analogs.* F&H.

Feldman, H.W. *et al. Angel Dust.* FAB: 1979.

Flexner, S.B. *I Hear America Talking.* SBF: 1976; *Listening to America.* SBF: 1982.

Florio, J. *A Worlde of Words.* JF: 1598.

Folb, E.A. *A Comparative Study of Urban Black Argot.* EAF: 1972; *Runnin' Down Some Lines.* EAF: 1980.

Fort, J. "The Treatment of Sedative, Stimulant, Marijuana, and LSD Abuse," JF: 1972.

Foster, H.L. *Ribbin', Jivin', and Playin' the Dozens.* HLF: 1974.

Franklin, B. "Silence Dogwood." BF: 1722; "A Drinker's Dictionary." BF: 1737.

Franklyn, J. *Dictionary of Rhyming Slang.* DRS.

Fraser, E., and Gibbons, J. *Soldier and Sailor Words and Phrases.* F&G: 1925.

Frykman, J.H. *A New Connection.* JHF: 1971.

Gallo, C. *Language of the Puerto Rican Street.* CG: 1980.

Geller, A., and Boas, M. *The Drug Beat.* G&B: 1969.

Gilmore, R. *Drug Education Handbook.* RG: 1970.

Gold, R.S. *A Jazz Lexicon.* RSG: 1964.

Goldin, H. *et al. Dictionary of American Underworld Lingo.* GOL: 1950.

Goldsmith, M. "Slang Used by USAF Personnel: Vietnam and California." MG: 1970.

Gove, P.B. *Webster's Third New International Dictionary of the English Language.* MW: 1961.

Grant, W., and Murison, D.D. *Scottish National Dictionary.* SND.

Granville, W. *The Theatre Dictionary.* WG: 1952; *Dictionary of Sailor's Slang.* WG: 1962.

Green, B.W. *Word-Book of Virginia Folk-Speech.* BWG: 1899.

Grose, F. *A Classical Dictionary of the Vulgar Tongue.* FG: 1785, FG: 1788, FG: 1796, FG: 1811, FG: 1823.

Hageman, E.R. "A 1926 Glossary of Criminal Slang." ERH: 1982.

Hall, B.A. *A Collection of College Words and Customs.* BHH: 1856.

Halliwell, J.O. *A Dictionary of Archaic and Provincial Words.* JOH: 1901.

Halpern, S. *Drug Abuse and Your Company.* SH: 1972.

Hamann, F. "Stillers' Argot." FH: 1946.

Hamilton, D.W. "Pacific War Language." DWH: 1947.

Harder, K.B. Review of *Language of the Underworld.* KBH: 1982.

Hardin, A. "Volstead English." AH: 1931.

Hardy, R.E., and Cull, J.G. *Drug Language and Lore.* H&C: 1975.

Harman, T. *A Caveat.* TH: 1567.

Harvey, B.T. "Word List From the Northwest." BTH: 1914.

Hayden, M.G. "Terms of Disparagement." MGH: 1915.

Holm, J.A. *Dictionary of Bahamian English.* JAH: 1982.

Homer, J. *Jargon.* JH: 1979.

Horman, R.E., and Fox, A.M. *Drug Awareness.* DA: 1970.

Hornadge, B. *The Australian Slanguage.* BH: 1980.

Hotten, J.C. *The Slang Dictionary.* JCH: 1859, JCH: 1864, JCH: 1887.

Irwin, G. *American Tramp and Underworld Slang.* GI: 1931.

Kane, E. "The Jargon of the Underworld." EK: 1927.

Kay, M.W. *Webster's Collegiate Thesaurus.* WT: 1976.

Kay, M.W., *et al.* *6,000 Words.* MW: 1976.

Keeley, M.P. "A.E.F. English." MPK: 1930.

Keller, M., and McCormick, M. *A Dictionary of Words About Alcohol.* K&M: 1968.

Kemp, P.K. *The Oxford Companion to Ships and the Sea.* PKK: 1976.

Kephart, H. "A Word List From the Mountains of Western North Carolina." HK: 1917.

Kerouac, J. *On the Road.* JK: 1957.

Klein, N. "Hobo Lingo." NK: 1926.

Kuethe, J.L. "Prison Parlance." JLK: 1934.

Landy, E.E. *The Underground Dictionary.* EEL: 1971.

Lee, F.B. "Jerseyisms." FBL: 1898.

Lehman, B.H. "California Word List." BHL: 1920.

Lighter, J. "The Slang of the American Expeditionary Forces in Europe." JL: 1972.

Lingeman, R.R. *Drugs From A to Z.* RRL: 1969, RRL: 1974.

Little, B. "Prison Lingo." BL: 1982.

Long, T.H. *Longman Dictionary of English Idioms.* LDEI: 1979.

Lumiansky, R.M. "Opium Argot: New Orleans, 1887." RML: 1948; "New Orleans Slang in the 1880s." RML: 1950.

Major, C. *Dictionary of Afro-American Slang.* CM: 1970.

Manchon, J. *Le Slang.* JM: 1923.

Marks, G.A., and Johnson, C.B. *The New English-French Dictionary of Slang and Colloquialisms.* M&J: 1975; *Harrap's French and English Dictionary of Slang and Colloquialisms.* M&J: 1980.

Martin, J.S. *Dictionary of CB Lingo.* EE: 1976.

Martin, W.C. *Operation Drug Prevention: A Curriculum Guide K-12.* WCM: 1972.

Mathews, M. *A Dictionary of Americanisms on Historical Principles.* DA.

Matsell, G.W. *Vocabulum.* GWM: 1859.

Maurer, D.W. "The Argot of the Underworld." DWM: 1931; "Junker Lingo, By-Product of Underworld Lingo." DWM: 1933; "The Lingo of the Good-People." DWM: 1935; "Argot of the Underworld Narcotics Addict, (Part One)." DWM: 1936; "Argot of the Underworld Narcotics Addict, (Part two)" DWM: 1938; "Marijuana Users and Their Lingo." DWM: 1946.

Maurer, D.W., and Vogel, V.H. *Narcotics and Narcotic Addiction.* M&V: 1954, M&V: 1967, M&V: 1973.

Maurer, D.W., with Baker, S.J. "Australian Rhyming Argot in the American Underworld." M&B: 1944.

Maxfield, E.K. "Maine List." EKM: 1926.

Mayhew, H. Works cited in F&H.

McCulloch, W.F. *Woods Words.* WFM: 1958.

Mead, W.E., and Chase, G.D. "A Central Connecticut Word-List." M&C: 1905.

Melville, H. Novels cited in OED.

Mencken, H.L. *The American Language.* HLM: 1982.

Mezzrow, M., and Wolfe, B. *Really the Blues.* M&W: 1946.

Milburn, G. "Convicts Jargon." GM: 1931.

Miller, D.E. *The Book of Jargon.* DEM: 1981.

Mish, F.C. *Webster's Ninth New Collegiate Dictionary.* MW: 1983.

Monteleone, V.J. *Criminal Slang.* VJM: 1949.

Morris, W., and Morris, M. *Morris Dictionary of Word and Phrase Origins.* M&M: 1977.

Morse, W.R. "Stanford Expressions." WM: 1927.

Mulvey, R. "Pitchman's Cant." RM: 1942.

Murray, J.A.H. *Oxford English Dictionary.* OED.

Murtagh, J.M., and Harris, S. *Who Live in Shadow.* M&H: 1959.

Neaman, J.S. *Kind Words.* N&S: 1983.

Neilson, W.A. *Webster's New International Dictionary of the English Language.* MW: 1934.

Nelson, V.F. "Addenda to 'Junker Lingo'." VFN: 1933.

O'Shaughnessy, P. *Market Trader's Slang.* POS: 1979.

Onions, C.T. *Shorter Oxford Dictionary.* SOD.

Orkin, M.M. *Speaking Canadian English.* MMO: 1970.

Partridge, E. *Dictionary of Forces Slang.* EP: 1948; *A Dictionary of the Underworld.* DU, DUS; *Smaller Slang Dictionary.* SSD; *A Dictionary of Slang and Unconventional English.* DSUE.

Payne, L.W. "A Word-List From East Alabama." LWP: 1908.

Pearl, A. *Dictionary of Popular Slang.* AP: 1980.

Pederson, L. "An Approach to Urban Word Geography." LP: 1971a; "Chicago Words." LP: 1971b; "The Randy Sons of Nancy Whisky." LP: 1977.

Pollock, A.J. *The Underworld Speaks.* AJP: 1935.

Pradhan, S.N. *Drug Abuse.* SNP: 1977.

Pratt, J. *Harrap's Slang Dictionary.* HSD: 1984.

Preble, E.A., and Casey, J.R. "Taking Care of Business." P&C: 1969.

Prenner, M. "Slang Synonyms for Drunk." MP: 1928.

Randolph, V. "Wet Words in Kansas." VR: 1929.

Randolph, V., and Pingry, C. "Kansas University Slang." R&P: 1928.

Roback, A.A. *A Dictionary of International Slurs.* AAR: 1944.

Roberts, H.E. *The Third Ear: A Black Glossary.* HER: 1971.

Rodgers, B. *The Queen's Vernacular: A Gay Lexicon.* BR: 1972.

Rollins, H.E. "A West Texas Word List." HER: 1915.

Rose, H.N. *A Thesaurus of Slang.* HNR: 1934.

Rosensweig, J.B. *Calo: Gutter Spanish.* JBR: 1973.

Rosten, L. *The Joys of Yiddish.* LR: 1968.

Ruppenthal, J.C. "A Word List From Kansas." JCR: 1914.

Russell, I. W., and Porter, M.G. "Among the New Words." R&P: 1982.

Russell, J.A. "Colgate University Slang." JAR: 1930.

Samolar, C. "The Argot of the Vagabond." CS: 1927.

Saul, V.W. "The Vocabulary of Bums." VWS: 1929.

Savage, H.J. "College Slang." HJS: 1922.

Schmidt, J.E. *Narcotics Lingo and Lore.* JES: 1959.

Shakespeare, W. Various works cited in F&H, OED.

Sherman, G. "Mexican Monkey on Our Back." GS: 1959.

Shidler, J.A. "More Stanford Expressions." JAS: 1932.

Shipley, J.T. *Dictionary of Word Origins.* DWO.

Simmons, J.L., and Winograd, B. *It's Happening.* S&W: 1966.

Simons, H. "A Prison Dictionary (Expurgated)." HS: 1933.

Smith, D.E. "The Trip - There and Back." DES: 1972.

Smith, D.E., and Rose, A.J. "LSD, Its Use, Abuse, and Suggested Treatment." S&R: 1972.

Smith, D.E., and Wesson, D.R. *Uppers and Downers.* S&W: 1973.

Smollett, T. Works cited in F&H, OED.

Spears, R.A. *Slang and Euphemism.* S&E: 1981.

Spradley, J.P. *You Owe Yourself a Drunk.* JPS: 1970.

Stevens, J. "Logger Talk." JS: 1925.

Stone, N. *et al. Cocaine: Seduction and Solution.* S&F: 1984.

Tak, M. *Truck Talk.* MT: 1971.

Tamony, P. "Tripping out From San Francisco." PT: 1981.

Taylor, John, the "water poet," i.e., a boatman turned poet. Works cited by F&H, OED.

Thornton, R.H. *An American Glossary.* RHT: 1912.

Underwood, G. "Razorback Slang." GU: 1975.

Urdang, L. *Picturesque Expressions.* PE: 1980.

Walton, R.P. *Marijuana.* RPW: 1938.

Ware, J.R. *Passing English of the Victorian Era.* JRW: 1909.

Watts, P. *A Dictionary of the Old West, 1850-1900.* PW: 1977.

Webster, N. *An American Dictionary of the English Language.* NW: 1828.

Weingarten, J. *An American Dictionary of Slang and Colloquial Speech.* JW: 1954.

Wells, W.H. "Terms Used in the Drug Traffic." WHW: 1922.

Wentworth, H. *American Dialect Dictionary.* ADD.

Wentworth, H., and Flexner, S.B. *Dictionary of American Slang.* W&F: 1960, W&F: 1967, W&F: 1975.

Weseen, M.H. *Dictionary of American Slang.* MHW: 1934.

Wesson, D.R., and Smith, D.E. *Barbiturates.* W&S: 1977.

Wilkes, G.A. *Dictionary of Australian Colloquialisms.* GAW: 1978.

Williams, J.B. *Narcotics and Hallucinogens.* JBW: 1967.

Wolfe, T. *The Electric Kool-aid Acid Test.* TW: 1968.

Wolff, P.O. *Marihuana in Latin America.* POW: 1949.

Woodward, B. *Wired: The short Life and Fast Times of John Belushi.* BW: 1984.

Wright, J. *The English Dialect Dictionary.* EDD.

Wright, P. *The Language of British Industry.* PW: 1974.

Yenne, H. "Prison Lingo." HY: 1927.

Young, L. *Recreational Drugs.* YKB: 1977.

Yule, H., and Burnell, A.C. *Hobson-Jobson.* Y&B: 1902.

Synonym Directory

The left side of each column lists the topics which are represented by lists of related terms or related subjects. The right side of each column lists the entry words where the lists of terms can be found. For instance, terms meaning acid will be found at *L.S.D.* Terms meaning addict will be found at *junky*.

Topic	Entry
acid	L.S.D.
addict	junky
addict, opium	campfire boy
addicted	hooked
addiction	habit
agents, drug	fuzz
alcohol	booze
alcohol, homemade	moonshine
ale	ale
amphetamines	amps
amyl nitrite	snapper
Amytal	blue
arrested	busted
bad beer	queer–beer
bad drug experience	bad trip
bad whiskey	rotgut
bar	bar
barbiturate	barbs
bartender	bartender
beer	beer
Benzedrine	benz
booze	booze
brandy	brandy
break a drug habit	kick
buy drugs	score
cannabis	hash, pot
champagne	cham
cigarette butt	brad
cigarette, marijuana	joint
cigarette rolling paper	paper
cigarette, tobacco	nail
cocaine	cocaine
cocaine user	kokomo
codeine	codeine
delirium tremens	D.T.s
Demerol	demies
Dexedrine	dex
Dilaudid	dids
dilute, to	cut
diluted	cut
doctor	croaker
Dolophine	dolo
dope	dope
Doriden	dories
dose of a drug	dose
downers	barbs, tranks
Drinamyl	Drinamyl
drink much liquor	guzzle
drink of liquor	nip
drink to drunkenness	mug oneself
drinker, heavy	sot
drinking spree	spree
drug addict	junky
drug combination	set
drug experience, bad	bad trip
drug habit	habit
drug habit, small	chippy habit
drug injection	shot
drug intoxicated	stoned
drug runner	mule
drug rush	rush
drug seller	dealer
drug seller, aggressive	pusher
drug smoking device	bong
drug use equipment	outfit
drug user	user
drugs	dope
drugs, phony	blank
drunk	drunk
drunkard	sot
Durophet	Durophet
empty bottle	dead soldier
fake drug spasm	brody
get drunk	mug oneself
gin	gin
hangover	hangover

hashish	hash
hashish oil	oil
heroin	heroin
hypodermic syringe	monkey pump
inebriated	drunk
inject drugs, to	shoot
injection of drugs	shot
injector of drugs	bangster
intoxicated with alcohol	drunk
intoxicated with cocaine	cocainized
intoxicated with drugs	stoned
intoxicated with marijuana	wasted
knock-out drink	Mickey Finn
L.S.D.	L.S.D.
L.S.D. guide	sitter
liquor	booze
liquor flask	flask
liquor store	L.I.Q.
liquor, illegal seller	bootlegger
low drinking place	dive
marijuana	pot
marijuana butt holder	crutch
marijuana cigarette	joint
marijuana cigarette stub	roach
marijuana intoxicated	wasted
marijuana smoker	toker
mescaline	peyote
methadone	dolo
methamphetamine	speed
methaqualone	ludes
methyl alcohol	methyl
moonshine	moonshine
morning glory seeds	seeds
morphine	morphine
narcotics	dope
narcotics addict	junky
needle	needle
needle marks	tracks
Nembutal	nemb
nondrinker	dry
off drugs	off
opium	opium
opium addict	campfire boy
opium den	opium den
opium pipe	hop stick
opium smoker	campfire boy
overdose	O.D.
P.C.P.	P.C.P.
paregoric	goric
Percodan	Percodan
peyote	peyote
physician	croaker
pimple from drinking	gin bud
place for drug use	pad
place to conceal drugs	stash
Placidyl	plass
police	fuzz
port wine	port
porter's ale	porter
portion of a drug	dose, load
powdered drugs	powder
Preludin	preludin
prohibition, national	prohibition
psilocybin	psilocybin
puff marijuana	toke
Quaalude	ludes
rolling paper	paper
rum	rum
rush, drug	rush
Seconal	sec
secret tavern	sly grogshop
sell drugs, to	push
sherry	sherry
smoke marijuana	hit the hay
smoke opium	suck bamboo
snort or sniff drugs	snort
snuff	snoose
sober	sober
speakeasy	speak
speed	speed
square person	square
stout	stout
strong whiskey	rotgut
syringe	monkey pump
T.H.C.	T.H.C.
take a drink of liquor	irrigate
tobacco	fogus
tobacco cigarette	nail
tobacco pipe	pipe
tobacco, fine cut	freckles
tobacco, hunk	quid
tranquilizers	tranks
Tuinal	tooies
undiluted	neat
user, drug	user
Valium	vals
weak beer	queer-beer
whiskey	whiskey
whiskey, bad	rotgut
wine	wine
wine drunkard	wino